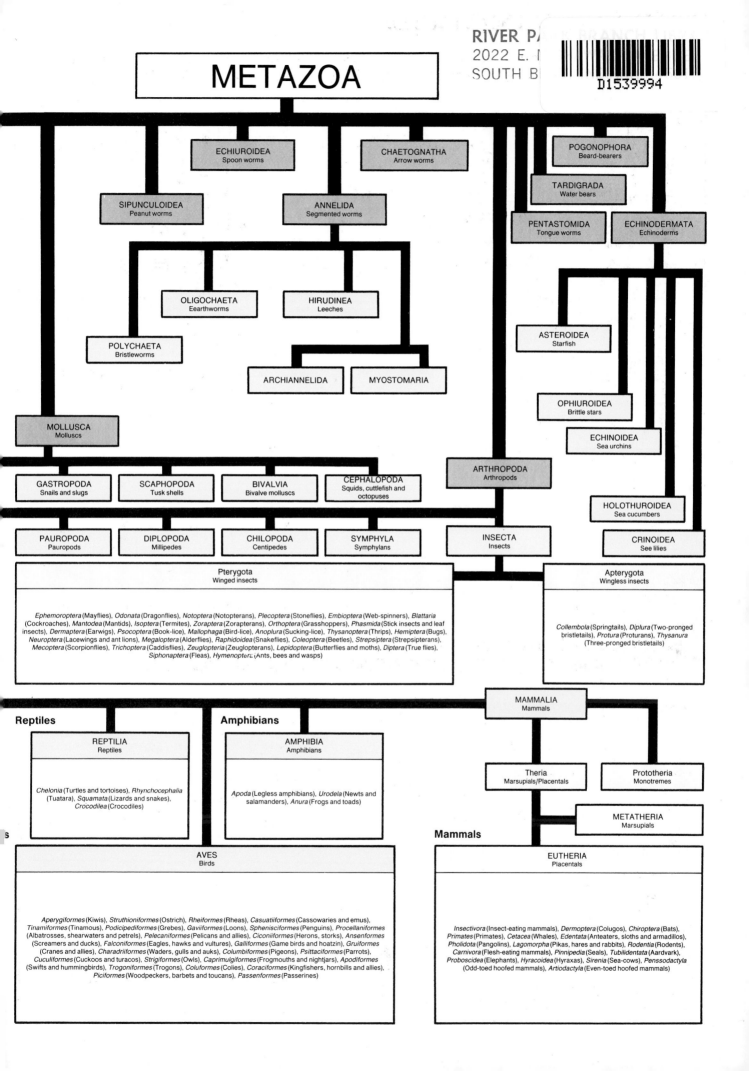

THE
GUINNESS
BOOK OF
ANSWERS

5th edition

GENERAL EDITOR
Norris McWhirter

GUINNESS BOOKS

CONTRIBUTORS

John Arblaster
Dr James Bevan
Robert Dearling
Julian Farino
Stan Greenberg

Peter Johnson
John Marshall
Peter Matthews
David Mondey
Patrick Moore, O.B.E.
Edward Pyatt

Colin C. Smith
Michael Stephenson
Andrew Thomas
H. A. Thompson B.Sc
G. L. Wood FZS

Illustrators: Eddie Botchway, Christine Darter, Pat Gibbon,
Don Roberts
Map work: McCombie/Skinner
Index: Anna Pavord
Design: Alan Hamp

The Guinness book of answers: a handbook of
  general knowledge.—5th ed.
  1. Encyclopedias and dictionaries
  I. McWhirter, Norris
  032.02   AE6

ISBN 0–85112–263–9

Printed and bound in Great Britain by
William Clowes Limited, Beccles and London

CONTENTS

The Calendar

Days of the week

ENGLISH	LATIN	SAXON
Sunday	Dies Solis	Sun's Day
Monday	Dies Lunae	Moon's Day
Tuesday	Dies Martis	Tiu's Day
Wednesday	Dies Mercurii	Woden's Day
Thursday	Dies Jovis	Thor's Day
Friday	Dies Veneris	Frigg's Day
Saturday	Dies Saturni	Saeternes' Day

Tiu was the Anglo-Saxon counterpart of the Nordic Tyr, son of Odin, God of War, who came closest to Mars (Greek, Ares) son of the Roman God Jupiter (Greek, Zeus). Woden was the Anglo-Saxon counterpart of Odin, Nordic dispenser of victory, who came closest to Mercury (Greek, Hermes), the Roman messenger of victory. Thor was the Nordic God of Thunder, eldest son of Odin and nearest to the Roman Jupiter (Greek, Zeus), who was armed with thunder and lightning. Frigg (or Freyja), wife of Odin, was the Nordic Goddess of Love, and equivalent to Venus (Greek, Aphrodite), Goddess of Love in Roman mythology. Thus four of the middle days of the week are named after a mythological husband and wife and their two sons.

The seasons

The four seasons in the northern hemisphere are astronomically speaking:

Spring   from the vernal equinox (20 Mar.) to summer solstice (21 June till AD 2000).

Summer   from the summer solstice (21 June) to the autumnal equinox (23 Sept. in 1985).

Autumn   (or Fall in USA) from the autumnal equinox (23 Sept.) to the winter solstice (21 Dec. or 22 Dec.).

Winter   from the winter solstice (21 Dec.) to the vernal equinox (20 Mar. in 1985).

In the southern hemisphere, of course, autumn corresponds to spring, winter to summer, spring to autumn and summer to winter.

The solstices (from Latin *sol*, sun; *stitium*, standing) are the two times in the year when the sun is farthest from the equator and appears to be still. The equinoxes (from Latin *aequus*, equal; *nox*, night) are the two times in the year when day and night are of equal length when the sun crosses the equator.

The longest day (day with the longest interval between sunrise and sunset) is the day on which the *solstice* falls and in the northern hemisphere occurs on 21 June, or more rarely on 22 June.

Old style (Julian) and new style (Gregorian) dates

The Julian Calendar, introduced by Julius Caesar in 45 BC, on the advice of the Egyptian astronomer Sosigenes, was in use throughout Europe until 1582 when Pope Gregory XIII ordained that 5 Oct. should be called 15 Oct. The discrepancy occurred because of the Augustinian ruling of AD 4 that every fourth year shall be of 366 days and hence include a Leap Day.

Countries switched from the Old Style (Julian) to the New Style (Gregorian) system as follows:

1582	Italy, France, Portugal, Spain
1583	Flanders, Holland, Prussia, Switzerland, and the Roman Catholic states in Germany
1586	Poland
1587	Hungary
1600	Scotland (except St Kilda till 1912)
1700	Denmark and the Protestant states in Germany
1700–40	Sweden (by gradual process)
1752	England and Wales, Ireland and the Colonies, including North America (11-day lag)
1872	Japan (12-day lag)
1912	China (13-day lag)
1915	Bulgaria (13-day lag)
1917	Turkey and the USSR (13-day lag)
1919	Romania and Yugoslavia (13-day lag)
1923	Greece (13-day lag)

LEAP YEAR

Leap years occur in every year the number of which is divisible by four, e.g. 1980, except centennial years, e.g. 1700, 1800, or 1900, which are treated as common or non-leap years *unless* the number of the *century* is divisible by four, e.g. 1600 was a leap year and 2000 will be a leap year.

The whole process is one of compensation for over-retrenchment of the discrepancy between the calendar year of 365 days and the mean solar year of 365·24219878 days. The date when it will be necessary to suppress a further leap year, sometimes assumed to be AD 4000, AD 8000, etc., is not in fact yet clearly specifiable, owing to minute variations in the earth-sun relationship.

The word 'leap' derives from the Old Norse *hlaupár*, indicating a leap in the sense of a jump. The origin probably derives from the observation that in a bissextile (i.e. leap) year any fixed day festival falls on the next day of the week but one to that on which it fell in the preceding year, and not on the next day of the week as happens in common years.

The term bissextile derives literally from a double (bis) day inserted after the sixth (sextile) day before the calends of March. Thus the Julian calendar compensated (albeit inaccurately) for the discrepancy between its year and the mean solar year.

EASTER DAY

Easter, the Sunday on which the resurrection of Christ is celebrated in the Christian world is, unlike Christmas which is fixed, a 'moveable feast'.

The celebration of Easter is believed to have begun in about AD 68. The English word Easter probably derives from *Eostre*, a Saxon goddess whose festival was celebrated about the time of the vernal equinox.

EASTER DAYS AND LEAP YEARS 1980–2000
(Years in bold type are leap years)

1980	6 Apr.	1987	19 Apr.	1994	3 Apr.
1981	19 Apr.	**1988**	3 Apr.	1995	16 Apr.
1982	11 Apr.	1989	26 Mar.	**1996**	7 Apr.
1983	3 Apr.	1990	15 Apr.	1997	30 Mar.
1984	22 Apr.	1991	31 Mar.	1998	12 Apr.
1985	7 Apr.	**1992**	19 Apr.	1999	4 Apr.
1986	30 Mar.	1993	11 Apr.	**2000**	23 Apr.

The date of Easter has been a matter of constant dispute between the eastern and western Christian churches. Much of the calendar of the Christian religion revolves around the date upon which, in any given year, Easter falls and repercussions extend in Christian countries into civil life.

The United Nations in 1949 considered the establishment of a perpetual world calendar, which would automatically and incidentally have fixed Easter, but the proposals were shelved indefinitely in 1956.

The Vatican Council in Rome in October 1963 approved the resolution to fix the date of Easter, subject to the agreement of other Christian churches, by 2058 votes to nine against.

The boldest scheme for calendar reform, which is winning increasing support, is that the year should be divided into four quarters of thirteen weeks, with each day of the year being assigned a fixed day of the week. By this scheme it is thought likely that Easter would always fall on Sunday, 8 Apr. For this calendar to conform with the mean solar year, a 'blank day' would be required each year in addition to the intercalary day in a leap year.

THE ZODIAC

The zodiac (from the Greek *zōdiakos kyklos*, circle of animals) is an unscientific and astrological system devised in Mesopotamia *c.* 3000 BC.

The zodiac is an imaginary belt of pictorial constellations which lie as a backdrop quite arbitrarily 8 degrees on either side of the annual path or ecliptic of the sun. It is divided into twelve sections each of 30 degrees. Each has been allocated a name from the constellation which at one time coincided with that sector. The present lack of coincidence of the zodiacal sectors with the constellations from which they are named, has been caused mainly by the lack of proper allowance for leap days. The old order is nonetheless adhered to.

The traditional 'signs' are:
Aries, the Ram 21 Mar.–19 Apr.
Taurus, the Bull 20 Apr.–20 May
Gemini, the Twins 21 May–21 June
Cancer, the Crab 22 June–22 July
Leo, the Lion 23 July–22 Aug.
Virgo, the Virgin 23 Aug.–22 Sept.
Libra, the Balance 23 Sept.–23 Oct.
Scorpio, the Scorpion 24 Oct.–21 Nov.
Sagittarius, the Archer 22 Nov.–21 Dec.
Capricornus, the Goat 22 Dec.–19 Jan.
Aquarius, the Water Carrier 20 Jan.–18 Feb.
Pisces, the Fishes 19 Feb.–20 Mar.

STANDARD TIME

Until the last quarter of last century the time kept was a local affair, or, in the smaller countries, based on the time kept in the capital city. But the spread of railways across the vaster countries caused great time-keeping confusion to the various railway companies and their passengers. In 1880 Greenwich Mean Time (GMT) became the legal time in the British Isles and by 1884 the movement to establish international time zones was successful.

The world, for this purpose, is divided into 24 zones, or segments, each of 15° of longitude, with twelve that, being to the east, are fast on Greenwich time, and twelve that, being to the west, are slow on Greenwich time, due to the West-to-East rotation of the Earth.

Each zone is 7½° on either side of its central meridian. The International Date Line – with some variations due to the convenience of political geography – runs down the 180° meridian. Sunday becomes Saturday when crossing the date line travelling eastward while Sunday becomes Monday when travelling westward.

A very few countries or divisions of countries do not adhere to the Greenwich system at all and in others no zoning system is used, i.e. the whole nation, despite spanning more than one of the 24 segments, elects to keep the same time. Yet a third group (e.g. India) uses differences of half an hour.

Europe has three zones, part keeping GMT, others mid-European time (i.e. GMT + 1) and the remainder east European time (GMT + 2).

In the United States there are four zones: Eastern, Central, Mountain and Pacific, and these are 5, 6, 7 and 8 hours respectively slow on Greenwich.

The authoritative and complete reference, where the method of time keeping in every place in the world can be found, is *The Nautical Almanac*, published annually by HMSO.

WATCHES AT SEA

A watch at sea is four hours except the period between 4 p.m. and 8 p.m., which is, in the Royal Navy, divided into two short watches termed the first dog watch and the last dog watch. The word dog is here a corruption of 'dodge'. The object of these is to prevent the same men always being on duty during the same hours each day.

Midnight–4 a.m.	Middle Watch
4 a.m.–8 a.m.	Morning Watch
8 a.m.–noon	Forenoon Watch
noon–4 p.m.	Afternoon Watch
4 p.m.–6 p.m.	First Dog Watch
6 p.m.–8 p.m.	*Last Dog Watch
8 p.m.–Midnight	First Watch

* Called Second Dog in Merchant Navy.

Time is marked by bells – one stroke for each half-hour elapsed during a watch which thus ends on 8 bells or 4 bells for a dog watch. The New Year is brought in with 16 bells.

SUNRISE, SUNSET AND TWILIGHT
The Nautical Almanac gives the GMT of sunrise and sunset for each two degrees of latitude for every third day in the year. The sunrise is the instant when the rim of the sun appears above the horizon, and the sunset when the last segment disappears below the horizon. But because of the Earth's atmosphere, the transition from day to night and vice versa is a gradual process, the length of which varies according to the declination of the sun and the latitude of the observer. The intermediate stages are called twilight.

There are three sorts of twilight:

Civil twilight. This occurs when the centre of the sun is 6° below the horizon. Before this moment in the morning and after it in the evening ordinary outdoor activities are impossible without artificial light.

Nautical twilight. This occurs when the sun is 12° below the horizon. Before this time in the morning and after it in the evening the sea horizon is invisible.

Astronomical twilight. This is the moment when the centre of the sun is 18° below the horizon. Before this time in the morning or after it in the evening there is a complete absence of sunlight.

WEDDING ANNIVERSARIES
The choice of object or material attached to specific anniversaries is in no sense 'official'. The list below is a combination of commercial and traditional usage.

First/Cotton	**Fourteenth**/Ivory
Second/Paper	**Fifteenth**/Crystal
Third/Leather	**Twentieth**/China
Fourth/Fruit, flowers	**Twenty-fifth**/Silver
Fifth/Wooden	**Thirtieth**/Pearl
Sixth/Sugar	**Thirty-fifth**/Coral
Seventh/Wool, copper	**Fortieth**/Ruby
Eighth/Bronze, pottery	**Forty-fifth**/Sapphire
Ninth/Pottery, willow	**Fiftieth**/Golden
Tenth/Tin	**Fifty-fifth**/Emerald
Eleventh/Steel	**Sixtieth**/Diamond
Twelfth/Silk, linen	**Seventieth**/Platinum
Thirteenth/Lace	

Days of the year: births, deaths & events

Below are given selected dates of birth and death, where accurately known, of people generally accepted as being famous or infamous. Also included are the dates of some notable events.

Note: b., born; d., died; bapt., baptized (where birth-date not established)

JANUARY (31 days)

DERIVATION: Latin, *Januarius*, or *Ianuarius*, named after Janus, the two-faced Roman god of doorways (*ianuae*) and archways (*iani*), as presiding over the 'entrance', or beginning, of the year.

1 *Daily Universal Register* became *The Times* 1788; Baron Pierre de Coubertin b. 1863; E M Forster b. 1879
2 Titus Livius (Livy) d. AD 18; Publius Ovidius Naso (Ovid) d. AD 18
3 Marcus Tullius Cicero b. 106 BC; Clement (later Earl) Attlee b. 1883
4 Louis Braille b. 1809; Augustus John b. 1878; T S Eliot d. 1965
5 Edward the Confessor d. 1066; German National Socialist Party founded 1919
6 Joan of Arc b. *c.* 1412; Louis Braille d. 1852; Jet propulsion invented 1944
7 Sir Thomas Lawrence d. 1830; St Bernadette of Lourdes b. 1844
8 Marco Polo d. 1324; Galileo Galilei d. 1642; Lord Baden-Powell d. 1941
9 Ex-Emperor Napoleon III d. 1873; Richard Nixon b. 1913
10 Penny Post began in Britain 1840; League of Nations founded 1920
11 Alexander Hamilton b. 1755; Thomas Hardy d. 1928
12 Edmund Burke b. 1729; Jack London b. 1876; Agatha Christie d. 1975
13 George Fox b. 1691; James Joyce d. 1941
14 Albert Schweitzer b. 1875; Charles Lutwidge Dodgson (alias Lewis Carroll) d. 1898; Earl of Avon d. 1977
15 Act of Supremacy 1535; Ivor Novello b. 1893; Martin Luther King b. 1929
16 Ivan the Terrible crowned 1547; Federal prohibition of alcohol introduced, USA 1920
17 Benjamin Franklin b. 1706; David Lloyd George b. 1863
18 A A Milne b. 1822; Scott reached South Pole 1912; Rudyard Kipling d. 1936
19 James Watt b. 1736; Edgar Allan Poe b. 1809; Paul Cézanne b. 1839
20 David Garrick b. 1779; John Ruskin d. 1900; King George V d. 1936
21 Vladimir Ulyanov (Lenin) d. 1924; Eric Blair (George Orwell) d. 1950
22 Francis Bacon (later Viscount St Albans) b. 1561; George (later Lord) Byron b. 1788; Queen Victoria d. 1901
23 William Pitt (the younger) d. 1806; Edouard Manet b. 1832
24 Frederick the Great of Prussia b. 1712; Gold discovered in California 1848; Sir Winston Churchill d. 1965
25 Robert Burns b. 1759; Somerset Maugham b. 1874
26 Douglas MacArthur b. 1880; Gen. Charles Gordon killed 1885; Baird's first demonstration of TV, London 1926
27 Wolfgang Amadeus Mozart b. 1756; Giuseppe Verdi d. 1901
28 Charlemagne d. 814; King Henry VIII d. 1547; Sir Francis Drake d. 1596
29 Victoria Cross instituted 1856; Anton Chekhov b. 1860; W C Fields b. 1880
30 King Charles I executed 1649; Franklin Roosevelt b. 1882; Mohandas Gandhi assassinated 1948; Stanley Holloway d. 1982
31 Franz Schubert b. 1797; *Great Eastern* launched 1858; Anna Pavlova b. 1881

FEBRUARY (28 or 29 days)

DERIVATION: Latin, *Februarius* (*februare*, to purify), from *februa*, a festival of purification held on 15 Feb.

1 Victor Herbert b. 1859; British State Labour Exchanges opened 1910
2 Nell Gwyn b. 1650; Fritz Kreisler b. 1875; Jascha Heifetz b. 1901; German capitulation at Stalingrad 1943
3 Felix Mendelssohn-Bartholdy b. 1809; Yalta conference began 1945
4 Thomas Carlyle b. 1881; Submarine warfare begun by Germany 1915
5 Sir Robert Peel b. 1788; John Dunlop b. 1840
6 King Charles II d. 1685; Ronald Reagan b. 1911; King George VI d. and Queen Elizabeth II succeeded to throne 1952; Ben Nicholson d. 1982
7 Sir Thomas More b. 1478; Charles Dickens b. 1812
8 Mary, Queen of Scots, executed 1587; Russo-Japanese War began 1904
9 Edward (later Lord) Carson b. 1854; Fyodor Dostoyevsky d. 1881
10 Académie Française founded 1635; Charles Lamb b. 1775; Harold Macmillan b. 1894; Bertolt Brecht b. 1898
11 Thomas Alva Edison b. 1847; Vatican City established 1929
12 Last invasion of Britain 1797; Abraham Lincoln b. 1809; Charles Darwin b. 1809; Marie Lloyd b. 1870
13 Massacre of the MacDonald clan at Glencoe 1692; Richard Wagner d. 1883; Yuri Andropov d. 1984
14 Nicolaus Copernicus b. 1473; Robert Malthus b. 1766; Captain James Cook killed 1779
15 Galileo Galilei b. 1564; Jeremy Bentham b. 1748; Ernest Shackleton b. 1874
16 Heinrich Heine d. 1856; George Macaulay Trevelyan b. 1876; John McEnroe b. 1959
17 Molière d. 1673; Edward German b. 1862; Geronimo d. 1909
18 Martin Luther d. 1546; Michelangelo d. 1564; John Bunyan's *Pilgrim's Progress* published 1678
19 David Garrick b. 1717; André Gide d. 1951
20 King James I of Scotland murdered 1437; Jimmy Greaves b. 1940; Percy Grainger d. 1961
21 John Henry Newman b. 1801; W H Auden b. 1907
22 George Washington b. 1732; Robert (later Lord) Baden-Powell b. 1857; Oskar Kokoschka d. 1980
23 Samuel Pepys b. 1633; George Frideric Handel b. 1685; John Keats d. 1821
24 Emperor Charles V b. 1500; Henry Cavendish d. 1810
25 Sir Christopher Wren d. 1723; Enrico Caruso b. 1873
26 Victor Hugo b. 1802; William F Cody ('Buffalo Bill') b. 1846
27 Henry Wadsworth Longfellow b. 1807; British Labour Party founded 1900
28 Vatslav Nijinsky b. 1890; Relief of Ladysmith 1900; Henry James d. 1916
29 Gioacchino Rossini b. 1792

MARCH (31 days)

DERIVATION: Latin, *Martius*, the month of Mars, the Roman god of war and the protector of vegetation.

1 Frédéric Chopin b. 1810; Oskar Kokoschka b. 1886; Robert Lowell b. 1917
2 John Wesley d. 1791; Kurt Weill b. 1900; D H Lawrence d. 1930
3 Robert Adam d. 1792; Alexander Graham Bell b. 1847; Russian serfs freed 1861; Henry Wood b. 1869
4 Saladin d. 1193; US Constitution in force 1789; Comintern formed 1919
5 William (later Lord) Beveridge b. 1879; Churchill's Iron Curtain speech 1946; Marshal Iosif Stalin d. 1953
6 Michelangelo b. 1475; Elizabeth Barrett Browning b. 1806; Ivor Novello d. 1951
7 Maurice Ravel b. 1875; Bell's telephone patented 1876
8 King William III d. 1702; Hector Berlioz d. 1869; Sir Thomas Beecham d. 1961; Sir William Walton d. 1983
9 Amerigo Vespucci b. 1454; William Cobbett b. 1763; Yuri Gagarin b. 1934
10 First telephone call 1876; Arthur Honegger b. 1892; Jan Masaryk d. 1948
11 Sir Harold Wilson b. 1916; German troops entered Austria 1938; Sir Alexander Fleming d. 1955
12 Cesare Borgia killed 1507; Russian revolution began 1917; Sun Yat-sen d. 1925
13 Tsar Alexander II of Russia assassinated 1881
14 Johann Strauss (the elder) b. 1804; Mrs Isabella Beeton b. 1836; Albert Einstein b. 1879; Karl Marx d. 1883; First trans-Atlantic broadcast 1925
15 Julius Caesar assassinated 44 BC; Andrew Jackson b. 1767
16 Tiberius, Emperor of Rome, d. AD 37; Lord Beveridge d. 1963

17 Marcus Aurelius d. AD 180; Edmund Kean b. 1787
18 Ivan the Terrible d. 1584; Sir Robert Walpole, Earl of Orford, d. 1745
19 David Livingstone b. 1813; Sergey Diaghilev b. 1872
20 Sir Isaac Newton d. 1727; Napoleon's 'Hundred Days' began 1815
21 Johann Sebastian Bach b. 1685; Modest Mussorgsky b. 1839
22 Anthony van Dyck b. 1599; Wolfgang von Goethe d. 1832
23 Stamp Act 1765; Stendhal d. 1842; Alfred (later Viscount) Milner b. 1854
24 Queen Elizabeth I d. 1603; Union of English and Scottish Crowns 1603
25 Béla Bartók b. 1881; Claude Debussy d. 1918; Treaty of Rome signed by six countries to found EEC 1957
26 Ludwig van Beethoven d. 1827; Earl Lloyd-George of Dwyfor d. 1945
27 King James I d. 1625; James Callaghan b. 1912; Arnold Bennett d. 1931
28 Britain and France entered Crimean War 1854; Spanish Civil War ended 1939; Dwight Eisenhower d. 1969
29 Charles Wesley d. 1788; Sir William Walton b. 1902
30 Francisco de Goya b. 1746; Vincent van Gogh b. 1853; Séan O'Casey b. 1880
31 Joseph Haydn b. 1732; John Constable d. 1837; Charlotte Brontë d. 1855; Jesse Owens d. 1980

APRIL (30 days)

DERIVATION: Latin, *Aprilis*, from *aperire* (to open), the season when trees and flowers begin to 'open'.

1 Prince Otto von Bismarck b. 1815; Royal Air Force formed 1918
2 Charlemagne b. 742; Hans Christian Andersen b. 1805; Emile Zola b. 1840
3 Pony Express established in USA 1860; Johannes Brahms d. 1897
4 Oliver Goldsmith d. 1774; North Atlantic Treaty signed 1949
5 Joseph (later Lord) Lister b. 1827; Algernon Charles Swinburne b. 1837
6 King Richard I d. 1199; Raphael prob. b. 1483, d. 1520; USA entered First World War 1917; PAYE introduced in Britain 1944; Igor Stravinsky d. 1971
7 Dick Turpin hanged 1739; William Wordsworth b. 1770
8 Entente Cordiale signed 1904; Vatslav Nijinsky d. 1950; Pablo Picasso d. 1973
9 Francis Bacon (Viscount St Albans) d. 1626; US Civil War ended 1865
10 William Booth b. 1829; Algernon Charles Swinburne d. 1909
11 Treaty of Utrecht 1713; Sir Gerald du Maurier d. 1934
12 US Civil War began 1861; Franklin Roosevelt d. 1945; Yuri Gagarin made first manned Earth orbit 1961; Joe Louis d. 1981
13 John Dryden became first Poet Laureate 1668; Thomas Jefferson b. 1743
14 George Frideric Handel d. 1759; Ernest Bevin d. 1951
15 Leonardo da Vinci b. 1452; Abraham Lincoln d. 1865 (wounded by assassin); *Titanic* sank 1912; Jean-Paul Sartre d. 1980
16 Battle of Culloden 1746; Francisco de Goya d. 1828; Charles Chaplin b. 1889
17 John Pierpoint Morgan b. 1837; Nikita Khrushchev b. 1894
18 Judge Jeffreys d. 1689; San Francisco earthquake 1906; Republic of Ireland established 1949; Albert Einstein d. 1955; Zimbabwe independent 1980
19 Lord Byron d. 1824; Benjamin Disraeli (Earl of Beaconsfield) d. 1881; Charles Darwin d. 1882; Pierre Curie b. 1906
20 Napoleon III b. 1808; Adolf Hitler b. 1889; Bram Stoker d. 1912
21 Foundation of Rome 753 BC; Charlotte Brontë b. 1816; Mark Twain d. 1910; Queen Elizabeth II b. 1926

22 Vladimir Ulyanov (Lenin) b. 1870; Yehudi Menuhin b. 1916
23 William Shakespeare prob b. 1564, d. 1616; William Wordsworth d. 1850
24 Daniel Defoe d. 1731; Anthony Trollope b. 1815; Stafford Cripps b. 1889
25 Oliver Cromwell b. 1599; Guglielmo Marconi b. 1874
26 Marcus Aurelius b. AD 121; David Hume b. 1711; Emma, Lady Hamilton b. 1765
27 Edward Gibbon b. 1737; Samuel Morse b. 1791; Herbert Spencer b. 1820; Ulysses S. Grant b. 1822
28 Mutiny on the *Bounty* began 1789; Benito Mussolini killed 1945; Japan regained independence 1952
29 William Randolph Hearst b. 1863; Emperor Hirohito of Japan b. 1901; Sir Alfred Hitchcock d. 1980
30 George Washington became first US President 1789; Adolf Hitler committed suicide 1945

MAY (31 days)

DERIVATION: Latin, *Maius*, either from Maia, an obscure goddess, or from *maiores* (elders), on the grounds that the month honoured old people, as June honoured the young.

1 Duke of Wellington b. 1769; Great Exhibition opened at Crystal Palace 1851; David Livingstone d. 1873
2 Leonardo da Vinci d. 1519; Catherine the Great of Russia b. 1729
3 Niccolò Machiavelli b. 1469; Golda Meir b. 1898; King George VI opened Festival of Britain 1951
4 Epsom Derby first run 1780; Thomas Huxley b. 1825; General Strike began 1926; Marshal Tito d. 1980
5 Søren Kierkegaard b. 1813; Karl Marx b. 1818; Napoleon Bonaparte d. 1821
6 Sigmund Freud b. 1856; First 4 min. mile by Roger Bannister, Oxford 1954
7 Robert Browning b. 1812; Johannes Brahms b. 1833; Pyotr Tchaikovsky b. 1840; *Lusitania* sunk 1915
8 John Stuart Mill d. 1873; Harry Truman b. 1884; Paul Gauguin d. 1903; VE-Day in Britain 1945
9 John Brown b. 1800; J M (later Sir James) Barrie b. 1860
10 Winston Churchill became Prime Minister 1940
11 William Pitt, Earl of Chatham, d. 1778; Irving Berlin b. 1888; Bob Marley d. 1981
12 Florence Nightingale b. 1820; General Strike ended 1926
13 Arthur Sullivan b. 1842; Viscount Milner d. 1925; Fridtjof Nansen d. 1930
14 Home Guard formed in Britain 1940; State of Israel proclaimed 1948
15 Judge Jeffreys b. 1645; Pierre Curie b. 1859; Sir Robert Menzies d. 1978
16 First film 'Oscars' awarded 1929; Dambusters' raid 1943
17 Edward Jenner b. 1749; Mafeking relieved 1900; Ayatollah Ruhollah Khomeini b. 1900
18 Bertrand (later 3rd Earl) Russel b. 1872; Gustav Mahler d. 1911; Pope John Paul II b. 1920
19 St Dunstan d. 988; Anne Boleyn executed 1536; W E Gladstone d. 1898
20 Christopher Columbus d. 1506; John Stuart Mill b. 1806
21 Alexander Pope b. 1688; Elizabeth Fry b. 1780; Charles Lindbergh completed first solo trans-Atlantic flight 1927
22 Richard Wagner b. 1813; Arthur Conan Doyle b. 1859
23 Thomas Hood b. 1799; Kit Carson d. 1868; Henrik Ibsen d. 1906
24 Nicolaus Copernicus d. 1543; Queen Victoria b. 1819
25 Ralph Waldo Emerson b. 1803; Max Aitken (later Lord Beaverbrook) b. 1879; Josip Broz (Tito) b. 1892

26 John Churchill (later Duke of Marlborough) b. 1650; Samuel Pepys d. 1703; Al Jolson d. 1886
27 John Calvin d. 1564; Habeas Corpus Act 1679; Dunkirk evacuation began 1940; Jawaharlal Nehru d. 1964
28 King George I b. 1660; William Pitt (the younger) b. 1759; 1st Earl Russell d. 1878; Duke of Windsor d. 1972
29 John F Kennedy b. 1917; Mount Everest first climbed 1953
30 Joan of Arc executed 1431; Peter Paul Rubens d. 1640; Voltaire d. 1778
31 Pepys' Diary ends 1669; Joseph Haydn d. 1809; Battle of Jutland 1916

JUNE (30 days)

DERIVATION: Latin, *Junius*, either from the goddess Juno or from *iuniores* (young people), on the grounds that the month is dedicated to youth.

1 Brigham Young b. 1801; John Masefield b. 1878
2 Thomas Hardy b. 1840; Coronation of Queen Elizabeth II 1953
3 Johann Strauss (the younger) d. 1899
4 King George III b. 1738; Giacomo Casanova d. 1798; Ex-Kaiser Wilhelm II d. 1941; Rome liberated 1944
5 Adam Smith bapt. 1723; John Maynard Keynes b. 1883; Marshall Plan launched 1947
6 Aleksandr Pushkin b. 1799; Thomas Mann b. 1875; D-Day 1944; Bjorn Borg b. 1956
7 Robert I ('The Bruce') d. 1329; George ('Beau') Brummell b. 1778
8 Muhammad d. 632; Edward, the Black Prince, d. 1376; Thomas Paine d. 1809
9 Peter the Great of Russia b. 1672; George Stephenson b. 1781; Charles Dickens d. 1870; Cole Porter d. 1893
10 Prince Philip, Duke of Edinburgh, b. 1921; Frederick Delius d. 1934
11 Ben Jonson b. 1573; John Constable b. 1776; Richard Strauss b. 1864
12 Charles Kingsley b. 1819; Anthony Eden (later Earl of Avon) b. 1897
13 Alexander the Great d. 323 BC; W B Yeats b. 1865; Boxer Rising in China 1900
14 Battle of Naseby 1645; G K Chesterton d. 1936; John Logie Baird d. 1946; Battle of the Falkland Islands ends 1982
15 Magna Carta sealed 1215; Edward, the Black Prince, b. 1330
16 Duke of Marlborough d. 1722; Earl Alexander of Tunis d. 1969
17 John Wesley b. 1703; Battle of Bunker Hill 1775; Igor Stravinsky b. 1882
18 USA declared war on Britain 1812; Battle of Waterloo 1815
19 Douglas (later Earl) Haig b. 1861; Sir James Barrie d. 1937
20 British captives held in Black Hole of Calcutta 1756; Jacques Offenbach b. 1819; King William IV d. 1837
21 Niccolò Machiavelli d. 1527; Inigo Jones d. 1652; Jean-Paul Sartre b. 1905; Nikolay Rimsky-Korsakov d. 1908; Prince William b. 1982
22 Germany invaded the USSR 1941; Darius Milhaud d. 1974
23 Battle of Plassey 1757; King Edward VIII (later Duke of Windsor) b. 1894
24 Battle of Bannockburn 1314; Lucrezia Borgia d. 1519; John Hampden d. 1643
25 Custer's Last Stand 1876; Louis of Battenberg (later Earl Mountbatten of Burma) b. 1900; Korean War began 1950
26 King George IV d. 1830; Corn Laws repealed 1846; UN Charter signed 1945
27 Charles Stewart Parnell b. 1846; First colour TV 1929
28 Peter Paul Rubens b. 1577; Archduke Franz Ferdinand assassinated 1914
29 Elizabeth Barrett Browning d. 1861; Thomas Huxley d. 1895
30 John Gay b. 1685; Stanley Spencer b. 1891; Nancy Mitford d. 1973

JULY (31 days)

DERIVATION; Latin, *Julius*, after Gaius Julius Caesar (b. 12 July, probably in 100 BC, d. 15 March 44 BC), the Roman soldier and statesman (Formerly known by the Romans as *Quintilis*, the fifth month.)

1 Aurore Dupin (alias George Sand) b. 1804; Louis Blériot b. 1872; Princess of Wales b. 1961
2 Thomas Cranmer b. 1489; Sir Robert Peel d. 1850; Joseph Chamberlain d. 1914; Ernest Hemingway d. 1961
3 Robert Adam b. 1728; Joel Chandler Harris ('Uncle Remus') d. 1908
4 US Declaration of Independence approved 1776; Thomas Jefferson d. 1826
5 Cecil Rhodes b. 1853; Britain's National Health Service inaugurated 1948
6 King Henry II d. 1189; Guy de Maupassant d. 1893; Aneurin Bevan d. 1960; William Faulkner d. 1962
7 King Edward I d. 1307; Gustav Mahler b. 1860; Marc Chagall b. 1887; Sir Arthur Conan Doyle d. 1930
8 Edmund Burke d. 1797; Percy Bysshe Shelley d. 1822; Joseph Chamberlain b. 1836; John D Rockefeller b. 1839
9 Edward Heath b. 1916; King Hassan II of Morocco b. 1929
10 Rodrigo Díaz de Vivar ('El Cid') d. 1099; John Calvin b. 1509
11 Robert I ('The Bruce') b. 1274; George Gershwin d. 1937; *Skylab I* disintegrated 1979
12 Julius Caesar b. 100 BC; Erasmus d. 1536; Amedeo Modigliani b. 1884
13 Arnold Schoenberg d. 1951
14 Storming of the Bastille began 1789; Gerald Ford b. 1913
15 Inigo Jones b. 1573; Rembrandt van Rijn b. 1606; Anton Chekhov d. 1904
16 Joshua Reynolds b. 1723; First atomic bomb exploded 1945
17 Adam Smith b. 1790; *Punch* published 1841; Spanish Civil War began 1936
18 Petrarch d. 1374; William Makepeace Thackeray b. 1811; Jane Austen d. 1817
19 Lady Jane Grey deposed 1553; Edgar Degas b. 1834
20 Petrarch b. 1304; Guglielmo Marconi d. 1937; First Moon landing by man 1969
21 Robert Burns d. 1796; Ernest Hemingway b. 1899; Dame Ellen Terry d. 1928
22 Battle of Salamanca 1812
23 Alan Brooke (later Viscount Alanbrooke) b. 1883; Gen. Ulysses S Grant d. 1885
24 Simón Bolívar b. 1783; Alexandre Dumas b. 1802; Robert Graves b. 1895
25 Arthur Balfour b. 1848; Louis Blériot flew Channel 1909
26 George Bernard Shaw b. 1856; Carl Jung b. 1875; Aldous Huxley b. 1894
27 Hilaire Belloc b. 1870; Gertrude Stein d. 1946; Korean War ended 1953; Tongshan earthquake 1976
28 Antonio Vivaldi d. 1741; Johann Sebastian Bach d. 1750
29 Spanish Armada defeated 1588; Robert Schumann d. 1856; Benito Mussolini b. 1833; Vincent van Gogh d. 1890; Prince Charles and Lady Diana Spencer m. 1981
30 William Penn d. 1718; Henry Ford b. 1863; Prince Otto von Bismarck d. 1898
31 St Ignatius of Loyola d. 1556; Franz Liszt d. 1886

AUGUST (31 days)

DERIVATION: Latin, *Augustus*, after Augustus Caesar (born Gaius Octavius), the first Roman emperor. (Originally called *Sextilis*, the sixth month.)

1 Queen Anne d. 1714; Battle of the Nile 1798; Herman Melville b. 1819
2 King William II d. 1100; Thomas Gainsborough d. 1788; Enrico Caruso d. 1921
3 Rupert Brooke b. 1887; Joseph Conrad d. 1924; Colette d. 1954
4 Percy Bysshe Shelley b. 1792; Queen Elizabeth the Queen Mother b. 1900; Britain declared war on German 1914
5 Guy de Maupassant b. 1850; Naum Gabo b. 1890; Neil Armstrong b. 1930; Richard Burton d. 1984
6 Alfred (later Lord) Tennyson b. 1809; Alexander Fleming b. 1881; Atomic bomb dropped on Hiroshima 1945
7 British Summer Time Act 1925; Konstantin Stanislavsky d. 1938
8 Mont Blanc first climbed 1786; Emiliano Zapata b. 1879; Battle of Britain began 1940; Great Train Robbery 1963
9 John Dryden b. 1631; Atomic bomb dropped on Nagasaki 1945; US President Richard Nixon resigned 1974
10 Royal Observatory founded at Greenwich 1675; Herbert Hoover b. 1874
11 Cardinal John Henry Newman b. 1890; Andrew Carnegie d. 1919
12 Robert Southey b. 1774; George Stephenson d. 1848; Tokyo air crash 1985
13 Battle of Blenheim 1704; Florence Nightingale d. 1910; Fidel Castro b. 1927; H G Wells d. 1946
14 John Galsworthy b. 1867; Viscount Northcliffe d. 1922; W R Hearst d. 1951; Bertolt Brecht d. 1956; J B Priestley d. 1984
15 Napoleon Bonaparte b. 1769; Panama Canal opened 1014; VJ-Day 1945; India and Pakistan independent 1947
16 Peterloo Massacre 1819; Menachem Begin b. 1913; Cyprus became independent 1960; Elvis Presley d. 1977
17 Frederick the Great d. 1786; Davy Crockett b. 1786; Mae West b. 1892
18 Lord John (later 1st Earl Russell) b. 1792; Berlin Wall completed 1961
19 Blaise Pascal b. 1662; James Watt d. 1819; Sir Jacob Epstein d. 1959
20 St Bernard of Clairvaux d. 1153; Gen. William Booth d. 1912; Groucho Marx d. 1977
21 Princess Margaret b. 1930; Leo Trotsky d. 1940 (wounded by assassin); Invasion of Czechoslovakia 1968
22 English Civil War began 1642; Claude Debussy b. 1862
23 Rudolph Valentino d. 1926; World Council of Churches formed 1948
24 Vesuvius erupted AD 79; William Wilberforce b. 1759
25 David Hume d. 1776; Michael Faraday d. 1867; Paris liberated 1944
26 Battle of Crécy 1346; Sir Robert Walpole b. 1676; Prince Albert b. 1819
27 Confucius b. 551 BC; Titian d. 1576; Krakatoa erupted 1883; Man Ray b. 1890; Sir Donald Bradman b. 1908; Earl Mountbatten assassinated 1979
28 St Augustine of Hippo d. 430; Wolfgang von Goethe b. 1749
29 John Locke b. 1632; Frans Hals d. 1666; Eamon de Valera d. 1975
30 Mary Shelley b. 1797; Ernest (later Lord) Rutherford b. 1871
31 John Bunyan d. 1688; Clive Lloyd b. 1944

SEPTEMBER (30 days)

DERIVATION: Latin, from *septem* (seven), as it was originally the seventh month.

1 King Louis XIV of France d. 1715; Germany invaded Poland 1939
2 Great Fire of London began 1666; Thomas Telford d. 1834
3 Oliver Cromwell d. 1658; Britain declared war on Germany 1939
4 Anton Bruckner b. 1824; Edvard Grieg d. 1907; Albert Schweitzer d. 1965
5 King Louis XIV of France b. 1638; Jesse James b. 1847
6 *Mayflower* sailed from Plymouth 1620
7 Queen Elizabeth I b. 1533; London Blitz began 1940
8 King Richard I b. 1157; Antonín Dvořák b. 1841; First V2 rocket landed in England 1944; Richard Strauss d. 1949

9 William the Conqueror d. 1087; Battle of Flodden Field 1513; Cardinal Richelieu b. 1585; Leo Tolstoy b. 1828; Mao Zedong (Mao Tse-tung) d. 1976
10 Mungo Park b. 1771
11 D H Lawrence b. 1885; Jan Smuts d. 1950
12 Herbert Asquith b. 1852; Jesse Owens b. 1913; Robert Lowell d. 1977
13 Gen. James Wolfe d. 1759; J B Priestley b. 1894
14 Gregorian Calendar adopted in Britain 1752; Duke of Wellington d. 1852
15 James Fenimore Cooper b. 1789; Isambard Kingdom Brunel d. 1859; Prince Henry (Harry) b. 1984
16 King Henry V b. 1387; Andrew Bonar Law b. 1858; Maria Callas d. 1977
17 Francis Chichester b. 1901; NATO established 1949
18 Samuel Johnson b. 1709; Greta Garbo b. 1905
19 Battle of Poitiers 1356; Dr. Thomas Barnardo d. 1905; Emil Zátopek b. 1922
20 Eton College founded 1440; George Robey b. 1869; Jean Sibelius d. 1957
21 John McAdam b. 1756; Sir Walter Scott d. 1832; H G Wells b. 1866
22 Michael Faraday b. 1791; Commercial television began in Britain 1955
23 Augustus, Emperor of Rome, b. 63 BC; Sigmund Freud d. 1939
24 Horatio (Horace) Walpole b. 1717
25 Samuel Butler d. 1680; Relief of Lucknow 1857; William Faulkner b. 1897; Dmitri Shostakovich b. 1906
26 T S Eliot b. 1888; *Queen Mary* launched 1934
27 St Vincent de Paul d. 1660; Stockton–Darlington Railway opened 1825; *Queen Elizabeth* launched 1938
28 Georges Clemenceau b. 1841; Louis Pasteur d. 1895; W H Auden d. 1973
29 Battle of Marathon 490 BC; Robert (later Lord) Clive b. 1725; Horatio Nelson b. 1758; Emile Zole d. 1902
30 St Thérèse d. 1897; David Oistrakh b. 1908; First BBC TV broadcast 1929

OCTOBER (31 days)

DERIVATION: Latin, from *octo* (eight), originally the eighth month.

1 Vladimir Horowitz b. 1904; Jimmy Carter b. 1924
2 Mohandas Gandhi b. 1869; Groucho Marx b. 1890; Graham Greene b. 1904
3 St Francis of Assisi d. 1226; William Morris d. 1896
4 Rembrandt van Rijn d. 1669; Damon Runyon b. 1884; Buster Keaton b. 1895; *Sputnik I* launched 1957
5 Jacques Offenbach d. 1880; Tea rationing ended in Britain 1952
6 Charles Stewart Parnell d. 1891; Lord Tennyson d. 1892; President Anwar Sadat assassinated 1981
7 William Laud b. 1573; Edgar Allan Poe d. 1849; Niels Bohr b. 1885
8 Henry Fielding d. 1754; Juan Perón b. 1895; Earl Attlee d. 1967
9 Camille Saint-Saëns b. 1835; Battle of Ypres began 1914; Pope Pius XII d. 1958; Ché Guevara killed 1967
10 Henry Cavendish b. 1731; Giuseppe Verdi b. 1813; Fridtjof Nansen b. 1861
11 H J Heinz b. 1844; Anton Bruckner d. 1896; Bobby Charlton b. 1937
12 Robert E Lee d. 1870; Ralph Vaughan Williams b. 1872; Nurse Edith Cavell executed 1915
13 Emilie Le Breton (Lillie Langtry) b. 1853; Sir Henry Irving d. 1905; Margaret Thatcher b. 1925
14 Battle of Hastings 1066; William Penn b. 1644; Dwight Eisenhower b. 1890
15 Publius Vergilius Maro (Virgil) b. 70 BC; Friedrich Wilhelm Nietzsche b. 1844; Marie Stopes b. 1880
16 Marie Antoinette executed 1793; Oscar

Wilde b. 1854; Eugene O'Neill b. 1888; Pope John Paul II elected 1978

17 Sir Philip Sidney d. 1586; Frédéric Chopin d. 1849
18 Viscount Palmerston d. 1865; Charles Gounod d. 1893; Thomas Alva Edison d. 1931; Martina Navratilova b. 1956
19 King John d. 1216; Jonathan Swift d. 1745; Lord Rutherford d. 1937
20 Sir Christopher Wren b. 1632; Viscount Palmerston b. 1784
21 Samuel Taylor Coleridge b. 1772; Battle of Trafalgar (Nelson d.) 1805
22 Franz Liszt b. 1811; Sarah Bernhardt b. 1844; Pablo Casals d. 1973
23 W G Grace b. 1915; Edson Pelé b. 1940; Battle of El Alamein began 1942; Al Jolson d. 1950
24 Sybil Thorndike b. 1882; UN Organization established 1945
25 Battle of Agincourt 1415; Charge of the Light Brigade at Balaklava 1854
26 King Alfred d. 899; William Hogarth d. 1764; Lev Bronstein (Trotsky) b. 1879
27 Erasmus b. 1466; Capt. James Cook b. 1728; Theodore Roosevelt b. 1858
28 John Locke d. 1704; Evelyn Waugh b. 1903
29 Sir Walter Raleigh executed 1618; James Boswell b. 1740; A J Ayer b. 1910; New York stock market crash 1929
30 King George II b. 1683; John Adams b. 1735; Andrew Bonar Law d. 1923
31 John Keats b. 1795; Chiang Kai-shek b. 1887; Augustus John d. 1961; Indira Ghandi assassinated 1984

NOVEMBER (30 days)

DERIVATION: Latin, from *novem* (nine), originally the ninth month.

1 Benvenuto Cellini b. 1500; First hydrogen bomb exploded 1952
2 Marie Antoinette b. 1755; George Bernard Shaw d. 1950
3 André Malraux b. 1901; Henri Matisse d. 1954
4 Felix Mendelssohn-Bartholdy d. 1847; Wilfred Owen killed 1918; Jacques Tati d. 1982
5 Gunpowder Plot 1605; Maurice Utrillo d. 1955; Lester Piggott b. 1935
6 John Philip Sousa b. 1854; Pyotr Tchaikovsky d. 1893
7 Marja Sklodowska (later Marie Curie) b. 1867; Bolshevik revolution 1917
8 John Milton d. 1674; César Franck d. 1890; Munich Putsch 1923
9 Neville Chamberlain d. 1940; General Charles de Gaulle d. 1970
10 Martin Luther b. 1483; H M Stanley met David Livingstone at Ujiji 1871; Leonid Brezhnev d. 1982

11 Fyodor Dostoyevsky b. 1821; Armistice Day 1918; Space shuttle *Columbia* launched 1982
12 King Canute d. 1035; Sir John Hawkins d. 1595; Auguste Rodin b. 1840
13 St Augustine b. 354; Edward III b. 1312; Robert Louis Stevenson b. 1850
14 Nell Gwyn d. 1687; Jawaharlal Nehru b. 1889; Prince of Wales b. 1948
15 William Pitt (the elder) b. 1708
16 Tiberius b. 42 BC; King Henry III d. 1272; Suez Canal opened 1869
17 Catherine the Great b. 1796; Bernard (later Viscount) Montgomery b. 1887
18 W S (later Sir William) Gilbert b. 1836; Amelita Galli-Curci b. 1889
19 Charles I b. 1600; Franz Schubert d. 1828; Mrs Indira Gandhi b. 1917
20 Count Leo Tolstoy d. 1910; Wedding of Princess (now Queen) Elizabeth 1947
21 François-Marie Arouet (Voltaire) b. 1694; Henry Purcell d. 1695
22 André Gide b. 1869; Charles de Gaulle b. 1890; Sir Arthur Sullivan d. 1900; John F Kennedy assassinated 1963
23 Billy the Kid b. 1859; Manuel de Falla b. 1876; André Malraux d. 1976
24 John Knox d. 1572; Charles Darwin's *Origin of Species* published 1859
25 Andrew Carnegie b. 1835; Dame Myra Hess d. 1965
26 William Cowper b. 1731; John McAdam d. 1836; Amelita Galli-Curci d. 1963
27 Quintus Horatius Flaccus (Horace) d. 8 BC; Alexander Dubček b. 1921
28 Royal Society founded 1660; William Blake b. 1757
29 Cardinal Thomas Wolsey d. 1530; Louisa May Alcott b. 1832
30 Jonathan Swift b. 1667; Samuel Clemens (Mark Twain) b. 1835; Winston Churchill b. 1874; Oscar Wilde d. 1900

DECEMBER (31 days)

DERIVATION: Latin, from *decem* (ten), originally the tenth month.

1 King Henry I d. 1135; Queen Alexandra b. 1844; Beveridge Report 1942
2 Hernán Cortés d. 1547; Battle of Austerlitz 1805; Maria Callas b. 1923; First nuclear chain reaction 1942
3 Samuel Crompton b. 1753; Sir Rowland Hill b. 1795; Joseph Conrad b. 1857; R L Stevenson d. 1894
4 Thomas Carlyle b. 1795; Samuel Butler b. 1835; Francisco Franco b. 1892
5 Wolfgang Amadeus Mozart d. 1791; Claude Monet d. 1926
6 Warren Hastings b. 1732; Anthony Trollope d. 1882

7 Mary, Queen of Scots, b. 1542; Japanese attacked Pearl Harbor 1941
8 Jean Sibelius b. 1865; James Thurber b. 1894; Golda Meir d. 1978; John Lennon murdered 1980
9 John Milton b. 1608; Joel Chandler Harris ('Uncle Remus') b. 1848
10 Royal Academy founded 1768; César Franck b. 1822; Alfred Nobel d. 1896
11 Hector Berlioz b. 1803; Aleksandr Solzhenitsyn b. 1918; King Edward VIII abdicated 1936
12 Robert Browning d. 1889; First trans-Atlantic radio signal 1901
13 Donatello d. 1466; Jan Vermeer d. 1675; Dr Samuel Johnson d. 1784; Heinrich Heine b. 1797
14 George Washington d. 1799; Roald Amundsen reached South Pole 1911
15 Sitting Bull killed 1890; Walt Disney d. 1966
16 Boston Tea Party 1773; Jane Austen b. 1775; Noël Coward b. 1899
17 Ludwig van Beethoven bapt. 1770; Sir Humphry Davy b. 1778; First powered aircraft flight 1903
18 Antonio Stradivari d. 1737; Slavery abolished in USA 1865
19 Carl Wilhelm von Scheele b. 1742; J M W Turner d. 1851; Leonid Brezhnev b. 1906; Jean Genet b. 1910
20 Robert Menzies b. 1894; John Steinbeck d. 1968; Artur Rubenstein d. 1982
21 Pilgrim Fathers landed 1620; Benjamin Disraeli b. 1804; Iosif Stalin b. 1879
22 Jean Racine b. 1639; James Wolfe b. 1726; Giacomo Puccini b. 1858
23 Richard Arkwright b. 1732; Robert Malthus d. 1834; Helmut Schmidt b. 1918
24 St Ignatius of Loyola b. 1491; Vasco da Gama d. 1524; Matthew Arnold b. 1822
25 Isaac Newton b. 1642; Anwar Sadat b. 1918; W C Fields d. 1946; Sir Charles Chaplin d. 1977
26 Thomas Gray b. 1716; Mao Zedong (Mao Tse-tung) b. 1893; Radium discovered by the Curies 1898; Harry Truman d. 1972
27 Johannes Kepler b. 1571; Louis Pasteur b. 1822; Charles Lamb d. 1834
28 Queen Mary II b. 1694; Woodrow Wilson b. 1856; Lord Macaulay d. 1859
29 St Thomas à Becket killed 1170; Madame de Pompadour b. 1721; William E Gladstone b. 1809; Jameson Raid 1895
30 Rudyard Kipling b. 1865; Grigori Rasputin assassinated 1916
31 John Wycliffe d. 1384; Charles Edward Stuart (the Young Pretender) b. 1720; Henri Matisse b. 1869

The Earth

Mass, density and volume
The Earth, including its atmosphere, has a mass estimated in 1979 to be 5 880 000 000 000 000 000 000 tons $5 \cdot 974 \times 10^{21}$ *tonnes* and has a density 5·515 times that of water to an accuracy of 0·06%. The volume of the Earth has been estimated at 259 875 300 000 miles³ *1 083 207 000 000 km³*.

Dimensions
Its equatorial circumference is 24 901·47 miles *40 075,03 km* with a polar or meridianal circumference of 24 859·75 miles *40 007,89 km* indicating that the Earth is not a true sphere but flattened at the poles and hence an ellipsoid. The Earth also has a slight ellipticity at the equator since its long axis (about longitude 37°) is 174 yd *159 m* greater than the short axis. Artificial satellite measurements have also revealed further departures from this biaxial ellipsoid form in minor protuberances and depressions varying between extremes of 244 ft *74 m* in the area of Papua New Guinea and a depression of 354 ft *108 m* south of Sri Lanka

(formerly Ceylon) in the Indian Ocean. The equatorial diameter of the Earth is 7926·385 miles *12 756,280 km* and the polar diameter 7899·809 miles *12 713,510 km*.

Land and sea surfaces
The estimated total surface area of the Earth is 196 937 400 miles² *510 065 600 km²* of which the sea or hydrosphere covers five sevenths or more accurately 70·92 per cent and the land or lithosphere two sevenths or 29·08 per cent. The mean depth of the hydrosphere is 11 660 ft

3554 m. The total volume of the oceans is 308 400 000 miles^3 or *1 285 600 000 km^3*, or 0·022 per cent by weight of the whole earth, viz. $1·3 \times 10^{18}$ tons.

The oceans and seas

The strictest interpretations permit only three oceans – The Pacific, Atlantic and Indian. The so-called Seven Seas would require the three undisputed oceans to be divided by the equator into North and South and the addition of the Arctic Sea. The term Antarctic Ocean is not recognised by the International Hydrographic Bureau.

The Continents

There is every increasing evidence that the Earth's land surface once comprised a single primaeval land mass, now called Pangaea, and that this split during the Upper Cretaceous period (65 000 000 to 100 000 000 years ago) into two super-continents, called Laurasia in the North and Gondwanaland in the South. (See also The Plate Tectonic Theory.) The Earth's land surface embraces seven continents, each with their attendant islands. Europe, Africa and Asia, though politically distinct, physically form one land mass known as Afro-Eurasia. Central America is often included in North America (Canada, the USA and Greenland). Europe includes all the USSR territory west of the Ural Mountains. Oceania embraces Australasia (Australia and New Zealand) and the non-Asian Pacific Islands.

Oceans

Ocean with adjacent seas	Area in millions miles^2	Area in millions km^2	Percentage of world area	Greatest depth (ft)	Greatest depth (m)	Greatest depth location	Average depth (ft)	Average depth (m)
Pacific	69·96	*81,20*	35·52	35 840	*10 924*	Mariana Trench	13 740	*4188*
Atlantic	41·11	*106,48*	20·88	31 037	*9460*	Puerto Rico Trench	12 257	*3736*
Indian	28·59	*74,06*	14·52	24 744	*7542*	Java Trench	12 703	*3872*
Total	139·67	*361,74*	70·92					

If the adjacent seas are detached and the Arctic Sea regarded as an ocean, the oceanic areas may be listed thus:

	Area (miles^2)	Area (km^2)	Percentage of sea area
Pacific	64 190 000	*166 240 000*	46·0
Atlantic	33 420 000	*86 560 000*	23·9
Indian	28 350 000	*73 430 000*	20·3
Arctic	5 110 000	*13 230 000*	3·7
Other Seas	8 600 000	*22 280 000*	6·1
	139 670 000	*361 740 000*	100·0

Ocean depths are zoned by oceanographers as bathyl (down to 6560 ft or *2000 m*); abyssal (between 6560 ft and 19 685 ft *2000 m* and *6000 m*) and hadal (below 19 685 ft *6000 m*).

Seas

Principal seas	Area (miles^2)	Area (km^2)	Average depth (ft)	Average depth (m)
1. South China*	1 148 500	*2 974 600*	4000	*1200*
2. Caribbean Sea	1 063 000	*2 753 000*	8000	*2400*
3. Mediterranean Sea	966 750	*2 503 000*	4875	*1485*
4. Bering Sea	875 750	*2 268 180*	4700	*1400*
5. Gulf of Mexico	595 750	*1 542 985*	5000	*1500*
6. Sea of Okhotsk	589 800	*1 527 570*	2750	*840*
7. East China Sea	482 300	*1 249 150*	600	*180*
8. Hudson Bay	475 800	*1 232 300*	400	*120*
9. Sea of Japan	389 000	*1 007 500*	4500	*1370*
10. Andaman Sea	308 000	*797 700*	2850	*865*
11. North Sea	222 125	*575 300*	300	*90*
12. Black Sea	178 375	*461 980*	3600	*1100*
13. Red Sea	169 000	*437 700*	1610	*490*
14. Baltic Sea	163 000	*422 160*	190	*55*
15. Persian Gulf†	92 200	*238 790*	80	*24*
16. Gulf of St Lawrence	91 800	*237 760*	400	*120*
17. Gulf of California	62 530	*162 000*	2660	*810*
18. English Channel	34 700	*89 900*	177	*54*
19. Irish Sea	34 200	*88 550*	197	*60*
20. Bass Strait	28 950	*75 000*	230	*70*

* The Malayan Sea, which embraces the South China Sea and the Straits of Malacca (3 144 000 miles^2 *8 142 000 km^2*), is not now an entity accepted by the International Hydrographic Bureau.
† Also referred to as the Arabian Gulf.

Peninsulas

	Area in miles^2	Area in km^2		Area in miles^2	Area in km^2
Arabia	1 250 000	*3 250 000*	Labrador	500 000	*1 300 000*
Southern India	800 000	*2 072 000*	Scandinavia	309 000	*800 300*
Alaska	580 000	*1 500 000*	Iberian Peninsula	225 500	*584 000*

World's largest islands

All illustrations are to scale

	Area in miles²	Area in km²
* Australia	2 941 526	7 618 493

* Geographically regarded as a continental land mass, as are Antarctica, Afro-Eurasia, and America.

1. Greenland
Area in miles²
840 000
Area in km²
2 175 600
Location
Arctic Ocean

2. New Guinea
Area in miles²
300 000
Area in km²
777 000
Location
W Pacific

3. Borneo
Area in miles²
280 100
Area in km²
725 545
Location
Indian Ocean

4. Madagascar
Area in miles²
227 800
Area in km²
590 000
Location
Indian Ocean

7. Honshū
Area in miles²
88 031
Area in km²
228 000
Location
NW Pacific

10. Ellesmere Island
Area in miles²
75 767
Area in km²
196 236
Location
Arctic Ocean

13. Java
Area in miles²
48 763
Area in km²
126 295
Location
Indian Ocean

17. Luzon
Area in miles²
40 420
Area in km²
104 688
Location
W Pacific

21. Hokkaido
Area in miles²
30 077
Area in km²
77 900
Location
NW Pacific

14. North Island, New Zealand
Area in miles²
44 281
Area in km²
114 687
Location
SW Pacific

18. Iceland
Area in miles²
39 769
Area in km²
103 000
Location
North Atlantic

22. Hispaniola (Dominican Republic and Haiti)
Area in miles²
29 418
Area in km²
76 192
Location
Caribbean Sea

5. Baffin Island
Area in miles²
183 810
Area in km²
476 065
Location
Arctic Ocean

8. Great Britain
Area in miles²
84 186
Area in km²
218 041
Location
North Atlantic

11. Celebes (Sulawesi)
Area in miles²
72 987
Area in km²
189 035
Location
Indian Ocean

15. Cuba
Area in miles²
44 217
Area in km²
114 522
Location
Caribbean Sea

19. Mindanao
Area in miles²
36 381
Area in km²
94 226
Location
W Pacific

23. Sakhalin
Area in miles²
28 597
Area in km²
74 060
Location
NW Pacific

6. Sumatra
Area in miles²
182 860
Area in km²
473 600
Location
Indian Ocean

9. Victoria Island
Area in miles²
81 930
Area in km²
212 197
Location
Arctic Ocean

12. South Island, New Zealand
Area in miles²
58 093
Area in km²
150 460
Location
SW Pacific

16. Newfoundland
Area in miles²
43 359
Area in km²
112 300
Location
North-West Atlantic

20. Ireland (Northern Ireland and the Republic of Ireland)
Area in miles²
31 839
Area in km²
82 460
Location
North Atlantic

24. Tasmania
Area in miles²
26 215
Area in km²
67 900
Location
SW Pacific

25. Sri Lanka
Area in miles²
25 332
Area in km²
65 600
Location
Indian Ocean

Deep-sea trenches

Length (miles)	Length (km)	Name	Deepest point	Depth (ft)	Depth (m)
1400	2250	Mariana Trench,* W Pacific	Challenger Deep†	35 840	10 924
1600	2575	Tonga-Kermadec Trench,‡ S Pacific	Vityaz 11 (Tonga)	35 598	10 850
1400	2250	Kuril-Kamchatka Trench,* W Pacific		34 587	10 542
825	1325	Philippine Trench, W Pacific	Galathea Deep	34 578	10 539
		Idzu-Bonin Trench (sometimes included in the Japan Trench, see below)		32 196	9810
200+	320+	New Hebrides Trench, S Pacific	North Trench	30 080	9165
400	640	Solomon or New Britain Trench, S Pacific		29 988	9140
500	800	Puerto Rico Trench, W Atlantic	Milwaukee Deep	28 374	8648
350	560	Yap Trench,* W Pacific		27 976	8527
1000	1600	Japan Trench,* W Pacific		27 591	8412
600	965	South Sandwich Trench, S Atlantic	Meteor Deep	27 112	8263
2000	3200	Aleutian Trench, N Pacific		26 574	8100
2200	3540	Peru-Chile (Atacama) Trench, E Pacific	Bartholomew Deep	26 454	8064
		Palau Trench (sometimes included in the Yap Trench)		26 420	8050
600	965	Romanche Trench, N-S Atlantic		25 800	7864
1400	2250	Java (Sunda) Trench, Indian Ocean	Planet Deep	25 344	7725
600	965	Cayman Trench, Caribbean		24 720	7535
650	1040	Nansei Shotó (Ryukyu) Trench, W Pacific		24 630	7505
150	240	Banda Trench, Banda Sea		24 155	7360

* These four trenches are sometimes regarded as a single 4600 mile *7400 km* long system.
† Subsequent visits to the Challenger Deep since 1951 have produced claims for greater depths in this same longitude and latitude. In Mar. 1959 the USSR research ship Vityaz claimed 36 198 ft *11 033 m*, using echo-sounding only.
‡ Kermadec Trench is sometimes considered to be a separate feature. Depth 32 974 ft *10 047 m*.

The continents

Continent	Area in miles²	Area in km²	Greatest distance between extremities of land masses			
			North to South (miles)	North to South (km)	East to West (miles)	East to West (km)
Asia	16 988 000	43 998 000	4000	6435	4700	7560
America	16 185 000	41 918 000				
North America	*8 305 000*	*21 510 000*	*4080*	*6565*	*3750*	*6035*
Central America	*1 060 000*	*2 745 000*	*820*	*1320*	*950*	*1530*
South America	*6 795 000*	*17 598 000*	*4500*	*7240*	*3200*	*5150*
Africa	11 506 000	29 800 000	4400	7080	3750	6035
Antarctica	c. 5 500 000	c.13 600 000	—	—	2700*	4340
Europe†	3 745 000	9 699 000	1800	2900	2500	4000
Australia	2 941 526	7 618 493	1870	3000	2300	3700

* Greatest transit from coast to coast.
† Includes 2 151 000 miles² *5 571 000 km²* of USSR territory west of the Urals.

Deserts

Name	Approx. area in miles²	Approx. area in km²	Territories
The Sahara	3 250 000	8 400 000	Algeria, Chad, Libya, Mali, Mauritania, Niger, Sudan, Tunisia, Egypt, Morocco. Embraces the Libyan Desert (600 000 miles² *1 550 000 km²*) and the Nubian Desert (100 000 miles² *260 000 km²*)
Australian Desert	600 000	1 550 000	Australia. Embraces the Great Sandy (or Warburton) (160 000 miles² *420 000 km²*), Great Victoria (125 000 miles² *325 000 km²*), Simpson (Arunta) (120 000 miles² *310 000 km²*), Gibson (85 000 miles² *220 000 km²*) and Sturt Deserts
Arabian Desert	500 000	1 300 000	Southern Arabia, Saudi Arabia, Yemen. Includes the Ar Rab'al Khali or Empty Quarter (250 000 miles² *647 500 km²*), Syrian (125 000 miles² *325 000 km²*) and An Nafud (50 000 miles² *129 500 km²*) Deserts
The Gobi	400 000	1 040 000	Mongolia and China (Inner Mongolia)
Kalahari Desert	200 000	520 000	Botswana
Takla Makan	125 000	320 000	Sinkiang, China
Sonoran Desert	120 000	310 000	Arizona and California, USA and Mexico

Name	Approx. area in miles²	Approx. area in km²	Territories
Namib Desert	120 000	*310 000*	In SW Africa (Namibia)
Kara Kum*	105 000	*270 000*	Turkmenistan, USSR
Thar Desert	100 000	*260 000*	North-western India and Pakistan
Somali Desert	100 000	*260 000*	Somalia
Atacama Desert	70 000	*180 000*	Northern Chile
Kyzyl Kum*	70 000	*180 000*	Uzbekistan-Kazakhstan, USSR
Dasht-e Lut	20 000	*52 000*	Eastern Iran (sometimes called Iranian Desert)
Mojave Desert	13 500	*35 000*	Southern California, USA
Desierto de Sechura	10 000	*26 000*	North-west Peru

* Together known as the Turkestan Desert.

Mountains

Key to Ranges: H = Himalaya   K = Karakoram   KS = Kunlun Shan   HK = Hindu Kush   P = Pamir   S = in Sikiang, China.

Subsidiary peaks or tops in the same mountain massif are italicized

Mountain	Height (ft)	Height (m)	Range	Date of First Ascent (if any)
Mount Everest [Qomolangma-feng (Chinese); Sagarmatha (Nepalese); Mi-ti gu-ti cha-pu long-na (Tibetan)]	29 028	*8848*	H	29 May 1953
Everest South Summit	*28 707*	*8750*	*H*	*26 May 1953*
K2 (Chogori)	28 250	*8610*	K	31 July 1954
Kangchenjunga	28 208	*8597*	H	25 May 1955
Lhotse	27 923	*8511*	H	18 May 1956
Subsidiary Peak	*27 591*	*8410*	*H*	*unclimbed*
Yalung Kang (Kangchenjunga West)	27 894	*8502*	H	14 May 1973
Kangchenjunga South Peak	27 848	*8488*	H	19 May 1978
Makalu I	27 824	*8481*	H	15 May 1955
Kangchenjunga Middle Peak	27 806	*8475*	H	22 May 1978
Lhotse Shar	27 504	*8383*	H	12 May 1970
Dhaulagiri I	26 795	*8167*	H	13 May 1960
Manaslu I (Kutang I)	26 760	*8156*	H	9 May 1956
Cho Oyu	26 750	*8153*	H	19 Oct 1954
Nanga Parbat (Diamir)	26 660	*8124*	H	3 July 1953
Annapurna I	26 546	*8091*	H	3 June 1950
Gasherbrum I (Hidden Peak)	26 470	*8068*	K	5 July 1958
Broad Peak I	26 400	*8047*	K	9 June 1957
Shisha Pangma (Gosainthan)	26 291	*8046*	H	2 May 1964
Gasherbrum II	26 360	*8034*	H	7 July 1956
Broad Peak Middle	*26 300*	*8016*	*K*	*28 July 1975*
Annapurna East	26 280	*8010*	H	29 Apr 1974
Makalu South-East	26 280	*8010*	H	Unclimbed
Broad Peak Central	26 246	*8000*	K	28 July 1975
Gasherbrum III	26 090	*7952*	K	11 Aug 1975
Annapurna II	26 041	*7937*	H	17 May 1960
Gasherbrum IV	26 000	*7923*	K	6 Aug 1958
Gyachung Kang	25 990	*7921*	H	10 Apr 1964
Nanga Parbat Vorgipfel	25 951	*7910*	H	11 July 1971
Kangbachen	25 925	*7902*	H	26 May 1974
Disteghil Sar	25 868	*7884*	K	9 June 1960
Nuptse	25 850	*7879*	H	16 May 1961
Himalchuli	25 801	*7864*	H	24 May 1960
Khinyang Chchish	25 762	*7852*	K	26 Aug 1971
Manaslu II (Peak 29) Dakuro, Dunapurna	25 705	*7835*	H	Oct 1970
Masherbrum East	25 660	*7821*	K	6 July 1960
Nanda Devi West	25 643	*7816*	H	29 Aug 1936
Nanga Parbat North	25 643	*7816*	H	Unclimbed
Chomo Lönzo	25 640	*7815*	H	30 Oct 1954
Ngojumba Ri I (Cho Oyu II)	25 610	*7805*	H	5 May 1965
Masherbrum West	*25 610*	*7805*	*K*	*unclimbed*
Rakaposhi	25 550	*7788*	K	25 June 1958
Batura Muztagh I	25 542	*7785*	K	30 July 1976
Zemu Gap Peak	25 526	*7780*	H	Unclimbed
Gasherbrum II East	*25 500*	*7772*	*K*	*unclimbed*
Kanjut Sar	25 460	*7760*	K	19 July 1959
Kamet	25 447	*7756*	H	21 June 1931
Namcha Barwa	25 445	*7756*	H	Unclimbed
Dhaulagiri II	25 429	*7751*	H	18 May 1971
Saltoro Kangri I	25 400	*7741*	K	24 July 1962
Batura Muztagh II	25 361	*7730*	K	1978
Gurla Mandhata	25 355	*7728*	H	Unclimbed
Ulugh Muztagh	25 340	*7725*	KS	Unclimbed
Qungur II (Kongur)	25 326	*7719*	P	12 July 1981

Mountain	Height (ft)	Height (m)	Range	Date of First Ascent (if any)
Dhaulagiri III	25 318	*7715*	H	23 Oct 1973
Jannu	25 294	*7709*	H	27 Apr 1962
Tirich Mir	25 282	*7706*	HK	21 July 1950
Saltoro Kangri II	25 280	*7705*	K	Unclimbed
Molamenqing	25 272	*7703*	H	Unclimbed
Disteghil Sar E	25 262	*7700*	K	Unclimbed
Trich Mir, East Peak	*25 236*	*7691*	*HK*	*25 July 1963*
Saser Kangri I	25 170	*7672*	K	5 June 1973
Chogolisa South West	25 148	*7665*	K	2 Aug 1975
Phola Gangchhen	25 135	*7661*	H	Unclimbed
Dhaulagiri IV	25 134	*7661*	H	9 May 1975
Shahkang Sham	25 131	*7660*		Unclimbed
Chogolisa North-East ('Bride Peak')	25 110	*7653*	K	4 Aug 1958
Trivor	25 098	*7650*	K	17 Aug 1960
Fang	25 088	*7647*	H	17 May 1980
Ngojumba Ri II	25 085	*7646*		24 Apr 1965
Makalu II (Kangshungtse)	25 066	*7640*	H	22 Oct 1954
Khinyang Chchish South	25 000	*7620*	K	Unclimbed
Shisparé	24 997	*7619*	K	21 July 1974
Dhaulagiri V	24 993	*7618*	H	1 May 1975
Broad Peak North	*24 935*	*7600*	*K*	*unclimbed*
Amne Machin	24 974	*7612*	S	2 June 1960
Qungur I (Kongur Tiubie)	24 918	*7595*	P	16 Aug 1956
Peak 38 (Lhotse II)	24 898	*7589*	H	Unclimbed
Minya Konka	24 891	*7587*	S	28 Oct 1932
Annapurna III	24 787	*7555*	H	6 May 1961
Khula Kangri I	24 784	*7554*	H	Unclimbed
Changtse (North Peak)	24 780	*7552*	H	Unclimbed
Muztagh Ata	24 757	*7546*	P	Unclimbed
Skyang Kangri	24 751	*7544*	K	11 Aug 1976
Khula Kangri II	24 740	*7541*	H	Unclimbed
Khula Kangri III	24 710	*7532*	H	Unclimbed
Yalung Peak	24 710	*7532*	H	Unclimbed
Yukshin Gardas Sar	24 705	*7530*	K	Unclimbed
Mamostong Kangri	24 692	*7526*	K	Unclimbed
Annapurna IV	24 688	*7525*	H	30 May 1955
Khula Kangri IV	24 659	*7516*	H	Unclimbed
Saser Kangri II (K24)	24 649	*7513*	K	Unclimbed
Shartse	24 612	*7502*	H	23 May 1974

South America

The mountains of the Cordillera de los Andes are headed by Aconcagua at 22 834 ft *6960 m* (first climbed on 14 Jan. 1897), which has the distinction of being the highest mountain in the world outside the great ranges of Central Asia.

Name	Height (ft)	Height (m)	Country
1. Cerro Aconcagua	22 834	*6960*	Argentina
2. Ojos de Salado	22 588	*6885*	Argentina–Chile
3. Nevado de Pissis	22 244	*6780*	Argentina–Chile
4. Huascarán, Sur	22 205	*6768*	Peru
5. Llullaillaco	22 057	*6723*	Argentina–Chile
6. Mercadario	21 884	*6670*	Argentina–Chile
7. Huascarán Norte	21 834	*6655*	Peru
8. Yerupajá	21 765	*6634*	Peru
9. Nevados de Tres Crucés	21 270	*6620*	Argentina–Chile
10. Coropuna	21 696	*6613*	Peru
11. Nevado Incahuasi	21 657	*6601*	Argentina–Chile
12. Tupungato	21 490	*6550*	Argentina–Chile
13. Sajama	21 463	*6542*	Bolivia
14. Nevado Gonzalez	21 326	*6500*	Argentina
15. Cerro del Nacimiento	21 302	*6493*	Argentina

Name	Height (ft)	Height (m)	Country
16. Illimani	21 200	6462	Bolivia
17. El Muerto	21 246	6476	Argentina–Chile
18. Ancohuma (Sorata N)	21 086	6427	Bolivia
19. Nevado Bonete	21 031	6410	Argentina
20. Cerro de Ramada	21 031	6410	Argentina

North and Central America

Mt McKinley (first ascent 1913) is the only peak in excess of 20 000 ft 6100 m in the entire North American continent. It was first climbed on 7 June 1913. The native name is Denali.

Name	Height (ft)	Height (m)	Country
1. McKinley, South Peak	20 320	6194	Alaska
2. Logan	19 850	6050	Canada
3. Citlaltépetl (Orizaba)	18 700	5699	Mexico
4. St Elias	18 008	5489	Alaska–Canada
5. Popocatépetl	17 887	5452	Mexico
6. Foraker	17 400	5304	Alaska
7. Ixtaccihuatl	17 342	5286	Mexico
8. Lucania	17 150	5227	Alaska
9. King Peak	17 130	5221	Alaska
10. Blackburn	16 522	5036	Alaska
11. Steele	16 440	5011	Alaska
12. Bona	16 420	5005	Alaska
13. Sanford	16 207	4940	Alaska
14. Wood	15 879	4840	Canada

Note: Mt McKinley, North Peak, is 19 470 ft 5934 m.

Africa

All the peaks listed in Zaïre and Uganda are in the Ruwenzori group.

Name	Height (ft)	Height (m)	Location
1. Kilimanjaro (Uhuru Point,* Kibo)	19 340	5894	Tanzania
Hans Meyer Peak, Mawenzi	16 890	5148	
Shira Peak	13 139	4005	
2. Mount Kenya (Batian)	17 058	5199	Kenya
3. Ngaliema (Mount Stanley) (Margherita Peak)	16 763	5109	Zaïre–Uganda
4. Duwoni or Mt Speke (Vittorio Emanuele Peak)	16 062	4896	Uganda
5. Mount Baker (Edward Peak)	15 889	4843	Uganda
6. Mount Emin (Umberto Peak)	15 741	4798	Zaïre
7. Mount Gessi (Iolanda Peak)	15 470	4715	Uganda
8. Mount Luigi di Savoia (Sella Peak)	15 179	4626	Uganda
9. Ras Dashan (Rasdajan)	15 158	4620	Semien Mts, Ethiopia
10. Humphreys Peak	15 021	4578	Uganda

* Formerly called Kaiser Wilhelm Spitze.

Highest European Alps

The highest point in Italian territory is a shoulder of the main summit of Mont Blanc (Monte Bianco) through which a 4760 m 15 616 ft contour passes. The highest top exclusively in Italian territory is Picco Luigi Amedeo (4460 m 14 632 ft) to the south of the main Mont Blanc peak, which is itself exclusively in French territory.

Subsidiary peaks or tops on the same massif have been omitted except in the case of Mont Blanc and Monte Rosa, where they have been indented in italic type.

Name	Height (m)	Height (ft)	Country	First Ascent
1. Mont Blanc	4807	15 771	France	1786
Monte Bianco di Courmayeur	4748	15 577	France	1877
2. Monte Rosa				
Dufourspitze	4634·0	15 203	Switzerland	1855
Nordend	4609	15 121	Swiss–Italian border	1861
Ostspitze	4596	15 078	Swiss–Italian border	1854
Zumstein Spitze	4563	14 970	Swiss–Italian border	1820
Signal Kuppe	4556	14 947	Swiss–Italian border	1842
3. Dom	4545·4	14 911	Switzerland	1858
4. Lyskamm (Liskamm)	4527·2	14 853	Swiss–Italian border	1861
5. Weisshorn	4505·5	14 780	Switzerland	1861
6. Täschhorn	4490·7	14 733	Switzerland	1862
7. Matterhorn	4475·5	14 683	Swiss–Italian border	1865

Name	Height (m)	Height (ft)	Country	First Ascent
Matterhorn cont.				
Le Mont Maudit (Mont Blanc)	4465	14 649	Italy–France	1878
Picco Luigi Amedeo (Mont Blanc)	4460	14 632	Italy	
8. La Dent Blanche	4356·6	14 293	Switzerland	1862
9. Nadelhorn	4327·0	14 196	Switzerland	1858
10. Le Grand Combin de Grafaneire	4314	14 153	Switzerland	1859
Dôme du Goûter (Mont Blanc)	4304	14 120	France	1784
11. Lenzspitze	4294	14 087	Switzerland	1870
12. Finsteraarhorn	4273·8	14 021	Switzerland	1829*

* Also reported climbed in 1812 but evidence lacking.
Note: In the Dunlop Book (1st Edition) this list was extended to include the 24 additional Alps over 4000 m 13 123 ft.

Europe

The Caucasus range, along the spine of which runs the traditional geographical boundary between Asia and Europe, includes the following peaks which are higher than Mont Blanc (15 771 ft 4807 m).

Name	Height (ft)	Height (m)
1. El'brus, West Peak	18 481	5663
El'brus, East Peak	18 356	5595
2. Dykh Tau	17 070	5203
3. Shkhara	17 063	5201
4. Pik Shota Rustaveli	17 028	5190
5. Koshtantau	16 876	5144
6. Pik Pushkin	16 732	5100
7. Jangi Tau, West Peak	16 572	5051
Janga, East Peak	16 529	5038
8. Dzhangi Tau	16 565	5049
9. Kazbek	16 558	5047
10. Katyn Tau (Adish)	16 355	4985
11. Pik Rustaveli	16 272	4960
12. Mishirgi, West Peak	16 148	4922
Mishirgitau, East Peak	16 135	4917
13. Kunjum Mishirgi	16 011	4880
14. Gestola	15 944	4860
15. Tetnuld	15 921	4853

Antarctica

Areas of Eastern Antarctica remain unsurveyed. Immense areas of the ice cap around the Pole of Inaccessibility lie over 12 000 ft 3650 m above sea-level rising to 14 000 ft 4265 m in 82° 25′ S 65° 30′ E.

Name	Height (ft)	Height (m)
1. Vinson Massif	16 863	5140
2. Mt Tyree	16 289	4965
3. Mt Shinn	15 750*	4800*
4. Mt Gardner	15 387	4690
5. Mt Epperley	15 098	4602
6. Mt Kirkpatrick	14 799	4511
7. Mt Elizabeth	14 698	4480
8. Mt Markham	14 271	4350
9. Mt MacKellar	14 074	4290
10. Mt Kaplan	13 943	4250
11. Mt Sidley	13 850*	4221*
12. Mt Ostenso	13 713	4180
13. Mt Minto	13 648	4160
14. Mt Long Gables	13 615	4150
15. Mt Miller	13 600	4145
16. Mt Falla	13 500	4115
17. Mt Giovinetto	13 408	4087
18. Mt Lister	13 353	4070
19. Mt Fisher	13 340	4066
20. Mt Wade	13 330	4063
21. Mt Fridtjof Nansen	13 156	4010

* Volcanic as is Erebus 12 447 ft 3794 m.

Oceania

The nomenclature of New Guinean mountains remains extremely confused.

Name	Height (ft)	Height (m)	Location
1. Puncak Jayakusumu (formerly Peak Sukarno, Carstensz Pyramid)	16 023	4884	West Irian
Ngga Pulu	15 950	4861	West Irian
Sunday Peak	15 945	4860	West Irian
2. Oost Carstensz top	15 879	4840	West Irian
3. Peak Trikora (formerly Sukarno, formerly Wilhelmina)	15 518	4730	West Irian
4. Enggea (Idenburg top)	15 475	4717	West Irian
5. Peak Mandala (formerly Juliana)	15 223	4640	West Irian

Name	Height (ft)	Height (m)	Location	Name	Height (ft)	Height (m)	Location
6. Mt Wilhelm	15 091	4600	New Guinea	16. Mt Sarawaket	13 451	4100	New Guinea
7. Peak Wisnumurti	15 075	4595	New Guinea	17. Mt Giluwe	13 385	4088	New Guinea
8. Point (unnamed)	14 271	4350	New Guinea	18. Mt Victoria	13 362	4073	Owen Stanley Range
9. Mt Kubor	14 107	4300	New Guinea				
10. Mt Leonard Darwin	13 891	4234	New Guinea	19. Mt Hogan	13 123	4000	New Guinea
11. Mt Herbert	13 999	4267	New Guinea				
12. *Mauna Kea	13 796	4205	Hawaii*				
13. *Mauna Loa	13 680	4170	Hawaii*				
14. Mt Bangeta	13 474	4107	New Guinea				
15. Mt Kinabalu	13 454	4101	Sabah (Borneo)				

* Politically part of the USA since 21 Aug. 1959.
Note: The highest mountain in North Island, New Zealand is the volcano Ruapehu (9176 ft *2797 m*). Mt Cook (12 349 ft *3764 m*) in South Island is the highest in New Zealand and is called Aorangi by the Maoris.
Australia's highest point is Mt Kosciusko (7316 ft *2230 m*) in the Snowy Mtns, New South Wales.

World's greatest mountain ranges

The greatest mountain system is the Himalaya–Karakoram–Hindu Kush–Pamir range with 104 peaks over 24 000 ft *7315 m*. The second greatest range is the Andes with 54 peaks over 20 000 ft *6096 m*.

Length (miles)	Length (km)	Name	Location	Culminating Peak	Height (ft)	Height (m)
4500	7200	Cordillera de Los Andes	W South America	Aconcagua	22 834	6960
3000	4800	Rocky Mountains	W North America	Mt Elbert (Colorado)‡	14 433	4400
2400	3800	Himalaya–Karakoram–Hindu Kush	S Central Asia	Mt Everest	29 028	8848
2250	3600	Great Dividing Range	E Australia	Kosciusko	7 310	2228
2200	3500	Trans-Antarctic Mts	Antarctica	Mt Kirkpatrick	14 860	4529
1900	3000	Brazilian Atlantic Coast Range	E Brazil	Pico de Bandeira	9 482	2890
1800	2900	West Sumatran–Javan Range	W Sumatra and Java	Kerintji	12 484	3805
1650*	2650	Aleutian Range	Alaska and NW Pacific	Shishaldin	9 387	2861
1400	2250	Tien Shan	S Central Asia	Pik Pobeda	24 406	7439
1250	2000	Central New Guinea Range	Irian Jaya–Papua/ N Guinea	Jayakusumu†	16 020	4883
1250	2000	Altai Mountains	Central Asia	Gora Belukha	14 783	4505
1250	2010	Uralskiy Khrebet	Russian SFSR	Gora Narodnaya	6 214	1894
1200	1930	Range in Kamchatka§	E Russian SFSR	Klyuchevskaya Sopka	15 910	4850
1200	1930	Atlas Mountains	NW Africa	Jebel Toubkal	13 665	4165
1000	1610	Verkhoyanskiy Khrebet	E Russian SFSR	Gora Mas Khaya	9 708	2959
1000	1610	Western Ghats	W India	Anai Madi	8 841	2694
950	1530	Sierra Madre Oriental	Mexico	Citlaltépetl (Orizaba)	18 700	5699
950	1530	Kūhhā-ye-Zāgros	Iran	Zard Kūh	14 921	4547
950	1530	Scandinavian Range	W Norway	Galdhopiggen	8 104	2470
900	1450	Ethiopian Highlands	Ethiopia	Ras Dashan	c. 15 100	c. 4600
900	1450	Sierra Madre Occidental	Mexico	Nevado de Colima	13 993	4265
850	1370	Malagasy Range	Madagascar	Maromokotro	9 436	2876
800	1290	Drakensberg (edge of plateau)	SE Africa	Thabana Ntlenyana	11 425	3482
800	1290	Khrebet Cherskogo	E Russian SFSR	Gora Pobeda	10 325	3147
750	1200	Caucasus	Georgia, USSR	El'brus, West Peak	18 481	5633
700	1130	Alaska Range	Alaska, USA	Mt McKinley, South Peak	20 320	6193
700	1130	Assam–Burma Range	Assam–W Burma	Hkakabo Razi	19 296	5881
700	1130	Cascade Range	Northwest USA–Canada	Mt Rainier	14 410	4392
700	1130	Central Borneo Range	Central Borneo	Kinabalu	13 455	4101
700	1130	Tihāmat ash Shām	SW Arabia	Jebel Hadhar	12 336	3760
700	1130	Appennini	Italy	Corno Grande	9 617	2931
700	1130	Appalachians	Eastern USA–Canada	Mt Mitchell	6 684	2037
650	1050	Alpa	Central Europe	Mt Blanc	15 771	4807
600	965	Sierra Madre del Sur	Mexico	Teotepec	12 149	3703
600	965	Khrebet Kolymskiy (Gydan)	E Russian SFSR	—	7 290	2221

* Continuous mainland length (excluding islands) 450 miles *720 km*.
§ Comprises the Sredinnyy and Koryakskiy Krebets.
† Also known (before 1970) as Ngga Pulu, Mount Sukarno and Cartensz Pyramide.
‡ Mt Robson 12 872 ft *3954 m* is the highest mountain in the Canadian Rockies.

Volcanoes

It is estimated that there are about 850 active volcanoes of which 80 are submarine. Vulcanologists classify volcanoes as extinct, dormant or active (which includes rumbling, steaming or erupting). Areas of volcanoes and seismic activity are well defined, notably around the shores of the N Pacific and the eastern shores of the S Pacific, down the Mid-Atlantic range, the Africa Rift Valley and across from Greece and Turkey into Central Asia, the Himalayas and Meghalaya (Assam).

Cerro Aconcagua (22 834 ft *6960 m*), the highest Andean peak, is an extinct volcano, while Kilimanjaro (19 340 ft *5895 m*) in Africa, and Volcán Llullaillaco in Chile (22 057 ft *6723 m*) are classified as dormant. The highest point on the Equator lies on the shoulder of the dormant Cayambe (18 982 ft *5786 m*) in Ecuador on the 4875 m *15 994 ft* contour. Among the principal volcanoes active in recent times are:

Name	Height (ft)	Height (m)	Range or Location	Country	Date of Last Notified Eruption
Ojos del Salado	22 588	6885	Andes	Argentina–Chile	1981–Steams
Guallatiri	19 882	6060	Andes	Chile	1960
Cotopaxi	19 347	5897	Andes	Ecuador	1975
Lascar	18 507	5641	Andes	Chile	1968
Tupungatito	18 504	5640	Andes	Chile	1964
Popocatépetl	17 887	5451	Altiplano de Mexico	Mexico	1920–Steams
Sangay	17 159	5230	Andes	Ecuador	1976
Klyuchevskaya sopka	15 913	4850	Sredinnyy Khrebet (Kamchatka Peninsula)	USSR	1974
Purace	15 059	4590	Andes	Colombia	1977
Tajumulco	13 881	4220		Guatemala	Rumbles
Mauna Loa	13 680	4170	Hawaii	USA	1978
Tacaná	13 379	4078	Sierra Madre	Guatemala	Rumbles
Cameroon Mt	13 350	4070	(monarch)	Cameroon	1959

Name	Height (ft)	Height (m)	Range or Location	Country	Date of Last Notified Eruption
Erebus	12 450	3795	Ross I	Antarctica	1975
Rindjani	12 224	3726	Lombok	Indonesia	1966
Pico de Teide	12 198	3718	Tenerife, Canary Is	Spain	1909
Semeru	12 060	3676	Java	Indonesia	1976
Nyiragongo	11 385	3470	Virunga	Zaïre	1977
Koryakskaya	11 339	3456	Kamchatka Peninsula	USSR	1957
Irazu	11 325	3452	Cordillera Central	Costa Rica	1967
Slamat	11 247	3428	Java	Indonesia	1967
Mt Spurr	11 070	3374	Alaska Range	USA	1953
Mt Etna	10 853	3308	Sicily	Italy	1979

Other Notable Active Volcanoes

Name	Height (ft)	Height (m)	Range or Location	Country	Date of Last Notified Eruption
Lassen Peak	10 453	3186	Cascade Range, California	USA	1915
Mt St Helens	9677	2949	Cascade Range, Washington	USA	1980
Tambora	9351	2850	Sumbawa	Indonesia	1913
The Peak	6760	2060	Tristan da Cunha	S Atlantic	1962
Mt Lamington	5535	1687		Papua New Guinea	1951
Mt Pelée	4800	1463		Martinique	1929–32
Hekla	4747	1447		Iceland	1980
La Soufrière	c.4200	1280	St Vincent Island	Atlantic	1979
Vesuvius	4198	1280	Bay of Naples	Italy	1944
Kilauea	4077	1240	Hawaii	USA	1977
Faial	3421	1043	Azores	Azores	1968
Stromboli	3038	926	Island	Mediterranean	1975
Santorini	1960	584	Thera	Greece	1956
Vulcano	1637	499	Lipari Islands	Mediterranean	1888–90
Paricutin	1213	370		Mexico	1943
Surtsey	568	173	off SW Iceland	Iceland	1963–65
Anak Krakatau	510	155	Island	Indonesia	1960

Depressions & glaciers

World's deepest depressions

	Maximum depth below sea level (ft)	(m)
Dead Sea, Jordan–Israel	1296	395
Turfan Depression, Sinkiang, China	505	153
Munkhafad el Qattâra (Qattâra Depression), Egypt	436	132
Poluostrov Mangyshlak, Kazakh SSR, USSR	433	131
Danakil Depression, Ethiopia	383	116
Death Valley, California, USA	282	86
Salton Sink, California, USA	235	71
Zapadnyy Chink Ustyurta, Kazakh SSR	230	70
Prikaspiyskaya Nizmennost', Russian SFSR and Kazakh SSR	220	67
Ozera Sarykamysh, Uzbek and Turkmen SSR	148	45
El Faiyûm, Egypt	147	44
Península Valdiés Lago Enriquillo, Dominican Republic	131	40

Note: Immense areas of West Antarctica would be below sea level if stripped of their ice sheet. The deepest estimated crypto-depression is the bed rock on the Hollick–Kenyon plateau beneath the Marie Byrd Land ice cap (84° 37′ S 110° W) at – 8100 ft *2468 m*. The bed of Lake Baykal (USSR) is 4872 ft *1484 m* below sea-level and the bed of the Dead Sea is 2600 ft *792 m* below sea-level. The ground surface of large areas of Central Greenland under the overburden of ice up to 11 190 ft *341 m* thick are depressed to 1200 ft *365 m* below sea-level. The world's largest exposed depression is the Prikaspiyskaya Nizmennost' stretching the whole northern third of the Caspian Sea (which is itself 92 ft *28 m* below sea-level) up to 250 miles *400 km* inland. The Qattâra Depression extends for 340 miles *547 km* and is up to 80 miles *128 km* wide.

World's longest glaciers

miles	km	
c.320	515	Lambert-Fisher Ice Passage, Antarctica (disc. 1956–7)
260	418	Novaya Zemlya, North Island, USSR (1160 miles² 3004 km²)
225	362	Arctic Institute Ice Passage, Victoria Land, E Antarctica
180	289	Nimrod–Lennox–King Ice Passage, E Antarctica
150	241	Denman glacier, E Antarctica
140	225	Beardmore Glacier, E Antarctica (disc. 1908)
140	225	Recovery Glacier, W Antarctica
124	200	*Petermanns Gletscher, Knud Rasmussen Land, Greenland
120	193	Unnamed Glacier, SW Ross Ice Shelf, W Antarctica
115	185	Slessor Glacier, W Antarctica

* Petermanns Gletscher is the largest in the Northern hemisphere: it extends 24·8 miles *40 km* out to sea.

Other Notable Glaciers

Name	Location	Length (miles)	Length (km)	Area (miles²)	Area (km²)
Vatnajökull	Iceland	88	141	3400	8800
Malaspina Glacier	Alaska	26	41	1480	3830
Nabesna Glacier	Alaska	43½	70	770	1990
Fedtschenko	Pamirs	47	75	520	1346
Siachen Glacier	Karakoram	47	75	444	1150
Jostedalsbre	Norway	62	100	415	1075
Hispar-Biafo Ice Passage	Karakoram	76	122	125 240	323 620
Kangchenjunga	Himalaya	12	19	177	458
Tasman Glacier	New Zealand	18	29	53	137
Aletschgletscher	Alps	16·5	26·5	44	114

Quarayaq Glacier, Greenland, flows at a velocity of 20 to 24 m *(65 to 80 ft)* a day – this is the fastest major glacier.
Hassanabad Glacier, Karakoram advanced 15·3 miles *9,5 km* in 'several months' c. 1900.

Glaciated areas of the world

It is estimated that 6 020 000 miles² *15 600 000 km²* or about 10·4 per cent of the world's land surface is permanently covered with ice, thus:

	miles²	km²
South Polar Regions	5 250 000	13 597 000
North Polar Regions (inc Greenland with 695 500)	758 500	1 965 000
Alaska–Canada	22 700	58 800
Asia	14 600	37 800
South America	4 600	11 900
Europe	4 128	10 700
New Zealand	380	984
Africa	92	238

World's deepest caves

Depth ft	m		
4773	1455	Reseau du Foillis, Haute Savoie	France
4334	1321	Reseau de la Pierre St. Martin, Haute Savoie	France
4200	1280	Snezhnaya, Caucasus	USSR
4002	1220	Sistema Huautla	Mexico
3930	1198	Gouffre Berger	France
3887	1185	Sima de Ukendi	Spain
3772	1150	Avenc B15, Pyrenees	Spain
3645	1111	Schneeloch, Salzburg	Austria
3602	1098	Sima G.E.S. Malaga	Spain
3359	1024	Lamprechtsofen	Austria
3339	1018	Reseau Felix Trombe	France
1010	308	Ogof Ffynnon Ddu, Powys	Wales
702	214	Giant's Hole – Oxlow Caverns, Derbyshire	England
587	179	Reyfad Pot, Fermanagh	Ireland, N
459	140	Carrowmore Cavern	Ireland, Republic

Note: The most extensive cave system is the Mammoth Cave system in Kentucky, USA, discovered in 1799 and in 1972 linked with the Flint Ridge system so making a combined mapped length of 213·3 miles *345 km*. The largest known cavern is the Sarawak Chamber, Lobang Nasip Bagus, Sarawak, surveyed in 1980, which has measurements of 2300 ft *700 m* in length, 980 ft *300 m* in average width and with a minimum height of 230 ft *70 m*.

World's greatest rivers

The importance of rivers still tends to be judged on their length rather than by the more significant factors – their basin areas and volume of flow. In this compilation all the world's river systems with a watercourse of a length of 1500 miles *2400 km* or more are listed with all three criteria where ascertainable.

Length (miles)	(km)	Name of Watercourse	Source	Course and Outflow	Basin Area (miles²)	(km²)	Mean Discharge Rate (ft³/s)	(m³/s)	Notes
1 4145	*6670*	Nile (Bahr-el-Nil)–White Nile (Bahr el Jabel)–Albert Nile–Victoria Nile–Victoria Nyanza–Kagera-Luvironza	Burundi: Luvironza branch of the Kagera, a feeder of the Victoria Nyanza	Through Tanzania (Kagera), Uganda (Victoria Nile and Albert Nile), Sudan (White Nile), Egypt to eastern Mediterranean	1 293 000	*3 350 000*	110 000	*3120*	Navigable length to first cataract (Aswan) 960 miles *1545 km*. UAR Irrigation Dept. states length as 4164 miles *6700 km*. Discharge 93 200 ft³/s *2600 m³/s* near Aswan. Delta is 9250 miles² *23 960 km²*
2 4007	*6448*	Amazon (Amazonas)	Peru: Lago Villafro, head of the Apurimac branch of the Ucayali, which joins the Marañon to form the Amazonas	Through Colombia to Equatorial Brazil (Solimões) to South Atlantic (Canal do Sul)	2 722 000	*7 050 000*	6 350 000	*180 000*	Total of 15 000 tributaries, ten over 1000 miles *1600 km* including Madeira (2100 miles *3380 km*). Navigable 2300 miles *3700 km* up stream. Delta extends 250 miles *400 km* inland
3 3710	*5970*	Mississippi-Missouri–Jefferson-Beaverhead–Red Rock	Beaverhead County, southern Montana, USA	Through N. Dakota, S. Dakota, Nebraska–Iowa, Missouri–Kansas, Illinois, Kentucky, Tennessee, Arkansas, Mississippi, Louisiana, South West Pass into Gulf of Mexico	1 245 000	*3 224 000*	650 000	*18 400*	Missouri is 2315 miles *3725 km* the Jefferson–Beaverhead–Red Rock is 217 miles *349 km*. Lower Mississippi is 1171 miles *1884 km*. Total Mississippi from Lake Itasca, Minn., is 2348 miles *3778 km*. Longest river in one country. Delta is 13 900 miles² *36 000 km²*
4 3442	*5540*	Yenisey-Angara-Selenga	Mongolia: Ideriin branch of Selenga (Selenge)	Through Buryat ASSR (Selenga feeder) into Ozero Baykal, thence *via* Angara to Yenisey confluence at Strelka to Kara Sea, northern USSR	996 000	*2 580 000*	670 000	*19 000*	Estuary 240 miles *386 km* long. Yenisey is 2200 miles *3540 km* long and has a basin of 792 000 miles² *2 050 000 km²*. The length of the Angara is 1150 miles *1850 km*
5 3436	*5530*	Yangtze Kiang (Chang' Chiang)	Western China, Kunlun Shan Mts. (as Dre Che and T'ungt'ien)	Begins at T'ungt'ien, then Chinsha, through Yünnan Szechwan, Hupeh, Anhwei, Kiangsu, to Yellow Sea	756 000	*1 960 000*	770 000	*21 800*	Flood rate (1931) of 3 000 000 ft³/s *85 000 m³/s*. Estuary 120 miles *190 km* long
6 3362	*5410*	Ob'-Irtysh	Mongolia: Kara (Black) Irtysh *via* northern China (Sin Kiang) feeder of Ozero Zaysan	Through Kazakhstan into Russian SFSR to Ob' confluence at Khanty Mansiysk, thence Ob' to Kara Sea, northern USSR	1 150 000	*2 978 000*	550 000	*15 600*	Estuary (Obskaya Guba) is 450 miles *725 km* long. Ob' is 2286 miles *3679 km* long, Irtysh 1840 miles *2960 km* long
7 3000	*4830*	Hwang Ho (Yellow River)	China: Tsaring-nor, Tsinghai Province	Through Kansu, Inner Mongolia, Honan, Shantung to Po Hai (Gulf of Chili), Yellow Sea, North Pacific	378 000	*979 000*	100 000 to 800 000	*2800 to 22 650*	Changed mouth by 250 miles *400 km* in 1852. Only last 25 miles *40 km* navigable. Longest river in one country in Asia
8 2920	*4700*	Zaïre (Congo)	Zambia–Zaïre border, as Lualaba	Through Zaïre as Lualaba along to Zaïre (Congo) border to N.W. Angola mouth into the South Atlantic	1 314 000	*3 400 000*	1 450 000	*41 000*	Navigable for 1075 miles *1730 km* from Kisangani to Kinshasa (formerly Léopoldville). Estuary 60 miles *96 km* long
9 2734	*4400*	Lena-Kirenga	USSR Hinterland of west central shores of Ozero Baykal as Kirenga	Northwards through Eastern Russia to Lapter Sea, Arctic Ocean	960 000	*2 490 000*	575 000	*16 300*	Lena Delta (17 375 miles² *45 000 km²*) extends 110 miles *177 km* inland, frozen 15 Oct. to 10 July. Second longest solely Russian river
10 2700	*4345*	Amur-Argun' (He lung Chiang)	Northern China in Khingan Ranges (as Argun')	North along Inner Mongolian–USSR and Manchuria–USSR border for 2326 miles *3743 km* to Tartar Strait, Sea of Okhotsk, North Pacific	787 000	*2 038 000*	438 000	*12 400*	Amur is 1771 miles *2850 km* long (711 600 basin and 388 000 flow): *China Handbook* claims total length to be 2903 miles *4670 km* of which only 575 miles *925 km* is exclusively in USSR territory
11 2635	*4240*	Mackenzie-Peace	Tatlatui Lake, Skeena Mts, Rockies, British Columbia, Canada (as River Finlay)	Flows as Finlay for 250 miles *400 km* to confluence with Peace. Thence 1050 miles *1690 km* to join Slave (258 miles *415 km*) which feeds Great Slave Lake whence flows Mackenzie (1077 miles *1733 km*) to Beaufort Sea	711 000	*1 841 000*	400 000	*11 300*	Peace 1195 miles *1923 km*
12 2600	*4180*	Mekong (Me Nam Kong)	Central Tibet (as Lants'ang), slopes of Dza-Nag-Lung-Mong, 16 700 ft *5000 m*	Flows into China, thence south to form Burma-Laotian and most of Thai-Laotian frontiers, thence through Cambodia to Vietnam into South China Sea	381 000	*987 000*	388 000	*11 000*	Max flood discharge 1 700 000 ft³/s *48 000 m³/s*
13 2600	*4184*	Niger	Guinea: Loma Mts near Sierra Leone border	Flows through Mali, Niger and along Benin border into Nigeria and Atlantic	730 000	*1 890 000*	415 000	*11 750*	Delta extends 80 miles *128 km* inland and 130 miles *200 km* in coastal length
14 2485	*4000*	Rió de la Plata-Paraná	Brazil: as Paranáiba. Flows south to eastern Paraguay border and into eastern Argentina	Emerges into confluence with River Uruguay to form Rio de la Plata, South Atlantic	1 600 000	*4 145 000*	970 000	*27 500*	After the 75 mile *120 km* long Delta estuary, the river shares the 210 mile *340 km* long estuary of the Uruguay called Rio de la Plata (River Plate)
15 2330	*3750*	Murray-Darling	Queensland, Australia: as the Culgoa continuation of the Condamine, which is an extension of the Balonne-branch of the Darling	Balonne (intermittent flow) crosses into New South Wales to join Darling, which itself joins the Murray on the New South Wales–Victoria border and flows west into Lake Alexandrina, in South Australia	408 000	*1 059 000*	14 000	*400*	Darling c. 1700 miles *2740 km* Murray 1609 miles *2590 km* or 1160 miles *1870 km*
16 2293	*3690*	Volga	USSR	Flows south and east in a great curve and empties in a delta into the north of the Caspian Sea	525 000	*1 360 000*	287 000	*8200*	Delta exceeds 175 miles *280 km* inland and arguably 280 miles *450 km*
17 2200	*3540*	Zambezi (Zambeze)	Zimbabwe: north-west extremity, as Zambezi	Flows after 45 miles *72 km* across eastern Angola for 220 miles *354 km* and back into Zimbabwe (as Zambezi), later forming border with eastern end of	514 000	*1 330 000*	250 000	*7000*	Navigable 380 miles *610 km* up to Quebrabasa Rapids and thereafter in stretches totalling another 1200 miles *1930 km*

Length (miles)	(km)	Name of Watercourse	Source	Course and Outflow	Basin Area (miles²)	(km²)	Mean Discharge Rate (ft³/s)	(m³/s)	Notes
				Caprivi strip of Namibia, thence over Victoria Falls (Mosi-Oa-tunya) into Kariba Lake. Thereafter into Mozambique and out into southern Indian Ocean					
2100	3380	Madeira–Mamoré–Grande (Guapay)	Bolivia: rises on the Beni near Illimani	Flows north and east into Brazil to join Amazon at the Ilha Tupinambaram	Tributary of No. 2		530 000	15 000	World's longest tributary, navigable for 663 miles 1070 km
2000	3200	Purus (formerly Coxiuara)	Peru: as the Alto Purus	Flows north and east into Brazil to join Amazon below Beruri	Tributary of No. 2		—	—	World's second longest tributary. Navigable for 1600 miles 2575 km. Pronounced meanders
18 1979	3185	Yukon-Teslin	North-west British Columbia, Canada, as the Teslin	Flows north into Yukon Territory and into west Alaska, USA, and thence into Bering Sea	330 000	855 000	—	—	Delta 85 miles 136 km inland, navigable (shallow draft) for 1775 miles 2855 km
19 1945	3130	St Lawrence	Head of St Louis River, Minn. USA	Flows into Lake Superior, thence Lakes Huron, Erie, Ontario to Gulf of St Lawrence and North Atlantic	532 000	1 378 000	360 000	10 200	Estuary 253 miles 407 km long or 383 miles 616 km to Anticosti Island. Discovered 1535 by Jacques Cartier
20 1885	3033	Rio Grande (Rio Bravo del Norte)	South-western Colorado, USA; San Juan Mts	Flows south through New Mexico, USA, and along Texas–Mexico border into Gulf of Mexico, Atlantic Ocean	172 000	445 000	3000	85	
21 1800	2900	Ganges–Brahmaputra	South-western Tibet as Matsang (Tsangpo)	Flows east 770 miles 1240 km south, then west through Assam, north-eastern India, joins Ganges (as Jamuna) to flow into Bay of Bengal, Indian Ocean	626 000	1 620 000	1 360 000	38 500	Joint delta with Ganges extends 225 miles 360 km across and 205 miles 330 km inland. Area 30 800 mile² 80 000 km² the world's largest. Navigable 800 miles 1290 km
22 1800	2900	São Francisco	Brazil: Serra da Canastra	Flows north and east into South Atlantic	270 000	700 000	—	—	Navigable 148 miles 238 km
23 1790	2880	Indus	Tibet: as Sengge	Flows west through Kashmir, into Pakistan and out into northern Arabian Sea	450 000	1 166 000	195 000	5500	Delta (area 3100 miles² 8000 km²) extends 75 miles 120 km inland
24 1770	2850	Danube	South-western Germany: Black Forest as Breg and Brigach	Flows (as Donau) east into Austria, along Czech–Hungarian border as Dunaj into Hungary (273 miles 440 km) as Duna, to Yugoslavia as Dunav along Romania–Bulgaria border and through Romania as Dunărea to Romania–USSR border as Dunay, into the Black Sea	315 000	815 000	250 000	7000	Delta extends 60 miles 96 km inland. Flows in territory of 8 countries
25 1750	2810	Salween (Nu Chiang)	Tibet in Tanglha range	Flows (as Nu) east and south into western China, into eastern Burma and along Thailand border and out into Gulf of Martaban, Andaman Sea	125 000	325 000	—	—	
26 = 1700	2740	Tigris–Euphrates (Shatt al-Arab)	Eastern Turkey as Murat	Flows west joining the Firat, thence into Syria as Al Furāt and south and east into Iraq joining Tigris flowing into Persian Gulf at Iran–Iraq border as Shatt al-Arab	430 000	1 115 000	50 000	400 low 2700 high	
26 = 1700	2740	Tocantins	Brazil: near Brazilia as Paraná	Flows north to join Pará in the Estuary Báia de Marajó and the South Atlantic	350 000	905 000	360 000	10 000	Not properly regarded as an Amazon tributary. Estuary 275 miles 440 km in length
26 = 1700	2740	Orinoco	South-eastern Venezuela	Flows north and west to Colombia border, thence north and east to north-eastern Venezuela and the Atlantic	400 000	1 036 000	—	—	
29 1650	2650	Si Kiang (Hsi-Chiang)	China: in Yünnan plateau as Nanp'an	Flows east as the Hungshui and later as the Hsün to emerge as the Hsi in the South China Sea, west of Hong Kong	232 300	602 000	—	—	Delta exceeds 90 miles 145 km inland and includes the Pearl River or Chu
30 1616	2600	Kolyma	USSR: in Khrebet Suntarkhayata (as Kulu)	Flows north across Arctic Circle into eastern Siberian Sea	206 000	534 000	134 000	3800	
31 = 1600	2575	Amu-Dar'ya (Oxus)	Wakhan, Afghanistan, on the border with Sinkiang China	Flows west to form Tadzhik SSR–Afghan border as Pyandzh for 680 km 420 miles and into Turkmen SSR as Amu-Dar'ya. Flows north and west into Aral'skoye More (Aral Sea)	179 500	465 000	—	—	
31 = 1600	2575	Nelson–Saskatchewan	Canada: Bow Lake, British Colombia	Flows north and east through Saskatchewan and into Manitoba through Cedar Lake into Lake Winnipeg and out through northern feeder as Nelson to Hudson Bay	414 000	1 072 000	80 000	2250	Saskatchewan 1205 miles 1940 km in length
33 1575	2540	Ural	USSR: South-central Urals	Flows south and west into the Caspian Sea	84 900	220 000	—	—	
1500	2410	Japurá	South-west Colombia in Cordillera Oriental as the Caquetá	Flows east into Brazil as Japurá, thence forms a left bank tributary of the Amazon opposite Tefé	Tributary of No. 2		—	—	
34 1500	2410	Paraguay	Brazil: in the Mato Grosso as Paraguai	Flows south to touch first Bolivian then Paraguayan border, then across Paraguay and then on to form border with Argentina. Joins the Paraná south of Humaitá	440 000 Tributary of No. 14	1 150 000	—	—	

Other Rivers of 1000 miles *1600 km* or Longer

Miles	km	Name and Location	Area of Basin (miles²)	(km²)
1450	2335	Arkansas, USA	Tributary of No. 3	
1450	2335	Colorado, USA	228 000	590 000
1420	2285	Dnepr (Dnieper), USSR	194 200	503 000
1400	2255	Rio Negro, Colombia–Brazil	Tributary of No. 2	
1360	2188	Orange (Oranje), South Africa	394 000	1 020 000
1343	2160	Olenek, USSR	95 000	246 000
1330	2140	Syr-Dar'ya, USSR	175 000	453 000
1306	2100	Ohio–Allegheny, USA	Tributary of No. 3	
1250	2010	Irrawaddy, China–Burma	166 000	430 000
1224	1969	Don, USSR	163 000	422 000

Miles	km	Name and Location	Area of Basin (miles²)	(km²)
1210	1950	Columbia-Snake, Canada–USA	258 000	668 000
1180	1900	Indigirka-Khastakh, USSR	139 000	360 000
1150	1850	Sungari (or Sunghua), China	Tributary of No. 10	
1150	1850	Tigris, Turkey–Iraq	Included in No. 26	
1112	1790	Pechora, USSR	126 000	326 000
1018	1638	Red River, USA	Tributary of No. 3	
1000	1600	Churchill, Canada	150 000	390 000
1000	1600	Uruguay, Brazil–Uruguay–Argentina	Included in No. 14	
1000	1600	Pilcomayo, Bolivia–Argentina–Paraguay	Tributary of Paraguay and sub-tributary of Paraná	

Note: Some sources state that the Amazon tributary the Juruá is over 1133 miles *1823 km* long and the Lena tributary, the Vitim, is 1200 miles *1931 km* long.

Waterfalls

World's Greatest Waterfalls – By Height

	Name	Total Drop (ft)	(m)	River	Location
1.	Angel (highest fall – 2648 ft *807* m*)	3212	979	Carrao, an upper tributary of the Caroni	Venezuela
2.	Tugela (5 falls) (highest fall – 1350 ft *410 m*)	3110	947	Tugela	Natal, S. Africa
3.	Utigård (highest fall – 1970 ft *600 m*)	2625	800	Jostedal Glacier	Nesdale, Norway
4.	Mongefossen	2540	774	Monge	Mongebekk, Norway
5.	Yosemite (Upper Yosemite – 1430 ft *435 m*; Cascades in middle section – 675 ft *205 m*; Lower Yosemite – 320 ft *97 m*)	2425	739	Yosemite Creek, a tributary of the Merced	Yosemite Valley, Yosemite National Park, Cal., USA
6.	Østre Mardøla Foss (highest fall – 974 ft *296 m*)	2154	656	Mardals	Eikisdal, W. Norway
7.	Tyssestrengane (highest fall – 948 ft *289 m*)	2120	646	Tysso	Hardanger, Norway
8.	Kukenaam (or Cuquenán)	2000	610	Arabopó, upper tributary of the Caroni	Venezuela
9.	Sutherland (highest fall – 815 ft *248 m*)	1904	580	Arthur	nr. Milford Sound, Otago, S. Island, New Zealand
10.	Kile (or Kjellfossen) (highest fall – 490 ft *149 m*)†	1841	561	Naerö fjord feeder	nr. Gudvangen, Norway
11.	Takkakaw (highest fall – 1200 ft *365 m*)	1650	502	A tributary of the Yoho	Daly Glacier, British Columbia, Canada
12.	Ribbon	1612	491	Ribbon Fall Stream	3 miles west of Yosemite Falls, Yosemite National Park, Cal., USA
13.	King George VI	1600	487	Utshi, upper tributary of the Mazaruni	Guyana
14.	Roraima	1500	457	An upper tributary of the Mazaruni	Guyana
15.	Cleve-Garth	1476	449	—	New Zealand
16.	Kalambo	1400	426	S.E. feeder of Lake Tanganyika	Tanzania–Zambia
17.	Gavarnie	1384	421	Gave de Pau	Pyrénées Glaciers, France
18.	Glass	1325	403	Iguazú	Brazil
19.	Krimmler fälle (4 falls, upper fall 460 ft *140 m*)	1280	390	Krimml Glacier	Salzburg, Austria
20.	Lofoi	1259	383	—	Zaïre
21.	Silver Strand (Widow's Tears)	1170	356	Merced tributary	Yosemite National Park, Cal., USA

* There are other very high but seemingly unnamed waterfalls in this area.
† Some authorities would regard this as no more than a 'Bridal Veil' waterfall, *i.e.*, of such low volume that the fall atomizes.

World's Greatest Waterfalls – By Volume of Water

Name	Maximum Height (ft)	(m)	Width (ft)	(m)	Mean Annual Flow (ft³/s)	(m³/s)	Location
Boyoma (formerly Stanley) (7 cataracts)	200 (total)	60	2400(7th)	730	c.600 000	17 000	Zaïre River nr. Kisangani
Guaíra (or Salto dos Sete Quedas) ('Seven Falls')	374	114	15 900	4846	470 000*	13 000	Alto Paraná, River Brazil–Paraguay
Khône	70	21	35 000	10 670	400 000 to 420 000	11 000 to 12 000	Mekong River, Laos
Niagara:					212 000	6000	
Horseshoe (Canadian)	160	48	2500	760	(Horseshoe – 94%)		Niagara River, Lake Erie to Lake Ontario
American	167	50	1000	300			Niagara River, Lake Erie to Lake Ontario
Paulo Afonso	192	58	—	—	100 000	2800	São Francisco River, Brazil
Urubu-punga	40	12	—	—	97 000	2700	Alto Paraná River, Brazil
Cataratas del Iguazú (Quedas do Iguaçu)	308	93	c.13 000	c.4000	61 660	1700	Iguazú (or Iguaçu) River, Brazil–Argentina
Patos–Maribondo	115	35	—	—	53 000	1500	Rio Grande, Brazil
Victoria (Mosi-oa-tunya): Leaping Water	355	108	108	33			Zambezi River, Zambia
Main Fall	(maximum)		2694	821	38 430	1100	Zimbabwe
Rainbow Falls			1800	550			
Churchill (formerly Grand)	245	75	—	—	30 000 to 40 000	850 to 1100	Churchill (formerly Hamilton) River, Canada
Kaieteur (Köituök)	741	225	300 to 350	90 to 105	23 400	660	Potaro River, Guyana

* The peak flow has reached 1 750 000 ft³/s *50 000 m³/s*.

Lakes of the World

Name	Country	Area (miles²)	Area (km²)	Length (miles)	Length (km)	Maximum Depth (ft)	Maximum Depth (m)	Average Depth (ft)	Average Depth (m)	Height of Surface above Sea-level (ft)	Height of Surface above Sea-level (m)
1. Caspian Sea	USSR and Iran	143 550	*371 800*	760	*1225*	3215	*980*	675	*205*	−92	*−28*
2. Superior	Canada and USA	31 800	*82 350*	350	*560*	1333	*406*	485	*147*	600·4	*183*
3. Victoria Nyanza	Uganda, Tanzania, and Kenya	26 828	*69 500*	225	*360*	265	*80*	130	*39*	3720	*1134*
4. Aral'skoye More (Aral Sea)	USSR	25 300	*65 500*	280	*450*	223	*68*	52	*15,8*	174	*53*
5. Huron	Canada and USA	23 010	*59 600*	206	*330*	750	*228*	196	*59*	579	*176*
6. Michigan	USA	22 400	*58 000*	307	*494*	923	*281*	275	*83*	579	*176*
7. Tanganyika	Zaire, Tanzania, Zambia and Burundi	12 700	*32 900*	450	*725*	4708	*1435*	—	—	2534	*772*
8. Great Bear	Canada	12 275	*31 800*	232	*373*	270	*82*	240	*73*	390	*118*
9. Ozero Baykal	USSR	11 780	*30 500*	385	*620*	6365	*1940*	2300	*700*	1493	*455*
10. Malawi (formerly Nyasa)	Tanzania, Malawi, and Mozambique	11 430	*29 600*	360	*580*	2226	*678*	895	*272*	1550	*472*
11. Great Slave	Canada	10 980	*28 500*	298	*480*	535	*163*	240	*73*	512	*156*
12. Erie	Canada and USA	9930	*25 700*	241	*387*	210	*64*	60	*18,2*	572	*174*
13. Winnipeg	Canada	9464	*24 500*	266	*428*	120	*36*	50	*15*	713	*217*
14. Ontario	Canada and USA	7520	*19 500*	193	*310*	780	*237*	260	*79*	246	*75*
15. Ozero Ladozhskoye (Lake Ladoga)	USSR	6835	*17 700*	120	*193*	738	*225*	170	*51*	13	*3,9*
16. Ozero Balkhash	USSR	6720	*17 400*	300	*482*	85	*26*	—	—	1112	*339*
17. Lac Tchad (Chad)	Niger, Nigeria, Chad and Cameroon	6300*	*16 300*	130	*209*	13–24	*3,9–7,3*	5	*1,5*	787	*240*
18. Ozero Onezhskoye (Onega)	USSR	3710	*9600*	145	*233*	361	*110*	105	*32*	108	*33*
19. Eyre	Australia	3700†	*9580*	115	*185*	65	*19,8*	—	—	−39	*−11,8*
20. Lago Titicaca	Peru and Bolivia	3200	*8300*	130	*209*	913	*278*	328	*100*	12 506	*3811*
21. Athabasca	Canada	3120	*8100*	208	*334*	407	*124*	—	—	699	*213*
22. Saimaa complex‡	Finland	c. 3100	*c. 8030*	203	*326*	—	—	—	—	249	*75*
23. Lago de Nicaragua	Nicaragua	3089	*8000*	100	*160*	200	*60*	—	—	110	*33*

* Highly variable area between 4250 and 8500 miles² *11 000 and 22 000 km²*.
† Highly variable area between 3100 and 5800 miles² *8030 and 15 000 km²*.
‡ The Saimaa proper (The Lake of a Thousand Isles) is, excluding the islands, c. 500 miles² *1300 km²*.

Lakes under 3000 miles² *770 km²* but over 2000 miles² *5180 km²*

Area (miles²)	(km²)	Name	Country	Area (miles²)	(km²)	Name	Country
2473	6400	Turkana (formerly Rudolf)	Kenya and Ethiopia	2105	5450	Winnipegosis	Canada
2465	6380	Reindeer	Canada	2075	5375	Mobutu Sese Seko (formerly Albert)	Uganda and Zaire
2355	6100	*Issyk Kul'	USSR				
2230	5775	Torrens	Australia	2050	5300	Kariba (dammed)	Zimbabwe and Zambia
2149	5565	Vänern	Sweden				

* Has a maximum depth of 2303 feet *700 m* and an average depth of 1050 ft *320 m*. The height of the surface above sea-level is 5279 ft *1600 m*.

Geology

Rocks of the Earth's crust
These are grouped in three principal classes:

(1) Igneous rocks have been solidified from molten *Magma*. These are divided into extrusive rock, viz. lava and pumice, or intrusive rock, such as some granites or gabbro which is high in calcium and magnesium and low in silicon. It should be noted that extreme metamorphism can also produce granitic rocks from sediment.

(2) Sedimentary rocks are classically formed by the deposition of sediment in water, viz. conglomerates (e.g. gravel, shingle, pebbles), sandstones and shales (layered clay and claystone). Peat, lignite, bituminous coal and anthracite are the result of the deposition of organic matter. Gypsum, chalk and limestone are examples of chemical sedimentation.

(3) Metamorphic rocks were originally igneous or sedimentary but have been metamorphosed (transformed) by the agency of intense heat, pressure or the action of water. Gneiss is metamorphosed granite; marble is metamorphosed limestone; and slate is highly pressurised shale. Metamorphic rocks made cleavable by intense heat and pressure are known generically as schist. Their foliate characteristics are shared by both gneiss and slate.

Geochemical abundances of the elements

	Lithosphere* (Parts per Mill. ‰)	Hydrosphere (Parts per Mill. ‰)
Oxygen	466·0	857·0
Silicon	277·2	0·003 to 0·00002
Aluminium	81·3	0·00001
Iron	50·0	0·00001
Calcium	36·3	0·40
Sodium	28·3	10·50
Potassium	25·9	0·38
Magnesium	20·9	1·35
Titanium	4·4	—
Hydrogen	1·40	103·0
Manganese	0·95	0·000002
Phosphorus	0·70	0·00007
Fluorine	0·65	0·0013
Sulfur	0·26	0·88
Carbon	0·25	0·028
Zirconium	0·17	—
Chlorine	0·13	19·0
Rubidium	0·09	0·0001
Nitrogen	0·02	0·0005
Chromium	0·01	0·00000005

* Assessment based on igneous rock.

Geo-chronology
Christian teaching as enunciated by Archbishop Ussher in the 17th century dated the creation of the Earth as occurring in the year 4004 BC. Lord Kelvin (1824–1907) calculated in 1899 that the earth was of the order of possibly some hundreds of millions of years old. In 1905 Lord Rutherford suggested radioactive decay could be used as a measurement and in 1907 Boltwood showed that a sample of pre-Cambrian rock dated from 1640 million years before the present (BP) measured by the uranium-lead method.

Modern dating methods, using the duration of radioisotopic half-lives, include also the contrasts obtained from thorium-lead, potassium-argon, rubidium-strontium, rhenium-osmium, helium-uranium and in the recent range of up to 40 000 years BP carbon-14. Other methods include thermoluminescence since 1968 and racemisation of amino acids since 1972 which latter is dependant upon the change from optically active to inactive forms which decline varies with the elapse of time.

Geo-Chronology

For early phases of the Earth's history, radiometric dating is the main method of dating events. Before a thousand million years ago dates may err as much as 10 per cent. When fossils became abundant at the start of the Palaeozoic era, the sequence is best defined by those fossils in stratigraphic sequence and assigning radiometric dates to these. Then, by interpolation, a date can be put forward for a geological event, or for the bed in which a fossil has been found. The table below is based on revisions up to 1982 of the timescale put forward by the US Geological Survey of 1980. Myr = one million years ago.

The four main geological divisions, going backwards in time, are: The Cenozoic (Gk. *kainos*, new or recent, *zo-os*, living), the Mesozoic (Gk. *mesos*, middle), the Palaeozoic (Gk. *palaios*, ancient) and the Proterozoic (Gk. *protos*, first). The earliest known life forms, spherical microfossils, date back to 3400 Myr.

Late Mammal Stages (Europe)	
Late Pliocene	
Early Villafranchian	3·25 Myr
Late Villafranchian	2·60 Myr
Pleistocene	
Early Biharian	1·90 Myr (?1·80 Myr)
Middle Biharian	c. 1·5 Myr
Late Biharian	730 000 yr
Toringian	480 000 yr

Gemstones

Gemstones are minerals possessing a rarity and usually a hardness, colour or translucency which gives them strong aesthetic appeal. Diamond, emerald, ruby and sapphire used to be classed as 'precious stones' and all others as 'semiprecious'. This distinction is no longer generally applied. The principal gemstones in order of hardness are listed below with data in the following order: – name; birthstone (if any); chemical formula; classic colour; degree of hardness on Mohs' Scale 10–1; principal localities where found and brief notes on outstanding specimens. A metric carat is ⅕th of a gram.

Diamond: (birthstone for April); C (pure crystalline isotope); fiery bluish-white; Mohs 10·0; S, SW and E Africa and India with alluvial deposits in Australia, Brazil, Congo, India, Indonesia, Liberia, Sierra Leone and USSR (Urals). Largest uncut: *Cullinan* 3106 carats (over 20 oz) by Capt M F Wells, Premier Mine, Pretoria, S Africa on 26 Jan. 1905. Cut by Jacob Asscher of Amsterdam 1909. Largest cut: *Cullinan I* or *Star of Africa* from the above in British Royal Sceptre at 530·2 carats. *Koh-i-nor* originally 186 now re-cut to 106 carats; also in British Crown Jewels. The largest blue diamond is the 44·4 carat vivid blue *Hope Diamond* from Killur, Golconda, India *ante* 1642 in the Smithsonian Institution, Washington DC since November 1958. The rarest colour is blood red.

Diamonds can be produced by 1400°C *2500°F* and 600 000 atmospheres. About 55 000 000 carats are mined annually with Antwerp the world's largest market with an annual turnover of £1000 million.

It takes an average 280 tons of diamond bearing ore to yield a 1 carat stone. The average diamond mined is 0·8 of a carat and less than 15% are used for jewellery (1 carat = 0·2 g).

DATES OF STARTS OF PHASES IN THE GEOLOGICAL TIMESCALE
(Myr = 1 million years ago)

	Myr		Myr		Myr
Hadean era	est. 4450	Late Carboniferous		Late Cretaceous	
Archean era	3800	Namurian	335	Cenomanian	96
Proterozoic era		Westphalian	316	Turonian	92
Early Proterozoic	2500	Stephanian	306	Coniacian	89
Middle Proterozoic	1600	Early Permian		Santonian	88
Late Proterozoic	900	Sakmarian	290	Campanian	84
Paleozoic era		Artinskian	278	Maastrichtian	72
Early Cambrian		Kungurian	268	**Cenozoic era**	
Georgian	570	Late Permian		Tertiary period	
Middle Cambrian		Kazanian	256		
Acadian	550	Tatarian	249	Early Paleocene	
Late Cambrian		**Mesozoic era**		Danian	67
Potsdamian	530	Early Triassic		Late Paleocene	
Early Ordovician		Scythian	245	Thanetian	61
Tremadocian	520	Middle Triassic		Early Eocene	
Arenigian	507	Anisian	240	Ypresian	55
Llanvirnian	493	Ladinian	235	Middle Eocene	
Llandeilian	476	Late Triassic		Lutetian	50
Late Ordovician		Karnian	230	Bartonian	45
Caradocian	458	Norian	225	Late Eocene	
Ashgillian	447	Rhaetian	216	Priabonian	41
Silurian		Early Jurassic		Early Oligocene	
Llandoverian	435	Hettangian	208	Rupelian	37
Wenlockian	430	Sinemurian	205	Late Oligocene	
Ludlovian	423	Pliensbachian	197	Chattian	33
Downtonian	417	Toarcian	188	Early Miocene	
Early Devonian		Aalenian	182	Aquitanian	25
Gedinnian	410	Middle Jurassic		Burdigalian	19·5
Siegenian	399	Bajocian	177	Middle Miocene	
Emsian	394	Bathonian	170	Langhian	14·7
Middle Devonian		Late Jurassic		Serravallian	13·3
Eifelian/Couvinian	389	Callovian	164	Late Miocene	
Givetian	383	Oxfordian	159	Tortonian	11·5
Late Devonian		Kimmeridgian	154	Messinian	6·7
Frasnian	378	Tithonian	145	Early Pliocene	
Famennian	370	Early Cretaceous		Zanclean, etc.	5·3
Early Carboniferous		Berriasian	138	Late Pliocene	
Tournaisian	360	Valanginian	133	Piacenzian	3·25
Visean	348	Hauterivian	126	Quaternary period	
		Barremian	123		
		Aptian	120	Early Pleistocene	1·8
		Albian	114	Late Pleistocene	730 000 yr
				Holocene	10 300 yr

Ruby: (birthstone for July); Al_2O_3 (red corundum with trace of chromic oxide); 9·0; Brazil, Burma, Sri Lanka, Thailand. Largest recorded gem ruby from Burma *ante* 1886 weighed 400 carats. Most valuable of all gems per carat.

Sapphire: (birthstone for September); Al_2O_3 (corundum); any colour but red, classically dark blue; 9·0; Australia, Burma, Sri Lanka, Kashmir, USA (Montana). Largest cut blue star: *Star of India*, 563·5 carats from Sri Lanka now in American Museum of Natural History, New York City. Largest star sapphire: 733 carat Black Star of Queensland from 1165 carat rough, found in 1934, owned by Kazanjian Foundation, Los Angeles.

Alexandrite: $Al_2[BeO_4]$ (chrysoberyl with chromium traces); green (daylight) but red (artificial light); 8·5; Brazil, Moravia, Sri Lanka, USSR (Urals), Zimbabwe.

Cat's Eye: $Al_2[BEO_4]$ (chrysoberyl) yellowish to brownish-green with narrow silken ray; 8·5.

Topaz: (birthstone for November); $Al_2SiO_4F_2$; tea coloured; 8·0; Australia, Brazil, Sri Lanka, Germany, Namibia, USSR. The largest recorded is of 596 lb from Brazil.

Spinel: $MgAl_2O_4$ with trace of FE_2O_3; red; 8·0; mainly Burma, Sri Lanka, India and Thailand.

Emerald: (birthstone for May); $Al_2Be_3Si_6O_{18}$ (beryl); vivid green; 7·5–8·0; Austria, Colombia, Norway, USA (N Carolina), USSR (Urals), Zambia; largest recorded beryl prism (non-gem quality) 135 lb *61,2 kg* from Urals; largest beryl crystal 16 200 carats; Musó, Columbia. Devonshire stone of 1383·95 carats presented in 1831, is from same area.

Aquamarine: (birthstone for March); $Al_2Be_3Si_6O_{18}$ (beryl), pale limpid blue; 7·5–8·0; found in Brazil, Malagasy and USSR and elsewhere, including N. Ireland; largest recorded 243 lb *110 kg* near Marambaia, Brazil 1910.

Garnet: (birthstone for January); silicates of Al, Ca, Cr, Fe, Mg, Ti, V, Zr, purplish-red (Almandine, $Fe_3Al_2[SiO_4]_3$; 7·5–8·0; India, Sri Lanka, USA (Arizona); green (Demantoid, $Ca_3Fe_2[SiO_4]_3$; 6·5–7·0; USSR (Siberia and Urals); black (Malanite, $TiCa_3 (Fe, Ti, Al)_2 [SiO_4]_3$, 6·5.

Zircon: Zr (SiO_4); colourless but also blue and red-brown (hyacinth); 7·0–7·5; Australia (NSW), Burma, France, Norway, Sri Lanka, India, North America, Thailand, USSR (Siberia).

Tourmaline: complex boro-silicate of Al, Mg alkalis; notably deep green, bluish green, deep red; 7·0–7·25; Brazil, Sri Lanka, USA, USSR (Siberia).

Rock Crystal: (birthstone for April, alternative to diamond); SiO_2; Colourless; 7·0; Brazil, Burma, France, Madagascar, Switzerland, USA (Arkansas). The largest recorded crystal ball is one of 106 lb *48 kg* from Burma now in the US National Museum, Washington DC.

Rose quartz: SiO_2; coarsely granular pale pink; 7·0; Bavaria, Brazil, Finland, Namibia, USA (Maine); USSR (Urals).

Cairngorm: (Smoky quartz); SiO_2; smoky yellow to brownish; 7·0; Brazil, Madagascar, Manchuria, Scotland (Cairngorm Mountains), Switzerland, USA (Colorado), USSR (Urals).

Amethyst: (birthstone for February); SiO_2; purple 7·0; Brazil, Sri Lanka, Germany, Madagascar, Uruguay, USSR (Urals).

Chrysoprase (Chalcedony form); (birthstone for

May, alternative to emerald); SiO_2 with nickel hydroxide impurity; apple green (opaque); 6·5–7·0; Germany, USA.

Jade: Jadeite $Na(Al,Fe^{+3})Si_2O_6$; dark to leek green; 6·5–7·0; Burma, China, Tibet (pale green and less valuable form is nephrite, $Ca_2(Mg,Fe^{+2})_5Si_8O_{22}(OH)_2$; China, Canada, New Zealand, USA.

Cornelian (Chalcedony form); often (wrongly) spelt carnelian; (birthstone for July, alternative to ruby); SiO_2 with ferric oxide impurity; blood red to yellowish-brown; 6·5–7·0; widespread, including Great Britain.

Agate (Striped chalcedony) SiO_2; opaque white to pale grey, blue; 6·6–7·0; variety is moss agate (milky white with moss like inclusions, often green); Brazil, Germany, India, Madagascar, Scotland.

Onyx: a black and white banded agate (see Agate).

Sardonyx: (birthstone for August, alternative to Peridot); a reddish-brown and white-banded agate (see Agate).

Jasper: (Chalcedony); SiO_2 with impurities; brown (manganese oxide), red (ferric oxide), yellow (hydrated ferric oxide); opaque; 6·5–7·0; Egypt, India.

Peridot (Green Olivine); (birthstone for August); $(Mg, Fe)_2[SiO_4]$ green; 6·5–7·0; Australia (Queensland); Brazil, Burma, Norway, St John's Island (Red Sea) now Zabargad Island, USA (Arizona).

Bloodstone or Blood Jasper: (Chalcedony): (birthstone for March, alternative to aquamarine); SiO_2; dark green with red spots (oxide of iron); 6·0–7·0.

Moonstone: (Feldspar): (birthstone for June, alternative to pearl); $K[AlSi_3O_8]$; white to bluish, iridescent; 6·0–6·5; Brazil, Burma, Sri Lanka.

Opal: (birthstone for October); $SiO_2.nH_2O$: rainbow colours on white background; other varieties include fire opal, water opal, black opal; 5·0–6·5; Australia, Mexico and formerly Hungary, USA. The largest recorded is one of 34 215 carats named *Desert Flame of Andamooka* found in Australia in 1969.

Turquoise: (birthstone for December); $CuAl_6[(OH)_8(PO_4)_4]5H_2O$; sky blue; 5·5–6·0; Egypt (Sinai Peninsula), Iran, Turkey, USA (California, Nevada, New Mexico, Texas).

Lapis Lazuli: (birthstone for September, alternative to sapphire); $(Na,Ca)_8[(S,Cl,SO_4)_2(AlSiO_4)_6]$; deep azure blue, opaque; 5·5–5·75; Afghanistan, Chile, Tibet, USSR (Lake Baykal area).

Obsidian: (glassy lava); green or yellowish-brown; 5·0–5·5; volcanic areas.

Non-mineral gem material

Amber (organic): about $C_{40}H_{64}O_4$; honey yellow; clear; or paler yellow, cloudy; 2·0–2·5; Mainly Baltic and Sicily coasts. A variety is fly amber in which the body of an insect is encased.

Coral (polyps of *Coelenterata*): varied colourations including Blood or Red Coral; Australasia, Pacific and Indian Oceans.

Pearl: (birthstone for June); (secretions of molluscs, notably of the sea-water mussel genus *Pinctada* and the fresh-water mussel *Quadrula*); Western Pacific and Indian Oceans; largest recorded is the *Hope Pearl* weighing nearly 3 oz *85 g*, circumference 4½ in *114 mm*. A nacreous mass of 14 lb 2 oz *6,4 kg* from a giant clam (*Tridacna gigas*) was recovered in the Philippines in 1934 and is known as the 'Pearl of Allah'.

Earthquakes

It is estimated that each year there are some 500 000 detectable seismic or micro-seismic disturbances of which 100 000 can be felt and 1000 cause damage.

It was not until as recently as 1874 that subterranean slippage along overstressed faults became generally accepted as the cause of tectonic earthquakes. The collapse of caverns, or mine-workings, volcanic action, and also possibly the very rare event of a major meteoric impact can also cause tremors. The study of earthquakes is called seismology.

The two great seismic systems are the Alps-Himalaya great circle and the circum-Pacific belt. The foci below the epicentres are classified as shallow (<50 km deep), intermediate (50–200 km) and deep (200–700 km).

In 1954 the Gutenberg-Richter scale was introduced to compare the strengths of seismic shocks. The scale measures the magnitude Mw. $Mw = \frac{2}{3}[\log_{10}(2E \times 10^4) - 10·7]$ where E is the energy released in dyne/cm. In 1977 the more satisfactory Kanamori scale, using the concept of seismic moment, devised by K-Aki (Japan) in 1966, was adopted. It measures the magnitude M_s. $M_s = \frac{2}{3}(\log_{10}E - 11·8)$. The Lebu shock, south of Concepción, Chile on 22 May 1960 uniquely registered 9·5 on the Kanamori scale indicating on estimated energy of 10^{26} ergs. No earthquake has ever reached 9 in the Gutenberg-Richter scale. It has been estimated however that the Great Lisbon Earthquake of 1 Nov. 1755, 98 years before the invention of seismographs would have rated between 8¾ and 9. The death roll was 60 000.

HISTORIC EARTHQUAKES

The five earthquakes in which the known loss of life has exceeded 100 000 have been:

c. 1·1 m	E. Mediterranean	c. July 1201
830 000	Shensi Province, China	2 Feb. 1556
300 000	Calcutta, India	11 Oct. 1737
242 000*	Tangshan, China (8·2R)	27 July 1976
180 000	Kansu Province, China (landslides) (8·6R)	16 Dec. 1920
142 807	Kwanto Plain, Honshū, Japan (8·3R)	1 Sept. 1923

* Unaccountably reduced to this figure on 22 Nov. 1979 from 655 237 unannounced on 4 Jan. 1977.

The material damage done in the Kwanto Plain, which includes Tōkyō, was estimated at £1 000 000 000.

Other notable earthquakes during this century, with loss of life have been:

1906	Colombian coast (31 Jan) (8·6R; 8·8K)	
1906	San Francisco, USA (18 Apr.) (452) (8·3R)	
1908	Messina, Italy (28 Dec.) (80 000) (7·5R)	
1915	Avezzano, Italy (13 Jan.) (29 970)	
1932	Gansu Province, China (26 Dec.) (70 000) (7·6R)	
1935	Quetta, India (31 May) (60 000) (7·5R)	
1939	Erzincan, Turkey (27 Dec.) (30 000) (7·9R)	
1950	Assam, India (15 Aug.) (1500) (8·6R; 8·6K)	
1952	Kamchatka, USSR (4 Nov.) (8·5R; 9·0K)	
1957	Andreanol, Aleutian Is. USA (9 Mar) (8·3R; 9·1K)	
1960	Agadir, Morocco (29 Feb.) (12 000) (5·8R)	
1960	Lebu, Chile (22 May) (8·3R; 9·5K)	
1964	Anchorage, Alaska (28 Mar.) (131) (8·5R)	
1970	Northern Peru (31 May) (66 800) (7·7R)	
1971	Los Angeles (9 Feb.) (64) (6.5K)	
1972	Nicaragua (23 Dec.) (5000) (6·2R)	
1976	Guatemala (4 Feb.) (22 700) (7·5R)	
1976	Tangshan, China (27 July) (see above) (8·2R)	
1977	Buchárest, Romania (4 Mar.) (1541) (7·5R)	
1978	Tabas, N.E. Iran (16 Sept.) (25 000) (7·7R)	
1980	El Asnam, Algeria (10 Oct.) (2327) (7.5R)	
1980	Potenza, Italy (23 Nov.) (c. 3000) (6·8R)	
1982	North Yemen (13 Dec.) (2800) (6·0R)	
1983	Eastern Turkey (30 Oct.) (1233) (7·1R)	

R = Richter-Gutenberg scale   K = Kanamori scale

Attendant phenomena include:
(i) *Tsunami* (wrongly called tidal waves) or gravity waves which radiate in long, low oscillations from submarine disturbances at speeds of 450–490 mph *725–790 km/h*. The 1883 Krakatoa *tsunami* reached a height of 135 ft *41 m* and that off Valdez, Alaska in 1964 attained a height of 220 ft *67 m*. The word *tsu* (wild), *nami* (wave) is Japanese.
(ii) *Seiches* (a Swiss-French term of doubtful origin, pronounced sāsh). Seismic oscillations in landlocked water. Loch Lomond had a 2 ft *60 cm* seiche for 1 hr from the 1755 Lisbon 'quake.
(iii) *Fore and After Shocks*. These often occur before major 'quakes and may persist after these for months or years.

BRITISH EARTHQUAKES

The earliest British earthquake of which there is undisputable evidence was that of AD 974 felt over England. The earliest precisely recorded was that of 1 May 1048, in Worcester. British earthquakes of an intensity sufficient to have raised or moved the chair of the observer (Scale 8 on the locally used Davison's scale) have been recorded thus:

25 Apr.	1180	Nottinghamshire
15 Apr.	1185	Lincoln
1 June	1246	Canterbury, Kent
21 Dec.	1246	Wells
19 Feb.	1249	South Wales
11 Sept.	1275	Somerset
21 May	1382	Canterbury, Kent
28 Dec.	1480	Norfolk
26 Feb.	1575	York to Bristol
6 Apr.	1580*	London
30 Apr.	1736	Menstrie, Clackmannan
1 May	1736	Menstrie, Clackmannan
14 Nov.	1769†	Inverness
18 Nov.	1795	Derbyshire
13 Aug.	1816‡	Inverness
23 Oct.	1839	Comrie, Perth
30 July	1841	Comrie, Perth
6 Oct.	1863	Hereford
22 Apr.	1884§	Colchester
17 Dec.	1896	Hereford
18 Sept.	1901	Inverness
27 June	1906‖	Swansea
30 July	1926	Jersey
15 Aug.	1926	Hereford
7 June	1931	Dogger Bank (5·6R)
11 Feb.	1957	Midlands
26 Dec.	1979	Longtown, Cumbria
19 July	1984	W. Areas & Ireland (5·5R)

* About 6 p.m. First recorded fatality – an apprentice killed by masonry falling from Christ Church.
† 'Several people' reported killed. Parish register indicates not more than one. Date believed to be 14th.
‡ At 10.45 p.m. Heard in Aberdeen (83 miles *133 km*), felt in Glasgow (115 miles *185 km*). Strongest ever in Scotland.
§ At 9.18 a.m. Heard in Oxford (108 miles *174 km*), felt in Exeter and Ostend, Belgium (95 miles *152 km*). At least 3, possibly 5, killed. Strongest ever in British Isles at 6 on the Richter scale.
‖ At 9.45 a.m. Strongest in Wales. Felt over 37 800 miles² *98 000 km²*.

OTHER MAJOR NATURAL DISASTERS

Landslides caused by earthquakes in the Kansu Province of China on 16 Dec. 1920 killed 180 000 people.

The Peruvian snow avalanches at Huarás (13 Dec. 1941) and from Huascarán (10 Jan. 1962) killed 5000 and 3000 people respectively. The Huascarán alluvion flood triggered by the earthquake of 31 May 1970 wiped out 25 000.

Both floods and famines have wreaked a greater toll of human life than have earthquakes. The greatest river floods on record are those of the Hwang-ho, China. From September into October 1887 some 900 000 people were drowned. The flood of August 1931 was reputed to have drowned or killed 3 700 000 people. A typhoon flood at Haiphong in Viet Nam (formerly Indo-China) on 8 Oct. 1881 killed an estimated 300 000 people. The cyclone of 12–13 Nov. 1970 which struck the Ganges Delta Islands, Bangladesh drowned an estimated 1 000 000 people.

History's worst famines have occurred in Asia. In 1770 nearly one third of India's total population died with ten million dead in Bengal alone. It was revealed in May 1981 that the death toll from the northern Chinese famines of 1969–71 totalled some 20 000 000.

The Krakatoa eruptions of 26–28 Aug. 1883 killed 36 000 mostly due to a *tsunami*. The Mont Pelée volcanic eruption in Martinique on 8 May 1902 killed over 30 000.

Petroleum

Most deposits of petroleum are found in sedimentary rocks representing deposition in shallow new seas which once supported flora and fauna. The assumption that oil is a downward migration of such organic decay is now modified by the abiogenic theory which maintains that some of the heavy hydrocarbons may have sprung, already polymerised, from deep layers of hot magma.

Exploration in the North Sea began on 26 Dec. 1964 from the drilling rig 'Mr Cap'. The first show of methane (CH_4) gas came on 20 Sept. 1965 from the drill of British Petroleum's 'Sea Gem' 42 miles east of the Humber estuary.

It was estimated that at 1 Jan. 1985 the world's total proved oil reserves were 96 100 000 000 tonnes or 707 200 000 000 bbl. World consumption ran at 58 870 000 barrels a day from 1 Apr. 1984 to 31 Mar. 1985 or 2844·5 million tonnes in the 12 months. World production was at the lesser rate of 57 800 000 bbl a day or 2826·1 million tonnes in the year, thus running down stocks. Unless more oil is discovered, and even if the world's consumption stays at the present level, the world's oil resources will run dry on 13 Jan. 2019 at 12.12 p.m.

Meteorology

Phenomena and Terms

Ball Lightning
A very rare phenomenon. A spheroid glowing mass of energised air, usually about one ft *30 cm* in diameter. On striking an earthed object it seems to disappear, hence giving the impression that it has passed through it. Only one photograph exists of the phenomenon, taken in August 1961.

'Blue Moon'
The diffraction of light through very high clouds of dust or smoke, as might be caused by volcanic eruptions (notably Krakatoa, 27 Aug. 1883) or major forest fires (notably in British Columbia, 26 Sept. 1950), can change the colour of the Sun (normally white overhead and yellow or reddish at sunrise or sunset) and the Moon (normally whitish) on such rare occasions to other colours, notably green and even blue.

Brocken Spectre
A person standing with his (or her) back to the Sun and looking down from higher ground onto a lower bank of fog or cloud, casts a shadow known by this name.

Coronae
When the Sun's or Moon's light is diffracted by water droplet cloud, a ring of light (sometimes two or more) which is blue on the inside and reddish brown on the outside, may be seen closely and concentrically around the Sun or Moon.

Cyclone
A violent circular storm in the northern part of the Indian Ocean (see also Hurricane and Typhoon). The term was originally used for any low-pressure system, in contrast to the Anticyclone or high-pressure system. The cyclone of 12–13 Nov. 1970 in the Ganges Delta area, Bangladesh, resulted in about 1 000 000 deaths mainly from drowning. Cyclone Tracy which struck the Darwin area of N. Australia on 24–25 Dec. 1974 produced measured wind speeds of 134·8 mph *216,9 km/h*.

Depression
A depression is a low pressure circulation in the temperate latitudes whose mean wind speeds are usually less than Beaufort force 8.

Fogbow
In rainbow conditions, when the refracting droplets of water are very small, as in fog, the colours of the rainbow may overlap and so the bow appears white. Alternative names for this phenomenon are a *Cloudbow* and *Ulloa's Ring*.

Flachenblitz
A rare form of lightning which strikes upwards from the top of Cumulonimbus clouds and ends in clear air.

Glory
A *glory* is a ring of light like a *corona* seen around a *Brocken Spectre*. It probably results from multiple reflection within tiny drops of water and then diffraction on the return of light to the eye. A *glory* can only be seen around an observer's own shadow, but people standing alongside each other can all see each other's shadow.

Haloes
When the Sun's light is refracted by ice crystals in Cirrus or Cirrostratus clouds, a bright ring of light, usually reddish on the inside and white on the outside, may be seen round the Sun with a 22° radius. Much more rarely a 46° *halo* may appear, and, very rarely indeed, haloes of other sizes with radii of 7° upwards. Halo phenomena may also be seen round the Moon. Sun haloes must not be studied by direct observation owing to the danger to eyesight.

Hurricanes
A violent circular storm in the southern part of the North Atlantic, notably the Caribbean Sea (see also Cyclone and Typhoon). Hurricane Betsy in 1965 caused damage estimated at more than $1000 million on which $750 million was paid out in insurance.

Iridescence (or Irisation)
The name given to the colouring at the edge of coronae.

Mirages
Mirages are cause by the refraction of light when layers of the atmosphere have sharply differing densities (due to contrasting temperature). There are two types of mirages: within the *inferior mirage* – the more common of the two – an object near the horizon appears to be refracted as in a pool of water; with the *superior mirage* the object near – or even beyond – the horizon appears to float above its true position.

Nacreous Clouds
Nacreous, or mother-of-pearl, clouds probably consisting of supercooled water droplets occasionally appear after sunset over mountainous areas, at a height of from 60 000–80 000 ft *8300–24 400 m*. These are lit by sunlight from below the horizon, so may be seen hundreds of miles away, for example in Scotland over Scandinavia.

Noctilucent 'clouds' are phenomena, possibly formed by cosmic dust, that appear bluish in colour at a very great height of 300 000 ft, say 60 miles or *100 km*. This phenomenon is reported from Shetland (Lat. 60° N) more than 30 times in some years e.g. 1967 (34) and 1976 (36).

Parhelia, mock or sun dogs
In halo conditions the ice crystals when orientated in a particular way can refract light so as to produce one or more *mock suns* or *parhelia* on either or both sides of the Sun and usually 22° away from it.

Rainbows
If an observer stands with his back to the Sun and looks out on a mass of falling raindrops lit by the Sun, he will see a *rainbow*. A *primary bow* is vividly coloured with violet on the inside, followed by blue, green, yellow, orange, and red. A *secondary bow*, which, if visible, is only about a tenth of the intensity of its primary, has its colour sequence reversed. Further bows, even more feeble, can on very rare occasions be seen.

Saint Elmo's Fire (or Corposants)
A luminous electrical discharge in the atmosphere which emanates from protruding objects, such as ships' mastheads, lightning conductors and windvanes.

Sun Pillars
A *Sun Pillar* is a column of light above or below a low elevation sun and is caused by reflection in ice crystals which are inclined slightly to the horizontal. Being reflected light a *sun pillar* has the same colour as the Sun.

Thunderbolts
These do not in fact exist, but the effect of the intense heating of a lightning strike may fuse various materials and so give the false impression that a solid object in fact hit the ground. A lightning strike may boil water almost instantaneously and so, for example, shatter damp masonry, so giving the appearance that it has been struck by a solid object.

Tornado
A *tornado* results most usually from intense convection, which produces a violent whirlwind extending downwards from a storm cloud base, often reaching the ground. The width varies between about 50 m *164 ft* and 400 m *1312 ft* and it moves across country at speeds varying from 10 to 30 mph *15–50 km/h* causing great damage. The British frequency is about 12 per annum, one in 1638 causing 4 deaths and more than 50 injured at Widecombe, Devon. On 18 Mar. 1925 tornadoes in the south central states of the USA killed 689. At Wichita Falls, Texas on 2 Apr. 1958, a wind speed of 280 mph *450 km/h* was recorded.

Typhoon
A violent circular storm in the south-western part of the North Pacific and especially the China Sea (see also Cyclone and Hurricane). A barometer pressure as low as 870 millibars (25·69 in) was recorded 300 miles *480 km* west of Guam in the Pacific on 12 Oct. 1979.

Waterspout
The same phenomenon as a tornado, except that it occurs over the sea, or inland water. These may reach an extreme height of a mile > *1600 m.*

Whiteout
When land is totally covered by snow, the intensity of the light reflected off it may be the same as that reflected off overhead cloud. This results in the obliteration of the horizon, and makes land and sky indistinguishable.

Fog
The international meteorological definition of fog is a 'cloud touching the ground and reducing visibility to less than one kilometer (1100 yd).' For road traffic reports visibility below 600 ft *180 m* is described as 'fog'.

Fog requires the coincidence of three conditions:
(i) Minute hygroscopic particles to act as nuclei. The most usual source over land is from factory or domestic chimneys, whereas at sea, salt particles serve the same purpose. Such particles exist everywhere, but where they are plentiful the fog is thickest.
(ii) Condensation of water vapour by saturation.
(iii) The temperature at or below dew point. This may arise in two ways. The air temperature may simply drop to dew point, or the dew point may rise because of increase amounts of water vapour.

Sea fog persists for up to 120 days in a year on the Grand Banks, off Newfoundland. London has twice been beset by 114 hours continuous fog relatively recently – 26 Nov. to 1 Dec. 1948 and 5–9 Dec. 1952.

Thunder and Lightning
At any given moment there are some 2200 thunderstorms on the Earth's surface which are audible at ranges of up to 18 miles *29 km*. The world's most thundery location is Bogor (for-merly Buitenzorg), Java, Indonesia, which in 1916–19 averaged 322 days per year with thunder heard. The extreme in the United Kingdom is 38 days at Stonyhurst, Lancashire in 1912, and in Huddersfield, West Yorkshire in 1967.

Thunder arises after the separation of electrical charges in Cumulonimbus (q.v.) clouds. In the bipolar thundercloud the positive charge is in the upper layer. Thunder is an audible compression wave, the source of which is the

Beaufort Scale
A scale of numbers, designated Force 0 to Force 12, was originally devised by Commander Francis Beaufort (1774–1857) (later Rear-Admiral Sir Francis Beaufort, KCB, FRS) in 1805. Force numbers 13 to 17 were added in 1955 by the US Weather Bureau but are not in international use since they are regarded as impracticably precise.

Force No.	Descriptive term	Wind speed mph	knots
0	Calm	0–1	0–1
1	Light air	1–3	1–3
2	Light breeze	4–7	4–6
3	Gentle breeze	8–12	7–10
4	Moderate breeze	13–18	11–16
5	Fresh breeze	19–24	17–21
6	Strong breeze	25–31	22–27
7	Near gale	32–38	28–33
8	Gale	39–46	34–40
9	Strong gale	47–54	41–47
10	Storm	55–63	48–55
11	Violent storm	64–75	56–65
12	Hurricane	76–82	66–71
13	Hurricane	83–92	72–80
14	Hurricane	93–103	81–89
16	Hurricane	115–125	100–108
17	Hurricane	126–136	109–118

Constituents of Air

Gas	Formula	% By volume
Invariable component gases of dry carbon dioxide-free air		
Nitrogen	N_2	78·110
Oxygen	O_2	20·953
Argon	A	0·934
Neon	Ne	0·001818
Helium	He	0·000524
Methane	CH_4	0·0002
Krypton	Kr	0·000114
Hydrogen	H_2	0·00005
Nitrous Oxide	N_2O	0·00005
Xenon	Xe	0·0000087
		99·9997647 %
Variable components		
Water Vapour	H_2O	0 to 7·0*
Carbon dioxide	CO_2	0·01 to 0·10 average 0·034
Ozone	O_3	0 to 0·000007
Contaminants		
Sulfur dioxide	SO_2	up to 0·0001
Nitrogen dioxide	NO_2	up to 0·000002
Ammonia	NH_3	trace
Carbon monoxide	CO	trace

* This percentage can be reached at a relative humidity of 100 per cent at a shade temperature of 40°C *104°F*

Cloud Classification

Genus (with abbreviation)	Ht of base (ft)	(m)	Temp at base level (°C)	Official description
Cirrus (Ci)	16 500 to 45 000	5000 to 13 700	−20 to −60	Detached clouds in the form of white delicate filaments, or white or mostly white patches or narrow bands. They have a fibrous (hair-like) appearance or a silky sheen, or both. They are the highest of the standard forms averaging 27 000 ft *8 250 m*.
Cirrocumulus (Cc)	16 500 to 45 000	5000 to 13 700	−20 to −60	Thin, white sheet or layer of cloud without shading, composed of very small elements in the form of grains, ripples, etc., merged or separate, and more or less regularly arranged.
Cirrostratus (Cs)	16 500 to 45 000	5000 to 13 700	−20 to −60	Transparent, whitish cloud veil of fibrous or smooth appearance, totally or partly covering the sky, and generally producing halo phenomena.
Altocumulus (Ac)	6500 to 23 000	2000 to 7000	+10 to −30	White or grey, or both white and grey, patch, sheet or layer of cloud, generally with shading, composed of laminae, rounded masses, rolls, etc. which are sometimes partly fibrous or diffuse, and which may or may not be merged.
Altostratus (As)	6500 to 23 000	2000 to 7000	+10 to −30	Greyish or bluish cloud sheet or layer of striated, fibrous or uniform appearance, totally or partly covering the sky, and having parts thin enough to reveal the sun at least vaguely.
Nimbostratus (Ns)	3000 to 10 000	900 to 3000	+10 to −15	Grey cloud layer, often dark, the appearance of which is rendered diffuse by more or less continually falling rain or snow which in most cases reaches the ground. It is thick enough throughout to blot out the sun. Low, ragged clouds frequently occur below the layer with which they may or may not merge.
Stratocumulus (Sc)	1500 to 6500	460 to 2000	+15 to −5	Grey or whitish, or both grey and whitish, patch, sheet or layer of cloud which almost always has dark parts, composed of tessellations, rounded masses, rolls, etc., which are non-fibrous (except for virga) and which may or may not be merged.
Stratus (St)	surface to 1500	surface to 460	+20 to −5	Generally grey cloud layer with a fairly low uniform base below 3500 ft *1050 m*, which may give drizzle, ice prisms or snow grains. When the sun is visible through the cloud its outline is clearly discernible. Stratus does not produce halo phenomena (except possibly at very low temperatures). Sometimes stratus appears in the form of ragged patches.
Cumulus (Cu)	1500 to 6500	460 to 2000	+15 to −5	Detached clouds, generally dense and with sharp outlines, developing vertically in the form of rising mounds, domes or towers, of which the bulging upper part often resembles a cauliflower. The sunlit parts of these clouds are mostly brilliant white; their bases are relative dark and nearly horizontal.
Cumulonimbus (Cb)	1500 to 6500	460 to 2000	+15 to −5	Heavy and dense cloud, with a considerable vertical extent, in the form of a mountain or huge towers up to 20 000 m *68 000 ft* in the tropics. At least part of its upper portion is usually smooth, or fibrous or striated, and nearly always flattened; this part often spreads out in the shape of an anvil or vast plume. Under the base of this cloud, which is often very dark, there are frequently low ragged clouds either merged with it or not, and precipitation, sometimes in the form of virga – (fallstreaks or trails or precipitation attached to the underside of clouds).

Note: The rare nacreous or mother-of-pearl formation sometimes attains an extreme height of 80 000 ft *24 000 m*.

rapid heating of the air by a return lightning stroke.

Lightning. The speed of lightning varies greatly. The downward leader strokes vary between 100 and 1000 miles per second *150 to 1500 km/s.* In the case of the powerful return stroke a speed of 87 000 miles per second *140 000 km/s,* nearly half the speed of light) is attained. The length of stroke varies with cloud height and thus between 300 ft *90 m* and 4 miles *6 km* lateral strokes as long as 20 miles *32 km* have been recorded. The central core of a lightning channel is extremely narrow – perhaps as little as a half-inch, *12 mm.* In the case of the more 'positive giant' stroke the temperature reaches c. 30 000°C *54 000° F* or over five times that of the sun's surface. In Britain the frequency of strikes is only 6 per mile[2] *2·3 per km[2]* per annum. British fatalities have averaged 11·8 per annum this century with 31 in 1914 but nil in 1937.

World and UK Meteorological Absolutes and Averages

Temperature: The world's overall average annual day side temperature is 59°F *15°C.* Highest shade (**world**): 136·4°F *58°C* Al'Aziziyah, Libya, 13 Sept. 1922. **UK:** 98·2°F *36,7°C* Rounds, Northants; Epsom, Surrey; Canterbury, Kent, 9 Aug. 1911. The hottest place (**world**) on annual average is Dallol, Ethiopia with 94°F *34,4°C* (1960–66) and in **UK** Penzance, Cornwall, and Isles of Scilly, both 52·7°F *11,5°C.* Annual Means: England 50·3°F *10,1°C;* Scotland 47·6°F *8,6°C.*

Lowest Screen (**world**): −128·6°F *−89,2°C* Vostok, Antarctica, 21 July 1983. **UK:** −17°F *−27,2°C* Braemar, Grampian, 11 Feb. 1895 and 9 Jan. 1982 (NB – Temperature of −23°F *−30,5°C* at Blackadder, Borders, in 1879 and of −20°F *−28,8°C* at Grantown-on-Spey, in 1955 were not standard exposures.) The coldest place (**world**) on annual average is the Pole of Cold, 150 miles *240 km* west of Vostok, Antarctica at −72°F *−57,8°C* and in the **UK** at Braemar, Aberdeen, Grampian 43·43°F *6,35°C* (1959–81).

Barometric Pressure: The world's average barometric pressure is 1013 mb. Highest (**world**): 1083·8 mb (32·00 in), Agata, Siberia, USSR, 31 Dec. 1968 and **UK**: 1054·7 mb (31·15 in) at Aberdeen, 31 Jan. 1902.

Lowest (**world**): 870 mb (25·69 in), recorded at sea 300 miles *480 km* W of Guam, Pacific Ocean, 12 Oct. 1979 and **UK**: 925·5 mb (27·33 in), Ochtertyre, near Crieff, Tayside, 26 Jan. 1884.

Wind Strength: Highest sustained surface speed (**world**) 231 mph *371 km/h,* (200·6 knots) Mt Washington (6288 ft *1916 m*), New Hampshire, USA, 24 Apr. 1934. **UK**: 144 mph *231 km/h* (125 knots). Coire Cas ski lift (3525 ft *1074 m*) Cairngorm, Highland, 6 Mar. 1967. (NB – The 201 mph *175 kts* reading reported from Saxa

The Earth's Atmospheric Layers

Troposphere
The realm of clouds, rain and snow in contact with the lithosphere (land) and hydrosphere (sea). The upper limit, known as the tropopause, is 17 km *11 miles* (58 000 ft) at the equator or 6–8 km *3·7–4·9 miles* (19 700–25 000 ft) at the Poles. In middle latitudes in high pressure conditions the limits may be extended between 13 km *8 miles* to 7 km *4 miles* in low pressure conditions. Aviation in the troposphere is affected by jet streams, strong, narrow air currents with velocities above 60 knots and by CAT (Clear Air Turbulence) which if violent can endanger aircraft.

Stratosphere
The second region of the atmosphere marked by a constant increase in temperature with altitude up to a maximum of −3°C at about 50 km *30 miles* (160 000 ft).

Mesosphere
The third region of the atmosphere about 50 km *30 miles* (160 000 ft) marked by a rapid decrease in temperature with altitude to a minimum value even below −113°C at about 85 km *55 miles* (290 000 ft) known as the mesopause.

Thermosphere
The fourth region of the atmosphere above the mesosphere characterised by an unremitting rise in temperature up to a night maximum during minimum solar activity of 225°C at about 230 km *140 miles* to above 1480°C in a day of maximum solar activity at 500 km *310 miles.* This region is sometimes termed the heterosphere because of the widely differing conditions in night and day and during solar calm and solar flare.

Exosphere
This is the fifth and final stage at 500 km *310 miles* in which the upper atmosphere becomes space and in which temperature no longer has the customary terrestrial meaning.

Note: The Appleton layer in the ionosphere at some 300 km is now referred to as the F_2 layer. The Heaviside layer at c. 100 km is now termed the E layer. They were named after the physicists Oliver Heaviside (1850–1925) and Sir Edward Appleton (1892–1965) and have importance in the reflection of radio waves.

Northern and Southern Lights

Polar lights are known as Aurora Borealis in the northern hemisphere and Aurora Australis in the southern hemisphere. These luminous phenomena are caused by electrical solar discharges between altitudes of 620 miles *1000 km* and 45 miles *72,5 km* and are usually visible only in the higher latitudes.

It is believed that in an auroral display some 100 million protons (hydrogen nuclei) strike each square centimetre of space in the exosphere or of atmosphere in the meso or thermospheres each second. Colours vary from yellow-green (attenuated oxygen), reddish (very low pressure oxygen), red below green (molecular nitrogen below ionised oxygen) or bluish (ionised nitrogen). Displays, which occur on every dark night in the year above 70°N or below 70°S (eg Northern Canada or Antarctica), vary in frequency with the 11-year sunspot cycle. Edinburgh may expect perhaps 25 displays a year against 7 in London, and Malta once a decade. The most striking recent displays over Britain occurred on 25 Jan. 1938 and 4–5 Sept. 1958. On 1 Sept. 1909, a display was reported from just above the equator at Singapore (1° 12′N) but is not uncritically accepted. In 1957 203 displays were recorded in the Shetland Islands (geometric Lat. 63°N).

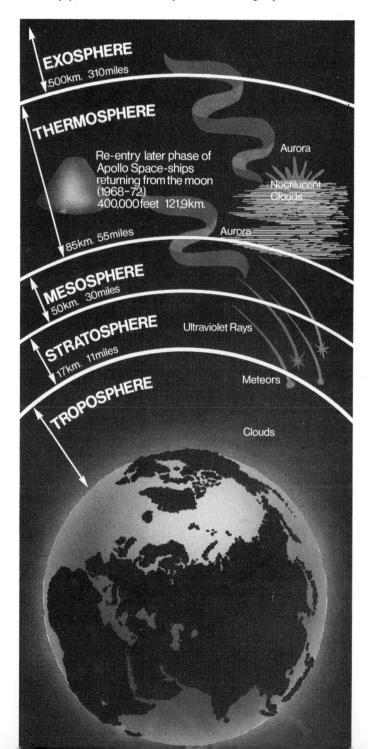

EXOSPHERE
500km. 310 miles

THERMOSPHERE
Re-entry later phase of Apollo Space-ships returning from the moon (1968–72) 400,000 feet 121,9km.
85km. 55miles

Aurora
Noctilucent Clouds
Aurora

MESOSPHERE
50km. 30miles

STRATOSPHERE
17km. 11miles
Ultraviolet Rays

TROPOSPHERE
Meteors
Clouds

Vord, Unst, Shetland, on 3 Mar. 1979 has *not* been accepted.) Windiest place (**world**): Commonwealth Bay, George V coast, Antarctica, several 200 mph *320 km/h* gales each year. **UK**: Fair Isle, Shetland annual average 20·7 mph *33,3 km/h.*

Rainfall: Highest (**world**) **Minute:** 1·23 in *31,2 mm* Unionville, Maryland, USA, 4 July 1956; **24 hr:** 73·62 in *1870 mm* Cilaos, La Réunion Island, Indian Ocean on 15–16 March 1952; **12 months:** 1041·78 in *26 461 mm* Cherrapunji, Assam, 1 Aug. 1860 to 31 July 1861. Highest (**UK**) **24 hrs:** 11·00 in *279 mm* Martinstown, Dorset, 18–19 July 1955; **Year:** 257·0 in *6527 mm* Sprinkling Tarn, Cumbria, in 1954. Wettest Place (**world**): Mt Wai-'ale'ale (5148 ft *1569 m*), Kauai I, Hawaiian Islands, annual average 451 in *11 455 mm* (1920–72). Most rainy days in a year (**world**) up to 350 on Mt. Wai-'ale'ale; **British Isles:** 309 at Ballynahinch, Galway, Ireland, in 1923.
Lowest (**world**) at places in the Desierto de Atacama of Chile, including Calama, where no rain has ever been recorded in the *c.* 400 years to 1971 since when there has been some rain. Lowest (**UK**) Year: 9·29 in *236 mm* Margate, Kent, in 1921. Longest Drought: 73 days from 4 March to 15 May 1893 at Mile End, Greater London.

Snowfall: Greatest (**world**) **Single Storm:** 189 in *4800 mm* Mt Shasta, California; **24 hr:** 76 in *1930 mm* Silver Lake, Colorado, 14–15 Apr. 1921; **Year:** 1224·5 in *31 102 mm* Paradise Ranger Station, Mt Rainier, Washington, USA, in 1971–2. **UK:** Annual days of snowfall vary between extremes of 40 in the Shetland Islands and 5 in Penzance, Cornwall. The gulleys on Ben Nevis (4406 ft *1342 m*) were snowless only 7 times in the 31 years 1933–64. An accumulated level of 60 in *1524 mm* was recorded in February 1947 in both Upper Teesdale and the Clwyd Hills of North Wales.

Sunshine: Maximum (**world**): in parts of the eastern Sahara the sun shines strongly enough to cast a shadow for 4300 hours in a year or 97 per cent of possible. **UK:** The highest percentage for a month is 78·3 per cent (382 hours) at Pendennis Castle, Falmouth, Cornwall, June 1925. Minimum (**world**): the longest periods of total darkness occur at the North Pole (over 9000 ft *2740 m* less altitude than South Pole) with 186 days. **UK:** the lowest monthly reading has been at Westminster, London, in Dec. 1890.

Ice Ages

A new method of dating events over the past million years has been established and relies on the precision with which ice-age cycles follow variations in the Earth's position in space and the shape of its orbit. These are calculated by established astronomical methods, and are observed in the Milankovitch theory as climatic rhythms. These rhythms correspond with cycles of about 90 000 years (changes in orbital configuration), 41 000 years (axis tilt) and 23 000 and 19 000 years (axis wobble or precession of the equinoxes). Ocean bed cores provide evidence of the last magnetic reversal 730 000 years ago, and give an important dating monitor. From these one can correlate the climatic phases or 'core stages', evident from marine fossils, with the orbital variations, and arrive at a timescale.

Although the 90 000 year cycle became regular only 800 000 years ago a count of 28 ice ages between 3 250 000 years and the start of an ice age 649 000 years ago gives a mean average between each ice age of 92 900 years. Seven more ice ages to the present can thus be computed to the present day. In the table below the figures are rounded off.

Ice age number	Start (rounded)
29	650 000 yr
30	550 000 yr
31	475 000 yr
32	350 000 yr
33	280 000 yr
34	188 000 yr
35	72 000 yr
36	due soon

The Solar System: its planets and their moons

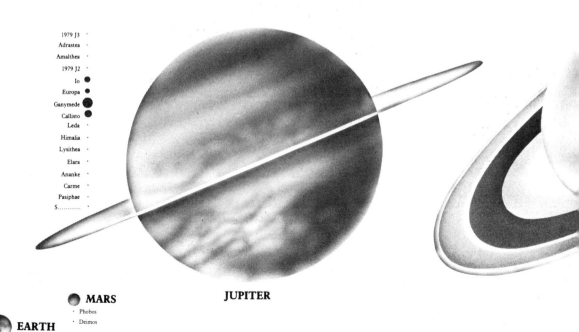

Astronomy

A guide to the scale of the Solar System and the Universe

If the Sun were reduced to the size of a beach ball of 1 ft *30,48 cm* in diameter, following on the same scale the nine planets would be represented *relatively* thus:
(1) Mercury = a grain of mustard seed 50 ft *15,2 m* away
(2) Venus = a pea 78 ft *23,7 m* away
(3) Earth = a pea 106 ft *32,3 m* away
    Moon = a grain of mustard seed 3½ in *8,5 cm* out from the Earth
(4) Mars = a currant 164 ft *49,9 m* away
(5) Jupiter = an orange 560 ft *170,6 m* away
(6) Saturn = a tangerine 1024 ft *312,1 m* away
(7) Uranus = a plum 2060 ft *627,8 m* away
(8) Neptune = a plum 3230 ft *984,5 m* away
(9) Pluto = a pinhead up to a mile *1,6 km* away.

The utter remoteness of the solar system from all other heavenly bodies is stressed by the fact that, still using this same scale of a 1 ft *30,48 cm* Sun, which for this purpose we shall place in the centre of London, the nearest stars, the triple Alpha Centauri system, would lie 5350 miles *8609,9 km* away, say near San Francisco with the largest member having a 2 ft *60,96 cm* diameter. Only the next six nearest stars in our Milky Way galaxy could, even on this scale, be accommodated on the Earth's surface.

Human imagination must boggle at distances greater than these, so it is necessary to switch to a much vaster scale of measurement.

Light travels at 186 282·397 miles/sec or *299 792,458 km/s* in vacuo. Thus, in the course of a tropical year (i.e. 365·242 198 78 mean solar days at January 0, 12 hours Ephemeris time in AD 1900) light will travel 5 878 499 814 000 miles or *9 460 528 405 000 km*. This distance has conveniently, since March 1888, been called a light year.

Light will thus travel to the Earth from the following heavenly bodies in the approximate times given:

From the Moon (reflected light)	1·25 sec
From the Sun (at perihelion)	8 min 27·3 sec
From Pluto (variable)	about 6 hrs
From nearest star (excepting the Sun)	4·28 yrs
From Rigel	900 yrs
From most distant star in the Milky Way	75 000 yrs
From nearest major extra-galactic body (Larger Magellanic cloud)	160 000 yrs
From Andromeda (limit of naked eye vision)	2 200 000 yrs
Limit of observable horizon (radio-located quasars)	c. 15 000 000 000 yrs

The stars

NUMBER OF STARS

There are 5776 stars visible to the naked eye, It is estimated that our own galaxy, the Milky Way galaxy, contains some 100 000 million (10^{11}) stars and that there are between 100 000 and 1 000 000 million (10^{11} to 10^{12}) galaxies in the detectable universe. This would indicate a total of 10^{22} to 10^{23} stars. The Milky Way galaxy is of a lens-shaped spiral form with a diameter of some 70 000 light years. The Sun is some 28 000 light years from the centre and hence the most distant star in our own galaxy is about 75 000 light years distant.

AGE OF STARS

Being combustible, stars have a limited life. The Sun, which is classified as a G2 Spectrum Yellow Dwarf, functions like a controlled hydrogen bomb, losing four million tons in mass each second. It has been estimated that it has more than 5 000 million years to burn. It is not yet possible to give a precise value for the age of the universe. However, the Earth is *c.* 4600 million years old, and the universe itself has most recently (Aug. 1978) been estimated to be between 13 500 and 15 500 million years old.

The planets

MERCURY

The closest of the planets to the Sun, Mercury, is never visible with the naked eye except when close to the horizon. Surface details were hard to see from Earth, even with powerful telescopes, but in 1974 the US probe Mariner 10 disclosed that the surface features are remarkably similar to those of the Moon, with mountains, valleys and craters. Mercury is virtually devoid of atmosphere, but it does have a weak but appreciable magnetic field.

VENUS

Venus, almost identical in size with the Earth, is surrounded by a cloud-laden atmosphere, so that its actual surface is never visible telescopically. Research with unmanned probes has shown that the mean surface temperature is 865°F *480°C*, that the atmospheric ground pressure is about 100 times that on Earth, and that the main atmospheric constituent is carbon dioxide; the clouds contain corrosive sulphuric acid. The US Pioneer Venus probe of Dec. 1978 revealed that Mount Maxwell is 12 000 m *39 370 ft* and winds of 640 km/h *400 mph* occur. Venus rotates very slowly in a retrograde direction (i.e. in a sense opposite to that of the Earth).

MARS

Mars was long thought to be the one planet in the Solar System, apart from Earth, to be capable of supporting life, but results from space-probes are not encouraging. Mariner 9 (1971–2) sent back thousands of high-quality pictures, showing that Mars is a world of mountains, valleys, craters and giant volcanoes; one volcano, Olympus Mons, is some 15 miles high *over 24 000 m* and is crowned by a caldera 40 miles *64 km* in diameter. The Martian atmosphere is made up chiefly of carbon dioxide, and is very tenuous, with a ground pressure which is everywhere below ten millibars (cf. Earth's 1013 mb). The permanent polar caps are composed of ice. The Viking missions of 1976–7 disclosed no trace of organic material on Mars. The two dwarf satellites, Phobos and Deimos, were discovered by A. Hall in 1877; Mariner 9 pictures show that each is an irregular, crater-pitted lump of rocky material.

SATURN

- 1980 S 20
- 1980 S 27
- 1980 S 26
- 1980 S 1
- 1980 S 3
- Mimas
- Enceladus
- Tethys
- 1980 S 13 (Probable moon)
- Dione
- 1980 S 6
- Rhea
- Titan
- Hyperion
- Iapetus
- Phoebe

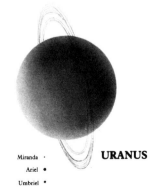

URANUS

Miranda
Ariel
Umbriel
Titania
Oberon

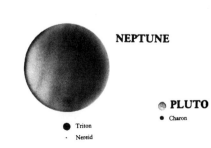

NEPTUNE

Triton
Nereid

PLUTO

Charon

JUPITER

Jupiter is the largest planet in the Solar System. The outer layers are gaseous, composed of hydrogen and hydrogen compounds; it is now thought that most of the planet is liquid, and that hydrogen predominates. The famous Great Red Spot has proved to be a kind of whirling storm, as was shown by the close-range photographs sent back by the US probe Pioneer 10 and 11. Jupiter has a strong magnetic field, and is surrounded by zones of lethal radiation.

SATURN

Saturn is basically similar to Jupiter, but is less dense and is, of course, colder. The rings which surround Saturn are composed of pieces of material (probably ices, or at least ice-covered) moving round the planet in the manner of dwarf satellites; the ring-system is 169 000 miles *270 000 km* wide, but less than 5 miles *8 km* thick. There are three main rings; two bright (A and B) and one dusky (C). Rings A and B are separated by the Cassini Division. However, the flyby of Voyager 1, in November 1980, showed that the rings are much more complicated than had been thought; there are hundreds of 'grooves', and there are thin rings even inside the Cassini Division. The new rings F and E lie outside the main ring system; F is 'braided'. Of Saturn's satellites, Titan is the most important; its diameter is about 2700 miles *4350 km*, and Voyager established that is has a dense nitrogen atmosphere, with a ground pressure 1½ times that of the Earth's air. Titan is permanently veiled by clouds; its surface may contain seas of liquid methane or even liquid nitrogen.

URANUS

Just visible to the naked eye, Uranus has the same low density as Jupiter and has a diameter nearly four times that of the Earth. Its axis is tilted at 98° compared with our 23° 27′ which means that the night and day must at some points last up to 21 years each. In 1977, indirect researches showed that there are eight rings round Uranus – too faint to be detected visually from Earth.

NEPTUNE

Neptune is rather denser and *slightly* smaller than Uranus. It requires nearly 165 years to make one revolution of the Sun against the 84 years of Uranus. Its axial tilt at 28° 48′ conforms more closely to those of the Earth (23° 27′), Mars (25° 12′), and Saturn (26° 44′).

PLUTO

Discovered by systematic photography in 1930. The 248-year orbit of this faint planet with only 8 per cent of the volume of the Earth is so eccentric that at perihelion is came inside the orbit of Neptune on 21 Jan. 1979. The existence of a moon, Charon, was announced on 22 June 1978 by James W. Christy of the US Naval Observatory, Flagstaff, Arizona.

THE SUN

The Sun (for statistics see Solar System table) is a yellow dwarf star (spectrum classification G2) with a luminosity of 3×10^{27} candle power such that each square inch of the surface emits 1.53×10^6 candelas. Sun spots appear to be darker because they are 2700°F (1500°C) cooler than the surface temperature of 10 220°F (5660°C). These may measure up to 7×10^9 miles² *1.8×10^{10} km²* and have to be 5×10^8 miles *1.3×10^9 km²* to be visible to the (*protected*) naked eye. During 1957 a record 263 were noted. Solar prominences may flare out to 365 000 miles *588 000 km* from the Sun's surface.

THE BRIGHTEST AND NEAREST STARS (EXCLUDING THE SUN)

Magnitude – a measure of stellar brightness such that the light of a star of any magnitude bears a ratio of 2·511 886 to that of the star of the next magnitude. Thus a fifth magnitude star is 2·511 886 times as bright, whilst one of the first magnitude is exactly 100 (or 2·511 886⁵) times as

bright as a sixth magnitude star. In the case of such exceptionally bright bodies as Sirius, Venus, the Moon (magnitude − 12·7) or the Sun (magnitude − 26·8) the magnitude is expressed as a minus quantity. Such a value for the Sun is its 'apparent magnitude' (m_v) which is the brightness as seen from the Earth, but for comparison the intrinsic brightness needs to be known and this is defined as the 'absolute magnitude' (M_v), the magnitude that would be observed if the star was placed at a distance of ten parsecs. On this basis the magnitude of the Sun is reduced to +4·8 or a four billionfold reduction in brightness.

The absolute magnitude of a star is related to its apparent magnitude and its distance in parsecs (d) by means of the equation:

$$M_v = m_v + 5 - 5 \log_{10}(d)$$

BRIGHTEST STARS

Name	Magnitude		Distance	
	Apparent	Absolute	Light years	Parsecs†
Sirius	−1·46	+1·4	8·65	2·65
Canopus*	−0·73	−4·6	200	60
Alpha Centauri*	−0·29	+4·1	4·38	1·34
Arcturus	−0·06	−0·3	36	11
Vega	+0·04	+0·5	26	8·1
Capella	+0·08	−0·5	42	13
Rigel	+0·10	−7·0	900	275
Procyon	+0·35	+2·6	11·4	3·5
Achernar*	+0·48	−2·5	127	39
Beta Centauri* (Agena)	+0·60	−4·6	490	150
Altair	+0·77	+2·3	16	5·0
Betelgeuse	+0·85 v	−5·7 v	650	200
Aldebaran	+0·85	−0·7	65	21
Alpha Crucis	+0·90	−3·7	270	85
Spica	+0·96	−3·6	260	80
Antares	+1·08	−4·5	430	130
Pollux	+1·15	+1·0	35	10·7
Fomalhaut	+1·16	+1·9	23	7·0
Deneb	+1·25	−7·1	1500	500
Beta Crucis	+1·25	−5·1	530	160
Regulus	+1·35	−0·7	85	26
Adhara	+1·50	−4·4	490	150

* Not visible from British Isles.
v = very variable apparent magnitude, average figure.
† A parsec (pc) = the distance at which 1 astronomical unit (AU) subtends an angle of 1 sec. of arc and = *c.*1.917×10^{13} miles. An AU = mean sun to Earth distance.

NEAREST STARS

Name	Distance		Magnitude			
	Light Years	Parsecs	Apparent		Absolute	
Proxima Centauri	4·22	1·30	11·05		15·49	
Alpha Centauri	4·35	1·33	A −0·01 B 1·33		A 4·37 B 5·71	
Barnard's Star	5·98	1·83	9·54		13·22	
Wolf 359	7·75	2·38	13·53		16·65	
Lalande 21185	8·22	2·52	7·50		10·49	
Luyten 726–8*	8·43	2·58	A 12·52 B 13·02		A 15·46 B 15·96	
Sirius	8·65	2·65	A −1·46 B 8·68		A 1·42 B 11·56	
Ross 154	9·45	2·90	10·6		13·3	
Ross 248	10·4	3·18	12·29		14·77	
Epsilon Eridani	10·8	3·31	3·73		6·13	
Ross 128	10·9	3·36	11·10		13·47	
61 Cygni	11·1	3·40	A 5·22 B 6·03		A 7·56 B 8·37	
Epsilon Indi	11·2	3·44	4·68		7·00	
Luyten 789–6	11·2	3·45	12·18		14·49	
Groombridge 34	11·2	3·45	A 8·08 B 11·06		A 10·39 B 13·37	
Procyon	11·4	3·51	A 0·37 B 10·7		A 2·64 B 13·0	
Sigma 2398	11·6	3·55	A 8·90 B 9·69		A 11·15 B 11·94	
Lacaille 9352	11·7	3·58	7·36		9·59	
Giclas 51–15	11·7	3·60	14·81		17·03	
Tau Ceti	11·8	3·61	3·50		5·71	
Luyten's Star	12·3	3·76	9·82		11·94	
Luyten 725–32	12·5	3·83	12·04		14·12	
Lacaille 8760	12·5	3·85	6·67		8·74	
Kapteyn's Star	12·7	3·91	8·81		10·85	
Kruger 60	12·9	3·95	A 9·85 B 11·3		A 11·87 B 13·3	

* The B star companion is known as UV Ceti.

Earth-Moon System

CREATION OF THE MOON

It was once believed that the Moon used to be part of the Earth, and that the original combined body broke in two as a result of tidal forces. This is not now believed to be the case. It may be that the Moon was once an independent body which was captured by the Earth; however, most authorities believe that it has always been associated with the Earth. Certainly the rocks brought back by the Apollo astronauts confirm that the age of the Moon is approximately the same as that of the Earth (c. 4600 million years).

CREATION OF THE EARTH

The long-popular theory that the Earth and

ELEMENTS OF THE PLANETARY ORBITS

Planet	Mean Distance From Sun miles km	Perihelion Distance miles km	Aphelion Distance miles km	Orbital Eccentricity	Orbital Inclination ° ′ ″	Sidereal Period days	Orbital Velocity Mean mph km/h	Maximum mph km/h	Minimum mph km/h
Mercury	35 983 100 *57 909 100*	28 584 000 *46 001 000*	43 382 000 *69 817 000*	0·205 630	7 00 15	87·9693	105 950 *170 500*	131 930 *212 310*	86 920 *139 890*
Venus	67 237 900 *108 208 900*	66 782 000 *107 475 000*	67 694 000 *108 943 000*	0·006 783	3 23 39	224·7008	78 340 *126 070*	78 870 *126 930*	77 810 *125 220*
Earth	92 955 800 *149 597 900*	91 402 000 *147 097 000*	94 510 000 *152 099 000*	0·016 718	— — —	365·2564	66 620 *107 220*	67 750 *109 030*	65 520 *105 450*
Mars	141 635 700 *227 940 500*	128 410 000 *206 656 000*	154 862 000 *249 226 000*	0·093 380	1 50 59	686·9797	53 860 *86 680*	59 270 *95 390*	49 150 *79 100*
Jupiter	483 634 000 *778 833 000*	460 280 000 *740 750 000*	506 990 000 *815 920 000*	0·048 286	1 18 16	4332·62	29 210 *47 000*	30 670 *49 360*	27 840 *44 810*
Saturn	886 683 000 *1 426 978 000*	837 000 000 *1 347 020 000*	936 370 000 *1 506 940 000*	0·056 037	2 29 21	10 759·06	21 560 *34 700*	22 820 *36 730*	20 400 *32 830*
Uranus	1 783 951 000 *2 870 991 000*	1 701 660 000 *2 738 560 000*	1 866 230 000 *3 003 400 000*	0·046 125	0 46 23	30 707·79	15 200 *24 460*	15 930 *25 630*	14 520 *23 370*
Neptune	2 794 350 000 *4 497 070 000*	2 766 270 000 *4 451 880 000*	2 822 430 000 *4 542 270 000*	0·010 050	1 46 20	60 199·63	12 150 *19 560*	12 270 *19 750*	12 030 *19 360*
Pluto	3 674 490 000 *5 913 510 000*	2 761 600 000 *4 444 400 000*	4 587 300 000 *7 382 600 000*	0·248 432	17 08 22	90 777·61	10 430 *16 790*	13 660 *21 980*	8220 *13 230*

PHYSICAL PARAMETERS OF THE SUN AND PLANETS

Sun or Planet		Diameter miles	km	Equatorial Sidereal Rotation Period d h m s	Equatorial Inclination	Mass tons	kg	Density g/cm³	Escape Velocity mps	km/s
Sun		865 270	*1 392 520*	25 09 07	7° 15′	1·958 × 10²⁷	*1,989 × 10³⁰*	*1,407*	383·65	*617,43*
Mercury		3031	*4878*	58 15 30 34	0°	3·250 × 10²⁰	*3,302 × 10²³*	*5,433*	2·64	*4,25*
Venus		7520	*12 102*	*243 00 14	178°	4·792 × 10²¹	*4,869 × 10²⁴*	*5,246*	6·44	*10,36*
Earth	Equ.	7926	*12 756*	23 56 04·091	23° 27′	5·2880 × 10²¹	*5,974 × 10²⁴*	*5,515*	6·95	*11,19*
	Polar	7900	*12 714*							
Mars	Equ.	4221	*6794*	24 37 22·663	25° 12′	6·318 × 10²⁰	*6,419 × 10²³*	*3,934*	3·12	*5,03*
	Polar	4196	*6752*							
Jupiter	Equ.	88 780	*142 880*	9 50 30·003	3° 04′	1·869 × 10²⁴	*1,899 × 10²⁷*	*1,330*	37·42	*60,23*
	Polar	82 980	*133 540*							
Saturn	Equ.	74 880	*120 500*	10 14	26° 44′	5·596 × 10²³	*5,686 × 10²⁶*	*0,687*	22·42	*36,09*
	Polar	67 640	*10 860*							
Uranus	Equ.	31 950	*51 400**	16 10	97° 53′	8·602 × 10²²	*8,740 × 10²⁵*	*1,26*	13·28	*21,38*
	Polar	31 250	*50 300*							
Neptune	Equ.	30 200	*48 600*	18 26	28° 48′	1·013 × 10²³	*1,029 × 10²⁶*	*1,75*	14·82	*23,84*
	Polar	29 500	*47 500*							
Pluto		1860	*3000*	6 09 18	90°	1·46 × 10¹⁹	*1,49 × 10²²*	*0,93*	0·67	*1,08*

* Retrograde.

Sun or Planet	Surface Temperature °C	Equatorial Diameter	On Scale Earth = 1 Volume	Mass	Surface Gravity	Mean Apparent Magnitude	Number of Satellites
Sun	5660	109·16	1 305 000	332 946·0	27·88	−26·8	—
Mercury	−180 to +420	0·3824	0·0561	0·055 27	0·3771	0·0	0
Venus	462	0·9487	0·8568	0·815 00	0·9034	−4·4	0
Earth	−88 to +58	1·0000	1·0000	** 1·000 00	1·0000	—	1
Mars	−125 to +30	0·5326	0·1506	0·107 45	0·3795	−2·0	2
Jupiter	−108	11·20	1318	317·89	2·644	−2·6	16
Saturn	−133	9·45	764	95·18	1·139	+0·7	16
Uranus	−160	4·03	64	14·63	0·912	+5·5	5
Neptune	−160	3·81	54	17·22	1·200	+7·8	2
Pluto	−220	0·24	0·013	0·025	0·040	+15·0	1

** The Earth-Moon system weighs 1·012 30 Earth masses.

other planets were globules thrown out from a molten Sun has long been discarded. Spectroscopic analysis has shown that the Sun consists of 98 per cent hydrogen and helium whereas the cores of planets are often a composite of heavy non-gaseous elements.

It is now thought that the planets including the Earth were formed by accretion from a cloud of material or 'solar nebula' which used to be associated with the Sun.

Eclipses

An eclipse (derived from the Greek *ekleipsis* 'failing to appear') occurs when the sight of a celestial body is either obliterated or reduced by the intervention of a second body.

There are two main varieties of eclipse.
(i) Those when the eclipsing body passes between the observer on Earth and the eclipsed body. Such eclipses are those of the Sun by the Moon; occultations of various stars by the moon; transits of Venus or Mercury across the face of the Sun; and the eclipses of binary stars.
(ii) Those when the eclipsing body passes between the Sun and the eclipsed body. These can only affect planets or satellites which are not self-luminous. Such are the eclipses of the Moon (by the Earth's shadow); and the eclipses of the satellites of Jupiter.

There is nothing in all the variety of natural phenomena that is quite so impressive as a total eclipse of the Sun.

Eclipses of the Sun (by the Moon) and of the Moon (by the Earth) have caused both wonder and sometimes terror since recorded history.

The element of rarity enhances the wonder of this event, which should on average only be seen from a given city or town once in about four hundred years. More specifically, Londoners saw no such eclipse between 20 March 1140 and 3 May 1715 – that is, about nineteen generations later. The next will be on 14 June 2151. The next total eclipse of the Sun visible from Great Britain will occur on 11 Aug. 1999 on the Cornish coast. Eclipses of the Sun are in fact commoner than those of the Moon but the area from which they can be seen is so much smaller that the number of possible spectators is infinitely smaller.

The places from which and the times at which solar eclipses have been seen have been worked out back as far as the year 4200 BC and can be worked out far into the future, with of course an increasing, but still slight, degree of inaccuracy. The precise date of actual historical events in the Assyrian, Chinese, Greek and Roman empires have been fixed or confirmed by eclipses. For example, the battle between the Lydians and the Medes, which is reported by Herodotus, can be fixed exactly as occurring on 28 May 585 BC, because a solar eclipse caused such awe that it stopped the fight. Modern astronomy has benefited from the study of ancient eclipses because they help to determine 'secular accelerations', that is, the progressive changes in celestial motions.

Solar Eclipses (i.e. of the Sun by the Moon)
Solar eclipses are of three sorts – Total, Partial and Annular. A *total* eclipse occurs when the Moon, which, of course, must be new, comes completely between the Sun's disc and the observer on Earth. The Moon's circular shadow – its umbra – with a maximum diameter of 170 miles *273 km.* sweeps across the face of the Earth from West to East. The maximum possible duration of totality for a stationary observer is 7 min 31 sec.

The dramatic events at the moment of totality are: sunlight vanishes in a few seconds; sudden darkness (but *not* as intense as that during a night even under a full moon); the brightest stars become visible; the Sun's corona is seen; there is a hush from the animal and bird world; cocks have been noted to crow when the light floods back.

The moon's partial shadow – its penumbra – which forms a much larger circle of about 2000 miles *3200 km* in diameter, causes a *partial* eclipse. Partial eclipses, of course, vary in their degree of completeness. There must be a minimum of two Solar eclipses each year.

An *annular* eclipse occurs when – owing to variations in the Sun's distance – the Moon's disc comes inside the Sun. In other words, the Moon's umbra stops short of the Earth's surface and an outer rim of the Sun surrounds the Moon. The maximum possible duration of containment is 12 min 24 sec.

Lunar Eclipses (i.e. of the Moon by the Earth's shadow)
Lunar eclipses are caused when the Moon – which, of course, must be full – passes through the shadow of the Earth and so loses its bright direct illumination by the Sun. A lunar eclipse is *partial* until the whole Moon passes into the Earth's umbra and so becomes *total*. After the Moon leaves the umbra it passes through the Earth's penumbra, which merely dims the moonlight so little that it is scarcely visible and is not even worth recording.

Other Observable Phenomena
I. During its movement across the sky the Moon may pass in front of a star, hiding or occulting it. Immersion takes place instantaneously, because the Moon has no atmosphere around its limb – in fact this was one of the earliest direct proofs of the Moon's lack of atmosphere. The emersion of the star is equally sudden. Planets may also be occulted, though in such cases both immersion and emersion are gradual because a planet presents an appreciable disk.
II. The two planets – Mercury and Venus – which are nearer the Sun than is the Earth, occasionally can be seen (with proper protection to the eyes) to pass slowly across the face of the Sun. These so-called Transits of Mercury occur on average about 14 times every century; Transits of Venus are far rarer with the last in 1882 and the next two on 8 June 2004 and 6 June 2012.
III. Some apparently single stars have been observed to vary sharply in brightness. They have been found in fact to be twin stars, revolving around each other and so eclipsing one another. Such stars are called *eclipsing binaries*, and the best-known examples are Algol and β Lyrae.

COMETS
Comets are Solar System bodies moving in orbits about the Sun. Records go back to the 7th century BC. The speeds of the estimated 2 000 000 comets vary from only 700 mph in the outer reaches to 1 250 000 mph (*1100-2 million km/h*) when near the Sun. The periods of revolution vary, according to the ellipticity of orbit, from 3·3 years (Encke's comet) to millions of years as in the case of Delavan's Comet of 1914 which is not expected to return for 24 million years. Comet Wilson-Harrington, discovered in Nov. 1949, had a calculated period of only 2·3 years but has not since been sighted.

Comets are tenuous to the point that 10 000 cubic miles *41 600 km³* of tail might embrace only a cubic inch of solid matter. Comets are not self luminous, hence only visible when in the inner part of the Solar System. They consist mainly of a head of dirty ice particles and a tail which always points more or less away from the Sun. In May 1910 the Earth probably passed through the tail of the famous Halley's Comet which is next due to return on 9 Feb. 1986 (perihelion). Lexell's Comet of 1770 approached to within 1 200 000 km *750 000 miles*. The 35 megaton explosion 40 miles *64 km* north of Vanavara, Siberia on 30 June 1908, known as the Tunguska event, was concluded in July 1977 to have been caused by a cometary collision.

Telescopes

The prototype of modern refracting telescopes was that made in 1608 by the Dutchman Hans Lippershey (or Lippersheim) after an accidental discovery of the magnifying power of spectacle lens when held apart. The principle of the reflecting telescope was expounded by the Scot, James Gregory in 1663 and the first successful reflector was built with a 5 cm *2 in* diameter mirror by Sir Isaac Newton for presentation to the Royal Society, London on 11 Jan. 1672.

The world's most powerful astronomical telescopes are now:

Diameter of Refractors (Lens)			Completion
Inches	cms		Date
40·0	102	Yerkes, Williams Bay, Wisconsin, USA	1897
36·0	91	Lick, Mt Hamilton, Cal., USA	1888
32·7	83	Paris Observatory, Meudon, France	1893
32·0	81	Astrophysical Observatory, Potsdam, Germany	1899
30·0	76	Nice Observatory, Nice, France	1880
30·0	76	Alleghany Observatory, Pittsburgh, Penn., USA	1914

Diameter of Reflectors (Mirror)			
Inches	cms		
236·2	600	Mount Semirodriki, Caucasus, USSR	1976
200·0	508	Hale, Mt Palomar, nr Pasadena, Cal., USA	1948
158·0	401	Kitt Peak Nat. Observatory, Tucson, Arizona, USA	1970
158·0	401	Cerro Tololo, Chile	1970
153·0	389	Siding Spring, Australia	1974
150·0	381	Mount Stromlo, Canberra, Australia	1972
150·0	381	La Cilla, Chile	1975
120·0	305	Lick, Mt Hamilton, Cal., USA	1959
107·0	272	McDonald Observatory, Fort Davis, Texas, USA	1968
104·0	264	Crimean Astrophysical Lab., Nauchny, USSR	1960
100·0	254	Hooker, Mt Wilson, Cal., USA	1917
98·0	249	Newton (Herstmonceux 1967) La Palma, Canary Is.	1983
88·0	223	Mauna Kea Observatory, Hawaii	1970

The Russian 600 cm *236·2 in* reflector is now the largest in the world; it may well remain so, as it is quite likely that future emphasis will be upon telescopes in space. The largest telescope in Great Britain was the 98 in *248 cm* reflector at the Royal Greenwich Observatory, Herstmonceux, known as the Isaac Newton Telescope of INT. However, this telescope was dismantled to be relocated on the island of La Palma in the Canary Isles in 1979 at the new La Palma Observatory.

RADIO TELESCOPE
The world's largest dish radio telescope is the non-steerable £3 750 000 ionospheric apparatus at Arecibo, Puerto Rico, completed in November 1963. It utilises a natural crater which is spanned by a dish 1000 ft *305 m* in diameter, covering an area of 18½ acres *7,28 ha*. Improvements and re-plating cost a further £4½ million in 1974.

RADIO ASTRONOMY
Radio astronomy became possible with the discovery in 1864 of radio waves by Dr M Loomis (USA). The earliest suggestion that extra-terrestrial radio waves might exist and be detected came from Thomas Edison (USA) who corresponded with Prof A E Kennelly on the subject on 2 Nov. 1890.

It was not until 1932 that Karl Guthe Jansky (1905–49) a US scientist of Czech descent first detected radio signals, from the Sagittarius constellation, at Holmdel, New Jersey. This 'cosmic static' was recorded on a 15-m wave length. The pioneer radio astronomer was Grote Reber (USA) (b. 1911) who built the world's first radio telescope, a 31 ft 5-in parabolic dish, in his back-yard at Wheaton, Illinois, in 1937. His first results were published in 1940.

Dr J S Hey (GB) discovered during war-time radar jamming research that sun spots emitted radio waves; that radio echoes come from meteor trails; and that the extra-galactic nebula Cygnus A was a discrete source of immense power.

In 1947 John G Bolton in Australia found that the Crab Nebula (M.1), a supernova remnant, is a strong radio source. Since then many more discrete sources have been found; some are supernova remnants in our Galaxy, while others are external galaxies and the mysterious, very remote quasars. Young science though it may be, radio astronomy is now of fundamental importance in our studies of the universe, and it has provided information which could never have been obtained in any other way.

Some milestones in astronomy

Aristotle (c. 385–325 BC) advanced the first argument against the flat Earth hypothesis. Eratosthenes of Cyrene (c. 285–203 BC) made the earliest estimate of the Earth's circumference in c. 230 BC. Ptolemy in c. AD 180 established the Ptolemic System, i.e. Earth was the centre of the universe.
Copernicus (1473–1543) established that both the Earth and Mars orbit the Sun.
Johannes Kepler published his first two laws of planetary motion in 1609: the third in 1619.
Galileo Galilei (1564–1642) harnessed in 1609 the use of the telescope and made astronomical observations with it. He was summoned by the Roman Church to adjure his heresy that the Earth went round the Sun.
Christiaan Huygens (1629–95) built a 210 ft *64 m* long refractor. In 1665 he described Saturn's rings, later observing the markings on Mars.
In the 1670s Cassini recalculated the Sun's distance at 86 million miles *138 million km*.
In 1675 Rømer measured the velocity of light. His inspired answer, ignored for more than 100 years and not believed by himself, was 186 000 miles per sec *300 000 km per sec*. Sir Isaac Newton (1642–1727) published his *Principia* in 1687.
In 1705 Halley predicted the return of Halley's

comet in 1758. This was confirmed in that year by Palitzsch.

Herschel discovered Uranus in 1781.

Giuseppe Piazzi observed the first asteroid in 1801, confirmed in 1802 and named *Ceres*.

Friedrich Bessel was one of the first to realise the vastness of our galaxy, measuring in 1835 *61 Cygni* to be 60 million million miles distant away.

The steady-state or continuous creation theory was postulated in 1948 by Professors H. Bondi and T. Gold but is now considered to be incorrect. Other theories of the universe currently under discussion are the evolutionary or 'big bang' theory, due to Abbé Lemaitre in 1927, and the oscillating theory of 1965 supported by Professor A. Sandage of the USA.

CHIRON

On 8 Nov. 1977 Charles Kowal at Palomar Observatory, California, discovered an exceptional object which may be about 500 miles *800 km* in diameter moving mainly between the orbits of Saturn and Uranus. It has been named Chiron. Its nature is still uncertain, and its size may have been over-estimated; it is thought to be rocky rather than icy, and may be classed as an exceptional asteroid.

CONSTELLATIONS

There are 31 accepted constellations in the northern and 52 in the southern hemispheres and 5 which appear at times in both hemispheres, making 88 in all. The International Astronomical Union completed the now accepted arc codification by 1945. The rectangular constellation Orion includes 15 stars above the 4th magnitude in its great quadrilateral – Rigel (bottom left, Mag. 0·08 variable), Betelgeuse (top right, Mag. 0·85 variable) and Bellatrix (top left, Mag. 1·64). For a complete list see *Guinness Book of Astronomy Facts and Feats* (pp. 169–170).

Meteorites

The term meteorite must now be confined to a fallen meteor, a meteoric mass of stone (aerolite) or nickel-iron (siderite). It is loosely and incorrectly used of a meteor or shooting star which is usually only the size of a pinhead. The existence of meteorites, owing to a religious bias, was first admitted as late as 26 Apr. 1803, after a shower of some 2500 aerolites fell around L'Aigle, near Paris, France.

The majority of meteorites inevitably fall into the sea (70·8 per cent of the Earth's surface) and are not recovered. Only eight meteorites exceeding ten tons have been located. All these are of the iron-nickel type. The largest recorded stone meteorite is the one which fell in the Kirin Province, Manchuria on 8 Mar. 1976 weighing 3894 lb *1766 kg*. The total number of strikes recorded since the mid-17th century is nearly 1700, including 22 in the British Isles.

The twenty largest asteroids

Asteroid		Diameter miles	km	Rotation Period hours	Absolute Visual Magnitude V(1,0)*	Discoverer	Date
(1)	Ceres	637	1025	9·087	3·63	G Piazzi	1 Jan. 1801
(2)	Pallas	362	583	7·811	4·36	H W Olbers	28 Mar. 1802
(4)	Vesta	345	555	5·342	3·46	H W Olbers	29 Mar. 1807
(10)	Hygeia	275	443	18	5·64	A De Gasparis	12 Apr. 1849
(704)	Interamnia	210	338	8·723	6·37	V Cerulli	2 Oct. 1910
(511)	Davida	208	335	5·17	6·48	R S Dugan	30 May 1903
(65)	Cybele	193	311	6·07	7·07	E W Tempel	8 Mar. 1861
(52)	Europa	181	291	11·258	6·61	H Goldschmidt	4 Feb. 1858
(451)	Patentia	175	281	20	6·89	A Charlois	4 Dec. 1899
(31)	Euphrosyne	168	270	5·531	7·03	J Ferguson	1 Sept. 1854
(15)	Eunomia	162	261	6·081	5·50	A De Gasparis	29 July 1851
(324)	Bamberga	159	256	29·4	7·07	J Palisa	25 Feb. 1892
(107)	Camilla	157	252	4·56	7·18	N R Pogson	17 Nov. 1868
(87)	Sylvia	156	251	5·186	7·19	N R Pogson	16 May 1866
(45)	Eugenia	155	250	5·700	7·43	H Goldschmidt	27 Jun. 1857
(24)	Themis	155	249	8·369	7·21	A De Gasparis	5 Apr. 1853
(3)	Juno	155	249	7·213	5·65	K Harding	1 Sept. 1804
(16)	Psyche	155	249	4·303	6·21	A De Gasparis	17 Mar. 1852
(13)	Egeria	152	245	7·045	6·81	A De Gasparis	2 Nov. 1850
(165)	Loreley	142	228	?	7·40	C H F Peters	9 Aug. 1876

* Magnitude reduced to unit distance (one astronomical unit)
Note: the total mass of the asteroids is about 3 × 10¹⁸ tons *3 × 10²¹ kg* or about one twenty-fifth of the mass of our Moon. The three largest asteroids account for over half of the total mass.

World's largest meteorites

		Approximate tonnage
Hoba	nr Grootfontein, South West Africa	60
Tent (Abnighito)	Cape York, West Greenland	30·4
Bacuberito	Mexico	27
Mbosi	Tanganyika	26
Willamette (1902)	Oregon, USA	14
Chupaero	Chihuahua, Mexico	14
Campo de Cielo	Argentina	13
Morito	Chihuahua, Mexico	11

The largest recorded in other continents are:

Australia	Cranbourne	3·5
Asia	Sikhote-Alin, USSR	1·7
Europe	Magura, Czechoslovakia	1·5

The largest British Isles meteorites of the 22 recorded have been:

Country and Location	Date	Weight	
Ireland			
Adare, Limerick	10 Sept. 1813	65 lb (total 106 lb)	*29,5 kg (total 48 kg)*
England			
World Cottage, nr Scarborough, North Yorkshire	13 Dec. 1795	56 lb	*25,4 kg*
Barwell, Leicestershire	24 Dec. 1965	17¾ lb (total 102 lb)	*7,8 kg (total 46,25 kg)*
Scotland			
Strathmore, Tayside	3 Dec. 1971	22¼ lb	*10,1 kg*
Wales			
Beddgelert, Gwynedd	21 Sept. 1949	25½ oz	*723 g*

Meteorite Craters

The most spectacular of all dry craters is the Coon Butte or Barringer crater near Canyon Diablo, Winslow, North Arizona, USA, discovered in 1891, which is now 575 ft *175 m* deep and 4150 ft *1265 m* in diameter. The next largest craters are Wolf's Creek, Western Australia (3000 ft *914 m* diameter, 170 ft *52 m* deep) and a crater discovered in N Chile in 1965 (1476 ft *450 m* diameter, 100 ft *30 m* deep). The New Quebec (formerly Chubb) 'crater' in North Ungava, Canada, discovered in June 1943, is 1325 ft *404 m* deep and 2·2 miles *3,5 km* in diameter, but is now regarded as a water-filled vulcanoid.

Ancient and oblique meteoric scars are much less spectacular though of far greater dimensions. These phenomena are known as astroblemes (Gk *astron*, a star; *blemma*, a glance).

World's largest meteorite craters

Name of Astrobleme	Diameter miles	km
Vredefort Ring, South Africa (meteoric origin disputed, 1963)	24·8	39,9
Nordlinger Ries, Germany	15·5	24,9
Deep Bay, Saskatchewan, Canada (discovered 1956)	8·5	13,6
Lake Bosumtibi, Ghana	6·2	9,9
Serpent Mound, Ohio, USA	3·98	6,4
Wells Creek, Tennessee, USA	2·97	4,7
Al Umchaimin, Iraq	1·98	3,1

Metrology

In essence, measurement involves *comparison:* the measurement of a physical quantity entails comparing it with an agreed and clearly defined *standard*. The result is expressed in terms of a *unit*, which is the name for a standard, preceded by a number which is the *ratio* of the measured quantity of the appropriate fixed unit.

A *system of units* is centred on a small number of *base units*. These relate to the fundamental standards of length, mass and time, together with a few others to extend the system to a wider range of physical measurements, e.g. to electrical and optical quantities. There are also two geometrical units which belong to a class known as *supplementary units*.

These few base units can be combined to form a large number of *derived units*. For example, units of area, velocity and acceleration are formed from units of length and time. Thus very many different kinds of measurement can be made and recorded employing very few base units.

For convenience, *multiples* and *submultiples* of both base and derived units are frequently used, eg kilometres and millimetres.

Historically, several systems of units have evolved: in Britain, the imperial system: in the United States, the US customary units; and forms of the metric system (CGS for centimetre-gram-second and MKS for metre-kilogram-second), employed universally in science and generally in very many countries of the world.

The International System of Units (Système International d'Unités or SI) is a modern form of the metric system. It was finally agreed at the Eleventh General Conference of Weights and Measures in October 1960 and is now being widely adopted throughout the scientific world.

Unit Definition

The yard (yd). This is equal to 0·9144 metre exactly (Weights and Measures Act, 1963).

The pound (lb). This is equal to 0·453 592 37 kilogram exactly (Weights and Measures Act, 1963).

The gallon (gal). 'The space occupied by 10 pounds weight of distilled water of density 0·998 859 gram per millilitre weighed in air of density 0·001 217 gram per millilitre against weights of density 8·136 gram per millilitre (Weights and Measures Act, 1963). The definition of the gallon in the meaning of the 1963 Weights and Measures Act uses the 1901 definition of the litre [1 litre (1901) = 1·000 028 dm³].

Other units of length employed are:

animal stature	the hand = 4 in. *NB* – a horse of 14 hands 3 in to the withers is often written 14·3 hands.
surveying	the link = 7·92 in or a hundreth part of a chain.
approximate	the span = 9 in (from the span of the hand).
biblical	the cubit = 18 in.
approximate	the pace = 30 in (from the stride).
nautical	the cable = 120 fathoms or 240 yd.
navigation	the UK nautical mile = 6080 ft at the Equator.
navigation	the International nautical mile (adopted also by the USA on 1 July 1954) = 6076·1 ft (0·99936 of a UK nautical mile).

The use of the metric system was legalised in the United Kingdom in 1897. The Halsbury Committee recommended the introduction of decimal currency in September 1963. The intention to switch to the metric system was declared on 24 May 1965 by the President of the Board of Trade 'within ten years'. The date for the official adoption of the metric system was announced on 1 Mar 1966 to be 'February 1971'. On Tuesday, 23 Mar 1976, the Government decided not to proceed with the second reading of the Weights and Measures (Metrication) Act.

Base units

Quantity	Unit	Symbol	Definition
length	metre	m	the length equal to 1 650 763·73 wavelengths in vacuum of the radiation corresponding to the transition between the levels $2p_{10}$ and $5d_5$ of the krypton-86 atom.
mass	kilogram	kg	the mass of the international prototype of the kilogram, which is in the custody of the Bureau International des Poids et Mésures (BIPM) at Sèvres near Paris, France.
time	second	s	the duration of 9 192 631 770 periods of the radiation corresponding to the transition between the two hyperfine levels of the ground state of the caesium-133 atom.
electric current	ampere	A	that constant current which, if maintained in two straight parallel conductors of infinite length of negligible circular cross-section, and placed 1 metre apart in vacuum, would produce between these conductors a force equal to 2×10^{-7} newton per metre of length.
thermodynamic temperature	kelvin	K	the fraction 1/273·15 of the thermodynamic temperature of the triple point of water. The triple point of water is the point where water, ice and water vapour are in equilibrium.
luminous intensity	candela	cd	the luminous intensity, in the perpendicular direction, of a surface of 1/600 000 square metre of a black body at the temperature of freezing platinum under a pressure of 101 325 pascals.
amount of substance	mole	mol	the amount of substance of a system which contains as many elementary entities as there are atoms in 0·012 kilogram of carbon-12.

Supplementary units

Quantity	Unit	Symbol	Definition
plane angle	radian	rad	the plane angle between two radii of a circle which cut off on the circumference an arc equal in length to the radius.
solid angle	steradian	sr	the solid angle which having its vertex in the centre of a sphere, cuts off an area of the surface of the sphere equal to that of a square having sides of length equal to the radius of the sphere.

Derived units

Quantity	Unit	Symbol	Expression in terms of other SI units
area	square metre	m²	—
volume	cubic metre	m³	—
velocity	metre per second	$m \cdot s^{-1}$	—
angular velocity	radian per second	rad s⁻¹	—
acceleration	metre per second squared	$m \cdot s^{-2}$	—
angular acceleration	radian per second squared	rad s⁻²	—
frequency	hertz	Hz	s⁻¹
density	kilogram per cubic metre	$kg \cdot m^{-3}$	—

Quantity	Unit	Symbol	Expression in terms of other SI units
momentum	kilogram metre per second	$kg \cdot m \cdot s^{-1}$	—
angular momentum	kilogram metre squared per second	$kg \cdot m^2 \cdot s^{-1}$	—
moment of inertia	kilogram metre squared	$kg \cdot m^2$	—
force	newton	N	$kg \cdot m \cdot s^{-2}$
pressure, stress	pascal	Pa	$N \cdot m^{-2} = kg \cdot m^{-1} \cdot s^{-2}$
work, energy, quantity of heat	joule	J	$N \cdot m = kg \cdot m^2 \cdot s^{-2}$
power	watt	W	$J \cdot s^{-1} = kg \cdot m^2 \cdot s^{-3}$
surface tension	newton per metre	$N \cdot m^{-1}$	$kg \cdot s^{-2}$
dynamic viscosity	newton second per metre squared	$N \cdot s \cdot m^{-2}$	$kg \cdot m^{-1} \cdot s^{-1}$
kinematic viscosity	metre squared per second	$m^2 \cdot s^{-1}$	—
temperature	degree Celsius	°C	—
thermal coefficient of linear expansion	per degree Celsius, or per kelvin	$°C^{-1}, K^{-1}$	—
thermal conductivity	watt per metre degree C	$W \cdot m^{-1} \cdot °C^{-1}$	$kg \cdot m \cdot s^{-3} \cdot °C^{-1}$
heat capacity	joule per kelvin	$J \cdot K^{-1}$	$kg \cdot m^2 \cdot s^{-2} \cdot K^{-1}$
specific heat capacity	joule per kilogram kelvin	$J \cdot kg^{-1} \cdot K^{-1}$	$m^2 \cdot s^{-2} \cdot K^{-1}$
specific latent heat	joule per kilogram	$J \, kg^{-1}$	$m^2 \cdot s^{-2}$
electric charge	coulomb	C	$A \cdot s$
electromotive force, potential difference	volt	V	$W \cdot A^{-1} = kg \cdot m^2 \cdot s^{-3} \cdot A^{-1}$
electric resistance	ohm	Ω	$V \cdot A^{-1} = kg \cdot m^2 \cdot s^{-3} \cdot A^{-2}$
electric conductance	siemens	S	$A \cdot V^{-1} = kg^{-1} \cdot m^{-2} \cdot s^3 \cdot A^2$
electric capacitance	farad	F	$A \cdot s \cdot V^{-1} = kg^{-1} \cdot m^{-2} \cdot s^4 \cdot A^2$
inductance	henry	H	$V \cdot s \cdot A^{-1} = kg \cdot m^2 \cdot s^{-2} \cdot A^{-2}$
magnetic flux	weber	Wb	$V \cdot s = kg \cdot m^2 \cdot s^{-2} \cdot A^{-1}$
magnetic flux density	tesla	T	$Wb \cdot m^{-2} = kg \cdot s^{-2} \cdot A^{-1}$
magnetomotive force	ampere	A	—
luminous flux	lumen	lm	$cd \cdot sr$
illumination	lux	lx	$lm \cdot m^{-2} = cd \cdot sr \cdot m^{-2}$
radiation activity	becquerel	Bq	s^{-1}
radiation absorbed dose	gray	Gy	$J \cdot kg^{-1} = m^2 \cdot s^{-2}$

Metric and Imperial Units and Conversions (* = exact)

Column One	Equivalent	Column Two	To convert Col. 2 to Col. 1 Multiply by	To convert Col. 1 to Col. 2 Multiply by
Length				
inch (in)	—	centimetre (cm)	0·393 700 78	2·54*
foot (ft)	12 in	metre	3·280 840	0·304 8*
yard (yd)	3 ft	metre	1·093 61	0·914 4*
mile	1760 yd	kilometre (km)	0·621 371 1	1·609 344*
fathom	6 ft	metre	0·546 80	1·828 8*
chain	22 yd	metre	0·049 70	20·116 8*
UK nautical mile	6080 ft	kilometre	0·539 611 8	1·853 184*
International nautical mile	6076·1 ft	kilometre	0·539 956 8	1·852*
angstrom unit (Å)	10^{-10} m	nanometre	10	10^{-1}
Area				
square inch	—	square centimetre	0·155 00	6·451 6*
square foot	144 sq. in.	square metre	10·763 9	0·092 903*
square yard	9 sq. ft.	square metre	1·195 99	0·836 127*
acre	4840 sq. yd.	hectare (ha) (10^4 m^2)	2·471 05	0·404 686*
square mile	640 acres	square kilometre	0·386 10	2·589 988*
Volume				
cubic inch	—	cubic centimetre	0·061 024	16·387 1*
cubic foot	1728 cu. in.	cubic metre	35·314 67	0·028 317*
cubic yard	27 cu. ft.	cubic metre	1·307 95	0·764 555*
Capacity				
litre	100 centilitres	cubic centimetre or millilitre	0·001*	1000*
pint	4 gills	litre	1·759 753	0·568 261
UK gallon	8 pints or 277·4 in³	litre	0·219 969	4·546 092
barrel (for beer)	36 gallons	hectolitre	0·611 026	1·636 59
US gallon	0·832 675 UK gallons	litre or dm³	0·264 172	3·785 412
US barrel (for petroleum)	42 US gallons	hectolitre	0·628 998	1·589 83
fluid ounce	0·05 pint	millilitre	0·035 195	28·413 074
Velocity				
feet per second (ft/s)	—	metres per second	3·280 840	0·304 8
miles per hour (m.p.h)	—	kilometres per hour	0·621 371	1·609 344
UK knot (1·00064 Int. knots)	nautical mile/hour	kilometres per hour	0·539 611 8	1·853 184
Acceleration				
foot per second per second (ft/s²)	—	metres per second per second (m/s²)	3·280 840	0·304 8*
Mass				
grain (gr)	a 1/480th of an oz troy	milligram (mg)	0·015 432 4	64·798 91
dram (dr)	27·3438 gr	gram	0·564 383	1·771 85
ounce (avoirdupois)	16 drams	gram	0·035 274 0	28·349 523 125
pound (avoirdupois)	16 ounces	kilogram	2·204 62*	0·453 592 37*
stone	14 pounds	kilogram	0·157 473 04	6·350 293 18*
quarter	28 pounds	kilogram	0·078 737 5	12·700 586 36*
hundredweight (cwt)	112 pounds	kilogram	0·019 684 1	50·802 345 44*
ton (long)	2240 pounds	tonne (= 1000 kg)	0·984 206 5	1·016 046 908 8

Note: A pound troy consists of 12 ounces troy each of 480 grains

Column One	Equivalent	Column Two	To convert Col. 2 to Col. 1 Multiply by	To convert Col. 1 to Col. 2 Multiply by
Density				
pounds per cubic inch	—	grams per cubic centimetre	0·036 127 2	27·679 9
pounds per cubic foot	—	kilograms per cubic metre	0·062 428 0	16·018 5
Force				
dyne (dyn)	10^{-5} Newton	Newton	10^5	10^{-5}
poundal (pdl)	—	Newton	7·233 01	0·138 255
pound-force (lbf)	—	Newton	0·224 809	4·448 22
tons-force	—	kilonewton (kN)	0·100 361	9·964 02
kilogram-force (kgf) (or kilopond)	—	Newton	0·101 972	9·806 65
Energy (Work, Heat)				
erg	10^{-7} Joule	Joule	10^7	10^{-7}
horse-power (hp) (550 ft/lbf/s)	—	kilowatt (kW)	1·341 02	0·745 700
therm	—	mega joule (MJ)	0·009 478 17	105·506
kilowatt hour (kWh)	—	mega joule (MJ)	0·277 778	3·6
calorie (international)	—	Joule	0·238 846*	4·186 8*
British thermal unit (Btu)	—	kilo-Joule (kJ)	0·947 817	1·055 06
Pressure, Stress				
millibar (mbar or mb)	1000 dynes/cm²	Pa	0·01*	100*
standard atmosphere (atm)	760 torrs	kPa	0·009 869 2	101·325
pounds per square inch (psi)	—	Pa	0·000 145 038	6894·76
pounds per square inch (psi)	—	kilogram-force per cm²	14·223 3	0·070 307 0

Millions and Billions

Some confusion has existed on the nomenclature of high numbers because of differing usage in various countries.

The position is that in the United Kingdom and in Germany it has been customary to advance by increments of a million thus:

million 1 000 000(10^6)
billion 1 000 000 000 000(10^{12})
trillion 1 000 000 000 000 000 000(10^{18})

In France and the United States it is the practice to advance in increments of a thousand thus:

million 1 000 000(10^6)
billion 1 000 000 000(10^9)
trillion 1 000 000 000 000(10^{12})

Thus a US trillion is equal to a classic British billion.

Billion began to be used in Britain, in the US sense, as early as 1951 but the latest supplement to the Oxford English Dictionary, published in 1972, states that the older sense 'prevails'. In France one thousand million is described as a milliard which term is also permissibly used in Britain, as is the even more rare milliardth.

On 20 Dec. 1974 the then Prime Minister (J H Wilson) announced that HM Treasury would adhere to their practice of using the billion (made more prevalent by inflationary trends) in financial statistics in the sense of £1000 million. The word million has been in use since 1370 and a trillion was first mentioned *c.*1484.

Multiples and Sub-Multiples

In the metric system the following decimal multiples and sub-multiples are used:

Prefix	Symbol	British Equivalent	Factor
atto- (Danish *atten* = eighteen)	a	trillionth part (US quintillionth)	$\times 10^{-18}$
femto- (Danish *femten* = fifteen)	f	thousand billionth part (US quadrillionth)	$\times 10^{-15}$
pico- (L. *pico* = minuscule)	p	billionth part (US trillionth)	$\times 10^{-12}$
nano- (L. *nanus* = dwarf)	n	thousand millionth part (US billionth)	$\times 10^{-9}$
micro- (Gk. *mikros* = small)	μ	millionth part	$\times 10^{-6}$
milli- (L. *mille* = thousand)	m	thousandth part	$\times 10^{-3}$
centi- (L. *centum* = hundred)	c	hundredth part	$\times 10^{-2}$
deci- (L. *decimus* = tenth)	d	tenth part	$\times 10^{-1}$
deca- (Gk. *deka* = ten)	da	tenfold	$\times 10$
hecto- (Gk. *hekaton* = hundred)	h	hundredfold	$\times 10^2$
kilo- (Gk. *chilioi* = thousand)	k	thousandfold	$\times 10^3$
mega- (Gk. *megas* = large)	M	millionfold	$\times 10^6$
giga- (Gk. *gigas* = mighty)	G	thousand millionfold (US billion)	$\times 10^9$
tera- (Gk. *teras* = monster)	T	billionfold (US trillion)	$\times 10^{12}$
peta- (Gk. *penta* = five)	P	thousand billionfold (US quadrillion)	$\times 10^{15}$
exa- (Gk. *hexa* = six)	E	trillionfold (US quintillion)	$\times 10^{18}$

The higher degrees of numbers in use together with the date of their earliest usage and number of zeroes are:

	First use	US	UK		First use	US	UK
quadrillion	(1674)	1×10^{15}	1×10^{24}	nonillion	(1828)	1×10^{30}	1×10^{54}
quintillion	(1674)	1×10^{18}	1×10^{30}	decillion	(1845)	1×10^{33}	1×10^{60}
sextillion	(1690)	1×10^{21}	1×10^{36}	vigintillion		1×10^{63}	1×10^{120}
septillion	(1690)	1×10^{24}	1×10^{42}	centillion		1×10^{303}	1×10^{600}
octillion	(1690)	1×10^{27}	1×10^{48}				

Mathematics

Odds on perfect deals

The number of possible hands with four players using a full pack of 52 cards is $\dfrac{52!}{(39!)(13!)}$ or 635 013 559 600. Thus the odds against a given player picking up a specific complete suit are 635 013 559 596 to 1 or *any* complete suit 158 753 389 899 to 1.

The number of possible deals is $\dfrac{52!}{(13!)^4 (4!)}$

or 2 235 197 406 895 366 368 301 559 999 or roughly $2·23 \times 10^{27}$. A complete suit is thus to be expected by any one of 4 players once in every 39 688 347 497 deals.

Cases throughout the world of single complete suits are in practice reported about once per year. This being so, cases of two players receiving complete suits could be expected with the present volume of card playing once every 2000 million years and this has only once been recorded.

Cases of all four players picking up complete suits might be expected once in 56 000 billion years. Odds against a perfect deal are however invariable and irrespective of any other deal. There have, however, been so many reported instances from all parts of the world in recent years that this goes far beyond straining credulity. What is happening is certain evidence of rigged shuffling or hoaxing.

Mathematical symbols

=	equal to	÷	divided by	r^n	r to the power n
≠	not equal to	( )[ ]{ }	brackets, square brackets, enveloping brackets	△	triangle, finite difference or increment
≡	identically equal to; congruent	‖	parallel	~	difference
>	greater than	∦	not parallel	Σ	summation
<	less than	#	numbers to follow (USA)	∫	integration sign
≯	not greater than	%	per cent(um) (hundred)	°'"	degree, minute, second
≮	not less than	‰	per mille (thousand)		($1° = 60'$, $1' = 60''$)
≥	equal to or greater than	∝	varies with	→	appropriate limit of; tends to
≤	equal to or less than	∞	infinity	∴	therefore
≃	approximately equal to	or $\left.\begin{matrix} r! \\ \lfloor r \end{matrix}\right\}$ factorial r		∵	because
+	plus			⇒	implies that
−	minus	√	square root	⇐	is implied by
±	plus or minus	$\sqrt[n]{}$	nth root	⇔	is equivalent to
×	multiplication (times)				

MENSURATION

Rectangle
Area $= \ell b$
Perimeter $= 2(\ell + b)$

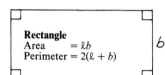

Square
Area $= \ell^2$
Perimeter $= 4\ell$

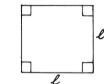

Parallelogram
Area $= bh$
Perimeter $= 2(a + b)$

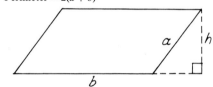

Triangle
Area $= \frac{1}{2} \cdot bh$
or $= \sqrt{[s(s-a)(s-b)(s-c)]}$
where $s = \dfrac{a+b+c}{2}$

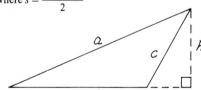

Trapezium
Area $= \frac{1}{2}(a+b)h$
i.e. $= \frac{1}{2}$ (sum of the parallel sides)
$\times$ perp. distance between them

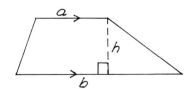

Note: "Square metres" and "Metres square" are not equivalent, e.g. 6 sq. m can refer to any shape, but 6 metres square only to a square. For this reason 'sq. m' or 'sq. km' and 'cu. m' or 'cu. cm' are preferred by some writers to m², km², m³ and cm³.

Rhombus
Area $= \frac{1}{2}(2a)(2b)$
i.e. $= \frac{1}{2}$ (product of the diagonals)
Perimeter $= 4\ell$

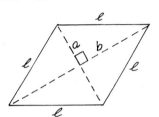

Circle
Circumference $= 2\pi r$ or πd
Area $= \pi r^2$

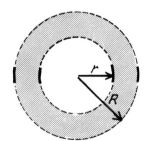

Radius
Sector
Segment
Chord
Diameter
Arc

Ring
Area $= \pi(R^2 - r^2)$
$= \pi(R-r)(R+r)$

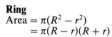

Rectangular block
Surface Area $= 2(\ell b + bh + h\ell)$
Volume $= \ell bh$
i.e. $=$ Area of the base $\times$ height
The volume of any solid whose sides are perpendicular to its base (or cross-section) and whose ends are parallel is always equal to the Area of the base $\times$ perpendicular height

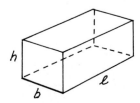

Pyramid
The volume of any pyramid (on a base of any shape) is always $= \frac{1}{3}$ (Volume of the surrounding solid)
Thus, the volume of a pyramid on a rectangular base $= \frac{1}{3}(\ell bh)$

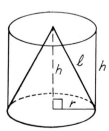

The volume of a pyramid within a triangular prism
$= \frac{1}{3}$ (Area of the triangular base $\times$ height)

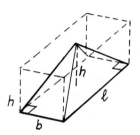

Cylinder
Curved Surface Area (C.S.A.) $= 2\pi rh$
Total Surface Area (T.S.A.) $= 2\pi r(h + r)$
(for a closed cylinder)
Volume $= \pi r^2 h$

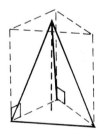

Cone
Curved Surface Area (C.S.A.)
$= \pi r \ell$ where $\ell =$ slant height
Total Surface Area
$= \pi r(\ell + r)$
Volume
$= \frac{1}{3}$ (Volume of the surrounding cylinder)
$= \frac{1}{3}\pi r^2 h$

Sphere
Surface Area $= 4\pi r^2$
Volume $\quad = \frac{4}{3}\pi r^3$

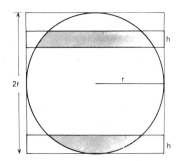

A little-known and interesting fact about the sphere is that the area of any zone of its curved surface lying between two parallel planes is exactly equal to the curved surface of the surrounding cylinder between the same two planes.

This applies to any belt of the sphere, or to a cap or to the whole sphere. It thus makes the calculation of what might appear to be a difficult area quite simple.

Thus, either shaded area of the sphere is equal to the curved surface area of a cylinder of radius a and height h, the height of the zone.
   i.e. $A = 2\pi rh$ and for the whole sphere
$$A = 2\pi r 2r$$
$$= 4\pi r^2 \text{ which we already know to be}$$
the surface area of a sphere.

Ellipse
Area $= \pi ab$

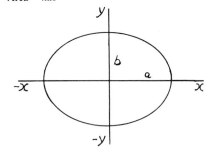

Parabola
Shaded area in the diagram $= \frac{1}{3}x_1 y_1$
i.e. one-third of the given rectangle

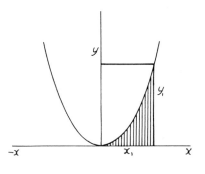

Area under any curve

(1) Trapezoidal Rule
$$\text{Area} = \left[\frac{y_1 + y_7}{2} + y_2 + y_3 + y_4 + y_5 + y_6\right]w$$
i.e. $=$ [half the sum of the first and last ordinates, $+$ all the others] $\times$ the width of a strip
The area may be divided into any number of equal strips

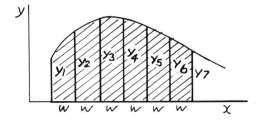

(2) Simpson's Rule
$$\text{Area} = \frac{w}{3}\left[y_1 + y_7 + 4(y_2 + y_4 + y_6) + 2(y_3 + y_5)\right]$$
i.e. $=$ one-third of the width of a strip, multiplied by the sum of the first and last ordinates, $+$ 4 times the even ordinates, $+$ twice the remaining odd ordinates.
For this rule the area must be divided into an *even* number of strips of equal width.

(3) Both the above rules give very good approximations, but the exact area is found by calculus provided the equation of the curve is known.

   Then, Area $= \displaystyle\int_{x_1}^{x_2} y\,dx$

Important curves (Conic Sections, so called because they can all be obtained by the intersection of a plane with a complete, or 'double' cone)

Circle
  General equation (centre at $-g, -f$) $x^2 + y^2 + 2gx + 2fy + c = 0$
  Basic equation (centre at the origin) $x^2 + y^2 = r^2$

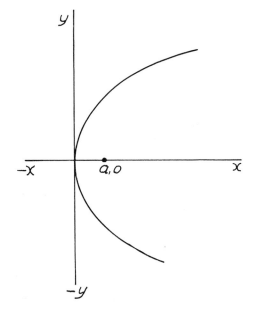

Parabola

Ellipse (see above)
  Basic equation (centre at the origin) $\dfrac{x^2}{a^2} + \dfrac{y^2}{b^2} = 1$

Parabola
  Basic equation [symmetrical about the x-axis, focus at $(a, 0)$]
$$y^2 = 4ax$$

Hyperbola
  Basic equation (centre at the origin) $\dfrac{x^2}{a^2} - \dfrac{y^2}{b^2} = 1$

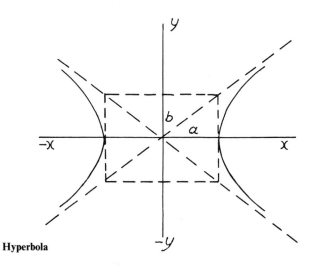

Hyperbola

Rectangular hyperbola (equal axes) $x^2 - y^2 = a^2$

Rectangular hyperbola (referred to the axes of coordinates as asymptotes) $xy = k^2$

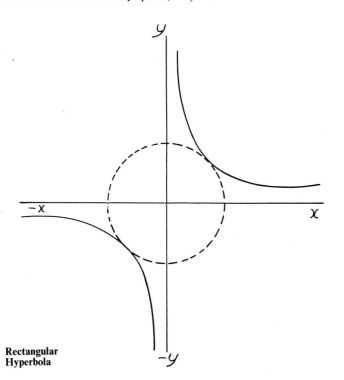

Rectangular Hyperbola

Basic Algebra

$$x^a \times x^b = x^{a+b} \qquad \frac{x^a}{x^b} = x^{a-b} \qquad (x^a)^b \text{ or } (x^b)^a = x^{ab} \qquad x^{-a} = \frac{1}{x^a} \qquad x^{1/n} = \sqrt[n]{x}$$

Important identities

$$(x \pm y)^2 \equiv x^2 \pm 2xy + y^2$$

$$[A]^2 - [B]^2 \equiv (A - B)(A + B) \qquad \text{A difference of two squares}$$

$$(x \pm y)^3 \equiv x^3 \pm 3x^2y + 3xy^2 \pm y^3$$

$$[A]^3 \pm [B]^3 \equiv (A \pm B)(A^2 \mp AB + B^2) \qquad \text{The sum or difference of two cubes}$$

The solutions of the standard quadratic equation $ax^2 + bx + c = 0$ are given by

$$x = \frac{-b \pm \sqrt{b^2 - 4ac}}{2a}$$

If b^2 is $> 4ac$ the roots are real and different
b^2 is $= 4ac$ the roots are real and equal
b^2 is $< 4ac$ the roots are imaginary (complex)
b is $= 0$ and c is $-ve$, the roots are real, equal and opposite
b is $= 0$ and c is $+ve$, the roots are imaginary (no real part)

If the roots are α and β, then $\alpha + \beta = -\dfrac{b}{a}$ and $\alpha\beta = \dfrac{c}{a}$

Logarithms

If N $= a^x$
then $\text{Log}_a N = x$ (i.e. Log N to the base 'a' $= x$)

$$\text{Log } NM = \text{Log } N + \text{Log } M \quad \text{and} \quad \text{Log } \frac{N}{M} = \text{Log } N - \text{Log } M$$

To change the base of a logarithm:

$$\text{Log}_b N = \frac{\text{Log}_a N}{\text{Log}_a b} \quad \text{or} \quad \text{Log}_a N \times \text{Log}_b a$$

$$\text{Log } N^p = p \text{ Log } N \qquad \text{Log}_a b = \frac{1}{\text{Log}_b a}$$

and $\text{Log} \sqrt[n]{N} = \dfrac{1}{n} \text{Log } N$

Basic Trigonometry

$$\text{Sin } C = \frac{AB}{AC} \qquad \text{Cosec } \theta = \frac{1}{\text{Sin } \theta}$$

$$\text{Cos } C = \frac{BC}{AC} \qquad \text{Sec } \theta = \frac{1}{\text{Cos } \theta}$$

$$\text{Tan } C = \frac{AB}{BC} \qquad \text{Cot } \theta = \frac{1}{\text{Tan } \theta}$$

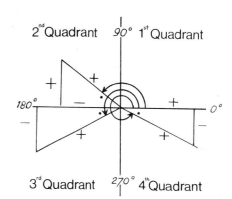

Trigonometrical equivalents of Pythagoras' Theorem (q.v.)

$$\text{Sin}^2 \theta + \text{Cos}^2 \theta = 1 \quad \text{Sec}^2\theta = 1 + \text{Tan}^2\theta \quad \text{Cosec}^2\theta = 1 + \text{Cot}^2\theta$$

Formulae for the solution of non-right-angled triangles:

Sine Rule
Given at least one side and the facing angle:

$$\frac{a}{\text{Sin } A} = \frac{b}{\text{Sin } B} = \frac{c}{\text{Sin } C} \ (= 2R)$$

where R = radius of the circumcircle
Area of a triangle $= \frac{1}{2}ab \text{ Sin } C$

Cosine Rules
(i) Given two sides and the included angle (b, c and the angle A)
$$a^2 = b^2 + c^2 - 2bc \text{ Cos } A$$
(ii) Given three sides
$$\text{Cos } A = \frac{b^2 + c^2 - a^2}{2bc}$$

Sines, cosines and tangents of angles greater than 90°

2nd quadrant
$90° < \theta < 180°$
$\text{Sin } \theta = \text{Sin } (180° - \theta)$
$\text{Cos } \theta = -\text{Cos } (180° - \theta)$
$\text{Tan } \theta = -\text{Tan } (180° - \theta)$

3rd quadrant
$180° < \theta < 270°$
$\text{Sin } \theta = -\text{Sin } (\theta - 180°)$
$\text{Cos } \theta = -\text{Cos } (\theta - 180°)$
$\text{Tan } \theta = \text{Tan } (\theta - 180°)$

4th quadrant
$270° < \theta < 360°$
$\text{Sin } \theta = -\text{Sin } (360° - \theta)$
$\text{Cos } \theta = \text{Cos } (360° - \theta)$
$\text{Tan } \theta = -\text{Tan } (360° - \theta)$

Radian measure
A radian is the angle subtended at the centre of a circle by a length of arc equal to the radius. Thus

1 radian $= \dfrac{180}{\pi}$ degrees or approx. 57.3° and π radians $= 180°$

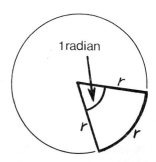

Length of an arc of a circle is given by:

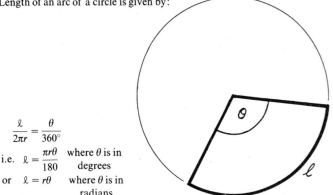

$$\frac{\ell}{2\pi r} = \frac{\theta}{360°}$$

i.e. $\ell = \dfrac{\pi r \theta}{180}$ where θ is in degrees

or $\ell = r\theta$ where θ is in radians

Area of the sector of a circle is given by:

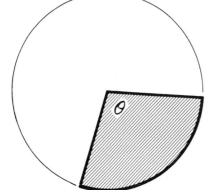

$$\frac{a}{\pi r^2} = \frac{\theta}{360°}$$

i.e. $a = \dfrac{\pi r^2 \theta}{360}$ where θ is in degrees

or $a = \dfrac{r^2 \theta}{2}$ where θ is in radians

Pythagoras' Theorem

In the triangle ABC right-angled at B

$$AC^2 = AB^2 + BC^2$$

Four useful sets of whole-number values which fit the theorem are:

3, 4, 5   5, 12, 13
8, 15, 17   and 7, 24, 25

Such whole-number sets are sometimes called 'Pythagorean Triples'.

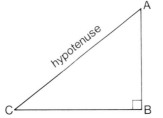

In words the theorem states that the area of the square drawn on the hypotenuse of a right-angled triangle is equal to the sum of the areas of the squares drawn on the other two sides.

Percentages

(1) $x\%$ of a number $(N) = \dfrac{x}{100} \times N$

(2) To find what percentage a quantity A is of a quantity B

$$\% = \frac{A}{B} \times 100$$

(3) To find the percentage increase or decrease of a quantity

$$\%\ \frac{\text{Increase}}{\text{Decrease}} = \frac{\text{Actual increase or decrease}}{\text{Original amount}} \times 100$$

(4) To find the percentage profit or loss

$$\%\ \frac{\text{Profit}}{\text{Loss}} = \frac{\text{Actual profit or loss}}{\text{Cost price}} \times 100$$

(5) To find 100% given that $x\% = N$

$$100\% = \frac{N}{x} \times 100$$

Note that percentages may not be added or subtracted unless they are percentages of the same quantity. Thus successive depreciations of 10% and 15% are not equivalent to a single depreciation of 25%.

Interest

Simple Interest = $\dfrac{PRT}{100}$ where P = principal (sum invested)
(Principal remains constant) R = rate % per annum
                                     T = time in years

Compound Interest (interest added to the principal each year)
$A = PR^n$ where A = Amount (i.e. Principal + Interest)

$$R = 1 + \frac{r}{100} \text{ where } r = \text{rate\% p.a.}$$

$$n = \text{number of years}$$

Polygons (many-sided figures)

Sum of the interior angles = $(2n - 4) \times 90°$ where n = number of sides.

Each interior angle of a regular polygon = $\dfrac{(2n - 4) \times 90°}{n}$

$$\text{or} = 180° - \frac{360°}{n}$$

Sum of the exterior angles of any polygon = 360°, regardless of the number of sides.

Some important polygons

Triangle	3 sides	Octagon	8 sides
Quadrilateral	4 sides	Nonagon	9 sides
Pentagon	5 sides	Decagon	10 sides
Hexagon	6 sides	Dodecagon	12 sides
Heptagon	7 sides		

The area of any regular polygon of side 'a' = $\frac{1}{4} n a^2 \text{Cot} \dfrac{180°}{n}$

where n = the number of sides

The Regular Solids (Polyhedra)

There are 5 principal regular solids

The Tetrahedron (triangular pyramid)	4 faces
The Cube	6 faces
The Octahedron	8 faces
The Dodecahedron	12 faces
The Icosahedron	20 faces

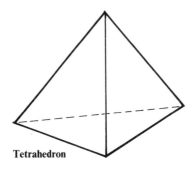

Tetrahedron

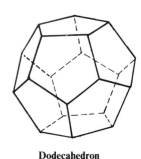

Dodecahedron

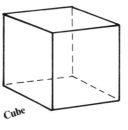

Cube

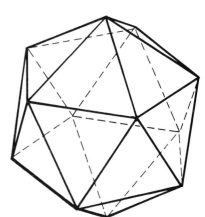

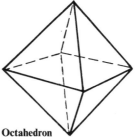

Octahedron   **Icosahedron**

In addition there are 4 much more complicated regular solids with star faces or vertices called the Kepler-Poinsot Polyhedra. They are

The Small Stellated Decahedron	The Great Dodecahedron
The Great Stellated Dodecahedron	The Great Icosahedron

The mathematician Euler made an interesting discovery about the relationship between the number of faces (F), vertices (V) and edges (E) of polyhedra. As far as is known, the equation $F + V - E = 2$ is true for all polyhedra except the two stellated ones mentioned above.

Furthermore, the same relationship is true for an area divided into any number of regions (R) by boundaries or arcs (A) which join at nodes (N).

Then $R + N - A = 2$

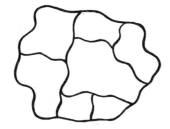

For the area shewn,
$R = 8$ (the surrounding space counts as a region)
$N = 12 \quad A = 18$
Thus $R + N - A$
$= 8 + 12 - 18$
$= 2$

Incidentally, for such a region, or indeed any map, no more than 4 colours are necessary so that no two adjoining regions have the same colour.

NETWORKS
A series of nodes joined by arcs is called a Network. A node is odd or even according to the number of arcs which are drawn from it. The network may represent a road or railway system, an electricity grid and so on. Such a system will be traversable (i.e. can be drawn without covering any arc twice or taking the pencil off the paper) if there are not more than 2 odd nodes. In which case the route must begin and end at an odd node. Here are two simplified networks, one of which is traversable and one is not. The latter was used by Euler to solve the famous Konigsberg Bridge problem.

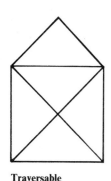

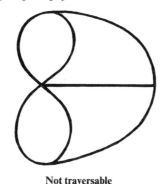

Traversable	Not traversable

MATRICES
A matrix is an array of numbers, of rectangular shape, which presents information in a concise form. Matrices serve many purposes, and according to the circumstances they may be multiplied or added or subtracted.

Two matrices may be multiplied if there are the same number of ROWS in the second matrix as there are COLUMNS in the first, but they may only be added or subtracted if they have the same number of rows and columns. A 2 × 3 matrix is one with 2 rows and 3 columns. Thus a 2 × 3 matrix may be multiplied by a 3 × 4 or a 3 × 2 or a 3 × n matrix where n is any number.

If $A = \begin{pmatrix} a & b \\ c & d \end{pmatrix}$ and $B = \begin{pmatrix} p & q \\ r & s \end{pmatrix}$

Then, $AB = \begin{pmatrix} a & b \\ c & d \end{pmatrix}\begin{pmatrix} p & q \\ r & s \end{pmatrix}$

$= \begin{pmatrix} ap + br & aq + bs \\ cp + dr & cq + ds \end{pmatrix}$

$A + B = \begin{pmatrix} a & b \\ c & d \end{pmatrix} + \begin{pmatrix} p & q \\ r & s \end{pmatrix}$

$= \begin{pmatrix} a + p & b + q \\ c + r & d + s \end{pmatrix}$

The Transformation Matrices change the position or shape of a geometrical figure, and sometimes both.
The following are the principal transformation matrices:

1. Reflection in the x-axis $\qquad \begin{pmatrix} 1 & 0 \\ 0 & -1 \end{pmatrix}$

2. Reflection in the y axis $\qquad \begin{pmatrix} -1 & 0 \\ 0 & 1 \end{pmatrix}$

3. Reflection in the line $y = x$ $\qquad \begin{pmatrix} 0 & 1 \\ 1 & 0 \end{pmatrix}$

4. Reflection in the line $y = -x$ $\qquad \begin{pmatrix} 0 & -1 \\ -1 & 0 \end{pmatrix}$

5. Rotation through 90° about the origin in a $+ve$ (anticlockwise) direction $\qquad \begin{pmatrix} 0 & -1 \\ 1 & 0 \end{pmatrix}$

6. Rotation through 180° ($+ve$ or $-ve$) $\qquad \begin{pmatrix} -1 & 0 \\ 0 & -1 \end{pmatrix}$

7. $+ve$ rotation of 270° ($-ve$ rotation of 90°) $\qquad \begin{pmatrix} 0 & 1 \\ -1 & 0 \end{pmatrix}$

8. $+ve$ rotation about the origin through an angle θ $\qquad \begin{pmatrix} \cos\theta & -\sin\theta \\ \sin\theta & \cos\theta \end{pmatrix}$

9. The IDENTITY MATRIX $\begin{pmatrix} 1 & 0 \\ 0 & 1 \end{pmatrix}$ leaves the elements of the multiplied matrix unchanged.

The following matrices change the shape of the figure.

10. An Enlargement, factor E $\begin{pmatrix} E & 0 \\ 0 & E \end{pmatrix}$ (e.g. if E = 3 the figure will have its linear dimensions trebled)

11. A Stretch, parallel to the x-axis, factor S $\qquad \begin{pmatrix} S & 0 \\ 0 & 1 \end{pmatrix}$

12. A Stretch, parallel to the y-axis, factor S $\qquad \begin{pmatrix} 1 & 0 \\ 0 & S \end{pmatrix}$

13. A two-way Stretch, parallel to the axes, factors S_1 and S_2 $\qquad \begin{pmatrix} S_1 & 0 \\ 0 & S_2 \end{pmatrix}$

14. A Shear, parallel to the x-axis $\qquad \begin{pmatrix} 1 & S \\ 0 & 1 \end{pmatrix}$

15. A Shear, parallel to the y-axis $\qquad \begin{pmatrix} 1 & 0 \\ S & 1 \end{pmatrix}$

The Inverse of matrix A above (denoted by A^{-1}) is $\dfrac{1}{(ad - bc)}\begin{pmatrix} d & -b \\ -c & a \end{pmatrix}$

The expression $(ad - bc)$ is called the Determinant of the matrix

The value of the Determinant of a matrix represents the ratio by which the area of the original figure has been changed. If the Determinant is zero, all the points will be moved to lie on a line, and the matrix is said to be 'singular'.

If a matrix is multiplied by its inverse the result is the Identity Matrix.

A transformation which does not change either the shape or the size of a figure is called an Isometric Transformation.

NUMBER BASES
Our familiar denary system of calculating undoubtedly arose because we have 5 'digits' on each hand. Had we been created with 4 instead, we should have been just as happily working in the Octal scale. A denary number may be easily converted to any other base simply by repeated division by the new base, the remainders being recorded at each step, thus:

$\begin{array}{l} 8)543_{10} \\ 8)67 \text{ r } 7 \\ 8)8 \text{ r } 3 \\ \quad 1 \text{ r } 0 \end{array}$ Reading from the bottom up, 543_{10} is equivalent to 1037_8 (Read 'one nought three seven base eight')

To convert a number in any other base into base 10, however, each digit must be given its appropriate place-value in the given base.

Thus, 1037_8
$= 1 \times 8^3 + 0 \times 8^2 + 3 \times 8^1 + 7$
$= 512 \quad + \quad 0 \quad + \quad 24 \quad + 7$
$= 543_{10}$

Base 2 or the Binary Scale is the most important non-denary base since it uses only the digits 0 and 1, and these can easily be related to the 'off' and 'on' of an electrical impulse and form the basis for the operation of electronic calculators and computers.

As before, a number may be converted to base 2 by repeated division.
Thus, to convert 217_{10}

$\begin{array}{l} 2)217 \\ 2)108 \text{ r } 1 \\ 2)54 \text{ r } 0 \\ 2)27 \text{ r } 0 \\ 2)13 \text{ r } 1 \\ 2) 6 \text{ r } 1 \\ 2) 3 \text{ r } 0 \\ \quad 1 \text{ r } 1 \end{array}$ i.e. 217_{10} $= 11011001_2$

The reverse process will be:

11011001_2

$= 1 \times 2^7 + 1 \times 2^6 + 0 \times 2^5 + 1 \times 2^4 + 1 \times 2^3$
$\quad + 0 \times 2^2 + 0 \times 2^1 + 1$

$= 128 + 64 + 0 + 16 + 8 + 0 + 0 + 1$

$= 217_{10}$

A denary-binary conversion table reveals some interesting points about binary numbers. Note the repetitive patterns in the columns of the successive numbers. Since odd numbers always end in 1 while even numbers end in 0, a number is doubled simply by adding a 0 (in the same way that a denary number is multiplied by 10 by adding a nought), and divided by 2, where possible, by removing a terminal 0. Denary numbers which are powers of 2 have a binary equivalent consisting of a 1 followed by the same number of zeros as the appropriate power of 2.

Denary	Binary
1	1
2 (2^1)	10
3	11
4 (2^2)	100
5	101
6	110
7	111
8 (2^3)	1000
9	1001
10	1010
11	1011
12	1100
13	1101
14	1110
15	1111
16 (2^4)	10000

Denary fractions are rendered as negative powers of 2.

Denary		Binary
0·5	(2^{-1})	0·1
0·25	(2^{-2})	0·01
0·125	(2^{-3})	0·001
0·0625	(2^{-4})	0·0001
0·03125	(2^{-5})	0·00001
0·015625	(2^{-6})	0·000001

Thus, to convert a 'bicimal' to a decimal,

$0·1101_2$

$= 0·5 + 0·25 + 0 + 0·0625$

$= 0·8125$

Converting from a decimal to a bicimal requires repeated *multiplication* of the *decimal part only* at each stage, the result being given by the whole-number parts read from the top. Thus, to convert 0·3 to a bicimal we proceed as follows:

$0·3 \times 2$
$\overline{0·6 \times 2}$
$1·2 \times 2$
$0·4 \times 4$
$0·8 \times 2$
$1·6 \times 2$
$1·2$ and so on.

Reading the whole-numbers from the top we have: 0·010011. Clearly this could go on until we have the required number of bicimal places or the process comes to a stop.

The check shows that we have only an approximate equivalence.

$0·010011_2$

$= 0 + 0·25 + 0 + 0 + 0·03125 + 0·015625$

$= 0·296875_{10}$

Some Important Series

Arithmetic Progression (A.P.)

$a, \quad a + d, \quad a + 2d, \quad a + 3d, \ldots [a + (n - 1)d]$

Sum to n terms $= \dfrac{n}{2}[2a + (n - 1)d]$

or $\qquad\qquad = \dfrac{n}{2}(a + \ell)$ where ℓ = last term

Geometric Series (G.P.)

$a, \quad ar, \quad ar^2, \quad ar^3 \ldots ar^{n-1}$

Sum to n terms $= a\dfrac{(1 - r^n)}{1 - r}$ if $r < 1$, or $\dfrac{a(r^n - 1)}{r - 1}$ if $r > 1$

When $r < 1$, the sum to infinity $S_\infty = \dfrac{a}{1 - r}$

The sum of the first n natural (counting) numbers

$1 + 2 + 3 + 4 + \cdots n$(i.e. an A.P. in which a = 1 and d = 1)

$= \dfrac{n}{2}(n + 1)$

The sum of the squares of the first n natural numbers

$1^2 + 2^2 + 3^2 + 4^2 \ldots n^2$

$= \dfrac{n}{6}(n + 1)(2n + 1)$

The sum of the cubes of the first n natural numbers

$1^3 + 2^3 + 3^3 + 4^3 \ldots n^3$

$= \left[\dfrac{n}{2}(n + 1)\right]^2$ i.e. the square of the sum of the first n natural numbers

The sum of the first n odd numbers

$1 + 3 + 5 + 7 \ldots$ to n terms.

$= n^2$ i.e. the square of the numbers of numbers

The sum of the first n even numbers

$2 + 4 + 6 + 8 \ldots$ to n terms

$= n(n + 1)$ i.e. twice the sum of an equal number of natural numbers.

Factorial n If a number is multiplied by all the successive numbers between it and 1, this is called Factorial *n*, and is denoted by $\underline{/n}$ or $n!$

Thus $\quad \underline{/6} = 6.5.4.3.2.1$

$\qquad\qquad = 720$

Exponential Series

$e^x = 1 + x + \dfrac{x^2}{\underline{/2}} + \dfrac{x^3}{\underline{/3}} + \dfrac{x^4}{\underline{/4}} + \cdots \dfrac{x^n}{\underline{/n}} + \cdots \infty$ for all values of x

Hence, when $x = 1$

$e = 1 + 1 + \dfrac{1}{\underline{/2}} + \dfrac{1}{\underline{/3}} + \dfrac{1}{\underline{/4}} + \cdots \infty = 2·71828$

More generally,

$e^{mx} = 1 + mx + \dfrac{(mx)^2}{\underline{/2}} + \dfrac{(mx)^3}{\underline{/3}} + \cdots \infty$

If $m = \log_e a$

$a^x = 1 + x \log_e a + \dfrac{(x \log_e a)^2}{\underline{/2}} + \dfrac{(x \log_e a)^3}{\underline{/3}} + \cdots \infty$

Logarithmic Series

$\mathrm{Log}_e(1 + x) = x - \dfrac{x^2}{2} + \dfrac{x^3}{3} - \dfrac{x^4}{4} \cdots (-1)^{n+1}\dfrac{x^n}{n}$ when $-1 < x \leqslant 1$

$\mathrm{Log}_e(1 - x) = -\left[x + \dfrac{x^2}{2} + \dfrac{x^3}{3} + \dfrac{x^4}{4} + \cdots\right]$ when $-1 \leqslant x < 1$

$\mathrm{Log}_e(n + 1) - \log_e n = 2\left[\dfrac{1}{2n + 1} + \dfrac{1}{3(2n + 1)^3} + \dfrac{1}{5(2n + 1)^5} + \cdots\right]$

Trigonometrical Series

$\mathrm{Sin}\,\theta = \theta - \dfrac{\theta^3}{\underline{/3}} + \dfrac{\theta^5}{\underline{/5}} - \dfrac{\theta^7}{\underline{/7}} + \cdots$

$\mathrm{Cos}\,\theta = 1 - \dfrac{\theta^2}{\underline{/2}} + \dfrac{\theta^4}{\underline{/4}} - \dfrac{\theta^6}{\underline{/6}} + \cdots$

where θ is in radians

Binomial Theorem

$(1 + x)^n = 1 + nx + \dfrac{n(n - 1)}{1.2}x^2 + \dfrac{n(n - 1)(n - 2)}{1.2.3}x^3 + \cdots$

If n is not a positive integer (whole number) the series is infinite and is only true if x is numerically < 1.

More generally,

$(a + x)^n = a^n + {}_nC_1 a^{n-1} x + {}_nC_2 a^{n-2} x^2 + \cdots {}_nC_r a^{n-r} x^r + \cdots x^n.$

where ${}_nC_r = \dfrac{n(n - 1)(n - 2) \cdots (n - r + 1)}{1.2.3 \ldots r}$

or $\qquad = \dfrac{\underline{/n}}{\underline{/r}\ \underline{/n - r}}$

NUMBER PATTERNS

Rectangular numbers — Numbers which have a pair of factors (i.e. which are not prime) and can therefore be represented in the form of a rectangle.

Thus $6 = \overset{\textstyle \cdots}{\textstyle \cdots}$

Square numbers — Numbers with a pair of equal factors, and may therefore be represented as a square

Thus $4 = \begin{smallmatrix}\cdot\ \cdot\\\cdot\ \cdot\end{smallmatrix} \qquad 9 = \begin{smallmatrix}\cdot\ \cdot\ \cdot\\\cdot\ \cdot\ \cdot\\\cdot\ \cdot\ \cdot\end{smallmatrix}$

1 4 9 16 25 36 49 64 81 100 121 144 169 are the squares of the first 13 numbers. Note that all square numbers are positive.

Triangular numbers — Numbers which can be formed into a series of equilateral triangles.

Thus $\quad 1 \qquad 3 \qquad 6 \qquad 10 \qquad 15$

The most important number pattern, however, is

Pascal's Triangle

Although it was known long before Pascal (who died in 1662) he was the first to make ingenious and wide use of its properties. It forms the basis of probability theory and has applications to statistics, insurance and other fields.

The numbers in each row are formed by adding the numbers above and to each side of it.

The numbers in the rows so formed are then the coefficients of the terms in the Binomial Theorem referred to above.

Thus the numbers in the 4th row (1 3 3 1) are the coefficients in the expansion of $(a + x)^3$, while those in the 6th would be those in the expansion of $(a + x)^5$, i.e.   1   5   10   10   5   1.

Note that if the rows are added horizontally, the results are all successive powers of 2,

	Totals
1	$1 = 2^0$
1 1	$2 = 2^1$
1 2 1	$4 = 2^2$
1 3 3 1	$8 = 2^3$
1 4 6 4 1	$16 = 2^4$
1 5 10 10 5 1	$32 = 2^5$

Permutations and Combinations

The number of permutations of a set of items i.e. the number of different *arrangements* of those items is denoted by $_nP_r$. The number of combinations of a set of items is the number of *groups* of those items (i.e. different arrangements do not count) and is denoted by $_nC_r$.

$_nP_r$ means the number of permutations of n things taken r at a time.

$_nP_n$ means the number of permutations of n things taken all at a time.

Thus $_nP_r = \dfrac{\underline{n}}{\underline{n-r}}$

$= n(n-1)(n-2)\dots(n-r+1)$

and $_nP_n = \underline{n}$, since $\underline{0} = 1$

Note that $_nC_r = \dfrac{_nP_r}{\underline{r}}$ i.e. the number of permutations of n things taken r at a time, divided by the number of permutations of all r things among themselves.

$= \dfrac{\underline{n}}{\underline{r}\ \underline{n-r}}$

The Real Number System

The Set of real numbers includes all the following:
1. The Natural or Counting numbers.
2. The Integers (whole numbers) both positive and negative.
3. The Fractions.

All the above are called Rational numbers since they can all be expressed as a Ratio.

4. The Irrational numbers, i.e. those which cannot be expressed as a ratio. For example $\sqrt{10}$, $\sqrt[3]{7}$ and so on.

All the real numbers can be located on a Number-line, and will in fact together form the solid line of Geometry.

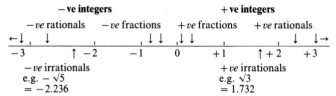

− ve integers	+ ve integers

− *ve* rationals   − *ve* fractions   + *ve* fractions   + *ve* rationals

$$\leftarrow\!\downarrow \quad \downarrow \qquad\qquad \downarrow\downarrow \ \ \downarrow\downarrow \qquad \downarrow \quad \downarrow\!\rightarrow$$
$$-3 \quad \uparrow -2 \qquad -1 \qquad 0 \qquad +1 \quad \uparrow +2 \qquad +3$$

− *ve* irrationals   + *ve* irrationals
e.g. − $\sqrt{5}$ e.g. $\sqrt{3}$
= − 2.236   = 1.732

In addition we have the Imaginary numbers e.g. $\sqrt{-1}$, $\sqrt{-3}$, which are part of the Complex numbers. These are part real and part imaginary and are generally represented by the expression

$x + iy$ where $i = \sqrt{-1}$

Thus x is the real part and iy the imaginary part

Complex numbers need to be located on a *plane*. This is done by an Argand diagram thus:

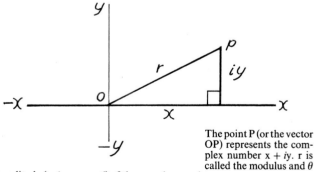

The point P (or the vector OP) represents the complex number $x + iy$. r is called the modulus and θ the amplitude (or 'argument') of the complex number,

where $r = \sqrt{(x^2 + y^2)}$ and $\operatorname{Tan}\theta = \dfrac{y}{x}$

Since $x = r\operatorname{Cos}\theta$ and $y = r\operatorname{Sin}\theta$ the complex number may also be rendered in the form $r(\operatorname{Cos}\theta + i\operatorname{Sin}\theta)$

Sets

Symbols: ξ or E   the universal set (i.e. containing all the elements under consideration)

        $A = \{\ \}$ defines a particular set within the universal set, the members of the set being enclosed within brackets

        $x \in A$ the element x is a member of the set A

        $y \notin A$ the element y is not a member of the set A

        $\bar{n}(A)$ the number of elements in the set A

        A' the set of elements *not* in the set A, or the 'complement' of the set A

        $A \cup B$ the union of all the elements in A and B

        $A \cap B$ the intersection of the elements of A and B, i.e. the elements which appear in both sets

        $A \subset B$ A is a sub-set of B, i.e. is part of the set B

        $B \supset A$ B contains A

[the above two symbols are 'corruptions' of the signs < (less than) and > (greater than) and may be remembered by this connection]

        ϕ an empty set i.e. a set with no members (e.g. the set of all odd numbers exactly divisible by 2)

        $\{x:\dots\}$ the set of values of x such that . . .

The relationship between sets may be conveniently represented on a Venn diagram. If the various sets to be represented are shaded differently and the general principle is that *Union* is represented by *everything* shaded and *Intersection* is represented by cross-hatched shading, quite complicated relationships may be easily clarified.

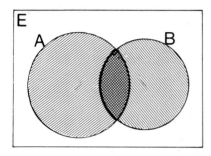

Thus $A \cup B$ = everything shaded and $A \cap B$ = cross-hatched shading and these two areas would contain the appropriate elements.

This illustrates that:
     $A \subset B$ and $A \cap B = A$
              and $A \cup B = B$

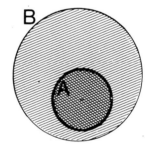

The shaded area represents A'

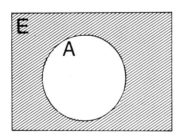

This shows that the elements in $A \cap B'$ will be found in the cross-hatched area. In this case the areas A and B' have been shaded.

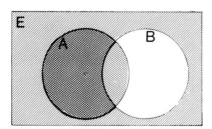

More complicated relationships between several sets may also be conveniently represented in this way, and the equivalence between apparently different relationships clearly illustrated.

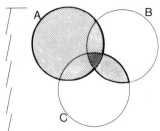

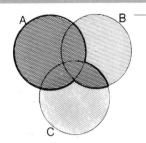

A **U** (B ∩ C)
Everything shaded

(A ∪ B) **∩** (A ∪ C)
Cross-hatched shading

Clearly these (bottom left) two are equivalent, but neither is equivalent to (A ∪ B) **∩** C illustrated in the third diagram (below).

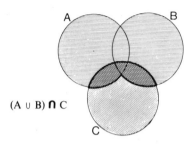

(A ∪ B) **∩** C

The reader should illustrate A **∩** (B ∪ C), (A ∩ B) **U** (A ∩ C) and (A ∩ B) **U** C in the same way.

BASIC CALCULUS

If y is any function of x, and Δy, Δx are corresponding increments of y and x, then the differential coefficient of y with respect to x

$$\left(\text{written } \frac{dy}{dx}\right) \text{ is defined as } \underset{\Delta x \to 0}{\text{Lt}} \frac{[f(x + \Delta x) - f(x)]}{\Delta x}$$

$\frac{dy}{dx}$ gives the gradient of a curve, i.e. it measures the rate of change of one variable with respect to another.

Thus, since velocity is the rate of change of distance with respect to time, it may be expressed in calculus terms as $\frac{dS}{dt}$ where S is the distance of a body from a fixed point and the equation of motion of the body is of the form S = f(t).

Similarly, since acceleration is the rate of change of *velocity* with time, it may be expressed as $\frac{dv}{dt}$ or as $\frac{d^2S}{dt^2}$, i.e. as the second differential of S with respect to t. Acceleration may also be expressed as $v\frac{dv}{ds}$, i.e. as the velocity multiplied by the rate of change of velocity with distance. In general, if
$$y = ax^n$$
then $\frac{dy}{dx} = nax^{n-1}$

Since $\frac{dy}{dx}$ gives the gradient of a curve it may be used to find the maximum and minimum values of a function.

Thus if y = f(x), then when $\frac{dy}{dx} = 0$, the tangents to the curve will be parallel to the x axis, and will indicate the positions of the critical values (the maximum or minimum) but without distinguishing them. However,

if $\frac{d^2y}{dx^2}$ is + ve the critical value of x gives a *minimum* value of the function

while if $\frac{d^2y}{dx^2}$ is − ve the critical value gives a *maximum* value of the function

and if $\frac{d^2y}{dx^2} = 0$, the curve is passing through a point of inflection

Minimum

$\frac{dy}{dx} = 0$ and $\frac{d^2y}{dx^2}$ is +*ve*

Maximum

$\frac{dy}{dx} = 0$ and $\frac{d^2y}{dx^2}$ is −*ve*

Point of inflection

$\frac{dy}{dx} = 0$ and $\frac{d^2y}{dx^2} = 0$

Differential coefficient of a product

If y = uv where u and v are functions of x,

then $\frac{dy}{dx} = u\frac{dv}{dx} + v\frac{du}{dx}$

Differential coefficient of a quotient

If $y = \frac{u}{v}$ where u and v are functions of x,

then $\frac{dy}{dx} = \frac{v\dfrac{du}{dx} - u\dfrac{dv}{dx}}{v^2}$

Integration

Integration is the reverse of differentiation.
In general, $\int ax^n dx$ where a is a constant,

$$= \frac{ax^{n+1}}{n+1} + c \text{ where c is constant.}$$

However, whereas in general differentiation is a straightforward process, integration may be difficult and require the knowledge of a number of standard results.

Integration may be used, among other things, for finding the area under a curve, the volume of revolution of a curve about an axis, and the length of the arc of a curve.

Thus, if the curve is represented by y = f(x), then the area between it and the x-axis between the limits x_1 and x_2 is given by

$$A = \int_{x_1}^{x_2} y dx.$$

The volume of revolution about the x-axis between the same limits is given by

$$V = \pi \int_{x_1}^{x_2} y^2 dx$$

and the length of arc between the same limits is given by

$$L = \int_{x_1}^{x_2} \sqrt{1 + \left(\frac{dy}{dx}\right)^2} \, dx$$

Among the various processes used in integration an important one is *Integration by Parts*

If u and $\frac{dv}{dx}$ are functions of x, then

$$\int \left(u\frac{dv}{dx}\right)dx = uv - \int \left(v\frac{du}{dx}\right)dx$$

For convenience in memorising this it may be abbreviated to

$$\int u dv = uv - \int v du$$

BASIC APPLIED MATHEMATICS

Newton's Laws of Motion were first published in his Principia in 1687.
1. Every body continues in its state of rest, or of uniform motion in a straight line, unless it be compelled by external impressed forces to change that state.
2. The rate of change of momentum is proportional to the impressed force, and takes place in the direction of the straight line in which the force acts.
3. To every action there is an equal and opposite reaction.
Newton's famous Law of Gravitation states that
Every particle of matter attracts every other particle of matter with a force which varies directly as the product of the masses of the particles, and inversely as the square of the distance between them. This may be expressed
as $F \propto \frac{m_1 m_2}{d^2}$
Law 2 leads to the definition of a unit of force as that which, acting on a unit of mass, generates in it unit acceleration.
This leads to the fundamental equation F = ma.

Basic Equations of Motion

$s = \dfrac{(u + v)}{2}$　　　　　　　　$v^2 = u^2 + 2as$

$v = u + at$　　　　　　　　　　$s = ut + \frac{1}{2}at^2$

where　u = initial velocity　　　v = final velocity
　　　　s = distance (space)　　　a = acceleration　　t = time
For constant velocity, Distance = velocity × time.

Relative Velocity

To find the velocity (and direction) of a body A relative to a body B, combine with the velocity of A a velocity equal and opposite to that of B.

The sides of the triangle represent the velocities in magnitude and direction.

Thus to a person on a ship B, the ship A would *appear* to be moving in the direction (and at the speed) represented by the double-arrowed line.

Triangle of Velocities

The triangle ABC shows how the track (i.e. the actual direction) and velocity relative to the ground (the ground speed) of an aircraft or boat may be found from the course set and the wind or current.

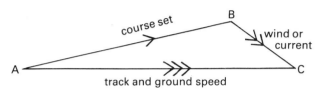

In vector terms, $\overrightarrow{AB} + \overrightarrow{BC} = \overrightarrow{AC}$

Note how, in the diagram, the sum of the arrows along AB + BC equals the number of arrows on AC.

Projectiles

For simple cases, in which air resistance is neglected (i.e. the horizontal component of the velocity is constant) and the vertical velocity is subject only to the force of gravity, the following results may be derived from the fundamental equations of motion:

1. The Time of Flight
$$T = \frac{2u \sin \theta}{g}$$

2. The Time to the greatest height
$$= \frac{T}{2}$$
$$= \frac{u \sin \theta}{g}$$

Parabolic flight path

3. The greatest height attained $\quad H = \dfrac{u^2 \sin^2 \theta}{2g}$

4. The Range on a horizontal plane $\quad R = \dfrac{u^2 \sin 2\theta}{g}$

For a given velocity of projection u there are, in general, two possible angles of projection to obtain a given horizontal range. These directions will make equal angles with the vertical and horizontal respectively. For maximum range the angle makes 45° with the horizontal, i.e. it bisects the angle between the two.

Note that (a) the time taken for a body moving freely under gravity is the same to rise as it is to descend.
(b) the velocity at any point on its upward path is equal to that at the same point on its downward path, and that consequently ...
(c) its velocity (and direction) on striking the ground at the same horizontal level are equal to that with which it was projected.

Impact of Elastic Bodies

If the bodies are smooth (e.g. two billiard balls) and only the forces between the bodies are considered, then the following equations will determine the velocities and directions of the bodies after the impact.
1. Momentum (i.e. product of the individual masses and velocities) along the line of centres after impact = momentum *in the same direction* before impact.
2. The velocity of separation = the velocity of approach (also measured along the line of centres) multiplied by the coefficient of elasticity between the two bodies.
If the impact is oblique (and the bodies are smooth) the velocities at right-angles to the line of centres are unchanged.
If u_1 and u_2, m_1 and m_2 are the initial velocities and masses of the two spheres, and α, β the angles these velocities make with the line of centres, and v_1 and v_2 the components of velocities *along the line of centres* after impact, then the above statements are represented by the following equations:

1. $m_1 v_1 + m_2 v_2 = m_1 u_1 \cos \alpha + m_2 u_2 \cos \beta$
2. $v_2 \pm v_1 = e(u_1 \cos \alpha - u_2 \cos \beta)$

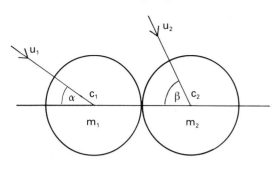

where e is the coefficient of elasticity between the two bodies. Note that in equation 2, v_1 and v_2 will be added or subtracted to get the 'velocity of separation' according to whether the bodies are considered to be going in the opposite or same direction respectively. The conditions of the problem will determine this for the 'velocity of approach'. In the example m_1 is 'catching up' on m_2 and therefore we take the difference in their velocities to obtain the velocity of approach.

Motion in a Circle

If a body is moving in a circle with uniform speed, then its linear velocity v is given by the equation $v = r\omega$ where r is the radius of the circle, and ω is the angular velocity. The body will nevertheless have an acceleration (since a force is acting on it to make it move in a circle) but this will be directed *towards* the centre.

The acceleration will be $\dfrac{v^2}{r}$ or $r\omega^2$ and the force producing it will be $\dfrac{mv^2}{r}$ or $mr\omega^2$ where m is the mass of the body.

Note that if a body is whirled round on the end of a string there is no tendency for it to move outwards along the *radius* of the circle. If the string breaks it will instead move straight on along the *tangent* to the circle.

In the case of a train going round a curve the necessary force is provided by the flanges on the wheels, while in the case of a car going round a track it is provided by the friction between the wheels and the ground. By banking the rails or road the weight of the train or car may be made to provide the necessary force.

The required angle to prevent any tendency to skid is given by the equation $\tan \theta = \dfrac{v^2}{gr}$ where θ is the angle made with the horizontal by the banking. It is the same angle by which a cyclist would have to lean over from the *vertical* when going round a corner.

Simple Harmonic Motion

If a particle moves so that its acceleration is directed towards a fixed point in its path, and is proportional to its distance from that point, it is said to move with simple harmonic motion.

The fundamental equation is $\dfrac{d^2x}{dt^2} = -\omega^2 x$, and by integrating the corresponding equation $v\dfrac{dv}{dx} = -\omega^2 x$ the velocity at any displacement x is given by $v = \omega\sqrt{a^2 - x^2}$ where a is the maximum value of x.

By solving the first equation we find that
$$x = a \cos \omega t \quad (\text{if } t = 0 \text{ when } x = a)$$
$$\text{or} \quad x = a \sin \omega t \quad (\text{if } t = 0 \text{ when } x = 0)$$

The period of the motion is given by $T = \dfrac{2\pi}{\omega}$

Some fundamental principles of **Statics** (the study of the forces acting on bodies at rest, as opposed to **Dynamics**, the study of bodies in motion) are:
1. The *moment of a force* about a point is the product of the force and the perpendicular distance of the line of action of the force from the point.
2. For a body to be at rest under a system of forces in one plane,
   (a) the algebraic sum of the resolved parts of the forces in any two directions which are not parallel must be zero, and
   (b) the algebraic sum of the moments of the forces about any point must be zero (i.e. clockwise moments = anticlockwise moments).
3. For a system of particles of weights w_1, w_2, w_3 etc. whose distances from a fixed axis are x_1, x_2, x_3, etc, the position of the centre of gravity from that axis is given by $x = \dfrac{\sum wx}{\sum w}$ where $\sum wx$ is the sum of all the moments of all the particles about the axis, and $\sum w$ is the sum of all the weights of the particles.

From this, the centres of gravity of irregular shapes, or shapes with portions missing, can be found by the principles that

the Moment of the whole = the sum of the moments of the parts
and the Moment of the remainder = the moment of the whole
— the sum of the moments of the parts removed

The positions of the centres of gravity of some important shapes are as follows:

(1) A triangle — at the intersection of the medians (i.e. the lines joining the vertices to the midpoints of the opposite sides) or at one-third of the length of the median from the base.

(2) Square, rectangle, parallelogram, rhombus — at the intersection of the diagonals.

(3) Sector of a circle of angle 2θ radians — at a distance $\dfrac{2}{3}\dfrac{r\,\text{Sin}\,\theta}{\theta}$ from the centre along the line bisecting the sector, where r = the radius,

For a semi-circle — $\theta = \dfrac{\pi}{2}$, and the distance of the centre of gravity from the centre of the circle will $= \dfrac{4r}{3\pi}$

(4) A solid pyramid on any base — at a point one-quarter of the height of the pyramid above the base

(5) A hollow cone — at a point one-third of the height from the base

(6) A solid hemisphere — at a point along the axis distant $\dfrac{3r}{8}$ from the centre where r is the radius.

(7) A hollow hemisphere — at a point distant $\dfrac{r}{2}$ along the axis from the centre

[Note that this is the same as for the centre of gravity of the cylinder which would surround, or contain, the hemisphere].

(8) A solid, or hollow closed cylinder — Half-way along the axis.

4. If a rigid body is in equilibrium under the action of three forces in a plane, the lines of action of these forces must either all be parallel, or must meet at a common point.

It must thus always be possible to draw a triangle to represent the forces.

5. The Laws of Friction.
   (a) The direction of the frictional force is opposite to that in which the body tends to move.
   (b) The magnitude of the friction is, up to a certain point, exactly equal to the force tending to produce motion.
   (c) Only a certain amount of friction can be called into play. This is called 'limiting friction'.
   (d) The magnitude of the limiting friction for a given pair of surfaces bears a constant ratio to the normal (i.e. perpendicular) pressure between the surfaces. This ratio is denoted by μ and is called the Coefficient of Friction.
   (e) The amount of friction is independent of the areas and shape of the surfaces in contact provided the normal pressure remains unaltered.
   (f) When motion takes place, the friction still opposes the motion. It is independent of the velocity, and is proportional to the normal pressure, but is less than the limiting friction.

If F is the limiting friction (i.e. the force of friction when motion is about to occur), and R is the normal (perpendicular) force, then

$$F = \mu R \quad \text{where } \mu \text{ is the coefficient of friction}$$

The resultant of the forces F and R makes an angle (usually denoted by λ) with R, and thus $\text{Tan}\,\lambda = \dfrac{F}{R}$

$$= \mu$$

λ is called the Angle of Friction.

These relationships are illustrated in the following diagrams:

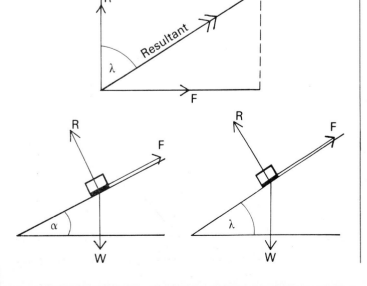

λ = Angle of Friction — If a body is placed on an inclined plane, then if the angle of the plane (α) is less than the angle of friction, it will not slide down.

If the angle of the plane is equal to λ, the angle of friction, the body will be just on the point of sliding. If the angle of the plane is greater than the angle of friction the body will slide.

The Units used in Applied Mathematics will be found on pp 34–6.

Fibonacci Numbers

Fibonacci Numbers were named in the 19th century after Leonardo Fibonacci of Pisa (b. *c.* 1170 d. *ante* 1240), who introduced Arabic figures 1 to 9 plus 0 in his *Liber abaci* in 1202. He earned the title of *Stupor mundi* (wonder of the world) from the Holy Roman Emperor. In 1225 he published a recursive sequence of his Arabic numbers 1, 1, 2, 3, 5, 8, 13, 21, 34, 55 etc. in which each number is the sum of the two preceding numbers. In the 19th century this sequence was found to occur in nature – the arrangement of leaf buds on a stem, animal horns, the genealogy of the male bee and spirals in sunflower heads and pine cones.

GLOSSARY OF COMPUTER TERMS

ALGOL	Computer language (ALGOrithmetic language).
analog	Pertaining to data of continuously variable physical quantities.
artificial language	A programming language whose rules and syntax are specifically developed beforehand.
auxiliary storage	A storage device controlled by a computer but not part of it, e.g. tape, disc.
B	Abbreviation in programming language for 'binary'.
BASIC	A computer language, used in home computers.
binary	Number system using two digits: 0 and 1.
bit	Short for 'binary digit'. The smallest unit of information that can be recognised by a computer.
block	A sequence of bytes grouped together to provide a complete unit of information.
bps	Bits per second.
buffer	Temporary storage of data between devices of differing speeds.
bug	Fault or error in a computer program.
byte	Smallest group of bits which can be called up individually. A byte usually contains eight bits. Each byte corresponds to one character of data; a single letter, number or symbol. A unit of measurement for computer storage capacity.
capacity	The amount of information that can be stored by a computer, e.g. 48K equals 48 kilobytes of data.
channel	That which connects a computer to its peripheral devices.
character	Any symbol capable of being stored and processed by a computer.
cps	Characters per second; the speed of operation of a character printer.
chip	Small piece of silicon etched with impurities in a pattern to form a logical circuit or circuits.
circuit	Complete path of an electrical current.
clear	To erase the contents of a storage device by replacing the contents with blanks or zeros.
closed	1. A switch is closed when turned on to allow the flow of current through it. 2. A file is closed when data cannot be read into it or written from it.
COBOL	Programming language for commercial data processing.
code	Instructions contained in a computer program.
coding	The process of writing program instructions.
command	Instructions to a program to perform some action or cause the execution of a certain program.
compatible	When two devices can work together without special hardware or software additions.
computer	Any device capable of accepting information, applying prescribed processes to the information, and supplying the results therefrom.
computer graphics	The processing and generation of visual information using a computer and a VDU.
console	A device that allows people to communicate directly with a computer.
CONTROL key	A keyboard key which, in conjunction with another key and both pressed at the same time, generates a function of the computer.
control panel	Part of the operator console that contains switches, lights and on/off buttons which control the computer system's various components.
control sequence	The sequence in which a program's instructions are carried out.
CP/M	Control Program for Microcomputers.
CPU	Central Processing Unit.
cursor	A small light pulse that traverses the VDU screen indicating where the next typed character will appear.
daisy wheel printer	Circular-element impact printer/printing one character at a time.
data	Factual information expressed in words and numbers.
database	A collection of data arranged in files used for more than one purpose.

data processing	Operations performed on data to achieve a desired objective.
debug	To locate and correct errors and their sources in a computer program.
decode	To determine the meaning of information in a message by the reversal of previous coding.
digital	1. Data in discreet quantities. 2. Pertaining to data in the form of digits.
disk	Computer memory device, either *hard* or *floppy*, in the shape of an audio record.
disk drive	Electromechanical device into which a disk is inserted to read or write information.
dot-matrix printer	A printing device that forms characters from a matrix of rows and columns of dots.
edit	To rearrange data or information.
enter	Computer keyboard key that is pressed at the end of each line to enter the contents of the line into the computer.
file	A collection of stored information, usually on disk or tape.
floppy disk	Made of non-rigid material.
hard copy	A printout on paper of computer output.
hardware	The physical components of a computer.
high-level language	A computer programming language permitting programs to be written without prior knowledge of the inner workings of a computer.
information	Data previously processed by a computer and produced as meaningful output.
input	Data fed into a computer for it to process.
interface	A boundary point where different elements of a system are linked together or between an operator and a computer system.
K	Represents 2^{10} or 1024. Usually represents a computer's byte capacity: e.g. 64K = 65,536 bytes of information. Short for kilobyte.
LED	Light Emitting Diode.
light pen	Small pen-like input device used with a VDU to select information or draw information etc.
liquid crystal display (LCD)	Video display type.
low-level languages	Symbolic programming languages coded at the same level of detail as machine code, and are translated in a ratio of one symbolic instruction to one machine code instruction.
machine code	The fundamental language of the computer, written in strips of binary Os and Is.
machine language	The binary code which a computer can immediately understand.
machine readable	Data recorded so that it can be read directly by the computer, e.g. data on tape or disk.
magnetic disk	Disk with magnetic surface on which data can be stored by selective magnetization of portions of the surface.
magnetic tape	Plastic tape with magnetic surface on which data can be stored by selective magnetization of portions of the surface.
mainframe	A large computer with a much greater capacity than that of a mini-computer.
malfunction	(Noun) Failure in a computer's hardware. (Verb) To operate incorrectly.
memory	That part of a computer system where data and instructions are stored.
menu	A list of options shown on a monitor screen or VDU during a computer program and from which the user must select an item. Such initial selection may subsequently present another menu.
merge	A process combining two or more sets of records with similarly ordered sets into one set that is arranged in the same order.
message	An item of data with a specific meaning transmitted through communication lines.
micro-computer	A computer whose processing unit is based on the microprocessor chip. Smaller than a mini-computer.
micro-processor	A complex chip that provides the CPU of a microcomputer system.
micro-program	Programs that are stored in RAM and are unalterable.
monitor	The screen of a VDU.
mouse	Hand-held object used to control the cursor on the monitor screen.
NEW	A command in BASIC that clears the memory and allows the operator to start typing a new program.
network	A system in which computers and terminals are so linked as to provide communications and data systems compatible with a user's needs.
node	Any terminal, station or communications computer in a computer network.
online	Under the direct control of the CPU, allowing data to be processed immediately.
online storage	Secondary storage devices, but under direct control of the CPU, so that it is immediately available when required.
open	1. A file is open when data can be transferred in or out of it. 2. When a switch is open it is turned off.
open loop	An information system that does not allow for automatic error correction or data modification, and requires the

	operator to make such adjustments.
open-ended system	Allows new programs, instructions, subroutines, modifications, terms or classifications without disturbing the original system.
operand	An item on which an operation is performed.
operating system	A collection of routines used in overseeing the input, and output processing, of a computer program.
operation	The action specified by a single computer instruction.
operator	Someone who controls a computer or a computer-related device.
output	Data that has been processed and made available for use.
pack	1. (Noun) Magnetic tape or disks or an assembly of such software. 2. (Verb) To compress data to conserve space in storage.
package	A self-contained collection of programs designed to serve a specific set of requirements.
page	A block or unit of fixed length of memory. A micro-computer page is normally 256 bytes.
PASCAL	A computer language which allows for different types of data.
password	A secret code of characters that a user must input to allow access to a computer system.
PEEK	A command that allows an operator to find out the contents of a specific location in a computer's memory.
peripherals	The mechanical and electric devides other than the computer which may be connected to it (terminals, VDU's, disk drives, printers, etc.)
portable program	One that can be used on more than one type of machine.
preprocessor	A program responsible for preparing data for further processing.
primary storage unit	The main memory unit of a digital computer.
printer	A peripheral output device which converts signals from a computer into hard copy on paper in readable form.
printout	Computer output printed on paper.
procedure	A computer program or routine.
processor	A microprocessor or central processor.
program	A set of instructions that a system follows to carry out tasks.
programming language	A communication system devised so that initial program writing in machine language binary code is obviated. (e.g. FORTRAN, BASIC, COBOL).
programming specifications	The precise steps to be taken to create a given application.
PROM	Programmable Read-Only Memory, a computer memory that can only be programmed once but not altered.
RAM	Random Access Memory. A memory device whereby any location in a memory system can be found as quickly as any other.
rated throughput	The maximum possible throughput of a computer.
raw data	Unprocessed data.
read head	A magnetic device that reads data from a storage tape or disk.
reader	Device able to transcribe data from an input medium.
ROM	Read-Only Memory. Memory that contains fixed information that does not need to be changed. A computer can read out of ROM, but ROM cannot be changed, deleted or added to.
readout	Processed information presented to the operator, usually on VDU, printer or plotter.
read/write head	A magnetic device that can read from or write into a storage medium.
real memory	A computer's actual memory which is directly addressable by CPU.
record	A collection of related data.
re-entry point	After a subroutine has been completed, the first instruction in the main program is addressed to the date being processed.
REM	A key word in BASIC used to announce the beginning of a comment.
remote station	Data terminal equipment used to communicate with a data processing system that is distant from the CPU.
resident	A program permanently stored in a computer's main memory or in a specific storage device.
resource sharing	The simultaneous use of computer facilities by several users (see time sharing).
response time	Time taken by a system to respond to an operator's commands.
retrieval	The process by which a requested data item is located in a file and subsequently displayed or printed on the appropriate terminal commanded by the operator.
row	A horizontal arrangement of characters, numbers, bits or other expressions.
RPG	Report Program Generator. A business programming language.
RUN	A command in BASIC which causes a currently stored program to go into output function.
scrolling	An operation that allows display data of larger capacity

than that which can appear on a specific display or VDU to be seen by 'rolling it upwards'. Input and output appear at the bottom of the screen and travel upwards as more lines of information are added. When the information reaches the top of the screen, it disappears to allow new material to be written in at the bottom of the screen.

secondary storage device	That which provides additional memory for a computer system (e.g. magnetic tape and disk storage units).
sequential file	The most straightforward method of file organization in which each record is written immediately after the previous one.
shared memory	A memory chip that can be accessed by two different CPUs.
shift register	A control signal where all the bits can be moved one place to the right or left by its activation.
silicon chip	A small piece of silicon on which complex miniaturized circuits are etched.
simulation	The process of representing one system by another.
skip	To ignore one or more instructions in a sequence of such instructions.
slave	Any device that is subject to the control of another.
soft copy	Output that appears on the screen of a VDU.
software	All the programs, computer languages and operations used to make a computer perform useful functions (see hardware).
software-compatible	Different makes or marks of computers are software-compatible if they can use the same machine language and, thus, can execute the same programs.
SOM	Start of Message
source program	High level programming language which must be translated into machine language before it can be used by a computer.
special symbol	Neither a letter nor a number (e.g. £, #).
station	Input or output point on a communication system.
storage capacity	Refers to the amount of information a system can store at any one time. A computer with 64K can store 65,5636 bytes in its inbuilt memory.
store	Transfer input data from the CPU to a memory device (tape or disk).
string	A group of characters stored in a computer.
STX	Start-of-Text; usually a coded control character.
subprogram	A section of a program that performs a specific function within it.
subroutine	A set of instructions given a specific name that will be carried out when a main program calls for it.
syntax	The set of rules in a programming language that specifies how the language symbols can be assembled to form meaningful statements.
system	A group of interrelated units that can function together. The CPU controls the other units.

systems program	A program for a computer (usually supplied with it) that allows the operator to use it easily and effectively. A collection of such programs constitutes the computer's operating system.
systems programmer	A person who plans, generates, extends and controls the use of an operating system.
systems analyst	A person who designs problems in data processing and indicates or writes directions for their solutions in data processing terms.
systems software	The software supplied with the computer which make it perform effectively.
tape	(See magnetic tape).
tape drive	Converts information stored on tape into signals that are sent to a computer, and receives information from the computer to be stored on tape.
terminal	A point in a system where data can either enter or exist.
test	The part of a message that contains the main body of information to be conveyed.
throughput	1. The rate at which information can be accurately transmitted when averaged out over a long period. 2. The time taken from an operation's beginning to its end.
time sharing	A computer system that allows several users to be connected simultaneously to one computer.
track	Concentric circles on a disk which store information. Each circle is a track.
transceiver	A device that both transmits and receives data, often simultaneously.
translator	A device that converts programs written in one language into another language.
up	A computer system is up when it is available for use.
update	To change, delete or add (or all three) data in a file or record.
user-friendly	A computing system that provides for the capabilities and limitations of an operator: a system requiring little expertise to operate.
VDU	Visual Display Unit.
verb	An instruction to action in a programming language (e.g. READ, WRITE, PRINT).
visual display unit	A peripheral device that displays information on a screen.
word processor	A computer-based system or software package that allows an operator to input text into the system which can then be edited or reformated at will before being printed out into hard copy.
wordstar	A popular brand of software package used in word processing.
write	To transfer data from a computer to an output device.
zap	To erase.

Physics

Milestones in physics

Physics is very much concerned with fundamental particles – the building blocks out of which the Universe is constructed – and the forces which bind and regulate them. Many theories have been proposed from time to time to provide a better understanding of the vast number of facts and observations which have accumulated. The main development of physics is essentially a series of unifications of these theories.

1687 Sir Isaac Newton (1642–1727) produced the great unifying theory of **gravitation** which linked the falling apple with the force which keeps the stars and planets in their courses. This made available for further scientific investigation one of the basic universal forces of nature, the force of gravity. The gravitational force, F, between two bodies of masses, m_1, m_2, distance, r, apart is given by

$$F = G\frac{m_1 m_2}{r^2}$$

where G is a Universal constant. Though he first derived his inverse square law of gravity in the

summer of 1666, at Woolsthorpe, Lincolnshire, Newton did not publish it until 1687 in his *Principia*.

By Newton's time there existed two rival theories to explain the passage of light from source to observer. One was the **particle theory** which maintained that light consists of vast numbers of minute particles ejected by the luminous body in all directions. Newton, who made so many brilliant advances in optics, favoured this theory. It accounted in a particularly simple way for the transmission of light through the vacuum of space, for its rectilinear propagation, and for the laws of reflection. The alternative was the **wave theory**, which assumed that light was transmitted by means of a wave motion. This would imply that light would bend round corners, but when it was discovered that the wavelength of the light was very small (about 1/2000th of a millimetre), it was realised that the effect would be small as is in fact observed. Light does not cast a perfectly sharp shadow. Further phenomena were discovered which demonstrated the wave nature of light and added support to that theory, e.g. interference and diffraction.

1820 Hans Christian Oersted (1777–1851) of Denmark discovered that the flow of electric current in a conductor would cause a nearby compass needle to be deflected.

1831 Michael Faraday (1791–1867) the English physicist, uncovered the principle of magnetic induction which led to the invention of the dynamo. He showed that a change in the magnetic field surrounding a conductor could cause a flow of electrical current.

1865 The unification between magnetism and electricity was brought to full flower by the Scottish physicist, James Clerk Maxwell (1831–79), in his great **electromagnetic theory**, which described every known kind of magnetic and electric behaviour. The set of equations named after him showed that electromagnetic waves travel at the velocity of light and confirmed that light is, in fact, an electromagnetic radiation. This provided further support for the wave theory of light.

1887 Heinrich Rudolph Hertz (1857–94), the German physicist, performed a classic experiment in which electromagnetic waves were produced and transmitted across the laboratory. This laid the foundation for radio transmission and provided ample vindication for Maxwell's theory.

As the 19th century drew to a close many of the problems of physics appeared to have been solved and there was a belief that, in principle, if all the observations and calculations could be made, the destiny of the universe could be revealed in full detail. However, following on Hertz's experiment, a quick succession of phenomena presented themselves which threatened to destroy the orderly structure which had been so painstakingly built up over the preceding centuries.

1895 X-rays were discovered by Wilhelm Konrad Röntgen (1845–1923) the German physicist. When experimenting with the passage of electrical discharges through gases, he noticed that fluorescent material near his apparatus glowed. He won the first Nobel prize for physics in 1901 for this work.

1896 Antoine Henri Becquerel (1852–1908), the French physicist, discovered that uranium salts, even in the dark, emit a radiation similar to Röntgen's X-rays and would fog a photographic plate. This was **radioactivity**.

1898 Marie Curie (1867–1934), of Poland, working with her French husband, Pierre, (1859–1906) announced the existence of two new chemical elements which powerfully emit radiation. She named the elements radium and polonium. The active phenomenon she gave the name radioactivity. She won the Nobel prize for physics in 1903 with Becquerel and her husband, and in 1911, for chemistry on her own.

Ernest Rutherford (1871–1937), New Zealand born British physicist and Frederick Soddy (1877–1956), British chemist, formulated a theory of radioactivity which forms the basis of our present understanding of the phenomenon. Three types of radioactivity were identified, α-rays, β-rays, and γ-rays. The γ-rays turned out to be like X-rays, more powerful than those of Röntgen. The β-rays were streams of fast moving electrons. The α-rays were found to consist of electrically charged particles being the nuclei of the element helium. The particles emitted from radioactive materials at such speed provided a means of investigating the structure of the atom itself, and enabled Rutherford to propose in 1911 a model of the atom which is the basis of our modern ideas of atomic structure.

A further important discovery which contributed to a revision of the ideas of classical physics was the **photoelectric effect**. It was observed that a polished zinc plate, when illuminated with ultra-violet light acquired a positive electric charge. In **1897** Joseph John Thomson (1856–1940), the British physicist, discovered the first of the fundamental particles, the **electron**, which is the basic unit of negative electricity. It became clear that the photoelectric effect was the result of electrons being knocked out of the metal surface by the incident light. It was further discovered that, firstly, the number of electrons emitted was greater for a greater intensity of light and, secondly, that their energy was related only to the wavelength of the light, being greater for shorter wavelengths. The first result was as expected but the second was a mystery.

MODERN PHYSICS

Modern physics could be said to have been born at the beginning of the 20th century, during the course of which a number of radical ideas have been formulated and developed into theories which have completely revolutionised the thinking in physics.

1900 The quantum theory was the first of these, put forward by the German physicist Max Karl Ernst Ludwig Planck (1858–1947). This arose out of yet another problem which had been insoluble up to that time. Calculations showed that the energy emitted from a hot body should be, at very short wavelengths, practically infinite: this was clearly not so. The calculations

THE FUNDAMENTAL PHYSICAL CONSTANTS

The constants are called 'fundamental' since they are used universally throughout all branches of science. Because of the unprecedented amount of new experimental and theoretical work being carried out, thorough revisions are now quite frequently published, the last being in 1973 and the next in 1982. Values are reported such that the figure in brackets following the last digit is the estimated uncertainty of that digit, e.g. the speed of light $c = 2·99792458(1) \times 10^8$ m s^{-1} could be written $c = (2·997\,924\,58 \pm 0·000\,000\,01) \times 10^8$ m s^{-1}. The unit m·s^{-1} represents m/s or metres per second.

	Quantity	Symbol	Value	Units
general constants	speed of light *in vacuo*	c	$2·99792458(1) \times 10^8$	m·s^{-1}
	elementary charge	e	$1·6021892(46) \times 10^{-19}$	C
	Planck's constant	h	$6·626176(36) \times 10^{-34}$	J·s
		$\hbar = h/2\pi$	$1·0545887(57) \times 10^{-34}$	J·s
	gravitational constant	G	$6·6720(41) \times 10^{-11}$	m^3·s^{-2}·kg^{-1}
matter in bulk	Avogadro constant	N_A	$6·022045(31) \times 10^{23}$	mol^{-1}
	atomic mass unit	$u = 1/N_A$	$1·6605655(86) \times 10^{-27}$	kg
			$9·315016(26) \times 10^2$	MeV
	faraday	$F = N_A e$	$9·648456(27) \times 10^4$	C·mol^{-1}
	normal volume of ideal gas	V_m	$2·241383(70) \times 10^{-2}$	m^3·mol^{-1}
	gas constant	R	$8·31441(26)$	J·mol^{-1}·K^{-1}
			$8·20568(26) \times 10^{-5}$	m^3·atm·mol^{-1}K^{-1}
	Boltzmann constant	$k = R/N_A$	$1·380662(44) \times 10^{-23}$	J·K^{-1}
electron	electron rest mass	m_e	$9·109534(47) \times 10^{-31}$	kg
			$0·5110034(14)$	MeV
	electron charge to mass ratio	e/m_e	$1·7588047(49) \times 10^{11}$	C·kg^{-1}
proton	proton rest mass	m_p	$1·6726485(86) \times 10^{-27}$	kg
			$9·382796(27) \times 10^2$	MeV
neutron	neutron rest mass	m_n	$1·6749543(86) \times 10^{-27}$	kg
			$9·395731(27) \times 10^2$	MeV
energy conversion	million electron volt unit	MeV	$1·7826758(51) \times 10^{-30}$	kg
			$1·6021892(46) \times 10^{-13}$	J

were satisfactory for radiation of longer wavelengths in that they agreed with experiment. To resolve this difficulty, Planck made the very novel suggestion that energy was radiated from the body, not in a continuous flow of waves as had been supposed up to then, but rather in distinct individual bundles. He called a bundle of energy a **quantum**. The energy of the quantum, E, is given by

$$E = \frac{hc}{\lambda}$$

where λ is the wavelength of the radiation, c is the velocity of light *in vacuo* and h is a fixed, universal constant called Planck's constant. On this theory, energy at the shorter wavelengths would require to be emitted in bigger bundles and thus there would be less of them available for emission in accordance with experimental results. Planck's constant is small and so quantum effects are also small, occurring only in the domain of atomic phenomena.

1905 Albert Einstein (1879–1955), a Swabian Jew, published his theory of the photoelectric effect and for which he was to win the Nobel prize in 1921. Einstein followed Planck's ideas and could see that the incident light must consist of a stream of quanta, that is, bundles of light, which came to be known as **photons**. A photon striking a metal surface is absorbed by an electron in it, the electron having more energy as a result. This causes it to jump from the surface, and since photons have greater energy at shorter wavelengths, so shorter wavelength light causes the emission of higher energy electrons. And, of course, the greater the intensity of the light the more quanta will be striking the surface and so more electrons will be emitted. Thus, the idea of the quantum enabled Einstein to account for the phenomena of the photoelectric effect and this was an early triumph for the new quantum theory which was to become a ground force in the subsequent developments in physics.

1905 This year also saw the publication of Einstein's **Special (or Restricted) Theory of Relativity**. It has been said that as a child he had wondered what would happen if it were possible to travel fast enough to catch a ray of light and that this led him some years later to formulate his celebrated theory. This theory arises from an apparent contradiction between two basic postulates:

1. The velocity of light *in vacuo* is a constant for all observers regardless of their state of motion relative to the light source.
2. The special principle of relativity which states that the laws of physics are the same for all observers in uniform motion relative to each other.

Imagine for a moment a train travelling with a uniform velocity v relative to the railway embankment, and a ray of light transmitted with velocity c along the embankment parallel, and in the direction of the train. For an observer in the train the velocity of the light should appear to be $c-v$: obviously less than c. But this violates the special principle of relativity above: the velocity of light must be the same for an observer on the embankment and an observer on the train. The reconciliation of these two apparently contradictory conclusions is the basis for the special theory and is achieved by surrendering the concepts of absolute time, absolute distance and of the absolute significance of simultaneity. From these ideas, fairly straightforward algebraic manipulation leads to equations which show that when a body is in uniform motion relative to an observer, the length of the body is diminished in the direction of travel and its mass is increased. The equations are:

$$l = l_0 \sqrt{(1 - v^2/c^2)} \quad \text{and} \quad m = \sqrt{\frac{m_0}{(1 - v^2/c^2)}}$$

where l and m are the length and mass respectively of a body as seen by an observer, and moving at velocity v in the direction of its length relative to him, l_0 is the velocity of the body at rest and m_0 is its mass at rest.

Thus, if a 20 m rocket came past you in space at 149 896 km per sec (i.e. 0·5c) it would (if you could measure it) be only about 17 m long.

If two observers are moving at a constant velocity relative to each other, it appears to each that the other's clocks are slowed down and this is expressed in the equation:

$$t = t_0 \sqrt{(1 - v^2/c^2)}$$

where t is one observer's time as read by the other, and t_0 is his own time as read by himself, v being the constant relative velocity of the two observers.

From the theory it can be shown that, at rest, a body possesses energy, E, given by

$$E = mc^2$$

Relativity theory thus confirms an important unification in physics between two of its very basic concepts: mass and energy with the former being a congealed form of the latter with a transmission constant being the speed of light (c) squared. This most famous of formulae was first published in Leipzig on 14 May 1907.

1911 Ernest Rutherford proposed a model of the atom which is the basis of our ideas of atomic structure to this day. He had from the first recognised the value of the fast moving α-particles emitted naturally from radioactive materials as probes for discovering the nature of the atom. He arranged for α-particles to bombard a thin gold foil and found that while many passed straight through a few were deflected at comparatively large angles, some even 'bouncing' back towards the source. He concluded from this that the mass of the atom was concentrated at its centre in a minute nucleus consisting of positively charged particles called **protons**. Around the nucleus and at a relatively large distance from it revolved the negatively charged electrons rather like a miniature solar system. The combined negative charges of the electrons exactly balanced the total positive charge of the nucleus. This important model of the atom suffered from a number of defects. One of these was that from Maxwell's electromagnetic theory the atom should produce light of all wavelengths whereas, in fact, atoms of each element emit light consisting of a number of definite wavelengths – a spectrum – which can be measured with great accuracy. The spectrum for each element is unique.

A further major difficulty was that the electrons, moving round the nucleus, should yield up their energy in the form of radiation and so would spiral into the nucleus bringing about the collapse of the atom. In fact, nothing of the sort occurs: under normal conditions an atom is a stable structure which does not emit radiation.

1913 The difficulties of the Rutherford atom were overcome by the Danish physicist, Neils Henrik David Bohr (1885–1962) who proposed that electrons were permitted only in certain orbits but could jump from one permitted orbit to another. In so jumping the electron would gain or lose energy in the form of photons, whose wavelength followed from Planck's rule:

$$\lambda = \frac{hc}{E}$$

In this way the spectrum of light emitted, or absorbed, by an atom would relate to its individual structure. The theoretical basis to Bohr's work was confirmed by Einstein in 1917 and the Bohr theory went on successfully to explain other atomic phenomena. However, after many outstanding successes over a number of years, an increasing number of small but important discrepancies appeared with which the Bohr theory could not cope.

1919 Rutherford performed the first artificial nuclear disintegration when he bombarded nitrogen atoms with α-particles from radon-C. He demonstrated that protons were emitted as a result of the disintegration and this confirmed that the proton was, indeed, a nuclear particle.

1924 Louis-Victor de Broglie (1892–1976), French physicist, postulated that the dual wave-particle nature of light might be shown by other particles and particularly by electrons. The wavelength, λ, would be given by

$$\lambda = \frac{h}{mv}$$

where m is the mass of the particle, and v is its velocity. Electron waves were demonstrated experimentally in 1927 by C. J. Davisson (1881–1958) and L. H. Germer (b. 1896) of the USA. Subsequently, de Broglie's idea of matter waves was extended to other particles, protons, neutrons, etc. All matter has an associated wave character, but for the larger bodies of classical

The forces of physics

There are considered to be four basic forces in nature which differ very considerably in strength. These are listed here in ascending order of strength, together with a fifth, the superstrong colour force, the theory of which came into being in the early part of this decade. Its existence is a matter of speculation but it is offering a satisfying explanation of some phenomena at the very heart of matter.

	range	force-carrying particle	
gravity	very long	graviton, g	acts on all matter; weak within the atom
weak force	short, about 10^{-15} cm	W-meson	acts on all the basic particles, leptons and quarks: involved in radioactive processes.
electromagnetic force	very long	photon γ	acts on all charged particles: provides the basis to the reactions of chemistry and biology.
strong force	short, 10^{-13} cm	meson	acts on the hadrons, e.g. the proton and neutron, and is responsible for binding the nucleus together. Is involved in nuclear reactions.
colour force	short, 10^{-13} cm	gluon	acts on the quarks, allowing them freedom of movement within the hadron, e.g. proton, but holding them firmly within it.

The particles of physics

THE QUANTA

	Symbol	Anti-particle symbol	Mass MeV	Spin	Electric charge	Strangeness	Charm
photon	γ		0	1	0		
graviton	g		0	2	0		

In addition to the quanta, there are thought to be only 2 families, the leptons and the quarks, which are elementary.

THE LEPTONS

	Symbol	Anti-particle symbol	Mass MeV	Spin	Electric charge	Strangeness	Charm
electron	e^-	e^+	0·511003	$\frac{1}{2}$	-1	0	0
muon	μ^-	μ^+	105·659	$\frac{1}{2}$	-1	0	0
electron neutrino	v_e	v_e	0	$\frac{1}{2}$	0	0	0
muon neutrino	v_μ	v_μ	0	$\frac{1}{2}$	0	0	0

THE QUARKS

	Symbol	Anti-particle symbol	Mass MeV	Spin	Electric charge	Strangeness	Charm
up	u	u	100	$\frac{1}{2}$	$+\frac{2}{3}$	0	0
down	d	d	100	$\frac{1}{2}$	$-\frac{1}{3}$	0	0
strange	s	s	400	$\frac{1}{2}$	$\frac{1}{3}$	-1	0
charmed	c	c	1500	$\frac{1}{2}$	$+\frac{2}{3}$		$+1$

THE HADRONS

The other particles belong to the family of hadrons, and are constructed from the quarks: the baryons from 3 quarks and the mesons from 2. The following lists a few baryons and mesons.

	Symbol	Anti-particle symbol	Composition	Mass MeV	Spin	Electric charge	Strangeness	Charm
THE BARYONS								
proton	p^+	p^-	uud	938·280	$\frac{1}{2}$	$+1$	0	0
neutron	n^0	n^0	udd	939·573	$\frac{1}{2}$	0	0	0
omega minus	Ω^-	Ω^+	sss	1672·2	$\frac{3}{2}$	-1	-3	0
THE MESONS								
charged pion	π^+	n^-	ud	139·567	0	$+1$	0	0
neutral pion	π^0		uu or dd	134·963	0	0	0	0
neutral psi	ψ		cc	3097	1	0	0	0
neutral D	D^0	D^0	cu	1863·3	0	0	0	$+1$

mechanics, the wavelengths are too small for their effects to be detectable.

1926 Erwin Schrödinger (1887–1961), a physicist from Vienna, took up the idea of de Broglie waves and applied them to the Bohr atom. The solutions to the resulting wave equation gave the allowed orbits or energy levels more accurately than the quantised orbits in the Bohr atom. Max Born (1882–1970), the German physicist, interpreted these solutions in terms of probability, i.e. they gave the probability of finding an electron in a given volume of space within the atom.

1927 The German physicist, Werner Karl Heisenberg (1901–76) formulated his celebrated and profound Uncertainty Principle: this states that there is a definite limit to the accuracy with which certain pairs of measurements can be made. The more accurate one quantity is known, the less accurate is our knowledge of the other. Position and momentum is an example of such

a pair of measurements. The more exactly we know the position of, say, an electron, the less will we know about its momentum. This can be expressed:

$$\Delta x . \Delta p \sim h$$

where Δx represents the uncertainty in position, Δp the uncertainty in momentum and h is Planck's constant. A further important example relates to time and energy: it is not possible to know how much energy E is possessed by a particle without allowing sufficient time t for the energy to be determined.

$$\Delta E . \Delta t \sim h$$

The uncertainty principle provides the main reason why the classical mechanics of Newton do not apply to atomic and subatomic phenomena.

1928 Paul Adrien Maurice Dirac (b. 1902), the Cambridge mathematician, introduced a theory of the electron which successfully brought together the ideas of quantum mechanics thus far developed with those of relativity. As a result of this, the important concept of electron spin previously advanced by Bohr became theoretically justified.

Dirac's equations revealed a negative quantity which led to the prediction of the existence of the antielectron, a particle identical to the electron, of the same mass but of opposite electric charge. This major idea, that there could exist **antimatter** in the universe composed of antiparticles arises from Dirac's bold prediction.

Heisenberg's uncertainty principle led to the idea of the instantaneous creation and annihilation of short-lived 'virtual' particles in the vicinity of stable particles. The basic uncertainty in the energy of a particle enables it to acquire a loan, as it were, of energy for a short time: the length of time, in fact, being inversely related to the amount of energy lent. Provided the loan is repaid in the time available, there is no violation of the law of conservation of energy. The action of forces could now be seen in terms of these 'virtual' particles, which behave as force-carriers travelling rapidly from one particle to the other. So, it comes about that particles, not in direct contact, respond each to the presence of the other.

1932 Ernest Orlando Lawrence (1901–58), an American physicist, developed the **cyclotron**. This was one of the first machines constructed for accelerating charged particles artificially to high velocities for research. The particles, which in the first instance were protons, were caused to move with ever increasing velocity in a spiral path by the suitable application of magnetic and electric fields. Lawrence was awarded the Nobel prize in 1939 for this work.

1932 Carl David Anderson (b. 1905), an American physicist of California, announced the discovery of the antielectron predicted a few years previously by Dirac. This was the first particle of antimatter to be discovered and he named it the **positron**.

1932 James Chadwick (1891–1974), the English physicist, discovered the **neutron**, a constituent of the atomic nucleus of zero charge and only slightly heavier than the proton.

1933 Wolfgang Pauli (1900–58) of Austria postulated the existence of the **neutrino**, a neutral particle of negligible mass in order to explain the fact that in β-emission in radioactivity, there was a rather greater loss of energy than could be otherwise explained.

In 1956 Fred Reines and Clyde Cowan in Los Alamos succeeded in detecting neutrinos (electron neutrinos). In 1962 Lederman and Melvin Schwarz of Columbia University demonstrated the existence of the other neutrino, the muon neutrino.

1934 Hideki Yukawa (b. 1907), the Japanese physicist, sought to explain the forces which held the particles in the nucleus together – the **strong force** – and called the force-carrying particles in this case **mesons**. The meson predicted by Yukawa, the **pion**, was discovered by Cecil F Powell of Bristol University in 1947.

1938 **Nuclear fission** was discovered by Otto Hahn (1879–1968) and Fritz Strassman (b. 1902) by bombarding uranium with neutrons, when trying to produce transuranic elements. They succeeded in producing elements lighter than uranium from the mineral of the periodic table. The incident neutron causes the target nucleus to split into two pieces of almost equal mass. Each of the fragments consists of protons and neutrons and an enormous amount of energy is released in the process. Enrico Fermi (1901–54) suggested that the neutrons released in fission could themselves induce further fission and that it should be possible to sustain a chain reaction.

1942 The first nuclear reactor, set up by Fermi in the University of Chicago, became critical.

1945 The first atomic explosion which was experimental took place in July followed by bombs dropped on Hiroshima and Nagasaki in August.

1952 The first hydrogen bomb was exploded in November. This derived its energy from the process of nuclear fusion in which two or more relatively light nuclei combined to form a heavier atomic nucleus releasing thereby a very considerable amount of energy. Considerable effort is being made to develop a fusion reactor and the main difficulty is the problem of containing the enormously high temperatures involved within the reactor for long enough to allow the reaction to proceed. In June 1954 the world's first nuclear powered generator produced electricity at Obnisk near Moscow, and in August 1956 the first large scale nuclear power generating station, Calder Hall, Cumberland (Cumbria), started up. It was officially opened by Her Majesty Queen Elizabeth II in October when power first flowed into the national grid.

By the 1950s a bewilderingly large number of apparently fundamental particles had been reported and their great number was becoming an embarrassment. Most particles then known fell into two classes: the **leptons** and the **hadrons** (see table on page 50).

Hadrons are complex and there was evidence that they themselves possessed an internal structure. Certain of the unstable hadrons were found to take very much longer to decay than expected. These were called **strange** particles.

1953 Murray Gell-Mann (b. 1929) of the USA, introduced a concept he called **strangeness**, a quality akin in some ways to electric charge, which helped to account for the increased lifetimes of the strange particles. Aided by this idea, it was found that particles could be fitted into patterns according to the amount of strangeness they possessed. This led to the prediction of the existence of a rather unusual particle and it was a great triumph for these theories when in 1964 the omega-minus particle was discovered.

1963 From considerations of these patterns, Gell-Mann was led to the idea that the hadrons were composed of more basic particles called **quarks** (a name he borrowed from the writings of the Irish author, James Joyce). There were three kinds of quark, 'up', 'down' and 'strange' and, for each, a corresponding antiquark. These combined in only one of two ways to form either **baryons** or **mesons** as the table shows. Thus the proton can be pictured as consisting of three quarks – 2 up quarks and 1 down quark held together by force-carrying particles called **gluons**.

A free quark has not yet been detected and there is speculation that it never will. But there is experimental evidence suggesting their existence within baryons.

Current theory suggests that the gluons carry an enormously strong force called the **colour force**. This is much stronger than the strong nuclear force and permits quarks in the proton, for example, freedom of movement over a very short distance but increases with distance to hold them firmly within the proton.

1974 A particularly heavy particle, a hadron, was discovered and called the J or psi particle. Up to this time, the rules for building hadrons from quarks accounted in a complete and satisfying way for every known hadron and so it was that there appeared to be no room for the new particle. However, it could be explained by assuming it to be composed of a new quark together with its antiquark. This new, fourth quark called the charmed quark had been proposed in 1970 by Sheldon Lee Glashow (b. 1932) for other theoretical reasons. Charm, a property similar to strangeness, was first suggested in 1964 by Glashow on aesthetic grounds: there were two pairs of leptons so the up and down quark also formed a pair leaving the strange quark without a companion. Now, the charmed quark completed the team and also explained this new particle.

However, the charm in this psi particle cancelled out because of the charm/anti-charm combination. The search was then for a particle exhibiting 'naked' charm, a particle containing

a charmed quark in combination with an up, down or strange quark.

1976 In May the D^0 meson was discovered by Gerson Goldhaber, co-discoverer of the psi particle, and Francoise Pierre at Stanford University. The D^0 particle consisted of a charmed quark and an anti-up quark.

In August, Wonyong Lee of Columbia University announced that a charmed antiproton had been detected, consisting of three antiquarks – up, down and charmed.

New particles were thus being discovered at this time with properties predicted by the charm theory.

1977 It was suggested that both quarks and leptons are combinations of more primitive fields known as preons. In November two very heavy Upsilon mesons with masses of 9400 MeV and 10 000 MeV were announced. These resonances indicated a massive new quark dubbed 'bottom' (symbol 'b').

Newton's laws of motion
These three self-evident principles were discovered experimentally before Newton's time but were first formulated by him.
Law 1. The law of inertia
A particle will either remain at rest or continue to move with uniform velocity unless acted upon by a force.
Law 2
The acceleration of a particle is directly proportional to the force producing it and inversely proportional to the mass of the particle.
Law 3. The law of action and reaction
Forces, the results of interactions of two bodies, always appear in pairs. In each pair the forces are equal in magnitude and opposite in direction.

Equations of motion (see also page 44)
Where
u is the initial velocity of a body;
v is its final velocity after time t;
s is the distance it travels in this time;
a is the uniform acceleration it undergoes, then

$$v = u + at$$
$$s = ut + \tfrac{1}{2}at^2$$
$$v^2 = u^2 + 2as$$

Laws of Thermodynamics
Thermodynamics (Greek, *thermos*, hot; *dynamis*, power) is the quantitative treatment of the relation of heat to natural and mechanical forms of energy.

There are three Laws of Thermodynamics.

The **First Law**, derived from the principle of Conservation of Energy, may be stated 'Energy can neither be created nor destroyed, so that a given system can gain or lose energy only to the extent that it takes it from or passes it to its environment'. This is expressed as

$$E_f - E_i = \Delta$$

where E_i is the initial energy, E_f the final content of energy and Δ the change of energy. The impossibility of useful mechanical perpetual motion follows directly from this. The law applies only to systems of constant mass.

The **Second Law** concerns the concept of entropy (Gk. *en*, into; *tropos*, a changing) which is the relation between the temperature of and the heat content within any system. A large amount of lukewarm water may contain the same amount of heat as a little boiling water. The levelling out (equalising) of heat within a system (i.e. the pouring of a kettle of boiling water into a lukewarm bath) is said to increase the entropy of that system of two vessels. Any system, including the Universe, naturally tends to increase its entropy, i.e. to distribute its heat. If the Universe can be regarded as a closed system, it follows from the Law that it will have a finite end, i.e. when it has finally dissipated or unwound itself to the point that its entropy attains a maximal level – this is referred to as the 'Heat Death' of the Universe. From this it would also follow that the Universe must then have had a finite beginning for if it had had a creation an infinite time ago heat death would by now inevitably have set in. The second Law, published in Berlin in 1850 by Rudolf Clausius (1822–88) states 'Heat cannot of itself pass from a colder to warmer body'. This is mathematically expressed by the inequality.

$$\Delta > 0$$

i.e. the change of entropy in any heat exchanging system and its surroundings taken together is always greater than zero.

The **Third Law** is not a general law but applies only to pure crystalline solids and states that at absolute zero the entropies of such substances are zero.

Celsius and Fahrenheit Compared

The two principal temperature scales are Celsius and Fahrenheit. The former was devised in 1743 by J P Christen (1683–1755) but is referred to by its present name because of the erroneous belief that it was invented by Anders Celsius (1701–44). In a meteorological context the scale is still referred to in the United Kingdom as Centigrade though the name was otherwise abandoned in 1948. The latter is named after Gabriel Daniel Fahrenheit (1686–1736), a German physicist.

To convert C to F, multiply the C reading by 9/5 and add 32.

To convert F to C, subtract 32 from the F reading and multiply by 5/9.

Useful comparisons are:

(1) Absolute Zero	=	−273·15°C	=	−459·67°F	
(2) Point of Equality	=	−40·0°C	=	−40·0°F	
(3) Zero Fahrenheit	=	−17·8°C	=	0·0°F	
(4) Freezing Point of water	=	0·0°C	=	32·0°F	
(5) Normal Human Blood Temperature	=	36·9°C	=	98·4°F	
(6) 100 Degrees F	=	37·8°C	=	100·0°F	
(7) Boiling Point of Water (at standard pressure)	=	100·0°C	=	212·0°F	

Scientists in a non-meteorological context most frequently employ the Kelvin Scale in which kelvin (K) = fraction 1/273·16 of the triple point of water (where ice, water and water vapour are in equilibrium). Thus absolute zero is zero K, the ice-point of water (0°C or 32°F) is 273·15 K and boiling point (100°C or 212°F) is 373·15 K.

NOBEL PRIZEWINNERS IN PHYSICS SINCE 1950

1984 Carlo Rubbia, Italian; Simon van der Meer, Dutch.
1983 Subrahmanyam Chandrasekhar, US; William A. Fowler, US.
1982 Kenneth G. Wilson, US.
1981 Nicolass Boembergen, Arthur Schlawlow, both US; Kai M. Siegbahn, Swedish.
1980 James W. Cronin, Val L. Fitch, both US.
1979 Steven Weinberg, Sheldon L. Glashow, both US; Abdus Salam, Pakistani.
1978 Pyotr Kapitsa, USSR; Arno Penzias, Robert Wilson, both US.
1977 John H. Van Vleck, Philip W. Anderson, both US; Nevill F. Mott, British.
1976 Burton Richter, US; Samuel C. C. Ting, US.
1975 James Rainwater, US; Ben Mottelson, US-Danish; Aage Bohr, Danish.
1974 Martin Ryle, British; Antony Hewish, British.
1973 Ivar Giaever, US; Leo Esaki, Japan; Brian D. Josephson, British.

1972 John Bardeen, US; Leon N. Cooper, US; John R. Schrieffer, US.
1971 Dennis Gabor, British.
1970 Louis Neel, French; Hannes Alfven, Swedish.
1969 Murray Gell-Mann, US.
1968 Luis W. Alvarez, US.
1967 Hans A. Bethe, US.
1966 Alfred Kastler, French.
1965 Richard P. Feynman, US; Julian S. Schwinger, US; Shinichiro Tomonaga, Japanese.
1964 Nikolai G. Basov, USSR; Aleksander M. Prochorov, USSR; Charles H. Townes, US.
1963 Maria Goeppert-Mayer, US; J. Hans D. Jensen, German; Eugene P. Wigner, US.
1962 Lev. D. Landau, USSR.
1961 Robert Hofstadter, US; Rudolf L. Mossbauer, German.
1960 Donald A. Glaser, US.
1959 Owen Chamberlain, US; Emilio G. Segre, US.
1958 Pavel Cherenkov, Ilya Frank, Igor Y. Tamm, all USSR.
1957 Tsung-dao Lee, Chen Ning Yang, both US.
1956 John Bardeen, US; Walter H. Brattain, US; William Shockley, US.
1955 Polykarp Kusch, US; Willis E. Lamb, US.
1954 Max Born, British; Walter Bothe, German.
1953 Frits Zernike, Dutch.
1952 Felix Bloch, US; Edward M. Purcell, US.
1951 Sir John D. Cockroft, British; Ernest T. S. Walton, Irish.
1950 Cecil F. Powell, British.

Chemistry

Inorganic chemistry

The nomenclature of chemistry is governed by the International Union of Pure and Applied Chemistry whose latest detailed and authoritative guidance was published in 1970 and was followed be a definitive interpretation by the Association of Science Education in 1972.

Because of the difficulties in trying to produce a systematic nomenclature which will adequately cover all aspects of inorganic chemistry, trivial names have not yet been completely discarded although, for example, the use of the familiar endings 'ous' and 'ic' to denote the lower and higher valency states of metal cations is to be discouraged in favour of the Stock System in which the oxidation number of the less electronegative constituent is indicated by Roman numerals in parentheses placed immediately after the name of the atom concerned, thus $FeCl_2$ is iron(II) chloride rather than ferrous chloride and $FeCl_3$ is iron(III) chloride rather than ferric chloride. For compounds consisting of simple molecules of known composition the stoichiometry determines the name using Greek or Roman multiplying affixes (see table below), thus P_4O_{10} is tetraphosphorus decaoxide. Trivial names for acids are still in use although such alchemical leftovers as 'Aquafortis' for nitric acid, 'Oil of Vitriol' for sulfuric acid, and 'Spirit of Salt' for hydrochloric acid have long (hopefully) been discarded.

Multiplying Affixes

½	hemi	8	octa	15	pentadeca
1	mono	9	nona (Latin)	16	hexadeca
1½	sesqui		ennea (Greek)	17	heptadeca
2	di	10	deca	18	octadeca
3	tri	11	undeca (Latin)	19	nonadeca
4	tetra		henadeca (Greek)	20	eicosa
5	penta	12	dodeca	24	tetracosa
6	hexa	13	trideca	30	triaconta
7	hepta	14	tetradeca	40	tetraconta

STABLE INORGANIC ACIDS OF THE NON-METALLIC ELEMENTS

Boron
boric acid (crystals) H_3BO_3

Arsenic
arsenious acid* H_3AsO_3
arsenic acid* H_3AsO_4

Bromine
hydrobromic acid (45%) HBr
hypobromous acid* HBrO
bromic acid* $HBrO_3$

Carbon
carbonic acid* H_2CO_3
carbolic acid (phenol) C_6H_5OH

Chlorine
hydrochloric acid (35%) HCl
hypochlorous acid* HClO
chlorous acid* $HClO_2$
chloric acid* $HClO_3$
perchloric acid (60%) $HClO_4$

Fluorine
hydrofluoric acid (40%) HF
fluoroboric acid (40%) HBF_4
fluorosilicic acid H_2SiF_6
fluorosulfonic acid (liquid) HSO_3F

Iodine
hydriodic acid (55%) HI
hypoiodic acid* HIO
iodic acid (crystals) HIO_3
periodic acid (crystals) HIO_4

Nitrogen
hyponitrous acid* $H_2N_2O_2$
nitrous acid* HNO_2
nitric acid (70%) HNO_3

Phosphorus
phosphinic acid (50%) H_3PO_2
(hypophosphorous acid)
phosphonic acid (crystals) H_3PO_3
(orthophosphorous acid)
diphosphonic acid (crystals) $H_4P_2O_5$
(pyrophosphorous acid)
diphosphoric acid (crystals) $H_4P_2O_6$
(hypophosphoric acid)
metaphosphoric acid (solid) $(HPO_3)_n$
orthophosphoric acid (85%) H_3PO_4
diphosphoric acid (crystals) $H_4P_2O_7$
(pyrophosphoric acid)

Selenium
selenious acid (crystals) H_2SeO_3
selenic acid (crystals) H_2SeO_4

Silicon
metasilicic acid (solid) $(H_2SiO_3)_n$
orthosilicic acid* H_4SiO_4

Sulfur
sulfurous acid* H_2SO_3
sulfuric acid (liquid) H_2SO_4

peroxomonosulfuric acid (crystals) H_2SO_5
(Caro's Acid)
dithionic acid* $H_2S_2O_6$
disulfuric acid (crystals) $H_2S_2O_7$
(pyrosulfuric acid)
peroxodisulfuric acid (crystals) $H_2S_2O_8$
(persulfuric acid)

Tellurium
tellurous acid (crystals) H_2TeO_3
orthotelluric acid (crystals) H_6TeO_6

---

* Stable only in aqueous solution
Values in parentheses indicate the concentration in aqueous solution of the usual commercial grades of the acid.

Organic chemistry

Organic chemistry is the chemistry of hydrocarbons and their derivatives. The original division between organic chemical compounds (meaning those occurring in the Animal and Plant Kingdoms) and inorganic chemical compounds (meaning those occurring in the mineral world) was made in 1675 by Lémery. This over-simplified division was upset when in 1828 Wöhler produced urea ($NH_2.CO.NH_2$) in an attempt to produce ammonium cyanate ($NH_4.CNO$) from inorganic sources and was ended with the synthesis of acetic acid (ethanoic acid) from its elements by Kolbe in 1845, and the synthesis of methane by Berthelot in 1856. Carbon has a valency number (from the Latin *valens* = worth) of 2 or 4, i.e. a combining power expressed in terms of the number of hydrogen atoms with which the atom of carbon can combine. In addition the carbon atom has the unique property of being able to join one to another to form chains, rings, double bonds and triple bonds.

Thus there are almost limitless numbers of organic compounds and since nearly four million are known then the transition to a strict system of nomenclature from the plethora of trivial names is an essential aim of the International Union of Pure and Applied Chemistry. When all the carbon valencies are utilised in bonding with other carbon or hydrogen atoms, with all the carbon linkages as single bonds, the hydrocarbons are said to be *saturated* and may be in the form of chains or rings. When the carbon atoms are joined together by double or triple bonds then these bonds are potentially available for completion of saturation and therefore such hydrocarbons are said to be *unsaturated*. Open chain compounds are called aliphatic from the Greek *aliphos*, fat, since the first compounds in this class to be studied were the so-called fatty acids.

Saturated hydrocarbons

Straight chain hydrocarbons necessarily conform to the formula C_nH_{2n+2} and are known collectively as **alkanes** or by their trivial name paraffins (form the Latin *parvum affinis*, small affinity, which refers to their low combining power with other substances). The first four alkanes retain their semi-trivial names:

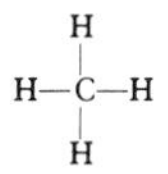

methane (CH_4) 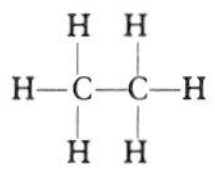   ethane (C_2H_6)

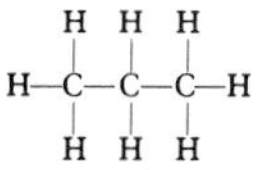

propane (C_3H_8) 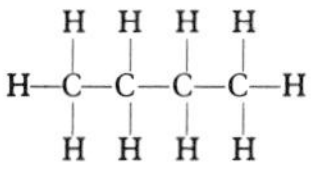   butane (C_4H_{10})

The higher alkanes are named by utilising the recommended multiplying affixes listed in the Inorganic Section to indicate the number of carbon atoms in the chain, i.e. C_5H_{12} is pentane, C_7H_{16} is heptane, and C_9H_{20} is nonane.

Ring compounds, in which the carbon atoms form a closed ring, are known as the **naphthene** family and of the formula C_nH_{2n}. They take their names from the corresponding alkanes by adding the prefix *cyclo-*, e.g.

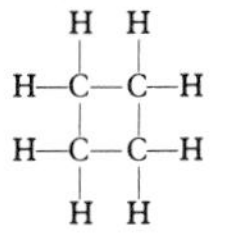

cyclobutane   cyclopropane
(C_4H_8)   (C_3H_6)

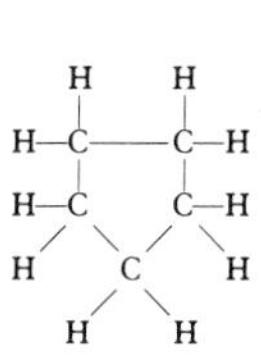

cyclopentane   cyclohexane
(C_5H_{10})   (C_6H_{12})

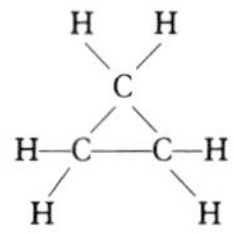

Unsaturated hydrocarbons

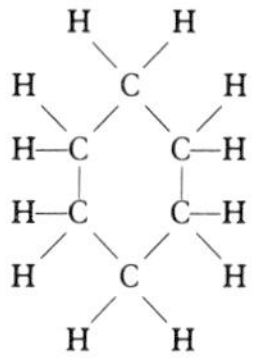

Compounds with one double bond are of the structure type $>C=C<$ and are of the formula C_nH_{2n}. They are known as **alkenes** or by the trivial name olefins (from the Latin *oleum*, oil, *faceo* = to make). They are named after their alkane equivalents by substituting the ending *-ene* to the root of the name, although the old system was to substitute the ending *-ylene*, e.g.

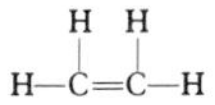

ethene   propene
(ethylene)   (propylene)
(C_2H_4)   (C_3H_6)

The higher alkenes are similarly named:

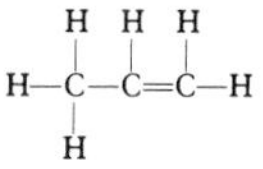

C_4H_8 butene (butylene)
C_5H_{10} pentene (pentylene)
C_6H_{12} hexene (hexylene) et seq.

where the letter ending 'a' in buta, penta, hexa, etc. is dropped for ease of pronunciation. When more than one double bond is present the endings *diene*, *triene*, etc. are used with the positions of the double bonds being carefully noted, i.e. $CH_2=CH-CH=CH_2$ is buta-1,3-diene.

Compounds with one triple bond are called **alkynes** or by their trivial name acetylenes (from the Latin *acetum* = vinegar) and are of the general formula C_nH_{2n-2}. The same rules for nomenclature are used with the ending *-yne* being added to the root of the name of the equivalent alkane. The first member of the group is named ethyne although the more common name acetylene still has a semi-trivial standing. Typical group members include:

ethyne (C_2H_2)   propyne (C_3H_4)

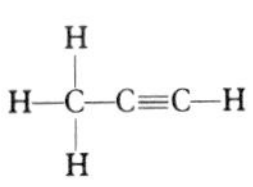

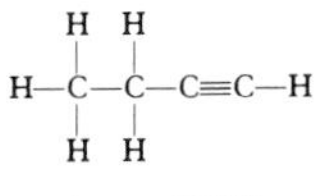

butyne (C_4H_6)

Aromatic hydrocarbons

Substances based on the hydrocarbon benzene C_6H_6 have the family name **aromatic** (from the Greek *aroma*, fragrant smell). They are characterised by the six membered ring represented as having alternating or conjugate double bonds as shown on the left below, although because the

double bonds have no fixed positions it is usual to symbolise the structure as shown on the right:

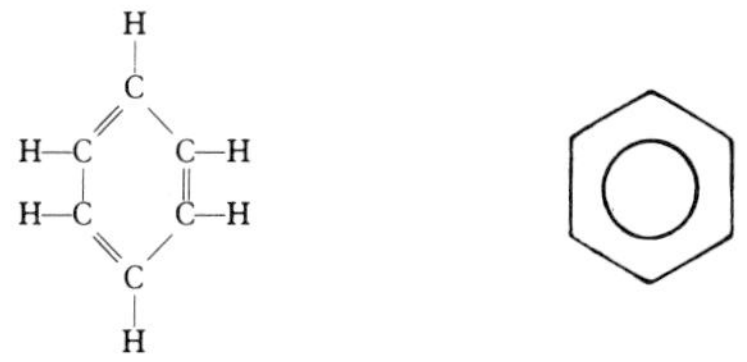

It is possible to produce multiple rings based on the benzene structure, e.g.

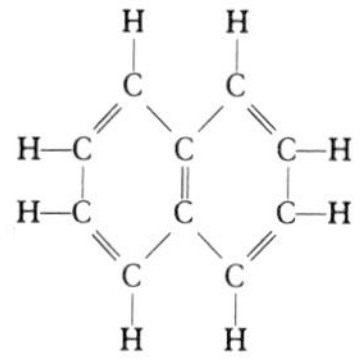

naphthalene ($C_{10}H_8$) 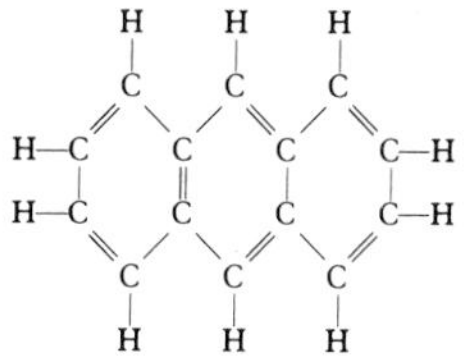   anthracene ($C_{14}H_{10}$)

Organic radicals

Removal of a hydrogen atom from hydrocarbon molecules forms a radical which is named by replacing the suffix *-ane* by *-yl*, e.g.

$(CH_3)^-$ *methyl*; from Greek *methy*, wine, *hyle* = wood
$(C_2H_5)^-$ *ethyl*; from Greek *aither*, clean air (i.e. odourless)
$(C_3H_7)^-$ *propyl*; from Greek *pro*, before, and *peon*, fat, hence radical of fatty acid
$(C_4H_9)^-$ *butyl*, from Greek *butyrum* = butter (rancid smell)

Higher radicals are again based on the use of multiplying affixes, i.e. pentane becomes pentyl $(C_5H_{11})^-$ and hexane becomes hexyl $(C_6H_{13})^-$. These radicals are generically known as **alkyls** and being covalent they can be substituted for hydrogen in other molecules.

The general designation for radicals of aromatic hydrocarbons is **aryl** and the monovalent radical formed from benzene $(C_6H_5)^-$ is called *phenyl* and not *benzyl* which is reserved for the radical $(C_6H_5CH_2)^-$. The use of these radical names leads to a better description of a molecule's structure, i.e. the semi-trivial name toluene does not immediately convey an indication of molecular structure but its systematic equivalent methyl benzene indicates the replacement of one of the hydrogen atoms in the benzene ring by a methyl group.

Isomers and organic nomenclature

It is evident that except in the cases of the simplest organic molecules, it is possible to rearrange the positions of carbon atoms along the molecule skeleton (chain isomerism), or to a limited extent reposition double and triple bonds along the chain, or substitute radicals for hydrogen atoms at specific points along the chain (position isomerism).

In the case of the alkanes (paraffins) methane, ethane, and propane exist only as single molecular species, but butane exists in two – the normal straight chain (n) and a branched isomeric chain (iso), and pentane in three – normal, isomeric, and neopentane:

$CH_3CH_2CH_2CH_3$
n-butane

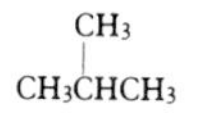

CH_3CHCH_3
$\quad$ CH_3
isobutane

$CH_3CH_2CH_2CH_2CH_3$
n-pentane

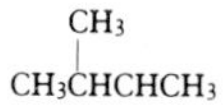

$CH_3CHCHCH_3$
$\quad$ CH_3
isopentane

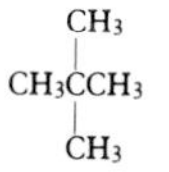

CH_3CCH_3
$\quad$ CH_3 (top)
$\quad$ CH_3 (bottom)
neopentane

From then on there is a rapid increase with the alkane $C_{15}H_{32}$ exhibiting no less than 4347 possible isomeric states!

However in the IUPAC system of nomenclature the use of these prefixes becomes unnecessary since the longest possible chain is chosen as the *parent* chain and the positions of sites on the chain are indicated by numbers, the direction of numbering being so chosen as to give the lowest series of numbers for the *side* chains. Thus isobutane becomes 2-methyl propane (since the methyl radical is attached to the second carbon atom in the chain), isopentane becomes 2-methyl butane for the same reason, and neopentane becomes 2,2-dimethyl propane (since two of the methyl radicals are regarded as forming a 'chain' with the central carbon atom and the two other methyl radicals are both attached to the 'second' carbon atom). For single bonding the treatment of more complex molecules is a simple extension of this principle with apparent side chains being regarded as belonging to the parent chain where necessary, e.g. the structure below is 3-methyl hexane and *not* 2-propyl butane:

$$CH_3CHCH_2CH_3$$
$$|$$
$$CH_2$$
$$|$$
$$CH_2$$
$$|$$
$$CH_3$$

For alkenes (olefins) and alkynes (acetylenes) the chain is always numbered from the end closest to the double or triple bond and the positions of these bonds are also specified:

$CH_3CH_2CH{=}CH_2$
but-1-ene
(α butylene)

CH_3
|
$C{=}CH_1$
|
CH_3
2-methyl propene
(isobutylene)

$CH_3CH_2C{\equiv}CH$
but-1-yne

$CH_3CH{=}CHCH_3$
but-2-ene
(β butylene)

$CH_3C{\equiv}CCH_3$
but-2-yne

In compounds containing mixed bonds the double bond takes preference over triple bonds in numbering the chain and double and triple bonds take preference over single bonds in deciding the length of the parent chain.

When there is more than one type of radical attached to the parent chain then these are listed in strict alphabetical order without regard to the position on the chain, e.g. for the first five radicals the order will be: butyl, ethyl, methyl, pentyl, and propyl. The multiplying affixes used to indicate the total number of a particular type of radical are ignored in this sequence, e.g. ethyl still precedes dimethyl and triethyl before methyl.

For radicals the same rules apply and apart from the prefixes *normal*, *iso*, and *neo* discussed previously, the old system also includes *secondary* (*sec*) isomers (so called because two hydrogen atoms have been repositioned from the principal carbon atom and their bonds replaced by two of the carbon bonds) and *tertiary* (*tert*) isomers (so called because three hydrogen atoms have been repositioned). In the IUPAC system these prefixes are no longer required since the longest chain principle is applied and numbering specified from the carbon atom which has the free valency. In the examples of the propyl and butyl isomers listed below the names isopropyl and isobutyl are still retained on a semi-trivial basis:

Trivial Name	Structure	IUPAC Name
n-propyl	$CH_3CH_2CH_2{-}$	propyl
iso-propyl	CH_3CHCH_3	1-methylethyl
n-butyl	$CH_3CH_2CH_2CH_2{-}$	butyl
iso-butyl	$(CH_3)_2CHCH_2{-}$	2-methylpropyl
sec-butyl	$CH_3CH_2CHCH_3$	1-methylpropyl
tert-butyl	$(CH_3)_3C{-}$	1,1-dimethylethyl

Common organic compounds

Common Name	Recommended Name	Formula
Acetaldehyde	Ethanal	$CH_3.CHO$
Acetic acid	Ethanoic acid	$CH_3.COOH$
Acetone	Propanone	$CH_3.CO.CH_3$
Acetylene	Ethyne	$CH{\equiv}CH$
Alcohol (ethyl)	Ethanol	$CH_3.CH_2OH$
Alcohol (wood)	Methanol	CH_3OH
Amyl acetate	Pentyl ethanoate	$CH_3.COO.C_5H_{11}$
Aniline	Phenylamine	$C_6H_5.NH_2$
Anthracene	no change	$C_{14}H_{10}$
Ascorbic acid (Vitamin C)	no change	$O.CO.C(OH){=}C(OH).CH.CHOH.CH_2OH$
Aspirin	Acetyl o-salicylic acid	$CH_3.COO.C_6H_4.COOH$
Aspirin (soluble)	Calcium salt of acetyl o-salicylic acid	$(CH_3.COO.C_6H_4.COO)_2Ca.2H_2O$
Benzaldehyde	Benzenecarbaldehyde	$C_6H_5.CHO$
Benzene	no change	C_6H_6
Benzoic acid	Benzenecarboxylic acid	$C_6H_5.COOH$
Bromoform	Tribromomethane	$CHBr_3$
Butane	no change	C_4H_{10}
Butylene	Butene	C_4H_8
Camphor	no change	$CO.CH_2CH[C(CH_3)_2].(CH_2)_2.C.CH_3$
Carbon tetrachloride	Tetrachloromethane	CCl_4
Celluloid	Poly(cellulose nitrate)	$[{-}C_6H_7O_2(OH)(ONO_2)_2{-}]_n$
Chloroform	Trichloromethane	$CHCl_3$
Citric acid	2-hydroxypropane-1,2,3-tricarboxylic acid	$(C(OH)(COOH)(CH_2.COOH)_2.H_2O$
Cyanogen	no change	$NC.CN$
Cyclohexane	no change	$CH_2.(CH_2)_4.CH_2$
Decane	no change	$C_{10}H_{22}$
Dimethylglyoxime	Butanedione dioxime	$(CH_3.C{=}N.OH)_2$
Diphenylamine	no change	$(C_6H_5)_2.NH$
Ethane	no change	C_2H_6
Ether (diethyl)	Ethoxyethane	$(CH_3.CH_2)_2O$
Ether (dimethyl)	Methoxymethane	$(CH_3)_2O$
Ethylene	Ethene	$CH_2{=}CH_2$
Ethyl mercaptan	Ethanethiol	$CH_3.CH_2SH$
Formaldehyde (Formalin)	Methanal	$H.CHO$
Formic acid	Methanoic acid	$H.COOH$
Fructose (Fruit Sugar)	no change	$O.CH_2(CHOH)_3C(OH).CH_2OH$
Glucose (Dextrose or Grape Sugar)	no change	$O.(CHOH)_4.CH.CH_2OH$
Glycerine (Glycerol)	Propane-1,2,3-triol	$CH_2OH.CHOH.CH_2OH$
Glycol	Ethane-1,2-diol	$CH_2OH.CH_2OH$
Heptane	no change	C_7H_{16}
Hexane	no change	C_6H_{14}
Indigo	Indigotin	$NH.C_6H_4.CO.C{=}C.CO.C_6H_4.NH$
Ketone, diethyl	Pentan-3-one	$(CH_3.CH_2)_2CO$
Ketone, ethylmethyl	Butanone	$CH_3.CO.CH_2.CH_3$
Lactic acid	2-hydroxypropanoic acid	$CH_3.CHOH.COOH$
Lactose (Milk Sugar)	no change	$C_{12}H_{22}O_{11}.H_2O$
Lead, tetraethyl	Tetraethyl lead (IV)	$(CH_3.CH_2)_4Pb$
Maltose (Malt Sugar)	no change	$C_{12}H_{22}O_{11}.H_2O$
Melamine	Tricyanodiamide	$NH_2.C{=}N.C(NH_2){=}N.C(NH_2){=}N$
Methane (Marsh Gas)	no change	CH_4
Mustard Gas	Dichlorodiethyl sulfide	$(ClCH_2.CH_2)_2S$

In the case of aromatic hydrocarbons, when two or more substituents are present in the benzene ring, the old nomenclature technique was to assign prefixes ortho, meta, and para to the name of the compound to indicate the differences in the positions of the radicals, i.e.

ortho (o)   *meta* (m)   *para* (p)

where ortho = neighbouring positions
     meta = one position between the groups
     para = opposite positions

In the IUPAC system these prefixes are again rendered unnecessary by simply numbering the benzene ring as shown below with the main functional group substituted usually assigned to position 1:

Thus a comparison of the different naming systems for the above examples clearly indicates the superiority of the IUPAC system:

Trivial Name	Semi-Trivial Name	IUPAC Name
o-xylene	o-dimethylbenzene	1,2,-dimethylbenzene
m-xylene	m-dimethylbenzene	1,3,-dimethylbenzene
p-xylene	p-dimethylbenzene	1,4-dimethylbenzene

Substitution radicals

(a) *Alcohols.* Replacement of hydrogen atoms by hydroxyl groups (OH) leads to the **alcohols**.

Common Name	Recommended Name	Formula
Naphthalene	no change	$C_{10}H_8$
Naphthol	Naphthalenol	$C_{10}H_7.OH$
Neoprene	Poly (2-chlorobuta-1,3-diene)	$[-CH_2.C(Cl){=}CH.CH_2-]_n$
Nitroglycerine	Propane-1,2,3-triyl trinitrate	$(O_2N.O)_3C_3H_5$
Nonane	no change	C_9H_{20}
Nylon	no change	$[-CO.(CH_2)_4.CO.NH.(CH_2)_6.NH-]_n$
Octane	no change	C_8H_{18}
Oxalic acid	Ethanedioic acid	$(COOH)_2$
Pentane	no change	C_5H_{12}
Phenol (Carbolic Acid)	no change	$C_6H_5.OH$
Phenolphthalein	no change	$O.CO.C_6H_4.C(C_6H_4.OH)_2$
Phosgene	Carbonyl chloride	$COCl_2$
Phthalic acid	Benzene-1,2-dicarboxylic acid	$C_6H_4(COOH)_2$
Picric acid	2,4,6-trinitrophenol	$(NO_2)_3.C_6H_2.OH$
Polystyrene	Poly (phenylethene)	$[-CH(C_6H_5).CH_2-]_n$
PTFE (Polytetrafluoroethylene) (Teflon)	Poly (tetrafluoroethene)	$[-CF_2.CF_2-]_n$
Polythene	Poly (ethene)	$[-CH_2.CH_2-]_n$
PVC (Polyvinyl chloride)	Poly (chloroethene)	$[-CH_2.CHCl-]_n$
Propane	no change	C_3H_6
Propionic acid	Propanoic acid	$CH_3.CH_2.COOH$
Propylene	Propene	C_3H_6
Prussic acid	Hydrocyanic acid	$HN{=}CH.NC$
Pyridine	no change	C_6H_5N
Rayon	Regenerated cellulose	$S{=}C(OR).SNa(R{=}cellulose[C_6H_{10}C_5]_n)$
Rochelle Salt	Potassium sodium 2,3-dihydroxy butanedioate	$COOK.(CHOH)_2COONa.4H_2O$
Saccharin (soluble)	Sodium salt of o-sulfobenzoicimide	$CO.C_6H_4.SO_2.NNa.2H_2O$
Salicylic acid	2-hydroxybenzenecarboxylic acid	$C_6H_4(OH).COOH$
Soap	Sodium or potassium salts of high molecular weight fatty acids such as palmitic acid (hexadecanoic acid) ($C_{15}H_{31}.COOH$) and stearic acid (octadecanoic acid) ($C_{17}H_{35}.COOH$)	$C_{15}H_{31}.COOR$ or $C_{17}H_{35}.COOR$ where $R{=}Na$ or K
Succinic acid	Butanedioic acid	$(CH_2.COOH)_2$
Sucrose (Cane Sugar or Beet Sugar)	no change	$C_{12}H_{22}O_{11}$
Tartaric acid	2,3-dihydroxybutanedioic acid	$(CHOH.COOH)_2$
Toluene	Methylbenzene	$C_6H_5.CH_3$
Trichloroethylene	Trichloroethene	$ClHC{=}CCl_2$
TNT (Trinitrotoluene)	Methyl-2,4,6-nitrobenzene	$(NO_2)_3.C_6H_2.CH_3$
Urea	Carbamide	$NH_2.CO.NH_2$
Valeric acid	Pentanoic acid	$CH_3.CH_2.CH_2.CH_2.COOH$
Xylene	Dimethylbenzene	$C_6H_5(NH_3)_2$

If the hydroxyl radical is the *principal* group (see end of this section) then the alcohol molecule is named after the hydrocarbon base with the ending *-ol* substituted for the ending *-e*, e.g. methanol (methyl alcohol) CH_3OH and ethanol (ethyl alcohol) C_2H_5OH. However, with longer chains the position of the attachment has to be specified and this is achieved by selecting the longest chain containing the hydroxyl group and assigning the lowest possible number to this side chain hydroxyl radical using the suffix *-ol*, e.g.

$CH_3CH_2CH_2OH$ propan-1-ol (propyl alcohol)
CH_3CHCH_3 propan-2-ol (isopropyl alcohol)
  |
  OH

This simplified procedure can be extended to much more complex alcohols provided that the hydroxyl radical is the principal group. To represent a number of alcohols present in a single molecule the multiplying affixes are used to obtain the endings *-diol*, *-triol*, etc.

In the case of aromatic hydrocarbons the single hydroxyl attachment is known as *phenol* whilst multi-hydroxyl groups are named on the *benzene . . . ol* system, even though the true aromatic alcohols are compounds containing the hydroxyl group in a side chain and may be regarded as aryl derivatives of the aliphatic alcohols, i.e. benzyl alcohol $C_6H_5CH_2OH$ is a true aromatic alcohol. Use of the new nomenclature gives a clearer understanding of molecular structure, e.g.

benzene-1,2-diol (catechol) benzene-1,3-diol (resorcinol) benzene-1,4-diol (quinol)

(*b*) *Ethers*. Derivatives of alcohols in which the hydrogen atoms in the hydroxyl groups are replaced by carbon are known as **ethers**. Thus $(C_6H_5)_2O$ is diphenyl ether and $CH_3.O.C_2H_5$ is ethylmethyl ether (using the rule that where there is no preference then the radicals are named alphabetically) but there is a tendency to treat the ether radical as a group (O.R) where 'R' is an alkyl radical part of the ether compound, so the above mixed radical compound would be methoxyethane since the group are known generically as **alkoxy** groups. Similarly $(C_2H_5)_2O$ becomes ethoxyethane rather than diethyl ether. When the two alkyl groups are the same the ether is said to be symmetrical or simple (i.e. ethoxyethane) but if the two alkyl groups are different the ether is said to be unsymmetrical or mixed (i.e. methoxyethane).

(*c*) *Aldehydes*. The substitution by the radical (CHO) leads to compounds known as the **aldehydes** although the suffix *carbaldehyde* is used if the carbon atom in the radical is not part of the base hydrocarbons, i.e. C_6H_5CHO is benzene carbaldehyde rather than its former name benzaldehyde. Where the carbon in the aldehyde is part of the original base hydrocarbon then the compound is named by substituting the ending *-al* for the hydrocarbon containing the same number of atoms in the parent group. Thus HCHO is methanal (formerly formaldehyde) and CH_3CHO is ethanal (formerly acetaldehyde).

(*d*) *Ketones*. Ketones are based on the double bonded (>CO) radical. The trivial naming technique is to add the name ketone to the ends of the names of the radicals connected by the bond, i.e. $(CH_3)_2CO$ is dimethyl ketone and $CH_3.CO.C_2H_5$ is ethyl methyl ketone. However the new recommended technique is to name the molecule after the longest structural chain by adding the ending *-one*. Thus dimethyl ketone or acetone is in reality propanone. For similar reasons ethyl methyl ketone becomes butanone, etc.

(*e*) *Acids*. The functional group (COOH) is known as carboxylic acid and is used as such if the carbon atom is not part of the main base hydrocarbon, e.g.

benzene carboxylic acid (benzoic acid) benzene-1,2-dicarboxylic acid (phthalic acid)

However if the carbon atom is part of the base chain then the acid molecule is named by substituting the ending *-oic* to the name of the hydrocarbon containing the same number of carbon atoms, i.e.

HCOOH   methanoic acid (formic acid)
CH_3COOH ethanoic acid (acetic acid)
CH_3CH_2COOH propanoic acid
$CH_3CH_2CH_2COOH$ butanoic acid

(*f*) *Amines*. Amines are formed by substituting (NH2) groups in place of hydrogen and the class name is added to the alkyl radical, i.e. CH_3NH_2 is methylamine. Further substitution can take place leading to dimethylamine $(CH_3)_2NH$ and even trimethylamine $(CH_3)_3N$. The aromatic amine $C_6H_5NH_2$ is phenylamine (aniline).

(*g*) *Principal Groups*. Since a large number of different radicals can attach to the base hydrocarbon it is important to produce an order of preference for listing these radicals. With a mixture of radicals the principal group is named as described above but the secondary groups are now named using prefixes to identify the type. Thus for hydroxy groups as secondary groups the ending *-ol* is dropped in favour of the prefix *hydroxy*. This occurs for many alcoholic compounds since this group is towards the bottom of the list. The carboxylic radical (COOH) heads the list and ethers, aldehydes, and ketones are intermediate.

Stereoisomerism
Where the carbon atoms are linked by double bonds, rotation of the kind exhibited by chain

and position isomerism is not possible. In this case isomerism can occur geometrically. For example, dichloroethene which has a double bond may occur in a *cis* form (from the Latin *cis*, on the near side) which indicates that the chlorine atoms are on the same side of the molecule, and a *trans* form (from the Latin *trans*, on the far side) which indicates that the atoms are diagonally opposed across the double bond, i.e.

cis-dichloroethene   trans-dichloroethene

The third class of isomerism is optical isomerism. In this the molecule of one is in one form but the molecule of the other is laterally inverted as in a mirror image. Using the instrument known as a *polarimeter* it can be shown that one isomer has the effect of twisting the plane of light shone through it to the right while its isomer twists it to the left. These optically active forms are known as the *d*-form (*dextro* or right rotating) and the *l*-form (*laevo* or left rotating). When the isomers are mixed in equal proportions the rotating effect is cancelled out to give an optically inactive or *racemic* form (from the Latin *racemus* = a bunch of grapes, because the mother liquid of fermented grape juice exhibits this characteristic). The practical importance of this phenomenon can be illustrated by the ability of yeast to convert *d*-grape sugar to alcohol and its powerlessness to affect the *l*-compound.

Carbohydrates

These are an important source of energy for living organisms as well as a means by which chemical energy can be stored. The name originally indicated the belief that compounds of this group could be represented as hydrates of carbon of general formula $C_x(H_2O)_y$ but it is now realised that many important carbohydrates do not have the required 2 to 1 hydrogen to oxygen ratio whilst other compounds which conform to this structure, such as methanal (formaldehyde) (HCHO) and ethanoic acid (acetic acid) (CH_3COOH) are obviously not of this group. Further, other carbohydrates contain sulfur and nitrogen as important constituents. Carbohydrates can be defined as polyhydroxy aldehydes or ketones or as a substance which yields these compounds on hydrolysis. Glucose and fructose (both of general formula $C_6H_{12}O_6$)

Table of the 109 elements

Atomic Number	Symbol	Name of Element	Derived From	Discoverers	Year
1	H	Hydrogen	Greek, 'hydor genes' = water producer	H Cavendish (UK)	1766
2	He	Helium	Greek, 'helios' = sun	J N Lockyer (UK) and P-J-C Jannsen (France)	1868
3	Li	Lithium	Greek, 'lithos' = stone	J A Arfwedson (Sweden)	1817
4	Be	Beryllium	Greek, 'beryllion' = beryl	N-L Vauquelin (France)	1798
5	B	Boron	Persian, 'burah' = borax	L-J Gay Lussac and L-J Thenard (France) and H Davy (UK)	1808
6	C	Carbon	Latin, *carbo* = charcoal	Prehistoric	—
7	N	Nitrogen	Greek, 'nitron genes' = saltpetre producer	D Rutherford (UK)	1772
8	O	Oxygen	Greek, 'oxys genes' = acid producer	C W Scheele (Sweden) and J Priestley (UK) (pub. 1774)	*c.* 1772
9	F	Fluorine	Latin *fluo* = flow	H Moissan (France)	1886
10	Ne	Neon	Greek, 'neos' = new	W Ramsay and M W Travers (UK)	1898
11	Na	Sodium (Natrium)	English, soda	H Davy (UK)	1807
12	Mg	Magnesium	Magnesia, a district in Thessaly	H Davy (UK)	1808
13	Al	Aluminium	Latin, *alumen* = alum	H C Oerstedt (Denmark) and F Wöhler (Germany)	1825-7
14	Si	Silicon	Latin, *silex* = flint	J J Berzelius (Sweden)	1824
15	P	Phosphorus	Greek, 'phosphorus' = light bringing	H Brand (Germany)	1669
16	S	Sulfur (Note 1)	Sanskrit, 'solvere'; Latin, *sulfurum*	Prehistoric	—
17	Cl	Chlorine	Greek, 'chloros' = green	C W Scheele (Sweden)	1774
18	Ar	Argon	Greek, 'argos' = inactive	W Ramsay and Lord Rayleigh (UK)	1894
19	K	Potassium (Kalium)	English, potash	H Davy (UK)	1807
20	Ca	Calcium	Latin, *calx* = lime	H Davy (UK)	1808
21	Sc	Scandium	Scandinavia	L F Nilson (Sweden)	1879
22	Ti	Titanium	Latin, *Titanes* = sons of the earth	M H Klaproth (Germany)	1795
23	V	Vanadium	Vanadis, a name give to Freyja, the Norse goddess of beauty and youth	N G Sefström (Sweden)	1830
24	Cr	Chromium	Greek, 'chromos' = colour	N-L Vauquelin (France)	1798
25	Mn	Manganese	Latin, *magnes* = magnet	J G Gahn (Sweden)	1774
26	Fe	Iron (Ferrum)	Anglo-Saxon, *iren*	Earliest smelting	*c.*4000 BC
27	Co	Cobalt	German, *kobold* = goblin	G Brandt (Sweden)	1737
28	Ni	Nickel	German, abbreviation of *kupfernickel* (devil's 'copper') or niccolite	A F Cronstedt (Sweden)	1751
29	Cu	Copper (Cuprum)	Cyprus	Prehistoric (earliest known use)	*c.* 8000 BC
30	Zn	Zinc	German, *zink*	A S Marggraf (Germany)	1746
31	Ga	Gallium	Latin, *Gallia* = France	L de Boisbaudran (France)	1875
32	Ge	Germanium	Latin, *Germania* = Germany	C A Winkler (Germany)	1886
33	As	Arsenic	Latin, *arsenicum*	Albertus Magnus (Germany)	*c.* 1220
34	Se	Selenium	Greek, 'selene' = moon	J J Berzelius (Sweden)	1818
35	Br	Bromine	Greek 'bromos' = stench	A-J Balard (France)	1826
36	Kr	Krypton	Greek, 'kryptos' = hidden	W Ramsay and M W Travers (UK)	1898
37	Rb	Rubidium	Latin, *rubidus* = red	R W Bunsen and G R Kirchhoff (Germany)	1861
38	Sr	Strontium	Strontian, a village in Highland region, Scotland	W Cruikshank (UK)	1787
39	Y	Yttrium	Ytterby, in Sweden	J Gadolin (Finland)	1794
40	Zr	Zirconium	Persion, 'zargun' = gold coloured	M H Klaproth (Germany)	1789
41	Nb	Niobium	Latin, *Niobe*, daughter of Tantalus	C Hatchett (UK)	1801
42	Mo	Molybdenum	Greek, 'molybdos' = lead	P J Hjelm (Sweden)	1781
43	Tc	Technetium	Greek, 'technetos' = artificial	C Perrier (France) and E Segré (Italy/USA)	1937

are typical examples, respectively of an 'aldose' and a 'ketose', e.g.

$$
\begin{array}{cc}
\text{glucose} & \text{fructose} \\
C_5H_{11}O_5.CHO & C_5H_{12}O_5.C{=}O
\end{array}
$$

Carbohydrates are defined by the number of carbon atoms in the molecule using the usual multiplying affixes, i.e. tetrose for 4 carbon atoms, pentose for 5, hexose for 6, etc. They are divided into two main groups known as sugars and polysaccharides, where the former is subdivided into monosaccharides of general formula $C_nH_{2n}O_n$ (where $n = 2$ to 10) which cannot be hydrolysed into smaller molecules, and oligosaccharides such as disaccharides ($C_{12}H_{22}O_{11}$), trisaccharides ($C_{18}H_{32}O_{16}$), and tetrasaccharides ($C_{24}H_{42}O_{21}$) which yield two, three, and four monosaccharide molecules respectively on hydrolysis.

The polysaccharides yield a large number of monosaccharides on hydrolysis and have molecular weights ranging from thousands to several million. The most widely spread polysaccharides are of the general formula $(C_6H_{10}O_5)_n$ and include *starch*, which occurs in all green plants and is obtained from maize, wheat, barley, rice and potatoes, and from which dextrins are produced by boiling with water under pressure; *glycogen*, which is the reserve carbohydrate of animals and is often known as 'animal starch'; and *cellulose*, the main constituent of the cell walls of plants.

Of the naturally-occurring sugars (which are all optically active), the most familiar monosaccharides are the dextrorotary (D+) aldohexose *glucose* (dextrose or grape sugar) and the laevorotary (D−) ketohexose *fructose* (laevulose or fruit sugar), both of formula $C_6H_{12}O_6$.

The most important disaccharides are those of the formula $C_{12}H_{22}O_{11}$ and include *sucrose* (cane sugar or beet sugar) obtained from sugar cane or sugar beet after chemical treatment; *maltose* (malt sugar) produced by the action of malt on starch; and *lactose* (milk sugar) which occurs naturally in the milk of all mammals.

Atomic Weight (Note 3)	Density at 20°C (unless otherwise stated) (g/cm³) (Note 4)	Melting Point °C (Note 5)	Boiling Point °C (Note 5)	Physical Description	Valency Number	Number of Nuclides
1.00794	0.0871 (solid at mp) 0.00008989 (gas at 0°C)	−259.192	−252.753	Colourless gas	1	3
4.00260	0.1908 (solid at mp) 0.0001785 (gas at 0°C)	−272.375 at 24.985 atm (Note 6)	−268.928	Colourless gas	0	7
6.941	0.5334	180.57	1344	Silvery-white metal	1	8
9.01218	1.846	1289	2476	Grey metal	2	9
10.811	2.297 (β Rhombohedral) 2.465 (α Rhombohedral) 2.396 (β Tetragonal)	2130	3865	Dark brown powder	3	11
12.011	2.266 (Graphite) 3.515 (Diamond)	3530 (Note 7)	3870	Colourless solid (diamond) or black solid (graphite)	2 or 4	13
14.0067	0.9426 (solid at mp) 0.001250 (gas at 0°C)	−210.004	−195.806	Colourless gas	3 or 5	11
15.9994	1.359 (solid at mp) 0.001429 (gas at 0°C)	−218.789	−182.962	Colourless gas	2	13
18.99840	1.780 (solid at mp) 0.001696 (gas at 0°C)	−219.669	−188.200	Pale greenish-yellow gas	1	13
20.179	1.434 (solid at mp) 0.0008999 (gas at 0°C)	−248.589	−246.048	Colourless gas	0	13
22.98977	0.9688	97.819	884	Silvery-white metal	1	17
24.305	1.737	649	1097	Silvery-white metal	2	15
26.98154	2.699	660.457	2525	Silvery-white metal	3	16
28.0855	2.329	1414	3225	Dark grey solid	4	16
30.97376	1.825 (white) 2.361 (violet) 2.708 (black)	44.14 597 at 45 atm 606 at 48 atm	277 431 sublimes 453 sublimes	White to yellow, violet to red, or black solid	3 or 5	17
32.066	2.068 (rhombic)	115.21	444.674	Pale yellow solid	2, 4, or 6	16
35.453	2.038 (solid at mp) 0.003214 (gas at 0°C)	−100.98	−33.99	Yellow-green gas	1, 3, 5, or 7	15
39.948	1.622 (solid at mp) 0.001784 (gas at 0°C)	−189.352	−185.855	Colourless gas	0	15
39.0983	0.8591	63.65	760	Silvery-white metal	1	20
40.078	1.526	840	1493	Silvery-white metal	2	18
44.95591	2.989	1541	2835	Metallic	3	14
47.88	4.504	1670	3360	Silvery metal	3 or 4	16
50.9415	6.119	1920	3425	Silvery-grey metal	2, 3, 4, or 5	15
51.9961	7.193	1860	2687	Silvery metal	2, 3, or 6	16
54.9380	7.472	1246	2065	Reddish-white metal	2, 3, 4, 6, or 7	14
55.847	7.874	1538	2865	Silvery-white metal	2 or 3	16
58.9332	8.834	1495	2900	Reddish-steel metal	2 or 3	12
58.69	8.905	1455	2885	Silvery-white metal	2 or 3	16
63.546	8.934	1084.88	2571	Reddish-bronze metal	1 or 2	17
65.39	7.140	419.58	908	Blue-white metal	2	23
69.723	5.912	29.772	2209	Grey metal	2 or 3	22
75.59	5.327	938.3	2835	Grey-white metal	4	22
74.9126	5.781	817 at 38 atm	603 sublimes	Steel-grey solid	3 or 5	22
78.96	4.810 (trigonal) 4.398 (α monoclinic) 4.352 (β monoclinic)	221.18	685	Greyish solid	2, 4, or 6	23
79.904	3.937 (solid at mp) 3.119 (liquid at 20°C)	−7.25	59.09	Red-brown liquid	1, 3, 5, or 7	23
83.80	2.801 (solid at mp) 0.003749 (gas at 0°C)	−157.386	−153.35	Colourless gas	0	25
85.4678	1.534	39.29	688	Silvery-white metal	1	27
87.62	2.582	768	1387	Silvery-white metal	2	24
88.9059	4.468	1522	3300	Steel-grey metal	3	23
91.224	6.506	1855	4340	Steel-white metal	4	22
92.9064	8.595	2473	4860	Grey metal	3 or 5	23
95.94	10.22	2624	4680	Silvery metal	2, 3, 4, 5, or 6	22
(97.9072)	11.40	2180	4270	Silvery-grey metal	2, 3, 4, 6, or 7	21

Atomic Number	Symbol	Name of Element	Derived From	Discoverers	Year
44	Ru	Ruthenium	Ruthenia (The Ukraine, in USSR)	K K Klaus (Estonia/USSR)	1844
45	Rh	Rhodium	Greek, 'rhodon' = rose	W H Wollaston (UK)	1804
46	Pd	Palladium	The asteroid Pallas (discovered 1802)	W H Wollaston (UK)	1803
47	Ag	Silver (Argentum)	Anglo-Saxon, *seolfor*	Prehistoric (earliest silversmithery)	*c.*4000 BC
48	Cd	Cadmium	Greek, 'kadmeia' = calamine	F Stromeyer (Germany)	1817
49	In	Indium	Its indigo spectrum	F Reich and H T Richter (Germany)	1863
50	Sn	Tin (Stannum)	Anglo-Saxon, *tin*	Prehistoric (intentionally alloyed with Cu to make Bronze)	*c.* 3500 BC
51	Sb	Antimony (Stibium)	Lower Latin, *antimonium*	Near Historic	*c.*1000 BC
52	Te	Tellurium	Latin, *tellus* = earth	F J Muller (Baron von Reichenstein) (Austria)	1783
53	I	Iodine	Greek, 'iodes' = violet	B Courtois (France)	1811
54	Xe	Xenon	Greek, 'xenos' = stranger	W Ramsay and M W Travers (UK)	1898
55	Cs	Caesium	Latin, *caesius* = bluish-grey	R W von Bunsen and G R Kirchoff (Germany)	1860
56	Ba	Barium	Greek, 'barys' = heavy	H Davy (UK)	1808
57	La	Lanthanum	Greek, 'lanthano' = conceal	C G Mosander (Sweden)	1839
58	Ce	Cerium	The asteroid Ceres (discovered 1801)	J J Berzelius and W Hisinger (Sweden); M H Klaproth (Germany)	1803
59	Pr	Praseodymium	Greek, 'prasios didymos' = green twin	C Auer von Welsbach (Austria)	1885
60	Nd	Neodymium	Greek, 'neos didymos' = new twin	C Auer von Welsbach (Austria)	1885
61	Pm	Promethium	Greek demi-god 'Prometheus' – the fire stealer	J Marinsky, L E Glendenin and C D Coryell (USA)	1945
62	Sm	Samarium	The mineral Samarskite, named after Col M Samarski, a Russian engineer	L de Boisbaudran (France)	1879
63	Eu	Europium	Europe	E A Demarçay (France)	1901
64	Gd	Gadolinium	Johan Gadolin (1760–1852)	J-C-G de Marignac (Switzerland)	1880
65	Tb	Terbium	Ytterby, in Sweden	C G Mosander (Sweden)	1843
66	Dy	Dysprosium	Greek, 'dysprositos' – hard to get at	L de Boisbaudran (France)	1886
67	Ho	Holmium	Holmia, a Latinised form of Stockholm	J-L Soret (France) and P T Cleve (Sweden)	1878–9
68	Er	Erbium	Ytterby, in Sweden	C G Mosander (Sweden)	1843
69	Tm	Thulium	Latin and Greek, 'Thule' = Northland	P T Cleve (Sweden)	1879
70	Yb	Ytterbium	Ytterby, in Sweden	J-C-G de Marignac (Switzerland)	1878
71	Lu	Lutetium	Lutetia, Roman name for the city of Paris	G Urbain (France)	1907
72	Hf	Hafnium	Hafnia = Copenhagen	D Coster (Netherlands) and G C de Hevesy (Hungary/Sweden)	1923
73	Ta	Tantalum	'Tantalus', a mythical Greek king	A G Ekeberg (Sweden)	1802
74	W	Tungsten (Wolfram)	Swedish, *tung sten* = heavy stone	J J de Elhuyar and F de Elhuyar (Spain)	1783
75	Re	Rhenium	Latin, *Rhenus* = the river Rhine	W Noddack, Fr I Tacke and O Berg (Germany)	1925
76	Os	Osmium	Greek, 'osme' = odour	S Tennant (UK)	1804
77	Ir	Iridium	Latin, *iris* = a rainbow	S Tennant (UK)	1804
78	Pt	Platinum	Spanish, *platina* = small silver	A de Ulloa (Spain)	1748
79	Au	Gold (Aurum)	Anglo-Saxon, *gold*	Prehistoric	—
80	Hg	Mercury (Hydrargyrum)	Assigned the alchemical sign of the Greek god 'Hermes' (Latin *Mercurius*), the divine patron of the occult sciences	Near Historic	*c.* 1600 BC
81	Tl	Thallium	Greek, 'thallos' = a budding twig	W Crookes (UK)	1861
82	Pb	Lead (Plumbum)	Anglo-Saxon, lead	Prehistoric	—
83	Bi	Bismuth	German, *weissmuth* = white matter	C-F Geoffroy (France)	1753
84	Po	Polonium	Poland	Mme M S Curie (Poland/France)	1898
85	At	Astatine	Greek, 'astos' = unstable	D R Corson (USA), K R Mackenzie (USA) and E Segrè (Italy/USA)	1940
86	RN	Radon	Latin, *radius* = ray	F E Dorn (Germany)	1900
87	Fr	Francium	France	Mlle M Perey (France)	1939
88	Ra	Radium	Latin, *radius* = ray	P Curie (France), Mme M S Curie (Poland/France) and M G Bemont (France)	1898
89	Ac	Actinium	Greek, 'aktinos', genitive of 'aktis' = a ray	A Debierne (France)	1899
90	Th	Thorium	Thor, the Norse god of thunder	J J Berzelius (Sweden)	1829
91	Pa	Protactinium	Greek, 'protos' = first, plus actinium	O Hahn (German) and Fr L Meitner (Austria); F Soddy and J A Cranston (UK)	1917
92	U	Uranium	The planet Uranus (discovered 1781)	M H Klaproth (Germany)	1789

Notes
1 The former spelling 'sulphur' is not recommended under International Union of Pure and Applied Chemistry rules on nomenclature.
2 Provisional International Union of Pure and Applied Chemistry names for elements 104 to 109.
3 A value in brackets is the atomic mass of the isotope with the longest known half-life (i.e. the period taken for its radioactivity to fall to half of its original value).

The transuranic elements (metallic)

Atomic Number	Symbol	Name of Element	Derived from	Year	Atomic Weight (Note 3)	Density at 20°C (g/cm³) (Note 4)	Melting Point °C (Note 5)	Boiling Point °C (Note 5)	Number of Nuclides
93	Np	Neptunium	The planet Neptune	1940	(237·0482)	20·47	637	4090	14
94	Pu	Plutonium	The planet Pluto	1940	(244·0642)	20·26	640	3330	15
95	Am	Americium	America	1944	(243·0614)	13·77	1176	2020	13
96	Cm	Curium	The Curies – Pierre (1859–1906) and Marie (1867–1934) of France	1944	(247·0703)	13·69	1340	3190	14
97	Bk	Berkelium	Berkeley, a town in California, USA	1949	(247·0703)	14·67	1050	710	11
98	Cf	Californium	California, USA	1950	(251·0796)	15·23	900	1470	18
99	Es	Einsteinium	Dr. Albert Einstein (1879–1955) (US citizen, b. Germany)	1953	(252·0828)	8·81	860	996	14
100	Fm	Fermium	Dr. Enrico Fermi (1901–54) of Italy	1953	(257·0951)	—	—	—	17
101	Md	Mendelevium	Dmitriy I Mendeleyev (1834–1907) (USSR)	1955	(258·0986)	—	—	—	11

Atomic Weight (Note 3)	Density at 20°C (unless otherwise stated) (g/cm³) (Note 4)	Melting Point °C (Note 5)	Boiling Point °C (Note 5)	Physical Description	Valency Number	Number of Nuclides
101·07	12·37	2334	4310	Bluish-white metal	3, 4, 6, or 8	23
102·9055	12·42	1963	3705	Steel-blue metal	3 or 4	21
106·42	12·01	1555·3	2975	Silvery-white metal	2 or 4	24
107·8682	10·50	961·93	2167	Lustrous white metal	1	28
112·41	8·648	321·108	768	Blue-white metal	2	28
114·82	7·289	156·635	2076	Bluish-silvery metal	1 or 3	31
118·710	7·288	231·968	2608	Silvery-white metal	2 or 4	32
121·75	6·693	630·755	1589	Silvery metal	3 or 5	29
127·60	6·237	449·87	989	Silver-grey solid	2, 4, or 6	33
126·9045	4·947	113·6	185·3	Grey-black solid	1, 3, 5, or 7	32
131·29	3·410 (solid at mp) 0·005 897 (gas at 0°C)	−111·760	−108·1	Colourless gas	0	36
132·9054	1·896	28·5	671	Silvery-white metal	1	35
137·33	3·595	729	1827	Silvery-white metal	2	31
138·9055	6·145	921	3435	Metallic	3	29
140·12	6·688 (beta) 6·770 (gamma)	799	3465	Steel-grey metal	3 or 4	30
140·9077	6·772	934	3480	Silvery-white metal	3	25
144·24	7·006	1021	3025	Yellowish-white metal	3	28
(144·9128)	7·135	1042	3000	Metallic	3	24
150·36	7·517	1077	1794	Light-grey metal	2 or 3	26
151·96	5·243	822	1560	Steel-grey metal	2 or 3	24
157·25	7·899	1313	3270	Silvery-white metal	3	25
158·9254	8·228	1356	3230	Silvery metal	3	22
162·50	8·549	1412	2573	Metallic	3	26
164·9304	8·794	1474	2700	Silvery metal	3	25
167·26	9·064	1529	2815	Greyish-silver metal	3	27
168·9342	9·319	1545	1950	Metallic	2 or 3	28
173·04	6·967	817	1227	Silvery metal	2 or 3	28
174·967	9·839	1665	3400	Metallic	3	32
178·49	13·28	2230	4630	Steel-grey metal	4	31
180·9479	16·67	3020	5520	Silvery metal	3 or 5	28
183·85	19·26	3420	5730	Grey metal	2, 4, 5, or 6	30
186·207	21·01	3185	5610	Whitish-grey metal	1, 4, or 7	31
190·2	22·59	3100	5020	Grey-blue metal	2, 3, 4, 6, or 8	34
192·22	22·56	2447	4730	Silvery-white metal	3 or 4	33
195·08	21·45	1768·7	3835	Bluish-white metal	2 or 4	34
196·9665	19·29	1064·43	2860	Lustrous yellow metal	1 or 3	32
200·59	14·17 (solid at mp) 13·55 (liquid at 20°C)	−38·836	356·661	Silvery metallic liquid	1 or 2	33
204·383	11·87	304	1475	Blue-grey metal	1 or 3	29
207·2	11·35	327·502	1753	Steel-blue metal	2 or 4	32
208·9804	9·807	271·442	1566	Reddish-silvery metal	3 or 5	28
(208·9824)	9·155	254	948	Metallic	2, 3, or 4	27
(209·9871)	∼7·0	302	377	Metallic	1, 3, 5, or 7	24
(222·0176)	∼4·7 (solid at mp) 0·010 04 (gas at 0°C)	−64·9	−61·2	Colourless gas	0	29
(223·0197)	∼2·8	24	657	Metallic	1	30
(226·0254)	5·50	707	1530	Silvery metal	2	25
(227·0278)	10·04	1050	3560	Metallic	3	24
232·0381	11·72	1760	4700	Grey metal	4	25
(231·0359)	15·41	1570	4490	Silvery metal	4 or 5	22
238·0289	19·05	1134	4160	Bluish-white metal	3, 4, 5, or 6	17

4 For the highly radioactive elements the density value has been calculated for the isotope with the longest known half-life.
5 All temperature values have been corrected to the International Practical Temperature Scale of 1968.
6 This value is the minimum pressure under which liquid helium can be solidified.
7 The melting point is for carbyne 6, the stable form of carbon above 3300°C. Recent evidence suggests that graphite is only metastable above 2300°C.

Atomic Number	Symbol	Name of Element	Derived from	Year	Atomic Weight (Note 3)	Density at 20°C (g/cm³) (Note 4)	Melting Point °C (Note 5)	Boiling Point °C (Note 5)	Number of Nuclides
102	No	Nobelium	Alfred B Nobel (1833–96) of Sweden	1958	(259·1009)	—	—	—	10
103	Lr	Lawrencium	Dr Ernest O Lawrence (1901–58)	1961	(260·1054)	—	—	—	8
104	Unq	Unnilquadium (Note 2)	Un-nil-quad (1–0–4)	1964 or 1969	(261·109)	—	—	—	9
105	Unp	Unnilpentium (Note 2)	Un-nil-pent (1–0–5)	1970	(262·114)	—	—	—	6
106	Unh	Unnilhexium (Note 2)	Un-nil-hex (1–0–6)	1974	(263·120)	—	—	—	4
107	Uns	Unnilseptium (Note 2)	Un-nil-sept (1–0–7)	1976	(262)	—	—	—	2 ?
108	Uno	Unniloctium	Un-nil-oct (1–0–8)	1984	(265)	—	—	—	3
109	Une	Unnilennium	Un-nil-enn (1–0–9)	1982	(266)	—	—	—	1

Nobel prizewinners in chemistry since 1950

1984 R. Bruce Merrifield, US
1983 Henry Taube, US
1982 Aaron Klug, S. African
1981 Kenichi Fukui, Japan; Roald Hoffmann, US
1980 Paul Berg, US; Walter Gilbert, US; Frederick Sanger, British
1979 Herbert C. Brown, US; George Wittig, German
1978 Peter Mitchell, British
1977 Ilya Prigogine, Belgian
1976 William N. Lipscomb, US
1975 John Cornforth, Austral.-Brit.; Vladimir Prelog, Yugo.-Switz.

1974 Paul J. Flory, US
1973 Ernst Otto Fischer, W. German; Geoffrey Wilkinson, British
1972 Christian B. Anfinsen, US; Stanford Moore, US; William H. Stein, US
1971 Gerhard Herzberg, Canadian
1970 Luis F. Leloir, Arg.
1969 Derek H. R. Barton, British; Odd Hassel, Norwegian
1968 Lars Onsager, US
1967 Manfred Eigen, German; Ronald G. W. Norrish, British; George Porter, British
1966 Robert S. Mulliken, US
1965 Robert B. Woodward, US
1964 Dorothy C. Hodgkin, British
1963 Giulio Natta, Italian; Karl Ziegler, German

1962 John C. Kendrew, British; Max F. Perutz, British
1961 Melvin Calvin, US
1960 Willard F. Libby, US
1959 Jaroslav Heyrovsky, Czech
1958 Frederick Sanger, British
1957 Sir Alexander R. Todd, British
1956 Sir Cyril N. Hinshelwood, British; Nikolai N. Semenov, USSR
1955 Vincent du Vigneaud, US
1954 Linus C. Pauling, US
1953 Hermann Staudinger, German
1952 Archer J. P. Martin, British; Richard L. M. Synge, British
1951 Edwin M. McMillan, US; Glen T. Seaborg, US
1950 Kurt Alder, German; Otto P. H. Diels, German

Anthropology

Anthropology, the study of the differences and similarities between the various races of mankind, contains two autonomous sciences: physical anthropology (the study of blood groups and genetic differences) and social anthropology or ethnology (the study of custom).

Physical Anthropology

The classification of the races or gene pools of man is complex and is vulnerable to political controversy. Many terms which have been used to describe racial groupings are hypothetical, being based either upon cultural and linguistic considerations which are not genetically linked (*e.g.* the term 'the Semitic race'), or upon physical similarities (*e.g.* the term negroid).

Formerly classifications of mankind were attempted based purely upon outward physical characteristics such as skin colour (black, brown, white, yellow); body proportions (anthropometry), the shape of the head (craniometry), hair form, teeth and eyelids. A widely adopted system was that based on hair form which recognised three main types: the straight haired, woolly haired and curly haired groups. Although this remains of value no modern description of race relies solely on hair form. External bodily differences are not ignored in the definition of races but are of less scientific importance to such simply inherited or single gene traits as can be easily and precisely quantified.

One of the major factors in modern anthropological studies is the blood group. Certain blood groups predominate in some races but are almost absent in others; *e.g.* B group is very rare in Amerinds. As well as blood groups various related factors are of racial consequence: abnormal haemoglobins and pigments and deficiencies in some type of cell are all known to be racially linked.

Many metabolic differences are now used in anthropological classification: abnormalities in the sense of taste (some races cannot taste phenylthiocarbamide), the incidence of colour blindness, differences in the secretion of amino acids and other biochemical traits have all been scientifically investigated and shown to be excellent aids in the definition of gene pools. Certain medical disorders of genetic origin are useful to the science; *e.g.* thalassemia is confined to the Mediterranean type of the Caucasoid race. The Japanese have studied earwax types and found them to be genetically significant. Thus blood and other genetic traits have taken first place over body measurements and hair types in the definition of races.

The study of genetically transmitted traits has allowed anthropologists to divide man into about ten major types – the exact number depends upon individual interpretation of the scientific evidence. These major divisions, often referred to as geographical races, account for over 99% of mankind. Each geographical race contains many local groupings which, although forming breeding units separate from others to a greater or lesser degree, are nevertheless genetically related to the whole. The remaining groups are sometimes (inaccurately) termed microraces and consist of either small local genetically distinct populations, (*e.g.* the Ainu of Hokkaido) or peoples whose place in the anthropological jigsaw is still the subject of much controversy (*e.g.* the Bushmen of southern Africa).

The Geographical Races

1. *The ASIATIC or MONGOLOID Race*
Extent: most of Asia north and east of India.
Classic appearance: 'yellow-brown' skin, straight hair, round head, high cheek bones and flat face.

A northern group includes Lapps, Yakuts and Koreans; a southern group – 'Oceanic Mongoloids' or Indonesians – is very mixed with a tendency to broader heads. The central (Pareoean) type with, in general, less prominent cheek bones and broader noses, includes both Chinese and Japanese.

2. *The AMERINDIAN Race*
Extent: the Americas.
Classic appearance: Similar to Asiatics though the Eskimos tend to have longer skulls, broader faces and narrower noses, and the Fuegans have curly hair.

Although there are undoubted links between the Indians of the New World and the Asiatics there is sufficient genetic reason to recognise them as separate races.

3. *The AFRICAN or NEGROID Race*
Extent: Africa south of the Sahara.
Classic appearance: tall, woolly hair, black or dark brown skin, broad nose, thickened lips.

Many sub-groups include Nilotics and the much shorter lighter skinned Pygmies (Negrillos). It is debatable whether the Bushmen belong to this geographical race.

4. *The POLYNESIAN Race*
Extent: Polynesia including New Zealand.
Classic appearance: similar to 'Oceanic Mongoloids' though with longer heads and some Caucasoid traits.

The ancestral home of the Polynesians was probably South-East Asia.

5. *The MELANESIAN Race*
Extent: Melanesia including New Guinea. Classic appearance: similar to Africans but some Melanesian islanders tend to be lighter skinned.

This group contains isolated pockets in Asia including Semang tribes in Sumatra and Malaysia, possibly the Andaman Island Negritos, and debatably the short Aeta of the Philippines.

6. *The MICRONESIAN Race*
Extent: Micronesia.
Classic appearance: slight of stature, light brown skins, curly hair.
Genetically related to 'Oceanic Mongoloids'.

7. *The AUSTRALOID Race*
Extent: mainland Australia.
Classic appearance: curly hair, dark brown to black skin, massive skull with protruding jaws and retreating forehead, slender limbs.

The Australian aboriginals are distantly related to the Indic race, in particular to the Veddah of Sri Lanka, but long isolation has resulted in some special features.

8. *The INDIC Race*
Extent: Indian sub-continent.
Classic appearance: medium height, curly hair, prominent forehead, light brown skin but considerable variation in colour.

Local races include the north Indian Caucasoid type, the south Indian 'Dravidians', Singhalese Veddah and some isolated peoples in Sumatra and Sulawesi.

9. *The CAUCASOID Race*
Extent: Europe, Asia west of India and north Africa. Also widely diffused to the Americas and Australasia.

Classic appearance: considerable variation in height and build, and hair colour and form although there is a tendency to curly hair; 'white' or light skin, prominent forehead.

Sub-groups include Proto-Nordics (from Turkestan), Somalis, Ethiops and other Caucasoid peoples of the Horn of Africa and the Red Sea, Eurafricans, Arabs (including Bedouins), the Mediterranean or Romance peoples, the Nordic peoples (of Britain, Scandinavia, the Low Countries and Germany), the Pamiri, the Eurasiatics (including the Alpine type) found from central Europe to the Himalayas, and possibly the Ainu of Hokkaido, who are often categorised as a 'microrace'.

Major anthropological discoveries

Year	Scientific Name	Period and Estimated Date BC	Location	Description	Anthropologist
1856[1]	*Homo neanderthalensis*	Late middle Palaeolithic 120 000	Neander Valley, nr Düsseldorf, Germany	skull, bones	Fuhlrott
1868[2]	*Homo sapiens* (Cromagnon man)	Upper Palaeolithic 35 000	Cromagnon, Les Eyzies, France	4 skeletons, 1 foetus	Lartet
1890	*Pithecanthropus erectus*	Upper Pleistocene 400 000	Kedung Brebus, Java	mandible, tooth	Dubois
1907	*Homo heidelbergensis*	Lower Palaeolithic 450 000	Mauer, nr Heidelberg, Germany	lower jaw	Schoetensack
1912[3]	*Eoanthropus dawsonii*	Holocene (Recent) (fraud)	Piltdown, East Sussex	composite skull	Dawson
1921	*Homo rhodesiensis*	Upper Gamblian *c.* 50 000	Broken Hill, Zambia	skull	Armstrong
1924	*Australopithecus africanus*	Early Pleistocene 1 000 000	Taung, Botswana	skull	Dart (Izod)
1926[4]	*Proconsul nyanzae*	Miocene *c.* 25 000 000	Koru, Kenya	fragments (non-hominoid)	Hopwood
1927	*Pithecanthropus pekinensis*	Lower Palaeolithic 400 000	Choukoutien, nr Peking, China	tooth	Bohlin
1929–34	*Neanderthaloid man*	Middle Palaeolithic or Mousterian 120 000	Mt Carmel, Israel	part 16 skeletons	Garrod
1932	*Ramapithecus*	Miocene *c.* 8–13 000 000	Siwalik Hills, N India	jaws, teeth	G. E. Lewis
1935[5]	*Homo sapiens fossilis*	Lower Palaeolithic 250 000	Boyn Hill, Swanscombe, Kent	parts skull	Marston
1935[6]	*Gigantopithecus blacki*	Middle Pleistocene 450 000	from Kwangsi, China (Hong Kong druggist)	teeth only	von Koenigswald
1936	*Pleisianthropus transvaalensis*	Early Pleistocene 1 000 000	Sterkfontein, Transvaal	skull, part femur	Broom (Barlow)
1938	*Paranthropus robustus*	Pleistocene 700 000	Kromdraai, Transvaal	skull part, bones	Broom (Terblanche)
1947	*Homo sapiens fossilis*	Middle Palaeolithic or Mousterian 125 000	Fontéchevade, France	*2 callottes*	Martin
1949	*Australopithecus prometheus*	Pleistocene 900 000	Makapansgat, Transvaal	fragments[7]	Dart
1953	*Telanthropus capensis*	Pleistocene 800 000	Swartkrans, Transvaal	jaw, skull parts	Broom
1954	*Atlanthropus*	Chelleo-Acheulian 500 000	Ternifine, Algeria	parietal, 3 mandibles	Arambourg
1957	*Neanderthaloid man*	Upper Palaeolithic 45 000	Shanidar, Iraq	skeletons	Solecki
1959	*Zinjanthropus boisei*	Pliocene-Pleistocene *c.* 1 750 000	Olduvai, Tanzania	skull	Mrs Mary Leakey
1960	*Homo habilis*	Pliocene-Pleistocene *ante supra*	Olduvai, Tanzania	fragments	Louis Leakey
1961	*Kenyapithecus wickeri*	Mid Miocene *c.* 14 000 000	Fort Ternan, Kenya	palate, teeth (non-hominoid)	Leakey (Mukiri)
1963	*Australopithecus robustus*	Middle Pleistocene 450 000	Chenchiawo, Lantien, NW China	jaw	
1964	*Sinanthropus lantianensis*	Middle Pleistocene *c.* 500 000	Kungwangling, Lantien, Shensi, China	skull cap and female jaw in 1963	Wu Ju Kang
1969	*Homo erectus*	Middle Pleistocene 500 000–1 000 000	Sangiran, Java	skull	Sartono
1972	*Homo?*	Plio–Pleistocene 2 000 000	East Turkana, Kenya	mandibular, cranial and limb bones	Richard Leakey
1974	*Australopithecus* or *Homo Australopithecus afarensis*	Pliocene 3–4 000 000	Hadar Afar region, Ethiopia	skull parts, jaws, teeth, skeleton known as 'Lucy'	Johanson and Taieb
1975	*Homo erectus*	Early Pleistocene 1 500 000	Turkana, Kenya	skull**	Richard Leakey
1975	*Homo*	Plio-Pleistocene 3 350 000–3 750 000	Laetoli, Tanzania	8 adults, 3 children	Mrs Mary Leakey
1976	*Homo*	Pleistocene 400 000	Halkidiki, Greece	complete skeleton	Greek Anthropological Society
1977	*Ramapithecus*	Mid-Miocene *c.* 9–11 million	Potwar Plateau, Pakistan	radius	Pilbeam
1978	*Hominid*	Plio-Pleistocene 3 500 000	Laetoli, Tanzania	footprints	Mrs Mary Leakey and Richard Hay
1980	*Homo sapiens*	Middle Pleistocene 120 000	Laetoli, Tanzania	skull	—

[1] Female skull discovered in Gibraltar in 1848 but unrecognised till 1864.
[2] Earliest specimen found at Engis, near Liége, Belgium, in 1832 by Schmerling.
[3] Exposed by X-Ray and radio-activity tests in Nov 1953 as an elaborate fraud.
[4] Non-hominoid. Complete skull discovered 1948 by Mrs Leakey.
[5] Further part discovered 1955.
[6] Since 1957 all the evidence is that these relate to a non-hominoid giant ape.
[7] Complete skull in 1958 (Kitching).
** Of great importance because of its uncanny resemblance to Peking man which Leakey believes is more correctly datable to triple the age advanced by the Chinese.

The 26 civilisations of man

If the duration of the evolution of Homo, now estimated at 3 750 000 years, is likened to a single year, then the earliest of all history's known civilisations began after 5 p.m. on 30 Dec. Put another way, 289/290ths of man's existence has been uncivilised.

Few historians have attempted to classify the world's civilisations because of the natural tendency to specialise. An early attempt was that of the Frenchman, Count de Gobineau, in his four-volume *L'Inégalité des Races Humaines* (Paris, 1853–5). His total was ten. Since that time western archaeologists have rescued five more ancient civilisations from oblivion – the Babylonic, the Hittite, the Mayan, the Minoan, and the Sumeric. This would have brought his total to 15 compared with a more modern contention of 26.

The most authoritative classification now available is the revised twelve-volume life work of Professor Arnold Joseph Toynbee, *A Study of History*, published between 1921 and 1961. This concludes that there have been 21 civilisations of which eight still survive. Those surviving are the Arabic (Islamic), the Far Eastern (began in AD 589 and now split into two), the Orthodox Christian (now also split into two), the Hindu (begun *c.* AD 775) the Western civilisation and the Communist civilisation. The term 'civilisa-tion' in the context of classifications relates purely to entities with separate imperial designs rather than a differing culture or ethos.

Archaeological discoveries in 1960 showed that the Yucatec and Mayan civilisations had the same cradle. The compilation below gives details. The Eskimo, Spartan, Polynesian, and Ottoman civilisations have been listed though Toynbee excludes these from his total on the grounds that they were 'arrested civilisations'. Spontaneous derivations, once favoured by 'isolationists', are under increasing attack by archaeologists of the 'diffusionist' school, who believe there were trans-oceanic contacts at very early dates.

(See over for table.)

The 26 civilisations of man

No.	Name	Dawn	Final Collapse	Duration in Centuries	Cradle	Dominant States	Religion and Philosophy	Derivation
1	Egyptiac	ante 4000 BC	c. AD 280	c. 43	Lower Nile	Middle Empire c. 2065–1660 BC	Osiris-worship Philosophy of Atonism	Spontaneous
2	Sumeric or Sumerian	ante 3500 BC	c. 1700 BC	c. 18	Euphrates-Tigris Delta	Sumer and Akkad Empire c. 2298–1905 BC	Tammuz-worship	Spontaneous
3	Indic	ante 3000 BC	c. AD 500	35	Mohenjo-Daro, Harappa, Indus and Ganges valleys	Mauryan Empire 322–185 BC Gupta Empire AD 390–475	Hinduism, Jainism, Hinayāna Buddhism	Possibly of Sumeric origin
4	Mayan[1]	c. 2500 BC	AD 1550	c. 45	Guatemalan forests	First Empire AD c. 300–690	Human sacrifice and human penitential self-mortification	Spontaneous
5	Minoan	ante 2000 BC	c. 1400 BC	6	Cnossus, Crete and the Cyclades	Thalassocracy of Minos c. 1750–1400 BC	?Orphism	Spontaneous
6	Hittite	2000 BC	c. 1200 BC	8	Boghazköi, Anatolia, Turkey	—	Pantheonism	Related to Minoan
7	Sinic	c. 1600 BC[3]	AD 220	18	Yellow River Basin	Ts'in and Han Empire 221 BC–AD 172	Mahāyāna Buddhism, Taoism, Confucianism	Believed unrelated
8	Babylonic	c. 1500 BC	538 BC	10	Lower Mesopotamia	Babylonian Empire 610–539 BC	Judaism, Zoroastrianism Astrology	Related to Sumeric
9	Hellenic	c. 1300 BC	AD 558	18½	Greek mainland and Aegean Is	Roman Empire 31 BC–AD 378	Mithraism, Platonism, Stoicism, Epicureanism Pantheonism, Christianity	Related to Minoan
10	Syriac	c. 1200 BC	AD 970	22	Eastern Cilicia	Achaemenian Empire c. 525–332 BC	Islam and Philosophy of Zervanism	Related to Minoan
11	Eskimo	c. 1100 BC	c. AD 1850	c. 30	Umnak, Aleutian Islands	Thule AD c. 1150–1850	Includes Sila, sky god; Sedna, seal goddess	—
12	Spartan	c. 900 BC	AD 396	13	Laconia	620–371 BC	—	Hellenic
13	Polynesian	c. 500 BC	c. AD 1775	22½	Samoa and Tonga	—	Ancestor spirits *Mana* – supernatural power	—
14	Andean	c. 100 BC	AD 1783	19	Chimu, N Peru and Nazca, S Peru	Inca Empire AD 1430–1533	Philosophy of Viracochaism	Spontaneous
15	Khmer[4]	c. AD 100	AD 1432	13	Cambodian coast	Angkor Kingdom AD 802–1432	Hinduism	Possibly related to Indic and Sinic
16	Far Eastern (main)	AD 589	Scarcely survives	14 to date	Si Ngan (Sian-fu) Wei Valley	Mongol Empire AD 1280–1351 Manchu Empire AD 1644–1912	Muhayaniah Buddhism	Related to Sinic
17	Far Eastern (Japan and Korea)	AD 645	Survives	13 to date	Yamato, Japan via Korea	Tokugawa Shogunate AD 1600–1868	Mikado-worship, Shintoism, Buddhism and Zen Philosophy	Related to Sinic
18	Western	c. AD 675	Flourishes	13 to date	Ireland	Habsburg Monarchy AD 1493–1918 and French (Napoleonic) Empire AD 1792–1815	Philosophy of Christianity	Related to Hellenic
19	Orthodox Christian (main)	c. AD 680	Survives	13 to date	Anatolia, Turkey	Byzantine Empire AD 395–1453	Bedreddinism Orthodox Church, Imāmi	Related to Hellenic and Western
20	Hindu	c. AD 775	Survives	11 to date	Kanauj, Jumna-Ganges Duab	Mughul Raj AD c. 1572–1707 British Raj 1818–1947	Hinduism, Sikhism	Related to Indic
21	Orthodox Christian (Russia)	c. AD 950	Survives	10 to date	Upper Dnieper Basin	Muscovite Empire AD 1478–1917	Orthodox Church Sectarianism	Related to Hellenic
22	Arabic	c. AD 975	AD 1525	5½	Arabia, Iraq, Syria	Abbasid Caliphate of Baghdad	Islām (post AD 1516)	Related to Syriac
23	Mexic	c. AD 1075	AD 1821	7½	Mexican Plateau	Aztec Empire AD 1375–1521	Quetzalcoatl	Related to Mayan
24	Ottoman	c. AD 1310	AD 1919	6	Turkey	Ottoman Empire AD 1372–1919	Islām	—
25	Iranic (now Islamic)	c. AD 1320	Survives	6½ to date	Oxus-Jaxartes Basin	—	Islām (post AD 1516)	Related to Syriac
26	Communist	1848	Flourishes		Western Europe	USSR and China	Atheism, Marxist-Leninism, Maoism	—

[1] Toynbee regards a Yucatec civilisation (c. AD 1075–1680) as a separate entity. Archaeological discoveries in 1960 indicate that Dzibilchaltan, on the Yucatan Peninsula, was in fact the cradle of the whole Mayan civilisation.
[2] There is evidence of links with Egyptiac. The early classic period at Tikal dates from c. AD 250–550.
[3] The earliest archaeologically acceptable dynasty was that of Shang, variously dated 1766–1558 BC. The historicity of the First, or Hsia dynasty, allegedly founded by Yü in 2205 BC, is in decided doubt.
[4] Not regarded by Toynbee as a separate civilisation but as an offshoot of the Hindu civilisation. Modern evidence shows, however, that the Khmer origins antedate those of the Hindu civilisation by 7 centuries.

The Living World

How life began

It is generally assumed by scientists who study the beginnings of life that its creation is a logical event, the result of conditions that existed on this planet more than 3 500 million years ago.

The raw materials and conditions for the creation of life must have been present at the time: temperature, humidity, chemicals, and the catalyst of violent electrical discharges, as in storms. After millions of years of the Earth's formation, the temperature of its atmosphere dropped to below 100°C, and the vapour or humidity fell as rain, making lakes and seas in which were dissolved the chemicals from the rocks forming a rich solution, or 'primeval soup'. In this 'soup' life was created.

Due to ultra-violet ray bombardment from the Sun, intense volcanic activity and electrical storms, parts of this 'soup' were chemically changed into the components of living things: proteins and nucleic acids. How these two essentials combined is still a matter of conjecture, but they probably existed alongside each other for a long time before combining together.

The first living organisms derived from this combination were probably similar to viruses, but able to reproduce themselves in the environment in which they existed. The development to a cellular existence requires a membrane and this could have been constructed out of the phosphates in the 'soup', forming phospholipids, which are present in modern cell structure.

The first true cells probably resembled bacteria. These would obtain energy by breaking down the chemicals in the 'soup', probably by a kind of fermentation. As they evolved, they would extract energy from the phosphates around them, as do modern cells.

The next prerequisite for the development of living organisms was their ability to photosynthesise, the process by which carbon dioxide and water are chemically changed by the action of sunlight into glucose, releasing oxygen into the surrounding atmosphere. At first the rocks and minerals of the Earth absorbed the oxygen, forming the oxides we find in the Earth today, but gradually the oxygen became part of the atmosphere and with it ozone, the three-atom structure of oxygen. Ozone absorbs ultra-violet light, and protects the Earth's surface from these rays. Although ultra-violet rays were necessary in the first instance, they are lethal to living cells. Thus the screen of ozone in the atmosphere ameliorated conditions on the planet for life to evolve. This allowed increased photosynthesis by the organisms, leading to the evolution of more advanced plants and animals.

The first organisms to employ photosynthesis probably resembled the blue-green algae today found in ponds. The oldest-known fossils, dated as far back as 3,100 million years ago, resemble these algae, which have no separate nucleus. Eukaryotic cells (those possessing a separate nucleus) probably evolved 1 300 million years ago. Between the period of the discovery of the earliest fossils of 3 100 million years ago, and the period when fossils are abundant, the Cambrian period of 570 million years ago, little fossil evidence has been found to show us the development of life, but the Cambrian period has yielded more than 600 different organisms to show that life was, by then, truly established on this planet.

Biological classification

The founder of modern taxonomy is usually regarded as Carolus Linnaeus of Sweden. He drew up rules for botanists and zoologists for the assigning of names to both plants and animals. The binomial system was introduced by him in 1758 with the still standard hierarchy of class, order and genus.

International codes were established for nomenclature in botany in 1901; in Zoology in 1906 and for bacteria and viruses in 1948. The Linnaean binomial system is not employed for viruses. The 5-kingdom Schemes of Classification is as follows:

Kingdom Procaryota

The organisms are characterised by an absence of distinct nuclei. Class Microtatobistes comprise viruses and the rickettsias, which are intermediate between viruses and bacteria in size and biochemistry.

Order Rickettsiales comprises some 60 species, four families, and were named after the virologist Howard T Ricketts (US) (1871–1910). No general classification of the 1000 plus viruses identified has yet been adopted. Eventual classification is expected to be based on the capsid (coat protein) symmetry in divisions between forms containing DNA (deoxyribonucleic acid) and RNA (ribonucleic acid). These infectious agents measure down to a minute $1·4 \times 10^{-5}$ mm in diameter.

Bacterial unicellular micro-organisms, often spherical or rod-like, generally range from a micron in diameter to filaments several millimetres in length. They belong to the class Schizomycetes (Greek *Schizo* = I split; *Mykes* = a fungus) in some 1500 species in ten orders.

Blue-green algae (Cyano phyta; Greek *Kyana* = corn-flower hence dark blue; *phyton* = a plant) have no motile flagellated cells and no sexual reproduction. Some 1500 species have been identified.

Kingdom Protista

This kingdom, first suggested by Ernst Haeckel in 1866, accommodates the mostly microscopic protozoa (Greek *protos* = first; *zoon* = an animal) of which some 30 000 unicellular species have been described embracing flagellates (Latin *Flagellum*, diminutive of *flagrum* = a whip), ciliates (Latin *Ciliatus* = furnished with hairs), amoeba, ciliates and parasitic forms.

Algae possessing the nuclear mitochondrial and chloroplast membranes are also included among the protophyta in this kingdom.

Kingdom Fungi

The fungus group of some 80 000 species because of dissimilarities to both plants and animals are now usually placed in a separate kingdom.

Sac fungi (Order Endomycetales) comprise yeasts (division mycota); moulds, mildews; truffles (class ascomycetes) and lichen (Order Lecanorales) which have both an algal and a fungal component.

Club fungi include smuts (Order Ustilaginales) so called because of black and dusty masses of spores; rusts (Order Uredinales) parasitic on vascular plants and hence destructive to agriculture; mushrooms (Order Agaricales); puff-balls (Order Lycoperdales and Order Sclerodermatales) and stinkhorns (Order Phallales).

The Plant Kingdom

(See front endpaper.)

Kingdom Plantae (Metaphyta) embraces mosses, liverworts, hornworts, whisk ferns, club mosses, horsetails, ferns, cycads, conifers and flowering plants in 11 divisions. These were listed together with their Greek or Latin derivatives on pp. 33–37 *Guinness Book of Answers* (2nd Edition). The most advanced clan among the vascular plants is Class Angiospermae.

Class Angiospermae (from Greek, *angeion* = receptacle; *sperma* = seed). The true flowering plants, of which there are more than 250 000 species. The Angiosperms have ovules enclosed within the ovary of a pistil (gynoecium) and the seeds are enclosed within the ripened ovary, which, when matured, becomes a fruit that may be single-seeded or many-seeded. The angiosperms usually have fibrous roots and soft herbaceous stem tissue. The leaves contain extensive mesophytic tissue (i.e. requiring only an average amount of moisture). The reproductive unit is the flower, which typically consists of a very short central axis bearing one or more apical megasporophylls, commonly called carpels, subtended by microsporophylls (termed stamens) and by two sets of sterile bract-like appendages collectively termed the perianth (composed of petals and sepals). In the simplest form of the flower, the ovules are borne along the inner margin of the megasporophyll – like peas in the pod. In all modern angiosperms the megasporophyll is closed and fused marginally, with the ovules in the loculus (cavity) thus formed. In this form, the carpel is termed the pistil and consists of the ovary (the ovule-containing organ) and its apical stigma (the pollen-receiving part). The microsporophylls are closed until maturity, when they open and their pollen is released. The pollen-producing part is the anther and the supporting stalk the filament. The fertilisation (which follows pollination) takes place entirely within the carpel of the flower. After the pollen grain (microgametophyte) reaches the receptive stigmatic surface of the pistil, a pollen tube is developed within, and into it moves the generative nucleus, which divides to form two male nuclei, each of which is a male gamete. Stimulated by the environment created in the stigma, the pollen tube grows through the wall of the pollen grain and into the tissue of the stigma and its style (i.e. the usually attenuated part of a pistil between the ovary and the stigma). This growth continues down the style until the tube penetrates the ovary. Growth continues and when the tube reaches the ovule it enters the micropyle (a pore at the tip of the ovule) or elsewhere through the integuments (i.e. the two outer layers of the ovule) and finally the female gametophyte (enclosed within the ovule). As pollen-tube growth progresses from stigma to female gametophyte it carries with it both male nuclei. On approach to the egg nucleus, within the female gametophyte, the two haploid male nuclei are released. One unites with the haploid egg nucleus and forms a diploid sporophyte, called the zygote, and the other unites with the polar nuclei to form a triploid endosperm nucleus. The zygote thus formed is a new generation, and becomes the embryo within the seed. The zygote (enclosed by a membrane) undergoes a series of divisions leading to wall formation (either transverse or longitudinal) separating the terminal cell from the basal cell. The terminal cell continues to divide to produce the axis or hypocotyl of the embryo, from which are later produced the cotyledons (Greek, *kotylēdon* = cup-shaped hollow) or seed leaves (either one or two – see below under sub-classes). The basal cell divides to form a chain of cells that functions as a suspensor, and the lowest is attached to the embryo and ultimately gives rise to the root and root cap of the embryo. The endosperm nucleus, together with the embryo sac, multiplies to form the endosperm tissue of the seed. This tissue multiplies as the embryo develops, but the bulk of it is digested by the embryo. The angiosperms may be divided into two groups:

Sub-class Dicotyledonae

(Greek, *di* = two). The dicotyledons – over 200 000 species. This sub-class contains angiosperms in which the embryo has two cotyledons (seed leaves). The stems produce a secondary growth by successive cylinders of xylem tissue (Greek, *xylē* = wood), the wood element which, in angiosperms, contains vessels for water conduction and wood fibres for support. The veins of the leaves are typically arranged in a network, i.e. reticular venation. Leaves may be simple, with entire or toothed margins, or compound with leaflets arranged on either side of, or radiating from a petiole, or footstalk. The petals and sepals of the flowers number mostly four or five, or multiples of four or five, and the pollen grains are mostly tricolpate (with three furrows). This group may be sub-divided into 40 or more orders. There are several families of dicotyledons which appear to have no direct relationship with any other group. These include the Salicaceae (willows and poplars), Fagaceae (beeches and oaks), the Proteaceae and the Casuarinaceae (not shown on the front endpaper chart).

Sub-class Monocotyledonae

(Greek, *monos* = one). The monocotyledons – about 50 000 species. The embryo has one cotyledon. The members of this sub-class have stems without any secondary thickening; the vascular strands are scattered through the stem and no cylinders of secondary xylem tissue are produced. The leaves have entire margins, the blades generally lack a petiole, and the veins are arranged in parallel form. The flower parts are always in multiples of three, and the sepals are often petal-like. The pollen grains are always monocolpate (i.e. with one furrow). This sub-class contains 15 orders, of which the Liliales (Lily order) is considered the most primitive, and the Orchidales (Orchid order) the most advanced. This sub-class also contains palms, grasses, and bamboos.

Fruit

Common name	Scientific name	Geographical origin	Date first described or known
Apple	*Malus pumila*	Southwestern Asia	Early times; Claudius 450 BC
Apricot	*Prunus armeniaca*	Central and western China	BC (Piling and Dioscoridês)
Avocado (Pear)	*Persea americana*	Mexico and Central America	Early Spanish explorers, Clusius 1601
Banana	*Musa sapientum*	Southern Asia	Intro: Africa 1st century AD, Canary Is 15th century
Cherry	*Prunus avium*	Europe (near Dardanelles)	Prehistoric times
Date	*Phoenix dactylifera*	unknown	Prehistoric times
Fig	*Ficus carica*	Syria westward to the Canary Is	c. 4000 BC (Egypt)
Grape	*Vitis vinifera*	around Caspian and Black Seas	c. 4000 BC
Grapefruit	*Citrus grandis*	Malay Archipelago and neighbouring islands	12th or 13th century
Lemon	*Citrus limon*	Southeastern Asia	11th–13th centuries
Lime	*Citrus aurantifolia*	Northern Burma	11th–13th centuries
Mandarin (Orange)	*Citrus reticulata*	China	220 BC in China; Europe 1805
Mango	*Mangifera indica*	Southeastern Asia	c. 16th century; Cult. India 4th or 5th century BC
Olive	*Olea europaea*	Syria to Greece	Prehistoric times
Orange	*Citrus sinensis*	China	2200 BC (Europe 15th century)
Papaya	*Carica papaya*	West Indian Islands or Mexican mainland	14th–15th centuries
Peach	*Prunus persica*	China?	300 BC (Greece)
Pear	*Pyrus communis*	Western Asia	Prehistoric times
Pineapple	*Ananas comosus*	Guadeloupe	c. 1493 (Columbus)
Plum	*Prunus domestica*	Western Asia	Possibly AD 100
Quince	*Cydonia oblonga*	Northern Iran	BC
Rhubarb	*Rheum rhaponticum*	Eastern Mediterranean lands and Asia Minor	2700 BC (China)
Water Melon	*Citrullus laratus*	Central Africa	c. 2000 BC (Egypt)

Vegetables

Common name	Scientific name	Geographical origin	Date first described or known
Asparagus	*Asparagus officinalis*	Eastern Mediterranean	c. 200 BC
Beetroot	*Beta vulgaris*	Mediterranean Area	2nd century BC
Broad Bean	*Vicia faba*	—	widely cultivated in prehistoric times
Broccoli	*Brassica oleracea* (variety *Italica*)	Eastern Mediterranean	1st century AD
Brussels Sprout	*Brassica oleracea* (variety *gemmifera*)	Northern Europe	1587 (Northern Europe)
Cabbage	*Brassica oleracea* (variety *capitata*)	Eastern Mediterranean lands and Asia Minor	c. 600 BC
Carrot	*Daucus carota*	Afghanistan	c. 500 BC
Cauliflower	*Brassica oleracea* (variety *botrytis*)	Eastern Mediterranean	6th century BC
Celery	*Apium graveolens*	Caucasus	c. 850 BC
Chive	*Allium schoenoprasum*	Eastern Mediterranean	c. 100 BC
Cucumber	*Cucumis sativus*	Northern India	2nd century BC (Egypt 1300 BC)
Egg plant	*Solanum melongena*	India, Assam, Burma	c. 450 AD (China)
Endive	*Cichorium endivia*	Eastern Mediterranean lands and Asia Minor	BC
Garden Pea	*Pisum sativum*	Central Asia	3000–2000 BC
Garlic	*Allium sativum*	Middle Asia	c. 900 BC (Homer)
Gherkin (W. Indian)	*Cucumis anguria*	Northern India	2nd century BC
Globe Artichoke	*Cynara scolymus*	Western and Central Mediterranean	c. 500 BC
Kale	*Brassica oleracea* (variety *acephala*)	Eastern Mediterranean lands and Asia Minor	c. 500 BC
Leek	*Allium porrum*	Middle Asia	c. 1000 BC
Lettuce	*Lactuca sativa*	Asia Minor, Iran and Turkistan	4500 BC (Egyptian tomb)
Marrow	*Cucurbita pepo*	America?	16th–17th century (Mexican sites 7000–5500 BC)
Musk Melon	*Cucumis melo*	Iran	2900 BC (Egypt)
Onion	*Allium cepa*	Middle Asia	c. 3000 BC (Egypt)
Parsnip	*Pastinaca sativa*	Caucasus	1st century BC
Pepper	*Capsicum frutescens*	Peru	Early burial sites, Peru; intro: Europe 1493
Potato	*Solanum tuberosum*	Southern Chile	c. 1530 Intro: Ireland 1565
Pumpkin	*Cucurbita maxima*	Northen Andean Argentina	1591
Radish	*Raphanus sativus*	Western Asia, Egypt	c. 3000 BC
Runner Bean	*Phaseolus vulgaris*	Central America	c. 1500 (known from Mexican sites 7000–5000 BC)
Soybean	*Soja max*	China	c. 2850 BC
Spinach	*Spinacia oleracea*	Iran	AD 647 in Nepal
Swede	*Brassica napobrassica*	Europe	1620
Sweet Corn	*Zea mays*	Andes	Cult. early times in America: intro: Europe after 1492
Tomato	*Lycopersicon esculentum*	Bolivia-Ecuador-Peru area	Italy c. 1550
Turnip	*Brassica rapa*	Greece	2000 BC

The Animal Kingdom

(See back endpaper.)

The Animal Kingdom Metazoa (greek, *meta* = later in time, *zoon* = an animal) is composed of multicellular animals that may lose their boundaries in the adult state, and with at least two layers of cells. The Kingdom contains 21 Phyla, with over a million species identified and described. Animals inhabit most of the planet's seas and land surfaces. As far as its classification is concerned, an animal's full modern hierarchy can extend to 20 strata:

Kingdom	Order
Sub-kingdom	Sub-order
Phylum	Super-family
Sub-phylum	*Family*
Super-class	Sub-family
Class	Tribe
Sub-class	Genus
Infra-class	*Species*
Cohort	Sub-species
Super-order	

Animal dimensions by species

Mollusca – 128 000 species: ranging in size between the minute coin shell *Neolepton sykesi* 1,2mm *0·047 in* long, and a giant octopus weighing 6–7 tons, which is the heaviest of all invertebrates.

Insecta – 950 000 (1974) described species of a suspected total of perhaps some 3 million: ranging in size between the Battledore wing fairy fly (*Hymenoptera mymaridae*) 0,2 mm *0·008 in* long to the bulky 100 g *3·5 oz* African goliath beetle (*Goliathus goliathus*).

Crustacea – 25 000 species: ranging in size from the water flea *Alonella* weighing at 0,25 mm *0·01 in* long to the Giant Japanese Spider crab (*Macrocheira kaempferi*) with a spread of 3,66 m *12 ft* between claws.

Pisces – 30 000 species: ranging in size between the 12–16 mm *0·47–0·63 in* long *Schindleria praematurus* at 2 mg or 17·750 to the oz and the 43 tonne 18,5 m *60 ft* long Whale shark (*Rhiniodon typus*).

Amphibia – 3000 species: ranging in size between minute poisonous frogs 12,5 mm *0·05 in* long and the 1,5 m *5 ft* long giant salamander (*Andrias davidianus*) weighing up to 45 kg *100 lb*.

Reptilia – 6000 species: ranging in size between 38 mm *1·5 in* long geckoes and the South American snake anaconda (*Eunectes murinus*), which has been reported to attain 13,7 m *45 ft* in length.

Aves – c. 8950 species: ranging in size from the 1,6 g *0·06 oz* Bee humming bird (*Calypte helenae*) up to the 156,5 kg *345 lb*, 2,7 m *9 ft* tall ostrich (*Struthio camelus*).

Mammalia – c. 4500 species: ranging in size, on land, between the 2 g *0·07 oz* Kitt's hog-nosed bat (*Craseonycteris thonglongyai*) and the African elephant (*Loxodonta africana africana*) which may very rarely attain 12 tons; and, at sea, between the 35 kg *77 lb* Commerson's dolphin (*Cephalorhynchus commersoni*) and the 190 tonne *187 ton* Blue Whale (*Balaenoptera musculus*).

Animal longevity

Age determination based on ring-producing structures (e.g. teeth) or length of time animal kept in captivity.

Maximum life span (years)		Species
152+	(a)	Marion's tortoise (*Testudo sumeirii*)
c. 150		Quahog (*Venus mercenaria*)
116+		Spur-thighed tortoise (*Testudo graeca*)
115+		Man (*Homo sapiens*) – highest proven age
c. 100		Deep sea clam (*Tindaria callistiformis*)
>90		Killer whale (*Orcinus orca*)
80–90		Sea anemone (*Cereus pedunculatus*)
88		European eel (*Anguilla anguilla*)
82	(b)	Lake sturgeon (*Acipenser fulvescens*)
70–80		Freshwater mussel (*Margaritana margaritifera*)
89		Asiatic elephant (*Elephas maximus*)
77		Tuatara (*Sphenodon punctatus*)
72+	(a)	Andean condor (*Vultur gryphus*)
c. 70		African elephant (*Loxodonta africana*)
69½		Sterlet (*Acipenser ruthenus*)
68+		Great eagle-owl (*Bubo bubo*)
66		American alligator (*Alligator mississipiensis*)
64		Blue macaw (*Ara macao*)
62+		Siberian white crane (*Grus leucogeranus*)
62		Horse (*Equus caballus*)
62		Ostrich (*Struthio camelus*)
60+		European catfish (*Silurus glanis*)
58¾		Alligator snapping turtle (*Macrochelys temminckii*)
57+		Orang-utan (*Pongo pygmaeus*)
56	(c)	Sulphur-crested cockatoo (*Cacatua galerita*)
55		Pike (*Esox lucius*)
54½		Hippopotamus (*Hippopotamus amphibius*)
54+		Slow-worm (*Anguis fragilis*)
53¼		Stinkpot (*Sternotherus odoratus*)
52+	(d)	Royal albatross (*Diomedea immutabilis*)
51+		Japanese giant salamander (*Andrias japonicus*)
51+	(d)	Chimpanzee (*Pan troglodytes*)
51		White pelican (*Pelecanus onocrotalus*)

Maximum life span (years)		Species
50+		Green turtle (*Chelonia mydas*)
50+	(d)	Gorilla (*Gorilla gorilla*)
>50		Koi carp (*Cyprinus carpio*)
c. 50		North American lobster (*Homarus americanus*)
49¾		Domestic goose (*Anser a. domesticus*)
49+		Short-nosed echidna (*Tachyglossus aculeatus*)
49	(e)	Grey parrot (*Psittacus erythacus*)
49		Indian rhinoceros (*Rhinoceros unicornis*)
47		European brown bear (*Ursus a. arctos*)
46+		White-throated capuchin (*Cebus capucinus*)
46+		Grey seal (*Halichoerus gypus*)
c. 46		Mandrill (*Mandrillus sphinx*)
c. 45		Blue whale (*Balaenoptera musculus*)
44		Herring gull (*Larus argentatus*)
42+	(d)	Emu (*Dromaius novaehollandiae*)
42		Metallic wood borer (*Buprestis aurulenta*)
41		Goldfish (*Carassius auratus*)
40½		Common boa (*Boa constrictor*)
>40		Common toad (*Bufo bufo*)
36¼		Cape giraffe (*Giraffa camelopardalis*)
35+		Bactrian camel (*Camelus ferus*)
34+		Hoffman's two-toed sloth (*Choloepus hoffmanni*)
34		Domestic cat (*Felis catus*)
34		Canary (*Serivus canaria*)
33		American bison (*Bison bison*)
32½		Bobcat (*Lynx rufus*)
32+		Australian school shark (*Galeorhinus australis*)
31+		Indian flying fox (*Pteropus giganteus*)
30+	(d)	American manatee (*Trichechus manatus*)
c. 30		Red kangaroo (*Macropus rufus*)
29¼		African buffalo (*Syncerus caffer*)
20½		Domestic dog (*Canis familiaris*)
29+		Budgerigar (*Melopsittacus undulatus*)
29+		Neptune crab (*Neptunus pelagines*)
c. 29		Lion (*Panthera leo*)
28		African civet (*Viverra civetta*)
c. 28		Theraphosid spider (*Mygalomorphae*)
27½		Sumatran crested porcupine (*Hystrix brachyura*)
27		Medicinal leech (*Hirudo medicinalis*)
27		Domestic pig (*Sus scrofa*)
26½		Red deer (*Cervus elephus*)
26¼		Tiger (*Panthera tigris*)
26+	(d)	Giant panda (*Ailuropoda melanoleuca*)
26		Common wombat (*Vombatus ursinus*)
24¼		Vicuna (*Vicugna vicugna*)
23¼		Grey squirrel (*Sciurus carolinensis*)
21+		Coyote (*Canis latrans*)
21		Canadian otter (*Lutra canadensis*)
20¾		Domestic goat (*Capra hircus domesticus*)
20¼		Blue sheep (*Pseudois nayaur*)
20+		Feather-star (*Promachocrinus kerguelensis*)
18+		Queen ant (*Myrmecina graminicola*)
18+		Common rabbit (*Oryctolagus cuniculus*)
15		Land snail (*Helix spiriplana*)
c. 15		Brittlestar (*Amphiura chiajei*)
14¾		Guinea pig (*Cavia porcellus*)
14		Hedgehog (*Erinaceus europaeus*)
13½		Indian pangolin (*Manis crassicaudata*)
12		Capybara (*Hydrochoerus hydrochoaeris*)
11½		Philippine tree shrew (*Urogale everetti*)
>10		Giant centipede (*Scolopendra gigantea*)
10		Golden hamster (*Mesocricetus auratus*)
9+		Purse-web spider (*Atypus affinis*)
8½		Fat dormouse (*Glis glis*)
8+		Greater Egyptian gerbil (*Gerbillus pyramidum*)
7+		Spiny starfish (*Marthasterias glacialis*)
7		Millipede (*Cylindroiulus londinensis*)
6		House mouse (*Mus musculus*)
5+		Segmented worm (*Allolobophora longa*)
4½		Moonrat (*Echinosorex gymnurus*)
3½		Siberian flying squirrel (*Pteromys volans*)
2		Pygmy white-toothed shrew (*Suncus etruscus*)
1½		Monarch butterfly (*Danaus plexippus*)
0·5		Bedbug (*Cimex lectularius*)
0·27	(f)	Black widow spider (*Latrodectus mactans*)
0·04		Common housefly (*Musca domestica*)

(a) Fully mature at time of capture
(b) Still actively growing when caught
(c) Unconfirmed claims up to 120 years
(d) Still alive
(e) Another less well substantiated record of 72 years
(f) males

Velocity of animal movement

The data on this topic are notoriously unreliable because of the many inherent difficulties of timing the movement of most animals – whether running, flying, or swimming – and because of the absence of any standardisation of the method of timing, of the distance over which the performance is measured, or of allowance for wind conditions.

The most that can be said is that a specimen of the species below has been timed to have attained a maximum the speed given.

mph	km/h		Species
225	362	(a)	Peregrine falcon (*Falco peregrinus*)
150+	240+	(b)	Golden eagle (*Aquila chrysaetos*)
106·25	171		White-throated spinetail swift (*Hirundapus caudacutus*)
c. 100	c. 160		Alpine swift (*Apus melba*)
95·7	154		Magnificent frigatebird (*Fregata magnificens*)
88	142		Spur-winged goose (*Plectropterus gambensis*)
80	129		Red-breasted merganser (*Mergus serrator*)
77	124		White-rumped swift (*Apus caffer*)
72	116		Canvasback duck (*Aythya valisineria*)
70	113		Common eider (*Somateria mollissima*)
60–70	96,5–113	(c)	Racing pigeon (*Columba livia*)
68	109		Sailfish (*Istiophorus platypterus*)
65	105		Mallard (*Anas platyrhynchos*)
60+	96,5+		Cheetah (*Acinonyx jubatus*)
60	96,5		Golden plover (*Pluvialis apricaria*)
57	92		Common quail (*Coturnix coturnix*)
57	92		Common swift (*Apus apus*)
56	90		Red grouse (*Lagopus lagopus*)
55+	88,5+		Pronghorn antelope (*Antilocapra americana*)
55	88,5		Green violetear (*Colibri thalassinus*)
55	88,5		Whooper swan (*Cygnus cygnus*)
53	85		Grey partridge (*Perdix perdix*)
50+	80+		Blackbuck (*Antilope cervicapra*)
50+	80+		Mongolian gazelle (*Procapra gutturosa*)
50	80		House martin (*Delichon urbica*)
50	80		Marlin (*Istophoridae*)
50	80		Springbok (*Antidorcas marsupialis*)
49	79		Royal albatross (*Diomedea epomophora*)
48·15	77,48		Wahoo (*Acanthocybium solandri*)
47·2	75,9		Long-tailed sylph (*Aglaiocercus kingi*)
47	75,5		Grant's gazelle (*Gazella granti*)
46·61	75		Yellowfin tuna (*Thunnus albacares*)
45	72		Ostrich (*Struthio camelus*)
45	72		Brown hare (*Lepus europaeus*)
43·4	69,8	(d)	Bluefin tuna (*Thunnus thynnus*)
43·26	69,62	(e)	Race horse (*Equus caballus*) (mounted)
42	67,5		Red deer (*Cervus elephus*)
41·72	67,14	(f)	Greyhound (*Canis familiaris*)
40+	64+		Red fox (*Vulpes vulpes*)
40	64		Bonefish (*Albula vulpes*)
40	64	(g)	Eastern grey kangaroo (*Macropus giganteus*)
40	64		Emu (*Dromaius novahollandiae*)
40	c.64		Mountain zebra (*Equus zebra*)
c.40	c.64		Swordfish (*Xiphias gladius*)
35–40	56–64		American free-tailed bat (*Tadarida brasiliensis*)
38	61		Barn swallow (*Hirundo rustica*)
37	59,5		Blue wildebeeste (*Connochaetes taurinus*)
36	58		Dragonfly (*Austrophlebia costalis*)
35·5	57		Whippet (*Canis familiaris*)
35	56		Coyote (*Canis latrans*)
30–35	48–56		Deer bot-fly (*Cephenemyia pratti*)
34·5	55,5		Killer whale (*Orcinus orca*)
33·5	53,9		Hawk-moth (*Sphingidae*)
32	51,5		Giraffe (*Giraffa camelopardalis*)
31·25	50,2		Horse-fly (*Tabanus bovinus*)
31	49,8		Mako shark (*Isurus oxyrinchus*)
30+	48		Butterfly (*Prepona*)
28·75	46		Minke whale (*Balaenoptera acutorostrata*)
28	45		Black rhinoceros (*Diceros bicornis*)
27·89	44,88	(h)	Man (*Homo sapiens*)
27·6	44,4		Common dolphin (*Delphinus delphis*)
25·3	40,7		Short-finned pilot whale (*Globicephala macrorhynchus*)
25	40		Californian sea-lion (*Zalophus californianus*)
24·5	39		African elephant (*Loxodonta africana*)
23	37		Salmon (*Salmo salar*)
22·8	36,5		Blue whale (*Balaenoptera musculus*)
21	34		Mountain goat (*Oreamnos americanus*)
20	32		Arabian camel (*Camelus dromedarius*)
c.18	c.29		Pacific leatherback turtle (*Dermochelys coriacea schlegeli*)
18	29		Six-lined race-runner (*Cnemidophorus sexlineatus*)
c.17	c.27		Gentoo penguin (*Pygosterlis papua*)
13·39	21,5		Hornet (*Vespa crabro*)
11·8	18,9		Crabeater seal (*Lobodon carcinophagus*) (land)
10–11	16–17,5		Black mamba (*Dendroaspis polylepsis*)
10	16		N American porcupine (*Erithizon dorsatum*)
7·26	11,5		Honey-bee (*Apis mellifera*)
6	9,5		House rat (*Ratus rattus*)
5·12	8,23		Common house-fly (*Musca domestica*)
4·5	7,24		Common flea (*Pulex irritans*) (jumping)
2·5	4,02		Common shrew (*Sorex araneus*)
2·24	3,6		Yellow-bellied sea snake (*Pelamis platurus*) (swimming)
1·17	1,88		House spider (*Tegenaria atrica*)
1·12	1,80		Centipede (*Scutiger coleoptrata*)
1·07	1,72		Millipede (*Diopsilus regressus*) (jumping)
0·23	0,37		Giant tortoise (*Geochelone gigantea*)
0·224	0,36		Rosy boa (*Lichanura roseofusca*)
0·068–	0,109–		Three-toed sloth (*Bradypus tridactylus*)
0·098	0,151	(i)	
0·031	0,049		Common garden snail (*Helix aspersa*)
0·000 39	0,000 62	(j)	Neptune crab (*Neptunus pelagines*)

(a) 45-deg angle of stoop in courtship display. Cannot exceed 62·5 mph 100,5 km/h in level flight.
(b) Vertical dive.
(c) Wind-assisted speeds up to 110·07 mph 177,1 km/h recorded.
(d) Credited with burst speeds up to 65 mph 104 km/h.
(e) Average over 440 yd 402 m.
(f) Average over 410 yd 375 m.
(g) Young mature females.
(h) Over 15 yd 13,7 m (flying start)
(i) Can double this speed in an emergency.
(j) Travelled 101·5 miles 163,3 km/h in 29 years.

World crop productions and main producers

Commodity	World total, Tons (000)	Chief producer	Tons (000)
Wheat	481 050	USSR	87 000
Rice	411 597	China	68 000
Maize	455 351	USA	213 302
Barley	160 288	USSR	41 000
Oats	45 278	USSR	14 000
Rye	30 126	USSR	12 500
Millet	29 166	India	9 000
Sorghum	69 113	USA	21 364
Potatoes	254 861	USSR	78 000
Cassava	128 944	Brazil	24 492
Sugar	101 403	Brazil	9 420
Tomatoes	53 892	USA	7 862

Commodity	World total, Tons (000)	Chief producer	Tons (000)
Oranges	53 892	Brazil	9 587
Apples	39 391	USSR	7 400
Grapes	70 605	France	11 230
Soyabeans	92 982	USA	62 584
Groundnuts	18 580	India	5 700
Sunflower seeds	16 046	USSR	5 300
Olives	10 577	Spain	3 174
Coffee	4 934	Brazil	1 003
Cocoa	1 587	Ivory Coast	390
Tea	1 925	India	565
Tobacco	6 058	China	1 500

Commodity	World total, Tons (000)	Chief producer	Tons (000)
Rubber	3 903	Malaysia	1 550
Cotton	14 697	China	3 598
Jute	3 950	India	1 220
Wool	1 716	Australia	436
Milk	437 909	USSR	89 600
Meat	144 615	USA	24 401
Fish	74 760	Japan	10 657
Timber*	3 143 000*	USA	411 292*

*Cubic metres (000)

The Human World

World population figures (in millions)

	1983	1984 (estimated)
World	4685	4763
Africa	521	537
N. America	390	395
S. America	257	263
Asia	2731	2777
Europe	489	490
Oceania	24	24
USSR	273	276

Prediction of Human Stature

The table below shows the average mean percentage of mature height for both boys and girls at each age from birth to 18 years. These percentages, taken from large samples, essentially reflect the proven average expectation of ultimate height.

Age in Years	Boys	Girls
Birth	28·6%	30·9%
$\frac{1}{4}$	33·9%	36·0%
$\frac{1}{2}$	37·7%	39·8%
$\frac{3}{4}$	40·1%	42·2%
1	42·2%	44·7%
1½	45·6%	48·8%
2	49·5%	52·8%
2½	51·6%	54·8%
3	53·8%	57·0%
4	58·0%	61·8%
5	61·8%	66·2%
6	65·2%	70·3%
7	69·0%	74·0%
8	72·0%	77·5%
9	75·0%	80·7%
10	78·0%	84·4%
11	81·1%	88·4%
12	84·7%	92·9%
13	87·3%	96·5%
14	91·5%	98·3%
15	96·1%	99·1%
16	98·3%	99·6%
17	99·3%	100·0%
18	99·8%	100·0%

Thus a boy measuring 137 cm *54 in* on his ninth birthday could be expected to be

$$137 \,(54) \times \frac{100}{75\cdot0} = 183 \text{ cm} \,(72\,in) \text{ as a man.}$$

In practice because of maternal factors, the prediction of adult stature becomes of value only after the age of 2 or 2½ years. After the age of 9½ prediction is more accurately based on skeletal rather than chronological age. The accuracy tends to be greater throughout for girls than for boys, who, at 14 are subject to a standard deviation of error of 4 per cent, *viz.* the 91·5 per cent figure can be 95·8 per cent for a physically advanced boy, and 87·6 per cent for a retarded one.

Human Expenditure of Energy

The 'calorie' used by dieticians is the kilo-calorie based on 15°C, written as $kcal_{15}$, *i.e.* the heat energy necessary to raise 1 kg of water from 14·5°C to 15·5°C and thus equal to 4·1868 kilojoules. The FAO reference man weighs 65 kg *143·3 lb*, is aged 25 years and is 'moderately active', requiring 3200 cal per diem. The reference woman weighs 55 kg *121·2 lb* and requires 2300 cal also living at an annual mean of 10°C or 50°F.

	Rate in calories per hour
Rest in bed (basal metabolic rate)	60
Sitting at ease (man)	108
Sitting and writing	114
Standing at ease	118
Driving a car	168
Washing up (woman)	198
Driving a motor cycle	204
Dressing, washing, shaving	212
Bed making (woman)	420
Walking 6,4 km/h 4 mph	492
Climbing 15 cm *6 in* stairs at 2,4 km/h *1·5 mph*	620
Tree felling	640
Bicycling at 13 mph	660
Running at 5 mph	850
Running at 7½ mph	975
Rowing at 33 strokes/min	1140
Swimming breaststroke at 56 strokes/min	1212
Nordic skiing (level snow) at 9·15 mph	1572

Note: Women expend less calories in performing the same activity. e.g. a man washing up would expend 275 cals./hour.

Sense of Smell

According to the stereochemical theory of olfaction there are for man seven primary odours each associated with a typical shape of molecule:

1. camphoraceous — spherical molecules
2. ethereal — very small or thin molecules
3. floral — kite shaped molecules
4. musky — disc shaped molecules
5. peppermint — wedge shaped molecules
6. pungent — undetermined
7. putrid — undetermined

Other smells are complexes of the above basic seven, e.g. almonds are a complex of 1, 3 and 5.

Somatotypes

One of the systems used for classifying human physique is somatotyping (from the Greek *soma*, body) first published in 1940 by Sheldon of the USA.

The three components used, some degree of which is present in everyone, are: (1) Endomorphy (a tendency to globularity); (2) Mesomorphy (a tendency to muscularity); and (3) Ectomorphy (a tendency to linearity). The degrees of tendency range from 1 to an extreme of 7.

Extreme endomorphics would be 7—1—1; Hercules would be 1—7—1, and the extreme in ectomorphics would be 1—1—7. In practice such extremes are rarely encountered. The commonest somatotypes are 3—4—4, 4—3—3, and 3—5—2. The components are oblique, not orthogonal, i.e. not independent of each other to the point where it would be impossible to have a 5—5—5 or a 7—7—1.

Research (Tanner, 1964) into a sample of Olympic athletes shows that mean Endomorphy varies between 2·0 (steeplechasers) and 3·8 (shot putters); Mesomorphy between 4·1 (high jumpers) and 6·2 (discus throwers); and Ectomorphy between 4·5 (steeplechasers) and 2·0 (shot and discus throwers). Sprinters averaged 2·5—5·5—2·9 while milers have a mean rating of 2·5—4·3—4·3.

Inflammatory conditions

The suffix -itis is the feminine form of the Greek -ites, meaning connected with. Originally, for example, carditis was termed carditis nosus, meaning the disease connected with the heart. Soon the nosus was dropped and the -itis suffix was used to indicate, more narrowly, an inflammation of a part of the body.

adenitis lymphatic glands
angiitis blood vessels
appendicitis vermiform appendix
arteritis arteries
arthritis joints
blepharitis eyelid
bronchiolitis bronchioles
bronchitis bronchial tubes
bursitis bursa
capsulitis joint ligaments ('frozen' shoulder)
carditis heart
cellulitis subcutaneous tissues
cervicitis neck of the uterus
cheilitis lip
cholecystitis gall bladder

chondritis cartilage
colitis colon
conjunctivitis conjunctiva
coxitis hip joint
cystitis bladder
dermatitis skin
diverticulitis diverticulae of colon
duodenitis duodenum
encephalitis brain
encystitis 'an encysted tumour'
endocarditis endocardium
endometritis uterine lining
enteritis bowels
entero-colitis colon and small intestine
epididymitis epididymis
ethmoiditis ethmoid sinuses
fibrositis fibrous tissues
gastritis stomach
gingivitis gums
glossitis tongue
hepatitis liver
hyalitis vitreous humour of the eye
ileitis ileum
iritis iris
keratitis cornea
laminitis part of a vertebra
laryngitis larynx
mastitis the breast
mastoiditis mastoid process
meningitis meninges
meningomyelitis meninges and spinal cord
mesenteritis mesentery
metritis uterus
myelitis spinal cord
myocarditis myocardium
myositis muscle
nephritis kidneys
neuritis nerves
œsophagitis œsophagus
omphalitis navel
oophoritis ovary
ophthalmitis whole eye
orchitis testes
osteitis bone
otitis ear
ovaritis ovary
pancreatitis pancreas
parotitis parotid glands (e.g. mumps)
pericarditis pericardium
periodontitis jaw (part around the tooth)
periostitis periosteum
peritonitis peritoneum
pharyngitis pharynx
phlebitis vein
pleuritis pleura
pneumonitis lungs
poliomyelitis inflammation of grey matter of spinal cord (or paralysis due to this)
proctitis rectum
prostatitis prostate gland
pyelitis pelvis of the kidney
rachitis spine
rectitis rectum
retinitis retina
rhinitis nose
salpingitis salpinx
sclerotitis sclera
scrotitis scrotum
sigmoiditis sigmoid colon
sinusitis sinus
sphenoiditis air cavity in the sphenoid bone
splenitis spleen
spondylitis vertebrae
stomatitis mouth
synovitis synovial membrane
tonsillitis tonsils
tracheitis trachea
tympanitis ear-drum
ulitis gums
ureteritis ureter
urethritis urethra
uteritis womb
vaginitis vagina
vulvitis vulva

The Hippocratic oath

A form of the following oath, attributed to Hippocrates (*c.*460–377 BC), the Greek physician called the 'Father of Medicine', is sworn to at some medical schools on the occasion of taking a degree.

'I swear by Apollo the healer, invoking all the gods and goddesses to be my witnesses, that I will fulfil this oath and this written covenant to the best of my ability and judgement.

'I will look upon him who shall have taught me this art even as one of my own parents. I will share my substance with him, and I will supply his necessities if he be in need, I will regard his offspring even as my own brethren, and I will teach them this art, if they would learn it, without fee or covenant. I will impart this art by precept, by lecture and by every mode of teaching, not only to my own sons but to the sons of him who has taught me, and to disciples bound by covenant and oath, according to the law of medicine.

'The regimen I adopt shall be for the benefit of the patients according to my ability and judgement, and not for their hurt or for any wrong. I will give no deadly drug to any, though it be asked of me, nor will I counsel such, and especially I will not aid a woman to procure abortion. Whatsoever house I enter, there will I go for the benefit of the sick, refraining from all wrongdoing or corruption, and especially from any act of seduction, of male or female, of bond or free. Whatsoever things I see or hear concerning the life of men, in my attendance on the sick or even apart therefrom, which ought not to be noised abroad, I will keep silence thereon, counting such things to be as sacred secrets. Pure and holy will I keep my life and my art.'

Human dentition

Man normally has two sets of teeth during his life span. The primary (milk or deciduous) set of 20 is usually acquired between the ages of 6 and 24 months. The secondary (or permanent) dentition of 32 teeth grows in usually from about the sixth year.

The four principal types of teeth are: –

Incisors (Lat. *incidere* – to cut into) total eight. Two upper central, flanked by two upper lateral with four lower.

Canine (Lat. *canis* – a dog) total four. These are next to the lateral incisors and are thus the third teeth from the mid-line in each quadrant of the mouth. These are also referred to as *cuspids* (Lat. *cuspis* – a point).

Pre-Molars (Lat. *molare* – to grind) total eight. These are next in line back from the incisors, two in each quadrant. Because these have two cusps these are alternatively known as bicuspids.

Molars (see above) total twelve. These are the furthest back in the mouth – three in each quadrant. The upper molars often have four cusps and the lower five cusps for grinding. The third (hindermost) molars are known also as 'wisdom teeth' and do not usually appear until the age of 18 to 20.

Human genetics

The normal human has 46 chromosomes. The chromosome is the microscopic thread-like body within cells which carries hereditary factors or genes. These are classified as 22 pairs of non-sex chromosomes (one of each pair derived from the father and one from the mother) and two sex chromosomes making 46. In a female both sex chromosomes are Xs, one from the father and one from the mother. In a male they are an X from the mother and a Y from the father. The X chromosome is much larger than the Y, thus women possess four per cent more deoxyribonucleic acid than males. This may have a bearing on their greater longevity.

The human sometimes exhibits 47 or more chromosomes. One such instance is the XXX female in which the supernumerary is an extra X. In some cases of hermaphroditism the supernumerary is a Y.

Chimpanzees, gorillas, and orang-outangs have 48 chromosomes. It has been suggested that man's emergence from the primitive man-ape population may have occurred by a process known as 'reciprocal translocation'. This is a mechanism whereby two dissimilar chromosomes break and two of the four dissimilar parts join with the possible net loss of one chromosome. It is possible that 47 and 46 chromosome hominoids enjoyed a bipedal advantage on forest edges over brachiating apes and thus the evolution of man began from this point.

Skin

The skin is by far the largest single organ of the human body. It weighs about 16 per cent of the total body weight and in an average adult male has a surface area of $18\,000\,cm^2$ *2800 in*^{2}. The three main groups into which Man is divided by the colour of his skin are *Leukoderms* (white-skinned), *Melanoderms* (black-skinned) and *Xanthoderms* (yellow-skinned). Pigment producing cells in the basal layers of the epidermis are called melanoblasts (Greek *melas* – black; *blastos* – bud).

The number (up to 4000 per sq cm) and the size do not vary significantly in white and negro skin but are more active and productive in the latter so protecting the iris and the retina against the brightness of the sun.

The human brain

It is estimated that a human brain, weighing about 1·36 kg *3 lb* contains 10 000 000 000 nerve cells. Each of these deploys a potential 25 000 interconnections with other cells. Compared with this the most advanced computers are giant electronic morons.

Sex ratio

In the United Kingdom about 1056 boys are born to every 1000 girls.

Medical and surgical specialties

There are in medicine many specialties. It is possible to have Departments of Neurology, Paediatrics and Paediatric-Neurology in the same hospital. This list provides an explanation of medical departments.

Allergy – reaction of a patient to an outside substance, e.g. pollen or Penicillin, producing symptoms which may vary between being inconvenient e.g. hay fever or rashes to fatal, e.g. asthma.
Anaesthetics – the skill of putting a patient to sleep with drugs.
Anatomy – the study of the structure of the body.
Anthropology – the study of man in his environment. Physical anthropology embraces blood grouping and genetic variations.
Apothecary – a pharmacist or, in its old-fashioned sense, a general practitioner was once described as an apothecary.
Audiology – the assessment of hearing.
Aurology – the study of ear disease.
Bacteriology – the study of bacterial infections. This usually includes viruses.
Biochemistry – the study of the variation of salts and chemicals in the body.
Bio-engineering – the study of the mechanical workings of the body, particularly with reference to artificial limbs and powered appliances which the body can use.
Biophysics – the study of electrical impulses from the body. This can be seen with assessment of muscle disease etc.
Cardiology — the study of heart disease.
Community medicine – the prevention of the spread of disease and the increase of physical and mental well being within a community.
Cryo-surgery – the use of freezing techniques in surgery.
Cytogenetics – the understanding of the particles within a cell which help to reproduce the same type of being.
Cytology – the microscopic study of body cells.
Dentistry – the treatment and extraction of teeth.
Dermatology – the treatment of skin diseases.
Diabetics – the treatment of diabetes.
Embryology – the study of the growth of the baby from the moment of conception to about the 20th week.
Endocrinology – the study of the diseases of the glands which produce hormones.
E.N.T. *see* Otorhinolaryngology
Entomology – the study of insects, moths, with

particular reference to their transmission of disease.

Epidemiology – the study of epidemics and the way that diseases travel from one person to another.

Forensic medicine – the study of injury and disease caused by criminal activity and the detection of crime by medical knowledge.

Gastro-enterology – the study of stomach and intestinal diseases.

Genetics – the study of inherited characteristics, disease and malformations.

Genito-urinary disease – the study of diseases of the sexual and urine-producing organs.

Geriatrics – the study of diseases and condition of elderly people.

Gerontology – the study of diseases of elderly people and in particular the study of the ageing process.

Gynaecology – the study of diseases of women.

Haematology – the study of blood diseases.

Histochemistry – the study of the chemical environment of the body cells.

Histology – the microscopic study of cells.

Histopathology – the microscopic study of diseased or abnormal cells.

Homeopathy – is a form of treatment by administering minute doses which in larger doses would reproduce the symptoms of the disease that is being treated. The theory is that the body is thereby stimulated into coping with the problem by itself.

Immunology – the study of the way the body reacts to outside harmful diseases and influences, e.g. the production of body proteins to overcome such diseases as diphtheria or the rejection of foreign substances like transplanted kidneys.

Laryngology – the study of throat diseases.

Metabolic disease – diseases of the interior workings of the body, e.g. disorders of calcium absorption, etc., thyroid disease or adrenal gland disease.

Microbiology – the study of the workings of cells.

Nephrology – the study of kidney disease.

Neurology – the study of a wide range of diseases of the brain or nervous system.

Neurosurgery – operations on the brain or nervous system.

Nuclear medicine – treatment of diseases with radio-active substances.

Obstetrics – the care of the pregnant mother and the delivery of the child.

Oncology – study of cancer.

Ophthalmic Optician (Optometrist) – a practitioner specially trained to assess any visual disorder and examine eyes and provide corrective treatment in the form of visual aids, e.g. spectacles, contact lenses.

Optician, dispensing – a registered dispensing optician is only allowed to dispense spectacles. The prescription is provided either by an Optometrist or an Ophthalmic Medical Practitioner.

Orthodontology – a dental approach to producing teeth that are straight.

Orthopaedics – fractures and bone diseases.

Orthoptics – treatment of squints of the eye (by an orthoptist-medically unqualified but trained practitioner).

Orthotist – an orthopaedic appliance technician.

Otology – the study of diseases of the ear.

Otorhinolaryngology – the study of diseases of the ear, nose and throat often referred to as E.N.T.

Paediatrics – diseases of children.

Parasitology – the study of infections of the body by worms and insects.

Pathology – the study of dead disease by *post mortem* examination either under the microscope or the whole organ.

Pharmacology – the study of the use of drugs in relation to medicine.

Physical medicine – the treatment of damaged parts of the body with exercises, electrical treatments, etc., or the preparation of the body for surgery, e.g. breathing exercises and leg exercises.

Physiology – the study and understanding of the normal workings of the body.

Physiotherapist – a trained person who works in the physical medicine department.

Plastic surgery – the reconstruction and alteration of damaged or normal parts of the body.

Proctology – the study of diseases of the rectum or back passage.

Prosthetics – the making of artificial limbs and appliances.

Psychiatry – the study and treatment of mental disease.

Psycho-analysis – the investigation of the formation of mental illness by long-term repeated discussion.

Psychology – the study of the mind with particular reference to the measurement of intellectual activity.

Psychotherapy – treatment of mental disorder.

Radiobiology – the treatment or investigation of disease using radio-active substances.

Radiography – the taking of X-rays.

Radiology – the study of X-rays.

Radiotherapy – the treatment of disease with X-rays.

Renal diseases – the diseases of the kidney or urinary tract.

Rheumatology – the study of diseases of muscles and joints.

Rhinology – the study of diseases of the nose.

Therapeutics – curative medicine, the healing of physical and/or mental disorder.

Thoracic surgery – surgery on the chest or heart.

Toxicology – the understanding and analysis of poisons.

Urology – the study of diseases of the kidney or urinary tract.

Vascular disease – diseases of the blood vessels.

Venereology – the study of sexually transmitted disease.

Virology – the study of virus diseases.

VACCINES

Anthrax – a killed vaccine which is recommended for workers at particular risk, e.g. farmers, and butchers. Doses should be given yearly.

Bubonic Plague – killed and live vaccines can be used to limit epidemics. They give about six months' protection.

Cholera – two injections of the killed organism should be given 10 days apart and will give 3–6 months' protection. Thereafter injections should be given six-monthly. It only gives moderate protection.

Diphtheria – the toxoid is given in a course of 3 injections to infants and a booster dose at the age of 5 will give long-lasting immunity. Antitoxin is used for those who have caught diphtheria. It gives temporary protection.

German Measles (Rubella) – a modified living vaccine is recommended to be given to all girls between the age of 11 and 13, i.e. before the onset of menstruation, and protects against infection of the foetus and thus congenital malformations.

Influenza – killed vaccines will give about 70 per cent protection for 9 months to a year in epidemics of a similar virus. They are particularly useful in those who tend to have respiratory illness, the infirm or elderly. Modified living virus vaccines are at present under assessment.

Jaundice (Infective Hapatitis) – a vaccine against one of the varieties (hepatitis B) is now being assessed and will soon be available.

Measles – a modified living vaccine is given in the second year of life and will give prolonged protection and, in about 50 per cent, will produce a very mild feverish illness. It does not produce encephalitis.

Meningococcal meningitis – killed vaccines of both types A and C have been produced. They help in the prevention of the spread of epidemics.

Mumps – a modified living vaccine gives long-lasting protection. It is often used for adults who have not had the natural infection.

Pneumonia – (when due to the pneumococcus bacteria). A vaccine is now available for use in the elderly and others vulnerable to this infection. Reimmunisation every 2–3 years is recommended.

Poliomyelitis – Sabin modified living oral vaccine gives long-term protection. It is usually given in 3 doses to infants, and a booster dose at the age of 5, and sometimes in the early teens. It rarely causes cases of clinical poliomyelitis. Salk vaccine is the killed virus and gives short-term protection. It is seldom used nowadays.

Rabies – protection is obtained with 3 injections of a vaccine at one and six months apart. If a person has been bitten injections should be given at once and on the third, seventh and fourteenth days, and then one and three months.

Smallpox – From 1st January 1980 the World Health Organization has declared the world free from smallpox. Vaccination is only needed for research scientists working with the virus.

Tetanus – the toxoid is usually given in 3 injections combined with diphtheria and sometimes whooping cough. A booster dose at the age of 5 and then boosters every 5 years. Antitoxin (A.T.S.) is given to those in immediate danger of developing tetanus.

Tuberculosis – Bacille Calmette-Guerin (BCG) is a modified living organism which is given to those aged between 10 and 13 in the UK by the school health authorities. It gives lifelong immunity.

Typhoid and Paratyphoid – the vaccine containing the killed organisms of Paratyphoid A & B does not give protection against these infections. A Typhoid vaccine protects about 50% of those immunised with two injections at 4–6 weeks apart. Booster injections are given yearly to those living in areas where the disease is common and every 2–3 years to those less at risk.

Typhus – highly effective killed vaccines will give protection for about a year.

Whooping Cough – this is usually combined in 3 injections with diphtheria and tetanus. There is evidence that it rarely causes brain damage and for this reason some infants should not have the injections. However the risk of damage in healthy infants from the natural disease is greater than that from immunisation.

Yellow Fever – a modified living vaccine will give 10 years' protection and this is recognised on an international vaccination certificate.

PHARMACOLOGY

Below are listed a selection of drugs which have been, or are important in medical practice. They are listed in order of the date of their introduction to show the development of modern therapeutics.

Principal drugs in order of their discovery

BC ante

c. 2100 *Ethyl alcohol* or *ethanol* (C_2H_5OH). One of the earliest drugs used to stupefy.

AD

c. 1550 *Digitalis*, a mixture of compounds from the leaf of the Foxglove (*Digitalis purpurea* and *D. lanata*), used to treat congestive heart failure. Employed by herbalists since the 16th century and introduced into scientific medicine by William Withering (GB) in 1785. Its components, particularly digoxin, are still in use.

1805 *Morphine*. Addictive narcotic analgesic, an alkaloid of opium which is the dried latex from the unripe capsules of the poppy (*Papaver somniferum*). First recognised by Friedrich Sertürner (Germany) in 1805 but not used in medical practice till 1821. Synthesised in 1952.

1818 *Quinine*. Obtained from Cinchona tree bark. Separated by P J Pelletier and J B Caventou (France) 1818 to 1820. Antimalarial use.

1819 *Atropine*. An anticholinergic agent isolated in 1819 by Rudolph Brandes from belladonna (*Atropa belladonna*). The related drug hyocine is used to prevent motion sickness.

1820 *Colchicine*. Drug derived from meadow saffron (*Colchicum autumnale*), used particularly in the treatment of gout. Isolated in 1820 by P J Pelletier and J B Caventou.

1821 *Codeine*. Occurs naturally in opium and is a derivative of morphine (q.v.). Antitussive, weak analgesic.

1842 *Ether* (diethyl ether). General anaesthetic. First administered by Dr C W Long (1815–78) in Jefferson, Georgia, on 30 Mar. 1842 for a cystectomy.

1844 *Nitrous Oxide* (N_2O) (Laughing Gas). Short-acting general anaesthetic used in dentistry and obstetrics. Discovered in 1776 by Joseph Priestley (GB). First used as anaesthetic in 1844 by an American dentist, Horace Wells.

1846 *Glyceryl Trinitrate* (nitroglycerin). Known mainly as an explosive. Used as a vasolidator in easing cardiac pains in angina pectoris. First prepared in 1846 by Ascanio Sobrero of Italy.

1847 *Chloroform*. Introduced as an anaesthetic by Sir James Simpson (UK) but rarely used today.

1859 *Cocaine* (from the Peruvian coca bean (*Erythroxylon coca* and *E. truxillense*)). First separated by Niemann. Formula established by Wöhler in 1860. Local anaesthetic, which results in dependence.

1867 *Phenol* (Carbolic acid (C_6H_5OH)). Earliest bactericide and disinfectant, discovered by Lister in 1867. Antiseptic and antipruritic.

1891 *Thyroid Extract*. First used as injection in treatment for myxoedema by George Murray in 1891. The active principles are *tri-iodothyronine* and *thyroxine*.

1893 *Aspirin* (acetylsalicylic acid). A non-steroidal anti-inflammatory and analgesic drug, introduced in 1893 by Hermann Dresser.

1893 *Paracetamol* (Acetaminophen). First used in medicine by Joseph von Mering in 1893, but only gained popularity as an antipyretic analgesic in 1949.

1901 *Adrenaline* (epinephrine). Hormone secreted by medulla of adrenal gland in response to stress. It mimics the effects of stimulation of the sympathetic (adrenergic) autonomic nervous system. First isolated in 1901 by J Takamine (1854–1922) and T B Aldrick and synthesised in 1904 by Friedrich Stolz (1860–1936).

1903 *Barbitone*. Early example of barbituric acid derivatives (barbiturates) with hypnotic, sedative and anti-convulsant properties, e.g. phenobarbitone (long-acting), pentobarbitone (intermediate), thiopentone (short-acting).

1906 *Vitamins*. F G Hopkins (1861–1947) established essentiality of vitamins. Principal vitamins now administered are Vitamin A, B_1, B_2, B_6, B_{12}, C, D, K, M and PP.

1906 *Procaine* (Novocaine). Local anaesthetic, a non-habit forming substitute for cocaine introduced by Alfred Einhorn. Largely superseded by lignocaine.

1907 *Histamine*. Isolated by Adolf Windus (1876–1959) and Karl Vogt (b. 1880). One of a number of substances released by body tissues as part of allergic or inflammatory responses. The earliest anti-histamine was 933 F discovered by G Ungar (France) *et al.* in 1937.

1912 *Acriflavine*. Introduced as an antiseptic by Paul Ehrlich.

1917 *Oxygen*. The most plentiful element in the Earth's crust. Discovered 1771 by the Swede, Carl Wilhelm Scheele and independently in 1774 by Joseph Priestley (GB). First used therapeutically by J S Haldane in 1917.

1921 *Ergometrine*. One of a mixture of ergot alkaloids found in rye grain infected with the fungus *Claviceps purpurea*. Used as a uterine stimulant. First isolated by K Spiro and A Stoll (Germany) in 1921. Another component *Ergotamine* is used to treat migraine.

1921 *Insulin*, the specific antidiabetic hormone from the mammalian pancreas. Isolated by Sir Frederick Banting (1891–1941) and Dr C H Best (1899–1978),

Toronto, Canada, in 1921. First synthesised in 1964.

1929 *Progesterone*. Female steroid hormone secreted by ovary following ovulation to prepare uterus for, and to maintain, pregnancy. Isolated by G Corner and W Allen in 1929. Related compounds are used with oestrogen, or alone, in oral contraceptives.

1929 *Testosterone*. Androgenic (masculinising) hormone. First obtained in 1929 by C Moore, T. Gallagher and F. Koch. Related anabolic (muscle-building) steroids abused by participants in sporting activities.

1930 *Mepacrine (quinacrine)*. Antimalarial. Now replaced by Chloroquine.

1933 *Adrenocorticotrophic hormone* (ACTH). First isolated by J B Collip (b. 1892) *et al.* Active against arthritis.

1935 *Thiopentone*. Very short-acting barbiturate intravenous anaesthetic.

1935 *Tubocurarine*. Alkaloid isolated from curare (a S. American Indian arrow-poison) in 1935 by Harold King, used as a skeletal-muscle relaxant.

1936 *Oestradiol*. The principal oestrogenic female hormone, isolated by D MacCorquodale in 1936.

1937 *Dapsone*. Bacteriostatic drug, effects in treatment of leprosy noted in 1937.

1937 *Sulphonamides*. Analogues of p-aminobenzoic acid with antibacterial activity. The most used early 'sulpha' drug was sulphapyridine (May and Baker 693), from 1937 (Dr Arthur Ewins).

1938 *Phenytoin*. Anticonvulsant introduced in 1938 by Merritt and Pulman for most types of epilepsy.

1939 *DDT* (Dichloro-diphenyl-trichloro-ethane). A powerful insecticide developed by Dr Paul Müller which has vastly lowered the malarial death rate by killing the malaria-carrying mosquitoes.

1939 *Pethidine*. A narcotic analgesic used particularly during childbirth. Introduced 1939 by Hoechst. Synthesised by Eisleb and Schaumann.

1940 *Penicillins*. Group of antibacterial substances (e.g. penicillin G, the benzyl derivative). Discovered in 1928 by Sir Alexander Fleming (1881–1955) by the chance contamination of a petri dish at St Mary's Hospital, London. First concentrated in 1940 by Sir Howard Florey (1898–1968) and E B Chain (1906–79). Not identified as *Penicillium notatum* until 1930. Penicillin G introduced 1946. In 1961 Chain *et al.* isolated *p-amino-penicillanic acid* which is the nucleus for many semi-synthetic derivatives.

1943 *LSD* (Lysergic acid diethylamide). A hallucinogen, discovered by Albert Hofman (Switzerland) in Apr. 1943. Now has no recognised therapeutic use.

c. 1943 *Dimercaprol (BAL)* (formerly British Anti-Lewisite). Developed during the war by L Stocken and R Thompson, to combat lethal war gas, lewisite. Later uses discovered as antidote to poisoning by arsenic, gold or mercury.

1944 *Mepyramine (Pyrilamine)*. First acceptable antihistamine.

1944 *Amphetamine*. A central nervous system stimulant, formerly widely abused.

1944 *Streptomycin*. An antibiotic discovered by S A Waksman (Russian born, USA) in 1944. Important for its activity against tuberculosis.

c. 1944 *Paludrine* (proguanil hydrochloride). An antimalarial drug.

1947 *Chloramphenicol*. An antibiotic from *Streptomyces venezuelae* used for treatment of typhoid. First isolated by Buckholder (USA) in 1947 and first synthesised in 1949.

1948 *Chlortetracycline (Aureomycin)*. An antibiotic first isolated in 1948 at Pearl River, NY, USA, by Dr Benjamin M Duggar.

1948 *Imipramine*. A benzodiazepine derivative, synthesised by Häfliger in 1948. An antidepressant.

1949 *Cortisone*. One of a number of steroid hormones from adrenal cortical extracts so named in 1939. First used in treatment of rheumatoid arthritis in 1949 leading to development of many anti-inflammatory steroids.

1951 *Halothane* ($C_2HBrClF_3$). General anaesthetic first synthesised in 1951 by Suckling.

1952 *Chlorpromazine*. Potent tranquilliser first synthesised by Charpentier in 1952. Acts selectively upon higher centre in brain as a central nervous system depressant.

1952 *Isoniazid* (Isonicotinic Acid Hydrazide, INH). Used in the treatment of tuberculosis, reported on by Edward Robitzek in 1952.

1954 *Methyldopa*. Used in treatment of hypertension. Effects first noted in 1954 by Sourkes.

1954 *Reserpine*. Tranquilliser from Rauwolfia, a genus of plant in the dogbane family, used in treatment of high blood pressure. Effects noted in modern times by Kline in 1954.

1955 *Oral Contraceptives*. The first reported field studies of a pill containing synthetic hormones that prevent ovulation were those by Pincus using Enovid in 1955, in Puerto Rico.

1955 *Metronidazole*. Based on discovery of Azomycin in 1955 by Nakamura. Used in treatment of trichomoniasis, and other protozoal infections.

1956 *Amphotericin*. An antifungal antibiotic used topically. Elucidated in 1956 by Vandeputte *et al.*

1957 *Interferon*. A group of proteins produced by virus-infected cells. They inhibit the multiplication of viruses.

c. 1960 *Tolbutamide*. Reduces blood sugar level in diabetics.

1960 *Chlordiazepoxide* ('Librium'). Tranquilliser for treatment of anxiety and tension states, convulsive states and neuromuscular and cardiovascular disorders. Effects first noted in 1960 by Randall *et al.* Related drug *Diazepam* ('Valium') also used in anxiety states and as premedication for surgery.

c. 1960 *Frusemide*. A diuretic.

1961 *Thiabendazole*. Efficacy in dealing with intestinal tract infestations noted by Brown *et al.* in 1961. Used to treat various worm infections.

1962–3 *Clofibrate*. Lowers the fatty acid and cholesterol levels in the blood. Effects noted in 1962–3 by Thorp and Waring.

1963 *Allopurinol*. Used in treatment of gout, it slows rate at which body forms uric acid. Reported on by Hitchings, Elion *et al.* in 1963.

1963 *Cephalosporins*. Antibiotics discovered in 1945 in Sardinia by Prof Brotzu. First utilised in 1963. Developed by Sir Howard (later Lord) Florey and Glaxo Laboratories.

1964 *Tolnaftate*. An anti-fungal agent announced October 1964. Highly effective against epidermiphytosis (athlete's foot).

1965 *Niridazole*. Discovered in 1961 (announced December 1965) by Dr Paul Schmidt of CIBA, Basle. Treatment of debilitating liver-infestation disease Bilharzia (250 million world incidence).

1966 *Pralidoxime*. Antidote for poisoning by cholinesterase inhibitors, particularly organophosphorus compounds, which are used as insecticides and 'nerve gases'.

1966 *Trometamol* (Tromethamine). A diuretic used to treat acidosis, especially after surgery.

1967 *Nitrazepam* ('Mogadon'). Tranquilliser and hypnotic.

1967 *Laevo-dopa* (L-Dopa). Naturally occurring amino acid reported on by Cotzias and others in 1967. Used in treatment of Parkinson's Disease.

1968 *Propranolol.* A β-adrenergic blocking drug used to treat hypertension. More recent related drugs include pindolol, sotalol, timolol.

1969 *Ibuprofen.* First of the proprionic acid derivatives; a non-steroidal anti-rheumatic.

1969 *Salbutamol.* Useful in asthma for its selective bronchodilator effects, whereas earlier unselective drugs were more dangerous in evaluating the heart rate.

1970 *Inosine Pranobex.* Immunomodulator/anti-viral used in the treatment of herpes simplex.

1972 *Prostaglandins.* The name given by von Euler in 1935 to a group of related substances found in the body, based on prostonoic acid. Prostaglandin $F_{2\alpha}$ was the first to be used therapeutically, in 1972, for induction of labour.

1976 *Cimetidine.* Selective antihistamine which prevents excessive acid secretion in the stomach, often the cause of ulcers.

1981 *Captopril.* The first anti-hypertensive drug which acts by inhibiting the formation of the hormone, angiotensin.

1981 *Acyclovir.* The first specific anti-viral: used in the treatment of herpes infections.

Normal pulse rates

	Beats per minute
Embryo 5 months	156
6 months	154
7 months	150
8 months	142
9 months	145
Newborn (premature)	110–185
Newborn (full term)	135
2 years	110
4 years	105
6 years	95
8 years	90
10 years	87
15 years	83
20 years	71
21–25	74
25–30	72
30–35	70
35–40	72
40–45	72
45–50	72
50–55	72
55–60	75
60–65	73
65–70	75
70–75	75
75–80	72
>80	78
Lying down (adult)	66
Sitting (adult)	73
Standing (adult)	82
Sleeping (adult)	♂59 ♀65
Waking (adult)	♂78 ♀84

Average height and weight at birth

	Boys					Girls				
	Length		Weight			Length		Weight		
Nationality	cm	in	kg	lb	oz	cm	in	kg	lb	oz
British	51,05	20·1	3,35	7	6·4	50,80	20·0	3,31	7	4·8
German	50,80	20·0	3,49	7	11·2	50,29	19·8	3,31	7	4·8
Swiss	50,80	20,0	3,31	7	4·8	50,03	19·7	3,08	6	12·8
American (White)	50,54	19·9	3,53	7	12·8	50,03	19·7	3,44	7	9·6
Japanese	50,03	19·7	3,04	6	11·5	49,27	19·4	2,96	6	8·6
French	49,78	19·6	3,08	6	12·8	49,02	19·3	3,08	6	12·8
American (Black)	49,53	19·5	3,22	7	1·6	48,51	19·1	3,08	6	12·8
Russian	48,51	19·1	3,40	7	8	48,51	19·1	3,31	7	4·8
Chinese	48,00	18·9	3,08	6	12·8	48,00	18·9	2,99	6	9·6
African (Pygmy)	45,72	18·0	3,58	7	14·4	46,22	18·2	3,71	8	3·2

Phobias

Acerophobia	Sourness
Acrophobia	Sharpness (pinnacles)
Agoraphobia	Open spaces
Aichurophobia	Points
Ailourophobia	Cats
Akousticophobia	Sound
Algophobia	Pain
Altophobia	Heights
Amathophobia	Dust
Ancraophobia	Wind
Androphobia	Men
Anginophobia	Narrowness
Anglophobia	England or things English
Anthropophobia	Human beings
Antlophobia	Flood
Apeirophobia	Infinity
Apiphobia	Bees
Arachnophobia	Spiders
Asthenophobia	Weakness
Astraphobia	Lightning
Atelophobia	Imperfection
Atephobia	Ruin
Aulophobia	Flute
Auroraphobia	Auroral lights
Bacilliphobia	Microbes
Barophobia	Gravity
Bathophobia	Depth
Batophobia	Walking
Batrachophobia	Reptiles
Belonephobia	Needles
Bibliophobia	Books
Blennophobia	Slime
Brontophobia	Thunder

Carcinophobia	Cancer
Cardiophobia	Heart condition
Chaetophobia	Hair
Cheimatophobia	Cold
Cherophobia	Cheerfulness
Chionophobia	Snow
Chrometophobia	Money
Chromophobia	Colour
Chronophobia	Duration
Claustrophobia	Enclosed spaces
Clinophobia	Going to bed
Cnidophobia	Stings
Coprophobia	Faeces
Cryophobia	Ice, frost
Crystallophobia	Crystals
Cymophobia	Sea swell
Cynophobia	Dogs
Demophobia	Crowds
Demonophobia	Demons
Dendrophobia	Trees
Dermatophobia	Skin
Dikephobia	Justice
Doraphobia	Fur
Dromophobia	Crossing streets
Eisoptrophobia	Mirrors
Elektrophobia	Electricity
Eleutherophobia	Freedom
Enetephobia	Pins
Entomophobia	Insects
Eosophobia	Dawn
Eremitophobia	Solitude
Ergophobia	Work
Erythrophobia	Blushing
Gallophobia	France or things French

Gametophobia	Marriage
Genophobia	Sex
Germanophobia	Germany or things German
Geumatophobia	Taste
Graphophobia	Writing
Gymnophobia	Nudity
Gynophobia	Women
Haematophobia	Blood
Haptophobia	Touch
Harpaxophobia	Robbers
Hedonophobia	Pleasure
Hippophobia	Horses
Hodophobia	Travel
Homichlophobia	Fog
Hormephobia	Shock
Hyalinopygophobia	Glass Bottoms
Hydrophobia	Water
Hygrophobia	Dampness
Hypegiaphobia	Responsibility
Hypnophobia	Sleep
Hypsophobia	High place
Ideophobia	Ideas
Kakorraphiaphobia	Failure
Katagelophobia	Ridicule
Kenophobia	Void
Keraunothnetophobia	Fall of man-made satellites
Kinesophobia (Kinetophobia)	Motion
Kleptophobia	Stealing
Koniphobia	Dust
Kopophobia	Fatigue
Kyphophobia	Stooping
Lalophobia	Speech
Limnophobia	Lakes
Linonophobia	String
Logophobia	Words
Lyssophobia	Insanity
Maniaphobia	Insanity
Mastigophobia	Flogging
Mechanophobia	Machinery
Metallophobia	Metals
Meteorophobia	Meteors
Monophobia	One thing
Musophobia	Mice
Musicophobia	Music
Mysophobia	Dirt
Myxophobia	Slime
Necrophobia	Corpses
Negrophobia	Negroes
Nelophobia	Glass
Neophobia	New
Nephophobia	Clouds
Nosophobia	Disease
Nyctophobia	Darkness
Ochlophobia	Crowds
Ochophobia	Vehicles
Odontophobia	Teeth
Oikophobia	Home
Olfactophobia	Smell
Ommetaphobia	Eyes
Oneirophobia	Dreams
Ophiophobia	Snakes
Ornithophobia	Birds
Ouranophobia	Heaven
Panphobia (Pantophobia)	Everything
Parthenophobia	Young girls
Pathophobia	Disease
Patroiophobia	Heredity
Peccatophobia	Sinning
Pediculophobia	Lice
Peniaphobia	Poverty
Phagophobia	Swallowing
Phasmophobia	Ghosts
Pharmacophobia	Drugs
Phobophobia	Fears
Phonophobia	Speaking aloud
Photophobia	Strong light
Phronemophobia	Thinking
Phyllophobia	Leaves
Pnigerophobia	Smothering
Pogonophobia	Beards
Poinephobia	Punishment
Polyphobia	Many things
Potophobia	Drink
Pteronophobia	Feathers
Pyrophobia	Fire
Russophobia	Russia or things Russian
Rypophobia	Soiling
Satanophobia	Satan
Sciophobia	Shadows
Selaphobia	Flashes
Siderodromophobia	Travelling by train
Siderophobia	Stars
Sinophobia	China or things Chinese
Sitophobia	Food
Spermophobia (Spermatophobia)	Germs
Stasophobia	Standing
Stygiophobia (Hadephobia)	Hell
Syphilophobia	Syphilis
Tachophobia	Speed
Taphophobia	Burial alive
Teratophobia	Monsters
Terdekaphobia	Number thirteen
Thaasophobia	Sitting idle
Thalassophobia	Sea
Thanatophobia	Death
Theophobia	God
Thermophobia	Heat
Thixophobia	Touching
Tocophobia	Childbirth
Toxiphobia	Poison
Traumatophobia	Wounds, injury
Tremophobia	Trembling
Trypanophobia	Inoculations, injections
Xenophobia (Zenophobia)	Foreigners
Zoöphobia	Animals

Bones in the human body

Skull	Number
Occipital	1
Parietal – 1 pair	2
Sphenoid	1
Ethmoid	1
Inferior Nasal Conchae – 1 pair	2
Frontal – 1 pair, fused	1
Nasal – 1 pair	2
Lacrimal – 1 pair	2
Temporal – 1 pair	2
Macilla – 1 pair	2
Zygomatic – 1 pair	2
Vomer	1
Palatine – 1 pair	2
Mandible – 1 pair, fused	1
	22

The Ears	
Malleus	2
Incus	2
Stapes	2
	6

Vertebrae	
Cervical	7
Thoracic	12
Lumbar	5
Sacral – 5, fused to form the Sacrum	1
Coccyx – between 3 and 5, fused	1
	26

Vertebral Ribs	
Ribs, 'true' – 7 pairs	14
Ribs, 'false' – 5 pairs of which 2 pairs are floating	10
	24

Sternum	
Manubrium	1
'The Body' (sternebrae)	1
Xiphisternum	1
	3

Hyoid (in the throat)	1

Pectoral Girdle	
Clavicle – 1 pair	2
Scapula – (including Coracoid) – 1 pair	2
	4

Upper Extremity (each arm)	
Humerus	1
Radius	1
Ulna	1
Carpus:	
Scaphoid	1
Lunate	1
Triquetral	1
Pisiform	1
Trapezium	1
Trapezoid	1
Capitate	1
Hamate	1
Metacarpals	5
Phalanges:	
First Digit	2
Second Digit	3
Third Digit	3
Fourth Digit	3
Fifth Digit	3
	30

Pelvic Girdle	
Ilium, Ischium and Pubis (combined) – 1 pair of hip bones, innominate	2

Lower Extremity (each leg)	
Femur	1
Tibia	1
Fibula	1
Tarsus:	
Talus	1
Calcaneus	1
Navicular	1
Cuneiform medial	1
Cuneiform, intermediate	1
Cuneiform, lateral	1
Cuboid	1
Metatarsals	5
Phalanges:	
First Digit	2
Second Digit	3
Third Digit	3
Fourth Digit	3
Fifth Digit	3
	29

Total	
Skull	22
The Ears	6
Vertebrae	26
Vertebral Ribs	24
Sternum	3
Throat	1
Pectoral Girdle	4
Upper Extremity (arms) – 2 × 30	60
Hip Bones	2
Lower Extremity (legs) – 2 × 29	58
	206

In human beings the musculature normally accounts for some 40 per cent of the total body-weight. There are 639 named muscles in the human anatomy.

Nobel prizewinners in physiology and medicine since 1950

1984 Cesar Milstein, British/Argentine; Georges J. F. Kohler, W. German; Neils K. Jerne, British/Danish

1983 Barbara McClintock, US

1982 Sune Bergstrom, Bengt Samuelsson, both Swedish; John R. Vane, British

1981 Roger W. Sperry, David H. Hubel, Tosten N. Wiesel, all US

1980 Baruj Benacerraf, George Snell, both US; Jean Dausset, France

1979 Allan M. Cormack, US, Geoffrey N. Hounsfield, British

1978 Daniel Nathans, Hamilton O. Smith, both US; Werner Arber, Swiss

1977 Rosalyn S. Yalow, Roger C. L. Guillemin, Andrew V. Schally, all US

1976 Baruch S. Blumberg, US; Daniel Carleton Gajdusek, US

1975 David Baltimore, Howard Temin, both US; Renato Dulbecco, Ital.-US

1974 Albert Claude, Lux.-US; George Emil Palade, Rom.-US; Christian Rene de Duve, Belg.

1973 Karl von Frisch, Ger.; Konrad Lorenz, Ger.-Austrian; Nikolaas Tinbergen, Brit.

1972 Gerald M. Edelman, US; Rodney R. Porter, British

1971 Earl W. Sutherland Jr., US

1970 Julius Axelrod, US; Sir Bernard Katz, British; Ulf von Euler, Swedish

1969 Max Delbruck, Alfred D. Hershey, Salvador Luria, all US

1968 Robert W. Holley, H. Gobind Khorana, Marshall W. Nirenberg, all US

1967 Ragnar Granit, Swedish; Haldan Keffer Hartline, US; George Wald, US

1966 Charles B. Huggins, Francis Peyton Rous, both US

1965 Francois Jacob, André Lwoff, Jacques Monod, all French

1964 Konrad E. Bloch, US; Feodor Lynen, German

1963 Sir John C. Eccles, Australian; Alan L. Hodgkin, British; Andrew F. Huxley, British

1962 Francis H. C. Crick, British; James D. Watson, US; Maurice H. F. Wilkins, British

1961 Georg von Bekesy, US

1960 Sir F. MacFarlane Burnet, Australian; Peter B. Medawar, British

1959 Arthur Kornberg, US; Severo Ochoa, US

1958 George W. Beadle, US; Edward L. Tatum, US; Joshua Lederberg, US

1957 Daniel Bovet, Italian

1956 André F. Cournand, US; Werner Forssmann, German; Dickinson W. Richards, Jr, US

1955 Alex H. T. Theorell, Swedish

1954 John F. Enders, Frederick C. Robbins, Thomas H. Weller, all US

1953 Hans A. Krebs, British; Fritz A. Lipmann, US

1952 Selman A. Waksman, US

1951 Max Theiler, US

1950 Philip S. Hench, Edward C. Kendall, both US; Tadeus Reischstein, Swiss

Philosophy

'Philosophy' is a word derived from the Greek words meaning 'love of wisdom', and philosophy in the Western world began with the ancient Greeks. It is used to cover a wide area: the scientific arrangement of those principles which underlie all knowledge and existence.

The sphere of philosophy can be roughly delineated by stating how it is distinct from other areas of thought. It differs from religion since its quest for the underlying causes and principles of being and thinking does not depend on dogma and faith; and from science, since it does not depend solely on fact, but leans heavily on speculation. Its inter-relation with both science and religion can be seen in the large number of philosophers who were also either theologians or scientists, and the few such as Blaise Pascal and Roger Bacon, who were all three. Philosophy developed from religion, becoming distinct when thinkers sought truth independent of theological considerations. Science in turn developed from philosophy, and eventually, all the branches of science from physics to psychology broke away – psychology being the last to do so in the 20th century.

Philosophy can be split into three particularly important categories: ethics, metaphysics and epistemology. Such a division leaves out some important areas of philosophical speculation, including logic, which is the increasingly formalised technique of exact analysis of reasoning, but it serves to introduce a few of the most important writings.

1. **Ethics** is the study of human conduct and morality. Philosophers have held many points of view about ideal human conduct but their opinions tend to resolve into an opposition between two main schools. One school, the 'Idealist', considers that the goodness or badness of a course of action must be judged by standards dictated from the other world – from God or from some force for good – external to man. The second school, who might be grouped under the term 'Utilitarians', feels that the effect which a course of action produces in this world makes it good or bad.

The Idealist school was represented quite early in the history of Western philosophy by the Greek philosopher Plato, who wrote in the 4th century BC. Plato, in a series of dialogues, has his ex-teacher Socrates discuss the problems of philosophy with friends and opponents.

Socrates' procedure is to draw out the wisdom from the gentleman with whom he is discussing the question. Socrates, in fact, rarely makes a statement. He prefers what advertising men call 'the soft sell'. That is to say, he asks questions which compel the others either to make the statement he wants them to make or to appear foolish.

In three of these dialogues, especially – *The Protagoras, The Phaedo,* and *The Gorgias* – Plato develops a system of ethics which is essentially idealistic. Socrates propounds that the good comes from the realm of 'ideas' or 'forms'. This is a sort of perfect other world which projects distorted copies of everything good down to the world we have to contend with. For Plato, individual conduct is good in so far as it is governed by the emanated spirit from above. Plato does not, of course, use the word 'heaven' for the world of ideas, but he was adapted – after being modified by Aristotle, Plotinus, and others – for Christian purposes. One of the ways in which the knowledge from the realm of the 'ideas' was communicated to mortals was by a voice or 'demon'. In the *Apology*, Socrates describes how this individual conscience has prevented him from wrongdoing.

Another important work which has to be classed with the idealists is Aristotle's *Nicomachean Ethics*. Aristotle was a pupil of Plato, and, like Plato, he thinks of the good as a divine emanation, or overflow, but his ethics have a

more 'practical' bent. He equates happiness with the good and is responsible for the doctrine of the 'golden mean'. This states that every virtue is a mean, or middle-point, between two vices. Generosity, for instance, is the mean between prodigality and stinginess.

A more cynical approach was introduced by Niccolò Machiavelli, founder of the modern science of politics. In his famous book, *The Prince*, Machiavelli drew his conclusions from the very nature of man.

The same tendency to give idealism a practical bent is found in a more modern philosopher, Immanuel Kant. His idealistic aspect may be compared with Socrates' 'demon'. Kant maintains that there is in each man a voice which guides him as to right or wrong.

But the part of Kant's ethics which is most famous is that connected with the phrase 'categorical imperative'. In Kant's own words: 'Act only according to a maxim by which you can at the same time will that it shall become a general law'. In other words, before acting in a certain way, the individual must ask himself: 'If everybody did the same thing what would be the moral condition of the universe?' This is a practical consideration in the sense that it concerns the *result* of an action, but Kant's concern is for the morality of the universe and not its happiness or earthly welfare. Kant's principal ethical works are *The Critique of Pure Reason, The Critique of Practical Reason, The Metaphysics of Morality,* and *The Metaphysics of Ethics*.

The opposing group of 'utilitarian' ethics is concerned with the matter of earthly welfare. The earliest Western philosopher to represent this tradition is Epicurus, a Greek philosopher of the 4th century BC.

Instead of deriving ideas of right and wrong from above, as did the Socratics for example, Epicurus maintained that 'we call pleasure the beginning and end of the blessed life'. The term 'Epicurean' was used – and often still is used – to describe one who indulges in excessive pleasure, but this usage is neither accurate nor just. Epicurus did not condone excesses. On the contrary, he said that pleasure was only good when moderate or 'passive'. 'Dynamic' pleasure, which caused painful after-effects, was not good.

The utilitarian tradition has on the whole had more adherents than the idealistic tradition in modern philosophy. Jeremy Bentham, for example, writing in the 18th century, acknowledged his debt to Epicurus in his *Principles of Morals and Legislation*. Bentham agreed that pain and pleasure were the 'sovereign masters' governing man's conduct. He added to this a doctrine of *utility* which argued that 'the greatest happiness of the greatest number is the measure of right and wrong'.

John Stuart Mill is perhaps the most famous of the Utilitarians. He extended Bentham's doctrines pointing out that there were different *qualities* of pleasure and pain; and that 'some *kinds* of pleasure are more valuable than others'. These articles were later put out in book form: *Utilitarianism*.

In the USA the Utilitarians made an impact on the Pragmatists, who held that 'the *right* is only the expedient in our way of thinking' – to quote William James, whose *Pragmatism* is the best-known book produced by this school.

2. **Metaphysics.** The term 'metaphysics' originated as the title of one of Aristotle's treatises. It probably meant only that he wrote it after his *Physics*, but it was once thought to signify study beyond the realm of physics. Today it is usually employed to describe the speculation as to the ultimate nature of reality and the structure of the universe.

The sort of questions asked by metaphysicians concern the origin and condition of the universe in which man lives, and, as we might expect,

they came up early in the history of philosophy. Before Aristotle had invented the term 'metaphysics' – as early as the 6th Century BC – pre-Socratic Greek philosophers were offering their solutions of the mysteries of the universe.

Much of the speculation of these pre-Socratic philosophers was centred on speculation about the four *elements* which they thought made up the universe. Empedocles, who, according to legend, threw himself into the volcano at Mt Etna to prove his immortality – and failed – first defined earth, air, fire and water as the four basic elements. Others attempted to make one of these the most important, or *primary*, element from which the others were derived. Thales – one of the seven wise men of Greece – thought water was on top. Heraclitus' primary element was fire. Anaximander reasoned that none of the four was primary. They must, he said, exist in perpetual balance.

3. **Epistemology** is the study of the nature, grounds and validity of man's knowing – how we come to know and how far we can rely on what we think we have discovered.

Epistemologists assert that knowledge is born in the individual and has only to be drawn forth. The other point of view is that at birth the mind is a *tabula rasa* – blank sheet – on which knowledge is imprinted.

The first school is represented classically by Plato. In the *Theaetetus* especially, he discusses various theories of knowledge and discards those built on the shifting sands of sense perception. The senses are, he feels, too fallible. True knowledge comes from those general notions which are derived from the realm of the *ideas* – which the soul possesses prior to birth.

The classic representative of the second school is John Locke – a 17th century English philosopher. In his *Essay Concerning Human Understanding*, Locke defines what is really the opposite point of view to Plato's. He is the pioneer proponent of the *tabula rasa*. Locke regards the mind at birth as comparable to an empty cabinet with two compartments. As we live, one compartment is filled with our *perceptions* and the other with our *sensations*. From these two combined we get our *ideas*.

This theory tends to make knowledge a matter of experience and mental processing rather than one of religious insight. As one might expect, Locke's theories are important influences in those fields which investigate the processes of mental activity – such as psychology and education.

Schools and Theories

Since the days of the early Greeks, philosophers have been divided into different schools and have advanced opposing theories. Among the many basic outlooks and theories not already discussed but which have developed since Thales of Miletus (624–550 BC) first questioned the nature of ultimate reality, the following may be listed:

1. *Absolutism:* the theory that there is an ultimate reality in which all differences are reconciled.

2. *Agnosticism:* the position that the ultimate answer to all fundamental inquries is that we do not know.

3. *Altruism:* the principle of living and acting in the interest of others rather than oneself.

4. *Asceticism:* the belief that withdrawal from the physical world into the inner world of the spirit is the highest good attainable.

5. *Atheism:* rejection of the concept of God as a workable hypothesis.

6. *Atomism:* the belief that the entire universe is composed of distinct and indivisible units.

7. *Conceptualism:* the doctrine that universal ideas are neither created by finite (human)

minds, nor entirely apart from an absolute mind (God).

8. *Critical Idealism:* the concept that man cannot determine whether there is anything beyond his own experience.

9. *Critical Realism:* the theory that reality is tripartite, that in addition to the mental and physical aspects of reality, there is a third aspect called essences.

10. *Criticism:* the theory that the path to knowledge lies midway between dogmatism and scepticism.

11. *Determinism:* the belief that the universe follows a fixed or pre-determined pattern.

12. *Dialectical Materialism:* the theory that reality is strictly material and is based on a struggle between opposing forces, with occasional interludes of harmony.

13. *Dogmatism:* assertion of a belief without authoritative support.

14. *Dualism:* the belief that the world consists of two radically independant and absolute elements, e.g. good and evil, spirit and matter.

15. *Egoism:* in ethics the belief that the serving of one's own interests is the highest end.

16. *Empiricism:* rejection of all *a priori* knowledge in favour of experience and induction.

17. *Evolutionism:* the concept of the universe as a progression of inter-related phenomena.

18. *Existentialism:* denial of objective universal values – man must create values for himself through action; the self is the ultimate reality.

19. *Hedonism:* the doctrine that pleasure is the highest good.

20. *Humanism:* any system that regards human interest and the human mind as paramount in the universe.

21. *Idealism:* any system that regards thought or the idea as the basis either of knowledge or existence; in ethics, the search for the best or the highest.

22. *Instrumentalism:* the concept of ideas as instruments, rather than as goals of living.

23. *Intuitionism:* the doctrine that the perception of truth is by intuition, not analysis.

24. *Materialism:* the doctrine that denies the independent existence of spirit, and asserts the existence of only one substance – matter; belief that physical well-being is paramount.

25. *Meliorism:* the belief that the world is capable of improvement, and that man has the power of helping in its betterment, a position between optimism and pessimism.

26. *Monism:* belief in only one ultimate reality, whatever its nature.

27. *Mysticism:* belief that the ultimate reality lies in direct contact with the divine.

28. *Naturalism:* a position that seeks to explain all phenomena by means of strictly natural (as opposed to supernatural) categories.

29. *Neutral Monism:* theory that reality is neither physical nor spiritual, but capable of expressing itself as either.

30. *Nominalism:* the doctrine that general terms have no corresponding reality either in or out of the mind, and are, in effect, nothing more than words. (*c.f.* Realism).

31. *Optimism:* any system that holds that the universe is the best of all possible ones, and that all will work out for the best.

32. *Pantheism:* the belief that God is identical with the universe.

33. *Personalism:* theory that ultimate reality consists of a plurality of spiritual beings or independent persons.

34. *Pessimism:* belief that the universe is the worst possible and that all is doomed to evil.

35. *Phenomenalism:* theory that reality is only appearance.

36. *Pluralism:* belief that there are more than two irreducible components of reality.

37. *Positivism:* the doctrine that man can have no knowledge except of phenomena, and that the knowledge of phenomena is relative, not absolute.

38. *Pragmatism:* a method that makes practical consequences the test of truth.

39. *Rationalism:* the theory that reason alone, without the aid of experience, can arrive at the basic reality of the universe.

40. *Realism:* the doctrine that general terms have a real existence. *c.f.* Nominalism.

41. *Relativism:* rejection of the concept of the absolute.

42. *Scepticism:* the doctrine that no facts can be certainly known.

43. *Theism:* acceptance of the concept of God as a workable hypothesis.

44. *Transcendentalism:* belief in an ultimate reality that transcends human experience.

45. *Voluntarism:* the theory that will is the determining factor in the universe.

Philosophers through the ages

Pre-Socratic Greeks

Thales of Miletas (624–550 BC). Regarded as the starting point of Western philosophy; the first exponent of monism.

Anaximander (611–547 BC). Continued Thales' quest for universal substance, but reasoned that that substance need not resemble known substances.

Anaximenes (588–524 BC). Regarded air as the ultimate reality.

Pythagoras (572–497 BC). Taught a dualism of body and soul.

Heraclitus (533–475 BC). Opposed concept of a single ultimate reality; held that one permanent thing is change.

Parmenides (*c.* 495 BC). Formulated the basic doctrine of idealism; member of Eleatic school, so called because based at Elea in southern Italy.

Anaxogorus (500–428 BC). Believed in an indefinite number of basic substances.

Zeno of Elea (*c.* 495–430 BC). Argued that plurality and change are appearances, not realities.

Empedocles (*c.* 495–435 BC). Held that there were four irreducible substances (water, fire, earth and air) and two forces (love and hate).

Protagoras (481–411 BC). An early relativist and humanist; doubted human ability to attain absolute truth.

Classic Greek Philosophers

Socrates (*c.* 470–399 BC). Developed Socratic method of inquiry; teacher of Plato, through whose writings his idealistic philosophy was disseminated.

Democritus (460–370 BC). Began tradition in Western thought of explaining universe in mechanistic terms.

Antisthenes (*c.* 450–*c.* 360 BC). Chief of group known as the Cynics; stressed discipline and work as the essential good.

Plato (*c.* 428–347 BC). Founded the Academy at Athens; developed the idealism of his teacher Socrates; teacher of Aristotle.

Diogenes of Sinope (*c.* 412–*c.* 325 BC). Famous Cynic.

Aristotle (384–322 BC). Taught that there are four factors in causation: the interrelated factors of form and matter; motive cause, which produces change; and the end, for which a process of change occurs. Perhaps the greatest influence on western civilization.

Hellenistic Period

Pyrrho of Elis (*c.* 365–275 BC). Initiated the Sceptic school of philosophy; believed that man could not know anything for certain.

Epicurus (341–270 BC). Taught that the test of truth is in sensation; proponent of atomism and hedonism.

Zeno of Citium [Cyprus] (*c.* 335–263 BC). Chief of the Stoics, so called because they met in the Stoa Poikile or Painted Porch at Athens; proponent of pantheism, evolutionism; taught that man's role is to accept nature and all it offers, good or bad.

Plotinus (AD 205–270). Chief expounder of Neo-Platonism, a combining of the teachings of Plato with Oriental concepts.

Augustine (AD 354–430). Known to history as St Augustine; expounder of optimism and

absolutism; believed that God transcends human comprehension; one of greatest influences on medieval Christian thought.

Boethius (*c.* AD 480–524). Late Roman statesman and philosopher. A Neo-Platonist, his great work, *The Consolations of Philosophy*, served to transmit Greek philosophy to medieval Europe.

Medieval Period

Avicenna (980–1037). Arabic follower of Aristotle and Neo-Platonism; his works led to a revival of interest in Aristotle in 13th century Europe.

Anselm (1033–1109). Italian Augustinian; known to history as St. Anselm; a realist, he is famous for his examination of the proof of God's existence.

Peter Abelard (1079–1142). Leading theologian and philosopher of medieval France; his nominalism caused him to be declared a heretic by the Church.

Averroes (1126–98). Great philosopher of Mohammedan Spain, and leading commentator on Aristotle; regarded religion as allegory for the common man, philosophy as the path to truth.

Moses Maimonides (1135–1204). Leading Jewish student of Aristle in medieval Mohammedan world; sought to combine Aristotelian teaching with that of the Bible.

Roger Bacon (*c* 1214–1292). English student of Aristotle, advocated return to Hebrew and Greek versions of Scripture; an empiricist.

St Bonaventure (*c.* 1217–74). Born John of Fidanza in Italy; friend of Thomas Aquinas; student of Plato and Aristotle; a mystic and ascetic.

St Thomas Aquinas (1225–74). Italian; leading philosopher of the Scholastics or Christian philosophers of the Middle Ages; evolved a compromise between Aristotle and Scripture, based on the belief that faith and reason are in agreement; his philosophical system is known as Thomism.

The Renaissance

Desiderius Erasmus (1466–1536). Greatest of the humanists, he helped spread the ideas of the Renaissance in his native Holland and throughout Northern Europe.

Niccolò Machiavelli (1469–1527). Italian politician and political thinker; a realist, he placed the state as the paramount power in human affairs.

Thomas More (1478–1535). Statesman and later saint; early influence in the English Renaissance. Stressed a return to Greek sources and political and social reform. All these traits appeared in his famous *Utopia* (1516).

Transition to Modern Thought

Francis Bacon (1561–1626). English statesman and philosopher of science; in his major work, *Novum Organum*, he sought to replace the deductive logic of Aristotle with an inductive system in interpreting nature.

Thomas Hobbes (1588–1679). English materialist who believed the natural state of man is war; outlined a theory of human government in his book *Leviathan*, whereby the state and men's subordination to it form the sole solution to human selfishness and aggressiveness.

René Descartes (1596–1650). French; dualist, rationalist, theist. Descartes and his system, Cartesianism, are at the base of all modern knowledge. What he furnished is a theory of knowledge that underlies modern science and philosophy. 'All the sciences are conjoined with one another and interdependent' he wrote.

Blaise Pascal (1623–52). French theist who held that sense and reason are mutually deceptive; truth lies between dogmatism and scepticism.

Benedict de Spinoza (1632–77). Dutch rationalist metaphysician, he developed ideas of Descartes while rejecting his dualism.

John Locke (1632–1704). English dualist, empiricist; in his great *Essay Concerning Human Understanding* he sought to refute the rationalist view that all knowledge derives from first

a. Plato (c. 428–347 BC) See page 73.

b. Aristotle (384–322 BC). See page 73.

c. Niccolò Machiavelli (1469–1527). See page 73.

d. Augustine of Hippo (AD 354–430). See page 73.

e. St. Thomas Aquinas (1225–74). See page 73.

f. Sir Thomas More (1478–1535). See page 73.

g. Adam Smith (1723–90). See right.

h. Immanuel Kant (1724–1804). See right.

i. Georg Wilhelm Hegel (1770–1831). See right.

j. Thomas Hobbes (1588–1679). See page 73.

k. John Stuart Mill (1806–73). See page 75.

l. Bertrand Russell (1872–1970). See page 75.

Photographs: a–k BBC Hulton Picture Library; l Popperfoto.

principles. His influence in political, religious, educational and philosophical thought was wide and deep.

18th Century

Gottfried Wilhelm von Leibniz (1646–1716). German idealist, absolutist, optimist (his view that this is the best of all possible worlds was ridiculed by Voltaire in *Candide*); held that reality consisted of units of force called monads.

George Berkeley (1685–1753). Irish idealist and theist of English ancestry who taught that material things exist only in being perceived; his system of subjective idealism is called Berkeleianism.

Emmanuel Swedenborg (1688–1772). Swedish mystic, scientist, theologian; author of *Principia Rerum Naturalium*, 1734.

David Hume (1711–76). Scottish philosopher and historian. An empiricist who carried on ideas of Locke, but developed a system of scepticism (Humism) according to which human knowledge is limited to experience of ideas and sensations, whose truth cannot be verified.

Jean-Jacques Rousseau (1712–78). French political philosopher whose concepts have had a profound influence on modern thought; advocated a 'return to nature' to counteract the inequality among men brought about by civilized society.

Adam Smith (1723–90). Founder of modern political economy and a leader of the 'Scottish Renaissance'. His *Wealth of Nations* (1776), with its emphasis on economic liberalism and natural liberty, has had a more profound influence than almost any other philosophical work.

Immanuel Kant (1724–1804). German founder of critical philosophy. At first influenced by Leibniz, then by Hume, he sought to find an alternative approach to the rationalism of the former and the scepticism of the latter; in ethics, formulated the Categorical Imperative – which states that what applies to oneself must apply to everyone else unconditionally – a restatement of the Christian precept 'Do unto others as you would have them do unto you'.

Jeremy Bentham (1748–1832). English Utilitarian. Believed, like Kant, that the interests of the individual are one with those of society, but regarded fear of consequences rather than basic principle as the motivation for right action.

Johann Gottlieb Fichte (1762–1814). German; formulated a philosophy of absolute idealism based on Kant's ethical concepts.

19th Century

Georg Wilhelm Friedrich Hegel (1770–1831). German; his metaphysical system, known as Hegelianism, was rationalist and absolutist, based on the belief that thought and being are one, and nature is the manifestation of an Absolute Idea.

Arthur Schopenhauer (1788–1860). German who gave the will a leading place in his metaphysics. The foremost expounder of pessimism, expressed in *The World as Will and Idea*. Rejected absolute idealism as wishful thinking, and taught that the only tenable attitude lay in utter indifference to an irrational world; an idealist who held that the highest ideal was nothingness.

Auguste Comte (1798–1857). French founder of positivism, a system which denied transcendant metaphysics and stated that the Divinity

f.

h.

i.

k.

l.

g.

j.

and man were one, that altruism is man's highest duty, and that scientific principles explain all phenomena.

John Stuart Mill (1806–73). English; major exponent of Utilitarianism, who differed from Bentham by recognizing differences in quality as well as quantity in pleasure. Most famous work *On Liberty* (1859).

Søren Kierkegaard (1813–55). Danish religious existentialist, whose thought is the basis of modern (atheistic) existentialism; taught that 'existence precedes essence' that only existence has reality, and the individual has a unique value.

Karl Marx (1818–83). German revolutionist, from whom the movement known as Marxism derives its name and many of its ideas; his works became, in the late 19th century, the basis of European socialism; published *The Communist Manifesto* with Friedrich Engels in 1848.

Herbert Spencer (1820–1903). English evolutionist whose 'synthetic philosophy' interpreted all phenomena according to the principle of evolutionary progress.

Charles S Pierce (1839–1914). American physicist and mathematician who founded philosophical school called pragmatism; regarded logic as the basis of philosophy and taught that the test of an idea is whether it works.

William James (1842–1910). American psychologist and pragmatist who held that reality is always in the making and that each man should choose the philosophy best suited to him.

Friedrich Wilhelm Nietzsche (1844–1900). German philosopher and poet. An evolutionist who held that the 'will to power' is basic in life, that the spontaneous is to be preferred to the orderly; attacked Christianity as a system that fostered the weak, whereas the function of evolution is to evolve 'supermen'.

20th Century

Edmund Husserl (1859–1938). German who developed a system called 'phenomenology', which asserts that realities other than mere appearance exist – called essences.

Henri Bergson (1859–1941). French evolutionist who asserted the existence of a 'vital impulse' that carries the universe forward, with no fixed beginning and no fixed end – the future is determined by the choice of alternatives made in the present.

John Dewey (1859–1952). American; basically a pragmatist, he developed a system known as instrumentalism. Saw man as continuous with but distinct from nature.

Alfred North Whitehead (1861–1947). British evolutionist and mathematician who held that reality must not be interpreted in atomistic terms, but in terms of events; that God is intimately present in the universe, yet distinct from it, a view called panentheism, as opposed to pantheism, which simply equates God and Nature.

George Santayana (1863–1952). American born in Spain; a foremost critical realist who held that the ultimate substance of the world is matter in motion – and the mind itself is a product of matter in motion.

Benedetto Croce (1866–1952). The best-known Italian philosopher of 20th century. Noted for his role in revival of historical realism in Italy 1900–1920.

Bertrand Russell (1872–1970). British agnostic who adhered to many systems of philosophy before becoming chief expounder of scientism, the view that all knowledge is solely attainable by the scientific method.

George Edward Moore (1873–1958). Rigorous British moral scientist. Developed doctrine of Ideal Utilitarianism in *Principia Ethica*, 1903.

Karl Jaspers (1883–1969). German existentialist who approached the subject from man's practical concern with his own existence.

Ludwig Wittgenstein (1889–1951). Austrian; developed the philosophy of language.

Martin Heidegger (1889–1976). German student of Husserl, he furthered development of phenomenology and greatly influenced atheistic existentialists.

Friedrich von Hayek (b. 1899). Austrian economist and philosopher. Argues that social science must not try to ape the method of physics. What can be predicted and used for analysis is an abstract pattern which leaves the details unspecified.

Karl Popper (b. 1902). British of Austrian extraction. Exponent of critical rationalism arguing that scientific laws can never be proved to be true; the most that can be claimed is that they have survived attempts to disprove them. Writer from liberal and individualistic standpoint.

Jean-Paul Sartre (1905–1980). French; developed existentialist thought of Heidegger; atheistic supporter of a subjective, irrational human existence, as opposed to an orderly overall reality.

Alfred J. Ayer (b. 1910). British, principal advocate of logical positivism, a modern extension of the thinking of Hume and Comte.

Religion

Religions of The World

(estimates in millions)

Christian	1056
Roman Catholic	*621*
Eastern Orthodox	*65*
Protestant	*369*
Muslim (Islam)	555
Hindu	462
Buddhist	251
Confucian	163
Shinto	33
Taoist	20
Jewish	17·3

The main religions of the world below are listed in order of their chronological appearance.

Judaism

The word Jew is derived through the Latin *Judaeus*, from the Hebrew *Yehudhi*, signifying a descendant of Judah, the fourth son of Jacob whose tribe, with that of his half brother, Benjamin, made up the peoples of the kingdom of Judah. This kingdom was separate from the remaining tribes of Israel. The exodus of the Israelites from Egypt is believed to have occurred *c.* 1400 BC.

Judaism is monotheistic and based on the covenant that Israel is the bearer of the belief in the one and only God.

From 311 until 1790 Jews existed under severe disabilities and discrimination in most Christian and Moslem areas. Jewish emancipation began with the enfranchisement of Jews in France in Sept. 1791. This touched off antisemitism which in return fired Zionism. The first Zionist Congress was held in Basle, Switzerland, in Aug. 1897.

The Balfour letter written on 2 Nov. 1917 by Arthur Balfour, British foreign secretary, addressed to Lord Rothschild declared 'His Majesty's Government view with favour the establishment of Palestine as a natural home for the Jewish people. . . .'

On 24 July 1922 the League of Nations approved a British mandate over Palestine. These policies led to bitter Arab resistance which revolts in 1929 and 1936–39 claiming the right of self-determination. The irreconcilable aims of Arab nationalism and Zionism led to partition with the creation of Israel (*q.v.*) on 14 May 1948 and the internationalizing of Jerusalem.

There are over 25 000 Thalessa Jews living in Ethiopia and the Horn of Africa.

Jewish holidays including *Pesach* (Passover), celebrating the Exodus, *Shabuoth* (Pentecost), *Rosh Hashana* (New Year) and *Yom Kippur* (Day of Atonement) devoted to fasting, meditation and prayer.

Yiddish, an Eastern Vernacular form of mediaeval German, is unrelated to Semitic Hebrew.

Hinduism

The precise date of the origin of Hinduism, or Sanatān-Dharma (ancient way of life) or Arya-Dharma (Aryan way of life) is not known, although the early Indus and Gangetic civilisations (approx: 3500 BC) may have made some contributions. There are no beliefs common to all Hindus and Hinduism is indeed very diverse for it covers 'Bhakti' (devotion) as well as 'Gyān' (knowledge). The Hindu caste system originally started as division of labour, but later, especially during non-Hindu domination it became very rigid. The Vedas (divine or sacred knowledge) was passed on by the Rishis and Munis (learned sages) to the people in the form of Mantras (Sanskrit verses). Brahma, Vishnu and Shiva represent Creation, preservation and destruction. To be reunited either with the Nirākār (form-less) or Sākār (with form), depending upon one's choice, one could either follow the path of devotion (Bhakti) or knowledge (Gyān) or a mixture of both.

The living status in the next life, if any, is determined by Karma (actions) in present life. When one's Karma are righteous, then, upon death there is unity with the supreme, and Moksha (freedom) from the birth and death cycle. If the way of life is not righteous, the birth and death cycle continues. Life is divided into (1) Brahmacharya (celibate period) (2) Grahastha (householder) (3) Vānprastha (retired stage) (4) Sanyās (renunciation).

Hinduism is not an organised religion. There is absolute freedom with regard to the choice and mode of one's philosophy. It is understood that while choosing one's own philosophy one has to follow basic human rules which are universal and can be summed up in an ancient Sanskrit phrase 'Vasudhaiv Kutumbakam' which means 'the whole world is one family'.

Hinduism and the problems within the present social system of the Hindus are entirely separate matters. Gandhian 'Ahimsa' (non-violence) was inspired by the Hindu philosophy as well. Generally speaking the Hindu philosophy could be summed up in the following translated verse (original in Sanskrit) from the ancient 'Bhagvad-Gītā' 'One has control over one's actions but not over the results'.

The recent interest in Hindu culture and philosophy in Europe and America, e.g. The International Society for Krishna Consciousness, or various other organisations is a modern facet of Hinduism, absolutely without any parallel in its entire history.

Buddhism

Buddhism is based on the teaching of the Indian prince, Siddhartha (later called Gautama) (*c.* 563–483 BC) of the Gautama clan of the Sakyas, later named Gautama Buddha (*buddha* meaning 'the enlightened one'). Aśoka, a 3rd Century BC King of Magadha [Gonyes] is regarded as a progenitor of Buddhism. After seeing in *c.* 534 BC for the first time a sick man, an old man, a holy man and a dead man, he wandered fruitlessly for six years, after which he meditated for 49 days under a Bodhi tree at Gaya in Magadha. He achieved enlightenment or *nirvana* and taught salvation in Bihar, west of Bengal, until he died, aged 80. Gautama's teaching was essentially a protesting offshoot of early Hinduism. It contains four Noble Truths: (1) Man suffers from one life to the next; (2) the Origin of suffering is craving; craving for pleasure, possessions and the cessation of pain; (3) the cure for craving is non-attachment to all things including self; (4) the way to non-attachment is the Eight-fold path of right conduct, right effort, right intentions, right livelihood, right meditations, right mindfulness, right speech and right views.

Buddhism makes no provisions for God and hence has no element of divine judgement or messianic expectation. It provides an inexorable law or *dharma* of cause and effect which determines the individual's fate.

The vast body or *sangha* of monks and nuns practise celibacy, non-violence, poverty and vegetarianism. Under the *Hinayana*, or Lesser Vehicle, tradition of India only they have hope of attaining *nirvana*. Under the *Mahayana*, or Greater Vehicle, as practised in Indo-China, China and Japan, laymen as well may attain the highest ideal of *bodhisattva*, the enlightened one who liberates himself by personal sacrifice. Under Zen Buddhism enlightenment or *satori* is achieved only by prolonged meditation and mental and physical shock.

Confucianism

Confucius (551–479 BC) was not the sole founder of Confucianism but was rather a member of the founding group of *Ju* or meek ones. Confucius is the Latinized version of K'ung Fu-tzo or Master K'ung who was a keeper of accounts from the province of Lu. He became the first teacher in Chinese history to instruct the people of all ranks in the six arts: ceremonies, music, archery, charioteering, history and numbers.

Confucius taught that the main ethic is *jen* (benevolence), and that truth involves the knowledge of one's own faults. He believed in altruism and insisted on filial piety. He decided that people could be led by example and aimed at the rulers of his own time imitating those in a former period of history, where he attributed the prosperity of the people to the leadership of the Emperors. Confucianism included the worship of Heaven and revered ancestors and great men, though Confucius himself did not advocate prayer, believing that man should direct his own destiny.

Confucianism can be better described as a religious philosophy or code of social behaviour, rather than a religion in the accepted sense, since it has no church or clergy and is in no way an institution. For many years it had a great hold over education, its object being to emphasize the development of human nature and the person. During the early 19th century attempts were made by followers to promote Confucianism to being a state religion, and though this failed, a good deal of the Confucian teachings still remain despite the onslaught of Communist ideology in the traditional area of its influence.

Christianity

The religion Christianity takes its name from Jesus Christ*, son of the Virgin Mary, whose subsequent husband, Joseph of Nazareth, was 27 generations descended from David. His birth is now regarded as occurring at Bethlehem in the summer of 4 BC or earlier. The discrepancy is due to an error in the 6th century by Dionysius Exiguus in establishing the dating of the Christian era.

The principles of Christianity are proclaimed in the New Testament which was written in Syriac-Aramaic and of which the earliest complete surviving manuscript dates from AD *c.* 350.

Christ was crucified in the reign of the Roman emperor Tiberius during the procuratorship in Judaea of Pontius Pilate in AD 29 or according to the Roman Catholic chronology, 7 April, AD 30.

The primary commandment of Jesus was to believe in God, and to love Him. His second commandment (Mark xii, 31) was to 'love thy neighbour' in a way that outward performance alone did not suffice.

Hate was prohibited and not only adultery but evil lust (Matt. v, 21).

Unselfishness and compassion are central themes in Christianity.

Jesus appointed twelve disciples; the following are common to the lists in the books of Matthew, Mark, Luke and the Acts.

1. Peter, Saint Peter (brother of Andrew).
2. Andrew, Saint Andrew (brother of Peter).
3. James, son of Zebedee (brother of John).
4. John, Saint John (the Apostle) (brother of James).
5. Philip.
6. Bartholomew.
7. Thomas.
8. Matthew, Saint Matthew.
9. James, of Alphaeus.
10. Simon the Canaanean (in Matthew and Mark) or Simon Zelotes (in Luke and the Acts).

11. Judas Iscariot (not an apostle).

Thaddaeus in the book of Matthew and Mark is the twelfth disciple, while in Luke and the Acts the twelfth is Judas of James. The former may have been a nickname or place name to distinguish Judas of James from the Iscariot. Matthias succeeded to the place of the betrayer Judas Iscariot.

* Jesus (the Saviour, from Hebrew root *yasha'*, to 'save') Christ (the anointed one, from Greek, Χριω, *chrio*, to anoint).

Roman Catholicism

Roman Catholic Christianity is that practised by those who acknowledge the supreme jurisdiction of the bishop of Rome (the Pope) and recognize him as the lawful successor of St. Peter who was appointed by Christ Himself to be head of the church. Peter visited Rome *c.* AD 42 and was martyred there *c.* AD 67. Pope John Paul II is his 263rd successor.

The Roman Catholic Church claims catholicity inasmuch as she was charged (*de jure*) by Christ to 'teach all nations' and *de facto* since her adherents are by far the most numerous among Christians. The Roman Catholic Church is regarded as the infallible interpreter both of the written (5 of the 12 apostles wrote) and the unwritten word of God. The organization of the Church is the Curia, the work of which is done by 11 permanent departments or congregations.

The great majority of Catholics are of the Roman rite and use the Roman liturgy. While acknowledging the hierarchical supremacy of the Holy See other Eastern Churches or Uniate Rites enjoy an autonomy. These include (1) the Byzantine or Greek rite, (2) the Armenian rite, and (3) the Coptic rite.

The doctrine of the Immaculate Conception was proclaimed on 8 Dec. 1854, and that of Papal Infallibility was adopted by the Ecumenical Council by 547 votes to 2 on 18 July 1870. The 21st Council was convened by Pope John XXIII. The election of Popes is by the College Cardinals.

Eastern Orthodox

The church officially described as 'The Holy Orthodox Catholic Apostolic Eastern Church' consists of those churches which accepted all the decrees of the first seven General Councils and such churches as have since sprung up in that tradition.

The origin arises from the splitting of the old Roman Empire into a Western or Latin half, centred on Rome, and an Eastern or Greek half, centred on Constantinople.

The Orthodox Church has no creed or dogma. Some features of this branch of Christianity are that bishops must be unmarried; the dogma of the immaculate conception is not admitted; icons are in the churches but the only 'graven image' is the crucifix; and fasts are frequent and rigorous.

Protestant

The term 'protestant' had never been used officially in the style of any church until the Anglican community in North America called themselves the 'Protestant Episcopal Church' during the 17th century. The name has never been officially used by the Church of England.

Islam (Mohammedanism)

Islām is the world's second largest religion with its emphasis on an uncompromising monotheism and a strict adherence to certain religious practices. It belongs to the Semitic family and was founded by Muhammad (Mohammed or Mahomet) (AD 575–632) and on 16 July AD 622 at Yathrib, now known as Al Madīnah, (Medina) in Saudi Arabia.

Muhammad, a member of the Koreish tribe, was a caravan conductor and later became a shop-keeper in Mekkah (Mecca). There is some evidence that he was semi-literate, at least in early manhood. He did not become a public preacher until 616. Soon after 622 [AH (anno Hegirae or the year of exile) 1] Muhammad turned the direction of his prayer southward from Jerusalem and an Israeli God to the pagan temple at Mecca and the God Allah. Muhammad soon became an administrator, general, judge and legislator in addition to being one through whom divine revelation was communicated.

The Arabic term *islām* literally meaning 'surrender' points to the fundamental religious idea of Islām namely that the believer, called a Muslim, accepts 'surrender to the Will of Allāh', who is viewed as the unique God. The Will of Allah is made known through the Qur'ān (Koran), the Book revealed to his messenger Muhammad. The basic belief of Islām is expressed in the *Shahādah*, the Muslim confession of faith: 'There is no God but Allah and Muhammad is his Prophet!' From this fundamental belief are derived beliefs in (1) angels, (particularly Gabriel), (2) the revealed Books (Jewish, Christian, Zoroastrian and Hindu in addition to the Qur'ān), (3) a series of prophets and (4) the Last Day, the Day of Judgement. Acceptance of this essential creed involves further duties that are to be strictly observed: five daily prayer sessions, a welfare tax called the zakāt, fasting during the month of Ramadān and a pilgrimage (*hajj*) to Mecca, all of which – including the profession of faith – are called the Five Pillars. Ramadān is the ninth month of the Muslim lunar calendar.

Shī'ism and Sunnism are the two main forms of Islām, others being Sufism, Mu'tazilah, Khārijism and other minor forms. Although the majority of Muslims are Sunnis, the Shī'ah (who number only about 40 000 000) are the most important surviving sect (the population of Iran is about 93% Shī'i). Shī'ism has exerted a great influence on Sunni Islām, although their doctrines differ greatly. Besides the main body of Twelver (Ithnā 'Asharīyah) Shī'ah, Shī'ism has produced a variety of extremist sects, the most conspicuous being the Ismā'īlī.

Though the sheer variety of races and cultures embraced by Islām has produced differences, all segments of Muslim society are bound by a common faith and a sense of belonging to a single community. With the loss of political power during the period of Western colonialism in the 19th and early 20th centuries, the concept of the Islāmic community, instead of weakening, became stronger. This, in harness with the discovery of immense oil reserves, helped various Muslim peoples in their struggle to gain political freedom and sovereignty in the mid-20th century.

Shinto

Shintō ('the teaching' or 'the way of the gods') came into practice during the 6th century AD to distinguish the Japanese religion from Buddhism which was reaching the islands by way of the mainland. The early forms of Shintō were a simple nature worship, and a religion for those who were not impelled by any complicated religious lore. The help of the deities was sought for the physical and spiritual needs of the people and there was great stress laid upon purification and truthfulness.

The more important national shrines were dedicated to well-known national figures, but there were also those set up for the worship of deities of mountain and forest.

During the 19th century, thirteen Sect Shintō denominations were formed and these were dependent on private support for their teaching and organization. They have very little in common and varied widely in beliefs and practices. Some adhered to the traditional Shintō deites while others did not. Of the 13 denominations *Tenrikyō* is the one with the greatest following outside Japan.

Theories of Shintō have been greatly influenced by Confucianism, Taoism and Buddhism. In 1868, however, the Department of Shintō was established and attempts were made to do away with the Shintō and Buddhist coexistence, and in 1871 Shintō was proclaimed the Japanese national religion. Following World War II the status was discontinued.

Taoism

Lao-tzu (Lao-tze or Lao-tse), the Chinese philosopher and founder of Taoism, was, according to tradition, born in the sixth century BC. Lao-tzu taught that Taoism (Tao = the Ultimate and Unconditioned Being) could be attained by virtue if thrift, humility and compassion were practised.

Taoism has the following features – numerous gods (though Lao-tzu did not himself permit this); a still persisting, though now decreasing, body of superstition; and two now declining schools – the 13th-century Northern School with its emphasis on man's life, and the Southern School, probably of 10th century origin, stressing the nature of man. Various Taoist societies have been formed more recently by laymen, who though worshipping deities of many religions, promote charity and a more moral culture. The moral principles of Taoism consist of simplicity, patience, contentment and harmony. Since the decline of its espousal by the T'ang dynasty (AD 618–906), it has proved to be chiefly the religion of the semi-literate.

Philosophical Taoism or Tao-chia advocates naturalism and is thus opposed to regulations and organization of any kind. After the 4th century BC when Buddhism and Taoism began to influence each other there was a weakening of this anti-collectivist strain but the philosophy still has a strong hold over the way of life and culture in parts of China.

The religion imitates Buddhism in the matter of clergy and temple, the chief of which is the White Cloud temple in Peking, China.

Art and Architecture

Drawing is the process of artistic depiction on a two-dimensional surface by linear (and sometimes tonal) means, of objects or abstractions.

Painting is the visual and aesthetic expression of ideas and emotions primarily in two dimensions, using colour, line, shapes, texture and tones.

Sculpture describes the processes of carving, or engraving, modelling and casting so as to produce representations or abstraction of an artistic nature in relief, in intaglio, or in the round.

PALAEOLITHIC ART
from 24 000 BC
Cave painting of the Perigordian (Aurignacian period) and the later Solutrean and Magdalenian periods (18 000–11 000 BC) first discovered at Chaffaud, Vienne, France in 1834. Lascaux examples discovered 1940. Cave painting also discovered in Czechoslovakia, the Urals, USSR, India, Australia (Mootwingie dates from c. 1500 BC) and North Africa (earliest is from the Bubulus period in the Sahara *post* 5400 BC).

MESOPOTAMIAN ART 3600–600 BC
Covering the Sumerian, Assyrian and Babylonian epochs, it is epitomised by many styles which incorporate figures, animals, plants and mythical animals. Is seen now mainly in the sculptural works on palaces (Nineveh) and on tiles.

EGYPTIAN ART (3100–341 BC)
It is essentially a decorative tomb art, based on the notion of immortality, and provided that a deceased was recorded and equipped for the after-life in writing (heiroglyph), pictures and material wealth and goods.

ANCIENT GREEK 2000–27 BC
Minoan and Mycenaean art (2800–1100 BC) consists mainly of sculptured engravings, decorated pottery and some frescoes. The Archaic period (800–500 BC) saw the development of sculpture, especially human figures. This tendency was developed in the Classical period (500–323 BC) where the body was glorified and drapery carved to imitate movement. The Hellenistic period (323–27 BC) expressed the emotions and was noticeable for its portraits. Throughout the entire period pottery was decorated with figures and scenes from story and legend.

ROMAN ART (100 BC – 400 AD)
Based on Greek art, it excelled in copying Greek sculpture and relief carving of a very high quality. Portraiture also was popular. Roman painting was mainly executed in fresco in a naturalistic style (Pompeii). Mosaic floors were also highly decorative.

EARLY CHRISTIAN AD 200
Funerary fresco painting in the Roman catacombs ended with Constantine.

MIGRATION PERIOD 150–1000
A general term covering the art of the Huns with strong Asian influence and the Revised post-Roman Celtic art in Ireland and Britain, the pre-Carolingian Frankish art and the art of the Vikings.

BYZANTINE ART c. 330–c. 1450
At first an admixture of Hellenic, Roman, Middle Eastern and Oriental styles, it dates from and has its first centre in the establishment of Constantinople as capital of the Roman Empire in the East. The First Golden Age was reached in the 6th century, when Hagia Sophia (St Sophia) was built in the city. The Second Golden Age occurred between 1051 and 1185 when Western Europe was influenced by its severe, spiritually uplifted style. These two Ages are chiefly artistically dominated by the use of mosaic work, but by the Third Golden Age (1261–1450) this expensive medium was being replaced by fresco painting.

ISLAMIC ART 7th century–17th century
Originally based on superb Koranic calligraphy, it is a highly decorative art form which reaches its apotheosis in the miniature painting, the ceramic tile, and carpetmaking in which floral and geometric motives reach a high peak of formal perfection.

ROMANESQUE ART 1050–1200
A widespread European style, mainly architectural, distinguished by the use of rounded arches. The sculpture is mainly church work intended to inspire awe of the divine power by depicting scenes of heaven and hell, demons and angels and the omnipotent deity. Illuminated manuscripts of high quality include the Winchester Bible.

GOTHIC ART (1125–1450)
The style of architecture, painting and sculpture which succeeded Romanesque art in Europe. The first Gothic building was St Denis, outside Paris, which differed from the previous style mainly by having ribbed vaulting to its roofs which were held up by pointed arches. The sculpture is narrative and realistic, in painting the style evolved more slowly and is seen in manuscripts, which developed into the most decorative style seen in International Gothic.

INTERNATIONAL GOTHIC c. 1380–c. 1470
A mixture of styles of painting and sculpture in Europe due to the movements of notable peripatetic artists and the increase in trade, travel and court rivalry. The main influences were Northern France, The Netherlands and Italy, and its main features are rich and decorative colouring and detail, and flowing line.

THE RENAISSANCE c. 1435–1545
Meaning 'rebirth', the term describes the revival of classical learning and art. At first centred in Florence, it marked the end of the Middle Ages and was probably the outstanding creative period in the history of the arts. Architecture, painting, sculpture, deriving from Greek and Roman models, moved into an unparalleled vigour and prominence, and the artist gained a role in society hitherto unknown, mainly due to the rival city states that employed them. Artistic invention included perspective and painting with oil. Latterly, the Renaissance style moved towards Mannerism.

MANNERISM c. 1520–1700
A style emerging from the Renaissance, it exaggerated the styles of Michaelangelo and Raphael into contorted and extravagantly gestured figures, to achieve a more intense emotional effect. This style influenced the later Baroque movement.

THE BAROQUE c. 1600–1720
Centred on the new stability of the Roman Catholic faith, its main artistic aim was to unite the main parts of building, sculpture and painting into an overall dramatic effect. It is mainly 'frontal', that is it is best seen from one, rather than many, viewpoints. Its exuberance and monumentality make it one of the most robust movements in art history.

ROCOCO c. 1735–65
A mainly French style, it is characterised by a wealth of elaborate and superficial decoration. Elegance was the keynote and Rococo reflected the extravagance and brilliance of Court Life.

NEO-CLASSICISM (c. 1750–1850)
More of a discipline than a movement, it expresses the qualities of harmony, clarity and order associated with Greek and Roman art. The antithesis of Romanticism, it espouses accepted notions of beauty and rejects individual inspiration.

ROMANTICISM c. 1780–1850
A mainly literary movement, it was a reaction to Classicism and the growing Industrial Revolution. Deriving its inspiration from untamed nature, the Romantic belief centred on the importance of spontaneity of individual feeling towards the natural world.

THE PRE-RAPHAELITE BROTHERHOOD 1848–1856
A brotherhood of seven London artists formed to make a return to the pre-Raphael (hence the name) Italian forms as a protest against the frivolity of the prevailing English School of the day. The founders and most important demonstrators of the style were William Holman Hunt, John Everett Millais and Dante Gabriel Rossetti.

ARTS AND CRAFTS MOVEMENT c. 1870–1900
Based on the revival of interest in the mediaeval craft system led by William Morris, its aims were to fuse the functional and the decorative, and to restore the worth of handmade crafts in the face of the growing mass-produced wares of the late 19th century.

SYMBOLISM c. 1880–1905
Influenced by the Pre-Raphaelites and the Romantics, it was a movement that provided an intellectual alternative to the straight visual work of the Impressionists. Its twin sources were either literary or pictorially formal and the results were intended to engage the emotions. Symbolism influenced the Surrealists and was the forerunner of Expressionist and abstract art.

IMPRESSIONISM 1875–1886
The term was inadvertently introduced by the journalist Leroy in *Charivari* to describe the work of Monet, Sisley, Pissarro and others, taking the name from Monet's *Impression: Soleil levant*. The painters in this manner were concerned with light and its effects, and the use of 'broken' colour.

POINTILLISM c. 1880–1915
Based on the colour theories of Chevreul, its aim was to achieve greater pictorial luminosity by placing small marks of pure primary colour on the surface, allowing them to merge at a viewing distance to create an optical mixture. Sometimes called Divisionism.

POST-IMPRESSIONISM c. 1880–1910
Term used to describe any breakaway tendencies from pure impressionism that took place during the period, and embraces Pointillism and the beginnings of Expressionism, especially the works of Gauguin, Van Gogh and Cézanne.

ART NOUVEAU c. 1890–1915
A decorative style deriving from the Arts and Crafts movement of the UK, it is represented by two streams, one of fluid asymmetry and flowing linear rhythms inspired by nature, the other of a geometrical austerity. Called Jugendstil (Germany) and Sezessionstil (Austria).

20th century forms

FAUVISM c. 1905–7
A short-lived but highly influential French movement of artists surrounding Matisse, it is summarised by the daring and spontaneous handling of paint in bold, brilliant, sometimes non-representational colour, in a subjective,

joyous response to the visual world. 'Fauve' means 'wild beast', a critic's response to seeing paintings by Matisse and others at the 1905 Salon d'Automne.

DIE BRUCKE (The Bridge) c. 1905–13
A group of German Expressionist artists, including Kirchner, whose manifesto was to overthrow the concept of art as an end in itself and to integrate art and life by using art as a means of communication. Influenced by tribal art and Van Gogh, the founders lived and worked communally, forcing the intensity of their work by using clashing colours and aggressive distortions.

EXPRESSIONISM c. 1905–25
Used loosely, a term that denotes an emphasis on pictorial distortion or chromatic exaggeration within a work of art of any given period. More specifically it is used to define certain 20th century North European art where the emphasis is on stress or heightened emotion, as portrayed through the artists' subjective vision. Influenced by Gauguin, Van Gogh, Munch and Fauvism, the movement includes the most specific groups of Die Brucke and Der Blaue Reiter.

CUBISM c. 1907–23
The style formulated from investigations by Picasso and Braque into Cezanne's late works and African tribal sculpture. The first painting to combine these influences was Picasso's 'Les Demoiselles d'Avignon'. The term 'Cubist' was coined by a French critic on seeing Braque's work in that style of 1908. 'Analytic' (early) Cubism presents the subject from a variety of viewpoints: 'Synthetic' (late) Cubism introduced decorative elements such as lettering and applied materials such as newspaper (collage) to achieve a balance between the depiction of reality and the picture as an object in its own right. The movement had many followers, but in a few years Picasso and Braque moved away from it to independent paths.

FUTURISM c. 1909–19
Initially a literary movement, its manifesto concerned itself with incorporating the thrust of modern technology with art. Anti art-establishment, it approached abstract art, especially cubism, to express its dynamism. Its founder-member Marinetti described speed as 'a new form of beauty'.

SCHOOL OF PARIS c. 1910–50
Term used to distinguish the large international group of Paris-based artists which made the city the centre of the Art World until the emergence of the New York School.

DER BLAUE REITER (the Blue Rider) c. 1911–14
A loosely-knit group of Expressionist painters including Kandinsky, Klee and Marc, united by a dictum of Kandinsky that stated 'the creative spirit is concealed within matter'.

DADA c. 1915–23
A total rejection of established values; anti-aesthetic and anti-rational, by European and American artists, sculptors and photographers.

BAUHAUS c. 1919–33
A post-First World War resolution to re-integrate the disparate visual arts and crafts within the discipline of architecture, function dictating the form. It exerted, and still exerts a profound influence on 20th century architecture and crafts.

SURREALISM c. 1924–
A French avant-garde movement of literary origin inspired by Dada, and greatly influenced by Freud's theories of psychoanalysis. Irrational association, spontaneous techniques and an elimination of premeditation to free the workings of the unconscious mind, as well as an interest in dreams, were the main motivations of its practitioners.

KINETIC ART c. 1930–
A term which broadly covers art which incorporates movement, in the work in space, generated by air currents, motors, artificial lights, etc.

ABSTRACT IMPRESSIONISM c. 1940–
Placing emphasis on spontaneous personal expression, it rejects contemporary, social and aesthetic values. Recognised as the first movement in the USA to develop independently of and actually influence Europe. Notable practitioners include Jackson Pollock and De Kooning. Includes Action Painting (USA), and Tachisme (Europe).

NEW YORK SCHOOL c. 1945–60
A group of avant-garde artists whose aim was to find a uniquely American mode of expression. The group included such artists as Pollock, De Kooning and Rothko.

OP ART c. 1950–
An abstract art that bases itself on creating optical effects which appear to move on a flat surface.

POP ART c. 1955–
A reaction against Abstract Expressionism, the movement started almost simultaneously in UK and USA and uses the images of mass media, advertising and pop culture, presenting the common, everyday object as art.

MINIMAL ART c. 1960–
A rejection of the aesthetic qualities of art in favour of the physical reality of the art object. The material used is important, as are their strictly geometrical formats and placings within settings. A famous (some might say, notorious) example was Andre's *Equivalent VIII*, 120 firebricks arranged in a solid rectangle on the Tate Gallery floor in 1966.

Media

ACRYLIC RESIN
A quick-drying waterproof emulsion that can be mixed with dry pigments to give paints that can be applied with heavy knife-laid impasto or diluted with water to wash-like consistency.

ETCHING
The process of biting out a design on a metal plate with acid, so that the resultant indentations hold ink, which will subsequently print the image onto paper.

FRESCO
(Ital.: *fresco*, fresh.) Developed by Minoan and other ancient civilisations. *Buon fresco* is executed with pigments ground in water or lime-water on to a freshly prepared lime-plaster wall while the plaster is still damp.

GOUACHE
A water-colour painting carried out with opaque colours as opposed to pure water colour which employs transparent colours.

INKS
Liquids for drawing or painting; generally the colours are in suspension or present as a dye. Sometimes, as with Indian ink or white ink, there may be opaque pigments in suspension. Inks may be applied with different types of pen or soft hair brushes.

INTAGLIO
Any method where a metal plate is bitten into, etched or cut to hold ink for a design to be printed from it. Engraving, Drypoint, Etching, Aquatint and Mezzotint fall into this category.

LITHOGRAPHY
Planar printing method where design is drawn on limestone or metal plate with greasy ink or crayon. The surface is then wetted; the ink applied to it adheres only to the greasy part, the wetted part repelling it. A print is then taken from the surface.

MONOTYPE
Single print taken from a design painted on a flat surface while the paint is still wet.

OIL
Dry pigments ground in an oil; this is generally linseed, but may be poppy, walnut or other similar oils. It is a technique that gradually evolved during the latter part of the Middle Ages. The Van Eyck brothers did much to perfect the medium.

PASTEL
A stick of colour made from powdered pigment bound with gum. Applied dry to paper the colours can be blended and mixed but the result can be fragile and impermanent unless fixed with spray varnish (fixative).

TEMPERA
A loose term in painting in which the dry pigments are mixed with such substances as egg white, egg yolk, glue, gelatine or casein. True tempera is when the colours are ground with egg yolk only.

WATER COLOUR
Pigments are ground with gum arabic and thinned in use with water. The technique as used today started with Albrecht Dürer but did not achieve widespread use until the emergence of the English School of water-colourists in the first half of the 19th century. Applied with squirrel or sable brushes on white or tinted paper.

WOODCUT
Design incised on wood, the grain of which runs lengthwise. The negative areas are cut away, leaving the raised design to take ink, from which is taken the paper print. The Japanese perfected this medium.

WOOD ENGRAVING
As in woodcut, except that the printing surface is on the end grain of the wood block, allowing fine detail to be cut with a graver or burin. Extensively used in book illustration until the invention of photo-mechanical engraving.

Renowned painters by country

Some of the world's most renowned painters with well-known examples of their work.

AUSTRALIA
Nolan, Sidney (b. 1917) *Themes from the Career of Ned Kelly.*

AUSTRIA
Klimt, Gustav (1862–1918) *Mosaic mural for the Palais Stoclet in Brussels.*
Kokoschka, Oskar (b. 1886) *View of the Thames.*
Schiele, Egon (1890–1918) *The Artist's Mother Sleeping.*

BELGIUM
Brueghel, Pieter (The Elder) (c. 1525–69) *The Adoration of the Kings, The Peasant Dance.*
Ensor, James (1860–1949) *Entry of Christ into Brussels.*
Gossaert, Jan (c. 1478–1533) *Adoration.*
Jordaens, Jacob (1593–1678) *The Bean King.*
Magritte, Rene (1898–1967) *The Key of Dreams.*
Memlinc, Hans (c. 1430–94) *Mystic Marriage of St. Catherine.*
Rubens, Peter Paul (1577–1640) *Adoration of the Magi, Battle of the Amazons.*
Teniers, David (The Younger) (1610–90) *Peasants Playing Bowls.*
Van der Weyden, Rogier (c. 1400–64) *Deposition, The Magdalen Reading.*
Van Dyck, Anthony (1599–1641) *Charles I of England, Elena Grimaldi-Cattaneo.*

Van Dyck, Hubert (*c.* 1370–*c.* 1426) Jan (*c.* 1390–1441) *Ghent Altarpiece, The Three Mary's at the Open Sepulchre.* Jan alone *The Arnolfini Marriage, Adoration of the Lamb.*

CZECHOSLOVAKIA
Kupka, Frank (Frantisek) (1871–1957) *Amorpha, fugue in two colours.*

FRANCE
Arp, Hans (Jean) (1887–1966) *Berger et Nuage.*
Bonnard, Pierre (1867–1947) *The Window.*
Boucher, François (1703–70) *Diana Bathing.*
Braque, Georges (1882–1963) *Vase of Anemones.*
Cézanne, Paul (1839–1906) *Mont Sainte-Victoire, Bathers.*
Chagall, Marc (1887–1985) *I and the Village, Calvary.*
Chardin, Jean-Baptiste Siméon (1699–1779) *The Skate, The Lesson.*
Corot, Jean-Baptiste Camille (1796–1875) *Ponte de Mantes, Sens Cathedral.*
Courbet, Gustave (1819–77) *A Burial at Ornans.*
Daumier, Honoré (1808–79) *The Third-Class Carriage.*
David, Jacques Louis (1748–1825) *The Rape of the Sabines.*
Degas, Hilaire-Germain-Edgar (1834–1917) *La Danseuse au Bouquet.*
Delacroix, Eugène (1798–1863) *The Massacre of Chios.*
Derain, André (1880–1954) *Mountains at Collioure.*
Fouquet, Jean (*c.* 1420–*c.* 1480) *Etienne Chevalier with St Stephen.*
Fragonard, Jean-Honoré (1732–1806) *The Love Letter, Baigneuses.*
Gauguin, Paul (1848–1903) *Ta Matete.*
Gellée, Claude (called Claude Lorraine) (1600–82) *Ascanius and the Stag.*
Gericault, Theodore (1791–1824) *The Raft of the Medusa.*
Ingres, Jean-Auguste Dominique (1780–1867) *Odalisque.*
La Tour, George de (1593–1652) *St. Sebastian tended by the Holy Women.*
Leger, Fernand (1881–1955) *Three Women.*
Lorraine, Claude (1600–82) *Embarkation of St Ursula.*
Manet, Edouard (1823–83) *Déjeuner sur l'Herbe.*
Matisse, Henri (1869–1954) *Odalisque.*
Millet, Jean-François (1814–75) *Man with the Hoe, Angelus.*
Monet, Claude (1840–1926) *Rouen Cathedral, Water-lilies.*
Pissarro, Camille (1830–1903) *The Harvest, Montfoucault.*
Poussin, Nicholas (1593/4–1665) *Worship of the Golden Calf.* (Damaged Mar. 1978)
Renoir, Pierre Auguste (1841–1919) *Luncheon of the Boating Party.*
Rouault, Georges (1871–1958) *Christ Mocked.*
Rousseau, Henri Julien ('Le Douanier') (1844–1910) *The Dream.*
Seurat, Georges (1859–91) *Sunday Afternoon on the Grande Jatte.*
Stael, Nicholas de (1914–55) *The Roofs.*
Toulouse-Lautrec, Henri de (1864–1901) *At the Moulin Rouge.*
Utrillo, Maurice (1883–1955) *Port St Martin.*
Vlaminck, Maurice de (1876–1958) *The Bridge at Chatou.*
Watteau, Antoine (1684–1721) *The Embarkation for Cythera.*

GERMANY
Altdorfer, Albrecht (*c.* 1480–1538) *Battle of Arbela.*
Beckmann, Max (1884–1950) *The Night.*
Beuys, Joseph (b. 1921) *Fond IV/4.*
Cranach, Lucas (The Elder) (1472–1553) *Venus, Rest on Flight into Egypt.*
Dix, Otto (1891–1969) *The War.*
Ernst, Max (1891–1976) *The Elephant Celebes.*
Durer, Albrecht (1471–1528) *The Four Apostles, Apocalypse.*
Friedrich, Caspar David (1774–1840) *The Cross in the Mountains.*
Grosz, George (1893–1959) *Suicide.*
Grunewald, Mathias (*c.* 1460–1528) *Isenheim Altarpiece.*

Holbein, Hans (The Younger) (*c.* 1497–1543) *Henry VIII, The Ambassadors.*
Kirchner, Ernst Ludwig (1880–1938) *Self-portrait with Model.*
Marc, Franz (1880–1916) *The Blue Horse.*
Nolde, Emil (Emil Hansen) (1867–1956) *Masks and Dahlias.*

GREAT BRITAIN
Auerbach, Frank (b. 1931) *E.O.W. Nude.*
Bacon, Francis (b. 1909) *Three Studies at the Base of a Crucifixion.*
Blake, William (1757–1827) *The Book of Job: Divine Comedy.*
Bonington, Richard Parkes (1801–28) *A Sea Piece.*
Constable, John (1776–1837) *The Hay Wain.*
Crome, John (1768–1821) *The Slate Quarries.*
Dobson, William (1610–46) *Endymion Porter.*
Freud, Lucian (b. 1922) *Francis Bacon.*
Fuseli, Henry (Johann Heinrich Fussli) (1741–1825) *Nightmare.*
Gainsborough, Thomas (1727–88) *Blue Boy.*
Girtin, Thomas (1775–1802) *Kirkstall Abbey: Evening.*
Hamilton, Richard (b. 1922) *Portrait of Hugh Gaitskell as a Famous Monster of Filmland.*
Hilliard, Nicholas (*c.* 1537–1619) *Elizabeth I, Sir Walter Raleigh.*
Hockney, David (b. 1937) *Mr. & Mrs. Clark and Percy.*
Hogarth, William (1697–1764) *Rake's Progress, Marriage à la Mode.*
Hunt, William Holman (1827–1910) *The Scapegoat, Light of the World.*
John, Augustus Edwin (1878–1961) *The Smiling Woman.*
John, Gwen (1876–1939) *Self Portrait.*
Landseer, Sir Edwin (1802–73) *The Old Shepherd's Chief Mourner, Shoeing.*
Millais, Sir John Everett (1829–96) *Order of Release.*
Nash, Paul (1889–1946) *British. Dead Sea.*
Nicholson, Ben (b. 1894) *White Relief.*
Raeburn, Sir Henry (1756–1823) *Sir John Sinclair.*
Ramsay, Allan (1713–84) *The Artist's Wife.*
Reynolds, Sir Joshua (1723–92) *Mrs Siddons as the Tragic Muse, The Three Graces.*
Rossetti, Dante Gabriel (1828–82) *Beata Beatrix.*
Sickert, Walter Richard (1860–1942) *Ennui.*
Sisley, Alfred (1839–99) *Flood at Port Marly.*
Smith, Sir Matthew (1879–1959) *Fitzroy Street Nudes.*
Spencer, Sir Stanley (1891–1959) *The Resurrection, Cookham.*
Stubbs, George (1724–1806) *Horse frightened by a Lion.*
Sutherland, Graham (1903–80) *Christ in Glory, Coventry Cathedral.*
Turner, Joseph Mallord William (1775–1851) *The Grand Canal, Venice, Shipwreck, Juliet and Her Nurse.*
Wilson, Richard (1713–82) *Okehampton Castle.*

HUNGARY
Moholy-Nagy, Laszlo (1895–1946) *Light prop.*
Vasarely, Victor (b. 1908) *Timbres II.*

ITALY
Balla, Giacomo (1871–1958) *Dynamism of a Dog on a Leash.*
Bellini, Giovanni (*c.* 1429–1561) *Pieta, Coronation of the Virgin, Agony in the Garden.*
Botticelli, Sandro (Alessandro di Mariano Filipepi) (1445–1510) *Birth of Venus, Mystic Nativity.*
Canaletto, Giovanni Antonio Canal (1697–1768) *Venice: A Regatta on the Grand Canal.*
Carra, Carlo (1881–1966) *Metaphysical Muse.*
Caravaggio, Michelangelo Merisi (1573–1610) *St Matthew, Deposition.*
Del Castagno, Andrea (Andrea di Bartolo di Bargilla) (1421–57) *The Vision of St. Jerome.*
Chirico, Giorgio de (1888–1978) *Mystery and Melancholy of a Street: Nostalgia of the Infinite.*
Correggio, Antonio Allegri (*c.* 1489–1534) *Jupiter and Io, Assumption of the Virgin, The Magdalene reading* (attributed but spurious).

Duccio (Di Buoninsegna) (active 1278–1318) *The Rucellai Madonna.*
Da Fabriano Gentile (1370–1427) *The Adoration of the Magi.*
Francesca, Piero della (*c.* 1415–92) *Nativity.*
Fra Angelico, Giovanni da Fiesole (1387–1455) *Annunciation.*
Fra Filippo Lippi (*c.* 1406–69) *Tarquinia Madonna.*
Giorgione, Giorgio da Castelfranco (1475–1510) *Sleeping Venus.*
Giotto di Bondone (*c.* 1267–1337) *Life of St. Francis.*
Leonardo da Vinci (1452–1519) *Mona Lisa (La Gioconda), Last Supper, Cinerva de' Benci, Benois Madonna.*
Lorenzetti, Ambrogio (active *c.* 1319–48?) *Good and Bad Government, Palazzo Pubblico, Siena.*
Mantegna, Andrea (*c.* 1430–1506) *The Triumph of Caesar.*
Martini, Simone (*c.* 1285–1344) *Annunciation.*
Masaccio (Tommaso di Set Giovanni di Mone) (1401–28?) *Scenes from the Life of St. Peter, Brancacci Chapel.*
Da Messina, Antonello (1430–79) *Salvador Mundi.*
Michelangelo, Buonarroti (1475–1564) *Creation of Adam.*
Modigliani, Amedeo (1884–1920) *Portrait of Madame Zborowski.*
Morandi, Giorgio (1890–1964) *Still Life.*
Orcagna (Andrea di Cione) (active 1343–68) *The Redeemer with the Madonna and Saints.*
Parmigianino (Girolamo Francesco Maria Mazzola) (1503–40) *The Vision of St. Jerome.*
Raphael (1483–1520) *Sistine Madonna, Panshanger Madonna, The Colonna altarpiece, Ansidei Madonna.*
Romano, Giulio (1499?–1546) *The Hall of the Giants.*
Del Sarto, Andrea (Andrea d'Agnolo) (1486–1530) *The Madonna of the Harpies: A Young Man.*
Signorelli, Luca (active 1470–1523) *The Last Judgment, Orvieto.*
Tiepolo, Giovanni Battista (1696–1770) *The Finding of Moses.*
Tintoretto, Jacopo Robusti (1518–94) *Last Supper, Il Paradiso.*
Titian (*c.* 1487–1576) *The Tribute Money, Bacchus and Ariadne.*
Uccello, Paolo (1396/7–1475) *The Battle of San Romano: The Night Hunt.*
Veronese, Paolo Caliari (1528–88) *Marriage at Cana.*

JAPAN
Hiroshige, Ando (1797–1858) *A Hundred Famous Views of Edo.*
Hokusai, Katsushika (1760–1849) *Thirty-six Views of Mount Fuji.*
Motonobu, Kano (1476–1559) *Eight Views of Hsiao-hsiang.*
Utamaro, Kitagawa (1753–1806) *Mushierabi (Book of Insects).*

MEXICO
Orozco, Jose Clemente (1883–1949) *Hidalgo and Castillo.*
Rivera, Diego (1886–1957) *Creation.*
Siqueiros, David Alfaro (1896–1974) *The March of Humanity on Earth: Towards the Cosmos.*

NETHERLANDS
Appel, Karel (b. 1921) *Cry of Liberty.*
Bosch, Hieronymus (*c.* 1450–1516) *Christ Crowned with Thorns, The Garden of Earthly Delights.*
Hals, Frans (*c.* 1580–1666) *Laughing Cavalier.*
Hooch, Pieter de (1629–83) *An Interior.*
Leyden, Lucas van (1494–1533) *Last Judgment.*
Mondrian, Piet (1872–1944) *Composition.*
Rembrandt, Harmensz van Rijn (1606–69) *The Night Watch, The Anatomy Lesson, Aristotle contemplating the Bust of Homer, The Mill.*
Ruisdael, Jacob van (*c.* 1628–82) *View of Haarlem.*
Van Gogh, Vincent (1853–90) *Road with Cypresses, Old Peasant, L'Eglise d'Auvers.*

Vermeer, Jan (1632–75) *Woman with a Water Jug.*
Weyden, Rogier van der (1399/1400–1464) *The Deposition.*

NORWAY
Munch, Edvard (1863–1944) *Dance of Death, Shriek.*

RUSSIA
Kandinsky, Wassily (1866–1944) *Compositions, Improvisations and Impressions.*
Larionov, Mikhail Fedorovich (1881–1964) *Glass.*
Malevich, Kasimir Severinovich (1878–1935) *Black Square.*
Soutine, Chaim (1893–1943) *The Madwoman.*
Tatlin, Vladimir (1885–1953) *Constructivist Sculptures.*

SPAIN
Dali, Salvador (b. 1904) *Crucifixion, The Persistence of Memory.*
El Greco (1541–1614) *The Burial of Count Orgaz, View of Toledo.*
Goya, Francisco de (1746–1828) *The Naked Maja, The Shootings of May 3rd.*
Gris, Juan (Jose Gonsalez) (1887–1927) *Violin and Fruit Dish.*
Murillo, Bartolomé Esteban (1617–82) *Virgin and Child, Immaculate Conception.*
Picasso, Pablo (1881–1973) *Guernica, Les Demoiselles d'Avignon.*
Ribera, José (1591–1652) *The Martyrdom of St. Bartholomew.*
Tapies, Antonio (b. 1923) *Large Painting.*
Velazquez, Diego (1599–1660) *Rokeby Venus, The Water-Carrier, Juan de Pareja.*

SWITZERLAND
Klee, Paul (1879–1940) *Twittering Machine.*

UNITED STATES OF AMERICA
Audubon, John James (1785–1851) *Birds of America.*
Cassatt, Mary (1845–1926) *The Bath.*
Eakins, Thomas (1844–1916) *The Gross Clinic.*
Homer, Winslow (1836–1910) *Northeaster.*
O'Keeffe, Georgia (b. 1887) *Cityscapes of New York.*
De Kooning, Willem (b. 1904) *Woman Series.*
Lichtenstein, Roy (b. 1923) *Wham!*
Moses, Grandma (Anna Mary Robertson) (1860–1961) *The Thanksgiving Turkey.*
Pollock, Jackson (1912–56) *Autumn Rhythm.*
Rauschenberg, Robert (b. 1925) *Monogram.*
Rothko, Mark (1903–70) *Green on Blue.*
Sargent, John Singer (1856–1925) *Carnation, Lily, Lily, Rose.*
Warhol, Andy (b. 1930) *Campbell's Soupcans.*
Whistler, James Abbott McNeill (1834–1903) *Arrangement in Grey and Black – The Artist's Mother.*

Renowned sculptors by country

FRANCE
Brancusi, Constantin (1876–1957) Romanian French.
Gaudier-Brzeska, Henri (1891–1915) French.
Pevsner, Antoine (1886–1962) French.
Pigalle, Jean-Baptiste (1714–85) French.
Rodin, Auguste (1840–1917) French.
Roubiliac, Louis-Francois (c. 1705–62) French.

GREAT BRITAIN
Caro, Anthony (b. 1924) British.
Epstein, Sir Jacob (1880–1959) English.
Flaxman, John (1755–1826) English.
Hepworth, Barbara (1903–75) British.
Moore, Henry (b. 1898) British.
Paolozzi, Eduardo (b. 1924) British.

GREECE
Phidias (died c. 432 BC) Greek.
Praxiteles (active mid-4th century BC) Greek.

ITALY
Bernini, Gianlorenzo (1598–1680) Italian.
Cellini, Benvenuto (1500–71) Italian.
Donatello (Donato di Niccolo) (1386–1466) Italian.
Ghiberti, Lorenzo (1378–1455) Italian.
Michelangelo, Buonarroti (1475–1564) Italian.
Pisano, Giovanni (active c. 1265–1314) Italian.
Pisano, Nicola (active c. 1258–84) Italian.
Robbia, Luca della (1400–82) Italian.

RUSSIA
Archipenko, Alexander (1887–1964) Russian.
Gabo, Naum (Naum Neemia Pevsner) (1890–1977) Russian.
Zadkine, Ossip (1890–1967) Russian.

SPAIN
Gonzalez, Julio (1876–1942) Spanish.

SWITZERLAND
Giacometti, Alberto (1901–66) Swiss.

UNITED STATES OF AMERICA
Calder, Alexander (1898–1976) American.
Nevelson, Louise (b. 1900) American.
Smith, David (1906–65) American.

Photography

The camera obscura (Latin, 'darkened room') and its principles were familiar as far back in time as the 4th century BC, when Aristotle observed that if a very small aperture was made in one wall of an otherwise light-free room, the scene outside the wall was cast, but inverted, on the opposite inside wall of the room. Perfected with lenses in the aperture during the 19th century, this device was used as an aid to artists.

In 1725 the German, Johann Heinrich Schultze, discovered that silver salts darken in ratio to the strength of light exposed to them. The first actual use of this phenomenon was made in England by Thomas Wedgwood and Sir Humphrey Davy, who coated silver salts onto paper and produced silhouette images on it from leaves and other natural sources. They published a joint paper on their findings in 1802.

In 1826, a Frenchman, Joseph Nicéphore Niepce, made and fixed permanently the first photographic image, a view from his workroom. His camera obscura lens resolved the image onto a bituminous, light-sensitive coating supported by a plate of pewter. Development of the image was obtained by acid etching the unexposed bitumen, the relief image left on the pewter giving a printing surface to obtain copies. Niepce then went into partnership with Louis Jacques Maudé Daguerre. Adapting Schultze's discovery, they used copper plates covered with silver iodide. In 1835 Daguerre succeeded in developing his images with mercury vapour; two years later he was able to permanently fix the images by immersing the plates in a solution of common salt (sodium chloride). Announcing his discovery in 1839, he patented it, using the name Daguerrotype, for which the French government awarded him an annual pension on condition that his process be made public.

Numerous experiments using silver salts then took place, the most important being those of William Henry Fox Talbot in England who, by using impregnated paper with silver salts, obtained negative images from which multiple positives could be made. The process was called Calotype, but was not as sharp and brilliant as Daguerrotype, which remained the more popular.

In 1850 an English sculptor, Frederick Scott Archer, invented the wet-plate process. The image was formed on a glass plate coated with light-sensitive collodion, a jelly-like substance that remained wet for some time. While still wet, the plate was exposed in the camera and straightway developed. Such methods were cumbersome and technical and it was not until the introduction of the dry-plate process, in-

vented in 1871 by Englishman, Richard L. Maddox, did amateur photography catch on.

By 1884 George Eastman in the United States was manufacturing silver bromide printing papers; in 1891 the Belgian, Leo Backland, marketed the first commercially successful contact papers, calling them Velox papers.

Dry-plate photography, though a great improvement on previous processes, was still awkward and cumbersome. John Carbutt, an American, coated sheets of celluloid with emulsion. Eastman was quick to realise its commercial aspects and in 1880 introduced the first Kodak, a simple hand camera already loaded at the factory with celluloid film for 100 shots. After the film was exposed the whole equipment was returned to the factory; the film developed and printed, and the camera reloaded. Eastman introduced paper-backed roll film for daylight loading in 1891, and, together with camera improvements, photography became a hobby for the masses.

Colour in photography is based on the principle that an admixture in varying ratios of the three primary colours, red, blue and green, will give any colour in the spectrum. In 1810 a German physicist found that wet silver chloride exposed to a spectrum would reproduce faintly the spectrum colours but would disappear when the image was dried. In 1860 James Clark Maxwell, a British physicist, made three wet-collodion photographs of a tartan ribbon, each one through a red, blue and green filter. He then projected them through similar filters, superimposing the images on a screen. A crude colour reproduction resulted, but lacking in sensitivity to red and green.

After various experiments the three-layer emulsion method, each layer being sensitive to a different primary colour, was perfected in the Kodachrome film, marketed in 1935. The film was developed layer by layer, each being dyed in the appropriate complementary colours yellow, magenta and cyan blue, thus giving a transparency of the true image colours. About the same time Agfacolour was introduced, the difference between it and Kodachrome being that the three layers contained not only the sensitive emulsions but also colour formers, all of which reacted with a special developer to produce an accurate colour image in one step, instead of the separate three-step development of Kodachrome. From these two methods, most modern colour film has been developed.

CAMERAS
From the camera obscura to a light-free box with a lens was an obvious step. Camera development followed that of the development of the image plate, and it was not until dryplate and celluloid roll film was introduced that the camera became truly portable. However, the first single-lens reflex camera had been patented in 1861 by Thomas Sutton, and in 1880 the British firm of R. & J. Beck produced a twinlens reflex camera. A roll-film camera, the Kodak, was brought out in 1888 by George Eastman, followed in 1895 by the folding 'Brownie' camera.

In 1914 Oscar Bernak of Germany invented the Leica principle, a small precision instrument of considerable sophistication using 35 mm roll film. This was marketed successfully in 1925 and is still the most widely used format, there being a host of refinements from Germany and later Japan up to the present day. Beck's twin-lens reflex camera was marketed in 1928 under the name Rolleiflex.

In 1963 Edwin Land introduced the revolutionary Polaroid camera, which was able to produce black-and-white and colour pictures in less than a minute after exposure. After the picture is taken, the negative forms a sandwich with the positive, which is passed through rollers that break open plastic pods containing developer and fixer. After an appropriate time lapse, the camera back is opened and the print is peeled away from the negative, giving a positive image of the picture.

Architecture

Architecture is a reflection of the life of the people, countries and civilizations who build it. The earliest architecture, built of mud, brick and wood, has long since vanished; only stone-built buildings and those hewn out of rock have left any traces to tell us what the first architecture may have looked like. Egyptian tombs, dating from 2700 BC are the first remnants; the mastabas, a small flat-topped building with sloping sides, and pyramids, the first built at Sakkara about 2700 BC. The rise of the Egyptian civilisation along the Nile saw the building of the great pyramids and, latterly (1600 BC), the great temples. Roughly parallel in time the Babylonians of Mesopotamia were building temples whose decoration reflected their religion. In Crete, the palace of Knossos was built in about 1600 BC and this was the prelude to the magnificent flowering of Greek architecture.

Greek architecture is characterised by three orders which manifest themselves in the design of the columns supporting the roof structures and the entablatures above the columns. The Doric order is simple and sturdy, very often undecorated. The Ionic order, possibly of Asiatic origin, was more slender, and carried scrolls and simple decoration on the capitals. The columns were also fluted. The Corinthian order has an elaborate capital decorated with stylised acanthus leaves. Temples and public buildings were built in these styles, and their position shows that the Greeks were adept and skilful in town planning.

The spread of the Roman Empire brought Greek influence to Roman architecture but the Romans added one architectural feature of outstanding importance – the arch. Arch construction enabled the Romans to supply their cities with water from outside by building aqueducts, which were arched to carry the load. From the arch they developed the cross-vault: the point where two tunnel-shaped roofs meet and cross each other at right angles.

The Middle Ages saw the rise of the Byzantine empire in Eastern Europe and the Middle East (330 AD) and the development of the dome. In the West, architecture scarcely moved forward until the beginning of the 11th century, when the Romanesque style, using cross-vaulting techniques and the plan of the early Christian Roman basilica was adopted.

About the middle of the 12th century the Romanesque style gave way to Gothic. This saw the invention or development of five features: the pointed arch, the rib (which supported the arch), the buttress on the outside of the building, the tracery widow, and architectural decoration of a high order. In this style, especially in France and Britain, abbeys and cathedrals sprang up of immense ambition and scale. The style continually developed, mainly in the art of decoration. The Decorated style (14th century) moved to the Flamboyant style in France, where the decorative stone was carved in flame-like patterns, and in England to the Perpendicular style, with its huge windows with flattened pointed arches and elaborate fan vaulting of the roofs.

The Renaissance period in Italy (early 15th century) was generated by powerful and rich families in the city-states in and around Florence, notably the Medicis. Drawing upon the styles of the Roman and Byzantine periods the architects of the early Renaissance (the first whose names we actually know with certainty) developed the dome (Brunelleschi, Florence Cathedral) and the design of the multi-storied town house or 'palazzo' (Palazzo Pitti, Florence). For the next 400 years the Renaissance movement spread rapidly through Europe, a peak being represented in St Peter's, Rome, which took 150 years to build to designs and alterations by 14 architects, including Bramante, Michelangelo (The Dome) and Maderna.

In and around Venice in the mid-16th century Palladio was designing elegant churches and exquisite houses, and in France the Loire Chateaux or hunting lodges of the French kings were being built in elaborate and fantastic styles, with turrets, pinnacles and chimneys. Such a flowering of ideas did not produce a coherent style as such until the 17th century, when the Classical style emerged in France with the building of the Louvre and Versailles. In England these influences were late in taking hold, but the first Renaissance building, the Queen's House, Greenwich, was built to designs by Inigo Jones after he had visited Italy in 1613. This was the starting point for such architects as Wren, Vanbrugh and Hawksmoor, whose churches and country houses represent a high point in English Architecture. At the same time in Italy, Spain, Austria and southern Germany, the Baroque style predominated, characterised by its bold, curving lines, large-scale planning and dramatic effects bordering on the theatrical, as exemplified by the piazza in St Peter's, Rome (Bernini) and the Belvedere Palace in Vienna, which is decorated inside in the Rococo style. The style was most restrained in England, and in the 18th century gave way to the Palladian style, derived from Palladio's villas around Venice. Domestic architecture in England became classical in the mid-1750s onward in the style popularly known as Georgian.

From then onward, in Europe and to a lesser extent in America, the various Renaissance styles were adapted or modified until the Gothic revival of the 1830s in Britain, where the Gothic and the Classical styles were equally prominent. A new building material was cast iron (the Crystal Palace, London), but which did not change the appearance of architecture.

The Modern Movement came out of the development of the steel frame, from which hung the masonry walls. Its first use in Chicago at the end of the 19th century was the start of a revolutionary change in the look of cities throughout the world. Within a generation reinforced concrete was invented and from then on the skyscrapers of America and elsewhere sprang into being. The strength of reinforced concrete allowed cantilevering and the construction of thin skins of vast area, and building styles were freed to take on sweeping and sculptured shapes. After the Second World War the large-scale use of glass for curtain walls gave a transparent and airy quality to skyscrapers, factories and public buildings.

Some terms used in architecture

abacus Flat top of the capital of a column.
apse Semicircular termination or recess at the end of a church chancel.
architrave The beam which extends across the top of the columns in classical architecture.
baptistry Building used for baptisms. Sometimes merely a bay or chapel reserved for baptisms.
bay Compartment or unit of division of an interior or of a façade – usually between one window or pillar and the next.
belvedere Open-sided structure designed to offer extensive views, usually in a formal garden.
boss Projection, usually carved, at the intersection of stone ribs of Gothic vaults and ceilings.
buttress. Vertical mass of masonry built against a wall to strengthen it and to resist the outward pressure of a vault.
campanile Bell-tower.
capital Top of a column, usually carved.
caryatid Sculptured female figure serving as a supporting column.

cornice Projecting upper part of the entablature in classical architecture.
dado Lower part of an interior wall when panelled or painted separately from the main part.
drum Cylindrical lower part of a dome or cupola.
entablature In classical architecture, the beam-like division above the columns, comprising architrave, freize and cornice.
flying buttress Arch conveying the thrust of a vault towards an isolated buttress.
frieze Decorated central division of an entablature, between the architrave and the cornice.
keystone Central, wedge-shaped stone of an arch, so called because the arch cannot stand up until it is in position.
lancet window Window with a single, sharply pointed arch. The style is associated with the Early English period of Gothic architecture, around the 13th century.
mezzanine Low storey introduced between two loftier ones, usually the ground and first floors.
order Basic elements of classical and Renaissance architecture, comprising the base, column, capital and entablature.
oriel Bay window on an upper floor, supported by projecting stonework.
pediment In classical architecture, the low-pitched gable above the entablature, usually filled with sculpture.
pier Vertical masonry support for a wall arch.
rustication Heavy stonework with the surface left rough, or with deeply channelled joints, used principally on Renaissance buildings.
spandrel Triangular space between the curves of two adjacent arches and the horizontal moulding above them.
tracery Ornamental stonework in the upper part of a Gothic window.
tympanum Triangular surface bounded by the mouldings of a pediment; also, the space, often carved, between the lintel and arch of a Gothic doorway.
vault A roof or ceiling built in stone, brick or concrete, as opposed to wood.

SOME NOTABLE ARCHITECTS

Aalto, Alvar (1898–1976) Finnish.
Adam, Robert (1728–1772) Scottish.
Alberti, Leone Battista (1404–72) Italian.
Barry, Sir Charles (1795–1860) English.
Bernini, Gianlorenzo (1598–1680) Italian.
Borromini, Francesco (1599–1667) Italian.
Brunelleschi, Filippo (1377–1446) Italian.
Burlington, Richard Boyle (Earl of) (1694–1753) English.
Campbell, Colen (1660?–1729) Scottish.
Gibbs, James (1682–1754) Scottish.
Hawksmoor, Nicholas (1661–1736) English.
Jones, Inigo (1573–1652) English.
Kent, William (1685–1748) English.
Le Corbusier (Charles Edouard Jeanmerat) (1887–1965) French.
Le Vau, Louis (1612–70) French.
Maderna, Carlo (1556–1629) Italian.
Mansart, François (1598–1666) French.
Mansart, Jules (1646–1708) French.
Michelangelo, Buonarroti (1475–1564) Italian.
Mies van der Rohe, Ludwig (1886–1969) German.
Nash, John (1752–1835) English.
Neimeyer, Oscar (b. 1907) Brazilian.
Palladio, Andrea (1508–1580) Italian.
Paxton, Sir Joseph (1801–1865) English.
Pugin, Augustus (1812–1852) English.
Saarinen, Eero (1910–1961) Finnish.
Soane, Sir John (1753–1837) English.
Vanbrugh, Sir John (1664–1726) English.
Wren, Sir Christopher (1632–1723) English.
Wright, Frank Lloyd (1869–1959) American.
Wyatt, James (1746–1813) English.

Music and The Dance

Orchestral instruments

(Woodwind 1–9; Brass 10–13; Percussion 14–23; Strings 24–28; Keyboard 29–30.)

1 Piccolo or Octave Flute
Earliest concerto: Vivaldi, *c.* 1735. *Earliest orchestral use:* 1717 Handel's Water Music. *History:* Name 'piccolo' dates from 1856, but the origin goes back to prehistory via flute and sopranino recorder.

2 Flute – transverse or cross-blown
Earliest concerto Vivaldi, *c.* 1729. *Earlist orchestral use:* 1672 Lully. *History:* Prehistoric (*c.* 18,000 BC); the modern Boehm flute dates from 1832.

3 Oboe
Earliest concerto: Marcheselli, 1708. *Earliest orchestral use:* 1657 Lully's *L'amour malade*. *History:* Originated Middle Ages in the schalmey family. The name comes from Fr. *hautbois* (1511) = high wood.

4 Clarinet
Earliest concerto: Vivaldi, *c.* 1740?: 2 clarinets; Molter, *c.* 1747: 1 clarinet. *Earliest orchestral use:* 1726 Faber: Mass. *History:* Developed by J C Denner (1655–1707) from the recorder and schalmey families.

5 Cor anglais
Earliest concerto: J M Haydn, *c.* 1755? *Earliest orchestral use:* 1760 in Vienna. *History:* Purcell wrote for 'tenor oboe' *c.* 1690; this *may* have originated the name English Horn. Alternatively, it may be from 'angled horn', referring to its crooked shape.

6 Bass Clarinet
Earliest orchestral use: 1838 Meyerbeer's *Les Huguenots*. *History:* Prototype made in 1772 by Gilles Lot of Paris. Modern Boehm form from 1838.

7 Bassoon
Earliest concerto: Vivaldi, *c.* 1730? *Earliest orchestral use:* *c.* 1619. *History:* Introduced in Italy *c.* 1540 as the lowest of the double-reed group.

8 Double Bassoon
Earliest orchestral use: *c.* 1730 Handel. *History:* 'Borrowed' from military bands for elemental effects in opera.

9 Saxophone
Earliest concerto: Debussy's *Rhapsody*, 1903. *Earliest orchestral use:* 1844 Kastner's *Last King of Judah*. *History:* Invented by Adolphe Sax, *c.* 1840.

10 Trumpet
Earliest concerto: Torelli, before 1700, Haydn, 1796: keyed trumpet. *Earliest orchestral use:* *c.* 1800 keyed trumpet. *Earliest orchestral use:* *c.* 1800 keyed, 1835 valved, in Halévy's *La Juive*. *History:* The natural trumpet is of prehistoric origin; it formed the basis of the earliest orchestras.

11 Trombone
Earliest concerto: Wagenseil, *c.* 1760. *Earliest orchestral use:* *c.* 1600, as part of bass-line. *History:* From Roman *buccina* or slide-trumpet, via the mediaeval sackbut to its modern form *c.* 1500.

12 Horn
Earliest concerto: Bach, 1717–21, or Vivaldi, Bach . . . Vivaldi: 2 horns; Telemann, before 1721: 1 horn. *Earliest orchestral use:* 1639, Cavalli. *History:* Prehistoric. The earliest music horns were the German helical horns of the mid-16th century. Rotary valve horn patented in 1832.

13 Tuba
Earliest concerto: Vaughan Williams, 1954. *Earliest orchestral use:* 1830, Berlioz' *Symphonie Fantastique*. *History:* Patented by W Wieprecht and Moritz, Berlin, 1835.

14 Timpani/Kettle Drum
Earliest concerto: Masek, *c.* 1790: 1 set, Tausch, *c.* 1870: 6 timpani. *Earliest orchestral use:* 1607, Monteverdi's *Orfeo*. *History:* Originated in the ancient Orient.

15 Bass Drum
Earliest orchestral use: 1748, Rameau's *Zais*. *History:* As timpani.

16 Side or Snare Drum
Earliest orchestral use: 1749, Handel's *Fireworks Music*. *History:* Derived from the small drums of prehistory, via the mediaeval tabor. Achieved its modern form in the 18th century.

17 Tenor Drum
Earliest orchestral use: 1842.

18 Tambourine
Earliest orchestral use: 1820. *History:* Dates back to the mediaeval Arabs; prototype used by Assyrians and Egyptians. Earliest use of the word 1579.

19 Cymbals
Earliest orchestral use: 1680, Strungk's *Esther*. *History:* From Turkish military bands of antiquity.

20 Triangle
Earliest orchestral use: 1774, Glantz: Turkish Symphony. *History:* As cymbals.

21 Xylophone
Earliest orchestral use: 1873, Lumbye's *Traumbilder*. *History:* Primitive; earliest 'art' mention 1511.

22 Gong or Tam tam
Earliest orchestral use: 1791, Gossec's *Funeral March*. *History:* Originating in the ancient Far East.

23 Glockenspiel
Earliest orchestral use: 1739, Handel's *Saul*. *History:* Today strictly a keyboard instrument, in the 19th century the metal plates were struck by hand-held hammers. The original instrument dates from 4th century Rome.

24 Violin
Earliest concerto: Torelli, 1709. *Earliest orchestral use:* *c.* 1600. *History:* Descended from the Lyre via the 6th century crwth, rebec and fiddle. Modern instrument of Lombardic origin *c.* 1545. The words violin and fiddle derive ultimately from Roman *vitulari* ('to skip like a calf').

25 Violoncello
Earliest concerto: Jacchini, 1701. *Earliest orchestral use:* *c.* 1600. *History:* As violin.

26 Viola
Earliest concerto: Telemann *ante* 1722. *Earliest orchestral use:* *c.* 1600. *History:* As violin.

27 Double Bass
Earliest concerto: Vanhal, *c.* 1770. *Earliest orchestral use:* *c.* 1600. *History:* Developed alongside the violin family, but is a closer relative to the bass viol or Violone.

28 Harp
Earliest concerto: Handel, 1738. *Earliest orchestral use:* *c.* 1600. *History:* Possibly prehistoric: attained its modern form by 1792.

29 Vibraphone
Earliest orchestral use: 1934. *History:* First used in dance bands in the 1920s.

30 Celesta
Earliest orchestral use: 1880, Widor's *Der Korrigane*. *History:* Invented by Mustel in 1880.

Popular and folk instruments

Accordion/concertina
Accordion invented (as Handäoline) in Germany, 1822. Concertina invented in England, 1829. The accordion produces two notes, one drawn, the other pressed, to a key, the concertina only one; further, the accordion sometimes has a keyboard, the concertina never has.

Bagpipes
A prehistoric Middle Eastern or Chinese instrument made by shepherds of a lamb or goat skin with pipes attached. The bag acts as a bellows to actuate chanter and drone pipes. First concerto, 1755. Much used today as a military instrument in Scotland and elsewhere.

Balalaika
East European (predominantly Russian) triangular development of the long-necked lute, reaching its present form about a century ago. Currently made in six sizes, each with three strings.

Guitar
A fretted, six-stringed development of the antique lute (qv), possibly introduced into Europe by the Moors (8th century) and settling as Spain's national instrument, attaining its present basic form *c.* 1750. Earliest printed music, 1546. Earliest concerto, 1808.

Harmonium
Invented (as *orgue expressif*) in France, 1830s. A bellows reed organ, perfected during the 1840s as a modest-sized keyboard instrument for church, cinema and home use (known in England sometimes as 'cottage organ').

Harpsicord
Evolved from the psaltery during the 14th century; earliest surviving example dated 1521. Mainly a domestic instrument, it also supported the bass line in early orchestras. First solo

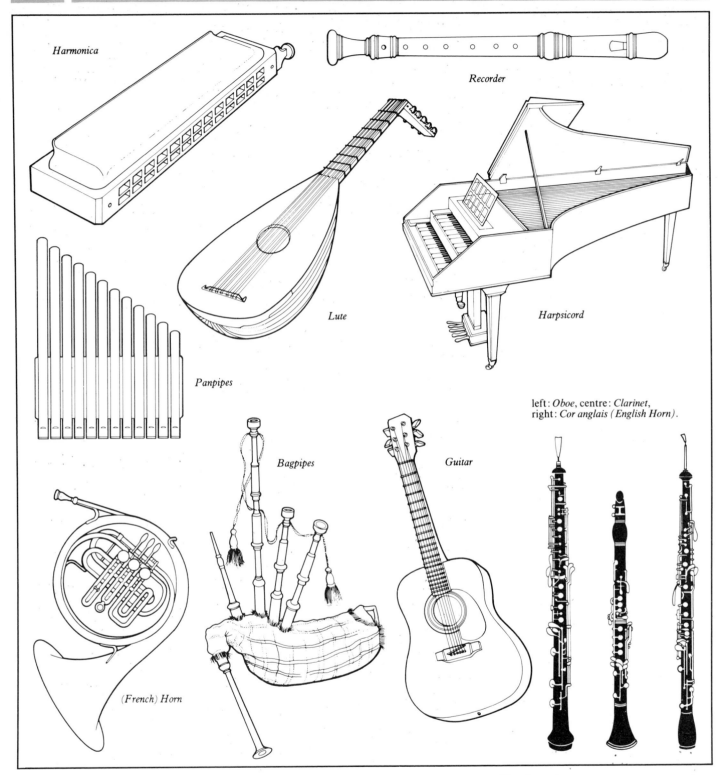

Harmonica

Recorder

Lute

Harpsicord

Panpipes

left: *Oboe*, centre: *Clarinet*, right: *Cor anglais (English Horn)*.

Bagpipes

Guitar

(French) Horn

concerto, *c*. 1720. Eclipsed *c*. 1800 by pianoforte (qv), but reintroduced progressively since 1903.

Lute
Extremely ancient (*c*. 3000 BC or before) source of all subsequent bowed and plucked stringed instruments, including violin, guitar, sitar, mandolin, etc. Earliest published music, 1507. Popularity subsided during 18th century, but currently revived for performance of early music.

Synthesiser
Electronic device, invented *c*. 1950 to create pitch, tone-colour and duration of any note or notes or sounds. Used especially in popular and jazz music, where it is often attached to a keyboard.

Mouth organ/harmonica
The most popular of all instruments. Invented in Germany, 1821. First concerto, 1951.

Organ
Ultimate origin lies in the antique panpipes (qv), but subsequent developments make it the biggest and most powerful of all instruments. First concerto by Handel, *c*. 1730. Saint-Saëns first used it in a symphony, 1886.

Panpipes
The simplest and most primitive organ, each pipe producing only one note. Named after the god Pan. An important instrument in Balkan folk music, it has recently achieved more widespread recognition.

Pianoforte
Descended from the dulcimer. Invented by Cristofori, *c*. 1709. Earliest printed music, 1732; first concert use in London, 1767; first concerto by J C Bach, 1776. Attained its modern basic form, *c*. 1850.

Keyboards
Generic term for keyboard instrument(s) connected to electronic device which produces extensive variations in tone-colour and note duration.

Recorder
End-blown flute, developed from prehistoric pipes. First mentioned, 1388. Popular during 17th and 18th centuries until being succeeded by the transverse flute.

Viola   *Violin*

Violoncello

Double Bass

The history and development of music

PREHISTORIC
Improvisatory music-making. Music and magic virtually synonymous.

PRIMITIVE (Ancient Greece and Rome; Byzantium) 8th century BC to 4th century AD
Improvisatory music-making in domestic surroundings. Competitive music-making in the arena.

AMBROSIAN (4th to 6th century AD)
The beginnings of plainsong and the establishment of order in liturgical music.

Principal composer
Bishop Ambrose of Milan (*c.* 333–97) established four scales.

GREGORIAN (6th to 10 century)
Church music subjected to strict rules, e.g.: melodies sung only in unison.

Principal composer
Pope Gregory I, 'The Great' (540–604) extended the number of established scales to eight.

MEDIAEVAL (1100–1300)
Guido d'Arezzo (*c.* 980–1050) was called the 'inventor of music': his teaching methods and invention of a method of writing music transformed the art. Beginning of organised instrumental music; start of polyphony in church music.

Principal composers
Minstrels (10th–13th centuries). Goliards (travelling singers of Latin songs: 11th–12th centuries). Troubadours (*c.* 1100–1210). Trouvères (from 1100).
Bernart de Ventadorn (*c.* 1150–95) encouraged singing in the vernacular.

RENAISSANCE (1300–1600)
The great age of polyphonic church music. Gradual emergence of instrumental music. Appearance of Madrigals, chansons, etc. The beginnings of true organisation in music and instruments.

Principal composers
Guillaume de Machut (*c.* 1300–77)
John Dunstable (d. 1453)
Guillaume Dufay (*c.* 1400–74)
Johannes Ockeghem (1430–95)
Josquin des Prés (*c.* 1450–1521)
John Taverner (*c.* 1495–1545)
Giovanni da Palestrina (*c.* 1525–94)
Orlando di Lasso (*c.* 1530–94)
Thomas Morley (1557–1603)
John Dowland (1563–1626)
Michael Praetorius (1571–1621)

BAROQUE (1600–1750)
Beginnings of opera and oratorio. Rise of instrumental music; the first orchestras, used at first in the opera house but gradually attaining separate existence. Beginnings of sonata, concerto, suite, and symphony. The peak of polyphonic writing.

Principal composers
Giovanni Gabrieli (1557–1612)
Claudio Monteverdi (1567–1643)
Orlando Gibbons (1583–1625)
Pietro Cavalli (1602–76)
Jean-Baptiste Lully (1632–87)
Arcangelo Corelli (1653–1713)
Henry Purcell (*c.* 1659–95)
Alessandro Scarlatti (1660–1725)
François Couperin (1668–1733)
Reinhard Keiser (1674–1739)
Antonio Lucio Vivaldi (1678–1741)
Georg Philipp Telemann (1681–1767)
Jean-Philippe Rameau (1683–1764)
Domenico Scarlatti (1685–1757)
Johann Sebastian Bach (1685–1750)
George Frideric Handel (1685–1759)

CLASSICAL (1750–1800+)
The age of the concert symphony and concerto. Beginning of the string quarter and sinfonia concertante. Decline of church music. Important developments in opera.

Principal composers
Giovanni Battista Sammartini (*c.* 1700–75)
Christoph Willibald von Gluck (1714–87)
Carl Philipp Emanuel Bach (1714–88)
Franz Joseph Haydn (1732–1809)
Wolfgang Amadeus Mozart (1756–91)
Luigi Cherubini (1760–1842)

EARLY ROMANTIC (1800–50)
High maturity of the symphony and concerto, etc. in classical style. Romantic opera. The age of the piano virtuosi. Invention of the Nocturne. Beginnings of the symphonic poem. Lieder. Beginnings of nationalism.

Principal composers
Ludwig van Beethoven (1770–1827)
Nicolo Paganini (1782–1840)
Carl Maria von Weber (1786–1826)
Gioacchino Rossini (1792–1868)
Franz Schubert (1797–1828)
Hector Berlioz (1803–69)
Mikhail Glinka (1804–57)
Jakob Ludwig Felix Mendelssohn Bartholdy (1809–47)
Frédéric François Chopin (1810–49)
Robert Schumann (1810–56)

HIGH ROMANTICISM (1850–1900)
The development of nationalism. Maturity of the symphonic and tone poems. Emergence of music drama.

Principal composers
Franz Liszt (1811–86)
Richard Wagner (1813–83)
Giuseppe Verdi (1813–1901)
César Franck (1822–90)
Bedřich Smetana (1824–84)
Anton Bruckner (1824–96)
Johannes Brahms (1833–97)
Pyotr Il'ich Tchaikovsky (1840–93)
Antonin Dvořák (1841–1904)
Edvard Hagerup Grieg (1843–1907)
Gustav Mahler (1860–1911)

MODERN (1900–)
Impressionism and post-romanticism. Gigantism. Neo-classicism and other reactionary movements. Atonalism.

Principal composers
Giacomo Puccini (1858–1924)
Claude Debussy (1862–1918)
Richard Strauss (1864–1949)
Carl Nielsen (1865–1931)
Jean Sibelius (1865–1957)
Alexander Skryabin (1872–1915)
Ralph Vaughan Williams (1872–1958)
Sergei Rakhmaninoff (1873–1943)
Arnold Schoenberg (1874–1951)
Charles Ives (1874–1954)
Maurice Ravel (1875–1937)
Béla Bartók (1881–1945)
Igor Stravinsky (1882–1971)
Anton Webern (1883–1945)
Alban Berg (1885–1935)
Sergei Prokofiev (1891–1953)
Aaron Copland (b 1990)
Sir William Walton (1902–82)
Sir Michael Tippett (b 1905)
Dimitri Shostakovich (1906–75)
Samuel Barber (b. 1910)
Benjamin Britten (1913–77)

AVANT-GARDE (Today)
Avant-Garde is history in the making and any list of composers would be arbitrary since one cannot tell which of the many directions taken by modern music will prove most influential. There have always been avant-garde composers, without which the art of music would never have developed: we would take many names from the

above chart as good examples. Here are some names of avant-gardistes of prominence.

Principal composers
Luigi Dallapiccola (1904–75)
Oliver Messiaen (b. 1908)
John Cage (b. 1912)
Witold Lutostawski (b. 1913)
Iannis Xenakis (b. 1922)
Luigi Nono (b. 1924)
Pierre Boulez (b. 1925)
Hans Werner Henze (b. 1926)
Karlheinz Stockhausen (b. 1928)
Steve Reich (b. 1936)

A chart of the main works of 72 of history's major composers from the 13th to the 20th century was published in the Guinness Book of Answers (2nd Edition) at pages 94–97.

Some musical comedy composers

Kern, Jerome (1885–1945) *Show Boat*; *Swing Time*
Berlin, Irving (b. 1888) *Annie Get Your Gun*; *Call Me Madam*
Porter, Cole (1891–1964) *Kiss Me Kate*; *Can Can*
Novello, Ivor (1893–69) *The Dancing Years*; *King's Rhapsody*
Gershwin, George (1898–1937) *Lady Be Good*; *Porgy and Bess*
Coward, Noel (1899–1973) *Bitter Sweet*; *Sail Away*
Weill, Kurt (1900–50) *Threepenny Opera*; *One Touch of Venus*
Rogers, Richard (b. 1902) *The King and I*; *Oklahoma*
Loesser, Frank (1910–69) *Guys and Dolls*
Bernstein, Leonard (b. 1918) *On the Town*; *West Side Story*
Wilson, Sandy (b. 1924) *The Boy Friend*
Sondheim, Stephen (b. 1930) *Company*; *A Little Night Music*
Lloyd Webber, Andrew (b. 1948) *Jesus Christ Superstar*; *Evita*

Some jazz musicians and composers

Handy, (W)illiam (C)hristopher (1873–1958) Composer
Bolden, Buddy (1878–1931) Cornet
Morton, (Ferdinand la Menthe) 'Jellyroll' (1885–1941) Piano
Oliver, Joe 'King' (1885–1938) Cornet
Ory, Edward 'Kid' (1886–1973) Trombone
Bechet, Sidney (1897–1959) Soprano saxophone
Smith, Bessie (1895–1937) Singer
Ellington, Edward Kennedy (Duke) (1899–1974) Pianist, bandleader
Armstrong, Louis 'Satchmo' (1900–1971) Trumpet, singer
Beiderbecke, Leon 'Bix' (1903–31) Cornet
Basie, William 'Count' (1904–84) Pianist, bandleader
Dorsey, Thomas (Tommy) (1905–56) Trombone, bandleader
Goodman, Benjamin David, 'Benny' (b. 1909) Clarinet, bandleader
Tatum, Arthur 'Art' (1910–56) Piano
Herman, Woodrow Charles, 'Woody' (b. 1913) Clarinet, bandleader
Holiday, Billie (1915–59) Singer
Monk, Theolonius Sphere (1917–82) Piano
Gillespie, John Birks, 'Dizzy' (b. 1917) Trumpet
Fitzgerald, Ella (b. 1918) Singer
Parker, Charles Christopher 'Bird' (1920–55) Saxophone
Peterson, Oscar Emmanuel (b. 1925) Piano
Roach, Maxwell, 'Max' (b. 1925) Drums
Coltrane, John (1926–67) Saxophone
Davis, Miles (b. 1926) Trumpet

Some popular singers and pop groups

Abba (formed 1971)
Baez, Joan (b. 1941)
The Beatles (formed 1960–1970)
Bowie, David (b. 1947)
Cash, Johnny (b. 1932)
Charles, Ray (b. 1930)
Crosby, Bing (1904–1977)
Dylan, Bob (b. 1941)
Haley, Bill (1925–1981)
Hendrix, Jimi (1942–1970)
John, Elton (b. 1947)
Holly, Buddy (1936–1959)
Marley, Bob (1945–1981)
Mitchell, Joni (b. 1943)
Parton, Dolly, (b. 1946)
Presley, Elvis (1935–1977)
Ross, Diana (b. 1944)
Richard, Cliff (b. 1940)
The Rolling Stones (formed 1962)
Sinatra, Frank (b. 1915)
Wonder, Stevie (b. 1950)

Musical terms

adagio slow and leisurely.
aleatory music Allowing performers freedom of interpretation or which introduces other random elements.
allegro Quick, lively.
andante Gently moving, flowing.
anthem Church choral work.
aria Solo song in opera or oratorio.
arpeggio Notes of a chord played upward or downward in quick succession.
atonal music Use of all twelve semitones; having no key.
cadence Musical punctuation used to end phrases, sections or complete works.
cadenza Solo virtuoso piece before the final cadence in an aria, or at any stated place in a concerto.
canon Repetition of tune or tunes that overlap each other.
chord Notes played together simultaneously.
chromatic relating to notes and chords comprising the twelve-note scale.
coda Theme introduced at the end of a movement to emphasise its finality.
concrete music (Musique concrète). Music constructed from previously recorded natural sounds.
continuo Keyboard augmentation of a 17th or 18th century orchestral work.
counterpoint Two or more independent tunes sung or played at the same time.
diatonic Relating to notes of the major and minor scales.
dominant key Key whose keynote is the fifth note of the tonic key.
electronic music Consisting of electronically produced sounds.
forte (f) Loudly.
fortissimo (ff) Very loudly.
fugue A polyphonic composition. The first tune is in the tonic; the second, introduced later, in the dominant key, and so on.
interval Difference in pitch between two notes.
largo Slow, stately.
libretto Text of oratoria or opera.
lieder German romantic songs of the 19th century.
madrigal Secular composition for voices.
Mass Roman Catholic sung service of Communion.
motet Unaccompanied part song of a religious nature.
movement A division of a long musical work.
obbligato Accompaniment by solo instrument.

opera Drama set to music.
operetta Light opera, often with dialogue.
oratorio Religious equivalent of opera without costume or scenery.
overture Instrumental introduction to opera or oratorio.
pentatonic scale A primitive five-note octave.
piano (p) Soft.
pianissimo (pp) Very soft.
pitch The height or depth of a note, measured according to its vibration (e.g. A above middle C equals 440 vibrations a second).
pizzicato Notes played by plucking strings of normally bowed instruments.
polyphonic 'Many voiced', combining independent melodic lines. As in motets and fugues.
recitative Solo vocal music that follows speech patterns.
Requiem Mass for the dead.
rondo Musical composition where the first and main section returns alternatively after different contrasting sections.
scherzo Lively movement.
serial music Compositions of the twelve-tone scale using all notes with equal importance, and each one once only before all have been used.
sonata form A form of musical composition developed during the 18th century. The first part sets out two main themes, each in a different key. The second part develops these two themes. The third is a recapitulation in which both themes are presented in the key of the first theme.
suite A work made up of several movements.
syncopation Accentuation of a beat in each bar that is normally not accentuated.
symphony Major orchestral work, usually made up of four movements.
tempo Pace at which a work is performed.
tertiary form A simple three-part musical structure in which the central part contrasts with the first and third, which are similar (ABA form).
theme A basic tune.
tutti Passage for whole orchestra.
vibrato Wavering of a note's pitch in singing, string playing and wind playing, to give vibrancy.
vivace Lively.

Ballet terms

à terre Steps which do not entail high jumps. They include the *glissade*, *pas balloné* and *pas brisé*.
battement Ballet exercises
batterie, battu Jump during which a dancer beats the calves sharply together.
corps de ballet Group of dancers who support the principal dancers.
divertissement Self-contained dance within a ballet, designed purely as entertainment or to show off a dancer's technique.
elevation Any high jump in ballet. Elevations include the *entrechat, rivoltade, pas de chat* and *cabriole*.
enchaînement. Sequence of steps linked to make a harmonious whole.
entrechat Vertical jump during which the dancer changes the position of the legs after beating the calves together.
fouetté Spectacular pirouette in which the dancer throws his raised leg to the front and side in order to achieve momentum for another turn.
jeté Jump from one leg to the other, basic to many ballet steps. These include the *grand jeté en avant*, in which the dancer leaps forward as if clearing an obstacle, and the *jeté foutté* where the dancer performs a complete turn in mid-air.
pas Basic ballet step in which the weight is transferred from one leg to another. The term is also used in combination to indicate the

The Dance

MAIN TRENDS	TYPES OF DANCE POPULAR AT THE TIME (*Basic rhythmic pulse in brackets*)
Pre-history Unorganised or loosely organised dances for warlike and communal purposes.	
c. 50 BC Mimes: dancing and singing spectacles (Rome).	
14th Century Danse basse: low, slow gliding steps. Hault danse: with high fast steps.	Pavane (4); derived from instrumental music from Padua; possibly the first stylised dance. Galliard (3), also from Italy, where the name implies gaiety.
15th Century First true ballet, with settings by Leonardo da Vinci, danced at Tortona, 1489. Introduced at the court of Henry VIII of England as Masque.	Court ballet: Branle (2), English clog dance with circular figures. Allemande (2,4,), i.e. 'from Germany'. Courante (3), i.e. 'running', from It. *corrente* (current). Volta (3), very lively (It. *volta*: vault).
16th Century Ballet comique. First complete printed account (15 Oct. 1581) of a ballet to celebrate the marriage of duc de Joyeuse and Marguerite of Lorraine. It was based on the story of Circe and choreographed by Baldassarino de Belgiojoso.	Morris dance, from Morocco.
17th Century Ballet Masquerade, often with hideous and elaborate masks. Playford's *English Dancing Master* published 1651; a collection of tunes and steps. First waltz, developed from minuet and Ländler in 1660; word 'waltz' first used in 1754 in Austria. Ballet systematique: Louis XIV established the Academie Royale de Danse 1661. Five classic positions codified; first history of dancing published in 1682.	Gigue (3,6,12), originally from English jig, the word from German *Geige*: 'fiddle'. Sarabande (3), slow and graceful, introduced to Spain *c.* 1588 from Morocco or West Indies. Bouree (4), lively dance, starting on the upbeat. Chaconne (3), graceful dance introduced from Peru (*guacones, c.* 1580) via Spain. Gavotte (2), medium pace, from Provencale: *gavoto:* a native of the Alps. Minuet (3), 'small steps'; rustic minuets occur in Strasbourg in 1682, but origin in the 15th century Branle. Passacaglia (3), as chaconne above, but in minor key. Rigaudon; Rigaudon: Rigadoon (2,4), lively French dance. Ländler (3), rustic dance, from *Ländl:* 'small country'. Matelot (2), Dutch sailors' clog dance. Contredanse (2,4) from Eng. 'country dance', but mistranslated as 'counter-dance', i.e. for opposing groups, and re-introduced into England in this form. Cotillion (6), from French word for 'petticoat', for 2 groups of 4 pairs each; developed into quadrille at the end of the 19th century.
18th Century Ballet steps on toe-tips (on point) (*c.* 1800).	Reel (4), stylised form of Scottish dance.
19th Century Square dance (*c.* 1815).	

MAIN TRENDS	TYPES OF DANCE POPULAR AT THE TIME (*Basic rhythmic pulse in brackets*)
Can-can (*c.* 1835); high-kicking exhibitionist female dance popular on Parisian stages.	Quadrille (2,4).
Age of the great waltz composers: Josef Lanner; Johann Strauss; Emil Waldteufel, etc.	Polka (2), introduced to Paris in 1843 from Bohemian courtship dance (1-2-3-hop). Cakewalk (2), graceful walking dance of competitive type with cakes as prizes, popular in Black America in 1872; introduced into ballrooms *c.* 1900.
20th Century Ballets Russes established in Paris by Diaghilev, 1909. New free dance forms emerging. Ballroom dance craze, mostly couples dancing to small instrumental groups (*c.* 1920). Growth of very energetic dancing, often to jazz or pseudo-jazz groups (from 1939). Modern Discotheque style, i.e. recorded music for dancing; originated in Parisian clubs (*c.* 1951). Popularity of dances closely linked to the 'hit-parade' progress of popular music and the consequent invention of many new dance styles.	Samba (2), emerged from Brazil, 1885; known *c.* 1920 as Maxixe; resumed name 'samba' *c.* 1940. Quickstep (2), invented in America 1900; reached peak of popularity in 1920s. Tango (2), earliest contest in Nice, France, in 1907. Barn dance (4), associated in America with festivities surrounding the completion of a new barn. Two-step (2). Boston (2), predecessor of the foxtrot. Turkey Trot (2). Foxtrot (4), slow and quick varieties, introduced in 1912 in America, allegedly named after Harry Fox. The slow foxtrot evolved *c.* 1927 into the 'blues' dance. Charleston (2), side kick from the knee. Named after a Mack and Johnson song (1923) about the town that saw the first ballet in America in 1735. Pasodoble (2), Spanish-style two-step. Rumba (8, i.e. 3 + 3 + 2), authentic Cuban dance popularised in 1923. Black Bottom (4), first mentioned in New York Times (19 Dec. 1926), a type of athletic and jerky foxtrot. Conga (4, i.e. 1–2–3–kick), single-file dance developed in 1935 from Rumba and from aboriginal African dances. Jive (2,4) derived from Jitterbug. Mambo (8), an off-beat Rumba (1948) of Cuban origin. Rock 'n' Roll (2), introduced in 1953 by Bill Haley and his Comets in America; heavy beat and simple melody for energetic and free dancing. Cha cha cha (2,4) (1954), a variation of the Mambo, couples dancing with lightly linked hands. Twist (2) (1961), body-torsion and knee-flexing lively dance, with partners rarely in contact. Bossa nova (2), lively Latin American dance. Go-go (2,4) (1965), repetitious dance of verve, often exhibitionist. Reggae (4) (1969), introduced from Jamaica, strong accentuations off-beat. Pogo (2) (1976), introduced by 'Punk Rockers'. Dancers rise vertically from the floor in imitation of a pogo stick. Robotic-dancers imitate clockwork dolls with rigid limb movements. 1980 Break dancing; dancers perform acrobatic feats while dancing.

number of performers in a dance; a *pas seul* is a solo and a *pas de deux* a dance for a pair of dancers.

pirouette Complete turn on one leg, performed either on the ball of the foot or on the toes.

plié Bending the legs from a standing position; *demi-plié* involves bending the knees as far as possible while keeping the heels on the ground.

relevé Bending the body from the waist to one side or the other during a turn or a pirouette.

rivoltade, revoltade Step in which a dancer raises one leg in front, jumps from the other and turns in the air, landing in his original position but facing the other way.

saut A plain jump into the air without embellishment.

soutenu Movement executed at a slower tempo than usual.

sur les pointes On the toes.

variation Solo by a male dancer in a *pas de deux*.

Some well known ballet companies

Royal Danish Ballet
Founded 1748
Bolshoi Ballet
Founded in Moscow in 1776
Kirov Ballet Formerly the Imperial Russian

Ballet of St. Petersburg (Leningrad)
Founded 1860
Ballets Russes
Founded by Diaghilev in Paris 1909
Martha Graham Dance Company
Founded by Graham in 1930
Ballet Rambert
Founded by Marie Rambert in 1930

Vic-Wells Ballet (afterwards, Sadlers Wells Ballet)
Founded in 1931 by Ninette de Valois
Ballets Jooss
Founded by Kurt Jooss in 1932
New York City Ballet
Founded in 1934

American Ballet Theatre
Founded in 1940 by Lucia Chase
Merce Cunningham Dance Company
Founded by Cunningham in 1952
Royal Ballet   Successor to Sadlers Wells Ballet.
Founded 1956

Language and Literature

World's principal languages

The world's total of languages and dialects is now estimated to be about 5000. The most widely spoken, together with the countries in which they are used, are as follows.

1. Guoyu (standardised Northern Chinese or Běifānghuà
Alphabetised into *Zhùyīn fùhào* (37 letters) in 1918 and converted to the *Pinyin* system of phonetic pronunciation in 1958. Spoken in China (Mainland). Language family: Sino-Tibetan. 700 000 000.

2. English
Evolved from an Anglo-Saxon, Norman-French and Latin amalgam *c.* 1350. Spoken in Australia, Bahamas, Canada, Sri Lanka (3rd), Cyprus (3rd), The Gambia, Ghana, Guyana, India (non-constitutional), Ireland, Jamaica, Kenya (official with Swahili), Malaysia, Malta (official with Maltese), New Zealand, Nigeria (official), Pakistan (now only 1 per cent), Sierra Leone (official), Singapore (2nd at 24 per cent), South Africa (38 per cent of white population), Tanzania (official with Swahili), Trinidad and Tobago, Uganda (official), UK, USA, Zimbabwe and also widely as the second language of educated Europeans and of citizens of the USSR. Language family: Indo-European. 395 000 000.

3. Great Russian
The foremost of the official languages used in the USSR and spoken as the first language by 60 per cent of the population. Language family: Indo-European. 250 000 000.

4. Spanish
Dates from the 10th century AD; spoken in Argentina, Bolivia, Canary Islands, Chile, Colombia, Costa Rica, Cuba, Dominican Republic, Ecuador, El Salvador, Guatemala, Honduras, Mexico, Nicaragua, Panama, Paraguay, Peru, The Philippines, Puerto Rico, Spain, Uruguay, Venezuela. Language family: Indo-European. 230 000 000.

5. Hindustani (a combination of Hindi and Urdu) foremost of the 845 languages of India of which 15 are 'constitutional'. Hindi (official) is spoken by more than 25 per cent, Urdu by nearly 4 per cent and Hindustani, as such, by 10 per cent. In Pakistan, Hindustani is the third most prevalent language (7½ per cent). Language family: Indo-European. 220 000 000.

=6. Bengali
Widely spoken in the Ganges delta area of India and Bangladesh. Language family: Indo-European. 135 000 000.

=6. Arabic
Dates from the early 6th century. Spoken in Algeria, Bahrain, Egypt, Iraq (81 per cent), Israel (16 per cent), Jordan, Kuwait, Lebanon, Libya, Maldives, Morocco (65 per cent), Oman, Qatar, Saudi Arabia, Somalia, Sudan (52 per cent), Syria, Tunisia, United Arab Emirates and both Yemens. Language family: Hamito-Semitic. 135 000 000.

=6. Portuguese
Distinct from Spanish by 14th century and, unlike it, was more influenced by French than by Arabic. Spoken in Angola, Brazil, Goa, Macao, Mozambique, Portugal, East Timor (Indonesia). Language family: Indo-European. 135 000 000.

9. German
Known in written form since the 8th century AD. Spoken in the Federal Republic of Germany (West) and the German Democratic Republic (East), Austria, Liechtenstein, Luxembourg and Switzerland plus minorities in the USA, USSR, Hungary, Poland, Romania and in formerly colonised German territories in eastern and southern Africa and the Pacific. Language family: Indo-European. 120 000 000.

10. Japanese
Earliest inscription (in Chinese characters) dates from the 5th century. Spoken in Japan, Formosa (Taiwan), Hawaii and some formerly colonised Pacific Islands. Unrelated to any other language. 110 000 000.

11. Malay-Indonesian
Originated in Northern Sumatra, spoken in Indonesia (form called Bahasa is official), Malaysia, Sabah, Sarawak, Thailand (southernmost parts). Language family: Malayo-Polynesian. 100 000 000.

12. French
Developed in 9th century as a result of Frankish influence on Gaulish substratum. Fixed by Académie Française from 17th century. Spoken in France, French Pacific Is., Belgium, Guadeloupe, Haiti, Luxembourg, Martinique, Monaco, Switzerland, the Italian region of Aosta, Canada, USA (Louisiana) and widely in former French colonies in Africa. Language family: Indo-European. 95 000 000.

=13. Italian
Became very distinct from Latin by 10th century. Spoken in Eritrea, Italy, Libya, Switzerland and widely retained in USA among Italian population. Language family: Indo-European. 60 000 000.

=13. Punjabi
One of the 15 constitutional languages of India spoken by the region of that name. Also spoken in parts of Pakistan. 60 000 000.

=13. Urdu
One of the 15 official languages of India. Also spoken in parts of Pakistan and Bangladesh. 60 000 000.

16. Korean
Not known to be related to any other tongue. 55 000 000.

=17. Cantonese
A distinctive dialect of Chinese spoken in the Kwang-tung area. Language family: Sino-Tibetan. 50 000 000.

=17. Telugu
Used in south India. Known in a written, grammatic form from the 11th century. Language family: Dravidian. 50 000 000.

=17. Tamil
The second oldest written Indian language. Cave graffiti date from the 3rd century BC. Spoken in Sri Lanka, southern India, and among Tamils in Malaysia. Language family: Dravidian. 50 000 000.

=17. Marathi.
A language spoken in west and central India, including Goa and part of Hyderabad and Poona with written origins dating from about AD 500. Language family: Indo-European. 50 000 000.

21. Javanese
Closely related to Malay. Serves as the language of 50 per cent of Indonesian population. Language family: Malayo-Polynesian. 45 000 000.

=22. Ukrainian (Little Russian)
Distinction from Great Russian discernible by

11th century, literary zenith late 18th and early 19th century. Banned as written language in Russia 1876–1905. Discouraged since 1931 in USSR. Spoken in Ukrainian SSR, parts of Russian SFSR and Romania. Language family: Indo-European. 40 000 000.

=22. Wu
A dialect in China spoken, but not officially encouraged, in the Yang-tse delta area. Language family: Sino-Tibetan. 40 000 000.

=22. Min (Fukien)
A dialect in China which includes the now discouraged Amoy and Fuchow dialects and Hainanese. Language family: Sino-Tibetan. 40 000 000.

=22. Turkish
Spoken in European and Asian Turkey – a member of the Oghuz division of the Turkic group of languages. 40 000 000.

=26. Vietnamese
Used in the whole of eastern Indo-China. Classified as a Mon-Khmer by some and as a Thai language by other philologists. 35 000 000.

=26. Polish
A western Slavonic language with written records back to the 13th century, 300 years before its emergence as a modern literary language. Spoken in Poland, and western USSR and among émigré populations notably in the USA. Language family: Indo-European. 35 000 000.

Origins of the English language

The three Germanic dialects on which English is based are descended from the Indo-Germanic or Aryan family of languages, spoken since c. 3000 BC by the nomads of the Great Lowland Plain of Europe, which stretches from the Aral Sea in the Soviet Union to the Rhine in West Germany. Now only fragments of Old Lithuanian contain what is left of this ancestral tongue.

Of the three inherited Germanic dialects, the first was Jutish, brought into England in AD 449 from Jutland. This was followed 40 years later by Saxon, brought from Holstein, and Anglian, which came from the still later incursions from the area of Schleswig-Holstein.

These three dialects were superimposed on the 1000-year-old indigenous Celtic tongue, along with what Latin had survived in the towns from nearly 15 generations of Roman occupation

(AD 43–410). The next major event in the history of the English language was the first of many Viking invasions, beginning in 793, from Denmark and Norway. Norse and Danish left permanent influences on the Anglo-Frisian Old English, though Norse never survived as a separate tongue in England beyond 1035, the year of the death of King Canute (Cnut), who had then reigned for 19 years over England, 16 years over Denmark and 7 years over Norway.

The Scandinavian influence now receded before Norman French, though Norse still struggled on in remote parts of Scotland until about 1630 and in the Shetland Islands until c. 1750. The Normans were, however, themselves really Vikings, who in five generations had become converts to the Latin culture and language of northern France.

For three centuries after the Norman conquest of 1066 by William I, descendant of Rollo the Viking, England lived under a trilingual system. The mother tongue of all the first 13 Kings and Queens, from William I (1066–1087) until as late as Richard II (1377–99), was Norman. English became the language of court proceedings only during the reign of Edward III, in October 1362, and the language for teaching in the Universities of Oxford and Cambridge in c. 1380.

English did not really crystallise as an amalgam of Anglo-Saxon and Latin root forms until the 14th century, when William Langland (c.1330–c.1400), and Geoffrey Chaucer (c.1340–1400) were the pioneers of a literary tradition, which culminated in William Shakespeare, who died in 1616, just four years before the sailing of the *Mayflower*.

English Literature

Nothing definite has survived of the stories or songs possessed by the ancient Britons who were invaded by Julius Caesar on 26 Aug. 55 BC. Barely anything has survived from the 367-year Roman occupation until AD 410. English literature thus begins at least by being English.

The earliest known British born author was Pelagius (fl. 400–18) from whom survive some remains of theological disputations written in Rome.

The earliest English poem know to us is Widseth, about a wandering minstrel of the 6th century. In the Exeter Book 150 lines of this poem survive.

The oldest surviving record of a named English poet who composed on British soil is from the paraphrase by Bede (673–735) of a hymn attributed to Caedmon of Streaneshalch (Whitby, North Yorkshire), who was living in 670. This survives in the Cambridge manuscript

of Bede (or Baeda) in a hand possibly of the 18th century.

The first great book in English prose is the Anglo-Saxon Chronicle supervised by King Alfred until 892. Alfred himself translated some of the writings of Bede and of Gregory the Great's *Pastoral Care* into West Saxon.

The Lindisfarne Gospels, a beautiful vellum quarto Latin manuscript now in the British Library, London, was written c. 696–8. In c. 950 Alred, Bishop of Durham, added an interlinear gloss in Northumbrian dialect.

The leading authors of the Old English Period are:

Alfric	c. 955—c. 1020
King Alfred	849—99
Venerable Bede	c. 673–735
Caedmon	fl. 670
Cynewulf	? 9th century
Wulfstan	d. 1023

Bibliography

Below are brief notes and a list of the major works of the 10 British writers who have the longest entries in the *Oxford Dictionary of Quotations*. They are listed in order of length of their entry.

Shakespeare, William (1564–1616)
The greatest contribution to the world's store of poetry and drama has been made by William Shakespeare (1564–1616). Born at Stratford-upon-Avon, this eldest surviving child of an Alderman and trader produced in the space of the seventeen years between 1594 (*Titus Andronicus*) and 1611 (*The Tempest*) thirty-seven plays which total 814 780 words.

Shakespeare's outpouring of sheer genius has excited and amazed critics of every age since. His contemporary Ben Jonson called him 'The applause! delight! the wonder of our stage!' Milton refers to him as 'Sweetest Shakespeare, Fancy's child'. To Thomas Carlyle, looking at his massive brow, he was 'The greatest of intellects'. Matthew Arnold refers to him as 'out-topping' knowledge'.

Venus and Adonis (narrative poem)	1593
The Rape of Lucrece (narrative poem)	1594
Titus Andronicus	1594
*Henry VI Part 2**	1594
The Taming of the Shrew (see also 1623, First Folio)	1594
*Henry VI Part 3**	1595
Romeo and Juliet	1597
Richard II	1597
Richard III	1597
Henry IV Part I	1598

The Russian alphabet

The Russian alphabet is written in Cyrillic script, so called after St. Cyril, the 9th century monk who is reputed to have devised it. It contains thirty-three characters, including five hard and five soft vowels. Five other Cyrillic letters appear only in Bulgarian (one) and Serbian (four).

Capital	Lower case	Name	English equivalent	Capital	Lower case	Name	English equivalent
А	а	ah	ā	Т	т	teh	t
Б	б	beh	b	У	у	oo	oo
В	в	veh	v	Ф	ф	eff	f
Г	г	gheh	g	Х	х	hah	h
Д	д	deh	d	Ц	ц	tseh	ts
Е	е	yeh	ye	Ч	ч	cheh	ch
Ж	ж	zheh	j	Ш	ш	shah	sh
З	з	zeh	z	Щ	щ	shchah	shch
И	и	ee	ee	Ъ	ъ	(hard sign)	—
К	к	kah	k	Ы	ы	yerih	I
П	п	ell	l	Ь	ь	(soft sign)	—
М	м	em	m	Э	э	eh	e
Н	н	en	n	Ю	ю	you	yu
О	о	aw	aw	Я	я	ya	yā
П	п	peh	p				
Р	р	err	r	Е	е	yaw	yo
С	с	ess	s	Й	й	short й	elided 'y'

The Greek alphabet

The Greek alphabet consists of twenty-four letters – seven vowels and seventeen consonants. The seven vowels are alpha (short a), epsilon (short e), eta (long e), iota (short i), omicron (short o), upsilon (short u, usually transcribed y), and omega (long o).

Name	Capital	Lower case	English equivalent	Name	Capital	Lower case	English equivalent
Alpha	Α	α	a	Nu	Ν	ν	n
Beta	Β	β	b	Xi	Ξ	ξ	x
Gamma	Γ	γ	g	Omicron	Ο	ο	ō
Delta	Δ	δ	d	Pi	Π	π	p
Epsilon	Ε	ε	ĕ	Rho	Ρ	ρ	r
Zeta	Ζ	ζ	z	Sigma	Σ	σ ζ	s
Eta	Η	η	ē	Tau	Τ	τ	t
Theta	Θ	θ	th	Upsilon	Υ	υ	u or y
Iota	Ι	ι	i	Phi	Φ	φ	ph
Kappa	Κ	κ	k	Chi	Χ	χ	kh
Lambda	Λ	λ	l	Psi	Ψ	ψ	ps
Mu	Μ	μ	m	Omega	Ω	ω	o

Greek has no direct equivalent to our c, f, h, j, q, u, v, or w.

Love's Labour's Lost (Revised version, original (?1596) probably lost)	1598
Henry IV Part 2	1600
A Midsummer Night's Dream	1600
The Merchant of Venice	1600
Much Ado About Nothing	1600
Henry V (First 'true' text published 1623 in First Folio)	1600
*Sir John Falstaff and the Merry Wives of Windsor** (First 'true' text published in 1623 in First Folio)	1602
*Hamlet**	1603
Hamlet ('according to the true and perfect copy')	1604
King Lear	1608
Pericles, Prince of Tyre	1609
Troilus and Cressida	1609
Sonnets (1640 in 'Poems')	1609

* Bad quartos or unauthorised editions.

Posthumously Published
Othello	1622
First Folio – 36 plays in all including the first publication of *The Taming of the Shrew* (Shakespeare's revised version of the 1594 version)	1623

Henry VI Part I	*Macbeth*
The Two Gentlemen of Verona	*Timon of Athens*
The Comedy of Errors	*Antony and Cleopatra*
King John	*Coriolanus*
As You Like It	*Cymbeline*
Julius Ceasar	*A Winter's Tale*
Twelfth Night	*The Tempest*
Measure for Measure	*Henry VIII*
All's Well That Ends Well	

The Second Folio (1632), the Third Folio (1663 1st issue, 1664 2nd issue) and the Fourth Folio (1685) added nothing of authority to Heming and Condell's monumental First Folio.
Scientific study of Shakespeare began with Edward Capell (1713–81) and his researches published from 1768. The eminently honest and painstaking work of Alexander Dyce's edition of 1857 led to the publication in 1863–66 of what is regarded as the standard text, *The Cambridge Shakespeare*, edited by W C Clark and J Glover.

Tennyson, Alfred, First Baron (1809–92)
Poems [including *The Lotos Eaters* and *The Lady of Shalott* (dated 1833)]	1832
Poems (two volumes) (including *Ulysses, Sir Galahad, Morte d'Arthur, Locksley Hall*)	1842
In Memoriam A.H.H. (Arthur Henry Hallam)	1850
Ode on the Death of the Duke of Wellington	1852
Charge of the Light Brigade	1854
Maud and Other Poems	1859
Idylls of the King	1857–85
	(completed edition 1889)
Enoch Arden (including *Old Style*)	1864
Holy Grail	1869
The Revenge: A Ballad of the Fleet	1878
Becket	1884
Locksley Hall 60 Years After	1886
Demeter and Other Poems (including *Crossing the Bar*)	1889

Milton, John (1608–74)
On the Death of Fair Infant Dying of a Cough	1625
L'Allegro and Il Penseroso	1632
Arcades	1633
Comus (2 Masques)	1634
Lycidas	1638
A Tractate of Education	1644
Doctrine and Discipline of Divorce	1644
Areopagitica (a Tract)	1644
Tenure of Kings and Magistrates (a Pamphlet)	1649
Paradise Lost (written c. 1640–57)	1657
Paradise Regained (written 1665–66)	1671
Samson Agonistes	1671

Kipling, Joseph Rudyard (1865–1936)
Departmental Ditties	1886
Plain Tales from The Hills	1888
Soldiers Three	1888

Wee Willie Winkie	1888
The Light That Failed	1891
Barrack Room Ballads	1892
Many Inventions	1893
Jungle Books (Two volumes)	1894–95
The Seven Seas (including *Mandalay*)	1896
Captains Courageous	1897
Recessional	1897
Stalky & Co.	1899
Kim	1901
Just So Stories for Children	1902
Puck of Pook's Hill	1906
Rewards and Fairies	1910
A School History of England	1911

Wordsworth, William (1770–1850)
The Evening Walk (written 1787–92)	1793
Descriptive Sketches (written 1787–92)	1793
Guilt and Sorrow	1794
Lyrical Ballads (with Coleridge)	1798 & 1800
Prelude	1805
Poems in Two Volumes (including *Ode to Duty* and *Ode on Intimations of Immortality*)	1807
Excursion: a portion of the *Recluse*	1814
Poems, including the *Borderers*	1842

Shelley, Percy Bysshe (1792–1822)
Alastor	1816
Ode to The West Wind	1819
The Cenci	1819
Prometheus Unbound	1820
The Witch of Atlas	1820
To a Skylark	1820
The Cloud	1820
Epipsychidion	1821
Adonais	1821
Queen Mab	1821
Hellas	1822
Defence of Poetry (uncompleted)	

Johnson, Dr Samuel (1709–84)
A Voyage to Abyssinia by Father Jerome Lobo (Translation)	1735
London: a Poem, in Imitation of the Third Satire of Juvenal (anon.)	1738
Parliamentary Reports disguised as Debates in the Senate of Magna Lilliputia (Senate of Lilliput) July 1741–Mar. 1744	
Life of Savage	1744
Plan of a Dictionary of the English Language	1747
Irene (Theatrical tragedy produced by Garrick at Drury Lane)	1748
The Vanity of Human Wishes	1749
The Rambler (essays in 208 bi-weekly issues) Mar. 1750–Mar. 1752	
A Dictionary of the English Language (8 years' work, 1747–55)	1755
The Prince of Abyssinia, A Tale	1759
The Idler (essays in the *Universal Chronicle* or the *Weekly Gazette*) Apr. 1758–Apr. 1760	
Rasselas	1759
Shakespeare, a new Edition	1765
A Journey to the Western Highlands	1775
The Lives of the Poets vols. i–iv 1779, vols. v–x 1781	
Dr Johnson's Diary, posthumously published	1816

Browning, Robert (1812–89)
Paracelsus	1835
Sordello	1840
Christmas-Eve and Easter-Day	1850
Men and Women (including *One Word More* and *Bishop Blougram's Apology*)	1855
Dramatis Personae (including *Rabi ben Ezera* and *Caliban upon Setebos*)	1864
The Ring and The Book	1868–69
A Grammarian's Funeral	
Soliloquy of the Spanish Cloister	
The Pied Piper of Hamelin	
Asolando posthumously	1890
New Poems (with Elizabeth Barrett Browning) posthumously	1914

Byron, George Gordon, sixth baron (1788–1824)
Fugitive Pieces (privately printed) originally called *Juvenilia*	1806
Hours of Idleness (reprint of the above with amendments)	1807
English Bards and Scotch Reviewers	1809
Childe Harold (began at Janina, 1809), Cantos i and ii	1812
The Giaour	1813
The Corsair	1814
Lora	1814
The Siege of Corinth	1816
The Prisoner of Chillon	1816
Childe Harold (written in Switzerland), Canto iii	1816
Childe Harold (written in Venice), Canto iv	1817
Manfred	1817
Don Juan (first five cantos)	1818–20
Autobiography	(burnt 1824)
Cain	1821
Don Juan (later cantos)	1821–22
Contribution to *The Liberal* newspaper 'Vision of Judgement'	1822
The Island	1823
Heaven and Earth	1824

Dickens, Charles John Huffam (1812–70)
Sketches of Young Gentlemen, Sketches of Young Couples, The Mudfog Papers	unpublished
A Dinner at Poplar Walk (re-entitled *Mr. Minns and his Cousin*)	Dec. 1833
Sketches by Boz. Illustrative of Every Day Life and Every-Day People published in *Monthly Magazine* (1833–35) and *Evening Chronicle*	1835
The Posthumous Papers of the Pickwick Club	from Apr. 1836
Oliver Twist (in Bentley's *Miscellany*)	1837–39
Nicholas Nickleby (in monthly numbers)	1838–39
Master Humphrey's Clock (Barnaby Rudge and *The Old Curiosity Shop)*	1840–41
The Old Curiosity Shop (as a book)	1841
Barnaby Rudge (as a book)	1841
American Notes	1842
Martin Chuzzlewit (parts)	1843–44
A Christmas Carol	1843
The Chimes (written in Italy)	1844
The Cricket on the Hearth	1845
Pictures from Italy	1846
Daily News (later the *News Chronicle*) Editor	Jan.–Feb. 1846
The Battle of Life	1846
The Haunted Man	1847
Dombey and Son (parts) (written in Switzerland)	1847–48
Household Word (weekly periodical) Editor (included *Holly-Tree*)	1848–59
David Copperfield	1849–50
Bleak House (in parts)	1852–53
A Child's History of England (in three volumes)	1852–3–4
Hard Times. For These Times (book form)	1854
Little Dorrit	1857–58
All the Year Round (Periodical) Editor	1859–70
Great Expectations	1860–61
The Uncommercial Traveller (collected parts of *A Tale of Two Cities*)	1861
Our Mutual Friend	1864–65
The Mystery of Edwin Drood (unfinished)	1870

Other British writers (14th to 20th centuries)

The writers below are listed in chronological order of year of birth, together with their best known work or works.

14th Century

Langland, William (c. 1330–c. 1400). *Vision of Piers Plowman*.

Chaucer, Geoffrey (c. 1340–1400). *Canterbury Tales*.

above left: *William Shakespeare (1564–1616) (engraved by E. S. Scriven)*
left: *Jonathan Swift (1667–1745) (engraved by B. Holl)*
above: *Izaac Walton (1593–1683)*
above right: *The Rev. Charles Kingsley (1819–75)*
right: *Robert Browning (1812–89)*

Photographs: Mary Evans Picture Library

15th century
Malory, Sir Thomas (*c.* 1400–1470). *Morte d'Arthur*.
More, Sir Thomas (1478–1535). *Utopia*.

16th century
Leland or Leyland (*c.* 1506–1552) *Itinerary*.
Spenser, Edmund (1552–99). *The Faerie Queene*.
Lyly, John (*c.* 1554–1606). *Euphues*.
Sidney, Sir Philip (1554–86). *The Countesse of Pembrokes Arcadia; Astrophel and Stella; The Defence of Poesie*.
Bacon, Francis (Baron Verulam, Viscount St Albans) (1561–1626). *The Advancement of Learning*.
Marlowe, Christopher (1564–1593). *Tamburlaine The Great; Dr Faustus*.
Donne, John (1572–1631). *Poems; Songs and sonnets; Satyres; Elegies*.
Jonson, Benjamin (1572–1637). *Every Man in his humour* (produced 1598, published 1601); *Every Man out of his humour* (1600); *Volpone: or the foxe* (1607); *The Alchemist* (1610, published 1612); *Bartholomew Fayre* (1614, published 1631).
Burton, Robert (1577–1640). *Anatomy of Melancholy*.
Beaumont, Francis (1584–1616) and Fletcher, John (1579–1625). *The Scornful Lady; Philaster; The Maid's Tragedy; A King and No King*.
Hobbes, Thomas (1588–1679). *Leviathan; Behemoth*.
Herrick, Robert (1591–1674). *Hesperides*.
Walton, Izaak (1593–1683). *The Complete Angler*.

17th Century
Clarendon, Edward Hyde, Earl of (1608–74). *History of the Rebellion and Civil Wars in England*.
Butler, Samuel (1612–80). *Hudibras*.
Evelyn, John (1620–1706). *Diary*.
Bunyan, John (1628–88). *The Pilgrim's Progress*.
Dryden, John (1631–1700). *All For Love*.
Locke, John (1632–1704). *Essay Concerning Human Understanding*.
Pepys, Samuel (1633–1703). *Diary*.
Newton, Sir Isaac (1643–1727). *Philosophiae Naturalis Principia Mathematica; Opticks*.
Ottway, Thomas (1652–85). *Venice Preserved*.
Defoe, Daniel (1660–1731). *The Life and Adventures of Robinson Crusoe*.
Swift, Jonathan (1667–1745). *Gulliver's Travels*.
Congreve, William (1670–1729). *The Way of the World*.
Addison, Joseph (1672–1719). *The Spectator*.
Pope, Alexander (1688–1744). *An Essay on Criticism; The Rape of the Lock; The Dunciad; An Essay on Man*.
Richardson, Samuel (1689–1761). *Pamela; Clarissa*.

18th Century
Fielding, Henry (1707–54). *Tom Thumb; The History of Tom Jones*.
Sterne, Laurence (1713–68). *Tristram Shandy*.
Gray, Thomas (1716–71). *An Elegy Written in a Country Churchyard*.
Walpole, Horace, 4th Earl of Orford (1717–97). *Letters*.
Smollett, Tobias George (1721–71). *Roderick Random; Peregrine Pickle; Humphrey Clinker*.
Smith, Adam (1723–1790). *Wealth of Nations*.
Goldsmith, Oliver (1728–74). *The Vicar of Wakefield; She Stoops to Conquer; The Deserted Village*.
Burke, Edmund (1729–97). *Reflections on the Revolution in France*.
Cowper, William (1731–1800). *Poems*.
Gibbon, Edward (1737–94). *A History of the Decline and Fall of the Roman Empire*.
Paine, Thomas (1737–1809). *Rights of Man*.
Boswell, James (1740–95). *Life of Johnson*.
Burney, Frances 'Fanny' (Madame D'Arblay), (1752–1840). *Evelina*.
Sheridan, Richard Brinsley (1751–1816). *The Rivals; The School For Scandal*.
Blake, William (1757–1827). *Songs of Innocence; Songs of Experience*.
Burns, Robert (1759–96). *Poems chiefly in the Scottish dialect; Tam O'Shanter; The Cotters Saturday Night; The Jolly Beggars*.
Cobbett, William (1762–1835). *Rural Rides*.
Smith, Rev Sydney (1771–1845). *The Letters of Peter Plymley; Edinburgh Review*.
Scott, Sir Walter (1771–1832). *Waverley; Rob Roy; Ivanhoe; Kenilworth; Quentin Durward; Redgauntlet; Lady of the Lake*.
Coleridge, Samuel Taylor (1772–1834). *Lyrical Ballads (Ancient Mariner); The Kubla Khan*.
Southey, Robert (1774–1843). *Quarterly Review* (contributions); *Life of Nelson*.
Austen, Jane (1775–1817). *Sense and Sensibility; Pride and Prejudice; Mansfield Park; Emma; Northanger Abbey; Persuasion*.
Lamb, Charles (1775–1834). *Tales from Shakespeare* [largely by his sister, Mary Lamb (1764–1847)]; *Essays of Elia*.
Hazlitt, William (1778–1830). *My First Acquaintance with Poets; Table Talk; The Plain Speaker*.
Hunt, James Henry Leigh (1784–1859). *The Story of Rimini; Autobiography*.
De Quincey, Thomas (1785–1859). *Confessions of an English Opium Eater*.
Peacock, Thomas Love (1785–1866). *Headlong Hall; Nightmare Abbey*.
Marryat, Frederick (1792–1848). *Mr Midshipman Easy*.
Clare, John (1793–1864). *Poems Descriptive of Rural Life*.
Keats, John (1795–1821). *Endymion; Ode to a Nightingale; Ode on a Grecian Urn; Ode to Psyche; Ode to Autumn; Ode on Melancholy; La Belle Dame sans Merci; Isabella*.

from top: *Thomas Hardy (1840–1928)*
Oscar Wilde (1854–1900)
Sir Arthur Conan Doyle (1859–1930)
Dame Edith Sitwell DBE (1887–1964)

Carlyle, Thomas (1795–1881). *The French Revolution; Oliver Cromwell's Letters and Speeches.*

Hood, Thomas (1799–1845). *The Song of the Shirt; The Bridge of Sighs; To The Great Unknown.*

Shelley, Mary Wollstonecraft (Godwin) (1797–1851). *Frankenstein.*

Macaulay, Thomas Babington (Lord) (1800–59). *Lays of Ancient Rome; History of England.*

19th Century

Newman, John Henry, Cardinal (1801–90). *The Dream of Gerontius.*

Surtees, Robert Smith (1803–64). *Handley Cross.*

Borrow, George (1803–1881). *Lavengro.*

Disraeli, Benjamin (Earl of Beaconsfield) (1804–81). *Coningsby; Sybil; Tancred.*

Browning, Elizabeth Barrett (1806–61). *Poems; Aurora Leigh.*

Mill, John Stuart (1806–1873). *Liberty.*

Darwin, Charles Robert (1809–82). *On the Origin of Species; The Descent of Man.*

Fitzgerald, Edward (1809–83). *Rubáiyát of Omar Khayyám.*

Gaskell, Mrs (Elizabeth Cleghorn Stevenson) (1810–65). *Mary Barton; Cranford; North and South.*

Thackeray, William Makepeace (1811–63). *Vanity Fair; The History of Henry Esmond Esq.*

Smiles, Samuel (1812–1904). *Self-Help.*

Lear, Edward (1812–88). *A Book of Nonsense; Nonsense Songs.*

Read, Charles (1814–84). *The Cloister and the Hearth.*

Trollope, Anthony (1815–82). *The six Barsetshire novels (The Warden; Barchester Towers; Doctor Thorne; Framley Parsonage; The Small House at Allington; The Last Chronicle of Barset).*

Brontë, (later Nicholls), Charlotte (1816–55). *Jane Eyre; Shirley; Villette.*

Brontë, Emily Jane (1818–48). *Wuthering Heights.*

Ruskin, John (1819–1900). *Modern Painters.*

'Eliot, George' (Mary Ann [or Marian] Evans, later Mrs J W Cross) (1819–80). *Adam Bede; The Mill on the Floss; Silas Marner; Middlemarch.*

Kingsley, Charles (1819–75). *Westward Ho!; The Water Babies.*

Brontë, Anne (1820–49). *Tenant of Wildfell Hall.*

Arnold, Matthew (1822–88). *The Strayed Reveler; Poems.*

Collins, William Wilkie (1824–89). *The Woman in White; The Moonstone.*

Bagehot, Walter (1826–77). *The English Constitution.*

Meredith, George (1828–1909). *Modern Love; Diana of the Crossways.*

Rossetti, Dante Gabriel (1828–82). *Poems; Ballads and Sonnets.*

'Carroll, Lewis' (Rev. Charles Lutwidge Dodgson) (1832–98). *Alice's Adventures in Wonderland; Through The Looking Glass.*

Morris, William (1834–96) *News from Nowhere.*

Gilbert, Sir William Schwenck (1836–1911). *The Mikado; The Gondoliers; HMS Pinafore; The Pirates of Penzance; The Yeomen of the Guard; Patience.*

Swinburne, Algernon Charles (1837–1909). *Poems and Ballads; Rosamund.*

Hardy, Thomas (1840–1928). *Under The Greenwood Tree; Tess of the D'Urbervilles; Far From the Madding Crowd; The Return of the Native; The Mayor of Casterbridge; Jude the Obscure.*

Hudson, W(illiam) H(enry) (1841–1922). *Green Mansions.*

Bridges, Robert Seymour (1844–1930). *The Testament of Beauty.*

Hopkins, Gerard Manley (1844–89). *The Notebooks and Papers of Gerard Manley Hopkins.*

Stoker, Bram (Abraham) (1847–1912). *Dracula.*

Jefferies, Richard (1848–1887). *The Amateur Poacher.*

Stevenson, Robert Louis (1850–94). *Travels with a Donkey in the Cévennes; New Arabian Nights; Treasure Island; Strange Case of Dr Jekyll and Mr Hyde; Kidnapped; Catriona; The Black Arrow; The Master of Ballantrae; Weir of Hermiston (unfinished).*

Moore, George (1852–1933). *Esther Waters.*

Wilde, Oscar Fingal O'Flahertie Wills (1854–1900). *The Picture of Dorian Gray; Lady Windermere's Fan; The Importance of Being Ernest.*

Haggard, Sir Henry Rider (1856–1925). *King Solomon's Mines; She; Alain Quartermain.*

Shaw, George Bernard (1856–1950). *Plays Pleasant and Unpleasant (including Mrs Warren's Profession, Arms and the Man; Candida); Three Plays for Puritans (The Devil's Disciple, Caesar and Cleopatra and Captain Brassbound's Conversion); Man and Superman; John Bull's Other Island; Major Barbara; Androcles and the Lion; Pygmalion; Saint Joan; Essays in Fabian Socialism.*

Gissing, George (Robert) (1857–1903). *The Private Papers of Henry Ryecroft.*

Conrad, Joseph (né Teodor Józef Konrad Nalecz Korzeniowski) (1857–1924). *Almayer's Folly; An Outcast of the Islands; The Nigger of the 'Narcissus'; Lord Jim; Youth; Typhoon; Nostromo; The Secret Agent; Under Western Eyes.*

Doyle, Sir Arthur Conan (1859–1930). *The White Company; The Adventures of Sherlock Holmes; The Hound of the Baskervilles; The Exploits of Brigadier Gerard; The Lost World.*

Thompson, Francis (1859–1907). *The Hound of Heaven; The Kingdom of God.*

Housman, Alfred Edward (1859–1936). *A Shropshire Lad.*

Grahame, Kenneth (1859–1932). *The Wind in the Willows.*

Barrie, Sir James Matthew (1860–1937). *Quality Street; The Admirable Crichton; Peter Pan.*

Quiller-Couch, Sir Arthur Thomes ('Q') (1863–1944). *On the Art of Writing; Studies in Literature.*

Yeats, William Butler (1865–1939). *Collected Poems; The Tower; Last Poems; The Hour Glass.*

Wells, Herbert George (1866–1946). *The Invisible Man; The History of Mr Polly; Kipps; The Shape of Things to Come; The War of the Worlds.*

Murray, George Gilbert Aimé (1866–1957). *History of Ancient Greek Literature.*

Bennett, Enoch Arnold (1867–1931). *Anna of the Five Towns; The Old Wives' Tale; Clayhanger; The Card; Riceyman Steps.*

Galsworthy, John (1867–1933). *The Forsyte Saga; Modern Comedy; The White Monkey.*

Douglas, Norman (1868–1952). *Old Calabria; South Wind.*

Belloc, Joseph Hilaire Pierre (1870–1953). *The Path to Rome; The Bad Child's Book of Beasts; Cautionary Tales.*

Synge, John Millington (1871–1909). *The Playboy of the Western World.*

Beerbohm, Sir Max (1872–1956). *Zuleika Dobson.*

Powys, John Cowper (1872–1963). *Weymouth Sands.*

Ford, Ford Madox (1873–1939). *The Good Soldier.*

De La Mare, Walter (1873–1956). *Poems; Come Hither; O Lovely England.*

Chesterton, Gilbert Keith (1874–1936). *The Innocence of Father Brown; The Ballad of The White Horse.*

Churchill, Sir Winston Spencer (1874–1965). *Life of Marlborough; The Second World War; A History of The English-Speaking Peoples; The World Crisis.*

Maugham, William Somerset (1874–1965). *Of Human Bondage; The Moon and Sixpence; The Razor's Edge.*

Buchan, John (1st Baron Tweedsmuir) (1875–1940). *Montrose; The Thirty-Nine Steps; Greenmantle; Prester John; Huntingtower.*

Powys, Theodore Francis (1875–1953). *Mr Weston's Good Wine.*

Trevelyan, George Macaulay (1876–1962). *History of England; English Social History.*

Masefield, John (1878–1967). *Salt-Water Ballads; The Everlasting Mercy; So Long to Learn; Jim Davis; Collected Poems.*

Thomas, Edward (1878–1917). *Poems.*

Forster, Edward Morgan (1879–1970). *Where Angels Fear to Tread; A Room with a View;*

Howard's End; A Passage to India.

O'Casey, Sean (1880–1964). *Juno and the Paycock; The Plough and the Stars.*

Wodehouse, Sir Pelham Grenville (1881–1975). *Summer Lightning; Much Obliged Jeeves.*

Joyce, James (1882–1941). *Ulysses; Finnegans Wake; Portrait of the Artist as a Young Man.*

Woolf (*née* Stephen), Virginia (1882–1941). *The Voyage Out; Night and Day; Jacob's Room; The Years.*

Milne, Alan Alexander (1882–1956). *Winnie the Pooh; The House at Pooh Corner.*

Keynes, John Maynard (Baron) (1883–1946). *The Economic Consequences of the Peace; The General Theory of Employment.*

Mackenzie, Sir Compton (1883–1972). *Whisky Galore; Sinister Street.*

Lewis, (Percy) Wyndham (1884–1957). *The Apes of God.*

Ransome, Arthur Michell (1884–1967). *Swallows and Amazons.*

Walpole, Sir Hugh Seymour (1884–1941). *Herries Chronicle.*

Flecker, James Elroy (1884–1915). *The Golden Journey to Sarmarkand.*

Lawrence, David Herbert (1885–1930). *Sons and Lovers; Love Poems and Others.*

Sassoon, Siegfried (1886–1967). *Memoirs of a Fox-Hunting Man; Memoirs of an Infantry Officer.*

Sitwell, Dame Edith (1887–1964). *Collected Poems; Aspects of Modern Poetry.*

Brooke, Rupert Chawner (1887–1915). *1914 and Other Poems; Letters from America.*

Muir, Edwin (1887–1959). *First Poems.*

Cary, (Arthur) Joyce (Lunel) (1888–1957). *The Horse's Mouth.*

Eliot, Thomas Stearns (1888–1965). *Murder in the Cathedral; The Waste Land.*

Lawrence, Thomas Edward (later Shaw) (1888–1935). *Seven Pillars of Wisdom.*

Mansfield, Katherine (Beauchamp) (1888–1923). *In a German Pension: The Dove's Nest and Other Stories.*

Toynbee, Arnold Joseph (1889–1975). *A Study of History.*

Herbert, Sir Alan Patrick (1890–1971). *Misleading Cases.*

Rosenberg, Isaac (1890–1918). *Poems.*

Christie, Agatha Mary Clarissa (1891–1976). *The Murder of Roger Ackroyd.*

Tolkien, J(ohn) R(onald) R(euel) (1892–1973). *The Hobbit; The Lord of the Rings.*

Owen, Wilfred (1893–1918). *Poems.*

Sayers, Dorothy Leigh (1893–1957). *The Nine Tailors.*

Priestley, John Boynton (1894–1985). *The Good Companions; The Linden Tree; An Inspector Calls.*

Huxley, Aldous Leonard (1894–1963). *Brave New World; Point Counter Point.*

Hartley, Leslie Poles (1895–1972). *The Go-Between.*

Graves, Robert Ranke (b. 1895). *I Claudius; Goodbye to All That.*

Blunden, Edmund (1896–1974). *Poems 1914–1930.*

Sheriff, Robert Cedric (1896–1975). *Journey's End.*

Williamson, Henry (1897–1977). *Tarka the Otter.*

Coward, Sir Noel (1899–1973). *Hay Fever; Private Lives; Blithe Spirit.*

Hughes, Richard (1900–1976). *A High Wind in Jamaica.*

20th Century

Orwell, George (Eric Arthur Blair) (1903–50). *Animal Farm; 1984.*

Waugh, Evelyn (1903–66). *Scoop, Men at Arms; Officers and Gentlemen; Unconditional Surrender; Brideshead Revisited.*

Day-Lewis, Cecil (1904–72). *Collected Poems.*

Isherwood, Christopher (b. 1904). *Goodbye to Berlin.*

Greene, Graham (b. 1904). *Brighton Rock; Our Man in Havana; The Power and the Glory.*

Green, Henry (pseud. of Henry Vincent Yorke) (1905–1973). *Living; Loving; Concluding.*

Snow, Sir Charles Percy (1905–1980). *Strangers*

and Brothers.

Bates, Herbert Ernest (1905–74). *'Flying-Officer X' Stories.*

Powell, Anthony (b. 1905). *The Music of Time novel sequence.*

Beckett, Samuel (b. 1906). *Waiting for Godot.*

Betjeman, John (1906–84). *Mount Zion; Collected Poems.*

Fry, Christopher (b. 1907). *The Lady's Not for Burning; Venus Observed.*

MacNeice, Louis (1907–63). *Autumn Journal; Collected Poems.*

Auden, Wystan Hugh (1907–73). *Poems; Look Stranger; The Dance of Death.*

Fleming, Ian (Lancaster) (1908–65). *Dr No; Goldfinger.*

Lowry, (Clarence) Malcolm (1909–57). *Under the Volcano.*

Golding, William (b. 1911). *Lord of the Flies.*

Rattigan, Terence (1911–77). *French Without Tears; The Winslow Boy.*

Durrell, Lawrence (b. 1912). *Selected Poems; The Alexandria Quartet.*

Thomas, Dylan (1914–53). *Portrait of the Artist as a Young Dog; Under Milk Wood.*

Burgess, Anthony (b. 1910). *Clockwork Orange; Napoleon Symphony.*

White, Patrick (Victor Martindale) (b. 1912). *Voss.*

Wilson, Angus (b. 1913). *Hemlock and After; The Old Men at the Zoo.*

Lessing, Doris (May) (b. 1919). *Children of Violence; The Golden Notebooks.*

Murdoch, Iris (b. 1919). *An Unofficial Rose; The Italian Girl; An Accidental Man.*

Amis, Kingsley (b. 1922). *Lucky Jim.*

Larkin, Phillip (b. 1922). *High Windows.*

Osborne, John (b. 1929). *Look Back in Anger.*

Arden, John (b. 1930). *Serjeant Musgrave's Dance.*

Hughes, Ted (b. 1930). *The Hawk in the Rain; Lupercal.*

Pinter, Harold (b. 1930). *The Caretaker; The Birthday Party.*

Wesker, Arnold (b. 1932). *Roots; Chips with Everything.*

Stoppard, Tom (b. 1937). *Rosencrantz and Guildenstern are Dead; Dirty Linen.*

Ayckbourn, Alan (b. 1939). *How the Other Half Loves; The Norman Conquests.*

Poets Laureate

The office of poet laureate is one of great honour, conferred on a poet of distinction, In 1616, James I granted a pension to the poet Ben Jonson, but it was not until 1668 that the laureateship was created as a royal office. When the position of poet laureate falls vacant, the prime minister is responsible for putting forth names for a new laureate, to be chosen by the sovereign. The sovereign then commands the Lord Chamberlain to appoint the poet laureate, and he does so by issuing a warrant to the laureate-elect. The Chamberlain also arranges for the appointment – for life – to be announced in the *London Gazette.*

John Dryden (1631–1700; laureate 1668–88)

Thomas Shadwell (1642?–92; laureate 1688–92)

Nahum Tate (1652–1715); laureate 1692–1715)

Nicholas Rowe (1674–1718; laureate 1715–18)

Laurence Eusden (1688–1730; laureate 1718–30)

Colley Cibber (1671–1757; laureate 1730–57)

William Whitehead (1715–85; laureate 1757–85) (Appointed after Thomas Gray declined the offer)

Thomas Warton (1728–90; laureate 1785–90)

Henry James Pye (1745–1813; laureate 1790–1813)

Robert Southey (1774–1843; laureate 1813–43)

William Wordsworth (1770–1850; laureate 1843–50)

Alfred, Lord Tennyson (1809–92); laureate 1850–92) (Appointed after Samuel Russell declined the offer)

Alfred Austin (1835–1913; laureate 1896–1913)

Robert Bridges (1844–1930; laureate 1913–30)

top: *Harold Pinter (b. 1930) (Popperfoto)*
centre: *Robert Louis Stevenson (1850–94) (Popperfoto)*
above: *Virginia Woolf (1882–1941) (Mary Evans/ Sigmund Freud copyrights)*

John Masefield (1878–1967; laureate 1930–67)
Cecil Day-Lewis (1904–72; laureate 1968–72)
Sir John Betjeman (1906–84; laureate 1972–84)
Ted Hughes (b. 1930 laureate 1984–)

Some well-known writers

Listed by country

Argentina
Borges, Jorge Luis (b. 1899). *The Labyrinth; Ficciones.*

Austria
Kafka, Franz (1883–1924). *The Trial: The Castle.*

Belgium
Maeterlinck, Maurice (1862–1949). *The Blue Bird.*

Chile
Neruda, Pablo (pseud. of Neftali Ricardo Reyes) (b. 1904). *Poems.*

Colombia
Marques, Gabriel Garcia (b. 1920). *One Hundred Years of Solitude.*

Denmark
Anderson, Hans Christian (1807–75). *The Emperor's New Clothes.*

France
Rabelais, Francois (1494?–1553?). *Gargantua: Pantagruel.*
Corneille, Pierre (1606–84). *Le Cid.*
Moliere, nom de theatre of Jean-Baptiste Poquelin (1622–73). *Tartuffe; La Malade Imaginaire.*
Racine, Jean (1639–99). *Phèdre.*
Voltaire, pseud. of Francois-Marie Arouet (1694–1778). *Candide.*
Stendhal, pseud. of Henri Beyle (1783–1842). *The Red and the Black.*
Balzac, Honore de (1799–1850). *Hunchback of Notre Dame.*
Dumas, Alexandre (père) (1802–70). *The Three Musketeers.*
Hugo, Victor Marie (1802–85). *Les Miserables.*
Baudelaire, Charles-Pierre (1821–67). *Les Fleurs du Mal.*
Flaubert, Gustave (1821–1880). *Madame Bovary.*
Zola, Emile (1840–1902). *Nana: Germinal.*
Maupassant, Guy de (1850–93). *Stories.*
Rimbaud, Arthur (1854–91). *Illuminations.*
Gide, Andre (1869–1951). *Strait is the Gate.*
Proust, Marcel (1871–1922). *Remembrance of Things Past.*
Colette, Sidonie Gabrielle (1873–1954). *Cheri.*
Sartre, Jean Paul (1905–80). *The Age of Reason.*
Genet, Jean (b. 1910–). *Thiefs' Journal: The Maids.*

Germany
Goethe, Johann Wolfgang von (1749–1832). *Faust.*
Schiller, Friedrich (1759–1805). *Poems: Wallenstein.*
Heine, Heinrich (1797–1856). *Poems.*
Mann, Thomas (1875–1955). *Death in Venice; The Magic Mountain.*
Rilke, Rainer Maria (1875–1926). *Poems.*
Hesse, Hermann (1877–1962). *Steppenwolf.*
Brecht, Bertolt (1898–1956). *Mother Courage.*
Grass, Gunter (b. 1927–). *The Tin Drum.*

India
Tagore, Rabindranath (1861–1941). *Poems.*

Italy
Dante, Alighieri (1265–1321). *Divine Comedy.*
Petrarch (Petrarca) Francesco (1304–74). *Sonnets.*
Machiavelli, Niccolo (1469–1527). *The Prince.*
D'Annunzio, Gabriele (1863–1938). *Francesca da Rimini.*
Pirandello, Luigi (1867–1936). *Six Characters in Search of an Author; The Rules of the Game.*
Lampedusa, Giuseppe Tomasi de (1896–1957). *The Leopard.*
Silone, Ignazio, pseud. of Secondo Tranquilli (b. 1900–). *Bread and Wine.*
Moravia, Alberto, pseud. of Alberto Pincherle (b. 1907–). *The Woman of Rome.*
Calvino, Italo (b. 1923–). *Adam One Afternoon and Other Stories.*

Japan
Murasaki Shikibu (c. 980–c. 1030). *Tale of Genji.*
Sei Shonagon (fl. 1000). *The Pillow-Book of Sei Shonagon.*

Norway
Ibsen, Henrik (1828–1906). *Ghosts; A Doll's House; Hedda Gabler.*
Hamsun, Knut (1859–1952). *The Growth of the Soil.*

Russia
Pushkin, Aleksandr Sergeyevich (1799–1837). *Eugene Onegin; Stories.*
Turgenev, Ivan (1818–83). *A Month in the Country.*
Dostoyevsky, Fyodor Mikhailovich (1821–1881). *The Idiot; The Brothers Karamazov; Crime and Punishment.*
Tolstoy, Count Lev Nikolayevich (1828–1910). *War and Peace; Anna Karenina.*
Chekhov, Anton Pavlovich (1860–1904). *The Seagull; The Cherry Orchard.*
Pasternak, Boris Leonidovich (1890–1960). *Dr. Zhivago.*
Solzhenitsin, Aleksandr Isayevich (1918–). *One Day in the Life of Ivan Denisovich.*

Spain
Cervantes Saavedra, Miguel de (1547–1616). *Don Quixote.*
Lorca, Federico Garcia (1898–1936). *Poems; Blood Wedding.*

Sweden
Strindberg, August (1849–1912). *Miss Julie.*

United States
Hawthorne, Nathaniel (1804–64). *The Scarlet Letter.*
Longfellow, Henry Wadsworth (1807–82). *The Wreck of the Hesperus; The Song of Hiawatha.*
Poe, Edgar Allan (1809–49). *The Murders in the Rue Morgue; The Raven.*
Thoreau, Henry David (1817–62). *Walden.*
Melville, Herman (1819–91). *Moby Dick; Billy Budd.*
Whitman, Walt (1819–92). *Leaves of Grass.*
Twain, Mark (Samuel Langhorne Clemens) (1835–1910). *Adventures of Tom Sawyer; Adventures of Huckleberry Finn.*
James, Henry (1843–1916). *The Turn of the Screw; The Golden Bowl; Portrait of a Lady.*
Frost, Robert (1874–1963). *Poems.*
London, Jack (John Griffith London) (1876–1916). *The Call of the Wild; White Fang.*

O'Neill, Eugene (1888–1953). *The Iceman Cometh; Long Day's Journey into Night.*
Fitzgerald, F. Scott (1896–1940). *The Great Gatsby; Tender is the Night; The Last Tycoon.*
Faulkner, William (1897–1962). *The Sound and the Fury.*
Hemingway, Ernest (1898–1961). *A Farewell to Arms; For Whom the Bell Tolls; The Old Man and the Sea.*
Nabokov, Vladimir (b. 1899). *Pale Fire; Lolita.*
Pound, Ezra (1900–). *Pisan Cantos; Hugh Selwyn Mauberley.*
Steinbeck, John (1902–68). *The Grapes of Wrath; Of Mice and Men.*
O'Hara, John (1905–70). *Appointment in Samarra; Pal Joey.*
Williams, Tennessee (b. 1914). *Streetcar Named Desire; The Glass Menagerie.*
Bellow, Saul (b. 1915). *Herzog; The Dean's December.*
Miller, Arthur (b. 1915). *Death of a Salesman; The Crucible.*
Lowell, Robert (1917–80). *Poems.*
Mailer, Norman (b. 1923). *The Naked and the Dead.*
Roth, Philip (b. 1933). *Portnoy's Complaint; Letting Go.*

Nobel prizewinners in literature since 1950

1984 Jaroslav Seifert, Czechoslovakian.
1983 William Golding, British
1982 Gabriel Garcia Marquez, Colombian-Mex.
1981 Elias Canetti, Bulgarian-British
1980 Czeslaw Milosz, Polish-US
1979 Odysseus Elytis, Greek
1978 Isaac Bashevis Singer, US (Yiddish)
1977 Vincente Aleixandre, Spanish
1976 Saul Bellow, US
1975 Eugenio Montale, Ital.
1974 Eyvind Johnson, Harry Edmund Martinson, both Swedish
1973 Patrick White, Australian
1972 Heinrich Boll, W. German
1971 Pablo Naruda, Chilean
1970 Aleksandr I. Solzhenitsyn, Russ.
1969 Samuel Beckett, Irish
1968 Yasunari Kawabata, Japanese
1967 Miguel Angel Asturias, Guate.
1966 Samuel Joseph Agnon, Israeli
     Nelly Sachs, Swedish
1965 Mikhail Sholokhov, Russian
1964 Jean Paul Sartre, French (Prize declined)
1963 Giorgos Seferis, Greek
1962 John Steinbeck, US
1961 Ivo Andric, Yugoslavian
1960 Saint-Jean Perse, French
1959 Salvatore Quasimodo, Italian
1958 Boris L. Pasternak, Russian (Prize declined)
1957 Albert Camus, French
1956 Juan Ramon Jimenez, Puerto Rican-Span.
1955 Halldor K. Laxness, Icelandic
1954 Ernest Hemingway, US
1953 Sir Winston Churchill, British
1952 Francois Mauriac, French
1951 Par F. Lagerkvist, Swedish
1950 Bertrand Russell, British

Media and Communication

Cinema

ORIGINS OF THE CINEMA
The creation of the cinema as we know it today was preceded by various developments in photography and the study of movement that go back to the early 19th century. The illusion of movement was first obtained by projecting images mechanically in rapid succession and was used in toys made in the 1830s.

An English photographer, Edward Muybridge, used up to 36 still cameras to capture the movements of animals and humans in a series of experiments; the results he projected in succession. The first motion picture films were taken on a camera patented in Britain by French-born Louis Le Prince, who used sensitized paper rolls to obtain images taken in 1888. A year later Eastman celluloid film was available in Britain and Le Prince used this to develop the commercial aspects of his patent.

The kinetoscope, invented in 1891 at the laboratories of Edison in the USA was the first apparatus for viewing cine film: the intermittent 'gate', which holds each frame of film stationary while it is being exposed was invented in Britain by William Friese-Greene in 1888. Rapidly, all these experiments and inventions were integrated into one apparatus, a combined movie camera and projector, by the French brothers, Auguste and Louis Lumière. They started the first movie shows, the first public performance taking place in Paris on 22 March 1894. Meanwhile in New York, on 14 April 1894, the first commercial showing of motion pictures took place, using kinetoscopes. The cinema, as we know it, was born.

The public's interest in the new medium became unassuageable, and showmen were quick to exploit its commercial potential. Programmes were shown in fairgrounds and hired halls; soon purpose-built cinemas were being built and by 1910 there were over 5,000 in Britain alone.

At first, cinema presentations were confined to the showing of a number of short films, but in 1906 the first feature film was made in Australia. Lasting 60–70 minutes, it was made by Charles Tait and was called *The Story of the Kelly Gang*. Europe and the United States soon followed Tait's lead, and by the outbreak of World War I in 1914, 22 countries were producing feature films.

COLOUR MOVIES
Colour photography experiments were being carried out throughout the latter half of the 19th century, and in July 1906 the first commercially successful colour film was made. Developed by G. A. Smith in Britain, he called his process Kinemacolor, and the first public presentation of a film in his new process was shown in a programme of 21 films on 26 February 1909. Britain led the United States in the production of Kinemacolor films, producing the first full-length feature in colour in 1914. The first (non-subtractive) Technicolor film was made in the United States in 1917, using (like Kinemacolor) colour filters on both camera and projector. Two-colour subtractive Technicolor film was made and used in 1922.

By 1932, three-colour subtractive Technicolor film was available and was first used for a Walt Disney cartoon shown on 17 July 1932. Mean-while, two-colour processes continued to be developed, the most notable being Cinecolor. Eastman Color was introduced in 1952 and steadily displaced its rivals. It is now almost universally used in Western countries.

THE INTRODUCTION OF SOUND
Although *The Jazz Singer*, starring Al Jolson, made in Hollywood in 1927, is credited with being the first 'talkie', there is a long list of precedents stretching back to 1896. Short sound films were shown in Berlin in September of that year, using synchronised discs for the sound. Sound-on-disc continued to be used in various forms until 1929, and as far back as 1906 the first sound-on-film process was patented by French-born Eugene Lauste of London, but it was not until 1910 that he succeeded in recording and reproducing speech on film. By 1913 he had perfected the apparatus to record and reproduce sound on films, but World War I put an end to his hopes of commercially exploiting his invention. Sound track was added to Technicolor film in 1924. The first presentation of a sound-on-film production before a paying audience was shown in New York on 15 April 1923. *The Jazz Singer* takes its place in the record as being the first talking feature film, and used the sound-on-disc system. The first sound-on-film feature was shown on 1 September 1928, in New York: its title, *The Air Circus*.

Stereophonic sound was patented in France in 1932 and its first use was three years later. Sensurround was first used in 1974 in *Earthquake*, having not only all-round sound, but vibrations set up by low-frequency sound.

OTHER TECHNICAL DEVELOPMENTS
The first wide screen showings date back to the 1890s, when film stock of exceptional width was used. It was first used in a feature film in Italy in 1923. Anamorphic lenses – used to contract a wide image onto standard film (as in Cinemascope) – were first used in France in 1927. 70 mm film for use with a wide screen was used in the United States in 1929. The first system to combine wide-gauge film and anamorphic lenses was called Ultra-Panavision which was first used in 1957. Cinemascope was developed by the Frenchman, Henri Chretien, from an anamorphic system he invented in 1927. The patent rights were bought by the Hollywood Fox Studios and used in the first Cinemascope feature in 1953, *The Robe*.

Cinerama was shown at the New York World Fair in 1939, but was not launched commercially until 1952.

Three-dimensional films date from 1915, using red and green spectacles worn by the viewers. Intermittent attempts to popularize the development have not been successful. A Russian development in 1947 was the first to dispense successfully with spectacles, and used a specially designed corrugated screen to reflect the two images to the left and right eye.

Holography gives the illusion of three-dimensional substance without resort to spectacles or screens, and uses lasers to create an effect whereby a spectator can move from one position to another and 'see' the object projected from these different vantages or angles. It was first presented in Moscow in 1977.

CINEMAS
(more than 3000)

USSR	142 146	(1981)
USA	14 732	(1981)
Italy	7726	(1981)
India	6991	(1981)
France	4532	(1981)
China	4000	(1979)
Spain	3970	(1981)
W. Germany	3530	(1981)
Bulgaria	3006	(1981)
Japan	2298	(1981)
UK	1541	(1981)
Sweden	1239	(1981)
Argentina	1010	(1981)
South Africa	700	(1979)
Australia	564	(1979)
New Zealand	172	(1979)

ATTENDANCE IN MILLIONS OF SEATS PER YEAR

China	22 500	(1979)
India	3676	(1981)
USA	1067	(1981)
Italy	215	(1981)
France	187	(1981)
Japan	149	(1981)
West Germany	141	(1981)
UK	86	(1981)

FILM PRODUCTION
(Feature films of 1 hour or more)

India	737	(1981)
Japan	332	(1981)
France	231	(1981)
USA	226	(1981)
USSR	153	(1981)
Italy	143	(1981)
Philippines	143	(1975)
Spain	137	(1981)
Germany (E. & W.)	92	(1981)
Mexico	88	(1981)
Korean Republic	87	(1981)
Czechoslovakia	48	(1981)
Australia	43	(1975)
Sri Lanka	42	(1981)
UK	41	(1981)
Canada	32	(1980)

SOME NOTABLE CINEMA ACTORS, ACTRESSES AND DIRECTORS
Allen, Woody (b. 1935) American actor, director. *Manhattan*; *Annie Hall*

Antonioni, Michelangelo (b. 1912) Italian director. *La Notte*

Attenborough, Sir Richard (b. 1923) British actor, director. *A Bridge Too Far*; *Ghandi*

Barrymore, John (1882–1942) American actor. *Beau Brummel*

Barrymore, Lionel (1878–1954) American actor. *You Can't Take it with You*

Bergman, Ingmar (b. 1918) Swedish director. *The Seventh Seal*; *Fanny and Alexander*

Bergman, Ingrid (1915–82) Swedish actress. *Anastasia*; *Indiscreet*

Bogart, Humphrey (1899–1957) American actor. *The Big Sleep*; *Casablanca*

Bunuel, Luis (1900–83) Spanish director. *L'Age d'Or*; *Le Chien Andalou*

Burton, Richard (1925–1984) British actor. *Beckett*; *Who's Afraid of Virginia Woolf?*

Carné, Marcel (b. 1909) French director. *Les Enfants du Paradis*

Chaplin, Sir Charles (1889–1977) British actor, director. *The Gold Rush*; *City Lights*; *Modern Times*

Colman, Ronald (1891–1958) British actor. *Lost Horizon*

Cooper, Gary (1901–61) American actor. *High Noon*; *For Whom the Bell Tolls*

Coppola, Francis Ford (b. 1939) American director. *The Godfather*; *Apocalypse Now*

Cukor, George (1899–1983) American director. *My Fair Lady*

Curtiz, Michael (1888–1962) Hungarian born director. *Casablanca*

Davis, Bette (b. 1908) American actress. *All About Eve*

Dean, James (1931–55) American actor. *Rebel Without a Cause*

De Mille, Cecil B. (1881–1959) American director. *The Ten Commandments*

De Sica, Vittorio (1902–72) Italian director. *Bicycle Thieves*

Dietrich, Marlene (b. 1901) German actress. *The Blue Angel*

Disney, Walt (1901–66) American animator and director. *Mickey Mouse*; *Snow White and the Seven Dwarfs*

Dreyer, Carl (1889–1968) Danish director. *The Passion of Joan of Arc*

Eastwood, Clint (b. 1930) American actor, director. *A Fistful of Dollars*

Eisenstein, Sergei (1898–1948) Russian director. *The Battleship Potemkin*; *Alexander Nevsky*

Fairbanks, Douglas (1883–1939) American actor. *The Three Musketeers*

Fassbinder, Rainer Werner (1946–85) German director. *The Marriage of Maria Braun*

Fellini, Frederico (b. 1920) Italian director. *La Dolce Vita*

Fields, W. C. (1879–1946) American actor. *David Copperfield*; *Never give a Sucker an Even Break*

Flaherty, Robert (1884–1951) American director. *Man of Aran*

Fonda, Jane (b. 1937) American actress. *Klute*; *The China Syndrome*

Ford, John (1895–1973) American director. *Stagecoach*; *The Quiet Man*

Gabin, Jean (1904–76) French actor. *Le Jour se Leve*; *Pepe Le Moko*

Gable, Clark (1901–60) American actor. *Gone with the Wind*; *The Misfits*

Gance, Abel (1889–1982) French director. *Napoleon*

Garbo, Greta (b. 1905) Swedish actress. *Ninotchka*; *Camille*

Garland, Judy (1922–69) American actress. *The Wizard of Oz*; *A Star is Born*

Godard, Jean-Luc (b. 1930) French director. *Breathless*; *Une Femme Mariée*

Goldwyn, Samuel (1882–1974) American producer. *The Goldwyn Follies*; *Wuthering Heights*

Griffith, D. W. (1875–1948) American director. *Birth of a Nation*; *Intolerance*

Hepburn, Katherine (b. 1907) American actress. *The Lion in Winter*; *The African Queen*

Herzog, Werner (b. 1942) German director. *Nosferatu*; *Fitzcarraldo*

Hitchcock, Alfred (1899–1980) British director. *Rear Window*; *Psycho*

Huston, John (b. 1906) American director. *Treasure of the Sierra Madre*; *The Asphalt Jungle*

Kazan, Elia (b. 1909) American director. *On The Waterfront*; *East of Eden*

Keaton, Buster (1895–1966) American actor, director. *The Navigator*; *The General*

Kubrick, Stanley (b. 1928) American director. *2001: A Space Odyssey*; *Dr. Strangelove*

Kurosawa, Akira (b. 1910) Japanese director. *The Seven Samurai*; *Rashomon*

Lang, Fritz (1890–1976) Austrian director. *The Cabinet of Dr. Caligari*; *Metropolis*

Lean, David (b. 1908) British director. *Bridge on the River Kwai*; *Lawrence of Arabia*; *A Passage to India*

Leigh Vivien (1913–67) British actress. *Gone with the Wind*; *Streetcar Named Desire*

Loren, Sophia (b. 1934) Italian actress. *Two Women*

Losey, Joseph (1909–85) American director. *The Concrete Jungle*; *The Servant*

Lubitsch, Ernst (1892–1947) German director. *Ninotchka*; *Heaven Can Wait*

McQueen, Steve (1930–83) American actor. *Bullitt*; *The Magnificent Seven*

Magnani, Anna (b. 1908) Italian actress. *Open City*; *The Rose Tattoo*

Marx Brothers (Chico (1886–1961) Harpo (1888–1964) Groucho (1890–1977) American comedy actors. *Duck Soup*; *A Night at the Opera*

Mason, James (1909–84) British actor. *The Wicked Lady*; *Odd Man Out*

Méliès, Georges (1861–1938) French director. *A Trip to the Moon*

Mifune, Toshiro (b. 1920) Japanese actor. *Rashomon*; *Seven Samurai*

Monroe, Marilyn (1926–62) American actress. *Seven Year Itch*; *Some Like It Hot*

Newman, Paul (b. 1925) American actor. *Butch Cassidy and the Sundance Kid*

Nicholson, Jack (b. 1937) American actor. *Chinatown*; *One Flew over the Cuckoo's Nest*

Olivier, Laurence (Lord Olivier) (b. 1907) British actor, director. *Henry V*; *Hamlet*; *Richard III*; *The Entertainer*

Pickford, Mary (1893–1979) American actress. *America's Sweetheart*; *The Mary Pickford Story*

Polanski, Roman (b. 1933) Polish director. *Chinatown*; *Rosemary's Baby*

Porter, Edwin (1869–1941) American director. *The Great Train Robbery*

Ray, Satyajit (b. 1921) Indian director. *Pathar Panchali*; *The Chess Players*

Redford, Robert (b. 1937) American actor. *The Sting*; *All the President's Men*

Reed, Sir Carol (b. 1906) British director. *The Third Man*; *Our Man in Havana*

Renoir, Jean (1894–1979) French director. *La Grande Illusion*; *Le Regle du Jeu*

Rossellini, Roberto (1906–77) Italian director. *Open City*

Schlesinger, John (b. 1926) British director. *Midnight Cowboy*; *Darling*

Sennett, Mack (1880–1960) American director. *The Keystone Cops series*

Sternberg, Josef von (1894–1969) American director. *Shanghai Express*; *The Blue Angel*

Stewart, James (b. 1908) American actor. *Rear Window*; *Destry Rides Again*

Streep, Meryl (b. 1951) American actress. *The French Lieutenant's Woman*; *Kramer v. Kramer*

Stroheim, Erich von (1885–1957) Austrian director. *Sunset Boulevard*

Tati, Jacques (1908–84) French director, actor. *Jour de Fête*; *M. Hulot's Holiday*

Taylor, Elizabeth (b. 1932) British actress. *Cleopatra*; *Who's Afraid of Virginia Woolf?*

Tracy, Spencer (1900–67) American actor. *Adam's Rib*; *Bad Day at Black Rock*

Truffaut, Francois (1932–84) French director. *Day for Night*; *Jules et Jim*

Valentino, Rudolph (1895–1926) American actor. *The Sheik*; *Blood and Sand*

Vidor, King (1894–1982) American director. *Wizard of Oz*; *War and Peace*

Visconti, Luchino (b. 1906) Italian director. *The Leopard*; *The Damned*

Wajda, Andrzej (b. 1926) Polish director. *Kanal*; *Ashes and Diamonds*

Wayne, John (1907–79) American actor. *Stagecoach*; *True Grit*

Welles, Orson (b. 1915) American director, actor. *Citizen Kane*; *The Third Man*

Radio

The first advertised broadcast was on 24th December 1906 from Brant Rock, Mass., USA. The first regular broadcast entertainment in the UK started on 14th February 1922.

Radio sets (thousands)*

	1965	1970	1980
World	529 000	758 000	1 500 100
W Europe	116 500	153 400	281 800
USSR & E Europe	59 700	73 500	141 800
Middle East & N Africa	12 300	18 800	47 000
Africa (excl. N. Africa)	7 400	14 500	45 600
China	6 000	12 000	80 000
India	4 800	14 000	40 000

Television

The invention of television, the instantaneous viewing of distant objects by electrical transmission, was a process of successive discoveries. The first commercial cathode ray tube was introduced in 1897 by Karl Braun but was not linked to electronic vision until 1907 by Boris Rosing. A A Campbell Swinton published the basis of television transmission in a letter to *Nature* in 1908. The earliest public demonstration was given on 27 Jan 1926 by John Logie Baird (1888–1946). The potential of modern technical developments, such as satellite and cable television, video-discs and video-cassettes, is widely recognised.

RECEIVERS (THOUSANDS)*

	1965	1970	1980	1982
World	177 000	273 000	546 000	622 400
W Europe	49 400	81 900	139 400	149 100
USSR & E Europe	24 000	45 300	105 500	113 500
Middle East & N Africa	1 250	2 600	11 800	15 100
South Africa	—	—	2 000	3 000
Other African countries	98	237	2 400	10 200
China	70	300	7 000	15 000
India	2	16	1 000	2 000
Japan	18 000	23 000	60 000	65 000
Other Asian countries	700	2 700	18 900	25 900
Australasia, Pacific & Oceania	3 200	4 000	6 800	7 500
United States	68 000	89 000	140 000	160 000
Canada	5 000	7 200	12 000	13 000
Latin America	7 400	16 100	37 500	44 300
West Indies	101	725	1 500	1 800

* *Source : BBC.*

BROADCASTING RECEIVING LICENCES IN THE UK:

	total	radio only	monochrome	colour
31 Mar 1940	8 951 045	8 897 618	—	—
31 Mar 1950	12 219 448	11 819 190	343 882	—
31 Mar 1968	17 645 821	2 529 750	15 068 079	20 428
31 Mar 1975	17 700 815	—	10 120 493	7 580 322
31 Mar 1981	18 667 211	—	4 887 663	13 779 548
31 Mar 1982	18 554 200	—	4 293 668	14 260 552
31 Mar 1983	18 494 235	—	3 795 587	14 698 648
31 Mar 1984	18 631 753	—	3 261 273	15 370 481

	1965	1970	1980
Japan	27 000	60 000	100 000
Other Asian countries	13 300	27 600	192 000
Australasia, Pacific & Oceania	7 800	10 400	20 000
United States	230 000	304 000	500 000
Canada	14 000	20 000	30 000
Latin America	29 400	47 000	112 900
West Indies	860	2 700	118 400

* Source: BBC.

The amount of listening in the UK (1980–81) averaged 9 hours 25 minutes a week per head of population.

Frequencies

Frequencies are measured in hertz (Hz) (cycles per second). 1000 Hz equals 1 kilohertz (kHz). 1000 kHz equals 1 megahertz (MHz) or 1 million hertz. Low frequencies between 150 kHz (2000 metres) and 285 kHz (1053 metres) comprise the long-wave band. Medium frequencies between 525 kHz (571 metres) and 1605 kHz (187 metres) comprise the medium-wave band. High frequencies between 3 MHz (75 metres) and 30 MHz (10 metres) comprise the short-wave band.

BBC Local Radio

(BBC's network of local radio stations)

Bedfordshire	London
Bristol	Manchester
Cambridgeshire	Merseyside
Cleveland	Newcastle
Cornwall	Norfolk
Cumbria	Northampton
Derby	Nottingham
Devon	Oxford
Furness	Sheffield
Humberside	Shropshire
Kent	Solent
Lancashire	Stoke-on-Trent
Leeds	Sussex
Leicester	WM (Birmingham)
Lincolnshire	York

EXTERNAL RADIO BROADCASTING

Estimated total programme hours per week of some external broadcasters

	1950	1955	1960	1965	1970	1975	1980	1981	1982	1983
USSR	533	656	1015	1417	1908	2001	2094	2114	2180	2177
United States of America	497	1690	1495	1832	1907	2029	1901	1959	1975	2004
Chinese People's Republic	66	159	687	1027	1267	1423	1350	1304	1423	1424
German Federal Republic	—	105	315	671	779	767	804	786	786	789
United Kingdom (BBC)	643	558	589	667	723	719	719	741	729	721
North Korea	—	53	159	392	330	455	597	581	587	593
Albania	26	47	63	154	487	490	560	567	578	581
Egypt	—	100	301	505	540	635	546	518	544	523
Cuba	—	—	—	325	320	311	424	459	420	420
East Germany	—	9	185	308	274	342	375	427	415	408
India	116	117	157	175	271	326	389	396	396	401
Australia	181	226	257	299	350	379	333	336	336	336
Nigeria	—	—	—	63	62	61	170	342	322	322
Poland	131	359	232	280	334	340	337	130	335	320
France	198	191	326	183	200	108	125	125	275	301
Netherlands	127	120	178	235	335	400	289	290	293	288
Bulgaria	30	60	117	154	164	197	236	289	289	288
Iran	12	10	24	118	155	154	175	238	280	282
Turkey	40	100	77	91	88	172	199	206	221	263
Japan	—	91	203	249	259	259	259	263	259	259
Czechoslovakia	119	147	196	189	202	253	255	283	283	258
Israel	—	28	91	92	158	198	210	210	212	228
Spain	68	98	202	276	251	312	239	253	274	221
Portugal	46	102	133	273	295	190	214	214	214	214
South Africa	—	127	63	84	150	141	183	205	205	205
Romania	30	109	159	163	185	190	198	204	201	205
Italy	170	185	205	160	165	170	169	169	169	169
Canada	85	83	80	81	98	159	134	143	147	154
Sweden	28	128	114	142	140	154	155	145	144	144
Hungary	76	99	120	121	105	127	127	127	127	123
Yugoslavia	80	46	70	78	76	82	72	72	72	72

(i) USSR includes Radio Moscow, Radio Station Peace & Progress and regional stations.
(ii) USA includes Voice of America (977 hours per week), Radio Free Europe (562 hours per week) and Radio Liberty (465 hours per week). (1983 figures).
(iii) German Federal Republic includes Deutsche Welle (536 hours per week) and Deutschlandfunk (253 hours per week). (1983 figures).
(iv) The list includes fewer than half the world's external broadcasters. Among those excluded are Taiwan, Vietnam, South Korea, and various international commercial and religious stations, as well as clandestine radio stations. Certain countries transmit part of their domestic output externally on shortwaves; these broadcasts are mainly also excluded.
(v) All figures for December or nearest available month.
February 1984   International Broadcasting and Audience Research

IBA LOCAL RADIO STATIONS

Area	Company	Air date	Area	Company	Air date
Aberdeen	North Sound	27.7.81	Hereford/Worcester	Radio Wyvern	4.10.82
Aylesbury	to be appointed		Hertford & Harlow	to be appointed	
Ayr (with Girvan)	West Sound	16.10.81	Humberside	Viking Radio	17.4.84
Basingstoke & Andover	to be appointed		Inverness	Moray Firth Radio	23.2.82
Belfast	Downtown Radio	16.3.76	Ipswich	Radio Orwell	28.10.75
Birmingham	BRMB Radio	19.2.74	Leeds	Radio Aire	1.9.81
The Borders (Hawick) with Berwick	to be appointed		Leicester	Leicester Sound	7.9.84
Bournemouth	2CR	15.9.80	Liverpool	Radio City	21.10.74
Bradford/Huddersfield & Halifax	Pennine Radio	Bradford 16.9.75 Huddersfield & Halifax Late 1984	London	Capital Radio	16.10.73
			London	LBC	8.10.73
			Londonderry	to be appointed	
			Luton/Bedford	Chiltern Radio	Luton 11.10.81 Bedford 1.3.82
Brighton	Southern Sound	29.8.83	Maidstone & Medway	Invicta Sound (incorporating Northdown Radio)	Late 1984
Bristol	Radio West	27.10.81			
Bury St Edmunds	Saxon Radio	6.11.82			
Cambridge & Newmarket	to be appointed		Manchester	Piccadilly Radio	2.4.74
Cardiff	CBC	11.4.80	Milton Keynes*	to be appointed	
Coventry	Mercia Sound	23.5.80	Newport (Gwent)	Gwent Broadcasting	13.6.83
Derby	to be appointed		Northampton	Hereward Radio	Late 1984
Dorchester/Weymouth	to be appointed		North West Wales (Conway Bay)	to be appointed	
Dundee/Perth	Radio Tay	Dundee 17.10.80 Perth 14.11.80	Nottingham	Radio Trent	3.7.75
			Oxford/Banbury	to be appointed	
East Kent	Invicta Sound (incorporating Network East Kent)	Late 1984	Peterborough	Hereward Radio	10.7.80
			Plymouth	Plymouth Sound	19.5.75
Eastbourne/Hastings	to be appointed		Portsmouth	Radio Victory	14.10.75
Edinburgh	Radio Forth	22.1.75	Preston & Blackpool	Red Rose Radio	5.10.82
Exeter/Torbay	DevonAir Radio	Exeter 7.11.80 Torbay 12.12.80	Reading	Radio 210	8.3.76
			Redruth/Falmouth/ Penzance/Truro	to be appointed	
Glasgow	Radio Clyde	31.12.78	Reigate & Crawley	Radio Mercury	Late 1984
Gloucester & Cheltenham	Severn Sound	23.10.80	Sheffield & Rotherham/ Barnsley/Doncaster	Radio Hallam	Sheffield 1.10.74 Barnsley/ Doncaster Late 1985
Great Yarmouth & Norwich	Radio Broadland	Late 1984			
Guildford	County Sound	4.4.83	Shrewsbury & Telford	to be appointed	

IBA LOCAL RADIO STATIONS (Cont.)

Area	Company	Air date
Southampton	to be appointed	
Southend/Chelmsford	Essex Radio	Southend 12.9.81
		Chelmsford
		10.12.81
Stoke-on-Trent	Signal Radio	5.9.83
Stranraer/Dumfries/ Galloway	to be appointed	
Swansea	Swansea Sound	30.9.74
Swindon/West Wilts.	Wiltshire Radio	12.10.82

Area	Company	Air date
Teeside	Radio Tees	24.6.75
Tyne & Wear	Metro Radio	15.7.74
Whitehaven & Workington/Carlisle	to be appointed	
Wolverhampton & Black Country	Beacon Radio	12.4.76
Wrexham & Deeside	Marcher Sound	5.9.83
Yeovil/Taunton	to be appointed	

* Milton Keynes to have some form of association with Northampton

Telephones

Zone		In service	% of World	Per 100 pop.
1	North America	198 882 227	40·9	74·2
2	Africa	6 135 956	1·3	1·8
3,4	Europe	172 098 479	35·4	38·0
5	South and Central America	23 011 120	4·7	6·7
6	South Pacific	5 407 086	1·1	2·0
7	USSR	18 000 000		
8	Far East	71 296 677	14·7	26·5
9	Middle East and South East Asia	9 818 924	2·0	1·1
10	World Total	486 055 001	100	17·1

	Number of Phones	Per 100 pop.
USA	181 893 000	78·7
Japan	60 349 857	51·0
UK	28 375 982	50·7
W. Germany	30 122 023	48·8
USSR	23 707 000	8·8 (at Jan 81)
France	26 940 296	49·8
Italy	20 444 037	36·3
Canada	15 741 723	64·7

At January 1, 1982. *Source AT & T*

World Press

DAILY NEWSPAPERS

	Total	Estimated Total approx.	per 100 approx.
World	8 107	304 000 000	142
Africa	128	4 501 000	8·6
America, N. & S.	2 441	77 308 000	117
Asia	3 137	16 200 000	24
Europe	1 601	98 000 000	200
Oceania	110	6 300 000	262
USSR	690	102 000 000	369*

By Country (a selection)

	Total	Estimated approx. in 000s	approx. per 000 popula- tion
USA	1 787	62 223	282
India	1 087	13 033	20
Turkey	1 115	3 880	—
W Germany	380	20 410	339
USSR (see above)			
Japan	178	65 881	569

Scale Rates per 1000 inhabitants

Japan	569	Liechtenstein	477
Iceland	557	Norway	456
Sweden	528	Austria	453
E. Germany	517	Netherlands	432
Finland	480		

* at 1979

MAJOR DAILY NEWSPAPERS WITH CIRCULATIONS

		Circulation
Australia	Sun News Herald	646 454
Canada	Toronto Globe & Mail	310 069
China	People's Daily	6 000 000
Egypt	Al Akhbar	751 115
France	Le Figaro	361 363
	Le Monde	405 674
W. Germany	Die Welt	200 636
	Frankfurter Allgemeine Zeitung	345 194
	Bild Zeitung	5 966 369
Italy	Corriere della Sera	533 615
	La Stampa	358 005
Japan	Yomiuri Shimbun[1]	8 704 470
	Asahi Shimbun[1]	7 485 632
Spain	El Pais	296 167
USA	Washington Post	768 286
	Chicago Sun-Times	657 275
	Chicago Tribune	756 857
	New York Daily News	1 554 604
	New York Times	963 443
	Wall Street Journal[2]	1 798 416
	Los Angeles Times	1 024 322
USSR	Pravda	10 700 000

[1] all editions.
[2] national edition.

Christian Science Monitor
Financial Times
International Herald Tribune } Available worldwide
Wall Street Journal

UNITED KINGDOM

Principal national newspapers	Circulation
The Sun	4 170 026
Daily Mirror	3 365 293
Daily Express	1 981 675
Daily Mail	1 800 783
Daily Star	1 370 942
Daily Telegraph	1 259 519
Guardian	478 159
Times	381 075
Financial Times	166 950
Sporting Life	78 508
Morning Star	29 235

National Sundays

News of the World	4 252 281
Sunday Mirror	3 523 000
Sunday People	3 377 282
Sunday Express	2 602 933
Mail on Sunday	1 584 707
Sunday Times	1 313 337
Observer	773 883
Sunday Telegraph	737 265
Sunday Mail (Scotland)	808 252
Sunday Post	1 000 000[1]

* ABC Jan–June 1984
[1] Estimated, June 1984

Regional morning papers

(Glasgow) Daily Record	744 605
Glasgow Herald	110 170
(Aberdeen) Press and Journal	110 487
(Darlington) Northern Echo	89 921
(Leeds) Yorkshire Post	87 424
(Norwich) Eastern Daily Press	90 179
(Edinburgh) Scotsman	92 461
(Cardiff) Western Mail	76 263
(Newcastle Upon Tyne) The Journal	67 637
Liverpool Daily Post	69 845
(Bristol) Western Daily Press	62 644
(Plymouth) Western Morning News	59 582
Belfast Newsletter	44 643
(Belfast) Irish News	42 061
(Ipswich) East Anglian Daily Times	39 475
Birmingham Post	34 050

Evening papers

(London) Standard	479 609
Manchester Evening News	295 547
Birmingham Evening Mail (all eds)	275 528
Liverpool Echo	200 646
(Glasgow) Evening Times	117 247
(Leeds) Evening Post	140 762
(Newcastle upon Tyne) Evening Chronicle	149 313
Belfast Telegraph	143 396
(Sheffield) The Star	148 333

MAGAZINES

Largest UK circulation[1]

Radio Times	3 204 087
TV Times	3 109 059
Woman's Weekly	1 386 411
Reader's Digest	1 460 350
Woman's Own	1 284 559
Woman	1 222 659
Family Circle	536 358
Woman & Home	578 038

Largest US circulation

TV Guide	17 670 543
Reader's Digest	17 926 542
National Geographic	10 215 000
Family Circle	7 427 979
McCall's Magazine	6 266 090
National Enquirer	4 602 524
Time	4 337 988
Newsweek	2 960 073
Sports Illustrated	2 286 069

[1] ABC July–Dec 1983

Sport

Origins and Antiquity of Sports

Date	Sport	Location and Notes
BC		
c. 3000	Coursing	Egypt. Saluki dogs. Greyhounds used in England AD 1067. Waterloo Cup 1836.
c. 2700	Wrestling	Nintu Temple, Khafajé, Iraq; ancient Olympic games c. 708 BC, Greco-Roman style, France c. AD 1860; Internationalised 1912.
c. 2050	Hockey	Beni Hasan tomb, Egypt. Lincolnshire AD 1277. Modern forms c. 1875. Some claims to be of Persian origin in 2nd millennium BC.
c. 1600	Falconry	China-Shang dynasty. Earliest manuscript evidence points to Persian origin.
c. 1520	Boxing	Thera fresco, Greece. First ring rules 1743 England. Queensberry Rules 1867.
c. 1360	Fencing	Egyptians used masks and blunted swords. Established as a sport in Germany c. AD 1450. Hand guard invented c. 1510. Foil 17th century, épée mid-19th century, and sabre in Italy, late 19th century.
c. 1300	Athletics	Ancient Olympic Games. Modern revival c. 1810, Sandhurst, England.
c. 800	Ice Skating	Bone skates superseded by metal blades c. AD 1600.
c. 776	Gymnastics	Ancient Olympic Games. Modern Sport developed c. AD 1776 in Germany.
c. 648	Horse Racing	Thirty-third ancient Olympic Games. Roman diversion c. AD 210 Netherby, Cumbria. Chester course 1540.
c. 600	Equestrianism	Riding of horses dates from c. 3000 BC Persia. Show jumping London AD 1869.
c. 525	Polo	As *Pulu*, Persia. Possibly of Tibetan origin.
c. 10	Fly Fishing	Earliest reference by the Roman Martial.
ante 1	Jiu Jitsu	Pre-Christian Chinese origin, developed as a martial art by Japan.
AD		
c. 300	Archery	Known as a Mesolithic skill (as opposed to a sport), Natal, South Africa *ante* 46 000 BC. Practised by the Genoese. Internationalised 1931.
c. 1050	Tennis (Royal or Real)	Earliest surviving court, Paris, France, 1496. First 'world' champion c. 1740.
1278	Fox Hunting	Earliest reference in England. Popularised at end 18th century. Previously deer, boar or hare hunted.
ante 1300	Bowls	On grass in Britain, descended from the Roman game of boccie.
c. 1410	Football (Association)	*Calcio* in Italy. First modern rules, Cambridge University, 1846. Eleven-a-side standardised 1870. Chinese ball-kicking game *Tsu-chin* known c. 350 BC.
1429	Billiards	First treatise by Marot (France) c. 1550. Rubber cushions 1835, slate beds 1836.
c. 1450	Golf	Earliest reference: parliamentary prohibition in March 1457, Scotland. Rubber core balls 1902, steel shafts 1929.
1472	Shooting	Target shooting recorded in Zurich, Switzerland.
ante 1492	Lacrosse	Originally American Indian *baggataway*. First non-Indian club, Montreal, 1856.
c. 1550	Cricket	Earliest recorded match, Guildford, Surrey, England. Earliest depictment c. 1250. Eleven-a-side Sussex 1697. Earliest recorded women's match, Surrey, 1745.
c. 1560	Curling	Netherlands. Kilsyth, Scotland 1716.
1600	Ice Yachting	Earliest patent in Low Countries. Sand yacht reported Belgian beach 1595.
c. 1600	Ice Hockey	Netherlands. Kingston, Ontario, Canada 1855. Rules devised in Montreal 1879.
1603	Swimming	Inter-school contests in Japan by Imperial edict. Sea-bathing at Scarborough by 1660. Earliest bath, Liverpool in 1828.
1661	Yachting	First contest Thames (1 Sept.). Earliest club in Cork, Ireland, 1720.
c. 1676	Caving	Pioneer explorer, John Beaumont, Somerset, England.
1698	Mountaineering	Rock climbing in St Kilda. First major alpine ascent (Mont Blanc) 1786. Continuous history since only 1854. Fujiyama climbed *ante* AD 806.
c. 1700	Bull Fighting	Francisco Romero of Ronda, Andalusia, Spain. Referred to by Romans c. 300 BC.
c. 1700	Baseball	English provenance. Cartwright Rules codified 1845.
1716	Rowing	Earliest contest, sculling race on Thames (1 Aug.). First English regatta, 1775, Henley Regatta 1839.
c. 1750	Trotting	Harness racing sulky introduced 1829.
1760	Roller Skating	Developed by Joseph Merlin (Belgium). Modern type devised by J L Plimpton (USA) in 1863.
1765	Fives (Eton Type)	Buttress hand-ball, Babcary, Somerset. New Courts at Eton, 1840. Rules codified 1877.
c. 1770	Shinty	Inter-village or clan game, West and Central Highlands of Scotland as gaelic *lomain* (driving forward). Rules suggested 1879.
1771	Surfing	Canoe surfing first recorded by Capt. James Cook in the Hawaiian Islands. Board surfing reported by Lt. James King, 1779. Sport revived by 1900 at Waikiki, Honolulu.
1787	Beagling	Newcastle Harriers, England.
1793	Lawn Tennis	Field tennis, as opposed to Court tennis, first recorded in England (29 Sept.). Leamington Club founded 1872. Patent as *sphairistike* by Major W C Wingfield Feb. 1874.
1798	Rackets	Earliest covered court, recorded, Exter. Of 17th century origin.
1823	Rugby	Traditional inventor Rev William Webb Ellis (c. 1807–72) at Rugby School (Nov.). Game formulated at Cambridge, 1839. The Rugby Union founded in 1871.
c. 1835	Croquet	Ireland as 'Crokey'. Country house lawn game in England, c. 1856. First rules 1857. The word dated back to 1478.
1843	Skiing (Alpine)	Tromsö, Norway. Kiandra Club, New South Wales 1855. California 1860. Alps 1883.
1845	Bowling (Ten-Pin)	Connecticut State, USA, to evade ban on nine-pin bowling. *Kegel* – a German cloister sport known since 12th century.
1847	Rodeo	Sante Fe, New Mexico, USA. Steer wrestling, 1900.
c. 1850	Fives (Rugby Type)	Earliest inter-school matches c. 1872.
c. 1850	Squash Rackets	Evolved at Harrow School, England. First US championship 1906.
1853	Gliding	Earliest flight by coachman to Sir George Cayley (possibly John Appleby) Brompton Hall, Yorkshire. World championships 1948.
1853	Australian Rules Football	Ballarat goldfields, Australia.
1865	Canoeing	Pioneered by John Macgregor (Scotland).
1868	Cycling	First International Race 31 May, Parc de St Cloud, Paris.
1869	Water Polo	Developed in England from 'Water Soccer'. An Olympic event since 1900.
1869	Equestrianism (Show Jumping)	London. Pignatelli's academy, Naples c. 1580.
c. 1870	Badminton	Made famous at Badminton Hall, Avon, England. First rules codified India 1876.
1875	Snooker	Devised by Col Sir Neville Chamberlain, Ootacamund Club, India as a variant of 'black pool'.
1876	Greyhound Racing	Railed 'hare' and windlass, Hendon, North London (Sept.). Race with mechanical hare, Emeryville, California, USA, 1919. First race in UK, Manchester 24 July 1926.
1878	Motor Racing	Earliest competitive race Green Bay – Madison, Wisconsin, USA. First real race, Paris to Bordeaux and back 1895 (11–13 June).
1879	Tug of War	First rules framed by New York AC. 'Rope pulling' known in neolithic times.

Origins and Antiquity of Sports continued

Date	Sport	Location and Notes
1879	Ski Jumping	Huseby, near Oslo, Norway.
1881	Lugeing	First competition, Klosters, Switzerland.
1882	Judo	Devised (February) by Dr Jigoro Kano (Japan) from Jiu Jitsu (see above).
1884	Tobogganing	First toboggan contests, St Moritz, Switzerland. Referred to in 16th century.
1887	Softball	Invented by George Hancock, Chicago, USA.
1889	Bobsledding	First known bobsleigh race, Davos, Switzerland.
1889	Table Tennis	Devised by James Bigg as 'Gossima' from a game known in 1881. Ping Pong Association formed in London, 1902. Sport resuscitated, 1921.
1891	Weightlifting	First international contest, Cafe Monico, London (28 Mar.).
1891	Netball	Invented in USA. Introduced to England 1895.
1891	Basketball	Invented by Dr James A Naismith. First played 20 Jan. 1892, Springfield, Mass, USA. Mayan Indian game *Pok-ta-Pok* dated *c.* 1000 BC.
1895	Rugby League	Professional breakaway, 1895 (29 Aug.). Team reduced from 15 to 13 in 1906 (12 June).
1895	Volleyball	Invented by William G Morgan at Holyoke, Mass, USA as *Minnonette*. Internationalised 1947.
1896	Marathon Running	Marathon to Athens, 1896 Olympics. Standardised at 26 miles 385 yds, *42,195 km* in 1924. Named after the run from the Marathon battlefield, Greece by Pheidippides in 490 BC.
1897	Motorcycle Racing	Earliest race over a mile, Sheen House, Richmond, Surrey (29 Nov.).
c. 1900	Water Skiing	Aquaplaning, US Pacific coast; plank-riding behind motor boat, Scarborough, England 1914; shaped skis by Ralph Samuelson, Lake Pepin, Minnesota, USA, 1922; devised ramp jump at Miami, Florida, 1928.
1901	Small Bore Shooting	·22 calibre introduced as a Civilian Army training device.
1912	Modern Pentathlon	First formal contest, Stockholm Olympic Games.
1918	Orienteering	Invented by Major Ernst Killander, Sweden (based on military exercises of the 1890s).
1922	Skiing (Slalom)	Devised by Sir Arnold Lunne, Mürren, Switzerland (21 Jan.).
1923	Speedway	West Maitland, NSW, Australia (Nov.); first World Championships Sept. 1936.
1936	Trampoline	Developed by George Nissen (US). First championships 1948. Used in show-business since 1910.
1951	Sky Diving (Parachuting)	First world championships in Yugoslavia.
1952	Synchronised Swimming	Given international status by FINA: US championships 1945.
1958	Hang Gliding	Modern revival by Prof. Rogallo; origins attributable to Otto Lilienthal (Germany) 1893.
1960	Aerobatics	First world championships instituted. First aerobatic manoeuvre 1913.
1964	Board Sailing	First appearance in California, USA.
1966	Skate Boarding	First championship in USA; upsurge from 1975; motorized boards from 1977.

Human Limitations in Sport

The basic physiological limitations to human performance in physical achievement embrace the following:

1) No human can survive more than 18 days without food and water.
2) Speed limit for transmission of messages through the nervous system is 180 mph *228 km/h*.
3) No human can survive prolonged blood temperatures above 105·8°F *41°C* or below 60·8°F *16°C* unharmed.
4) No human (except perhaps some asthmatic children) can detect sounds of a frequency above 20 000 Hz.
5) No human can detect sounds below 2 × 10 pascal and the most sensitive a frequency below 2750 Hz.
6) The human eye cannot resolve an object smaller than 100 microns at 25,4 cm *10 in*.
7) Visual stimuli rapidly repeated appear fused or continuous at frequencies between 4 and 60 per second according to the level of luminance.
8) No human can detect a vibration with an amplitude of less than 0·02 micron.
9) The human lung volume or vital capacity at maturity tends to a limit of 5,5 litres with up to 300 million alveoli.
10) The heart, as a pump, has a limited capacity above the normal circulatory volume of 5 to 6 litres per minute of which 60 per cent is liquid plasma.

The Olympic Games

The Ancient Olympic Games were staged every four years at Olympia, 120 miles west of Athens. The earliest celebration of which there is a certain record is that of July 776 BC, from which all subsequent Games are dated. However, earlier Games were certainly held, perhaps dating back to 1370 BC. These early Games had considerable religious significance.

The Games grew in size and importance to the height of their fame in the 5th and 4th centuries BC. Events included running, jumping, wrestling, throwing the discus, boxing and chariot racing. They were much more than sporting contests, great artistic festivals upholding the Greek ideal of perfection of mind and body. Winners were awarded a branch of wild olive, the Greeks' sacred tree.

The final Olympic Games of the ancient era were held in 393 AD before the Emperor of Rome, Theodosius I, decreed the prohibition of the Games, which were not favoured by the early Christians and which were then long past their great days.

The first modern Games, in Athens in 1896, were at the instigation of Pierre de Fredi, Baron de Coubertin (1863–1937). A far cry from today's huge organisation, just 311 competitors (from 13 countries) took part, of whom 230 were from Greece and others were foreign tourists. By contrast, the 1984 Los Angeles Games, despite the absence of most of the eastern bloc, had record participants of 140 countries comprising 7 400 athletes, and record attendances totalling 5 767 923.

CELEBRATIONS OF THE MODERN OLYMPIC GAMES

	Year	Venue	Date	Countries	Competitors Male	Female
I	1896	Athens, Greece	6–15 Apr.	13	311	
II	1900	Paris, France	20 May–28 Oct.	22	1319	11
III	1904	St Louis, USA	1 July–23 Nov.	13[1]	617	8
*	1906	Athens, Greece	22 Apr.–2 May	20	877	7
IV	1908	London, England	27 Apr.–31 Oct.	22	2013	43
V	1912	Stockholm, Sweden	5 May–22 July	28	2491	55
VI	1916	Berlin, Germany	Not held due to war	—	—	—
VII	1920	Antwerp, Belgium	20 Apr.–12 Sept.	29	2618	74
VIII	1924	Paris, France	4 May–27 July	44	2956	136
IX	1928	Amsterdam, Netherlands	17 May–12 Aug.	46	2724	290
X	1932	Los Angeles, USA	30 July–14 Aug.	37	1281	127
XI	1936	Berlin, Germany	1–16 Aug.	49	3738	328
XII	1940	Tokyo, then Helsinki	Not held due to war	—	—	—

	Year	Venue	Date	Countries	Competitors Male	Female
XIII	1944	London, England	Not held due to war	—	—	—
XIV	1948	London, England	29 July–14 Aug.	59	3714	385
XV	1952	Helsinki, Finland	19 July–3 Aug.	69	4407	518
XVI	1956[2]	Melbourne, Australia	22 Nov.–8 Dec.	67	2958	384
XVII	1960	Rome, Italy	25 Aug.–11 Sept.	83	4738	610
XVIII	1964	Tokyo, Japan	10–24 Oct.	93	4457	683
XIX	1968	Mexico City, Mexico	12–27 Oct.	112	4749	781
XX	1972	Munich, FRG	26 Aug.–10 Sept.	122	6086	1070
XXI	1976	Montreal, Canada	17 July–1 Aug.	92	4834	1251
XXII	1980	Moscow, USSR	19 July–3 Aug.	81	4238	1088
XXIII	1984	Los Angeles, USA	28 July–12 Aug.	140		
XXIV	1988	Seoul, South Korea	20 Sept.–5 Oct.			

* This celebration to mark the tenth anniversary of the Modern Games was officially intercalated but is not numbered.
[1] Including newly discovered French national.

[2] The equestrian events were held in Stockholm, Sweden, 10–17 June with 158 competitors from 29 countries.

CELEBRATIONS OF THE WINTER GAMES

	Year	Venue	Date	Countries	Competitors Male	Female
I*	1924	Chamonix, France	25 Jan.–4 Feb.	16	281	13
II	1928	St Moritz, Switzerland	11–19 Feb.	25	468	27
III	1932	Lake Placid, USA	4–15 Feb.	17	274	32
IV	1936	Garmisch-Partenkirchen, Germany	6–16 Feb.	28	675	80
V	1948	St Moritz, Switzerland	30 Jan.–8 Feb.	28	636	77
VI	1952	Oslo, Norway	14–25 Feb.	22	623	109
VII	1956	Cortina d'Ampezzo, Italy	26 Jan.–5 Feb.	32	687	132

	Year	Venue	Date	Countries	Competitors Male	Female
VIII	1960	Squaw Valley, USA	18–28 Feb.	30	521	144
IX	1964	Innsbruck, Austria	29 Jan.–9 Feb.	36	893	200
X	1968	Grenoble, France	6–18 Feb.	37	1065	228
XI	1972	Sapporo, Japan	3–13 Feb.	35	1015	217
XII	1976	Innsbruck, Austria	4–15 Feb.	37	900	228
XIII	1980	Lake Placid, USA	13–24 Feb.	37	833	234
XIV	1984	Sarajevo, Yugoslavia	7–19 Feb.	49	1287	223
XV	1988	Calgary, Canada	23 Feb.–6 Mar.	—	—	—

* There were Winter Games events included in the Summer Games of 1908 (London and 1920 (Antwerp) which attracted six countries, 14 males and seven females for the first, and 10 countries, 73 males and 12 females for the latter.

TABLE OF OLYMPIC MEDAL WINNERS – SUMMER GAMES, 1896–1984

		Gold	Silver	Bronze	TOTAL
1.	USA	710	529	448	1687
2.	USSR	340	292	253	885
3.	Great Britain	168	212	197	577
4.	Germany[1]	146	193	192	531
5.	France	147	163	171	481
6.	Sweden	131	135	162	428
7.	Italy	141	117	120	378
8.	Hungary	113	106	130	349
9.	GDR[2]	116	94	97	307
10.	Finland	96	74	108	278
11.	Japan	83	72	75	230
12.	Australia	68	61	82	211
13.	Romania	48	53	76	177
14.	Poland	38	51	86	175
15.	Canada	36	60	68	164
16.	Switzerland	40	64	55	159
17.	Netherlands	41	45	58	144
18.	Denmark	31	57	52	140
19.	Czechoslovakia	42	45	47	134
20.	Belgium	35	48	40	123
21.	Bulgaria	27	50	39	116
22.	Norway	40	30	33	103
23.	Greece	22	39	38	99
24.	Austria	18	26	34	78
25.	Yugoslavia	23	25	23	71
26.	Cuba	23	21	15	59
27.	South Africa[3]	16	15	21	52
28.	Turkey	23	12	10	45
29.	Argentina	13	18	13	44
30.	New Zealand	23	4	15	42
31.	Mexico	9	12	16	37
32.	South Korea	7	12	18	37
33.	China	15	8	9	32
34.	Brazil	6	7	17	30
35.	Iran	4	10	15	29
36.	Kenya	6	7	9	22
37.	Estonia[4]	6	6	9	21
38.	Jamaica	4	8	8	20
39.	Spain	3	11	6	20
40.	Egypt	6	6	6	18
41.	India	8	3	3	14
42.	Ireland	4	4	5	13
43.	Portugal	1	4	7	12
44.	North Korea[5]	2	5	5	12

		Gold	Silver	Bronze	TOTAL
45.	Ethiopia	5	1	4	10
46.	Mongolia	0	5	5	10
47.	Uruguay	2	1	6	9
43.	Pakistan	3	3	2	8
49.	Venezuela	1	2	5	8
50.	Trinidad	1	2	4	7
51.	Chile	0	5	2	7
52.	Philippines	0	1	5	6
53.	Uganda	1	3	1	5
54.	Tunisia	1	2	2	5
=55.	Lebanon	0	2	2	4
=55.	Colombia	0	2	2	4
=57.	Puerto Rico	0	1	3	4
=57.	Nigeria	0	1	3	4
59.	Morocco	2	1	0	3
60.	Latvia[4]	0	2	1	3
=61.	Taipei	0	1	2	3
=61.	Ghana	0	1	2	3
=63.	Luxembourg	1	1	0	2
=63.	Peru	1	1	0	2
65.	Bahamas	1	0	1	2
66.	Tanzania	0	2	0	2
=67.	Cameroun	0	1	1	2
=67.	Haiti	0	1	1	2
=67.	Iceland	0	1	1	2
=67.	Thailand	0	1	1	2
=71.	Algeria	0	0	2	2
=71.	Panama	0	0	2	2
73.	Zimbabwe	1	0	0	1
=74.	Ivory Coast	0	1	0	1
=74.	Singapore	0	1	0	1
=74.	Sri Lanka	0	1	0	1
=74.	Syria	0	1	0	1
=78.	Bermuda	0	0	1	1
=78.	Dominican Repub.	0	0	1	1
=78.	Guyana	0	0	1	1
=78.	Iraq	0	0	1	1
=78.	Niger	0	0	1	1
=78.	Zambia	0	0	1	1

[1] Germany 1896–1964, West Germany from 1968.
[2] GDR, East Germany, from 1968.
[3] South Africa, up to 1960.
[4] Estonia and Latvia, up to 1936.
[5] North Korea, from 1964.

TABLE OF OLYMPIC MEDAL WINNERS – WINTER GAMES, 1924–84

		Gold	Silver	Bronze	TOTAL
1.	USSR	68	48	50	166
2.	Norway	54	57	52	163
3.	USA	40	46	31	117
4.	Finland	29	42	32	103
5.	Austria	25	33	30	88
6.	Sweden	32	25	29	86
7.	GDR[1]	30	26	29	85
8.	Germany[2]	24	22	21	67
9.	Switzerland	18	20	20	58
10.	Canada	14	10	15	39
11.	France	12	10	15	37
12.	Netherlands	10	15	10	35
13.	Italy	12	9	7	28
14.	Great Britain	7	4	10	21
15.	Czechoslovakia	2	7	11	20
16.	Liechtenstein	2	2	4	8
17.	Japan	1	4	1	6
18.	Hungary	—	2	4	6
=19.	Belgium	1	1	2	4
=19.	Poland	1	1	2	4
21.	Spain	1	0	0	1
=22.	North Korea[3]	0	1	0	1
=22.	Yugoslavia	0	1	0	1
=24.	Bulgaria	0	0	1	1
=24.	Romania	0	0	1	1

Totals include all first, second and third places, including those events not on the current schedule.
[1] GDR, East Germany, from 1968.
[2] Germany, 1924–64, West Germany from 1968.
[3] From 1964.

Speed in Sport

mph	km/h	Record	Name	Place	Date
739·666	1190,377	Highest land speed – unofficial	Stan Barrett (USA) in *Budweiser Rocket*	Edwards Air Force Base, California, USA	17 Dec. 1979
633·468	1019,467	Highest land speed (official one mile record, jet powered)	Richard Noble (UK) in *Thrust II*	Black Rock Desert, Nevada, USA	4 Oct. 1983
625·2	1006	Parachuting freefall in mesosphere (military research)	Capt J W Kittinger (USA)	Tularosa, New Mexico, USA	16 Aug. 1960
429·311	690,909	Highest land speed (wheel driven)	Donald Campbell (UK) in *Bluebird*	Lake Eyre, South Australia	17 July 1964
418·504	673,516	Highest land speed (4-wheel direct drive)	Robert Summers (USA) in *Goldenrod*	Bonneville Salt Flats, Utah, USA	12 Nov. 1965
345	556	Highest water borne speed – estimated	Ken Warby (Aus) in *The Spirit of Australia*	Blowering Dam, NSW, Australia	20 Nov. 1977
319·627	514,39	Official water speed record	Ken Warby (Aus) in *The Spirit of Australia*	Blowering Dam, NSW, Australia	8 Oct. 1978
318·866	513,165	Highest speed motor cycle	Don Vesco (USA)	Bonneville Salt Flats, Utah	28 Aug. 1978
250·958	403,878	Motor Racing – closed circuit	Dr Hans Liebold (FRG)	Nardo, Italy	5 May 1979
215·33	346,54	Hydroplane record (propeller driven)	Eddie Hill (USA)	Lake Irvine, California	5 June 1983
214·158	344,654	Motor Racing – race lap record	Mario Andretti (USA)	Texas World Speedway	6 Oct. 1973
188	302,5	Pelota (Fastest ball game)	Jose Areitio	Newport, Rhode Island	3 Aug. 1979
170	273	Golf ball		USA	1960
163·6	263	Lawn tennis – serve	Bill Tilden	USA	1931
156·62	252,05	Lap record (practice) 24 Hr Endurance Motor Racing	Hans Stuck (W. Germany)	Le Mans, France	14 June 1985
152·284	245,077	Cycling, motor paced	John Howard (USA)	Bonneville Salt Flats, Utah	20 July 1985
143·08	230,26	Water skiing	Christopher Massey (Aus)	Hawkesbury River, NSW, Australia	6 Mar. 1983
143	230	Ice yacht	John D Buckstaff (USA)	Lake Winnebago, Wisconsin, USA	1938
138	222	Lawn tennis – serve (modern equipment)	Steve Denton (USA)	Colorado, USA	29 July 1984
129·827	208,936	Alpine skiing – Downhill Schuss	Franz Weber (Austria)	Les Arcs, France	19 Apr. 1984
121·28	195,18	Gliding (*100 km* triangular course)	Ingo Renner (Aus) in a Nimbus 3	Tocumwal, NSW, Australia	14 Dec. 1982
118·3	190,3	Ice Hockey – puck slap shot	Bobby Hull (Canada)	Chicago, Illinois, USA	1965
113·67	182,93	Water skiing, Barefoot	Lee Kirk (USA)	Firebird Lake, Phoenix, USA	11 June 1977
100·9	162,3	Baseball (pitch)	Lynn Nolan Ryan (USA)	Anaheim, California, USA	20 Aug. 1974

mph	km/h	Record	Name	Place	Date
88·4	142,26	Sand Yacht	Nord Embroden (USA) in *Midnight at the Oasis*	Superior Dry Lake, California, USA	15 Apr. 1976
66·48	107	Sand Yacht – official record	Christian-Yves Nau (Fra) in *Mobil*	Le Touquet, France	22 Mar. 1981
64·95	104,53	Alpine Skiing – Olympic Downhill course (average)	William Johnson (USA)	Sarajevo, Yugoslavia	16 Feb. 1984
52·57	84,60	Speedway (4 laps of 430 yds *393 m*)	Scott Autrey	Exeter, England	19 June 1978
52·40	84,33	Tobogganing – Cresta Run (3977 ft *1212,25 m* course in 51·75 secs)	Franco Gansser (Sui)	St. Moritz, Switzerland	19 Feb. 1984
44·645	71,849	Track Cycling (200 m unpaced in 10·021 secs)	Lutz Hesslich (GDR)	Moscow, USSR	22 Aug. 1984
43·26	69,62	Horse racing (440 yds *402 m* in 20·8 secs)	Big Racket	Mexico City, Mexico	5 Feb. 1945
41·72	67,14	Greyhound racing (410 yds *374 m* straight in 26·13 secs)	The Shoe (Aus)	Richmond, NSW, Australia	25 Apr. 1968
41·50	66,78	Sailing (36·04 knots)	Tim Coleman (UK) in *Crossbow II*	Portland, Dorset, England	17 Nov. 1980
37·22	59,91	Boardsailing (in Force 9 wind)	Michael Pucher (Austria)	Marseille, France	17 Apr. 1985
35·06	56,42	Horse Racing – The Derby (1 mile 885 yds, *2,41 km*)	Mahmoud	Epsom, Surrey, England	27 May 1936
35	56	Boxing – speed of punch	Sugar Ray Robinson (USA)	USA	Jan. 1957
31·784	51,151	Cycling – 1 hour, unpaced	Francesco Moser (Italy)	Mexico City, Mexico	23 Jan. 1984
30·58	49,21	Speed skating on ice (500 m *546 yds* in 36·57 secs on 400 m *437 yds* rink)	Pavel Pegov (USSR)	Medeo, USSR	26 Mar. 1983
29·80	47,96	Steeplechasing – The Grand National (4 miles 856 yds, *7,280 km* in 9 min 1·9 sec)	Red Rum ridden by Brian Fletcher	Aintree, Liverpool, England	31 Mar. 1973
25·78	41,48	Roller skating (440 yds *402 m* in 34·9 secs)	Giuseppe Cantarella (Italy)	Catania, Sicily	28 Sept. 1963
25·13	40,45	Sprinting (during 100 m of 4 × 100 m relay)	Carl Lewis (USA)	Helsinki, Finland	14 Aug. 1983
13·676	22,009	Rowing (2000 m)	USA Eight	Lucerne, Switzerland	17 June 1984
12·36	19,90	Marathon run (average over 26 miles 385 yds *42,195 km*)	Carlos Lopes (Portugal)	R. Herdan, Netherlands	20 Apr. 1985
12·24	19,70	Canoeing (1000 m in 3 min 02·70 sec)	USSR Olympic K4	Moscow, USSR	31 July 1980
9·478	15,253	Walking, 1 hour	Ernesto Canto (Mexico)	Fana, Norway	5 May 1984
5·28	8,50	Swimming (50 yds) – short course in 19·36 secs	Robin Leamy (USA)	Austin, Texas, USA	27 Mar. 1981
4·56	7,35	Swimming (100 m) – long course in 48·95 secs	Matthew Biondi (USA)	Mission Viejo, Cal., USA	7 Aug. 1985
2·74	4,40	Channel swimming (effective speed)	Penny Dean (USA)	England to France	29 July 1978
0·00084	0,00135	Tug 'o War (2 hr 41 min pull – 12 ft *3,6 m*)	2nd Derbyshire Regt (UK)	Jubbulpore, India	12 Aug. 1889

AMERICAN FOOTBALL

Evolved at American universities in the second half of the 19th century as a descendant from soccer and rugby in Britain. The first professional game was played in 1895 at Latrobe, Pennsylvania; organisation into National Football League (NFL) took place in 1922 and was divided into two divisions. The American Football League (AFL) was formed in 1960. The two leagues merged in 1970, and under the NFL was reorganised into the National Football Conference (NFC) and the American Football Conference (AFC).

The major trophy is the Super Bowl, held annually since 1967 as a competition between firstly champions of the NFL and AFL, and since 1970 between the champions of the NFC and AFC.

The game is 11-a-side (12-a-side in Canada) with substitutes freely used. Pitch dimensions: 360 ft (*109·7 m*) × 160 ft (*48·8 m*). Ball length 280–6 mm (*11–11¼ ins*), weighing 397–425 g (*14–15 oz*).

ARCHERY

Although developed as an organised sport from the 3rd century AD, archery is portrayed, much earlier, as a skill in Mesolithic cave paintings. Internationalised as a sport in 1931 with the founding of the governing body, *Fédération Internationale de Tir à l'Arc* (FITA); FITA now has more than 45 affiliated countries, and is widespread in USA, UK and Japan. The most popular form of archery is termed Target Archery. Other forms are Field Archery, shooting at animal figures, and Flight Shooting, which has the sole object of achieving distance.

World Target Championships were first held in Poland in 1931, and biennially since 1957. Competitors shoot Double FITA rounds, 144 arrows from four different distances. An Olympic event in 1900, it disappeared between 1920 and 1972. The 1984 champions were: (men) Darrell Pace (USA), and (women) Seo Hyang-Soon (S. Korea).

ATHLETICS (TRACK AND FIELD)

There is evidence that running was involved in early Egyptian rituals at Memphis *c.* 3800 BC, but organised athletics is usually dated to the ancient Olympic Games *c.* 1370 BC. The earliest accurately known Olympiad was in July 776 BC, where Coroibos of Elis is recorded as winning the foot race, about 180–185 m (164–169 yds).

The modern Olympics were revived in 1896 (see Olympic section). The inaugural World Championships were held at Helsinki, Finland in August 1983 and attracted entries from 157 countries, making it the greatest number of nations represented at any sports meeting in history. The Championships are to be quadrennial, the next in Rome in 1987.

Marathon events, held since 1896, commemorate the legendary run of an unknown Greek courier, possibly Pheidippides, who in 490 BC ran some 24 miles (*38·6 km*) from the Plain of Marathon to Athens with news of a Greek victory over the numerically superior Persian army. Delivering his message – 'Rejoice! We have won' – he collapsed and died. Since 1908 the distance has been standardised as 26 miles 385 yds (*42,195 m*).

Dimensions in field events: Shot (men) – weight 7,26 kg (*16 lb*), diameter 110–130 mm (*4·33–5·12 ins*); Shot (women) – weight 4 kg (*8 lb 13 oz*), diameter 95–110 mm (*3·74–4·33 ins*); Discus (men) – weight 2 kg (*4·409 lb*), diameter 219–221 mm (*8·622–8·701 ins*); Discus (women) – weight 1 kg (*2·204 lb*), diameter 180–182 mm (*7·086–7·165 ins*). Hammer – weight 7,26 kg (*16 lb*), length 117,5–121,5 cm (*46·259–47·835 ins*), diameter of head 110–130 mm (*4·33–5·12 ins*); Javelin (men) – weight 800 g (*28·219 oz*), length 260–270 cm (*102·362–106·299 ins*); Javelin (women) – weight 600 g (*21·164 oz*) length 220–230 cm (*86·61–90·55 ins*).

AUSTRALIAN RULES FOOTBALL

Originally a hybrid of soccer, Gaelic football and rugby, laws were codified in 1866 in Melbourne, with the oval (rather than round) ball in use by 1867. The first football body in Australia, the Victoria Football Association, was formed in 1877 and the Australian Football Council (AFC) in 1906.

Teams are 18-a-side. Pitch dimensions are: width 110–155 m (*120–170 yds*), length 135–185 m (*150–200 yds*), encompassing an oval boundary line. The oval ball measures 736 mm (*29½ ins*) in length, 572 mm (*22½ in*) in diameter and weighs 452–482 g (*16–17 oz*).

BADMINTON

The modern game is believed to have evolved from Badminton Hall, Avon, England, *c.* 1870, or from a game played in India at about the same time. Modern rules were first codified in Poona, India in 1876. A similar game was played in China 2000 years earlier.

The International Badminton Federation was founded in 1934, with affiliations in over 70 countries. Main countries today: Canada, China, Denmark, India, Indonesia, Japan, Malaysia, New Zealand, S. Africa, USA, and the UK.

World Championships were instituted in 1977 and are held triennially. Previously, the All England Championships (instituted 1899) was considered premier. International men's teams compete for the Thomas Cup (first held 1949); and women's for the Uber Cup (first held 1957). Both are held triennially; the 1984 winners were Indonesia and China respectively. Court dimensions: 13·41 m (*44 ft*) × 6·1 m (*20 ft*) (singles game 3 ft narrower). The net is 5 ft high at the centre; two or four players.

BASEBALL

The modern rules, or Cartwright rules, were introduced in New Jersey on 19 June 1846, although a game of the same name had been played in England prior to 1700. Baseball is mainly played in America, where there are two leagues, the National (NL) and the American (AL), founded in 1876 and 1901 respectively. It is also very popular in Japan. The winners of each league meet annually in a best of seven series of games, the World Series, established permanently in 1905.

The game is 9-a-side. A standard ball weighs 5–5¼ oz (*148 g*) and is 9–9½ ins (*23 cm*) in circumference. Bats are up to 2¾ ins (*7 cm*) in diameter and up to 42 in (*1·07 m*) in length.

BASKETBALL

A game not dissimilar to Basketball was played in Mexico in the 10th century BC, but the modern game was devised by (Canadian born) Dr James Naismith in Massachusetts, December 1891.

The governing body is the Fédération Internationale de Basketball Amateur (FIBA), formed in 1932, and the game is played worldwide. By 1973, 133 national federations were members of FIBA. An Olympic sport since 1936 for men, for women since 1976. America won both 1984 titles. World titles for men (instituted 1950) and for women (instituted 1953) are held every four years. Russia won both golds in the last respective championships.

Teams are 5-a-side, with seven substitutes allowed. The rectangular court is 26·0 m (*85 ft*) in length, and 14·0 m (*46 ft*) wide, and the ball is 75–78 cms (*30 ins*) in circumference and weighs 600–650 grams.

BILLIARDS

Probably deriving from the old French word *billiard* (a stick with a curved end), an early reference exists, dated 1429, to the game played on grass. Louis XVI of France (1461–83) is believed to be the first to have played on a table. Rubber cushions were introduced in 1835, and slate beds in 1836.

World Professional and Amateur Championships have been held since 1870 and 1926 respectively.

Dimensions of table: 3·66 × 1·87 m (*12 ft × 6 ft*).

BOARDSAILING (WINDSURFING)

Following a High Court decision, Peter Chilvers has been credited with devising the prototype boardsail in 1958. As a sport, it was pioneered by Henry Hoyle Schweitzer and Jim Drake in California in 1968. World Championships were first held in 1973 and boardsailing was added to the Olympic Games in 1984.

BOBSLEIGH AND TOBOGGANING

Although the first sledge dates back to *c*. 6500 BC in Heinola, Finland, organised bobsleighing began in Davos, Switzerland in 1889.

The International Federation of Bobsleigh & Tobogganing was formed in 1923, followed by the International Bobsleigh Federation in 1957. There are less than a dozen major courses in the world.

World and Olympic Championships began in 1924, and competition is for crews of two or four. The driver steers whilst the rear man operates brakes and corrects skidding. With the four-man, the middle two riders alter weight transference for cornering.

The oldest tobogganing club is the St Moritz in Switzerland, founded in 1887, and home of the Cresta Run which dates to 1884. The course is 1212·25 m (*3977 ft*) long with a drop of 157 m (*514 ft*). A solo activity, speeds reach 145 km/h (*90 mph*). In Lugeing, the rider sits or lies back, as opposed to lying prone face down in tobogganing.

BOWLING (TEN-PIN)

Evolved from the ancient German game of ninepins, which having been exported to America was banned in Connecticut in 1847 and then in other States. Ten pins were introduced to beat the ban. Rules were first standardised by the American Bowling Congress (ABC), formed in September 1895.

Concentrated in the USA, the game is also very popular in Japan and Europe. World Championships were introduced for men in 1954 and women in 1963, under the Fédération Internationale des Quilleurs (FIQ), which governs a number of bowling games.

The ten pins are placed in a triangle at the end of a lane of total length 19·16 m (*62 ft 10⅚ in*), and width 1·06 m (*42 in*).

BOWLS

Outdoor bowls go back as far as 13th century England, but were forbidden by Edward III since its popularity threatened the practice of archery. The modern rules were not framed until 1848–9, in Scotland by William Mitchell. There are two types of greens, the crown and the level, the former being played almost exclusively in Northern England and the Midland counties.

Lawn bowls is played mostly in the UK and Commonwealth countries. The International Bowling Board was formed in July 1905. Men and Women's World Championships are held every four years, with singles, pairs, triples and fours events. World Championships for Indoor Bowls were introduced in 1979.

BOXING

Competitively, boxing began in Ancient Greece as one of the first Olympic sports. Boxing with gloves was first depicted on a fresco, however, from the Isle of Thera, *c*. 1520 BC. Prize-fighting rules were formed in England in 1743 by Jack Broughton, but modern day fights evolved from 1867 when the 8th Marquess of Queensberry gave his name to rules. Boxing only became a legal sport in 1901.

Professional boxing has two world governing bodies, the World Boxing Council and the World Boxing Association, based in Mexico City and Manila respectively. Each body has a world champion at each of 15 recognised weights: Light-flyweight (limit 108 lbs); Flyweight (limit 112 lbs); Super-flyweight (limit 115 lbs); Bantamweight (118 lbs); Light-featherweight (122 lbs); Featherweight (126 lbs); Junior Lightweight (130 lbs); Lightweight (135 lbs); Light Welterweight (140 lbs); Welterweight (147 lbs); Light middleweight (153½ lbs); Middleweight (160 lbs); Light Heavyweight (175 lbs); Cruiserweight (190 lbs) and Heavyweight.

CANOEING

Modern canoes and kayaks originated among the Indians and Eskimoes of North America, but canoeing as a sport is attributed to an English barrister, James MacGregor, who founded the Royal Canoe Club in 1866.

With a kayak, the paddler sits in a forward-facing position and uses a double-bladed paddle, whereas in a canoe the paddler kneels in a forward-facing position and propels with a single-bladed paddle. An Olympic sport since 1936, Olympic titles are now held in nine events for men – New Zealand took four golds at Los Angeles, Canada two – and three for women of which Sweden won two.

CHESS

Derived from the Persian word *Shah*, meaning a king or ruler, the game itself originated in India under the name Chaturanga, a military game (literally 'four corps'). The first chessmen, of ivory, found in Russia, are dated *c*. 200 AD. By the 10th century, chess was played in most European countries. There are today some 40 million enthusiasts in Russia alone. The governing body, founded in 1922, is the *Fédération Internationale des Echecs* (FIDE), which has been responsible for the World Chess Championship competitions since 1946, although official champions date from 1886 and unofficial before then.

Players are graded according to competitive results on the official ELO scoring system. Bobby Fischer (USA), world champion 1972–5, achieved the highest-ever rating of 2785.

CRICKET

A drawing dated *c*. 1250 shows a bat and ball game resembling cricket, although the formal origins are early 18th century. The formation of the MCC (Marylebone Cricket Club) in 1787 resulted in codified laws by 1835.

The International Cricket Conference (ICC), so called since 1965, having allowed membership from non-Commonwealth countries, now numbers seven. There are additionally 18 associate members. Recognised Test matches are played between England, Australia, West Indies, India, Pakistan, New Zealand and Sri Lanka.

There are four domestic competitions. The UK County Championship, a league of the 17 first class counties with matches over three days; the one-day knockouts of the Nat. West (previously Gillette) Trophy of 60-over matches and the Benson & Hedges of 55, and the one-day John Player League (40-over matches). The domestic competitions of Australia, New Zealand, India and the West Indies are the Sheffield Shield, the Shell Trophy, the Ranji Trophy and the Shell Shield respectively.

The World Cup, the international one day tournament, is held every four years, with the seven Test-playing countries plus the winner of the ICC Trophy which is competed for by non-Test playing countries. India won the 1983 tournament, the West Indies the first two.

Dimensions: Ball circumference 20·79–22·8 cms (*8 1/16 – 9 in*), weight 155–163 g (*5½–5¾ oz*); pitch 20·11 m (*22 yds*) from stump to stump.

CURLING

Similar to bowls on ice, curling dates from the 15th century although organised administration only began in 1838 with the Grand (later Royal) Caledonian Curling Club in Edinburgh. The sport is traditionally popular in Scotland and Canada. The International Curling Federation was formed in 1966, and curling is to be added to the 1988 Olympic Games as a demonstration sport.

CYCLING

The first known race was held over 2 km (*1·2 miles*) in Paris on 31 May 1868. The Road Record Association in Britain was formed in 1888, whilst F. T. Bidlake devised the time trial (by 1890) as a means of avoiding traffic congestion caused by ordinary mass road racing.

Competitive racing, popular worldwide, is now conducted both on road and track. The Tour de France (founded in 1903) is the longest lasting non-motorised sporting event in the world, taking 23 days to stage annually. The yellow jersey, to distinguish the leading rider, was introduced in 1919.

Included since the first of the modern Olympic Games in 1896, there were seven men's events in 1984 and one women's, the Individual Road Race.

DARTS

Brian Gamlin of Bury, Lancashire, is credited with devising the present numbering system on the board, although in non-sporting form darts began with the heavily weighted throwing arrows used in Roman and Greek warfare.

Immensely popular in the UK – there are today some 6 000 000 players – the sport is rapidly spreading in America and parts of Europe.

EQUESTRIANISM

Horse riding is some 5000 years old, but schools of horsemanship, or equitation, were not established until the 16th century, primarily in Italy and then in France. The earliest jumping competition was in Islington, London in 1869.

An Olympic sport since 1912, events are held in dressage, showjumping and Three Day Event, with team and individual titles for each. Dressage (the French term for the training of horses) is a test of riders' ability to control horses through various manoeuvres within an area of 60 × 20 m (*66 × 22 yds*). In showjumping riders jump a set course of fences, incurring four faults for knocking a fence down or landing (one or more feet) in the water, three faults for a first refusal, six faults then elimination for 2nd and 3rd, and eight for a fall. The Three Day event encompasses dressage, cross country and jumping.

The governing body is the Fédération Equestre Internationale, founded in May 1921.

FENCING

Fencing (fighting with single sticks) was practiced as a sport, or as part of a religious ceremony, in Egypt as early as 1360 BC. The modern sport developed directly from the duelling of the Middle Ages.

There are three types of sword used today. With the foil (introduced 17th century), only the trunk of the body is acceptable as a target. The épée (mid-19th century) is marginally heavier and more rigid and the whole body is a valid target. The sabre (late 19th century) has cutting edges on both sides of the blade and scores on the whole body from the waist upwards. Only with the sabre can points be scored with the edge of the blade rather than the tip.

For men, there are individual and team events for each type of sword in the Olympics. Women compete in foil only. Governed by the Fédération Internationale d'Escrine (f. 1913), the sport has taken off in the eastern bloc having once been dominated by France and Italy.

FIVES

Eton Fives originates from a handball game first recorded as being played against the buttress of Eton College Chapel in 1825. Rules were codified in 1877, and last amended in 1981.

Rugby Fives, a variation, dates from *c*. 1850. Both are more or less confined to the UK.

FOOTBALL (Association)

Tsu-Chu – Tsu meaning 'to kick the ball with feet' (*chu* means 'leather'), was played in China around 400 BC. Calcio, closer to the modern game, existed in Italy in 1410. Official references date to Edward II's reign in Britain – he banned the game in London in 1314. Later monarchs issued similar edicts. The first soccer rules were formulated at Cambridge University in 1846; previously football was brutal and lawless. The Football Association (FA) was founded in England on 26 October 1863. Eleven per side became standard in 1870.

The governing body, the Fédération Internationale de Football Association (FIFA) was founded in Paris on 21 May 1904; football is played throughout the world.

Professionally, domestic competitions in England are the League Championship (the Football League was formed in 1888 with 12 teams), today comprising four divisions totalling 92 teams; the FA Challenge Cup, inst. 1871; and the Milk (previously League) Cup, inst. 1960. 'Non-League' or semi-professional football is also widespread. Internationally, the World Cup has been held every four years since 1930 (not 1942 or 1946); the European Championship, instituted in 1958 as the Nations Cup, held every four years; the European Champions Club Cup, instituted in 1955 as the European Cup, contested annually by the League Champions of the member countries of the Union of European Football Associations (UEFA); the European Cup Winners Cup, instituted in 1960 for National Cup winners (or runners-up if the winners are in the European Cup); the UEFA Cup instituted in 1955 as the Inter-City Fairs Cup, held annually since 1960; the European Super Cup (inst. 1972) played between the winners of the European Champions Club Cup and the Cup Winners Cup; and the World Club Championship (inst. 1960) a contest between the winners of the European Cup and the Copa Libertadores (the S. American championship).

Football is an 11-a-side game; the ball's circumference is 68–71 cm (*27–28 ins*) and weight 396–453 g (*14–16 oz*). Pitch length 91–120 m (*100–130 yds*), width 45–91 m (*50–100 yds*).

The World Cup

Year	Winner	Venue
1930	Uruguay	Uruguay
1934	Italy	Italy
1938	Italy	France
1950	Uruguay	Brazil
1954	W. Germany	Switzerland
1958	Brazil	Sweden
1962	Brazil	Chile
1966	England	England
1970	Brazil	Mexico
1974	W. Germany	W. Germany
1978	Argentina	Argentina
1982	Italy	Spain
1986		Mexico

The FA Cup (UK)

The FA Cup, or Football Association Challenge Cup, was instituted in 1871, 17 years before the birth of the Football League. The first final was played at Kennington Oval, London in 1872, when the Wanderers defeated Royal Engineers 1–0. Southern amateur clubs dominated the early years and the Cup did not 'go north' until Blackburn Olympic won in 1883. The final has been played at Wembley Stadium since 1923, when Bolton Wanderers defeated West Ham.

1872	Wanderers
1873	Wanderers
1874	Oxford University
1875	Royal Engineers
1876	Wanderers
1877	Wanderers
1878	Wanderers
1879	Old Etonians
1880	Clapham Rovers
1881	Old Carthusians
1882	Old Etonians
1883	Blackburn Olympic
1884	Blackburn Rovers
1885	Blackburn Rovers
1886	Blackburn Rovers
1887	Aston Villa
1888	West Bromwich Albion
1889	Preston North End
1890	Blackburn Rovers
1891	Blackburn Rovers
1892	West Bromwich Albion
1893	Wolverhampton Wanderers
1894	Notts County
1895	Aston Villa
1896	Sheffield Wednesday
1897	Aston Villa
1898	Nottingham Forest
1899	Sheffield United
1900	Bury
1901	Tottenham Hotspur
1902	Sheffield United
1903	Bury
1904	Manchester City
1905	Aston Villa
1906	Everton
1907	Sheffield Wednesday
1908	Wolverhampton Wanderers
1909	Manchester United
1910	Newcastle United
1911	Bradford City
1912	Barnsley
1913	Aston Villa
1914	Burnley
1915	Sheffield United
1920	Aston Villa
1921	Tottenham Hotspur
1922	Huddersfield Town
1923	Bolton Wanderers
1924	Newcastle United
1925	Sheffield United
1926	Bolton Wanderers
1927	Cardiff City
1928	Blackburn Rovers
1929	Bolton Wanderers
1930	Arsenal
1931	West Bromwich Albion
1932	Newcastle United
1933	Everton
1934	Manchester City
1935	Sheffield Wednesday
1936	Arsenal
1937	Sunderland
1938	Preston North End
1939	Portsmouth
1946	Derby County
1947	Charlton Athletic
1948	Manchester United
1949	Wolverhampton Wanderers
1950	Arsenal
1951	Newcastle United
1952	Newcastle United
1953	Blackpool
1954	West Bromwich Albion
1955	Newcastle United
1956	Manchester City
1957	Aston Villa
1958	Bolton Wanderers
1959	Nottingham Forest
1960	Wolverhampton Wanderers
1961	Tottenham Hotspur
1962	Tottenham Hotspur
1963	Manchester United
1964	West Ham United
1965	Liverpool
1966	Everton
1967	Tottenham Hotspur
1968	West Bromwich Albion
1969	Manchester City
1970	Chelsea
1971	Arsenal
1972	Leeds United
1973	Sunderland
1974	Liverpool
1975	West Ham United
1976	Southampton
1977	Manchester United
1978	Ipswich Town
1979	Arsenal
1980	West Ham United
1981	Tottenham Hotspur
1982	Tottenham Hotspur
1983	Manchester United
1984	Everton
1985	Manchester United

GAELIC FOOTBALL

The game developed from inter-parish 'free for all' with no time limit, no defined playing area nor specific rules. The Gaelic Athletic Association established the game in its present form in 1884. Teams are 15-a-side. Played throughout Ireland.

GOLF

A prohibiting law passed by the Scottish Parliament in 1457, which declared 'goff be utterly cryit doune and not usit', is the earliest mention of golf, although games of similar principle date as far back as AD 400. Golf is today played worldwide.

Competition is either 'match play', contested by individuals or pairs and decided by the number of holes won, or 'stroke play' decided by the total number of strokes for a round. The modern golf course measures total distance 5500–6400 metres, divided into 18 holes of varying lengths. Clubs are currently limited to a maximum of 14, comprising 'irons' Nos. 1–10 (with the face of the club at increasingly acute angles), and 'woods' for driving. Golf balls in the UK have minimum diameter 41·55 mm (*1·62 ins*) and maximum weight 45·93 grams (*1·62 oz*). In America, the minimum diameter is 42·62 mm (*1·68 ins*).

Professionally, the four major tournaments are the British Open, the US Open, the US Masters and the US Professional Golfers' Association (USPGA).

The British Open Golf Championship

The oldest open championship in the world, 'The Open', was first held on 17 October 1860 at the Prestwick Club, Ayrshire. It was then over 36 holes; since 1892 it has been over 72 holes of stroke play. Since 1920, the Royal and Ancient Golf Club have managed the event.

		Score
1860	Willie Park, Sr	174
1861	Tom Morris, Sr	163
1862	Tom Morris, Sr	163
1863	Willie Park, Sr	168
1864	Tom Morris, Sr	167
1865	Andrew Strath	162
1866	Willie Park, Sr	169
1867	Tom Morris, Sr	170
1868	Tom Morris, Jr	170
1869	Tom Morris, Jr	154
1870	Tom Morris, Jr	149
1871	Not held	
1872	Tom Morris, Jr	166
1873	Tom Kidd	179
1874	Mungo Park	159
1875	Willie Park, Sr	166
1876	Robert Martin	176
1877	Jamie Anderson	160
1878	Jamie Anderson	157
1879	Jamie Anderson	170
1880	Robert Ferguson	162
1881	Robert Ferguson	170
1882	Robert Ferguson	171
1883	Willie Fernie	159
1884	Jack Simpson	160
1885	Bob Martin	171
1886	David Brown	157
1887	Willie Park, Jr	161
1888	Jack Burns	171
1889	Willie Park, Jr	155
1890	John Ball	164
1891	Hugh Kirkcaldy	169
1892	Harold Hilton	305
1893	William Auchterlonie	322
1894	John Taylor	326
1895	John Taylor	322
1896	Harry Vardon	316
1897	Harry Hilton	314
1898	Harry Vardon	307
1899	Harry Vardon	310
1900	John Taylor	309
1901	James Braid	309
1902	Alexander Herd	307
1903	Harry Vardon	300
1904	Jack White	296
1905	James Braid	318
1906	James Braid	300
1907	Arnaud Massy (Fra)	312

1908	James Braid	291
1909	John Taylor	295
1910	James Braid	299
1911	Harry Vardon	303
1912	Edward (Ted) Ray	295
1913	John Taylor	304
1914	Harry Vardon	306
1920	George Duncan	303
1921	Jock Hutchinson (USA)	296
1922	Walter Hagen (USA)	300
1923	Arthur Havers	295
1924	Walter Hagen (USA)	301
1925	James Barnes (USA)	300
1926	Robert T. Jones, Jr (USA)	291
1927	Robert T. Jones, Jr (USA)	285
1928	Walter Hagen (USA)	292
1929	Walter Hagen (USA)	292
1930	Robert T. Jones, Jr (USA)	291
1931	Tommy Armour (USA)	296
1932	Gene Sarazen (USA)	283
1933	Denny Shute (USA)	292
1934	Henry Cotton	283
1935	Alfred Perry	283
1936	Alfred Padgham	287
1937	Henry Cotton	283
1938	Reg Whitcombe	295
1939	Richard Burton	290
1946	Sam Snead (USA)	290
1947	Fred Daly	293
1948	Henry Cotton	284
1949	Bobby Locke (Saf)	283
1950	Bobby Locke (Saf)	279
1951	Max Faulkner	285
1952	Bobby Locke (Saf)	287
1953	Ben Hogan (USA)	282
1954	Peter Thomson (Aus)	283
1955	Peter Thomson (Aus)	281
1956	Peter Thomson (Aus)	286
1957	Bobby Locke (Saf)	279
1958	Peter Thomson (Aus)	278
1959	Gary Player (Saf)	284
1960	Kel Nagle (Aus)	278
1961	Arnold Palmer (USA)	284
1962	Arnold Palmer (USA)	276
1963	Bob Charles (NZ)	277
1964	Tony Lema (USA)	279
1965	Peter Thomson (Aus)	285
1966	Jack Nicklaus (USA)	282
1967	Roberto de Vicenzo (Arg)	278
1968	Gary Player (Saf)	299
1969	Tony Jacklin	280
1970	Jack Nicklaus (USA)	283
1971	Lee Trevino (USA)	278
1972	Lee Trevino (USA)	278
1973	Tom Weiskopf (USA)	276
1974	Gary Player (Saf)	282
1975	Tom Watson (USA)	279
1976	Johnny Miller (USA)	279
1977	Tom Watson (USA)	268
1978	Jack Nicklaus (USA)	281
1979	Severiano Ballesteros (Spa)	283
1980	Tom Watson (USA)	271
1981	Bill Rogers (USA)	276
1982	Tom Watson (USA)	284
1983	Tom Watson (USA)	275
1984	Severiano Ballesteros (Spa)	276
1985	Sandy Lyle	282

GLIDING

Leonardo da Vinci around 1500 AD defined the difference between gliding and powered flight in some drawings. However, the first authenticated man-carrying glider was designed by Sir George Cayley in 1853.

In competitive terms, gliders contest various events – pure distance, distance to a declared goal, to a declared goal and back, height gain and absolute altitude. World Championships were first held in 1937 and biennially from 1948.

Hang Gliding has flourished in recent years, boosted by the invention of the flexible 'wing' by Professor Francis Rogallo in the early 1960s. The first official World Championships were held in 1976.

GREYHOUND RACING

Greyhounds were first used in sport at coursing – chasing of hares by pairs of dogs – brought to England by the Normans in 1067. Use of mechanical devices was first practised in Eng-land, but the sport was popularised in the USA. The first regular track was opened at Emeryville, California in 1919.

Races are usually conducted over distances of between 210 m (*230 yds*) for the sprint and 1097 m (*1200 yds*) for the marathon. The Derby, the major race in Britain, was instituted in 1927.

GYMNASTICS

Tumbling and similar exercises were performed *c*. 2600 BC as religious rituals in China, but it was the ancient Greeks who coined the word gymnastics, which encompassed various athletic contests including boxing, weightlifting and wrestling. A primitive form was practised in the ancient Olympic Games, but the foundations of the modern sport were laid by German Johann Friedrich Simon in 1776, and the first national federation was formed in Germany in 1860.

The International Gymnastics Federation was founded in Belgium in 1881, and gymnastics was included in the first modern Olympic Games in 1896. Current events for men are: floor exercises, horse vaults, rings, pommel horse, parallel bars and horizontal bar, while for women are: floor exercises, horse vault, asymmetrical bars and balance beam. Rhythmic Gymnastics for women was introduced for the first time at the Los Angeles games. Russia, USA, Romania, China, and Japan are now the strongest nations.

HANDBALL

Handball, similar to soccer only using hands not feet, was first played at the end of the 19th century. A growing sport, by 1982 there were 80 countries affiliated to the International Handball Federation (founded 1946) and an estimated 10 million participants.

Handball was introduced into the Olympic Games at Berlin in 1936 as an 11-a-side outdoor game but on its reintroduction in 1972, it became indoor 7-a-side, the standard size of team since 1952. (In Britain it is often 5-a-side.) Yugoslavia won both men and women's events at the Los Angeles Olympics.

HARNESS RACING

Trotting races were held in Valkenburg, Netherlands in 1554 but harness racing developed and is most popular in North America. The sulky, the lightweight vehicle, first appeared in 1829. Horses may trot, moving their legs in diagonal pairs, or pace, moving fore and hind legs on one side simultaneously.

HOCKEY

Early Greek wall carvings *c*. 500 BC show hockey-like games, whilst curved-stick games appear on Egyptian tomb paintings *c*. 2050 BC. Hockey in its modern form, however, developed in England in the second half of the 19th century, with Teddington HC (formed 1871) standardising the rules. The English Hockey Association was founded in 1886; hockey was included in the 1908 and 1920 Olympic Games, and re-introduced on a permanent basis in 1928. Pakistan, Germany, and the Netherlands have joined India as the strong nations. The 1984 Olympic titles were taken by Pakistan (men) and Netherlands (women).

Dimensions: ball circumference 223–234 cm ($8\frac{3}{16}$–$9\frac{1}{4}$ins) and weight 155–163 g ($5\frac{1}{2}$–$5\frac{3}{4}$oz); pitch length 91·44 m (*100 yds*); width 50–55 m (*55–60 yds*).

HORSE RACING

Early organised racing appears to have been confined to chariots – Roman riders had a foot on each of two horses. The first horse-back racing was by the Greeks in the 33rd Ancient Olympiad in 648 BC. The first recognisable race meeting was held at Smithfield, London in 1174, whilst the first known prize money was a purse of gold presented by Richard I in 1195.

The Jockey Club is now the governing body of flat racing, steeplechasing and hurdle racing, having merged with the National Hunt Committee in 1968. The flat racing season in England takes place between late March and early November. Thoroughbreds may not run until they are two year olds. The five classic races are the Two Thousand Guineas and the One Thousand Guineas (Newmarket, 1600 m *one mile*), the Derby and the Oaks (Epsom, 2400 m *1½ miles*) and the St. Leger (Doncaster, 2800 m *1¾ miles*).

Steeplechase and hurdle races are run over distances of 2 or more miles, with at least one ditch and six birch fences for every mile. The National Hunt season can last from early August to 1st June, and the two most important steeplechases are the Grand National, first run in 1839, at Aintree over a course of 7220 m (*4 miles 856 yds*) with 30 jumps, and the Gold Cup at Cheltenham.

HURLING

An ancient game that has been played in Ireland since pre-Christian times, but standardised only since the founding of the Gaelic Athletic Association in 1884. The hurl, or stick, is similar to a hockey stick only flat on both sides. All-Ireland Championships have been held since 1887.

ICE HOCKEY

A game similar to hockey on ice was played in Holland in the early 16th century, but the birth of modern ice hockey took place in Canada, probably at Kingston, Ontario in 1855. Rules were first formulated by students of McGill University in Montreal who first formed a club, in 1880.

The International Ice Hockey Federation was formed in 1908, and World and Olympic Championships inaugurated in 1920. Russia have won five of the last six Olympic titles. The major professional competition is the National Hockey League (NHL) in North America, founded in 1917, whose teams contest the Stanley Cup.

Teams are 6-a-side; the ideal rink size is 61 m (*200 ft*) long and 26 m (*85 ft*) wide.

ICE AND SAND YACHTING

Ice, sand and land yachting require, in basic form, a wheeled chassis beneath a sailing dinghy. Dutch ice yachts date to 1768, but ice yachting today is mainly in North America. Land and sand yachts of Dutch construction go back even further to 1595. The sports are governed by the International Federation of Sand and Land Yacht Clubs who recognise speed records. International championships were first staged in 1914.

ICE SKATING

Second century Scandinavian literature refers to ice skating, although archaeological evidence points to origins ten centuries earlier. The first English account is dated 1180, while the first club, the Edinburgh Skating Club, was formed around 1742. Steel blades, allowing precision skating, were invented in America in 1850. The International Skating Union was founded in the Netherlands in 1892.

Competitively, ice skating is divided into figure skating, speed skating and ice dancing. Figure skating has been an Olympic event since the Winter Games were first organised in 1924, but there were also events at the 1908 and 1920 Games. Ice dancing was not included until 1976.

The first international speed skating competition was in Hamburg, Germany, in 1885, with World Championships officially dated from 1893. Included for men in the 1924 Olympics, women's events were included in 1960.

JUDO

Developed from a mixture of pre-Christian Japanese fighting arts, the most popular of which was ju-jitsu which is thought to be of ancient Chinese origin. 'Ju' means 'soft', i.e. the reliance on speed and skill as opposed to 'hard' brute force. Judo as a modern combat sport first devised in 1882 by Dr Jigoro Kano. Today, students are graded by belt colours from white to black, the 'master' belts. Grades of black belts are 'Dans', the highest attainable being Tenth Dan.

The Wimbledon Championships
Wimbledon, 'The All England Championships', date back to 1877 when it comprised just one event, the men's singles. Women's singles and men's doubles were introduced in 1884, with women's doubles and mixed doubles becoming full Championship events in 1913.

Champions since 1946

Men's Singles		*Women's Singles*
1946	Yvon Petra (Fra)	Pauline Betz (USA)
1947	Jack Kramer (USA)	Margaret Osborne (USA)
1948	Bob Falkenburg (USA)	Louise Brough (USA)
1949	Ted Schroeder (USA)	Louise Brough (USA)
1950	Budge Patty (USA)	Louise Brough (USA)
1951	Dick Savitt (USA)	Doris Hart (USA)
1952	Frank Sedgman (Aus)	Maureen Connolly (USA)
1953	Vic Seixas (USA)	Maureen Connolly (USA)
1954	Jaroslav Drobny (Cz)	Maureen Connolly (USA)
1955	Tony Trabert (USA)	Louise Brough (USA)
1956	Lew Hoad (Aus)	Shirley Fry (USA)
1957	Lew Hoad (Aus)	Althea Gibson (USA)
1958	Ashley Cooper (Aus)	Althea Gibson (USA)
1959	Alex Olmedo (USA)	Maria Bueno (Bra)
1960	Neale Fraser (Aus)	Maria Bueno (Bra)
1961	Rod Laver (Aus)	Angela Mortimer (GB)
1962	Rod Laver (Aus)	Karen Susman (USA)
1963	Chuck McKinley (USA)	Margaret Smith (Aus)
1964	Roy Emerson (Aus)	Maria Bueno (Bra)
1965	Roy Emerson (Aus)	Margaret Smith (Aus)
1966	Manuel Santana (Spa)	Billie Jean King (USA)
1967	John Newcombe (Aus)	Billie Jean King (USA)
1968	Rod Laver (Aus)	Billie Jean King (USA)
1969	Rod Laver (Aus)	Ann Jones (GB)
1970	John Newcombe (Aus)	Margaret Smith-Court (Aus)
1971	John Newcombe (Aus)	Evonne Goolagong (Aus)
1972	Stan Smith (USA)	Billie Jean King (USA)
1973	Jan Kodes (Cz)	Billie Jean King (USA)
1974	Jimmy Connors (USA)	Chris Evert (USA)
1975	Arthur Ashe (USA)	Billie Jean King (USA)
1976	Bjorn Borg (Swe)	Chris Evert (USA)
1977	Bjorn Borg (Swe)	Virginia Wade (GB)
1978	Bjorn Borg (Swe)	Martina Navratilova (Cz)
1979	Bjorn Borg (Swe)	Martina Navratilova (Cz)
1980	Bjorn Borg (Swe)	Evonne Goolagong-Cawley (Aus)
1981	John McEnroe (USA)	Chris Evert-Lloyd (USA)
1982	Jimmy Connors (USA)	Martina Navratilova (USA)
1983	John McEnroe (USA)	Martina Navratilova (USA)
1984	John McEnroe (USA)	Martina Navratilova (USA)
1985	Boris Becker (W. Germany)	Martina Navratilova (USA)

Women's Doubles
1946 Louise Brough & Margaret Osborne (USA)
1947 Pat Todd & Doris Hart (USA)
1948 Louise Brough & Margaret Osborne-du Pont (USA)
1949 Louise Brough & Margaret Osborne-du Pont (USA)
1950 Louise Brough & Margaret Osborne-du Pont (USA)
1951 Doris Hart & Shirley Fry (USA)
1952 Doris Hart & Shirley Fry (USA)
1953 Doris Hart & Shirley Fry (USA)
1954 Louise Brough & Margaret Osborne-du Pont (USA)
1955 Angela Mortimer & Anne Shilcock (GB)
1956 Angela Buxton (GB) & Althea Gibson (USA)
1957 Althea Gibson & Darlene Hard (USA)
1958 Maria Bueno (Bra) & Althea Gibson (USA)
1959 Jean Arth & Darlene Hard (USA)
1960 Maria Bueno (Bra) & Darlene Hard (USA)
1961 Karen Hantze & Billie Jean Moffitt (USA)
1962 Karen Hantze-Susman & Billie Jean Moffitt (USA)
1963 Maria Bueno (Bra) & Darlene Hard (USA)
1964 Margaret Smith & Lesley Turner (Aus)
1965 Maria Bueno (Bra) & Billie Jean Moffitt (USA)
1966 Maria Bueno (Bra) & Nancy Richey (USA)
1967 Rosemary Casals & Billie Jean Moffitt-King (USA)
1968 Billie Jean King & Rosemary Casals (USA)
1969 Margaret Smith-Court & Judy Tegart (Aus)
1970 Billie Jean King & Rosemary Casals (USA)
1971 Billie Jean King & Rosemary Casals (USA)
1972 Billie Jean King (USA) & Betty Stove (Hol)
1973 Billie Jean King & Rosemary Casals (USA)
1974 Evonne Goolagong (Aus) & Peggy Michel (USA)
1975 Ann Kiyomura (USA) & Kazuko Sawamatsu (Jap)
1976 Chris Evert (USA) & Martina Navratilova (Cz)
1977 Helen Cawley (Aus) & Joanne Russell (USA)
1978 Kerry Reid & Wendy Turnbull (Aus)
1979 Billie Jean King (USA) & Martina Navratilova (Cz)
1980 Kathy Jordan & Anne Smith (USA)
1981 Martina Navratilova (Cz) & Pam Shriver (USA)
1982 Martina Navratilova & Pam Shriver (USA)
1983 Martina Navratilova & Pam Shriver (USA)
1984 Martina Navratilova & Pam Shriver (USA)
1985 Kathy Jordan (USA) & Liz Smylie (Aus)

Men's Doubles
1946 Tom Brown & Jack Kramer (USA)
1947 Bob Falkenburg & Jack Kramer (USA)
1948 John Bromwich & Frank Sedgman (Aus)
1949 Ricardo Gonzales & Frank Parker (USA)
1950 John Bromwich & Adrian Quist (Aus)
1951 Ken McGregor & Frank Sedgman (Aus)
1952 Ken McGregor & Frank Sedgman (Aus)
1953 Lew Hoad & Ken Rosewall (Aus)
1954 Rex Hartwig & Mervyn Rose (Aus)
1955 Rex Hartwig & Lew Hoad (Aus)
1956 Lew Hoad & Ken Rosewall (Aus)
1957 Budge Patty & Gardnar Mulloy (USA)
1958 Sven Davidson & Ulf Schmidt (Swe)
1959 Roy Emerson & Neale Fraser (Aus)
1960 Rafael Osuna (Mex) & Dennis Ralston (USA)
1961 Roy Emerson & Neale Fraser (Aus)
1962 Bob Hewitt & Fred Stolle (Aus)
1963 Rafael Osuna & Antonio Palafox (Mex)
1964 Bob Hewitt & Fred Stolle (Aus)
1965 John Newcombe & Tony Roche (Aus)
1966 Ken Fletcher & John Newcombe (Aus)
1967 Bob Hewitt & Frew McMillan (Saf)
1968 John Newcombe & Tony Roche (Aus)
1969 John Newcombe & Tony Roche (Aus)
1970 John Newcombe & Tony Roche (Aus)
1971 Roy Emerson & Rod Laver (Aus)
1972 Bob Hewitt & Frew McMillan (Saf)
1973 Jimmy Connors (USA) & Ilie Nastase (Rom)
1974 John Newcombe & Tony Roche (Aus)
1975 Vitas Gerulaitis & Sandy Mayer (USA)
1976 Brian Gottfried (USA) & Raul Ramirez (Mex)
1977 Ross Case & Geoff Masters (Aus)
1978 Bob Hewitt & Frew McMillan (Saf)
1979 John McEnroe & Peter Fleming (USA)
1980 Peter McNamara & Paul McNamee (Aus)
1981 John McEnroe & Peter Fleming (USA)
1982 Peter McNamara & Paul McNamee (Aus)
1983 John McEnroe & Peter Fleming (USA)
1984 John McEnroe & Peter Fleming (USA)
1985 Balazs Taroczy (Hun) & Heinz Gunthardt (Switz)

Mixed Doubles
1946 Louise Brough & Tom Brown (USA)
1947 Louise Brough (USA) & John Bromwich (Aus)
1948 Louise Brough (USA) & John Bromwich (Aus)
1949 Sheila Summers & Eric Sturgess (Saf)
1950 Louise Brough (USA) & Eric Sturgess (Saf)
1951 Doris Hart (USA) & Frank Sedgman (Aus)
1952 Doris Hart (USA) & Frank Sedgman (Aus)
1953 Doris Hart & Vic Seixas (USA)
1954 Doris Hart & Vic Seixas (USA)
1955 Doris Hart & Vic Seixas (USA)
1956 Shirley Fry & Vic Seixas (USA)
1957 Darlene Hard (USA) & Mervyn Rose (Aus)
1958 Loraine Coghlan & Bob Howe (Aus)
1959 Darlene Hard (USA) & Rod Laver (Aus)
1960 Darlene Hard (USA) & Rod Laver (Aus)
1961 Lesley Turner & Fred Stolle (Aus)
1962 Margaret Osborne-du Pont (USA) & Neale Fraser (Aus)
1963 Margaret Smith & Ken Fletcher (Aus)
1964 Lesley Turner & Fred Stolle (Aus)
1965 Margaret Smith & Ken Fletcher (Aus)
1966 Margaret Smith & Ken Fletcher (Aus)
1967 Billie Jean Moffitt-King (USA) & Owen Davidson (Aus)
1968 Margaret Smith-Court & Ken Fletcher (Aus)
1969 Ann Jones (GB) & Fred Stolle (Aus)
1970 Rosemary Casals (USA) & Ilie Nastase (Rom)
1971 Billie Jean King (USA) & Owen Davidson (Aus)
1972 Rosemary Casals (USA) & Ilie Nastaste (Rom)
1973 Billie Jean King (USA) & Owen Davidson (Aus)
1974 Billie Jean King (USA) & Owen Davidson (Aus)
1975 Margaret Smith-Court (Aus) & Marty Reissen (USA)
1976 Françoise Durr (Fra) & Tony Roche (Aus)
1977 Greer Stevens & Bob Hewitt (Saf)
1978 Betty Stove (Hol) & Frew McMillan (Saf)
1979 Greer Stevens & Bob Hewitt (Saf)
1980 Tracy Austin & John Austin (USA)
1981 Betty Stove (Hol) & Frew McMillan (Saf)
1982 Anne Smith (USA) & Kevin Curren (Saf)
1983 Wendy Turnbull (Aus) & John Lloyd (GB)
1984 Wendy Turnbull (Aus) & John Lloyd (GB)
1985 Martina Navratilova (USA) & Paul McNamee (Aus)

The International Judo Federation was founded in 1951; World Championships were first held in Tokyo in 1956, with women competing from 1980. Included in the Olympics since 1964 (except 1968), there are currently eight weight divisions. Points are scored by throws, locks on joints, certain pressures on the neck, and immobilisations.

KARATE

Literally meaning 'empty hand' fighting, karate is based on techniques devised from the 6th century Chinese art of Shaolin boxing (Kempo), and was developed by an unarmed populace in Okinawa as a weapon against Japanese oppressors *c.* 1500. Transmitted to Japan in the 1920s by Funakoshi Gichin, the sport was refined and organised with competitive rules.

There are five major styles in Japan: Shotokan, Wado-ryu, Goju-ryu, Shito-ryu and Kyokushinkai, each placing different emphases on speed and power. The military form of Tae Kwon-do is a Korean equivalent of Karate. Wu shu is a comprehensive term embracing all Chinese martial arts. Kung fu is one aspect of these arts popularised by the cinema. Many forms of the martial arts have gained devotees in Europe and the Americas.

LACROSSE

North American Indians played *baggataway*, and a French clergyman likening the curved stick to a bishop's crozier called it *la crosse*. The French may also have named it after their game *Chouler a la crosse*, known in 1381. Certainly in its recognisable form the game had reached Europe by the 1830s, and was introduced into Britain in 1867.

The International Federation of Amateur Lacrosse (AFAL) was founded in 1928, but the game was not standardised sufficiently to hold World Championships until 1967 for men and 1969 for women. Now every four years, America won both titles in 1982. It was played in the Olympic Games of 1904 and 1908, and was a demonstration sport in 1928, 1932 and 1948.

The game is 10-a-side (12-a-side for women at international level); pitch dimensions 100 × 64 m (*110 × 70 yds*). Ball weight in England 142 g (*5 oz*), circumference 184–203·2 mm (*7¼–8 ins*), colour yellow; in USA weight 142–149 g (*5–5¼ oz*), circumference 196·9–203·2 mm (*7¾–8 ins*), colour orange or white.

LAWN TENNIS

Lawn tennis evolved from the indoor game of real tennis; 'field tennis' is mentioned in a 1793 magazine; Major Harry Gem founded the first club in Leamington Spa in 1872. The All England Croquet Club added Lawn Tennis to their title in 1877 and held their first Championships. The United States Lawn Tennis Association (now USLTA) was founded in 1881, the English in 1888. The International Lawn Tennis Federation was formed in Paris in March 1913.

The Wimbledon or All England, Championships have since 1877 been regarded as the most important in the world, alongside the US Open, French and Australian Opens. Together these four make up the 'Grand Slam', the elusive distinction of holding all four titles at once. The US Open (instituted 1881) is now held at Flushing Meadows, New York, and the French at Roland Garros, Paris. The Australian Championships were first held in 1905.

Men and women today compete in various 'circuits' in the second richest sport in the world to golf. 'Grand Prix' tournaments are scaled according to a standard, with points awarded for results, totted to decide world rankings. The international team competition for men is the Davis Cup, won most times by the USA. The Federation Cup (first held 1963) is the women's equivalent and has again been dominated by USA, and Australia. The Wightman Cup is an annual USA-GB match begun in 1923 when only these two showed interest in a multi-nation tournament.

Tennis was part of the Olympic programme until 1924, and was a demonstration sport at Mexico 1968 and Los Angeles 1984. It is likely to be re-instituted to the Games proper in 1988.

MODERN PENTATHLON AND BIATHLON

In the ancient Olympic Games, the Pentathlon was the most prestigious event. It then consisted of discus, javelin, running, jumping and wrestling. The modern pentathlon, introduced into the Olympics in 1912, consists of riding (an 800 m course with 15 fences, riders do not choose their mounts); fencing (épée), shooting, swimming (300 m freestyle) and finally a cross-country run of 4000 m. Each event is held on a different day, with scaled points awarded for each activity.

L'Union Internationale de Pentathlon Moderne et Biathlon (UIPMB) was founded in 1948. Originally the UIPM, the administration of Biathlon (cross-country skiing and shooting) was added in 1957. Biathlon has been an Olympic event since 1960.

MOTORCYCLE RACING

The earliest motorcycle race was held at Sheen House, Richmond, Surrey in 1897 over one mile (*1·6 km*) oval course. The first international motorcycle-only race (early races had included motorcars) was held in 1905, the International Cup Race, after the same race had been declared void in 1904 following bad organisation and underhand intrigues. The new Fédération Internationale des Clubs Motocyclistes (FICM) had organised the 1905 event, but have since been succeeded by the Fédération Internationale Motocycliste (FIM).

World Championships were started in 1949 by the FIM, in which competitors gain points from a series of Grand Prix races. Races are currently held for the following classes of bike: 50 cc, 125 cc, 250 cc, 350 cc, 500 cc and sidecars.

In road racing, the TT races (Auto-Cycle Union Tourist Trophy), first held in 1907, are the most important series. The 60·72 km (*37·73 miles*) 'Mountain' course, with 264 corners and curves, has been in use since 1911.

In Moto-Cross, or Scrambling, competitors race over rough country including steep climbs and drops, sharp turns, sand, mud and water. Originated at Camberley, Surrey in 1924; the Belgians have dominated in recent years.

MOTOR RACING

The first known race between automobiles was over 323 km (*201 miles*) in Wisconsin in 1878, but it is generally accepted that the first 'real' race was the Paris-Bordeaux-Paris run of 1178 km (*732 miles*) in 1895. Emile Levassor (Fra), the winner, averaged 24·15 km/h (*15·01 mph*). The first closed circuit race was at Rhode Island, 1896; the oldest Grand Prix is the French, inaugurated in 1906.

Competition in the highest bracket, the Formula One, is over the series of Grand Prix races (each usually about 200 miles in length) held worldwide, scoring points according to placing. The first World Championships were held in 1950, with the Manufacturers' Championships starting in 1958. Formula Two and Three Championships are held for cars with lesser cubic capacities.

Other forms of competition include the Le Mans circuit, a 24-hour race for touring cars; 'rallying' over public roads through several thousand miles, and drag racing, a test of sheer acceleration, most firmly established in USA.

NETBALL

Modern netball grew out of basketball, and reached England in 1895 having been invented in America in 1891. Rings instead of baskets date to 1897, and the term netball was coined in 1901 in England. National Associations date to 1924 and 1926 in New Zealand and England; the International Federation was formed in 1960. World Championships are held every four years, since 1963, with Australia winning in 1983 and maintaining their dominance.

Netball is no-contact, 7-a-side and played almost exclusively by females. The court measures 30·48 × 15·24 m (*100 × 50 ft*); ball circumference 68–71 cms (*27–28 ins*), weight 397–454 g (*14–16 oz*).

ORIENTEERING

'Orienteering' was first used to describe an event held in Oslo in 1900, based on military exercises, but the founding of the modern sport is credited to Major Ernst Killander (Swe) in 1918.

Basically a combination of cross-country running and map-reading, the sport is very popular in Scandinavia and has a keen band of followers in Britain. The International Orienteering Federation was founded in 1961, with World Championships from 1966, largely dominated by Sweden.

PELOTA VASCA (Jaï Alaï)

The sport, which originated in Italy as *longue paume* and was introduced into France in the 13th century, is said to be the fastest of all ball games. Various forms of pelota are played according to national character or local custom throughout the world. 'Gloves' and 'chisteras' (curved frames attached to a glove) are of varying sizes, and courts can be open or enclosed with wide differences in dimensions and detail. The Federacion Internacional de Pelota Vasca has staged World Championships every four years since 1952.

PÉTANQUE

Pétanque, or *boules*, originated in France from its parent game Jeu Provencal, where it is still immensely popular. Origins go back over 2000 years, but it was not until 1945 that the Fédération Français de Pétanque et Jeu Provencal was formed, and subsequently the Fédération Internationale (FIPJP).

POLO

Thought to be of Persian origin, having been played as *Pulu c.* 525. Brought to England from India in 1869. Teams are 4-a-side, mounted on horses of any type.

POWERBOAT RACING

Steamboat races date from 1827, petrol engines from 1865, but actual powerboat racing started in about 1900. International racing was largely established by the presentation of a Challenge Trophy by Sir Alfred Harmsworth in 1903, heralding thereafter 'circuit' or shorter course competition (America has been the most prominent winner of the trophy). Offshore events for (planing) cruises began in 1958, and speed records are recognised in various categories by the various governing bodies.

REAL TENNIS

Evolved from the game *jeu de paume* ('game of the palm') played in French monasteries in the 11th century, using the hands. The long-handled racket was not invented until about 1500. The world championship at real tennis is the oldest world championship of any sport, dating to approximately 1740. Today, real tennis is only played in five countries – England, Scotland, USA, France and Australia and the total number of courts in use throughout the world has dwindled to approximately 30.

ROLLER SKATING

The first roller skate was devised by Jean-Joseph Merlin of Belgium in 1760, but proved disastrous in demonstration. The present four-wheeled type was patented by New Yorker James L. Plimpton in 1863. Competition is along similar lines to ice skating – speed, figure and dance.

ROWING

A literary reference to rowing is made by the Roman poet Virgil in the *Aeneid*, published after his death in 19 BC; regattas were held in Venice *c.* 300 AD. The earliest established sculling race is the Doggett's Coat and Badge, first rowed in August 1716 from London Bridge to Chelsea, and still contested annually.

The governing body, the Fédération Internationale de Sociétés d'Aviron was founded in 1892, with the first major international meeting, the European Championships, held a year later.

Olympic Championships were first held in 1900 for men and 1976 for women. Current events are held for: (men) single, double and coxless quadruple sculls, coxless and coxed pairs, coxless and coxed fours and eights; (women) single and double skulls, coxless pairs, coxless quadruple sculls, coxed fours and eights. With sculling, the sculler has a smaller oar in each hand rather than pulling one oar with both hands.

The Oxford-Cambridge Boat Race was first held in 1829, from Hambledon Lock to Henley Bridge, and won by Oxford. The current course, used continuously since 1864, is from Putney to Mortlake and measures 6·779 km (*4 miles 374 yds*). To 1985, there has been only one dead heat, in 1877.

RUGBY LEAGUE

The game originated as a breakaway from Rugby Union on 29 August 1895, on account of the governing body forbidding northern clubs paying players, who thus lost Saturday wages. Three years later full professionalism came into being. In 1906 the major change from 15-a-side to 13 was made, and the title 'Rugby League' was created in 1922.

Rugby League is played principally in Great Britain, Australia, New Zealand and France. Major trophies in England are the Challenge Cup (inst. 1897), the League Championship (inst. 1907), the Premiership Trophy (inst. 1975) and the John Player Trophy (inst. 1972).

Dimensions: Pitch length maximum 100·58 m (*110 yds*), width maximum 68·58 m (*75 yds*). Ball length 27·3–29·2 cms (*10¾–11½ins*), circumference at widest point 584–610 mm (*23–24 ins*).

RUGBY UNION

Developed at Rugby School, England. A traditional yarn tells of William Webb Ellis illegally picking up the ball and running with it during a football game, although this may be apocryphal. Certainly the game was known to have been played at Cambridge University by 1839. The Rugby Football Union was formed on 26 January 1871.

The International Rugby Football Board was formed in 1890. Teams representing the British Isles have toured Australia, New Zealand and South Africa since 1888, although they were not composed of players from all the Home Countries until 1924, when the term 'British Lions' was first coined.

The International Championship – between England, Ireland, Scotland, and Wales – was first held in 1884, with France included from 1910. Now also known as the Five Nations tournament, the 'Grand Slam' is prized for winning all four matches. The 'Triple Crown' is achieved for a Home Countries side defeating the other three.

The game is 15-a-side. Dimensions: pitch of maximum 68·58 m (*75 yds*) width, and 91·44 m (*100 yds*) between goal lines. Ball length 27·9–28·5 cms (*10¾–11½ in*) and weight 382–439 g (*13½–15½ oz*).

SHINTY

Shinty (from the Gaelic *sinteag*, a bound) goes back some 2000 years to Celtic history and legend, to the ancient game of *camanachd*, the sport of the curved stick. Having been introduced by the invading Irish Gaels it kept close associations with hurling but is essentially native to Scotland. The governing body, the Camanachd Association, was set up in 1893.

SHOOTING

The first recorded club for gun enthusiasts was the Lucerne Shooting Guild in Switzerland, dating from *c.* 1466, and the first known shooting match took place in Zurich in 1472. The National Rifle Association in Britain was founded in 1860; the Clay Pigeon Shooting Association developed from trap shooting in the USA and descended from the Inanimate Bird S.A. Skeet shooting is a form of clay pigeon designed to simulate a range of bird game-shot

and was invented in the USA in 1915. Pistol events, like air rifle, are judged by accuracy in scoring on a fixed target, from various distances and positions.

Shooting events for men were held in the first modern Olympic Games in 1896, but the 1984 Games included two mixed events for the first time. Only two other Olympic sports have mixed competition, equestrianism and yachting.

SKIING

A well preserved ski found in Sweden is thought to be 4500 years old, and various other evidence from Russia and Scandinavia chronicles primitive skiing, but the modern sport did not develop until 1843 with a competition in Tromsö, Norway. The first modern slalom was held at Murren, Switzerland in 1922. The International Ski Federation (FIS) was founded in 1924.

Alpine skiing is racing on prepared slopes, against the clock, whereas Nordic skiing is either cross-country or ski jumping. Alpine world championships date to 1931, and have been included in the Olympics since 1936, as a combination event, but events are now split into Slalom, Giant Slalom and Downhill. Nordic events date to the 1924 Olympics, and include a combination event of cross-country and jump.

SNOOKER

Colonel Sir Neville Chamberlain concocted the game of snooker as a cross between 'Black Pool', 'Pyramids' and billiards, in 1875 at Madras, India. The term 'Snooker' came from the nickname given to first-year cadets at the Royal Military Academy, Woolwich. The game reached England in 1885 via world billiards champion, John Roberts who had been introduced to snooker in India.

Rules were codified in 1919, and the World Professional Championship instituted in 1927. Since 1970 the professional game has been controlled by the World Professional Billiards and Snooker Association.

A full size table measures 3·66 × 1·87 m (*12 × 6 ft*); ball values are: red (1), yellow (2), green (3), brown (4), blue (5), pink (6) and black (7).

SOFTBALL

Softball, the indoor derivative of baseball, was invented by George Hancock in Chicago, USA in 1887, and rules were first codified in Minnesota in 1895. The name softball was not adopted until 1930. A 9-a-side game (except in the USA) softball is played in Canada, Japan, the Philippines, most of Latin America, New Zealand and Australia. The ball is as hard as a baseball, but as distinct from baseball must be pitched underarm and released below hip level. The pitching distance is 14 m (*45 ft 11 ins*) for men, 11·11 m (*36 ft 5¼ ins*) for women and 18·3 m (*60 ft ¼ in*) between bases for both. 'Slow pitch' softball is a modern variation.

SPEEDWAY

Motorcycle racing on dust track surfaces has been traced back to 1902 in the USA, but the first 'short track' races were in Australia in 1923. Evolving in Britain in the 1920s, the National League was instituted in 1932. The first World Championships were held in September 1936 at Wembley under the auspices of the Fédération Internationale Motocycliste (FIM). A team competition was inaugurated only as late as 1960. Each race is contested by four riders (six in Australia) over four laps; the bikes have no brakes, one gear and are limited to 500 cc.

SQUASH

Squash developed at Harrow School, England in 1817 from a game used for practising rackets but substituted a softer, 'squashy' ball. There was no recognised champion of any country however until 1907 in America. A rapidly growing game in modern times, World Open Championships have been held since 1976, and since 1979 the ISRF (International Squash Rackets Federation), previously for amateurs only, has been open to all players and includes a team event won always by either Australia,

Great Britain or Pakistan. The British Open has been held since 1922 for women and 1930 for men.

Court dimensions: 9·75 m (*31 ft 11¾ ins*) long and 6·40 m (*21 ft*) wide, with front wall height 4·75 m (*15 ft 7 ins*) up to the boundary line. The 'tin' runs along the bottom of the front wall, above which the ball must be hit.

SURFING

Originating in Polynesia, the first reference to surfing on a board dates to 1779 by a Naval Officer in Hawaii. Revived in the early 20th century in Australia; hollow boards were introduced in 1929. World Amateur Championships began in 1964.

SWIMMING

Competitive swimming dates to 36 BC in Japan, the first country to seriously adopt the sport, Emperor G-Yozei decreeing its introduction in schools. In Britain, organised competitive swimming was only introduced in 1837 when the National Swimming Society was formed. Australia led modern developments with an unofficial world 100 yd championship in 1858 at Melbourne.

The first widely-used technique (possibly excepting the 'doggy paddle') was the breaststroke. From this developed the side-stroke, a similar action performed sideways, last used by an Olympic Champion, Emil Rausch (Ger) to win the 1904 one mile event. A style resembling the front crawl had been seen in various parts of the world by travellers in the mid-19th century. Backstroke developed as inverted breaststroke, which modified towards inverted crawl. Butterfly began as an exploitation of a loophole in the rules for breaststroke allowing the recovery of arms from the water, and was recognised as a separate stroke in 1952. The medley event, using all four strokes in turn, came from America in the 1930s.

The world governing body for swimming, diving, water polo and synchronised swimming is the Fédération Internationale de Natation Amateur (FINA), founded in 1908. World Championships in swimming were first held in 1973, and are now held quadrennially. Last held in 1982, East Germany dominated the women's events, America and Russia the men's.

Swimming has been an integral part of the Olympics since 1896, the first modern Olympic Games, with 100 m, 400 m, 1500 m and 100 m (sailors) freestyle events for men. Women first competed in 1912. Diving was introduced in 1904 (1912 for women), and water polo in 1900. Current events are: (Men) 100 m, 200 m, 400 m and 1500 m freestyle; 100 m, 200 m backstroke, breaststroke and butterfly; 200 m and 400 m medley; 4 × 100 m medley relay; 4 × 100 m and 4 × 200 m freestyle relay; springboard diving; high diving and water polo. (Women) 100 m, 200 m, 400 m and 800 m freestyle; 100 m and 200 m backstroke, breaststroke and butterfly; 200 m and 400 m medley; 4 × 100 m medley relay; 4 × 100 m freestyle medley; springboard diving, high diving, and solo and duet synchronised swimming.

Synchronised swimming, a form of water ballet, was first recognised internationally in 1952 and was included in the first World Championships in 1973. It appeared in the Olympics for the first time in 1984.

TABLE TENNIS

Earliest evidence of a game resembling table tennis goes back to London sports goods manufacturers in the 1880s. Known as *gossima*, it was the introduction of the celluloid ball and the noise it made when hit that brought the name 'ping pong' and the Ping Pong Association in 1902. Interest declined until the use of attached rubber mats to the wooden bats (allowing spin) in the early 1920s. The International Table Tennis Association was founded in 1926, with World Championships held since 1927. The Swaythling and Corbillon Cups are held as world team championships, instituted in 1927 and 1934 for men and women respectively. China has been particularly dominant in recent years. Dimensions: ball diameter 37·2–38·2 mm (*1·46–1·5 in*), weight 2·4–2·53 g, table length 2·74 m (*9 ft*); 1·525 m (*5 ft*) wide.

TRAMPOLINING

Equipment similar to today's trampoline was used by a show business group, 'The Walloons', just prior to World War I. The word originates from the Spanish *trampolin*, a springboard, and indeed springboards date to circus acrobats of the Middle Ages. The birth of the sport follows the invention of the prototype 'T' type by the American, George Nissen in 1936. World Championships, administered by the International Trampolining Association, were instituted in 1964 and held biennially since 1968.

VOLLEYBALL

Although an Italian game *pallone* was played in the 16th century, the modern game was invented as *Minnonette* in 1895 by William Morgan at Massachusetts, USA, as a game for those who found basketball too strenuous. The name volleyball came a year later. The game spread rapidly worldwide and reached Britain in 1914. The first international tournament was the inaugural European Championship in 1948, the year after the founding of the International Volleyball Federation.

Although proposed for the 1924 Games by the USA, volleyball was not included in the Olympics until 1964. America won the 1984 men's title, although Russia have dominated the World (instituted 1949) and European Championships in recent years. China won the women's Olympic event and also the 1982 World Championship (instituted 1959). The two are equated in Olympic year.

Court dimensions are 18 × 9 m (*89 ft 0¾ins × 29 ft 6⅜ins*); ball circumference 65–67 cm (*25½–26⅜ins*), 250–260 g (*8·85–9·9 oz*) in weight. Net height is 2·43 m (*7 ft 11¾ins*) for men and 2·24 m (*7 ft 4¼ins*) for women.

WALKING

Walking races have been included in the Olympic events since 1906 but walking matches have been known since 1859. Walking as a sport is defined as 'progression by steps so that unbroken contact with the ground is maintained'. Road walking has become more prevalent than track walking, and the Olympic distances are currently 20 km and 50 km.

WATER SKIING

Water skiing as we now know it was pioneered by Ralph Samuelson (USA) on Lake Pepin, Minnesota in 1922. Having tried and failed with snow skies, he gave exhibitions with pine board skis culminating in the first jump, off a greased ramp, in 1925. The Union Internationale de Ski Nautique was set up in July 1946 and the British Water Ski Federation was formed in 1954.

Competitively, the sport is divided into trick skiing, slalom and skijumping. (Trick skiing, performed at lower speeds, involves gymnastic feats rewarded according to difficulty.) The World Championships, begun in 1947 and held biennially, include an overall title, in which the USA have figured prominently in recent years, both for men and women.

Skiing barefoot brought a new element to the sport and competitions are held for straight speed records.

WEIGHTLIFTING

In China during the Chou Dynasty, which ended in 249 BC, weightlifting became a necessary military test, and as an exercise could date as far back as 3500 BC. Competitions for lifting weights of stone were held in the ancient Olympic Games. The amateur sport, however, is of modern vintage with competitions dating to *c*.1850 and the first championship termed 'world' to 1891. The International Weightlifting Federation was established in 1920, and their first official championships held in 1922 in Estonia.

Weightlifting was included in the first modern Olympics in 1896, and then from 1920. In 1984 there were ten weight divisions, from up to 52 kg to over 110. Competition is decided by aggregate of two forms of lifting, the snatch and the clean and jerk. A third form, the press, was dropped in 1976 because of the difficulty in judging it. The Eastern bloc, especially Russia, have dominated the sport in which world records are broken more frequently than in any other.

Powerlifting involves different techniques which perhaps have greater emphasis on sheer strength rather than technique. The three basic lifts are the squat (or deep knee bend), bench press and dead lift. The International Powerlifting Federation was founded in 1972, with the USA recently dominant as world record holders in the 11 weight divisions stretching to 125+ kg.

WRESTLING

One of the oldest sports in the world, organised wrestling may date to *c*. 2750–2600 BC; certainly it was the most popular sport in the ancient Olympic Games, and victors were recorded from 708 BC. Wrestling developed in varying forms in varying countries, with the classical Greco-Roman style popular in Europe, and free style more to the liking of countries in the East and the Americas. The main distinction is that in Greco-Roman the wrestler cannot seize his opponent below the hips nor grip with the legs. The International Amateur Wrestling Federation (FILA) also recognises Sambo wrestling, akin to judo and popular in the USSR. FILA was founded in 1912, although the sport was in the first modern Olympics in 1896. There are currently ten weight divisions in both free-style and Greco-Roman events at the Games.

Sumo wrestling is a traditional form in Japan dating to 23 BC. Conducted with ceremony and mysticism, weight and bulk are vital since the object is to force the opponent out of the circular ring, using any hold.

YACHTING

Yachting dates to the race for a £100 wager between Charles II and his brother James, Duke of York, on the Thames in 1661 from Greenwich to Gravesend and back. The first recorded regatta was held in 1720 by the Cork Harbour Water Club (later Royal Cork Yacht Club), the oldest club, but did not prosper until the seas became safe after the Napoleonic Wars in 1815. That year the Yacht Club (later the Royal Yacht Squadron) was formed and organised races at Cowes, Isle of Wight, the beginning of modern yacht racing. The International Yacht Racing Union (IYRU) was established in 1907.

Yachting forms an Olympic event for six classes of boat; other competitions include the Admiral's Cup, a biennial inter-nation, 200 mile Channel and inshore race from Cowes to Fastnet Rock, Ireland and back to Plymouth, and the Whitbread Round the World Race, instituted in 1973 and quadrennial. The America's Cup was originally won as an outright prize by the schooner *America* on 22 August 1851 at Cowes and later offered by the New York Yacht Club as a challenge trophy. Since 1870 the Cup has been challenged by Great Britain in 16 contests, by Canada in two and seven times by Australia, but the USA were undefeated until 1983 when *Australia II* defeated the American boat *Liberty*.

Inventions

The invention and discovery of drugs, and musical instruments are treated separately (see Index)

Object	Year	Inventor	Notes
Adding Machine	1623	Wilhelm Schickard (Ger)	Earliest commercial machine devised by William Burroughs (US) in St Louis, Missouri, in 1885
Aeroplane	1903	Orville (1871–1948) and Wilbur Wright (1867–1912) (US)	Kitty Hawk, North Carolina (17 Dec). First sustained controlled flight
Airship (non-rigid)	1852	Henri Giffard (Fr) (1825–82)	Steam-powered propeller, near Paris (24 Sept.)
(rigid)	1900	Graf Ferdinand von Zeppelin (Ger) (1838–1917)	Bodensee (2 July) Getafe, Spain (9 Jan.)
Bakelite	1907	Leo H Baekeland (Belg/US) (1863–1944)	First use, electrical insulation by Loando & Co, Boonton, New Jersey
Balloon	1783	Jacques (1745–99) and Joseph Montgolfier (1740–1810) (Fr)	Tethered flight, Paris (15 Oct.) manned free flight, Paris, (21 Nov.) by François de Rozier and Marquis d'Arlandes. Father Bartolomeu de Gusmão (*né* Lourenço) (b. Brazil, 1685) demonstrated hot air balloon in Portugal on 8 Aug. 1709
Ball-Point Pen	1888	John J Loud (US)	First practical and low cost models by Lazlo and Georg Biro (Hungary) in 1938

Object	Year	Inventor	Notes
Barbed Wire	1867	Lucien B Smith (patentee) (25 June)	Introduced to Britain in 1880 by 5th Earl Spencer in Leicestershire
Barometer	1644	Evangelista Torricelli (It) (1608–47)	Referred to in a letter of 11 June
Battery (Electric)	1800	Alessandro Volta (1745–1827)	Demonstrated to Napoleon in 1801
Bicycle	1839–40	Kirkpatrick Macmillan (Scot) (1810–78)	Pedal-driven cranks. First direct drive in March 1861 by Ernest Michaux (Fr)
Bicycle Tyres (pneumatic)	1888	John Boyd Dunlop (GB) (1840–1921)	Principle patented but undeveloped by Robert William Thomson (GB), 10 June 1845. First motor car pneumatic tyres adapted by André and Edouard Michelin (Fr) 1895 (see Rubber tyres)
Bifocal Lens	1780	Benjamin Franklin (1706–90) (US)	His earliest experiments began c. 1760
Bronze (copper with tin) Working	c.2800 BC	SW Asia and Mediterranean	Copper smelting with arsenical ores was practised earlier
Bunsen Burner	1855	Robert Willhelm von Bunsen (1811–99) (Ger) at Heidelberg	Michael Faraday (1791–1867) (UK) had previously designed an adjustable burner
Burglar Alarm	1858	Edwin T Holmes (US)	Electric installed, Boston, Mass (21 Feb.)
Car (steam)	1769	Nicolas Cugnot (Fr) (1725–1804)	Three-wheeled miliary tractor. Oldest surviving automobile is the Italian Bordino (1854) in Turin
(petrol)	1888	Karl Benz (Ger) (1844–1929)	First run Mannheim Nov. or Dec. Patented 29 Jan. 1886. First powered hand cart with internal combustion engine was by Siegfried Marcus (Austria), c. (1864)
Carburettor	1876	Gottlieb Daimler (Ger) (1834–1900)	Carburettor spray: Charles E Duryea (US) (1892)
Carpet Sweeper	1876	Melville R Bissell (US)	Grand Rapids, Mich (Patent, 19 Sept.)
Cash Register	1879	James Ritty (US) (Patent 4 Nov.)	Built in Dayton, Ohio. Taken over by National Cash Register Co 1884
Cellophane	1908	Dr Jacques Brandenberger (Switz), Zurich	Machine production not before 1911
Celluloid	1861	Alexander Parkes (GB) (1813–90)	Invented in Birmingham, England; developed and trade marked by J W Hyatt (US) in 1870
Cement (Portland)	1824	Joseph Aspdin (GB) (1779–1855)	Wakefield, Yorkshire (21 Oct.)
Chronometer	1735	John Harrison (GB) (1693–1776)	Received in 1772 Government's £20 000 prize on offer since 1714
Cinema (see also Film)	1895	Auguste Marie Louis Nicolas Lumière (1862–1954) and Louis Jean Lumière (1864–1948) (Fr)	Development pioneers were Etienne Jules Marey (Fr) (1830–1903) and Thomas A Edison (US) (1847–1931). First public showing, Blvd. des Capucines, Paris (28 Dec.)
Clock (mechanical)	725	I-Hsing and Liang-Tsan (China)	Earliest escapement, 600 years before Europe
(pendulum)	1656	Christiaan Huygens (Neth) (1629–95)	
Copper working	c.4500 BC	Earliest smelting sites	Rudna Glava, Yugoslavia (Vinça culture)
Dental Plate	1817	Anthony A Plantson (US) (1774–1837)	
Dental Plate (rubber)	1855	Charles Goodyear (US) (1800–1860)	
Diesel Engine	1895	Rudolf Diesel (Ger) (1858–1913)	Lower pressure oil engine patent by Stuart Akroyd, 1890. Diesel's first commercial success, Augsburg, 1897
Disc Brake	1902	Dr F Lanchester (GB) (1868–1946)	First used on aircraft 1953 (Dunlop Rubber Co)
Dynamo	1832	Hypolite Pixii (Fr), demonstrated, Paris 3 Sept.	Rotative dynamo, demonstrated by Joseph Saxton, Cambridge, England June 1833
Electric Blanket	1883	Exhibited Vienna, Austria Exhibition	
Electric Flat Iron	1882	H W Seeley (US)	New York City, USA (Patent 6 June)
Electric Lamp	1879	Thomas Alva Edison (US) (1847–1931)	First practical demonstration at Menlo Park, New Jersey, USA, 20 Dec. Pioneer work on carbon filaments, Sir Joseph Swan (1828–1914), 1860
Electric motor (DC)	1873	Zénobe Gramme (Belg) (1826–1901)	Exhibited in Vienna. First demonstrated by Michael Faraday (1791–1867) in 1821. Patent by Thomas Davenport (US) of Vermont, 25 Feb. 1837
Electric motor (AC)	1888	Nikola Tesla (b. Yugoslavia) (US) (1856–1943)	
Electromagnet	1824	William Sturgeon (GB) (1783–1850)	Improved by Joseph Henry (US) (1797–1878)
Electronic Computer (see also Micro-processor)	1943	Dr Alan M Turing (GB) (1912–54)	Designed 'Colossus' for decyphering German codes, Bletchley Park, Herts, England: Alterable stored programme Manchester University Mark I by Sir Frederick Williams and Prof T Kilburn 1948: Point-contact transistor announced by John Bardeen and Walter Brattain, July 1948. Junction transistor announced by R L Wallace, Morgan Sparks and Dr William Shockley in early 1951
Film (moving outlines)	1885	Louis le Prince	Institute for the Deaf, Washington Hts, NY, USA
(talking)	1922	Josef Engl, Josef Mussolle and Hans Vogt (Germany)	*Der Brandstifter*, Alhambra, Berlin (17 Sept.)
(musical sound)	1923	Dr Lee de Forest (US) (1873–1961)	New York demonstration (13 Mar.)
Fountain Pen	1884	Lewis E Waterman (US) (1837–1901)	Patented by D Hyde (US), 1830, undeveloped
Galvanometer	1834	André-Marie Ampère (1755–1836)	First measurement of flow of electricity with a free-moving needle
Gas Lighting	1792	William Murdock (GB) (1754–1839)	Private house in Cornwall, 1792; Factory Birmingham, 1798; London Streets, 1807
Glass (stained)	c.1080	Augsburg, Germany	Earliest English, c. 1150, York Minster
Glassware	c.1500 BC	Egypt and Mesopotamia	Glass blowing Syria, c. 50 BC
Glider	1853	Sir George Cayley (GB) (1773–1857)	Near Brompton Hall, Yorkshire. Passenger possibly John Appleby. Emmanuel Swedenborg (1688–1772) sketches dated c. 1714
Gramophone	1878	Thomas Alva Edison (US) (1847–1931)	Hand-cranked cylinder at Menlo Park, NJ. Patent, 19 Feb. First described on 30 Apr 1877 by Charles Cros (1842–88) (Fr)
Gyro-compass	1911	Elmer A Sperry (US) (1860–1930)	Tested on USS *Delaware*, (28 Aug.). Gyroscope devised 1852 by Jean Foucault (Fr) (1819–68)
Helicopter	1924	Etienne Oehmichen (Fr)	First FAI world record set on 14 Apr. 1924. Earliest drawing of principle Le Mans Museum, France c. 1460. First servicable machine by Igor Sikorsky (US), 1939

Object	Year	Inventor	Notes
Hovercraft	1955	Sir Christopher Cockerell (GB) (b. 1910)	Patented 12 Dec. Earliest air-cushion vehicle patent was in 1877 by J I Thornycroft (1843–1928) (GB). First 'flight' Saunders Roe SRN-1 at Cowes, England, 30 May 1959
Iron Working (Carburized iron)	*c.*1200 BC	Cyprus and Northern Palestine	Introduced into Britain, *c.* 550 BC
Jet Engine	1937	Sir Frank Whittle (GB) (b. 1907)	First test bed run (12 Apr.). Principles announced by Merconnet (Fr) 1909 and Maxime Guillaume (Fr) 1921. First flight 27 Aug. 1939 by Heinkel He-178
Laser	1960	Dr Charles H Townes (US) (b. 1915). First demonstration by Theodore Maiman (US) (b. 1927)	Demonstrated at Hughes Research, Malibu, California in July. Abbreviation for Light amplification by stimulated emission of radiation
Launderette	1934	J F Cantrell (US)	Fort Worth, Texas (18 Apr.)
Lift (Mechanical)	1852	Elisha G Otis (US) (1811–61)	Earliest elevator at Yonkers, NY
Lightning Conductor	1752	Benjamin Franklin (US) (1706–90)	Philadelphia, Pennsylvania, USA in Sept.
Linoleum	1860	Frederick Walton (GB)	
Locomotive	1804	Richard Trevithick (GB) (1771–1833)	Penydarren, Wales, 9 miles *14,4 km* (21 Feb.)
Loom, power	1785	Edmund Cartwright (GB) (1743–1823)	
Loudspeaker	1900	Horace Short (GB) Patentee in 1898	A compressed air Auxetophone. First used atop the Eiffel Tower, Summer 1900. Earliest open-air electric public address system used by Bell Telephone on Staten Island, NY on 30 June 1916
Machine Gun	1718	James Puckle (GB) patentee, 15 May 1718. White Cron Alley factory in use 1721	Richard Gatling (US) (1818–1903) model dates from 1861
Maps	*c.*3800 BC	Sumerian (clay tablets of river Euphrates)	Earliest measurement by Eratosthenes *c.* 220 BC. Earliest printed map printed in Bologna, Italy, 1477
Margarine	1869	Hippolyte Mège-Mouries (Fr)	Patented 15 July
Match, safety	1826	John Walker (GB), Stockton, Teeside	
Microphone	1876	Alexander Graham Bell (1847–1922) (US)	Name coined 1878 by Prof David Hughes, who gave demonstration in London in January 1878
Micro-processor	1971	Drs Robert Noyce and Gordon Moore (USA)	Launched by US company Intel
Microscope	1590	Zacharias Janssen (Neth)	Compound convex-concave lens
Motor Cycle	1885	Gottlieb Daimler (1834–1900) of Cannstatt, Germany, patent 29 Aug.	First rider Paul Daimler (10 Nov. 1885); first woman rider Mrs Edward Butler near Erith, Kent, 1888
Neon Lamp	1910	Georges Claude (Fr) (1871–1960)	First installation at Paris Motor Show (3 Dec.)
Night Club	1843	Paris, France	First was Le Bal des Anglais, Paris 5me. (Closed *c.* 1960)
Nylon	1937	Dr Wallace H Carothers (US) (1896–1937) at Du Pont Labs, Seaford, Delaware, USA (Patent, 16 Feb.)	First stockings made about 1937. Bristle production 24 Feb. 1938. Yarn production December 1939
Paper	AD 105	Mulberry based fibre, China	Introduced to West *via* Samarkand, 14th century
Parachute	1785	Jean-Pierre F Blanchard (Fr) (1753–1809)	Dropped small mammal over London. Earliest jump from aircraft 1 Mar. 1912 by Albert Berry (US) over St Louis, Missouri, USA
Parchment	*c.*1300 BC	Egypt	Modern name from Pergamum (now Bergama), Asia Minor, *c.* 250 BC
Parking Meter	1935	Carlton C Magee (US)	Oklahoma City (16 July)
Pasteurization	1867	Louis Pasteur (1822–1895)	Destruction of pathogenic micro-organisms by heat. Effective against tuberculous milk

above: *Rudolf Diesel (1858–1913) inventor of the diesel engine.*
right: *Count Alessandro Volta (1745–1827), the physicist who invented the electric battery in 1800, demonstrating it to Napoleon Bonaparte in 1801. The volt was named in his honour.*

Photographs: Popperfoto

Object	Year	Inventor	Notes
Photography (on metal)	1826	J Nicéphore Niépce (Fr) (1765–1833)	Sensitised pewter plate, 8 hr exposure at Chalon-sur-Saône, France
(on paper)	1835	W H Fox Talbot (GB) (1807–1877)	Lacock Abbey, Wiltshire (August)
(on film)	1888	John Carbutt (US)	Kodak by George Eastman (US) (1854–1932), August 1888
Plastics	c.1852	Alexander Parks (1813–90)	Discovered pyroxylin, the first plastic
Porcelain	851	Earliest report from China	Reached Baghdad in ninth century
Potter's Wheel	c.6500 BC	Asia Minor	Used in Mesopotamia c. 3000 BC
Printing Press	c.1455	Johann Gutenberg (Ger) (c. 1400–68)	Hand printing known in Korea by 704
Printing (rotary)	1846	Richard Hoe (US) 1812–86)	Philadelphia Public Ledger rotary printed, 1847
Propeller (ship)	1837	Francis Smith (GB) (1808–74)	Hand propellor screw used in 1776 submarine (q.v.)
Pyramid	2650 BC	Imhotep	Earliest was Zoser step pyramid, Saqqâra
Radar	1922	Dr Albert H Taylor and Leo C Young	Radio reflection effect first noted. First harnessed by Dr Rudolph Kühnold, Kiel, Germany 20 Mar. 1934. Word coined in 1940 by Cdr S M Tucker USN
Radio Telegraphy	1864	Dr Mahlon Loomis (US) demonstrated over 14 miles *22 km* Bear's Den, Loudoun County, Virginia (October)	First advertised radio broadcast by Prof R A Fessenden (b. Canada, 1868–1932) at Brant Rock, Massachusetts on 24 Dec. 1906
Radio Telegraphy (Transatlantic)	1901	Guglielmo Marconi (It) (1874–1937)	Morse signals from Poldhu, Cornwall, to St John's, Newfoundland (12 Dec.)
Rayon	1883	Sir Joseph Swan (1828–1914) (GB)	Production at Courtauld's Ltd, Coventry, England November 1905. Name 'Rayon' adopted in 1924
Razor (electric)	1931	Col Jacob Schick (US)	First manufactured Stamford, Conn (18 Mar.)
(safety)	1895	King C Gillette (US) Patented 2 Dec. 1901	First throw-away blades. Earliest fixed safety razor by Kampfe
Record (long-playing)	1948	Dr Peter Goldmark (US)	Micro-groove developed in the CBS Research Labs and launched 21 June by Columbia, so ending 78 rpm market supremacy
Refrigerator	1850	James Harrison (GB) and Alexander Catlin Twining (US)	Simultaneous development at Rodey Point, Victoria, Australia and in Cleveland, Ohio. Earliest domestic refrigerator 1913 in Chicago, Illinois
Rubber (latex foam)	1928	Dunlop Rubber Co (GB)	Team led by E A Murphy at Fort Dunlop, Birmingham
(tyres)	1846	Thomas Hancock (GB) (1786–1865)	Introduced solid rubber tyres for vehicles (1847) (*see also* Bicycle)
(vulcanised)	1841	Charles Goodyear (US) (1800–60)	
(waterproof)	1823	Charles Macintosh (GB) (1766–1843) Patent	First experiments in Glasgow with James Syme. G Fox in 1821 had marketed a Gambroon cloth, but no detail has survived
Rubik Cube	1975	Prof. Ernö Rubik (Hungary)	Patented device with $4·3 \times 10^{22}$ combinations
Safety Pin	1849	Walter Hunt (US)	First manufactured New York City, NY (10 Apr.)
Scotch Tape	1930	Richard Drew (US) (1899–1980)	Developed from opaque masking tape
Self-Starter	1911	Charles F Kettering (US) (1876–1958)	Developed at Dayton, Ohio, sold to Cadillac

left: *Lazlo Biro, who, with his brother Georg, made the first practical model of the ball-point pen in 1938.*

above: *Guglielmo Marconi (1874–1937) pioneer of transatlantic Radio Telegraphy in 1901.*

Photographs: Popperfoto

Object	Year	Inventor	Notes
Sewing Machine	1829	Barthélemy Thimmonnier (Fr) (1793–1854)	A patent by Thomas Saint (GB) dated 17 July 1790 for an apparently undeveloped machine was found in 1874. Earliest practical domestic machine by Isaac M Singer (1811–75) of Pittstown, NY, USA, in 1851. AB Wilson machine of 1850, Farrington Museum, Conn., USA, Sept. 1938
Ship (sea-going)	*c.*40 000 BC	Possibly double dug-out canoes	Traversed Indonesia to Australia
(steam)	1775	J C Périer (Fr) (1742–1818)	On the Seine, near Paris. Propulsion achieved on river Saône, France by Marquis d'Abbans, 1783. First sea-going Phoenix by John Stevens (1749–1838) built 1808. Clement Fulton first commercially successful
(turbine)	1894	Hon Sir Charles Parsons (GB) (1854–1931)	*SS Turbinia* attained 34·5 knots on first trial. Built at Heaton, Tyne and Wear
Silk Manufacture	*c.* 50 BC	Reeling machines devised, China	Silk mills in Italy *c.* 1250, world's earliest factories
Skyscraper	1882	William Le Baron Jenny (US)	Home Insurance Co Building, Chicago, Ill, 10 storey (top 4 steel beams)
Slide Rule	1621	William Oughtred (1575–1660) (Eng)	Earliest slide between fixed stock by Robert Bissaker, 1654
Spectacles	1289	Venice, Italy (convex)	Concave lens for myopia not developed till *c.* 1450
Spinning Frame	1769	Sir Richard Arkwright (GB) (1732–92)	
Spinning Jenny	1764	James Hargreaves (GB) (1745–78)	
Spinning Mule	1779	Samuel Crompton (GB) (1753–1827)	
Steam Engine	1698	Thomas Savery (GB) (*c.* 1650–1715)	Recorded on 25 July. Denis Papin (Fr) (1647–1712) invented the pressure cooker 1679
Steam Engine (piston)	1712	Thomas Newcomen (GB) (1663–1729)	
Steam Engine (condenser)	1765	James Watt (Scot) (1736–1819)	
Steel Production	1855	Henry Bessemer (GB) (1813–1898)	At St Pancras, London. Cementation of wrought iron bars by charcoal contact known to Chalybes people of Asia Minor *c.* 1400 BC
Steel (stainless)	1913	Harry Brearley (GB)	First cast at Sheffield (Eng) (20 Aug.). Krupp patent, Oct. 1912 for chromium carbon steel; failed to recognise corrosion resistance
Submarine	1776	David Bushnell (US), Saybrook, Conn	Hand propelled screw, one man crew, used off New York. A twelve man wooden and leather submersible devised by Cornelius Drebbel (Neth) demonstrated in Thames in 1624
Tank	1914	Sir Ernest Swinton (GB) (1868–1951)	Built at Lincoln, designed by William Tritton. Tested 8 Sept. 1915
Telegraph	1787	M Lammond (Fr) demonstrated a working model, Paris	
Telegraph Code	1837	Samuel F B Morse (US) (1791–1872)	The real credit belonged largely to his assistant Alfred Vail (US) who first transmitted at Morristown, NJ on 8 Jan. 1838
Telephone	1849	Antonio Meucci (It) in Havana, Cuba	Caveat not filed until 1871. Instrument worked imperfectly by electrical impulses
	1876	Alexander Graham Bell (US) (1847–1922) Patented 7 Mar. 1876	First exchange at Boston, Mass, 1878
Telescope (refractor)	1608	Hans Lippershey (Neth)	(2 Oct.)
Television (mechanical)	1926	John Logie Baird (GB) (1888–1946)	First successful experiment 30 Oct. 1925. First public demonstration 27 Jan. 1926, London, of moving image with gradations of light and shade at 22 Frith Street, London. First transmission in colour on 3 July 1928 at 133 Long Acre, London
Television (electronic)	1927	Philo Taylor Farnsworth (US) (1906–71)	First images (Nov.) 202 Green St, Los Angeles. Patent granted 26 Aug. 1930
Terylene	1941	J R Whinfield (1901–66), J T Dickson (GB) at Accrington, Lancashire	First available 1950, marketed in USA as 'Dacron'
Thermometer	1593	Galileo Galilei (It) (1564–1642)	Gas thermoscope built at Royal Institution, London (29 Aug.)
Transformer	1831	Michael Faraday (GB) (1791–1867)	
Transistor	1948	John Bardeen, William Shockley and Walter Brattain (US)	Researched at Bell Telephone Laboratories. First application for a patent was by Dr Julius E Lilienfeld in Canada on October 1925 (*see* Electronic Computer)
Typewriter	1808	Pellegrine Tarri (It)	First practical 27 character keyed machine with carbon paper built in Reggio Emilia, Italy
Washing Machine (electric)	1907	Hurley Machine Co (US)	Marketed under the name of 'Thor' in Chicago, Illinois, USA
Watch	1462	Bartholomew Manfredi (It)	Earliest mention of a named watchmaker (November) but in reference to an earlier watchmaker
Water Closet	1589	Designed by Sir John Harington (GB)	Installed at Kelston, near Bath. Built by 'T C' (full name unknown)
Welder (electric)	1877	Elisha Thomson (US) (1853–1937)	
Wheel	*c.*3300 BC	Sumerian civilisation	Spoked as opposed to solid wheels *c.* 1900 BC
Windmill	*c.* 600	Persian corn grinding	Oldest known English post mill, 1191, Bury St Edmunds
Writing	*c.*3500 BC	Sumarian civilisation	Earliest evidence found in SE Iran, 1970
X-Ray	1895	Wilhelm Konrad Röntgen (Ger) (1845–1923)	University of Wurzburg (8 Nov.)
Zip Fastener	1891	Whitcomb L Judson (US) Exhibition 1893 at Chicago Exposition	First practical fastener invented in USA by Gideon Sundback (Sweden) in 1913

Transport

Shipping

WORLD'S LARGEST SHIPS

The largest liner of all-time was *Queen Elizabeth* (UK) of 82 998 gross tons and 1031 ft *314 m* completed in 1940 and destroyed by fire in Hong Kong as *Seawise University* on 9 Jan. 1972. The largest and active liner is the *Norway* of 70 202·19 grt and 315,66 m *1035 ft 7½ in* in length. She was built as the *France* in 1961 and put out of service in 1975. In June 1979 she was bought by the Norwegian Knut Kloster, renamed *Norway*, and recommissioned as a cruise ship in August 1979.

SHIPPING TONNAGES

There are four tonnage systems in use, viz. gross tonnage (GRT), net tonnage (NRT), deadweight tonnage (DWT) and displacement tonnage.

(1) *Gross Registered Tonnage*, used for merchantmen, is the sum in cubic ft of all the enclosed spaces divided by 100, such that 1 grt = 100 ft^3 of enclosed space.

(2) *Net Registered Tonnage*, also used for merchantmen, is the gross tonnage (above) less deductions for crew spaces, engine rooms and ballast which cannot be utilised for paying passengers or cargo.

(3) *Deadweight Tonnage*, mainly used for tramp ships and oil tankers, is the number of UK long tons (of 2240 lb) of cargo, stores, bunkers and, where necessary, passengers which is required to bring down a ship from her height line to her load-water line, i.e. the carrying capacity of a ship.

(4) *Displacement Tonnage*, used for warships and US merchantmen, is the numbers of tons (each 35 ft^3) of sea water displaced by a vessel charged to its load-water line, i.e. the weight of the vessel and its contents in tons.

Oil tankers (over 450 000 tons dwt)

Name	*Flag*	*High Dwt*	*Grt*	*Ft*	*M*	*Ft*	*M*
Seawise Giant	Liberia	564 763	238 558	1504	*458*	209	*63*
Pierre Guillaumat	France	555 051	274 838	1359	*414*	206	*62*
Prairial	France	554 974	274 838	1359	*414*	206	*62*
Bellamya	France	553 662	275 276	1359	*414*	206	*62*
Batillus	France	553 662	273 550	1358	*413*	206	*62*
Esso Atlantic	Liberia	516 893	234 638	1333	*406*	233	*71*
Esso Pacific	Liberia	516 423	234 626	1333	*406*	233	*71*
Nanny	Sweden	491 120	245 140	1194	*363*	259	*78*
Nissei Maru	Japan	484 337	238 517	1243	*378*	203	*61*
Globtik London	Liberia	483 933	213 894	1243	*378*	203	*61*
Globtik Tokyo	Liberia	483 662	213 886	1243	*378*	203	*61*
Burmah Enterprise	UK	457 927	231 629	1241	*378*	224	*68*
Burmah Endeavour	UK	457 841	231 629	1241	*378*	223	*67*

Bulk, Ore, Bulk Oil and Ore Oil Carriers (over 250 000 tons dwt)

				Length		*Breadth*	
Name	*Flag*	*High Dwt*	*Grt*	*Ft*	*M*	*Ft*	*M*
World Gala	Liberia	282 462	133 748	1109	*338*	179	*54*
Weser Ore	Liberia	278 734	139 410	1099	*334*	170	*51*
Docecanyon	Liberia	275 589	131 473	1113	*339*	180	*54*
Jose Bonifacio	Brazil	270 355	126 760	1106	*337*	179	*54*
Licorne Pacifique	France	269 007	132 809	1111	*338*	176	*53*
Usa Maru	Japan	268 767	142 246	1105	*336*	179	*54*
Mary R Koch	Liberia	264 999	136 991	1099	*334*	170	*51*
Cast Narwhal	Liberia	268 728	132 305	1101	*335*	176	*53*
Rhine Ore	Panama	264 999	139 406	1099	*334*	170	*51*
Lauderdale	UK	264 591	143 959	1101	*335*	176	*53*
Licorne Atlantic	France	262 411	131 619	1101	*335*	176	*53*

Aircraft

MAIN COMMERCIAL AIRCRAFT IN AIRLINE SERVICE 1982

*Aircraft**	*Nationality*	*Number in Service (1 May 1981)*	*Wingspan*	*Length*	*Maximum cruising speed*	*Range with maximum payload*	*Maximum take-off weight*	*Maximum seating capacity*
Boeing 727 (−200)	USA	1618	108 ft 0 in (*32,92 m*)	153 ft 2 in (*46,69 m*)	520 knots (*964 km/h*)	2140 naut miles (*3966 km*)	209 500 lb (*95 025 kg*)	189
McDonnell Douglas DC-9 (Super 81)	USA	943	107 ft 10 in (*32,87 m*)	147 ft 10 in (*45,06 m*)	487 knots (*902 km/h*)	2657 naut miles[1] (*4925 km*)	140 000 lb (*63 500 kg*)	172
Antonov An-24/-26 (An-26)	USSR	850**	95 ft 9½ in (*29,20 m*)	78 ft 1 in (*23,80 m*)	237 knots (*440 km/h*)	594 naut miles (*1100 km*)	52 911 lb (*24 000 kg*)	40
Yakovlev Yak-40	USSR	750**	82 ft 0¼ in (*25,00 m*)	66 ft 9½ in (*20,36 m*)	297 knots (*550 km/h*)	782 naut miles (*1450 km*)	35 275 lb (*16 000 kg*)	32
Boeing 737 (−200)	USA	665	93 ft 0 in (*28,35 m*)	100 ft 2 in (*30,53 m*)	500 knots (*927 km/h*)	2300 naut miles (*4262 km*)	124 500 lb (*56 472 kg*)	130
Boeing 707/720 (707-320)	USA	546	145 ft 9 in (*44,42 m*)	152 ft 11 in (*46,61 m*)	525 knots (*973 km/h*)	5000 naut miles[2] (*9265 km*)	333 600 lb (*151 315 kg*)	219
Tupolev Tu-134 (Tu-134A)	USSR	500**	95 ft 1¾ in (*29,00 m*)	121 ft 6½ in (*37,05 m*)	477 knots (*884 km/h*)	1020 naut miles (*1890 km*)	103 600 lb (*47 000 kg*)	84
Boeing 747 (−200)	USA	463	195 ft 8 in (*59,64 m*)	231 ft 10 in (*70,66 m*)	520 knots (*964 km/h*)	5700 naut miles[3] (*10 562 km*)	833 000 lb (*377 840 kg*)	516
Tupolev Tu-154 (−154B)	USSR	420**	123 ft 2½ in (*37,55 m*)	157 ft 1¾ in (*47,90 m*)	513 knots (*950 km/h*)	1485 naut miles (*2750 km*)	211 650 lb (*96 000 kg*)	169
Ilyushin Il-18 (Il-18D)	USSR	380**	122 ft 8½ in (*37,40 m*)	117 ft 9½ in (*35,90 m*)	364 knots (*675 km/h*)	1997 naut miles (*3700 km*)	141 095 lb (*64 000 kg*)	110[4]
McDonnell Douglas DC-8 (Srs 63)	USA	361	148 ft 5 in (*45,23 m*)	187 ft 5 in (*57,12 m*)	521 knots (*965 km/h*)	3907 naut miles (*7240 km*)	350 000 lb (*158 000 kg*)	259

Aircraft*	Nationality	Number in Service (1 May 1981)	Wingspan	Length	Maximum cruising speed	Range with maximum payload	Maximum take-off weight	Maximum seating capacity
McDonnell Douglas DC-10 (Srs 40)	USA	341	165 ft 4½ in (50,41 m)	182 ft 1 in (55,50 m)	498 knots (922 km/h)	4050 naut miles (7505 km)	572 000 lb (259 450 kg)	380
Fokker F27 (Mk 500)	Netherlands	282	95 ft 1¾ in (29,00 m)	82 ft 2½ in (25,06 m)	259 knots (480 km/h)	935 naut miles (1741 km)	45 000 lb (20 410 kg)	60
Lockheed L-1011 TriStar (−500)	USA	200	155 ft 4 in (47,34 m)	164 ft 2½ in (50,05 m)	525 knots (973 km/h)	5209 naut miles (9653 km)	496 000 lb (224 980 kg)	400
BAC One-Eleven (Srs 500)	UK	153	93 ft 6 in (28,50 m)	107 ft 0 in (32,61 m)	470 knots (871 km/h)	1480 naut miles (2744 km)	104 500 lb (47 400 kg)	119
Airbus A300B (A300B4-200)	International	138	147 ft 1 in (44,84 m)	175 ft 11 in (53,62 m)	492 knots (911 km/h)	2750 naut miles[6] (5095 km)	363 760 lb (165 000 kg)	336
Fokker F28 (Mk 4000)	Netherlands	125	82 ft 3 in (25,07 m)	97 ft 1¾ in (29,61 m)	455 knots (843 km/h)	900 naut miles (1667 km)	73 000 lb (33 110 kg)	85
BAC/Aérospatiale Concorde	International	13	83 ft 10 in (25,56 m)	203 ft 9 in (62,10 m)	1176 knots (2179 km/h)	3360 naut miles (6230 km)	408 000 lb (185 065 kg)	128

* Scheduled and non-scheduled services, including all-freight. Specification details apply to version noted in brackets.
** Figure approximate
[1] range quoted is with maximum fuel   [2] with 147 passengers   [3] with 442 passengers   [4] 122 seats in summer with wardrobes deleted   [5] with 52 passengers   [6] with 269 passengers

MAJOR WORLD AIRLINES (1980 IATA STATISTICS)

Airline	Passenger km (000)*	Aircraft km (000)*	Passengers carried (000)**	Aircraft departures*	Scheduled route network (km)
Aeroflot, USSR[1]	150 707 000	na	101 900	na	565 000
United Airlines (UAL), USA	61 826 916	643 810	32 806	466 136	na
Eastern Air Lines, USA	46 019 300	503 104	39 522	554 971	na
Trans World Airlines (TWA), USA	45 822 426	370 966	20 597	254 948	336 373
American Airlines, USA	45 346 947	509 786	25 729	341 681	315 388
Delta Air Lines, USA[2]	42 023 356	424 163	40 274	549 058	na
British Airways, UK	40 140 169	271 133	16 133	206 523	571 123
Pan American World Airways, USA[2]	36 652 383	206 877	9 248	79 701	na
Japan Air Lines (JAL), Japan	28 876 005	177 747	13 279	80 151	298 207
Air France, France	25 391 779	194 299	10 921	142 683	636 172
Air Canada, Canada	23 751 863	215 629	12 959	192 282	308 978
Northwest Airlines, USA[2]	21 395 686	186 809	11 634	168 609	na
Lufthansa, Germany	21 056 127	196 219	13 046	187 277	405 152
Braniff International, USA	19 150 612	213 106	12 153	198 442	77 897
Western Air Lines, USA[2]	16 456 333	175 875	11 937	168 915	na
Qantas Airways, Australia	15 768 885	59 026	1 961	15 647	180 692
Continental Air Lines, USA[2]	15 253 476	174 835	9 910	157 916	na
All Nippon Airways (ANA), Japan[3]	15 165 275	110 272	20 371	168 476	na
Iberia, Lineas Aereas de Espana, Spain	14 817 659	154 353	13 837	187 963	370 850
KLM-Royal Dutch Airlines, Netherlands	14 058 136	98 277	3 849	65 192	373 030
National Airlines, USA	13 295 611	136 831	6 552	102 502	na
Alitalia, Italy	12 876 600	118 184	7 310	108 079	353 782
Singapore Airlines (SIA), Singapore[2]	12 048 900	68 791	3 377	32 833	na
Scandinavian Airlines (SAS), Sweden	10 955 907	118 570	8 301	158 660	223 863
Swissair, Switzerland	10 830 530	97 815	5 930	97 454	270 884
Saudi Arabian Airlines, Saudi Arabia	9 937 985	91 332	9 241	94 355	na
CP Air, Canada	9 329 496	64 940	3 337	44 942	165 951
Korean Air Lines, South Korea[2]	9 110 479	59 932	3 726	39 842	na
South African Airways (SAA), South Africa	8 843 038	64 012	3 983	56 513	224 885
US Air (formerly Allegheny Airlines), USA[2]	8 123 388	131 777	14 058	288 177	na
Varig International, Brasil[2]	8 104 101	92 324	4 447	75 334	na
Mexicana, Mexico	7 444 866	75 543	7 336	81 339	89 963
Aerolineas Argentinas, Argentina	6 926 778	71 641	3 968	71 540	226 302
Air India, India	6 596 513	39 760	1 355	14 961	221 197
Aeromexico, Mexico	6 354 887	77 618	5 339	85 290	109 787
Philippine Airlines, Philippine Islands[2]	6 033 347	43 166	3 314	50 296	na

* Scheduled and non-scheduled services, including all-freight   ** Scheduled services only   [1] Data approximate   [2] ICAO 1979 statistics   [3] ICAO 1978 statistics

WORLD'S MAJOR AIRPORTS 1980

Name and location	Terminal passengers (000s)	International* passengers (000s)	Air transport movements (000s)	Cargo (tonnes) (000s)	Date opened to scheduled traffic	Distance from city centre miles (km)
O'Hare International, Chicago, Illinois, USA	44 425	2 883	624	816	1 Oct. 1955	18 (29)
Hartfield International, Atlanta, Georgia, USA	40 180	829	559	330	3 May 1961	12·5 (20·1)
Los Angeles International, California, USA	33 038	5 652	411	882	9 Dec. 1946	10 (16·1)
Heathrow Airport, London, UK	27 472	23 367	273	469	31 May 1946	15 (24·1)
John F. Kennedy International, New York, USA	26 796	13 029	236	92	1 July 1948	15 (24·1)
Dallas/Fort Worth Regional, Texas, USA	21 951	355	436	198	13 Jan. 1974	17 (27·4)
San Francisco International, California, USA	21 338	2 649	297	319	7 June 1927	16 (25·7)
Stapleton International, Denver, Colorado, USA	20 849	225	374	118	1 May 1961	5 (8)
Haneda International, Tokyo, Honshu, Japan	20 810	Na	Na	194	July 1952	8·7 (14)
Miami International Airport, Florida, USA	20 505	8 438	278	581	1 Feb. 1959	9 (14·5)
LaGuardia Airport, New York, USA	17 459	Nil	225	32	2 Dec. 1939	5 (8)
Flughafen Frankfurt Main, Frankfurt am Main, Germany	16 874	11 856	209	605	8 July 1936	7·5 (12)
Osaka International Airport, Osaka, Japan	16 434	2 551	127	198	17 Mar. 1958	9·9 (16)
Aéroport de Paris, Orly, Paris, France	15 670	8 507	175	167	8 Mar. 1961	8·7 (14)
Logan International, Boston, Massachusetts, USA	14 722	2 159	258	180	8 Sept. 1923	3 (4·8)
Washington National, Washington, DC, USA	14 294	Na	203	26	16 June 1941	3·4 (5·5)
Honolulu International Airport, Oahu, USA	14 036	2 115	198	160	11 Nov. 1929	4 (6·4)
Toronto International (Malton), Toronto, Canada	13 707	6 370	198	181	18 Oct. 1938	17 (27·4)
Greater Pittsburgh International, Pa, USA	11 453	96	344	Na	31 May 1952	18·6 (30)
Aeroporto Roma (Fiumicino), Rome, Italy	10 707	6 503	144	149	16 Jan. 1961	21·7 (35)

* Represents the international component of the total terminal passengers

BAC One-Eleven 107 ft *32,61 m*

Boeing '707' 152 ft 11 in *46,61 m*

Lockheed L-1011 Tristar 164 ft $2\frac{1}{2}$ in *50,05 m*

Airbus A300 B4 175 ft 11 in *53,62 m*

McDonnell Douglas DC10 182 ft 1 in *55,50 m*

BAE-Aérospatiale Concorde 203 ft 9 in *62,10 m*

Boeing '747' (Jumbo Jet) 231 ft 10 in *70,66 m*

MILESTONES IN AVIATION

1717	Earliest 'rational' design published by Emmanuel Swedenborg (1688–1772) in Sweden.
1785	7 Jan. First crossing of English Channel by balloon Jean Pierre Blanchard (FRA) and Dr John J Jeffries (USA).
1852	24 Sept. First flight by navigable airship, in France.
1900	2 July. First flight by German Zeppelin airship.
1903	17 Dec. First sustained flight in an aeroplane, by Wright Brothers, near Kitty Hawk, N. Carolina, United States.
1906	12 Nov. First public aeroplane flight in Europe. Alberto Santos-Dumont covers a distance of 220 m *722 ft* near Paris, France.
1909	25 July. Louis Blériot (FRA) completes first aeroplane crossing of the English Channel in 36½ min.
1910	27–8 Aug. Louis Paulhan completes first flight from London to Manchester, in 4 hr 12 min with an overnight stop.
1919	14–15 June. Capt John William Alcock and Lieut Arthur Whitten Brown complete first non-stop crossing of the Atlantic in 16 hr 27 min.
1919	12 Nov.–10 Dec. Capt Ross Smith and Lieut Keith Smith complete first flight from United Kingdom (Hounslow) to Australia (Darwin).
1924	1 Apr. Imperial Airways formed in Great Britain.
1927	20–21 May. First solo non-stop trans-atlantic flight (eastbound) by Charles A Lindbergh (US) in Ryan monoplane in 33 hr 29½ min.
1928	15 May. Inauguration of Australia's Flying Doctor Service.
1928	31 May–9 June. First trans-Pacific flight from San Francisco to Brisbane, by Capt Charles Kingsford Smith and C T P Ulm.
1929	30 March. First commercial air route between London and Karachi inaugurated by Imperial Airways.
1929	8–29 Aug. The first airship flight around the world was made by the German *Graf Zeppelin*, commanded by Dr Hugo Eckener.
1934	8 Dec. The first weekly air mail service between England and Australia was started.
1935	13 April. The first through passenger service by air from England to Australia was initiated.
1935	22 Nov. The first scheduled air mail flight across the Pacific was flown, from San Francisco to Manila, Philippines.
1937	12 Apr. First test-bed run of a jet engine by Fl Off Frank Whittle (GB).
1939	28 June. Inauguration of Pan American's transatlantic New York–Southampton flying-boat service.
1939	27 Aug. First turbo-jet test flight by Fl Kapt Erich Warsitz in He 178 at Marienche, Germany.
1947	14 Oct. First supersonic flight by Capt Charles E Yeager USAF in Bell XS-1 over Maroc, California, USA.
1949	21 June. First flight of a turbojet-powered airliner, the de Havilland Comet 1. (Entered service 2 May 1952.)
1950	29 July. A Vickers Viscount made the world's first scheduled passenger service by a turbine-powered airliner.
1957	19 Dec. The first transatlantic passenger service to be flown by turbine-powered airliners was inaugurated by BOAC with Bristol Britannia aircraft.
1958	4 Oct. The first transatlantic service to be flown by a turbojet-powered airliner was inaugurated by a de Havilland Comet 4 of BOAC.
1968	31 Dec. First flight of the Russian supersonic airliner, the Tupolev TU-144.
1969	9 Feb. First flight of the Boeing 747 'Jumbo-jet'. (Entered service 21 Jan. 1970.)
1969	2 March. First flight of BAC/Aérospatiale Concorde. (Entered scheduled service with Air France and British Airways 21 Jan. 1976.)
1974	1 Sept. Lockheed SR-71A flew the North Atlantic in 1 hr 54 min 56·4 sec.
1977	26 Sept. Laker Airways inaugurated transatlantic cheap fare Skytrain.
1978	12–17 Aug. First crossing of the North Atlantic by a balloon, the American Yost HB-72 *Double Eagle II*, crewed by Ben L Abruzzo, Maxie L Anderson and Larry M Newman.
1979	12 June. First crossing of the English Channel by a man-powered aircraft, Dr Paul MacCready's *Gossamer Albatross*, powered/piloted by Bryan Allen.
1980	5 Dec. Dr Paul MacCready's solar-powered aircraft, *Solar Challenger*, recorded a first significant solar-powered flight of 1 hr 32 min.
1981	14 Apr. The NASA space shuttle *Columbia* made an unpowered, but otherwise conventional landing by a heavier-than-air craft, on the dry bed of Rogers Lake at Edwards Air Force Base, California, after a space mission involving 54 hr 20 min in Earth orbit.
1981	7 July. Piloted by Steve Ptacek, Dr Paul MacCready's *Solar Challenger* became the first solar-powered aircraft to make a crossing of the English Channel, flying from Cormeille-en-Vexin, France, to Manston, Kent.

Rail

A railway may be defined as a track which guides vehicles travelling along it. Such tracks, formed of parallel lines of stone blocks with grooves in the centres, date back to Babylonian times, about 2245 BC, and can still be found in south-eastern Europe. The word 'railway' was first recorded in 1681 at Pensnett near Stourbridge, West Midlands. 'Railroad' was first used at Rowton near Coalport, Shropshire, in 1702. Both words were used in Britain until about 1850 after which 'railway' was adopted. In the USA 'railroad' became widely, though not universally, used. The first positive record of the use of steam power on a railway was in 1804 when a locomotive built by Richard Trevithick hauled a train at Penydarren Ironworks in South Wales. The first railway to be operated entirely by steam engines from its opening was the Liverpool & Manchester, on 15 September 1830.

The 'standard guage' of 1435 mm (4 ft 8½ in) was first established on the Willington Colliery wagonway near Newcastle upon Tyne in 1764–5. Today this guage is standard in Great Britain, Canada, the USA, Mexico, Europe (except Ireland, Spain, Portugal, Finland and the USSR), North Africa, the Near East countries, Australian National Railways and New South Wales, China, Korea and the Japanese Shinkansen lines. In South America it is found in Paraguay, Uraguay, the Argentine Urquiza system, Central and Southern Railways of Peru, Venezuela and short lines in Brazil.

The modern standard system of railway electrification at 25 kV 50 Hz was first used in France in 1950 and in England, on the Colchester – Clacton – Walton lines, in 1959.

PRINCIPAL RAILWAY SYSTEMS OF THE WORLD

Railway system	Year of first railway	Gauge mm	ft	in	Route length km	miles
Argentina	1857	1676	5	6	22 101	13 733
		1435	4	8½	3 088	1 919
		1000	3	3⅜	11 844	7 359
		750	2	5½	285	177
					37 318	23 188
Australia	1854	1600	5	3	8 396	5 217
		1435	4	8½	14 243	8 850
		1067	3	6	16 749	10 407
					39 388	24 474
Brazil	1854	1600	5	3	3 385	2 104
		1000	3	3⅜	25 330	15 739
		762	2	6	202	126
					28 917	17 969
Canada	1836	1435	4	8½	68 023	42 267
		1067	3	6	1 146	712
		915	3	0	178	111
					69 347	43 090

Railway system	Year of first railway	Gauge mm	ft	in	Route length km	miles
Chile	1851	1676	5	6	4 282	2 661
		1435	4	8½	370	230
		1000	3	3⅜	3 300	2 050
					7 952	4 941
China	1880	1435	4	8½	c. 50 000	c. 31 000
Czechoslovakia	1839	1435	4	8½	13 029	8 095
France	1832	1435	4	8½	34 362	21 351
Germany	1835					
Federal (West)		1435	4	8½	28 450	17 678
State (East)		1435	4	8½	14 215	8 833
					42 665	26 511
Great Britain	1830	1435	4	8½	17 229	10 706
		600	1	11½	19	12

Railway system	Year of first railway	Gauge mm	ft	in	Route length km	miles
India	1853	1676	5	6	31 789	19 753
		1000	3	3⅜	25 209	15 664
		762	2	6	3 521	2 188
		610	2	0	390	242
					60 909	37 847
Italy	1839	1435	4	8½	16 133	10 024
Japan	1872	1435	4	8½	1 177	731
		1067	3	6	20 145	12 517
					21 322	13 248
Mexico	1850	1435	4	8½	14 223	8 838
		913	3	0	451	280
					14 674	9 118
Pakistan	1861	1676	5	6	7 754	4 818
		1000	3	3⅜	444	276
		762	2	6	610	379
					8 808	5 473
Poland	1842	1435	4	8½	23 855	14 822

Railway system	Year of first railway	Gauge mm	ft	in	Route length km	miles
Roumania	1869	1435	4	8½	10 515	6 534
		762	2	6	568	353
		610	2	0		
					11 083	6 887
South Africa	1860	1065	3	6	22 891	14 223
		610	2	0	705	438
					23 596	14 661
Spain	1848	1668	5	6	13 531	8 407
Sweden	1856	1435	4	8½	11 158	6 933
		891	2	11	182	113
					11 340	7 046
Turkey	1896	1435	4	8½	8 140	5 857
USA	1830	1435	4	8½	294 625	183 077
USSR	1837	1520	4	11	c. 140 000	c. 87 000
Yugoslavia	1846	1435	4	8½	9 762	6 066

Road Transport

Average Mileage
The average estimated mileage for a car rose from 8700 miles in 1970 to 9500 miles in 1978. Car ownership rose in the same period from 593 per 1000 households to 691 while 4 star petrol rose from 32½p to 76½p per gallon. In July 1979 it rose to 120p.

Accidents
The cumulative total of fatalities since the first in the United Kingdom on 17 Aug. 1896 surpassed 250 000 in 1959 and by the end of 1978 reached about 370 000. There are only estimated figures for Northern Ireland in the period 1923–30. The peak reached was 1941 with 9444 killed or 26 per day in Great Britain only. L plates were introduced in May 1935.

Traffic signals: dates of introduction
1868 Parliament Square, Westminster, London, semaphore-arms with red and green gas lamps for night use.
1925 Piccadilly Circus, London, police-operated.
1926 Wolverhampton, Staffordshire, modern type electric.
1932 First vehicle actuation sets introduced.

Right and Left Hand Driving
Of the 221 separately administered countries and territories in the world 58 drive on the left and 163 on the right. In Britain it is believed that left hand driving is a legacy from the preference of passing an approaching horseman or carriage right side to right side to facilitate right armed defence against sudden attack. On the Continent postillions were mounted on the rearmost left horse in a team and thus preferred to pass left side to left side. While some countries have transferred from left to right the only case recorded of a transfer from right to left is in Okinawa on 30 July 1978.

Purchase and Value Added Tax on cars

		%			%
Oct.	1940	33⅓	Nov.	1962	25
June	1947	33⅓*	July	1966	27½
Apr.	1950	33⅓	Apr.	1973	
Apr.	1951	66⅔	*Purchase tax*		
Apr.	1953	50	*replaced by VAT*		
Oct.	1955	60	Apr.	1973	10
Apr.	1959	50	Apr.	1974	10
July	1961	55	July	1974	8
Apr.	1962	45	June	1979	15

* 66⅔% if retail value exceeded £1280.

UNITED KINGDOM MOTOR VEHICLES AND ROADS

Year	No. of Vehicles (Sept.)	Road (31 Mar.) Miles	km	Miles	km	Road per Vehicle Yds	m	Fatalities
1904	c. 18 000	—		—	—	—	—	—
1914	388 860	c. 176 000	283 200	—	—	796	727,8	—
1920	c. 652 000	c. 176 000	283 200	—	—	475	434,3	—
1925	1 538 235	c. 178 000	286 400	—	—	203	185,6	—
1930	2 309 515	179 286	288 532	—	—	136·7	124,9	c. 7400
1935	2 612 093	178 507	287 279	—	—	120·3	110	6625
1939	3 208 410	180 527	290 530	—	—	99·0	90,5	8419
1945	1 654 364	c. 183 000	294 500	—	—	194·7	178	5380
1950	4 511 626	197 076	317 163	—	—	77·1	70,5	5156
1955	6 567 393	201 724	324 643	—	—	54·1	49,4	5686
1960	9 610 432	207 939	334 645	(95	152,8)*	38·1	34,8	7142
1961	10 148 714	208 986	336 330	(136	218,8)*	36·3	33,1	7077
1962	10 763 502	209 937	337 860	(151	243)*	34·3	31,3	6866
1963	11 729 675	212 275	341 623	(200	321,8)*	31·8	29	7098
1964	12 671 817	213 602	343 759	(298	479,5)*	29·7	27,1	8039
1965	13 263 537	214 958	345 941	(368	592,2)*	28·5	26	8143
1970	15 322 533	222 000	354 055	(704	1132,9)*	25·5	23,3	7771
1974	17 626 273	221 009	355 679	(1231	1981,1)*	22·1	20,2	7192
1975	17 870 654	220 690	355 166	(1320	2124,3)*	21·7	19,8	6664
1976	18 218 219	221 665	356 735	(1430	2301,3)*	21·4	19,5	6870
1977	18 070 057	222 752	358 484	(1490	2397,9)*	21·6	19,7	6968
1978	18 198 956	223 633	359 902	(1568	2523,4)*	21·6	19,7	7119
1979	18 625 000	224 612	361 401	(1537	2473,5)*	21·2	19,4	(GB) 6351

* Figures in brackets indicate the miles/*km* of motorways within the total.

Notes: Vehicles surpassed 1 million early in 1923. Cars surpassed 1 million early in 1930, 5 million early in 1949. Motor cycles (including mopeds, scooters and three-wheelers) surpassed 1 million in 1953. Trams reached their peak in 1927 with 14 413 and sank by 1965 to 110. Diesel vehicles surpassed 25% of all goods vehicles in 1961 (2·1% in 1935) and 35% in 1965. The road mileage includes Trunk roads, Class I, Class II and Unclassified. Statistics prior to 1925 apply to Great Britain only. The earliest dual carriageway was the Southend arterial in 1937 though parts of both the Great West Road and the Kingston by-pass were converted to separate carriageways in 1936.

Engineering

Seven wonders of the world

The seven Wonders of the World were first designated by Antipater of Sidon in the second century BC. They are, or were:

Name	Location	Built (circa)	Fate
1. Three Pyramids of Giza (El Gîzeh)*	near El Gîzeh, Egypt	from 2580 BC	still stand
2. Hanging Gardens of Semiramis, Babylon	Babylon, Iraq	600 BC	no trace
3. Statue of Zeus (Jupiter) by Phidias	Olympia, Greece	*post* 432 BC	destroyed by fire
4. Temple of Artemis (Diana) of the Ephesians	Ephesus, Turkey	*ante* 350 BC	destroyed by Goths AD 262
5. Tomb of King Mausolus of Caria	Halicarnassus (now Bodrum), Turkey	*post* 353 BC	fragments survive
6. Statue of Helios (Apollo) by Charles of Lindus, called the Colossus of Rhodes (117 ft *36 m* tall)	Rhodes, Aegean Sea	292–280 BC	destroyed by earthquakes 224 BC
7. Lighthouse (400 ft *122 m*) on island of Pharos	off Alexandria, Egypt	270 BC	destroyed by earthquakes AD 400 and 1375

* Built by the Fourth Dynasty Pharaohs, Hwfw (Khufu or Cheops), Kha-f-Ra (Khafre or Khefren) and Menkaure (Mycerinus). The Great pyramid ('Horizon of Khufu') originally had a height of 480 ft 11 in *146·5 m* now, since the loss of its topmost stone or pyramidion, reduced to 449 ft 6 in *137 m*), Khafre's pyramid was 470 ft 9 in *143 m*, and Menkaure's was 218 ft *66 m* tall. The estimated weight of the 2 300 000 limestone blocks is 5 840 000 metric tonnes.

World's tallest inhabited buildings

Height (ft)	Height (m)	No of storeys	Building	Location
1454	443	110	Sears Tower (1974)	Wacker Drive, Chicago, Illinois
1350	412	110	World Trade Centre (1973)[1]	Barclay and Liberty Sts, New York City
1250	381	102	Empire State Building (1930)[2]	5th Av and 34th St, New York City
1136	346	80	Standard Oil Building (1973)	Chicago, Illinois
1127	343	100	John Hancock Center (1968)	Chicago, Illinois
1046	319	77	Chrysler Building (1930)	Lexington Av and 42nd St, New York City
1002	305	75	Texas Commercial Plaza	Houston, Texas
985	300	71	Allied Bank Plaza	1000 Louisiana, Houston, Texas
954	290	76	Columbia Center	Seattle, Washington State
952	290	72	First Bank Tower	First Canadian Place, Toronto, Ontario
939	286	73	Main Center	901 Main St, Dallas, Texas
927	282	71	40 Wall Tower	New York City
914	279	59	Citicorp Center (1977)	New York City
899	274	64	Transco Tower	Houston, Texas
886	270	68	Scotia Squava	Toronto, Ontario
859	262	74	Water Tower Plaza (1975)[3]	Chicago, Illinois
858	261	62	United California Bank (1974)	Los Angeles, California
853	259	48	Transamerica Pyramid	San Francisco, California
851	259	66	United California Bank	New York City
850	259	70	RCA Building	Rockefeller Centre, 5th Av, New York City
844	257	60	First National Bank of Chicago (1969)	Chicago, Illinois
841	256	64	US Steel Building (1971)	Pittsburgh, Pennsylvania
838	255	66	Bank of Nova Scotia	Toronto, Ontario
813	248	60	One Chase Manhattan Plaza	Liberty St and Nassau St, New York City
808	246	59	Pan American Building (1963)	Park Av, and 43rd St, New York City
800	244	68	MLC Office Tower (1977)	Sydney, Australia
794	242	60	Rialto Tower†	Collins St, Melbourne, Australia
792	241	57	Woolworth Building (1911–13)	233 Broadway, New York City
790	241	60	John Hancock Tower	Boston, Mass
790	241	42	Palace of Culture and Science	Warsaw, Poland
787	240	60	Sunshine 60 (1978)	Tokyo, Japan
787	240	28	Mikhail Lomonosov University	Moscow, USSR

[1] Two TV antennae bring the overall height to 1559 ft *475,18 m*.
[2] Between 27 July 1950 and 1 May 1951 a 222 ft TV tower was added.
[3] World's tallest reinforced concrete building.
† Under construction.

World's tallest structures

Height (ft)	Height (m)	Structure	Location
2120	646	Warszawa Radio Mast (May 1974)	Konstantynow, nr Płock, Poland
2063	629	KTHI-TV (December 1963)	Fargo, North Dakota, USA
1815	553	CN Tower, Metro Centre (April 1975)	Toronto, Canada
1762	537	Ostankino TV Tower (1967) (*4 m* added in 1973)	near Moscow, USSR
1749	533	WRBL-TV & WTVM (May 1962)	Columbus, Georgia, USA
1749	533	WBIR-TV (September 1963)	Knoxville, Tennessee, USA
1732	528	Moscow TV Tower	Moscow, USSR
1673	510	KFVS-TV (June 1960)	Cape Girardeau, Missouri, USA
1638	499	WPSD-TV	Paducah, Kentucky, USA
1619	493	WGAN-TV (September 1959)	Portland, Maine, USA
1610*	490	KSWS-TV (December 1956)	Roswell, New Mexico, USA
1600	487	WKY-TV	Oklahoma City, Okla, USA
1572	479	KW-TV (November 1954)	Oklahoma City, Okla, USA
1527	465	BREN Tower (unshielded atomic reactor) (April 1962)	Nevada, USA

* Fell in a gale, 1960; re-erected.

Below: left to right

Warszawa
Radio Mast
Poland
2120 ft 646 m

GPO Tower
London
619 ft 188 m

Sears Tower
Chicago USA
1454 ft 443 m

CN Tower
Toronto Canada
1815 ft 553 m

OTHER TALL STRUCTURES

Height (ft)	Height (m)	Structure	Location
1345	410	Danish Govt Navigation Mast	Greenland
1312	399	Peking Radio Mast	Peking, China
1272†	387	Anglia TV Mast (1965–September 1967)	Belmont, Lincolnshire
1271	387	Tower Zero (1967)	North West Cape, W Australia
1253	382	Lopik Radio Mast	Netherlands
1251	381	International Nickel Co Chimney (1970)	Sudbury, Ontario, Canada
1212	369	Thule Radio Mast (1953)	Thule, Greenland
1206	368	American Electric Power Smokestack (1969)	Cresap, West Virginia, USA

Height (ft)	Height (m)	Structure	Location
1200	366	Kennecott Copper Corp Chimney (1975)	Magna, Utah, USA
1179	359	Television Centre	Moscow
1150	350	TV Tower	Vinnitsa, Ukraine, USSR
1093	333	CHTV Channel II Mast	Hamilton, Ontario, Canada
1092	332	Tokyo Television Mast	Tokyo, Japan
1080	329	IBA Transmitter Tower (September 1971)	Emley Moor, West Yorkshire
1065	325	Leningrad TV Mast	Leningrad, USSR
1052	320	La Tour Eiffel (1887–9)	Paris, France

† Highest structure in Great Britain.

Tallest smokestacks and towers in the United Kingdom

Height (ft)	Height (m)	Building	Location
850	259	Drax Power Station	Drax, N. Yorkshire
800	244	Grain Power Station	Isle of Grain, Kent
700	213	Pembroke Power Station	Pembroke, Dyfed
670	204	Littlebrook 'D'	Dartford, Kent
670	204	Ironbridge 'B' Power Station (1 chimney)	Ironbridge, Salop
654	199	Didcot Power Station	Didcot, Oxfordshire
650	198	Eggborough Power Station (1 chimney)	Eggborough, N. Humberside
650	198	Ferrybridge 'C' Power Station (2 chimneys) (1 completed, 1966)	Ferrybridge, W. Yorkshire
650	198	Fiddler's Ferry	Cuerdley, Warrington
650	198	Kingsnorth Power Station (1 chimney)	Kingsnorth, Kent
650	198	Fawley Power Station (1 chimney)	Fawley, Hampshire
650	198	West Fife Power Station (2 chimneys)	West Fife
619	188	GPO Tower (1963)	Cleveland Mews, London, W1
600	182	West Burton Power Station (2 chimneys)	Retford, Nottinghamshire
558	170	Tilbury 'B' Power Station (2 chimneys)	Tilbury, Essex
550	167	Drakelow 'C' Power Station (2 chimneys)	Burton-on-Trent, Derbyshire

OTHER TALL STRUCTURES IN THE UNITED KINGDOM

Height (ft)	Height (m)	Structure	Location
820	250	Post Office Radio Masts (1925)	Rugby, Warwickshire
630	192	Transmission line pylons	West Thurrock, Thames Estuary
600·3	183	National Westminster Bank (1971–1979)	Old Broad Street–Bishopsgate, London
533	162	Humber Estuary Bridge Towers	Hessle and Barton
518·7	158,1	Blackpool Tower (1894)	Blackpool, Lancashire
512	156	Forth Road Bridge (1964)	Lothian–Fife, Scotland
488	148	Transmission line pylons	Severn Estuary
450	137	St John's Beacon	Liverpool
404	123	Salisbury Cathedral (_ante_ 1305)	Salisbury, Wiltshire
399	121	Co-operative Insurance Society Building (1962)	Miller Street, Manchester
387	118	Vickers Building (1959–63)	Millbank, London
385	117	Centre Point (1966)	St Giles Circus, London
380	116	Penta Hotel (1971–73)	Kensington, London
370	113	Forth Rail Bridge (1882–90)	Lothian–Fife, Scotland
365	111	St Paul's Cathedral (1675–1710)	London
365	111	Stock Exchange (1972)	London
343	104	Shell Upstream Tower (1957–61)	South Bank, London
340	103	Victoria Tower (1840–67)	Palace of Westminster, London
328	100	Hilton Hotel (1960–63)	Park Lane, London
327	99	Portland House	Victoria, London

Note: The 474 ft _144 m_ Townsend's stack, Port Dundas, Glasgow (1857–9) was demolished in 1928. The 455 ft _139 m_ Tennant's Stalk, St Rollox, Glasgow (1841–2) has also been demolished. No power stations of or below 400 ft _122 m_ are listed. Battersea Power Station, London, is 337 ft _103 m_.

Longest bridge spans in the world

STEEL ARCH BRIDGES

Steel was first used in bridge construction in 1828 (Danube Canal Bridge, Vienna) but the first all-steel bridge was the Chicago and Alton Railway Bridge over the Missouri at Glasgow, South Dakota, USA, in 1878. The longest concrete arch bridge is the KRK Island Bridge, Yugoslavia with a span of 390 m _1280 ft._

Length (ft)	Length (m)	Name	Year of completion	Location
1700	518,2	New River Gorge	1977	Fayetteville, West Virginia, USA
1652	503,5	Bayonne (Kill Van Kull)	1931	Bayonne, NJ-Staten I, NY, USA
1650	502,9	Sydney Harbour	1932	Sydney, Australia
1255	382,5	Fremont	1972	Portland, Oregon, USA
1200	365,7	Port Mann	1964	Vancouver, BC, Canada
1128	343,8	Thatcher Ferry	1962	Balboa, Panama

Length (ft)	Length (m)	Name	Year of completion	Location
1100	335,2	Laviolette (St Lawrence)	1967	Trois-Rivières, Quebec, Canada
1090	332,2	Zdakov	1967	Vltava River, Czechoslovakia
1082	330,0	Runcorn–Widnes	1961	Runcorn, Cheshire–Widnes, Lancashire, England
1080	329,2	Birchenough	1935	Sabi River, Rhodesia

CANTILEVER BRIDGE

The term cantilever came in only in 1883 (from _cant_ and _lever_, an inclined or projecting lever). The earlier bridges of this type were termed Gerber bridges from Heinrich Gerber, engineer, of the 425 ft _129,5 m_ Hassfurt am Main, Germany, bridge completed in 1867.

Length (ft)	Length (m)	Name	Year of completion	Location
1800	548,6	Quebec*	1917	St Lawrence, Canada
1710	521,2	Firth of Forth*	1890	Firth of Forth, Scotland
1673	510,0	Minato	1974	Osaka, Japan
1644	501,0	Commodore Barry Delaware River	1970	Chester, Pennsylvania, USA
1575	480,0	Greater New Orleans	1958	Algiers, Mississippi River, Louisiana, USA
1500	457,2	Howrah	1943	Calcutta, India
1400	426,7	Transbay (Oakland)	1936	San Francisco, California, USA

Length (ft)	Length (m)	Name	Year of completion	Location
1235	376,4	Baton Rouge	1968	Mississippi River, Louisiana, USA
1235	376,4	Astoria	1966	Oregon, USA
1212	369,4	Nyack-Tarrytown (Tappan Zee)	1955	Hudson River, NY, USA
1200	365,7	Longview	1930	Columbia River, Washington, USA
1200	365,7	Baltimore	1976	Maryland, USA
1182	360,2	Queensboro	1909	East River, NY City, USA
1100	335,2	Carquinez Strait†	1927	nr San Francisco, California, USA
1100	335,2	Second Narrows	1959	Burrard Inlet, Vancouver, BC, Canada

* Rail bridge. † New parallel bridge completed 1958.

SUSPENSION BRIDGES

The suspension principle was introduced in 1741 with a 70 ft *21 m* span iron bridge over the Tees, England. Ever since 1816 the world's longest span bridges have been of this construction except for the reign of the Forth Bridge (1889–1917) and Quebec Bridge (1917–29).

Length (ft)	Length (m)	Name	Year of completion	Location
5840	1780	Akashi-Kaikyo†	1988	Honshu-Shikoku, Japan
4626	1410	Humber Estuary Bridge	1980	Humber, England
4260	1298	Verrazano-Narrows (6+6 lanes)	1964	Brooklyn-Staten I, USA
4200	1280	Golden Gate	1937	San Francisco Bay, USA
3800	1158	Mackinac Straits	1957	Straits of Mackinac, Mich, USA
3524	1074	Bosphorus Bridge	1973	Bosphorus, Istanbul, Turkey
3500	1067	George Washington (2 decks, lower has 6 lanes, upper has 8 lanes since 1962)	1931	Hudson River, NY City, USA
3323	1013	Ponte 25 Abril (Tagus) (4 lanes)	1966	Lisbon, Portugal
3300	1006	Firth of Forth Road Bridge	1964	Firth of Forth, Scotland
3240	988	Severn-Wye River (4 lanes)	1966	Severn Estuary, England
2874	876	Ohnaruto*	1983	Kobe-Naruto Route, Japan
2800	853	Tacoma Narrows II	1952	Washington, USA
2526	770	Innoshima*	1982	Onomichi-Impari Route, Japan
2336	712	Angostura	1967	Ciudad Bolívar, Venezuela
2336	712	Kammon Straits	1973	Shimonoseki, Japan
2310	704	Transbay (2 spans)	1936	San Francisco-Oakland, Calif, USA
2300	701	Bronx-Whitestone (Belt parkway)	1939	East River, NY City, USA
2190	668	Pierre Laporte Bridge	1970	Quebec City, Canada
2150	655	Delaware Memorial I	1951	Wilmington, Delaware, USA
2150	655	Delaware Memorial II	1968	Wilmington, Delaware, USA
2000	610	Melville Gaspipe	1951	Atchafalaya River, Louisiana, USA
2000	610	Walt Whitman	1957	Philadelphia, Pennsylvania, USA
1995	608	Tancarville	1959	Seine, Le Havre, France
1968	600	Lillebaelt	1970	Lillebaelt, Denmark

† Under design. * Under construction.

LONGEST BRIDGING

Length (miles)	Length (km)	Name	Date Built	Location
23·87	38,422	Lake Pontchartrain Causeway II	1969	Mandeville-Jefferson, Louisiana, USA
23·83	38,352	Lake Pontchartrain Causeway I	1956	Mandeville-Jefferson, Louisiana, USA
17·99	28,952	Swampland Expressway	1973	Louisiana, USA
17·65	28,400	Chesapeake Bay Bridge-Tunnel	1964	Delmarva Peninsula-Norfolk, Virginia, USA
11·85*	19,070	Great Salt Lake Viaduct (Lucin cut-off)	1904	Great Salt Lake, Utah, USA
7·5	12,102	Ponte President Costa e Silva	1974	Rio de Janeiro-Niteroi, Brazil
6·7	10,78	San Mateo-Hayward	1967	San Francisco, California, USA

Other notable bridging

Length (miles)	Length (km)	Name	Date Built	Location
5·40	8,69	Lake Pontchartrain	1963	Slidell, Louisiana, USA
4·23	6,81	Sunshine Skyway I	1954	Lower Tampa Bay, Florida, USA
4·23	6,81	Sunshine Skyway II	1970	Lower Tampa Bay, Florida, USA
4·2	6,8	Nanking	1968–9	Yangtze Kiang, China
4·03	6,48	Chesapeake Bay I	1952	Maryland, USA
4·0	6,43	Champlain	1962	Montreal, Canada
3·98	6,41	Chesapeake Bay II	1972	Maryland, USA
3·77	6,06	Oeland	1972	Sweden
3·75	6,03	London Bridge-Deptford Creek (878 brick arches)	1836	London
3·5	5,63	North Beveland to Schouwen Duiveland (52 arches)	1966	Netherlands
3·12	5,02	Oosterschelde	1965	Middelburg-Zierikzee, Netherlands
2·38	3,83	Evergreen Point	1963	Seattle, Washington
2·28*	3,67	Lower Zambesi (46 spans)	1935	Dona Ana-Vila de Sena, Mozambique
2·24*	3,60	Lake of Venice (222 arches)	1846	Mestre-Venice, Italy
2·21*	3,55	New Tay Bridge (85 spans)	1887	Wormit, Fife-Dundee, Tayside, Scotland
2·2	3,54	Laveka Bay Causeway	1961	Texas, USA
2·13	3,42	Newport Bridge	1969	Rhode Island, USA
1·99	3,20	Storstrom (3 arches, 51 piers)	1937	Sjaelland-Falster, Denmark
1·9	3,1	Upper Sone	1900	Sone River, India

* Rail viaduct.

Canals

A canal, from the Latin *canalis* – a water channel – is an artificial channel used for purposes of drainage, irrigation, water supply, navigation or a combination of these purposes.

Navigation canals were originally only for specially designed barges, but were later constructed for sea-going vessels. This important latter category consists either of improved barge canals, or, since the pioneering of the Suez in 1859–69, canals specially constructed for ocean-going vessels.

The world's major deep-draught ship canals (of at least 5 m *16·4 ft* depth) in order of length

Length of Waterway (miles)	Length of Waterway (km)	Name	Year Opened	Minimum Depth (ft)	Minimum Depth (m)	No of Locks	Achievement and Notes
141	227	White Sea (Beloye More)–Baltic (formerly Stalin) Canal	1933	16·5	5,0	19	Links with Barents Sea and White Sea to the Baltic with a chain of a lake, canalised river, and 32 miles *51,5 km* of canal.
100·6	162	Suez Canal	1869	39·3	12,9	Nil	Eliminates the necessity for 'rounding the Cape'. Deepening in progress.
62·2	100	V I Lenin Volga–Don Canal	1952	—	—	13	Interconnects Black, Azov and Caspian Seas.
60·9	98	North Sea (or Kiel) Canal	1895	45	13,7	2	Shortens the North Sea–Baltic passage; south of German–Danish border. Major reconstruction 1914.
56·7	91	Houston (Texas) Canal	1940	34	10,4	Nil	Makes Houston, although 50 miles from the coast, the United States' eighth busiest port.
53	85	Alphonse XIII Canal	1926	25	7,6	13	Makes sea access to Seville safe. True canal only 4 miles, *6,4 km* in length.
50·71	82	Panama Canal	1914	41	12,5	6	Eliminates the necessity for 'rounding the Horn'. 49 miles *78,9 km* of the length was excavated.
39·7	64	Manchester Ship Canal	1894	28	8,5	4	Makes Manchester, although 54 miles *86,9 km* from the open sea, Britain's third busiest port.
28·0	45	Welland Canal	1931	29	8,8	7	Circumvents Niagara Falls and Niagara River rapids.
19·8	32	Brussels or Rupel Sea Canal	1922	21	6,4	4	Makes Brussels an inland port.

Notes: (1) The Volga–Baltic canal system runs 1850 miles *2300 km* from Leningrad *via* Lake Ladoga, Gor'kiy, Kuybyshev and the Volga River to Astrakhan. The Grand Canal of China, completed in the 13th century over a length of 1107 miles *1780 km* from Peking to Hangchou had silted up to a maximum depth of 6 ft *1,8 m* by 1950 but is now being reconstructed.
(2) the world's longest inland navigation route is the St Lawrence Seaway of 2342 miles *3769 km* from the North Atlantic up the St Lawrence estuary and across the Great Lakes to Duluth, Minnesota, USA. It was opened on 26 Apr. 1959.

World's highest dams

Name	River	Country	Completion	Height (ft)	Height (m)
Rogunsky	Vakhsh	USSR	Building	1066	325
Nurek	Vakhsh	USSR	Building	1040	317
Grande Dixence	Dixence-Rhône	Switzerland	1962	935	285
Ingurskaya	Inguri	USSR	Building	892	272
Chicoasen	Grijalva	Mexico	1980	869	265
Vajont	Piave	Italy	1961	858	262
Tehri	Upper Ganges	India	Building (1989)	856	261
Mica	Columbia	Canada	1976	794	242

Name	River	Country	Completion	Height (ft)	Height (m)
Sayano-Shushenskaya	Yenisey	USSR	1980	794	242
Patia	Patia	Colombia	Building	787	240
Chivor	Bata	Colombia	1975	778	237
Mauvoisin	Rhône	Switzerland	1957	777	237
Oroville	Feather-Sacramento	USA	1968	770	235
Chirkyi	Sulak-Caspian Sea	USSR	1975	764	233

World's most massive earth and rock dams

Name	Volume (millions of cubic yards)	Volume (millions of cubic metres)
New Cornelia Tailings, Arizona (1973)	274·0	209,4
Tarbela, Indus, Pakistan (1975)	159·2	121,7
Fort Peck, Missouri, Montana, USA (1940)	125·6	96,0
Guri, Caroni, Venezuela*	102·0	78,0
Oahe, Missouri, S Dakota, USA (1963)	92·0	70,0
Oosterschelde, Netherlands (1980)	91·5	70,0
Mangla, Jhelum, Pakistan (1967)	85·8	65,6
Gardiner, South Saskatchewan, Canada (1968)	85·6	65,4
Afsluitdijk, Netherlands (1932)	82·9	63,3
Rogunsky, Vakhsh, Tadjikistan, USSR*	81·0	62,0
Yacyreta-Apípe, Paraguay–Argentina*	80·0	61,2
Oroville, Feather, Calif, USA (1968)	78·0	60,0
San Luis, Calif, USA (1967)	77·9	59,5
Nurek, Vakhsh, Tadjikistan, USSR*	75·8	57,9
Garrison, Missouri, N Dakota, USA (1956)	66·5	50,8
Cochiti, USA (1975)	62·1	47,5
Tabka, Syria (1976)	60·1	45,9
W A C Bennett (formerly Portage Mt), Peace River, BC, Canada (1967)	57·2	43,7
Kiev, Dnieper, Ukraine, USSR (1964)	56·0	42,7
Aswan High Dam (Sadd-el-Aali), Nile river, Egypt (1970)	55·7	41,3

* under construction.

World's greatest man-made lakes

Name of Dam	Capacity miles³	Capacity km³
Owen Falls, Uganda (1964)	49·16	204,9
Bratsk, Angara River, USSR (1964)	40·59	169,2
Aswan High Dam (Sadd-el-Aali), Nile, Egypt (1970)	39·36	164
Kariba, Rhodesia-Zambia (1959)	39·38	160
Akosombo, Volta, Ghana (1965)†	35·5	148
Daniel Johnson, Manicouagan, Quebec, Canada (1968)	34·07	142
Guri (Raul Leon), Caroni-Orinoco, Venezuela*	32·66	131,1
Krasnoyarsk, Yenisey, USSR	17·58	73,3
WAC Bennett (Portage Mt) Peace River, BC, Canada (1967)	16·79	70
Zeya, E Siberia, USSR*	16·41	68,4
Wadi Tharthar, Tigris, Iraq (1956)	16	66,7
Ust-Ilim, Angara, USSR*	14·23	59,3

† Lake Volta, Ghana is the largest artificial lake measured by area (3275 miles² *8482 km²*).
*. under construction.
Note: Owen Falls Dam regulates the natural Victoria Nyanza which is the world's third largest by area.

World's longest vehicular tunnels

Miles	km		
33·49	53,9	Seikan (rail) 1972–85*	Tsugaru Channel, Japan
19·07	30,7	Moscow Metro (1979)	Belyaevo to Medvedkovo, Moscow, USSR
17·30	27,84	Northern Line (Tube) 1939	East Finchley-Morden, London
13·78	22,17	Oshimizu 1981	Honshū, Japan
12·31	19,82	Simplon II (rail) 1918–22	Brigue, Switzerland-Iselle, Italy
12·30	19,80	Simplon I (rail) 1898–1906	Brigue, Switzerland-Iselle, Italy
11·61	18,68	Shin-Kanmon (rail) 1975	Kanmon Strait, Japan
11·49	18,49	Great Apennine (rail) 1923–34	Vernio, Italy
10·14	16,32	St Gotthard (road) 1971–80	Göschenen-Airolo, Switzerland
10·00	16,0	Rokko (rail) 1972	Japan
9·94	16,0	Hong Kong Subway (1975–80)	Hong Kong
9·85	15,8	Henderson (rail) 1975	Rocky Mts, Colorado, USA
9·26	14,9	St Gotthard (rail) 1872–82	Göschenen-Airolo, Switzerland
9·03	14,5	Lötschberg (rail) 1906–13	Kandersteg-Goppenstein, Switzerland
8·7	14,0	Arlberg (road) (1978)	Langen-St Anton, Austria
8·61	13,85	Hokkuriku (rail) 1957–62	Tsuruga-Imajo-Japan
8·5	13,6	Mont Cenis (rail extension) (1857–81)	Modane, France-Bardonecchia, Italy
8·3	13,35	Shin-shimizu (rail) (1967)	Japan
8·1	13,03	Aki (rail) (1975)	Japan
7·99	12,87	Fréjus II (road) 1974–80	Lanslebourg, France-Susa, Italy
7·78	12,52	Cascade (rail) 1925–29	Berne-Senic, Washington, USA
7·27	11,69	Mont Blanc (road) 1959–65	Pèlerins, France-Entrèves, Italy

* under construction

World's long non-vehicular tunnels

Miles	km		
105	168,9	Delaware Aqueduct 1937–44	New York State, USA
51·5	82,9	Orange-Fish Irrigation 1974	South Africa
49·7	80	Blomen water tunnel	Blomen, Sweden
44	70,8	West Delaware 1960	New York City, USA
31	50	Central Outfall 1975	Mexico City, Mexico
29·8	48	Arpa-Sevan hydro-electric*	Armenia, USSR
20·2	32.1	Kielder water tunnel	Tyne, Wear, Tees, England
18·8	30,3	Thames-Lea Water Supply 1960	Hampton-Walthamstow, London
18·1	29,1	Shandfaken Aqueduct 1923	Catskill, New York State
18·0	29	San Jacinto Aqueduct 1938	California, USA
17·7	28,5	Rendalen hydro-electric*	Norway
17·5	28,2	Kielder Aqueduct 1980	Tyne-Tees, England
15	24,1	Lochaber-hydro-electric 1930	Ben Nevis, Scotland
14·6	23,4	Encumbene-Snowy hydro-electric	New South Wales, Australia
13·7	22	Third Water Tunnel 1970–7	New York City, USA
13	20,9	Florence lake Tunnel 1925	California, USA
13	20,9	Continental Divide Tunnel 1946	Colorado, USA
12	20	Ely-Ouse 1969	Cambridgeshire, England

* under construction
Note: The Chicago Tunnels and Reservoir Plan (TARP), Illinois, USA involves 120 miles *193 km* of sewerage tunnelling. The Majes hydro-electric and water supply in Peru comprises 60·9 miles *98 km* of tunnels. The whole Snowy Mountain system New South Wales, Australia comprises 30·9 miles *49,7 km* of tunnels. It was completed in 1966.

Defence

APPROXIMATE COST OF THE TWO WORLD WARS TO THE MAIN CONTESTANTS IN PEOPLE AND MONEY

	Mobilised (000)	Military Killed (000)	Civilians Killed (000)	Cost in $ million (000)		Mobilised (000)	Military Killed (000)	Civilians Killed (000)	Cost in $ million (000)
World War I					**World War II**				
The Central Powers					*The Axis Powers*				
Germany	11 000	1808	760	58	Germany	11 000	3 250	3810	300
Austria Hungary	7 800	1200	300	24	Italy	4 500	330	500	50
Turkey	2 850	325	2150	3·5	Japan	6 095	1 700	360	100
Bulgaria	1 200	87	275	1					
The Allied Powers					British Empire	8 720	452	80	150
British Empire	8 904	908	30	52	France	6 000	250	360	100
France	8 410	1357	40	50	Poland	1 000	120	5 300	na
Russia (USSR post-1917)	12 000	1700	2000	25·6	USSR	12 500	7 500	17 500	200
Serbia	707	45	650	2·5	USA[1]	14 900	407	Small	350
Italy	5 615	650	Small	18	China[1]	8 000	1 500	7 800	na
USA	4 355	126	Small	33					
Other Allied Powers	2 200	365	—	—					
Total all countries involved	65 000	8500	6642	282	Total from above countries	72 700	15 600	35 800[2]	1600

[1] 1937–45. Figures highly speculative. [2] Does not include full total of victims of wartime genocides. na – not available.

THE TWO GREAT WARS
History's two greatest wars have both been fought in the 20th century. World War I (1914–18) resulted in 9 700 000 fatalities including 765 399 from the United Kingdom. World War II (1939–45) resulted in 54·8 million battle and civilian deaths including 25 million in the USSR, and 6 028 000 or 22·2% of her population in Poland. The UK losses were 265 000.

NAVAL FORCES
Apart from contributing to the nuclear deterrent, navies continue to pursue their time honoured role of maintaining an armed presence at sea while contributing to the protection of trade and of anti-submarine warfare.

LAND AND AIR FORCES
The many confrontations since World War II have been combined action by land and air forces with a minor naval role. The arbiters of decision since the 1930s have been close support aircraft and armoured fighting vehicles, of which the predominant weapon has been the tank.

PRINCIPAL WARS SINCE 1945
1945– China and Taiwan: Nationalist Chinese (with US assistance) *versus* Communist Chinese. Intensive phase lapsed in 1949 with establishment of Communist state.

1946–79 Indo-China/Vietnam: French/South Vietnamese and then USA and South Vietnamese *versus* Communists and North Vietnamese. China *versus* Vietnam 1979; Cambodian (Kampuchean) genocide under Pol Pot regime 1976–79.

1947–71 Indian sub-continent: India *versus* Pakistan, intermittently in Kashmir, plus short intensive confrontations in 1947, 1965 and 3–16 Dec. 1971.

1948–73 Middle East: Israel *versus* Arab States (with interventions by Britain and France). Continuous state of war with intensive confrontations in 1948, 1956, 5–10 June 1967 (6-day war) and 6–24 Oct. 1973.

1950–1953 Korea: North Korea and China *versus* United nations forces. 25 June 1950 invasion of South Korea. Armistice signed 27 July 1953.

1979 Afghanistan: USSR military incursion 24 Dec. 1979. Occupation continues.

Strategic nuclear delivery vehicles
For over three decades a factor in the deterrence from world war has been the threat of nuclear attack by one or other of the major powers linked to the achievement of a measure approaching parity in the means of delivery. It is now possible for many nations to use tactical nuclear missiles on the battlefield by means of aircraft, rockets, artillery or from mines. For strategic delivery six major systems are available:

Inter-continental ballistic missiles with ranges in excess of 4000 miles *6400 km* ICBM

Intermediate-range ballistic missiles with ranges between 1500 and 4000 miles *2400–6400 km* IRBM

Medium-range ballistic missiles with ranges between 500 and 1500 miles *800–2400 km* MRBM

Short-range ballistic missiles with ranges less than 500 miles *800 km* SRBM

Long-range bombers with ranges over 6000 miles *9650 km*

Medium-range bombers with ranges between 3500 and 6000 miles *5600–9650 km*

Ballistic missiles can be launched from ground sites or submarines.

The warheads may be productive of explosions ranging between 25 Megaton (MT) in the largest SS 9 Scarp (USSR) ICBM, with its range of 7500 miles *12 000 km* to 50 kiloton (kT) in the SRBMs. One kT is equivalent to 1000 tons of TNT and one MT or megaton to one million tons of TNT. The USSR SS-18 has 10 'Mirved' warheads (multiple independently targetable re-entry vehicles) each of 1 MT.

Air-launched medium-range nuclear weapons (1984–85)*

USA	USSR
1008	0

Ground-launched medium-range nuclear weapons (1984–85)*

USA/NATO	USSR
48	0

Land-based medium-range nuclear weapons (1984–85)*

USA/NATO	USSR
48	620

Long-range (strategic) nuclear-capable aircraft (1984–85)*

	No. deployed	Range, km
USA		
B-52G	151	12 000
B-52H	90	16 000
TOTAL	241	
USSR		
TU-95	100	12 800
MYA-4	43	11 200
TOTAL	143	

* Source *The Military Balance 1984–85*, International Institute for Strategic Studies, London

Conventional armed force comparisons (1984–85)*

	NATO	Warsaw Pact
Total uniformed manpower	5 024 000	6 169 000
Total reserves	5 424 000	7 119 000
Total manpower deployed in Europe	1 767 000	1 960 000
Main battle tanks	20 742	50 500
Submarines	188	193
Surface ships	1 110	1 132
Naval aircraft	1 458	786
Land-based aircraft	4 382	11 325

* Source *The Military Balance 1984–85*, International Institute for Strategic Studies

Sea-based long-range (strategic) nuclear weapons (1984–85)*

	Total missiles	Total warheads
USA	592	5344
UK	64	384†
France	80	80
TOTAL	736	5808
USSR TOTAL	980*	2–3000

* Source *The Military Balance 1984–85*, International Institute of Strategic Studies, London
† assumes completion of the Chevaline improvements to Polaris in which three warheads per launcher have been replaced by six per launcher

Abbreviations

AAM	air-to-air missile
AB	airburst
ABM	anti-ballistic missile
ACDA	Arms Control and Disarmament Agency
ACHDF	Air Command Home Defence Forces
ACM	Advanced Cruise missile
ADM	atomic demolition munition
AEA	Atomic Energy Authority
AEC	Atomic Energy Commission
AERE	Atomic Energy Research Establishment
AEW	airborne early warning
AFAP	artillery-fired atomic projectile
AfP	Atoms for Peace
AGM	air-to-ground missile
AGR	advanced gas-cooled reactor
ALBM	air-launched ballistic missile
ALCM	air-launched cruise missile
ASALM	advanced strategic air-launched missile
ASAT	anti-satellite
ASBM	air-to-surface ballistic missile

ASC	American Security Council
ASM	air-to-surface missile
ASROC	anti-submarine rocket
ASW	anti-submarine warfare
ATB	advanced technology bomber (Stealth)
AUR	all-up round
AWACS	airborne warning and control system
AWDREY	atomic weapons detection, recognition, and estimation of yield
AWRE	Atomic Weapons Research Establishment
BIT	built-in test
BMD	ballistic missile defence
BMEWS	ballistic missile early warning system
BWR	boiling water reactor
C^3I	command, control, communication and intelligence
CCD	Conference of the Committee on Disarmament
CD	Committee on Disarmament
CDS	command disable system
CEP	circular error probable
CINCUSEUR	Commander in Chief, US Forces, Europe
CM	Cruise missile
CMP	counter military potential
CND	Campaign for Nuclear Disarmament
CPS	Coalition for Peace through Strength
CSCE	Conference on Security and Cooperation in Europe
CTB	comprehensive test ban
DDRE	Directorate of Defense Research and Engineering (US)
DGZ	desired ground zero
DMA	Defense Mapping Agency (US)
DP	deep basing
DSMAC	digital scene matching area correlation
ECM	electronic counter-measures
ELINT	electronic intelligence
EMt	equivalent megatonnage
EMP	electromagnetic pulse
END	European Nuclear Disarmament
ENDC	Eighteen Nation Disarmament Committee
ER-RB	enhanced radiation-reduced blast
ERW	enhanced radiation weapon
FBR	fast-breeder reactor
FBS	forward based systems
FOBS	fractional orbital bombardment system
FOST	Force Océanique Stratégique
FROD	functionally related observable differences
GAMA	GLCM alert and maintenance area
GAO	General Accounting Office (US Congress)
GB	ground burst
GCI	ground-controlled intercept
GLCM	ground-launched cruise missile
GZ	ground zero
HLG	High Level Group (NATO)
IAEA	International Atomic Energy Agency
ICBM	intercontinental ballistic missile
IISS	International Institute of Strategic Studies
INF	intermediate-range nuclear force
IOC	initial operational capability
IRBM	intermediate-range ballistic missile
ISMA	International Satellite Monitoring Agency
JANE	Journalists Against Nuclear Extermination

JCMPO	Joint Cruise Missile Project Office
kT	kiloton
LCC	launch control centre
LNO	limited nuclear options
LNW	limited nuclear war
LORAN	long-range navigation
LOW	launch-on warning
LRTNF	long-range theatre nuclear force
LRTNW	long-range theatre nuclear weapons
LTA	launch-through attack
LWR	light water reactor
MAD	mutual assured destruction
MAPW	Medical Association for Prevention of War
MARV	manoeuvring re-entry vehicle
MBFR	mutual and balanced force reductions
MCANW	Medical Campaign Against Nuclear War
MIRV	multiple independently retargetable re-entry vehicle
MLF	multi-lateral force
MRASM	Medium-range air-to-surface missile
MRBM	medium-range ballistic missile
MRL	multiple rocket launchers
MRTNF	medium-range theatre nuclear force
MRV	multiple re-entry vehicle
MT	megaton
M-X	missile experimental
NATO	North Atlantic Treaty Organisation
NFZ	nuclear free zone
NND	non-nuclear defence
NOP	nuclear operations plans
NORAD	North American Aerospace Defense Command
NPG	Nuclear Planning Group (NATO)
NPT	Non-Proliferation Treaty
NVDA	non-violent direct action
OPANAL	Agency for the Prohibition of Nuclear Weapons in Latin America
PAL	permissive action link
PBV	post-boost vehicle
PGW	precision guided weapon
PLS	pre-launch survivability
PNET	Peaceful Nuclear Explosions Treaty
PTBT	Partial Test Ban Treaty
PTP	probability to penetrate
QRA	quick reaction alert
RW	radiological weapon
RV	re-entry vehicle

SAC	Strategic Air Command (USAF)
SACEUR	Supreme Allied Command, Europe (NATO)
SALT	Strategic Arms Limitation Talks
SAM	surface-to-air missile
SANA	Scientists against Nuclear Arms
SCC	Standing Consultative Commission
SCG	Special Consultative Group (NATO)
SEO	selective employment options
SHAPE	Supreme Headquarters Allied Powers, Europe (NATO)
SICBM	small intercontinental ballistic missile
SIOP	single integrated operational plan
SIPRI	Stockholm International Peace Research Institute
SLBM	submarine-launched ballistic missile
SLCM	sea-launched cruise missile
SOSUS	sound surveillance system
SRAM	short-range attack missile
SRBM	short-range ballistic missile
SRDB	Scientific Research and Development Branch (of UK Home Office)
SSBN	nuclear-powered ballistic missile submarine
SSPK	single shot probability of kill
SSM	surface-to-surface missile
SSN	nuclear-powered attack submarine
START	Strategic Arms Reductions Talks
SUBROC	submarine rocket
TAC	Tactical Air Command
TEL	transporter-erector-launcher
TERCOM	terrain contour matching
TNF	theatre nuclear forces
TNW	theatre nuclear war
TTBT	Threshold Test Ban Treaty
UNA	United Nations Association
UNSSD	United Nations Special Session on Disarmament
USAF	United States Air Force
VLS	vertical launch system
WDC	World Disarmament Campaign
WTO	Warsaw Treaty Organisation

Force comparisons of major nuclear systems

Land-based long-range (strategic) nuclear weapons*

	Total no of launchers	Yield of warhead	Number of warheads per launcher	Accuracy, m (circle of error probable)	Range, km
USA					
Titan II	37	9MT	1	1500	15 000
Minuteman II	450	1.2MT	1	370	11 300
Minuteman III (1970)	250	170kT	3	280	14 800
Minuteman III (1980)	300	335kT	3	220	12 900
TOTAL	1037		2137		
USSR					
SS11	520	1MT/300kT	3 or 1†	1200	8–10 000
SS13	60	750kT	1	2000	10 000
SS17	150	20kT/1MT	4 or 1	450	10 000
SS18	308	900kT/20MT	8 or 1	300–450	10 000
SS19	360	550kT/5MT	6 or 1	300	10 000
TOTAL	1398		approx. 6000		

* Source *The Military Balance 1984–85* (published annually by The International Institute for Strategic Studies, London)
† Many Soviet missiles are produced in a range of modes, each with differing configurations of numbers and yields of warheads

International Organisations

The United Nations

'A general international organisation . . . for the maintenance of international peace and security' was recognised as desirable in Clause 4 of the proposals of the Four-Nation Conference of Foreign Ministers signed in Moscow on 30 Oct. 1943 by R Anthony Eden, later the Earl of Avon (1897–1977) (UK), Cordell Hull (1871–1955) (USA), Vyacheslav M Skryabin, *alias* Molotov (b. 1890) (USSR), and Ambassador Foo Pingsheung (China).

Ways and means were resolved at the mansion of Dumbarton Oaks, Washington, DC, USA, between 21 Aug. and 7 Oct. 1944. A final step was taken at San Francisco, California, USA, between 25 Apr. and 26 June 1945 when delegates of 50 participating states signed the Charter (Poland signed on 15 Oct. 1945). This came into force on 24 Oct. 1945, when the four above-mentioned states, plus France and a majority of the other 46 states, had ratified the Charter. The first regular session was held in London on 10 Jan.–14 Feb. 1946.

Of the 168 *de facto* sovereign states of the world, 158 are now in membership including the two USSR republics of Byelorussia and the Ukraine which have separate membership.
The non-members are:
Andorra
China (Taiwan)
Kiribati
Korea, Democratic People's Republic of
Korea, Republic of
Liechtenstein
Monaco
Nauru
San Marino
Switzerland
Tonga
Tuvalu
Vatican City (Holy See)

The United Nations' principal organs are:

The General Assembly consisting of all member nations, each with up to five delegates but one vote, and meeting annually in regular sessions with provision for special sessions. The Assembly has seven main committees, on which there is the right of representation by all member nations. These are (1) Political and Security, (2) Economic and Financial, (3) Social, Humanitarian and Cultural, (4) Decolonisation, (5) Administration and Budgetary, (6) Legal, and the Special Political.

The Security Council, consisting of 15 members, each with one representative, of whom there are five permanent members (China, France, the USSR, the United Kingdom and the USA) and 10 elected members serving a two-year term. Apart from procedural questions, an affirmative majority vote of at least nine must include that of all five permanent members. It is from this stipulation that the so-called veto arises.

The Economic and Social Council, consisting of 54 members elected for three-year terms, is responsible for carrying out the functions of the General Assembly's second and third Committees, viz. economic, social, educational, health and cultural matters. It had the following Functional Commissions in 1983: (1) Statistical,

(2) Population, (3) Social Development, (4) Narcotic Drugs, (5) Human Rights, (6) Status of Women. The Council has also established Economic Commissions, as follows: (1) for Europe (ECE), (2) for Asia and the Pacific (ESCAP), (3) for Latin America (ECLA), (4) for Africa (ECA) and (5) for Western Asia (ECWA).

The International Court of Justice or World Court, comprising 15 Judges (quorum of nine) of different nations, each serving a nine-year term and meeting at 's Gravenhage (The Hague), Netherlands. All members of the UN plus Liechtenstein, San Marino and Switzerland are parties to the Statute of the Court. Only States may be parties in contentious cases. In the event of a party's failing to adhere to a judgment, the other party may have recourse to the Security Council. Judgments are final and without appeal but can be reopened on grounds of a new decisive factor within ten years.

The Secretariat. The principal administrative officer is the Secretary General who is appointed by the General Assembly for a five-year term. This office has been held thus:
Trygve Halvdan Lie (1896–1968) (Norway) 1 Feb. 1946–10 Nov. 1952.
Dag Hjalmar Agne Carl Hammarskjöld (1905–61) (Sweden) 10 Apr. 1953–18 Sept. 1961.
U Maung Thant (1909–74) (Burma) (acting) 3 Nov. 1961–30 Nov. 1962, (permanent) 30 Nov. 1962–31 Dec. 1971.
Kurt Waldheim (b. 21 Dec. 1918) (Austria) 1 Jan. 1972–31 Dec. 1981.
Javier Pérez de Cuéllar (b. 19 Jan. 1920) (Peru) 1 Jan. 1982 (in office).

Specialised Agencies of the United nations
There are 15 specialised agencies, which in order of absorption or creation are as follows:

ILO
International Labour Organisation (Headquarters – Geneva). Founded 11 Apr. 1919 in connection with the League of Nations. Re-established as the senior UN specialised agency, 14 Dec. 1946. Especially concerned with social justice, hours of work, unemployment, wages, industrial sickness, and protection of foreign workers.

FAO
Food and Agriculture Organisation of the United Nations (Headquarters – Rome). Established, 16 Oct. 1945. Became UN agency, 14 Dec. 1946. Objects: to raise levels of nutrition and standards of living; to improve the production and distribution of agricultural products. FAO provides an Intelligence Service on Agriculture, Forestry and Fisheries.

UNESCO
United Nations Educational, Scientific and Cultural Organisation (Headquarters – Paris). Established, 4 Nov. 1946. Objects: to stimulate popular education and the spread of culture, and to diffuse knowledge through all means of mass communication; to further universal respect for justice, the rule of law, human rights and fundamental freedoms. Became a UN agency, 14 Dec. 1946.

ICAO
International Civil Aviation Organisation (Headquarters – Montreal). Established, 4 Apr. 1947. Objects: to study the problems of international civil aviation; to encourage safety measures and co-ordinate facilities required for safe international flight. A UN agency from 13 May 1947.

IBRD
International Bank for Reconstruction and Development (The World Bank) (Headquarters – Washington). Established, 27 Dec. 1945. Objects: to assist in the reconstruction and development of territories of members by aiding capital investment. Because a UN agency, 15 Nov. 1947.

The trusteeship council

This council administers territories under UN trusteeship. Twelve territories have been under UN trusteeship:

Original Trust Territory	Subsequent Status
Tanganyika (UK)	Independent, 9 Dec. 1961; merged with Zanzibar, 26 Apr. 1964, as Tanzania
Ruanda–Urundi (Belgium)	Two independent states, 1 July 1962
Somaliland (Italy)	Independent, 1 July 1960
Cameroons (UK)	Northern part joined Nigeria, 1 June 1961; southern part joined Cameroon, 1 Oct. 1961.
Cameroons (France)	Independent republic of Cameroon, 1 Jan. 1960
Togoland (UK)	United with Gold Coast, to form Ghana, 6 Mar. 1957
Togoland (France)	Independent republic of Togo, 27 Apr. 1960
Western Samoa (NZ)	Independent, 1 Jan. 1962
Nauru (Australia, NZ and UK)	Independent, 31 Jan. 1968
New Guinea (Australia)	Merged with Papua to form Papua New Guinea, independent 16 Sept. 1975
Pacific Islands (USA) comprising the Carolines, Marshalls and Marianas (excepting Guam)	The Northern Mariana Islands became a Commonwealth territory of the USA on 9 Jan. 1978 but remain legally part of the Trust Territory until the termination of the trusteeship. The other islands are grouped in three territories which are to enter into 'free association' with the USA.

IMF
International Monetary Fund (Headquarters – Washington). Established, 27 Dec. 1945. Objects: to promote international monetary co-operation, the expansion of international trade and stability of exchange rates. A UN agency from 15 Nov. 1947.

UPU
Universal Postal Union (Headquarters – Berne, Switzerland). Established 1 July 1875; became a UN specialised agency, 1 July 1948. Objects: to unite members in a single postal territory.

WHO
World Health Organisation (Headquarters – Geneva). Established, 7 Apr. 1948. Objects: to promote the attainment by all peoples of the highest possible standard of health. Its services are both advisory and technical. A UN agency from 10 July 1948.

ITU
International Telecommunication Union (Headquarters – Geneva). Founded 17 May 1865; incorporated in the United Nations, 10 Jan. 1949. Objects: to seek the standardisation of procedures concerning greater efficacy of telecommunications and to allocate frequencies.

WMO
World Meteorological Organisation (Headquarters – Geneva). Established 11 Oct 1947. Objects: to standardise meteorological observations; to secure their publication, and apply the information for the greater safety of aviation and shipping and benefit of agriculture, etc. A UN agency from 20 Dec. 1951.

IFC
International Finance Corporation (Headquarters – Washington). Established, 24 July 1956. Objects: to promote the flow of private capital internationally and to stimulate the capital markets. Membership is open only to those countries that are members of the World Bank. A UN agency from 20 Feb. 1957.

IMCO
Inter-Governmental Maritime Consultative Organisation (Headquarters – London). Established 17 Mar. 1958. Objects: to co-ordinate safety at sea and to secure the freedom of passage. A UN agency from 13 Jan. 1959.

IDA
International Development Association (Headquarters – Washington). Established, 24 Sept 1960. Object: to assist less developed countries by providing credits on special terms. Membership limited as in IFC. A UN agency from 27 Mar. 1961.

WIPO
World Intellectual Property Organisation (Headquarters – Geneva). Established, 26 Apr. 1970; became a UN specialised agency, 17 Dec. 1974. Objects: to promote the protection of intellectual property (inventions, designs, copyright, etc.) and to centralise administration of its legal and technical aspects.

IFAD
International Fund for Agricultural Development (Headquarters – Rome). Established, 30 Nov. 1977; became a UN specialised agency, 15 Dec. 1977. Objects: to mobilise substantial additional resources (grants or loans) on concessional terms to increase food production in developing countries.

NATO

North Atlantic Treaty Organisation
NATO, an idea first broached by the Secretary of State for External Affairs for Canada on 28 Apr. 1948, came into existence on 4 Apr. 1949 and into force on 24 Aug. 1949, with Belgium, Canada, Denmark, France, Iceland, Italy, Luxembourg, the Netherlands, Norway, Portugal, the United Kingdom and the USA. Greece and Turkey were admitted on 18 Feb. 1952, the Federal Republic of Germany on 5 May 1955, and Spain on 30 May 1982 bringing the total of countries to 16. France withdrew from NATO's military affairs on 1 July 1966 and the HQ was moved from Paris to Brussels. Greece left the military command structure on 14 Aug. 1974 but its re-integration was approved by NATO's Defence Planning Committee on 20 Oct. 1980.

OECD

Organisation for Economic Co-operation and Development
Founded as a European body (OEEC) on 20 Sept. 1961, the Organisation after 14 years was reconstituted to embrace other Western countries. It now comprises 24 countries: Australia, Austria, Belgium, Canada, Denmark, Finland, France, Federal Republic of Germany, Greece, Iceland, Ireland, Italy, Japan, Luxembourg, Netherlands, New Zealand, Norway, Portugal, Spain, Sweden, Switzerland, Turkey, United Kingdom and USA, with Yugoslavia (special status).

Headquarters are in Paris. The aims are to achieve the highest sustainable economic growth and level of employment with a rising standard of living compatible with financial stability.

EFTA

European Free Trade Association
Established 3 May 1960.
With the departure of the United Kingdom and Denmark, EFTA comprised six countries, viz. Austria, Iceland, Norway, Portugal, Sweden and Switzerland, with Finland as an associate member. EFTA was established on 27 Mar. 1961.

The EFTA countries (except Norway) signed a free trade agreement with the EEC on 22 July 1972 and Norway did so on 14 May 1973.

OAU

Organisation of African Unity
In Addis Ababa, Ethiopia, on 25 May 1963, 32 African countries established the organisation for common defence of independence, the elimination of colonialism and co-ordination of economic policies. By 1980 the OAU had 50 members. English and French are recognised as official languages in addition to African languages.

OPEC

Organization of the Petroleum Exporting Countries
Established 21 Jan. 1961. Founded by a group of 13 major oil exporting countries to represent their interests in dealings with the major oil companies, it sets price levels per barrel of crude oil for their markets that effectively control the world market price. Members include Algeria, Ecuador, Gabon, Indonesia, Iran, Iraq, Kuwait, Libya, Nigeria, Qatar, Saudi Arabia, United Arab Emirates, Venezuela.

The European Communities

ECSC
European Coal and Steel Community

EEC
European Economic Community

EURATOM
European Atomic Energy Community
The ECSC was established by a treaty signed on 18 April 1951, effective from 25 July 1952. The founding members were Belgium, France, the Federal Republic of Germany, Italy, Luxembourg and the Netherlands. These six countries were also the original members of the EEC (or Common Market) and EURATOM, established by two treaties signed in Rome on 25 March 1957, both effective from 1 Jan. 1958. Common institutions for the three Communities were established by a treaty signed on 8 April 1965, effective from 1 July 1967. The six original members established a complete customs union, and introduced a common external tariff, on 1 July 1968.

Denmark, Ireland and the United Kingdom joined the three Communities on 1 Jan. 1973, having signed a treaty of accession on 22 Jan. 1972. The first direct elections to the European Parliament were held on 7–10 June 1979, when 410 members were elected.

Greece signed a treaty of accession on 28 May 1979 and joined the Communities on 1 Jan. 1981, increasing the membership to 10. The European Parliament was increased to 434 members with 24 elected from Greece on 18 Oct. 1981. Spain's and Portugal's applications have been accepted, with accession in January 1986.

The Council of Europe

The Council of Europe, with headquarters in Strasbourg (France), was established in May 1949. It was founded in the wake of the trauma of World War II caused by extremist political régimes in Germany and Italy. Its object was to achieve greater unity between its member nations to safeguard their European heritage and to facilitate both economic and social progress.

The principal organ of the Council is its Committee of Ministers, consisting of the Foreign Ministers of the 21 member countries.

The Council's principal achievement has been the signing of the European convention for the Protection of Human Rights and Fundamental Freedoms in 1950, under which was established the European Commission and the European Court of Human Rights. All the member states' inhabitants (about 390 million at mid-1980) are thus protected against their own Governments on matters of basic human rights such as the right to life; freedom from torture; right to liberty and security of person; right to respect for private and family life; freedom of thought, conscience and religion; freedom of expression; freedom of association and the right to marry.

The 21 member nations and their dates of adherence are:

Austria	1957	Liechtenstein	1978
Belgium	1950	Luxembourg	1950
Cyprus	1961	Malta	1966
Denmark	1950	Netherlands	1950
France	1950	Norway	1950
Germany		Portugal	1978
(Fed. Rep.)	1950	Spain	1978
Greece	1950	Sweden	1950
Iceland	1950	Switzerland	1972
Ireland	1950	Turkey	1950
Italy	1950	United Kingdom	1950

Countries of the World

NON-SOVEREIGN COUNTRIES

The trend towards full national sovereign status has substantially reduced the total number of non-sovereign territories. With a few obvious exceptions, these territories now tend to have too small a population and/or resources to sustain statehood.

The non-sovereign territories are divided below into four parts:
  (a) Territories administered by the United Kingdom.
  (b) Territories administered by Australia or New Zealand.
  (c) Territories administered by the United States of America.
  (d) Other non-sovereign territories.

TERRITORIES ADMINISTERED BY THE UNITED KINGDOM

(excluding the Channel Islands and the Isle of Man)

Anguilla

Location: Anguilla (with Scrub I. and other offshore islands) lies about 5 miles *8 km* north of St Martin, in the Leeward Islands, West Indies. Sombrero I. lies about 30 miles *48 km* north of Anguilla.
Area: 37 miles² *96 km²* (Anguilla 35 miles² *91 km²*, Sombrero 2 miles² *5 km²*).
Population: 6500 (1977 estimate).
Capital: The Valley.

Bermuda

Location: The Bermudas (or Somers Islands) are a group of islands in the western North Atlantic Ocean, about 570 miles *917 km* east of Cape Hatteras in North Carolina, USA.
Area: 20·59 miles² *53,3 km²*.
Population: 58 525 (census of 29 Oct. 1970); 67 761 (census of 12 May 1980). 20 islands are inhabited.
Capital: Hamilton (population about 3000 in 1980), on Bermuda I.

British Antarctic Territory

Location: Comprises all the land south of latitude 60°S, situated between longitude 20°W and 80°W. This includes the South Shetland Islands, the South Orkney Islands, Graham Land and a part of the mainland of Antarctica.
Area: The total area within the sector is about 2 095 000 miles² *5 425 000 km²*, of which land (excluding ice-shelves) occupies about 150 000 miles² *388 498 km²*. The South Shetland Is. are about 130 miles² *336 km²* and the South Orkney Is. 240 miles² *621 km²*.
Population: There are no permanent inhabitants. The only occupants are scientific workers, of whom UK personnel number about 100.
Capital: There being no settlements, the Territory is administered from Stanley, Falkland Is. (*q.v.*).

British Indian Ocean Territory

Location: The territory is now confined to the Chagos Archipelago (or Oil Islands) which is 1180 miles *1899 km* north-east of (and formerly administered by) Mauritius. The islands of Aldabra, Farquhar and Desroches (originally parts of the territory) were restored to Seychelles when the latter became independent on 29 June 1976.
Area: about 20 miles² *52 km²*.
Population: 747 (30 June 1962). The territory has a 'floating' population of contract labourers, but no permanent population.

British Virgin Islands

Location and Composition: Comprises the eastern part of the Virgin Islands group (the western part is a US colony), and lies to the east of Puerto Rico, in the West Indies.
Area: About 59 miles² *153 km²* (Tortola 21 miles² *54 km²*, Virgin Gorda 8¼ miles² *21 km²*, Anegada 15 miles² *39 km²*, Jost van Dyke 3¼ miles² *8 km²*).
Population: 12 034 in 1980 (Tortola 9322; Virgin Gorda 1443; Anegada 169; Jost van Dyke 136; other islands 82; marine population 220; institutional population 662).
Capital: Road Town (population 3976 in 1980); on Tortola.

Cayman Islands

Location: A group of three islands, in the Caribbean Sea, south of Cuba. The principal island, Grand Cayman, is 178 miles *286 km* west of Jamaica.
Area: approximately 100 miles² *259 km²* (Grand Cayman 76 miles² *197 km²*, Cayman Brac 14 miles² *36 km²*, Little Cayman 10 miles² *26 km²*).
Population: 10 460 (Grand Cayman 9151, Cayman Brac 1289, Little Cayman 20) at census of 7 Apr. 1970; 16 677 (census of 1 July 1979).
Capital: George Town (population 7617 in 1979).

Falkland Islands and Dependencies

Location: A group of islands in the south-western Atlantic Ocean, about 480 miles *772 km* north-east of Cape Horn, South America. The Dependencies are South Georgia, an island 800 miles *1287 km* to the east, and the South Sandwich Islands, 470 miles *756 km* south-east of South Georgia.
Area: approximately 6280 miles² *16 265 km²*, of which the Falklands are approximately 4700 miles² *12 173 km²* (East Falkland and adjacent islands 2610 miles² *6760 km²*, West Falkland, etc., 2090 miles² *5413 km²*). South Georgia is 1450 miles² *3755 km²* and the Sandwich Is. 130 miles² *336 km²*.
Population: Falkland Islands 1855 (census of 7 Dec. 1980). South Goergia has a small population (22 residents in 1980) which is highest during the summer whaling season.
Capital: Port Stanley (population 1079 in 1972), on East Falkland.

City of Gibraltar

Location: A narrow peninsula on the south coast of Spain, commanding the north side of the Atlantic entrance to the Mediterranean Sea.
Area: 2·1 miles² *5,5 km²* (2¾ miles *4,4 km* long, greatest breadth nearly 1 mile *1,6 km*).
Population: 31 183 (1982 estimate).
Chief (and only) Town: Gibraltar, at north-western corner of the Rock.

Hong Kong

Location: A peninsula in the central south coast of the Guangdong (Kwangtung) province of southern China, the island of Hong Kong and some 235 other islands, the largest of which is Lantao (58 miles² *150 km²*).
Area: 409·2 miles² *1059,8 km²* (Hong Kong Island 30·1 miles² *78,0 km²*, Kowloon peninsula 4·1 miles² *10,5 km²*, Stonecutters Island ¼ mile² *0,6 km²*, New Territories (leased) 374·8 miles² *970,7 km²*). Including the ocean area within administrative boundaries, the total is 1126 miles² *2916 km²*.
Population: 5 313 000 (1983 estimate). About 98% are Chinese, many being British subjects by virtue of birth in the Colony.
Languages: Mainly Chinese (Cantonese); English 8·5%.
Religion: Predominantly Buddhist.
Capital City and Other Principal Towns (population at Census, 1971): Victoria (520 932), on Hong Kong Island; Kowloon; New Kowloon; North Point; Tsuen Wan; Cheung Chau (an island).
Status and Government: A Crown Colony with the Governor assisted by an Executive Council (16 in 1980) and a Legislative Council (47, including 26 elected, in 1980).
Recent History: British colony, 1841. New Territories leased in 1898 for 99 years. Attacked by Japan, 8 Dec. 1941. Surrendered, 25 Dec. 1941. Recaptured by UK forces, 30 Aug. 1945. UK military administration, 3 Sept. 1945 to May 1946. Formal Japanese surrender, 16 Sept. 1945. Many refugees during Chinese civil war 1948–50, and subsequently, notably on 1–25 May 1962.
Economic Situation: The principal occupations are manufacturing (notably cotton piece goods, shirts, electric products, cameras, toys and games, footwear), services and commerce. Agriculture (poultry and pigs), fishing and mining (notably iron) are carried on.
Currency: 100 cents = 1 Hong Kong dollar (£1 sterling = HK $ 9·431 at 26 April 1985).
Climate: The sub-tropical summer (28°C *82°F* July) is hot and humid with the winter cool and dry (15°C *59°F* February). The average annual rainfall is 2160 mm *85 in*, three-quarters of which falls from June to August in the south-west monsoon season.

Montserrat

Location: An island about 35 miles *56 km* north of Basse Terre, Guadeloupe, in the Leeward Islands, West Indies.
Area: 38 miles² *98 km²*.
Population: 11 698 (census of 7 Apr. 1970); 12 073 (census of 12 May 1980).
Capital: Plymouth (population 3200 in 1980), on south-west coast.

Location of Commonwealth and other non-sovereign Countries of the World

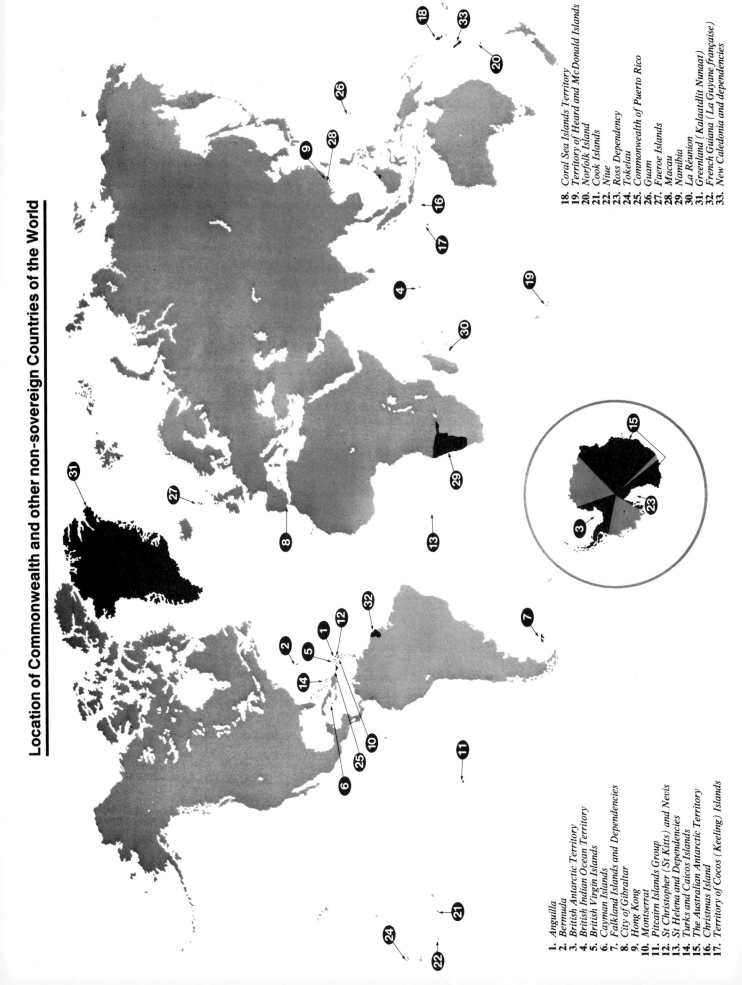

1. Anguilla
2. Bermuda
3. British Antarctic Territory
4. British Indian Ocean Territory
5. British Virgin Islands
6. Cayman Islands
7. Falkland Islands and Dependencies
8. City of Gibraltar
9. Hong Kong
10. Montserrat
11. Pitcairn Islands Group
12. St Christopher (St Kitts) and Nevis
13. St Helena and Dependencies
14. Turks and Caicos Islands
15. The Australian Antarctic Territory
16. Christmas Island
17. Territory of Cocos (Keeling) Islands
18. Coral Sea Islands Territory
19. Territory of Heard and McDonald Islands
20. Norfolk Island
21. Cook Islands
22. Niue
23. Ross Dependency
24. Tokelau
25. Commonwealth of Puerto Rico
26. Guam
27. Faeroe Islands
28. Macau
29. Namibia
30. La Réunion
31. Greenland (Kalaatdlit Nunaat)
32. French Guiana (La Guyane française)
33. New Caledonia and dependencies

Pitcairn Islands Group

Location: Four islands in the south Pacific Ocean, about 3000 miles *4828 km* east of New Zealand and 3500 miles *5632 km* south-west of Panama: Pitcairn, Henderson, Ducie, Oeno.
Area: 18·5 miles² *48 km²*, including Pitcairn 1·75 miles² *4,5 km²*.
Population: Pitcairn 61 (1983 count).
Principal settlement: Adamstown.

St Christopher (St Kitts) and Nevis

Location: In the northern part of the Leeward Islands, in the West Indies. The main island is St Christopher (or St Kitts), with Nevis 3 miles *5 km* to the south-east.
Area: 101 miles² *262 km²* (St Christopher 65 miles² *168 km²*, Nevis 36 miles² *93 km²*).
Population: 44 404 in 1980.
Capital: Basse-terre (population 14 725 in 1980), on coast of St Christopher.

St Helena and Dependencies

Location and Composition: An island in the South Atlantic Ocean, 1200 miles *1931 km* west of Africa. The dependencies are: (*a*) Ascension, an island 700 miles *1126 km* to the north-west; (*b*) the Tristan da Cunha group, comprising: Tristan da Cunha, 1320 miles *2124 km* south-west of St Helena; Inaccessible Island, 20 miles *32 km* west of Tristan; the three Nightingale Islands (Nightingale, Middle Island and Stoltenhoff Island), 20 miles *32 km* south of Tristan; Gough Island (Diego Alvarez), 220 miles *354 km* south of Tristan.
Area: 162 miles² *419 km²* (St Helena 47·3 miles² *122 km²*. Ascension 34 miles² *88 km²*, Tristan da Cunha 38 miles² *98 km²*, Gough 35 miles² *90 km²*, Inaccessible 4 miles² *10 km²*, Nightingale ¾ mile² *2 km²*).
Population: St Helena 5499 (1982); Ascension 1625; Tristan da Cunha 325.
Capital: Jamestown (population 1862 at 31 Dec. 1978).
Principal Settlements: Ascension – Georgetown (or Garrison); Tristan da Cunha – Edinburgh.

Turks and Caicos Islands

Location: Two groups of islands at the south-eastern end of the Bahamas, 120 miles *193 km* north of Hispaniola (Haiti and Dominican Republic), in the West Indies. There are over 30 islands, including eight Turks Islands.
Area: 166 miles² *430 km²*.
Population: 7436 (1980 census). There are six inhabited islands (two in the Turks Islands, four in the Caicos Islands).
Capital: Cockburn Town, on Grand Turk Island (population 2897 in 1978).

TERRITORIES ADMINISTERED BY AUSTRALIA OR NEW ZEALAND
Australian Dependencies

The Australian Antarctic Territory

Location: Comprises all land south of latitude 60°S, between 45°E and 160°E, except for French territory of Terre Adélie, whose boundaries were fixed on 1 Apr. 1938 as between 136°E and 142°E.
Area: 2 333 624 miles² *6 044 068 km²* of land and 29 251 miles² *75 759 km²* of ice shelf.

Christmas Island

Location: In the Indian Ocean, 223 miles *360 km* south of Java Head.
Area: Approximately 52 miles² *135 km²*.
Population: 2691 (census of 30 June 1971); 3000 (1820 Chinese, 750 Malays, 350 Europeans, 90 others) (estimate).
Principal settlement: Flying Fish Cove.

Territory of Cocos (Keeling) Islands

Location: In the Indian Ocean, about 1720 miles *2768 km* north-west of Perth. The territory contains 27 islands. North Keeling Island lies about 15 miles *24 km* north of the main group.
Area: Approximately 5½ miles² *14 km²*.
Population: 579 (Home Island 363, West Island 216) at 30 June 1983.
Principal settlement: Bantam Village (on Home Island).

Coral Sea Islands Territory

Location: East of Queensland, between the Great Barrier Reef and 157° 10′ E longitude.
Population: 3 meteorologists on an island in the Willis Group.

Territory of Heard and MacDonald Islands

Location: In the southern Indian Ocean, south-east of the Kerguelen Islands, and about 2500 miles *4023 km* south-west of Fremantle.
Area: 113 miles² *292 km²*. No permanent inhabitants.

Norfolk Island

Location: In south-west Pacific Ocean 1042 miles *1676 km* from Sydney and about 400 miles *643 km* from New Zealand. Philip Island is about 4 miles *6 km* south of Norfolk Island.
Area: 13·34 miles² *34,55 km²*.
Population: 1683 (census of 30 June 1971); 2180 (estimate for 30 June 1979). Figures include visitors. Philip Island and Nepean Island are uninhabited.
Seat of Government: Kingston.

New Zealand Dependencies

Cook Islands

Location: In the southern Pacific Ocean, between about 1750 miles *2816 km* and 2350 miles *3782 km* north-east of New Zealand, between 8°S and 23°S, and 156°W and 167°W. Comprises 15 atolls or islands (Northern group 7, Lower group 8).
Area: 90·3 miles² *234 km²*. Main islands are Rarotonga (16 602 acres *6718 ha*), Mangaia (12 800 acres *5180 ha*), Atiu (6654 acres *2693 ha*), Mitiaro (5500 acres *2226 ha*), Mauke (Parry Is.) (4552 acres *1842 ha*), Aitutaki (4461 acres *1805 ha*) and Penrhyn (Tongareva) (2432 acres *985 ha*).
Population: 17 754 (1981); approx. 24 500 Cook Islanders in New Zealand (1982).
Chief Town: Avarua, on Rarotonga Island.

Territories administered by the United States of America

Territory	Area (miles²)	Area (km²)	Population		Capital
North America					
Commonwealth of Puerto Rico	3435	*8897*	3 187 570	(1/4/80)	San Juan
Virgin Islands of the United States	133	*344*	95 214	(1/4/80)	Charlotte Amalie
Oceania					
American Samoa	76	*197*	32 395	(1/4/80)	Pago Pago
Guam	212	*549*	110 000	(1981 estimate)	Agaña
Johnston and Sand Islands	<½	*1*	300	(1978 estimate)	—
Midway Islands	2	*5*	2 256	(1975 estimate)	—
Wake Island	3	*8*	300	(1980 census)	—
Trust Territory of the Pacific Islands	687*	*1779**	116 974	(1980 census)	Saipan

* Inhabited dry land only.

Other non-sovereign territories

Territory	Administering Country	Area (miles²)	Area (km²)	Population		Capital
Europe						
Faeroe Islands	Denmark	540	*1399*	13 951	(31/12/81)	Thorshavn
Svalbard and Jan Mayen Islands	Norway	24 101	*62 422*	4012	(31/12/82)*	Ny Ålesund
Asia						
Macau (or Macao)	Portugal	6	*16*	261 680	(1981 census)	Macau
Africa						
French Southern and Antarctic Territories	France	2918	*7557*	168	(1983 estimate)	—
Mayotte†	France	144	*374*	47 246	(1982 estimate)	Dzaoudzi
Namibia (South West Africa)‡	South Africa§	318 261	*824 292*	1 039 800	(1982 estimate)	Windhoek
La Réunion	France	969	*2510*	515 814	(1982 census)	Saint-Denis
North America						
Greenland	Denmark	840 000	*2 175 600*	51 903	(1/1/83)	Godthåb (Nuuk)
St Pierre and Miquelon	France	93	*242*	6041	(1982 census)	St Pierre
Central America						
Guadeloupe and dependencies	France	687	*1779*	328 400	(1982 census)	Pointe-à-Pitre
Martinique	France	425	*1102*	328 566	(1982 census)	Fort-de-France
Netherlands Antilles	Netherlands	371	*961*	260 000	(1981)	Willemstad
South America						
French Guiana	France	35 000	*91 000*	73 022	(1982 census)	Cayenne
Oceania						
French Polynesia	France	c.1500	*c.4000*	148 000	(1983 estimate)	Papeete
New Caledonia and dependencies	France	7358	*19 058*	146 600	(1983 estimate)	Nouméa
Wallis and Futuna Islands	France	77	*200*	11 943	(1982 census)	Mata-Utu

* Inhabited only during winter season.
† Mayotte is part of the Comoros archipelago and is regarded by the Comoros government as part of its territory. However, since the Comoros declared independence in July 1975 the island of Mayotte has remained under French administration.
‡ Including data for Walvis Bay (area 434 miles² *1124 km²*, population 23 461 in 1970), an integral part of South Africa.
§ South Africa's jurisdiction is disputed by the UN, which claims a protectorate over the territory.

Niue

Location: Niue Island is in the southern Pacific Ocean, 1343 miles *2161 km* north of Auckland, New Zealand, between Tonga and the Cook Islands.
Area: 64 028 acres (100·04 miles² *259 km²*).
Population: 3298 (1981); approx. 10 000 Niueans in New Zealand (1982).
Capital: Alofi.

Ross Dependency

Location: All the land between 160°E and 150°W longitude (moving eastward) and south of 60°S latitude, comprising a sector of the mainland of Antarctica, including the Ross Ice Shelf, and some off-shore islands.
Area: The mainland area is estimated at 160 000 miles² *414 400 km²* and the permanent ice shelf at 130 000 miles² *336 700 km²*.
Population: No permanent inhabitants, but some bases are permanently occupied by scientific personnel.

Tokelau

Location: Tokelau (formerly known as Tokelau Islands) consist of three atolls in the central Pacific Ocean, about 300 miles *483 km* north of Western Samoa.
Area: Approximately 2500 acres *1010 ha* (Nukunonu 1350 acres *545 ha*, Fakaofo 650 acres *260 ha*, Atafu 500 acres *200 ha*), or about 4 miles² *10 km²*.
Population: 1572 (Nukunonu 368, Fakaofo 650, Atafu 554).

SOVEREIGN COUNTRIES
By 1985 there were 169 sovereign countries in the world. In this book the United Kingdom has been treated separately, and in the pages which follow, the salient details of the 168 other sovereign countries are given.

Afghanistan

Official name: De Afghanistan Democrateek Jamhuriat (Pushtu) or Jamhuriat Democrateek ye Afghanistan (Dari): The Democratic Republic of Afghanistan.
Population: 15 551 358 (census of 23 June 1979), including an estimate of 2 500 000 for Kuchies (nomads).
Area: 250 000 miles² *647 497 km²*.
Languages: Dari (a Persian dialect), Pushtu (Pushtu or Pakhto).
Religion: Muslim.
Capital city: Kabul, population 913 164 (including suburbs) at 1979 census.
Other principal towns (1979): Qandahar (Kandahar) 178 409; Herat 140 323; Mazar-i-Sharif 103 372; Jalalabad 53 915; Kunduz 53 251.
Highest point: Noshaq, 24 581 ft *7492 m* (first climbed 17 Aug. 1960).
Principal mountain ranges: Hindu Kush, Koh-i-Baba, Band-i-Baian, Band-i-Baba, Paropamisus, Paghman.

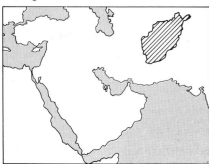

AFGHANISTAN

Principal rivers: Helmand, Bandihala-Khoulm, Kabul, Murghab, Kunduz, Hari Rud, Farah Rud, Ab-i-Panja.
Head of State: Babrak Karmal (b. 1929), President of the Revolutionary Council and General Secretary of the Central Committee of the People's Democratic Party.
Prime Minister: Soltan Ali Keshtmand (b. 1935).
Climate: Wide variations between highlands and lowlands. Average annual rainfall 300 mm *12 in*. In Kabul, July (16°C *61°F* to 33°C *92°F*) and August (15°C *59°F* to 33°C *91°F*) hottest; Jan. (−8°C *18°F* to 2°C *36°F*) coldest; March rainiest (7 days). Maximum temperature up to 49°C *120°F*; minimum below −23°C − *10°F*.
Labour force: 3 868 081 (settled population only) aged 8 and over (1979 census): Agriculture, forestry and fishing 61·3%; Industry (mining, manufacturing, utilities) 12·8% (manufacturing 10·9%); Services 24·6%. Figures exclude persons seeking work for the first time.
Gross national product: 156 000 million afghanis (at 1978 prices) in year ending 20 March 1979: Agriculture, forestry and fishing 58·7%; Industry 22·5%; Services 14·0%.
Exports: US$694·3 million in 1981: Natural gas 39·3%; Dried fruit and nuts 25·2%; Fresh fruit 7·3%; Raw cotton 3·3%.
Monetary unit: Afghani. 1 afghani = 100 puls (puli).
Denominations:
  Coins 25, 50 puls; 1, 2, 5 afghanis.
  Notes 10, 20, 50, 100, 500, 1000 afghanis.
Exchange rate to £ sterling: 99 (14 Jan. 1985).
Political history and government: Formerly an hereditary kingdom, under British influence until 1919. Afghanistan became a limited constitutional monarchy, without political parties, on 1 Oct. 1964. A bicameral parliament was inaugurated on 16 Oct. 1965. The last king was deposed by a military *coup* on 17 July 1973, when the Republic of Afghanistan was proclaimed, the constitution abrogated and parliament dissolved. The king abdicated on 24 Aug. 1973. Government was assumed by a 13-man Central Council of the Republic, led by Lt-Gen. Muhammad Da'ud, a former Prime Minister, who, became President. Da'ud was deposed and killed in another *coup* (known, from the month, as the 'Saur Revolution') on 27 Apr. 1978, when power was assumed by an Armed Forces Revolutionary Council (AFRC). On 30 Apr. 1978 the Democratic Republic of Afghanistan (DRA) was proclaimed and the AFRC incorporated into a new Revolutionary Council. Nur Muhammad Taraki, imprisoned leader of the formerly banned People's Democratic Party of Afghanistan (PDPA), was released and installed as President of the Revolutionary Council. The 1977 republican constitution was abolished. On 16 Sept. 1979 Taraki was overthrown and succeeded as President by the Prime Minister, Hafizullah Amin. On 27 Dec. 1979 Amin was deposed and killed in a Soviet-backed *coup* which brought Babrak Karmal into office as Head of State.

A provisional constitution, 'Basic Principles of the DRA', was ratified by the PDPA on 13 April 1980 and by the Revolutionary Council on the following day. This provided for the establishment of a *Loya Jirgah* (National Assembly), to be directly elected by adult suffrage. Pending elections to the Assembly, supreme power was vested in the 57-member Revolutionary Council. This body rules by decree and appoints the Council of Ministers. Political power is held by the Central Committee of the pro-Communist PDPA.

Afghanistan has 26 provinces, each administered by an appointed governor.
Telephones: 31 200 (1978).
Daily newspapers: 4 (1980).
Radio: 823 000 (1977).
Length of roadways: 11 652 miles *18 752 km* (31 Dec. 1978).
Universities: 2.
Adult illiteracy: 87·8% (males 80·8%; females 96·3%) in 1975 (population aged 6 and over).
Expectation of life: Males 39·9 years; females 40·7 years (UN estimates for 1970–75).

Defence: Military service two years; total armed forces 43 000 (1981 estimate); defence expenditure, 1978/79: $64 million.
Cinemas: 45 in 1977.
Foreign tourists: 117 083 in 1977.

Albania

Official name: Republika Populore Socialiste e Shqipërisë (Socialist People's Republic of Albania).
Population: 2 591 000 (census of Jan. 1979); 2 750 000 (estimate for 1982).
Area: 11 100 miles² *28 748 km²*.
Language: Albanian.
Religions: Muslim; eastern Orthodox; Roman Catholic (religious activity is officially forbidden).
Capital city: Tiranë (Tirana), population 198 000 (estimate for 1978).
Other principal towns (1978): Shkodër (Scutari) 62 500; Durrës (Durazzo) 61 000; Vlorë (Valona) 58 400; Elbasan 50 700; Korçë (Koritsa) 50 900; Berat 30 000; Fier 28 000.
Highest point: Mount Korabi, 9028 ft *2751 m*.
Principal mountain ranges: Albanian Alps, section of the Dinaric Alps.
Principal rivers: Semani (157 miles *253 km*), Drini (174 miles *280 km*), Vjosa (147 miles *236 km*), Mati (65 miles *105 km*), Shkumbini (91 miles *146 km*).
Head of State: Ramiz Alia, President of the Presidium of the People's Assembly.
Head of Government: Adil Carcani, Chairman of the Council of Ministers.
Climate: Mild, wet winters and dry, hot summers along coast; rainier and colder inland. Maximum temperature 45,3°C *113·5°F*, Lezhe, 23 Aug. 1939; minimum −25,0°C − *13·0°F*, Voskopje, 29 Jan. 1942.
Labour force: 730 762 (1960 census); 923 000 (mid-1970): Agriculture, forestry and fishing 66·2%; Industry 21·2%; Services 12·6% (ILO estimates).
Gross national product: $1930 million in 1978 (World Bank estimate).
Exports: 2996 million old leks (299·6 million new leks) in 1964: Foodstuff 23·1%; Fuels, minerals and metals 54·2%.
Monetary unit: Lek. 1 lek = 100 qindarka (qintars).
Denominations:
  Coins 5, 10, 20, 50 qintars; 1 lek.
  Notes 1, 3, 5, 10, 25, 50 and 100 leks.
Exchange rate to £ sterling: 11·50 (14 Jan. 1985).
Political history and government: Formerly part of Turkey's Ottoman Empire. On 28 Nov. 1912 a group of Albanians established a provisional government and declared the country's independence. Albania was occupied by Italy in 1914 but its independence was re-established in 1920. A republic was proclaimed on 22 Jan. 1925 and Ahmet Beg Zogu was elected President. He was proclaimed King Zog on 1 Sept. 1928 and reigned until invading Italian forces occupied Albania on 7 April 1939. Italian rule ended in 1943 but German forces then occupied

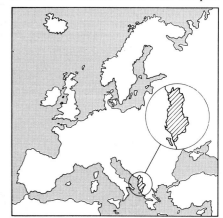

ALBANIA

Albania. After they withdrew a provisional government was established in October 1944. The Communist-led National Liberation Front, a wartime resistance group, took power on 29 Nov. 1944. A Communist-dominated assembly was elected on 2 Dec. 1945. This body proclaimed the People's Republic of Albania on 12 Jan. 1946. The new régime's first constitution was adopted in March 1946. The Communist Party was renamed the Albanian Party of Labour (APL) in 1948. A new constitution, introducing the country's present name, was adopted by the People's Assembly on 27 Dec. 1976. In April 1985 Enver Hoxha, who had led Albania since the Second World War, died. At the time of his death he was the world's longest serving head of state.

The supreme organ of state power is the unicameral People's Assembly, with 250 members elected for four years by universal adult suffrage. The assembly elects a Presidium (13 members) to be its permanent organ. Executive and administrative authority is held by the Council of Ministers, elected by the Assembly.

Political power is held by the APL (or Worker's Party), the only permitted political party, which dominates the Democratic Front. The Front presents a single list of approved candidates for elections to all representative bodies. The APL's highest authority is the Party Congress, convened every five years. The Congress elects a Central Committee (88 full members and 40 candidate members were elected on 7 Nov. 1981) to supervise Party work. To direct its policy the Committee elects a Political Bureau (Politburo), with 13 full and five candidate members.

For local government Albania is divided into 26 districts, each with a People's Council elected for three years.

Telephones: 10 150 (1963).
Daily newspapers: 2 (1976).
 Total circulation: 115 000.
Radio: 200 000 (1977).
TV: 4500 (1977).
Length of roadways: 1926 miles *3100 km*.
Length of railways: 142 miles *228 km*.
Universities: 1.
Adult illiteracy: 28·5% (males 20·1%; females 36·9%) in 1955 (population aged 9 and over).
Expectation of life: Males 67·0 years; females 69·9 years (UN estimates for 1970–75).
Defence: Military service: Army two years, Air Force, Navy and special units three years; total armed forces 40 000 (20 000 conscripts) in 1981; defence expenditure, 1980: $199 million (converted at $1 = 4·59 leks).
Cinemas: 450 in 1979 (incl. mobile).

Algeria

Offical name: El Djemhouria El Djazaïria Demokratia Echaabia, or la République algérienne démocratique et populaire (the Democratic and Popular Republic of Algeria).
Population: 19 535 560 (estimate for 1982) plus about 800 000 nationals living abroad.
Area: 919 595 miles² *2 381 741 km²*.
Languages: Arabic; Berber; French.
Religion: Muslim.
Capital city: El Djazaïr or Alger (Algiers), population 3 000 000 (1983 estimate).
Other principal towns (1977): Ouahran (Oran) 500 000; Qacentina (Constantine) 430 000; Annaba (Bône) 340 000; Tizi-Ouzou 230 000; El Boulaïda (Blida) 162 000; Sétif 160 000; Sidi-Bel-Abbès 158 000.
Highest point: Mt Atakor 9573 ft *2918 m*.
Principal mountain ranges: Atlas Saharien, Ahaggar (Hoggar), Hamada de Tinrhert.
Principal river: Chéliff (430 miles *692 km*).
Head of State: Col Bendjedid Chadli (b. 14 Apr. 1929), President.
Prime Minister: Abdelhamid Brahimi (b. 2 Apr. 1936).
Climate: Temperate (hot summers, fairly mild winters, adequate rainfall) along the coast, more extreme inland, hot and arid in the Sahara. In Algiers, August hottest (22°C *71°F* to 29°C

85°F), January coldest (9°C *49°F* to 15°C *59°F*), December rainiest (12 days). Maximum temperature 53·0°C *127·4°F*, Ouargla, 27 Aug. 1884.
Labour force: 3 260 000 (1981).
Gross domestic product: 68 692 million dinars in 1976: Mining and quarrying 26·4% (crude petroleum and natural gas 25·9%); Manufacturing 14·0%; Construction 14·3%; Trade, restaurants and hotels 12·2% (trade 11·3%); Government services 11·9%.
Exports: 62 405·828 million dinar: Crude oil 78%; Petroleum products 14%.
Monetary unit: Algerian dinar. 1 dinar = 100 centimes.
Denominations:
 Coins 1, 2, 5, 10, 20, 50 centimes; 1, 5, 10 dinars.
 Notes 5, 10, 100, 200 dinars.
Exchange rate to £ sterling: 5·80 (14 Jan. 1985).
Political history and government: A former French possession, 'attached' to metropolitan France. A nationalist revolt, led by the *Front de libération nationale* (FLN) or National Liberation Front, broke out on 1 Nov. 1954. This ended with a cease-fire and independence agreement on 18 March 1962. A provisional government was formed on 28 March 1962. Following a referendum on 1 July 1962, Algeria became independent on 3 July 1962. The provisional government transferred its functions to the Political Bureau of the FLN on 7 Aug. 1962. A National Constituent Assembly was elected, from a single list of candidates adopted by the Bureau, on 20 Sept. 1962. The Republic was proclaimed on 25 Sept. 1962 and a new government was formed with Ahmed Ben Bella as Prime Minister. The government's draft constitution, providing for a presidential régime with the FLN as sole party, was adopted by the Assembly on 28 Aug. 1963 and approved by popular referendum on 8 Sept. 1963. Ben Bella was elected President on 15 Sept. 1963 and a new National Assembly elected on 20 Sept. 1964. The President was deposed by a military *coup* on 19 June 1965, when the Assembly was dissolved and power was assumed by a Revolutionary Council, led by Col. Houari Boumédienne, Minister of Defence.

The régime's National Charter, proclaiming Algeria's adherence to socialism, was approved by referendum on 27 June 1976. A new constitution, embodying the principles of the Charter, was similarly approved on 19 Nov. 1976 and promulgated on 22 Nov. 1976. It continues the one-party system, with the FLN as sole party. Executive power is vested in the President, who is Head of State and Head of Government. He is nominated by the FLN and elected by universal adult suffrage. The President appoints the Council of Ministers. Legislative power is held by the National People's Assembly, with 261 members elected by popular vote for five years (subject to dissolution by the Head of State). Boumédienne was elected President (unopposed) on 10 Dec. 1976 and members of the Assembly elected (from 783 candidates – three per constituency – nominated by the FLN) on 25 Feb. 1977. President Boumédienne died on 27 Dec. 1978. His successor was elected on 7 Feb. 1979, and sworn in two days later. A Prime Minister was appointed on 8 Mar. 1979. Legislation approved on 30 June 1979 shortened the President's term of office from 6 to 5 years.

Algeria comprises 48 *wilayaat* (regions), each *wilaya* having an appointed governor (*wali*).
Telephones: 606 869 (1982).
Daily Newspapers: 4 (1977).
 Total circulation: 236 000.
Radio: 3 000 000 (1976).
TV: 560 000 (1977).
Length of roadways: 48 720 miles *78 408 km* (31 Dec. 1974).
Length of railways: 2417 miles *3890 km*.
Universities: 16.
Adult illiteracy: 73·6% (males 58·2%; females 87·4%) in 1971.
Expectation of life: Males 57·04 years; females 59·77 years.
Defence: Military service 24 months; total armed forces 136 300 (1984); defence expenditure,

1981: $914 million.
Cinemas: 304 in 1979.
Foreign tourists: 321 478 (1981).

Andorra

Official name: Les Valls d'Andorrà (Catalan); also Los Valles de Andorra (Spanish), or Les Vallées d'Andorre (French).
Population: 39 940 (1983).
Area: 175 miles² *453 km²*.
Languages: Catalan (official), French, Spanish.
Religion: Roman Catholic.
Capital city: Andorra la Vella, population 12 800 in 1979.
Other principal towns: Les Escaldes; Sant Julià de Lòria.
Highest point: Pla del'Estany, 9678 ft *3011 m*.
Principal mountain range: Pyrenees.
Principal river: Valira.
Head of State: Co-Princes (the Bishop of Urgel and the President of France), each represented by a Permanent Delegate and, in Andorra, by the Vegeur Episcopal and the Viguier Français.
First Syndic: Francesc Cerqueda-Pascuet.
Head of Government: Oscar Ribas-Reig.
Climate: Mild (cool summers, cold winters) and dry. May–October are rainiest months.
Monetary unit: French and Spanish currencies (*q.v.*).
Political history and government: In 1278 Andorra was placed under the joint suzerainty of the Bishop of Urgel, in Spain, and the Comte de Foix, in France. The rights of the Comte passed to France in 1589. Andorra is an autonomous principality (*seigneurie*) in which legislative

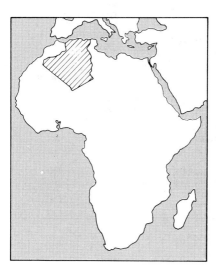

ALGERIA

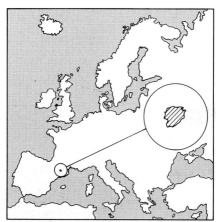

ANDORRA

power is held by the unicameral General Council of the Valleys, with 28 members (four from each of the seven parishes) elected by adult Andorran citizens for four years, half the seats being renewable every two years. Female suffrage was introduced by decree on 23 April 1970. The Council elects the First Syndic to act as chief executive for a three-year term. Political parties are technically illegal but one sought recognition in 1979.

In January 1982 an Executive Council was appointed, following elections held in 1981. Legislative and executive powers were thus separated.

Telephones: 17 719 (1982).
Radio: 7000 (1977).
TV: 3000 (1977).

Angola

Official name: A República Popular de Angola (the People's Republic of Angola).
Population: 5 646 166 (census of 15 Dec. 1970); 7 108 000 (1983 estimate).
Area: 481 354 miles² *1 246 700 km²*.
Languages: Portuguese (official), Ovimbundu, Kimbundu, Bakongo, Chokwe.
Religions: Catholic 38%; Protestant 12%; traditional beliefs 50%.
*Capital city: São Paulo de Luanda, population 480 613 (1970 census).
*Other principal towns (1970): Huambo (Nova Lisboa) 61 885; Lobito 59 258; Benguela 40 996; Lubango (Sá de Bandeira) 31 674; Malanje 31 559.
Highest point: Serra Môco, 8563 ft *2610 m*.
Principal mountain ranges: Rand Plateau, Benguela Plateau, Bié Plateau, Humpata Highlands, Chela mountains.
Principal rivers: Cunene (Kunene), Cuanza (Kwanza), Congo (Zaire), Cuando (Kwando), Cubango (Okavango), Zambezi, Cassai (Kasai).
Head of State: José Eduardo dos Santos (b. 28 Aug. 1942), President.
Climate: Tropical, tempered locally by altitude. Two distinct seasons (wet and dry) but with little variation in temperature. Very hot and rainy in lowlands, with lower temperatures inland. Rainy season October to May; average annual rainfall 1780 mm *70 in* Cabina, 280 mm *11 in* at Lobito. Average annual temperature 26°C *79°F* at Santo António do Zaire, 19°C *67°F* at Huambo.
Labour force: 1 421 966 (census of 30 Dec. 1960); 1 698 000 (1970): Agriculture, forestry and fishing 64·0% (ILO estimates).
Gross domestic product: $2701 million in 1975 (estimate).
Exports: 39 531 million kwanza in 1979: Crude petroleum 74%; Petroleum products 10%; Coffee 5%; Diamonds 10%.
Monetary unit: Kwanza. 1 kwanza = 100 lwei.

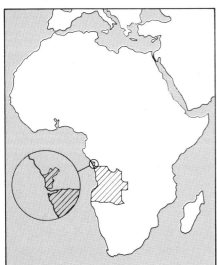

ANGOLA

Denominations:
Coins 50 lwei; 1, 2, 5, 10 kwanza.
Notes 20, 50, 100, 500, 1000 kwanza.
Exchange rate to £ sterling: 34·08 (14 Jan. 1985).
Political history and government: A former Portuguese territory, independent since 11 Nov. 1975. Before and after independence, rival nationalist groups fought for control of the country. By February 1976 the dominant group was the *Movimento Popular de Libertação de Angola* (MPLA), the Popular Movement for the Liberation of Angola, supported by troops from Cuba. The MPLA's first Congress, on 4–11 Dec. 1977, restructured the Movement into a Marxist-Leninist political party called MPLA-*Partido de Trabalho* (MPLA-PT) or MPLA-Party of Labour. No other parties are permitted. The supreme organ of state is the National People's Assembly, with 206 members serving a three-year term. Members are chosen by electoral colleges composed of representatives elected by 'loyal citizens'. The first Assembly was installed on 11 Nov. 1980. Executive power is vested in the President, who is also Chairman of the Council of Ministers and Chairman of the MPLA-PT. Angola has 18 provinces, each with a legislature elected by 'loyal citizens'.
Telephones: 29 796 (1978).
Daily newspapers: 5 (1976).
Total circulation: 119 000.
Radio: 125 000 (1980).
TV: 2000 (1980).
Length of roadways: 44 939 miles *72 323 km* (31 Dec. 1974).
Length of railways: 1739 miles *2798 km*.
Universities: 1.
Adult illiteracy: 70% plus.
Expectation of life: Males 37·0 years, females 40·1 years (UN estimates for 1970–75).
Defence: Military service two years; total armed forces 37 000 (1984); also about 19 000 Cuban and 2500 East German troops; defence expenditure, 1975: $98 million.
Cinemas: 48 (seating capacity 35 700) in 1972.
Foreign tourists: 156 000 in 1973.

* As a result of the civil war there have been large-scale movements of population. Later (March 1976) estimates suggest that Luanda has 800 000 inhabitants, Huambo over 100 000 and Lobito over 70 000.

Antigua and Barbuda

Population: 65 525 (census of 7 April 1970); 74 000 (1981 estimate).
Area: 170½ miles² *442 km²*.
Language: English.
Religion: Christian (mainly Anglican).
Capital city: St John's (St John City), population 24 000 in 1975.
Highest point: Boggy Peak, 1319 ft *402 m*.
Head of State: HM Queen Elizabeth II, represented by Sir Wilfred Ebenezer Jacobs, KCVO, OBE (b. 19 Oct. 1919), Governor-General.
Prime Minister: Vere Cornwall Bird (b. 7 Dec. 1910).
Climate: Generally warm and pleasant. Temperatures range from 15°C *60°F* to 34°C *93°F*, with an average of 27°C *81·5°F*. Average annual rainfall 1090 to 1140 mm *43 to 45 in*.
Labour force: 23 067 (1970 census): Agriculture, forestry and fishing 11·8%; Construction 13·9%; Trade, restaurants and hotels 16·5%; Community, social and personal services 31·9%.
Gross domestic product: EC$129·0 million (at factor cost) in 1977: Trade, restaurants and hotels 22·3% (trade 12·6%); Transport, storage and communications 18·8%; Owner-occupied dwellings 12·0%; Community, social and personal services (excl. government) 11·1%.
Exports: US$27·7 million in 1975: Petroleum products 87·2% (motor spirit 11·5%, residual fuel oils 64·8%).
Monetary unit: East Caribbean dollar (EC$). 1 dollar = 100 cents.
Denominations:
Coins 1, 2, 5, 10, 25, 50 cents.
Notes 1, 5, 20, 100 dollars.
Exchange rate to £ sterling: 3·051 (14 Jan. 1985).
Political history and government: A former British dependency, comprising Antigua, Bar-

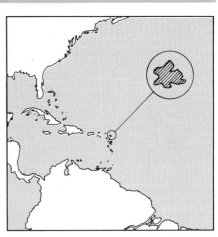

ANTIGUA AND BARBUDA

ARGENTINA

buda (formerly Dulcina) and Redonda. The islands (collectively known as Antigua) were administered as part of the Leeward Islands, under a federal arrangement. Antigua became a separate Crown Colony on 30 June 1956, although under the Governor of the Leeward Islands until 31 Dec. 1959. From 1 Jan. 1960 the colony had a new constitution, with its own Administrator. On 27 Feb. 1967 Antigua became one of the West Indies Associated States, with full internal self-government. The Administrator was replaced by a Governor and the Chief Minister was restyled Premier.

Following a constitutional conference on 4–16 Dec. 1980, the islands became fully independent, within the Commonwealth, on 1 Nov. 1981, when the Governor became Governor-General and the Premier took office as Prime Minister. Executive power is vested in the British monarch and is exercisable by the Governor-General, who is appointed on the advice of the Prime Minister and acts in almost all matters on the advice of the Cabinet. Legislative power is vested in the bicameral Parliament, comprising a Senate (17 members appointed by the Governor-General) and a House of Representatives (17 members elected by universal adult suffrage for 5 years, subject to dissolution). The Governor-General appoints the Prime Minister and, on the latter's recommendation, other Ministers. The Cabinet is responsible to the House.

Telephones: 6712 (1980).
Daily newspapers: 2 (1976).
Total circulation: 10 000.

Radio: 16 000 (1977).
TV: 15 000 (1976).
Length of roadways: 600 miles *960 km.*
Adult illiteracy: 11·3% (males 10·4%; females 12·0%) in 1960.
Expectation of life: Males 60·48 years; females 64·32 years (1959–61).
Defence: There are two U.S. military bases on Antigua.
Cinemas: 2 (seating capacity 1700) in 1966.
Foreign tourists: 86 512 (excluding cruise passengers) in 1979.

Argentina

Official name: La República Argentina (the Argentine Republic).
Population: 27 862 771 (census of 22 Sept. 1980).
Area: 1 072 163 miles² *2 776 889 km²*.
Language: Spanish.
Religion: Roman Catholic.
Capital city: Buenos Aires, population 2 908 000 (1980 census).
Other principal towns (1980): Córdoba 969 000; Rosario 750 455; La Plata 455 000; San Miguel de Tucumán 497 000; Mar de Plata 302 282; Santa Fé 287 000.
Highest point: Cerro Aconcagua, 22 834 ft *6960 m* (first climbed 14 Jan. 1897).
Principal mountain range: Cordillera de los Andes.
Principal rivers: Paraná (2485 miles *4000 km*), Negro, Salado.
Head of State: Dr Raul Alfonsin, President.
Climate: Sub-tropical in Chaco region (north), sunny and mild in pampas, cold and windy in southern Patagonia. In Buenos Aires, January hottest (17°C *63°F* to 29°C *85°F*), June coldest (5°C *41°F* to 14°C *57°F*), August, October and November rainiest (each 9 days). Absolute maximum temperature 48,8°C *119·8°F*, Rivadavia, 27 Nov. 1916; minimum −33,0°C *−27·4°F*, Sarmiento.
Labour force: 9 011 450 aged 10 and over (1970 census): Agriculture, forestry and fishing 16·2%; Manufacturing 21·5%; Trade, restaurants and hotels 16·1%; Community, social and personal services (incl. business services) 25·5%; 10 337 000 (estimate for 30 June 1979).
Gross domestic product: 1 345 000 million pesos in 1975: Agriculture, forestry and fishing 12·9%; Manufacturing 35·3%; Trade, restaurants and hotels 10·7%; Community, social and personal services 20·5%.
Exports: $8000 million in 1980.
Monetary unit: Argentine peso. 1 peso = 100 centavos.
Denominations:
Coins 1, 5, 10, 50, 100 pesos.
Notes 50, 100, 500, 1000, 5000, 10000, 100 000, 500 000 pesos.
Exchange rate to £ sterling: 215865 (14 Jan. 1985).
Political history and government: A federal republic of 22 states and two centrally administered territories. Lt-Gen. Juan Perón was elected President on 23 Sept. 1973 and took office on 12 Oct. 1973. Gen. Perón died on 1 July 1974 and was succeeded by his wife, the former Vice-President. She was deposed by an armed forces *coup* on 24 March 1976, when a three-man military junta took power. The bicameral Congress (a Senate and a Chamber of Deputies) and provincial legislatures were dissolved and political activities suspended. The junta's leader, Lt-Gen. Jorge Videla, was inaugurated as President on 29 March 1976. On 2 May 1978 the junta confirmed President Videla in office until 29 March 1981. On 1 Aug. 1978 he retired from the Army and ceased to be part of the junta. The junta chooses the President for a 3-year term and the President appoints the Cabinet. Each province is administered by an appointed Governor.
Telephones: 3 041 475 in 1982.
Daily newspapers: 297 in 1984.
Radio: 7 500 000 in 1984.
TV: 5 600 000 in 1984.

Length of roadways: 129 015 miles *207 630 km* (31 Dec. 1978).
Length of railways: 21 176 miles *34 079 km.*
Universities: 40.
Adult illiteracy: 7·4% (males 6·5%; females 8·3%) in 1970.
Expectation of life: Males 65·16 years; females 71·38 years (1970–75).
Defence: Military service: Army and Air Force one year, Navy 14 months; total armed forces 154 400 (118 000 conscripts) in 1984; defence expenditure, 1980: $3380 million.
Cinemas: 1794 in 1979.
Foreign tourists: 800 000 in 1982.

Australia

Official name: The Commonwealth of Australia.
Population: 13 915 000 (census of 30 June 1976); 15 276 100 (1982 estimate).
Area: 2 966 150 miles² *7 682 300 km²*.
Language: English.
Religions: Church of England; Roman Catholic; Methodist; Presbyterian.
Capital city: Canberra, population 241 300 at 30 June 1979.
Other principal towns (metropolitan areas, 1979): Sydney 3 193 300; Melbourne 2 739 700; Brisbane 1 015 200; Adelaide 933 300; Perth 883 600; Newcastle 379 800; Wollongong 224 000; Hobart 168 500; Geelong 141 100.
Highest point: Mt Kosciusko, 7316 ft *2230 m.*
Principal mountain ranges: Great Dividing Range, Macdonnell Ranges, Flinders Ranges, Australian Alps.
Principal rivers: Murray (with Darling), Flinders, Ashburton, Fitzroy.
Head of State: HM Queen Elizabeth II, represented by the Rt Hon. Sir Ninian Stephen, AK, GCMG, GCVO, KBE, Governor-General.
Prime Minister: The Rt. Hon. Robert Hawke.
Climate: Hot and dry, with average temperatures of about 27°C *80°F*. Very low rainfall in interior. In Sydney, January and February warmest (each average 18°C *65°F* to 25°C *78°F*), July coldest (8°C *46°F* to 15°C *60°F*), each month has an average of between 11 and 14 rainy days. In Perth, average daily maximum of 17°C *63°F* (July) to 29°C *85°F* (January, February), minimum 9°C *48°F* (July, August) to 17°C *63°F* (January, February), July and August rainiest (each 19 days), January and February driest (each 3 days). In Darwin, average maximum 30°C *87°F* (July) to 34°C *94°F* (November), minimum 19°C *67°F* (July) to 25°C *78°F* (November, December), January rainiest (20 days), no rainy days in July or August. Absolute maximum temperature 53,1°C *127·5°F*, Cloncurry, 13 Jan. 1889; absolute minimum −22,2°C *−8·0°F*, Charlotte Pass, 14 July 1945 and 22 Aug. 1947.
Labour force: 6 261 600 in 1983, excluding 718 600 unemployed: Agriculture, forestry and fishing 6·6%; Mining 1·6%; Manufacturing 18·4%; Construction 6·7%; Trade 19%; Finance, property and business services 9·2%; Community services 16·4%.
Gross domestic product: A$83 216 million in year ending 30 June 1977: Manufacturing 20·5%; Trade 14·7%; Finance, insurance, real estate and business services 10·4%; Community, social and personal services (incl. restaurants and hotels) 19·6%.
Exports: A$22 205·2 million in 1982–3: Meat 7·1%; Cereals 8·2%; Metal ores and metal scrap 16·9%; Coal, coke and briquettes 13·9%; Petroleum and products 5·9%; Non-ferrous metals 5·6%; Textile fibres and waste 8·7%.
Monetary unit: Australian dollar (A$). 1 dollar = 100 cents.
Denominations:
Coins 1, 2, 5, 10, 20, 50 cents.
Notes 1; 2, 5, 10, 20, 50 dollars.
Exchange rate to £ sterling: 1·97 (18 Apr. 1985).
Political history and government: Britain's six Australian colonies merged to form a federation

**AUSTRALIA—1. Western Australia   2. Northern Territory   3. Queensland
4. New South Wales   5. Victoria   6. Tasmania   7. South Australia.**

of states as the Commonwealth of Australia, a dominion under the British Crown, on 1 Jan. 1901. The Northern Territory was separated from South Australia, and the Australian Capital Territory was acquired from New South Wales, on 1 Jan. 1911. The capital was transferred from Melbourne to Canberra in May 1927. Australia became fully independent, within the Commonwealth, under the Statute of Westminster, a law promulgated in Britain on 11 Dec. 1931 and adopted by Australia on 9 Oct. 1942 (with effect from 3 Sept. 1939).

Executive power is vested in the Queen and exercised by her representative, the Governor-General, advised by the Federal Executive Council (the Cabinet), led by the Prime Minister. The Governor-General appoints the Prime Minister and, on the latter's recommendation, other Ministers. Legislative power is vested in the Federal Parliament. This consists of the Queen, represented by the Governor-General, and two chambers elected by universal adult suffrage (voting is compulsory). The Senate has 64 members (10 from each state and two from each of the federal territories) elected by proportional representation for six years (half the seats renewable every three years). The House of Representatives has 125 members elected for three years (subject to dissolution) from single-member constituencies. The Cabinet is responsible to Parliament. Australia comprises six states (each with its own Government and judicial system) and two federally-administered territories.
Telephones: 7 396 212 (1980).
Daily newspapers: 60 (1977).
   Total circulation: 4 365 000.
Radio: 14 600 000 (1977).
TV: 5 020 000 (1977).
Length of roadways: 523 274 miles *842 128 km* (30 June 1977).
Length of railways: 27 611 miles *44 435 km* (government 24 675 miles *39 710 km*, other 2936 miles *4725 km*) at 30 June 1978.
Universities: 19.
Expectation of life: Males 67·63 years; females 74·15 years (1965–67), excluding full-blooded aborigines.
Defence: Military service voluntary; total armed forces 72 354 (1983); defence expenditure, 1981–2: A$ 4135 million.
Cinemas: 900 (incl. drive-in) in 1978.
Foreign tourists: 954 674 in 1982.

NEW SOUTH WALES
Population: 4 914 300 (1976 census); 5 307 900 (1982 estimate).
Area: 309 500 miles² *801 600 km²*.
Capital city: Sydney, population 3 310 500 (1982 estimate).
Other principal towns (1982): Newcastle 410 250; Wollongong 233 650; Lake Macquarie 156 950; Wagga Wagga 48 950; Shoalhaven 48 600; Shellharbour 44 350; Albury 38 100.
Highest point: Mt Kosciusko, 7316 ft *2230 m*.
Principal mountain ranges: Great Dividing Range, Australian Alps, New England Range, Snowy Mountains, Blue Mountains, Liverpool Range.
Principal rivers: Darling, Murray.
Governor: Air Marshal Sir James Anthony Rowland, KBE, DFC, AFC (b. 1 Nov. 1922).
Premier: Neville Kenneth Wran.
Climate: Most of the state has hot summers and mild winters, with rainfall well distributed, but in the east drought and storms sometimes occur.
Telephones: 2 714 946 (including Australian Capital Territory) at 30 June 1979.
Length of roadways: 117 547 miles *189 173 km* (30 June 1978).
Length of railways: 6299 miles *10 138 km* (government railways only, 30 June 1978).
Universities: 6.

QUEENSLAND
Population: 2 111 700 (1976 census); 2 295 123 (1981 census).
Area: 666 875 miles² *1 727 200 km²*.
Capital city: Brisbane, population 1 096 200 (1981 census).

Other principal towns (1981): Gold Coast 143 090; Townsville 96 310; Sunshine Coast 65 320; Cairns 58 270; Rockhampton 55 260.
Highest point: Mt Bartle Frere, 5287 ft *1611 m*.
Principal mountain ranges: Great Dividing Range, Selwyn, Kirby.
Principal rivers: Brisbane, Mitchell, Fitzroy, Barcoo, Flinders.
Governor: Commodore Sir James Maxwell Ramsey, KCMG, CBE, DSC (b. 27 Aug. 1916).
Premier: Johannes Bjelke-Petersen (b. 13 Jan. 1911).
Telephones: 797 906 (30 June 1979).
Length of roadways: 100 877 miles *162 345 km* (30 June 1978).
Length of railways: 6081 miles *9787 km* (government railways only, 30 June 1978).
Universities: 3.

SOUTH AUSTRALIA
Population: 1 294 509 (1981 census).
Area: 379 925 miles² *984 000 km²*.
Capital city: Adelaide, population 960 000 (1982 estimate).
Other principal towns (1976): Whyalla 33 426; Mount Gambier 19 292; Port Pirie 15 005.
Principal mountain ranges: Middleback, Mt Lofty Range, Flinders Range, Musgrave Range.
Principal river: Murray.
Governor: Lt-Gen. Sir Donald Dunstan, KBE, CB.
Premier: John Charles Bannon.
Climate: Mediterranean type.
Telephones: 576 901 (including Northern Territory) at 30 June 1979.
Length of roadways: 62 466 miles *100 529 km* (30 June 1978).
Length of railways: 3793 miles *6105 km* (government railways only, 30 June 1978).
Universities: 2.

TASMANIA
Population: 427 300 (1981 census).
Area: 26 175 miles² *67 800 km²*.
Capital city: Hobart, population 178 800 (1982 estimate).
Other principal towns (1976): Launceston 63 629; Devonport 19 473; Burnie-Somerset 19 189.
Highest point: Cradle Mountain, 5069 ft *1545 m*.
Principal mountain range: Highlands.
Principal rivers: Derwent, Gordon, Tamar.
Governor: Sir James Plimsoll, AC, CBE.
Premier: R. Gray.
Telephones: 163 244 (30 June 1979).
Length of roadways: 13 811 miles *22 227 km* (30 June 1978).
Length of railways: 537 miles *864 km* (government railways only, 30 June 1978).
Universities: 1.

VICTORIA
Population: 3 994 122 (1982 estimate).
Area: 87 875 miles² *227 600 km²*.
Capital city: Melbourne, population 2 836 800 (1982 estimate).
Other principal towns (1981): Geelong 125 279; Ballarat 62 641; Bendigo 52 741; Shepparton-Mooroopna 28 373.
Principal mountain ranges: Australian Alps, Great Dividing Range.
Principal rivers: Murray, Yarra-Yarra.
Governor: Rear-Adm. Sir Brian Stewart Murray, KCMG.
Premier: John Cain.
Telephones: 1 909 119 (30 June 1979).
Length of roadways: 97 370 miles *156 701 km* (30 June 1978).
Length of railways: 3751 miles *6036 km* (government railways only, 30 June 1978).
Universities: 4.

WESTERN AUSTRALIA
Population: 1 299 100 (1982 census).
Area: 975 100 miles² *2 525 500 km²*.
Capital city: Perth, population 948 850 (1982 estimate).
Other principal towns (1981): Fremantle 23 360; Bunbury 21 749; Geraldton 20 895; Kalgoorlie-Boulder 19 848; Albany 15 222; Port Hedland 12 948.

Highest point: Mt Meharry, 4082 ft *1244 m*.
Principal mountain ranges: Darling, Hamersley.
Principal rivers: Fitzroy, Ashburton, Fortescue, Swan, Murchison.
Governor: Prof. Gordon Stanley Reid (b. 26 Sept. 1923).
Premier: Hon. Brian Thomas Burke.
Telephones: 514 460 (30 June 1979).
Length of roadways: 101 478 miles *163 313 km* (30 June 1977).
Length of railways: 4035 miles *6494 km* (government railways only, 30 June 1978).
Universities: 2.

THE NORTHERN TERRITORY OF AUSTRALIA
Population: 101 400 (1976 census); 125 900 (estimate for 31 Dec. 1980).
Area: 519 750 miles² *1 346 200 km²*.
Administrative Headquarters: Darwin, population 60 923 (1982 estimate).
Other principal town: Alice Springs, population 19 610 (1982 estimate).
Highest point: Mount Ziel, 4955 ft *1510 m*.
Principal mountain range: MacDonnell Ranges.
Principal rivers: Victoria, Roper.
Administrator: Commodore E E Johnston, OBE.
Chief Minister: Paul Anthony Edward Everingham (b. 4 Feb. 1943).
Climate: Tropical, but with considerable variations. Dry in the south, with very hot summers. On the coast, the rainy season is from November to April and the dry season from May to October.
Length of roadways: 12 652 miles *20 362 km* (30 June 1978).
Length of railways: 173 miles *278 km* (government railways only, 30 June 1978).

THE AUSTRALIAN CAPITAL TERRITORY
Population: 203 300 (1976 census); 230 200 (estimate for 1982).
Area: 925 miles² *2400 km²*.
Principal town: Canberra, population 251 000 (including Queanbeyan, NSW), 1982 estimate.
Principal river: Murrumbidgee.
Climate: (see New South Wales).
Length of roadways: 1356 miles *2182 km* (30 June 1978).
Length of railways: 5 miles *8 km* (government railways only, 30 June 1978).
Universities: 1.

Austria

Offical name: Republik Österreich (Republic of Austria).
Population: 7 551 842 (1983).
Area: 32 376 miles² *83 853 km²*.
Language: German.
Religions: Roman Catholic, Protestant minority.
Capital city: Wien (Vienna), population 1 531 346 (1981).
Other principal towns (1981): Graz 243 166; Linz 199 910; Salzburg 139 926; Innsbruck 117 287.
Highest point: Grossglockner, 12 462 ft *3798 m* (first climbed in 1800).
Principal mountain range: Alps.
Principal rivers: Donau (Danube) (1770 miles *2850 km*), Inn, Mur.
Head of State: Dr Rudolf Kirchschläger (b. 20 Mar. 1915), Federal President.
Head of Government: Dr Fred Sinowatz (b. 5 Feb. 1929), Federal Chancellor.
Climate: Generally cold, dry winters and warm summers, with considerable variations due to altitude. Average annual temperature 7°C *45°F* to 9°C *48°F*. Most of rain in summer. In Vienna, July hottest (15°C *59°F* to 24°C *75°F*), January coldest (−3°C *26°F* to 1°C *34°F*), August rainiest (10 days). Absolute maximum temperature 39,4°C *102·9°F*, Horn, 5 July 1957; absolute minimum −36,6°C *−33·9°F*, Zwettl, 11 Feb. 1929.
Labour force: 2 798 600 in 1981 (excludes 69 295 unemployed): Agriculture and forestry 7·8%; Industry and manufacturing 22·4%; Services 34·5%.
Gross domestic product: 1207·7 billion Schilling

in 1983: Agriculture and forestry 5%; Mining and material goods production 29·4%; Construction 6·9%; Commerce, hotels and restaurants 16·9%; Transport and communications 6·1%.
Exports: 277 120 million Schilling in 1983: Machinery and vehicles 30·2%; Semi-manufactured and manufactured goods 34·1%; Raw materials (excluding fuels) 6·6%; Food 4%.
Monetary unit: Schilling. 1 Schilling = 100 Groschen.
Denominations:
   Coins 2, 5, 10, 50 Groschen; 1, 5, 10, 20, 25, 50, 100, 500, 1000 Schilling.
   Notes 20, 50, 100, 500, 1000 Schilling.
Exchange rate to £ sterling: 26·96 (12 Apr. 1985).
Political history and government: Formerly the centre of the Austro-Hungarian Empire. In 1918 the Empire was dissolved and Austria proper became a republic. Troops from Nazi Germany entered Austria on 11 March 1938. It was annexed on 12 March 1938 and incorporated in the German Reich. After liberation by Allied forces, a provisional government was established on 27 April 1945. Austria was divided into four occupation zones, controlled by France, the USSR, the United Kingdom and the USA. It regained independence by the Austrian State Treaty, signed on 15 May 1955 and effective from 27 July 1955. Occupation forces were withdrawn on 25 Oct. 1955.
   Austria is a federal republic, divided into nine provinces. Legislative power is vested in the bicameral Federal Assembly, comprising the *Nationalrat* (National Council) of 183 members, directly elected by universal adult suffrage for four years (subject to dissolution), and the *Bundesrat* (Federal Council) of 58 members elected for varying terms by the provincial assemblies. The Federal President is a constitutional Head of State, elected by direct popular vote for six years. He normally acts on the advice of the Council of Ministers, led by the Federal Chancellor, which is responsible to the National Council. The President appoints the Chancellor and, on the latter's advice, other Ministers.
Telephones: 2 414 359 (1982).
Daily newspapers: 30 (1983).
Radio: 2 538 645 (1984).
TV: 2 359 130 (1984).
Length of roadways: 66 287 miles *106 679 km* (classified roads only, 31 Dec. 1979).
Length of railways: 4036 miles *6495 km*.
Universities: 18.
Expectation of life: Males 69 years; females 76 years (1983).
Defence: Military service six months, followed by 60 days' reservist training; total armed forces 50 000 (32 000 conscripts) in 1984; defence expenditure, 1983: $826 million.
Cinemas: 528 (1983).
Foreign tourists: 87 444 481 overnight stays in 1983.

The Bahamas

Official name: The Commonwealth of the Bahamas.
Population: 223 455 (census of 12 May 1980).
Area: 5382 miles² *13 939 km²*.
Languages: English.
Religions: Anglican, Baptist, Roman Catholic, Methodist, Saints of God and Church of God.
Capital city: Nassau (on New Providence Island), population of island 135 537 (1980).
Other principal islands (1980): Grand Bahama 33 102; Eleuthera 10 600; Abaco 7324; Andros 8397; Long Island 3358; Cat Island 2143.
Highest point: Mount Alvernia, Cat Island.
Head of State: HM Queen Elizabeth II, represented by Sir Gerald Christopher Cash, KCVO, OBE (b. 28 May 1917), Governor-General.
Prime Minister: The Rt Hon, Lynden Oscar Pindling (b. 22 Mar. 1930).
Climate: Equable. Winter averages of 21°C to 24°C *70°F to 75°F*. Summer averages of 26°C to 32°C *80°F to 90°F*. Highest recorded temperature is 34°C *94°F* and lowest ·10°C *51°F*. Rainfall mainly between May and September.
Labour force: 69 791 (including unemployed)

aged 14 and over (1970 census): Construction 13·6%; Trade, restaurants and hotels 25·9%; Community, social and personal services 27·1%; 84 288 (household survey, Oct. 1975).
Gross domestic product: B$1073·8 million in 1979.
Exports: B$2 444 000 in 1982.
Monetary unit: Bahamian dollar (B$). 1 dollar = 100 cents.
Denominations:
   Coins 1, 5, 10, 15, 25, 50 cents; B$ 1, 2, 5.
   Notes 50 cents; B$ 1, 3, 5, 10, 20, 50, 100.
Exchange rate to £ sterling: 1·254 (23 April 1985).
Political history and government: A former British colony, with internal self-government from 7 Jan. 1964. Following a constitutional conference on 12–20 Dec. 1972, the Bahamas became independent, within the Commonwealth, on 10 July 1973. Executive power is vested in the Queen and exercisable by her appointed representative, the Governor-General, advised by the Cabinet. The Governor-General appoints the Prime Minister and, on the latter's advice, other members of the Cabinet. Legislative power is vested in the bicameral Parliament, comprising the Senate (16 appointed members) and the House of Assembly, with 38 members elected for five years by universal adult suffrage. The Cabinet is responsible to Parliament.
Telephones: 75 071 (1982).
Daily newspapers: 2 (1977).
Radio: 97 000 (1977).
TV: 20 000 (1977).
Length of roadways: 1450 miles *2334 km*.
Adult illiteracy: 10·2% (males 9·8%; females 10·5%) in 1963.
Expectation of life: Males 64·0 years; females 67·3 years (1969–71).
Defence: A force was established in 1977.
Cinemas: 5 (seating capacity 4100) in 1971.
Foreign tourists: 1 947 742 in 1982.

Bahrain

Official name: Daulat al-Bahrain (State of Bahrain).
Population: 350 798 (1981 census).
Area: 240 miles² *622 km²*.
Language: Arabic.
Religions: Muslim, Christian minority.
Capital city: Manama, population 121 986 (1981 census).
Other principal towns (1981): Muharraq 61 853; Rifa'a 28 150; Isa Town 21 275; Hidd 7111.
Highest point: Jabal ad-Dukhan, 440 ft *134 m*.
Head of State: H H Shaikh Isa bin Sulman al-Khalifa, Hon GCMG (b. 3 July 1933), Amir.
Prime Minister: Shaikh Khalifa bin Sulman al-Khalifa (b. 1935).
Climate: Very hot and humid. Average maximum 20°C *68°F* (January) to 38°C *100°F* (August), minimum 14°C *57°F* (January) to 29°C *85°F* (July, August), December and February rainiest (each two days).
Labour force: 134 900 (April 1979): Construction 25·6%; Trade, restaurants and hotels 12·6%; Transport, storage and communications 11·1%; Community, social and personal services 29·7%.
Gross domestic product: 655·3 million Bahrain dinars in 1982.
Exports: 1424·8 million Bahrain dinars in 1982: non-oil products 17%.
Monetary unit: Bahrain dinar. 1 dinar = 1000 fils.
Denominations:
   Coins 1, 5, 10, 25, 50, 100, 250, 500 fils.
   Notes 500 fils; 1, 5, 10, 20 dinars.
Exchange rate to £ sterling: 0·4215 (15 Jan. 1985).
Political history and government: A shaikhdom under British protection from 1882 until full independence on 15 Aug. 1971. Now an amirate, with a Cabinet appointed by the Ruler. A new constitution came into force on 6 Dec. 1973. This provided for a National Assembly, containing Cabinet ministers and 30 elected members serving a four-year term. Elections were held on 7 Dec. 1973 but the Assembly was dissolved by

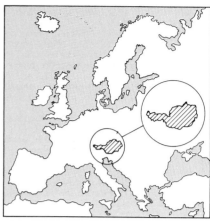

AUSTRIA

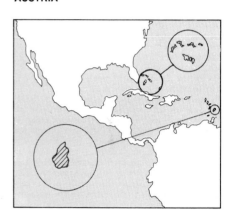

centre: **THE BAHAMAS**

right **BARBADOS**

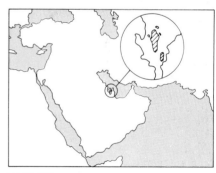

BAHRAIN

Amiri decree on 26 Aug. 1975.
Telephones: 84 593 (1982).
Daily newspapers: 4 (1979).
Radio: 93 500 (1978).
TV: 80 000 (1978).
Expectation of life: Males 54·8 years; females 58·2 years (UN estimates, average for Bahrain, Qatar and the United Arab Emirates, 1970–75).
Adult illiteracy: 59·8% (males 50·7%; females 71·5%) in 1971.
Defence: Military service voluntary; total armed forces 2600 (1984); defence expenditure, 1981: $135 million.
Cinemas: 10 (seating capacity 10 500) and 2 mobile units in 1974.

Bangladesh

Official name: Gana Praja Tantri Bangla Desh (People's republic of Bangladesh).
Population: 94 651 000 in 1983.
Area: 55 598 miles² *143 998 km²*.
Language: Bengali.
Religions: Muslim, with Hindu, Christian and Buddhist minorities.

Capital city: Dhaka (Dacca), population 3 458 602 (census 1981).
Other principal towns (1981): Chittagong 1 388 475; Khulna 623 184; Narayanganj 298 400; Rajshahi 171 600; Barisal 166 680.
Principal rivers: Ganga (Ganges), Jumna, Meghna.
Head of State: Lt-Gen. Hossain Mohammad Ershad, President.
Prime Minister: Ataur Rahman Khan.
Climate: Tropical and monsoon. Summer temperature about 30°C *86°F*; winter 20°C *68°F*. Rainfall is heavy, varying from 1270 to 3430 mm *50 in to 135 in* per year in different areas, and most falling from June to September (the monsoon season).
Labour force: 20 019 886 (excluding 502 706 unemployed) at 1974 census: Agriculture, forestry and fishing 79·0%; Community, social and personal services 10·3%.
Gross domestic product: 148 032 million taka in year ending 30 June 1979. Agriculture, forestry and fishing 52·5% (agriculture 44·4%); Trade 10·7%.
Exports: 12 000 million taka: Jute and jute products 64%.
Monetary unit: Taka. 1 taka = 1 paisa.
Denominations:
Coins 1, 2, 5, 10, 25, 50 paisa.
Notes 1, 5, 10, 50, 100 taka.
Exchange rate to £ sterling: 28·45 (14 Jan. 1985).
Political history and government: Formerly the eastern wing of Pakistan, formed by the partition of British India on 15 Aug. 1947. In elections for a Pakistan National Assembly on 7 Dec. 1970 the Awami League, led by Sheikh Mujibur Rahman, won all but two seats in East Pakistan and an overall majority in the Assembly. The League advocated autonomy for East Pakistan within a loose federation but this was unacceptable to the main party in West Pakistan. When constitutional talks failed, the League declared East Pakistan's independence as Bangladesh on 26 Mar. 1971. Civil war broke out and the League was outlawed. Mujib was arrested but the League announced on 11 Apr. 1971 that he was President of Bangladesh. After Indian

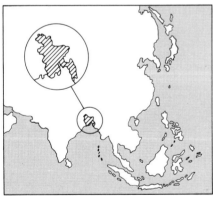

BANGLADESH

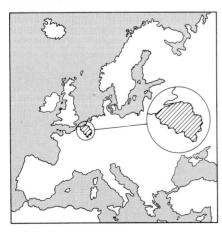

BELGIUM

intervention, Pakistani forces surrendered and Bangladesh's secession became effective on 16 Dec. 1971. Mujib was released and became Prime Minister on 12 Jan. 1972. Bangladesh joined the Commonwealth on 18 Apr. 1972. A state of emergency was proclaimed on 28 Dec. 1974. Mujib became an executive President on 25 Jan. 1975 and Bangladesh a one-party state on 25 Feb. 1975. Mujib was deposed by a *coup* and killed on 15 Aug. 1975, when martial law was imposed. Political parties were banned on 30 Aug. 1975. After an army mutiny on 3 Nov. 1975, the new President resigned on 6 Nov. 1975, when the Chief Justice of the Supreme Court became President and Chief Martial Law Administrator. He immediately dissolved Parliament and on the next day the mutiny was crushed. Political parties were again legalised by a regulation of 28 July 1976. The President's deputy, Maj-Gen. Ziaur Rahman, took over martial law powers on 29 Nov. 1976 and became President on 21 Apr. 1977. A Presidential proclamation of 22 Apr. 1977 amended the constitution to change Bangladesh from a secular to an Islamic state. A referendum on 30 May 1977 gave 99% support to President Zia. He was elected President by a large majority of the popular vote on 3 June 1978 and sworn in for a 5-year term on 12 June. On 29 June 1978 he formed a Cabinet in place of his Council of Advisers. Elections were held on 18 Feb. 1979 for 300 members to serve a 5-year term in a new *Jatiya Sangsad* (Parliament). In a further 30 seats, reserved for women, candidates were unopposed. Parliament first met on 2 Apr. 1979 and martial law was ended on 6 Apr. A new Cabinet, including the President, Vice-President and a Prime Minister, was formed on 15 Apr. 1979. The state of emergency was revoked on 27 Nov. 1979. President Zia was killed on 30 May 1981, during an attempted insurrection, and the Vice-President became acting Head of State. He was elected President on 15 Nov. 1981. The Cabinet is responsible to Parliament.

The elected President was deposed and the Jatiya Sangsad (Parliament) dissolved following promulgation of martial law and the take-over of power by Lt-Gen. H M Ershad on 24 March 1982. Gen. Ershad appointed a retired judge to be President on 27 March 1982, but assumed the Presidency himself on 11 December 1983.
Telephones: 122 190 (1982).
Daily newspapers: 53 (1981).
Radio: 770 000 (1982).
TV: 252 000 (1982).
Length of roadways: 3900 miles *6276 km*.
Length of railways: 1786 miles *2874 km* (1977).
Universities: 6.
Adult illiteracy: 74·2% in 1974.
Expectation of life: Males 45·8 years; females 46·6 years (1974).
Defence: Military service voluntary; total armed forces 73 000 (1983); estimated defence expenditure, 1983–4: 4169 million taka.
Cinemas: 230 in 1976.
Foreign tourists: 64 162 in 1980.

Barbados

Population: 246 082 (census of 12 May 1980); 270 000 (estimate 1981).
Area: 166 miles² *430 km²*.
Language: English.
Religions: Anglican, with Methodist, Roman Catholic and Moravian minorities.
Capital city: Bridgetown, population 7517 (parish of Bridgetown and St Michael 97 872) at 1980 census.
Other principal towns: Speightstown.
Highest point: Mount Hillaby, 1115 ft *340 m*.
Head of State: HM Queen Elizabeth II, represented by Sir Hugh Springer, GCMG, KA, CBE (b. 22 June 1913), Governor-General.
Prime Minister: The Rt Hon John Michael Geoffrey Manningham Adams (b. 24 Sept. 1931).
Climate: Pleasant, with temperatures rarely rising above 30°C *86°F* or falling below 18°C *67°F*. Average annual rainfall, which varies

from district to district, 1270 mm to 1778 mm *50 in to 75 in*. Subject to hurricanes.
Labour force: 111 600 (excluding 16 700 unemployed) at Dec. 1983: Agriculture 8%; Manufacturing 13·2%; Commerce 22·5%; Services (Government and other) 36·8%; Construction and quarrying 8·1%.
Gross domestic product: B$1 798 040 in 1982: Sugar 3·1%; Other agriculture 3·7%; Manufacturing 12·2%; Wholesale and retail trade 22·1%; Tourism 10·1%; Financial, insurance and business services 13·9%.
Exports: B$717·4 million in 1983: Electrical components 30·8%; Clothing 11·9%; Sugar 6·6%.
Monetary unit: Barbados dollar (B$). 1 dollar = 100 cents.
Denominations:
Coins 1, 5, 10, 25 cents; B$1.
Notes B$ 1, 2, 5, 10, 20, 100.
Exchange rate to £ sterling: 2·25 (February 1985).
Political history and government: A former British colony, with internal self-government from 16 Oct. 1961. A member of the West Indies Federation from 3 Jan. 1958 to 31 May 1962. Following a constitutional conference on 20 June–4 July 1966, Barbados became independent, within the Commonwealth, on 30 Nov. 1966. Executive power is vested in the Queen and exercisable by her appointed representative, the Governor-General, advised by the Cabinet. The Governor-General appoints the Prime Minister and, on the latter's advice, other members of the Cabinet. Legislative power is vested in the bicameral Parliament, comprising the Senate (21 appointed members) and the House of Assembly, with 27 members elected by universal adult suffrage for five years (subject to dissolution) from 27 constituencies. The Cabinet is responsible to Parliament.
Telephones: 53 002 (1983).
Daily newspapers: 2.
Total circulation: 43 000.
Radio: 120 000 (1983).
TV: 60 000 (1983).
Length of roadways: 1020 miles *1642 km*.
Universities: 1.
Adult illiteracy: 0·8% in 1970.
Expectation of life: Males 67 years; females 72·5 years (1982).
Defence: The Barbados Defence Force was established in April 1978 with 154 regular personnel.
Cinemas: 6 (seating capacity 4900), 2 mobile units and 2 drive-in (capacity 2300) in 1975.
Foreign tourists: 328 325 (1983).

Belgium

Official name: Royaume de Belgique (in French), Koninkrijk België (in Dutch) or Königreich Belgien (in German): Kingdom of Belgium.
Population: 9 650 944 (census of 31 Dec. 1970); 9 858 017 (estimate for 31 Dec. 1983).
Area: 11 783 miles² *30 519 km²*.
Languages: Dutch (Flemish), French, German.
Religion: Roman Catholic.
Capital city: Bruxelles (Brussel, Brussels), population 989 877 (including Anderlecht, Schaerbeek and other suburbs) at 1 Jan. 1983.
Other principal towns (1983): Gent (Gand, Ghent) 236 540; Charleroi 216 144; Liège (Luik) 207 496; Antwerpen (Anvers, Antwerp) 490 524; Schaerbeek (Schaarbeek) 118 950 (1970); Bruges (Brugge) 118 218; Anderlecht 103 796 (1970).
Highest point: Botrange, 2277 ft *694 m*.
Principal mountain range: Ardennes.
Principal rivers: Schelde, Meuse (575 miles *925 km*).
Head of State: HM Baudouin Albert Charles Léopold Axel Marie Gustave, KG (b. 7 Sept. 1930), King of the Belgians. The King's name is also written Boudewijn (in Dutch) or Balduin (in German).
Prime Minister: Wilfried Martens.
Climate: Mild and humid on coast. Hotter summers, colder winters inland. In Brussels, January coldest (−0,5°C *31°F* to 5°C *42°F*), July hottest (12°C *54°F* to 23°C *73°F*), December rainiest (13 days). Absolute maximum

temperature 40,0°C *104°F* on the coast, 27 June 1947; absolute minimum −29,8°C *−21·6°F*, Viesalm, 10 Dec. 1879.
Labour force: 4 088 000 (1982, not including armed forces), of which: Primary sector 107 000; Secondary sector 1 170 000; Tertiary sector 2 339 000; Job applicants 472 000.
Gross national product: 3 902·9 billion Belgian francs in 1982: Primary sector 3%; Secondary sector 33%; Tertiary sector 64%.
Exports: 2 394 billion Belgian francs (including Luxembourg) in 1982: Raw materials and semi-finished goods 57%; Fuels and energy 7%; Consumer goods 17%; Equipment goods 9%; Other products 10%.
Monetary unit: Belgian franc (frank). 1 franc = 100 centimes (centiemen).
Denominations:
  Coins 25, 50 centimes; 1, 5, 10, 20, 100, 250 francs.
  Notes 20, 50, 100, 500, 1000, 5000 francs.
Exchange rate to £ sterling: 76·40 (4 Apr. 1985).
Political history and government: A constitutional and hereditary monarchy, comprising nine provinces. Legislative power is vested in the King and the bicameral Parliament. comprising the Senate (181 members, including 106 directly elected by universal adult suffrage, 50 elected by provincial councils and 25 co-opted by the elected members) and the Chamber of Representatives (212 members directly elected, using proportional representation). Members of both Houses serve for up to four years. Executive power, nominally vested in the King, is exercised by the Cabinet. The King appoints the Prime Minister and, on the latter's advice, other Ministers. The Cabinet is responsible to Parliament.
Telephones: 3 818 626 (1982).
Daily newspapers: 38 in 1983, although some of them are only regional or local editions of larger dailies.
Radio: 4 622 649 receivers (1982).
TV: 2 978 689 sets (1982).
Length of roadways: 77 670 miles *125 000 km.*
Length of railways: 2646 miles *4259 km.*
Universities: 7.
Expectation of life: Males 67·79 years; females 74·21 years (1968–72).
Defence: Military service 8 months (in Germany) or 10 months (in Belgium); total armed forces 87 220 in 1984; defence expenditure, 1981: $3560 million.
Cinemas: 479 in 1982.

Belize

Population: 144 857 (census of 12 May 1980).
Area: 8867 miles² *22 965 km².*
Languages: English (official), Spanish.
Religion: Christian (Roman Catholic 55%, Protestant 43%).
Capital city: Belmopan, population 3000 (1984 estimate).
Other principal towns (1980): Belize City 39 771; Dangriga 6061; Orange Walk Town 8439; Corozal Town 6899; San Ignacio 5616.
Highest point: Victoria Peak, 3681 ft *1122 m.*
Principal mountain range: Maya Mountains.
Principal rivers: Hondo (on Mexican border), Belize, New River.
Head of State: HM Queen Elizabeth II, represented by Dr Minita Gordon, GCMG, Governor-General.
Prime Minister: Manuel Esquivel.
Climate: Sub-tropical. At Belize City, on the coast, temperatures range from 10°C *50°F* to 36°C *96°F*, with an annual average of 31°C *78·5°F*. There are greater variations inland. Rainfall increases from north (annual average 1295 mm *51 in* at Corozal) to south (4445 mm *175 in* at Toledo).
Labour force: 33 121 (census of 7 April 1970).
Gross domestic product: BZ$185 million in 1976: Agriculture, forestry and fishing 24% (agriculture 19%); Manufacturing 12%; Trade, restaurants and hotels 18%; Community, social and personal services 20%.

Exports: BZ$119·6 million in 1982.
Monetary unit: Belizean dollan (BZ$). 1 dollar = 100 cents.
Denominations:
  Coins 1, 5, 10, 25, 50 cents.
  Notes 1, 2, 5, 10, 20, 100 dollars.
Exchange rate to £ sterling: 2·222 (14 Jan. 1985).
Political history and government: Formerly British Honduras, a dependency of the United Kingdom. The colony was granted internal self-government on 1 Jan. 1964, when the First Minister became Premier. Renamed Belize on 1 June 1973.

Following a constitutional conference on 6–14 Apr. 1981, Belize became independent within the Commonwealth, on 21 Sept. 1981, when the Premier was restyled Prime Minister. Executive power is vested in the British monarch and is exercisable by the Governor-General, who is appointed on the advice of the Prime Minister and acts in almost all matters on the advice of the Cabinet. Legislative power is vested in the bicameral National Assembly, comprising a Senate (8 members appointed by the Governor-General) and a House of Representatives (28 members elected by universal adult suffrage for 5 years, subject to dissolution). The Governor-General appoints the Prime Minister and, on the latter's recommendation, other Ministers. The Cabinet is responsible to the House.
Telephones: 8100 (1983).
Daily newspapers: 2 (1976).
  Total circulation: 7000.
Radio: 85 000 (1977).
TV: 14 000 (1983).
Length of roadways: 2600 miles *4180 km.*
Adult illiteracy: 13·4% (males 12·5%; females 14·3%) in 1960.
Defence: The Belize Defence Force was formed on 1 Jan. 1978.
Cinemas: 8 (seating capacity 4500) in 1970.

Benin

Official name: La République populaire du Bénin (the People's Republic of Benin).
Population: 3 905 000 (1983 estimate).
Area: 43 484 miles² *112 622 km².*
Languages: French (official), Fon, Adja, Bariba, Yoruba.
Religions: Animist, with Christian and Muslim minorities.
Capital city: Porto-Novo, population 132 000 (1979 census).
Other Principal towns (1979): Cotonou 327 600; Natitingou 50,800; Abomey 41 000; Kandi 31 000; Ouidah 30 000.
Highest point: 2083 ft *635 m.*
Principal mountain range: Châine de l'Atakora.
Principal rivers: Ouémé, Niger (2600 miles *4184 km*) on frontier.
Head of State: Lt-Col. Mathieu Kerekou (b. 2 Sept. 1933), President and Head of the Government.
Climate: Tropical (hot and humid). Average temperatures 20°C *68°F* to 34°C *93°F*. Heavy rainfall near the coast, hotter and drier inland. In Cotonou the warmest month is April (daily average high 28°C *83°F*), coldest is August (23°C *73°F*).
Labour force: 1 317 000 (mid-1970): Agriculture, forestry and fishing 49·7%; Industry 11·8%; Services 38·5% (ILO estimates); 1 530 000 (1977).
Gross domestic product: 148 480 million CFA francs in 1977: Agriculture, forestry and fishing 42·6%; Trade, restaurants and hotels 25·2%.
Exports: $20·3 million in 1978: Food and live animals 38·3% (cocoa 29·7%); Raw cotton 35·7%; Palm kernel oil 11·7%.
Monetary unit: Franc de la Communauté financière africaine.
Denominations:
  Coins 1, 2, 5, 10, 25 CFA francs.
  Notes 50, 100, 500, 1000, 5000 CFA francs.
Exchange rate to £ sterling: 542·3 (14 Jan. 1985).
Political history and government: Formerly part of French West Africa, became independent as the Republic of Dahomey on 1 Aug. 1960. The

latest in a series of *coups* took place on 26 Oct. 1972, when power was assumed by army officers, led by Maj (later Lt-Col) Mathieu Kerekou. On 1 Sept. 1973 President Kerekou announced the creation of a National Council of the Revolution (CNR), with 69 members (including 30 civilians), under his leadership, to develop state policy. The military régime proclaimed its adherence to Marxist-Leninist principles and on 1 Dec. 1975 it introduced the country's present name, with a single ruling political party. In August 1977 the CNR adopted a *Loi fondamentale* (Fundamental Law) providing for the establishment of a National Revolutionary Assembly comprising 336 People's Commissioners representing socio-professional classes. The first Assembly was elected by universal adult suffrage on 20 Nov. 1979, from a single list of candidates, and the CNR was disbanded. The Assembly elects the President, who appoints the National Executive Council (Cabinet).
Telephones: 10 000 (1975).
Daily newspapers: 1 (1980).
  Total circulation: 10 000.
Radio: 65 000 (1981).
TV: 12 500 (1981).
Length of roadways: 4310 miles *6937 km* (31 Dec. 1974).
Length of railways: 360 miles *580 km.*
Universities: 1.
Adult illiteracy: 95·4% (males 92·3%; females 98·2%) in 1961.
Expectation of life: Males 41·8 years; females 45·0 years (UN estimates for 1970–75).
Defence: Total armed forces 33 100 (1984).
Cinemas: 4 (seating capacity 4400) in 1976 (cinemas exhibiting 35 mm films); also 1 mobile unit.
Foreign tourists: 23 033 in 1977.

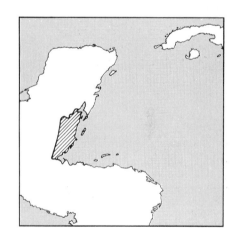

BELIZE

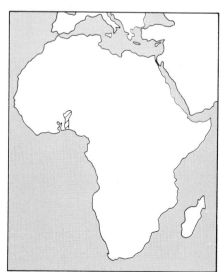

BENIN

Bhutan

Official name: Druk-yul or, in Tibetan, Druk Gyalkhap (Realm of the Dragon). The name Bhutan is Tibetan for 'the End of the Land'.
Population: 1 165 000 (mid-1981).
Area: 18 000 miles² *47 000 km²*.

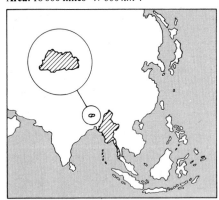

left: **BHUTAN** *right:* **BURMA**

left: **BOLIVIA** *right:* **BRAZIL**

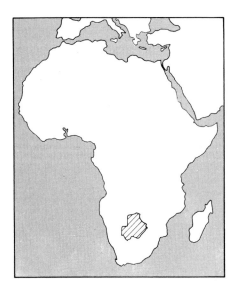

BOTSWANA

Languages: Dzongkha, Bumthangka, Sarchapkkha.
Religions: Buddhist, with Hindu minority.
Capital city: Thimphu, population 20 000 (Jan. 1985).
Other principal towns: Paro Dzong; Punakha; Tongsa Dzong.
Highest point: Khula Kangri 1, 24 784 ft *7554 m*.
Principal mountain range: Himalaya.
Principal rivers: Amo-Chu, Wang-chu, Machu, Manas.
Head of State: Jigme Singye Wangchuk (b. 11 Nov. 1955), Druk Gyalpo ('Dragon King').
Climate: Steamy hot in lowland foothills. Cold most of the year in higher areas.
Labour force: 521 000 (1970): Agriculture, forestry and fishing 94·3% (ILO estimates).
Gross domestic product: $104 million in 1975 (UN estimate).
Monetary unit: Ngultrum. 1 ngultrum = 100 chetrums (Indian currency is also legal tender).
Denominations:
   Coins 5, 10, 25, 50 chetrums; 1 ngultrum.
   Notes 1, 5, 10 and 100 ngultrums.
Exchange rate to £ sterling: 13·98 (14 Jan. 1985).
Political history and government: A hereditary monarchy, under the Wangchuk dynasty since 1907. The Treaty of Punakha in 1910 provided that Bhutan's external relations were to be guided by British India. After the independence of India in 1947, an Indo-Bhutan Treaty of 8 Aug. 1949 transferred this protection to India.

The King is Head of State and Head of Government but a Royal Advisory Council (nine members), established in 1965, is the principal policy-making body. Bhutan's first Cabinet was formed in May 1968. The government is assisted by the unicameral National Assembly (*Tsogdu*), established in 1953. The Assembly has 150 members, of whom 110 are indirectly elected by village headmen, 10 represent ecclesiastical bodies and 30 are appointed officials. Members of the Assembly serve a three-year term. The Royal Advisory Council and the Council of Ministers are responsible to the Assembly.
Telephones: 1900 (1982).
Radio: 8121 (1985).
Length of roadways: 1271 miles *2050 km* (1982).
Expectation of life: Males 47 years; females 50 years.
Defence: Army: 4000 men, Indian trained.
Cinemas: 3 (seating capacity 1500) in 1971.
Foreign tourists: 2000 in 1984.

Bolivia

Official name: República de Bolivia.
Population: 6 081 722 (1983 estimate).
Area: 424 164 miles² *1 098 581 km²*.
Languages: Spanish, Amyará, Quéchua.
Religion: Roman Catholic.
Capital city: La Paz de Ayacucho, population 835 283 (1983 estimate).
Other principal towns (1976): Santa Cruz de la Sierra 254 682; Cochabamba 204 684; Oruro 124 213; Potosí 77 397; Sucre (constitutional capital) 63 625.
Highest point: Nevado Sajama, 21 391 ft *6520 m* (first climbed in 1937).
Principal mountain ranges: Cordillera de los Andes, Cordillera Real, Cordillera Oriental, Cordillera Central.
Principal rivers: Beni, Mamoré, Pilcomayo, Paraguai (Paraguay) (1500 miles *2410 km*) on frontier.
Head of State: Hernan Silez, President.
Climate: Dry, with cold winds on Altiplano, hot and humid in eastern lowlands. In La Paz, average maximum 17°C *62°F* (June, July) to 19°C *67°F* (November), minimum 0,5°C *33°F* (July) to 6°C *43°F* (January, February), January rainiest (21 days).
Labour force: 1 501 391 (1976 census): Agriculture, forestry and fishing 48·1%; Manufacturing 10·1%; Community, social and personal services 19·6%.
Gross domestic product: 58 675 million pesos in 1976: Agriculture, forestry and fishing (excl.

government) 17·1% (agriculture 16·5%); Mining and quarrying 10·8%; manufacturing 13·3%; Trade, restaurants and hotels 18·9% (trade 18·7%); Community, social and personal services 15·3%.
Exports: US$898·18 million in 1982: Minerals 46·7%.
Monetary unit: Bolivian peso. 1 peso = 100 centavos.
Denominations:
   Coins 20, 25, 50 centavos; 1 peso.
   Notes 5, 10, 20, 50, 100 pesos.
Exchange rate to £ sterling: 9762·91 (14 Jan. 1985).
Political history and government: A republic, divided into nine departments. A series of military régimes held power from 1969 to 1979. Elections were held on 1 July 1979 for a President and for a bicameral Congress. No candidate gained a majority in the presidential election. Congress was convened on 1 Aug. 1979 but it also failed to give a majority to any presidential candidate. On 8 Aug. 1979 the President of the Senate was sworn in to serve as interim President. He was deposed by a military *coup* on 1 Nov. 1979. The *coup* leader resigned on 16 Nov. Congress elected the President of the Chamber of Deputies to be interim Head of State until fresh elections for a President and Congress, to hold office for four years. These were held on 29 June 1980 but the presidential election again proved inconclusive. Congress, comprising a Senate (27 members) and a Chamber of Deputies (130 members), was due to meet on 4 Aug. 1980 to elect a President but an armed forces junta again seized power on 17 July 1980. The *coup* leader, Gen Luis García Meza, was sworn in as President on the next day and Congress was suspended. On 4 Aug. 1981 President García resigned and ceded power to the junta. On 4 Sept. the junta transferred sole power to one of its members.
Telephones: 144 300 (1982).
Daily newspapers: 13 (1976).
   Total circulation: 150 000.
Radio: 440 000 (1977).
TV: 49 000 (1977).
Length of roadways: 23 185 miles *37 313 km* (1974).
Length of railways: 2298 miles *3698 km*.
Universities: 9.
Adult illiteracy: 37·3% in 1976.
Expectation of life: Males 46·5 years; females 51·1 years (UN estimates for 1970–75).
Defence: Military service 12 months, selective; total armed forces 28 000 in 1984; defence expenditure, 1980: $118 million.
Cinemas: 41 in 1976.
Foreign tourists: 179 500 in 1977.

Botswana

Official name: The Republic of Botswana.
Population: 941 027 (1981 census).
Area: 231 805 miles² *600 372 km²*.
Languages: Setswana, English.
Religions: Christian, ancestral beliefs.
Capital city: Gaborone, population 59 657 (1983 estimate).
Other principal towns (1980): Francistown 32 000; Selebi-Pikwe 29 000; Kanye 22 000; Lobatse 20 000; Mochudi 20 000; Molepole 19 000; Mahalapye 19 000; Maun 16 000.
Principal rivers: Chobe, Shashi.
Head of State: Dr Quett Ketumile Joni Masire (b. 23 July 1925), President.
Climate: Sub-tropical but variable. Hot summers. In winter, warm days and cold nights in higher parts. Average annual rainfall 457 mm *18 in*, varying from 635 mm *25 in* in north to 228 mm *9 in* or less in western Kalahari. Sand and dust blown by westerly wind in August.
Labour force: 384 000 in 1977: Agriculture 69%; Domestic service 2·9%; Employed outside Botswana 12%.
Gross domestic product: 298·2 million pula in year ending 30 June 1977: Agriculture, forestry and fishing 23·7%; Mining and quarrying 13·5%; Trade, restaurants and hotels 18·0%;

Government services 15·7%.
Exports: 442·3 million pula in 1982: Diamonds and copper-nickel matte 66% (76% in 1983); Beef and beef products 20%; Clothing and textiles 4%.
Monetary unit: Pula. 1 pula = 100 thebe.
Denominations:
  Coins 1, 5, 10, 25 and 50 thebe.
  Notes 1, 2, 5 and 10 pula.
Exchange rate to £ sterling: 2·178 (14 Jan. 1985).
Political history and government: Formerly the Bechuanaland Protectorate, under British rule. In February 1965 the seat of government was moved from Mafeking (now Mafikeng), in South Africa, to Gaberones (now Gaborone). The first elections were held on 1 Mar. 1965, when internal self-government was achieved, and the first Prime Minister was appointed two days later. Bechuanaland became the independent Republic of Botswana, within the Commonwealth, on 30 Sept. 1966, when the Prime Minister became President.
Legislative power is vested in the unicameral National Assembly, with 38 members, including 32 directly elected by universal adult suffrage from single-member constituencies. Members of the Assembly serve for up to five years. Executive power is vested in the President, who is leader of the majority party in the Assembly. He governs with the assistance of an appointed Cabinet, responsible to the Assembly. The government is also advised by the House of Chiefs, with 15 members, including the chiefs of the eight principal tribes, four sub-chiefs and three others.
Telephones: 11 214 (1979).
Daily newspapers: 2 (1977).
  Total circulation: 17 000.
Radio: 63 000 (1977).
Length of roadways: 6509 miles *10 476 km* (31 Dec. 1979).
Length of railways: 441 miles *710 km*.
Universities: 1.
Adult illiteracy: 67·1% (males 69·7%; females 65·0%) unable to read in 1964.
Expectation of life: Males 44·3 years; females 47·5 years (UN estimates for 1970–75).
Defence: Total armed forces 3000 (1984); defence expenditure, 1980: $22 million.
Cinemas: 1 (seating capacity 800) in 1975 (cinema exhibiting 35 mm films).
Foreign tourists: 82 193 in 1983.

Brazil

Official name: A República Federativa do Brasil (the Federative Republic of Brazil).
Population: 129 660 000 (1983 estimate).
Area: 3 286 488 miles² *8 511 965 km²*.
Language: Portuguese.
Religion: Roman Catholic.
Capital city: Brasília, population 1 434 000 (1983 estimate).
Other principal towns (1980): Sao Paulo 7 032 547; Rio de Janeiro 5 090 700; Salvador 1 491 642; Belo Horizonte 1 441 567; Recife 1 183 391; Porto Alegre 1 114 867; Curitiba 842 818; Belem 755 984; Goiãna 702 858; Fortaleza 647 917.
Highest point: Pico da Bandeira, 9482 ft *2890 m*.
Principal mountain ranges: Serra do Mar, Serra Geral, Serra de Mantiqueira.
Principal rivers: Amazonas (Amazon) (4007 miles *6448 km*) and tributaries, Paraná, São Francisco.
Head of State: Jose Sarney, President.
Climate: Hot and wet in tropical Amazon basin; sub-tropical in highlands; temperate (warm summers and mild winters) in southern uplands. In Rio de Janeiro, average maximum 24°C *75°F* (July, September) to 29°C *85°F* (February), minimum 17°C *63°F* (July) to 23°C *73°F* (January, February), December rainiest (14 days). In São Paulo, maximum 22°C *71°F* (June, July) to 28°C *82°F* (February), minimum 9°C *49°F* (July) to 18°C *64°F* (February), January rainiest (19 days). Absolute maximum temperature 43·9°C *111·0°F*, Ibipetuba, 16 Sept. 1927: absolute

minimum −11°C *+12·2°F*, Xanxerê, 14 July 1933.
Labour force: 29 557 224 (including unemployed) aged 10 and over (1970 census): Agriculture, forestry and fishing 45·4%; Manufacturing 11·2%; Community, social and personal services 22·6%; 36 311 800 (estimate for July 1977).
Gross domestic product: 3 410 018 million cruzeiros in 1978: Agriculture, forestry and fishing 11·4%; Manufacturing 28·3%; Trade 15·3%; Finance, insurance and real estate (incl. owner-occupied dwellings) 15·5%.
Exports: 3 368·8 billion cruzeiros in 1982: Coffee 16%; Iron ore 15%; Rolling stock and vehicles 15%; Soybean bran 14%; Machinery 11%.
Monetary unit: Cruzeiro. 1 cruzeiro = 100 centavos.
Denominations:
  Coins 1, 2, 5, 10, 20, 50 centavos; 1 cruzeiro.
  Notes 1, 5, 10, 50, 100, 500, 1000 cruzeiros.
Exchange rate to £ sterling: 3701·68 (14 Jan. 1985).
Political history and government: Under a military-backed government since the army revolution of 31 Mar.–1 Apr. 1964. Existing political parties were banned on 27 Oct. 1965. Two new parties (one pro-government, one against) were formed in Dec. 1965. New constitutions were introduced on 15 Mar. 1967 and 20 Oct. 1969. Brazil is a federal republic comprising 23 States, four Territories and a Federal District (Brasília). Legislative power is exercised by the National Congress, comprising the Chamber of Deputies (420 members, elected for four years) and the Federal Senate (66 members, elected in rotation for eight years). One-third of the Senate is elected indirectly. All literate adults may vote. Executive power is exercised by the President, elected for six years by an electoral college composed of members of Congress and representatives of State legislatures. He is assisted by a Vice-President and an appointed Cabinet. The President has far-reaching powers. On 22 Nov. 1979 Congress approved legislation to end the two-party system. Several opposition parties were later formed.
Telephones: 8 536 000 (1982).
Daily newspapers: 344 (1979).
Radio: 16 980 000 (1975).
TV: 11 000 000 (1977).
Length of roadways: 860 241 miles *1 384 423 km* (31 Dec. 1979).
Length of railways: 18 665 miles *30 039 km*.
Universities: 65.
Adult illiteracy: 24·3% (males 22·0%; females 26·5%) in 1976.
Expectation of life: Males 57·61 years; females 61·10 years (1960–70).
Defence: Military service one year; total armed forces 273 750 in 1983; defence expenditure, 215 billion cruzeiros in 1981.
Cinemas: 2937 in 1979.
Foreign tourists: 1 357 879 in 1981.

Brunei

Population: 191 770 (1981 census).
Area: 2226 miles² *5765 km²*.
Language: Malay, English.
Religion: Islam.
Capital city: Bandar Seri Begawan, population 75 000 (1976).
Principal river: Brunei River.
Head of State: HH Muda Sir Hassanal Bolkiah Mu'izzaddin Waddaulah, Sultan of Brunei (b. 15 July 1946).
Climate: Hot and wet, tropical marine, rainfall ranging from 2500 mm *100 inches* on the coast to 5000 mm *200 inches* inland. Bandar Seri Begawan, Jan. 27°C *80°F*, July 28°C *82°F*.
Exports: US$3171 million in 1982: Crude oil 62%; Liquefied natural gas 31%; Petroleum products 6%.
Currency: Brunei dollar = 100 cents.
Exchange rate to £ sterling: 2·4532 (14 Jan. 1985).
Political history and government: The Sultanate of Brunei once controlled all of the island of Borneo, as well as parts of the Sulu Islands and

the Philippines. After the 16th century its power declined until, by the middle of the 19th century, it had been reduced to its present boundaries, under the protection of Great Britain.
The present Sultan formed a constitution in 1959, whereby there would be a Privy Council, an Executive and a Legislative Council. On 6 Jan. 1965 amendments were made to the constitution so that elections could be made to the Legislative Council. The Executive Council was renamed the Council of Ministers. The Council of Ministers is presided over by the Sultan and consists of six ex-officio members and four other members, all of whom, except one, are members of the Legislative Council. The Mentri Besar, or Acting Chief Minister (one of the ex-officio members of the Legislative Council and the Council of Ministers) is responsible to the Sultan for the exercise of executive authority in the State.
On 7 Jan. 1979 the Sultan and the British government signed a treaty by which Brunei became an independent state on 31 December 1983.
Telephones: 21 928 (1982).
Radio: 38 000 (1980).
TV: 32 000 (1980).
Length of roadways: 916 miles *1474 km*.
Defence: Total armed forces, 3650 (1984).

Bulgaria

Official name: Narodna Republika Bulgariya (People's Republic of Bulgaria).
Population: 8 905 581 (1982 estimate).
Area: 42 823 miles² *110 912 km²*.
Languages: Bulgarian 88%; Turkish and Macedonian minorities.
Religions: Eastern Orthodox, with Muslim, Roman Catholic and Protestant minorities.
Capital city: Sofiya (Sofia), population 1 070 358 (1981 estimate).
Other principal towns (1981): Plovdiv 358 176; Varna 293 950; Ruse 176 013; Burgas 173 078; Stara Zagora 138 902; Pleven 131 690; Sliven 99 147.
Highest point: Musala, 9596 ft *2925 m*.
Principal mountain range: Stara Planina (Balkan Mountains).
Principal rivers: Dunav (Danube) (1770 miles *2850 km*), Iskŭr (Iskar) (229 miles *368 km*), Maritsa (326 miles *524 km*), Tundzha.
Head of State: Todor Zhivkov (b. 7 Sept. 1911), President of the State Council and General Secretary of the Central Committee of the Bulgarian Communist Party.
Head of Government: Grisha Filipov (b. 13 July 1919), Chairman of the Council of Ministers.
Climate: Mild in the south, more extreme in the north. In Sofia, July (14°C *57°F* to 28°C *82°F*), August (13°C *56°F* to 28°C *82°F*) hottest, January (−5°C *22°F* to 1°C *34°F*) coldest, May rainiest (11 days).
Labour force: 4 047 501 in 1981 (excluding peasants): Industry 34·3%; Agriculture and forestry 23·2%; Construction 8·6%.
Net material product: 16 337·9 million leva in

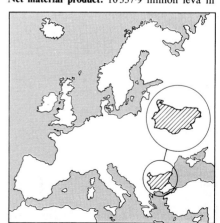

BULGARIA

1978: Agriculture and forestry 18·3% (agriculture 17·8%); Industry 55·1%.
Exports: 9958 million leva in 1981.
Monetary unit: Lev. 1 lev = 100 stotinki (singular: stotinka).
Denominations:
Coins 1, 2, 5, 10, 20, 50 stotinki; 1, 2, 5 leva.
Notes 1, 2, 5, 10, 20 leva.
Exchange rate to £ sterling: 1·2323 (14 Jan. 1985).
Political history and government: Formerly part of Turkey's Ottoman Empire, becoming an autonomous principality in 1878. Bulgaria became a fully independent kingdom on 22 Sept. 1908. The government allied with Nazi Germany in the Second World War. On 9 Sept. 1944 the Fatherland Front, a Communist-dominated coalition, seized power in a *coup*. The monarchy was abolished by a popular referendum on 8 Sept. 1946 and a republic proclaimed on 15 Sept. 1946. A constitution for a People's Republic was adopted on 4 Dec. 1947. A new constitution was promulgated, after approval by referendum, on 18 May 1971.

The supreme organ of state power is the unicameral National Assembly, with 400 members elected for five years (unopposed) by universal adult suffrage in single-member constituencies. The Assembly elects the State Council (28 members were elected on 17 June 1981) to be its permanent organ. The Council of Ministers, the highest organ of state administration, is elected by (and responsible to) the Assembly.

Political power is held by the Bulgarian Communist Party (BCP), which dominates the Fatherland Front. The Front presents an approved list of candidates for elections to all representative bodies. The BCP's highest authority is the Party Congress, convened every five years. The Congress elects a Central Committee (197 members were elected in April 1981) to supervise Party work. To direct its policy, the Committee elects a Political Bureau (Politburo), with 12 full members and three candidate members in 1981.

Bulgaria comprises 27 provinces and three cities, each with a People's Council elected for 2½ years.
Telephones: 1 382 076 (1981).
Daily newspapers: 14 (1981).
Total circulation: 2 200 000.
Radio: 2 115 059 (1981).
TV: 1 658 688 (1981).
Length of roadways: 20 108 miles *32 354 km* (1981).
Length of railways: 2698 miles *4341 km* (1983).
Universities: 3.
Adult illiteracy: 9·8% (males 4·8%; females 14·7%) in 1965.
Expectation of life: Males 68·68 years; females 73·91 years (1974–76).
Defence: Military service: Army and Air Force two years, Navy three years; total armed forces 164 000 in 1984; defence expenditure, 1981: $1340 million (converted at $1 = 0·69 lev).
Cinemas: 3529 in 1979.
Foreign tourists: 5 120 324 (including 2 124 746 visitors in transit) in 1979.

Burma

Official name: Pyidaungsu Socialist Thammada Myanma Nainggnan (The Socialist Republic of the Union of Burma).
Population: 35 313 905 (1983 census).
Area: 261 218 miles² *676 552 km²*.
Languages: Burmese, English.
Religions: Buddhist, with Muslim, Hindu and Animist minorities.
Capital city: Yangon (Rangoon), population 2 458 712 (1983 census).
Other principal towns (1977): Mandalay 458 000; Moulmein 188 000; Bassein 138 000; Pegu 135 000.
Highest Point: Hkakado Razi, 19 296 ft *5881 m*.
Principal mountain ranges: Arakan Yoma, Pegu Yoma.
Principal rivers: Irrawaddy (including Chind-

win), Salween, Sittang, Mekong (2600 miles *4180 km*) on frontier.
Head of State: Brig-Gen. U. San Yu (b. 1919), President.
Prime Minister: U Maung Maung Kha (b. 2 Nov. 1917).
Climate: Hot March–April, monsoon May–October, cool November–February. In Rangoon, average maximum 29°C *85°F* (July, August) to 36°C *97°F* (April), minimum 18°C *65°F* (January) to 25°C *77°F* (May), July (26 days) and August (25 days) rainiest. Absolute maximum temperature 45,56°C *114°F*, Mandalay, 29 Apr. 1906, Monywa, 15 May 1934; absolute minimum −0,56°C *31°F*, Maymyo, 29 Dec. 1913.
Labour force: 12 935 000 (excluding 512 000 unemployed) in 1979: Agriculture, forestry and fishing 70·3%; Trade, restaurants and hotels 10·0%.
Gross domestic product: 29 511 million kyats in year ending 30 Sept. 1978: Agriculture, forestry and fishing 46·1% (agriculture. excl. livestock, 37·3%); Trade 29·1%.
Exports: $192·6 million (excluding re-exports) in 1976: Food and live animals 64·2% (rice 55·2%); Wood, lumber and cork 26·4% (sawlogs and veneer logs 17·8%).
Monetary unit: Kyat. 1 kyat = 100 pyas.
Denominations:
Coins 1, 5, 10, 25, 50 pyas; 1 kyat.
Notes 1, 5, 10, 20, 25, 50, 100 kyats.
Exchange rate to £ sterling: 10·2341 (14 Jan. 1985).
Political history and government: Formerly part of British India. Burma became a separate British dependency, with limited self-government, in 1937. It was invaded and occupied by Japanese forces in February 1942 but re-occupied by British forces in May 1945. Burma became independent, outside the Commonwealth, on 4 Jan. 1948. The government was deposed by a military *coup* on 2 Mar. 1962 and Parliament was dissolved the next day. Power was assumed by a Revolutionary Council, led by Gen Ne Win. The military régime established the Burmese Socialist Programme Party (BSPP), the only permitted party since 28 Mar. 1964.

A new one-party constitution, approved by popular referendum on 15–31 Dec. 1973, was introduced on 4 Jan. 1974, when the country's present name was adopted. Legislative power is vested in the People's Assembly, with 475 members elected for four years by universal adult suffrage. The first Assembly was elected on 27 Jan.–10 Feb. 1974 and inaugurated on 2 Mar. 1974, when the Revolutionary Council was dissolved. The Assembly elects a Council of State (29 members) to be the country's main policy-making body. The Chairman of the Council of State is President of the Republic. The Council of Ministers, elected by the Assembly, has executive responsibility. Burma comprises 7 states and 7 administrative regions.
Telephones: 32 616 (1978).
Daily newspapers: 7 (1976).
Total circulation: 329 000.
Radio: 693 000 (1977).
Length of roadways: 16 812 miles *27 056 km* (1979).
Length of railways: 1949 miles *3137 km* (30 Sept. 1975).
Universities: 2.
Adult illiteracy: 40·3% in 1962.
Expectation of life: Males 48·6 years; females 51·5 years (UN estimates for 1970–75).
Defence: Military service voluntary; total armed forces 182 000 (1984); defence expenditure, 1980: $200 million.
Cinemas: 400 in 1979.
Foreign tourists: 23 845 in 1980.

Burundi

Official name: La République du Burundi or Republika y'Uburundi (the Republic of Burundi).
Population: 4 920 000 (1983 estimate).
Area: 10 747 miles² *27 834 km²*.

Languages: French, Kirundi, Kiswahili.
Religions: Roman Catholic, with Animist and Protestant minorities.
Capital city: Bujumbura (formerly Usumbura), population 144 040 (1979).
Other principal town: Gitega (Kitega), population 15 943 (1978).
Highest point: 8809 ft *2685 m*.
Principal rivers: Kagera, Ruzizi.
Head of State: Col Jean-Baptiste Bagaza (b. 29 Aug. 1946), President.
Climate: Hot and humid in lowlands, cool in highlands.
Labour force: 1 715 000 (1970): Agriculture, forestry and fishing 87·1% (ILO estimates); 1 882 000 (1979 estimate).
Gross domestic product: 56 132·5 million Burundi francs in 1978: Agriculture, forestry and fishing 55·9% (agriculture 52·6%).
Exports: 6260 million Burundi francs in 1981: Coffee 85·5%; Cotton 2·9%; Tea 2·9%.
Monetary unit: Burundi franc. 1 franc = 100 centimes.
Denominations:
Coins 1, 5, 10 francs.
Notes 10, 20, 50, 100, 500, 1000 francs.
Exchange rate to £ sterling: 144·75 (14 Jan. 1985).
Political history and government: Formerly a monarchy, ruled by a *Mwami* (King). Part of German East Africa from 1899. Occupied in 1916 by Belgian forces from the Congo (now Zaire). From 1920 Burundi was part of Ruanda–Urundi, administered by Belgium under a League of Nations mandate and later as a UN Trust Territory. Became independent on 1 July 1962. A one-party state since 24 Nov. 1966. The monarchy was overthrown, and a republic established, by a military *coup* on 28 Nov. 1966, when the Prime Minister, Col (later Lt-Gen) Michel Micombero, took power and became President. Another military *coup* deposed Micombero on 1 Nov. 1976. A Supreme Revolutionary Council (SRC) with 30 members, all military officers, was established on 2 Nov. 1976 and its leader became President of the Second Republic. The office of Prime Minister was abolished on 13 Oct. 1978. The ruling party's National Congress, opening on 26 Dec. 1979, elected a Central Committee to take over the SRC's functions.
Telephones: 5601 (1982).
Daily newspapers: 1 (1976).
Radio: 107 000 (1977).
Length of roadways: 4000 miles *6400 km*.
Universities: 1.
Adult illiteracy: 86·1% in 1962.
Expectation of life: Males 40 years; females 43 years (sample survey, 1970–71).
Defence: Total armed forces 5200 (1984); defence expenditure, 1980: $22 million.
Cinemas: 12 in 1977.
Foreign tourists: 31 410 (including 1643 Burundi nationals residing abroad) in 1976.

Cameroon

Official name: La République unie du Cameroun (the United Republic of Cameroon).
Population: 7 663 246 (census of 9 April 1976); 9 060 000 (1983 estimate).
Area: 183 569 miles² *475 442 km²*.
Languages: French, English (both official).
Religions: Animist, with Christian and Muslim minorities.
Capital city: Yaoundé, population 313 000 (1976).
Other principal towns (1976): Douala 458 426; Nkongsamba 71 298; Garoua 69 285; Maroua 67 187; Bamenda 67 184; Bafoussam 62 239; Foumban 59 701.
Highest point: Cameroon Mt, 13 350 ft *4069 m*.
Principal mountain range: Massif de Ladamaoua.
Principal rivers: Sanaga, Nyong.
Head of State: Paul Biya (b. 13 Feb. 1933), President.
Prime Minister: Luc Ayang.
Climate: Hot and rainy on the coast; cooler and drier inland. Average temperature 27°C *80°F*.

In Yaoundé average maximum 27°C *80°F* to 29°C *85°F*, minimum around 19°C *66°F*.

Labour force: 2 757 899 (Africans only) at 1976 census: Agriculture, forestry and fishing 79·4%.

Gross domestic product: 789 800 million CFA francs in year ending 30 June 1977: Agriculture, forestry and fishing 34·8% (agriculture 30·9%); Manufacturing 10·0%; Trade, restaurants and hotels 17·0%.

Exports: 299 717 million francs CFA in 1981: Coffee 23%; Cocoa 21%; Crude oil 31%; Timber 11%.

Monetary unit: Franc de la Communauté financière africain (CFA).

Denominations:
 Coins 1, 2, 5, 10, 25, 50, 100, 500 CFA francs.
 Notes 100, 500, 1000, 5000, 10 000 CFA francs.

Exchange rate to £ sterling: 542·25 (14 Jan. 1985).

Political history and government: The former German colony of Cameroon was divided into British and French zones, both parts becoming UN Trust Territories. The French zone became independent as the Republic of Cameroon on 1 Jan. 1960. The northern part of the British zone joined Nigeria on 1 June 1961 and the southern part became West Cameroon when it joined the former French zone (renamed East Cameroon) to form a federal republic on 1 Oct. 1961. A one-party state since 8 Sept. 1966. After approval by a referendum on 21 May 1972, the federal arrangement ended and Cameroon became a unitary state on 2 June 1972. The legislature is a unicameral National Assembly of 120 members elected for five years by universal suffrage. The President, elected by the people every five years, appoints the Prime Minister, other Ministers and a governor for each of the seven provinces.

Telephone: 14 321 (1978).

Daily newspapers: 3 (1976).
 Total circulation: 30 000.

Radio: 760 000 (1980).

Length of roadways: 16 730 miles.
 26 920 km (1977).

Length of railways: 729 miles *1173 km*.

Universities: 1.

Adult illiteracy: 81·1% in 1962.

Expectation of life: Males 41·9 years; females 45·1 years (UN estimates for 1970–75).

Defence: Total armed forces 7300 (1984); defence expenditure, 1980: $92 million.

Cinemas: 45 (seating capacity 25 000) and 17 mobile units (1977).

Foreign tourists: 126 337 in 1979.

Canada

Official name: Canada.

Population: 24 343 181 (1981 census).

Area: 3 851 809 miles² *9 976 139 km²*.

Languages: English 60·1%; French 26·9%; German 2·6%; Italian 2·5%; Ukrainian 1·4% (1971).

Religions: Roman Catholic, United Church of Canada, Anglican.

Capital city: Ottawa, population 717 978 (1981 census).

Other principal towns (1981): Toronto 2 998 947; Montreal 2 828 349; Vancouver 1 268 183; Edmonton 657 057; Winnipeg 584 842; Quebec 576 075; Hamilton 542 095; Calgary 592 743.

Highest point: Mt Logan, 19 850 ft *6050 m* (first climbed 23 June 1925).

Principal mountain ranges: Rocky Mts, Coast Mts, Mackenzie Mts.

Principal rivers: Mackenzie (2635 miles *4240 km*, including Peace 1195 miles *1923 km*), Yukon (1979 miles *3185 km*), St Lawrence (1945 miles *3130 km*), Nelson (1600 miles *2575 km*, including Saskatchewan 1205 miles *1940 km*), Columbia (1150 miles *1850 km*), Churchill (1000 miles *1609 km*).

Head of State: HM Queen Elizabeth II, represented by Mme Jeanne Sauvé (b. 1922), Governor-General.

Prime Minister: The Rt Hon Brian Mulroney (b. 1939).

Climate: Great extremes, especially inland. Average summer temperature 65°F, very cold winters. Light to moderate rainfall, heavy snowfalls. Below are listed a selection of towns showing the extreme monthly variations in average maximum and minimum daily temperatures and the month with the maximum number of rainy days.

Calgary: Average maximum −4°C *24°F* (January) to 24°C *76°F* (July). Average minimum −17°C *2°F* (January) to 8°C *47°F* (July). Rainiest month (rainy days) June (12).

Halifax: Average maximum −0,5°C *31°F* (February) to 23°C *74°F* (July, August). Average minimum −9°C *15°F* (January, February) to 13°C *56°F* (August). Rainiest month (rainy days) January (17).

Ottawa: Average maximum −6°C *21°F* (January) to 27°C *81°F* (July). Average minimum −16°C *3°F* (January, February) to 14°C *58°F* (July). Rainiest month (rainy days) December (14).

St John's: Average maximum −2°C *28°F* (February) to 20°C *69°F* (August). Average minimum −9°C *16°F* (February) to 12°C *53°F* (August). Rainiest months (rainy days) November, December (17).

Vancouver: Average maximum 5°C *41°F* (January) to 23°C *74°F* (July). Average minimum 0°C *32°F* (January) to 12°C *54°F* (July, August). Rainiest month (rainy days) December (22).

Winnipeg: Average maximum −14°C *7°F* (January) to 26°C *79°F* (July). Average minimum −25°C *−13°F* (January) to 13°C *55°F* (July). Rainiest months (rainy days) January, June (12).

Yellowknife: Average maximum −23°C *−10°F* (January) to 20°C *69°F* (July). Average minimum −33°C *−26°F* (January) to 11°C *52°F* (July). Rainiest month (rainy days) December (13).

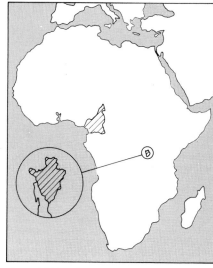

above: **CAMEROON**   *encircled:* **BURUNDI**

Absolute maximum temperature 46,1°C *115°F*, Gleichen, Alberta, 28 July 1903; absolute minimum −62,8°C *−81°F*, Snag, Yukon, 3 Feb. 1947.

Labour force: 10 354 000 (excluding 937 000 unemployed) in April 1980: Manufacturing 19·9%; Trade, restaurants and hotels 17·2%; Community, social and personal services 36·0%. Figures exclude Yukon Territory, the Northwest Territories, armed forces and Indians living on reservations.

Gross domestic product: C$234 215 million in

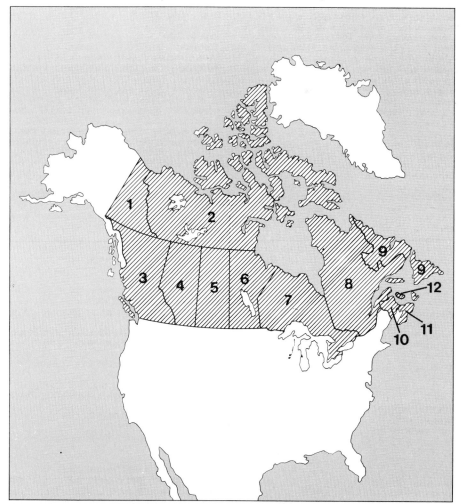

CANADA—1. Yukon Territory   2. Northwest Territories   3. British Columbia
4. Alberta   5. Saskatchewan   6. Manitoba   7. Ontario   8. Quebec   9. Newfoundland
10. New Brunswick   11. Nova Scotia   12. Prince Edward Island

1978: Manufacturing (excl. government) 20·7%; Trade (excl. government) 11·3%; Community, social and personal services (incl. restaurants, hotels and business services) 26·2% (government services 16·8%).
Exports: US$55 116·7 million in 1979: Mineral fuels, lubricants, etc. 13·2%; Machinery 10·7%; Transport equipment 19·4% (road motor vehicles and parts 17·4%).
Monetary unit: Canadian dollar (C$). One dollar = 100 cents.
Denominations:
Coins 1, 5, 10, 25, 50 cents; $1.
Notes $1, 2, 5, 10, 20, 50, 100, 500, 1000.
Exchange rate to £ sterling: 1·65 (10 April 1985).
Political history and government: The Dominion of Canada, under the British Crown, was established on 1 July 1867 by the British North America Act. It was originally a federation of four provinces (Quebec, Ontario, Nova Scotia and New Brunswick). These were later joined by Manitoba (15 July 1870), British Columbia (20 July 1871), Prince Edward Island (1 July 1873), Alberta and Saskatchewan (1 Sept. 1905). Canada acquired its Arctic islands from the United Kingdom on 1 Sept. 1880. The country achieved full independence, within the Commonwealth, by the Statute of Westminster on 11 Dec. 1931. Newfoundland, previously a separate British dependency, became the tenth province on 1 Apr. 1949.

In November 1981 the Canadian government agreed on the provisions of an amended constitution, to the end that it should replace the British North America Act and that its future amendment should be the prerogative of Canada. These proposals were adopted by the Parliament of Canada and were enacted by the UK Parliament as the Canada Act of 1982.

The Act gave to Canada the power to amend the Constitution according to procedures determined by the Constitutional Act 1982, which was proclaimed in force by the Queen on 17 April 1982. The Constitution Act 1982 added to the Canadian Constitution a charter of Rights and Freedoms, and provisions which recognize the nation's multi-cultural heritage, affirm the existing rights of native peoples, confirm the principle of equalization of benefits among the provinces, and strengthen provincial ownership of natural resources.

Canada is a federal parliamentary state. Executive power is vested in the Queen and exercisable by her representative, the Governor-General, whom she appoints on the advice of the Canadian Prime Minister. The Federal Parliament comprises the Queen, a nominated Senate (104 members, appointed on a regional basis) and a House of Commons (282 members elected by universal adult suffrage). A Parliament may last no longer than 5 years. The Governor-General appoints the Prime Minister and, on the latter's recommendation, other Ministers to form the Cabinet. The Prime Minister must have majority support in Parliament, to which the Cabinet is responsible. Canada contains 10 provinces (each with a Lieutenant-Governor and a legislature from which a Premier is chosen) and two centrally-administered territories.
Telephones: 16 248 428 (1983).
Daily newspapers: 120 (1982).
Total circulation: 5 150 000.
Radio: 24 270 000 (1977).
TV: 11 000 000 (1979).
Length of roadways: 575 520 miles *928 258 km* (1981).
Length of railways: 41 150 miles *66 370 km*.
Universities: 47.
Expectation of life: Males 69·34 years; females 76·36 years (1970–72).
Defence: Military service voluntary; total armed forces 82 000 (1983); defence expenditure, 1981/82: US $4990 million.
Cinemas: 1322 in 1981.
Foreign tourists: 34 406 501 in 1982.

ALBERTA
Population: 2 237 724 (1981 census).
Area: 255 285 miles² *661 199 km²*.

Languages: English, German, Ukrainian, French.
Religions: United Church of Canada, Roman Catholic, Anglican, Lutheran.
Capital city: Edmonton, population 657 057.
Other principal towns (1981): Calgary 592 743; Lethbridge 58 086; Red Deer 50 257; Medicine Hat 41 167.
Principal mountain range: Rocky Mountains.
Principal rivers: Peace, Athabasca.
Lieutenant-Governor: Helen Hunley.
Premier: (Edgar) Peter Lougheed (b. 26 July 1928).
Telephones: 1 046 040 (1983).
Daily newspapers: 7 (1974).
Length of roadways: 86 347 miles *138 962 km*.
Length of railways: 6244 miles *10 048 km*.
Universities: 4.

BRITISH COLUMBIA
Population: 2 744 467 (1981 census).
Area: 366 255 miles² *948 596 km²*.
Languages: English, German.
Religions: United Church of Canada, Anglican, Roman Catholic, Lutheran.
Capital city: Victoria, population 236 400 (1982 estimate).
Other principal towns (1982): Vancouver 1 268 183; Prince George 68 867; Kamloops 64 660; Kelowna 60 026; Nanaimo 49 139.
Principal mountain range: Rocky Mountains.
Principal rivers: Fraser, Thompson, Kootennay, Columbia.
Lieutenant-Governor: Robert Gordon Rogers.
Premier: William Richards Bennett (b. 14 April 1932).
Telephones: 1 300 000 (1982).
Daily newspapers: 19 (1974).
Length of roadways: 28 120 miles *45 254 km*.
Length of railways: 4826 miles *7766 km*.
Universities: 3.

MANITOBA
Population: 1 026 241 (1981 census).
Area: 251 000 miles² *650 087 km²*.
Languages: English, Ukrainian, German, French.
Religions: United Church of Canada, Roman Catholic, Anglican, Lutheran.
Capital city: Winnipeg, population 584 842 (1981 census).
Other principal towns (1981): Brandon 35 894; Thompson 14 102; Portage la Prairie 12 959.
Highest point: Duck Mountain, 2727 ft *831 m*.
Lieutenant-Governor: Pearl McGonigal.
Premier: Howard Pawley.
Telephones: 748 170 (1982).
Daily newspapers: 8 (1974).
Length of roadways: 11 300 miles *18 185 km*.
Length of railways: 4900 miles *7886 km*.
Universities: 3.

NEW BRUNSWICK
Population: 696 403 (1981 census).
Area: 28 354 miles² *73 437 km²*.
Languages: English, French.
Religions: Roman Catholic, Baptist, United Church of Canada, Anglican.
Capital city: Fredericton, population 45 248 (1976 census).
Other principal towns (1976): Saint John 85 956; Moncton 55 934; Bathurst 16 301; Edmundston 12 710.
Highest point: Mt Carleton, 2690 ft *820 m*.
Principal river: St John.
Lieutenant-Governor: George F. S. Stanley.
Premier: Richard Bennett Hatfield (b. 9 Apr. 1931).
Telephones: 389 466 (1980).
Daily newspapers: 5 (1983).
Length of roadways: 12 854 miles *20 686 km*.
Universities: 4.

NEWFOUNDLAND (Terre-Neuve)
Population: 567 681 (1981 census).
Area: 156 185 miles² *404 517 km²*.
Language: English.
Religions: Roman Catholic, Anglican, United Church of Canada, Salvation Army.
Capital city: St John's, population 154 820 (1981

census).
Other principal towns (1981): Corner Brook 24 339; Labrador City 11 538; Gander 10 404; Stephenville 8876.
Highest point: Mt Gras Morne, 2666 ft *812 m*.
Principal mountain range: Long Range Mountain.
Principal rivers: Humber, Exploits, Gander.
Lieutenant-Governor: Dr William Anthony Paddon (b. 10 July 1914).
Premier: (Alfred) Brian Peckford (b. 27 Aug. 1942).
Telephones: 265 436 (1981).
Daily newspapers: 3 (1974).
Length of railways: 1085 miles *1746 km*.
Universities: 1.

NOVA SCOTIA
Population: 847 442 (1981 census).
Area: 21 425 miles² *55 490 km²*.
Language: English.
Religions: Roman Catholic, United Church of Canada, Anglican, Baptist.
Capital city: Halifax, population 114 594 (1981 census).
Other principal towns (1981): Dartmouth 62 277; Sydney 29 444; Glace Bay 21 466; Truro 12 552.
Lieutenant-Governor: Alan R. Abraham.
Premier: John MacLennan Buchanan (b. 22 April 1931).
Telephones: 352 867 (1973).
Daily newspapers: 6 (1974).
Length of roadways: 15 443 miles *24 853 km* (excluding cities and towns).
Length of railways: 1750 miles *2816 km*.
Universities: 8.

ONTARIO
Population: 8 625 107 (1981 census).
Area: 412 582 miles² *1 068 582 km²*.
Languages: English, French, Italian, German.
Religions: Roman Catholic, United Church of Canada, Anglican, Presbyterian.
Capital city: Toronto, population 2 998 847 (1981 census).
Other principal towns (1981): Hamilton 542 095; Ottawa 717 978; London 254 280; Windsor 192 083.
Principal rivers: St Lawrence, Ottawa.
Lieutenant-Governor: John Black Aird (b. 5 May 1923).
Premier: Frank Miller.
Telephones: 6 416 200 (1982).
Daily newspapers: 51 (1974).
Length of roadways: 12 990 miles *20 900 km*.
Length of railways: 10 045 miles *16 166 km*.
Universities: 15.

PRINCE EDWARD ISLAND
Population: 122 506 (1981 census).
Area: 2184 miles² *5657 km²*.
Languages: English, French.
Religions: Roman Catholic, United Church of Canada, Presbyterian.
Capital city: Charlottetown, population 17 063 (1980).
Other principal town: Summerside 8532 (1980).
Lieutenant-Governor: Joseph Aubin-Doiron.
Premier: James M. Lee.
Telephones: 74 594 (1983).
Daily newspapers: 3 (1974).
Length of roadways: 3360 miles *5406 km*.
Length of railways: 283 miles *455 km*.
Universities: 1.

QUEBEC
Population: 6 438 403 (1981 census).
Area: 594 860 miles² *1 540 680 km²*.
Languages: French, English.
Religion: Roman Catholic.
Capital city: Quebec, population 576 075 (1981).
Other principal towns (1981): Montreal 2 828 349; Laval 268 335; Sherbrooke 74 075; Verdun 61 287; Hull 56 225; Trois-Rivières 50 466.
Highest point: Mt Jacques Cartier, 4160 ft *1268 m*.
Principal mountain ranges: Notre Dame, Appalachian.
Principal river: St Lawrence.
Lieutenant-Governor: Jean-Pierre Côté (b. 9 Jan. 1926).

Premier: René Lévesque (b. 24 Aug. 1922).
Telephones: 4 102 671 (1981).
Daily newspapers: 12 (1982).
Length of roadways: 45 994 miles *74 020 km.*
Length of railways: 5360 miles *8626 km.*
Universities: 7.

SASKATCHEWAN
Population: 968 313 (1981 census).
Area: 251 700 miles² *651 900 km².*
Languages: English, German, Ukrainian.
Religions: United Church of Canada, Roman Catholic, Lutheran, Anglican.
Capital city: Regina, population 167 900 (1983 estimate).
Other principal towns (1981): Saskatoon 154 210; Moose Jaw 33 951; Prince Albert 31 380; Yorkton 15 339; Swift Current 14 747.
Highest point: 4546 ft *1385 m.*
Principal rivers: N. Saskatchewan, Cree, Geokie.
Lieutenant-Governor: Frederick W. Johnson.
Premier: Grant Devine.
Telephones: 688 402 (1982).
Daily newspapers: 4 (1974).
Length of roadways: 128 125 miles *206 197 km.*
Length of railways: 8690 miles *13 985 km.*
Universities: 2.

NORTHWEST TERRITORIES
Population: 45 471 (1981 census).
Area: 1 304 903 miles² *3 379 683 km².*
Languages: Eskimo and Indian languages, English, French.
Religions: Roman Catholic, Anglican, United Church of Canada.
Capital city: Yellowknife, population 9731 (1980).
Other principal towns (1980): Hay River 3322; Inuvik 2918; Frobisher Bay 2444; Fort Smith 2265.
Principal mountain range: Mackenzie.
Principal river: Mackenzie.
Commissioner: John Havelock Parker (b. 2 Feb. 1929).
Telephones: 12 950 (1973).

YUKON TERRITORY
Population: 22 135 (1981 census).
Area: 207 076 miles² *536 324 km².*
Languages: English, Indian languages.
Religions: Anglican, Roman Catholic, United Church of Canada.
Capital city: Whitehorse, population 16 771 (1981).
Other principal town (1981): Faro 1972.
Highest point: Mt Logan, 19 850 ft *6050 m.*
Principal mountain range: St Elias.
Principal river: Yukon.
Commissioner: Douglas Bell.
Telephones: 9225 (1973).
Length of roadways: 2332 miles *3752 km.*

Cape Verde

Official name: A República de Cabo Verde (the Republic of Cape Verde).
Population: 296 093 (1980 census).
Area: 1557 miles² *4033 km².*
Languages: Portuguese, Crioulo (a patois).
Religion: Roman Catholic 98·7% (1965).
Capital city: Praia, population 37 500 (1980 census).
Other principal towns: Mindelo 28 797 (1970); São Filipe.
Highest point: 9285 ft *2829 m.*
Head of State: Aristides Maria Pereira (b. 17 Nov. 1924) President.
Prime Minister: Commandant Pedro Verona Rodrigues Pires (b. 29 Apr. 1934).
Climate: Hot and semi-arid, tempered by oceanic situation. Average temperature in Praia varies from 22°C *72°F* to 27°C *80°F.* Prevailing north-easterly wind. Rainfall is scarce (falling almost entirely between August and October) and drought sometimes chronic.
Labour force: 105 570 (census of 15 Dec. 1960).
Gross national product: $80 million in 1978

(World Bank estimate).
Exports: 170·5 million escudos Caboverdianos in 1980: Fish 32%; Salt 17%; Bananas 10%.
Monetary unit: Escudo Capoverdianos. 1 escudo = 100 centavos.
Denominations:
 Coins 20, 50 centavos; 1, 2½, 10, 20, 50 escudos.
 Notes 100, 500, 1000 escudos.
Exchange rate to £ sterling: 100·87 (14 Jan. 1985).
Political history and government: A former Portuguese territory, the Cape Verde Islands were part of Portuguese Guinea (now Guinea-Bissau) until 1879 and formed a separate territory from then until independence on 5 July 1975. The independence movement was dominated by the *Partido Africano da Independência da Guiné e Cabo Verde* (PAIGC), the African Party for the Independence of Guinea and Cape Verde. At independence Portugal transferred power to a PAIGC régime. The country's first constitution was approved on 7 Sept. 1980. Legislative power is vested in the National People's Assembly, with 56 members elected by universal adult suffrage for five years. Executive power is held by the President, elected for five years by the Assembly. He appoints and leads a Council of Ministers. Following the *coup* in Guinea-Bissau on 14 Nov. 1980, the Cape Verde branch of the PAIGC was renamed the African Party for the Independence of Cape Verde on 20 Jan. 1981. Constitutional articles relating to the proposed union with Guinea-Bassau were revoked on 12 Feb. 1981.
Telephones: 1739 (1981).
Radio: 42 000 (1982).
Length of roadways: 800 miles *1300 km* (1978).
Adult illiteracy: 63·1% (population aged 14 and over) in 1970.
Expectation of life: Males 56·3 years; females 60·0 years (UN estimates for 1970–75).
Defence: Popular Revolutionary Armed Forces (about 3000).
Cinemas: 6 (seating capacity 2800) in 1972.

The Central African Republic

Official name: La République centrafricaine.
Population: 2 520 000 (1983 estimate).
Area: 240 535 miles² *622 984 km².*
Languages: Sangho, French (official).
Religions: Protestant, Roman Catholic, Animist.
Capital city: Bangui, population 387 100 (1981).
Other principal towns (1981): Berberati 95 000; Bouar (51 000).
Highest point: Mt Gaou, 4659 ft *1420 m.*
Principal mountain range: Chaîne des Mongos.
Principal river: Oubangui.
Head of State: Gen. André Kolingba, Chairman of the Military Committee for National Recovery.
Climate: Tropical (hot and humid). Heavy rains June to October, especially in south-western forest areas. Average temperature 26°C *79°F.* Daily average high temperature 29°C *85°F* to 34°C *93°F,* low 19°C *66°F* to 22°C *71°F.*
Labour force: 900 000 (1970): Agriculture, forestry and fishing 91·3% (ILO estimates).
Gross domestic product: 56 983 million CFA francs in 1970: Agriculture, forestry and fishing 33·1%; Manufacturing (including diamond cutting) and utilities 14·4%; Trade, restaurants and hotels 21·3%; Government services 14·0%.
Exports: 24 384 francs CFA in 1980: Diamonds 25%; Timber 29%; Cotton 7%.
Monetary unit: Franc de la Communauté financière africaine.
Denominations:
 Coins 1, 2, 5, 10, 25, 50, 100 CFA francs.
 Notes 100, 500, 1000, 5000, 10 000 CFA francs.
Exchange rate to £ sterling: 542·25 (14 Jan. 1985).
Political history and government: Formerly Ubangi-Shari (Obangui-Chari), part of French Equatorial Africa. Became the Central African Republic (CAR) on achieving self-government, 1 Dec. 1958. Independent since 13 Aug. 1960.

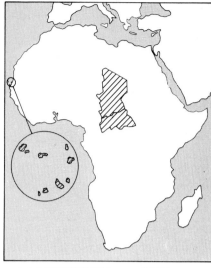

encircled: **CAPE VERDE** *top:* **CHAD**
immediately below: **THE CENTRAL AFRICAN REPUBLIC**

The first President, David Dacko, was deposed on 31 Dec. 1965 by a military *coup*, led by his uncle, Col (later Marshal) Jean-Bédel Bokassa. The National Assembly was dissolved on 1 Jan. 1966 and the constitution revoked on 4 Jan. Bokassa assumed full powers and became 'President for life' in Feb. 1972. On 4 Dec. 1976 he proclaimed the Central African Empire with himself as Emperor. He crowned himself on 4 Dec. 1977. Bokassa was deposed on 20–21 Sept. 1979, when ex-President Dacko and the CAR were restored. The imperial constitution was abrogated. A new constitution, providing for a multi-party system, was approved by referendum on 1 Feb. 1981 and promulgated on 6 Feb. Dacko was elected President on 15 March and sworn in for a six year term on 3 April. On 21 July he declared a 'state of siege', to be administered by Gen André Kolingba, the Army Chief of Staff. On 1 Sept. 1981 President Dacko was deposed in a military *coup* by Gen Kolingba as leader of a 23-man *Comité militaire pour le redressement national* (CMRN). The constitution and political parties were suspended, and all legislative and executive powers assumed by the CMRN. An all-military Council of Ministers was formed.
Telephones: 5000 (1973).
Daily newspapers: 1 (1972).
 Total circulation: 500.
Radio: 80 000 (1977).
TV: 200 (1977).
Length of roadways: 13 670 miles *22 000 km* (31 Dec. 1978).
Universities: 1.
Adult illiteracy: 97·9% (males 95·6%; females 99·8%) in 1959–60 (aged 14 and over).
Expectation of life: Males 41·9 years; females 45·1 years (UN estimates for 1970–75).
Defence: Total armed forces 2385 (1984); defence expenditure, 1980: $13·5 million.
Cinemas: 8 (1971).
Foreign tourists: 4077 in 1974.

Chad

Official name: La République du Tchad (the Republic of Chad).
Population: 4 970 000 (1983 estimate).
Area: 495 750 miles² *1 284 000 km².*
Languages: French (official), Arabic, African languages.
Religions: Muslim, Animist, Christian.
Capital city: N'Djaména (formerly Fort-Lamy), population 303 000 at 1 July 1979 (estimate).
Other principal towns (1979): Moundou 66 000; Sarh (Fort-Archambault) 65 000; Abéché 54 000.
Highest point: Emi Koussi, 11 204 ft *3415 m.*
Principal mountain ranges: Tibesti, Ennedi.
Principal rivers: Chari, Bahr Kéita.

CHILE

Head of State: Hissène Habré, President.

Climate: Hot and dry in the Sahara desert (in the north) but milder and very wet (annual rainfall 4980 mm *196 in*) in the south. In N'Djaména, average maximum 30°C *87°F* (August) to 42°C *107°F* (April), minimum 14°C *57°F* (December, January) to 25°C *77°F* (May), August rainiest (22 days).

Labour force: 1 738 000 in 1981: Agriculture, forestry and fishing 83%.

Gross domestice product: 148 570 million CFA francs in 1975: Agriculture, forestry and fishing 41·4% (agriculture 34·4%); Manufacturing 11·2%; Trade, restaurants and hotels 28·7% (trade 27·9%).

Exports: 6862 million francs CFA in 1977.

Monetary unit: Franc de la Communauté financière africaine.

Denominations:
Coins 1, 2, 5, 10, 25, 50, 100 CFA francs.
Notes 100, 500, 1000, 5000, 10 000 CFA francs.

Exchange rate to £ sterling: 542·25 (14 Jan. 1985).

Political history and government: Former province of French Equatorial Africa, independent since 11 Aug. 1960. From the time of independence the central government was opposed by Muslim rebels, who formed the *Front de libération nationale du Tchad* (FROLINAT), or Chad National Liberation Front, in 1966. The Front later split into several factions but most insurgent groups remained linked to it. On 13 April 1975 the central government was overthrown by a military *coup*. The new régime formed a Supreme Military Council (SMC), led by Gen Félix Malloum. On 25 Aug. 1978 the SMC signed a 'fundamental charter' with a section of one of Chad's rebel groups, the Northern Armed Forces Command Council (CCFAN). The charter was to serve as the country's interim constitution. On 29 Aug. 1978 the SMC was dissolved. Gen Malloum was confirmed as President and a CCFAN leader became Prime Minister. Following a peace conference between the various factions, the President and Prime Minister resigned on 23 Mar. 1979 and a Provisional State Council was formed. Fighting continued, however, and this body was replaced by a transitional Council of Ministers on 29 April 1979. After a further reconciliation conference, this Government resigned on 29 Aug. 1979 to make way for a new régime dominated by FROLINAT, whose Chairman Goukouni Oueddei, became Head of State. A Provisional Administrative Committee (including only northern guerrilla representatives) was set up on

3 Sept. 1979 but this was replaced on 10 Nov. by a Transitional Government of National Unity, including most faction leaders.

Telephones: 3850 (1978).

Daily newspapers: 4 (1976).
Total circulation: 1500 (1975).

Radio: 70 000 (1981).

Length of roadways: 19 092 miles *30 725 km* (31 Dec. 1974).

Universities: 1.

Adult illiteracy: 94·4% (males 87·9%; females 99·4%) in 1963–64.

Expectation of life: Males 40·0 years; females 42·6 years (UN estimates for 1970–75).

Defence: Total armed forces 4200 (1984); defence expenditure, 1980: $22 million.

Cinemas: 13 (seating capacity 12 400) and 3 mobile units (1977).

Foreign tourists: 16 691 (including 3173 excursionists) in 1973.

Chile

Official name: La República de Chile.

Population: 11 275 440 (1982 census); 11 682 260 (1983 estimate).

Area: 292 258 miles² *756 945 km²*.

Language: Spanish.

Religions: Roman Catholic, Protestant minority.

Capital city: Santiago, population 3 853 275 (estimate for 30 June 1980).

Other principal towns (1980): Viña del Mar 272 814; Valparaíso 266 280; Concepción 198 824; Talcahuano 185 744; Antofagasta 161 266; Temuco 155 683.

Highest point: Ojos del Salado, 22 588 ft *6885 m* (first climbed 1937).

Principal mountain range: Cordillera de los Andes.

Principal rivers: Loa (273 miles *439 km*), Maule, Bio-Bio, Valdiva.

Head of State: Gen Augusto Pinochet Ugarte (b. 25 Nov. 1915), President.

Climate: Considerable variation north (annual rainfall 1 mm *0·04 in*) to south (2665 mm *105 in*). Average temperatures 12°C *53°F* winter, 17°C *63°F* summer. In Santiago, December (10°C *51°F* to 28°C *83°F*), January (12°C *53°F* to 29°C *85°F*), and February (11°C *52°F* to 29°C *84°F*) hottest, June (3°C *37°F* to 14°C *58°F*) and July (3°C *37°F* to 15°C *59°F*) coldest and rainiest (6 days each). Absolute maximum temperature 41,6°C *106·9°F*, Los Angeles, February 1944; absolute minimum −21,2°C −6·16°F, Longuimay, July 1933.

Labour force: 3 253 600 (excluding 444 200 unemployed) at March 1980: Agriculture, forestry and fishing 18·1%; Manufacturing 18·4%; Commerce (trade, financing, insurance and real estate) 15·9%; Other services (including electricity, gas and water) 39·2%.

Gross domestic product: 321 188 million pesos in 1977: Agriculture, forestry and fishing 10·3%; Manufacturing 20·4%; Trade 29·0%; Community, social and personal services (incl. restaurants, hotels and business services) 17·1%.

Exports: US$3798 million in 1982: Copper 45·6%; Paper and pulp 6·1%; Iron ore 4·2%; Timber 3·2%; Nitrate 2%.

Monetary unit: Chilean peso. 1 peso = 100 centavos.

Denominations:
Coins 10, 50 centavos; 1 peso.
Notes 5, 10, 50, 100, 500, 1000 pesos.

Exchange rate to £ sterling: 148·43 (14 Jan. 1985).

Political history and government: A republic, divided into 25 provinces. The last civilian President was deposed by a military *coup* on 11 Sept. 1973. A 'state of siege' was proclaimed; the bicameral National Congress (a Senate and a Chamber of Deputies) was dissolved on 13 Sept. 1973, and the activities of political parties were suspended on 27 Sept. 1973. Power is held by the *Junta Militar de Gobierno*, whose leader was proclaimed President of the Republic on 17 Dec. 1974. All political parties were banned on 12 Mar. 1977. The state of siege was lifted on 11 Mar. 1978 but a state of emergency remained in

force. A new constitution was approved in a plebiscite on 11 Sept. 1980, signed by the President on 21 Oct. 1980 and entered into force on 11 Mar. 1981. It provided for the separation of the junta and presidency, with the military régime retaining power for a 'transitional' period of eight years. Legislative elections are scheduled for 1989, when the junta is to nominate a single presidential candidate.

Telephones: 595 108 (1982).

Daily newspapers: 42 (morning dailies only) in 1977.

Radio: 2 000 000 (1977).

TV: 710 000 (1976).

Length of roadways: 47 645 miles *76 677 km* (31 Dec. 1979).

Length of railways: 5446 miles *8764 km*.

Universities: 8.

Adult illiteracy: 8% (1980).

Expectation of life: 67·01 years (1980).

Defence: Military service one year (Army and Navy only); total armed forces 96 600 (30 000 conscripts) in 1984; defence expenditure, 1979: $726 million.

Cinemas: 160 in 1979.

Foreign tourists: 307 495 in 1982.

China (mainland)

Official name: Zhonghua Renmin Gongheguo (People's Republic of China).

Population: 1 008 200 000 (1982 census).

Area: 3 691 500 miles² *9 561 000 km²*.

Language: Chinese (predominantly Mandarin dialect).

Religions: Confucianism, Buddhism, Daoism (Taoism); Roman Catholic and Muslim minorities.

Capital city: Beijing (Pei-ching or Peking), population 9 230 000 (1982 census).

Other principal towns (1970): Shanghai (Shanghai) 11 890 000 (1982); Tianjin (T'ien-chin or Tientsin) 4 280 000; Shenyang (Shen-yang or Mukden) 2 800 000; Wuhan (Wu-han or Hankow) 2 560 000, Guangzhou (Kuang-chou or Canton) 2 500 000; Chongqing (Ch'ung-ch'ing or Chungking) 2 400 000; Nanjing (Nan-ching or Nanking) 1 750 000; Harbin (Ha-erh-pin) 1 670 000; Luda (Lü-ta) 1 650 000; Xian (Hsi-an or Sian) 1 600 000; Lanzhou (Lan-chou or Lanchow) 1 450 000 (UN estimates except for Shanghai and Tianjin).

Highest point: Mt Everest (on Tibet-Nepal border), 29 028 ft *8848 m* (first climbed 29 May 1953).

Principal mountain ranges: Himalaya, Kunlun Shan, Tien Shan, Nan Shan, Astin Tagh.

Principal rivers: Changjiang (Yangtze Kiang) (3436 miles *5530 km*), Huanghe (Yellow), Mekong.

Head of State: Marshal Ye Jianying (Yeh Chienying) (b. 14 May 1897), State President.

Political Leader: Hu Yaobang (Hu Yao-pang) (b. 1915), General Secretary of the Politburo.

Head of Government: Zhao Ziyang (Chao Tzuyang) (b. 1919), Premier of the State Council.

Climate: Extreme variations. Warm, humid summers and long cold winters in north (annual average below 10°C *50°F*); sub-tropical in extreme south; monsoons in the east; arid in the north-west. In Beijing, July hottest (22°C *71°F* to 32°C *89°F*) and rainiest (13 days), January coldest (−9°C *15°F* to 2°C *35°F*).

Labour force: 364 612 000 (1970): Agriculture, forestry and fishing 67·8%; Industry 20·4%; Services 11·9% (ILO estimates, including Taiwan).

Gross national product: $219 010 million in 1978 (World Bank estimate).

Exports: US$21 600 million in 1982.

Monetary unit: Yuan. 1 yuan = 10 jiao (chiao) = 100 fen.

Denominations:
Coins 1, 2, 5 fen.
Notes 1, 2, 5, jiao; 1, 2, 5, 10 yuan.

Exchange rate to £ sterling: 3·171 (14 Jan. 1985).

Political history and government: Under Communist rule since September 1949. The People's Republic was inaugurated on 1 Oct. 1949. The present constitution was adopted on 5 Mar. 1978. China is a unitary state comprising 21 provinces, 5 'autonomous' regions (including Tibet) and 3 municipalities. The Communist Part is 'the core of leadership' and the Chairman of the Party's Central Committee commands the People's Liberation Army (PLA), which includes naval and air forces. The highest organ of state power is the National People's Congress, with (in 1980) 3478 deputies indirectly elected for 5 years by provinces, regions, municipalities and the PLA. The Congress, under the leadership of the Party, elects a Standing Committee (196 members in March 1978) to be its permanent organ. The executive and administrative arm of government is the State Council (a Premier, Vice-Premiers and other Ministers), appointed by and accountable to the Congress.

Political power is held by the Communist Party of China (CPC). The CPC's highest authority is the Party Congress, convened normally every five years. The 11th Congress, meeting on 12–18 Aug. 1977, elected a Central Committee (201 full and 132 alternate members) to supervise Party work. To direct its policy, the Committee elects a Political Bureau (Politburo), with 24 full and two alternate members in 1980. The Politburo has a seven-member Standing Committee (the Chairman and six Vice-Chairmen).

A new constitution was introduced in 1982 which, among other things, restored the post of State President.

Telephones: 255 000 (1951).
Daily newspapers: 43 (1979).
 Total circulation: 34 million.
Radio: *c.* 12 000 000 (1970).
TV: 9 020 000 (1980).
Length of roadways: 553 000 miles *890 000 km* (1978).
Length of railways: 31 000 miles *50 000 km* (1978).
Universities: 37.
Adult illiteracy: 33% (1960 claim).
Expectation of life: Males 60·7 years; females 64·4 years (UN estimates for 1970–75, including Taiwan).
Defence: Military service selective (Army three years, Air and Army technicians four years, Navy five years); total regular forces 4 038 000 (1984).
Cinemas: 4000 in 1979.

China (Taiwan)

Official name: Chung-hua Min Kuo (Republic of China).
Population: 18 700 000 (1983 estimate).
Area: 13 892·5 miles² *35 981,4 km²*.
Language: Northern Chinese (Amoy dialect).
Religions: Buddhist, with Muslim and Christian minorities.
Capital city: Taipei, population 2 300 000 (1982 estimate).
Other principal towns (31 Dec. 1980): Kaohsiung 1 202 123; Taichung 593 427; Tainan 583 799; Panchiau 403 057; Keelung 344 867; Shanchung 327 001.
Highest point: Yü Shan (Mt Morrison), 13 113 ft *3997 m*.
Principal mountain range: Chunyang Shanmo.
Principal rivers: Hsia-tan-shui Chi (99 miles *159 km*), Choshui Chi (106 miles *170 km*), Tanshui Ho (89 miles *144 km*), Wu Chi (70 miles *113 km*).
Head of State: Gen Chiang Ching-kuo (b. 18 Mar. 1910) President.
Prime Minister: Sun Yun-suan (b. 11 Nov. 1913).
Climate: Rainy summers and mild winters, average temperature 23°C *73°F*, average annual rainfall 2565 mm *101 in*. In Taipei, July (24°C *76°F* to 34°C *93°F*) and August (24°C *75°F* to 33°C *91°F*) warmest, January (12°C *54°F* to 19°C *66°F*) and February (12°C *53°F* to 18°C *65°F*) coolest, April rainiest (14 days).
Labour force: 7 000 000 in 1982: Agriculture, forestry and fishing 18·6%; Industry 40%; Commerce 17·1%; Transport and communications 5·7%; Other services 18·6%.
Gross domestic product: NT$1 450 305 million in

1980: Manufacturing 40·8%; Trade 12·8%; Community, social and personal services (incl. restaurants and hotels) 14·1%.
Exports: US$22 204 million in 1982.
Monetary unit: New Taiwan dollar (NT $). 1 dollar = 100 cents.
Denominations:
 Coins 10, 20, 50 cents; 1, 5, dollars.
 Notes 1, 5, 10, 50, 100, 500, 1000 dollars.
Exchange rate to £ sterling: 44·52 (14 Jan. 1985).
Political history and government: After the Republic of China was overthrown by Communist forces on the mainland, the government withdrew to Taiwan on 8 Dec. 1949. As it claims to be the legitimate administration for all China, the régime continues to be dominated by mainlanders who came to the island in 1947–49. The first elections since the Communist victory were held in Taiwan on 23 Dec. 1972. There are five governing bodies (*yuans*). The highest legislative organ is the Legislative Yuan, comprising (in 1980) 320 life members and 48 elected for 3 years. This body submits proposals to the National Assembly (1128 life members and 62 elected for 6 years), which elects the President and Vice-President for 6 years. The Executive Yuan (Council of Ministers) is the highest administrative organ and is responsible to the Legislative Yuan.
Telephones: 4 356 765 (1982).
Daily newspapers: 31 (1977).
 Total circulation: 2 300 000.
Radio: 8 000 000 (1978).
TV: 3 992 675 (31 Dec. 1980).
Length of roadways: 10 732 miles *17 271 km* (31 Dec. 1979).
Length of railways: 2247 miles *3616 km* (1980).
Universities: 11.
Adult illiteracy: 27·6% (males 15·2%; females 42·0%) in 1966.
Expectation of life: Males 66·82 years; females 74·13 years (1977).
Defence: Military service two years; total armed forces 451 000 (1984); defence expenditure, 1977/78: US $ 1750 million.
Cinemas: 544 (capacity 490 000) in 1980.
Foreign tourists: 1 393 254 in 1980.

Colombia

Official name: La República de Colombia.
Population: 22 551 811 (census of 24 Oct. 1973); 27 185 000 (estimate for 1 July 1980).
Area: 439 737 miles² *1 138 914 km²*.
Language: Spanish.
Religion: Roman Catholic.
Capital city: Santa Fé de Bogotá, population 4 055 909 at 24 Oct. 1979 (estimate).
Other principal towns (1979): Medellín 1 506 661; Cali 1 316 137; Barranquilla 855 195; Cartagena de Indias 435 361; Bucaramanga 402 379; San José de Cúcuta 376 625.
Highest point: Pico Cristóbal Colón, 18 947 ft *5775 m* (first climbed 1939).
Principal mountain range: Cordillera de los Andes.
Principal rivers: Magdalena, Cauca, Amazonas (Amazon, 4007 miles *6448 km*) on frontier.
Head of State: Dr Belisario Betancur, President.
Climate: Hot and humid on the coasts and in the jungle lowlands, temperate in the Andean highlands, with rainy seasons March–May and September–November. In Bogotá, daily average low temperature 9°C *48°F* to 10°C *51°F*, high 18°C *64°F* to 20°C *68°F*, April and October rainiest (20 days).
Labour force: 5 118 475 (excluding 856 517 unemployed) aged 12 and over (1973 census); Agriculture, forestry and fishing 37·2%; Manufacturing 16·3%; Trade, restaurants and hotels 13·9%; Community, social and personal services 20·2%.
Gross domestic product: 895 767 million pesos in 1978: Agriculture, forestry and fishing 28·3% (agriculture 26·9%); Manufacturing 20·6%; Trade 18·6%.
Exports: US$3127 in 1981: Coffee 74·5%; Cotton 3·3%; Sugar 5·5%; Fuel oil 7·6%; Clothing and textiles 8·3%; Bananas 3·5%.

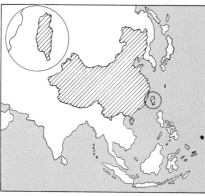

CHINA (MAINLAND)
encircled: **CHINA (TAIWAN)**

COLOMBIA

Monetary unit: Colombian peso. 1 peso = 100 centavos.
Denominations:
 Coins 1, 2, 5, 10, 20, 50 centavos.
 Notes 1, 5, 10, 20, 50, 100, 500 pesos.
Exchange rate to £ sterling: 148·43 (14 Jan. 1985).
Political history and government: A republic. Legislative power is vested in Congress, which is composed of the Senate (112 members) and the House of Representatives (199 members). Members of both Houses are elected for 4 years. Executive power is exercised by the President (elected for 4 years by universal adult suffrage), assisted by a Cabinet. The country is divided into 22 departments, 5 intendancies and 4 commissaries.
Telephones: 1 747 689 in 1982.
Daily newspapers: 42 (1976).
 Total circulation: 1 330 000 (35 dailies).
Radio: 2 930 000 (1977).
TV: 1 750 000 (1978).
Length of roadways: 40 469 miles *65 129 km* (31 Dec. 1979).
Length of railways: 2115 miles *3403 km*.
Universities: 37 (21 state, 16 private).
Adult illiteracy: 19·2% (males 18·0%; females 20·2%) in 1973.
Expectation of life: Males 58·5 years; females 61·2 years (UN estimates for 1970–75).
Defence: Military service two years; total armed forces 70 700 (28 500 conscripts) in 1984; defence expenditure, 1979: $125 million.
Cinemas: 1000 in 1980.
Foreign tourists: 1 300 000 in 1981.

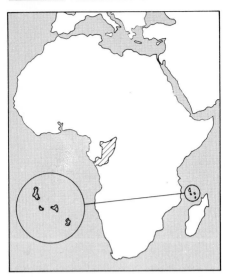

left : **THE CONGO**   *right :* **THE COMOROS**

The Comoros

Official name: La République fédérale islamique des Comores (the Federal Islamic Republic of the Comoros).
Population: 385 000 (1983 estimate).
Area: 838 miles² *2171 km²* (including Mayotte, 144 miles² *373 km²*).
Languages: French (official), Comoran (a blend of Swahili and Arabic).
Religions: Muslim, with a Christian minority.
Capital city: Moroni, population 16 000 (1978 estimate).
Other principal towns: Dzaoudzi (on Mayotte), Mutsamudu.
Highest point: Mt Kartala, 7746 ft *2361 m.*
Head of State: Ahmed Abdallah (b. 1918), President.
Prime Minister: Ali Mroudjae.
Climate: Tropical climate with two distinct seasons. Dry between May and October, hot and humid from November to April. Most rain in January (up to 380 mm *15 in*). Cyclones, water-spouts and tidal waves occur in the summer. The November monsoon brings the maximum temperature of 28°C *82°F*, while the minimum temperature (July) falls to 20°C *68°F.*
Labour force: 104 000 (mid-1970): Agriculture, forestry and fishing 67·1%; Industry 20·8%; Services 12·1% (ILO estimates).
Gross domestic product: $70 million (estimate) in 1975.
Exports: 2712 million francs CFA in 1980: Vanilla 27·1%; Essential oils 23·6%; Cloves 17%; Copra 7·6%.
Monetary unit: Franc de la Communauté financière africaine (French currency is used on Mayotte).
Denominations:
Coins 1, 2, 5, 10, 20 CFA francs.
Notes 50, 100, 500, 1000, 5000 CFA francs.
Exchange rate to £ sterling: 542·25 (14 Jan. 1985).
Political history and government: A former French dependency. Attached to Madagascar in 1912, the Comoro Islands became a separate French Overseas Territory in 1947. The Territory achieved internal self-government by a law of 29 Dec. 1961, with a Chamber of Deputies (in place of the Territorial Assembly) and a Government Council to control local administration. Ahmed Abdallah, President of the Council from 26 Dec. 1972, was restyled President of the Government on 15 June 1973. In a referendum on 22 Dec. 1974 the Comorans voted 95·6% in favour of independence, though on the island of Mayotte the vote was 65% against. The French Government wanted each island to ratify a new constitution separately by referendum. To avoid the expected separation of Mayotte, the Chamber of Deputies voted for immediate independence on 6 July 1975. A

unilateral declaration of independence, as the *Etate Comorien* (Comoran State), was made on the same day. On 7 July the Chamber elected Abdallah as President of the Comoros and constituted itself as the National Assembly. France kept its hold on Mayotte but the three other main islands achieved *de facto* independence. On 3 Aug. 1975 Abdallah was deposed in a *coup*. France recognized the independence of the three islands on 31 Dec. 1975. The new régime was overthrown by a *coup* on 12–13 May 1978. A Political-Military Directory was formed and on 23 May ex-President Abdallah and his former deputy were appointed its co-presidents. On 24 May 1978 the country's present name was announced. A new constitution was approved by referendum on 1 Oct. 1978 and Abdallah was elected President (unopposed) for a 6-year term on 22 Oct. 1978. A 39-member Federal Assembly was elected for a 5-year term on 8 and 15 Dec. 1978.

A referendum on Mayotte on 8 Feb. 1976 resulted in a 99·4% vote for retaining links with France. In a second referendum, on 11 Apr. 1976, Mayotte voted against remaining a French Overseas Territory. In Dec. 1976 France enacted legislation to give the island a special status as a *collectivité particulière*. On 6 Dec. 1979 this status was extended for a further five years, after which Mayotte will become a French Overseas Department if the residents still so desire. Meanwhile, Mayotte is governed by an appointed Prefect.
Telephones: 1378 (1975).
Radio: 37 750 (1982).
Length of roadways: 466 miles *750 km* (1973).
Adult illiteracy: 41·6% in 1966.
Expectation of life: Males 43·3 years; females 46·6 years (UN estimates for 1970–75).
Defence: About 1000 personnel.
Cinemas: 2 (seating capacity 800) in 1973.

The Congo

Official name: La République populaire du Congo (the People's Republic of the Congo).
Population: 1 660 000 (1983 estimate).
Area: 132 047 miles² *342 000 km².*
Languages: French (official), Bantu languages.
Religions: Animist, Christian minority.
Capital city: Brazzaville, population 422 402 (1980).
Other principal towns: Pointe-Noire 185 105 (1980); Loubomo 28 941 (1974); N'Kayi 28 326 (1974).
Highest point: 3412 ft *1040 m.*
Principal mountain range: Serro do Crystal.
Principal rivers: Zaïre (Congo) (2920 miles *4700 km*), Oubangui.
Head of State: Col Denis Sassou-Nguesso (b. 1943), President.
Prime Minister: Col Louis-Sylvain Goma (b. 28 June 1941).
Climate: Tropical (hot and humid). Equatorial rains for seven to eight months per year. In Brazzaville, daily average low temperature 17°C *63°F* to 21°C *70°F*, high 28°C *82°F* to 33°C *91°F.*
Labour force: 428 000 (1970): Agriculture, forestry and fishing 41·8%; Industry 21·5%; Services 36·7% (ILO estimates); 487 267 (1974 census).
Gross domestic product: 166 326 million CFA francs in 1976.
Exports: 192 000 million francs CFA in 1980: Petroleum 79·5%.
Monetary unit: Franc de la Communauté financière africaine.
Denominations:
Coins 1, 2, 5, 10, 25, 50, 100 CFA francs.
Notes 100, 500, 1000, 5000, 10 000 CFA francs.
Exchange rate to £ sterling: 542·25 (14 Jan. 1985).
Political history and government: Formerly, as Middle Congo, a part of French Equatorial Africa. Became independent as the Republic of the Congo on 15 Aug. 1960. A one-party state since 2 July 1964. Present name adopted on 3 Jan. 1970. On 18 Mar. 1977 the President was

assassinated and the Central Committee of the ruling party transferred its powers to an 11-member Military Committee. The new régime suspended the 1973 constitution on 5 Apr. 1977 and dissolved the National Assembly the next day. On 5 Feb. 1979 the Military Committee resigned and handed over powers to the party's Central Committee. On 8 July 1979 a new constitution was approved by referendum and a National People's Assembly of 89 members elected (unopposed). The Congress of the ruling party elects a Central Committee (60 members) whose Chairman is also the country's President (serving a five-year term). The President leads the Council of Ministers, including a Prime Minister who is responsible to the party. The Assembly is responsible to the Prime Minister.
Telephones: 8899 (1982).
Daily newspapers: 1 (1977).
Radio: 92 000 (1979).
TV: 3300 (1979).
Length of roadways: 5124 miles *8246 km* (31 Dec. 1977).
Length of railways: 494 miles *795 km.*
Universities: 1.
Adult illiteracy: 83·5% (males 76·2%; females 92·7%) in 1960–61.
Expectation of life: Males 41·9 years; females 45·1 years (UN estimates for 1970–75).
Defence: Military service voluntary; total armed forces 8750 (1984); defence expenditure, 1980: $78 million.
Cinemas: 7 (seating capacity 5100) in 1973.

Costa Rica

Official name: República de Costa Rica (the 'rich coast').
Population: 2 403 781 (1983 estimate).
Area: 19 600 miles² *50 700 km².*
Language: Spanish.
Religion: Roman Catholic.
Capital city: San José, population 271 873 (1983 estimate).
Other principal towns (1983): Limon (38 916; Puntarenas 34 613; Alajuela 42 579; Heredia 29 544; Cartago 27 929.
Highest point: Chirripó, 12 533 ft *3820 m.*
Principal mountain ranges: Cordillera del Guanacaste, Cordillera de Talamanca.
Principal river: Río Grande.
Head of State: Luis Alberto Monge, President.
Climate: Hot and wet on Caribbean coast, hot but drier on Pacific coast, cooler on central plateau. In San José, May hottest (17°C *62°F* to 27°C *80°F*), December and January coolest (14°C *58°F* to 24°C *75°F*), rainy season May–November, October rainiest (25 days). Absolute maximum temperature 42°C *107·6°F*, Las Cañas de Guanacaste, 26 Apr. 1952; absolute minimum −1·1°C *30°F*, Cerro Buena Vista, 11 Jan. 1949.
Labour force: 585 313 (including unemployed) aged 12 and over (1973 census): Agriculture, forestry and fishing 38·4%; Mining and manufacturing 12·9% (manufacturing 12·6%); Trade, restaurants and hotels 12·2%; Community, social and personal services 21·5%; 666 682 (household survey, March 1977).
Gross domestic product: 29 764·2 million colones in 1978: Agriculture, forestry and fishing 20·0% (agriculture 19·3%); Mining and manufacturing 18·2%; Trade, restaurants and hotels 20·2% (trade 18·7%); Government services 14·2%.
Exports: US$870·8 million in 1982: Manufactured goods and other products 14·5%; Coffee 27·2%; Bananas 26·9%; Sugar 1·5%.
Monetary unit: Costa Rican colón. 1 colón = 100 céntimos.
Denominations:
Coins 5, 10, 25, 50 céntimos; 1, 2 colones.
Notes 5, 10, 20, 50, 100, 500, 1000 colones.
Exchange rate to £ sterling: 53·96 (14 Jan. 1985).
Political history and government: A republic. Legislative power is vested in the unicameral Legislative Assembly (57 deputies elected for four years by compulsory adult suffrage). Executive power is vested in the President, similarly elected for four years. He is assisted by two Vice-Presidents and a Cabinet. There are 7 provinces, each administered by an appointed governor.

Telephones: 255 898 (1982).
Daily newspapers: 4 (1983).
Radio: 156 000 (1977).
TV: 277 694 (1980).
Length of roadways: 13 999 miles *22 530 km* (1980).
Length of railways: 608 miles *979 km*.
Universities: 3.
Adult illiteracy: 11·6% (males 11·4%; females 11·8%) in 1973. Highest rate of literacy in Central America.
Expectation of life: Males 66·26 years; females 70·49 years (1972–74).
Defence: There have been no armed forces since 1948. Paramilitary forces number about 5000.
Cinemas: 106 in 1979.
Foreign tourists: 345 470 in 1980.

Cuba

Official name: La República de Cuba.
Population: 9 706 369 (1981 census).
Area: 42 827 miles² *110 922 km²*.
Languages: Spanish, English.
Religions: Roman Catholic, Protestant minority.
Capital city: San Cristóbal de la Habana (Havana), population 1 924 886 (1981 census).
Other principal towns (1981): Santiago de Cuba 563 455; Santa Clara 525 402; Camaguey 480 620; Holguin 456 595; Guira de Melena 429 090; Matanzas 421 272.
Highest point: Pico Turquino, 6467 ft *1971 m*.
Principal mountain range: Sierra Maestra.
Principal river: Cauto (155 miles *249 km*).
Head of State: Dr Fidel Castro Ruz (b. 13 Aug. 1927), President of the State Council and Chairman of the Council of Ministers; also First Secretary of the Communist Party of Cuba.
Climate: Semi-tropical. Rainy season May–October. High winds, hurricanes frequent. In Havana, July and August warmest (24°C *75°F* to 32°C *89°F*), January and February coolest (18°C *65°F* to 26°C *79°F*), September and October rainiest (11 days each).
Labour force: 2 633 309 (excluding domestic servants) aged 10 and over (1970 census): Agriculture, forestry and fishing 30·4%; Manufacturing 19·7%; Trade, restaurants and hotels, storage and personal service 11·8%; Community and social services (including water), finance, insurance, real estate and business services 25·0%.
Gross material product: 7414·1 million pesos in 1974.
Exports: 4939 million pesos in 1982: Sugar 80% approx.
Monetary unit: Cuban peso. 1 peso = 100 centavos.
Denominations:
 Coins 1, 5, 20, 40 centavos.
 Notes 1, 5, 10, 20, 50, 100 pesos.
Exchange rate to £ sterling: 1·0275 (14 Jan. 1985).
Political history and government: On 1 Jan. 1959 the dictatorship of Gen Fulgencio Batista was overthrown by revolutionary forces, led by Dr Fidel Castro. The constitution was suspended and a Fundamental Law of the Republic was instituted from 7 Feb. 1959. Executive and legislative authority was vested in the Council of Ministers, led by a Prime Minister, which appointed the Head of State. A 'Marxist-Leninist programme' was proclaimed on 2 Dec. 1961 and revolutionary groups merged into a single political movement, called the Communist Party of Cuba (CPC) since 2 Oct. 1965. On 24 Nov. 1972 the government established an Executive Committee (including the President and Prime Minister) to supervise State administration. The first elections since the revolution were held for municipal offices in one province on 30 June 1974.

A new constitution, approved by referendum on 15 Feb. 1976 and in force from 24 Feb. 1976, provides for assemblies at municipal, provincial and national levels. On 10 Oct. 1976 elections were held for 169 municipal assemblies, with 'run-off' elections a week later. Members are elected by universal adult suffrage for 2½ years.

On 31 Oct. 1976 the municipal assemblies elected delegates to 14 provincial assemblies. On 2 Nov. 1976 the municipal assemblies elected 481 deputies to the National Assembly of People's Power, inaugurated on 2 Dec. 1976. The National Assembly, whose members hold office for five years, is the supreme organ of state. The Assembly elects 31 of its members to form a Council of State, its permanent organ. The Council's President is Head of State and Head of Government. Executive power is vested in the Council of Ministers, appointed by the National Assembly on the proposal of the Head of State, who presides over it.

The CPC, the only permitted political party, is 'the leading force of society and the state'. The first Congress of the CPC met on 17–22 Dec. 1975. The second Congress, held on 17–20 Dec. 1980, elected a new Central Committee (148 full and 77 alternate members) to supervise Party work. To direct its policy, the Committee elected a Political Bureau (Politburo), with 16 full and 11 alternate members.
Telephones: 406 355 (1982).
Daily newspapers: 14 (1980).
Radio: 1 895 000 (1977).
TV: 800 000 (1977).
Length of roadways: 18 357 miles *29 543 km* (1975).
Length of railways: 9242 miles *14 873 km*.
Universities: 4.
Adult illiteracy: estimated 4%.
Expectation of life: Males 68·5 years; females 71·8 years (1970).
Defence: Military service three years; total armed forces 147 000 (1984); defence expenditure, 1981: $1100 million.
Cinemas: 439 (seating capacity 294 300) and one drive-in (capacity 2000) in 1972; 458 and 637 mobile units (1976).
Foreign tourists: 100 000 in 1979.

Cyprus

Official name: Kypriaki Dimokratia (in Greek), or Kibris Cumhuriyeti (in Turkish), meaning Republic of Cyprus.
Population: 653 450 in 1983.
Area: 3572 miles² *9251 km²*.
Languages: Greek 77%; Turkish 18%; English 3% (1960).
Religions: Greek Orthodox 77·0%; Moslem 18·3%.
Capital city: Nicosia, population 161 100 (1982 estimate).
Other principal towns (1982): Limassol (107 200); Famagusta (39 500); Larnaca (48 400).
Principal mountain ranges: Troödos, Kyrenian Mts.
Principal rivers: Seranhis, Pedieas.
Head of State: Spyros Kyprianou (b. 28 Oct. 1932), President.
Climate: Generally equable. Average rainfall is about 380 mm *15 in* but the summers are often rainless. The average daily high temperature in Nicosia reaches 36°C *97°F* (July) and the average daily low 5°C *42°F* (January).
Labour force: 220 089 (in 1983): Agriculture, forestry, fishing 19·7%; Manufacturing 18·9%; Trade, restaurants and hotels 17·4%; Transport, storage and communication 4·8%; Services 18·1%.
Gross domestic product: C£1091·8 million in 1983: Agriculture 9·3%; Mining, manufacturing, electricity and gas 19·9%; Services 15·2%; Construction 12·0%; Transport 8·7%; Trade 14·8%; Banking 7·7%; Public administration 8·1%.
Exports: C£260·5 million (including re-exports) in 1983: Fruit and vegetables 15·4% (citrus fruit 5·2%; potatoes 4·8%); Alcoholic beverages 4·2%.
Monetary unit: Cyprus pound. C£1 = 100 cents.
Denominations:
 Coins ½, 1, 2, 5, 10, 20 cent.
 Notes 50 cent, £1, £5, £10.
Exchange rate to £ sterling: 0·75 (March 1985).
Political history and government: A former British dependency, independent since 16 August 1960 and a member of the Commonwealth

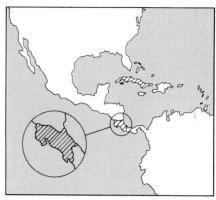

above: **CUBA**   *below:* **COSTA RICA**

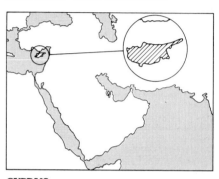

CYPRUS

since 13 March 1961. Under the 1960 constitution, Cyprus is a unitary republic with executive authority vested in one President (who must be a Greek Cypriot) and the Vice-President (who must be a Turkish Cypriot). They are elected for 5 years by universal suffrage (among the Greek and Turkish communities respectively) and jointly appoint a Council of Ministers (seven Greeks, three Turks). The national legislature is the unicameral House of Representatives, comprising 50 members (35 Greek and 15 Turkish, separately elected for 5 years). Each community was also to have a communal chamber.

The first President of Cyprus was Archbishop Makarios III, who proposed amendments to the constitution on 30 November 1963. These were unacceptable to the Turks, who have ceased to participate in the central government since December 1963. After the Turkish withdrawal, the all-Greek House of Representatives abolished the Greek Communal Chamber and the separate electoral rolls. The Turkish community continued to elect a Vice-President for Cyprus (not recognised by the Greeks) and established separate administrative, legal and judicial organs.

After the temporary overthrow of President Makarios in a coup in July 1974, the armed forces of Turkey intervened and occupied northern Cyprus. On 17 February 1975 the Turkish Cypriots unilaterally proclaimed this area the Turkish Federated State of Cyprus, for which a constitution was approved by referendum on 8 June 1975. Makarios died on 3 August 1977, when Spyros Kyprianou, President of the House of Representatives, became acting Head of State. On 31 August 1977 he was elected unopposed to complete Makarios's term of office. He was returned unopposed as President on 26 January 1978 and inaugurated on 1 March. He was again re-elected for a further five year term on 13 February 1983.

In November 1983 the Turkish Cypriot leadership declared the Turkish-held area of Cyprus to be the Turkish Republic of Northern Cyprus. To date this action remains unrecognised by the world community. UN sponsored talks between the Greek and the Turkish Cypriot sides have made no progress in resolving the Cyprus problem.
Telephones: 109 861 (1983).
Daily newspapers: 9 (1985).

Radio: 212 000 (1977).
TV: 66 000 licences (1973).
Length of roadways: 6130 miles *9866 km* (31 Dec. 1978).
Adult illiteracy: 9·5% (1976).
Expectation of life: Males 72·3 years; females 76·0 years (1978–81).
Defence: *Greek Cypriots:* military service 26 months; total armed forces 8000 (1981); defence expenditure, 1981: $27·0 million. *Turkish Cypriots:* Security Force of about 4500 (1981).
Cinemas: 74.
Foreign tourists: 620 726 plus 6866 excursionists (1983).

Czechoslovakia

Official name: Československá Socialistická Republika (Czechoslovak Socialist Republic).
Population: 15 344 679 (31 Dec. 1981).
Area: 49 375 miles² *127 881 km²*.
Languages: Czech 64%; Slovak 30%; Hungarian 4%.
Religions: Roman Catholic 70%; Protestant 15%.
Capital city: Praha (Prague), population 1 186 253 at 1 Jan. 1984.
Other principal towns (1 Jan. 1984): Bratislava 401 383; Brno 380 871; Ostrava 323 732; Košice 214 270; Plzeň 174 094.
Principal mountain ranges: Bohemian–Moravian Highlands, Krkonoše (Giant Mountains), High Tatras, Low Tatras.
Principal rivers: Labe (Elbe, 525 miles *845 km*), Vltava (Moldau), Dunaj (Danube, 1770 miles *2850 km*), Morava, Váh, Nitra, Hron.
Head of State: Dr Gustáv Husák (b. 10 Jan. 1913), President; also General Secretary of the Central Committee of the Communist Party of Czechoslovakia.
Prime Minister: Dr L'ubomír Štrougal (b. 19 Oct. 1924).
Climate: Cold winters and warm, rainy summers. Average temperature 9°C *49°F*. In Prague, July warmest (14°C *58°F* to 23°C *74°F*), January coldest (−4°C *25°F* to 1°C *34°F*), June and July rainiest (14 days each). Absolute maximum temperature 39,0°C *102·2°F*, Hurbanovo, 5 Aug. 1905; absolute minimum −41,0°C *−41·8°F*, Vigľaš-Pstruša, 11 Feb. 1929.
Labour force: 7 262 572 registered employed aged 15 and over in 1981: Industry 38·5%; Agriculture 13·2%; Building 8·7%; Commerce 9·2%; Services 24·8%.
Exports: Kčs 95 562 million in 1982: Machinery 52%; Industrial consumer goods 17%; Raw materials and fuel 28%.
Monetary unit: Koruna (Kčs) or Czechoslovak crown. 1 koruna = 100 haléřu (singular: halér̆).
Denominations:
Coins 5, 10, 20, 50 haléřu; 1, 2, 5 korunas.
Notes 10, 20, 50, 100, 500 korunas.
Exchange rate to £ sterling: 14·63 (14 Jan. 1985).
Political history and government: Formerly part of Austria-Hungary, independent since 28 Oct. 1918. Under the Munich agreement, made on

29 Sept. 1938 by France, German, Italy and the United Kingdom, Czechoslovakia ceded the Sudetenland to Germany and other areas to Hungary and Poland. German forces entered Czechoslovakia on 1 Oct. 1938. In 16 Mar. 1939 Germany invaded and occupied the rest of the country. At the end of the Second World War in May 1945 the pre-1938 frontiers were restored but Czechoslovakia ceded Ruthenia to the U.S.S.R. in June 1945. The Communist Party won 38% of the vote at the 1946 election and dominated the government. After Ministers of other parties resigned, Communist control became complete on 25 Feb. 1948. A People's Republic was established on 9 June 1948. A new constitution, introducing the country's present name, was proclaimed on 11 July 1960. Czechoslovakia has been a federal republic since 1 Jan. 1969.

The country comprises two nations, the Czechs and the Slovaks, each forming a republic with its own elected National Council and government. Czechoslovakia comprises 10 administrative regions and two cities.

The supreme organ of state power is the bicameral Federal Assembly, elected for 5 years by universal adult suffrage. Its permanent organ is the elected Presidium. The Assembly comprises the Chamber of the People, with 200 members (136 Czechs and 64 Slovaks), and the Chamber of Nations, with 150 members (75 from each republic). The Assembly elects the President of the Republic for a 5-year term and he appoints the Federal Government, led by the Chairman of the Government (Prime Minister), to hold executive authority. Ministers are responsible to the Assembly.

Political power is held by the Communist Party of Czechoslovakia, which dominates the National Front (including four other minor parties). All candidates for representative bodies are sponsored by the Front. The Communist Party's highest authority is the Party Congress, which elects the Central Committee to supervise Party work. The Committee elects a Presidium (12 full members and one alternate member were elected in April 1981) to direct policy.
Telephones: 3 401 775 (1983).
Daily newspapers: 59 (1982).
Radio: 4 100 000 licences in 1981.
TV: 4 300 000 licences in 1981.
Length of roadways: 45 694 miles *73 538 km* (excluding local roads) at 31 Dec. 1974.
Length of railways: 8229 miles *13 243 km*.
Universities: 5 (plus 7 technical universities).
Adult illiteracy: under 1%.
Expectation of life: Males 66·7 years; females 73·6 years (1977).
Defence: Military service: Army 2 years, Air Force 3 years; total regular forces 204 000 in 1984; defence expenditure, 1980: $3520 million (converted at $1 = 6·36 korunas).
Cinemas: 2866 in 1983.
Foreign tourists: 14 301 839 in 1983.

Denmark

Official name: Kongeriget Danmark (Kingdom of Denmark).
Population: 5 116 464 (1 Jan. 1983).
Area: 16 632 miles² *43 076 km²*.
Language: Danish.
Religions: Evangelical Lutheran 94%, other Christian minorities.
Capital city: København (Copenhagen), population 641 904 (1 Jan. 1983); including suburbs 1 372 019.
Other principal towns (1 Jan. 1983): Aarhus 248 509; Odense 170 648; Aalborg 154 755; Esbjerg 80 317.
Highest point: Yding Skovhøj, 568 ft *173 m*.
Principal river: Gudenå.
Head of State: HM Queen Margrethe II (b. 16 Apr. 1940).
Prime Minister: Poul Schlüter (b. 3 Apr. 1929).
Climate: Temperate: Mild summers (seldom above 21°C *70°F*) and cold winters (although seldom below freezing). The days are often foggy and damp. In Copenhagen, July warmest (13°C

55°F to 22°C *72°F*), February coldest (−2°C 28°F to 2°C *36°F*), August rainiest (12 days). Absolute maximum temperature 35,8°C *96.4°F*, Antvorskov, 13 Aug. 1911; absolute minimum −31,0°C *−23.8°F*, Løndal, 26 Jan. 1942.
Labour force: 1 779 000 aged 15 to 74 in 1983: Agriculture, fishing, raw material extraction 2·1%; Manufacturing 20·3%; Building and construction 5·6%; Commerce 13·2%.
Gross domestice product: 568·5 billion kroner in 1984.
Exports: 157·75 billion kroner in 1984: Industrial products 65·7%; Agricultural exports 24·4%; Fish and fur 5·7%.
Monetary unit: Danish krone. 1 krone = 100 øre.
Denominations:
Coins 5, 10, 25 øre; 1, 5, 10 kroner.
Notes 2, 10, 50, 100, 500, 1000 kroner.
Exchange rate to £ sterling: 13·62, (10 Apr. 1985).
Political history and government: A constitutional monarchy since 1849. Under the constitutional charter (*Grundlov*) of 5 June 1953, legislative power is held jointly by the hereditary monarch (who has no personal political power) and the unicameral Parliament (*Folketing*), with 179 members (175 from metropolitan Denmark and two each from the Faeroe Islands and Greenland). Members are elected by universal adult suffrage for 4 years (subject to dissolution), using proportional representation. Executive power is exercised by the monarch through a Cabinet, led by the Prime Minister, which is responsible to Parliament. Denmark comprises 14 counties, one city and one borough.
Telephones: 3 483 323 (1981).
Daily newspapers: 47 (1982).
Total circulation: 1 820 000.
Radio: 1 950 000 (1981).
TV: 2 130 000 (1981).
Length of roadways: 42 374 miles *68 194 km* (31 Dec. 1979).
Length of railways: 1586 miles *2552 km*.
Universities: 5 (plus 3 technical universities).
Adult illiteracy: under 1%.
Expectation of life: Males 71·1 years; females 76·8 years (1975–76).
Defence: Military service nine months; total armed forces 39 300 in 1984; defence expenditure, 1981: $1520 million.
Cinemas: 463 in 1982.
Foreign tourists: 16 231 862 (including excursionists and local frontier crossings), excluding arrivals from other Nordic countries (1976).

Djibouti

Official name: Jumhuriya Jibuti (Arabic) or République de Djibouti (French): Republic of Djibouti.
Population: 350 000 (1981 estimate).
Area: 8880 miles² *23 000 km²*.
Languages: Arabic (official), Somali, Afar.
Religions: Muslim; Christian minority.
Capital city: Djibouti (Jibuti), population 150 000 (1981 estimate).
Other principal towns: Tadjoura, Obock, Dikhil, Ali-Sabieh.
Head of State: Hassan Gouled Aptidon (b. 1916), President.
Prime Minister: Barket Gourad Hamadou.
Climate: Very hot and dry.
Gross domestic product: 17 000 million Djibouti francs in 1977.
Exports: 20 348 million Djibouti francs in 1981.
Monetary unit: Djibouti franc. 1 franc = 100 centimes.
Denominations:
Coins 1, 2, 5, 10, 20, 50, 100 francs.
Notes 500, 1000, 5000 francs.
Exchange rate to £ sterling: 195 (14 Jan. 1985).
Political history and government: Formerly a dependency of France. Known as French Somaliland until 5 July 1967 and from then until independence as the French Territory of the Afars and the Issas. Also in 1967 the Territorial Assembly became the Chamber of Deputies. A provisional independence agreement was signed

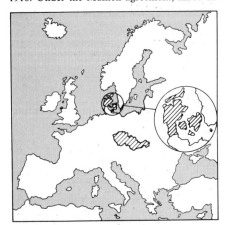

above: **DENMARK**
below: **CZECHOSLOVAKIA**

on 8 June 1976. A popular referendum approved independence on 8 May 1977, when an enlarged Chamber of Deputies (65 members) was also elected. The Chamber elected a Prime Minister on 16 May 1977. The Territory became independent on 27 June 1977, when the Prime Minister became President and the Chamber became a Constituent Assembly. Executive power is held by the President, directly elected for a six-year term as Head of State and Head of Government. The President appoints the Prime Minister and, on the latter's recommendation, other members of the Council of Ministers. The Assembly is to draw up a new constitution.

Telephones: 4348 (1980).
Radio: 17 200 (1982).
TV: 10 550 (1982).
Length of roadways: 1250 miles *2000 km.*
Length of railways: 62 miles *100 km.*
Defence: Total armed forces 2700 (1984).
Cinemas: 4 (seating capacity 5800) and 3 mobile units (1975).

Dominica

Official name: The Commonwealth of Dominica.
Population: 74 859 (census of 1981).
Area: 298·8 miles² *751 km².*
Language: English.
Religion: Roman Catholic 80%.
Capital city: Roseau, population 20 000 (1981).
Other principal towns: Portsmouth, Marigot.
Highest point: Imray's View, 4747 ft *1447 m.*
Principal river: Layou.
Head of State: Clarence A. Seignoret, President.
Prime Minister: Mary Eugenia Charles (b. 1919).
Climate: Warm and pleasant. Cool from December to May. Rainy season generally June to October, dry February to May. Sometimes in the path of severe hurricanes.
Labour force: 21 171 (1970 census).
Gross domestic product: EC$85 million in 1977: Agriculture, forestry and fishing 39·8% (Agriculture 38·9%); Government services 20·4%.
Exports: EC$61 516 134 in 1982.
Monetary unit: East Caribbean dollar (EC$). 1 dollar = 100 cents.
Denominations:
Coins 1, 2, 5, 10, 25, 50 cents.
Notes 1, 5, 20, 100 dollars.
Exchange rate to £ sterling: 3·00 (29 Jan. 1985).
Political history and government: A former British dependency, Dominica was part of the Leeward Islands until 31 Dec. 1939, when it was transferred to the Windward Islands. The federal arrangement in the British-ruled Windward Islands ended on 31 Dec. 1959. Under a new constitution, effective from 1 Jan. 1960, Dominica achieved a separate status, with its own Administrator. On 1 Mar. 1967 Dominica became one of the West Indies Associated States, gaining full autonomy in internal affairs. The Administrator became Governor and the Chief Minister was restyled Premier.

Dominica became an independent republic on 3 Nov. 1978, with the Premier as Prime Minister. Legislative power is vested in the unicameral House of Assembly, with 31 members (21 elected by universal adult suffrage, 9 appointed by the President and 1 *ex officio*) serving a term of five years (subject to dissolution). Executive authority is vested in the President, elected by the House, but he generally acts on the advice of the Cabinet. The President appoints the Prime Minister, who must be supported by a majority in the House, and (on the Prime Minister's recommendation) other Ministers. The Cabinet effectively controls government and is responsible to the House.
Telephones: 3193 (1983).
Radio: 13 405 (1982).
Length of roadways: 467 miles *752 km* (31 Dec. 1976).
Adult illiteracy: 4·7% in 1970.
Expectation of life: Males 56·97 years; females 59·18 years (1958–62).
Cinemas: 2 (1982).
Foreign tourists: 10 419 (1982).

The Dominican Republic

Official name: La República Dominicana.
Population: 5 982 000 (1983 estimate).
Area: 18 703 miles² *48 442 km².*
Language: Spanish.
Religion: Roman Catholic.
Capital city: Santo Domingo de Guzmán, population 1 313 172 (1981 census).
Other principal towns (1981): Santiago de los Caballeros 278 638; La Romana 91 571; San Pedro de Macoris 78 562; San Francisco de Macoris 64 906; La Vega 52 432.
Highest point: Pico Duarte (formerly Pico Trujillo), 10 417 ft *3175 m.*
Principal mountain range: Cordillera Central.
Principal river: Yaque del Norte.
Head of State: Dr Salvador Jorge Blanco, President.
Climate: Sub-tropical. Average temperature 27°C *80°F.* The west and south-west are arid. In the path of tropical cyclones. In Santo Domingo, August is hottest (23°C *73°F* to 31°C *88°F*), January coolest (19°C *66°F* to 29°C *84°F*), June rainiest (12 days). Absolute maximum temperature 43°C *109·4°F,* Valverde, 31 Aug. 1954; absolute minimum −3,5°C *+25·7°F,* Valle Nuevo, 2 Mar. 1959.
Labour force: 1 107 468 (1970 census): Agriculture, forestry and fishing 54·9%; Manufacturing 10·7%; Community, social and personal services 16·1%; 1 592 072 (estimate for 1 July 1979).
Gross domestic product: RD$6·4 billion in 1980..
Exports: RD$767·7 in 1982: Sugar and byproducts 31·6%; Coffee 6·3%; Ferronickel 12%.
Monetary unit: Dominican Republic peso. 1 peso = 100 centavos.
Denominations:
Coins 1, 5, 10, 25, 50 centavos; 1 peso.
Notes 1, 5, 10, 20, 50, 100, 500, 1000 pesos.
Exchange rate to £ sterling: 1·254 (23 April 1985).
Political history and government: A republic comprising 27 provinces (each administered by an appointed governor) and a *Distrito Nacional* (DN) containing the capital. Legislative power is exercised by the bicameral National Congress, with a Senate of 28 members (one for each province and one for the DN) and a Chamber of Deputies (91 members). Members of both houses are elected for four years by universal adult suffrage. Executive power lies with the President, elected by direct popular vote for four years. He is assisted by a Vice-President and an appointed Cabinet containing Secretaries of State.
Telephones: 175 054 (1982).
Daily newspapers: 7 (1978).
Total circulation: 40 000.
Radio: 210 000 (1977).
TV: 385 000 (1983).
Length of roadways: 7360 miles *11 844 km* (31 Dec. 1975).
Length of railways: 365 miles *588 km.*
Universities: 4 (plus 1 technical university).
Adult illiteracy: 29% in 1983.
Expectation of life: 62 years for both males and females.
Defence: In 1984 the armed forces totalled 23 000: Army 14 000; Navy 4500; Air force 4500; defence expenditure in 1982 estimated as US$103 million.
Cinemas: 150 in 1980.
Foreign tourists: 613 774 in 1981.

Ecuador

Official name: La República del Ecuador ('the equator').
Population: 9 250 000 (1983 estimate).
Area: 109 484 miles² *283 561 km².*
Language: Spanish.
Religion: Roman Catholic.
Capital city: Quito, population 635 713 at 1974 census.
Other principal towns (1974): Guayaquil 941 009; Cuenca 110 600; Ambato 77 062; Machala 68 379; Esmeraldas 60 132; Portoviejo 59 404; Riobamba 58 029.
Highest point: Chimborazo, 20 561 ft *6267 m*

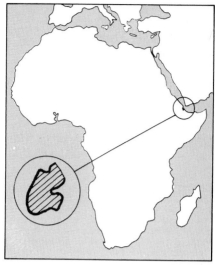

DJIBOUTI

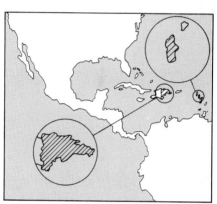

left: **THE DOMINICAN REPUBLIC**
right: **DOMINICA**

(first climbed 1879).
Principal mountain range: Cordillera de los Andes.
Principal rivers: Napo, Pastaza, Curaray, Daule.
Head of State: Osvaldo Hurtado Larrea (b. 1940), President.
Climate: Tropical (hot and humid) in coastal lowlands. Temperate (mild days, cool nights) in highlands, average temperature 13°C *55°F,* rainy season November–May. In Quito, average maximum 21°C *70°F* (April, May) to 23°C *73°F* (August, September), minimum 7°C *44°F* (July) to 8°C *47°F* (February–May), April rainiest (22 days). Absolute maximum temperature 38°C *100·4°F,* Babahoyo, 4 Jan. 1954; absolute minimum −3,6°C *25·5°F,* Cotopaxi, 9 Sept. 1962.
Labour force: 1 940 628 (including 61 408 unemployed) at 1974 census: Agriculture, forestry and fishing 49·4%; Manufacturing 12·5%; Trade, restaurants and hotels 10·4%; Community, social and personal services 18·1%.
Gross domestic product: 187 057 million sucres in 1978: Agriculture, forestry and fishing 21·0%; Mining and quarrying 11·1%; Manufacturing 17·2%; Trade, restaurants and hotels 13·3%; Community, social and personal services 14·0%.
Exports: US$2140 million in 1982: Petroleum 55·3%; Bananas 10%; Cocoa 3%; Coffee 6·5%.
Monetary unit: Sucre. 1 sucre = 100 centavos.
Denominations:
Coins 5, 10, 20, 50 centavos; 1 sucre.
Notes 5, 10, 20, 50, 100, 1000 sucres.
Exchange rate to £ sterling: 136·76 (14 Jan. 1985).
Political history and government: A republic comprising 19 provinces (each administered by an appointed governor) and a National Territory, the Archipiélago de Colón (the Galapagos Islands). On 22 June 1970 the President dismissed the National Congress (a Senate of 54 members and a 72-member Chamber of

Deputies) and assumed dictatorial powers. He was deposed by the armed forces on 15 Feb. 1972 and a National Military Government was formed. All political activity was suspended on 11 July 1974. A three-man military junta took power on 11 Jan. 1976 as the Supreme Council of Government. On 2 June 1976 the régime announced plans for a return to civilian rule. A referendum on 15 Jan. 1978 approved a new constitution providing for an executive President and a unicameral Congress with legislative power, both to be directly elected by universal adult suffrage. A presidential election was held on 16 July 1978 but no candidate obtained a majority of the votes. A 'run-off' election between the two leading candidates was held on 29 Apr. 1979, when the new Congress (69 members) was also elected. Jaime Roldós Aguilera was elected President and took office for a 4-year term on 10 Aug. 1979, when the Congress was inaugurated and the new constitution came into force. President Roldós was killed in an air crash on 24 May 1981 and his Vice-President succeeded him for the remainder of his term. The President appoints and leads the Council of Ministers.
Telephones: 260 000 (1980).
Daily newspapers: 37 (1978).
   Total circulation: 350 000.

ECUADOR

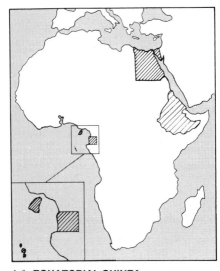

left: **EQUATORIAL GUINEA**
top right: **EGYPT** *lower right:* **ETHIOPIA**

Radio: 1 700 000 (1971).
TV: 340 000 (1977).
Length of roadways: 11 042 miles *17 770 km* (1980).
Length of railways: 600 miles *965 km* (1977).
Universities: 8 (plus 8 technical universities).
Adult illiteracy: 25·8% (males 21·8%; females 29·6%) in 1974.
Expectation of life: Males 54·89 years; females 58·07 years (1962–74, excluding nomadic Indian tribes).
Defence: Military service: two years, selective; total armed forces 36 100 (1984); defence expenditure, 1980: $194 million.
Cinemas: 330 in 1977.
Foreign tourists: 239 000 in 1981.

Egypt

Official name: Jumhuriyat Misr al-'Arabiya (Arab Republic of Egypt).
Population: 46 000 000 (1984 estimate).
Area: 386 662 miles² *1 001 449 km².*
Language: Arabic.
Religions: Muslim 92·6% Christian 7·3% (1960).
Capital city: El Qahira (Cairo), population 8 540 000 (1979 estimate).
Other principal towns (1976): El Iskandariyah (Alexandria) 2 318 655; El Giza 1 246 713; Subra-El Khema 393 700; El Mahalla el Kubra 292 853; Tanta 284 636; Bur Sa'id (Port Said) 262 620; El Mansura 257 866.
Highest point: Jebel Katherina, 8651 ft *2609 m.*
Principal mountain ranges: Sinai, Eastern Coastal Range.
Principal river: Nile (4145 miles *6670 km*).
Head of State: Lt-Gen. (Muhammad) Husni Mubarak (b. 1928), President and Prime Minister.
Climate: Hot and dry. Over 90% is arid desert. Annual rainfall generally less than 50 mm *2 in,* except on Mediterranean coast (maximum of 200 mm *8 in* around Alexandria). Mild winters. In Cairo, average maximum 18°C *65°F* (January) to 35°C *96°F* (July), minimum 8°C *47°F* (January) to 22°C *71°F* (August). In Luxor, average maximum 23°C *74°F* (January) to 42°C *107°F* (July), minimum 5°C *42°F* (January) to 23°C *73°F* (July, August), rain negligible.
Labour force: 9 448 000 (excluding 354 500 unemployed) aged 12 to 64 years (May 1978): Agriculture, forestry and fishing 43·4%; Manufacturing 15·6%; Community, social and personal services 19·5%. Including persons outside this age range, the total labour force was 10 743 300. All figures exclude aliens.
Gross domestic product: £E7341·0 million in 1977: Agriculture, forestry and fishing 27·6%; Manufacturing, mining and quarrying 24·4%; Trade, restaurants and hotels (incl. finance and insurance services) 12·3%; Community, social and personal services 20·5%.
Exports: £E2184 million in 1982: Raw cotton and cotton products 34%; Crude oil 31%; Petroleum products 11%.
Monetary unit: Egyptian pound (£E). £E1 = 100 piastres = 1000 millièmes.
Denominations:
   Coins 1, 5 millièmes; 1, 2, 5, 10, 20 piastres.
   Notes 5, 10, 25, 50 piastres; 1, 5, 10, 20, 100 pounds.
Exchange rate to £ sterling: 1·35 (14 Jan. 1985).
Political history and government: A former British protectorate, Egypt became independent, with the Sultan as King, on 28 Feb. 1922. Army officers staged a *coup* on 23 July 1952 and the King abdicated, in favour of his son, on 26 July 1952. Political parties were dissolved on 16 Jan. 1953. The young King was deposed, and a republic proclaimed, on 18 June 1953. Egypt merged with Syria to form the United Arab Republic on 1 Feb. 1958. Syria broke away and resumed independence on 29 Sept. 1961 but Egypt retained the union's title until the present name was adopted on 2 Sept. 1971. A new constitution, proclaiming socialist principles, was approved by referendum on 11 Sept. 1971. Legislative authority rests with the unicameral People's Assembly of 392 members (10 ap-

pointed and 382 elected by universal adult suffrage for 5 years). Half the elected members must be workers or peasants. The Assembly nominates the President, who is elected by popular referendum for six years. He has executive authority and appoints one or more Vice-Presidents, a Prime Minister and a Council of Ministers to perform administrative functions. The Arab Socialist Union (ASU), created on 7 Dec. 1962, was the only recognised political organisation of the state until the formation of political parties was again legalised on 29 June 1977. The three parties initially permitted were based on the three 'platforms' of the ASU which presented separate candidates at the Assembly elections of 28 Oct. and 4 Nov. 1976. The country is composed of 25 governorates (5 cities, 16 provinces, 4 frontier districts).
Telephones: 521 625 (1982).
Daily newspapers: 10 (1976).
   Total circulation: 3 012 000.
Radio: 15 275 000 (1977).
TV: 1 000 000 (1977).
Length of roadways: 17 964 miles *28 910 km* (main and secondary roads only) at 31 Dec. 1979.
Length of railways: 3018 miles *4857 km.*
Universities: 18.
Adult illiteracy: 56·5% (males 43·2%; females 71·0%) in 1976 (population aged 10 and over).
Expectation of life: Males 51·6 years; females 53·8 years (1960).
Defence: Military service; 3 years (selective); total armed forces 362 000 (1984); defence expenditure, 1979/80: $2168 million.
Cinemas: 215 in 1979.
Foreign tourists: 1 500 000 in 1983.

El Salvador

Offical name: La República de El Salvador ('The Saviour').
Population: 4 672 900 (1981 census).
Area: 8124 miles² *21 041 km².*
Language: Spanish.
Religion: Roman Catholic.
Capital city: San Salvador, population 884 093 (1981 census).
Other principal towns (1981): Santa Ana 208 322; San Miguel 161 156; Zacatecoluca 69 355; Usulutain 65 462; San Vicente 63 660.
Highest point: 9200 ft *2804 m.*
Principal rivers: Lempa (250 miles *402 km*), San Miguel.
Head of State: José Napoleón Duarte, President.
Climate: Tropical (hot and humid) in coastal lowlands, temperate in uplands. In San Salvador, maximum temperature is 32°C *90°F* (April and May), minimum around 15°C *60°F* (December, January, February).
Labour force: 1 437 600 in 1980: Agriculture 39·7%; Manufacturing 15·2%; Commerce 18·9%; Services 17·4%.
Gross domestic product: 7325·3 million colones in 1980: Agriculture, forestry and fishing 30·7%; Manufacturing 17·7%; Commerce 27·5%; Public administration 12·1%; Personal services 7·7%.
Exports: 1845·6 million colones in 1982: Coffee 57%.
Monetary unit: Salvadorian colón. 1 colón = 100 centavos.
Denominations:
   Coins 1, 5, 10, 25, 50 centavos.
   Notes 1, 2, 5, 10, 25, 100 colones.
Exchange rate to £ sterling: 4·6838 (14 Jan. 1985).
Political history and government: A republic composed of 14 departments. From 1932 a series of military officers held power, either as elected Presidents (often after disputed polls) or by means of a *coup.* On 20 Feb. 1977 Gen Carlos Humberto Romero Mena was elected President (despite allegations of fraud) and on 1 July 1977 he was sworn in. On 15 Oct. 1979 President Romero was deposed in a military *coup.* The unicameral Legislative Assembly was dissolved. The new régime formed a 5-member junta (including 3 civilians). On 15 Oct. 1980 the junta

announced that elections to a constituent assembly would be held in 1982 and general elections in 1983. On 22 Dec. 1980 two members of the junta were sworn in as President and Vice-President.
Telephones: 86 316 (1982).
Daily newspapers: 5 (1985).
Radio: 1 415 000 (1977).
TV: 148 000 (1977).
Length of roadways: 5216 miles *8394 km.*
Length of railways: 374 miles *602 km* (1979).
Universities: 12.
Adult illiteracy: 31·5% (1979).
Expectation of life: Males 62·9 years; females 66·4 years (1980–5).
Defence: Total armed forces 22 000 (1984); defence expenditure, 1979: $72 million.
Cinemas: 72 (1974).
Foreign tourists: 69 111 (1981).

Equatorial Guinea

Official name: La República de Guinea Ecuatorial.
Population: 380 000 (1982 estimate).
Area: 10 831 miles² *28 051 km².*
Languages: Spanish (official), Fang, Bubi.
Religions: Roman Catholic, Protestant minority.
Capital city: Malabo (formerly Santa Isabel), population 37 237 at 1960 census.
Other principal town: Bata, population 27 024 (1960).
Highest point: Pico de Moca (Moka), 9350 ft *2850 km.*
Principal rivers: Campo, Benito, Muni.
Head of State: Lt-Col Teodoro Obiang Nguema Mbasogo (b. 1946), Chairman of the Supreme Military Council.
Climate: Tropical (hot and humid), with average temperatures of over 26°C *80°F* and heavy rainfall (about 2000 mm *80 in* per year).
Labour force: 87 000 (mid-1970): Agriculture, forestry and fishing 79·9%; Services 12·6% (ILO estimates).
Gross domestic product: 3311 million ekuele (at 1962 prices) in 1967; $112 million (estimate) in 1975.
Exports: 1740·9 million ekuele in 1970: Cocoa 66·2% (cocoa beans 65·3%); Coffee 24·2%.
Monetary unit: Ekuele. 1 ekuele = 100 céntimos.
Denominations:
  Coins 5, 10, 50 céntimos; 1, 2½, 5, 25, 50, 100 ekuele.
  Notes 50, 100, 500, 1000, 5000 ekuele.
Exchange rate to £ sterling: 279·54 (14 Jan. 1985).
Political history and government: Formed on 20 Dec. 1963 by a merger of two Spanish territories, Río Muni on the African mainland and the adjacent islands of Fernando Póo (later renamed Macías Nguema Biyogo, then Bioko) and Annobón (now Pagalu). Became an independent republic, as a federation of two provinces, on 12 Oct. 1968. All political parties were merged into one on 2 Feb. 1970. The first President, Francisco Macías Nguema, was proclaimed 'President for Life' on 14 July 1972. A revised constitution, approved by referendum on 29 July 1973 and effective from 4 Aug. 1973, gave absolute power to the President and established a unitary state, abolishing the provincial autonomy of the islands. President Macías was deposed by a *coup* on 3 Aug. 1979, when a Supreme Military Council assumed power.
Telephones: 1451 (1969).
Daily newspapers: 2 (1976).
Radio: 82 000 (1977).
TV: 1000 (1977).
Length of roadways: 730 miles *1175 km.*
Expectation of life: Males 41·9 years; females 45·1 years (UN estimates for 1970–75).
Defence: A paramilitary force.
Cinemas: 10 (seating capacity 4500) in 1977.

Ethiopia

Official name: Socialist Ethiopia.
Population: 33 008 000 (1983 estimate).

Area: 471 800 miles² *1 221 900 km².*
Languages: Amharic, Galla, Somali.
Religions: Muslim 50%, Christian (mainly Coptic).
Capital city: Addis Ababa ('New Flower'), population 1 277 159 (1980 estimate).
Other principal towns (1980): Asmara 424 532; Dire Dawa 82 024; Gondar 76 932; Dessie 75 616; Nazret 69 865; Jimma 63 837; Harar 62 921; Bahr Dar 52 188.
Highest point: Ras Dashen, 15 158 ft *4620 m.*
Principal mountain ranges: Eritrean highlands, Tigre Plateau, Eastern Highlands, Semien mountains.
Principal rivers: Abbay, Tekeze, Awash, Omo, Sagan, Webi, Shebele.
Head of State: Lt-Col Mengistu Haile Mariam (b. 1937), President of the Derg (Provisional Military Administrative Council).
Climate: Mainly temperate and cool on the high plateau, with average annual temperature of 13°C *55°F*, abundant rainfall (June to August) and low humidity. Very hot and dry in desert lowlands and valley gorges. In Addis Ababa, average maximum 21°C *69°F* (July, August) to 25°C *77°F* (March–May), minimum 5°C *41°F* (December) to 10°C *50°F* (April–August). Absolute maximum 47,5°C *117·5°F*, Kelaffo, May 1959; absolute minimum −5,6°C *−22·0°F*, Maichew, November 1956.
Labour force: 10 823 000 (mid-1970): Agriculture, forestry and fishing 84·1%; Services 10·1% (ILO estimates); 13 889 200 (official estimate, 1978).
Gross domestic product: 6004·0 million birr in year ending 7 July 1976: Agriculture, forestry and fishing 49·5% (agriculture 47·3%); Manufacturing 10·5%; Community, social and personal services (incl. restaurants, hotels and business services) 12·4%.
Exports: US$374·1 million in 1981.
Monetary unit: Birr (formerly Ethiopian dollar). 1 birr = 100 cents.
Denominations:
  Coins 1, 5, 10, 25, 50 cents.
  Notes 1, 2, 10, 50, 100 birr.
Exchange rate to £ sterling: 390·90 (14 Jan. 1985).
Political history and government: Formerly a monarchy, ruled by an Emperor with near-autocratic powers. Political parties were not permitted. The former Italian colony of Eritrea was merged with Ethiopia, under a federal arrangement, on 15 Sept. 1952. Its federal status was ended on 14 Nov. 1962.
The last Emperor was deposed by the armed forces on 12 Sept. 1974. The constitution and the bicameral Parliament (a Senate and a Chamber of Deputies) were suspended. The *coup* was engineered by the Armed Forces Coordinating Committee (the Derg). The Committee established a Provisional Military Government and on 28 Nov. 1974 created the Provisional Military Administrative Council (PMAC) as its executive arm. Ethiopia was declared a socialist state on 20 Dec. 1974 and the monarchy was abolished on 21 Mar. 1975. Under a government re-organisation, announced on 29 Dec. 1976 and modified by proclamation on 11 Feb. 1977, the PMAC was renamed the Derg and was re-constituted with three organs: a General Congress (all members of the Derg) to determine national policy; a Central Committee (32 members of the Derg elected by the Congress) to supervise policy; and a Standing Committee (16 members), elected from the Central Committee by the Congress. The President of the Derg is Head of State and Chairman of the General Congress and the two committees. The Council of Ministers is appointed by, and responsible to, the Derg. Ethiopia has 14 provinces.
Telephones: 100 783 (1982).
Daily newspapers: 3 (1984).
  Total circulation: 45 000.
Radio: 250 000 (1980).
TV: 45 000 (1982).
Length of roadways: 23 172 miles *37 291 km* (31 Dec. 1979).
Length of railways: 614 miles *988 km.*

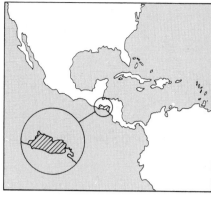

EL SALVADOR

Universities: 2.
Adult illiteracy: 54% (1983).
Expectation of life: Males 37·0 years; females 40·1 years (UN estimates for 1970–75).
Defence: Military service: conscription; total armed forces 249 500 (including 150 000 People's Militia) in 1984; defence expenditure, 1980; $385 million (converted at $1 = 2·86 birr).
Cinemas: 31 (seating capacity 25 600) in 1974.
Foreign tourists: 55 000 in 1982.

Fiji

Population: 588 068 (census of 13 Sept. 1976); 646 561 (estimate for 30 June 1980).
Area: 7056 miles² *18 274 km².*
Languages: English, Fijian, Hindi.
Religions: Christian 50·8% (mainly Methodist), Hindu 40·3%, Muslim 7·8% (1966).
Capital city: Suva, population 68 178 (1981 estimate).
Other principal towns: Lautoka, Vatukoula, Ba, Labasa, Levuka.
Highest point: Mt Victoria (Tomaniivi) on Viti Levu, 4341 ft *1323 m.*
Principal rivers: Rewa, Sigatoka, Navua, Nadi, Ba.
Head of State: HM Queen Elizabeth II, represented by Ratu Sir Penaia Ganilau, GCMG, KCVO, KBE, CMG, CVO, Governor General.
Prime Minister: Ratu the Rt Hon Sir Kamisese Kapaiwai Tuimacilai Mara, GCMG, KBE (b. 13 May 1920).
Climate: Temperate, with temperatures rarely falling below 15,5°C *60°F* or rising above 32,2°C *90°F*. Copious rainfall on windward side; dry on leeward side. Rainy season Nov.–March, driest month July.
Labour force: 203 000 (including 23 000 unemployed) in 1980: Manufacturing 6·8%; Wholesale and retail trades and restaurants 4·9%; Construction 4·4%; Community, social and personal services 11·8%.
Gross domestic product: $1084·5 million in 1981.
Exports: $475 591 000 in 1982: Mineral fuels 28·8%; Machinery and transport 17·2%; Food 14·9%; Manufactured goods 16·5%.
Monetary unit: Fiji dollar (F$). 1 dollar = 100 cents.
Denominations:
  Coins 1, 2, 5, 10, 20, 50 cents.
  Notes 1, 2, 5, 10, 20 dollars.
Exchange rate to £ sterling: 1·293 (14 Jan. 1985).
Political history and government: A former British colony, an independent member of the Commonwealth since 10 Oct. 1970. Executive power is vested in the Queen and exercisable by her personal representative, the Governor-General, appointed on the recommendation of the Cabinet. The Governor-General normally acts in accordance with the Cabinet's advice. The bicameral legislature comprises a Senate (22 members nominated for staggered six-year terms) and a House of Representatives (52 members elected for five years, subject to dissolution). Elections to the House are on three rolls: Fijian (22), Indian (22) and general (8). The Cabinet, which effectively directs the

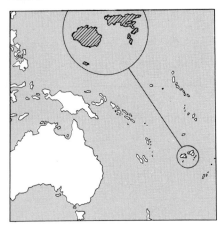

FIJI

government, is responsible to the legislature. The Prime Minister is chosen by the House and other Ministers are appointed on his recommendation. There are 14 provinces, each headed by a chairman.
Telephones: 48 069 (1982).
Daily newspapers: 2 (1982).
   Total circulation: 38 000.
Radio: 308 000 (1977).
Length of roadways: 1518 miles *2443 km.*
Length of railways: 400 miles *644 km.*
Universities: 1.
Expectation of life: Males 68·5 years; females 71·7 years (UN estimates for 1970–75).
Defence: Military service voluntary; total armed forces 2671 (1984); defence expenditure, 1980: US$9·9 million.
Cinemas: 50 (seating capacity 40 000) in 1976.
Foreign tourists: 273 406 (including 69 770 cruise passengers) in 1982.

Finland

Official name: Suomen Tasavalta (Republic of Finland).
Population: 4 869 858 (31 Dec. 1983) 4 898 000 (estimate for 31 Dec. 1984).
Area: 130 557 miles² *338 145 km².*
Languages: Finnish 93·6%; Swedish 6·2%.
Religions: Lutheran 90·1%; Orthodox 1·1%.
Capital city: Helsinki (Helsingfors), population 484 471 (31 Dec. 1983).
Other principal towns (1983): Tampere (Tammerfors) 167 344; Turku (Åbo) 163 002; Espoo (Esbo) 149 057; Vantaa (Vandu) 139 202; Lahti 94 466; Oulu (Uleåborg) 96 243.
Highest point: Haltiatunturi, 4344 ft *1324 m.*
Principal mountain ranges: Suomenselkä, Maanselkä.
Principal rivers: Paatsjoki, Torniojoki, Kemijoki, Kokemäenjoki.
Head of State: Dr Mauno Henrik Koivisto (b. 25 Nov. 1923), President.
Climate: Warm summers, very cold winters. Average annual temperature 17°C *62°F.* Winters are long and extreme in the north. In Helsinki, July warmest (14°C *57°F* to 22°C *71°F*), February coldest (−9°C *15°F* to −3°C *26°F*), August and October rainiest (12 days each). Absolute maximum temperature 35,9°C *96·6°F,* Turku, 9 July 1914; absolute minimum −48,8°C −55·8°F, Sodankylä, January 1868.
Labour force: 2 390 000 (excluding 156 000 unemployed) aged 15 to 74 years (1983): Agriculture, forestry and fishing 12·6%; Manufacturing 25·4%; Trade, restaurants and hotels 14·1%; Community, social and personal services 27·0%.
Gross domestic product: 275 084 million markkaa in 1983; Manufacturing 25·5%; Community, social and personal services 21·1% (government services 15·5%).
Exports: $12 512·1 million in 1983: Paper and paperboard 22·5%; Machinery and transport equipment 24·6%.
Monetary unit: Markka (Finnmark). 1 markka = 100 penniä (singular: penni).

Denominations:
   Coins 5, 10, 20, 50 penniä; 1, 5, 10 markkaa.
   Notes 5, 10, 50, 100, 500 markkaa.
Exchange rate to £ sterling: 8·06 (23 April 1985).
Political history and government: Formerly a Grand Duchy within the Russian Empire. After the Bolshevik revolution in Russia, Finland's independence was declared on 6 Dec. 1917. A republic was established by the constitution of 17 July 1919. This combines a parliamentary system with a strong presidency. The unicameral Parliament (*Eduskunta*) has 200 members elected by universal adult suffrage for 4 years (subject to dissolution by the President), using proportional representation. The President, entrusted with supreme executive power, is elected for 6 years by a college of 301 electors, chosen by popular vote in the same manner as members of Parliament. Legislative power is exercised by Parliament in conjunction with the President. For a general administration the President appoints a Council of State (Cabinet), headed by a Prime Minister, which is responsible to Parliament. Finland has 12 provinces, each administered by an appointed Governor.
Telephone: 2 777 073 (1983).
Daily newspapers: 66 (1982).
   Total circulation: 3 million.
TV: 1 737 810 (1983).
Length of roadways: 46 881 miles *75 448 km* (excluding urban streets) at 1 Jan. 1983.
Length of railways: 3789 miles *6097 km.*
Universities: 17 universities of science, 3 universities of art and 1 educational institution for social work at third level.
Adult illiteracy: Under 1%.
Expectation of life: Males 70·08 years; females 78·13 years (1982).
Defence: Military service: 8 to 11 months; total armed forces 39 900 (29 000 conscripts) in 1983; defence expenditure, 1983; $816 million.
Cinemas: 368 in 1983.
Tourism: Foreign exchange receipts on travel and ticket balances totalled $3993 million in 1983.

France

Official name: La République française (the French Republic).
Population: 54 453 000 (1983 estimate).
Area: 211 208 miles² *547 026 km².*
Language: French; Breton and Basque minorities.
Religions: Roman Catholic, Protestant, Jewish.
Capital city: Paris, population 8 549 898 (1975 census).
Other principal towns (1975): Lyon 1 170 660; Marseille 1 070 912; Lille 935 882; Bordeaux 612 456; Toulouse 509 939; Nantes 453 500; Nice 437 566; Grenoble 389 088; Rouen 388 711; Toulon 378 430; Strasbourg 365 323; Valenciennes 350 599; St-Étienne 334 846; Lens 328 741; Nancy 280 569; Le Havre 264 422; Cannes 258 479; Clermont-Ferrand 253 244; Tours 245 631; Rennes 229 310; Mulhouse 218 743; Montpellier 211 430; Douai 210 508; Orléans 209 234; Dijon 208 432; Reims 197 021.
Highest point: Mont Blanc, 15 771 ft *4807 m* (first climbed on 8 Aug. 1786).
Principal mountain ranges: Alps, Massif Central, Pyrenees, Jura Mts, Vosges, Cévennes.
Principal rivers: Rhône, Seine, Loire (625 miles *1006 km*), Garonne, Rhin (Rhine).
Head of State: François Maurice Marie Mitterand (b. 26 Oct. 1916), President.
Prime Minister: Laurent Fabius.
Climate: Generally temperate, with cool summers in the west and warm summers elsewhere. Mediterranean climate (warm summers, mild winters) in the south. In Paris, average maximum 5°C *42°F* (January) to 24°C *76°F* (July), minimum 0°C *32°F* (January) to 13°C *55°F* (July, August), December rainiest (17 days). Absolute maximum temperature 44,0°C *111·2°F,* Toulouse, 8 Aug. 1923; absolute minimum −33°C −27·4°F, Langres, 9 Dec. 1879.
Labour force: 21 403 600 (excluding persons on compulsory military service and 1 357 400 un-

employed) in 1979: Manufacturing 25·7%; Trade, restaurants and hotels 15·8%; Community, social and personal services 26·6%.
Gross domestic product: 1 870 341 million francs in 1977: Manufacturing 29·0%; Trade, restaurants and hotels 13·4% (trade 11·6%); Community, social and personal services 19·8% (government services 12·3%).
Exports: $97 958·8 million (including Monaco) in 1979: Food and live animals 11·4%; Chemicals 12·2%; Machinery 20·0% (non-electric machinery 12·8%); Transport equipment 16·3% (road motor vehicles and parts 12·1%).
Monetary unit: French franc. 1 franc = 100 centimes.
Denominations:
   Coins 5, 10, 20, 50 centimes; 1, 2, 5, 10 francs.
   Notes 10, 50, 100, 500 francs.
Exchange rate to £ sterling: 11·74 (22 Apr. 1985).
Political history and government: A republic whose present constitution (establishing the Fifth Republic and the French Community) was approved by referendum on 28 Sept. 1958 and promulgated on 6 Oct. 1958. Legislative power is held by a bicameral Parliament. The Senate has 318 members (298 for metropolitan France, 12 for the overseas departments and territories and 8 for French nationals abroad) indirectly elected for 9 years (one third renewable every three years). The National Assembly has 491 members (474 for metropolitan France and 17 for overseas departments) directly elected by universal adult suffrage (using two ballots if necessary) for 5 years, subject to dissolution. Executive power is held by the President. Since 1962 the President has been directly elected by universal adult suffrage (using two ballots if necessary) for 7 years. The President appoints a Council of Ministers, headed by the Prime Minister, which administers the country and is responsible to Parliament. Metropolitan France comprises 22 administrative regions containing 96 departments. There are also five overseas departments (French Guiana, Guadeloupe, Martinique, La Réunion and St. Pierre and Miquelon) which are integral parts of the French Republic. Each department is administered by an elected President of the Regional Council.
Telephones: 26 940 296 (1982).
Daily newspapers: 96 (1977).
   Total circulation: 10 863 000.
Radio: 17 442 000 licences (1976).
TV: 19 000 000 (1981).
Length of roadways: 498 896 miles *802 896 km* plus 435 000 miles *700 000 km* of rural roads (31 Dec. 1979).
Length of railways: 21 503 miles *34 599 km.*
Universities: 69.
Expectation of life: Males 70·2 years; females 78·5 years.
Defence: Military service; 12 months (18 months for overseas); total armed forces 721 123; defence expenditure, 1983; 141 505 million francs.
Cinemas: 5386 (seating capacity 1 601 400) in 1977; also 6 drive-in (1974).
Foreign tourists: 26 265 000 in 1977.

Gabon

Official name: La République gabonaise (the Gabonese Republic).
Population: 1 232 000 in 1984.
Area: 103 347 miles² *267 667 km².*
Languages: French (official), Fang, Eshira, Mbété.
Religions: Christian 60%, Animist minority.
Capital city: Libreville, population 251 400 (1974).
Other principal towns (1974): Port-Gentil 77 611; Lambaréné 22 682.
Highest point: Mont Iboundji, 5185 ft *1580 m.*
Principal river: Ogooué (Ogowe).
Head of State: *El Hadj* Omar Bongo (b. Albert-Bernard Bongo, 30 Dec. 1935), President and Head of Government.
Prime Minister: Léon Mébiame (b. 1 Sept. 1934).
Climate: Tropical (hot and humid). Average temperature 26°C *79°F.* Heavy rainfall (annual

average 2490 mm *98 in*). In Libreville, average maximum 30°C *86°F* to 34°C *94°F*, minimum 18°C *65°F* to 22°C *71°F*.
Labour force: 220 000 (31 Dec. 1963); 250 000 (mid-1970): Agriculture, forestry and fishing 81·4%; Services 10·2% (ILO estimates).
Gross domestic product: 600 203 million CFA francs in 1978: Mining and quarrying (excluding government) 36·3% (crude petroleum and natural gas 30·2%); Construction 14·1%.
Exports: 477 760 million CFA francs in 1980: Petroleum 72%; metals 18%; timber 6%.
Monetary unit: Franc de la Communauté financière africaine.
Denominations:
   Coins 1, 2, 5, 10, 25, 50, 100 CFA francs.
   Notes 100, 500, 1000, 5000, 10 000 CFA francs.
Exchange rate to £ sterling: 542·25 (14 Jan. 1985).
Political history and government: Formerly part of French Equatorial Africa, independent since 17 Aug. 1960. A one-party state since March 1968. The legislature is a unicameral National Assembly of 93 members, of whom nine are nominated by the President and 84 directly elected by universal adult suffrage for five years. Executive power is held by the President, directly elected for seven years. He appoints, and presides over, a Council of Ministers, including a Prime Minister. Gabon comprises nine regions, each administered by an appointed Prefect.
Telephones: 11 133 (1982).
Daily newspapers: 1 (1976).
Radio: 98 000 (1982).
TV: 10 000 (1982).
Length of roadways: 4511 miles *7276 km* (1981).
Length of railways: 200 miles *325 km*.
Universities: 1.
Adult illiteracy: 87·6% in 1960.
Expectation of life: Males 39·4 years; females 42·6 years (UN estimates for 1970–75).
Defence: Military service voluntary; total armed forces 2170 (1984); defence expenditure, 1978: $52·6 million.
Cinemas: 6 (seating capacity 4100) in 1974.
Foreign tourists: 52 453 (1973).

The Gambia

Official name: The Republic of the Gambia.
Population: 680 000 (1983 census, excluding seasonal farming immigrants).
Area: 4361 miles² *11 295 km²*.
Languages: English (official), Mandinka, Fula, Wollof.
Religions: Muslim, Christian minority.
Capital city: Banjul (formerly Bathurst), population 65 000 (1983 census).
Other principal towns: Brikama; Salikeni; Bakau; Gunjur.
Principal river: Gambia.
Head of State: *Alhaji* Sir Dawda Kairaba Jawara (b. 11 May 1924), President.
Climate: Long dry season, normally November to May, with pleasant weather on coast (best in West Africa) due to effect of the *harmattan*, a northerly wind. Hotter up-river, especially February to May. Average annual rainfall 1000 mm *40 in* on coast, less inland. Rainy season June to October. Average annual temperature in Banjul 27°C *80°F*.
Labour force: 345 000 (1983).
Gross domestic product: $148 million (1983).
Exports: 86 million dalasi; Food and live animals 11%; Oil seeds, oil nuts and oil kernels 56% (groundnuts 55%); Groundnut oil 30%.
Monetary unit: Dalasi. 1 dalasi = 100 butut.
Denominations:
   Coins 1, 5, 10, 25, 50 butut; 1 dalasi.
   Notes 1, 5, 10, 25 dalasi.
Exchange rate to £ sterling: 5·00 (14 Jan. 1985).
Political history and government: A former British dependency, an independent member of the Commonwealth since 18 Feb. 1965. A republic since 24 April 1970. Legislative power is held by a unicameral House of Representatives containing 43 members (35 directly elected for 5

years by universal adult suffrage, 4 Chiefs' Representative Members elected by the Chiefs in Assembly, 3 non-voting nominated members and the Attorney-General). Executive power is held by the President, the leader of the majority party in the House. He appoints a Vice-President (who is leader of government business in the House) and a Cabinet from elected members of the House. The country has four political parties. On 1 Feb. 1982 The Gambia and Senegal formed a confederation named Senegambia.
Telephones: 3476 (1980).
Radio: 66 000 (1983).
Length of roadways: 1858 miles *2990 km* (Jan. 1974).
Adult illiteracy: 94% in 1962.
Expectation of life: Males 39·4 years; females 42·5 years (UN estimates for 1970–75).
Defence: Gambia Army.
Cinemas: 9 and 9 part-time (1976).
Foreign tourists: 40 000 in year ending June 1984.

Germany (East)

Official name: Deutsche Demokratische Republik (German Democratic Republic).
Population: 16 705 635 (census of 31 Dec. 1981); 16 701 487 (estimate for 31 Dec. 1983).
Area: 41 767 miles² *108 177 km²*.
Language: German.
Religions: Protestant 50%, Roman Catholic 8%.
Capital city: (East) Berlin, population 1 179 442 (estimate for 30 June 1982).
Other principal towns (mid-1982): Leipzig 557 474; Dresden 521 773; Karl-Marx-Stadt (Chemnitz) 319 053; Magdeburg 288 728; Rostock 240 751; Halle 235 448.
Highest point: Fichtelberg, 3983 ft *1214 m*.
Principal mountain ranges: Thüringer Wald, Erz Gebirge.
Principal rivers: Elbe (525 miles *845 km*) (with Havel and Saale), Oder (with Neisse).
Head of State: Erich Honecker (b. 25 Aug. 1912), Chairman of the Council of State; also General Secretary of the Central Committee of the Socialist Unity Party.
Head of Government: Willi Stoph (b. 9 July 1914), Chairman of the Council of Ministers.
Climate: Temperate (warm summers, cool winters), greater range inland. In Berlin, July warmest (13°C *55°F* to 23°C *74°F*), January coldest (−3°C *26°F* to 2°C *35°F*), December rainiest (11 days). Absolute maximum temperature 38,3°C *102·7°F*, Blankenberg, 7 July 1957; absolute minimum −33,8°C *−28·8°F*, Zittau-Hirschfelde, 11 Feb. 1939.
Labour force: 8 445 300 (1983, excluding apprentices): Industry and crafts 41%; Construction 6·9%; Agriculture and forestry 10·7%; Transport, posts and telecommunications 7·4%; Trade and other productive branches 13·3%; Non-productive sectors 20·7%.
Gross domestic product: 563 792 million DDR-marks (1982): Industry 70·2%; Construction 5·8%; Agriculture and forestry 7·7%; Transport, posts and telecommunications 4·1%; Domestic trade 9·1%; Other productive sectors 3%.
Exports: 84 227 million Valuta marks (1983): Machinery 47·8%; Fuels, mineral raw materials, metals 17·7%; Other raw materials and semi-manufactured goods 7·9%; Industrial consumer goods 14·1%; Chemical products, building materials and other goods 12·5%.
Monetary unit: Mark der Deutschen Demokratischen Republik (DDR-Mark). 1 Mark = 100 Pfennige.
Denominations:
   Coins 1, 5, 10, 20, 50 Pfennige; 1, 2, 5, 10, 20 DDR-Marks.
   Notes 5, 10, 20, 50, 100 DDR-Marks.
Exchange rate to £ sterling: 3·856 (15 Apr. 1985).
Political history and government: The territory was the USSR's Zone of Occupation in Germany from May 1945. The republic, a 'people's democracy' on the Soviet pattern, was proclaimed on 7 Oct. 1949. The USSR granted full sovereignty on 25 Mar. 1954. The present constitution was promulgated on 9 Apr. 1968.

left: **FRANCE**   *right:* **FINLAND**

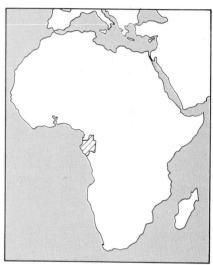

GABON

The supreme organ of state power is the *Volkskammer* (People's Chamber), with 500 members elected for 5 years by universal adult suffrage (from a single list of candidates). The Chamber elects a 24-member *Staatsrat* (Council of State) to be its permanent organ. The executive branch of government is the *Ministerrat* (Council of Ministers), under a Chairman (Minister-President) appointed by the Chamber, which also approves his appointed Ministers. The Council's work is directed by a Presidium of 16 members. Political power is held by the (Communist) Socialist Unity Party of Germany (SED), formed in 1946 by a merger of the Communist Party and the Social Democratic Party in the Soviet Zone. The SED dominates the National Front of Democratic Germany, which also includes four minor parties and four mass organisations. The SED's highest authority is the Party Congress. The Congress elects the Central Committee to supervise Party work (on 15 Apr. 1981 the Congress elected a Committee of 156 full members and 57 candidate members). The Central Committee elects a Political Committee (Politburo), with 17 full members and eight candidate members in 1981, to direct its policy. The country is divided into 14 districts (*Bezirke*) and the city of East Berlin.
Telephones: 3 071 515 (1980).
Daily newspapers: 39 (1978).
   Total circulation: 7 100 000.
Radio: 15 000 000 (1977).
TV: 5 928 000 licences (1983).
Length of roadways (classified): 29 375 miles *47 380 km* (1983).
Length of railways: 8820 miles *14 226 km* (1983).
Universities: 7.
Expectation of life: Males 68·82 years; females 74·42 years (1976).
Defence: Military service 18–24 months; total

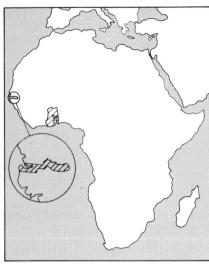

encircled left: **THE GAMBIA**
GHANA

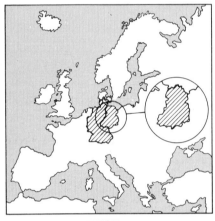

left: **GERMANY (WEST)**
encircled right: **GERMANY (EAST)**

regular forces 169 000 (92 000 conscripts) in 1984; defence expenditure, 1981: $6960 million (converted at $1 = 2·03 Marks).
Cinemas: 824 in 1983.
Foreign tourists: 1 100 799 plus 17 143 481 frontier arrivals (stays of less than 24 hours) in 1977.

Germany (West)

Official name: Bundesrepublik Deutschland (Federal Republic of Germany).
Population: 61 306 669 (estimate for 31 Dec. 1983).
Area: 96 025 miles² *248 706 km²*.
Language: German.
Religions: Protestant 49%, Roman Catholic 44·6%.
Capital city: Bonn, population 291 509 (estimate for 31 Dec. 1983).
Other principal towns (1983): Berlin (West) 1 854 502; Hamburg 1 609 531; München (Munich) 1 283 457; Köln (Cologne) 940 663; Frankfurt 610 244; Dortmund 589 955; Dusseldorf 575 805; Stuttgart 567 020; Bremen 540 442; Duisberg 536 402; Hannover (Hanover) 523 033; Nürnberg (Nuremberg) 424 290; Bochum 389 064; Wuppertal 383 775; Bielefeld 305 481; Mannheim 298 042; Gelsenkirchen 293 329; Wiesbaden 270 444; Münster 273 453; Karlsruhe 269 389; Mönchengladbach 257 636; Braunschweig (Brunswick) 256 931.
Highest point: Zugspitze, 9721 ft *2963 m* (first climbed 1820).
Principal mountain ranges: Alps, Schwarzwald (Black Forest).

Principal rivers: Rhein (Rhine) (820 miles *1320 km*), Ems, Weser, Elbe, Donau (Danube) (1770 miles *2850 km*).
Head of State: Dr Richard Von Weizsäcker (b. 15 Mar. 1920), Federal President.
Head of Government: Dr Helmut Kohl (b. 3 April 1930), Federal Chancellor.
Climate: Generally temperate (average annual temperature 9°C *48°F*) with considerable variations from northern coastal plain (mild) to Bavarian Alps (cool summers, cold winters). In Hamburg, July warmest (13°C *56°F* to 20°C *69°F*), January coolest (−2°C *28°F* to 2°C *35°F*), January, July and December rainiest (each 12 days). Absolute maximum temperature 39,8°C *103·6°F*, Amberg, 18 Aug. 1892; absolute minimum −35,4°C *−31·7°F*, 12 Feb. 1929.
Labour force: 25 668 000 in 1982.
Gross domestic product: 1 602 500 million DM in 1982: Agriculture and forestry 2·3%; Producing industries 42%; Trade, transport and communications 14·9%; Services 24·7%.
Exports: 427 741 million DM in 1982: Road vehicles 16·9%; Products of mechanical engineering 15·5%; Chemicals 12·6%.
Monetary unit: Deutsche Mark (DM). 1 Deutsche Mark = 100 Pfennige.
Denominations:
   Coins 1, 2, 5, 10, 50 Pfennige; 1, 2, 5 DM.
   Notes 5, 10, 20, 50, 100, 500, 1000 DM.
Exchange rate to £ sterling: 3·856 (15 Apr. 1985).
Political history and government: The territory was the British, French and US Zones of Occupation in Germany from May 1945. A provisional constitution, the *Grundgesetz* (Basic Law), came into force in the three Zones (excluding Saarland) on 23 May 1949 and the Federal Republic of Germany (FRG) was established on 21 Sept. 1949. Sovereignty was limited by the continuing military occupation, and subsequent defence agreements, until 5 May 1955, when the FRG became fully independent. Saarland (under French occupation) was rejoined with the FRG administratively on 1 Jan. 1957 and economically incorporated on 6 July 1959. The FRG is composed of 10 states (*Länder*) – each *Land* having its own constitution, parliament and government – plus the city of West Berlin which retains a separate status. The country has a parliamentary regime, with a bicameral legislature. The Upper House is the *Bundesrat* (Federal Council) with 45 seats, including 41 members of *Land* governments (which appoint and recall them) and 4 non-voting representatives appointed by the West Berlin Senate. The term of office varies with *Land* election dates. The Lower House, and the FRG's main legislative organ, is the *Bundestag* (Federal Assembly), with 519 deputies, including 497 elected for four years by universal adult suffrage (using a mixed system of proportional representation and direct voting) and 22 members (with limited voting rights) elected by the West Berlin House of Representatives. Executive authority rests with the *Bundesregierung* (Federal Government), led by the *Bundeskanzler* (Federal Chancellor) who is elected by an absolute majority of the *Bundestag* and appoints the other Ministers. The Head of State, who normally acts on the Chancellor's advice, is elected for a five-year term by a Federal Convention, consisting of the *Bundestag* and an equal number of members elected by the *Land* parliaments.
Telephones: 30 122 023 (1982).
Daily newspapers: 412 (1977).
   Total circulation: 25 968 000.
Radio: 24 158 000 (1982).
TV: 21 836 000 (1982).
Length of roadways: 299 501 miles *482 000 km* (31 Dec. 1979).
Length of railways: 19 441 miles *31 280 km* (1982).
Universities: 48 (and 10 technical universities).
Expectation of life: Males 69·9 years; females 76·6 years (1981).
Defence: Military service 15 months; total armed forces 495 000 (225 000 conscripts) in 1984; defence expenditure, 1981: $25 000 million.
Cinemas: 3110 in 1979.
Foreign tourists: 10 300 000 in 1979.

Ghana

Official name: The Republic of Ghana ('land of gold').
Population: 12 205 574 (1984 census).
Area: 92 100 miles² *238 537 km²*.
Languages: English (official), Asante, Ewe, Fante.
Religions: Christian, Muslim, Animist.
Capital city: Accra, population 564 194 (1970 census).
Other principal towns (1970): Kumasi 260 286; Tamale 83 653; Tema 60 767; Takoradi 58 161; Cape Coast 51 653; Sekondi 33 713.
Highest point: Vogag, 2989 ft *911 m*.
Principal rivers: Volta (formed by the confluence of the Black Volta and the White Volta) and its tributaries (principally the Oti, Tano, Ofin).
Head of State: Flight-Lieutenant Jerry John Rawlings (b. 1947), Chairman Provisional National Defence Council.
Climate: Tropical. In north hot and dry. Forest areas hot and humid. Eastern coastal belt warm and fairly dry. In Accra average maximum 27°C *80°F* (August) to 31°C *88°F* (February to April and December), average minimum 22°C *71°F* (August) to 24°C *76°F* (March, April), June rainiest (10 days).
Labour force: 3 331 618 (including 198 571 unemployed) aged 15 and over (1970 census); 3 351 000 (mid-1970): Agriculture forestry and fishing 58·4%; Industry 16·7%; Services 24·9% (ILO estimates).
Gross domestic product: 6526·2 million new cedis in 1976: Agriculture, forestry and fishing (excluding government) 50·3% (agriculture 43·3%); Industry 19·1% (manufacturing 13·1%); Trade, restaurants and hotels 13·1% (trade 12·3%).
Exports: $766·4 million in 1981: Cocoa 72·9% (cocoa, beans 62·1%, cocoa butter and paste 10·8%).
Monetary unit: New cedi. 1 cedi = 100 pesewas.
Denominations:
   Coins ½, 1, 2½, 5, 10, 20 pesewas; 1 cedi.
   Notes 1, 2, 5, 10, 50 cedis.
Exchange rate to £ sterling: 55·625 (14 Jan. 1985).
Political history and government: On 6 Mar. 1957 the British dependency of the Gold Coast merged with British Togoland to become independent, and a member of the Commonwealth, as Ghana. Became a republic on 1 July 1960. The President, Dr Kwame Nkrumah, was deposed by a military *coup* on 24 Feb. 1966. Civilian rule was restored on 30 Sept. 1969 but again overthrown by the armed forces on 13 Jan. 1972. The 1969 constitution was abolished, the National Assembly dissolved and political parties banned. Power was assumed by the National Redemption Council (NRC), comprising military commanders and Commissioners of State with ministerial responsibilities. The first Chairman of the NRC was Lt-Col (later Gen) Ignatius Acheampong. On 14 Oct. 1975 a 7-man Supreme Military Council (led by Acheampong) was established, with full legislative and administrative authority, to direct the NRC. Acheampong was removed from office by the SMC on 5 July 1978. A constitutional drafting commission, appointed by the military government, reported on 17 Nov. 1978. Its recommendations were debated by a Constitutional Assembly of 120 members (64 elected by local councils, the remainder nominated by the SMC and other national bodies), which was inaugurated on 21 Dec. 1978 and presented its final report on 15 May 1979. The ban on political parties had been lifted on 1 Jan. 1979 and the return to civilian rule planned for 1 July. The régime was overthrown by another military *coup* on 4 June 1979, when an Armed Forces Revolutionary council (AFRC) took power. The AFRC postponed the return to civilian rule but on 14 June it promulgated the new constitution, providing for an executive President (serving a four-year term) and a unicameral parliament (with a five-year term) both to be elected by universal adult suffrage. Elections were held on 18 June 1979 for a President and the 140 members of Parliament. No presidential candidate received

a majority of votes and a 'run-off' election between the two leading candidates was held on 9 July. Civilian rule was restored, and the President took office, on 24 Sept. 1979, but was subsequently overthrown in a bloodless coup by Flt-Lt Rawlings on 31 Dec. 1981. Ghana comprises nine regions, each the responsibility of a Minister.
Telephones: 70 653 (1982).
Daily newspapers: 4 (1976).
　　Total circulation: 435 000.
Radio: 1 880 000 (1982).
TV: 60 000 (1982).
Length of roadways: 20 000 miles *32 200 km* (31 Dec. 1977).
Length of railways: 592 miles *953 km*.
Universities: 3.
Adult illiteracy: 69·8% in 1970.
Expectation of life: Males 41·9 years; females 45·1 years (UN estimates for 1970–75).
Defence: Military service voluntary; total armed forces 12 740 (1984); defence expenditure, 1981: $140 million.
Cinemas: 8 (seating capacity 13 200) in 1977.
Foreign tourists: 48 000 in 1979.

Greece

Official name: Elleniki Dimokratia (Hellenic Republic).
Population: 9 740 417 (1981 census).
Areas: 50 944 miles² *131 944 km²*.
Language: Greek.
Religions: Eastern Orthodox Church 97%; Roman Catholic and other minorities.
Capital city: Athínai (Athens), population 3 027 331 (1981).
Other principal towns (1981): Thessaloniki (Salonika) 402 443; Patras 140 878; Heraklion 101 668; Larisa 103 263; Volos 70 967; Kavála 56 260; Piraeus (1971) 187 362.
Highest point: Óros Ólimbos (Olympus), 9550 ft *2911 m*.
Principal mountain range: Pindus Mountains.
Principal rivers: Aliákmon (195 miles *314 km*), Piniós, Akhelóös.
Head of State: Christos Sartzetatis (b. 1929), President.
Prime Minister: Andreas Georgios Papandreou (b. 5 Feb. 1919).
Climate: Mediterranean (hot, dry summers and mild, wet winters). Colder in the north and on higher ground. In Athens, July and August hottest (22°C *72°F* to 32°C *90°F*), January coolest (5°C *42°F* to 12°C *54°F*), December and January rainiest (seven days each). Absolute maximum temperature 45,7°C *114·3°F*, Heraklion, Crete, 16 June 1914; absolute minimum − 25°C *− 13°F*, Kavála, 27 Jan. 1954.
Labour force: 3 491 300 (1982).
Gross domestic product: 1 157 670 million drachmae in 1978: Agriculture, forestry and fishing 17·2% (agriculture 16·5%); Manufacturing 18·9%; Trade 12·9%; Community, social and personal services (including restaurants, hotels and business services) 21·7%.
Exports: 286 281 million drachmae in 1982.
Monetary unit: Drachma. 1 drachma = 100 leptae (singular: lepta).
Denominations:
　　Coins 10, 20, 50 leptae; 1, 2, 5, 10, 20 drachmae.
　　Notes 50, 100, 500, 1000 drachmae.
Exchange rate to £ sterling: 168 (16 Apr. 1985).
Political history and government: While Greece was a monarchy a *coup* by army officers, led by Col Georgios Papadopoulos, deposed the constitutional government on 21 Apr. 1967. Parliament was suspended and political parties banned. Papadopoulos became Prime Minister on 13 Dec. 1967, a Regent was appointed and the King left the country the next day. A Republic was proclaimed on 1 June 1973 and Papadopoulos became President. He was deposed by another military *coup* on 25 Nov. 1973. Civilian rule was re-established on 24 July 1974, when a Government of National Salvation took office. The ban on political parties was lifted and free elections for a Parliament were held on

17 Nov. 1974. A referendum on 8 Dec. 1974 rejected the return of the monarchy. A new republican constitution, providing for a parliamentary democracy, came into force on 11 June 1975. Executive power rests with the President, elected for 5 years by the legislature, a unicameral parliament (*Vouli*) of 300 members directly elected by universal adult suffrage for 4 years. The President appoints a Prime Minister and, on his recommendation, the other Ministers to form a Cabinet to govern the country. The Cabinet is accountable to Parliament. The country is divided into 51 prefectures (*Nomoi*). The district of Mount Athos, with its autonomous monastic community, has a privileged status as a self-governing part of the Greek state.
Telephones: 2 956 663 (1982).
Daily newspapers: 112 (1977).
　　Total circulation: 962 000 (104 dailies in 1974).
Radio: 5 000 000 (1982).
TV: 1 400 000 (1982).
Length of roadways: 22 999 miles *37 013 km* (main and secondary roads only) at 30 Apr. 1979.
Length of railways: 1583 miles *2548 km*.
Universities: 6.
Adult illiteracy: 15·6% (males 6·9%; females 23·7%) in 1971.
Expectation of life: males 70·13 years; females 73·64 years (1970).
Defence: Military service 22–26 months; total armed forces 186 000 in 1984; defence expenditure 1982: 134 694 million drachmai.
Cinemas: 1504 in 1979.
Foreign tourists: 5 232 973 (including Greek nationals residing abroad) plus 565 387 cruise passengers (1979).

Grenada

Official name: State of Grenada.
Population: 115 000 (1981 estimate).
Area: 133 miles² *344 km²*.
Language: English.
Religion: Christian.
Capital city: St. George's, population 30 813 (1978 estimate).
Other principal towns: Grenville, Victoria, Sauteurs, Gouyare (Charlotte Town), Hillsborough.
Highest point: Mount St Catherine's, 2756 ft *840 m*.
Head of State: HM Queen Elizabeth II, represented by Sir Paul Scoon, GCMG, OBE (b. 4 July 1935), Governor-General.
Prime Minister: H. A. Blaiz.
Climate: Tropical maritime, with equable temperature averaging 28°C *82°F* in the lowlands. Annual rainfall averages 1524 mm *60 in* in coastal area and 3810–5080 mm *150–200 in* in mountain areas. Rainy season June to December (November wettest), dry season January to May.
Labour force: 28 682 (1970 census).
Gross domestic product: EC$80·5 million (at factor cost) in 1975: Agriculture, forestry and fishing 28·7% (agriculture 24·3%); Trade, restaurants and hotels 18·1% (trade 15·8%); Community, social and personal services 18·9%.
Exports: EC$50 275 362 in 1981.
Monetary unit: East Caribbean dollar (EC$). 1 dollar = 100 cents.
Denominations:
　　Coins 1, 2, 5, 10, 25, 50 cents.
　　Notes 1, 5, 20, 100 dollars.
Exchange rate to £ sterling: 3·051 (14 Jan. 1985).
Political history and government: A former British dependency. An Associated State, with internal self-government, from 3 Mar. 1967 until becoming fully independent, within the Commonwealth, on 7 Feb. 1974. Executive power is vested in the Queen and exercised by the Governor-General, who acts on the advice of the Cabinet, led by the Prime Minister. At independence the Grenada United Labour Party (GULP) was in power. The GULP government was overthrown on 13 Mar. 1979 in a *coup* by supporters of the main opposition party, the New Jewel Movement. A 'People's Revolutionary Government' took power, dissolved Parliament, suspended the constitution and

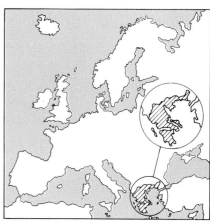

GREECE

announced plans to create a People's Consultative Assembly to draft a new one. Maurice Bishop, the Prime Minister was subsequently killed in a power struggle, whereupon the army took control (19 Oct. 1983). At the request of other Caribbean countries, the US then led an invasion of the island, and a state of emergency was declared. An interim government took over, to be succeeded by an elected government in November 1984.
Telephones: 5648.
Daily newspapers: 1.
Radio: 63 500 (1978).
Length of roadways: 610 miles *982 km*.
Adult illiteracy: 2·2% in 1970.
Expectation of life: Males 60·14 years; females 65·60 years (1959–61).
Defence: People's Revolutionary Army of about 6500 in 1983.
Cinemas: 6 (seating capacity 4000), 3 mobile units and 1 drive-in (capacity 600) in 1975.
Foreign tourists: 102 668 in 1981.

Guatemala

Official name: República de Guatemala.
Population: 6 043 559 (1983).
Area: 42 042 miles² *108 889 km²*.
Languages: Spanish, with some twenty Indian dialects (most important is Quiché).
Religion: Roman Catholic 90%.
Capital city: Ciudad de Guatemala (Guatemala City), population 1 300 000 (1983 estimate).
Other principal towns (1983): Quezaltenango 65 733; Puerto Barrios 38 956; Mazatenango 38 319; Antigua 26 631; Zacapa 35 769; Coban 43 538.
Highest point: Volcán Tajumulco, 13 881 ft *4220 m*.
Principal mountain ranges: Sierra Madre, Sierra de las Minas, Sierra de los Cuchumatanes, Sierra de Chuacús.
Principal rivers: Motagua (249 miles *400 km*), Usumacinta (688 miles *1107 km*).
Head of State: Brig.-Gen. Oscar Humberto Mejía Victores, President.
Climate: Tropical (hot and humid) on coastal lowlands, with average temperature of 28°C *83°F*. More temperate in central highlands, with average of 21°C *68°F*. Mountains cool. In Guatemala City, average maximum 22°C *72°F* (December) to 29°C *84°F* (May), minimum 12°C *53°F* (January) to 16°C *61°F* (June), June rainiest (23 days). Absolute maximum temperature 45°C *113°F*, Guatemala City, 17 Dec. 1957; absolute minimum −7,1°C *19·2°F*, Quezaltenango, 15 Jan. 1956.
Labour force: 2 092 337 (excluding institutional households) in 1979: Agriculture, forestry and fishing 58·4%; Manufacturing 14·0%; Services 23·0%.
Gross domestic product: 2874·6 million quetzales (at 1958 prices) in 1978: Agriculture, forestry and fishing 25·9%; Manufacturing 16·2%; Trade 28·2%; Community, social and personal services (including restaurants and hotels) 10·6%.
Exports: 1281·2 million quetzals in 1981: Cotton

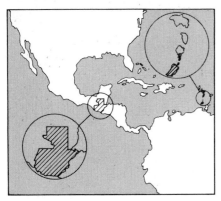

left: **GUATEMALA**
right: **GRENADA**

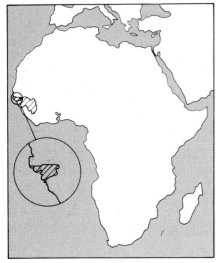

encircled left: **GUINEA-BISSAU**
right: **GUINEA**

10·9%; Sugar 4·6%; Coffee 30·5%.
Monetary unit: Quetzal. 1 quetzal = 100 centavos.
Denominations:
  Coins 1, 5, 10, 25 centavos.
  Notes 50 centavos; 1, 5, 10, 20, 50, 100 quetzales.
Exchange rate to £ sterling: 1·254 (23 April 1985).
Political history and government: A republic comprising 22 departments. Under the constitution, promulgated on 15 Sept. 1965 and effective from 1 July 1966, legislative power is vested in the unicameral National Congress, with 61 members elected for 4 years by universal adult suffrage. Executive power is held by the President, also directly elected for 4 years. If no candidate obtains an absolute majority of votes, the President is chosen by Congress. He is assisted by a Vice-President and an appointed Cabinet.
Telephones: 97 670 (1982).
Daily newspapers: 8 (1980).
Radio: 280 000 (1978).
TV: 192 000 (1982).
Length of roadways: 10 736 miles *17 278 km* (31 Dec. 1979).
Length of railways: 601 miles *967 km.*
Universities: 5.
Adult illiteracy: 53·9% (males 46·1%; females 61·5%) in 1973.
Expectation of life: Males 48·29 years; females 49·74 years (1963–65).
Defence: Military service: 2 years; total armed forces 21 150 (1984); defence expenditure, 1980: $77 million.
Cinemas: 106 (seating capacity 75 200) in 1973; 104 and 22 mobile units (1976).
Foreign tourists: 466 041 (1980).

Guinea

Official name: La République populaire et révolutionnaire de Guinée (the People's Revolutionary Republic of Guinea).
Population: 5 412 000 (1983 estimate).
Area: 94 926 miles² *245 857 km².*
Languages: French (official), Fulani (Poular), Susu, Malinké.
Religions: Muslim, Animist minority.
Capital city: Conakry, population 763 000 (1980 estimate).
Other principal towns (1972); Kankan 85 310; Kindia 79 861; Labé 79 670; N'Zérékoré 23 000.
Highest point: Mt Nimba, 5748 ft *1752 m.*
Principal mountain range: Fouta Djalon.
Principal rivers: Niger (2600 miles *4184 km*), Bafing, Konkouré, Kogon.
Head of State: Col. Lansana Konté.
Prime Minister: Col. Diarra Traore.
Climate: Hot and moist, with heavy rainfall in coastal areas. Cooler in higher interior. In Conakry, average maximum 28°C *82°F* to 32°C *90°F*, minimum around 23°C *74°F*, annual rainfall 4300 mm *169 in.*
Labour force: 1 870 000 (mid-1970): Agriculture, forestry and fishing 84·7% (ILO estimates).
Gross domestic product: $723 million in 1975 (UN estimate).
Exports: 7000 million sylis in 1979: Bauxite 58%; Alumina 30%.
Monetary unit: Syli. 1 syli = 100 cauris (corilles).
Denominations:
  Coins 50 cauris; 1, 2, 5 sylis.
  Notes 10, 25, 50, 100 sylis.
Exchange rate to £ sterling: 28·58 (14 Jan. 1985).
Political history and government: Formerly French Guinea, part of French West Africa. Became independent as the Republic of Guinea, outside the French Community, on 2 Oct. 1958. A provisional constitution was adopted on 12 Nov. 1958. Legislative power is vested in the unicameral National Assembly, with 210 members elected by universal adult suffrage for 7 years. The Assembly elects a Commission to be its permanent organ. Full executive authority is vested in the President, also directly elected for 7 years. He appoints and leads a Cabinet, including a Prime Minister. Guinea has a single political party, the *Parti démocratique de Guinée* (PDG), which exercises 'sovereign and exclusive control of all sections of national life'. The party's directing organ is the Central Committee, 25 members elected for 5 years at Congress. The PDG Congress of 17–22 Nov. 1978 decided to alter the country's name from 1 Jan. 1979. It was also decided to increase the PDG Central Committee to 75. The Congress elected a 15-member Political Bureau.
Telephones: 10 000 (1977).
Daily newspapers: 1 (1976).
  Total circulation: 10 000.
Radio: 121 000 (1979).
Length of roadways: 17 650 miles *28 400 km.*
Length of railways: 584 miles *940 km.*
Adult illiteracy: 91·4% (estimate) in 1965.
Expectation of life: Males 39·4 years; females 42·6 years (UN estimates for 1970–75).
Defence: Military service voluntary; total armed forces 9900 (1984).
Cinemas: 16 (1959).

Guinea-Bissau

Official name: A República da Guiné-Bissau (the Republic of Guinea-Bissau).
Population: 826 000 (1983 estimate).
Area: 13 948 miles² *36 125 km².*
Languages: Portuguese (official), Creole, Balante, Fulani, Malinké.
Religions: Animist; Muslim minority.
Capital city: Bissau, population 109 486 (1979 census).
Other principal towns: Bolama, Cacheu.
Principal rivers: Cacheu, Mansôa, Gêba, Corubel.
Head of State: Maj. João Bernardo Vieira (b. 1939), President of the Council of the Revolution.

Climate: Tropical, with an average annual temperature of 25°C *77°F.* Rainy season June to November. In dry season (December to May) the northerly *harmattan*, a dust-laden wind, blows from the Sahara.
Labour force: 158 000 (1970): Agriculture, forestry and fishing 87·0% (ILO estimates).
Gross domestic product: $177 million in 1975 (UN estimate).
Exports: 368 million pesos in 1980.
Monetary unit: Guinea peso. 1 peso = 100 centavos.
Denominations:
  Coins 5, 10, 20, 50 centavos; 1, 2½, 5, 10, 20 pesos.
  Notes 50, 100, 500 pesos.
Exchange rate to £ sterling: 97·31 (14 Jan. 1985).
Political history and government: Formerly Portuguese Guinea. Independence declared on 24 Sept. 1973, recognized by Portugal on 10 Sept. 1974. The independence movement was dominated by the *Partido Africano da Independência da Guiné e Cabo Verde* (PAIGC), the African Party for the Independence of Guinea and Cape Verde. In 1973 the PAIGC established a National People's Assembly as the supreme organ of the state and formulated the independence constitution, which provided for the eventual union of Guinea-Bissau with Cape Verde (*q.v.*). In elections held between 19 Dec. 1976 and January 1977 voters chose regional councils from which a new National Assembly of 150 members was subsequently selected. The Assembly, to hold office for up to four years, was convened on 13 Mar. 1977. The Head of State was elected for a four-year term by the Assembly. The constitution proclaimed the PAIGC, the only permitted party, to be 'the supreme expression of the sovereign will of the people'. Executive power was vested in the State Council, with 15 members elected for three years from deputies to the Assembly. Administrative authority lay with the Council of State Commissioners, appointed by the Head of State. On 10 Nov. 1980 the Assembly approved a new constitution, increasing the powers of the Head of State, but on 14 Nov. he was overthrown in a *coup.* A nine-member Revolutionary council, led by the former Chief State Commissioner, took power. The Assembly and State Council were dissolved on 19 Nov. 1980 and a Provisional Government announced on the next day.
Telephones: 3000 (1973).
Daily newspapers: 1 (1976).
  Total circulation: 6000.
Radio: 15 000 (1977).
Length of roadways: 2175 miles *3500 km* (1979).
Adult illiteracy: 95·1% in 1962.
Expectation of life: Males 37·0 years; females 40·1 years (UN estimates for 1970–75).
Defence: Total armed forces 6300 (1984).
Cinemas: 7 (seating capacity 3000) in 1972.

Guyana

Official name: The Co-operative Republic of Guyana.
Population: 900 000 (1983 estimate).
Area: 83 000 miles² *214 969 km².*
Languages: English (official), Hindu, Urdu.
Religions: Christian 56·7%; Hindu 33·4%; Muslim 8·8% (1960).
Capital city: Georgetown, population 188 000 (1983 estimate).
Other principal towns (1970): Linden 29 000; New Amsterdam 23 000; Mackenzie 20 000; Corriverton 17 000.
Highest point: Mt Roraima (9094 ft *2772 m*), on the Brazil-Venezuela frontier.
Principal mountain ranges: Pakaraima, Serra Acarai, Kanuku, Kamoa.
Principal rivers: Essequibo, Courantyne (on the frontier with Suriname), Mazaruni, Berbice, Demarara.
Head of State: (Linden) Forbes Sampson Burnham (b. 20 Feb. 1923), President.
Prime Minister: Dr Ptolemy Alexander Reid (b. 8 May 1918).
Climate: Generally warm and pleasant. Average

temperature 27°C *80°F*, with daily range of about 10°C *18°F* on coast, increasing inland. Average annual rainfall 2360 mm *93 in*, 2030–2540 mm *80 to 100 in* on coast (mainly April to August and November to January), 1520 mm *60 in* inland (May to August).
Labour force: 174 772 (including unemployed) in March 1965: Agriculture, forestry and fishing 33·5%; Manufacturing 17·2%; Commerce 13·3%; 177 164 (1970 census); 204 000 (mid-1970): Agriculture, forestry and fishing 28·1%; Industry 32·7%; Services 39·2% (ILO estimates).
Gross domestic product: $G 1117·5 million in 1976: Agriculture, forestry and fishing 23·0% (agriculture 21·1%); Mining and quarrying 14·1%; Manufacturing (excluding engineering), electricity, gas and water 13·2%; Trade 10·5%; Government services 17·6%.
Exports: G$755 544 161 in 1982: Sugar 33·6%; Rice 11·3%; Bauxite 34·6%; Alumina and alumina hydrate 9·4%; Rum 2·5%; Timber 1·6%.
Monetary unit: Guyana dollar ($G). 1 dollar = 100 cents.
Denominations:
   Coins 1, 5, 10, 25, 50 cents.
   Notes 1, 5, 10, 20 dollars.
Exchange rate to £ sterling: 4·695 (14 Jan. 1985).
Political history and government: Formerly the colony of British Guiana. Became independent, within the Commonwealth, on 26 May 1966, taking the name Guyana. A republic since 23 Feb. 1970. Legislative power is held by the unicameral National Assembly. Following a referendum on 10 July 1978, which gave the Assembly power to amend the constitution, elections to the Assembly were postponed for 15 months. It assumed the role of a Constituent Assembly, established on 6 Nov. 1978, to draft a new constitution. On 24 Oct. 1979 elections were postponed for a further year. A new constitution was promulgated on 6 Oct. 1980. The National Assembly has 65 members, including 12 regional representatives and 53 members elected for five years by universal adult suffrage, using proportional representation. Executive power is vested in the President, who is leader of the majority party in the Assembly and holds office for its duration. The President appoints and leads a Cabinet, responsible to the Assembly.
Telephones: 28 468 (1982).
Daily newspapers: 1 (1982).
   Total circulation: 42 000.
Radio: 300 000 (1977).
Length of roadways: 5000 miles *8000 km*.
Length of railways: 116 miles *187 km*.
Universities: 1.
Adult illiteracy: 8·7% in 1970.
Expectation of life: males 59·03 years; females 63·01 years (1959–61, excluding Amerindians).
Defence: Total armed forces 7000 (1981); defence expenditure, 1978: US$17 million.
Cinemas: 50 (seating capacity 40 000), 9 mobile units and 1 drive-in (capacity 1500) in 1977.
Foreign tourists: 24 887 in 1970.

Haiti

Official name: République d'Haïti.
Population: 4 583 785 (1975 census); 5 009 000 (estimate for 30 June 1980).
Area: 10 714 miles² *27 750 km²*.
Languages: French (official), Créole 90%.
Religions: Roman Catholic, Vodum (Voodoo).
Capital city: Port-au-Prince, population 745 700 at 30 June 1978 (estimate).
Other principal towns (1975): Cap Haïtien 54 691; Gonaïves 36 736; Les Cayes 27 222; Port de Paix 21 733.
Highest point: Pic La Selle, 8793 ft *2680 m*.
Principal mountain range: Massif de la Hotte.
Principal river: Artibonite (147 miles *237 km*).
Head of State: Jean-Claude Duvalier (b. 3 July 1951), President.
Climate: Tropical but cooled by sea winds. Rainy season May to September. North warmer than south. In Port-au-Prince, average maximum 31°C *87°F* (December, January) to 34°C *94°F* (July), minimum 20°C *68°F* (January, February)

to 23°C *74°F* (July), May rainiest (13 days).
Labour force: 2 326 201 (1971 census): Agriculture, forestry and fishing 73·8%; Trade, restaurants and hotels 10·0%.
Gross domestic product: 2303·6 million gourdes (at 1955 prices) in year ending 30 Sep. 1978: Agriculture, forestry and fishing 40·6% (agriculture, excluding, livestock, 36·1%); Manufacturing 11·7%; Trade 10·3%; Community, social and personal services (incl. restaurants and hotels) 17·3%.
Exports: US$150 million in 1982.
Monetary unit: Gourde. 1 gourde = 100 centimes.
Denominations:
   Coins 5, 10, 20, 50 centimes.
   Notes 1, 2, 5, 10, 50, 100, 250, 500 gourdes.
Exchange rate to £ sterling: 5·555 (14 Jan. 1985).
Political history and government: A republic comprising 9 departments. Dr François Duvalier was elected President on 22 Sept. 1957 and took office on 22 Oct. 1957. Under the constitution of June 1964, the unicameral Legislative Chamber has 58 members elected for 6 years by universal adult suffrage. The constitution granted absolute power to the President, who took office for life on 22 June 1964. On 14 Jan. 1971 the constitution was amended to allow the President to nominate his own successor. The President named his son, Jean-Claude, to succeed him as President for life. Dr Duvalier died on 21 Apr. 1971 and his son was sworn in on the following day. Only one political party is officially recognised.
Telephones: 34 900 (1980).
Daily newspapers: 6 (1982).
Radio: 105 000 (1982).
TV: 65 000 (1982).
Length of roadways: 2500 miles *400 km*.
Universities: 1.
Adult illiteracy: 76·7% (males 71·3%; females 81·6%) in 1971.
Expectation of life: Males 47·1 years; females 50·0 years (UN estimates for 1970–75).
Defence: Total armed forces 7500 (1984); defence expenditure 1979/80: $15 million.
Cinemas: 19 exhibiting 35 mm films (seating capacity 2800) a 4 drive-in (1977).
Foreign tourists: 112 000 in 1978.

Honduras

Official name: Republica de Honduras.
Population: 4 094 000 (1983).
Area: 43 277 miles² *112 088 km*.
Language: Spanish, some Indian dialects.
Religion: Roman Catholic.
Capital city: Tegucigalpa, population 510 000 (1984).
Other principal towns (1983): San Pedro Sula 325 000; La Ceiba 60 000; El Progreso 52 000; Puerto Cortes 38 000; Choluteca 52 000.
Highest point: Cerro las Minas 9400 ft *2865 m*.
Principal rivers: Patuca, Ulúa.
Head of State: Dr Roberto Suazo Cordova.
Climate: Tropical (hot and humid) and wet on coastal plains. Rainy season May to November. More moderate in central highlands. In Tegucigalpa, average maximum 25°C *77°F* (December, January) to 30°C *86°F* (June), September and October rainiest (each 14 days). Absolute maximum temperature 43,3°C *110°F*, Neuva Octepeque, 13 Mar. 1958; absolute minimum −0·6°C *31°F*, La Esperanza, 17 Feb. 1956.
Labour force: 970 508 (30 June 1977): Agriculture, forestry and fishing 60·8%; Manufacturing 11·8%; Community, social and personal services 11·5%; 1 044 433 (estimate for 30 June 1979).
Gross domestic product: 3638 million lempiras in 1977: Agriculture, forestry and fishing 31·5%; Manufacturing 17·0; Trade 12·3%; Community, social and personal services (incl. restaurants and hotels) 12·4%.
Exports: 1360·6 million lempiras: Bananas 30·5%; Coffee 22·2%; Timber 5·8%; Frozen meat 4·6%; Shellfish 5%.
Monetary unit: Lempira. 1 lempira = 100 centavos.
   Coins 1, 2, 5, 10, 20, 50 centavos.

GUYANA

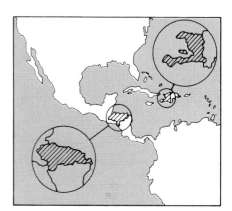

left: **HONDURAS**   *right:* **HAITI**

   Notes 1, 2, 5, 10, 20, 50, 100 lempiras.
Exchange rate to £ sterling: 2·3246 (14 Jan. 1985).
Political history and government: A republic comprising 18 departments. The last elected President was deposed on 4 Dec. 1972 by a military *coup*, led by a former President, Brig-Gen Oswaldo López Arellano. The military regime suspended the legislature, a unicameral Congress of Deputies, and introduced government by decree. On 22 Apr. 1975 Gen López was overthrown by army officers and replaced by Col (later Gen) Juan Melgar Castro. On 7 Aug. 1978 Gen Melgar was deposed by another *coup* and a 3-man military junta took power. Its leader became President and rules with the assistance of an appointed Cabinet. On 20 Apr. 1980 a 71-member Constituent Assembly was elected by universal adult suffrage. On 20 July 1980 the junta transferred power to the Assembly and on 25 July the Assembly elected the President to continue in office as interim Head of State. A presidential election on 29 Nov. 1981 was won by Dr Roberto Suazo Córdova, who took office on 27 Jan. 1982.
Telephones: 33 667 (1982).
Daily newspapers: 8 (1976).
   Total circulation: 140 000 (5 dailies).
Radio: 173 000 (1978).
TV: 27 000 (1979).
Length of roadways: 5162 miles *8308 km* (1978).
Length of railways: 1106 miles *1780 km*.
Universities: 1.
Adult illiteracy: 43·1% (males 41·1%; females 44·9%) in 1974.
Expectation of life: Males 52·4 years; females

55·9 years (UN estimates for 1970–75).
Defence: Military service: 14 months; total armed forces 14 700 (1984); defence expenditure, 1980; $45 million.
Cinemas: *c.* 100 in 1979.
Foreign tourists: 162 024 (1982).

Hungary

Official name: Magyar Népkőztársaság (Hungarian People's Republic).
Population: 10 679 000 (1 Jan. 1984).
Area: 35 921 miles² *93 036 km²*.
Language: Magyar.
Religions: Roman Catholic; Protestant, Orthodox and Jewish minorities.
Capital city: Budapest, population 2 064 000 (1 Jan. 1983).
Other principal towns (1 Jan. 1983): Miskolc 212 000; Debrecen 205 000; Szeged 176 000; Pécs 175 000; Győr 128 000; Nyíregyháza 114 000; Székesfehérvár 109 000; Kecskemét 102 000.
Highest point: Kékes, 3330 ft *1015 m.*
Principal mountain ranges: Cserhát, Mátra, Bükk, Bakony.
Principal rivers: Duna (Danube) (1770 miles *2850 km*, 273 miles *439 km* in Hungary), with its tributaries (Drava, Tisza, Rba).
Head of State: Pál Losonczi (b. 18 Sept. 1919), President of the Presidential Council.
Political Leader: János Kádár (b. 22 May 1912), First Secretary of the Central Committee of the Hungarian Socialist Workers' Party.
Head of Government: György Lázár (b. 15 Sept. 1924), Chairman of the Council of Ministers.
Climate: Continental (long, dry, hot summers, cold winters). In Budapest, July warmest (16°C *61°F* to 28°C *82°F*), January coldest (−3°C *26°F* to 2°C *35°F*), May and December rainiest (each nine days). Absolute maximum temperature 41,3°C *106·3°F*, Pécs, 5 July 1950; absolute minimum −34,9°C *−30·8°F*, Asófügöd, 16 Feb. 1940.
Labour force: 4 970 100 in 1983: Industry 31·7%; Agriculture and forestry 21·8%; Trade 10%; Sanitary, social and cultural services 10·7%.
Net material product: 744 000 million forints in 1983: Agriculture, forestry and fishing 18·8%;

HUNGARY

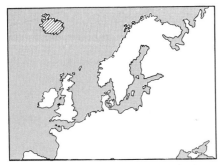

ICELAND

Industry 45%; Construction 12%; Trade 14%.
Exports: 374 000 million forints in 1983: Machinery, transport equipment and other capital goods 28%; Industrial consumer goods 14·6%; Food products 14·7%; Semi-finished products 16·9%.
Monetary unit: Forint. 1 forint = 100 fillér.
Coins 10, 20, 50 fillér; 1, 2, 5, 10, 20 forints.
Notes 20, 50, 100, 500, 1000 forints.
Exchange rate to £ sterling: 57·964 (14 Jan. 1985).
Political history and government: After occupation by Nazi Germany, a Hungarian provisional government signed an armistice on 20 Jan. 1945. Following elections in October 1945, a republic was proclaimed on 1 Feb. 1946. The Communist Party took power in May–June 1947. A new constitution was introduced on 18 Aug. 1949 and a People's Republic established two days later.
The highest organ of state power is the unicameral National Assembly, with 352 members elected for 5 years by universal adult suffrage (at the last election, on 8 June 1980, 337 members were elected unopposed while 15 seats were each contested by two or more candidates). The Assembly elects from its members a Presidential Council (21 members) to be its permanent organ and the state's executive authority, responsible to the Assembly. The Council of Ministers, the highest organ of state administration, is elected by the Assembly on the recommendation of the Presidential Council.
Political power is held by the (Communist) Hungarian Socialist Workers' party (HSWP), the only legal party, which dominates the Patriotic People's Front. The Front presents an approved list of candidates for elections to representative bodies. The HSWP's highest authority is the Party Congress, which elects a Central Committee to supervise Party work (the 12th Congress, held on 24–27 Mar. 1980, elected a Central Committee of 127). the Central Committee elects a Political Committee (Politburo) of 13 members to direct policy.
Hungary comprises 19 counties and the capital city.
Telephones: 1 296 682 (1982).
Daily newspapers: 29 (1978).
Total circulation: 2 941 900.
TV: 2 864 000 (1983).
Length of roadways: 18 449 miles *29 684 km* (1983).
Length of railways: 4822 miles *7759 km.*
Universities: 10 (plus 9 technical universities).
Adult illiteracy: 2·0% (males 1·6%; females 2·4%) in 1970.
Expectation of life: Males 66·1 years; females 73·7 years (1983).
Defence: Military service: 18 months; total regular forces 105 500 (50 000 conscripts) in 1984; defence expenditure, 1981: $1240 million (converted at $1 = 15·37 forints).
Cinemas: 3700 (1983).
Foreign tourists: 10 463 000 (1983).

Iceland

Official name: Lýđveldiđ Island (Republic of Iceland).
Population: 237 894 (1 Dec. 1983).
Area: 39 769 miles² *103 000 km².*
Language: Icelandic.
Religion: Lutheran.
Capital city: Reykyavik ('Bay of Smokes'), population 87 106 (1 Dec. 1983).
Other principal towns (1983): Kópavogur 14 433; Akureyri 13 742; Hafnarfjordur 12 700; Keflavik 6874; Akranes 5351; Gardbaer 4731; Vestmannaeyjar 4743.
Highest point: Hvannadalshnúkur, 6952 ft *2119 m.*
Principal rivers: Thjórsá (120 miles *193 km*), Skjálfandafljót, Jökulsa á Fjöllum.
Head of State: Mme Vigdís Finnbogadóttir (b. 15 Apr. 1930), President.
Prime Minister: Gunnar Thoroddsen (b. 29 Dec. 1910).
Climate: Cold. Long winters with average

temperature of 1°C *34°F.* Short, cool summers with average of 10°C *50°F.* Storms are frequent. In Reykjavík, average maximum 2°C *36°F* (January) to 14°C *58°F* (July), minimum −2°C *28°F* (January, February) to 9°C *48°F*, (July), December rainiest (21 days). Absolute maximum temperature 32,8°C *91·0°F* Mödrudalur, 26 July 1901; absolute minimum −44,6°C *−48·2°F*, Grímsstaoir, 22 Mar. 1918.
Labour force: 111 405 in 1981: Agriculture 7·4%; Fishing 5%; Fish processing 9·1%; Other manufacturing 16·6%; Construction 9·8%; Trade, finance and services 19%; Other services 27·6%; Transport 5·5%.
Gross domestic product: 5907 million new krónur in 1978.
Exports: 27 456 million kronur in 1983: Fish products 68%; Aluminium 17·6%; Other manufacturing products 11·7%.
Monetary unit: New Icelandic króna. 1 króna = 100 aurar (singular: eyrir).
Denominations:
Coins 5, 10, 50 aurar; 1, 5 krónur.
Notes 10, 50, 100, 500 krönur.
Exchange rate to £ sterling: 45·65 (14 Jan. 1985).
Political history and government: Formerly ruled by Denmark. Iceland became a sovereign state, under the Danish Crown, on 1 Dec. 1918. An independent republic was declared on 17 June 1944. Legislative power is held jointly by the President (elected for 4 years by universal adult suffrage) and the Althing (Parliament), with 60 members elected by universal suffrage for 4 years (subject to dissolution by the President), using a mixed system of proportional representation. The Althing chooses 20 of its members to form the Upper House, the other 40 forming the Lower House. For some purposes, the two Houses sit jointly as the United Althing. Executive power is held jointly by the President and the Cabinet, although the President's functions are mainly titular. The President appoints the Prime Minister and, on the latter's recommendation, other Ministers. The Cabinet is responsible to the Althing. Iceland has seven administrative districts.
Telephones: 116 856 (1982).
Daily newspapers: 5 (1982).
Total circulation: 125 000.
Radio: 70 059 (1982).
TV: 62 623 (1982).
Length of roadways: 7238 miles *11 649 km* (31 Dec. 1979).
Universities: 1.
Expectation of life: males 73·9 years; females 79·5 years (1981–2).
Defence: Iceland has no forces but is a member of NATO.
Cinemas: 25 in 1979.
Foreign tourists: 72 600 in 1982.

India

Official name: Bharatiya Ganrajya or Bharat ka Ganatantra (the Republic of India). India is called Bharat in the Hindi language.
Population: 685 184 692 (census of 1 Mar. 1981).
Area: 1 269 213 miles² *3 287 263 km²* (provisional, 31 March 1982).
Languages: Assamese; Bengali 7%; Gujarati; Hindi (official) 24%; Kannada; Kashmiri; Malayalam; Marathi 6%; Oriya; Punjabi; Sanskrit; Sindhi; Tamil; Telugu 7%; Urdu.
Religions: Hinduism 82·7%; Islam 11·2%; Christianity 2·6%; Sikhism 1·9%; Buddhism 0·7%; Jainism 0·5%; plus others (1971).
Capital city: New Delhi, population 6 220 406 (1981 census).
Other principal towns (1981): Mumbai (Bombay) 8 243 405; Calcutta 3 305 006; Madras 3 276 622; Bangalore 2 921 751; Ahmedabad 2 548 057; Hyderabad 2 545 836; Pune (Poona) 1 686 109; Kanpur 1 639 064; Nagpur 1 302 066; Jaipur 1 015 160; Lucknow 1 007 604; Indore 970 410; Patna 918 903; Surat 913 806; Madurai 907 732; Varanasi (Benares) 797 162; Jabalpur 757 303; Agra 747 318; Vadodara 744 881; Howrah 744 429; Cochin 685 836; Allahabad 650 070.
Highest point: Nanda Devi, 25 645 ft *7816 m*

(first climbed 29 Aug. 1936), excluding Kashmir.
Principal mountain ranges: Himalaya, Gravalti, Sappura, Vindhya, Western Ghats, Chota Nagpur.
Principal rivers: Ganga (Ganges) (1560 miles *2510 km*) and tributaries, Brahmaputra (1800 miles *2900 km*), Sutlej, Narmeda, Tapti, Godavari, Krishna, Cauvery.
Head of State: Giani Zail Singh (b. 5 May 1916), President.
Prime Minister: Rajiv Gandhi (b. 20 August 1944).
Climate: Ranges from temperate in the north (very cold in the Himalayas) to tropical in the south. The average summer temperature in the plains is about 29°C *85°F*. The full weight of the monsoon season is felt in June and July but the rainfall figures vary widely according to locality. Average daily high temperature in Bombay 28°C *83°F* (January, February) to 33°C *91°F* (May); average daily low temperature 19°C *67°F* (January, February) to 27°C *80°F* (May); rainiest, month July (21 days). Average daily high temperature in Calcutta 26°C *79°F* (December) to 36°C *97°F* (April); average daily low 13°C *55°F* (December, January) to 26°C *79°F* (June, July); rainiest months July, August (each 18 days).
Labour force: 220 100 000 (excluding unemployed) at 1981 census: Agriculture 66%; Manufacturing 3%.
Gross domestic product: 532 290 million rupees (provisional) in year ending 31 March 1982: Agriculture, forestry, fishing, mining, 40·1%; Manufacturing, construction, electricity, gas and water, 21·8%; Transport, communications and trade, 19·3%.
Exports: 78 095 million rupees (1981–2): Handicrafts, 14·5%; Engineering goods, 10·9%; Ready-made garments, 7·6%.
Monetary unit: Indian rupee. 1 rupee = 100 paisa (singular: paise).
Denominations:
   Coins 5, 10, 20, 25, 50 paisa; 1 rupee.
   Notes 1, 2, 5, 10, 20, 50, 100 rupees.
Exchange rate to £ sterling: 13·98 (14 Jan. 1985).
Political history and government: On 15 Aug. 1947 former British India was divided on broadly religious lines into two independent countries, India and Pakistan, within the Commonwealth.

India was formed as a Union of States, with a federal structure. A republican constitution was passed by the Constituent Assembly on 26 Nov. 1949 and India became a republic, under its present name, on 26 Jan. 1950. France transferred sovereignty of its five Indian settlements on 2 May 1950 (Chandernagore) and 1 Nov. 1954 (Pondicherry, Karikal, Yanam and Mahé). The Portuguese territories of Goa, Daman and Diu were invaded by Indian forces on 19 Dec. 1961 and incorporated in India. Sikkim, formerly an Associated State, became a State of India on 26 Apr. 1975.

Legislative power is vested in a Parliament, consisting of the President and two Houses. The Council of States (*Rajya Sabha*) has 244 members, including 236 indirectly elected by the State Assemblies for 6 years (one-third retiring every two years) and 8 nominated by the President. The House of the People (*Lok Sabha*) has 544 members, including 542 elected by universal adult suffrage for 5 years (subject to dissolution) and two nominated. The President is a constitutional Head of State elected for 5 years by an electoral college comprising elected members of both Houses of Parliament and the State legislatures. He exercises executive power on the advice of the Council of Ministers, which is responsible to Parliament. The President appoints the Prime Minister and, on the latter's recommendation, other Ministers.

India comprises 22 self-governing States (including the disputed territory of Jammu-Kashmir) and 9 Union Territories. Each State has a Governor (appointed by the President for 5 years), a legislature elected for 6 years (to be reduced to 5 years under legislation of 30 Apr. 1979) and a Council of Ministers. The Union Territories are administered by officials appointed by the President.

Telephones: 2 981 609 (1982).
Newspapers: 1173 (1981).
   Circulation: 13·2 million.
Radio: 10 178 552 (1981).
TV: 1 672 627 (1981).
Length of roadways: 951 080 miles *1 534 000 km* (1980).
Length of railways: 37 950 miles *61 230 km* (1982).
Universities: 120.
Adult literacy: 36·23% (1981): Males 46·89%; Females 24·82%.
Expectation of life: Males 50·8 years; Females 50 years (1981).
Defence: Military service voluntary: Army 944 000; Air Force 113 000; Navy 45 000 (1982).
Cinemas: 11 682 (1983): Permanent 7149; Touring 4533.
Foreign tourists: 1 288 162 (1982).

Indonesia

Official name: Republik Indonesia.
*Population: 147 383 075 (census of 31 Oct. 1980).
*Area: 735 272 miles² *1 904 345 km²*.
Languages: Bahasa Indonesia (official), Javanese, Madurese, Sundanese.
Religions: Muslim 85%; Christian, Buddhist and Hindu minorities.
Capital city: Jakarta, population 4 576 009 (1971 census).
Other principal towns (1971): Surabaja 1 556 255; Bandung 1 201 730; Semarang 646 590; Medan 635 562; Palembang 582 961; Ujungpandang (Makasar) 434 766; Malang 422 428; Surakarta 414 285; Yogyakarta (Jogjakarta) 342 267.
Highest point: Putjak Djaja (formerly Ngga Pulu and Mt Sukarno), 16 020 ft *4883 m* (first climbed on 13 Feb. 1962).
Principal mountain ranges: Bukit, Barisan, Pegunungan Djajawidjaja.
Principal rivers: Kapuas (715 miles *1150 km*), Digul (557 miles *896 km*), Barito (560 miles *900 km*), Mahakam, Kajan, Hari.
Head of State: Gen Suharto (b. 8 June 1921), President and Prime Minister.
Climate: Tropical (hot and rainy). Average temperature 27°C *80°F*. Mountain areas cooler. In Jakarta, average maximum 29°C *84°F* (January, February) to 31°C *88°F* (September), minimum 23°C *73°F* (July, August) to 24°C *75°F* (April, May) January rainiest (18 days).
Labour force: 53 443 668 (excluding 1 046 617 unemployed) in 1976: Agriculture, forestry and fishing 67·0%; Trade, restaurants and hotels 11·9%.
Gross domestic product: 21 788 400 million rupiahs in 1978: Agriculture, forestry and fishing 31·1% (agriculture 26·5%); Mining and quarrying 17·8%.
Exports: US$23 120 million in 1981: Oil 67·4%; Coffee 2·7%; Rubber 4·1%; Wood 7·8%; Tea 3·6%.
Monetary unit: Rupiah. 1 rupiah = 100 sen.
Denominations:
   Coins 1, 5, 10, 25, 50 sen.
   Notes 1, 2½, 5, 10, 25, 50, 100, 500, 1000, 5000, 10 000 rupiahs.
Exchange rate to £ sterling: 1220·40 (14 Jan. 1985).
Political history and government: Excluding East Timor (see below), Indonesia was formerly the Netherlands East Indies. The islands were occupied by Japanese forces in March 1942. On 17 Aug. 1945, three days after the Japanese surrender, a group of nationalists proclaimed the independence of the Republic of Indonesia. The Netherlands transferred sovereignty (except for West New Guinea) on 27 Dec. 1949. West New Guinea remained under Dutch control until 1 Oct. 1962, when a UN Temporary Executive Authority took over administration of the territory until it was transferred to Indonesia on 1 May 1963.

Military commanders, led by Gen Suharto, assumed emergency executive powers on 11–12 Mar. 1966. The President handed all power to Suharto on 22 Feb. 1967. On 12 Mar. 1967 the

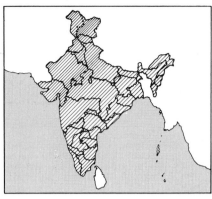

INDIA

People's Consultative Assembly removed the President from office and named Gen Suharto as acting President. He became Prime Minister on 11 Oct. 1967 and, after being elected by the Assembly, was inaugurated as President on 27 Mar. 1968.

The highest authority of the state is the People's Consultative Assembly, with 920 members who serve for 5 years. The Assembly, which elects the President and Vice-President for 5 years, includes 460 members of the People's Representation Council (House of Representatives), which is the legislative organ. The council has 100 appointed members, 351 directly elected and 9 representatives from West Irian (West New Guinea) chosen in indirect elections. The remaining 460 members of the Assembly include 207 appointed by the government, 130 elected by regional assemblies, 121 allocated to parties and groups in proportion to their elected seats in the Council and 2 allocated to minor parties. The President is assisted by an appointed Cabinet.

Indonesia comprises 27 provinces, including East (formerly Portuguese) Timor, unilaterally annexed on 17 July 1976.
Telephones: 600 643 (1982).
Daily newspapers: 178 (1976).
   Total circulation: 2 358 000 (50 dailies).
Radio: 5 250 000 (1977).
TV: 1 000 000 (1977).
Length of roadways: 52 749 miles *84 891 km* (31 Dec. 1972).
Length of railways: 4273 miles *6877 km*.
Universities: 53 (29 state, 24 private).
Adult illiteracy: 43·4% (males 30·5%; females 55·4%) in 1971.
Expectation of life: males 46·4 years; females 48·7 years (UN estimates for 1970–75).
Defence: Military service selective; total armed forces 275 000 (1984); defence expenditure, 1981: $2387 million.
Cinemas: 406 in 1977.
Foreign tourists: 561 000 in 1980.
* Figures exclude East (formerly Portuguese) Timor, annexed in 1976.

INDONESIA

Iran

Official name: Jomhori-e-Islami-e-Irân (Islamic Republic of Iran).
Population: 40 550 000 (1982 estimate).
Area: 636 296 miles² *1 648 000 km²*.
Languages: Farsi (Persian), Azerbaizhani, Kurdish, Arabic.
Religions: Muslim 98%; Christian, Jewish, Zoroastrian minorites.
Capital city: Tehrān (Teheran), population 4 496 159 (1976 census).
Other principal towns (1976): Eṣfāhān (Isfahan) 671 825; Mashhad (Meshed) 670 180; Tabriz 598 576; Shīrāz 416 408; Ahvez (Ahwaz) 329 006; Abādān 296 081; Kermanshah 290 861; Qom (Ghom) 246 831.
Highest point: Qolleh-ye Damāvand (Mt Demavend), 18 386 ft *5604 m*.
Principal mountain ranges: Reshteh-ye Alborz (Elburz Mts), Kūhhā-ye-Zāgros (Zagros Mts).
Principal rivers: Kārūn, Safid (Sefid Rud), Atrak, Karkheh, Zāyandeh.
National Leader: Ayatollah Ruhollah Khomeini (b. 17 May 1900), *Wali Faqih*.
President: Hojatoleslam Ali Khamenei (b. 1939).
Prime Minister: Hossein Mousavi (b. 1941).
Climate: Extremely hot on Persian Gulf, cooler and dry on central plateau, subtropical on shore of Caspian Sea. In Teheran, July hottest (25°C *77°F* to 37°C *99°F*), January coldest (−3°C *27°F* to 7°C *45°F*), March rainiest (5 days). Absolute maximum temperature 52°C *126°F*, Abādān, 6 July 1951.
Labour force: 8 788 894 (excluding 943 614 unemployed) at 1976 census (5% sample): Agriculture, forestry and fishing 34·3%; Manufacturing 19·1%; Construction 13·6%; Community, social and personal services 17·8%.
Gross domestic product: 4 689 200 million rials in year ending 20 Mar. 1977: Petroleum production 38·0%; Other mining and manufacturing 10·7%; Community, social and personal services (incl. restaurants, hotels and business services) 12·9%.
Exports: 963 500 million rials in 1980: Crude oil 73%; Refined petroleum products 21%.
Monetary unit: Iranian rial. 1 rial = 100 dinars.
Denominations:
  Coins 50 dinars; 1, 2, 5, 10, 20 rials.
  Notes 5, 10, 20, 50, 100, 200, 500, 1000, 5000, 10 000 rials.
Exchange rate to £ sterling: 105·50 (14 Jan. 1985).
Political history and government: Formerly the Empire of Persia, renamed Iran on 21 Mar. 1935. The country was an absolute monarchy until the adoption of the first constitution, approved by the Shah (Emperor) on 30 Dec. 1906. On 31 Oct. 1925 the National Assembly deposed the Shah and handed power to the Prime Minister, Reza Khan. He was elected Shah on 13 Dec. 1925 and took the title Reza Shah Pahlavi. During the Second World War Reza Shah favoured Nazi Germany. British and Soviet forces entered Iran on 25 Aug. 1941, forcing the Shah to abdicate in favour of his son, Mohammad Reza Pahlavi, on 16 Sept. 1941.

Under the Pahlavi dynasty, Iran was a limited constitutional monarchy and executive power remained with the Shah. On 2 Mar. 1975 Shah Mohammad dissolved existing political parties and announced the formation of a single party.

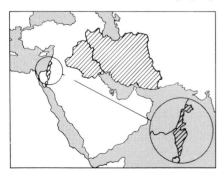

encircled: **ISRAEL** *centre:* **IRAQ** *right:* **IRAN**

Opposition to the Shah's rule later grew and, in response to increasing political violence and demonstrations, other parties were granted the freedom to resume their activities on 29 Aug. 1978. Protests against the Shah intensified and a mainly military government was appointed on 6 Nov. 1978. After further unrest, another civilian Prime Minister was appointed on 4 Jan. 1979. The new Cabinet was approved by the legislature on 16 Jan., when the Shah left the country. Popular opposition to the Shah grouped behind the Islamic traditionalist movement, dominated by the Ayatollah Ruhollah Khomenei, a spiritual leader of the Shi'a Muslims, who had been exiled by the Shah since 1963. Khomeini established a Revolutionary Islamic Council on 13 Jan. 1979, returned to Iran on 1 Feb. and appointed a provisional government on 5 Feb. After heavy fighting, the Shah's government fell, and power was surrendered to Khomeini's movement, on 11 Feb. 1979. Both houses of Parliament requested their own dissolution.

Following a referendum on 30–31 Mar., a republic was proclaimed on 1 Apr. 1979. A draft constitution officially published on 18 June, was submitted to a Constituent Council of Experts, with 73 members elected by popular vote on 3 Aug. 1979. The council, inaugurated on 19 Aug., completed its work on 14 Nov. 1979. The constitution, including the Council's far-reaching amendments, was approved by a referendum on 2–3 Dec. 1979. In accordance with Ayotollah Khomeini's principle of *Wilayat e Faqih* ('Rule of the Theologian'), supreme authority is vested in the *Wali Faqih*, a religious leader (initially Khomeini) agreed by the Muslim clergy, with no fixed term of office. The President is chief executive, elected by universal adult suffrage for a four-year term. Legislative power is vested in the unicameral Islamic Consultative Assembly (*Majlis*), with 270 members, also directly elected for four years. A 12-member Council of Guardians ensures that legislation conforms with Islamic precepts. Abolhasan Bani-Sadr was elected first President on 25 Jan. 1980 and assumed office on 4 Feb. The *Majlis* was elected on 14 Mar. and 9 May 1980.

The Prime Minister appointed by Khomeini had resigned on 5 Nov. 1979. On the next day power was assumed by the 14-man Revolutionary Council. After the transfer of legislative power from this Council to the *Majlis*, the President was formally sworn in on 22 July 1980. The *Majlis* approved a new Prime Minister, Muhammad Ali Rajai, on 11 Aug. 1980 and he was appointed on 20 Aug. A list of Ministers was approved on 10 Sept. 1980 and the Revolutionary Council dissolved itself. After a dispute between the *Majlis* and President Bani-Sadr, the *Wali Faqih* dismissed the President on 22 June 1981. Rajai was elected President on 24 July and sworn in by the *Majlis* on 3 Aug. President Rajai and his Prime Minister were assassinated on 30 Aug. Another presidential election was held on 2 Oct. and the winning candidate sworn in on 13 Oct. A new Prime Minister was approved by the *Majlis* on 29 Oct. 1981.
Telephones: 1 041 939 (1982).
Daily newspapers: 17 (1982).
Radio: 10 000 000 (1980).
TV: 2 100 000 (1980).
Length of roadways: 26 994 miles *43 442 km* (31 Dec. 1972).
Length of railways: 2838 miles *4567 km*.
Universities: 17.
Adult illiteracy: 63·1% (males 52·3%; females 74·5%) in 1971 (population aged 6 and over).
Expectation of life: Males 57·63 years; females 57·44 years (1973–76).
Defence: Military service 24 months; total armed forces 205 000 (1984); defence expenditure, 1980: $4200 million.
Cinemas: 438 in 1976.
Foreign tourists: 690 550 in 1977.

Iraq

Official name: Al-Jumhuriya al-'Iraqiya (the

Republic of Iraq).
Population: 14 000 000 (1982 estimate).
Area: 167 925 miles² *434 924 km²*.
Languages (1965): Arabic 81·1%; Kurdish 15·5%; Turkoman 1·7%.
Religions: Muslim, Christian minority.
Capital city: Baghdad, population 2 183 760 (1970 census).
Other principal towns (1970): Al-Basrah 333 684; Mosul 293 079; Kirkuk 207 852; An-Najaf 179 160; Al-Hillah 128 811; Karbala 107 496; Irbil 107 355.
Highest point: 12 000 ft *3658 km*.
Principal mountain ranges: Kurdistan Mts.
Principal rivers: Tigris, Euphrates (1700 miles *2740 km*).
Head of State: Saddam Husain (b. 1937), President and Prime Minister.
Climate: Extremely hot, dry summers, humid near coast. Cold, damp winters with severe frosts in highlands. In Baghdad, average maximum 15°C *60°F* (January) to 43°C *110°F* (July, August), minimum −1°C *39°F* (January) to 24°C *76°F* (July, August), December rainiest (5 days). Absolute maximum temperature 52°C *125°F*, Shaiba, 8 Aug. 1937; minimum −14°C *6°F*, Ar Rutbah, 6 Jan. 1942.
Labour force: 3 059 214 (excl. 74 725 unemployed) at 1977 census: Agriculture, forestry and fishing 31·5% Construction 10·7%; Community, social and personal services 31·9%.
Gross domestic product: 4022·4 million dinars in 1975: Mining and quarrying 57·6%; Community, social and personal services (incl. business services) 13·8%.
Exports: 7782 million Iraqi dinars in 1980: Crude oil 99%.
Monetary unit: Iraqi dinar. 1 dinar = 5 riyals = 20 dirhams = 1000 fils.
Denominations:
  Coins 1, 5, 10, 25, 50, 100 fils.
  Notes 250, 5000 fils; 1, 5, 10 dinars.
Exchange rate to £ sterling: 0·3480 (14 Jan. 1985).
Political history and government: Formerly part of Turkey's Ottoman Empire, captured by British forces during the 1914–18 war. After the war Iraq became a Kingdom under a League of Nations mandate, administered by Britain. The mandate was ended on 3 Oct. 1932, when Iraq became independent. In an army-led revolution on 14 July 1958 the King was murdered, the bicameral parliament dissolved and a republic established. A succession of military régimes then held power. The latest of these was established on 17 July 1968. A provisional constitution, proclaiming socialist principles, was introduced on 16 July 1970. A National Charter, to be the basis of a permanent constitution, was issued on 15 Nov. 1971.

An elected National Assembly was envisaged but, before it was formed, the highest authority in the state was the Revolutionary Command Council (RCC). Legislation published on 5 Dec. 1979, and ratified by the RCC on 16 Mar. 1980, provided for a National Assembly, with a four-year term, to perform legislative duties alongside the RCC. The 250 members of the Assembly were elected on 20 June 1980. Executive power remains with the RCC, whose President is Head of State and Supreme Commander of the Armed Forces. The RCC, whose membership was increased to 22 on 4 Sept. 1977, elects the President and the Vice-President. The President appoints and leads a Council of Ministers to control administration. The dominant political organization is the Arab Socialist Renaissance (Ba'ath) Party.

Iraq comprises 18 governorates, each administered by an appointed governor. Three of the governorates form the (Kurdish) Autonomous Region, which has an elected Legislative Council.
Telephones: 319 591 (1976).
Daily newspapers: 7 (1976).
  Total circulation: 202 000 (5 dailies).
Radio: 2 000 000 (1977).
TV: 475 000 (1977).
Length of roadways: 6022 miles *9292 km* (31 Dec. 1975).

Length of railways: 1571 miles *2528 km* (1971).
Universities: 6.
Adult illiteracy: 75·7% (males 64·4%; females 87·1%) in 1965.
Expectation of life: Males 51·2 years; females 54·3 years (UN estimates for 1970–75).
Defence: Military service 21–24 months; total armed forces 523 000 in 1984; defence expenditure, 1980: $2700 million.
Cinemas: 87 in 1979.
Foreign tourists: 721 577 (incl. short-stay visits).

Ireland

Official name: Poblacht na h'Éireann (Republic of Ireland), abbreviated to Éire (Ireland).
Population: 3 443 405 (1 Apr. 1981).
Area: 27 136·3 miles² *70 282·6 km²*.
Languages: English, Irish Gaelic.
Religions: Roman Catholic 94·9% (1961); Church of Ireland, Presbyterian, Methodist, Jewish minorities.
Capital city: Dublin (Baile Átha Cliath), population 525 882 (1981 census).
Other principal towns (1981): Cork (Corcaigh) 136 344; Limerick (Luimneach) 60 736; Dun Laoghaire 54 496; Galway (Gaillimh) 37 835; Waterford (Port Lairge) 38 473.
Highest point: Carrantuohill, 3414 ft *1041 m*, in Co. Kerry.
Principal mountain ranges: Macgillycuddy's Reeks, Wicklow Mts.
Principal rivers: Shannon (224 miles *360 km*), Suir (85 miles *136 km*), Boyne (70 miles *112 km*), Barrow (119 miles *191 km*), Erne (72 miles *115 km*).
Head of State: Dr Patrick John Hillery (Pádraig Ó hIrighile) (b. 2 May 1923), *An Uachtaran* (President).
Head of Government: Dr Garret FitzGerald (Gearóid MacGearailt) (b. 9 Feb. 1926), *Taoiseach* (Prime Minister).
Climate: Mild (generally between 0°C *32°F* and 21°C *70°F*). In Dublin, average maximum 8°C *47°F* (December, January, February) to 19°C *67°F* (July, August), minimum 2°C *35°F* (January, February) to 10°C *51°F* (July, August); December rainiest (14 days). Absolute maximum temperature 33°C *92°F*, Dublin (Phoenix Park), 16 July 1876; absolute minimum −19°C −2°F, Markee Castle, Co. Sligo, 16 Jan. 1881.
Labour force: 1 283 000 at mid-April 1982, of which 137 000 were out of work.
Gross domestic product: IR$16·1 billion in 1984: Agriculture, forestry and fishing 18·2%; Industry and construction 39·1%; Trade, transport, etc. 42·8%.
Exports: IR$8·75 billion in 1984: Meat, other food and live animals 24%; Chemicals 14%; Machinery and transport equipment 39%.
Monetary unit: Irish pound (punt or IR£). 1 pound = 100 pence.
Denominations:
   Coins ½, 1, 2, 5, 10, 50 pence.
   Notes 1, 5, 10, 20, 50, 100 pounds.
Exchange rate to £ sterling: 1·234 (15 Apr. 1985).
Political history and government: The whole of Ireland was formerly part of the United Kingdom. During an insurrection against British rule in April 1916 a republic was proclaimed but the movement was suppressed. After an armed struggle, beginning in 1919, a peace agreement was signed on 6 Dec. 1921 and became operative on 15 Jan. 1922. It provided that the six Ulster counties of Northern Ireland should remain part of the UK while the remaining 26 counties should become a dominion under the British Crown. Southern Ireland duly achieved this status as the Irish Free State on 6 Dec. 1922. A new constitution, giving full sovereignty within the Commonwealth, became effective on 29 Dec. 1937. Formal ties with the Commonwealth were ended on 18 Apr. 1949, when the 26 counties became a republic.
   Legislative power is vested in the bicameral National Parliament (*Oireachtas*): a Senate (*Seanad Éireann*) of 60 members (11 nominated by the Prime Minister, 49 indirectly elected for 5 years) with restricted powers; and a House of Representatives (*Dáil Eireann*) with 166 members elected by universal adult suffrage for 5 years (subject to dissolution), using proportional representation. The President is a constitutional Head of State elected by universal adult suffrage for 7 years. Executive power is held by the Cabinet, led by a Prime Minister, appointed by the President on the nomination of the *Dáil*. The President appoints other Ministers on the nomination of the Prime Minister with the previous approval of the *Dáil*. The Cabinet is responsible to the *Dáil*.
Telephones: 580 000 (1982).
Daily newspapers: 7 (1983).
   Total circulation: 711 319.
Radio: 949 000 (1976).
TV: 695 500 (1982).
Length of roadways: 57 349 miles *92 294 km* (31 Dec. 1977).
Length of railways: 1993 miles *3207 km*.
Universities: 4.
Expectation of life: Males 68·77 years; females 73·52 years (1970–72).
Defence: Military service voluntary; total armed forces 18 000 (1984); defence expenditure, 1980: $285 million.
Cinemas: 124 in 1982.
Foreign tourists: 9 794 000 in 1982.

Israel

Official name: Medinat Israel (State of Israel).
Population: 4 060 000 (1983 estimate; includes East Jerusalem and Israeli residents in other occupied territories).
Area: 8019 miles² *20 770 km*.
Languages (1961): Hebrew (official) 65·9%; Arabic 15·9%; Yiddish 4·8%.
Religions (1961): Jewish 88·7%; Muslim 7·8%.
Capital city: Yerushalayim (Jerusalem), population 424 400 (1982 estimate), including East Jerusalem (Jordanian territory under Israeli occupation since 1967).
Other principal towns (1982): Tel Aviv/Jaffa 325 700; Haifa 226 100; Ramat Gan 118 300; Bat-Yam 134 500; Holon 134 600; Petach Tikva 124 000; Beersheba 112 600.
Highest point: Mt Atzmon (Har Meron), 3963 ft *1208 m*.
Lowest point: The Dead Sea, 1296 ft *395 m* below sea level.
Principal mountain range: Mts of Judea.
Principal rivers: Jordan (200 miles *321 km*), Qishon.
Head of State: Chaim Herzog, President.
Prime Minister: Shimon Peres.
Climate: Mediterranean (hot, dry summers and mild, rainy winters). More extreme in the south. Sub-tropical on coast. In Jerusalem, average maximum 12°C *55°F* (January) to 30°C *87°F* (July, August), minimum 5°C *41°F* (January) to 17°C *64°F* (August), February rainiest (11 days). Absolute maximum temperature 54°C *129°F*, Tirat Zevi, 22 June 1942; absolute minimum −16°C *2°F*, Tel ha Tanim, 8 Nov. 1950.
Labour force: 1 241 000 (excluding armed forces and 37 000 unemployed) aged 14 and over (1977): Mining and manufacturing 24·3%; Trade, restaurants and hotels 11·8%; Community, social and personal services 35·7%. Figures cover also certain occupied territories.
Gross domestic product: 25 225 million shekels in 1978: Mining and manufacturing 23·3%; Trade, restaurants and hotels 11·5%; Finance, insurance, real estate and business services 13·1%; Community services (incl. all government services) 19·4%.
Exports: US$5017 million in 1982: Diamonds 23%; Chemical and oil products 11·6%; Food, beverages and tobacco 6·6%; Citrus fruit 3·7%.
Monetary unit: Shekel. 1 shekel = 100 agorot (singular: agora).
Denominations:
   Coins 1, 5, 10, 50 agorot.
   Notes 1, 5, 10, 50 shekels.
Exchange rate to £ sterling: 1150 (22 April 1985).
Political history and government: Palestine (of which Israel forms part) was formerly part of Turkey's Ottoman Empire. During the First

IRELAND

World War (1914–18) Palestine was occupied by British forces. After the war it was administered by Britain as part of a League of Nations mandate, established in 1922. The British Government terminated its Palestine mandate on 14 May 1948, when Jewish leaders proclaimed the State of Israel. After armed conflict with neighbouring Arab states, Israel's borders were fixed by armistice agreements in 1949. During the war of 5–10 June 1967 Israeli forces occupied parts of Egypt, Syria and Jordan, including East Jerusalem (which Israel unilaterally incorporated into its territory by legislation passed on 27 June 1967).
   Israel is a republic. Supreme authority rests with the unicameral *Knesset* (Assembly), with 120 members elected by universal suffrage for 4 years, using proportional representation. The *Knesset* elects the President, a constitutional Head of State, for 5 years. Executive power rests with the Cabinet, led by the Prime Minister. The Cabinet takes office after receiving a vote of confidence in the *Knesset*, to which it is responsible. Israel comprises 6 administrative districts.
Telephones: 1 302 000 (1982).
Daily newspapers: 36 (1979).
Radio: 750 000 (1977).
TV: 475 000 licences (1976).
Length of roadways: 2824 miles *4545 km* (31 Dec. 1979).
Length of railways: 343 miles *552 km*.
Universities: 6 (plus 2 specialized).
Adult illiteracy: 12·1% (males 7·4%; females 16·7%) in 1971.
Expectation of life: Males 71·32 years; females 74·68 years (1977, including East Jerusalem).
Defence: Military service: men 36 months, women 24 months (Jews and Druses only), Christians may volunteer; annual training for reservists thereafter up to age 54 for men, 38 (or marriage) for women; total armed forces 172 000 (120 300 conscripts) in 1984; defence expenditure, 1981: $7340 million.
Cinemas: 230 in 1980.
Foreign tourists: 893 883 plus 92 651 cruise passengers (1977).

Italy

Official name: Repubblica Italiana (Italian Republic), abbreviated to Italia.
Population: 53 744 737 (*de facto*, census of 24 Oct. 1971); 56 929 101 (estimate Dec. 1983).
Area: 116 318 miles² *301 263 km²*.
Languages: Italian; small German and other minorities.
Religions; Roman Catholic; Protestant and Jewish minorities.
Capital city: Roma (Rome), population 3 722 053 (estimate Dec. 1983).
Other principal towns (31 Dec. 1983): Milano (Milan) 1 561 438; Napoli (Naples) 1 208 545; Torino (Turin) 1 069 013; Genova (Genoa) 746 785; Palermo 712 342; Bologna 447 971; Firenze (Florence) 440 910; Catania 380 370; Bari 369 576; Venezia (Venice) 340 873; Messina

263 924; Verona 261 947; Trieste 246 315.
Highest point: On Monte Bianco (Mont Blanc), 15 616 ft *4760 m.*
Principal mountain ranges: Appennini (Appennines), Alps.
Principal rivers: Po (418 miles *672 km*), Tevere (Tiber), Arno, Volturno, Garigliano.
Head of State; Alessandro Pertini (b. 25 Sep. 1896), President.
Head of Government: Bettino Craxi (b. 24 Feb. 1934), President of the Council of Ministers (Prime Minister).
Climate; Generally Mediterranean, with warm, dry summers (average maximum 26°C *80°F*) and mild winters. Cooler and rainier in the Po Valley and the Alps. In Rome, average maximum 12°C *54°F* (January) to 31°C *88°F* (July, August), minimum 4°C *39°F* (January, February) to 17°C *64°F* (July, August), February rainiest (11 days). Absolute maximum temperature 46°C *114°F*, Foggia, 6 Sept. 1946; absolute

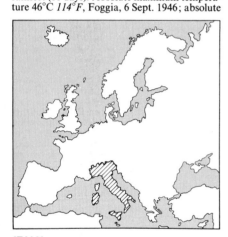

ITALY

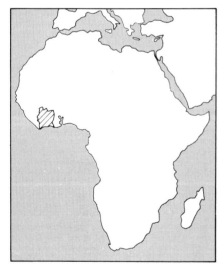

THE IVORY COAST

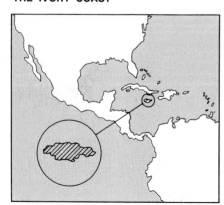

JAMAICA

minimum −34°C −*29°F*, Pian Rosa, 14 Feb. 1956.
Labour force: 20·1 million persons employed, 1·9 million unemployed (April 1982).
Gross domestic product: 172 988 000 million lire in 1977: Industry 34·2%; Trade, restaurants and hotels (including repairs) 14·1% (trade and repairs 12·2%); Government services 10·4%.
Exports: 99 246 476 million lire in 1982.
Monetary unit; Italian lira. 1 lira = 100 centesimi.
Denominations:
  Coins 1, 2, 5, 10, 20, 50, 100, 500, 1000 lire.
  Notes 500, 1000, 2000, 5000, 10000, 20000, 50 000, 100 000 lire.
Exchange rate to £ sterling: 2420 (9 April 1985).
Political history and government: Formerly several independent states. The Kingdom of Italy, under the House of Savoy, was proclaimed in 1861 and the country unified in 1870. Italy was under Fascist rule from 28 Oct. 1922 to 25 July 1943. A referendum on 2 June 1946 voted to abolish the monarchy and Italy became a republic on 10 June 1946. A new constitution took effect on 1 Jan. 1948.

Legislative power is held by the bicameral Parliament (*Parlamento*), elected by universal suffrage for 5 years (subject to dissolution), using proportional representation. The Senate has 315 elected members (seats allocated on a regional basis) and 7 life Senators. The Chamber of Deputies has 630 members. The minimum voting age is 25 years for the Senate and 18 for the Chamber. The two houses have equal power. The President of the Republic is a constitutional Head of State elected for 7 years by an electoral college comprising both Houses of Parliament and 58 regional representatives. Executive power is exercised by the Council of Ministers. The Head of State appoints the President of the Council (Prime Minister) and, on the latter's recommendation, other Ministers. The Council is responsible to Parliament.

Italy has 20 administrative regions, each with an elected legislature and a regional executive.
Telephones: 21 680 000 (1982).
Daily newspapers: 79 (1982).
Radio/TV licences: 14 022 738 in 1982.
Length of roadways: 184 131 miles *296 986 km.*
Length of railways: 12 211 miles *19 652 km.*
Universities: 59.
Adult illiteracy: 3%, and only among over-60s.
Expectation of life: Males 68·97 years; females 74·88 years (1970–72).
Defence: Military service: Army and Air Force 12 months, Navy 18 months; total armed forces 370 600 in 1984; defence expenditure, 1981: $8887 million.
Cinemas: 7014 in 1982.
Foreign tourists: 18 475 660 in 1983 (provisional).

The Ivory Coast

Official name: La République de la Côte d'Ivoire (the Republic of the Ivory Coast).
Population: 6 702 866 (census of 30 Apr. 1975); 9 273 167 (estimate 1983).
Area: 124 504 miles² *322 463 km².*
Languages: French (official), many African languages.
Religions: Animist, Muslim, Christian.
Capital city: Yamoussoukro, population 70 000 in 1983.
Other principal towns (1983): Abidjan 1 000 000; Bouaké 200 000; Daloa 70 000; Man 50 000; Gagnoa 45 000.
Highest point: Mont Toukui, *c.* 6900 ft *2100 m.*
Principal mountain ranges: Man Mountains, Guinea Highlands.
Principal rivers: Bandama, Sassandra, Komoé.
Head of State: Félix Houphouët-Boigny (b. 18 Oct. 1905), President.
Climate: Generally hot, wet and humid. Temperatures from 14°C *57°F* to 39°C *103°F*. Rainy seasons May to July, October to November. In Abidjan, average maximum 28°C *82°F* to 32°C *90°F*, minimum around 23°C *74°F.*
Labour force: 2 301 000 (1970): Agriculture, forestry and fishing 84·5%; Services 12·9% (ILO

estimates); 2 831 705 (excl. unpaid family workers) at 1975 census.
Gross domestic product: 1 539 265 million CFA francs in 1977: Agriculture, forestry and fishing 26·2% (agriculture 22·2%); Manufacturing 11·4%; Trade, restaurants and hotels 30·9% (trade 30·5%).
Exports: 689 000 million CFA francs in 1981: Coffee 18%; Cocoa 34%; Timber 14%; Petroleum products 8%.
Monetary unit: Franc de la Communauté financière africaine.
Denominations:
  Coins 1, 2, 5, 10, 25, 50, 100 CFA francs.
  Notes 100, 500, 1000, 5000, 10000 CFA francs.
Exchange rate to £ sterling: 542·25 (14 Jan. 1985).
Political history and government: Formerly part of French West Africa, independent since 7 Aug. 1960. The ruling *Parti démocratique de la Côte d'Ivoire* has been the only organised political party since its establishment in 1946.

Under the constitution, promulgated on 31 Oct. 1960, legislative power is vested in the unicameral National Assembly, elected for five years by universal adult suffrage. The first multicandidate elections were held in two rounds on 9 and 23 Nov. 1980, the Assembly being increased from 120 to 147 members. Executive power is held by the President, also directly elected for five years. On 25 Nov. 1980 the Assembly adopted a constitutional amendment creating the post of Vice-President. The President rules with the assistance of an appointed council of Ministers, responsible to him. The country comprises 34 departments.
Telephones: 78 370 (1980).
Daily newspapers: 3 (1976).
  Total circulation; 63 000.
Radio: 800 000 (1977).
TV: 300 000 (1977).
Length of roadways: 28 095 miles *45 214 km* (31 Dec. 1977).
Length of railways: 407 miles *655 km.*
Universities: 1.
Adult illiteracy: 95% (males 92%; females 98%) in 1962 (UNESCO estimates).
Expectation of life: males 41·9 years; females 45·1 years (UN estimates for 1970–75).
Defence: Military service voluntary; total armed forces 5120 (1984); defence expenditure, 1980: $245 million.
Cinemas: 60 (seating capacity 41 000) and 6 mobile units (1977).
Foreign tourists: 137 750 in 1980.

Jamaica

Population: 1 848 512 (census of 7 Apr. 1970); 2 230 000 (1982 estimate).
Area: 4411 miles² *11 425 km².*
Language: English.
Religion: Christian (Anglican and Baptist in majority).
Capital city; Kingston, population 750 000 (1982 estimate).
Other principal towns (1982): Montego Bay 60 000; Spanish Town 41 600.
Highest point: Blue Mountain Peak (7402 ft *2256 m*).
Principal mountain range: Blue Mountains.
Principal river: Black River.
Head of State: HM Queen Elizabeth II, represented by Sir Florizel Augustus Glasspole, GCMG (b. 25 Sept. 1909), Governor-General.
Prime Minister: Edward Philip George Seaga (b. 28 May 1930).
Climate: The average rainfall is 1956 mm *77 in,* and the rainfall is far greater in the mountains than on the coast. In Kingston, average maximum 30°C *86°F* (January to March) to 32°C *90°F* (July, August), minimum 19°C *67°F* (January, February) to 23°C *74°F* (June), wettest month is October (nine days). In the uplands the climate is pleasantly equable.
Labour force: 1 019 000 in 1983.
Gross domestic product: J$2965·5 million in 1977: Mining and quarrying 10·2%; Manufac-

turing 18·5%; Trade, restaurants and hotels 15·8% (trade 13·9%); Community, social and personal services 18·0% (public administration and defence 14·3%).
Exports: US$ 736·6 million (excluding re-exports) in 1978: Food and live animals 15·5%; Bauxite and aluminium concentrates 19·8%; Aluminium oxide and hydroxide 52·8%.
Monetary unit: Jamaican dollar (J$). 1 dollar = 100 cents.
Denominations:
 Coins 1, 5, 10, 20, 25, 50 cents.
 Notes 50 cents; 1, 2, 5, 10, 20 dollars.
Exchange rate to £ sterling: 4·74 (14 Jan. 1985).
Political history and government: A former British colony. Became independent, within the Commonwealth, on 6 Aug. 1962. Executive power is vested in the British monarch and exercised by the Governor-General, who is appointed on the recommendation of the Prime Minister and acts in almost all matters on the advice of the Cabinet. Legislative power is held by the bicameral Parliament: the Senate has 21 members, appointed by the Governor-General (13 on the advice of the Prime Minister and 8 on that of the Leader of the Opposition), and the House of Representatives has 60 members elected by universal adult suffrage for 5 years (subject to dissolution) in single-member constituencies. The Governor-General appoints the Prime Minister and, on the latter's recommendation, other Ministers. The Cabinet is responsible to the House.
Telephones: 124 258 (1982).
Daily newspapers: 2 (1985).
Radio: 850 000 (1984).
TV: 200 000 (1984).
Length of roadways: 10 206 miles *16 425 km.*
Length of railways: 232 miles *373 km.*
Universities: 1.
Adult illiteracy: 4·6% (1970).
Expectation of life: Males 62·65 years; females 66·63 years (1959–61).
Defence: Total armed forces 3000 (1984); defence expenditure, 1978: US$17 million.
Cinemas: 25 and 3 drive-in cinemas (1981).
Foreign tourists: 782 436 plus 209 646 cruise passengers (1983).

Japan

Official name: Nippon or Nihon (land of the Rising Sun).
Population: 118 693 000 (1982 census).
Area: 143 751 miles² *372 313 km²*.
Language: Japanese.
Religions: Shintō, Buddhist.
Capital city: Tōkyō, population 8 139 000 (1982 census).
Other principal towns (1982): Yokohama 2 823 000; Osaka 2 542 000; Nagoya 2 053 000; Kyoto 1 458 000; Sapporo 1 419 000; Kobe 1 361 000; Fukuoka 1 065 000; Kitakyushu 1 055 000; Kawasaki 1 027 000.
Highest point: Fuji, 12 388 ft *3776 m* (first climbed before AD 806).
Principal mountain range: Hida.
Principal rivers: Tone (200 miles *321 km*), Ishikari (227 miles *365 km*), Shinano (229 miles *368 km*), Kitakami (156 miles *251 km*).
Head of State: HIM Hirohito (b. 29 Apr. 1901), *Nihon-koku Tennō* (Emperor of Japan).
Prime Minister: Yasuhiro Nakasone.
Climate: Great variation, from north (warm summers with long, cold winters) to south (hot, rainy summers with mild winters). In Tokyo, August warmest (22°C *72°F* to 30°C *86°F*), January coldest (−6°C *20°F* to 8°C *47°F*), June and September rainiest (each 12 days). Absolute maximum temperature 41°C *105°F*, Yamagata, 25 July 1933; absolute minimum −41°C −42°F, Asahikawa, 25 Jan. 1902.
Labour force: 55 800 000 in 1981: Agriculture and forestry 9·1%; Fishing 0·8%; Construction 9·7%; Manufacturing 24·9%; Commerce and finance 26·3%; Transport and other public utilities 6·7%; Services 18·5%; Government work 3·5%.
Gross domestic product: 204 976 000 million yen

in 1978: Manufacturing 28·6%; Trade 14·0%; Community, social and personal services (including restaurants and hotels) 19·3%.
Exports: US$131 931 million in 1982.
Monetary unit: Yen. 1 yen = 100 sen.
Denominations:
 Coins 1, 5, 10, 50, 100 yen.
 Notes 500, 1000, 5000, 10 000 yen.
Exchange rate to £ sterling: 317·64 (22 Apr. 1985).
Political history and government: An hereditary monarchy, with an Emperor as Head of State. After being defeated in the Second World War, Japanese forces surrendered on 14 Aug. 1945. Japan signed an armistice on 2 Sept. 1945, agreeing to give up many outer islands, and the country was placed under US military occupation. A new constitution was promulgated on 3 Nov. 1946 and took effect from 3 May 1947. Following the peace treaty of 8 Sept. 1951, Japan regained its sovereignty on 28 Apr. 1952. The Tokara Archipelago and the Amami Islands (parts of the Ryukyu group) were restored on 5 Dec. 1951 and 25 Dec. 1953 respectively. The Bonin Islands were restored on 26 June 1968 and the rest of the Ryukyu Islands (including Okinawa) on 15 May 1972.
Japan is a constitutional monarchy, with the Emperor as a symbol of the state. He has formal prerogatives but no power relating to government. Legislative power is vested in the bicameral Diet (*Kokkai*), elected by universal adult suffrage. The House of Councillors (*Sangiin*), with limited delaying powers, has 252 members elected for 6 years (half retiring every three years) and the House of Representatives (*Shugiin*) has 511 members elected for 4 years (subject to dissolution). Executive power is vested in the Cabinet. The Prime Minister is appointed by the Emperor (on designation by the Diet) and himself appoints the other Ministers. The Cabinet is responsible to the Diet.
Japan has 47 prefectures, each administered by an elected Governor.
Telephones: 58 678 000 (1982).
Daily newspapers: 125 (1981).
 Total circulation: 67 292 563.
Radio: 64 978 793 (1977).
TV: 60 000 000 (1979).
Length of roadways: 687 337 miles *1 106 161 km* (31 Mar. 1979).
Length of railways: 16 727 miles *26 914 km.*
Universities: 122 (59 national, 12 municipal, 51 private).
Adult illiteracy; 2·2% (males 1·0%; females 3·3%) in 1960.
Expectation of life: Males 72·15 years; females 77·35 years (Japanese nationals only, 1976).
Defence: Military service voluntary; total armed forces 269 400 (1984); defence expenditure, 1983: 4 818 631 million yen.
Cinemas: 2364 in 1980.
Foreign tourists: 1 583 000 in 1981.

Jordan

Official name: Al-Mamlaka al-Urduniya al-Hashimiyah (the Hashemite Kingdom of Jordan).
Population: 3 253 408 (1984 estimate).
Area: 37 738 miles² *97 740 km²*.
Language: Arabic.
Religions: Muslim, Christian minority.
Capital city: 'Ammān, population 956 720 (1984 estimate).
Other principal towns: Az Zarqa (Zarka) 215 687 (1979); Irbid 112 954 (1979); Bait Lahm (Bethlehem) 68 009 (1961); Ariha (Jericho) 66 839 (1961); Al Quds ash Sharif (Jerusalem) 60 337 (Jordanian sector, 1961).
Highest point: Jabal Ramm, 5755 ft *1754 m.*
Principal river: Jordan (200 miles *321 km*).
Head of State: HM King Husain ibn Talal, GCVO (b. 14 Nov. 1935).
Prime Minister: Ahmed Obeidat.
Climate: Hot and dry, average temperature 15°C *60°F* with wide diurnal variations. Cool winters, rainy season December to March. In Ammān, August hottest (average maximum 32°C *90°F*),

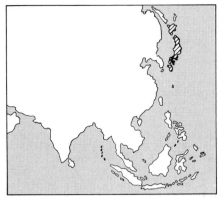

JAPAN

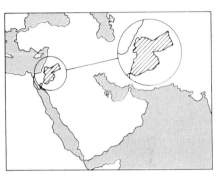

JORDAN

January coolest (average minimum −1°C *39°F*). Absolute maximum temperature 51°C *124°F*, Dead Sea North, 22 June 1942; absolute minimum −7°C *18°F*, Ammān, 28 Feb. 1959.
Labour force: 565 000 (1970): Agriculture, forestry and fishing 33·9%; Industry 32·8%; Services 33·4% (ILO estimates).
Gross domestic product: 477·6 million dinars (East Bank only) in 1977: Agriculture, forestry and fishing 10·4%; Manufacturing 12·7%; Trade, restaurants and hotels 17·1%; Transport, storage and communication 10·5%; Community, social and personal services 23·2% (public administration and defence 21·0%).
Exports: $296·7 million in 1978. Fruit and vegetables 19·9% (fresh and simply preserved vegetables 10·7%); Natural phosphates 21·4%; Machinery and transport equipment 13·5%.
Monetary unit: Jordanian dinar. 1 dinar = 1000 fils.
Denominations:
 Coins 1, 5, 10, 20, 25, 50, 100, 250 fils.
 Notes 500 fils; 1, 5, 10 dinars.
Exchange rate to £ sterling: 0·453 (14 Jan. 1985).
Political history and government: Formerly part of Turkey's Ottoman Empire, Turkish forces were expelled in 1918. Palestine and Transjordan were administered by Britain under League of Nations mandate, established in 1922. Transjordan became an independent monarchy, under an Amir, on 22 Mar. 1946. The Amir became King, and the country's present name was adopted, on 25 May 1946. In the Arab-Israeli war of 1948 Jordanian forces occupied part of Palestine, annexed in December 1949 and fully incorporated on 24 Apr. 1950. This territory was captured by Israel in the war of 5–10 June 1967.
Under the constitution, adopted on 7 Nov. 1951, legislative power is vested in a bicameral National Assembly comprising a Chamber of Notables (30 members appointed by the King for 8 years, half retiring every 4 years) and a Chamber of Deputies with 60 members (50 Muslims and 10 Christians) elected by universal adult suffrage for 4 years (subject to dissolution). In each Chamber there is equal representation for the East Bank and the (occupied) West Bank. Executive power is vested in the King, who rules with the assistance of an appointed Council of Ministers, responsible to the Assembly. On 9 Nov. 1974 both Chambers of the Assembly

approved constitutional amendments which empowered the King to dissolve the Assembly and to postpone elections for up to 12 months. The Assembly was dissolved on 22 Nov. 1974 and reconvened on 5–7 Feb. 1976, when it approved a constitutional amendment giving the King power to postpone elections indefinitely and to convene the Assembly as required. A royal decree of 19 Apr. 1978 provided for the creation of a National Consultative Council, with 60 members appointed by the King, on the Prime Minister's recommendation, to debate proposed legislation. The Council, whose members serve for two years (subject to dissolution by the King), first met on 24 Apr. 1978 and was renewed on 20 Apr. 1980.

Jordan comprises 8 administrative districts, including 3 on the West Bank (under Israeli occupation since June 1967).
Telephones: 60 533 (1980).
Daily newspapers: 4 (1980).
Radio: 532 000 (East Bank only) in 1977.
TV: 165 000 (East Bank only) in 1977.
Length of roadways: 3683 miles *5927 km* (East Bank only) at 31 Dec. 1979.
Length of railways: 384 miles *618 km*.
Universities: 4.
Adult illiteracy: 67·6% (males 49·9%; females 84·8%) in 1961.
Expectation of life: Males 52·6 years; females 52·0 years (1969–63).
Defence: Military service: selective conscription; total armed forces 72 800 in 1984; defence expenditure, 1981: $420 million.
Cinemas: 43 plus 2 mobile units (East Bank only) in 1977.
Foreign tourists: 2 200 000 in 1981.

Kampuchea

Official name: Sathearanakrath Pracheachon Kampuchea (People's Republic of Kampuchea).
Population: 6 682 000 (1981 estimate).

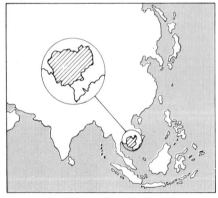

KAMPUCHEA

KENYA

Area: 69 898 miles² *181 035 km²*.
Languages: Khmer (official), French.
Religion: Buddhist.
Capital city: Phnom-Penh, population 500 000 (1983 estimate).
Other principal towns: Battambang, Kompong Chhnang, Kompong Cham, Kompong Som (Sihanoukville).
Highest point: Mt Ka-Kup, 5722 ft *1774 m*.
Principal mountain range: Chaîne des Cardamomes.
Principal river: Mekong (2600 miles *4184 km*).
Head of State: Heng Samrin (b. 1934), Chairman of the People's Revolutionary Council; also Secretary-General of the Kampuchean People's Revolutionary Party.
Prime Minister: Chan Si.
Climate: Tropical and humid. Rainy season June–November. In Phnom-Penh, average maximum 30°C *86°F* (November, December) to 34°C *94°F* (April), minimum 21°C *70°F* (January) to 24°C *76°F* (April–October), September rainiest (19 days).
Labour force: 2 499 735 aged 10 and over (1962 census); 2 849 000 (1970): Agriculture, forestry and fishing 78·2%; Services 17·6% (ILO estimates).
Gross domestic product: 32 000 million riels in 1966 (when $1 = 35 riels); $1192 million (estimate) in 1975.
Exports: $65·0 million in 1969: Cereals and cereal preparations 23·6% (rice 17·1%); Fruit and vegetables 11·1%; Natural rubber 40·3%.
Monetary unit: New riel. 1 riel = 100 sen.
Denominations:
   Coins 5 sen.
   Notes 10, 20, 50 sen; 1, 5, 10, 20, 50 riels.
Exchange rate to £ sterling: approx. 7·7 (30 June 1981).
Political history and government: As Cambodia, formerly a monarchy and part of French Indo-China. Norodom Sihanouk became King on 26 Apr. 1941. On 6 May 1947 he promulgated a constitution providing for a bicameral Parliament, including an elected National Assembly. Cambodia became an Associate State of the French Union on 8 Nov. 1949 and a fully independent kingdom on 9 Nov. 1953. Sihanouk abdicated on 2 Mar. 1955 in favour of his father, Norodom Suramarit. King Suramarit died on 3 Apr. 1960 and Parliament elected Prince Sihanouk to become Head of State (without taking the title of King) on 20 June 1960.

On 18 Mar. 1970 Prince Sihanouk was deposed by his Prime Minister, Lt-Gen (later Marshal) Lon Nol, who proclaimed the Khmer Republic on 8 Oct. 1970. Sihanouk went into exile and formed a Royal Government of National Union, supported by the pro-Communist *Khmers Rouges* ('Red Cambodians'). Sihanoukists and the *Khmers Rouges* formed the National United Front of Cambodia (NUFC). Their combined forces defeated the republicans and Phnom-Penh surrendered on 17 April 1975, when the Royal Government took power. On 14 Dec. 1975 a congress of the NUFC approved a new republican constitution, promulgated on 5 Jan. 1976, when the name of the country was changed to Democratic Kampuchea. Elections were held on 20 March 1976 for the People's Representative Assembly (250 members). Prince Sihanouk resigned as Head of State on 4 April 1976. In his place the Assembly chose a three-man State Presidium on 11 April 1976. Pol Pot was appointed Prime Minister two days later. On 27 Sep. 1977 it was officially revealed that the ruling organization was the Communist Party of Kampuchea, with Pol Pot as its Secretary. Rival Communists, opponents of Pol Pot, established the Kampuchean National United Front for National Salvation (KNUFNS), announced on 3 Dec. 1978. After a year of border fighting, Vietnamese forces, supporting the KNUFNS, invaded Cambodia on 25 Dec. 1978, capturing the capital on 7 Jan. 1979. The next day the KNUFNS established the People's Revolutionary Council (8 members) and on 10 Jan. 1979 the country's present name was adopted. The second Congress of the KNUFNS, held on 29–30 Sept. 1979, elected a

Central Committee of 35 members.

Elections were held on 1 May 1981 for 117 members of a new National Assembly. The Assembly began its first session on 24 June 1981 and ratified a new constitution on 27 June. The supreme organ of state power is the unicameral Assembly, elected by universal adult suffrage for a five-year term. The Assembly chooses seven of its members to form the Council of State, its permanent organ, which appoints the Council of Ministers. The new régime is based on the Kampuchean People's Revolutionary Party.
Telephones: 71 000 (1975).
Daily newspapers: 1 (1979).
Radio: 110 000 (1975).
TV: 35 000 (1977).
Length of roadways: c. 6835 miles *c. 11 000 km*.
Length of railways: 403 miles *649 km*.
Adult illiteracy: 63·9% (males 37·7%; females 89·6%) in 1962.
Expectation of life: Males 44·0 years; females 46·9 years (UN estimates for 1970–75).
Defence: Military service: conscription; total armed forces about 20 000 (1981), also about 200 000 Vietnamese troops.
Cinemas: Nil in 1979.
Foreign tourists: 16 505 in 1973.

Kenya

Official name: Jamhuri ya Kenya (Republic of Kenya).
Population: 15 322 000 (census of Aug. 1979); 19 000 000 (1985 estimate).
Area: 224 961 miles² *582 646 km²*.
Languages: Swahili (official), English, Kikuyu, Luo.
Religions; Christian 58% (1962), Muslim.
Capital city: Nairobi, population 1 100 000 (1985 estimate).
Other principal towns (1985 estimates): Mombasa 478 000; Nakuru 130 000; Kisumu 215 000; Machakos 117 000; Meru 98 000; Eldoret 71 000; Thika 57 000.
Highest point: Mount Kenya (17 058 ft *5199 m*).
Principal mountain range: Aberdare Mountains.
Principal rivers: Tana, Umba, Athi, Mathioya.
Head of State: Daniel Toroitich arap Moi (b. Sept. 1924), President.
Climate: Varies with altitude. Hot and humid on coast, with average temperatures of 20°C *69°F* to 32°C *90°F*, falling to 7°C *45°F* to 27°C *80°F* on land over 5000 ft *1524 m*. Ample rainfall in the west and on highlands, but very dry in the north. In Nairobi, average maximum 20°C *69°F* (July) to 26°C *79°F* (February), minimum 10°C *51°F* (July) to 14°C *58°F* (April), May rainiest (17 days).
Labour force: 1 024 000 in 1981: Agriculture, forestry and fishing 17%; Rest of private sector 35·8%; Public sector 47·3%.
Gross domestic product: 51 640 million shillings in 1981: Agriculture 30·7%; Manufacturing 13·3%; Government services 15·2%.
Exports: 9248 million shillings in 1981 (excluding re-exports): Coffee 21·3%; Petroleum products 30·7%; Tea 11·9%.
Monetary unit; Kenya shilling. 1 shilling = 100 cents.
Denominations:
   Coins 5, 10, 50 cents; 1 shilling.
   Notes 5, 10, 20, 100 shillings.
Exchange rate to £ sterling: 17·625 (14 Jan. 1985).
Political history and government: Formerly a British colony and protectorate. Became independent, within the Commonwealth, on 12 Dec. 1963 and a republic on 12 Dec. 1964. A one-party state since 30 Oct. 1969. Legislative power is held by the unicameral National Assembly, with 172 members (158 elected by universal adult suffrage, the Attorney-General, the Speaker and 12 members nominated by the President) serving a term of five years (subject to dissolution). Executive power is held by the President, also directly elected for five years. He is assisted by an appointed Vice-President and Cabinet. Kenya has 40 districts, each with a

District Development Committee responsible for all development projects.
Telephones: 198 294 (1981).
Daily newspapers: 4 (1983).
 Total circulation: 270 000.
Radio: 700 000 (1981).
TV: 80 000 (1981).
Length of roadways: 33 298 miles *53 577 km* (1981).
Length of railways: 1658 miles *2668 km.*
Universities: 2.
Adult illiteracy: 80·5% (males 70%; females 90%) in 1962 (UNESCO estimate).
Expectation of life: Males 46·9 years; females 51·2 years (1969).
Defence: Military service voluntary; total armed forces 15 650 (1984); defence expenditure, 1977: $168 million.
Cinemas: 35 in 1979.
Foreign tourists: 407 878 (including visitors in transit) in 1981.

Kiribati

Population: 56 213 (census of 12 Dec. 1978); 60 302 (estimate 1982).
Area: 277 miles² *717 km².*
Languages: Kiribati (Gilbertese), English.
Religion: Christian (Anglican, Methodist, Roman Catholic, Mormons, Seventh Day Adventists).
Capital city: Tarawa atoll, population 20 148 at 1978 census.
Highest point: 265 ft *81 m,* on Banaba (Ocean Island).
Head of State: Ieremia T Tabai, GCMG (b. 16 Dec. 1950), Beretitenti (President).
Climate: Warm and pleasant, with day temperatures between 27°C *80°F* and 32°C *90°F* and a minimum of about 23°C *77°F* at night. Average annual rainfall varies widely between atolls, ranging from 30 in *762 mm* to 150 in *3810 mm.* Rainy season December to February, dry from August to October.
Labour force: 9539 (approx. 15–49 age group) in Dec. 1978.
Gross domestic product: A$24 million (1982 estimate).
Exports: A$13 500 000 (1984 estimate): Copra 52%.
Monetary unit: Australian currency (*q.v.*).
Political history and government: In 1892 a United Kingdom protectorate was established over the 16 atolls of the Gilbert Islands and the 9 Ellice Islands (now Tuvalu) the two groups being administered together. Ocean Island (now Banaba) was annexed on 28 Nov. 1900. The Gilbert and Ellice Islands were annexed on 10 Nov. 1915, effective from 12 Jan. 1916, when the protectorate became a colony. Later in 1916 the new Gilbert and Ellice Islands Colony (GEIC) was extended to include Ocean Island and two of the Line Islands. Christmas Island (now Kiritimati), in the Line Islands, was annexed in 1919 and the 8 Phoenix Islands on 18 Mar. 1937. Two of the Phoenix Islands, Canton (now Kanton) and Enderbury, were also claimed by the USA and a joint British-US administration was agreed on 6 Apr. 1939. The 5 uninhabited Central and Southern Line islands became part of the GEIC on 1 Jan. 1972. The Ellice Islands were allowed to form a separate territory, named Tuvalu, on 1 Oct. 1975. The remainder of the GEIC was renamed the Gilbert Islands and obtained self-government on 1 Jan. 1977. Following a constitutional conference on 21 Nov.–7 Dec. 1978, this territory became an independent republic, within the Commonwealth, on 12 July 1979, taking the name Kiribati (pronounced 'Kiribass'). The USA has agreed to renounce its claim to Kanton and Enderbury Islands under a 1982 Treaty of Friendship.

Legislative power is vested in the Maneaba ni Maungatabu, a unicameral body. It has 35 members elected by universal adult suffrage for 4 years (subject to dissolution), one nominated representative of the Banaban community and, if he is not an elected member, the Attorney-General as an *ex officio* member. The 35 elected members of the pre-independence House of Assembly took office as members of the first Maneaba. Executive power is vested in the Beretitenti (President), who is Head of State and Head of Government. The pre-independence Chief Minister became the first Beretitenti but in future the Beretitenti is to be elected. After each general election for the Maneaba, it will nominate, from among its members, three or four candidates from whom the Beretitenti will be elected by universal adult suffrage. The Maneaba is empowered to remove the Beretitenti from office.

The Beretitenti governs with the assistance of a Kauoman-ni-Beretitenti (Vice-President) and Cabinet, whom he appoints from among members of the Maneaba. The Cabinet is responsible to the Maneaba.
Telephones: 821 (1982).
Radio: 8000 (1977).
Length of roadways: 400 miles *640 km.*
Expectation of life: Males 56·9 years; females 59·0 years (1958–62, including Tuvalu).

Korea (North)

Official name: Chosun Minchu-chui Inmin Konghwa-guk (Democratic People's Republic of Korea).
Population: 18 490 000 (1983 estimate).
Area: 46 540 miles² *120 538 km²* (excluding demilitarised zone).
Language: Korean.
Religions: Buddhist, Confucian, Taoist.
Capital city: Pyongyang, population 1 280 000 (1981 estimate).
Other principal towns (1976): Ch'ongjin 300 000; Hungnam 260 000; Kaesong 240 000.
Highest point: Pektu San (Pait'ou Shan), 9003 ft *2744 m* (first climbed 1886).
Principal mountain range: Nangnim Sanmaek.
Principal rivers: Imjin, Ch'ongch'ŏn, Yalu (300 miles *482 km*) on frontier.
Head of State: Marshall Kim Il Sung (*né* Kim Sung Chu, b. 15 Apr. 1912), President; also General Secretary of the Central Committee of the Korean Workers' Party.
Head of Government: Li Jong Ok, Premier of the Administration Council.
Climate; Continental; hot, humid, rainy summers (average temperature 25°C *77°F*) and cold, dry winters (average −6°C *21°F*).
Labour force: 5 993 000 (1970): Agriculture, forestry and fishing 54·7%; Industry 27·6%; Services 17·7% (ILO estimate).
Gross national product: $17 040 million in 1978 (World Bank estimate).
Exports: US$1610 million in 1981: Manufactured goods 59%.
Monetary unit: Won. 1 won = 100 chon (jun).
Denominations:
 Coins 1, 5, 10 chon.
 Notes 50 chon; 1, 5, 10, 50, 100 won.
Exchange rate to £ sterling: 1·57 (14 Jan. 1985).
Political history and government: Korea was formerly a kingdom, for long under Chinese suzerainty. Independence was established on 17 Apr. 1895. Korea was occupied by Japanese forces in Nov. 1905 and formally annexed by Japan on 22 Aug. 1910, when the monarch was deposed. After Japan's defeat in the Second World War, Korea was divided at the 38th parallel into military occupation zones, with Soviet forces in the North and US forces in the South. After the failure of negotiations in 1946 and 1947, the country remained divided. With Soviet backing, a Communist-dominated administration was established in the North. Elections were held on 25 Aug. 1948 and the Democratic People's Republic of Korea was proclaimed on 9 Sept. 1948. After the Korean War of 1950–53 a cease-fire line replaced the 38th parallel as the border between North and South.

In North Korea a new constitution was adopted on 27 Dec. 1972. The highest organ of state power is the unicameral Supreme People's Assembly, with 579 members elected (unopposed) for four years by universal adult suffrage. The Assembly elects for its duration the President of the Republic and, on the latter's recommendation, other members of the Central People's Committee to direct the government. The Assembly appoints the Premier and the Committee appoints other Ministers to form the Administration Council, led by the President.

Political power is held by the (Communist) Korean Workers' Party (KWP), which dominates the Democratic Front for the Reunification of the Fatherland (including two other minor parties). The Front presents an approved list of candidates for elections to representative bodies. The KWP's highest authority is the Party Congress. The sixth Congress met on 10–14 Oct. 1980 and elected a new Central Committee to supervise Party work. To direct its policy, the Committee elects a Political Bureau (19 full and 15 alternate members were elected on 14 Oct. 1980. The five-member Presidium of the Political Bureau is the Party's most powerful policy-making body.

North Korea comprises nine provinces and two cities, each with an elected People's Assembly.
Daily newspapers: 11 (1976).
Radio: 600 000 (1961).
TV: 200 000 (1982).
Length of railways: 2722 miles *4380 km* (1974).
Universities: 3.
Adult illiteracy: 10% (est.).
Expectation of life: 74 years (1982).
Defence: Military service: Army, Navy 5 years, Air Force 3–4 years; total armed forces 869 000 (1984); defence expenditure, 1981: $1470 million (converted at $1 = 2·05 won).

Korea (South)

Official name: Daehan-Minkuk (Republic of Korea).
Population: 37 449 000 (1980 census); 39 331 000 (1982 estimate).
Area: 38 221 miles² *98 992 km².*
Language: Korean.

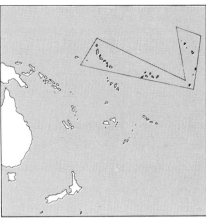

KIRIBATI

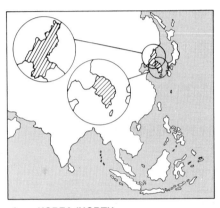

above: **KOREA (NORTH**
below: **KOREA (SOUTH)**

Religions: Buddhist, Christian, Confucian, Chundo Kyo.
Capital city: Sǒul (Seoul), population 8 366 756 at 1980 census.
Other principal towns (1980): Pusan (Busan) 3 160 276; Taegu (Daegu) 1 607 458; Inchǒ'n (Incheon) 1 084 730; Kwangchu (Gwangju) 727 627; Taejǒn (Daejeon) 651 642; Ulsan 418 415; Masan 386 773; Seongnam 376 447; Chonchu (Jeonju) 366 997; Suweon 310 757.
Highest point: Halla-san, 6398 ft *1950 m*.
Principal rivers: Han, Naktong (with Nam), Kum, Somjin, Yongsan.
Head of State: Gen Chun Doo Hwan (b. 23 Jan. 1931), President.
Prime Minister: Chin Jee Chong (b. 13 Dec. 1921).
Climate: Hot, humid summers (average temperature 25°C *77°F*) and cold, dry winters (average −6°C *21°F*). In Seoul, August hottest (22°C *71°F* to 30°C *87°F*), January coldest (−9°C *15°F* to 0°C *32°F*), July rainiest (16 days). Absolute maximum temperature 40°C *104°F*, Taegu, 1 Aug. 1942; absolute minimum −43,6°C −46·5°F, Chungkangjin, 12 Jan. 1933.
Labour force: 14 515 000 in 1983 (excluding 613 000 unemployed): Agriculture, forestry and fishing 29·7%; Mining and manufacturing 23·3%; Services 47%.
Gross domestic product: 58 279·7 billion won in 1983: Agriculture, forestry and fishing 14%; Mining and manufacturing 29·5%; Others 56·5%.
Exports: US$24·3 billion in 1983: Food and live animals 4·4%; Manufactured goods 28·3%; Machinery and transport equipment 32·1%; Miscellaneous manufactured articles 27·8%.
Monetary unit: Won. 1 won = 100 chun (jeon).
Denominations:
Coins 1, 5, 10, 50, 100, 500 won.
Notes 500, 5000, 10 000 won.
Exchange rate to £ sterling: 928·58 (14 Jan. 1985).
Political history and government: (For events before partition, *see* North Korea, above). After UN-supervised elections for a National Assembly on 10 May 1948, South Korea adopted a constitution and became the independent Republic of Korea on 15 Aug. 1948. North Korean forces invaded the South on 25 June 1950 and

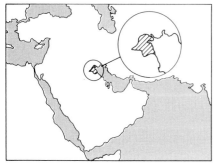

KUWAIT

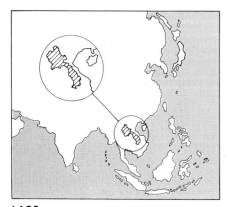

LAOS

war ensued until 27 July 1953, when an armistice established a cease-fire line (roughly along the 38th parallel) between North and South. This has become effectively an international frontier.

On 16 May 1961 South Korea's government was overthrown by a military *coup*, led by Maj-Gen Pak Chung Hi, who assumed power, dissolved the National Assembly, suspended the constitution and disbanded political parties. A new constitution was approved by referendum on 17 Dec. 1962. Gen Pak was elected President on 15 Oct. 1963 and inaugurated on 17 Dec. 1963, when a newly-elected National Assembly was convened. Martial law was imposed on 17 Oct. 1972 and another constitution approved by referendum on 21 Nov. 1972. This *Yushin* ('Revitalising') Constitution provided for the President to be elected indirectly by a 'National Conference for Unification' (NCU), comprising delegates elected by popular vote. The National Assembly had two-thirds of its members directly elected and one-third nominated by the NCU. Emergency Decree No. 9, issued on 13 May 1975, banned virtually all opposition activities.

President Pak was assassinated on 26 Oct. 1979. On the next day, martial law was introduced (with the Army Chief of Staff as martial law administrator), except on the island of Cheju, and the Prime Minister, Choi Kyu Ha, became Acting President. On 6 Dec. 1979 he was elected President by the NCU and on the next day he rescinded Emergency Decree No. 9. In a virtual *coup* on 12–13 Dec. 1979 the martial law administrator and other officers were arrested by troops under Lt-Gen (later Gen) Chun Doo Hwan, head of the Army Security Command. President Choi was inaugurated on 21 Dec. 1979 to complete his predecessor's last term (1978–84). Following a wave of strikes and demonstrations, martial law was extended throughout the country on 17 May 1980. All political activities were banned and the national Assembly was closed on 19 May. The Cabinet resigned on 20 May and a new Prime Minister was appointed the next day. On 31 May 1980 the government established a Special Committee for National Security Measures, an advisory body controlled by the armed forces, which assumed political power. Following a 'purification' campaign, involving mass arrests and purges, President Choi resigned on 16 Aug. 1980. To succeed him, Gen Chun was endorsed by the armed services and (after retiring from the Army) was elected unopposed on 27 Aug. He was sworn in on 1 Sept. and a new Cabinet was formed.

A new constitution was approved by referendum on 22 Oct. 1980 and came into effect on 27 Oct., when the 'Fifth Republic' was inaugurated. The National Assembly and existing political parties were dissolved. Martial law was lifted on 24 Jan. 1981.

Executive power is held by the President, indirectly elected for a single seven-year term by a presidential electoral college whose members are elected by universal adult suffrage. The first college (5278 members) was elected on 11 Feb. 1981. The college elected President Chun on 25 Feb. and he was sworn in on 3 March, when the college was dissolved. The President rules with the assistance of an appointed State Council (Cabinet), led by a Prime Minister. Legislative power is vested in the unicameral National Assembly, popularly elected for a four-year term. On 25 Mar. 1981 voting took place for an Assembly of 276 members: 184 directly elected (two each from 92 districts, though no party could have more than one candidate per district) and 92 additional members (61 for the party gaining the most seats by direct election, the remaining 31 for other parties in proportion to seats won directly).
Telephones: 4 268 270 (1980).
Daily newspapers: 44 (1977).
Total circulation: 7 169 000.
Radio: 10 250 000 (1983).
TV: 7 200 000 (1983).
Length of roadways: 31 284 miles *50 336 km*.
Length of railways: 1940 miles *3121 km*.
Universities: 41.

Adult illiteracy: 8% (1983).
Expectation of life: Males 64·2 years; females 70·6 years (1983).
Defence: Military service: Army and Marines 2½ years, Navy and Air Force 3 years; total armed forces 619 600 (1984); defence expenditure, 1981: $4400 million.
Cinemas: 443 in 1981.
Foreign tourists: 1 194 551 in 1982.

Kuwait

Official name: Daulat al-Kuwait (State of Kuwait). Kuwait means 'little fort'.
Population: 1 466 431 (1981 census).
Area: 6880 miles² *17 818 km²*.
Language: Arabic.
Religions: Muslim; Christian minority.
Capital city: Kuwait City, population 276 356 (1981 census).
Other principal towns (1975): Hawalli 130 565; Salmiya 113 943; Abraq Kheetan 59 443; Farawaniya 44 875.
Highest point: 951 ft *289 m*.
Head of State: HH Shaikh Jabir al-Ahmad al-Jabir as-Sabah (b. 1928), Amir.
Prime Minister: HH Shaikh Saad al-Abdullah as-Salim as-Sabah.
Climate: Humid, average temperature 24°C *75°F*. In Kuwait City, maximum recorded temperature 51°C *124°F*, July 1954; minimum −2·6°C *+27·3°F*, January 1964.
Labour force: 304 582 (including unemployed) aged 12 and over (1975 census): Construction 10·8%; Trade, restaurants and hotels 13·3%; Community, social and personal services 53·7%.
Gross domestic product: 3279 million dinars in year ending 31 Mar. 1976: Mining and quarrying 70·0%.
Exports: 4363 million Kuwait dinar in 1981: Crude oil and petroleum products 80%.
Monetary unit: Kuwait dinar. 1 dinar = 1000 fils.
Denominations:
Coins 1, 5, 10, 20, 50, 100 fils.
Notes 250, 500 fils; 1, 5, 10 dinars.
Exchange rate to £ sterling: 0·341 (14 Jan. 1985).
Political history and government: A monarchy formerly ruled by a Shaikh. Under British protection from 23 Jan. 1899 until achieving full independence, with the ruling Shaikh as Amir, on 19 June 1961. Present constitution adopted on 16 Dec. 1962. Executive power is vested in the Amir (chosen by and from members of the ruling family) and is exercised through a Council of Ministers. The Amir appoints the Prime Minister and, on the latter's recommendation, other Ministers. Legislative power is vested in the unicameral National Assembly, whose members serve for four years (subject to dissolution) and are elected by literate civilian adult male Kuwaiti citizens. On 29 Aug. 1976 the Amir dissolved the Assembly and suspended parts of the constitution, including provisions for fresh elections. In accordance with an Amiri decree of 24 Aug. 1980, a new 50-seat National Assembly (two deputies from each of 25 constituencies) was elected on 23 Feb. 1981. The Assembly's first session opened on 9 Mar. 1981. Political parties are not legally permitted. Kuwait comprises three governorates.
Telephones: 231 643 (1982).
Daily newspapers: 7 (1977).
Total circulation: 180 000.
Radio: 550 000 (1977).
TV: 540 000 (1977).
Length of roadways: 1491 miles *2400 km* (31 Dec. 1978).
Universities: 1.
Adult illiteracy: 40·4% (males 32·0%; females 52·0%) in 1975.
Expectation of life: males 66·4 years; females 71·5 years (1970).
Defence: Military service 18 months; total armed forces 11 900 (1984); defence expenditure, 1980: $1100 million.
Cinemas: 10 in 1979.

Laos

Official name: Saathiaranagrŏat Prachhathippatay Prachhachhon Lao (Lao People's Democratic Republic).
Population; 3 427 000 (estimate for 31 Dec. 1977).
Area: 91 400 miles² *236 800 km²*.
Languages: Lao (official), French.
Religions: Buddhist, tribal.
Capital city: Viengchane (Vientiane), population 176 637 (1973).
Other principal towns (1973): Savannakhet 50 690; Pakse 44 860; Luang Prabang 44 244.
Highest point: Phou Bia, 9252 ft *2820 m*.
Principal mountain range: Annamitic Range.
Principal river: Mekong (2600 miles *4184 km*).
Head of State: Souphanouvong (b. 1902), President.
Prime Minister: Kaysone Phomvihane (b. 13 Dec. 1920), also General Secretary of the Lao People's Revolutionary Party.
Climate: Tropical (warm and humid). Rainy monsoon season May–October. In Vientiane, average maximum 28°C *83°F* (December, January) to 34°C *93°F* (April), minimum 14°C *57°F* (January) to 24°C *75°F* (June to September), July and August rainiest (each 18 days). Maximum recorded temperature 44,8°C *112·6°F*, Luang Prabang, April 1960; minimum 0,8°C *33·4°F*, Luang Prabang, January 1924.
Labour force: 1 495 000 (1970); Agriculture, forestry and fishing 78·8%; Services 15·9% (ILO estimates).
Gross domestic product: $300 million in 1975 (UN estimate).
Exports: US$48 million in 1981.
Monetary unit: New kip. 1 kip = 100 at.
Denominations:
  Notes 1, 5, 10, 20 kips.
Exchange rate to £ sterling: 38·885 (14 Jan. 1985).
Political history and government: Formerly the three principalities of Luang Prabang, Vientiane and Champassac. Became a French protectorate in 1893. The three principalities were merged in 1946 and an hereditary constitutional monarchy, under the Luang Prabang dynasty, was established on 11 May 1947. The Kingdom of Laos became independent, within the French Union, on 19 July 1949. Full sovereignty was recognized by France on 23 Oct. 1953. After nearly 20 years of almost continuous civil war between the Royal Government and the *Neo Lao Hak Sat* (Lao Patriotic Front or LPF), a Communist-led insurgent movement whose armed forces were known as the *Pathet Lao*, a peace agreement was signed on 21 Feb. 1973. A joint administration was established on 5 Apr. 1974 but the LPF became increasingly dominant. The National Assembly was dissolved on 13 Apr. 1975. The King abdicated on 29 Nov. 1975 and on 1 Dec. 1975 a National Congress of People's Representatives (264 delegates elected by local authorities) proclaimed the Lao People's Democratic Republic, with Prince Souphanouvong, Chairman of the LPF, as President. The Congress installed a Council of Ministers, led by a Prime Minister, and appointed a Supreme People's Council (SPC) of 45 members, chaired by the President, to draft a new constitution. The SPC held its first plenary session on 12–17 June 1976.

Political power is held by the Lao People's Revolutionary Party (LPRP), formerly called the People's Party of Laos. The Communist LPRP has a Central Committee with 14 full and 6 alternate members, headed by a seven-member Political Bureau.
Telephones: 7000 (1977).
Daily newspapers: 3 (1976).
Radio: 200 000 (1977).
Length of roadways: 10 408 miles *16 750 km* (1979).
Universities: 1.
Adult illiteracy: 15% (1981).
Expectation of life: Males 39·1 years; females 41·8 years (UN estimates for 1970–75).
Defence: Military service: 18 months; total armed forces 52 550 (1984); defence expenditure, 1979: $38 million.

Cinemas: 16 (seating capacity 8200) in 1969.
Foreign tourists: 23 102 plus 25 280 excursionists (1973).

Lebanon

Official name: Al-Jumhuriya al-Lubnaniya (the Lebanese Republic), abbreviated to al-Lubnan.
Population: 2 126 325 (survey of 15 Nov. 1970), excluding Palestinian refugees in camps (registered Palestinian refugees numbered 187 529 at 30 June 1973); 2 600 000 (1980 estimate).
Area: 3950 miles² *10 400 km²*.
Languages: Arabic (official), French, Armenian, English.
Religions: Christian (Roman Catholic, Orthodox), Muslim.
Capital city: Beirut, population 702 000 (1980 estimate).
Other principal towns (1980): Tripoli 175 000; Zahlé 46 800; Saida (Sidon) 24 740; Tyre 14 000.
Highest point: Qurnat as-Sawdā, 10 131 ft *3088 m*.
Principal mountain ranges: Lebanon, Jabal ash-Sharqī (Anti-Lebanon).
Principal river: Nahr al-Litāni (Leontes).
Head of State: Shaikh Amin Gemayel, President.
Prime Minister: Rashid Karami.
Climate: Coastal lowlands are hot and humid in summer, mild (cool and damp) in winter. Mountains cool in summer, heavy snowfall in winter. In Beirut, average maximum 16°C *62°F* (January) to 32°C *89°F* (August), minimum 10°C *51°F* (January, February) to 23°C *74°F* (August), January rainiest (15 days).
Labour force: 538 410 (excluding 33 345 unemployed) at November 1970 survey: Agriculture, forestry and fishing 19·0%; Mining, quarrying and manufacturing 17·8% (manufacturing 17·7%); Trade, restaurants and hotels 17·1%; Community, social and personal services 27·9%.
Gross domestic product: £L6365 million in 1972: Mining, quarrying and manufacturing 13·9%; Trade, restaurants and hotels 31·5%; Community, social and personal services 18·1%.
Exports: £Leb 1639 million in 1978.
Monetary unit: Lebanese pound (£L). 1 pound = 100 piastres.
Denominations:
  Coins 1, 2½, 5, 10, 25, 50 piastres; 1 pound.
  Notes 1, 5, 10, 25, 50, 100, 250 pounds.
Exchange rate to £ sterling: 10·71 (14 Jan. 1985).
Political history and government: Formerly part of Turkey's Ottoman Empire. Turkish forces were expelled in 1918 by British and French troops, with Arab help. Administered by France under League of Nations mandate from 1 Sept. 1920. Independence declared on 26 Nov. 1941. A republic was established in 1943 and French powers transferred on 1 Jan. 1944. All foreign troops left by December 1946.

Legislative power was vested in the unicameral Chamber of Deputies, with 99 members elected by universal adult suffrage for 4 years (subject to dissolution), using proportional representation. Seats are allocated on a religious basis (53 Christian, 45 Muslim). Elections to the Chamber due in April 1976 were postponed because of civil disorder. On 15 Mar. 1979 the Chamber renamed itself the National Assembly. On 15 Mar. 1980 the term of the Assembly was extended, for a third time, until the end of 1981. Executive power is vested in the President, elected for 6 years by the Assembly. He appoints a Prime Minister and other Ministers to form a Cabinet, responsible to the Assembly. By convention, the President is a Maronite Christian, the Prime Minister a Sunni Muslim, and the Speaker of Parliament a Shiite Muslim.
Telephones: 231 000 (1977).
Daily newspapers: 33 (1976).
  Total circulation: 281 000 (15 dailies).
Radio: 1 600 000 (1976).
TV: 450 000 (1977).
Length of roadways: 4598 miles *7400 km* (31 Dec. 1971).
Length of railways: 138 miles *222 km*.
Universities: 5.
Adult illiteracy: Males 21·5%; females 42·1%

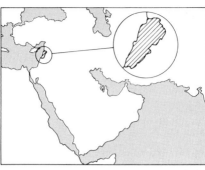

LEBANON
(population aged 10 and over, 1970).
Expectation of life: Males 61·4 years; females 65·1 years (UN estimates for 1970–75).
Defence: Military service: voluntary; total armed forces 23 750 (1981); defence expenditure, 1981: $253 million.
Cinemas: 170 (seating capacity 86 600) and 2 drive-ins (1972).

Lesotho

Official name: The Kingdom of Lesotho.
Population: 1 700 000 (1983 estimate).
Area: 11 720 miles² *30 355 km²*.
Languages: Sesotho, English.
Religion: Christian 73·4% (1966).
Capital city: Maseru, population 45 000 (1976 census).
Other principal towns: Mafeteng, Leribe, Mohale's Hoek.
Highest point: Thabana Ntlenyana (Thadentsonyane), 11 425 ft *3482 m*.
Principal mountain range: Drakensberg.
Principal rivers: Orange, Caledon (on northern frontier).
Head of State: King Motlotlehi Moshoeshoe II (b. 2 May 1938).
Prime Minister: Chief (Joseph) Leabua Jonathan (b. 30 Oct. 1914).
Climate: In lowlands, maximum temperature in summer 32°C *90°F*, winter minimum −6°C *20°F*. Range wider in highlands. Average annual rainfall 29 in *736 mm*. Rainy season October–April.
Labour force: 436 696 (excluding absentee workers) aged 15 and over (1966 census); 581 000 (mid-1970); Agriculture, forestry and fishing 89·7% (ILO estimates).
Gross domestic product: 95·0 million maloti in year ending 31 Mar. 1975: Agriculture, forestry and fishing 47·5%; Trade, restaurants and hotels 17·4% (trade 14·3%); Owner-occupied dwellings 11·3%.
Exports: 38 million maloti in 1982.
Monetary unit: Loti (plutal: maloti). 1 loti = 100 lisente.
Denominations:
  Coins 1, 2, 5, 10, 25, 50 lisente; 1 loti.
  Notes 2, 5, 10 maloti.
Exchange rate to £ sterling: 2·5905 (14 Jan. 1985).
Political history and government: An hereditary monarchy, formerly the British colony of Basutoland. Granted internal self-government, with the Paramount Chief as King, on 30 April 1965. Became independent (under present name), within the Commonwealth, on 4 Oct. 1966. Under the constitution, legislative power was vested in a bicameral Parliament, comprising a Senate of 33 members (22 Chiefs and 11 Senators nominated by the King for 5-year terms) and a National Assembly of 60 members elected by universal adult suffrage for 5 years (subject to dissolution). Executive power is exercised by the Cabinet, led by the Prime Minister, which is responsible to Parliament. The Assembly elections of 27 Jan. 1970 were annulled three days later by the Prime Minister, who declared a state of emergency and suspended the constitution. The Cabinet assumed full power. No more elections have been held but an interim National Assembly of 93 members (the former Senate and

60 nominated members) was inaugurated on 27 Apr. 1973. Lesotho comprises 9 administrative districts, each under an appointed District Administrator.
Telephones: 5409 (1983).
Daily newspapers: 1 (1976).
Total circulation: 1300.
Radio: 37 786.
Length of roadways: 2485 miles *4000 km* (31 Dec. 1979).
Length of railways: 1 mile *1½km.*
Universities: 1.
Adult illiteracy: 41·2% (males 55·9%; females 32·2%) in 1966 (excl. absentee workers).
Expectation of life: Males 46·7 years; females 48·9 years (UN estimates for 1970–75).
Defence: Plans to form an army were announced in 1979.
Cinemas: 2 (seating capacity 800) in 1971.
Foreign tourists: 150 000 in 1980.

Liberia

Official name: The Republic of Liberia.
Population: 1 900 000 (1981 estimate).
Area: 43 000 miles² *111 369 km².*
Languages: English (official), tribal languages.
Religions: Christian; Muslim and Animist minorities.
Capital city: Monrovia, population 306 460 (1981 estimate).
Other principal towns: Harbel, Buchanan, Greenville (Sinoe), Harper (Cape Palmas).
Highest point: On Mt Nimba, 4500 ft *1372 m.*
Principal mountain range: Guinea Highlands.
Principal rivers: St Paul, St John, Cess.
Head of State: Master Sgt Samuel Kanyon Doe (b. 6 May 1952), Chairman of the People's Redemption Council.
Climate: Tropical (hot and humid), with temperatures from 13°C *55°F* to 49°C *120°F.* Rainy season April to October. In Monrovia, average maximum 27°C *80°F* (July, August) to 30°C *87°F* (March, April), minimum 22°C *72°F* to 23°C *74°F* all year round, June and September rainiest (each 26 days).
Labour force: 409 372 (excl. 23 499 persons seeking work for the first time) at 1974 census: Agriculture, forestry and fishing 75·7%; Community, social and personal services 10·6%.
Gross domestic product: L$699·7 million in 1977: Agriculture, forestry and fishing 16·0%; Mining and quarrying 22·6%; Trade, restaurants and hotels 10·9%; Community, social and personal services (incl. all government services) 16·6%.
Exports: US$529·2 million in 1981: Coffee 3·7%; Cocoa 2·6%; Iron ore and concentrates 61·5%; Logs and lumber 7%.
Monetary unit: Liberian dollar (L$). 1 dollar = 100 cents.

Denominations:
Coins 1, 2, 5, 10, 25, 50 cents; 1, 5 Liberian dollar.
Notes 1, 5, 10, 20 US dollars (There are no Liberian banknotes).
Exchange rate to £ sterling: 1·254 (23 April 1985).
Political history and government: Settled in 1822 by freed slaves from the USA. Became independent on 26 July 1847. The constitution was modelled on that of the USA. Legislative power was vested in a bicameral Congress, comprising a Senate and a House of Representatives, both chambers elected by universal adult suffrage. Executive power was vested in the President, also directly elected. On 26 Apr. 1979, following anti-government riots, Congress granted the President emergency powers for one year. Leaders of opposition party were arrested on 9 Mar. 1980 and charged with attempting to overthrow the government. They were due to face trial on 14 Apr. but on 12 Apr. the President was deposed and killed in a military *coup.* Power was assumed by a People's Redemption Council (PRC), which released the former President's opponents. On 25 Apr. 1980 the PRC suspended the constitution and imposed martial law. Executive power was vested in the PRC, which appoints the Cabinet. On 26 July 1981 members of the Cabinet (then mainly civilians) were all given military ranks.
Telephones: 7736 (1980).
Daily newspapers: 3 (1976).
Total circulation: 8000 (2 dailies).
Radio: 320 000 (1982).
TV: 21 000 (1982).
Length of roadways: 6971 miles *11 218 km* (31 Dec. 1977).
Length of railways: 304 miles *490 km.*
Universities: 1.
Adult illiteracy: 91·1% (males 86·1%; females 95·8%) illiterate in English in 1962.
Expectation of life: Males 45·8 years; females 44·0 years (1971).
Defence: Total armed forces 5600 (1984); defence expenditure, 1981: $21 million.
Cinemas: 19 (seating capacity 11 900) and 3 mobile units (1977).
Foreign tourists: 6000 in 1976.

Libya

Official name: Daulat Libiya al-'Arabiya al-Ishtrakiya al-Jumhuriya (Socialist People's Libyan Arab Jamahiriya – 'state of the masses').
Population: 3 500 000 (1982 estimate).
Area: 679 363 miles² *1 759 540 km².*
Language: Arabic.
Religion: Muslim.
Capital city: Tripoli (Tarābulus), population 980 000.
Other principal towns (1973): Benghazi 219 317; Misrātah (Misurata) 42 815; Az Zawiyah (Zawia) 39 382; Al Baida 31 796; Ajdabiyah (Agedabia) 31 047; Derna 30 241; Sabhah (Sebha) 28 714; Tubruq (Tobruk) 28 061.
Highest point: Pico Bette, 7500 ft *2286 m.*
Principal mountain ranges: Jabal as-Sawdā, Al Kufrah, Al Harūj al-Aswad, Jabal Nafūsah, Hamada de Tinrhert.
Principal river: Wādi al-Fārigh.
Head of State: Col Mu'ammar Muhammad Abdulsalam Abu Miniar al-Qadhafi (b. Sept. 1942), Revolutionary Leader.
Head of Government: Muhammad az-Zarruq Rajab, Secretary-General of the General People's Congress.
Climate: Very hot and dry, with average temperatures between 13°C *55°F* and 38°C *100°F.* Coast cooler than inland. In Tripoli, August hottest (22°C *72°F* to 30°C *86°F*), January coolest (8°C *47°F* to 16°C *61°F*). Absolute maximum temperature 57,3°C *135·1°F,* Al 'Aziziyah (El Azizia), 24 Aug. 1923; absolute minimum −9°C +*15·8°F,* Hon, 10 Jan. 1938.
Labour force: 773 200 (excl. armed forces and unemployed) in 1978: Agriculture, forestry and fishing 20·8%; Construction 23·1%; Community, social and personal services 26·9%.
Gross domestic product: 5911·5 million dinars in

1978: Mining and quarrying 56·1%; Construction 11·3%; Government services 11·1%.
Exports: US$15 466 million in 1981.
Monetary unit: Libyan dinar. 1 dinar = 1000 dirhams.
Denominations:
Coins 1, 5, 10, 20, 50, 100 dirhams.
Notes 250, 500 dirhams; 1, 5, 10 dinars.
Exchange rate to £ sterling: 0·329 (14 Jan. 1985).
Political history and Government: Formerly part of Turkey's Ottoman Empire. Became an Italian colony in September 1911. Italian forces were expelled in 1942–43 and the country was under British and French administration from 1943 until becoming an independent kingdom, under the Amir of Cyrenaica, on 24 Dec. 1951. The monarchy was overthrown by an army *coup* on 1 Sept. 1969, when a Revolutionary Command Council (RCC) took power and proclaimed the Libyan Arab Republic. The bicameral Parliament was abolished and political activity suspended. On 8 Sept. 1969 the RCC elected Col Mu'ammar al-Qadhafi as its Chairman. A provisional constitution, proclaimed in December 1969, vested supreme authority in the RCC, which appointed a Council of Ministers. On 11 June 1971 the Arab Socialist Union (ASU) was established as the sole political party. Under a decree of 13 Nov. 1975 provision was made for the creation of a 618-member General National Congress of the ASU. This later became the General People's Congress (GPC), comprising members of the RCC, leaders of existing 'people's congresses' and 'popular committees', and trade unions and professional organizations. The Congress held its first session on 5–18 Jan. 1976. On 2 Mar. 1977 the GPC approved a new constitution, which adopted the country's present name. Under the constitution, the RCC and Council of Ministers were abolished and power passed to the GPC, assisted by a General Secretariat. The Council of Ministers was replaced by a General People's Committee. The first Secretary-General of the GPC was Col Qadhafi. At a GPC meeting on 1–2 Mar. 1979 he relinquished this post, although remaining Supreme Commander of the Armed Forces. Libya is divided into 10 governorates.
Telephones: 64 000 (1973).
Daily newspapers: 1 (1983).
Total circulation: 40 000.
Radio: 150 000 (1982).
TV: 160 000 (1982).
Length of roadways: c. 3232 miles c. *5200 km.*
Universities: 2.
Adult illiteracy: 49·9% (males 33·1%; females 69·9%) in 1973 (population aged 10 and over).
Expectation of life: Males 51·4 years; females 54·5 years (UN estimates for 1970–75).
Defence: Military service: conscription; total armed forces 70 500 (1984); defence expenditure, 1978: $448 million.
Cinemas: 52 (seating capacity 31 000) in 1977.
Foreign tourists: 125 692 (incl. short-stay visits) in 1977.

Liechtenstein

Official name: Fürstentum Liechtenstein (Principality of Liechtenstein).
Population: 25 215 (census of 1980); 26 380 (estimate for 1982).
Area: 61·8 miles² *160·0 km².*
Language: German.
Religions: Roman Catholic; Protestant minority.
Capital city: Vaduz, population 4904 in 1982 (estimate).
Other principal towns (1979): Schaan 4636; Balzers 3234; Triesen 2935; Eschen 2700; Mauren 2584; Triesenberg 2099.
Highest point: Grauspitze, 8526 ft *2599 m.*
Principal mountain range: Alps.
Principal rivers: Rhein (Rhine) (820 miles *1319 km,* 17 miles *27 km* in Liechtenstein), Samina.
Head of State: Prince Franz Josef II (b. 16 Aug. 1906).

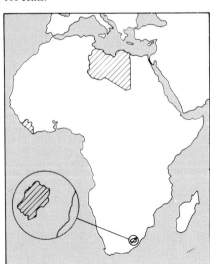

top: **LIBYA**
left: **LIBERIA**
encircled: **LESOTHO**

Head of Government: Hans Brunhart (b. 28 Mar. 1945).
Climate: Alpine, with mild winters. Temperature extremes for Sargans, in Switzerland, a few miles from the Liechtenstein border: absolute maximum 38,0°C *100·4°F*, 29 July 1947; absolute minimum −25,6°C −*14·1°F*, 12 Feb. 1929.
Labour force: 11 598 (excl. unemployed) in 1979: Industry, commerce and construction 54·6%; Other services 41·5%.
Exports: 894 million Swiss francs in 1982.
Monetary unit: Swiss currency (*q.v.*).
Political history and government: An hereditary principality, independent since 1866. Present constitution adopted on 5 Oct. 1921. Legislative power is exercised jointly by the Sovereign and the unicameral Diet (*Landtag*), with 15 members elected (by men only) for 4 years, using proportional representation. A 5-man Government (*Regierung*) is elected by the Diet for its duration and confirmed by the Sovereign.
Telephones: 10 986 (1982).
Daily newspapers: 2 (1982).
  Total circulation: 15 200.
Radio: 8068 (1982).
TV: 7608 (1982).
Length of railways: 11·5 miles *18·5 km*.
Cinemas: 3 (seating capacity 900) in 1971.
Foreign tourists: 73 657 in 1979.

Luxembourg

Official name: Grand-Duché de Luxembourg (French), Grouscherzogdem Lezebuurg (Luxembourgois) or Grossherzogtum Luxemburg (German): Grand Duchy of Luxembourg.
Population: 364 600 (1981 census); 365 800 (1983 estimate).
Area: 999 miles² *2586 km²*.
Languages: Letzeburgesch (Luxembourgois), French, German.
Religion: Roman Catholic.
Capital city: Luxembourg-Ville, population 78 900 (1981 census).
Other principal towns (1981): Esch-sur-Alzette 25 500; Differdange 17 100; Dudelange 14 100; Petange 12 300.
Highest point: Bourgplatz, 1833 ft *559 m*.
Principal mountain range: Ardennes.
Principal rivers: Mosel (Moselle), Sûre (107 miles *172 km*, 99 miles *159 km* in Luxembourg), Our, Alzette.
Head of State: HRH Prince Jean Benoît Guillaume Marie Robert Louis Antoine Adolphe Marc d'Aviano (b. 5 Jan. 1921), Grand Duke.
Head of Government: Jacques Santer (b. 18 May 1937), President of the Government (Prime Minister).
Climate: Temperate (cool summers and mild winters). Absolute maximum temperature 37,0°C *98·6°F*, Luxembourg-Ville, 28 July 1895, and Grevenmacher, 6 July 1957; absolute minimum −24,3°C −*11·7°F*, Wiltz, 5 Feb. 1917.
Labour force: 158 500 aged 15 and over in 1983: Agriculture 4·7%; Industry 36·7%; Services 58·6%.
Gross domestic product: 181 400 million francs in 1982: Mining and manufacturing 26·5% (manufacturing 26·4%); Trade, services and restaurants 29·8% (distributive trades, hotels and catering 16%, services, construction and transport 13·8%); Banking, finance and insurance 12%; Government services 12·3%; Other services 16%; Agriculture and forestry 3·4%.
Exports: 111 421 million Luxembourg francs in 1983: Iron and steel 43·9%; Plastic and rubber manufactures 14·2%; Textile products 6·4%; Animals and animal products 2·8%.
Monetary unit: Luxembourg franc. 1 franc = 100 centimes.
Denominations:
  Coins 25 centimes; 1, 5, 10, 20 Luxembourg francs.
  Notes 50, 100 Luxembourg francs; 50, 100, 500, 1000, 5000 Belgian francs.
Exchange rate to £ sterling: 77·87 (16 Apr. 1985).
Political history and government: An hereditary grand duchy, independent since 1867. Luxem-

bourg is a constitutional monarchy. Legislative power is exercised by the unicameral Chamber of Deputies, with 64 members elected by universal adult suffrage for 5 years (subject to dissolution) on the basis of proportional representation. Some legislative functions are also entrusted to the advisory Council of State, with 21 members appointed for life by the Grand Duke, but the Council can be overridden by the Chamber. Executive power is vested in the Grand Duke but is normally exercised by the Council of Ministers, led by the President of the Government. The Grand Duke appoints Ministers but they are responsible to the Chamber. Luxembourg is divided into 12 cantons.
Telephones: 142 134 (1983).
Daily newspapers: 6 (1982).
  Total circulation: 130 000.
Radio: 182 000 (1978).
TV: 122 470 (1981).
Length of roadways: 3205 miles *5157 km* (1983).
Length of railways: 170 miles *274 km*.
Universities: 1.
Expectation of life: Males 66·9 years; females 73·4 years (1982).
Defence: Military service voluntary; total armed forces 720 (1983); defence expenditure, 2103·6 million Luxembourg francs (1983).
Cinemas: 14 in 1984.

Madagascar

Official name: Repoblika Demokratika n'i Madagaskar (in Malagasy) or République démocratique de Madagascar (in French): Democratic Republic of Madagascar.
Population: 9 472 000 (1983 estimate).
Area: 226 658 miles² *587 041 km²*.
Languages: Malagasy, French (both official).
Religions: Animist, Christian, Muslim.
Capital city: Antananarivo (Tananarive), population 400 000 (1978 estimate).
Other principal towns (1978): Toamasina 59 100; Mahajanga 57 500; Fianarantsoa 55 500; Antseranana 48 000; Toliary 34 000.
Highest point: Maromokotro, 9436 ft *2876 m*.
Principal mountain ranges: Massif du Tsaratanan, Ankaratra.
Principal rivers: Ikopa, Mania, Mangoky.
Head of State: Lt-Cdr Didier Ratsiraka (b. 4 Nov. 1936), President.
Prime Minister: Lt-Col Désiré Rakotoarijaona (b. 19 June 1934).
Climate: Hot on coast (average daily maximum 32°C *90°F*), but cooler inland. Fairly dry in south, but monsoon rains (December to April) in north. In Antananarivo, average maximum 20°C *68°F* (July) to 27°C *81°F* (November), minimum 8°C *48°F* (July, August) to 16°C *61°F* (January, February), January rainiest (21 days). Absolute maximum temperature 44·4°C *111·9°F*, Behara, 20 Nov. 1940; absolute minimum −6·3°C +*20·7°F*, Antsirabé, 18 June 1945.
Labour force: 3 622 000 (1970): Agriculture, forestry and fishing 89·4% (ILO estimates); 4 177 000 (official estimate, 1975).
Gross domestic product: 372 853 million Malagasy francs in 1974: Agriculture, forestry and fishing 42·8%; Manufacturing 12·2%; Trade 11·2%; Government services 11·6%.
Exports: 84 781 million Malagasy francs in 1980: Coffee 53%; Cloves 8%.
Monetary unit: Franc malgache (Malagasy franc). 1 franc = 100 centimes.
Denominations:
  Coins 1, 2, 5, 10, 50, 100 francs.
  Notes 50, 100, 500, 1000, 5000 francs.
Exchange rate to £ sterling: 725·70 (14 Jan. 1985).
Political history and government: Formerly a French colony, Madagascar became the Malagasy Republic on achieving self-government, within the French community, on 14 Oct. 1958. It became fully independent on 26 June 1960. Following disturbances, the President handed over full powers to the army commander on 18 May 1972, when Parliament was dissolved. A

LIECHTENSTEIN

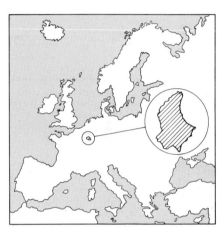
LUXEMBOURG

National Military Directorate was formed on 12 Feb. 1975 and suspended all political parties. On 15 June 1975 the Directorate elected Lt-Cdr Didier Ratsiraka to be Head of State, as President of the Supreme Revolutionary Council (SRC). A referendum on 21 Dec. 1975 approved a draft constitution and the appointment of Ratsiraka as Head of State for 7 years. The Democratic Republic of Madagascar was proclaimed on 30 Dec. 1975 and Ratsiraka took office as President of the Republic on 4 Jan. 1976.

Executive power is vested in the President, who rules with the assistance of the SRC and an appointed Council of Ministers. Legislative power is vested in the National People's Assembly, with 137 members elected by universal adult suffrage for 5 years. The Assembly was first elected on 30 June 1977, with a single list of candidates presented by the *Front national pour la défense de la révolution malgache*, a pro-government alliance of political parties. The country is divided into 6 provinces.
Telephones: 28 686 (1978).
Daily newspapers: 12 (1977).
  Total circulation: 59 000 (9 dailies in 1974).
Radio: 1 150 000 (1979).
TV: 9000 (1980).
Length of roadways: 17 092 miles *27 507 km* (31 Dec. 1976).
Length of railways: 549 miles *884 km* (1978).
Universities: 1.
Adult illiteracy: 66·5% (males 59·2%; females 73·0%) illiterate in Malagasy in 1953 (indigenous population aged 14 and over).
Expectation of life: Males 41·9 years; females 45·1 years (UN estimates for 1970–75).
Defence: Military service 18 months; total armed forces 21 100 (1984); defence expenditure, 1979: $102 million.
Cinemas: 31 (seating capacity 12 400) in 1974.
Foreign tourists: 9089 in 1977.

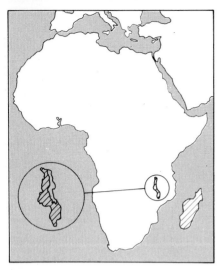

encircled: **MALAWI**
right: **MADAGASCAR**

Malawi

Official name: The Republic of Malaŵi.
Population: 5 547 460 (census of 20 Sept. 1977); 6 838 800 (estimate for 1 July 1984).
Area: 45 747 miles² *118 484 km²*.
Languages: English (official), Chichewa.
Religions: Mainly traditional beliefs; Christians form 33% of population; Moslem minority.
Capital city: Lilongwe, population 124 000 (1982 estimate).
Other principal towns (1982 estimate): Blantyre 258 000; Zomba 38 000; Mzuzu 39 000.
Highest point: Mount Sapitwa, 9843 ft *3000 m*.
Principal river: Shire.
Head of State: Dr Hastings Kamuzu Banda (b. 14 May 1906), President.
Climate: In the low-lying Shire valley temperatures can rise to 46°C *115°F* in October and November, but above 3000 ft *910 m* the climate is much more temperate and at the greatest heights the nights can be frosty. Dry season May to September, very wet season late December to March. Annual rainfall in the highlands is about 1270 mm *50 in* and in the lowlands 900 mm *35 in.*
Labour force: 2 288 351 (1977 census): Agriculture, forestry and fishing 86·2%.
Gross domestic product: 826 million Kwacha in 1983: Agriculture, forestry and fishing (including all non-monetary output) about 43%.
Exports: K247 886 000 in 1982: Food and live animals 30% (tea 18%); tobacco (unmanufactured) 59%.
Monetary unit: Malawi kwacha. 1 kwacha = 100 tambala.
Denominations:
  Coins 1, 2, 5, 10, 20 tambala.
  Notes 50 tambala; 1, 5, 10 kwacha.
Exchange rate to £ sterling: 0·5609 in 1984.
Political history and government: Formerly the British protectorate of Nyasaland. Granted internal self-government on 1 Feb. 1963 and became independent, within the Commonwealth, on 6 July 1964, taking the name Malawi. Became a republic, and a one-party state, on 6 July 1966, when Dr Hastings Banda (Prime Minister since 1963) became President. Under a constitutional amendment of Nov. 1970, he became President for life on 6 July 1971. Legislative power is held by the unicameral National Assembly, with 87 members elected by universal adult suffrage for 5 years (subject to dissolution) and up to 15 additional members nominated by the President. All members must belong to the ruling Malawi Congress Party. All candidates were returned unopposed in 1964, 1971 and 1976 but on 29 June 1978 voting took place (for 47 seats) for the first time since 1961. Executive power is vested in the President, who rules with the assistance of an appointed Cabinet. Malawi has three administrative

regions, each the responsibility of a Cabinet Minister.
Telephones: 36 557 in 1982.
Daily newspapers: 1 (1984).
  Total circulation: 14 000.
Radios: 26 760 (1981).
Length of roadways: 6680 miles *10 772 km* (1982).
Length of railways: 415 miles *677 km* (1982).
Universities: 1 (with five constituent colleges).
Adult illiteracy: 75% (males 60%; females 80%) in 1982.
Expectation of Life: Males 46 years; females 50 years (Africans only, 1982).
Defence: Total armed forces 4000 (1984); defence expenditure in 1984: K25 million.
Cinemas: 4 (seating capacity 2300), 13 mobile units and 2 drive-ins (capacity 2400) in 1984.
Foreign tourists: 52 569 in 1982.

Malaysia

Official name: Persekutuan Tanah Melaysiu (Federation of Malaysia).
Population: 14 420 000 (1982 estimate).
Area: 127 581 miles² *330 433 km²*.
Languages: Malay (official), Chinese, Tamil, Iban, English.
Religions (1970): Muslim 50·0%; Buddhist 25·7%; Hindu; Christian.
Capital city: Kuala Lumpur, population 937 875 (1980 census).
Other principal towns (1980): Ipoh 300 727; Georgetown 250 578; Johore Bharu 249 880; Kuala Trengganu 186 608; Kota Bharu 170 559; Kuantan 136 625; Seremban 136 252; Kuching 120 000.
Highest point: Mount Kinabalu, 13 455 ft *4101 m*, in Sabah.
Principal mountain range: Trengganu Highlands.
Principal rivers: Pahang, Kelantan.
Head of State: HM Sultan Mahmood Iskandar ibni Al-Marhum Sultan Ismail DK, SPMJ, SPDK, DK (Brunei) SSIJ, PIS, BSI, *Yang di-Pertuan Agong* (Supreme Head of State).
Prime Minister: Dato Seri Dr Mahathir bin Mohamad (b. 20 Dec. 1925).
Climate: Peninsular Malaysia is hot and humid, with daytime temperatures around 29°C *85°F* and little variation throughout the year. The average daily range on the coast is 22°C *72°F* to 33°C *92°F*. Rainfall is regular and often heavy. Maximum recorded temperature 39,4°C *103·0°F*, Pulau Langkawi, 27 Mar. 1931; minimum 2,2°C *36·0°F*, Cameron Highlands, 6 Jan. 1937.
  Sabah is generally fairly humid but relatively cool. In Kota Kinabalu, average temperatures are 23°C *74°F* to 31°C *87°F*, average annual rainfall 2640 mm *104 in.* The north-east monsoon is from mid-October to March or April, the south-west monsoon from May to August.
  Sarawak is humid, with temperatures generally 22°C *72°F* to 31°C *88°F*, sometimes reaching 36°C *96°F*. It has heavy rainfall (annual average 3050 mm *120 in* to 4060 mm *160 in*), especially in the north-east monsoon season (October to March).
Labour force: 3 455 318 (including unemployed) aged 10 and over (1970 census): Agriculture, forestry and fishing 53·5%; Commerce 10·2%.
Gross domestic product: 12 955 million ringgit (Peninsular Malaysia only) in 1971: Agriculture, forestry and fishing 29·0% (agriculture 20·0%); Manufacturing 14·8%; Trade, restaurants and hotels 13·9% (trade 12·8%); Community, social and personal services 14·3% (government services 12·1%).
Exports: US$6079·3 million in 1977: Natural rubber 22·6%; Wood, lumber and cork 15·8% (sawlogs and veneer logs 10·1%); Petroleum and petroleum products 14·3% (crude petroleum 12·7%); Palm oil 11·2%; Tin metal 11·4%.
Monetary unit: Ringgit (Malaysian dollar). 1 ringgit = 100 sen.
Denominations:
  Coins 1, 5, 10, 20, 50 sen; 1, 5, 10, 15, 25, 100, 200, 250, 500 ringgit.
  Notes 1, 5, 10, 50, 100, 1000 ringgit.

Exchange rate to £ sterling: 2·7782 (14 Jan. 1985).
Political history and government: Peninsular (West) Malaysia comprises 11 states (nine with hereditary rulers, two with Governors) formerly under British protection. They were united as the Malayan Union on 1 Apr. 1946 and became the Federation of Malaya on 1 Feb. 1948. The Federation became independent, within the Commonwealth, on 31 Aug. 1957. On 16 Sept. 1963 the Federation (renamed the States of Malaya) was merged with Singapore (*q.v.*), Sarawak (a British colony) and Sabah (formerly the colony of British North Borneo) to form the independent Federation of Malaysia, still in the Commonwealth. On 9 Aug. 1965 Singapore seceded from the Federation. On 5 Aug. 1966 the States of Malaya were renamed West Malaysia, now known as Peninsular Malaysia.
  Malaysia is an elective monarchy. The nine state rulers of Peninsula Malaysia choose from their number a Supreme Head of State and a Deputy, to hold office for 5 years. Executive power is vested in the Head of State but is normally exercised on the advice of the Cabinet. Legislative power is held by the bicameral Parliament. The Senate (*Dewan Negara*), with limited powers, has 58 members, including 32 appointed by the Head of State and 26 (two from each state) elected by State Legislative Assemblies for 6 years. The House of Representatives (*Dewan Rakyat*) has 154 members (114 from Peninsular Malaysia, 16 from Sabah and 24 from Sarawak) elected by universal adult suffrage for 5 years (subject to dissolution). The Head of State appoints the Prime Minister and, on the latter's recommendation, other Ministers. The cabinet is responsible to Parliament.
  Malaysia comprises 13 states and, since 1 Feb. 1974, the Federal Territory of Kuala Lumpur. Each state has a unicameral Legislative Assembly, elected by universal adult suffrage.
Telephones: 946 367 (1982).
Daily newspapers: 37 (1976).
  Total circulation: 1 834 000 (35 dailies).
Radio: 1 500 000 (1977).
TV: 665 000 (1977).
Length of roadways: 25 766 miles *41 458 km* (1982).
Length of railways: 1103 miles *1775 km*.
Universities: 5.
Adult illiteracy: 42·0% (males 30·9%; females 53·2%) in 1970 (population aged 10 and over): Peninsular Malaysia 39·2%; Sabah 55·7%; Sarawak 61·7%.
Expectation of life: Males 57·3 years; females 60·9 years (UN estimates for 1970–75).
Defence: Military service voluntary; total armed forces 102 000 (1984); defence expenditure, 1981: US$2250 million.
Cinemas: 425 plus 350 mobile units (1977).
Foreign tourists: 1 462 000 (Peninsula Malaysia only) in 1979, excluding visitors from Singapore by road through Johore Bahru.

Maldives

Official name: Dhivehi Jumhuriya (Republic of Maldives).
Population: 143 046 (census of 1 Jan. 1978); 158 500 (1983 estimate).
Area: 115 miles² *298 km²*.
Language: Dhivehi (Maldivian).
Religion: Muslim.
Capital city: Malé, population 29 555 at 1978 census.
Head of State: Maumoon Abdul Gayoom (b. 29 Dec. 1937), President.
Climate: Very warm and humid. Average temperature 27°C *80°F*, with little daily variation. Annual rainfall 2540–3800 mm *100–150 in.*
Labour force: 60 259 (Dec. 1977).
Gross domestic product: $10 million in 1975 (UN estimate).
Exports: 23·0 million Maldivian rupees in 1979: Fresh fish 56·1%; Dried salt fish 36·4%.
Monetary unit: Rufiyaa (Maldivian rupee). 1 rufiyaa = 100 laaris (larees).

Denominations:
Notes 1, 2, 5, 10, 50, 100 rufiyaa.
Exchange rate to £ sterling: 8·388 (14 Jan. 1985).
Political history and government: Formerly an elective sultanate, called the Maldive Islands. Under British protection, with internal self-government, from December 1887 until achieving full independence, outside the Commonwealth, on 26 July 1965. Following a referendum in March 1968, the islands became a republic on 11 Nov. 1968, with Ibrahim Nasir (Prime Minister since 1954) as President. Name changed to Maldives in April 1969. Legislative power is held by the unicameral Citizens' Council (*Majilis*), with 48 members, including eight appointed by the President and 40 (two from each of 20 districts) elected for five years by universal adult suffrage. Executive power is vested in the President, also directly elected for five years. He rules with the assistance of an appointed Cabinet, responsible to the *Majilis*. Near the end of his second term, President Nasir announced his wish to retire. The *Majilis* chose a single candidate who was approved by referendum on 28 July 1978 and sworn in on 11 Nov. 1978. There are no political parties. The country has 20 administrative districts: the capital is centrally administered while each of the 19 atoll groups is governed by an appointed atoll chief (*verin*) who is appointed by the President and advised by an elected committee.
Telephones: 1540 (1982).
Daily newspapers: 1 (1977).
Radio: 2900 (1977).
Cinemas: 2 (seating capacity 800) in 1969.
Foreign tourists: 33 140 in 1979.

Mali

Official name: La République du Mali (the Republic of Mali).
Population: 7 492 000 (1983 estimate).
Area: 478 767 miles² *1 240 000 km²*.
Languages: French (official language); Bambara 60%; Fulani.
Religions: Sunni Muslim 65%; traditional beliefs 30%.
Capital city: Bamako, population 404 022 (including suburbs) at 1976 census.
Other principal towns (1976): Ségou 65 000; Mopti 54 000; Sikasso 47 000; Kayes 45 000.
Highest point: Hombori Tondo, 3789 ft *1155 m*.
Principal mountain ranges: Mandingué Plateau, Adrar des Iforas.
Principal rivers: Sénégal, Niger, Faléme.
Head of State: Gen. Moussa Traoré (b. 25 Sept. 1936), President; also President of the Government (Prime Minister).
Climate: Hot. Very dry in the north, wetter in the south (rainy season June to Oct.). Average temperatures in the south 24°C *75°F* to 32°C *90°F*, higher in the Sahara. In Bamako, average maximum 30°C *87°F* (August) to 39°C *103°F* (April), minimum 16°C *61°F* to 24°C *76°F*. In Timbuktu, average maximum 30°C *87°F* (August) to 43°C *110°F* (May), minimum 13°C *55°F* (Jan.) to 26°C *80°F* (June), July and August rainiest (each 9 days).
Labour force: 2 850 000 (1970): Agriculture, forestry and fishing 91·0% (ILO estimates).
Gross domestic product: 166 900 million Mali francs in 1971; $507 million (estimate) in 1975.
Exports: 83 830 million Mali francs in 1981.
Monetary unit: Franc malien (Mali franc).
Denominations:
Coins 5, 10, 25 francs.
Notes 50, 100, 500, 1000, 5000, 10 000 francs.
Exchange rate to £ sterling: 542·25 (14 Jan. 1985).
Political history and government: Formerly French Sudan, part of French West Africa. Joined Senegal to form the Federation of Mali on 4 Apr. 1959. By agreement with France, signed on 4 Apr. 1960, the Federation became independent on 20 June 1960. Senegal seceded on 20 Aug. 1960 and the remnant of the Federation was proclaimed the Republic of Mali on 22 Sept. 1960. The elected National Assembly was dissolved on 17 Jan. 1968. The government

was overthrown by an army *coup* on 19 Nov. 1968, when a Military Committee for National Liberation (CMLN), led by Lt (later Brig-Gen) Moussa Traoré, was established. The constitution was abrogated and political parties banned. The CMLN ruled by decree with the assistance of an appointed Council of Ministers. The President of the CMLN assumed the functions of Head of State on 6 Dec. 1968 and became also Prime Minister on 19 Sept. 1969. The CMLN published a new constitution on 26 Apr. 1974 and it was approved by referendum on 2 June 1974. This provides for a one-party state with an elected President and National Assembly, with the CMLN remaining in power for a transitional period of five years. The formation of the ruling party, the *Union démocratique du peuple malien* (UDPM), was announced on 22 Sept. 1976. The UDPM was formally constituted on 30 Mar. 1979 and nominated Traoré as presidential candidate on 18 May. Elections were held on 19 June 1979 for a National Assembly (82 members serving a four-year term) and for a President (with a five-year term). Mali has eight administrative regions.
Telephones: 8485 (1982).
Daily newspapers: 2 (1976).
Total circulation: 3000 (1 daily in 1974).
Radio: 95 000 (1982).
Length of roadways: 9137 miles *14 704 km* (31 Dec. 1976).
Length of railways: 398 miles *640 km*.
Adult illiteracy: 97·5% (males 96%; females 99%) in 1962 (UNESCO estimates).
Expectation of life: Males 39·4 years; females 42·5 years (UN estimates for 1970–75).
Defence: Military service voluntary; total armed forces 4950 (1984); defence expenditure, 1980: $33·4 million.
Cinemas: 19 (seating capacity 17 100) in 1968.
Foreign tourists: 19 853 in 1976.

Malta

Official name: Repubblika ta Malta (Republic of Malta).
Population: 314 765 (census of 26 Nov. 1967); 326 178 (estimate for 31 Dec. 1982).
Area: 122 miles² *316 km²*, including Gozo (25·9 miles² *67 km²*) and Comino (1·07 miles² *2,77 km²*).
Languages: Maltese, English, Italian.
Religion: Roman Catholic.
Capital city: Valletta, population 14 527 (1982).
Other principal town: Sliema, population 20 120 in 1973.
Highest point: 816 ft *249 m*.
Head of State: Miss Agatha Barbara, President.
Prime Minister: Dr Carmelo Mifsud Bonnici.
Climate: Basically healthy without extremes. The temperature rarely drops below 4°C *40°F* and in most years does not rise above 38°C *100°F*. The average annual rainfall in Valletta is 576 mm *22·7 in*. In the summer the nights are cool except when the *Sirocco* desert wind blows from the south-east.
Labour force: 214 252 in Dec. 1982: Agriculture and fisheries 3%; Manufacturing 14%; Services 16·9%.
Gross domestic product: £M277·6 million in 1978: Manufacturing 33·6%; Trade 15·6%; Government services 14·8%.
Exports: £M169 036 000 in 1982: Manufactures 60%; Machinery and transport 11·5%; Semi-manufactures 10·3%.
Monetary unit: Maltese pound (£M). 1 pound = 100 cents = 1000 mils.
Denominations:
Coins 2, 3, 5 mils; 1, 2, 5, 10, 25, 50 cents.
Notes 1, 5, 10 pounds.
Exchange rate to £ sterling: 0·545 (14 Jan. 1985).
Political history and government: A former British colony. Became independent, within the Commonwealth, on 21 Sept. 1964. A republic since 13 Dec. 1974, when the Governor-General became President. Legislative power is held by the unicameral House of Representatives, with 65 members elected for 5 years (subject to dissolution) by universal adult suffrage, using

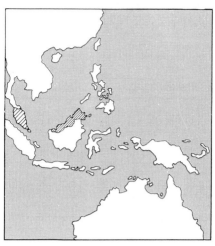

MALAYSIA

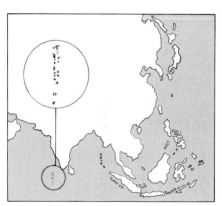

MALDIVES

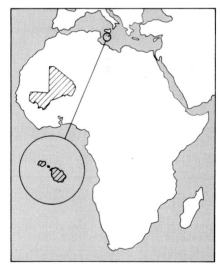

left: **MALI**

encircled: **MALTA**

proportional representation. The President is a constitutional Head of State, elected for 5 years by the House, and executive power is exercised by the Cabinet. The President appoints the Prime Minister and, on the latter's recommendation, other Ministers. The Cabinet is responsible to the House.
Telephones: 98 125 (1982)
Daily newspapers: 4 (1982).
Radio: 85 000 (1977).
TV: 178 000 (1976).
Length of roadways: 799 miles *1278 km* (1979).
Universities: 1.
Adult illiteracy: 33·5% (males 31%; females 36%) in 1963 (UNESCO estimates).
Expectation of life: Males 68·27 years; females 73·10 years (1976).

Defence: Military service voluntary; total armed forces 800 (1984); defence expenditure, 1981: $8·8 million.
Cinemas: 29 in 1981.
Foreign tourists: 705 710 in 1981.

Mauritania

Official name: République Islamique de Mauritanie (French) or Jumhuriyat Muritaniya al-Islamiya (Arabic): Islamic Republic of Mauritania.
Population: 1 781 000 (1983 estimate).
Area: 397 955 miles² *1 030 700 km²*.
Languages: Arabic, Hassaniya, French.
Religion: Muslim.
Capital city: Nouakchott, population 134 986 (including suburbs) at 1976 census.
Other principal towns (1976): Nouadhibou (Port-Etienne) 21 961; Kaédi 20 848; Zouérate 17 474; Rosso 16 466; Atar 16 326.
Highest point: Kediet Ijill, 3002 ft *915 m*.
Principal river: Sénégal.
Head of State: Lt-Col Mohamed Khouna Ould Haidalla (Kaydalla) (b. 1939), Chairman of the Military Committee for National Salvation.
Prime Minister: Lt-Col Maouya Ould Sidi Ahmed Taya (b. 1943).
Climate: Hot and dry, with breezes on coast. In Nouakchott, average maximum 28°C *83°F* to 34°C *93°F*. In interior, F'Derik has average July maximum of 43°C *109°F*.
Labour force: 363 000 (1970): Agriculture, forestry and fishing 87·5% (ILO estimates).
Gross domestic product: 25 127 million ouguiya in 1978: Agriculture, forestry and fishing 27·2% (agriculture 22·3%); Mining and quarrying 13·1%; Government services 21·4%.
Exports: 12 505 million ouguiya in 1981: Iron ore 65%; Salted and dried fish 35%.
Monetary unit: Ouguiya. 1 ouguiya = 5 khoums.
Denominations:
 Coins 1 khoum; 1, 5, 10, 20 ouguiya.
 Notes 100, 200, 1000 ouguiya.
Exchange rate to £ sterling: 75·90 (14 Jan. 1985).
Political history and government: Formerly part of French West Africa, Mauritania became a self-governing member of the French Community on 28 Nov. 1958. Moktar Ould Daddah became Prime Minister on 23 June 1959. The country became fully independent on 28 Nov. 1960, with Daddah as Head of State. Under the constitution of 20 May 1961, Daddah became President on 20 Aug. 1961. A one-party state, under the Mauritanian People's Party (PPM), was introduced in 1964. On 28 Feb. 1976 Spain ceded Spanish Sahara to Mauritania and Morocco, to be apportioned between them. Mauritania occupied the southern part of this territory, which it named Tiris el-Gharbia.
President Daddah was deposed by the armed forces on 10 July 1978, when power was assumed by a Military Committee for National Recovery (CMRN), led by Lt-Col Moustapha Ould Mohamed Salek. The constitution was suspended and the National Assembly and ruling party dissolved. On 20 July 1978 the new regime published a Constitutional Charter, under which the Chairman of the CMRN would exercise executive authority. On 6 Apr. 1979 the CMRN was replaced by a Military Committee for National Salvation (CMSN), also led by Salek, but he relinquished the post of Prime Minister to Lt-Col Ahmed Ould Bouceif (Bousseif). On 11 Apr. 1979 the CMSN adopted a new Constitution Charter, assuming legislative power for itself and separating the roles of Head of State and Head of Government. Bouceif was killed in an air crash on 27 May and the CMSN appointed a new Prime Minister, Lt-Col Mohamed Khouna Ould Haidalla, on 31 May. Salek, then only titular Head of State, resigned on 3 June 1979, being replaced by Lt-Col Mohamed Mahmoud Ould Ahmed Louly.
Following negotiations with the *Frente Popular para la Liberación de Sakiet el Hamra y Río de Oro* (the Polisario Front), a Saharan nationalist group, Mauritania signed an agreement on 5 Aug. 1979 providing for its withdrawal from its portion of Western (formerly Spanish) Sahara. It formally withdrew on 15 Aug. 1979, although Morocco had previously announced its annexation of the area (in addition to the northern part which it already held).
On 4 Jan. 1980 Louly was deposed by Haidalla, who (despite the previous separation of powers) became Head of State while remaining Prime Minister. He relinquished the premiership on 15 Dec. 1980, when an almost entirely civilian Cabinet was formed. This was replaced on 25 Apr. 1982, when the Army Chief of Staff became Prime Minister.
On 19 Dec. 1980 the CMSN published a draft constitution, to be submitted to a referendum. The constitution envisages a National Assembly, elected for four years, and a President serving a single six-year term. Executive power would be held by the Prime Minister, to be designated by the President (from among the majority in the Assembly) and approved by the Assembly. Political parties would be permitted but the PPM would remain banned.
Telephones: 2000 (1977).
Daily newspapers: 1 (1974).
 Total circulation: 3000.
Radio: 95 000 (1976).
Length of roadways: 4290 miles *6904 km* (31 Dec. 1972).
Length of railways: 404 miles *650 km* (31 Dec. 1977).
Adult illiteracy: 82·6% (population aged 6 and over) in 1977.
Expectation of life: Males 39·4 years; females 42·5 years (UN estimates for 1970–75).
Defence: Total armed forces 8470 (1984); defence expenditure, 1981: $29 million.
Cinemas: 12 (seating capacity 8800) in 1977.
Foreign tourists: 20 700 in 1975.

Mauritius

Population: 851 335 (Mauritius and Rodrigues 850 968, other islands 367) at census of 30 June 1972; 994 000 at 31 Dec. 1982 (estimate).
Area: 789·5 miles² *2045 km²*.
Languages (1962): Hindi 35·5%; Creole 31·0%; Urdu 13·2%, French 6·8%; Tamil 6·3%; Chinese 2·8%; Telugu 2·3%; Marathi 1·6%. The official language is English.
Religions (1962): Hindu 52%; Christian 30%; Muslim 16%.
Capital city: Port Louis, population 149 000 at 31 Dec. 1982 (estimate).
Other principal towns (1979): Beau Bassin-Rose Hill 84 728; Curepipe 55 175; Quatre Bornes 54 509; Vacoas-Phoenix 52 793.
Highest point: Piton de la Rivière Noire (Black River Mountain), 2711 ft *826 m*.
Head of State: HM Queen Elizabeth II, represented by Sir Seewoosagur Ramgoolan (b. 18 Sept. 1900), Governor-General.

Prime Minister: Anerood Jugnauth.
Climate: Generally humid, with south-east trade winds. Average temperatures between 19°C *66°F* at 2000 ft *610 m* and 23°C *75°F* at sea-level. At Vacoas, 1394 ft *425 m*, maximum 37°C *98·6°F*, minimum 8°C *46·4°F*. Average annual rainfall between 890 mm *35 in* and 5080 mm *200 in* on highest parts. Wettest months are January to March. Tropical cyclones between September and May.
Labour force: 260 749 (including unemployed) at 1972 census (island of Mauritius only): Agriculture, forestry and fishing 33·0%; Manufacturing 13·6%; Community, social and personal services 24·7%. The island of Rodrigues had a labour force of 8206.
Gross domestic product: 10 650 million rupees in 1983: Agriculture, forestry and fishing (excl. government) 19·1% (agriculture 18·6%); Manufacturing 21·6%; Trade, restaurants and hotels 12·5% (trade 10·8%); Community, social and personal services 16·1%.
Exports: US$368 million in 1983: Sugar 62%; Molasses 1·5%; Tea 2·3%; Clothing 21·4%.
Monetary unit: Mauritian rupee. 1 rupee = 100 cents.
Denominations:
 Coins 1, 2, 5, 10, 25, 50 cents; 1 rupee.
 Notes 5, 10, 25, 50 rupees.
Exchange rate to £ sterling: 17·525 (14 Jan. 1985).
Political history and government: A former British colony. On 12 Mar. 1964 the Chief Minister became Premier. On 8 Nov. 1965 the United Kingdom transferred the Chagos Archipelago, a Mauritian dependency, to the newly-created British Indian Ocean Territory. A new constitution was adopted, and Mauritius achieved self-government, on 12 Aug. 1967, when the Premier became Prime Minister. Following communal riots, a state of emergency was declared on 21–22 Jan. 1968. Mauritius became independent, within the Commonwealth, on 12 Mar. 1968.
Executive power is vested in the British monarch and exercisable by the Governor-General, who is appointed on the recommendation of the Prime Minister and acts in almost all matters on the advice of the Council of Ministers. Legislative power is held by the unicameral Legislative Assembly, with 71 members: the Speaker, 62 members elected by universal adult suffrage for 5 years and 8 'additional' members (the most successful losing candidates of each community). The Governor-General appoints the Prime Minister and, on the latter's recommendation, other Ministers. The Council of Ministers is responsible to the Assembly.
By a constitutional amendment of 18 Nov. 1969, the term of the Assembly (elected on 7 Aug. 1967) was extended by four years and the election due in 1972 was not held until 20 Dec. 1976. The state of emergency was lifted on 31 Dec. 1970 but, after industrial unrest, it was reimposed on 16 Dec. 1971.
Telephones: 48 462 (1983).
Daily newspapers: 6 (1983).
 Total circulation: 60 000.
Radio: 125 625 (1983).
TV: 95 458 (1983).
Length of roadways: 1103 miles *1775 km* (31 Dec. 1979).
Universities: 1.
Adult illiteracy: 39·2% (males 28·5%; females 49·9%) in 1962 (population aged 13 and over).
Expectation of life: Males 60·68 years; females 65·31 years (island of Mauritius only) in 1971–73.
Defence: No standing force.
Cinemas: 46 (seating capacity 45 000) in 1981.
Foreign tourists: 118 300 in 1982.

Mexico

Official name: Estados Unidos Mexicanos (United Mexican States).
Population: 76 791 819 (projection from 1980 national census).
Area: 756 062 miles² *1 958 201 km²*.

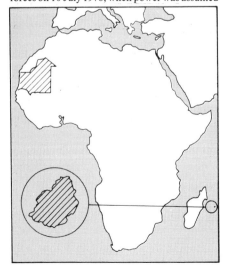

left: **MAURITANIA**
encircled: **MAURITIUS**

Languages: Spanish 90%, indigenous.
Religion: Roman Catholic 96%.
Capital city: Ciudad de México (Mexico City), population 9 191 295 at 30 June 1979 (estimate).
Other principal towns (1979): Nezahualcóyotl 2 231 351; Guadalajara 1 906 145; Monterrey 1 064 629; Heróica Puebla de Zaragoza (Puebla) 710 833; Ciudad Juárez 625 040; León 624 816; Tijuana 566 344; Acapulco de Juárez 462 144; Chihuahua 385 953; Mexicali 348 528; San Luis Potosí 327 333; Hermosillo 324 292; Veracruz Llave 319 257; Culiacán Rosales 306 843.
Highest point: Pico de Orizaba (Volcán Citlaltepetl), 18 405 ft *5610 m*.
Principal mountain ranges: Sierra Madre Occidental, Sierra Madre Oriental, Sierra Madre del Sur, Sistema Volcánico Transversal.
Principal rivers: Río Bravo del Norte (Río Grande) (1885 miles *3033 km*), Balsas, Grijalva, Pánuco.
Head of State; Miguel De la Madrid (b. 12 December 1934), President.
Climate: Tropical (hot and wet) on coastal lowlands and in south, with average temperature of 18°C *64°F*. Temperate on highlands of central plateau. Arid in north and west. In Mexico City, average maximum 19°C *66°F* (December, January) to 25°C *78°F* (May), minimum 5°C *42°F* (January) to 13°C *55°F* (June), July and August rainiest (27 days each). Absolute maximum temperature 58°C *136°F*, San Luis Potosí, 11 Aug. 1933; absolute minimum −28°C *−19°F*, Balerio, 30 Jan. 1949.
Labour force: 22 066 084 (June 1980): Agriculture, forestry and fishing 25%; Mining 2%; Manufacturing 11·7%; Building industry 5·9%; Commerce, restaurants and hotels 7·8%; Transport and communications 3%; Personal, social and communal services 10·9%.
Gross domestic product: 9 417 089 million pesos in 1982: Agriculture, forestry and fishing 7·3%; Mining 9·9%; Manufacturing 21·2%; Building industry 6·3%; Commerce, restaurants and hotels 22·8%; Transport and communications 6·4%; Finance, insurance and real estate 7·5%; Personal, social and communal services 18·8%.
Exports: US$21 398·8 million (1983): Agriculture, livestock and fishing 5%; Crude oil and natural gas 72·9%; Manufacturing industries (including oil products and petrochemicals) 21%.
Monetary unit: Mexican peso. 1 peso = 100 centavos.
Denominations:
 Coins 20 and 50 centavos; 1, 5, 10, 20, 25, 50 and 100 pesos.
 Notes 50, 100, 500, 1000, 5000 and 10 000 pesos.
Exchange rate to £ sterling: 302·56 (1 April 1985).
Political history and government: A federal republic of 31 states and Federal District (around the capital). Present constitution was proclaimed on 5 Feb. 1917. Legislative power is vested in the bicameral National Congress. The Senate has 64 members – two from each state and the Federal District – elected by universal adult suffrage for 6 years. The Chamber of Deputies, directly elected for 3 years, has 400 seats, of which 300 are filled from single-member constituencies. The remaining 100 seats, allocated by proportional representation, are filled from minority parties' lists. Executive power is held by the President, elected for 6 years by universal adult suffrage at the same time as the Senate. He appoints and leads a Cabinet to assist him. Each state is administered by a Governor (elected for 6 years) and an elected Chamber of Deputies.
Telephones: 6 409 161 (1983).
Daily newspapers: 268 (1976).
 Total circulation: 3 994 000 (146 dailies).
Radio: 10 338 024 (1982).
TV: 4 589 170 (1982).
Length of roadways: 134 043 miles *214 470 km* (1983).
Length of railways: 16 034 miles *25 799 km*.
Universities: 47 plus 2 technical universities.
Adult illiteracy: 17% (males 13·8%, females 20·2%) in 1980.
Expectation of life: 65 years (1980).
Defence: Military service: voluntary, with part-time conscript militia; total regular armed forces

127 670 (1984); defence expenditure 1981: $1166 million.
Cinemas: 2005 in 1982.
Foreign tourists: 4 749 000 in 1983.

Monaco

Official name: Principauté de Monaco (Principality of Monaco).
Population: 28 000 (1980).
Area: 0·70 mile² *1,81 km²*.
Language: French.
Religion: Mainly Roman Catholic.
Capital city: Monaco-Ville, population 2422.
Other principal towns: Monte Carlo, population 9948 (1968).
Highest point: On Chemin de Révoirés, 533 ft *162 m*.
Principal river: Vésubie.
Head of State: HSH Prince Rainier III (b. 31 May 1923).
Minister of State: Jean Lucien Emile Herly (b. 15 Sept. 1920).
Climate: Mediterranean, with warm summers (average July maximum 28°C *83°F*) and very mild winters (average January minimum 3°C *37°F*), 62 rainy days a year (monthly average maximum seven days in winter). Absolute maximum temperature 34°C *93°F*, 29 June 1945 and 3 Aug. 1949; absolute minimum −2,3°C *27·8°F*.
Labour force: 10 093 (excluding 232 unemployed) aged 15 and over (census of 1 Mar. 1968): Industry 21·9% (manufacturing 14·8%); Services 77·9% (commerce 18·7%).
Monetary unit: French currency (*q.v.*).
Political history and government: An hereditary principality, in close association with France since 2 Feb. 1861. Monaco became a constitutional monarchy on 5 Jan. 1911. The present constitution was promulgated on 17 Dec. 1962. Legislative power is held jointly by the Sovereign and the unicameral National Council, with 18 members elected by universal adult suffrage for 5 years. The electorate comprises only true-born Monégasque citizens aged 25 years or over. Executive power is vested in the Sovereign and exercised jointly with a 4-man Council of Government, headed by a Minister of State (a French civil servant chosen by the Sovereign). Monaco comprises 3 *quartiers*.
Telephones: 45 000 (1980).
Daily newspapers: 3 (1977).
 Total circulation: 11 000.
Radio: 7500 (1976).
TV: 16 000 (1977).
Length of railways: 1·1 miles *1,7 km*.
Cinemas: 3 (seating capacity 800) in 1981.
Foreign tourists: 218 243 in 1979.

Mongolia

Official name: Bügd Nairamdakh Mongol Ard Uls (Mongolian People's Republic).
Population: 1 594 800 (census of 5 Jan. 1979); 1 820 400 (estimate for 1984).
Area: 604 250 miles² *1 565 000 km²*.
Language: Khalkh Mongolian.
Religion: Buddhist.
Capital city: Ulan Bator (Ulaan Baatar), population 470 500 (1984 estimate).
Other principal towns (1984): Darhan 63 600; Erdenet 40 500.
Highest point: Mönh Hayrhan Uul, 14 311 ft *4362 m*.
Principal mountain ranges: Altai Mts, Hangayn Nuruu.
Principal rivers: Selenge (Selenga) with Orhon, Hereleng (Kerulen).
Head of State: Jambyn Batmunkh (b. 10 Mar. 1926), Chairman of the Praesidium of the Peoples' Great Hural.
Head of Government: Dumaagyn Sodnom (b. 14 July 1933), Chairman of the Council of Ministers.
Climate: Dry. Summers generally mild, winters very cold. In Ulan Bator, July warmest (10°C *51°F* to 22°C *71°F*) and rainiest (10 days),

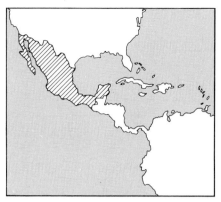

MEXICO

MONACO
January coldest (−32°C *−26°F* to −18°C *−2°F*).
Labour force: 365 000 (estimate for 1983): Agriculture and forestry 36·3%; Industry 17·8%; Construction 7·2%; Non-productive sector 25·2%.
Gross national product: $1100 million in 1978 (World Bank estimate).
Exports: 1816 tugriks in 1983: Fuel, mineral raw materials and metals 39·2%; Raw materials and products of its processing 25·6%; Foodstuffs 12·1%; Industrial consumer goods 13·5%.
Monetary unit: Tugrik. 1 tugrik = 100 möngö.
Denominations:
 Coins 1, 2, 5, 10, 15, 20, 50 möngö; 1 tugrik.
 Notes 1, 2, 5, 10, 25, 50, 100 tugrik.
Exchange rate to £ sterling: 4·56 (14 Jan. 1985).
Political history and government: Formerly Outer Mongolia, a province of China. With backing from the USSR, the Mongolian People's (Communist) Party – called the Mongolian People's Revolutionary Party (MPRP) since 1921 – established a Provisional People's Government on 31 Mar. 1921. After nationalist forces, with Soviet help, overthrew Chinese rule in the capital, independence was proclaimed on 11 July 1921. The USSR recognized the People's Government on 5 Nov. 1921. The Mongolian People's Republic was proclaimed on 26 Nov. 1924 but was not recognized by China. A plebiscite on 20 Oct. 1945 voted 100% for independence, recognized by China on 5 Jan. 1946. A new constitution was adopted on 6 July 1960.
 The supreme organ of state power is the People's Great Hural (Assembly), with 370 members elected (unopposed) by universal adult suffrage for five years. The Assembly usually meets only twice a year but elects a Presidium (9 members) to be its permanent organ. The Chairman of the Presidium is Head of State. The highest executive body is the Council of Ministers, appointed by (and responsible to) the Assembly.
 Political power is held by the MPRP, the only legal party. The MPRP presents a single list of approved candidates for elections to all representative bodies. The MPRP's highest authority

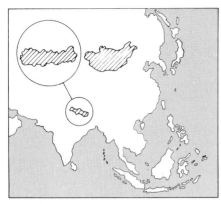

top: **MONGOLIA**   *below:* **NEPAL**

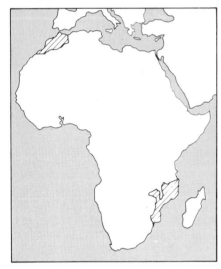

top left: **MOROCCO**
bottom right: **MOZAMBIQUE**

is the Party Congress, which elects the Central Committee (91 full members and 71 candidate members were elected in May 1981) to supervise Party work. The Committee elects a Political Bureau (8 full members and 2 candidate members) to direct its policy.

For local administration, Mongolia is divided into 18 provinces and 3 municipalities.
Telephones: 44 600 (1983).
Daily newspapers: 37 (1983).
Total circulation: 112 000.
Radio: 169 700 (1983).
TV: 70 700 (1983).
Length of roadways: *c.* 46 602 miles *c. 75 000 km.*
Length of railways: 1056 miles *1700 km.*
Universities: 1.
Adult illiteracy: 4·6% (population aged 9 to 50) in 1956.
Expectation of life: Males 59·1 years; females 62·3 years (UN estimates for 1970–75).
Defence: Military service: 2 years; total armed forces 33 100 (1981); defence expenditure, 1980: $127 million (converted at $1 = 3·37 tugrik).
Cinemas: 60 in 1977.
Foreign tourists: 170 000 (1984).

Morocco

Official name: Al-Mamlaka al-Maghribiya (the Kingdom of Morocco).
*Population: 20 255 687 (Sept. 1982 census).
*Area: 177 115 miles² *458 730 km².*
Languages: Arabic, Berber, French, Spanish.
Religions: Muslim; Christian minority.
Capital city: Rabat, population 1 020 001 (1982 census).
Other principal towns (1982): Casablanca 2 436 664; Marrakech 1 266 695; Fes 805 464; Meknes 626 868; Tanger 436 227; Oujda 780 762; Tetouan 704 205; Kenitra 715 967; Safi 706 618.

Highest point: Jebel Toubkal, 13 665 ft *4165 m* (first climbed in 1923).
Principal mountain ranges: Haut (Grand) Atlas, Moyen (Middle) Atlas, Anti Atlas.
Principal rivers: Oued Dra (335 miles *539 km*), Oued Oum-er-Rbia, Oued Moulouya (320 miles *515 km*), Sebou (280 miles *450 km*).
Head of State: HM King Hassan II (b. 9 July 1929).
Prime Minister: Mohamed Karim Lamrani.
Climate: Semi-tropical. Warm and sunny on coast, very hot inland. Rainy season November to March. Absolute maximum temperature 51,7°C *125·0°F*, Agadir, 17 Aug. 1940; absolute minimum −24°C −*11·2°F*, Ifrane, 11 Feb. 1935.
Labour force: 3 636 618 (excluding 343 900 unemployed) at 1971 census: Agriculture, forestry and fishing 57·1%; Manufacturing 10·6%; Community, social and personal services 14·4%. Figures for females exclude unreported family helpers in agriculture.
Gross domestic product: 70 161 million dirhams in 1980: Agriculture, forestry and fishing 18·1%; Commerce 13%; Restaurants and hotels 1·5%; Community and social services 12·2%.
Exports: 12 440 million dirhams in 1982: Phosphates 27·7%; Fresh fruit 8·7%; Clothes 4·4%.
Monetary unit: Dirham. 1 dirham = 100 francs (centimes).
Denominations:
Coins 1, 2, 5, 10, 20, 50 francs; 1, 5 dirhams.
Notes 5, 10, 50, 100 dirhams.
Exchange rate to £ sterling: 10·70 (14 Jan. 1985).
Political history and government: An hereditary monarchy, formerly ruled by a Sultan. Most of Morocco (excluding the former Spanish Sahara) became a French protectorate on 30 Mar. 1912. A smaller part in the north became a Spanish protectorate on 27 Nov. 1912. Tangier became an international zone on 18 Dec. 1923. The French protectorate became independent on 2 Mar. 1956 and was joined by the Spanish protectorate on 7 Apr. 1956. The Tangier zone was abolished on 29 Oct. 1956. The Sultan became King on 18 Aug. 1957. The northern strip of Spanish Sahara was ceded to Morocco on 10 Apr. 1958 and the Spanish enclave of Ifni was ceded on 30 June 1969. On 28 Feb. 1976 the rest of Spanish Sahara was ceded to Morocco and Mauritania, to be apportioned between them. After Mauritania announced its intention to withdraw from Tiris el-Gharbia, its section of Western (formerly Spanish) Sahara, Morocco annexed that portion also (and renamed it Oued Eddahab) on 14 Aug. 1979.

A new constitution, approved by referendum on 1 Mar. 1972 and promulgated on 10 Mar. 1972, provides for a modified constitutional monarchy. Legislative power is vested in a unicameral Chamber of Representatives, which, after the elections of 14 September 1984, had 306 members, of which 204 are elected directly and 102 chosen by an electoral college.

Executive power is vested in the King, who appoints (and may dismiss) the Prime Minister and other members of the Cabinet. The King can also dissolve the Chamber.
Telephones: 241 000 (1982).
Daily newspapers: 11 (1984).
Radio: 1 600 000 (1977).
TV: 605 000 licences (1978).
Length of roadways: 16 592 miles *26 702 km* (31 Dec. 1976).
Length of railways: 1091 miles *1756 km* (1975).
Universities: 6.
Adult illiteracy: 78·6% (males 66·4%; females 90·2%) in 1971.
Expectation of life: Males 51·4 years; females 54·5 years (UN estimates for 1970–75).
Defence: Military service: 18 months; total armed forces 136 800 (1984); defence expenditure, 1981: $1210 million.
Cinemas: 276 in 1974.
Foreign tourists: 1 815 435 (including 526 927 Moroccan nationals residing abroad) in 1982.

---

* Figures exclude Western (formerly Spanish) Sahara, with an area of 97 343 miles² *252 120 km²* and a 1982 population of 163 868.

Mozambique

Official name: A República Popular de Moçambique (the People's Republic of Mozambique).
Population: 13 140 000 (1983 estimate).
Area: 309 496 miles² *801 590 km².*
Languages: Portuguese (official), many African languages.
Religions: Animist; Christian and Muslim minorities.
Capital city: Maputo (formerly Lourenço Marques), population 850 000 (1982 estimate).
Other principal towns (1970): Nampula 126 126; Beira 113 770.
Highest point: Monte Binga, 7992 ft *2436 m.*
Principal mountain range: Lebombo Range.
Principal rivers: Limpopo, Zambezi, Rovuma, Shire.
Head of State: Samora Moïsés Machel (b. 29 Sept. 1933), President.
Climate: Varies from tropical to sub-tropical except in a few upland areas. Rainfall is irregular but the rainy season is usually from November to March, with an average temperature of 28°C *83°F* in Maputo. In the dry season, average temperatures 18°C *65°F* to 20°C *68°F.*
Labour force: 2 875 597 (excluding 21 689 persons on compulsory military service and 30 320 unemployed) at 1970 census: Agriculture, forestry and fishing 74·3%.
Gross domestic product: $2722 million in 1975 (UN estimate).
Exports: 12 700 million meticais in 1979: Cashew nuts 30%; Textiles 9%; Tea 8%.
Monetary unit: Metical (plural:¨ meticais). 1 metical = 100 centavos.
Denominations:
Coins 10, 20, 50 centavos; 1, 2½, 5, 10, 20 meticais.
Notes 50, 100, 500, 1000 meticais.
Exchange rate to £ sterling: 49·83 (14 Jan. 1985).
Political history and government: Formerly a Portuguese colony, independent since 25 June 1975. The independence movement was dominated by the *Frente de Libertação de Moçambique* (Frelimo), the Mozambique Liberation Front. Before independence Frelimo was recognized by Portugal and its leader became the first President. The independence constitution proclaims that Frelimo is the directing power of the state and of society. At its third Congress, in February 1977, Frelimo was reconstituted as the Frelimo Party, a 'Marxist-Leninist vanguard party'. Legislative power is vested in the People's Assembly, with 210 members, mainly Frelimo Party officials, indirectly elected on 1–4 Dec. 1977. Executive power is held by the President, who appoints and leads a Council of Ministers. Mozambique has 11 provinces.
Telephones: 56 305 (1982).
Daily newspapers: 2 (1976).
Total circulation: 42 000.
Radio: 255 000 (1979).
TV: 1500 (1979).
Length of roadways: 24 341 miles *39 173 km* (31 Dec. 1974).
Length of railways: 2388 miles *3843 km.*
Universities: 1.
Adult illiteracy: 88·6% (males 85%; females 92%) in 1962 (UNESCO estimates).
Expectation of life: Males 41·9 years; females 45·1 years (UN estimates for 1970–75).
Defence: Military service: two years (including women); total armed forces 12 000 (1984); defence expenditure, 1981: $198 million (converted at $1 = 28·3 meticais).
Cinemas: 28 (seating capacity 19 500) in 1971.
Foreign tourists: 68 826 in 1974.

Nauru

Official name: The Republic of Nauru (Naoero).
Population: 8421 (1983 estimate).
Area: 8·2 miles² *21 km².*
Languages: English, Nauruan.
Religions: Protestant, Roman Catholic.
Highest point: 225 ft *68 m.*
Head of State: Hammer DeRoburt, OBE (b. 25 Sept. 1922), President.

Climate: Tropical; day temperature 30°C *85°F*; rainfall variable, averaging 2000 mm *80 inches*; wettest periods Nov. to Feb.
Labour force: 2504 aged 15 and over (1966 census).
Monetary unit: Australian currency (*q.v.*).
Political history and government: Annexed by Germany in October 1888. Captured by Australian forces in November 1914. Administered by Australia under League of Nations mandate (17 Dec. 1920) and later as UN Trust Territory. A new constitution was adopted on 29 Jan. 1968 and Nauru became independent on 31 Jan. 1968. Hammer DeRoburt, Head Chief of Nauru since 1956, was elected the country's first President on 19 May 1968. Under an agreement announced on 29 Nov. 1968, Nauru became a 'special member' of the Commonwealth. Legislative power is held by a unicameral Parliament, with 18 members elected by universal adult suffrage for three years (subject to dissolution). Executive power is held by the President, who is elected by Parliament for its duration and rules with the assistance of an appointed Cabinet, responsible to Parliament. Nauru's first political party was formed in 1976.
Telephones: 1600 (1980).
Radio: 3600 (1977).
Length of roadways: 12 miles *19 km*.
Length of railways: 3·2 miles *5,2 km*.
Cinemas: 7 in 1978.

Nepal

Official name: Sri Nepāla Sarkār (Kingdom of Nepal).
Population: 16 000 000 (1982 estimate).
Area: 54 362 miles² *140 797 km²*.
Languages (1971): Nepali (official) 52·4%; Maithir 11·5%; Bhojpuri 7·0%; Tamang 4·8%; Tharu 4·3%; Newari 3·9%; Abadhi 2·7%; Magar 2·5%; Raikirati 2·0%.
Religions (1971): Hindu 89·4%; Buddhist 7·5%; Muslim 3·0%.
Capital city: Kathmandu, population 150 402 (1971); 353 756 (incl. suburbs).
Other principal towns (1971, including suburbs): Morang 301 557; Lalitpur 154 998; Patan 135 230; Bhaktapur 110 157.
Highest point: Mount Everest, 29 028 ft *8848 m* (on Chinese border). First climbed 29 May 1953.
Principal mountain range: Nepal Himalaya (Mahabharat Range).
Principal rivers: Karnali, Naryani, Kosi.
Head of State: HM King Birenda Bir Bikram Shah Dev (b. 28 Dec. 1945).
Prime Minister: Lokendra Bahadur Chand.
Climate: Varies sharply with altitude, from Arctic in Himalaya to humid sub-tropical in the central Vale of Kathmandu (annual average 11°C *52°F*), which is warm and sunny in summer. Rainy season June to October. In Kathmandu, average maximum 18°C *65°F* (January) to 30°C *86°F* (May), minimum 2°C *35°F* (January) to 20°C *68°F* (July, August), July (21 days) and August (20 days) rainiest. Maximum temperature recorded in Kathmandu is 37°C *99°F* (2 May 1960) and minimum is −3°C *26°F* (20 Jan. 1964).
Labour force: 4 852 524 (1971 census): Agriculture, forestry and fishing 94·4%.
Gross domestic product: 17 344 million rupees in year ending 15 July 1977: Agriculture, forestry and fishing 62·3%; Manufacturing (incl. cottage industries) 10·4%.
Exports: 1492 million rupees in 1982.
Monetary unit: Nepalese rupee. 1 rupee = 100 paisa.
Denominations:
  Coins 1, 5, 10, 25, 50 paisa; 1 rupee.
  Notes 1, 5, 10, 100, 500, 1000 rupees.
Exchange rate to £ sterling: 18·90 (14 Jan. 1985).
Political history and government: An hereditary kingdom. A limited constitutional monarchy was proclaimed on 18 Feb. 1951. In a royal *coup* on 15 Dec. 1960 the King dismissed the Cabinet and dissolved Parliament. A royal proclamation of 5 Jan. 1961 banned political parties. A new constitution, adopted on 16 Dec. 1962, vested executive power in the King and established a National Assembly (*Rashtriya Panchayat*) whose members (most of them indirectly elected, the remainder nominated by the King) had only consultative functions. A referendum held on 2 May 1980 approved the retention of the non-party system. Under a decree of 15 Dec. 1980, the constitution was amended to provide for a National Assembly of 140 members (112 directly elected by universal adult suffrage for five years, 28 nominated by the King). Voting for the elective seats took place on 9 May 1981. The Prime Minister is elected by the Assembly, with other members of the Council of Ministers appointed by the King on the Prime Minister's recommendation. The Council is responsible to the Assembly.
  Nepal comprises 14 zones, each administered by an appointed Commissioner.
Telephones: 9425 (1978).
Daily newspapers: 29 (1976).
  Total circulation: 96 000 (13 dailies).
Radio: 200 000 (1977).
Length of roadways: 2858 miles *4600 km* (31 Dec. 1978).
Length of railways: 63 miles *101 km*.
Universities: 1.
Adult illiteracy: 80·8% (males 66·6%; females 95·0%) in 1975.
Expectation of life: Males 42·2 years; females 45·0 years (UN estimates for 1970–75).
Defence: Military service voluntary; total armed forces 25 000 (1984); defence expenditure, 1980: $22 million.
Foreign tourists: 162 276 in 1979.

The Netherlands

Official name: Koninkrijk der Nederlanden (Kingdom of the Netherlands).
Population: 14 420 000 (estimate for 1 Jul. 1984).
Area: 15 770 miles² *40 844 km²*.
Language: Dutch.
Religions: Roman Catholic 40%; Protestant 33%.
Capital city: Amsterdam, population 936 410 at 1 Jan. 1983 (estimate). The seat of government is 's Gravenhage (Den Haag or The Hague), population 674 546 (1 Jan. 1983).
Other principal towns (1 Jan. 1983): Rotterdam 1 024 702; Utrecht 498 877; Eindhoven 373 877; Arnhem 290 746; Heerlen-Kerkrade 264 988; Enschede-Hengelo 247 759; Nijmegen 229 408; Tilburg 220 852; Haarlem 219 350.
Highest point: Vaalserberg, 1053 ft *321 m*.
Principal rivers: Mass (Meuse), Waal (Rhine) (820 miles *1319 km*), IJssel.
Head of State: HM Queen Beatrix Wilhelmina Armgard (b. 31 Jan. 1938).
Prime Minister: Ruud F. M. Lubbers.
Climate: Temperate, generally between −17°C 0°F and 21°C *70°F*. Often foggy and windy. In Amsterdam, average maximum 4°C *40°F* (January) to 20°C *69°F* (July), minimum 1°C *34°F* (January, February) to 15°C *59°F* (July, August). November, December, January rainiest (each 19 days). Absolute maximum temperature 38,6°C *101·5°F*, Warnsveld, 23 Aug. 1944; absolute minimum −27,4°C *−17·3°F*, Winterswijk, 27 Jan. 1942.
Labour force: 5 934 000 in Nov. 1984; registered unemployed 825 000.
Gross domestic product: 283·5 billion guilders in 1983: Agriculture and fisheries 4%; Industry 35%; Services 45%.
Exports: 212·1 billion guilders in 1984 (estimate); Natural gas 7·9%.
Monetary unit: Netherlands gulden (guilder) or florin. 1 guilder = 100 cents.
Denominations:
  Coins 1, 5, 10, 25 cents; 1, 2½ guilders.
  Notes 1, 2½, 5, 10, 25, 100, 1000 guilders.
Exchange rate to £ sterling: 4·317 (11 Apr. 1985).
Political history and government: A constitutional and hereditary monarchy. Legislative power is held by the bicameral States-General. The First Chamber has 75 members indirectly elected for 4 years by the 11 Provincial Councils. The Second Chamber has 150 members directly

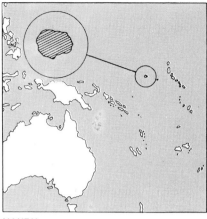

NAURU

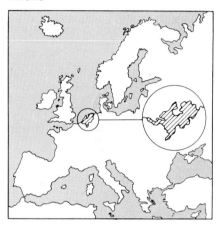

THE NETHERLANDS

elected by universal suffrage for 4 years (subject to dissolution), using proportional representation. The Head of State has mainly formal prerogatives and executive power is exercised by the Council of Ministers, which is responsible to the States-General. The monarch appoints the Prime Minister and, on the latter's recommendation, other Ministers. Each of the 11 provinces is administered by an appointed Governor and an elected Council.
Telephones: 5 462 000 (1983).
Daily newspapers: 83 (1982).
  Total circulation: 4 500 000.
Radio: 4 636 000 (1983).
TV: 4 454 000 (1983).
Length of roadways: 58 990 miles *95 146 km* (1983).
Length of railways: 1921 miles *3092 km*.
Universities: 9 (plus 3 technical universities and 4 colleges of university standing).
Expectation of life: Males 69·7 years; females 74·9 years (1983).
Defence: Military service: Army 14 months, Navy and Air Force 14–17 months; total armed forces 106 300 (1984); defence expenditure, 1981: $4930 million.
Cinemas: 546 in 1983.
Foreign tourists: 2 991 000 (hotel arrivals only) in 1983.

New Zealand

Official name: Dominion of New Zealand.
Population: 3 175 737 (1981 census); 3 270 000 (1984 estimate).
Area: 103 736 miles² *268 676 km²*.
Languages: English, Maori.
Religions: Church of England, Presbyterian, Roman Catholic.
Capital city: Wellington, population 133 700 at 31 March 1983; including suburbs 342 500.
Other principal towns (1983): Auckland 800 100; Christchurch 322 200; Hamilton 164 700; Dunedin 112 000; Napier-Hastings 114 400; Palmerston North 93 700.

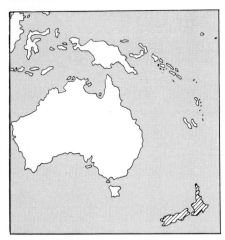

NEW ZEALAND

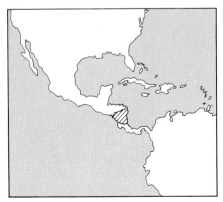

NICARAGUA

Highest point: Mt Cook, 12 349 ft *3764 m*.
Principal mountain range: Southern Alps.
Principal rivers: Waikato, Clutha (210 miles *338 km*), Waihou, Rangitaiki, Mokau, Wanganui, Rangitikei, Manawatu.
Head of State: HM Queen Elizabeth II, represented by Sir David Stuart Beattie, GCMG (b. 29 Feb. 1924), Governor-General.
Prime Minister: The Rt Hon. David Russell Lange (b. 1942).
Climate: Temperate and moist. Moderate temperatures (annual average 11°C *52°F*) except in the hotter far north. Small seasonal variations. In Wellington, January and February warmest (13°C *56°F* to 20°C *69°F*), July coolest (5°C *42°F* to 12°C *53°F*) and rainiest (18 days), February driest (nine days). In Auckland, average maximum 13°C *56°F* (July) to 23°C *73°F* (January, February), minimum 8°C *46°F* (July, August) to 15°C *60°F* (January, February), July rainiest (21 days).
Labour force: 1 340 000 (excluding armed forces overseas) aged 15 and over (1982 estimate): Agriculture, forestry and fishing 11·83%; Manufacturing 23·33%; Trade, restaurants and hotels 16·19%; Community, social and personal services 22·29%.
Gross domestic product: NZ$32 240 million in year ended 31 March 1983: Manufacturing 22·8%; Trade, restaurants and hotels 22%; Central government services 11·4%.
Exports: NZ$7694·3 million for the year ended 30 June 1983: Meat and meat preparations 24·3%; Dairy products 19·3%; Wool 13·2%.
Monetary unit: New Zealand dollar ($NZ). 1 dollar = 100 cents.
Denominations:
    Coins 1, 2, 5, 10, 20, 50 cents.
    Notes 1, 2, 5, 10, 20, 50, 100 dollars.
Exchange rate to £ sterling: 2·3854 (16 Jan. 1985).
Political history and government: A former British colony. Became a dominion, under the British crown, on 26 Sept. 1907. Fully independent, within the Commonwealth, under the Statute of Westminster, promulgated in the United Kingdom on 11 Dec. 1931 and accepted by New Zealand on 25 Nov. 1947. Executive power is vested in the British monarch and exercisable by the Governor-General, who is appointed on the recommendation of the Prime Minister and acts in almost all matters on the advice of the Executive Council (Cabinet), led by the Prime Minister. Legislative power is held by the unicameral House of Representatives, with 95 members (including four Maoris) elected by universal adult suffrage for three years (subject to dissolution). The Governor-General appoints the Prime Minister and, on the latter's recommendation, other Ministers. The Cabinet is responsible to the House.
Telephones: 1 939 488 (1983).
Daily newspapers: 33 (1984).
    Total circulation: 1 090 280.
TV: 921 724 (1983).
Length of roadways: 57 733 miles *92 909 km* (main and secondary roads only) at 31 Mar. 1983.
Length of railways: 2692 miles *4332 km*.
Universities: 6.
Expectation of life: European males 70·34 years; European females 76·42 years; Maori males 65·44 years; Maori females 69·84 years (1980–2).
Defence: Military service: voluntary, supplemented by Territorial Army service of 12 weeks basic, 20 days per year; total armed forces 12 856 (1983); defence expenditure, 1983: NZ$652·13 million.
Cinemas: 154 in 1981.
Foreign tourists: 518 441 (incl. short-stay visits) in 1983.

Nicaragua

Official name: República de Nicaragua.
Population: 2 823 979 (1981 estimate).
Area: 50 193 miles² *130 000 km²*.
Language: Spanish.
Religion: Roman Catholic.
Capital city: Managua, population 819 679 (1981 estimate).
Other principal towns (1978): León 81 647; Granada 56 232; Masaya 47 276; Chinandega 44 435; Matagalpa 26 986; Esteli 26 892.
Highest point: Pico Mogotón, 6913 ft *2107 m*.
Principal mountain ranges: Cordillera Isabelia, Cordillera de Darién.
Principal rivers: Coco (Segovia) (300 miles *482 km*), Rio Grande, Escondido, San Juan.
Head of State: Daniel Ortega, President.
Climate: Tropical (hot and humid) with average annual temperature of 26°C *78°F*. Rainy season May–December. Annual rainfall 2540 mm *100 in* on east coast. In Managua, annual average over 27°C *80°F* all year round.
Labour force: 813 000 (excluding unemployed) in 1980: Agriculture, forestry and fishing 42%; Manufacturing 16%; Trade, restaurants and hotels 13%; Community, social and personal services 18%.
Gross domestic product: 14 988 million córdobas in 1978: Agriculture, forestry and fishing 24·7% (agriculture 23·3%); Manufacturing 21·0%; Trade 23·6%; Community, social and personal services (incl. restaurants, hotels and business services) 12·3%.
Exports: US$520 million in 1981.
Monetary unit: Córdoba. 1 córdoba = 100 centavos.
Denominations:
    Coins 5, 10, 25, 50 centavos; 1 córdoba.
    Notes 1, 2, 5, 10, 20, 50, 100, 500, 1000 córdobas.
Exchange rate to £ sterling: 11·16 (14 Jan. 1985).
Political history and government: A republic comprising 16 departments and one territory. At the government's request, US forces intervened in Nicaragua in 1912 and established bases. They left in 1925 but returned in 1927, when a guerrilla group, led by Augusto César Sandino, was organised to oppose the US occupation. The US forces finally left in 1933, when their role was assumed by a newly-created National Guard, commanded by Gen. Anastasio Somoza García. Sandino was assassinated in 1934, apparently on Somoza's orders, but his followers ('Sandinistas') remained active in opposing the new régime. Somoza became President in 1936 and, either in person or through nominees, held power until his assassination by a 'Sandinista' in 1956. Political power, exercised within a constitutional framework, was retained by a member of the Somoza family, either directly as President or as Commander of the National Guard. From 1960 the régime was opposed by a guerrilla group which in 1962 formed the *Frente Sandinista de Liberación Nacional* (FSLN), the Sandinist National Liberation Front, named after Sandino. General Anastasio Somoza Debayle, son of the former dictator, was President from 1967 to 1972 and again from 1 Dec. 1974. The FSLN allied with other opponents of the régime in 1977. Armed clashes with the National Guard developed into civil war. After 6 months of heavy fighting, President Somoza resigned and left the country on 17 July 1979. The President of the National Congress was nominated as interim President but he left after two days, when the capital fell to the Sandinistas.

The guerrilla groups had formed a provisional Junta of National Reconstruction (initially five members) on 16 June 1979. The Junta named a Provisional Governing Council on 16 July and this Council took office as the Government of National Reconstruction on 20 July 1979. The 1974 constitution was abrogated and the bicameral National Congress (a Senate and a Chamber of Deputies) dissolved. The National Guard was also dissolved, being replaced by the 'Sandinista People's Army', officially established on 22 Aug. 1979.

On taking office, the junta published a Basic Statute, providing for the creation of an appointed 33-member Council of State to act as an interim legislature and to draft a new constitution. On 21 Aug. 1979 the junta issued a 'Statute on Rights and Guarantees for the Citizens of Nicaragua', promising a wide range of democratic reforms. The initial membership of the Council of State, announced on 21 Apr. 1980, was increased to 47. The Council first convened on 4 May 1980 and was increased to 51 members on 4 May 1981. A decree banning electoral activity until Jan. 1984 was issued on 27 Aug. 1980. The ruling junta was reduced from five to three members on 4 Mar. 1981, and elections took place in March 1985.
Telephones: 51 237 (1982).
Daily newspapers: 3 (1983).
    Total circulation: 105 000.
Radio: 140 000 (1981).
TV: 180 000 (1981).
Length of roadways: 11 210 miles *18 040 km* (1977).
Length of railways: 232 miles *373 km* (1977).
Universities: 3.
Adult illiteracy: 42·5% (males 42·0%; females 42·9%) in 1971.
Expectation of life: Males 51·2 years; females 54·6 years (UN estimates for 1970–75).
Defence: Total armed forces 23 000 (1984); defence expenditure, 1979: $5·4 million.
Cinemas: 85 in 1972.
Foreign tourists: 207 000 in 1976.

Niger

Official name: République du Niger.
Population: 6 040 000 (1983 estimate).
Area: 489 191 miles² *1 267 000 km²*.
Languages: French (official), Hausa, Tuareg, Djerma, Fulani.
Religions: Muslim 85%; Animist, Christian.
Capital city: Niamey, population 225 314 (1977).
Other principal towns (1977): Zinder 58 436; Maradi 45 852; Tahoua 31 265; Agadez 20 475.
Highest point: Mont Gréboun, 6562 ft *2000 m*.
Principal mountain ranges: Aïr (Azbine), Plateau du Djado.
Principal rivers: Niger (370 miles *595 km* in Niger), Dillia.
Head of State: Col Seyni Kountché (b. 1930),

President of the Supreme Military Council and Chairman of the Council of Ministers.
Climate: Hot and dry. Average temperature 29°C *84°F*. In Niamey, average maximum 34°C *93°F* (January) to 42°C *108°F* (April). ·
Labour force: 1 280 000 (mid-1970): Agriculture, forestry and fishing 92·8% (ILO estimates); 2 530 000 (official estimate for 1978).
Gross domestic product: 97 808 million CFA francs in 1969: Agriculture, forestry and fishing 51·2%; Trade, restaurants and hotels 14·7%; $736 million (estimate) in 1975.
Exports: 97 000 million francs CFA in 1980: Uranium 76%.
Monetary unit: Franc de la Communauté financière africaine.
·**Denominations:**
 Coins 1, 2, 5, 10, 25, 50, 100 CFA francs.
 Notes 50, 100, 500, 1000, 5000 CFA francs.
Exchange rate to £ sterling: 542·25 (14 Jan. 1985).
Political history and government: Formerly part of French West Africa, independent since 3 Aug. 1960. Under military rule since 15 Apr. 1974, when the constitution was suspended and the National Assembly dissolved. Niger is ruled by a Supreme Military Council, composed of army officers, which has appointed a provisional government. The country has 16 administrative districts.
Telephones: 8147 (1977).
Daily newspapers: 1 (1982).
 Total circulation: 3000.
Radio: 200 000 (1979).
TV: 500 (1979).
Length of roadways: 4757 miles *7656 km* (31 Dec. 1978).
Universities: 1.
Adult illiteracy: 98·6% (males 98%; females 99%) in 1962 (UNESCO estimates).
Expectation of life: Males 39·4 years; females 42·5 years (UN estimates for 1970–75).
Defence: Total armed forces 2220 (1984); defence expenditure, 1980: $18 million.
Cinemas: 4 (seating capacity 3800) in 1970.

Nigeria

Official name: The Federal Republic of Nigeria.
Population: 82 390 000 (1983 estimate).
Area: 356 669 miles² *923 768 km²*.
Languages: English (official), Hausa, Ibo, Yoruba and other linguistic groups.
Religions: Muslim, Christian.
Capital city: Lagos, population 1 060 848 at 1 July 1975 (estimate).
Other principal towns (1975): Ibadan 847 000; Ogbomosho 432 000; Kano 399 000; Oshogbo 282 000; Ilorin 282 000; Abeokuta 253 000; Port Harcourt 242 000; Zaria 224 000; Ilesha 224 000; Onitsha 220 000; Iwo 214 000; Ado-Ekiti 213 000; Kaduna 202 000; Mushin 197 000.
Highest point: Dimlang, 6700 ft *2042 m*.
Principal mountain range: Jos Plateau.
Principal rivers: Niger (2600 miles *4184 km* in total length), Benue, Cross.
Head of State: Maj.-Gen. Mohammed Buhari.
Climate: On the coast it is hot (average daily maximum temperature at Lagos 32°C *89°F*) and unpleasantly humid. In the north it is drier and semi-tropical. Annual rainfall ranges from 625 to 3800 mm *25 to 150 in*.
Labour force: 22 278 000 (mid-1970): Agriculture, forestry and fishing 62·1%; Industry 13·8%; Services 24·1% (ILO estimates).
Gross domestic product: 32 359·6 million naira in year ending 31 Mar. 1978: Agriculture, forestry and fishing 23·4% (agriculture 17·6%); Mining and quarrying 24·7% (crude petroleum and natural gas 22·1%); Trade, restaurants and hotels 21·4% (trade 21·2%).
Exports: 7215·9 million naira in 1982: Crude oil 95%.
Monetary unit: Naira. 1 naira = 100 kobo.
Denominations:
 Coins ½, 1, 5, 10, 25 kobo.
 Notes 50 kobo; 1, 5, 10, 20 naira.
Exchange rate to £ sterling: 1·09877 (14 Jan. 1985).

Political history and government: In 1914 the British dependencies of Northern and Southern Nigeria were unified. In 1947 the United Kingdom introduced a new Nigerian constitution, establishing a federal system of government based on three regions. The Federation of Nigeria became independent, within the Commonwealth, on 1 Oct. 1960. The northern part of the British-administered Trust Territory of Cameroon was incorporated into the Northern Region of Nigeria on 1 June 1961. A fourth region was created by dividing the Western Region under legislation approved on 8 Aug. 1963. The country became a republic, under its present name, on 1 Oct. 1963. The government was overthrown by a military *coup* on 15 Jan. 1966 and power was assumed by a Supreme Military Council (SMC), ruling by decree. Political parties were banned on 24 May 1966. The four regions were replaced by 12 States on 1 April 1968. These were reorganised into 19 States on 17 Mar. 1976.
 The SMC published a draft constitution on 7 Oct. 1976. Local government councils were elected (directly in some States, indirectly in others) in Nov.–Dec. 1976. A constituent assembly of 233 members (203 selected by the local councils on 31 Aug. 1977, 22 nominated by the SMC and 8 from the constitutional drafting committee) was inaugurated on 6 Oct. 1977 to finalise the constitution in preparation for a return to civilian rule. The assembly closed on 5 June 1978. A new constitution was issued on 21 Sept. 1978, when the régime ended the ban on political parties and the state of emergency in force since 1966.
 Under the constitution, the federal legislature is a bicameral National Assembly, comprising a Senate of 95 members (5 for each State) and a House of Representatives (449 members). Both chambers are elected by universal adult suffrage for 4 years. Executive power is vested in the President, similarly elected (with a Vice-President) for 4 years. The President appoints and leads the Federal Executive Council (Cabinet). Each State has an elected Governor and unicameral House of Assembly. In 1979 elections were held for the Senate on 7 July, for the House of Representatives on 14 July, for the State legislatures on 21 July, for State Governors on 28 July and for the President on 11 Aug. The constitution came into force on 1 Oct. 1979, when military rule was ended and the civilian President sworn in. The National Assembly opened on 9 Oct. 1979. Elections were held in August 1983, but in December 1983 the military took over control again, and in January 1984 an 18-member Supreme Military Council was sworn in. The constitution provides for the future establishment of a Federal Capital Territory, to be represented by one member in the Senate and one in the House.
Telephones: 708 390 (1982).
Daily newspapers: 19 (1976).
 Total circulation: 527 000 (8 dailies).
Radio: 5 600 000 (1980).
TV: 450 000 (1980).
Length of roadways: 65 244 miles *105 000 km* (31 Dec. 1977).
Length of railways: 2178 miles *3505 km*.
Universities: 13.
Adult illiteracy: 88·5% in 1952–53 (population aged 7 and over); 84·6% (males 75%; females 94%) in 1962 (UNESCO estimates).
Expectation of life: Males 43·4 years; females 46·6 years (UN estimates for 1970–75).
Defence: Military service voluntary; total armed forces 133 100 (1984); defence expenditure, 1980: $1702 million.
Cinemas: 131 in 1979.
Foreign tourists: 113 827 in 1976.

Norway

Official name: Kongeriket Norge (Kingdom of Norway).
Population: 4 106 651 (1 Jan. 1983).
Area: 149 411 miles² *386 975 km²*.
Languages: Norwegian; small Lapp minority.

top: **NIGER** *immediately below:* **NIGERIA**

NORWAY

Religion: Lutheran.
Capital city: Oslo, population 448 747 at 1 Jan. 1983.
Other principal towns (1 Jan. 1983): Bergen 207 232; Trondheim 134 652; Stavanger 92 012; Kristiansand 61 834; Drammen 50 605.
Highest point: Glittertinden 8110 ft *2472 m*.
Principal mountain range: Langfjellene.
Principal rivers: Glomma (Glama) (380 miles *611 km*), Lågen (224 miles *360 km*), Tanaelv (213 miles *342 km*).
Head of State: HM King Olav V, KG, KT, GCB, GCVO (b. 2 July 1903).
Prime Minister: Kåre Isaachsen Willoch (b. 3 Oct. 1928).
Climate: Temperate on coast, but cooler inland. In Oslo, average maximum −1°C *30°F* (January) to 23°C *73°F* (July), minimum −7°C *20°F* (January, February) to 13°C *56°F* (July), August rainiest (11 days). Absolute maximum temperature 35°C *95°F*, Oslo, 21 July 1901, and Trondheim, 22 July 1901; absolute minimum −51,4°C *−60·5°F*, Karasjok, 1 Jan. 1886.
Labour force: 1 946 000 (excluding 41 390 unemployed) in 1982: Agriculture, forestry and fishing 8·1%; Manufacturing, mining and quarrying 21·5%; Construction 7·9%; Trade, hotels and restaurants 17·3%.
Gross domestic product: 401 769 million kroner in 1983: Agriculture, forestry and fishing 3·8%; Crude petroleum and natural gas 16·8%; Manufacturing 13·7%; Construction 5·5%; Wholesale and retail trade 12·1%.
Exports: 131 397 million kroner in 1983: Petroleum and petroleum products 34%; Natural gas 17·6%; Manufactured goods 18·3%; Machinery and transport equipment 13·3%.
Monetary unit: Norwegian krone (plural: kroner). 1 krone = 100 øre.

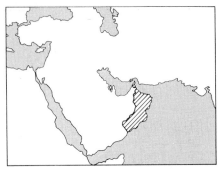

OMAN

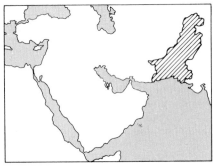

PAKISTAN

Denominations:
Coins 50 øre; 1, 5 kroner.
Notes 10, 50, 100, 500, 1000 kroner.
Exchange rate to £ sterling: 11·16 (15 Apr. 1985).
Political history and government: Formerly linked with Sweden. Independence declared on 7 June 1905; union with Sweden ended on 26 Oct. 1905. Norway is a constitutional monarchy, headed by an hereditary King. Legislative power is held by the unicameral Parliament (*Storting*), with 155 members elected for 4 years by universal adult suffrage, using proportional representation. For the consideration of legislative proposals, the *Storting* divides itself into two chambers by choosing one quarter of its members to form the *Lagting* (upper house), the remainder forming the *Odelsting* (lower house). Executive power is nominally held by the King but is exercised by the Council of Ministers (*Statsråd*), led by the Prime Minister, who are appointed by the King in accordance with the will of the *Storting*, to which the Council is responsible. Norway comprises 19 counties.
Telephones: 2 394 712 (1983).
Daily newspapers: 65 (1983).
Total circulation: 1 848 000.
Radio: 1 318 022 licences (1977).
TV: 1 295 267 (1982).
Length of roadways: 50 276 miles *80 911 km* (31 Dec. 1979).
Length of railways: 2651 miles *4266 km.*
Universities: 4.
Expectation of life: Males 72·64 years; females 79·41 years (1981–2).
Defence: Military service: Army 12 months; Navy and Air Force 12/15 months; total armed forces 30 370 in 1983; defence expenditure 12 062·2 million kroner.
Cinemas: 446 in 1982.

Oman

Official name: Sultanat 'Uman (Sultanate of Oman).
Population: 1 500 000 (1980 estimate).
Area: 82 030 miles² *212 457 km².*
Language: Arabic.
Religion: Muslim.
Capital city: Masqat (Muscat), population 80 000 (with port of Matrah).
Other principal towns: Matrah; Salalah.
Highest point: Jabal ash Sham, 10 400 ft *3170 m.*
Principal mountain range: Jabal Akhdas ('Green Mountains').
Head of State: Sultan Qabus ibn Sa'id (b. 18 Nov. 1940).
Climate: Extremely hot summers (temperatures rising to 55°C *130°F*) and mild winters, Cooler in the mountains. Average annual rainfall 75 to 150 mm *3 to 6 in.*
Gross domestic product: 892·8 million rials in 1978: Mining and quarrying 55·8%; Public administration and defence 11·9%.
Exports: $4696 million in 1981: Crude and partly refined petroleum 94·1%.
Monetary unit: Rial Omani. 1 rial = 1000 baiza.
Denominations:
Coins 2, 5, 10, 25, 50, 100 baiza.
Notes 100, 250, 500 baiza; 1, 5, 10 rials.
Exchange rate to £ sterling: 0·386 (14 Jan. 1985).
Political history and government: A sultanate, formerly called Muscat and Oman, under British influence since the 19th century. Full independence was recognised by the treaty of friendship with the UK on 20 Dec. 1951. The port and peninsula of Gwadur were ceded to Pakistan on 8 Sept. 1958. Sultan Sa'id ibn Taimur was deposed by his son, Qabus, on 23 July 1970 and the country adopted its present name on 9 Aug. 1970. The Sultan is an absolute ruler and legislates by decree. He is advised by an appointed Cabinet. On 20 Oct. 1981 Sultan Qabus issued decrees creating a State Advisory Council, with 45 members nominated for 2 years. There are no political parties.
Telephones: 27 296 (1984).
Length of roadways: 7425 miles *11 950 km.*
Expectation of life: Males 43·7 years; females 45·9 years (UN estimates for 1970–75).
Defence: Military service voluntary; total armed forces 24 100 (1984); defence expenditure, 1980: $879 million.
Cinemas: 12 (seating capacity 800) in 1976.

Pakistan

Official name: Islami Jamhuria-e-Pakistan (Islamic Republic of Pakistan). 'Pakistan' means 'land of the pure' in the Urdu language.
***Population:** 83 780 000 (1981 census).
***Area:** 310 404 miles² *803 943 km².*
Languages: Urdu (national), Punjabi, Pashto, Baluchi, Sindhi, English (official).
Religions: Muslim 97·1%; Hindu 1·6%; Christian 1·3% (1961).
Capital city: Islamabad, population 251 000 (1981 census).
Other principal towns (1981): Karachi 5 103 000; Lahore 2 922 000; Faisalabad 1 092 000; Rawalpindi 806 000; Hyderabad 795 000; Multan 730 000; Gujranwala 597 000; Peshawar 555 000.
Highest point: K2 (Mt Godwin Austen), 28 250 ft *8611 m* (first climbed 31 July 1954).
Principal mountain ranges: Hindu Kush, Pamirs, Karakoram.
Principal rivers: Indus and tributaries (Sutlej, Chenab, Ravi, Jhelum).
Head of State: Gen Mohammad Zia ul-Haq (b. 1924), President and Chief Martial Law Administrator.
Climate: Dry, and generally hot, with average temperature of 27°C *80°F* except in the mountains, which have very cold winters. Temperatures range from −1°C *30°F* in winter to 49°C *120°F* in summer. In Karachi, June warmest (average 28°C to 34°C *82°F to 93°F*), January coolest (13°C to 25°C *55°F to 77°F*), rainfall negligible throughout the year. In Lahore, average maximum 21°C *69°F* (January) to 41°C *106°F* (June), minimum 5°C *40°F* (December, January) to 27°C *80°F* (July), July and August rainiest (each six days). Absolute maximum temperature 53°C *127°F*, Jacobabad, 12 June 1919.
Labour force: 26 060 000 in 1982–3: Agriculture 55·5%; Manufacturing 13·74%.
Gross domestic product: 329·8 billion rupees in 1982–3: Agriculture 29·7%; Manufacturing (includes mining and quarrying) 18·1%; Construction 4·9%; Wholesale and retail trade 14·6%.
Exports: $2628 million in 1982–3: Raw cotton 11·7%; Rice 11%; Cotton fabrics 10·7%; Cotton yarn and thread 9·9%; Carpets and rugs 5·7%.
Monetary unit: Pakistani rupee. 1 rupee = 100 paisa.
Denominations:
Coins 1, 2, 5, 10, 25, 50 paisa; 1 rupee.
Notes 5, 10, 50, 100 rupees.
Exchange rate to £ sterling: 17·02 (14 Jan. 1985).
Political history and government: Pakistan was created as an independent dominion within the Commonwealth on 15 Aug. 1947, when former British India was partitioned. Originally in two parts, East and West Pakistan, the country became a republic on 23 Mar. 1956. The port and peninsula of Gwadur were ceded to Pakistan by Muscat and Oman (now Oman) on 8 Sept. 1958. Military rule was imposed on 27 Oct. 1958. Elections for a Constituent Assembly were held on 7 Dec. 1970, giving a majority to the Awami League, which sought autonomy for East Pakistan. After negotiations on a coalition government failed, East Pakistan declared independence as Bangladesh on 26 Mar. 1971. Following Indian intervention on behalf of the Bengalis, Pakistan's forces surrendered on 16 Dec. 1971, when Bangladesh's independence became a reality. Pakistan was confined to the former western wing. Military rule ended on 20 Dec. 1971. Zulfiqar Ali Bhutto became President and Prime Minister. Pakistan left the Commonwealth on 30 Jan. 1972. A new constitution came into force on 14 Aug. 1973. Under this constitution, Pakistan became a federal republic comprising four provinces (each under a Governor) plus the Federal Capital Territory and 'tribal areas' under federal administration. President Bhutto took office as executive Prime Minister, whose advice was binding on the constitutional President. On 5 July 1977 the government was deposed by a military *coup*. A martial law régime was established, with Gen Mohammad Zia ul-Haq, the Army Chief of Staff, as Chief Martial Law Administrator. The constitution was suspended, although the President remained in office, and a 4-man Military Council was formed to direct the government. The Federal Legislature (a Senate and a National Assembly) and provincial Assemblies were dissolved. Gen Zia appointed a mainly civilian Cabinet on 5 July 1978. The President resigned on 16 Sept. 1978, when Gen Zia assumed his office. He announced on 23 Mar. 1979 that general elections would be held on 17 Nov. Bhutto, the former Prime Minister, was executed (following conviction on a murder charge) on 4 Apr. 1979. Local elections, on a non-party basis, were held on 20–27 Sept. 1979. The President announced on 16 Oct. 1979 that general elections were postponed indefinitely, political parties dissolved and political activity banned. On 24 Mar. 1981 he promulgated an interim constitution. This provided for an advisory Federal Council, to be nominated by the President. On 24 Oct. 1981 President Zia announced that the Council would draft a new constitution.
Telephones: 393 010 (1982).
Daily newspapers: 121 (1983).
Radio: 5 000 000 (1982).
TV: 850 000 (1982).
Length of roadways: 53 801 miles *86 585 km* (30 June 1979).
Length of railways: 5473 miles *8808 km.*
Universities: 20.
Adult illiteracy: 76·7% (1981).
Expectation of life: Males 49·4 years; females 49·2 years (UN estimates for 1970–75).
Defence: Military service voluntary; total armed forces 483 800 (1984); defence expenditure, 1980: $1540 million.
Cinemas: 650 plus 220 mobile units and 1 drive-in (capacity 400) in 1975.
Foreign tourists: 292 000 (1980).

* Excluding the disputed territory of Jammu and Kashmir. The Pakistan-held part has an area of 32 358 miles² *83 807 km².*

Panama

Official name: La República de Panamá.
Population: 1 830 175 (census of 11 May 1980); 1 970 000 (1983 estimate).

Area: 29 762 miles² *77 082 km²*.
Language: Spanish.
Religions: Roman Catholic, Protestant minority.
Capital city: Panamá (City), population 388 638 at 1980 census.
Other principal town: Colón, population 59 832 (1980).
Highest point: Volcán de Chiriquí, 11 410 ft *3477 m*.
Principal mountain ranges: Serrania de Tabasará, Cordillera de San Blas.
Principal rivers: Tuira (with Chucunaque), Bayano, Santa María.
Head of State: Nicolas Ardito Barletta, President.
Climate: Warm, humid days with cool nights. Little seasonal temperature change. Absolute maximum temperature 36,7°C *98°F* at Madden Dam, in the former Canal Zone, 13 Apr. 1920, and Panamá (City), 16 Apr. 1958; absolute minimum 15°C *59°F* at Madden Dam, 4 Feb. 1924.
Labour force: 466 530 (including unemployed) aged 10 and over (1970 census): Agriculture, forestry and fishing 42·2%; Trade, restaurants and hotels 13·0%; Community, social and personal services 22·9%. Figures exclude 21 805 persons working in the Canal Zone.
Gross domestic product: 2154·2 million balboas (excl. former Canal Zone) in 1977: Agriculture, forestry and fishing 17·0%; Manufacturing 13·9%; Trade, restaurants and hotels 17·1% (trade 14·5%); Community, social and personal services 22·1%.
Exports: 407 million balboas in 1980; Crustacea and molluscs 12%; Fruit and vegetables 30%; Other food 19%; Petroleum products 23%.
Monetary unit: Balboa. 1 balboa = 100 centésimos.
Denominations:
  Coins 1, 5, 10, 25, 50 centésimos; 1 and 100 balboas.
  Notes US$1, 2, 5, 10, 20, 50, 100 (there are no Panamanian bank notes).
Exchange rate to £ sterling: 1·254 (23 April 1985).
Political history and government: Formerly part of Colombia, independence declared on 3 Nov. 1903. The elected President was deposed by a *coup* on 11–12 Oct. 1968, when power was seized by the National Guard, led by Col (later Brig-Gen) Omar Torrijos Herrera. A Provisional Junta was established, the National Assembly dissolved and political activity suspended. Political parties were abolished in February 1969. On 6 Aug. 1972 elections were held for a National Assembly of Community Representatives (505 members to hold office for six years) to approve a new constitution. The Assembly elects a President and Vice-President. On 13 Sept. 1972 the Assembly approved measures to legalise, for a transitional period of six years from 11 Oct. 1972, the assumption of full executive authority by Gen Torrijos as Chief of Government and Supreme Leader of the Panamanian Revolution. A new Assembly was elected on 6 Aug. 1978, although political parties were still banned. On 11 Oct. 1978 Torrijos resigned as Chief of Government (although remaining Commander of the National Guard until his death in an air crash on 31 July 1981) and the Assembly elected a new President, with full governing powers, for six years. Three political parties were legally registered in Mar.–June 1979. The National Legislative Council, which performs the National Assembly's functions when the Assembly is not in session, was increased from 38 members (all appointed from the Assembly) when elections were held on 28 Sept. 1980 for 19 additional seats, with political parties contesting for the first time since 1968. Full legislative elections and a direct presidential election took place in 1984.

Territorial jurisdiction over the Canal Zone was granted to the USA 'in perpetuity' by treaty of 18 Nov. 1903. Treaties to restore Panamanian rule were signed on 7 Sept. 1977 and approved by a referendum in Panama on 23 Oct. 1977. Under these treaties, ratified on 16 June 1978, the Zone reverted to Panama on 1 Oct. 1979. The Panama Canal itself is to be administered by a joint US-Panamanian commission until 31 Dec. 1999.
Telephones: 212 992 (1982).
Daily newspapers: 6 (1976).
  Total circulation: 136 000.
Radio: 280 000 (1978).
TV: 206 000 (1977).
Length of roadways: 5063 miles *8148 km* (31 Dec. 1978).
Length of railways: 290 miles *467 km*.
Universities: 2.
Adult illiteracy: 21·7% (males 21·1%; females 22·3%) in 1970.
Expectation of life: Males 64·26 years; females 67·50 years (1970, excluding former Canal Zone and tribal Indians).
Defence: Total armed forces (including a paramilitary National Guard) 10 000 (1984).
Cinemas: 45 (seating capacity 39 800) in 1971, excluding former Canal Zone (7 cinemas – capacity 3800 – in 1974).
Foreign tourists: 392 062 in 1980.

Papua New Guinea

Official name: The Independent State of Papua New Guinea.
Population: 3 006 799 (census of Aug. 1980).
Area: 178 704 miles² *462 840 km²*.
Languages: English (official), Pidgin, Moru.
Religion: Christian 92·8% (1966).
Capital city: Port Moresby, population 123 624 (1980 census).
Other principal towns (1980): Lae 61 617; Rabaul 14 954; Madang 21 335; Mt Hagen 13 441.
Highest point: Mt Wilhelm, 15 400 ft *4694 m*.
Principal mountain range: Bismarck Range.
Principal rivers: Fly (with Strickland), Sepik (690 miles *1110 km*).
Head of State: HM Queen Elizabeth II, represented by Sir Kingsford Dibela, KGM, Governor-General.
Prime Minister: Michael Somare.
Climate: Generally hot and humid, cooler in highlands. Average annual rainfall between 1000 and 6350 mm *40 and 250 in*. In Port Moresby, average maximum temperature 28°C *82°F* (August) to 32°C 90°F (December), minimum 23°C *73°F* (July, August) to 25°C *76°F* (November to March), rainiest month is March (9 days).
Labour force: 733 000 employed in 1980.
Gross domestic product: 1009·1 million kina (provisional) in year ending 30 June 1975: Agriculture, forestry and fishing 30·5%; Mining and quarrying 13·8%; Community, social and personal services (including restaurants and hotels) 18·9%. Revised total is 1004·0 million kina.
Exports: K570 247 000 in 1982: Coconut and copra products 4·5%; Coffee 13·6%; Cocoa 5·6%; Forest and timber products 10·4%; Copper concentrate 52·3%.
Monetary unit: Kina. 1 kina = 100 toea.
Denominations:
  Coins 1, 2, 5, 10, 20 toea; 1 kina.
  Notes 2, 5, 10, 20 kina.
Exchange rate to £ sterling: 1·0679 (14 Jan. 1985).
Political history and government: Formed by a merger of the Territory of Papua (under Australian rule from 1906) and the Trust Territory of New Guinea, administered by Australia from 1914, later under a trusteeship agreement with the United Nations. A joint administration for the two territories was established by Australia on 1 July 1949. The combined territory achieved self-government on 1 Dec. 1973 and became independent, within the Commonwealth, on 16 Sept. 1975. Executive authority is vested in the British monarch and exercisable by the Governor-General, who is appointed on the recommendation of the Prime Minister and acts in almost all matters on the advice of the National Executive Council (the Cabinet). Legislative power is vested in the unicameral National Parliament (109 members directly elected for four years by universal adult suffrage). The pre-independence House of Assembly became the

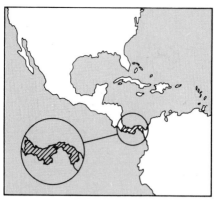

PANAMA

PAPUA NEW GUINEA

first Parliament. The Cabinet is responsible to Parliament, where the Prime Minister, appointed by the Governor-General on Parliament's proposal, must command majority support. Other Ministers are appointed on the Prime Minister's proposal. The country comprises 19 provinces.
Telephones: 50 050 (1982).
Daily newspapers: 4 (1985).
Radio: 125 000 (1977).
Length of roadways: 10 713 miles *17 241 km* (June 1977).
Universities: 2.
Adult illiteracy: 67·9% (males 60·7%; females 75·6%) in 1971.
Expectation of life: Males 47·5 years; females 47·0 years (UN estimates for 1970–75).
Defence: Military service voluntary; total armed forces 3800 (1984); defence expenditure, 1981: $36 million.
Cinemas: 28 (seating capacity 18 800) and 1 drive-in (capacity 3000) in 1972.
Foreign tourists: 40 000 (1984 estimate).

Paraguay

Official name: La República del Paraguay.
Population: 3 023 092 (1982 census).
Area: 157 048 miles² *406 752 km²*.
Languages: Spanish (official), Guaraní.
Religion: Roman Catholic.
Capital city: Asunción, population 455 517 (1982 census).
Other principal towns (1982): San Lorenzo 74 632; Fernando de la Mora 66 810; Lambaré 61 722; Presidente Stroessner 39 676; Pedro Juan Caballero 37 331; Encarnación 27 632.
Highest point: Cerro Tatug, 2297 ft *700 m*.
Principal mountain ranges: Cordillera Amambay, Sierra de Maracaju.
Principal rivers: Paraguay (1500 miles *2414 km*), Paraná (2500 miles *4023 km*), Pilcomayo (1000 miles *1609 km*).
Head of State: Gen Alfredo Stroessner Mattiauda (b. 3 Nov. 1912), President.
Climate: Sub-tropical and humid, average temperatures 18°C to 29°C *65°F to 85°F*. Hot

left: **PERU** *centre:* **PARAGUAY**

THE PHILIPPINES

December–March. Cool season May–September. Wet season March–May. In Asunción, average maximum 22°C *72°F* (June) to 35°C *95°F* (January), minimum 12°C *53°F* (June, July) to 22°C *72°F* (January, February), October, November and January rainiest (each 8 days).
Labour force: 1 111 442 (1980): Agriculture, forestry and fishing (incl. mining and quarrying) 43·5%; Manfacturing 17·7%; Trade, restaurants and hotels 13·2%; Community, social and personal services 14·7%.
Gross domestic product: 322 542 million guaranies in 1978: Agriculture, forestry and fishing 32·1% (agriculture 29·0%); Manufacturing 16·9%; Trade, finance and insurance 26·0%; Community, social and personal services (incl. restaurants, hotels and business services) 11·8%.
Exports: US$295 million in 1981: Fruit 28%; Cotton 24%; Sugar 13%; Soybeans 8%; Timber 6%; Yerba maté 6%.
Monetary unit: Guaraní. 1 guaraní = 100 céntimos.
Denominations:
  Coins (issued only for commemorative purposes).
  Notes 1, 5, 10, 50, 100, 500, 1000, 5000, 10 000 guaraníes.
Exchange rate to £ sterling: 443·52 (14 Jan. 1985).
Political history and government: A republic comprising 16 departments. Gen Alfredo Stroessner Mattiauda assumed power by a military *coup* on 5 May 1954. He was elected President on 11 July 1954 to complete his predecessor's term. President Stroessner was re-elected in 1958, 1963, 1968, 1973 and 1978. A new constitution

was promulgated on 25 Aug. 1967 and took effect in 1968. Legislative power is held by a bicameral National Congress, whose members serve for 5 years. The Senate has 30 members and the Chamber of Deputies 60 members. The party receiving the largest number of votes (since 1947 the National Republican Association, known as the Colorado Party) is allotted two-thirds of the seats in each chamber, the remaining seats being divided proportionately among the other contending parties. Executive power is held by the President, directly elected for 5 years at the same time as the Congress. He rules with the assistance of an appointed Council of Ministers.
Telephones: 58 713 (1981).
Daily newspapers: 5 (1980).
  Total circulation: 200 000.
Radio: 187 000 (1977).
TV: 56 000 (1978).
Length of roadways: 9915 miles *15 956 km* (31 Dec. 1973).
Length of railways: 274 miles *441 km.*
Universities: 2.
Adult illiteracy: 19·9% (males 14·9%; females 24·5%) in 1972.
Expectation of life: Males 60·3 years; females 63·6 years (UN estimates for 1970–75).
Defence: Military service: 18 months (Navy 2 years); total armed forces 16 000 (1984); defence expenditure, 1980: $64 million.
Cinemas: 65 in Asunción (1974).
Foreign tourists: 178 454 in 1982.

Peru

Official name: La República del Perú.
Population: 17 762 231 (1981 census).
Area: 496 225 miles^2 *1 285 216 km^2.*
Languages: Spanish, Quéchua, Aymará.
Religion: Roman Catholic.
Capital city: Lima, population 4 164 597 (1981 census).
Other principal towns (1981): Callao 296 220 (1972): Arequipa 447 431; Trujillo 354 557; Chiclayo 280 244; Chimbote 216 406; Piura 186 354; Cuzco 181 604; Huancayo 115 693 (1972); Iquitos 173 629.
Highest point: Huascarán, 22 205 ft *6768 m.*
Principal mountain ranges: Cordillera de los Andes (C. Oriental, C. Occidental, C. Blanca).
Principal rivers: Amazonas (Amazon), with Ucayali.
Head of State: Fernando Belaúnde Terry (b. 7 Oct. 1913), President.
Prime Minister: Sandro Mariategui.
Climate: Varies with altitude. Daily fluctuations greater than seasonal. Rainy season October–April. Heavy rains in tropical forests. In Lima, average maximum 19°C *66°F* (August) to 28°C *83°F* (February, March), minimum 13°C *56°F* (August) to 19°C *67°F* (February), August rainiest (two days). Absolute maximum temperature 38,5°C *101·3°F*, Iquitos, 19 June 1948; absolute minimum −20,2°C *−4·4F*, Imata, 1 Aug. 1947.
Labour force: 5 613 500 (mid-1980): Agriculture, forestry and fishing 40·0%; Manufacturing 12·6%; Trade, restaurants and hotels 15·1%; Community, social and personal services 20·2%.
Gross domestic product: 1 132 678 million soles in 1977: Agriculture, forestry and fishing 11·8% (agriculture and forestry 11·1%); Manufacturing 25·9%; Trade, restaurants and hotels 16·2% (trade 15·3%); Community, social and personal services (incl. all government services) 16·5%.
Exports: US$3212 million in 1982.
Monetary unit: Sol. 1 sol = 100 centavos.
Denominations:
  Coins 50 centavos; 1, 5, 10 soles.
  Notes 5, 10, 50, 100, 200, 500, 1000, 5000 soles.
Exchange rate to £ sterling: 6587·40 (14 Jan. 1985).
Political history and government: A republic comprising 23 departments and one province. Following disputed presidential elections on 10 June 1962, a military junta took power in a *coup* on 18 July 1962 and annulled the election results.

Congressional and presidential elections were held again on 9 June 1963. Fernando Belaúnde Terry, runner-up in 1956 and 1962, was elected President and took office for a six-year term on 28 July 1963, when military rule ended. On 3 Oct. 1968 President Belaúnde was deposed by another military *coup*, led by the army commander, Gen Juan Velasco Alvarado. The bicameral National Congress was abolished, political activity suspended and a revolutionary government of military officers took power, with Gen Velasco as President. Executive and legislative powers were exercised by the armed forces through the President, ruling by decree with the assistance of an appointed Council of Ministers. On 29 Aug. 1975 President Velasco was deposed by the Prime Minister, Gen Francisco Morales Bermúdez.
On 28 July 1977 President Morales announced plans for the restoration of civilian rule. On 18 June 1978 a Constituent Assembly of 100 members was elected by literate adults, using proportional representation. The Assembly was convened on 28 July 1978. It adopted a new constitution on 12 July 1979 and dissolved itself two days later. The constitution vests executive power in a President, elected for a five-year term by universal adult suffrage (including illiterates for the first time). Legislative power is vested in a bicameral National Congress, also directly elected for five years. The Congress comprises the Senate (60 members chosen on a regional basis plus ex-Presidents of constitutional governments) and the Chamber of Deputies (180 members chosen on the basis of proportional representation). Congressional and presidential elections were held on 18 May 1980, when ex-President Belaúnde was re-elected Head of State. Power was transferred to the new civilian authorities on 28 July 1980, when the new constitution came into force. Each department is administered by an appointed official.
Telephones: 629 742 (1981).
Daily newspapers: 30 (1977).
  Total circulation: 828 000.
Radio: 2 200 000 (1977).
TV: 825 000 (1977).
Length of roadways: 31 485 miles *50 670 km* (31 Dec. 1974).
Length of railways: 1012 miles *1628 km.*
Universities: 32.
Adult illiteracy: 27·5% (males 16·7%; females 38·2%) in 1972.
Expectation of life: Males 52·59 years; females 55·48 years (1960–65).
Defence: Military service: two years, selective; total armed forces 130 000 (51 000 conscripts) in 1984; defence expenditure, 1979: $431 million.
Cinemas: 400 in 1977.
Foreign tourists: 336 000 in 1981.

The Philippines

Official name: República de Filipinas (in Spanish) or Repúblika ñg Pilipinas (in Tagalog): Republic of the Philippines.
Population: 50 350 000 (1984 estimate).
Area: 115 831 miles^2 *300 000 km^2.*
Languages (1960): Cebuano; Tagalog; Ilocano; Panay-Hiligaynon; Bikol; many others. The national language, Pilipino, is based on Tagalog.
Religions (1960): Roman Catholic 84%; Aglipayan 5%; Muslim 5%; Protestant 3%.
Capital city: Manila, population 5 925 884 (1980 estimate).
Other principal towns (1980): Quezon City 1 165 865; Davao 610 375; Cebu 490 281; Zamboanga 343 722; Pasay 287 770; Bacolod 262 415; Iloilo 244 827; San Carlos (on Pangasinan) 101 243; San Carlos (on Negros Occidental) 91 627.
Highest point: Mt Apo (on Mindanao), 9690 ft *2953 m.*
Principal mountain ranges: Cordillera Central (on Luzon), Diuata Range (on Mindanao).
Principal rivers: Cagayan (180 miles *290 km*) Pampanga, Abra, Agusan, Magat, Laoang, Agno.
Head of State: Ferdinand Edralin Marcos

(b. 11 Sept. 1917), President.
Prime Minister: Cesar E. A. Virata (b. 12 Dec. 1930).
Climate: Tropical. Hot and humid, except in mountains. Heavy rainfall, frequent typhoons. In Manila, average maximum 30°C *86°F* (December January) to 34°C *93°F* (April, May), minimum 21°C *69°F* (January, February) to 24°C *75°F* (May–August), July rainiest (24 days). Absolute maximum temperature 42,2°C *108·0°F*, Tuguegarao, 29 Apr. 1912; absolute minimum 7,3°C *45·1°F*, Baguio City, 1 Feb. 1930 and 11 Jan. 1932.
Labour force: 14 323 000 (excluding armed forces, institutional households and 671 000 unemployed) at Oct.–Dec. 1977): Agriculture, forestry and fishing 51·5%; Manufacturing 11·0%; Services 33·2%.
Gross domestic product: 172 854 million pesos in 1978: Agriculture, forestry and fishing 27·3% (agriculture 19·6%); Manufacturing 24·6%; Trade, restaurants and hotels 15·3% (trade 14·1%).
Exports: US$5021 million in 1982: Electronics 19·2%; Clothes 10·8%; Sugar 8·3%; Coconut oil 8%; Copper concentrates 6·2%.
Monetary unit: Philippine peso. 1 peso = 100 centavos.
Denominations:
Coins 1, 5, 10, 25, 50 centavos; 1, 5 pesos.
Notes 2, 5, 10, 20, 50, 100 pesos.
Exchange rate to £ sterling: 20·38 (18 Jan. 1985).
Political history and government: Formerly a Spanish colony. After the Spanish-American War, Spain ceded the Philippines to the USA (10 Dec. 1898). A constitution, ratified by plebiscite on 14 May 1935, gave the Philippines self-government and provided for independence after 10 years. The islands were occupied by Japanese forces in 1942–45. After the restoration of US rule, the Philippines became an independent republic on 4 July 1946.

Ferdinand Marcos was elected President on 9 Nov. 1965 and inaugurated on 30 Dec. 1965. He was re-elected in 1969. Before completing his (then) maximum of two four-year terms, President Marcos proclaimed martial law, and suspended the bicameral Congress, on 23 Sept. 1972. On 2 Jan. 1973 the President ordered the formation of 'citizens' assemblies', open to all persons over 15. After discussion by these assemblies, a new constitution was ratified by the President on 17 Jan. 1973. This provided for a unicameral National Assembly and a constitutional President (both elected for 6 years), with executive power held by a Prime Minister, to be elected by the Assembly. Pending its full implementation, transitional provisions gave the incumbent President the combined authority of the Presidency (under the 1935 constitution) and the Premiership under the new constitution, without any fixed term of office. Under martial law the definitive provisions of the constitution remained in abeyance. A referendum on 27–28 July 1973 approved the President's continuation in office beyond his elected term. Another referendum, on 27 Feb. 1975, approved the continuation of martial law, enabling the President to rule by decree. A referendum on 16–17 Oct. 1976 approved the further continuation of martial law and constitutional amendments, including a provision for the formation of an interim assembly. On 27 Oct. 1976 a Presidential decree amended the constitution in accordance with the referendum results. On 18 Dec. 1977 a fourth referendum approved Marcos's continuation in office. Elections were held on 7 Apr. 1978 for 165 members of an interim National Assembly (*Batasang Pambansa*). The 192-member Assembly (including 14 representatives of sectoral organisations and 13 Cabinet Ministers appointed by the President) was inaugurated for a 6-year term on 12 June 1978, when Marcos was sworn in as Prime Minister. Martial law remained in force and the President retained power to legislate by decree. On 17 Jan. 1981 President Marcos announced the lifting of martial law. Two days later he transferred his legislative powers to the National Assembly. On 7 Apr. 1981 a referendum approved constitu-

tional amendments providing for a mixed presidential-parliamentary form of government, including the election by direct popular vote of a President with increased powers. President Marcos was re-elected on 16 June 1981 and took office for a 6 year term on 30 June. On 3 July 1981 he appointed a new Prime Minister, who was approved by the Assembly on 28 July.

The country is divided into 12 regions and 72 provinces.
Telephones: 794 569 in 1982.
Daily newspapers: 4.
Total circulation: 1 100 000.
Radio: 1 936 000 (1977).
TV: 850 000 (1977).
Length of roadways: 79 007 miles *127 150 km* (June 1979).
Length of railways: 711 miles *1144 km*.
Universities: 45.
Adult illiteracy: 17·4% (males 15·7%; females 19·1%) in 1970.
Expectation of life: Males 56·9 years; females 60·0 years (UN estimates for 1970–75).
Defence: Military service: selective; total armed forces 100 300 (1984); defence expenditure, 1981: $863 million.
Cinemas: 1200 in 1980.
Foreign tourists: 890 807 in 1982.

Poland

Official name: Polska Rzeczpospolita Ludowa (Polish People's Republic).
Population: 32 642 270 (census 8 Dec. 1970); 37 063 300 (estimate for 31 Dec. 1984).
Area: 120 727 miles² *312 683 km²*.
Language: Polish.
Religion: Roman Catholic (over 70%).
Capital city: Warszawa (Warsaw), population 1 649 050 at 31 Dec. 1984.
Other principal towns (31 Dec. 1984): Łódź 849 460; Kraków (Cracow) 740 260; Wrocław (Breslau) 635 950; Poznań (Posen) 574 070; Gdańsk (Danzig) 467 170; Szczecin (Stettin) 370 780; Katowice 363 270; Bydgoszcz (Bromberg) 361 390; Lublin 324 150.
Highest point: Rysy, 8199 ft *2499 m*.
Principal mountain ranges: Carpathian Mountains (Tatra range), Beskids.
Principal rivers: Wisła (Vistula) with Narew, Odra (Oder).
Head of State: Dr Henryk Jabłoński (b. 27 Dec. 1909), Chairman of the Council of State.
Head of Government: Gen. Wojciech Jaruzelski (b. 6 July 1923), Chairman of the Council of Ministers, also First Secretary of the Central Committee of the Polish United Worker's Party.
Climate: Temperate in west, continental in east. Short, rainy summers, but occasional dry spells; cold, snowy winters. In Warsaw, average maximum −0,4°C *31°F* (January) to 24°C *75°F* (July), minimum −6°C *21°F* (January) to 15°C *59°F* (July), June, July and August rainiest (each 6 days). Absolute maximum temperature 40·2°C *104·4°F*, Prószków, 29 July 1921; absolute minimum −40·6°C *−41·1°F*, Żywiec, 10 Feb. 1929.
Labour force: 17 163 800 aged 15 and over (31 Dec. 1984): Agriculture and forestry 30·8%; Industry (mining, quarrying, manufacturing, electricity, gas and water) 29·1%; Services 7·7%.
Net material product: 4 855 600 million złotys (in domestic prices) in 1983: Industry 49·1%; Agriculture, forestry 18·1%; Construction 11·1%; Trade 15·5%.
Exports: $11 750 million in 1984: Coal, coke and briquettes 15·1% (coal 14·3%); Machinery and transport equipment 39·3%.
Monetary unit: Złoty. 1 złoty = 100 groszy.
Denominations:
Coins 1, 2, 5, 10, 20, 50 groszy; 1, 2, 5, 10, 20, 50 złotys.
Notes 50, 100, 200, 500, 1000, 2000, 5000 złotys.
Exchange rate to £ sterling: 152·36 (18 March 1985).
Political history and government: Formerly partitioned between Austria, Prussia and Russia. After the First World War an independent

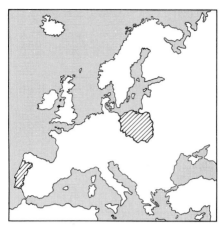

left: **PORTUGAL** *right:* **POLAND**

republic was declared on 11 Nov. 1918. Parliamentary government was overthrown in May 1926 by military leaders who ruled until 1939, when invasions by Nazi Germany (1 Sept.) and the USSR (17 Sept.) led to another partition (29 Sept.). After Germany declared war on the USSR (June 1941) its forces occupied the whole of Poland but they were driven out by Soviet forces in March 1945. With the end of the Second World War (May 1945) Poland's frontiers were redrawn. A provisional government was formed on 28 June 1945. A Communist régime took power after the elections of 19 Jan. 1947 and a People's Republic was established on 19 Feb. 1947. At a congress on 15–21 Dec. 1948 the Polish Workers' (Communist) Party merged with the Polish Socialist Party to form the Polish United Workers' Party (PUWP). A new constitution was adopted on 22 July 1952.

The supreme organ of state power is the unicameral Parliament (*Sejm*), with 460 members elected by universal adult suffrage for four years (in the elections of 23 Mar. 1980 there were 646 candidates). The *Sejm* elects a Council of State (17 members) to be its permanent organ. The highest executive and administrative body is the Council of Ministers, appointed by (and responsible to) the *Sejm*.

Political power is held by the Communist PUWP, which dominates the Front of National Unity (including two other smaller parties). The Front presents an approved list of candidates for elections to representative bodies. The PUWP's highest authority is the Party Congress, normally convened every four years. The Congress elects a Central Committee (200 members were elected on 17 July 1981) to supervise Party work. To direct its policy the Committee elects a Political Bureau (Politburo), with 15 full members (including the Committee's First Secretary) and two alternate members in 1981.

On 13 Dec. 1981 the régime declared martial law and established a 20-member military council for national salvation led by the Chairman of the Council of Ministers.
Telephones: 4 028 385 (1984).
Daily newspapers: 44 (1983).
Total circulation: 7 841 000.
Radio: 9 286 663 licences (31 Dec. 1984).
TV: 8 764 768 licences (31 Dec. 1984).
Length of roadways: 157 786 miles *253 878 km* (excluding forest, factory and agricultural roads) at 31 Dec. 1984.
Length of railways: 16 871 miles *27 145 km*.
Universities: 10 (plus 18 technical universities).
Adult illiteracy: 1·2% (males 0·7%; females 1·7%) in 1978.
Expectation of life: Males 67·0 years; females 75·2 years (1983).
Defence: Military service: Army, internal security forces and Air Force 2 years, Navy and special services 3 years; total regular forces 340 500 in 1984; defence expenditure, 1980: $4670 million (converted at $1 = 15·06 złotys).
Cinemas: 1769 (seating capacity 478 214) and 292 mobile units (1984).
Foreign tourists: 2 997 031 in 1984.

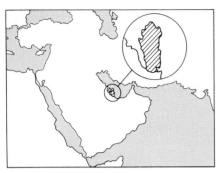

QATAR

Portugal

Official name: A República Portuguesa (the Portuguese Republic).
*Population: 9 806 333 (1981 census).
*Area: 35 553 miles² *92 082 km²*.
Language: Portuguese.
Religion: Roman Catholic.
Capital city: Lisboa (Lisbon), population 817 600 (1981 census).
Other principal towns (1981): Oporto 330 100; Amadora 93 700; Coimbra 71 800; Setubal 76 800.
*Highest point: 7713 ft *2351 m*.
Principal mountain range: Serra da Estréla.
Principal river: Rio Tejo (Tagus).
Head of State: Gen António dos Santos Ramalho Eanes (b. 25 Jan. 1935), President.
Prime Minister: Dr Mario Alberto Nobre Lopes Soares.
Climate: Mild and temperate. Average annual temperature 16°C *61°F*, drier and hotter inland. Hot summers, rainy winters in central areas, warm and very dry in south. In Lisbon, average maximum 13°C *56°F* (January) to 27°C *80°F* (August), minimum 8°C *46°F* (January) to 18°C *64°F* (August); March, November and December rainiest (each 10 days). Absolute maximum temperature 45,8°C *114·4°F*, Coimbra, 31 July 1944; absolute minimum −11,0°C *12·2°F*, Penhas Douradas, 25 Jan. 1947.
Labour force: 3 943 000 in 1981, excluding 325 000 unemployed: Agriculture, forestry and fishing 26·7%; Extractive and manufacturing industries 26·3%; Construction 9·8%; Commerce, restaurants and hotels 12·6%; Transport and communications 3·9%; Other services 11%.
Gross domestic product: 2289·6 billion escudos in 1983: Agriculture, forestry and fishing 8·4%; Mining and manufacturing industries 30·2%; Construction 7·4%; Services 55·7%.
Exports: 506·3 billion escudos in 1983: Agricultural goods and processed agricultural goods 11·6%; Mineral products 9%; Chemical and allied products 5%; Products of wood and cork 13·4%; Clothing and shoes 33%; Machinery and transport equipment 15·3%.
Monetary unit: Portuguese escudo. 1 escudo = 100 centavos.
Denominations:
　Coins 10, 20, 50 centavos; 1, 2½, 5, 10, 25 escudos.
　Notes 20, 50, 100, 500, 1000, 5000 escudos.
Exchange rate to £ sterling: 206·00 (19 Apr. 1985).
Political history and government: Formerly a kingdom. An anti-monarchist uprising deposed the King on 5 Oct. 1910, when a republic was proclaimed. The parliamentary regime was overthrown by a military *coup* on 28 May 1926. Dr António Salazar became Prime Minister, with dictatorial powers, on 5 July 1932. A new constitution, establishing a corporate state, was adopted on 19 Mar. 1933. Dr Salazar retained power until illness forced his retirement on 26 Sept. 1968. His successor, Dr Marcello Caetano, was deposed on 25 Apr. 1974 by a military *coup*, initiated by the Armed Forces Movement. Military leaders formed a Junta of National Salvation and appointed one of its members as President. He appointed a Prime Minister and, on the latter's recommendation, other Ministers

to form a provisional government. The 1933 constitution was suspended and the bicameral Parliament dissolved.

On 14 Mar. 1975 the Junta was dissolved and three days later a Supreme Revolutionary Council (SRC) was established to exercise authority until a new constitution took effect. A Constitutional Assembly was elected on 25 Apr. 1975 to formulate a new constitution. After approval by the SRC, the constitution, committing Portugal to make a transition to socialism, was promulgated on 2 Apr. 1976. It provides for a unicameral legislature, the Assembly of the Republic, elected by universal adult suffrage for 4 years (subject to dissolution). The first Assembly, with 263 members, was elected on 25 Apr. 1976, when the constitution entered into force. The SRC was renamed the Council of the Revolution, becoming a consultative body, headed by the President, with powers to delay legislation and the right of veto in military matters. Executive power is vested in the President, directly elected for 5 years. A new President was elected on 27 June and inaugurated on 14 July 1976. The President appoints a Prime Minister to lead a Council of Ministers, responsible to the Assembly. Legislation approved on 2 Oct. 1978 reduced the Assembly to 250 members (including four representing Portugal abroad) at the next elections. The Assembly was dissolved by the President on 11 Sept. 1979 and new elections held on 2 Dec. 1979 to complete the Assembly's term, ending in Oct. 1980. A new Assembly, also with 250 members, was elected on 5 Oct. 1980.
Telephones: 1 455 805 (1982).
Daily newspapers: 32 (1982).
　Total circulation: 188 836.
Radio: 1 575 000 (1979).
TV: 1 460 902 (1981).
Length of roadways: 31 510 miles *50 710 km* (31 Dec. 1978).
Length of railways: 2229 miles *3588 km*.
Universities: 11.
Adult illiteracy: 29·0% (males 22·4%; females 34·7%) in 1970.
Expectation of life: Males 65·29 years; females 72·03 years (1974).
Defence: Military service: Army 16 months, Navy and Air Force 24 months; total armed forces 70 000 (18 000 conscripts) in 1984; defence expenditure, 1981; $944 million.
Cinemas: 435 with seating capacity for 240 874 in 1979.
Foreign tourists: 7 299 000 in 1982.

* Metropolitan Portugal, including the Azores and Maideira Islands.

Qatar

Official name: Dawlat Qatar (State of Qatar).
Population: 257 081 (estimate 1982).
Area: 4416 miles² *11 437 km²*.
Language: Arabic.
Religion: Muslim.
Capital city: Ad Dauhah (Doha), population 190 000 (estimate 1982).
Other principal towns: Dukhan, Umm Said.
Highest point: 240 ft *73 m*.
Head of State: Shaikh Khalifa ibn Hamad al-Thani (b. 1932), Amir and Prime Minister.
Climate: Very hot, with high humidity on the coast. Temperatures reach 49°C *120°F* in summer.
Labour force: 109 436 (1983).
Gross domestic product: 23 365 million Qatar riyals in 1983: Mining and quarrying 45·8%; Manufacturing 5·9%; Building and construction 7·1%; Trade, restaurants and hotels 6·8%; Finance, insurance, real estate and business services 9%.
Exports: 21 272 million Qatar riyals in 1981: crude oil 94%.
Monetary unit: Qatar riyal. 1 riyal = 100 dirhams.
Denominations:
　Coins 1, 5, 10, 25, 50 dirhams.
　Notes 1, 5, 10, 50, 100, 500 riyals.
Exchange rate to £ sterling: 4·06 (19 Jan. 1985).
Political history and government: Became part of

Turkey's Ottoman Empire in 1872. Turkish forces evacuated Qatar at the beginning of the First World War. The UK entered into treaty relations with the ruling Shaikh on 3 Nov. 1916. A provisional constitution was adopted on 2 Apr. 1970. Qatar remained under British protection until achieving full independence on 1 Sept. 1971. On 22 Feb. 1972 the ruler was deposed by his deputy, the Prime Minister.

Qatar is an absolute monarchy, with full powers vested in the ruler (called Amir since independence). It has no parliament or political parties. The ruler appoints and leads a Council of Ministers to exercise executive power. The Ministers are assisted by a nominated Consultative Council with 20 members (increased to 30 in Dec. 1975), whose term was extended for 3 years in May 1975 and for a further 3 years in May 1978.
Telephones: 96 000 (1983).
Daily newspapers: 1.
　Total circulation: 7000.
Radio: 40 000 (1976).
TV: 200 000 (1977).
Universities: 1.
Expectation of life: Males 54·8 years; females 58·2 years (UN estimates, average for Bahrain, Qatar and the United Arab Emirates, 1970–75).
Defence: Total armed forces 5700 (1984); defence expenditure, 1980: $59·5 million.
Cinemas: 4 in 1983.

Romania

Official name: Republica Socialistă România (Socialist Republic of Romania).
Population: 22 600 000 (1984 estimate).
Area: 91 699 miles² *237 500 km²*.
Languages (1966): Romanian 87·8%; Hungarian 8·6%; German 2·0%.
Religions: Romanian Orthodox (85% of believers), Roman Catholic, Reformed (Calvinist).
Capital city: Bucureşti (Bucharest), population 2 211 460 (1982).
Other principal towns (1980): Braşov 304 670; Timişoara 287 543; Cluj-Napoca 283 647; Constanţa 283 629; Iaşi 271 441; Galaţi 260 898; Craiova 227 444; Brăila 214 940; Ploieşti 211 505.
Highest point: Negoiu, 8360 ft *2548 m*.
Principal mountain ranges: Carpathian Mountains, Transylvanian Alps.
Principal rivers: Dunărea (Danube) (1777 miles *2860 km*, 668 miles *1075 km* in Romania), Mureş (446 miles *718 km*), Prut (437 miles *703 km*).
Head of State: Nicolae Ceauşescu (b. 26 Jan. 1918), President; also General Secretary of the Central Committee of the Romanian Communist Party.
Head of Government: Constantin Dăscălescu, Chairman of the Council of Ministers.
Climate: Hot and humid summers (average temperature 21°C *70°F*); cold, windy, snowy winters (average −2°C *28°F*). Moderate rainfall. Absolute maximum temperature 44,5°C *112·1°F*, Ion Sion, 10 Aug. 1951; minimum −38,5°C *−37·3°F*, Bod, near Braşov, 25 Jan. 1942.
Labour force: 10 362 300 (excluding persons seeking work for the first time) aged 14 and over (census of 15 Mar. 1966): Agriculture and forestry 57·2%; Mining, quarrying, manufacturing and fishing 19·4%; 11 342 000 (mid-1970): Agriculture, forestry and fishing 56·0%; Industry 26·3%; Services 17·7% (ILO estimates).
Gross national product: $36 190 million in 1978 (World Bank estimate).
Exports: 151 837 million lei in 1982.
Monetary unit: Leu (plural: lei). 1 leu = 100 bani.
Denominations:
　Coins 5, 10, 15, 25 bani; 1, 3, 5 lei.
　Notes 1, 5, 10, 25, 50, 100 lei.
Exchange rate to £ sterling: 14·47 (14 Jan. 1985).
Political history and government: Formerly a monarchy. Under the Fascist 'Iron Guard' movement, Romania entered the Second World War as an ally of Nazi Germany. Soviet forces entered Romania in 1944. The Iron Guard

régime was overthrown on 23 Aug. 1944 and a predominantly Communist government took power on 6 Mar. 1945. The Romanian Communist Party (RCP) merged with the Social Democratic Party, to form the Romanian Workers' Party (RWP), on 1 Oct. 1947. The King was forced to abdicate on 30 Dec. 1947, when the Romanian People's Republic was proclaimed. The RWP became the RCP again on 2 June 1965. A new constitution, introducing the country's present name, was adopted on 21 Aug. 1965.

The supreme organ of state power is the unicameral Grand National Assembly, with 369 members elected by universal adult suffrage for five years. The Assembly elects from its number the State Council (25 members were appointed on 29 Mar. 1980) to be its permanent organ. The President of the Republic, elected by the Assembly for its duration, is also President of the State Council. The Council of Ministers, the highest organ of state administration, is elected by (and responsible to) the Assembly.

Political power is held by the RCP, the only legal party, which dominates the Front of Socialist Unity. The Front presents an approved list of candidates for elections to representative bodies. The Head of State is General Secretary of the RCP and Chairman of the Front. The RCP's highest authority is the Party Congress, convened every five years. The Congress elects a Central Committee (245 full members and 163 alternate members were elected on 23 Nov. 1979) to supervise Party work. The Central Committee elects from its members an Executive Political Committee (27 full members and 18 alternate members) to direct policy. The Executive Committee has a 15-member Permanent Bureau (including the President), which is the Party's most powerful policy-making body.

Romania comprises 40 administrative districts, each with a People's Council elected for five years.

Telephones: 1 748 000 (1982).
Daily newspapers: 34 (1977).
  Total circulation: 3 711 000.
Radio: 3 200 000 (1982).
TV: 3 860 000 (1982).
Length of roadways: 45 584 miles *73 361 km* (31 Dec. 1978).
Length of railways: 6914 miles *11 127 km*.
Universities: 7 (plus 4 technical universities).
Adult illiteracy: 11·4% (males 6·1%; females 16·3%) in 1956.
Expectation of life: Males 67·4 years; females 72·4 years (1982).
Defence: Military service: Army and Air Force 16 months, Navy 2 years; total armed forces 192 500 in 1984; defence expenditure, 1981: $1350 million (converted at $1 = 7·7 lei).
Cinemas: 578 in 1977.
Foreign tourists: 3 684 854 in 1977.

Rwanda

Official name: La République rwandaise (in French) or Republika y'u Rwanda (in Kinyarwanda).
Population: 5 576 000 (1983 estimate).
Area: 10 169 miles² *26 338 km²*.
Languages: French, Kinyarwanda (both official), Kiswahili.
Religions: Roman Catholic, Animist; Protestant and Muslim minorities.
Capital city: Kigali, population 117 749 at 1978 census.
Other principal towns (1978): Butare 21 691; Ruhengeri 16 025; Gisenyi 12 436.
Highest point: Mt Karisimbi, 14 787 ft *4507 m*.
Principal mountain range: Chaîne des Mitumba.
Principal river: Luvironza (headwaters of the Nile).
Head of State: Maj-Gen Juvénal Habyarimana (b. 8 Mar. 1937), President.
Climate: Tropical, tempered by altitude. Average temperature at 4800 ft *1463 m* is 23°C *73°F*. Hot and humid in lowlands, cool in highlands. Average annual rainfall 785 mm *31 in*. Main rainy season from February to May, dry season

May to September.
Labour force: 1 988 000 (mid-1970): Agriculture, forestry and fishing 93·2% (ILO estimates).
Gross domestic product: 71 600 million Rwanda francs in 1977: Agriculture, forestry and fishing 47·9% (agriculture 45·8%); Manufacturing 14·7%; Trade, restaurants and hotels 15·3% (trade 15·2%).
Exports: 7025 million Rwanda francs in 1980: Coffee 55%; Tea 18%; Tin 8%.
Monetary unit: Franc rwandais (Rwanda franc). 1 franc = 100 centimes.
Denominations:
  Coins 50 centimes; 1, 2, 5, 10, 20, 50 francs.
  Notes 20, 50, 100, 500, 1000 francs.
Exchange rate to £ sterling: 120·24 (14 Jan. 1985).
Political history and government: Formerly a monarchy, ruled by a *Mwami* (King). Part of German East Africa from 1899. Occupied in 1916 by Belgian forces from the Congo (now Zaire). From 1920 Rwanda was part of Ruanda-Urundi, administered by Belgium under League of Nations mandate and later as a UN Trust Territory. Following a referendum on 25 Sept. 1961, the monarchy was abolished and the republic which had been proclaimed on 28 Jan. 1961 was recognised by Belgium on 2 Oct. 1961. Rwanda became independent on 1 July 1962. On 5 July 1973 the government was overthrown by a military *coup*, led by Maj-Gen Juvénal Habyarimana, who became President. The National Assembly was dissolved and political activity suspended. On 5 July 1975 President Habyarimana established a new ruling party, the *Mouvement révolutionnaire national pour le développement* (MRND), the National Revolutionary Movement for Development. A referendum on 17 Dec. 1978 approved a new constitution legalising Habyarimana's régime. Executive power is vested in the President, elected by universal adult suffrage for a five-year term. The constitution provides for a 50-member National Development Council (NDC), also to be directly elected for five years. The NDC is granted limited legislative powers but is unable to change government policy. The MRND became the sole political organisation. Habyarimana was elected (unopposed) on 24 Dec. 1978 to continue as President. The President appoints and leads a Council of Ministers. A congress of the MRND on 17–21 Dec. 1980 decided that elections to the NDC should be held in 1981. Rwanda comprises 10 prefectures, each administered by an appointed official.
Telephones: 4543 (1978).
Daily newspapers: 1 (1977).
  Total circulation: 200.
Radio: 152 000 (1979).
Length of roadways: 4088 miles *6579 km* (31 Dec. 1979).
Universities: 1.
Adult illiteracy: 83·6% (males 76%; females 91%) in 1962 (UNESCO estimates).
Expectation of life: Males 41·8 years; females 45·0 years (UN estimates for 1970–75).
Defence: Total armed forces 5150 (1984); defence expenditure, 1980: $22 million.
Cinemas: 3 (seating capacity 1000) in 1975.

Saint Lucia

Population: 124 000 (1981).
Area: 238 miles² *616 km²*.
Language: English.
Religion: Christian (mainly Roman Catholic, also Anglican and Methodist).
Capital city: Castries, population 48 782 (1981).
Other principal town: Vieux Fort, Sarfriere.
Highest point: Morne (Mt.) Gimie, 3145 ft *959 m*.
Head of State: HM Queen Elizabeth II, represented by Sir Allen Lewis GCMG.
Prime Minister: The Rt Hon. John Compton.
Climate: Warm and moist. Dry season Jan.–Apr., rainy May–Aug. In Castries, average annual temperature 28°C *82°F*, rainfall 2235 mm *88 in*, rising to 3480 mm *137 in* inland.
Labour force: 48 012 (1981).
Gross domestic product: US$210 million in 1980:

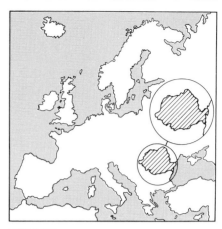

ROMANIA

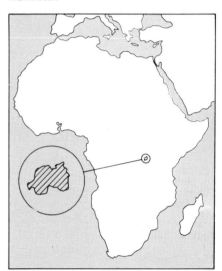

RWANDA

Agriculture 14·7%; Manufacturing 8·4%; Construction 11%; Government services 20·1%.
Exports: EC$40·4 million in 1980.
Monetary unit: East Caribbean dollars (EC$). 1 dollar = 100 cents.
Denominations:
  Coins 1, 2, 5, 10, 25, 50 cents.
  Notes 1, 5, 20, 100 dollars.
Exchange rate to £ sterling: 3·43 (28 Jan. 1985).
Political history and government: A former British dependency, St. Lucia was administered by the Governor of the Windward Islands until 31 Dec. 1959. From 1 Jan. 1960 it had a new constitution, with its own Administrator. On 1 Mar. 1967 St. Lucia became one of the West Indies Associated States, with full internal self-government. The Administrator became Governor and the Chief Minister was restyled Premier. After a constitutional conference on 24–27 July 1978, Saint Lucia (as it was restyled) became fully independent, within the Commonwealth, on 22 Feb. 1979. The Governor became Governor-General and the Premier took office as Prime Minister.

Saint Lucia is a constitutional monarchy. Executive power is vested in the British monarch and is exercisable by the Governor-General, who is appointed on the advice of the Prime Minister and acts in almost all matters on the advice of the Cabinet. Legislative power is vested in a bicameral Parliament, comprising a Senate (11 members appointed by the Governor-General) and a House of Assembly (initially 17 members) elected from single-member constituencies by universal adult suffrage for 5 years (subject to dissolution). The Governor-General appoints the Prime Minister and, on the latter's recommendation, other Ministers from among members of the Senate and the House. The Cabinet is responsible to the House.
Telephones: 9500 (1982).

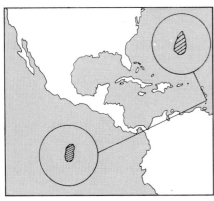

top: **SAINT LUCIA**
below: **SAINT VINCENT AND THE GRENADINES**

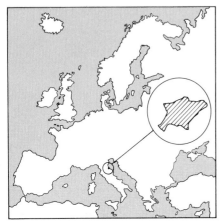

SAN MARINO

Daily newspapers: 1 (1976).
  Total circulation: 4000.
Radio: 84 000 (1977).
TV: 1700 (1976).
Length of roadways: 500 miles *800 km*.
Adult illiteracy: 14·8% (population aged 10 and over) in 1970.
Expectation of life: Males 65 years; females 71 years (1983).
Cinemas: 9 (seating capacity 9500) in 1970.
Foreign tourists: 142 855 in 1981.

Saint Vincent and the Grenadines

Population: 123 000 (1984 estimate).
Area: 150·3 miles² *389 km²*.
Language: English.
Religion: Christian (mainly Anglican).
Capital: Kingstown, population 29 831 (1977 estimate).
Other principal towns: Georgetown, Barrouaillie, Chateaubelair, Layou.
Highest point: Soufrière, 4048 ft *1234 m*.
Head of State: HM Queen Elizabeth II, represented by Sir Sydney Douglas Gun-Munro, MBE (b. 29 Nov. 1916), Governor-General.
Prime Minister: The Rt Hon. James Mitchell.
Climate: Warm and moist, with average temperatures between 19°C *67°F* and 32°C *89°F*.
Labour force: 40 000 (1983).
Gross domestic product: US$42 million (1979).
Exports: EC$87 371 560 in 1982: Bananas 26·9%; Root crops 10%; Coconut oil 1·4%.
Monetary unit: East Caribbean dollar (EC$). 1 dollar = 100 cents.
Denominations:
  Coins 1, 2, 5, 10, 25, 50 cents.
  Notes 1, 5, 20, 100 dollars.
Exchange rate to £ sterling: 3·45 (28 Jan. 1985).
Political history and government: A former British dependency. The islands, collectively known as St Vincent, were administered by the

Governor of the Windward Islands until 31 Dec. 1959. From 1 Jan. 1960 St Vincent had a new constitution, with its own Administrator. On 27 Oct. 1969 it became one of the West Indies Associated States, with full internal self-government. The Administrator became Governor and the Chief Minister was restyled Premier. After a constitutional conference on 18–21 Sept. 1978, the islands, under their present name, became fully independent, as a 'special member' of the Commonwealth, on 27 Oct. 1979. The Governor became Governor-General and the Premier took office as Prime Minister.

  The country is a constitutional monarchy. Executive power is vested in the British monarch and is exercisable by the Governor-General, who is appointed on the advice of the Prime Minister and acts in almost all matters on the advice of the Cabinet. Legislative power is vested in the unicameral House of Assembly, with 19 members serving for 5 years (subject to dissolution). The House has 6 Senators (nominated by the Governor-General) and 13 members elected by universal adult suffrage from single-member constituencies. The 13 members of the pre-independence House took office as the elective members of the new House. The Governor-General appoints the Prime Minister and, on the latter's recommendation, other Ministers from among members of the House. The Cabinet is responsible to the House.
Telephones: 6047 (1982).
Radio: 30 000 (1974).
TV: 600 (1974).
Length of roadways: 633 miles *1019 km*.
Expectation of life: Males 58·46 years; females 59·67 years (1959–61).
Cinemas: 3 (seating capacity 2400), 1 mobile unit and 1 drive-in (capacity 1000) in 1974.
Foreign tourists: 63 440 in 1979.

San Marino

Official name: Serenissima Repubblica di San Marino (Most Serene Republic of San Marino).
Population: 19 149 (census of 30 Nov. 1976); 22 206 (estimate for 30 Sept. 1984).
Area: 23·4 miles² *60,5 km²*.
Language: Italian.
Religion: Roman Catholic.
Capital city: San Marino, population 4620 at 31 Dec. 1984.
Highest point: Mt Titano, 2424 ft *739 m*.
Head of State: There are two Captains-Regent (*Capitani reggenti*) appointed every six months.
Climate: Warm summers, average maximum 29°C *85°F*; dry, cold winters.
Monetary unit: Italian currency (*q.v.*) and San Marino currency.
Political history and government: Founded as a city-state in AD 301. In customs union with Italy since 1862. Legislative power is vested in the unicameral Great and General Council, with 60 members elected by universal adult suffrage for 5 years (subject to dissolution). Women have had the right to vote since 1960 and to stand for election since 1973. The Council elects two of its members (one representing the capital, one the rest of the country) to act jointly as Captains-Regent, with the functions of Head of State and Government, for 6 months at a time. The first female Captain-Regent took office on 1 Apr. 1981. Executive power is held by the Congress of State, with 10 members elected by the Council for the duration of its term. San Marino comprises nine administrative areas, called 'castles', each with an elected committee led by the 'Captain of the Castle', chosen for a 6-month term.
Telephones: 8712 (1982).
Daily newspapers: 3 (1976).
  Total circulation: 1300.
Radio: 6000 licences (1976).
TV: 4000 licences (1976).
Length of roadways: 137 miles *220 km*.
Cinemas: 6 (seating capacity 2600) for 35 mm films (1977).
Foreign tourists: 2 561 221 in 1984.

São Tomé and Príncipe

Official name: A República Democrática de São Tomé e Príncipe (the Democratic Republic of São Tomé and Príncipe).
Population: 100 000 (1983 estimate).
Area: 372 miles² *964 km²*.
Language: Portuguese (official).
Religion: Roman Catholic.
Capital city: São Tomé, population 5714 at 15 Dec. 1960.
Other principal town: Santo António.
Highest point: Pico Gago Coutinho (Pico de São Tomé), 6640 ft *2024 m*.
Head of State: Dr Manuel Pinto da Costa (b. 1910), President.
Climate: Warm and humid, with an average temperature of 27°C *80°F*.
Gross domestic product: 724·6 million dobra in 1974: Agriculture, forestry and fishing (excluding government) 56·0% (agriculture 49·1%); Trade, restaurants and hotels 14·2% (trade 13·3%); Community, social and personal services 14·3%.
Exports: 180·432 million dobras in 1975: Cocoa 87%; Copra 8%.
Monetary unit: Dobra. 1 dobra = 100 centavos.
Denominations:
  Coins 10, 20, 50 centavos; 1, 2½, 5, 10, 20, 50 dobra.
  Notes 20, 50, 100, 500, 1000 dobra.
Exchange rate to £ sterling: 52·39 (14 Jan. 1985).
Political history and government: A former Portuguese territory, independent since 12 July 1975. Before independence, Portugal recognised the islands' Liberation Movement (MLSTP), whose leader became first President. A Constitutional Assembly, elected on 6 July 1975, approved a new constitution on 12 Dec. 1975. Under the constitution, the MLSTP is 'the leading political force of the nation'. The supreme organ of state is the People's Assembly, with 33 members (mostly MLSTP officials) serving a 4-year term. Executive power is vested in the President, elected for 4 years by the Assembly on the proposal of the MLSTP. He directs the government and appoints Ministers. The government is responsible to the Assembly. The post of Prime Minister was abolished in April 1979.
Telephones: 850 (1980).
Radio: 21 000 (1977).
Length of roadways: 178 miles *287 km* (1973).
Cinemas: 1 (seating capacity 1000) in 1972.
Defence: Total armed forces 160 in 1976.

Saudi Arabia

Official name: Al-Mamlaka al-'Arabiya as-Sa'udiya (the Kingdom of Saudi Arabia).
Population: 9 320 000 (1982 estimate).
Area: 830 000 miles² *2 149 690 km²*.
Language: Arabic.
Religion: Muslim.
Capital city: Ar Riyād (Riyadh), population 666 840 at 1974 census.
Other principal towns (1974): Jidda (Jeddah) 561 104; Makkah (Mecca) 366 801; At Ta'if 204 857; Al Madinah (Medina) 198 186; Ad Dammam 127 844; Al Hufuf 101 271.
Highest point: Jebel Razikh, 12 002 ft *3658 m*.
Principal mountain range: Tihā matash Shām.
Principal rivers: The flows are seasonal only.
Head of State and Prime Minister: HM King Fahd bin Abdulaziz.
Climate: Very hot and dry. Mostly desert; frequent sandstorms. Average summer temperature 38°C *100°F* to 49°C *120°F* on coast, up to 54°C *130°F* inland. High humidity. Some places have droughts for years. In Riyadh, average maximum is 42°C *107°F* June–August; January coldest (4°C *40°F* to 21°C *70°F*). In Jeddah, average maximum 29°C *84°F* (January, February) to 37°C *99°F* (July, August), minimum 18°C *65°F* (February) to 27°C *80°F* (August), rainiest month is November (two days).
Labour force: 2 121 000 (mid-1970): Agriculture, forestry and fishing 66·0%; Industry 11·7%;

Services 22·3% (ILO estimates).
Gross domestic product: 223 747 million riyals in year ending 30 June 1978: Mining and quarrying 56·8%; Construction 14·3%.
Exports: 405 481 million rials in 1981: Petroleum and petroleum products 97%.
Monetary unit: Saudi riyal. 1 riyal = 20 qursh = 100 halalah.
Denominations:
  Coins 1, 5, 10, 25, 50 halalah; 1, 2, 4 qursh.
  Notes 1, 5, 10, 50, 100 riyals.
Exchange rate to £ sterling: 4·619 (23 Apr. 1985).
Political history and government: Formerly part of Turkey's Ottoman Empire. In 1913 the Sultan of Nejd overthrew Turkish rule in central Arabia. Between 1919 and 1925 he gained control of the Hijaz and was proclaimed King there on 8 Jan. 1926. On 23 Sept. 1932 the Hijaz and Nejd were combined and named Saudi Arabia. The country is an absolute monarchy, with no parliament or political parties. The King rules in accordance with the *Sharia*, the sacred law of Islam. He appoints and leads a Council of Ministers, which serves as the instrument of royal authority in both legislative and executive matters. The King is also assisted by advisory councils, nominated or approved by him.
Telephones: 788 576 (1982).
Daily newspapers: 10 (1983).
Radio: 2 700 000 (1982).
TV: 1 700 000 (1982).
Length of roadways: 23 300 miles *37 500 km* (31 Dec. 1978).
Length of railways: 355 miles *571 km*.
Universities: 6.
Adult illiteracy: 97·5% (males 95%; females 100%) in 1962 (UNESCO estimates).
Expectation of life: Males 44·2 years; females 46·5 years (UN estimates for 1970–75).
Defence: Military service voluntary; total armed forces 49 000 (1984); defence expenditure, 1981/82; $27 695 million.
Foreign tourists: 2 000 000 Muslim pilgrims to Mecca in 1982.

Senegal

Official name: La République du Sénégal.
Population: 5 085 388 (census of 16 Apr. 1976); 6 177 000 (estimate for 1983).
Area: 75 954 miles^2 *196 722 km^2*.
Languages: French (official), Wolof, Fulani (Peulh), Serer, Toucouleur.
Religions: Muslim 90%; Christian (mainly Roman Catholic) 5%.
Capital city: Dakar, population 978 553 (1979 estimate).
Other principal towns (1979): Thiès 126 886; Kaolack 115 679; Saint-Louis 96 594; Ziguinchor 79 464; Diourbel 55 307.
Highest point: Gounou Mt, 4970 ft *1515 m*.
Principal mountain range: Fouta Djalon.
Principal rivers: Gambie (Gambia), Casamance, Sénégal.
Head of State: Abdou Diuof (b. 7 Sept. 1935), President.
Climate: Tropical. Hot, with long dry season and short wet season. Average annual temperature about 29°C *84°F*. Heavy rainfall on coast. Average maximum 32°C *90°F* to 42°C *108°F* in interior; average minimum about 15°C *60°F*. In Dakar, on coast, average maximum 26°C *79°F* (January) to 32°C *89°F* (September, October); minimum 17°C *63°F* (February) to 24°C *76°F* (July to Oct.); rainiest month is Aug. (13 days).
Labour force: 2 558 000 (1982): Agriculture, forestry and fishing 79·7%; Services 13·8% (ILO estimates).
Gross domestic product: 823·6 billion CFA francs in 1982: Agriculture, forestry and fishing 30·2%; Industry (mining, manufacturing, utilities) 19·6%; Trade, restaurants and hotels 20·1%; Public administration and defence 10·8%.
Exports: 100 767 million CFA francs in 1980: Fisheries 24%; Petroleum products 18%; Phosphates 16%; Peanut oil 12%.

Monetary unit: Franc de la Communauté financière africaine.
Denominations:
  Coins 1, 2, 5, 10, 25, 50, 100 CFA francs.
  Notes 50, 100, 500, 1000, 5000 CFA francs.
Exchange rate to £ sterling: 542·25 (14 Jan. 1985).
Political history and government: Formerly part of French West Africa, Senegal joined French Sudan (now the Republic of Mali) to form the Federation of Mali on 4 Apr. 1959. By agreement with France, signed on 4 Apr. 1960, the Federation became independent on 20 June 1960. Senegal seceded, and became a separate independent state, on 20 Aug. 1960. The Republic of Senegal was proclaimed on 5 Sept. 1960, with Léopold-Sédar Senghor as first President. A new constitution was promulgated on 7 Mar. 1963. Senegal became a one-party state in 1966 but two legal opposition parties were subsequently formed (in July 1974 and Feb. 1976). A constitutional amendment, approved by the government on 10 Mar. 1976, fixed the maximum number of permitted parties at three. On 3 Apr. 1978 the President announced that a fourth party would be permitted. Legislative power rests with the unicameral National Assembly, with 100 members elected for 5 years by universal adult suffrage (the elections of 26 Feb. 1978 were contested by three parties). Executive power is held by the President, also directly elected for 5 years at the same time as the Assembly. He appoints and leads a Cabinet, including a Prime Minister. President Senghor retired on 31 Dec. 1980 and was succeeded by the Prime Minister, Abdou Diouf. On 24 Apr. 1981 the National Assembly adopted a constitutional amendment, effective from 6 May, lifting restrictions on political parties. By July a further 7 parties had registered. On 1 Feb. 1982 Senegal and The Gambia formed a confederation named Senegambia, led by President Diouf.
Telephones: 42 105 (1978).
Daily newspapers: 1 (1976).
  Total circulation: 25 000.
Radio: 300 000 (1981).
TV: 4000 (1981).
Length of roadways: 8270 miles *13 309 km* (31 Dec. 1979).
Length of railways: 642 miles *1034 km*.
Universities: 2.
Adult illiteracy: 94·4% (males 89·6%; females 98·9%) illiterate in French (Africans, 1961).
Expectation of life: Males 39·4 years; females 42·5 years (UN estimates for 1970–75).
Defence: Military service: two years, selective; total armed forces 9380 (1984); defence expenditure, 1980: $71 million.
Cinemas: 75 (1979).
Foreign tourists: 198 433 (1979).

Seychelles

Official name: The Republic of Seychelles.
Population: 69 000 (1983 estimate).
Area: 119 miles^2 *308 km2*.
Languages: Creole 94·4%; English 3·0%; French 1·9% (census of 5 May 1971).
Religions: Christian (mainly Roman Catholic) 98·2% (1971).
Capital city: Victoria (formerly Port Victoria), population 13 736 (including suburbs) at 1971 census.
Other principal town: Takamaka.
Highest point: Morne Seychellois, 2992 ft *912 m*.
Head of State: (France) Albert René (b. 16 Nov. 1935), President.
Climate: Warm and pleasant, with temperatures generally between 24°C *75°F* and 30°C *85°F*, cooler on high ground. Hottest during northwest monsoon, December to May. South-east monsoon is from June to November. Average annual rainfall on Mahé between 1780 mm *70 in* and 3430 mm *135 in*. In Victoria, average annual temperature 29°C *84°F*, rainfall 2300 mm *91 in*.
Labour force: 25 947 (including 2608 unemployed) at 1977 census: Agriculture, forestry and fishing 20·2%; Construction 18·2%; Trade, restaurants and hotels 16·2%; Community, social

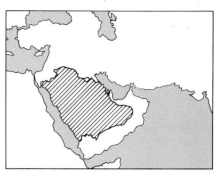

SAUDI ARABIA

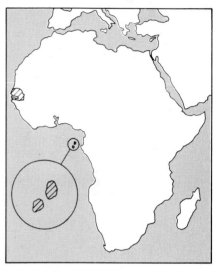

left: **SENEGAL**
encircled: **SÃO TOMÉ AND PRÍNCIPE**

and personal services 28·2%.
Gross domestic product: 482·4 million rupees in 1977: Agriculture, forestry and fishing 15·4% (agriculture 11·7%); Trade, restaurants and hotels 21·0% (trade 10·9%, restaurants and hotels 10·1%); Transport, storage and communication 13·1%; Government services 17·1%.
Exports: 20·4 million Seychelles rupees in 1982: Copra 43·1%; Frozen fish 36·3%; Cinnamon bark 14·7%.
Monetary unit: Seychelles rupee. 1 rupee = 100 cents.
Denominations:
  Coins 1, 5, 25, 50 cents; 1, 5, 10 rupees.
  Notes 5, 10, 20, 50, 100 rupees.
Exchange rate to £ sterling: 8·20 (14 Jan. 1985).
Political history and government: Formerly a British colony, with internal self-government from 1 Oct. 1975. Following a constitutional conference on 19–22 Jan. 1976, Seychelles became an independent republic, within the Commonwealth, on 29 June 1976. At the same time three islands which formed part of the British Indian Ocean territory (established on 8 Nov. 1965) were returned to Seychelles. The pre-independence Prime Minister, James Mancham, became the first President, leading a coalition government comprising members of his own Seychelles Democratic Party and of the Seychelles People's United Party (SPUP), formerly in opposition. The SPUP leader, Albert René, became Prime Minister. President Mancham was deposed on 5 June 1977 in a *coup* by armed opponents of his rule. At the request of the *coup* leaders, René became President. The constitution was suspended and the elected National Assembly dissolved. President René assumed power to rule by decree. In May 1978 the SPUP was renamed the Seychelles People's Progressive Front (SPPF). A new constitution was proclaimed on 26 Mar. 1979 and took effect from 5 June. It provides for a one-party state, with a unicameral People's Assembly of 25 members (two nominated to represent uninhabited islands and 23 elected by universal adult

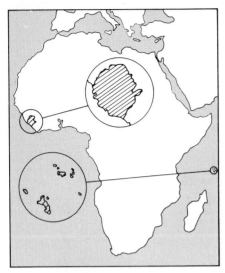

above: **SIERRA LEONE**
below: **SEYCHELLES**

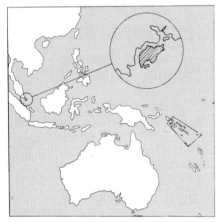

top encircled: **SINGAPORE**
below: **SOLOMON ISLANDS**

suffrage), serving a four-year term. Executive power is vested in the President, directly elected for five years. Elections for the President (with René as sole candidate) and the Assembly (all candidates being from the SPPF) were held on 23–26 June 1979. The President appoints and leads the Cabinet, his nominations being subject to ratification by the Assembly.

Telephones: 4008 (1981).
Daily newspapers: 1 (1977).
  Total circulation: 4000.
Radio: 18 000 (1979).
Length of roadways: 139 miles *224 km.*
Adult illiteracy: 42·3% (males 44·4%; females 40·2%) in 1971.
Expectation of life: Males 61·9 years; females 68·0 years (1970–72).
Defence: People's Liberation Army (about 750 members in 1984) formed in 1977.
Cinemas: 2 (seating capacity 800) and 4 mobile units (1975).
Foreign tourists: 47 280 in 1982.

Sierra Leone

Official name: The Republic of Sierra Leone.
Population: 2 735 159 (census of 8 Dec. 1974); 3 470 000 (1980 estimate).
Area: 27 699 miles² *71 740 km².*
Languages: English (official), Krio, Mende, Temne.
Religions: Animist; Muslim and Christian minorities.
Capital city: Freetown, population 316 312 (1974 census).
Other principal towns (1974): Makeni 1 046 000; Kenema 773 500; Bo 597 000.

Highest point: Bintimani and Kundukonko peaks, 6390 ft *1948 m.*
Principal mountain range: Loma.
Principal rivers: Siwa, Jong, Rokel.
Head of State: Dr Siaka Probyn Stevens (b. 24 Aug. 1905), President.
Climate: Generally hot with two main seasons: wet (May–October), when humidity is tryingly high, and dry (November–April). The average annual rainfall at Freetown is 3505 mm *138 in* and the average daily high temperature nearly 29°C *85°F.*
Labour force: 908 147 (excluding 29 590 not at work) at census of 1 Apr. 1963 (excluding 5% underenumeration); 1 055 000 (mid-1970): Agriculture, forestry and fishing 71·5%; Industry 14·8%; Services 13·6% (ILO estimates).
Gross domestic product: 814·7 million leones in year ending 30 June 1978: Agriculture, forestry and fishing 38·7%; Trade, restaurants and hotels 13·1%; Transport, storage and communication 10·3%.
Exports: 133·25 million leone in 1982.
Monetary unit: Leone. 1 leone = 100 cents.
Denominations:
  Coins 1, 5, 10, 20, 50 cents.
  Notes 50 cents, 1, 2, 5, 10, 20 leones.
Exchange rate to £ sterling: 2·85 (14 Jan. 1985).
Political history and government: A former British dependency which became independent, within the Commonwealth, on 27 Apr. 1961. At independence the Sierra Leone People's Party was in power, with the All-People's Congress (APC) in opposition. Following disputed elections, the army assumed power on 21 Mar. 1967. Two days later, in a counter-*coup*, another group of officers established a National Reformation Council (NRC), which suspended the constitution. The NRC was overthrown on 17–18 Apr. 1968 by junior officers who restored constitutional government and civilian rule on 26 Apr. 1968, when Dr Siaka Stevens of the APC, appointed Prime Minister in 1967, was sworn in. A republic was established on 19 April 1971 and two days later Dr Stevens was elected President and took office. Legislative power is held by the unicameral House of Representatives, with 104 members: 85 elected by universal adult suffrage for 5 years (subject to dissolution), 12 Paramount Chiefs (one from each District) and 7 members appointed by the President. A constitutional amendment bill, published on 13 May 1978, provided for the repeal of the 1971 constitution and for the introduction of one-party government under the APC; for an extension of the President's term of office from 5 to 7 years; and for the abolition of the office of Prime Minister. After approving the bill, the House was prorogued on 26 May 1978. A referendum on 5–12 June 1978 supported the proposed changes and President Stevens was sworn in on 14 June for a 7-year term. Under the new constitution, the President, formerly elected by the House, is elected by the National Delegates' Conference of the APC. He holds executive power and he appoints and leads the Cabinet.

Telephones: 220 000 (1981).
Daily newspapers: 2 (1975).
  Total circulation: 30 000.
Radio: 500 000 (1981).
TV: 20 000 (1981).
Length of roadways: 4595 miles *7395 km* (31 Dec. 1979).
Universities: 1.
Adult illiteracy: 93·3% (males 90·4%; females 96·1%) in 1963.
Expectation of life: Males 41·8 years; females 45·0 years (UN estimates for 1970–75).
Defence: Total armed forces 3180 (1984): defence expenditure, 1979: $11 million.
Cinemas: 10 (seating capacity 5500) in 1969.
Foreign tourists: 32 299 (including short-stay visits) in 1976.

Singapore

Official name: Hsing-chia p'o Kung-ho Kuo (Chinese) or Republik Singapura (Malay): Re-

public of Singapore.
Population: 2 502 000 (1983).
Area: 238·6 miles² *618·1 km².*
Languages: Malay, Mandarin Chinese, Tamil, English.
Religions: Muslim, Buddhist, Hindu, Christian.
Capital city: Singapore City, population 1 327 500 at 30 June 1974 (estimate).
Highest point: Bukit Timah (Hill of Tin), 581 ft *177 m.*
Principal river: Sungei Seletar (9 miles *14 km*).
Head of State: Chengara Veetil Devan Nair (b. 5 Aug. 1923), President.
Prime Minister: Lee Kuan Yew (b. 16 Sept. 1923).
Climate: Hot and humid throughout the year, with average maximum of 30°C *86°F* to 32°C *89°F,* minimum 23°C *73°F* to 24°C *75°F.* Frequent rainfall (between 11 and 19 days each month).
Labour force: 1 186 400 aged 15–64 years (1983): Manufacturing 28·9%; Trade, restaurants and hotels 23·3%; Transport, storage and communication 11·7%; Community, social and personal services 21·2%.
Gross domestic product: S$32·25 billion in 1983: Manufacturing (excluding government) 25%; Trade, restaurants and hotels 26%; Transport, storage and communication 13%; Community, social and personal services 10%.
Exports: S$44·47 billion in 1983: Petroleum and petroleum products 23%; Machinery and transport equipment 26%.
Monetary unit: Singapore dollar (S$). 1 dollar = 100 cents.
Denominations:
  Coins 1, 5, 10, 20, 50 cents; 1 dollar.
  Notes 1, 5, 10, 20, 25, 50, 100, 500, 1000, 10 000 dollars.
Exchange rate to £ sterling: 2·45 (14 Jan. 1985).
Political history and government: A former British colony, with internal self-government from 3 June 1959. Singapore became a constituent state of the independent Federation of Malaysia, within the Commonwealth, on 16 Sept. 1963 but seceded and became a separate independent country on 9 Aug. 1965. The new state joined the Commonwealth on 16 Oct. 1965 and became a republic on 22 Dec. 1965. Legislative power rests with the unicameral Parliament, with 75 members elected by universal adult suffrage (voting being compulsory) from single-member constituencies for 5 years (subject to dissolution). The President is elected by Parliament for a 4-year term as constitutional Head of State. Effective executive authority rests with the Cabinet, led by the Prime Minister, which is appointed by the President and responsible to Parliament.

Telephones: 851 952 (1983).
Daily newspapers: 9 (1983).
  Total circulation: 631 593.
Radio: 430 604 licences (31 Dec. 1979).
TV: 658 000 (1977).
Length of roadways: 1572 miles *2529 km* (1983).
Length of railways: 16 miles *26 km* (1978).
Universities: 1.
Adult illiteracy: 14·8% (1983).
Expectation of life: Males 65·1 years; females 70·0 years (1970).
Defence: Military service: 24–36 months; total armed forces 54 000 (1984); defence expenditure, 1980: US$574 million.
Cinemas: 73 (seating capacity 67 400) and 1 drive-in (capacity 3600) in 1979.
Foreign tourists: 2 956 690 in 1982.

Solomon Islands

Population: 196 825 (census of 1980); 267 265 (estimate for 1985).
Area: 10 983 miles² *28 446 km².*
Languages: English (official), Pidgin English (national) and 87 local (mainly Melanesian) languages.
Religion: mainly Christian (Anglican and Roman Catholic).
Capital city: Honiara, population 21 277 (1980).
Other principal towns: Gizo, Auki, Kirakira.

Highest point: Mt Makarakombou, 8028 ft *2447 m*.
Head of State: HM Queen Elizabeth II, represented by Sir Baddeley Devisi, GCMG, GCVO (b. 16 Oct. 1941), Governor-General.
Prime Minister: The Rt Hon. Sir Peter Kenilorea, KBE.
Climate: Warm season during north-west trade winds, Nov.–Apr.; cooler during south-east season, Apr.–Nov. In Honiara, average annual temperature is 27°C *80°F*, average annual rainfall about 2160 mm *85 in*.
Gross domestic product: SI$175 million in 1983.
Exports: SI$71·2 million in 1983: Fish preparations 5·5%; Fish, fresh and frozen 28·7%; oil seeds, nuts and kernels 12·2%; copra 16·7%; wood products 29·7%.
Monetary unit: Solomon Islands dollar (SI$). 1 dollar = 100 cents.
Denominations:
Coins 1, 2, 5, 10, 20 cents; 1 dollar.
Notes 2, 5, 10, 20 dollars.
Exchange rate to £ sterling: 1·51 (18 Jan. 1985).
Political history and government: The Northern Solomon Islands became a German protectorate in 1885 and the Southern Solomons a British protectorate in 1893. Germany ceded most of the Northern Solomons to the United Kingdom between 1898 and 1900. The combined territory was named the British Solomon Islands Protectorate. The first Chief Minister was appointed on 28 Aug. 1974. In June 1975 the territory was renamed the Solomon Islands, although retaining protectorate status. Full internal self-government was achieved on 2 Jan. 1976. After a constitutional conference on 6–16 Sept. 1977, Solomon Islands (as it was restyled) became independent, within the Commonwealth, on 7 July 1978, with the Chief Minister as the first Prime Minister.

Legislative power is vested in the unicameral National Parliament, with 38 members elected by universal adult suffrage for 4 years (subject to dissolution). The pre-independence Legislative Assembly became the first Parliament. Executive power is vested in the British monarch and is exercisable by the Governor-General, who is appointed for up to 5 years on the advice of Parliament and acts in almost all matters on the advice of the Cabinet. The Prime Minister is elected by and from members of Parliament. Other Ministers are appointed by the Governor-General, on the Prime Minister's recommendation, from members of Parliament. The Cabinet is responsible to Parliament. The country comprises seven provinces.
Telephones: 3980.
Radio: 15 000 (1984).
Length of roadways: 1425 miles *2300 km*.
Cinemas: 3 (seating capacity 900) in 1984.

Somalia

Official name: Jamhuuriyadda Dimuqraadiga Soomaaliya (Somali Democratic Republic).
Population: 3 862 000 (1982 estimate).
Area: 246 201 miles² *637 657 km²*.
Language: Somali, Arabic (both official); English, Italian.
Religions: Sunni Muslim; Christian minority.
Capital city: Muqdisho (Mogadishu or Mogadiscio), population 377 000 (1982 estimate).
Other principal towns (1982): Hargeisa 70 000; Kisimayu 70 000; Merca 60 000; Berbera 55 000.
Highest point: Surud Ad, 7894 ft *2406 m*.
Principal mountain range: Guban.
Principal rivers: Juba (Giuba), Shebelle (Scebeli).
Head of State: Maj-Gen Muhammad Siyad Barrah (b. 1919), President and Prime Minister.
Climate: Hot and dry. Average temperature of 27°C *80°F*. Average maximum over 32°C *90°F* in interior and on Gulf of Aden. Cooler on Indian Ocean coast. Average rainfall less than 430 mm *17 in*. In Mogadishu, average maximum 28°C *83°F* (July, August) to 32°C *90°F* (April), minimum 23°C *73°F* (January, July, August) to 25°C *78°F* (April), rainiest month is July (20 days).

Labour force: 1 084 000 (mid-1970): Agriculture, forestry and fishing 84·7% (ILO estimates).
Gross domestic product: $492 million in 1975 (UN estimate).
Exports: 1104 million Somali shillings in 1981.
Monetary unit: Somali shilling. 1 shilling = 100 centesimi.
Denominations:
Coins 1, 5, 10, 50 centesimi; 1 shilling.
Notes 1, 5, 10, 20, 100 shillings.
Exchange rate to £ sterling: 28·886 (14 Jan. 1985).
Political history and government: Formed on 1 July 1960 as an independent country, called the Somali Republic, by a merger of the Trust Territory of Somaliland, under Italian protection, with British Somaliland (a protectorate until 26 June 1960). Following the assassination of the President on 15 Oct. 1969, the government was overthrown by a military *coup* on 21 Oct. 1969, when the constitution and political parties were abolished and the National Assembly dissolved. A Supreme Revolutionary Council (SRC) was established and the country's present name adopted on 22 Oct. 1969. The President of the SRC, Maj-Gen Muhammad Siyad Barrah, became Head of State. On 1 July 1976 the SRC was dissolved and its power transferred to the newly-formed Somali Revolutionary Socialist Party (SRSP). All members of the SRC became members of the ruling party's central committee and the President is the party's secretary-general.

A meeting of the SRSP on 20–25 Jan. 1979 produced a draft constitution, endorsed by the SRSP Central Committee on 20 May 1979. After approval by referendum on 25 Aug. 1979, the constitution was promulgated on 29 Aug. and came into force on 23 Sept. 1979. It defines the SRSP as the sole political party and the country's 'supreme authority'. Legislative power is vested in the People's Assembly, with six members appointed by the President and 171 elected by universal adult suffrage for 5 years (subject to dissolution). Elections to the Assembly were first held on 30 Dec. 1979 and its first session opened on 24 Jan. 1980. Executive power is vested in the President, nominated by the SRSP Central Committee and elected by the Assembly for 6 years. He appoints and leads the Council of Ministers. On 26 Jan. 1980 Gen Siyad Barrah was elected President. On 21 Oct. 1980 he declared a state of emergency and reinstituted the SRC, with extensive powers. The SRC's 17 members are all officers in the armed forces.
Telephones: 5000 (1970).
Daily newspapers: 2 (1973).
Total circulation: 4000.
Radio: 87 000 (1981).
Length of roadways: 10 702 miles *17 233 km* (1971).
Universities: 1.
Adult illiteracy: 98·5% (males 97%; females 100%) in 1962 (UNESCO estimates); 40% (claimed after the 1974–75 literacy campaign).
Expectation of life: Males 39·4 years; females 42·6 years (UN estimates for 1970–75).
Defence: Military service voluntary; total armed forces 62 550 (1984); defence expenditure, 1979: $95 million.
Cinemas: 26 (seating capacity 23 000) in 1970.

South Africa

Official name: Republic of South Africa, or Republiek van Suid-Afrika.
Population: 26 124 000 (1983 estimate).
Area: 471 445 miles² *1 221 037 km²* (excluding Walvis Bay, area 434 miles² *1124 km²*).
Languages: Afrikaans, English, Xhosa, Zulu, Sesuto (Sesotho), Tswana (Setswana), Sepedi.
Religions: Christian; Muslim and Hindu minorities.
Capital city: Administrative: Pretoria, population 528 407 (1980 census). Legislative: Cape Town (Kaapstad), population 213 830 (1980 census).
Other principal towns (1980): Johannesburg 1 536 457; Durban 505 963; Port Elizabeth 492 140; Kempton Park 289 815; Bloemfontein

right: **SOMALIA**
below: **SOUTH AFRICA**

230 688; Alberton 230 667; Benoni 206 810; Pietermaritzburg 178 972; Welkom 176 608; Roodepoort Maraisburg 165 315; East London 160 582; Germiston 155 435; Boksburg 150 287.
Highest point: Injasuti, 11 182 ft *3408 m*.
Principal mountain range: Drakensberg.
Principal rivers: Orange (Oranje), 1300 miles *2092 km*; Limpopo; Vaal.
Head of State: Marais Viljoen (b. 2 Dec. 1915), State President.
Prime Minister: Pieter Willem Botha (b. 12 Jan. 1916).
Climate: Generally temperate (cool summers, mild winters). Average temperatures about 17°C *63°F*. In Cape Town, average maximum 17°C *63°F* (July) to 26°C *79°F* (February), minimum 7°C *45°F* (July) to 15°C *60°F* (January, February), rainiest month is July (10 days). In Johannesburg, average maximum 17°C *62°F* (June) to 25°C *78°F* (December, January), minimum 4°C *39°F* (June, July) to 14°C *58°F* (January, February), rainiest month is January (12 days). Absolute maximum temperature 51·56°C *124·8°F*, Main, 28 Jan. 1903; absolute minimum −14·7°C *5·5°F*, Carolina, 23 July 1926.
Labour force: 7 556 930 (excluding 429 290 unemployed) at 1970 census (sample tabulation): Agriculture, forestry and fishing 30·9%; Manufacturing 14·1%; Community, social and personal services 21·7%.
Gross domestic product: 39 727 million rand (including South West Africa) in 1978: Mining and quarrying 15·0%; Manufacturing 21·7%; Trade, restaurants and hotels 12·9%.
Exports: 19 082 million rand in 1982 (excluding exports of gold): Base metals and metal manufactures 9%; Mineral products 11%; Vegetables and products 5%. Figures include the trade of South Africa, Botswana, Lesotho, Swaziland and Transkei.
Monetary unit: Rand. 1 rand = 100 cents.
Denominations:
Coins 1, 2, 5, 10, 20, 50 cents.
Notes 1, 2, 5, 10, 20 rand.
Exchange rate to £ sterling: 2·35 (24 April 1985).
Political history and government: After the Boer War of 1899–1902 two former Boer republics, the Transvaal and the Orange Free State, became part of the British Empire. On 31 May 1910 they were merged with the British territories of Natal and Cape Colony (now Cape Province) to form the Union of South Africa, a dominion under the British crown. Under the Statute of Westminster, passed by the British Parliament in December 1931 and accepted by South Africa in June 1934, the Union was recognised as an independent country within the Commonwealth. Following a referendum among white voters on 5 Oct. 1960, South Africa became a republic, outside the Commonwealth, on 31 May 1961. Under the initial republican constitution, legislative power was vested in a bicameral Parliament, made up exclusively of European (white) members holding office for 5

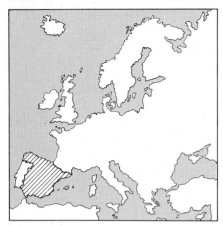

SPAIN

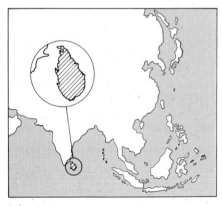

SRI LANKA

years (subject to dissolution). Under constitutional changes approved on 12 June 1980, the Senate was abolished from 1 Jan. 1981, leaving the House of Assembly as the sole legislative chamber. The House has 165 members directly elected by Europeans only. From 1 Jan. 1981 an additional eight members are chosen by the elected members while another four members are nominated by the President. Executive power is vested in the State President, elected by Parliament for a 7-year term as constitutional Head of State. He acts on the advice of the Executive Council (Cabinet), led by the Prime Minister, which is appointed by the President and responsible to Parliament. The constitutional changes introduced on 1 Jan. 1981 created the office of Vice State President (with a 7-year term) and established an advisory President's Council, with 56 non-African members (41 European, seven Coloured, seven Indian and one Chinese) nominated by the State President for a 5-year term. The Council, chaired by the Vice State President, was inaugurated on 3 Feb. 1981.

Each of the four provinces has an Administrator appointed by the President for 5 years and a provincial council elected (by whites only) for 5 years.

South Africa has granted independence to the Transkei (26 Oct. 1976), Bophuthatswana (6 Dec. 1977), Venda (13 Sept. 1979) and the Ciskei (4 Dec. 1981), African 'homelands' established by the government, but these acts have not received international recognition.

Telephones: 3 356 833 (1982).
Daily newspapers: 22 (1983).
Radio: 2 300 000 (1980).
TV: 1 450 000 (1980).
Length of roadways: 115 036 miles *185 133 km* (31 Mar. 1976).
Length of railways: 14 217 miles *22 876 km.*
Universities: 17.
Adult illiteracy: 59·7% (males 59·3%; females 60·2%) in 1960 (Africans only).
Expectation of life:
All races: Males 56·6 years; females 59·4 years (UN estimates for 1970–75).

For non-Africans (1959–61):
Asiatic: Males 57·70 years; females 59·57 years.
Coloured: Males 49·62 years; females 54·28 years.
White: Males 64·73 years; females 71·67 years.
Defence: Military service: 24 months; total armed forces 84 200 in 1984; defence expenditure, 1981–2: 3017·5 million rand.
Cinemas: 700 in 1971.
Foreign tourists: 702 794 in 1980.

Spain

Official name: The Kingdom of Spain.
*Population: 37 746 260 at the census of 1 Mar. 1981; 37 974 000 estimate for 31 Dec. 1982.
*Area: 194 897 miles² *504 782 km².*
Languages: Spanish (Castilian), Catalan, Basque, Galician.
Religion: Roman Catholic.
Capital city: Madrid, population 3 188 297 (1981 census).
Other principal towns (1981): Barcelona 1 745 900; Valencia 751 734; Sevilla 653 833; Zaragoza 590 750; Malaga 503 251; Bilbao 433 030; Las Palmas 366 454; Valladolid 330 242; Palma de Mallorca 304 422; Hospitalet 294 033; Cordoba 284 737.
Highest point: Mt Teide (Canary Is), 12 190 ft *3716 m.*
Principal mountain ranges: Pyrenees, Cordillera Cantábrica.
Principal rivers: Ebro (556 miles *895 km*), Duero (Douro), Tajo (Tagus), Guadiana, Guadalquivir.
Head of State: HM King Juan Carlos (b. 5 Jan. 1938).
Head of Government: Felipe Gonzalez (b. 5 Mar. 1942), President of the Government (Prime Minister).
Climate: Cool summers and rainy winters on north coast; hot summers and cold winters in interior; hot summers and mild winters on south coast. In Madrid, average maximum 8°C *47°F* (January) to 30°C *87°F* (July), minimum 0,5°C *33°F* (January) to 17°C *62°F* (July, August), rainiest month is March (11 days). In Barcelona, average maximum 13°C *56°F* (January) to 28°C *82°F* (August), minimum 5°C *42°F* (January) to 20°C *69°F* (July, August), rainiest months are April, May, October (each 8 days). Absolute maximum temperature 46,2°C *115 2°F*, Gualulcacin, 17 July 1943; absolute minimum – 32,0°C *– 25·6°F*, Estangento, 2 Feb. 1956.
Labour force: Fully employed 13 212 200 (unemployed 2 500 000) in 1982: Industry 24·1%; Construction 9·5%; Services 43·5%.
Gross domestic product: 15 219 600 million pesetas in 1980.
Exports: 2 260 198 million pesetas in 1982: Iron and steel castings 12%; Vehicles 10·9%; Boilers, machinery and mechanical hardware 9·6%; Refined petroleum and related products 7%; Citrus and other fruits 4·7%.
Monetary unit: Spanish peseta. 1 peseta = 100 céntimos.
Denominations:
Coins 1, 5, 10, 25, 50, 100 pesetas.
Notes 100, 200, 500, 1000, 2000, 5000 pesetas.
Exchange rate to £ sterling: 213 (10 Apr. 1985).
Political history and government: In the civil war of 1936–39 the forces of the republic (established on 14 Apr. 1931) were defeated. Gen Francisco Franco, leader of the successful insurgent forces, acted as Head of State until his death on 20 Nov. 1975. The legislature, traditionally designated the *Cortes* (Courts), was revived in 1942 as a unicameral body, with strictly limited powers, named *Las Cortes Españolas*. In accordance with the 1947 Law of Succession, Prince Juan Carlos de Borbón, grandson of the last reigning monarch, became King on 22 Nov. 1975. The government's Political Reform Bill, passed by the *Cortes* on 18 Nov. 1976, was approved by a popular referendum on 15 Dec. 1976. This provided for a new bicameral *Cortes*, comprising a Congress of Deputies (350 elected members) and a Senate of 248 members (207 elected, 41 nominated by the King). Elections for the new

Cortes were held on 15 June 1977. The old *Cortes* expired on 30 June 1977; the new legislature was inaugurated on 13 July and formally opened on 23 July 1977.

In 1978 a new constitution was approved by both Houses of the *Cortes* on 31 Oct., endorsed by a referendum on 6 Dec. and ratified by the King on 27 Dec. It entered into force on 29 Dec. 1978 and the *Cortes* was dissolved on 2 Jan. 1979. The constitution confirmed Spain as a parliamentary monarchy, with freedom for political parties, and it recognised and guaranteed the right of Spain's 'nationalities and regions' to autonomy. All the 'fundamental laws' of the Franco régime were repealed and the Roman Catholic Church was disestablished. The monarchy is hereditary, with the King having mainly formal prerogatives. Legislative power is vested in the bicameral *Cortes Generales*, comprising a Senate and a Congress of Deputies, both Houses elected by universal adult suffrage for 4 years (subject to dissolution). Members of the Congress are elected on the basis of proportional representation. For the elections of 1 Mar. 1979 the Congress had 350 seats and the Senate 208: 188 for continental Spain (4 for each of the 47 provinces), 5 for the Balearic islands, 11 for the Canary Islands (2 provinces) and 2 each for the African enclaves of Ceuta and Melilla. Executive power is held by the Council of Ministers, led by the President of the Government (Prime Minister), who is appointed by the King with the approval of the *Cortes*. Other Ministers are appointed on the Prime Minister's recommendation. The Government is responsible to the Congress. Spain comprises 50 provinces, each with its own Assembly (*Diputación Provincial*) and an appointed Civil Governor.
Telephones: 12 350 058 (1982).
Daily newspapers: approx. 100 (1981).
Total circulation: approx. 5 million.
Radio: 9 600 000 (1982).
TV: 9 400 000 (1982).
Length of roadways: 143 795 miles *231 416 km* (31 Dec. 1979).
Length of railways: 9934 miles *15 988 km.*
Universities: 33.
Adult illiteracy: 9·9% (males 5·7%; females 13·7%) in 1970.
Expectation of life: Males 69·69 years; females 74·96 years (1970, excluding Ceuta and Melilla).
Defence: Military service: 12 months; total armed forces 356 250 in 1984; defence expenditure, 1982: 478 332 million pesetas.
Cinemas: 3970 (1981).
Foreign tourists: 40 129 323 in 1981: Visitors with passports 35 569 413; Excursionists and cruise passengers 2 824 591; Spanish nationals residing abroad 1 735 319.

* Figures refer to Metropolitan Spain, including the Canary Islands and Spanish North Africa (Ceuta and Melilla).

Sri Lanka

Official name: Sri Lanka Prajatantrika Samajawadi Janarajaya (Democratic Socialist Republic of Sri Lanka – 'Exalted Ceylon').
Population: 14 850 001 (census of 17 Mar. 1981).
Area: 25 332 miles² *65 610 km².*
Languages: Sinhala (official) 69%; Tamil 23%; English.
Religions (1981): Buddhist 69·3%; Hindu 15·5%; Muslim 7·6%; Christian 7·5%.
Capital city: Colombo, population 585 776 at 1981 census.
Other principal towns (1981): Dehiwela-Mt Lavinia 174 385; Moratuwa 135 610; Jaffna 118 215; Kotte 101 563; Kandy 101 281; Galle 77 183; Negombo 61 376; Trincomalee 44 913.
Highest point: Pidurutalagala, 8292 ft *2527 m.*
Principal rivers: Mahaweli Ganga (203 miles *327 km*), Kelani Ganga.
Head of State: Junius Richard Jayawardene (b. 17 Sept. 1906), President.
Prime Minister: Ranasinghe Premadasa (b. 23 June 1924).
Climate: Tropical, with average temperature of about 27°C *80°F*. Monsoon strikes the south-

west of the island. In Colombo, average maximum 29°C *85°F* (June to December) to 31°C *88°F* (March, April); minimum 22°C *72°F* (December, January, February) to 25°C *78°F* (May); May and October rainiest (each 19 days).
Labour force: 3 648 875 (excluding 839 264 unemployed) at 1971 census: Agriculture, forestry and fishing 54·8%; Manufacturing 10·2%; Trade, restaurants and hotels 10·3%; Community, social and personal services 14·8%.
Gross domestic product: 40 532·5 million rupees in 1978: Agriculture, forestry and fishing 37·8% (agriculture 33·8%); Manufacturing 13·0%; Trade, restaurants and hotels 19·2% (trade 18·1%).
Exports: 20 728·5 million Sri Lankan rupees in 1982: Tea 30·6%; Rubber 11·2%; Coconut and coconut products 4·8%; Other crops 7·9%; Textiles and garments 16·9%; Precious and semi-precious stones 3·3%.
Monetary unit: Sri Lanka rupee. 1 rupee = 100 cents.
Denominations:
  Coins 1, 2, 5, 10, 25, 50 cents; 1, 2, 5 rupees.
  Notes 2, 5, 10, 20, 50, 100, 500, 1000 rupees.
Exchange rate to £ sterling: 29·24 (14 Jan. 1985).
Political history and government: Formerly, as Ceylon, a British dependency. It became independent, as a monarchy within the Commonwealth, on 4 Feb. 1948. The country's name and status were changed on 22 May 1972, when it became the Republic of Sri Lanka. Under the first republican constitution, the President was a non-executive Head of State and direction of the government was vested in the Cabinet. Legislative power was vested in the unicameral National State Assembly (formerly the House of Representatives), with 168 members elected for 6 years by universal adult suffrage. On 4 Oct. 1977 the Assembly adopted an amendment to the constitution to provide for a directly elected executive President. Under the amendment, signed into law on 20 Oct. 1977, the Prime Minister in office (J. R. Jayawardene) became President. It provided for the President to be Head of Government but also to appoint a Prime Minister. Jayawardene was sworn in as President for a 6-year term on 4 Feb. 1978.

A new constitution was adopted by the Assembly on 16 Aug. 1978 and came into force on 7 Sept. 1978. The country's present name was introduced and the Assembly renamed Parliament. Future elections to Parliament are to be on the basis of proportional representation and Parliament is to have 196 members elected for 6 years (subject to dissolution). The President appoints the Prime Minister and other Ministers from among the members of Parliament. The President is not responsible to Parliament and may dissolve it. Sri Lanka comprises 24 administrative districts, each with a development council, first elected on 4 June 1981.
Telephones: 109 900 (1982).
Daily newspapers: 14 (1983).
Radio: 1 000 000 (1977).
Length of roadways: 15 479 miles *24 911 km* (31 Dec. 1978).
Length of railways: 903 miles *1453 km.*
Universities: 6.
Adult illiteracy: 22·4% (males 14·0%; females 31·5%) in 1971.
Expectation of life: Males 64·8 years; females 66·9 years (1967).
Defence: Military service voluntary; total armed forces 16 460 (1981); defence expenditure, 1980: $63 million.
Cinemas: 352 (seating capacity 185 500) in 1977.
Foreign tourists: 407 230 in 1982.

Sudan

Official name: Al Jumhuriyat as-Sudan al-Dimuqratiya (the Democratic Republic of Sudan).
Population: 18 900 000 (1981 estimate).
Area: 967 500 miles² *2 505 813 km².*
Languages: Arabic, Nilotic, others.
Religions: Muslim (in North), Animist (in South).

Capital city: El Khartum (Khartoum), population 333 906 at 1973 census.
Other principal towns (1973): Umm Durman (Omdurman) 299 399; El Khartum Bahri (Khartoum North) 150 989; Bur Sudan (Port Sudan) 132 632; Wadi Medani 106 715; El Obeid 90 073.
Highest point: Mt Kinyeti, 10 456 ft *3187 m.*
Principal mountain ranges: Darfur Highlands, Nubian Mts.
Principal rivers: Nile (the Blue Nile and White Nile join at Khartoum), 4145 miles *6670 km.*
Head of State: Gen. Abdel Rahman Swareldahab, President.
Climate: Hot and dry in desert areas of north (average maximum up to 44°C *111°F*); rainy and humid in tropical south. Average temperature about 21°C *70°F.* In Khartoum, average maximum 32°C *90°F* (January) to 42°C *107°F* (May), minimum 15°C *59°F* (January) to 26°C *79°F* (June); rainiest month is August (6 days). Absolute maximum 49,0°C *120·2°F*, Wadi Halfa, 7 and 8 June 1932, 9 and 13 June 1933, 19 June 1941; absolute minimum −0,8°C *30·6°F*, Zalingei, 6 Feb. 1957.
Labour force: 4 442 921 (1973 census): Agriculture, forestry and fishing 71·5%; Community, social and personal services 11·0%.
Gross domestic product: £S1848·0 million in year ending 30 June 1976: Agriculture, forestry and fishing 35·7%; Trade, restaurants and hotels 17·9%; Transport, storage and communication 10·9%.
Exports: US$796 million in 1981.
Monetary unit: Sudanese pound (£S). 1 pound = 100 piastras = 1000 millièmes.
Denominations:
  Coins 1, 2, 5, 10 millièmes; 2, 5, 10 piastres.
  Notes 25, 50 piastres; 1, 5, 10, 20 pounds.
Exchange rate to £ sterling: 1·4615 (14 Jan. 1985).
Political history and government: An Anglo-Egyptian condominium from 19 Jan. 1899 until becoming an independent parliamentary republic on 1 Jan. 1956. On 25 May 1969 the civilian government was overthrown by army officers, under Col (promoted Maj-Gen) Ga'afar an-Numairi, who established a Revolutionary Command Council (RCC) and introduced the country's present name. Gen Numairi became Prime Minister on 28 Oct. 1969. On 13 Aug. 1971 the RCC promulgated a provisional constitution, proclaiming socialist principles. Gen Numairi was elected President (unopposed) in September 1971 and inaugurated for a 6-year term on 12 Oct. 1971. The RCC was dissolved and the Sudanese Socialist Union (SSU) established as the country's sole political party. A new definitive constitution was introduced on 8 May 1973. Executive power is vested in the President, nominated by the SSU, and he appoints a Council of Ministers. Gen (later Field Marshal) Numairi was re-elected President in April 1977. In March 1985 President Numairi was deposed while out of the country.

Legislative power is vested in the National People's Assembly, whose members serve a 4-year term. An Assembly of 366 members was elected in April 1980 but dissolved by the President on 5 Oct 1981. The next Assembly is due to have only 151 seats. The Southern Region also has an elected regional assembly. Sudan comprises 15 provinces, each administered by an appointed Commissioner.
Telephones: 68 503 (1982).
Daily newspapers: 4 (1976).
  Total circulation: 26 000 (2 dailies).
Radio: 1 400 000 (1982).
TV: 107 000 (1982).
Length of roadways: *c.* 31 070 miles *c. 50 000 km.*
Length of railways: 2974 miles *4786 km.*
Universities: 4 (plus the Khartoum branch of Cairo University).
Adult illiteracy: 85·3% (males 74·7%; females 96·3%) in 1966.
Expectation of life: Males 43·0 years; females 45·0 years (UN estimates for 1970–75).
Defence: Military service: conscription; total armed forces 58 000 (1984); defence expenditure, 1980: $245 million.
Cinemas: 58 (seating capacity 112 000) and 43

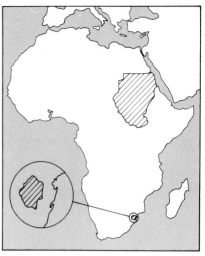

top: **SUDAN**
below: **SWAZILAND**

SURINAME

mobile units (1975).
Foreign tourists: 26 714 in 1977.

Suriname

Official name: Republiek Suriname (Republic of Suriname).
Population: 385 000 (1982 estimate).
Area: 63 037 miles² *163 265 km².*
Languages: Dutch 37·1%; Hindustani 31·7%; Javanese 15·4%; Creole 13·8% (1964).
Religions: Christian 45·1%; Hindu 27·8%; Muslim 20·2% (1964).
Capital city: Paramaribo, population 151 500 (1971).
Other principal towns: Nieuw Nickerie, Nieuw Amsterdam.
Highest point: Julianatop, 4218 ft *1286 m.*
Principal mountain ranges: Wilhelmina Gebergte, Kayser Gebergte.
Principal rivers: Corantijn, Nickerie, Coppename, Saramacca, Suriname, Commewijne, Maroni (Marowijne).
Head of State: Lt-Col. Deysi Bouterse, Chairman of the National Military Council.
Climate: Sub-tropical, with fairly heavy rainfall and average temperatures of 21°C to 30°C *73°F* to *88°F.*
Labour force: 72 152 (excluding armed forces, Amerindians and Bush Negroes living in tribes and 8047 unemployed) at census of 31 Mar. 1964: Agriculture, forestry and fishing 28·3%; Manufacturing 10·2%; Services 49·2% (commerce 12·6%); 92 000 (mid-1970): Agriculture, forestry and fishing 22·4%; Industry 24·2%; Services 53·4% (ILO estimates).

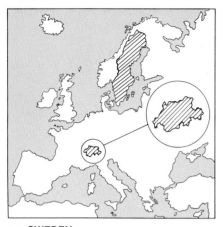

top: **SWEDEN**
encircled: **SWITZERLAND**

Gross domestic product: 1319·9 million guilders in 1977: Agriculture, forestry and fishing 10·7%; Mining and quarrying 20·2%; Trade, restaurants and hotels 15·4%; Government services 21·8%.
Exports: 918·2 million Suriname Guilders in 1980: Alumina 51%; Bauxite 12%; Aluminium 10%; Rice 7%; Plywood 1%; Bananas 1%; Shrimp 7%.
Monetary unit: Suriname gulden (guilder) or florin. 1 guilder = 100 cents.
Denominations:
Coins 1, 5, 10, 25 cents; 1 guilder.
Notes 1, 2½, 5, 10, 25, 100, 1000 guilders.
Exchange rate to £ sterling: 1·9885 (14 Jan. 1985).
Political history and government: Formerly a Dutch possession, with full internal autonomy from 29 Dec. 1954. Suriname became an independent republic on 25 Nov. 1975. The constitution vested legislative power in the *Staten* (Legislative Assembly) of 39 members, elected by universal adult suffrage for 4 years. The Assembly elected a constitutional President and Vice-President. Executive power was vested in the appointed Council of Ministers, led by the Prime Minister, which was responsible to the Assembly.
The government was overthrown in a *coup* on 25 Feb. 1980, when a National Military Council (NMC), comprising eight army officers, took power. The Cabinet resigned on the next day but the President remained in office. On 15 Mar. 1980 the NMC appointed a mainly civilian Cabinet, with Dr Henrik (Henk) Chin A Sen as Prime Minister. Elections to the *Staten*, planned for 27 Mar. 1980, were postponed until Oct. 1981, as originally due. On 15 Aug. 1980 the NMC dismissed the President and Dr Chin A Sen assumed this office while remaining Prime Minister. At the same time a state of emergency was declared and the constitution suspended. The *Staten* was replaced by an advisory assembly. On 20 Nov. 1980 Dr Chin A Sen became the country's first executive President and the office of Prime Minister was abolished. On 21 Dec. 1980 general elections were further postponed for 'at least two years'. In 1982 Dr Chin A Sen was dismissed by the NMC and in 1984 the subsequent Prime Minister was dismissed.
Suriname comprises nine districts.
Telephones: 27 495 (1982).
Daily newspapers: 1 (1983).
Radio: 182 000 (1977).
TV: 39 000 (1977).
Length of roadways: 2310 miles *3717 km*.
Length of railways: 104 miles *167 km*.
Universities: 1.
Adult illiteracy: 16·4% (males 16·0%; females 16·7%) in 1964.
Expectation of life: Males 62·5 years; females 66·7 years (1963).
Defence: Total armed forces about 5000 (1983).
Cinemas: 31 (seating capacity 19 000) and 1 drive-in (1973).
Foreign tourists: 54 673 (including 14 594 Suriname nationals residing abroad) in 1976.

Swaziland

Official name: The Kingdom of Swaziland.
Population: 494 534 (census of 25 Aug. 1976); 585 000 (estimate for 1982).
Area: 6704 miles² *17 363 km²*.
Languages: English, Siswati.
Religions: Christian 60%, Animist.
Capital city: Mbabane, population 22 262 at 1976 census.
Other principal towns (1976): Manzini 10 472; Havelock 5000; Big Bend 3500; Mhlame 2600; Pigg's Peak 2100.
Highest point: Emlembe, 6113 ft *1863 m*.
Principal mountain range: Lubombo.
Principal rivers: Usutu, Komati, Umbuluzi, Ingwavuma.
Head of State: HM Queen Regent Ntombi.
Prime Minister: Prince Bhekimpi Dlamini.
Climate: Rainy season October to March. Annual average at Mbabane, in high veld, 1395 mm *55 in*, in low veld 635 mm *25 in*. Average temperatures 11°C *52°F* to 22°C *72°F* at Mbabane, 13°C *56°F* to 27°C *80°F* at Manzini, warmer on low veld.
Labour force: 131 145 aged 15 and over (census of 24 May 1966); 198 000 (mid-1970): Agriculture, forestry and fishing 81·0%; Services 12·7% (ILO estimates).
Gross domestic product: 200·3 million emalangeni in 1981: Agriculture, forestry and fishing (excluding government) 30% (agriculture 25%); Manufacturing 25%; Trade, restaurants and hotels 11%; Community, social and personal services 10%.
Exports: 175·4 million emalangeni (excluding re-exports) in 1982: Sugar 35%; Wood pulp 16%; Asbestos 10%.
***Monetary unit:** Lilangeni (plural: emalangeni). 1 lilangeni = 100 cents.
Denominations:
Coins 1, 2, 5, 10, 20, 50 cents; 1 lilangeni.
Notes 1, 2, 5, 10, 20 emalangeni.
Exchange rate to £ sterling: 2·51 (14 Jan. 1985).
Political history and government: A former British protectorate, with internal self-government from 25 Apr. 1967 and full independence, within the Commonwealth, from 6 Sept. 1968. Swaziland is a monarchy, with executive authority vested in the King. He appoints a Cabinet, led by a Prime Minister. Under the independence constitution, legislative power was vested in a bicameral Parliament. On 12 Apr. 1973, in response to a motion passed by both Houses, the King repealed the constitution, suspended political activity and assumed all legislative, executive and judicial powers. On 24 Mar. 1977 the King announced the abolition of the parliamentary system and its replacement by traditional tribal communities called *tinkhundla*. A new constitution was promulgated on 13 Oct. 1978. The functions of the bicameral Parliament (*Libandla*), comprising a Senate (20 members) and a House of Assembly (50 members), are confined to debating government proposals and advising the King. No political parties are permitted. Elections were held on 27 Oct. 1978 to an 80-member electoral college which chose from its number 10 Senators and 40 members of the House. The King appointed a further 10 members to each chamber. The new Parliament opened on 19 Jan. 1979. Swaziland has 4 districts, each administered by an appointed District Commissioner.
Telephones: 15 357 (1982).
Daily newspapers: 1 (1976).
Total circulation: 5000.
Radio: 70 000 (1977).
Length of roadways: 1525 miles *2455 km* (31 Dec. 1977).
Length of railways: 196 miles *316 km*.
Universities: 1.
Adult illiteracy: males 68·7%; females 72·5% (1966).
Expectation of life: Males 41·8 years; females 45·0 years (UN estimates for 1970–75).
Defence: An army of 6250 (1982).
Cinemas: 5 in 1980.
Foreign tourists: 82 000 (1981).
* South African currency is also legal tender.

Sweden

Official name: Konungariket Sverige (Kingdom of Sweden).
Population: 8 330 500 (estimate for 1982).
Area: 173 654 miles² *449 793 km²*.
Languages: Swedish; Finnish and Lapp in north.
Religion: Lutheran 95%.
Capital city: Stockholm ('log island'), population 1 409 000 in 1982.
Other principal towns (1982): Göteborg 456 663; Malmö 226 849; Uppsala 101 969; Västerås 97 463; Örebro 84 721; Norrköping 83 940; Linköping 79 620; Helsingborg 77 332; Jönköping 75 999; Borås 63 179.
Highest point: Kebnekaise, 6965 ft *2123 m*.
Principal mountain ranges: Norrland Mountains, Smaland Highlands.
Principal rivers: Ume (310 miles *499 km*), Torne (354 miles *569 km*), Angerman (279 miles *449 km*), Klar (304 miles *489 km*), Dal (323 miles *520 km*).
Head of State: King Carl XVI Gustaf (b. 30 Apr. 1946).
Prime Minister: Olof Palme (b. 30 Jan. 1927).
Climate: Summers mild and warm; winters long and cold in north, more moderate in south. In Stockholm, average maximum −0,5°C *31°F* (January, February) to 21°C *70°F* (July), minimum −5°C *22°F* (February) to 12°C *55°F* (July), rainiest month is August (10 days). Absolute maximum temperature 38,0°C *100·4°F*, Ultana, 9 July 1933; absolute minimum −53,3°C *−63·9°F*, Laxbacken, 13 Dec. 1941.
Labour force: 4 230 000 in 1983: Agriculture, forestry and fishing 5·4%; Mining and manufacturing 23·5%; Trade, restaurants and hotels 13·8%; Communications 7%; Banking and insurance 7·1%; Public administration and other services 36·7%.
Gross domestic product: 695 billion kronor in 1983: Agriculture, forestry and fishing 3·8%; Mining and manufacturing 23·5%; Electricity, gas and waterworks 3·4%; Construction 7·7%; Private services 36·1%; Public services 25·5%.
Exports: 198 462 million kronor in 1983: Foodstuffs and beverages 6·6%; Raw materials 3·9%; Mineral fuels 23%; Manufactured goods 15·1%; Non-electrical machinery 14·6%; Electrical machinery 7·1%; Transport equipment 7·7%; Various finished goods 11·5%.
Monetary unit: Swedish krona (plural: kronor). 1 krona = 100 öre.
Denominations:
Coins 10, 50 öre; 1, 5 kronor.
Notes 5, 10, 50, 100, 1000, 10 000 kronor.
Exchange rate to £ sterling: 11·30 (16 Apr. 1985).
Political history and government: Sweden has been a constitutional monarchy, traditionally neutral, since the constitution of 6 June 1809. Parliamentary government was adopted in 1917 and universal adult suffrage introduced in 1921. A revised constitution was introduced on 1 Jan. 1975. The King is Head of State but has very limited formal prerogatives. Legislative power is held by the Parliament (*Riksdag*), which has been unicameral since 1 Jan. 1971. It has 349 members elected by universal adult suffrage for 3 years, using proportional representation. Executive power is held by the Cabinet, led by the Prime Minister, which is responsible to the *Riksdag*. Under the 1975 constitution, the Prime Minister is nominated by the Speaker of the *Riksdag* and later confirmed in office by the whole House. After approval, the Prime Minister appoints other members of the Cabinet. Sweden is divided into 24 counties, each administered by a nominated governor.
Telephones: 6 889 000 (1982).
Daily newspapers: 163 (1982).
Total circulation: 4 820 000.
Radio: 8 300 000 (1977).
TV: 3 236 000 licences in 1982.
Length of roadways: 80 198 miles *129 066 km* (1 Oct. 1979).
Length of railways: 7374 miles *11 864 km*.
Universities: 20.
Expectation of life: Males 75·79 years; females 81·76 years (1977–81).

Defence: Military service: Army and Navy $7\frac{1}{2}$ to 15 months; Air Force 8 to 12 months; total armed forces 82 780 in 1983; defence expenditure, 1982–3; 19 662 million kronor.
Cinemas: 1256 in 1983.

Switzerland

Official name: Schweizerische Eidgenossenschaft (German), Confédération Suisse (French), Confederazione Svizzera (Italian): Swiss Confederation.
Population: 6 482 000 (census 1983).
Area: 15 943 miles² *41 293 km²*.
Languages: German 65%; French 18%; Italian 10%; Romansch 1%; Others 6%.
Religions: Roman Catholic 48%; Protestant 44%.
Capital city: Bern (Berne), population 300 900 (1983 census).
Other principal towns (1983): Zurich 839 900; Basel (Bâle or Basle) 365 000; Genève (Genf or Geneva) 371 700; Lausanne 254 900; Winterthur 107 600; St Gallen (St Gall) 123 800; Luzern (Lucerne) 157 700; Biel 83 572.
Highest point: Dufourspitze (Monte Rosa), 15 203 ft *4634 m* (first climbed 1855).
Principal mountain range: Alps.
Principal rivers: Rhein (Rhine) and Aare, Rhône, Inn, Ticino.
Head of State: Dr Kurt Furgler (b. 1924), President for 1984.
Climate: Generally temperate, with wide variations due to altitude. Cooler in north, warm on southern slopes. In Zürich, average maximum 9°C *48°F* (January) to 30°C *86°F* (July), minimum −10°C *14°F* (January) to 10°C *51°F* (July), rainiest months are June and July (each 15 days). In Geneva, January coldest (−2°C *29°F* to 4°C *39°F*), July warmest (14°C *58°F* to 25°C *77°F*). Absolute maximum temperature 38,7°C *101·7°F*, Basel, 29 July 1947; absolute minimum −35,8°C *−34·4°F*, Jungfraujoch, 14 Feb. 1940.
Labour force: 2 993 700 (excluding 26 288 unemployed) in 1983: Agriculture 7·1%; Industry 37·9%; Services 55%.
Gross domestic product: 196 billion Swiss francs in 1983.
Exports: 53 723 million Swiss francs in 1983.
Monetary unit: Schweizer Franken (Swiss franc). 1 franc = 100 Rappen (centimes).
Denominations:
Coins 1, 2, 5, 10, 20, 50 centimes; 1, 2, 5 francs.
Notes 10, 20, 50, 100, 500, 1000 francs.
Exchange rate to £ sterling: 3·22 (16 Apr. 1985).
Political history and government: Since 1815 Switzerland has been a neutral confederation of autonomous cantons. The present constitution, establishing a republican form of government, was adopted on 29 May 1874. The cantons hold all powers not specifically delegated to the federal authorities. On 1 Jan. 1979 a new canton, the first since 1815, was established when the Jura seceded from Bern. Switzerland now has 20 cantons and 6 half-cantons.
Legislative power is held by the bicameral Federal Assembly: a Council of States with 46 members representing the cantons (two for each canton and one for each half-canton), elected for 3 to 4 years; and the National Council with 200 members directly elected by universal adult suffrage for 4 years, using proportional representation. The two Houses have equal rights. A referendum on 7 Feb. 1971 approved women's suffrage in federal elections. Executive power is held by the Federal Council, which has 7 members (not more than one from any canton) elected for 4 years by a joint session of the Federal Assembly. Each member of the Council, which is responsible to the Assembly, has ministerial responsibility as head of a Federal Department. The Assembly elects one Councillor to be President of the Confederation (also presiding over the Council) for one calendar year at a time. Each canton has a constitution, an elected unicameral legislature and an executive.
Telephones: 3 095 057 (1983).

Daily newspapers: 91 (1977).
Total circulation: 2 622 000.
Radio: 2 379 461 (1983).
TV: 2 094 787 (1983).
Length of roadways: 42 709 miles *68 718 km* (1981).
Length of railways: 3104 miles *4995 km.*
Universities: 7 (plus 2 technical universities).
Expectation of life: Males 70·29 years; females 76·22 years (1968–73).
Defence: Military service: 17 weeks recruit training, followed by reservist refresher training of three weeks per year for 8 out of 12 years, two weeks for 3 of 10 years, and one week for 2 of 8 years; total armed forces on mobilization: 625 000 in 1984; defence expenditure, 1982: 4537 million Swiss francs.
Cinemas: 494 (seating capacity 176 800) in 1977.
Foreign tourists: 6 901 500 in 1983.

Syria

Official name: Al-Jumhuriya al-'Arabiya as-Suriya (the Syrian Arab Republic).
Population: 9 171 622 (1981 census).
Area: 71 498 miles² *185 180 km²*.
Languages: Arabic (official); Kurdish; Armenian; Turkish; Circassian.
Religion: Muslim; Christian minority.
Capital city: Dimash'q (Damascus), population 1 042 000 (1981).
Other principal towns (1981): Halab (Aleppo) 1 523 000; Homs 629 000; Al Ladhiqiyah (Latakia, 1970) 389 552; Hama (1970) 514 748.
Highest point: Jabal ash-Shaikh (Mt Hermon), 9232 ft *2814 m*.
Principal mountain ranges: Ansariyah range, Jabal ar-Ruwā.
Principal rivers: Al Furat (Euphrates headwaters) (420 miles *676 km* out of 1400 miles *2253 km*), Asi (Orontes).
Head of State: Lt-Gen Hafiz al-Assad (b. 6 Oct. 1930), President.
Prime Minister: Dr Abdul Rauf al-Qasim (b. 1931).
Climate: Variable. Hot summers, mild winters and ample rainfall on coast. Inland it is arid with hot, dry summers and cold winters. In Damascus, average maximum 12°C *53°F* (January) to 37°C *99°F* (August), minimum 2°C *36°F* (January) to 18°C *64°F* (July, August), rainiest month is January (seven days).
Labour force: 2 124 496 (excluding 49 731 seeking work for the first time) in Sept. 1979: Agriculture, forestry and fishing 32·6%; Manufacturing 15·9%; Construction 14·0%; Trade, restaurants and hotels 10·4%; Community, social and personal services 19·9%.
Gross domestic product: S£30 641 million in 1978: Agriculture, forestry and fishing 19·9%; Manufacturing 10·8%; Trade 22·8%; Community, social and personal services (including restaurants, hotels and business services) 18·5%.
Exports: S£8254 million in 1981.
Monetary unit: Syrian pound (S£). 1 pound = 100 piastres.
Denominations:
Coins 2½, 5, 10, 25, 50 piastres; 1 pound.
Notes 1, 5, 10, 25, 50, 100, 500 pounds.
Exchange rate to £ sterling: 9·0 (14 Jan. 1985).
Political history and government: Formerly part of Turkey's Ottoman Empire. Turkish forces were defeated in the First World War (1914–18). In 1920 Syria was occupied by French forces, in accordance with a League of Nations mandate. Nationalists proclaimed an independent republic on 16 Sept. 1941. The first elected parliament met on 17 Aug. 1943, French powers were transferred on 1 Jan. 1944 and full independence achieved on 12 Apr. 1946. Syria merged with Egypt to form the United Arab Republic, proclaimed on 1 Feb. 1958 and established on 21 Feb. 1958. Following a military *coup* in Syria on 28 Sept. 1961, the country resumed separate independence, under its present name, on 29 Sept. 1961. Left-wing army officers overthrew the government on 8 Mar. 1963 and formed the National Council of the Revolutionary Command (NCRC), which took

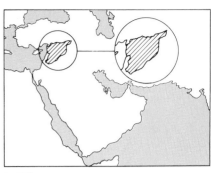

SYRIA

over all executive and legislative authority. The NCRC installed a Cabinet dominated by the Arab Socialist Renaissance (Ba'ath) Party. This party has held power ever since. Lt-Gen Hafiz al-Assad became Prime Minister on 18 Nov. 1970 and assumed Presidential powers on 22 Feb. 1971. His position was approved by popular referendum on 12 Mar. 1971 and he was sworn in for a 7-year term as President on 14 Mar. 1971. Legislative power is held by the People's Council, originally appointed for two years on 16 Feb. 1971 to draft a permanent constitution. The constitution, proclaiming socialist principles, was approved by referendum on 12 Mar. 1973 and adopted two days later. It declares that the Ba'ath party is 'the leading party in the State and society'. The People's Council became a full legislature after election by universal adult suffrage on 25–26 Mar. 1973. For the elections of 1–2 Aug. 1977 the Council was increased to 195 members. Political power is held by the Progressive Front of National Unity, formed on 7 Mar. 1972 by a merger of the Ba'ath Party and four others. The Head of State is leader of the Ba'ath Party and President of the Front. Syria has 14 administrative districts.
Telephones: 471 127 (1982).
Daily newspapers: 7 (1977).
Radio: 1 800 000 (1982).
TV: 387 000 (1982).
Length of roadways: 10 383 miles *16 710 km.*
Length of railways: 995 miles *1601 km.*
Universities: 4.
Adult illiteracy: 60·0% (males 40·4%; females 80·0%) in 1970.
Expectation of life: Males 54·49 years; females 58·73 years (1970).
Defence: Military service: 30 months; total armed forces 222 500 (1984); defence expenditure, 1981: $2389 million.
Cinemas: 70 in 1977.
Foreign tourists: 1 075 100 in 1981.

Tanzania

Official name: United Republic of Tanzania (Jamhuri ya Muungano wa Tanzania).
Population: 19 730 000 (1983 estimate).
Area: 364 900 miles² *945 087 km²*.
Languages: English, Swahili.
Religions: Traditional beliefs, Christian, Muslim.
Capital city: Dodoma, population 45 703 (1978 census).
Other principal towns (1978): Dar es Salaam (former capital) 757 346; Zanzibar Town 110 669; Mwanza 110 611; Tanga 103 409; Mbeya 76 606; Morogoro 61 890; Arusha 55 281.
Highest point: Mount Kilimanjaro, 19 340 ft *5894 m*.
Principal mountain range: Southern Highlands.
Principal rivers: Pangani (Ruvu), Rufiji, Rovuma.
Head of State: Dr Julius Kambarage Nyerere (b. April 1922), President.
Prime Minister: Cleopa David Msuya (b. 4 Jan. 1931).
Climate: Varies with altitude. Tropical (hot and humid) on Zanzibar, and on the coast and plains. Cool and semi-temperate in the highlands. In Dar es Salaam, average maximum 28°C *83°F* to 31°C *88°F*, minimum 19°C *66°F* to 25°C *77°F*.

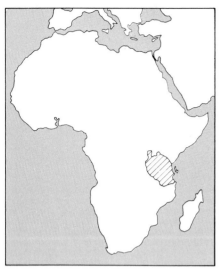

TANZANIA

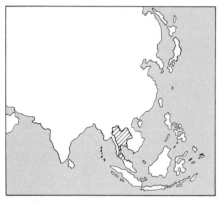

THAILAND

In Zanzibar Town, average maximum 28°C 82°F (July) to 33°C 91°F (February, March), minimum 22°C 72°F (July–September) to 25°C 77°F (March–April), average annual rainfall 1575 mm *62 in*, April rainiest (16 days), July driest (four days).
Labour force: 5 747 096 (census of 26 Aug. 1967): Agriculture, forestry and fishing 91·6%.
Gross domestic product: 33 466 million shillings in 1978 (Tanganyika only): Agriculture, forestry and fishing 50·1% (agriculture 45·8%); Trade, restaurants and hotels 12·0% (trade 11·8%); Community, social and personal services 10·6%.
Exports: 5248 million Tanzanian shillings in 1981: Coffee 27·7%; Cotton 13·1%; Cloves 7·9%; Sisal 5·5%; Tea 3·5%; Tobacco 3·1%.
Monetary unit: Tanzanian shilling. 1 shilling = 100 cents.
Denominations:
    Coins 5, 10, 20, 50 cents; 1, 5, 20 shillings.
    Notes 10, 20, 100 shillings.
Exchange rate to £ sterling: 20·27 (14 Jan. 1985).
Political history and government: Tanganyika became a German protectorate in 1885. During the First World War (1914–18) the territory was occupied by British and Belgian forces. In 1919 the United Kingdom was granted a League of Nations mandate over Tanganyika. On 13 Dec. 1946 it became a United Nations Trust Territory under British administration. Tanganyika became an independent member of the Commonwealth on 9 Dec. 1961 and a republic on 9 Dec. 1962. Zanzibar, a sultanate under British protection since 1890, became an independent constitutional monarchy within the Commonwealth on 10 Dec. 1963. The Sultan was overthrown by revolution on 12 Jan. 1964 and the People's Republic of Zanzibar proclaimed. A new constitution was decreed on 24 Feb. 1964. The two republics merged on 26 Apr. 1964 to form the United Republic of Tanganyika and Zanzibar (renamed Tanzania on 29 Oct. 1964) and remained in the Commonwealth.

An interim constitution, declaring Tanzania a one-party state, was approved by the legislature on 5 July 1965 and received the President's assent three days later. Legislative power was vested in the unicameral National Assembly, with a term of five years (subject to dissolution). Executive power lies with the President, elected by popular vote for five years. He appoints a First Vice-President (who is Chairman of the Zanzibar Revolutionary Council), a Prime Minister and a Cabinet.

At a joint conference the ruling parties of Tanganyika and Zanzibar decided on 21 Jan. 1977 to merge into a single party, *Chama Cha Mapinduzi* (CCM or Revolutionary Party), formed on 5 Feb. 1977. The Party's leading decision-making organ is the National Executive, elected by party members.

On 25 Apr. 1977 the National Assembly approved a permanent constitution for Tanzania. On 26 Oct. 1980 elections were held for 111 seats (101 in Tanganyika, 10 in Zanzibar) in the 239-member Assembly. The remaining 128 members include 32 appointees from Zanzibar, 25 regional commissioners (one for each of the 20 administrative regions in Tanganyika, five for the two Zanzibar regions), the President of Zanzibar, 30 members nominated by the Head of State and 40 others (25 regional members and 15 representing state bodies) chosen by the Assembly's elected members.

In Zanzibar, comprising the islands of Zanzibar and Pemba, a Revolutionary Council is responsible for internal government. On 13 Oct. 1979 this Council adopted a new constitution for the territory. A special session of the CCM approved the new Zanzibar constitution on 28 Dec. 1979 and legislation incorporating the necessary amendments to the Tanzanian constitution was approved on 2 Jan. 1980.
Telephones: 96 521 (1982).
Daily newspapers: 2 (morning dailies) in 1977.
    Total circulation: 133 000.
Radio: 500 000 (1979).
TV: 8840 (1978).
Length of roadways: 10 403 miles *16 742 km* (1969).
Length of railways: 2218 miles *3568 km*.
Universities: 1.
Adult illiteracy: 71·9% (males 57·3%; females 85·1%) in 1967.
Expectation of life: Males 46·4 years; females 49·7 years (UN estimates for 1970–75).
Defence: Military service voluntary; total armed forces 40 150 (1984); defence expenditure, 1980/81: $179 million.
Cinemas: 34 (seating capacity 13 400), 20 mobile units and 1 drive-in (capacity 2400) in 1977.
Foreign tourists: 91 600 in 1981.

Thailand

Official name: Prathet Thai (Kingdom of Thailand), also called Prades Thai or Muang-Thai (Thai means free).
Population: 48 846 927 (1982 estimate).
Area: 198 457 miles² *514 000 km²*.
Language: Thai.
Religions: Buddhist, Muslim minority.
Capital city: Krungt'ep (Bangkok), population 5 468 286 (1982 estimate).
Other principal towns (1979): Chiang Mai 105 230; Nakhon Ratchasima 87 371; Khon Kaen 80 286; Udon Thani 76 173; Pitsanulok 73 175; Hat Yai 67 117.
Highest point: Doi Inthanon, 8452 ft *2576 m*.
Principal rivers: Mekong (2600 miles *4184 km*), Chao Pyha (154 miles *247 km*).
Head of State: HM King Bhumibol Adulyadej (b. 5 Dec. 1927).
Prime Minister: Gen Prem Tinsulanond (b. 26 Aug. 1920).
Climate: Tropical monsoon climate (humid). Three seasons – hot, rainy and cool. Average temperature 29°C *85°F*. In Bangkok, average maximum 30°C 87°F (November, December) to 35°C 95°F (April), minimum 20°C 68°F (December, January) to 25°C 77°F (April, May), rainiest month is September (15 days). Absolute maxi-

mum temperature 44,1°C *111·4°F*, Mae Sariang, 25 Apr. 1958; absolute minimum 0,1°C *32·2°F*, Loey, 13 Jan. 1955.
Labour force: 21 736 500 (excluding 156 800 unemployed) at July–Sept. 1978: Agriculture, forestry and fishing 73·7%; Services 17·7%.
Gross domestic product: 444 196 million baht in 1978: Agriculture, forestry and fishing 27·1% (agriculture 23·1%); Manufacturing 19·1%; Trade, restaurants and hotels 22·9% (trade 19·8%).
Exports: 153 001 million baht in 1981: Rice 15%; Tapioca products 11%; Rubber 9%; Tin 9%; Maize 5%; Sugar 2%.
Monetary unit: Baht. 1 baht = 100 satangs.
Denominations:
    Coins 5, 10, 25, 50 satangs; 1, 5 baht.
    Notes 5, 10, 20, 100, 500 baht.
Exchange rate to £ sterling: 30·19 (14 Jan. 1985).
Political history and government: Thailand, called Siam before 1939, is a kingdom with an hereditary monarch as Head of State. The military régime established on 17 Nov. 1971 was forced to resign, following popular demonstrations, on 14 Oct. 1973. An interim government was formed and a new constitution, legalising political parties, was promulgated on 7 Oct. 1974. The constitutional government was overthrown on 6 Oct. 1976 by a military junta, the National Administrative Reform Council (NARC), which declared martial law, annulled the 1974 constitution, dissolved the bicameral National Assembly and banned political parties. A new constitution, promulgated on 22 Oct. 1976, provided for a National Administrative Reform Assembly (340 members appointed for 4 years by the King on 20 Nov. 1976). A new Prime Minister was appointed and the NARC became the Prime Minister's Advisory Council. On 20 Oct. 1977 a Revolutionary Council of military leaders (almost identical to the NARC) deposed the government, abrogated the 1976 constitution and abolished the Advisory Council. An interim constitution was promulgated on 9 Nov. 1977. It provided that the Revolutionary Council would become the National Policy Council (NPC) and that the Prime Minister would be appointed by the King on the advice of the NPC's chairman. General Kriangsak Chamanan, Supreme Commander of the Armed Forces and Secretary-General of the NPC, became Prime Minister on 11 Nov. 1977. Other Ministers were appointed by the King on the Prime Minister's recommendation. On 16 Nov. 1977 a National Legislative Assembly (NLA) of 360 members was nominated by the King on the advice of the NPC's chairman. On 23 Nov. the NLA opened and on 1 Dec. 1977 it appointed a 35-member committee to draft a new constitution.

A new constitution was approved by the NLA on 18 Dec. 1978 and promulgated on 22 Dec. 1978. Legislative power is vested in a bicameral National Assembly, comprising a House of Representatives (301 members elected for 4 years by universal adult suffrage) and a Senate (225 members appointed for 6 years by the King on the recommendation of the incumbent Prime Minister). The two chambers meet in joint session to appoint the Prime Minister and to debate motions of confidence. Elections to the House were held on 22 Apr. 1979. The nominated Senators were almost all military officers. On 11 May 1979 the Assembly invited Gen Kriangsak to continue as Prime Minister. After a new Cabinet was formed, the NPC was dissolved. Kriangsak resigned on 29 Feb. 1980. General Prem Tinsulanond, Minister of Defence and Army Commander-in-Chief, was nominated by the Assembly to become Prime Minister, and was appointed by the King, on 3 Mar. 1980.

Thailand comprises 71 provinces, each headed by an appointed governor.
Telephones: 529 106 (1982).
Daily newspapers: 20 (1979).
    Total circulation: 800 000.
Radio: 5 700 000 (1977).
TV: 765 000 (1977).
Length of roadways: 39 816 miles *64 078 km* (31 Dec. 1979).

Length of railways: 2339 miles *3765 km* (30 Sept. 1976).
Universities: 11 (plus 2 technical universities).
Adult illiteracy: 21·3% (males 12·7%; females 29·5%) in 1970.
Expectation of life: Males 53·6 years; females 58·7 years (1960).
Defence: Military service: 2 years; total armed forces 233 100 (1984); defence expenditure, 1981: $1279 million.
Cinemas: 415 in 1977.
Foreign tourists: 2 015 615 in 1981.

Togo

Official name: La République togolaise (the Togolese Republic).
Population: 2 963 000 (1983 estimate).
Area: 21 622 miles² *56 000 km²*.
Languages: French (official), Ewe, Kabiye.
Religions: Animist; Christian and Muslim minorities.
Capital city: Lomé, population 247 000 (1979 estimate).
Other principal towns (1 Jan. 1977): Sokodé 33 500; Palimé 25 500; Atakpamé 21 800; Bassari 17 500; Tsévié 15 900.
Highest point: 3018 ft *919 m*.
Principal rivers: Mono, Oti.
Head of State: Major-Gen Etienne Gnassingbe Eyadéma (b. 26 Dec. 1937), President.
Climate: Equatorial (hot and humid). On coast, average temperatures 24°C *76°F* to 28°C *82°F*, higher inland (average 36°C *97°F* in drier north).
Labour force: 719 308 (excluding unemployed) aged 15 and over (1970 census); 859 000 (mid-1970): Agriculture, forestry and fishing 73·3%; Industry 10·9%; Services 15·8% (ILO estimates).
Gross domestic product: 133 829 million CFA francs in 1976: Agriculture, forestry and fishing 28·0%; Industry 11·9%; Trade, restaurants and hotels 30·6%.
Exports: 71 285 million francs CFA: Phosphates 40%; Cocoa beans 12%; Coffee 8%.
Monetary unit: France de la Communauté financière africaine.
Denominations:
   Coins 1, 2, 5, 10, 25, 50, 100, 500 CFA francs.
   Notes 50, 100, 500, 1000, 5000 CFA francs.
Exchange rate to £ sterling: 542·25 (14 Jan. 1985).
Political history and government: Formerly a United Nations Trust Territory under French administration, an independent republic since 27 Apr. 1960. An army *coup* on 13 Jan. 1967 deposed the President and established military rule under Lieut-Col (later Major-Gen) Etienne Gnassingbe Eyadéma, who suspended the constitution and dissolved the National Assembly. Eyadéma proclaimed himself President on 14 Apr. 1967. Political parties were banned and the President ruled by decree through an appointed Council of Ministers. On 29 Nov. 1969 the President established a single ruling party, the *Rassemblement du peuple togolais* (RPT). A congress of the RPT on 27–29 Nov. 1979 approved a new constitution for Togo. This provides for a one-party state, with legislative power vested in a 67-member National Assembly (elected for five years by universal adult suffrage) while executive power is held by the President, directly elected for seven years. The constitution was approved by referendum on 30 Dec. 1979, when President Eyadéma was re-elected (unopposed) and the new Assembly elected (from a single list of RPT candidates). On 13 Jan. 1980 the President proclaimed the 'Third Republic'. Togo is divided into four regions, each administered by an appointed Inspector.
Telephones: 7870 (1981).
Daily newspapers: 1 (1983).
   Total circulation: 10 000.
Radio: 125 000 (1981).
TV: 5000 (1981).
Length of roadways: 4629 miles *7450 km* (31 Dec. 1978).
Length of railways: 325 miles *525 km*.
Universities: 1.

Adult illiteracy: 84·1% (males 73·1%; females 92·9%) in 1970.
Expectation of life: Males 41·9 years; females 45·1 years (UN estimates for 1970–75).
Defence: Total armed forces 4500 (1984); defence expenditure, 1979: $28 million.
Cinemas: 2 (seating capacity 2300) in 1964.
Foreign tourists: 117 000 in 1980.

Tonga

Official name: Pule'anga Fakatu'i 'o Tonga (Kingdom of Tonga).
Population: 98 750 (1983 estimate).
Area: 270 miles² *699 km²*.
Languages: Tongan, English.
Religion: Christian, mainly Wesleyan.
Capital city: Nuku'alofa, population 18 312 (including suburbs) at 1976 census.
Highest point: Kao, 3380 ft *1030 m*.
Head of State: HM King Taufa'ahau Tupou IV, GCMG, GCVO, KBE (b. 4 July 1918).
Prime Minister: HRH Prince Fatafehi Tu'ipelehake, KCMG, KBE (b. 7 Jan. 1922).
Climate: Warm and pleasant. Average annual temperature is 23°C *73°F*. Hot and humid from Jan. to March (32°C *90°F*). Average annual rainfall 1600 mm *63 in* on Tongatapu, 2080 mm *82 in* on Vava'u.
Labour force: 18 626 (excluding persons seeking work for the first time and 2809 other unemployed) at 1976 census: Agriculture, forestry and fishing 56·1%; Community, social and personal services 24·0%.
Gross domestic product: 13·3 million pa'anga in year ending 30 June 1971: Agriculture, forestry and fishing 52%; Trade, restaurants and hotels 10%; Community, social and personal services 17%.
Exports: 4 287 906 pa'anga in 1982.
Monetary unit: Pa'anga. 1 pa'anga = 100 seniti.
Denominations:
   Coins 1, 2, 5, 10, 20, 50 seniti; 1, 2 pa'anga.
   Notes 50 seniti; 1, 2, 5, 10 pa'anga.
Exchange rate to £ sterling: 1·3755 (14 Jan. 1985).
Political history and government: Tonga is a kingdom ruled by an hereditary monarch. It was under British protection from 18 May 1900 until becoming independent, within the Commonwealth, on 4 June 1970. The King is Head of State and Head of Government. He appoints, and presides over, a Privy Council which acts as the national Cabinet. Apart from the King, the Council includes six Ministers, led by the Prime Minister (currently the King's brother), and the Governors of two island groups. The unicameral Legislative Assembly comprises 23 members: the King, the Privy Council, seven hereditary nobles elected by their peers and seven representatives elected by literate adults (male voters must be tax-payers). Elected members hold office for three years. There are no political parties.
Telephones: 2608 (1982).
Radio: 11 000 (1975).
Length of roadways: 269 miles *433 km*.
Adult illiteracy: 0·4% (males 0·3%; females 0·5%) in 1976.
Expectation of life: 55·2 years (both sexes) in 1965.
Defence: Defence budget, 1972/73: 74 100 pa'anga.
Cinemas: 7 (seating capacity 7500) and 8 mobile units (1975).
Foreign tourists: 12 526 in 1977.

Trinidad and Tobago

Official name: The Republic of Trinidad and Tobago.
Population: 1 168 200 (1984).
Area: 1981 miles² *5130 km²*.
Languages: English (official), Hindi, French, Spanish.
Religions: Christian; Hindu and Moslem minorities.

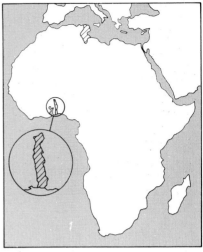

top: **TUNISIA**
encircled: **TOGO**

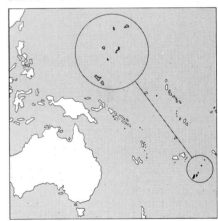

TONGA

Capital city: Port of Spain, population 120 000 (1983).
Other principal towns (1983): San Fernando 60 000; Arima 20 000.
Highest point: Cerro Aripo, 3085 ft *940 m*.
Principal mountain ranges: Northern and Southern, Central.
Principal rivers: Caroni, Ortoire, Oropuche.
Head of State: Ellis Emmanuel Innocent Clarke (b. 28 Dec. 1917), President.
Prime Minister: George Michael Chambers (b. 4 Oct. 1928).
Climate: Tropical, with an annual average temperature of 29°C *84°F*. The dry season is January to May.
Labour force: 470 936 in 1984 (including 60 383 unemployed): Petroleum, mining and quarrying 2·3%; Agriculture, forestry, fishing 6·4%; Manufacturing 10·6%; Construction 15·6%; Government utilities 5·8%; Government 11%.
Gross domestic product: TT$20 136 million (1983): Petroleum 24·6%; Manufacturing 6·6%; Agriculture 2·9%; Construction and quarrying 12·8%; Transportation 11·4%; Government services 14·1%.
Exports: TT$5728 million in 1983: Mineral fuel and lubricants 84%; Chemicals 8%; Manufactured goods 2%.
Monetary unit: Trinidad and Tobago dollar (TT$) 1 dollar = 100 cents.
Denominations:
   Coins 1, 5, 10, 25, 50 cents; 1 dollar.
   Notes 1, 5, 10, 20, 100 dollars.
Exchange rate to £ sterling: 2·69 (29 Jan. 1985).
Political history and government: Formerly a British dependency. The colony's first Chief Minister, Dr Eric Williams, took office on 28 Oct. 1956. A new constitution was introduced, with Dr Williams as Premier, on 20 July 1959. Internal self-government was granted after elections on 4 Dec. 1961. Following a constitutional conference on 28 May–8 June 1962,

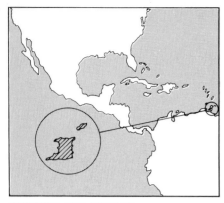

TRINIDAD AND TOBAGO

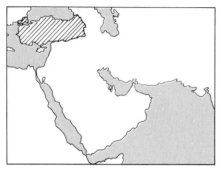

TURKEY

Trinidad and Tobago became an independent member of the Commonwealth, with the Premier as Prime Minister, on 31 Aug. 1962. The country became a republic on 1 Aug. 1976. Dr Williams, Prime Minister since independence, died on 29 Mar. 1981.

Legislative power is vested in a bicameral Parliament, comprising a Senate with 31 members, appointed for up to five years by the President (16 on the advice of the Prime Minister, 6 on the advice of the Leader of the Opposition and 9 at the President's own discretion), and a House of Representatives (36 members elected by universal adult suffrage for five years). The President is a constitutional Head of State elected for five years by both Houses of Parliament. He appoints the Prime Minister to form a Cabinet from members of Parliament. The Cabinet has effective control of the government and is responsible to Parliament.

Telephones: 74 908 (1978).
Daily newspapers: 3 (1976).
 Total circulation: 144 000 (2 dailies).
Radio: 500 000.
TV: 230 000.
Length of roadways: 4400 miles *7080 km* (1977).
University: 1 (shared with Jamaica, Barbados and other Caribbean territories).
Adult illiteracy: 7·8% (males 5·3%; females 10·3%) in 1970.
Expectation of life: Males 64 years; females 68 years (1979).
Defence: Army and Coast Guard amount to 800.
Cinemas: 68 in 1978.
Foreign tourists: 200 000 (1983).

Tunisia

Official name: Al-Jumhuriya at-Tunisiya (the Republic of Tunisia).
Population: 6 966 173 (March 1984).
Area: 63 170 miles² *163 610 km².*
Languages: Arabic, French.
Religions: Muslim; Jewish and Christian minorities.
Capital city: Tunis, population 596 654 (1984).
Other principal towns (1984): Sfax (Safaqis) 231 911; Bizerte 94 509; Djerba 92 269; Gabes 92 259; Sousse 83 509; Kairouan 72 254; Gafsa 60 970.

Highest point: Djebel Chambi, 5066 ft *1544 m.*
Principal river: Medjerda (300 miles *482 km*).
Head of State: Habib Ben Ali Bourguiba (b. 3 Aug. 1903), President.
Prime Minister: Mohamed Mzali (b. 23 Dec. 1925).
Climate: Temperate, with winter rain, on coast; hot and dry inland. In Tunis, August warmest (20°C *69°F* to 33°C *91°F*), January coolest (6°C *43°F* to 14°C *58°F*), December rainiest (14 days). Absolute maximum temperature 55,0°C *131·0°F*, Kébili, 7 Dec. 1931; absolute minimum −9,0°C *15·8°F*, Fort-Saint, 22 Dec. 1940.
Labour force: 1 621 820 aged 15 and over (1975 census, sample tabulation): Agriculture, forestry and fishing 39·0%; Manufacturing 17·8%; Construction 10·4%; Community, social and personal services 16·1%. In addition, the labour force included 107 240 persons aged 10 to 15.
Gross domestic product: 3992 million dinars in 1981: Agriculture, forestry and fishing 18·3% (agriculture and forestry 17·4%); Manufacturing 11·7%; Public administration and defence 14·3%.
Exports: 1154 million dinars in 1982: Petroleum and petroleum products 38·5% (crude and partly refined petroleum 36·7%); Chemicals 11·2%; Clothing (excluding footwear) 17·9%.
Monetary unit: Tunisian dinar. 1 dinar = 1000 millimes.
Denominations:
 Coins 1, 2, 5, 10, 20, 50, 100, 500 millimes; 1, 5 dinars.
 Notes 500 millimes; 1, 5, 10, 20 dinars.
Exchange rate to £ sterling: 0·97 (14 Jan. 1985).
Political history and government: Formerly a monarchy, ruled by the Bey of Tunis. A French protectorate from 1883 until independence on 20 Mar. 1956. The campaign for independence was led by the Neo-Destour Party (founded by Habib Bourguiba), since October 1964 called the *Parti Socialiste Destourien* (PSD), the Destourian (Constitutional) Socialist Party. Elections were held on 25 Mar. 1956 for a Constitutional Assembly, which met on 8 Apr. 1956 and appointed Bourguiba as Prime Minister two days later. On 25 July 1957 the Assembly deposed the Bey, abolished the monarchy and established a republic, with Bourguiba as President. A new constitution was promulgated on 1 June 1959. Legislative power is vested in the unicameral National Assembly, first elected on 8 Nov. 1959. The Assembly's members are elected by universal adult suffrage for five years. Executive power is held by the President, elected for five years by popular vote at the same time as the Assembly. On 3 Nov. 1974 President Bourguiba was re-elected for a fourth term of office but on 18 Mar. 1975 the Assembly proclaimed him 'President for life'. The President, who is Head of State and Head of Government, appoints a Council of Ministers, headed by a Prime Minister, which is responsible to him. From 1963 to 1981 the PSD was the only legal party. An 18-year ban on the Tunisian Communist Party was lifted on 18 July 1981. Elections were held on 1 Nov. 1981 for a new National Assembly, with 136 members chosen from 23 multi-member constituencies. Parties other than the PSD were permitted to contest the elections but none received the necessary 5% of the valid votes to achieve subsequent legal recognition.
Telephones: 188 476 (1981).
Daily newspapers: 5 (morning dailies).
Radio: 1 124 000 (1976).
TV: 255 700 (1979).
Length of roadways: 15 017 miles *24 168 km* (31 Dec. 1978).
Length of railways: 1251 miles *2013 km.*
Universities: 1.
Adult illiteracy: 62·0% (males 48·9%; females 72·2%) in 1975.
Expectation of life: Males 54·0 years; females 56·0 years (UN estimate for 1970–75).
Defence: Military service: 12 months, selective; total armed forces 27 600 (1984); defence expenditure, 1981: $262 million.
Cinemas: 73 in 1980.
Foreign tourists: 1 400 000 in 1984.

Turkey

Official name: Türkiye Cumhuriyeti (Republic of Turkey).
Population: 45 217 556 (census of 12 Oct. 1980).
Area: 301 382 miles² *780 576 km².*
Languages: Turkish 90·2%; Kurdish 6·9%; Arabic 1·2%; Zaza 0·5% (1965).
Religion: Muslim 98%.
Capital city: Ankara (Angora), population 2 316 333 in 1980.
Other principal towns (1980): Istanbul 3 033 810; Izmir (Smyrna) 776 954; Adana 644 435; Bursa 431 844; Gaziantep 394 640; Eskişehir 311 300; Konya 302 454.
Highest point: Büyük Ağridaği (Mt Ararat), 17 011 ft *5185 m.*
Principal mountain ranges: Armenian Plateau, Toros Dağlari (Taurus Mts), Kuzey Anadolu Dağlari.
Principal rivers: Firat (Euphrates), Dicle (Tigris), Kizilirmak (Halys), Sakarya.
Head of State: Gen Kenan Evren (b. 1918), Chairman of the National Security Council.
Prime Minister: Turgut Ozal.
Climate: Hot, dry summers and cold, snowy winters in interior plateau; mild winters and warm summers on Mediterranean coast. In Ankara, average maximum 4°C *30°F* (January) to 30°C *87°F* (August), minimum −4°C *24°F* (January) to 15°C *59°F* (July, August), rainiest month is December (9 days). In Istanbul, average maximum 7°C *45°F* (January) to 27°C *81°F* (July, August), minimum 2°C *36°F* (January) to 19°C *66°F* (August), rainiest month is December (15 days). Absolute maximum temperature 46,2°C *115·2°F,* Diyarbakir, 21 July 1937; absolute minimum −43,2°C *−45·8°F,* Karaköse, 13 Jan. 1940.
Labour force: 16 349 380 (1975 census): Agriculture, forestry and fishing 66·9%; Community, social and personal services 11·9%.
Gross domestic product: 1 215 955 million liras in 1978: Agriculture, forestry and fishing (excluding government) 25·8% (agriculture 24·7%); Manufacturing 19·2%; Trade 13·3%; Government services 11·1%.
Exports: US$5746 million in 1982: Cotton 5·4%; Hazelnuts 4·2%; Tobacco 6·1%; Textiles 18·4%; Raisins 1·8%; Cereals and pulses 5·9%.
Monetary unit: Turkish lira. 1 lira = 100 kuruş.
Denominations:
 Coins 25, 50 kuruş; 1, 2½, 5 liras.
 Notes 5, 10, 20, 50, 100, 500, 1000, 5000 liras.
Exchange rate to £ sterling: 510 (25 Jan. 1985).
Political history and government: Formerly a monarchy, ruled by a Sultan. Following the disintegration of the Ottoman Empire after the First World War, power passed to the Grand National Assembly, which first met on 23 Apr. 1920. The Assembly approved a new constitution on 20 Jan. 1921, vesting executive and legislative authority in itself. It abolished the sultanate on 1 Nov. 1922 and declared Turkey a republic on 29 Oct. 1923. The armed forces overthrew the government on 27 May 1960, the Assembly was dissolved and political activities suspended until 12 Jan. 1961. A new constitution was approved by referendum on 9 June 1961 and took effect on 25 Oct. 1961. Legislative power was vested in the bicameral Grand National Assembly, comprising the Senate of the Republic (with, in 1980, 19 life senators plus 150 elected and 15 appointed members serving a six-year term) and the National Assembly (450 members elected by universal adult suffrage for four years. The Grand National Assembly elected one of its members to be President of the Republic for a single seven-year term. The President appointed the Prime Minister from among members of the legislature.

Following a period of severe political violence, martial law was proclaimed on 26 Dec. 1978 in 13 of Turkey's 67 provinces. This was later extended to other provinces. The President's term of office ended on 6 Apr. 1980 but, despite more than 100 ballots in the Grand National Assembly, no candidate gained enough support to succeed him. On 11–12 Sept. 1980 a military

coup deposed the civilian government. Power was assumed by a five-member National Security Council (NSC), led by the Chief of the General Staff, Gen Kenan Evren. Martial law was extended to the whole country and the Grand National Assembly dissolved. General Evren became Head of State and the NSC was sworn in on 18 Sept. A mainly civilian Council of Ministers was appointed on 21 Sept. The NSC adopted a provisional constitution, giving itself unlimited powers, on 27 Oct. 1980. All political parties were dissolved on 16 Oct. 1981. A Consultative Assembly of 160 members (40 nominated by the NSC and 120 selected from provincial governors' lists), appointed to draft a new constitution, opened on 23 Oct. 1981.
Telephones: 2 104 113 (1982).
Daily newspapers: 493 (1977).
Radio: 4 283 753 (1950).
TV: 3 348 138 (1980).
Length of roadways: 144 259 miles *232 162 km* (31 Dec. 1979).
Length of railways: 5058 miles *8140 km* (1975).
Universities: 26.
Adult illiteracy: 39·7% (males 22·8%; females 56·9%) in 1975.
Expectation of life: Males 58·3 years; females 59·4 years (UN estimates for 1970–75).
Defence: Military service: 20 months; total armed forces 568 000 (489 000 conscripts) in 1984; defence expenditure, 1981: $3106 million.
Cinemas: 3000 (claimed) in 1979.
Foreign tourists: 1 400 000 in 1982.

Tuvalu

Population: 7349 (census of May 1979).
Area: 9·5 miles² *24,6 km²*.
Languages: Tuvaluan, English.
Religion: Christian (Congregational 97%).
Capital city: Fongafale (in Funafuti atoll, population 871 at census of 8 Dec. 1973).
Other principal atolls: Nanumea (population 977 in 1973), Niutau, Vaitupu.
Head of State: HM Queen Elizabeth II, represented by Sir (Fiatau) Penitala Teo, GCMG, ISO, MBE (b. 23 July 1911), Governor-General.
Prime Minister: The Rt. Hon. Dr Tomasi Puapua.
Climate: Warm and pleasant, with day temperatures between 27°C *80°F* and 32°C *90°F* and a minimum of about 21°C *70°F* at night. Average annual rainfall about 3050 mm *120 in.* Rainy season Dec.–Feb., dry Aug.–Oct.
Labour force: 2766 (1973 census).
Monetary unit: Australian currency (*q.v.*).
Political history and government: Formerly known as the Ellice (Lagoon) Islands. In Sept. 1892 the group became a United Kingdom protectorate and was linked administratively with the Gilbert Islands. The Gilbert and Ellice Islands were annexed by the UK on 10 Nov. 1915, effective from 12 Jan. 1916, when the protectorate became a colony. The Gilbert and Ellice Islands Colony (GEIC) was later expanded to include other groups. A referendum was held in the Ellice Islands in Aug.–Sept. 1974, when over 90% of voters favoured separation from the GEIC. The Ellice Islands, under the old native name of Tuvalu ('eight standing together'), became a separate British dependency on 1 Oct. 1975. The 8 Ellice representatives in the GEIC House of Assembly became the first elected members of the new Tuvalu House of Assembly. They elected one of their number to be Chief Minister. Tuvalu's first separate elections were held on 29 Aug. 1977, when the number of elective seats in the House was increased from 8 to 12. Following a 4-day conference in London, a new constitution was finalised on 17 Feb. 1978. Afer 5 months of internal self-government, Tuvalu became independent on 1 Oct. 1978, with the Chief Minister as the first Prime Minister. Tuvalu is a 'special member' of the Commonwealth and is not represented at meetings of Heads of Government.

Tuvalu is a constitutional monarchy. Executive power is vested in the British monarch and is exercisable by the Governor-General, who is appointed on the recommendation of the Prime Minister and acts in almost all matters on the advice of the Cabinet. Legislative power is vested in the unicameral Parliament, with 12 members elected by universal adult suffrage for 4 years (subject to dissolution). The pre-independence House of Assembly became the first Parliament. The Cabinet is led by the Prime Minister, elected by and from members of Parliament. Other Ministers are appointed by the Governor-General, on the Prime Minister's recommendation, from members of Parliament. The Cabinet is responsible to Parliament. Each of the 8 inhabited atolls has an elected Island Council.
Telephones: 92 (1982).
Expectation of life: Males 56·9 years; females 59·0 years (average for Kiribati and Tuvalu, 1958–62).

Uganda

Official name: The Republic of Uganda.
Population: 13 047 000 (1981 estimate).
Area: 91 134 miles² *236 036 km²*.
Languages: English (official), Luganda, Ateso, Runyankore.
Religions: Christian, Muslim, traditional beliefs.
Capital city: Kampala, population 454 974 (1981 estimate).
Other principal towns (1981): Jinja-Njeru 45 060; Mbale 28 039; Entebbe 20 472.
Highest point: Mount Stanley, 16 763 ft *5109 m* (first climbed 1900), on the border with Zaire.
Principal mountain range: Ruwenzori.
Principal rivers: Nile, Semliki.
Head of State: Dr (Apollo) Milton Obote (b. 28 Dec. 1925), President.
Prime Minister: E Otema Allimadi (b. 11 Feb. 1929).
Climate: Tropical, with an average temperature of 22°C *71°F*. There is a seasonal variation of only 11°C *20°F*.
Labour force: 4 262 000 (mid-1970): Agriculture, forestry and fishing 85·9% (ILO estimates).
Gross domestic product: 6890 million shillings in 1982: Agriculture 52%; Manufacturing 6%; Other industries 7%; Services 35%.
Exports: US$220 million in 1981: Coffee 99%.
Monetary unit: Uganda shilling. 1 shilling = 100 cents.
Denominations:
   Coins 5, 10, 50 cents; 1 shilling.
   Notes 5, 10, 20, 50, 100, 500, 1000 shillings.
Exchange rate to £ sterling: 577·50 (14 Jan. 1985).
Political history and government: Formerly a British dependency. The first Council of Ministers took office on 13 Apr. 1961 and the first Chief Minister was appointed on 2 July 1961. Uganda was granted internal self-government on 1 Mar. 1962, when the Chief Minister became Prime Minister. The leader of the Uganda People's Congress (UPC), Dr Milton Obote, became Prime Minister on 30 Apr. 1962. The country achieved independence, within the Commonwealth, on 9 Oct. 1962. Uganda became a republic, with a nominal President and Dr Obote continuing as executive Prime Minister, on 9 Oct. 1963. The constitution was suspended, and the President deposed, on 24 Feb. 1966. A provisional constitution, effective from 15 Apr. 1966, ended the former federal system and introduced an executive presidency, with Dr Obote as Head of State. A unitary republic was established on 8 Sept. 1967. After an assassination attempt against President Obote on 19 Dec. 1969, all parties other than the UPC were banned.

President Obote was deposed on 25 Jan. 1971 by an army *coup*, led by Major-Gen (later Field Marshal) Idi Amin Dada, who assumed full executive powers as Head of the Military Government and suspended political activity. The National Assembly was dissolved on 2 Feb. 1971, when Amin declared himself Head of State, took over legislative powers and suspended parts of the 1967 constitution. He was proclaimed President on 21 Feb. 1971 and ruled

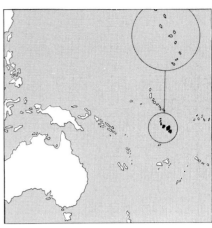

TUVALU

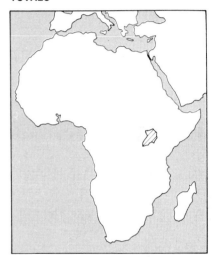

UGANDA

with the assistance of an appointed Council of Ministers. On 25 June 1976 the Defence Council appointed Amin 'President for Life'. No legislature was formed under Amin but a large advisory assembly, the National Consultative Forum, held its first meeting on 15–20 Jan. 1978.

After border fighting with Tanzanian forces in 1978, Ugandan troops captured the northern part of Tanzania. Amin announced Uganda's annexation of this territory on 1 Nov. 1978. Tanzania retaliated and its forces entered Uganda in Jan. 1979. Ugandan opponents of Amin met in Tanzania on 23–25 Mar. 1979, when 18 exile groups formed the Uganda National Liberation Front (UNLF), with Prof Yusufu Lule as leader of the 11-member executive council. The Ugandan capital fell to combined Tanzanian and UNLF forces on 10–11 April 1979 and Amin's rule was overthrown. On 11 Apr. 1979 the UNLF formed a provisional government, the National Executive Committee (NEC), and on 13 Apr. it was sworn in. Lule became Chairman of the NEC and Head of State. On 8 May 1979 the new régime announced a two-year ban on political parties. The UNLF, the sole authorised political organisation, formed a 30-member National Consultative Council (NCC) as a provisional parliament. By 3 June the anti-Amin forces had occupied the whole country. On 20 June the NCC replaced President Lule by Godfrey Binaisa. In Sept. 1979 the UNLF nominated members of 33 district councils. On 3 Oct. these councils elected 61 members of an expanded NCC. Additional members were appointed from the Uganda National Liberation Army (UNLA). The new NCC, with 127 members, was inaugurated on 6 Oct. 1979. General elections were due to be held, within a one-party UNLF framework, by June 1981.

On 12 May 1980 President Binaisa was relieved of his post when power was assumed by

THE UNION OF SOVIET SOCIALIST REPUBLICS

the UNLF's Military Commission, led by Paulo Muwanga. On 18 May the Military Commission issued a declaration, proclaiming its powers, and appointed a new Cabinet. On the next day Muwanga stated that the new régime was an interim one and committed to general elections. On 22 May a three-man Presidential Commission was appointed. On 23 June it was reported that four political parties, including the UPC (led by ex-President Obote) would be allowed to contest the elections. The NCC was dissolved on 8 Nov. 1980.

Voting took place on 10–11 Dec. 1980 for the 126 elective seats in a new National Assembly. Deputies to the Assembly, representing single-member constituencies, were elected by universal adult suffrage. The UPC gained a majority and, as the party's presidential candidate, Dr Obote was declared Head of State. He was sworn in on 15 Dec., when constitutional rule was restored. On 22 Dec. 1980 the government appointed 10 members of the armed forces to represent UNLA in the Assembly. The withdrawal of Tanzanian troops from Uganda was completed on 30 June 1981.

Telephones: 46 359 (1980).
Daily newspapers: 4 (1983).
   Total circulation: 40 000.
Radio: 275 000 (1982).
TV: 75 000 (1982).
Length of roadways: 17 337 miles *27 901 km* (31 Dec. 1979).
Length of railways: 799 miles *1286 kms* (1978).
Universities: 1.
Adult illiteracy: 52% (1983).
Expectation of life: Males 48·3 years; females 51·7 years (UN estimates for 1970–75).
Defence: Total armed forces 15 000 (1983).
Cinemas: 17 (seating capacity 10 000) exhibiting 35 mm films, and 1 drive-in (capacity 3400) in 1977.
Foreign tourists: 10 296 in 1974.

The Union of Soviet Socialist Republics

Official name: Soyuz Sovyetskikh Sotsialisticheskikh Respublik (abbreviation in Cyrillic script is CCCP), sometimes shortened to Sovyetskiy Soyuz (Soviet Union).
Population: 262 436 227 (census of 17 Jan. 1979); 271 200 000 (estimate for 1 Jan. 1983).
Area: 8 649 540 miles² *22 402 200 km²*. This official total includes two areas of ocean, the White

Sea (34 750 miles² *90 000 km²*) and the Sea of Azov (14 400 miles² *37 300 km²*).
Languages (1970): Russian (official) 58·7%; Ukrainian 14·6%; Uzbek 3·8%; Byelorussian 3·2%; Tatar 2·4%; Kazakh 2·2%; over 50 others.
Religions: No state religion. Christian with Jewish and Muslim minorities.
Capital city: Moskva (Moscow), population 8 396 000 at 1 Jan 1983.
Other principal towns (1 Jan. 1983): Leningrad 4 779 000; Kiev 2 355 000; Tashkent 1 944 000; Baku 1 638 000; Kharkov 1 519 000; Minsk 1 405 000; Gorky 1 382 000; Novosibirsk 1 370 000; Sverdlovsk 1 269 000; Kuibyshev 1 242 000; Dnepropetrovsk 1 128 000; Tbilisi 1 125 000; Odessa 1 097 000; Omsk 1 080 000; Yerevan 1 095 000; Chelyabinsk 1 077 000; Donetsk 1 055 000; Perm 1 037 000; Ufa 1 034 000; Kazan 1 031 000; Alma-Ata 1 023 000.
Highest point: Pik Kommunizma (Garmo, later Pik Stalin), 24 589 ft *7494 m* (first climbed 3 Sept. 1933).
Principal mountain ranges: Caucasus, Urals, Pamirs, Tien Shan.
Principal rivers: 14 rivers over 1000 miles *1609 km* in length (see pages 19–20).
Head of State: Mikhail S. Gorbachev, Chairman of the Presidium of the Supreme Soviet and General Secretary of the Communist Party of the Soviet Union.
Head of Government: Nikolay Aleksandrovich Tikhonov (b. 14 May 1905), Chairman of the Council of Ministers.
Climate: Great variations. Summers generally short and hot, winters long and cold. Very hot in central Asia, extremely cold in north-east Siberia. Average maximum and minimum temperatures for selected places:
Moscow: Average maximum −6°C *21°F* (January) to 24°C *76°F* (July). Average minimum −13°C *9°F* (January) to 13°C *55°F* (July). Rainiest months July, August (each 12 days).
Archangel: Average maximum −13°C *9°F* (January) to 18°C *64°F* (July). Average minimum −18°C *0°F* (February) to 10°C *51°F* (July). Rainiest month October (12 days).
Odessa: Average maximum −2°C *28°F* (January) to 26°C *79°F* (July). Average minimum −5°C *22°F* (January) to 18°C *65°F* (July, August). Rainiest months January and June (each 7 days).
Yakutsk: Average maximum −43°C *−45°F* (January) to 23°C *73°F* (July). Average minimum −47°C *−53°F* (January) to 12°C *54°F* (July). Rainiest months September, October, November (each 10 days).

Absolute maximum temperature 50,0°C *122·0°F*, Termez (Uzbekistan), July 1912; absolute minimum −71,1°C *−96·0°F*, Oymyakon, 1964.
Labour force: 117 027 575 at census of 15 Jan. 1970: Agriculture 26·4%; Industry (mining, manufacturing, electricity, gas and water), construction, transport and communications 45·3%; Education, cultural institutions, scientific and research institutes, public health 14·2%; 134 860 000 (1979 census, provisional).
Net material product: 438 300 million roubles in 1979: Agriculture, forestry and fishing 16·2%; Industry 51·6%; Construction 10·9%; Trade, restaurants, etc. 15·6%.
Exports: \$33 309·8 million in 1975: Petroleum and petroleum products 24·6% (crude petroleum 15·6%); Machinery and transport equipment 19·1%.
Monetary unit: Rubl' (ruble or rouble). 1 rouble = 100 kopeks.
Denominations:
   Coins 1, 2, 3, 5, 10, 20, 50 kopeks; 1 rouble.
   Notes 1, 3, 5, 10, 25, 50, 100 roubles.
Exchange rate to £ sterling: 1·016 (14 Jan. 1985).
Political history and government: Formerly the Russian Empire, ruled by an hereditary Tsar (of the Romanov dynasty from 1613). Prompted by discontent with autocratic rule and the privation caused by the First World War, a revolution broke out on 27 Feb. (12 March New Style) 1917, causing the abdication of the last Tsar three days later and the establishment of a provisional government. During the following months Soviets (councils) were elected by some groups of industrial workers and peasants. A republic was proclaimed on 1 Sept. (14 Sept. NS) 1917. A political struggle developed between government supporters and the Bolshevik Party (founded in 1903 and called the Communist Party from 1919), which advocated the assumption of power by the Soviets. On 25 Oct. (7 Nov. NS) 1917 the Bolsheviks led an insurrection, arrested the provisional government and transferred power to the All-Russian Congress of Soviets. The Bolsheviks won only 175 out of 707 seats in the elections of 25–27 Nov. 1917 for the Constituent Assembly. The Assembly met on 18 Jan. 1918 but was forcibly dissolved by the Bolsheviks, who proclaimed a 'dictatorship of the proletariat'. On 31 Jan. 1918 Russia was proclaimed a Republic of Soviets. A constitution for the Russian Soviet Federative Socialist Republic (RSFSR) was adopted on 10 July 1918. Armed resistance to Communist rule developed into civil war (1917–22) but was eventually crushed. During the war other Soviet Republics were set up in the Ukraine, Byelorussia (White Russia) and Transcaucasia. These were merged with the RSFSR by a Treaty of Union, establishing the USSR, on 30 Dec. 1922. The USSR's first constitution was adopted on 6 July 1923. By splitting the territory of the original four, two more Republics were added in 1925 and another in 1929. A new constitution was adopted on 5 Dec. 1936, when the number of Soviet Socialist Republics (SSRs) was raised from seven to eleven. On 31 Mar. 1940 territory ceded by Finland became part of the newly-formed Karelo-Finnish SSR. Territory ceded by Romania on 28 June 1940 became part of the new Moldavian SSR on 2 Aug. 1940. The three Baltic republics of Lithuania, Latvia and Estonia were annexed on 3–6 Aug. 1940, raising the number of Union Republics to 16. This was reduced to the present 15 on 16 July 1956, when the Karelo-Finnish SSR was merged with the RSFSR.

A new constitution took effect on 7 Oct. 1977. According to the constitution, the Communist Party is 'the leading and guiding force of Soviet society'. Early in 1978 new constitutions, modelled on that for the USSR, came into force in all 15 Union Republics.

The Soviet Union is formally a federal state comprising 15 Union (constituent) Republics of equal status, voluntarily linked and having the right to secede. Some of the 15 Union Republics contain Autonomous Republics and Autonomous Regions. The RSFSR also includes 10

National Areas. The highest organ of state power is the bicameral legislature, the Supreme Soviet of the USSR, comprising the Soviet (Council) of the Union, with 750 members elected from constituencies, and the Soviet (Council) of Nationalities, with 750 members (32 from each of the 15 Union Republics; 11 from each of the 20 Autonomous Republics; five from each of the eight Autonomous Regions; one from each of the 10 National Areas). Both houses have equal rights and powers and their terms run concurrently. Members are directly elected (from a single list of candidates) for five-year terms by universal adult suffrage. At a joint session the members elect the Presidium of the Supreme Soviet (39 members, including, as *ex officio* deputy chairmen, the 15 chairmen of the Supreme Soviets of the Union Republics) to be the legislature's permanent organ. The Chairman of the Presidium serves as Head of State. The Supreme Soviet also appoints the Council of Ministers (called People's Commissars until 16 Mar. 1946), headed by a Chairman, to form the executive and administrative branch of government, responsible to the Supreme Soviet.

Each of the 15 Union Republics has a constitution and state structure on the same pattern as the central government, with a unicameral Supreme Soviet and a Council of Ministers to deal with internal affairs. The Chairmen of the Councils of Ministers of the Union Republics are *ex officio* members of the USSR Council of Ministers. The Union Republics are entitled to maintain direct relations with foreign countries. Two of them, the Ukrainian and Byelorussian SSRs, are separately represented in the United Nations.

Throughout the whole country, real power is held by the highly centralised Communist Party of the Soviet Union (CPSU, the only legal party, which has an absolute monopoly of power in all political affairs and controls government at all levels. The Party had over 17 480 000 members in 1981. Its highest authority is, in theory, the Party Congress, which should be convened at least every five years (the 26th Congress was held on 23 Feb.–3 Mar. 1981). The Congress elects the Central Committee (319 full members and 151 candidates, i.e. non-voting, members were chosen on 2 Mar. 1981) which supervises Party work and directs state policy. The Committee, which meets twice a year, elects a Political Bureau (Politburo), which is the Party's most powerful policy-making body. In 1981 the Politburo had 14 full members (including the General Secretary) and eight candidate members. Apart from the RSFSR, each Union Republic has its own Communist Party, with a Central Committee led by a First Secretary, but they are subsidiary to, and form an integral part of, the CPSU.

Telephones: 26 400 000 (1982).
Daily newspapers: 686 (1977).
Total circulation: 102 462 000.
Radio: 66 000 000 (1982).
TV: 64 300 000 (1982).
Length of roadways: 873 400 miles *1 405 600 km* (31 Dec. 1976).
Length of railways: 87 690 miles *141 123 km.*
Universities: 66.
Adult illiteracy: 0·3% (males 0·2%; females 0·3%) in 1970.
Expectation of life: Males 64 years; females 74 years (1971–72).
Defence: Military service: Army and Air Force 2–3 years, Navy 5 years; total armed forces over 5 million; defence expenditure, 1983: 17·05 billion roubles.
Cinemas: 142 000 plus 9400 mobile units (1983).
Foreign tourists: 23 915 000 in 1981.

The United Arab Emirates

Official name: Al-Imarat Al-A'rabiya Al-Muttahida.
Population: 1 040 275 (census of Dec. 1980); 1 175 000 (1982 estimate).
Area: 32 278 miles[2] *83 600 km[2].*
Language: Arabic.

Religion: Muslim.
Capital city: Abu Dhabi, population 516 000 (1982 estimate).
Other principal towns (1982): Dubai 296 000; Sharjah 184 000; Ras al Kaimah 83 000.
Highest point: Western Al-Hajar, 3900 ft *1189 m.*
Principal mountain range: Al-Hajar.
Head of State: Shaikh Zayed bin Sultan Al-Nahayan (b. 1918), President.
Prime Minister: Shaikh Rashid bin Sa'id Al-Maktoum (b. 1914).
Climate: Very hot and humid, with summer temperatures of over 38°C *100°F;* cooler in the eastern mountains.
Labour force: 296 516 (1975 estimate); Construction 32·2%; Trade, restaurants and hotels 12·9%; Community, social and personal services 29·7%.
Gross domestic product: 53 338·1 million dirhams in 1978: Mining and quarrying 56·6%; Construction 10·1%.
Exports: US$21 792 million in 1981: Oil 95%.
Monetary unit: UAE dirham. 1 dirham = 100 fils.
Denominations:
Coins 1, 5, 10, 25, 50 fils; 1 dirham.
Notes 1, 5, 10, 50, 100 dirhams.
Exchange rate to £ sterling: 4·0925 (14 Jan. 1985).
Political history and government: Formerly the seven shaikhdoms of Trucial Oman (the Trucial States), under British protection. An independent federation (originally of six states), under a provisional constitution, since 2 Dec. 1971. The seventh, Ras al-Khaimah, joined the UAE on 11 Feb. 1972. The highest federal authority is the Supreme Council of the Union, comprising the hereditary rulers of the seven emirates (the rulers of Abu Dhabi and Dubai have the power of veto). From its seven members the Council elects a President and a Vice-President, each with a 5-year term. The President appoints a Prime Minister and a Union (Federal) Council of Ministers, responsible to the Supreme Council, to hold executive authority. The legislature is the Federal National Council, a consultative assembly (comprising 40 members appointed for two years by the rulers of the constituent emirates) which considers laws proposed by the Council of Ministers. The provisional constitution, originally in force for 5 years, was extended to 1981 by a decree of 28 Nov. 1976. There are no political parties. In local affairs each ruler has absolute power over his subjects.
Telephones: 240 167 (1982).
Daily newspapers: 3 (1977).
Total circulation: 2000.
Radio: 150 000 (1978).
TV: 80 000 (1977).
Universities: 1.
Adult illiteracy: 43·7% (males 39·6%; females 55·8%) in 1975 (population aged 10 and over).
Expectation of life: Males 54·8 years; females 58·2 years (UN estimates for 1970–75, average for Bahrain, Qatar and the United Arab Emirates).
Defence: Military service voluntary; total armed forces 50 000 (1984); defence expenditure, 1979; $750 million.
Cinemas: 74 (seating capacity 29 000) and 9 mobile units (1977).

The United States of America

Population: 227 658 000 (census of 1 Apr. 1980); 229 807 000 (1981 estimate).
Area: 3 615 122 miles[2] *9 363 123 km[2].*
Language: English.
Religions: Protestant, Roman Catholic, Jewish, Orthodox (*see* p. 204).
Capital city: Washington, D.C., population 635 185 at 1980 census.
Other principal towns (1980): New York 7 015 608; Chicago 2 969 570; Los Angeles 2 950 010; Philadelphia 1 680 235; Houston 1 554 992; Detroit 1 192 222; Dallas 901 450; San Diego 870 006; Baltimore 783 320; San Antonio 783 296; Phoenix 781 443; Indianapolis 695 040; San Francisco 674 063; Memphis 644 838; Milwaukee 632 989; San Jose 625 763; Cleveland

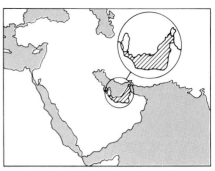

THE UNITED ARAB EMIRATES

572 532; Boston 562 118; Columbus 561 943; New Orleans 556 913; Jacksonville 541 269.
Head of State: Ronald Wilson Reagan (b. 6 Feb. 1911), President.
Climate: Its continental dimensions ensure extreme variety, ranging in temperature between the 56,7°C *134°F* recorded in Death Valley, California, on 10 July 1913, and the −60,0°C −76°F at Tanana, Alaska, in January 1886. Mean annual averages range between 24,7°C *76·6°F* at Key West, Florida, and −12,1°C *10·1°F* at Barrow, Alaska. Excluding Alaska and Hawaii, rainfall averages 736 mm *29 in* per year and ranges between 1412 mm *55·6 in* in Louisiana and 218 mm *8·6 in* in Nevada.
Climate in representative population centres are:
Anchorage, Alaska: Average daily high 18°C *65°F* July; −7°C *19°F* January. Average daily low −15°C *5°F* January; 9°C *49°F* July. Days with rain 15 in August; 4 in April.
San Francisco, Cal: Average daily high 20°C *69°F* September; 13°C *55°F* January. Average daily low 7°C *45°F* January; 13°C *55°F* September. Days with rain 11 in January–February; nil in July–August.
Washington, DC: Average daily high 30°C *87°F* July; 5°C *42°F* January. Average daily low −3°C *27°F* January; 20°C *68°F* July. Days with rain 12 in March, May; 8 in September–October.
Chicago, Illinois: Average daily high 27°C *81°F* July; 0°C *32°F* January. Average daily low −8°C *18°F* January; 19°C *66°F* July. Days with rain 12 in March, May; 9 in July–October.
Honolulu, Hawaii: Average daily high 28°C *83°F* August–September; 24°C *76°F* January–February. Average daily low 19°C *67°F* February–March; 23°C *74°F* September–October. Days with rain 15 in December; 11 in February, May.
New York, NY: Average daily high 28°C *82°F* July; 3°C *37°F* January. Average daily low −4°C *24°F* January–February; 19°C *66°F* July–August. Days with rain 12 in January, March, July; 9 in September–November.
Miami, Florida: Average daily high 31°C *88°F* July–August; 23°C *74°F* January. Average daily low 16°C *61°F* January–February; 24°C *76°F* July–August. Days with rain 18 in September; 6 in February.
Labour force: 100 397 000 aged 16 and over in 1981, excluding 2 142 000 in the armed forces and 8 273 000 unemployed: Agriculture, forestry and fishing 3·5%; Mining 1·1%; Construction 6%; Manufacturing 21·7%; Transportation and other public utilities 6·6%; Wholesale and retail trade 20·4%; Finance, insurance and real estate 6·1%; Professional and related services 20·1%; Other services 14·3%.
Gross domestic product: $2 112 365 million in 1978: Manufacturing 24·0%; Trade, restaurants and hotels 17·4% (trade and restaurants 16·8%); Finance, insurance, real estate and business services 11·2%; Government services 12·6%.
Exports: $150 236 million in 1982: Food and live animals 15·9%; Crude materials 12·8%; Machinery and transport equipment 58%; Chemicals 14·1%.
Monetary unit: US dollar ($). 1 dollar = 100 cents.

THE FIFTY STATES OF THE UNITED STATES OF AMERICA
(in order of admission)

1.	Delaware	26.	Michigan
2.	Pennsylvania	27.	Florida
3.	New Jersey	28.	Texas
4.	Georgia	29.	Iowa
5.	Connecticut	30.	Wisconsin
6.	Massachusetts	31.	California
7.	Maryland	32.	Minnesota
8.	South Carolina	33.	Oregon
9.	New Hampshire	34.	Kansas
10.	Virginia	35.	West Virginia
11.	New York	36.	Nevada
12.	North Carolina	37.	Nebraska
13.	Rhode Island	38.	Colorado
14.	Vermont	39.	North Dakota
15.	Kentucky	40.	South Dakota
16.	Tennessee	41.	Montana
17.	Ohio	42.	Washington
18.	Louisiana	43.	Idaho
19.	Indiana	44.	Wyoming
20.	Mississippi	45.	Utah
21.	Illinois	46.	Oklahoma
22.	Alabama	47.	New Mexico
23.	Maine	48.	Arizona
24.	Missouri	49.	Alaska
25.	Arkansas	50.	Hawaii (see note)

Note: The state of Hawaii consists of a chain of more than 100 islands (including 8 large ones) stretching for about 1600 miles *2575 km*. The map shows the island of Hawaii (largest and easternmost of the group) but about 80% of the population are on the island of Oahu, which contains Honolulu and Pearl Harbor.

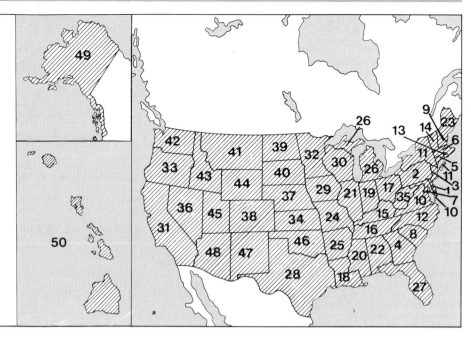

Denominations:
Coins 1, 5, 10, 25, 50 cents; 1 dollar.
Notes 1, 2, 5, 10, 20, 50, 100 dollars.
Exchange rate to £ sterling: 1·254 (23 April 1985).
Telephones: 182 558 000 (1980).
Daily newspapers: 1829 (1977).
Total circulation: 62 159 000.
Radio: 444 000 000 (1977).
TV: 135 000 000 (1979).
Length of roadways: 3 866 296 miles *6 220 870 km* (31 Dec. 1982).
Length of railways: 147 049 miles *236 602 km.*
Universities: over 3000 (including colleges) in 1978.
Adult illiteracy: 1·0% (males 1·1%; females 1·0%) in 1969.
Expectation of life: Males 68·7 years; females 76·5 years (1975).
Defence: Military service voluntary; total armed forces 3 492 129 (1983); defence expenditure, $205 012 million in 1983.
Cinemas: 16 965 in 1979.
Foreign tourists: 21 900 000 (including visits for study or transit) in 1982.

The United States of America ranks fourth in area (3 615 122 miles² *9 363 123 km²*), fourth in population (an estimated 229 807 000 in 1981) and first in economic production of all the countries in the world.

The area of the 48 coterminous states comprises 3 022 260 miles² *7 827 617 km².* The principal mountain ranges are listed on p. 17. The highest point is Mount McKinley (20 320 ft *6194 m*) in Alaska.

There are eight US river systems involving rivers in excess of 1000 miles *1609 km* in length, of which by far the vastest is the Mississippi–Missouri (see page 19).

At the 1980 census the declared racial origins of the population were: White 83·2%; Black 11·7%; Indigenous 0·6%; Asian and Pacific Islander 1·5%; Other 3·0%. The population of foreign origin included at March 1972:

Jewish	6 460 000
Italian	8 764 000
German	25 543 000
British (UK)	29 548 000
Polish	5 105 000
Russian	2 188 000
Irish (Republic)	16 408 000
Spanish and Spanish origin	9 178 000
French	5 420 000

The principal religious denominations in 1980 were (in millions):

Roman Catholic	51·2
Baptist	25·5
Methodist	13·7
Lutheran	5·6
Jewish	5·9
Presbyterian	3·2
Protestant Episcopal Church	2·8
Eastern Orthodox	3·9
Mormon	3·7
United Church of Christ	1·7

The capital city is Washington, District of Columbia (DC). The District of Columbia (population 631 000, 1981 estimate) is the seat of the US Federal Government, comprising 69 miles² *179 km²* from west central Maryland on the Potomac River opposite Virginia. The site was chosen in October 1790 by President Washington and the Capitol corner stone laid by him on 18 Sept. 1793. Washington became the capital (Philadelphia 1790–1800) on 10 June 1800.

Historical note: Evidence from the most recent radiometric dating has backdated human habitation of North America to *c.* 35 000 BC. This occupation was probably achieved via the Bering Bridge (now the 55 mile *88,5 km* wide Bering Strait) from north-east Asia.

The continent derived its name from the Italian explorer Amerigo Vespucci (1454–1512), discoverer of the north-east South American coastal regions in 1498. The German cartographer Martin Waldseemüller named the New World 'Terra America' in his atlas published in St Dié, France, in April 1507.

The earliest European landing on present US territory was on 27 Mar. 1513 by the Spaniard Juan Ponce de León in Florida. The discovery of the US Pacific coast was by Juan R Cabrillo who landed from Mexico on 28 Sept. 1542, near

20th Century Presidents

Name	Dates of Birth and Death	Party	Dates in Office
Theodore Roosevelt	27 Oct. 1858 to 6 Jan. 1919	Republican	1901–09
William Howard Taft	15 Sept. 1857 to 8 Mar. 1930	Republican	1909–13
Thomas Woodrow Wilson	28 Dec. 1856 to 3 Feb. 1924	Democratic	1913–21
Warren Gamaliel Harding	2 Nov. 1865 to 2 Aug. 1923	Republican	1921–23
John Calvin Coolidge	4 July 1872 to 5 Jan. 1933	Republican	1923–29
Herbert Clark Hoover	10 Aug. 1874 to 20 Oct. 1964	Republican	1929–33
Franklin Delano Roosevelt	30 Jan. 1882 to 12 Apr. 1945	Democratic	1933–45
Harry S Truman	8 May 1884 to 26 Dec. 1972	Democratic	1945–53
Dwight David Eisenhower	14 Oct. 1890 to 28 Mar. 1969	Republican	1953–61
John Fitzgerald Kennedy	29 May 1917 to 22 Nov. 1963	Democratic	1961–63
Lyndon Baines Johnson	27 Aug. 1908 to 22 Jan. 1973	Democratic	1963–69
Richard Milhous Nixon	b. 9 Jan. 1913	Republican	1969–74
Gerald Rudolph Ford	b. 14 July 1913	Republican	1974–77
James Earl Carter	b. 1 Oct. 1924	Democratic	1977–81
Ronald Wilson Reagan	b. 6 Feb. 1911	Republican	1981–

Presidential Elections
US Presidential elections occur on the first Tuesday after the first Monday of November in every fourth year – these coincide with leap years. Election is not by popular majority but by majority of votes in the Electoral College which comprises 538 Electors divided between the States on the basis of one Elector for each of the 100 Senators (upper house) and the 435 Representatives (lower house) plus, since 1964, three Electors for the District of Columbia. Thus a Presidential election victory is achieved by securing at least 270 votes. Recent results have been:

Year	Republican	Democrat	Plurality
1944	99	432	Roosevelt (D) over Dewey (R) by 333
1948	189	303	Truman (D) over Dewey (R) by 114
1952	442	89	Eisenhower (R) over Stevenson (D) by 353
1956	457	73	Eisenhower (R) over Stevenson (D) by 384
1960	219	303	Kennedy over Nixon (R) by 84
1964	52	486	Johnson (D) over Goldwater (R) by 434
1968	301	191	Nixon (R) over Humphrey (D) by 110
1972	521	17	Nixon (R) over McGovern (D) by 504
1976	241	297	Carter (D) over Ford (R) by 56
1980	489	49	Reagan (R) over Carter (D) by 440

San Diego, California. The oldest town of European origin is St Augustine, Florida, founded on 8 Sept. 1565 on the site of Seloy by Pedro Menéndez de Avilés with 1500 Spanish colonists. The British exploration of what is now US territory began with Philip Amadas and Arthur Barlowe in Virginia in 1584. Henry Hudson sailed into New York harbour in September 1609. The Plymouth Pilgrims reached Cape Cod 54 days out from Plymouth, England, in the *Mayflower* (101 passengers and 48 crew) on 9 Nov. 1620. On 6 May 1626 Peter Minuit bought Manhattan island for some trinkets valued at $39. In 1664 the area was seized by the British and granted to Charles II's brother, the Duke of York, and the city of New Amsterdam was renamed New York.

By the 18th century there were 13 British colonies along the Atlantic seaboard of North America. The American revolution and the War of Independence (total battle deaths 4435) occupied the years 1763–83. The incident of the Boston Tea Party occurred on 16 Dec. 1773 and the Battle of Bunker Hill on 17 June 1775. The Declaration of Independence was made on 4 July 1776. This was recognised by Britain in March 1782. General George Washington was chosen President in February 1789 and the first US Congress was called on 4 Mar. 1789, when the US Constitution took effect. Washington took office on 30 Apr. 1789.

The War of 1812 between the US and Great Britain was declared by Congress on 18 June 1812, because Britain seized US ships running her blockade of France, impressed 2800 seamen and armed Indians who raided US territory. In 1814 Maj-Gen Robert Ross burnt the Capitol and the White House in Washington. The war which inspired national unity cost only 2260 battle deaths. The Monroe Doctrine (the isolationism of the Americans from Europe) was declared on 2 Dec. 1823.

On 1 Nov. 1835 Texas proclaimed independence from Mexico. In the Alamo in San Antonio a US garrison was massacred (including Sen David Crockett) on 6 Mar. 1836.

The secession of States over the question of slave labour on cotton plantations began with South Carolina on 20 Dec. 1860. The Southern States of South Carolina, Georgia, Alabama, Mississippi, Louisiana and Florida formed the Confederate States of America on 8 Feb. 1861. War broke out on 12 Apr. 1861 with the bombardment of Fort Sumter in Charleston Harbor, South Carolina. The war culminated in the Battle of Gettysburg in July 1863 during which there was a total of 43 000 casualties. President Abraham Lincoln was assassinated on 14 Apr. 1865. Slavery was abolished by the adoption of the 13th Amendment (to the Constitution) on 18 Dec. 1865.

The total fatal casualties in the Civil War were *c.* 547 000 of which the Union forces (North) lost 140 400 in the field and the Confederates (South) 74 500 in battle and *c.* 28 500 in Union prisons. In 1867 the USA purchased Alaska from Russia. By 1890 the USA was in full possession of the continental territories which now comprise the 48 contiguous states (statehood being granted to all by 1912). Hawaii was annexed in 1898. The dates of the United States' entry into the World Wars of 1914–18 and 1939–45 respectively were 6 Apr. 1917 and 8 Dec. 1941. Alaska and Hawaii became the 49th and 50th states in 1959.

Government: The 1789 constitution established a federal republic in which extensive powers are reserved to the component states (originally 13, now 50).

At federal level, legislative power is held by the bicameral Congress of the United States. The upper house is the Senate, with 100 members (two from each state) elected by universal adult suffrage for six years (one-third retiring every two years). The second chamber is the House of Representatives, with 435 voting members directly elected from single-member constituencies for two years. The number of Representatives per state is determined periodically

THE 50 STATES OF THE UNITED STATES OF AMERICA

Name, with date and order of (original) admission into the Union. Nicknames	Area (inc inland water). Pop. at 1980 Census (with rankings). Population density per mile² per km². State Capital. Admin. divisions	Major Cities (with population at 1 Apr. 1980)
ALABAMA (Ala) 14 Dec. 1819 (22nd) 'Heart of Dixie' 'Cotton State' 'Yellowhammer State'	51 609 miles² *133 667 km²* (29th) 3 890 061 (22nd) 75·4 *29,1* Montgomery 67 counties	Birmingham (284 413) Mobile (200 452) Montgomery (178 157) Huntsville (142 513) Tuscaloosa (75 143) Dothan (48 750) Gadsden (47 565)
ALASKA (Aleut, 'Great Land') 3 Jan. 1959 (49th) 'The Last Frontier' 'Land of the Midnight Sun'	586 412 miles² *1 518 800 km²* (1st) 400 481 (50th) 0·7 *0,3* Juneau* 19 election districts	Anchorage (173 017) Kenai Peninsula borough (25 282) Fairbanks (22 645) Juneau (19 528)
ARIZONA (Ariz) 14 Feb. 1912 (48th) 'Grand Canyon State' 'Apache State'	113 909 miles² *295 023 km²* (6th) 2 717 866 (29th) 23·9 *9,2* Phoenix 14 counties	Phoenix (764 911) Tucson (330 537) Mesa (152 453) Tempe (106 743) Glendale (96 988)
ARKANSAS (Ark) 15 June 1836 (25th) 'Land of Opportunity' 'Wonder State' 'Bear State'	53 104 miles² *137 539 km²* (27th) 2 285 513 (33rd) 43·0 *16,6* Little Rock 75 counties	Little Rock (158 461) Fort Smith (71 384) North Little Rock (64 419) Pine Bluff (56 576) Fayetteville (36 604) Hot Springs (35 166)
CALIFORNIA (Cal) 9 Sept. 1850 (31st) 'Golden State'	158 693 miles² *411 013 km²* (3rd) 23 668 562 (1st) 149·1 *57,6* Sacramento 58 counties	Los Angeles City (2 966 763) San Diego (875 504) San Francisco (678 974) San Jose (636 550) Long Beach (361 334) Oakland (339 288) Sacramento (275 741) Anaheim (221 847) Fresno (218 202) Santa Ana (203 713)
	Sixteen other towns in California had a 1980 population of over 100 000: Riverside (170 876); Huntington Beach (170 505); Stockton (149 779); Glendale (139 060); Fremont (131 945); Torrance (131 497); Garden Grove (123 351); Pasadena (119 374); San Bernardino (118 057); Oxnard (108 195); Sunnyvale (106 618); Modesto (106 105); Bakersfield (105 611); Berkeley (103 328); Concord (103 251); Fullerton (102 034).	
COLORADO (Colo) 1 Aug. 1876 (38th) 'Centennial State'	104 247 miles² *269 998 km²* (8th) 2 888 834 (28th) 27·7 *10,7* Denver 63 counties	Denver (491 396) Colorado Springs (215 150) Aurora (158 588) Lakewood (112 848) Pueblo (101 686) Arvada (84 576) Boulder (76 658) Fort Collins (64 632)
CONNECTICUT (Conn) 9 Jan. 1788 (5th) 'Constitution State' 'Nutmeg State'	5009 miles² *12 973 km²* (48th) 3 107 576 (25th) 620·4 *239,5* Hartford 8 counties	Bridgeport (142 546) Hartford (136 392) New Haven (126 109) Waterbury (103 266) Stamford (102 453) Norwalk (77 767) New Britain (73 840)
DELAWARE (Del) 7 Dec. 1787 (1st) 'First State' 'Diamond State'	2057 miles² *5327 km²* (49th) 595 225 (47th) 289·4 *111,7* Dover 3 counties	Wilmington (70 195) Newark (25 247) Dover (23 512) Elsmere (6493) Milford (5358) Seaford (5256)
FLORIDA (Fla) 3 Mar. 1845 (27th) 'Sunshine State' 'Peninsula State'	58 560 miles² *151 670 km²* (22nd) 9 739 992 (7th) 163·3 *64,2* Tallahassee 67 counties	Jacksonville (540 898) Miami (346 931) Tampa (271 523) St Petersburg (236 898) Fort Lauderdale (153 256) Hialeah (145 254) Orlando (128 394) Hollywood (117 188)
GEORGIA (Ga) 2 Jan. 1788 (4th) 'Empire State of the South' 'Peach State'	58 876 miles² *152 488 km²* (21st) 5 464 265 (13th) 92·8 *35,8* Atlanta 159 counties	Atlanta (425 022) Columbus (169 441) Savannah (141 634) Macon (116 860) Albany (73 934) Augusta (47 532)

---

* On 4 Nov. 1976 Alaskan voters approved a proposal to move the state capital to Willow South.

Name, with date and order of (original) admission into the Union. Nicknames	Area (inc inland water). Pop. at 1980 Census (with rankings). Population density per mile² per km². State Capital. Admin. divisions	Major Cities (with population at 1 Apr. 1980)
HAWAII 21 Aug. 1959 (50th) 'Aloha State'	6450 miles² *16 705 km²* (47th) 965 000 (39th) 149·6 *57,8* Honolulu (on Oahu) 5 counties	Honolulu (365 048) Ewa (190 037) Koolaupoko (109 373) Wahiawa (41 562)
IDAHO 3 July 1890 (43rd) 'Gem State' 'Gem of the Mountains'	83 557 miles² *216 412 km²* (13th) 943 935 (41st) 11·3 *4,4* Boise City 44 counties, plus small part of Yellowstone Park	Boise City (102 451) Pocatello (46 340) Idaho Falls (39 590) Lewiston (27 986) Twin Falls (26 209) Nampa (25 112)
ILLINOIS (Ill) 3 Dec. 1818 (21st) 'Prairie State'	56 400 miles² *146 075 km²* (24th) 11 418 461 (5th) 202·5 *78,2* Springfield 102 counties	Chicago (3 005 072) Rockford (139 712) Peoria (124 160) Springfield (99 637) Decatur (94 081) Joliet (77 956) Evanston (73 706)
INDIANA (Ind) 11 Dec. 1816 (19th) 'Hoosier State'	36 291 miles² *93 993 km²* (38th) 5 490 179 (12th) 151·3 *58,4* Indianapolis 92 counties	Indianapolis (700 807) Fort Wayne (172 196) Gary (151 953) Evansville (130 496) South Bend (109 727) Hammond (93 714) Muncie (77 216)
IOWA (Ia) 28 Dec. 1846 (29th) 'Hawkeye State'	56 290 miles² *145 790 km²* (25th) 2 913 387 (27th) 51·8 *20,0* Des Moines 99 counties	Des Moines (191 003) Cedar Rapids (110 243) Davenport (103 264) Sioux City (82 003) Waterloo (75 985) Dubuque (62 321) Council Bluffs (56 449)
KANSAS (Kan) 29 Jan. 1861 (34th) 'Sunflower State' 'Jayhawk State'	82 264 miles² *213 063 km²* (14th) 2 363 208 (32nd) 28·7 *11,1* Topeka 105 counties	Wichita (279 272) Kansas City (161 087) Topeka (115 266) Overland Park (81 784) Lawrence (52 738) Salina (41 843)
KENTUCKY (Ky) (officially the Commonwealth of Kentucky) 1 June 1792 (15th) 'Bluegrass State'	40 395 miles² *104 623 km²* (37th) 3 661 433 (23rd) 90·6 *35,0* Frankfort 120 counties	Louisville (298 451) Lexington (204 165) Owensboro (54 450) Covington (49 013) Bowling Green (40 450) Paducah (29 315)
LOUISIANA (La) 30 Apr. 1812 (18th) 'Pelican State' 'Creole State' 'Sugar State' 'Bayou State'	48 523 miles² *125 674 km²* (31st) 4 203 972 (19th) 86·6 *33,5* Baton Rouge 64 parishes (counties)	New Orleans (557 482) Shreveport (205 815) Baton Rouge (219 486) Lafayette (81 961) Lake Charles (75 051)
MAINE (Me) 15 Mar. 1820 (23rd) 'Pine Tree State'	33 215 miles² *86 026 km²* (39th) 1 124 660 (38th) 33·9 *13,1* Augusta 16 counties	Portland (61 572) Lewiston (40 481) Bangor (31 643) Auburn (23 128)
MARYLAND (Md) 28 Apr. 1788 (7th) 'Old Line State' 'Free State'	10 577 miles² *27 394 km²* (42nd) 4 216 448 (18th) 398·6 *153,9* Annapolis 23 counties, plus the independent city of Baltimore	Baltimore (786 775) *Dundalk (85 377) *Towson (77 768) *Silver Spring (77 411) *Bethesda (71 621) *Wheaton (66 280)
MASSACHUSETTS (Mass) 6 Feb. 1788 (6th) 'Bay State' 'Old Colony State'	8257 miles² *21 385 km²* (45th) 5 737 037 (11th) 694·8 *268,3* Boston 14 counties	Boston (562 994) Worcester (161 799) Springfield (152 319) New Bedford (98 478) Cambridge (95 322)
MICHIGAN (Mich) 26 Jan. 1837 (26th) 'Wolverine State'	58 216 miles² *150 779 km²* (23rd) 9 258 344 (8th) 159·0 *61,4* Lansing 83 counties	Detroit (1 203 339) Grand Rapids (181 843) Warren (161 134) Flint (159 611) Lansing (130 414)

according to population but each state is entitled to at least one Representative. Since 1970 the District of Columbia has been represented by a non-voting delegate.

Federal executive power is vested in the President, who serves for a four-year term and (by a constitutional amendment ratified on 26 Feb. 1951) is limited to two terms in office. The President, with a Vice-President, is elected by an Electoral College composed of electors (themselves chosen by direct popular vote) from each state and the District of Columbia (see Presidential Elections in box above). Usually, the presidential candidate with a majority of popular votes in any state receives the whole of that state's Electoral College votes.

The President appoints a Cabinet which must be approved by the Senate. A presidential veto on legislative proposals may be overridden by a separate two-thirds vote in each house of the Congress.

Each state has a constitution modelled on the federal pattern, with its own legislature (all but one bicameral) and executive power held by a popularly elected Governor.

Name, with date and order of (original) admission into the Union. Nicknames	Area (inc inland water). Pop. at 1980 Census (with rankings). Population density per mile² per km². State Capital. Admin. divisions	Major Cities (with population at 1 Apr. 1980)
MINNESOTA (Minn) 11 May 1858 (32nd) 'North Star State' 'Gopher State'	84 068 miles² *217 735 km²* (12th) 4 077 148 (21st) 48·5 *18,7* St Paul 87 counties	Minneapolis (370 951) St Paul (270 230) Duluth (92 811) Bloomington (81 831) Rochester (57 855)
MISSISSIPPI (Miss) 10 Dec. 1817 (20th) 'Magnolia State'	47 716 miles² *123 584 km²* (32nd) 2 520 638 (31st) 52·8 *20,4* Jackson 82 counties	Jackson (202 895) Biloxi (49 311) Meridian (46 577) Hattiesburg (40 829) Greenville (40 613)
MISSOURI (Mo) 10 Aug. 1821 (24th) 'Show Me State'	69 686 miles² *180 486 km²* (19th) 4 917 444 (15th) 70·6 *27,2* Jefferson City 114 counties, plus the independent city of St Louis	St Louis (453 085) Kansas City (448 159) Springfield (133 116) Independence (111 806) St Joseph (76 691) Columbia (62 061)
MONTANA (Mont) 8 Nov. 1889 (41st) 'Treasure State'	147 138 miles² *381 086 km²* (4th) 786 690 (44th) 5·3 *2,1* Helena 56 counties, plus small part of Yellowstone National Park	Billings (66 798) Great Falls (56 725) Missoula (37 205) Butte (33 388) Helena (23 938)
NEBRASKA (Nebr) 1 Mar. 1867 (37th) 'Cornhusker State' 'Beef State' 'Tree Planter's State'	77 227 miles² *200 017 km²* (15th) 1 570 006 (35th) 20·3 *7,8* Lincoln 93 counties	Omaha (311 681) Lincoln (171 932) Grand Island (33 180) North Platte (24 479) Fremont (23 979)
NEVADA (Nev) 31 Oct. 1864 (36th) 'Sagebrush State' 'Silver State' 'Battle Born State'	110 540 miles² *286 297 km²* (7th) 799 184 (43rd) 7·2 *2,8* Carson City 17 counties	Las Vegas (164 674) Reno (100 756) North Las Vegas (42 739) Sparks (40 780) Carson City (32 022)
NEW HAMPSHIRE (NH) 21 June 1788 (9th) 'Granite State'	9304 miles² *24 097 km²* (44th) 920 610 (42nd) 98·9 *38,2* Concord 10 counties	Manchester (90 936) Nashua (67 865) Concord (30 400) Portsmouth (26 254)
NEW JERSEY (NJ) 18 Dec. 1787 (3rd) 'Garden State'	7836 miles² *20 295 km²* (46th) 7 364 158 (9th) 939·8 *362,9* Trenton 21 counties	Newark (329 248) Jersey City (223 532) Paterson (137 970) Elizabeth (106 201) Trenton (92 124) Camden (102 551) Woodbridge (90 074)
NEW MEXICO (NM) 6 Jan. 1912 (47th) 'Land of Enchantment' 'Sunshine State'	121 666 miles² *315 113 km²* (5th) 1 299 968 (37th) 10·7 *4,1* Santa Fe 32 counties	Albuquerque (331 767) Santa Fe (48 899) Las Cruces (45 086) Roswell (39 676) Clovis (31 194)
NEW YORK (NY) 26 July 1788 (11th) 'Empire State'	49 576 miles² *128 401 km²* (30th) 17 557 288 (2nd) 354·1 *136,7* Albany 62 counties	New York City (7 071 030) Buffalo (357 870) Rochester (241 741) Yonkers (195 351) Syracuse (170 105) Albany (101 727) Utica (75 632) Niagara Falls (71 384)
NORTH CAROLINA (NC) 21 Nov. 1789 (12th) 'Tar Heel State' 'Old North State'	52 586 miles² *136 197 km²* (28th) 5 874 429 (10th) 111·7 *43,1* Raleigh 100 counties	Charlotte (314 447) Greensboro (155 642) Raleigh (149 771) Winston-Salem (131 885) Durham (100 831) High Point (64 107) Fayetteville (59 507)
NORTH DAKOTA (ND) 2 Nov. 1889 (39th) 'Sioux State' 'Flickertail State'	70 665 miles² *183 022 km²* (17th) 652 695 (46th) 9·2 *3,6* Bismarck 53 counties	Fargo (61 308) Bismarck (44 485) Grand Forks (43 765) Minot (32 843) Jamestown (16 280)

Name, with date and order of (original) admission into the Union. Nicknames	Area (inc inland water). Pop. at 1980 Census (with rankings). Population density per mile² per km². State Capital. Admin. divisions	Major Cities (with population at 1 Apr. 1980)
OHIO 1 Mar. 1803 (17th) 'Buckeye State'	41 222 miles² *106 764 km²* (35th) 10 797 419 (6th) 261·9 *101,1* Columbus 88 counties	Cleveland (573 822) Columbus (564 871) Cincinnati (385 457) Toledo (354 635) Akron (237 177) Dayton (203 588) Youngstown (115 436) Canton (94 730)
OKLAHOMA (Okla) 16 Nov. 1907 (46th) 'Sooner State'	69 919 miles² *181 089 km²* (18th) 3 025 266 (26th) 43·3 *16,7* Oklahoma City 77 counties	Oklahoma City (403 213) Tulsa (360 919) Lawton (80 054) Norman (68 020) Enid (50 363) Midwest City (49 559)
OREGON (Ore) 14 Feb. 1859 (33rd) 'Beaver State'	96 981 miles² *251 180 km²* (10th) 2 632 663 (30th) 27·1 *10,5* Salem 36 counties	Portland (366 383) Eugene (105 624) Salem (89 233) Springfield (41 621)
PENNSYLVANIA (Pa) 12 Dec. 1787 (2nd) 'Keystone State'	45 333 miles² *117 412 km²* (33rd) 11 866 728 (4th) 261·8 *101,1* Harrisburg 67 counties	Philadelphia (1 688 210) Pittsburgh (423 938) Erie (119 123) Allentown (103 758) Scranton (88 117) Reading (78 686) Bethlehem (70 419)
RHODE ISLAND (RI) 29 May 1790 (13th) 'Little Rhody'	1214 miles² *3144 km²* (50th) 947 154 (40th) 780·2 *301,3* Providence 5 counties	Providence (156 804) Warwick (71 123) Cranston (71 992) Pawtucket (71 204) East Providence (50 980) Woonsocket (45 914) Newport (29 259)
SOUTH CAROLINA (SC) 23 May 1788 (8th) 'Palmetto State'	31 055 miles² *80 432 km²* (40th) 3 119 208 (24th) 100·4 *38,8* Columbia 46 counties	Columbia (99 296) Charleston (69 510) North Charleston (65 630) Greenville (58 242) Spartanburg (43 968)
SOUTH DAKOTA (SD) 2 Nov. 1889 (40th) 'Coyote State' 'Sunshine State'	77 047 miles² *199 551 km²* (16th) 690 178 (45th) 9·0 *3,5* Pierre 67 counties (64 county governments)	Sioux Falls (81 343) Rapid City (46 492) Aberdeen (25 956) Watertown (15 649) Brookings (14 951) Mitchell (13 916)
TENNESSEE (Tenn) 1 June 1796 (16th) 'Volunteer State'	42 244 miles² *109 411 km²* (34th) 4 590 750 (17th) 108·7 *42,0* Nashville 95 counties	Memphis (646 356) Nashville-Davidson (455 651) Knoxville (183 139) Chattanooga (169 565) Clarksville (54 777) Jackson (49 131)
TEXAS 29 Dec. 1845 (28th) 'Lone Star State'	267 338 miles² *692 402 km²* (2nd) 14 228 383 (3rd) 53·2 *20,5* Austin 254 counties	Houston (1 594 086) Dallas (904 078) San Antonio (785 410) El Paso (425 259) Fort Worth (385 141) Austin (345 496) Corpus Christi (231 999) Lubbock (173 979) Arlington (160 123) Amarillo (149 230) Garland (138 857) Beaumont (118 102) Pasadena (112 560)
UTAH 4 Jan. 1896 (45th) 'Beehive State'	84 916 miles² *219 931 km²* (11th) 1 461 037 (36th) 17·2 *6,6* Salt Lake City 29 counties	Salt Lake City (163 033) Provo (73 907) Ogden (64 407) Orem (52 399) Sandy City (51 022) Bountiful (32 877) Logan (26 844)
VERMONT (Vt) 4 Mar. 1791 (14th) 'Green Mountain State'	9609 miles² *24 887 km²* (43rd) 511 456 (48th) 53·2 *20,6* Montpelier 14 counties	Burlington (37 712) Rutland (18 436) Bennington (15 815) Essex (14 392) Colchester (12 629)

Name, with date and order of (original) admission into the Union. Nicknames	Area (inc inland water). Pop. at 1980 Census (with rankings). Population density per mile² per km². State Capital. Admin. divisions	Major Cities (with population at 1 Apr. 1980)
VIRGINIA (Va) (officially called the Commonwealth of Virginia) 26 June 1788 (10th) 'The Old Dominion' 'Cavalier State'	40 817 miles² *105 716 km²* (36th) 5 346 279 (14th) 131·0 *50,6* Richmond 98 counties, plus 32 independent cities	Norfolk (266 979) Virginia Beach (262 199) Richmond (219 214) Newport News (144 903) Hampton (122 617) Chesapeake (114 226) Portsmouth (104 577) Alexandria (103 217) Roanoke (100 427) Lynchburg (66 743)
WASHINGTON (Wash) 11 Nov. 1889 (42nd) 'Evergreen State' 'Chinook State'	68 192 miles² *176 616 km²* (20th) 4 130 163 (20th) 60·6 *23,4* Olympia 39 counties	Seattle (493 846) Spokane (171 300) Tacoma (158 501) Bellevue (73 903) Everett (54 413) Yakima (49 826) Bellingham (45 794) Vancouver (42 834) Bremerton (36 208)
WEST VIRGINIA (W Va) 20 June 1863 (35th) 'Mountain State' 'Panhandle State'	24 181 miles² *62 629 km²* (41st) 1 949 644 (34th) 80·6 *31,1* Charleston 55 counties	Charleston (63 968) Huntingdon (63 684) Wheeling (43 070) Parkersburg (39 967) Morgantown (27 605) Weirton (24 763) Fairmont (23 863)
WISCONSIN (Wisc) 29 May 1848 (30th) 'Badger State'	56 154 miles² *145 438 km²* (26th) 4 705 335 (16th) 83·8 *32,4* Madison 72 counties	Milwaukee (636 212) Madison (170 616) Green Bay (87 899) Racine (85 725) Kenosha (77 685) West Allis (63 982) Appleton (59 032)
WYOMING (Wyo) 10 July 1890 (44th) 'Equality State'	97 914 miles² *253 596 km²* (9th) 470 816 (49th) 4·8 *1,9* Cheyenne 23 counties, plus most of Yellowstone National Park	Casper (51 016) Cheyenne (47 283) Laramie (24 410) Rock Springs (19 458) Sheridan (15 146) Green River (12 807)

* 1970 census figures

Upper Volta

Official name: République de Haute-Volta (Republic of Upper Volta).
Population: 7 285 000 (1982 estimate).
Area: 105 869 miles² *274 200 km²*.
Languages: French (official), Mossi, other African languages.
Religions: Animist; Muslim and Christian minorities.
Capital city: Ouagadougou, population 286 453 (1982 estimate).
Other principal towns (1982): Bobo-Dioulasso 165 171; Koudougou 44 089; Ouahigouya 38 374.
Highest point: Mt Tema, 2457 ft *749 m*.
Principal rivers: Volta Noire (Black Volta), Volta Rouge (Red Volta), Volta Blanche (White Volta).
Head of State: Capt. Thomas Sankara, President.
Climate: Hot (average temperature 28°C *83°F*). Dry from November to March. Very dry in north and north-east. Rainy season June to October in south. In Ouagadougou, average maximum temperature 30°C *87°F* (August) to 40°C *104°F* (March), minimum 15°C *60°F* to 26°C *79°F*.
Labour force: 3 503 610 in 1982: Agriculture, forestry and fishing 85%.
Gross domestic product: 109 599 million CFA francs in 1974. Agriculture, forestry and fishing (excluding government) 43·6% (agriculture 37·5%); Manufacturing 10·9%; Trade, restaurants and hotels 16·1% (trade 15·9%); 186 425 million CFA francs in 1978.
Exports: 18 109 million francs CFA in 1982: Cotton 41·9%; Almonds 16%; Livestock 14·1%.

Monetary unit: Franc de la Communauté financière africaine.
Denominations:
   Coins 1, 2, 5, 10, 25, 50, 100 CFA francs.
   Notes 50, 100, 500, 1000, 5000 CFA francs.
Exchange rate to £ sterling: 542·25 (14 Jan. 1985).
Political history and government: Formerly a part of French West Africa, independent since 5 Aug. 1960. The civilian President was deposed on 3 Jan. 1966 in a military *coup* led by Lt-Col (later Maj-Gen) Sangoulé Lamizana, the army Chief of Staff. He took office as President and Prime Minister, the constitution was suspended, the National Assembly dissolved and a Supreme Council of the Armed Forces established. Political activities were suspended on 21 Sept. 1966 but the restriction was lifted in Nov. 1969. A new constitution was approved by popular referendum on 14 June 1970 and introduced on 21 June. This provided for a four-year transitional régime, under joint military and civilian control, leading to the return of civilian rule. Elections for a unicameral National Assembly of 57 members were held on 20 Dec. 1970. The leader of the majority party was appointed Prime Minister by the President, took office on 13 Feb. 1971 and formed a mixed civilian and military Council of Ministers. On 8 Feb. 1974, after a dispute between the Premier and the Assembly, the President dismissed the former and dissolved the latter. The army again assumed power, with the constitution and political activity suspended. The Head of State also became President of the Council of Ministers on 11 Feb. 1974. Political parties were banned on 30 May. The Assembly was replaced by a National Consultative Council for Renewal, formed on 2

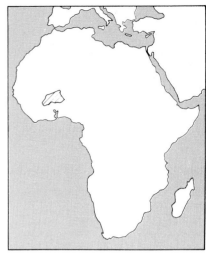

UPPER VOLTA

July 1974, with 65 members nominated by the President.
   Political parties were allowed to resume activities from 1 Oct. 1977. A referendum on 27 Nov. 1977 approved a draft constitution providing for a return to civilian democratic rule, with legislative elections on a multi-party basis, a President directly elected for a 5-year term and a separate Prime Minister nominated by the President. Elections were held on 30 Apr. 1978 for a new National Assembly (57 members serving a 5-year term). Under the constitution, only the three parties which obtained most votes were allowed to continue their activities (other parties being obliged to merge with them). A presidential election was held on 14 May 1978 but no candidate gained an overall majority. A 'run-off' election between the two leading candidates on 28 May was won by Lamizana. On 7 July 1978 the Assembly elected the President's nominee for Prime Minister. The President appointed other Ministers on the Prime Minister's recommendation. On 29 May 1979 the Assembly passed a law limiting the number of authorised political parties to the three strongest in the 1978 elections.
   On 25 Nov. 1980 the government was overthrown in a military *coup*, led by Col Saye Zerbo, military commander of the capital region. Power was assumed by a *Comité militaire de redressement pour le progrès national* (CMRPN), headed by Col Zerbo, which suspended the 1977 constitution and political parties, dissolved the National Assembly and banned political activity. Supreme political power now resides in a 12-member People's Salvation Council, which rules through an appointed Cabinet.
   Local government is through 10 *départements* and 5 autonomous municipal authorities.
Telephones: 3 564 (1978).
Daily newspapers: 3 (1983).
Radio: 90 000 (1981).
TV: 5500 (1981).
Length of roadways: 10 299 miles *16 574 km*.
Length of railways: 321 miles *517 km*.
Universities: 1.
Adult illiteracy: 98·5% (males 98%; females 99%) in 1962 (UNESCO estimates).
Expectation of life: Males 39·4 years; females 42·5 years (UN estimates for 1970–75).
Defence: Total armed forces 3775 (1984); defence expenditure, 1980: $33 million.
Cinemas: 6 (seating capacity 2000) and 3 part-time (capacity 700) in 1969.
Foreign tourists: 50 049 in 1982.

Uruguay

Official name: La República Oriental del Uruguay (the Eastern Republic of Uruguay).
Population: 2 991 341 (1981 estimate).
Area: 68 037 miles² *176 215 km²*.
Language: Spanish.
Religion: Roman Catholic.

URUGUAY

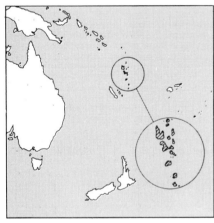

VANUATU

Capital city: Montevideo, population 1 345 858 (1980 estimate).
Other principal towns (1975): Salto 71 000; Paysandú 61 000; Las Piedras 53 000; Rivera 49 000; Melo 38 000; Mercedes 35 000; Minas 35 000.
Highest point: Cerro de las Animas, 1643 ft *500 m*.
Principal mountain range: Sierra de las Animas.
Principal river: Uruguay (1000 miles *1609 km*).
Head of State: Lt-Gen Gregorio C. Alvarez (b. 1926), President.
Climate: Temperate (average 16°C *61°F*). Warm summers and mild winters. Moderate rain. In Montevideo, average maximum 14°C *58°F* (July) to 28°C *83°F* (January), minimum 6°C *43°F* (June, July, August) to 17°C *62°F* (January), rainiest months are August and December (each 7 days). Maximum recorded temperature 44°C *111·2°F*, Rivera, February 1953; minimum −7°C *19·4°F*, Paysandú, June 1945.
Labour force: 1 077 468 (excluding 17 131 seeking work for the first time) at 1975 census: Agriculture, forestry and fishing 17·6%; Manufacturing 20·8%; Trade, restaurants and hotels 13·6%; Community, social and personal services 31·9%.
Gross domestic product: 30 314 million new pesos in 1978: Agriculture, forestry and fishing 11·2% (agriculture 10·9%); Manufacturing 28·8%; Trade, restaurants and hotels 17·4% (trade 14·2%); Community, social and personal services 13·4%.
Exports: US$975·8 million in 1982: Wool and manufactures 26·9%; Meat and meat products 17·5%; Vegetable products 15·1%; Hides, furs

and leather manufactures 13·9%.
Monetary unit: New Uruguayan peso. 1 new peso = 100 centésimos.
Denominations:
   Coins: 1, 2, 5, 10 new pesos.
   Notes 50, 100, 500, 1000 new pesos.
Exchange rate to £ sterling: 84·28 (14 Jan. 1985).
Political history and government: A republic comprising 19 departments. A new constitution approved by plebiscite on 27 Nov. 1966 and taking effect on 1 Mar. 1967, provided that elections by universal adult suffrage be held every five years for a President, a Vice-President and a bicameral legislature, the General Assembly (Congress), comprising a Senate (30 elected members plus the Vice-President) and a 99-member Chamber of Representatives. Elections to both Houses were on the basis of proportional representation.
   Executive power is held by the President, who appoints and leads the Council of Ministers. Juan María Bordaberry Arocena was elected President on 28 Nov. 1971 and took office on 1 Mar. 1972. The armed forces intervened on 8 Feb. 1973 to demand reforms and military participation in political affairs. On 13 Feb. President Bordaberry accepted the military programme. On 27 June the President dissolved both Houses of Congress. On 19 Dec. 1973 he appointed a new legislature, a 25-member Council of State, headed by a President, to control the executive and draft plans for constitutional reform. On 12 June 1976 the President was deposed by the armed forces and replaced by the Vice-President. On 27 June the new régime established the Council of the Nation, with 46 members (the Council of State and 21 officers of the armed forces). On 14 July the Council of the Nation elected a new President, who took office for a five-year term on 1 Sept. 1976. A proposed constitution, which would have institutionalised the role of the armed forces within a 'restricted democracy', was rejected in a referendum on 30 Nov. 1980. A new President, appointed by the Council of State, took office on 1 Sept. 1981 for a 3½-year term, to prepare for elections in 1985 and the return of civilian rule.
Telephones: 294 350 (1982).
Daily newspapers: 26 (1977).
   Total circulation: 637 000 (19 dailies, 1975).
Radio: 1 000 000 (1982).
TV: 440 000 (1982).
Length of roadways: 15 506 miles *24 954 km* (31 Dec. 1977).
Length of railways: 1867 miles *3004 km*.
Universities: 1.
Adult illiteracy: 6·1% (males 6·6%; females 5·7%) in 1975.
Expectation of life: Males 65·51 years; females 71·56 years (1963–64).
Defence: Military service voluntary; total armed forces 32 700 (1984); defence expenditure, 1978: $134·5 million.
Cinemas: 94 in 1979.
Foreign tourists: 480 900 in 1981.

Vanuatu

Official name: The Republic of Vanuatu.
Population: 117 000 (1980 estimate).
Area: 5700 miles² *14 763 km²*.
Languages: Bislama (ni-Vanuatu pidgin), English, French.
Religion: Christian.
Capital city: Port Vila, population 14 000 (1980 estimate).
Other principal town: Luganville (Santo).
Highest point: Mt Tabwebesana, 6195 ft *1888 m*.
Head of State: *Ati* George Sokomanu (né Kalkoa) MBE, President.
Prime Minister: Rev. Walter Hadye Lini, CBE (b. 1943).
Climate: Warm and generally pleasant. Southeast trade winds, May–Oct. Average annual rainfall from 1140 mm *45 in* in south to 6350 mm *250 in* in north. In Port Vila, average temperatures from 16°C *60°F* to 33°C *92°F*, average annual rainfall 2050 mm *81 in*.

Labour force: 35 133 (census of 28 May 1967).
Gross national product: $50 million in 1978 (World Bank estimate).
Exports: 2199 vatu in 1982: Copra 53%; Fish 29%; Beef 5%.
Monetary unit: Vatu (formerly New Hebrides franc). 1 vatu = 100 centimes.
Denominations:
   Coins 1, 2, 5, 10, 20, 50 vatu.
   Notes 100, 500, 1000 vatu.
Exchange rate to £ sterling: 112·35 (14 Jan. 1985).
Political history and government: Formerly the Anglo-French Condominium of the New Hebrides. The United Kingdom and France established a joint administration on 20 Oct. 1906, each power being represented by a Resident Commissioner. The first elections under universal adult suffrage were held for two municipal councils on 16 Aug. 1975. To increase the territory's autonomy, the administration's Advisory Council, established in 1957, was replaced by a Representative Assembly of 42 members (including 29 popularly elected on 10 Nov. 1975). The Assembly's first full working session was delayed until 29 Nov. 1976. Later it was reduced to 39 members, all directly elected. The Assembly chose the territory's first Chief Minister on 5 Dec. 1977 and he formed a Council of Ministers, with powers of internal self-government, on 13 Jan. 1978. A conference ending on 19 Sept. 1979 adopted a constitution providing for the islands to become an independent republic. The constitution was signed by the Resident Commissioners on 5 Oct. and its terms were agreed on 23 Oct. by an exchange of notes between the British and French governments. Elections were held on 14 Nov. for a new Representative Assembly with increased powers. On 29 Nov. 1979 the Assembly elected the Rev. Walter Lini to be Chief Minister. On 30 July 1980 the New Hebrides became independent, as Vanuatu ('our land'), and joined the Commonwealth. The Assembly was renamed Parliament and Lini became Prime Minister.
   Legislative power is vested in the unicameral Parliament, elected for a four-year term by universal adult suffrage, partly on the basis of proportional representation. The President is a constitutional Head of State elected for five years by an electoral college consisting of Parliament and the presidents of regional councils. The first President was the former Deputy Chief Minister, George Kalkoa, who was elected on 4 July 1980 and adopted the surname Sokomanu ('leader of thousands'). Executive power is vested in the Prime Minister, elected by and from members of Parliament. Other Ministers are appointed by the Prime Minister from among members of Parliament. The Council of Ministers is responsible to Parliament. The constitution also provides for a Council of Chiefs, composed of traditional tribal rulers, to safeguard Melanesian customs.
Telephones: 3000 (1981).
Radio: 16 000 (1977).
Length of roadways: 620 miles *1000 km*.
Cinemas: 3 (seating capacity 1300) in 1976 (former British administration only).
Foreign tourists: 22 000 in 1980.

The Vatican City

Official name: Stato della Città del Vaticano (State of the Vatican City).
Population: 728 (estimate for 1 July 1978).
Area: 108·7 acres *44 hectares*.
Languages: Italian, Latin.
Religion: Roman Catholic.
Head of State: Pope John Paul II (b. Karol Wojtyła, 18 May 1920).
Head of Government: Cardinal Agostino Casaroli (b. 24 Nov. 1914), Secretary of State.
Climate: See Italy for climate of Rome.
Monetary unit: Italian currency (*q.v.*).
Political history and government: An enclave in the city of Rome, established on 11 Feb. 1929 by the Lateran Treaty with Italy. The Vatican City is under the temporal jurisdiction of the

Pope, the Supreme Pontiff elected for life by a conclave comprising members of the Sacred College of Cardinals. He appoints a Pontifical Commission, headed by the Secretary of State, to conduct the administrative affairs of the Vatican, which serves as the international headquarters, and administrative centre, of the worldwide Roman Catholic Church.

The Holy See (a term designating Rome as the Pope's own bishopric) is a distinct, pre-existing entity. Both entities, although united in the person of the Pope, are subjects of international law. The Holy See has diplomatic relations with foreign states on the basis of its religious status.

The 'Apostolic Constitution' (*Regimini Ecclesiae Universae*) published on 15 Aug. 1967, and effective from 1 Mar. 1968, reformed the Roman Curia, the Papal Court which acts as the central administrative body of the Church. The Vatican City remains an absolute monarchy, with legislative, executive and judicial power vested in the Pope. The College of Cardinals, whose members are created by the Pope, serves as the chief advisory body (at the end of 1984 there were 124 Cardinals). An Apostolic Letter of 21 Nov. 1970 decreed that, from 1 Jan. 1971, Cardinals reaching the age of 80 would lose the right to elect the Pope. On 5 Mar. 1973 the Pope announced that the number of Cardinals permitted to participate in the conclave would be limited to 120. Rules governing the conclave, issued on 13 Nov. 1975, included these limits and also stipulated that, to be successful, a candidate should normally have a two-thirds majority plus one vote.

Daily newspapers: 1 (1976).
Total circulation: 70 000.
Lengths of railways: 0·54 mile *0·86 km.*
Universities: There are 5 pontifical universities in Rome.

Venezuela

Official name: La República de Venezuela ('Little Venice').
Population: 14 690 000 (1982 estimate).
Area: 352 144 miles² *912 050 km².*
Language: Spanish.
Religion: Roman Catholic.
Capital city: Santiago de León de los Caracas, population 2 576 000 (metropolitan area) at 30 June 1976 (estimate).
Other principal towns (1976): Maracaibo 792 000; Valencia 439 000; Barquisimeto 430 000; Maracay 301 000; Barcelona/Puerto La Cruz 242 000; San Cristóbal 241 000.
Highest point: La Pico Columna (Pico Bolívar), 16 427 ft *5007 m.*
Principal mountain ranges: Cordillera de Mérida, Sierra de Perijá, La Gran Sabana.
Principal river: Orinoco (1700 miles *2736 km*).
Head of State: Dr Jaime Lusinchi, President.
Climate: Varies with altitude from tropical in steamy lowlands to cool in highlands. Maximum recorded temperature 38°C *100·4°F*, minimum −6°C *21·2°F.* In Caracas, average temperature 20°C *69°F,* average maximum 20°C *75°F* (January) to 27°C *81°F* (April), minimum 13°C *56°F* (January, February) to 17°C *62°F* (May, June), rainiest months are July and August (each 15 days).
Labour force: 6 000 000 in 1983: Agriculture 19·5%; Manufacturing 18·8%; Construction 9·6%.
Gross domestic product: 170 323 million bolívares in 1978: Mining and quarrying 17·0%; Manufacturing 15·1%; Transport, storage and communication 12·1%; Government services 11·0%.
Exports: US$13 200 million in 1982.
Monetary unit: Bolívar. 1 bolívar = 100 céntimos.
Denominations:
Coins 5, 12·5, 25, 50 céntimos; 1, 2, 5 bolívares.
Notes 10, 20, 50, 100, 500 bolívares.
Exchange rate to £ sterling: 8·8475 (14 Jan. 1985).
Political history and government: A federal

republic of 20 states, two Federal Territories and a Federal District (containing the capital), each under an appointed Governor. The last military dictatorship was overthrown by popular revolt on 21–22 Jan. 1958, after which Venezuela returned to democratic rule. A new constitution was promulgated on 23 Jan. 1961. Legislative power is held by the bicameral National Congress, comprising a Senate (44 elected members plus ex-Presidents of the Republic) and a Chamber of Deputies (199 members). Executive authority rests with the President. Senators, Deputies and the President are all elected for 5 years by universal adult suffrage. Members of both houses of Congress, whose terms run concurrently with that of the President, are chosen partly by direct election and partly on the basis of proportional representation, with seats for minority parties. The President has wide powers and appoints a Council of Ministers to conduct the government. He may not have two consecutive terms of office.
Telephones: 1 377 630 (1982).
Daily newspapers: 54 (1977).
Total circulation: 2 263 000.
Radio: 5 273 000 (1977).
TV: 1 900 000 (1979).
Length of roadways: 38 417 miles *61 826 km.*
Length of railways: 109 miles *175 km.*
Universities: 14.
Adult illiteracy: 23·5% (males 20·3%; females 26·6%) in 1971.
Expectation of life: 66 years (1978).
Defence: Military service: 18 months, selective; total armed forces 41 000 (1984); defence expenditure, 1981: $1118 million.
Cinemas: 563 (seating capacity 256 000) and 25 drive-in (capacity 26 000) in 1977.
Foreign tourists: 652 423 in 1977.

Viet-Nam

Official name: Công hoa xã hôi chu nghia Viêt Nam (Socialist Republic of Viet-Nam).
Population: 52 741 766 (census of 1 Oct. 1979); 54 000 000 (estimate 1981).
Area: 128 402 miles² *332 559 km².*
Language: Vietnamese.
Religions: Buddhist, Taoist, Confucian, Christian.
Capital city: Hã-nôi (Hanoi), population 2 570 905 at 1979 census.
Other principal towns (1979): Ho Chi Minh City (formerly Saigon) 3 419 978 (including Cholon); Haiphong 1 279 067; Da-Nhang (Tourane) 492 194 (1973); Nha-trang 216 227 (1973); Qui-Nhon 213 757 (1973); Huê 209 043 (1973).
Highest point: Fan si Pan, 10 308 ft *3142 m.*
Principal rivers: Mekong (2600 miles *4184 km*), Songkoi (Red River), Songbo (Black River), Ma.
Head of State: Truong Chinh (formerly Dang Xuan Khu, b. 1908), Chairman of the Council of State.
Political Leader: Le Duan (b. 1908), First Secretary of the Central Committee of the Communist Party of Viet-Nam.
Prime Minister: Pham Van Dong (b. 1 Mar. 1906).
Climate: Hot and wet in the north, warm and humid in the south. The rainy monsoon season is from April or May to October. In Hanoi, average maximum temperature 20°C *68°F* (January) to 33°C *92°F* (June), minimum 13°C *56°F* to 25°C *78°F* (June, July, August); rainiest month August (16 days). In Ho Chi Minh City, average maximum 30°C *87°F* (November, December) to 35°C *95°F* (April), minimum 21°C *70°F* (January) to 24°C *76°F* (April, May); rainiest month July (23 days).
Labour force: 18 770 000 (mid-1970): Agriculture, forestry and fishing 76·4%; Services 17·0% (ILO estimates).
Gross national product: 20 742 million dông in 1978.
Exports: $535 million in 1979 (unofficial estimate).

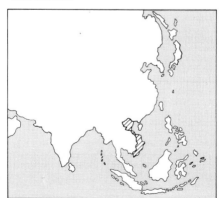

THE VATICAN CITY

VENEZUELA

VIET-NAM

Monetary unit: Dông. 1 dông = 10 hào = 100 xu.
Denominations:
Coins 1, 2, 5 xu.
Notes 2, 5 xu; 1, 2, 5 hào; 1, 2, 5, 10, 20, 30, 50, 100 dông.
Exchange rate to £ sterling: 12·015 (14 Jan. 1985).
Political history and government: Formerly part of French Indo-China, Viet-Nam was occupied by Japanese forces, with French co-operation, in Sept. 1940. On 6 June 1941 nationalist and revolutionary groups, including the Communist Party of Indo-China, formed the *Viet-Nam Doc-Lap Dong Minh Hoi* (Revolutionary League for

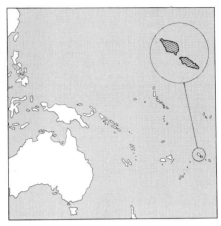

WESTERN SAMOA

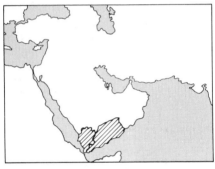

left: **THE YEMEN ARAB REPUBLIC**
right: **THE PEOPLE'S DEMOCRATIC REPUBLIC OF YEMEN**

the Independence of Viet-Nam), known as the *Viet-Minh*, to overthrow French rule. On 9 Mar. 1945 French administrative control was ended by a Japanese *coup* against their nominal allies. After Japan's surrender in Aug. 1945, *Viet-Minh* forces entered Hanoi and formed a provisional government under Ho Chi Minh, leader of the Communist Party. On 2 Sept. 1945 the new régime proclaimed independence, as the Democratic Republic of Viet-Nam (DRV), with Ho as President. On 6 Mar. 1946, after French forces re-entered Viet-Nam, an agreement between France and the DRV recognised Viet-Nam as a 'free' state within the French Union. The DRV government continued to press for complete independence but negotiations broke down and full-scale hostilities began on 19 Dec. 1946. The war continued until cease-fire agreements were made on 20–21 July 1954. These provided that DRV forces should regroup north of latitude 17°N. Thus the DRV was confined to North Viet-Nam.

On 8 Mar. 1949, during the first Indo-China war, the French government made an agreement with anti-Communist elements for the establishment of the State of Viet-Nam, under Bao Dai, Emperor of Annam. Originally within the French Union, the State made an independence agreement with France on 4 June 1954. After the cease-fire agreements of 20–21 July 1954 French forces withdrew, leaving the State's jurisdiction confined to the zone south of latitude 17°N. Complete sovereignty was transferred by France on 29 Dec. 1954. Following a referendum, Bao Dai was deposed and the Republic of Viet-Nam proclaimed on 26 Oct. 1955. In 1959 an insurgent movement, supported by North Viet-Nam, launched guerrilla warfare to overthrow the Republic. On 20 Dec. 1960 the insurgents formed the National Front for the Liberation of South Viet-Nam, known as the National Liberation Front (NLF). From 1961 the USA supported the Republic with troops, numbering over 500 000 by 1969. From 1964 regular forces from North Viet-Nam, numbering about 250 000 by 1975, moved south to support the NLF. On 10 June 1969 the NLF announced the formation of a Provisional Revolutionary

Government (PRG) to administer 'liberated' areas. A 'peace' agreement on 27 Jan. 1973 led to the withdrawal of US forces but fighting continued until the Republic surrendered to the PRG on 30 Apr. 1975. The territory was renamed the Republic of South Viet-Nam.

Following the PRG victory, it was agreed to merge North and South Viet-Nam. Elections were held on 25 Apr. 1976 for a single National Assembly (for both North and South) of 492 members. The new Assembly met on 24 June and the country was reunited as the Socialist Republic of Viet-Nam on 2 July 1976.

On 18 Dec. 1980 the National Assembly adopted a new constitution. The highest state authority is the Assembly, a unicameral body elected by universal adult suffrage for five years. The Assembly elects from its members a Council of State to be its permanent organ, with a term of office corresponding to that of the Assembly. The Council's Chairman serves as Head of State. The highest administrative organ is the Council of Ministers, headed by a Prime Minister, which is elected by, and responsible to, the Assembly. A new National Assembly was elected on 26 Apr. 1981, when 496 members were chosen from 93 constituencies. The first Chairman of the Council of State was elected on 4 July 1981.

Political power is held by the Communist Party of Viet-Nam, described by the constitution as 'the only force leading the state and society'. The Party was established on 20 Dec. 1976 in succession to the *Dang Lao Dong Viet-Nam* (Viet-Nam Workers' Party), formed in 1951. The Party Congress of 14–20 Dec. 1976 elected a Central Committee (101 full members and 32 alternate members) to supervise Party work. The Central Committee elected a Political Bureau (Politburo), with 14 full and three alternate members, to direct its policy.

On 6 July 1976 representatives of the former DRV's Communist-led National Fatherland Front, the NLF and other groups met to organise a united Viet-Nam Fatherland Front, formally launched during a congress on 31 Jan.–4 Feb. 1977. The Front presents an approved list of candidates for elections to all representative bodies.

Viet-Nam comprises 37 provinces and three cities.

Telephones: 47 000 (South only) in 1973.
Daily newspapers: 5 (1977).
   Total circulation: 250 000.
Radio: 1 000 000 in the North (1974); 1 550 000 in the South (1973).
TV: 2 000 000 (1980).
Length of roadways: 215 767 miles *347 243 km* (1980).
Length of railways: 1616 miles *2600 km.*
Universities: 3.
Adult illiteracy: 35·5% (population aged 12 and over) in the North (1960).
Expectation of life: Males 43·2 years; females 46·0 years (UN estimates for 1970–75).
Defence: Military service: 2 years minimum; total armed forces 1 216 000 (1984).
Cinemas: 145 in 1980.

Western Samoa

Official name: The Independent State of Western Samoa (Samoa i Sisifo).
Population: 156 350 (1981 census); 160 000 (1983 estimate).
Area: 1097 miles² *2842 km².*
Languages: Samoan, English.
Religions: Congregational, Roman Catholic, Methodist, Mormon.
Capital city: Apia, population 36 000 (1981 census).
Highest point: Mauga Silisli, 6094 ft *1857 m.*
Head of State: H H Malietoa Tanumafili II, CBE (b. 4 Jan. 1913).
Prime Minister: Tofilau Eti Alesana.
Climate: Warm all the year round. Rainy season November to April. In Apia, average maximum 29°C *84°F* to 30°C *86°F*, minimum 23°C *74°F* to 24°C *76°F*; rainiest month is January (22 days).
Labour force: 38 204 (excluding 45 unemployed)

at 1976 census: Agriculture, forestry and fishing 61·4%; Community, social and personal services 18·1%.
Gross domestic product: 30·3 million tala (at factor cost) in 1972: Agriculture, forestry and fishing (excluding government) 49·9% (agriculture 45·3%); Government services 21·6%.
Exports: 15 828 000 tala in 1980: Copra 53·1%; Cocoa 19%; Taro 6·6%; Timber 2%.
Monetary unit: Tala. 1 tala = 100 sene.
Denominations:
   Coins 1, 2, 5, 10, 20, 50 sene.
   Notes 1, 2, 10 tala.
Exchange rate to £ sterling: 2·46 (14 Jan. 1985).
Political history and government: The islands became a German protectorate in 1899. They were occupied by New Zealand forces during the First World War (1914–18). In 1919 New Zealand was granted a League of Nations mandate over the islands. In 1946 Western Samoa was made a United Nations Trust Territory, administered by New Zealand. An independence constitution, adopted by a Constitutional Convention on 28 Oct. 1960, was approved by a UN-supervised plebiscite in May 1961. The islands duly became independent on 1 Jan. 1962. The position of Head of State (*O le Ao o le Malo*) was held jointly by two tribal leaders, one of whom died on 5 Apr. 1963. The other remains Head of State for life, performing the duties of a constitutional monarch. In the absence of the Head of State, his functions are performed by a Council of Deputies. Future Heads of State will be elected for five years by the Legislative Assembly. The Assembly is a unicameral body of 47 members, including 45 Samoans elected by about 11 000 *matai* (elected clan chiefs) in 41 constituencies and two members popularly elected by voters (mainly Europeans) outside the *matai* system. Members hold office for three years (subject to dissolution). The country's first political party was formed by an anti-government group in Mar. 1979.

In most cases, executive power is held by the Cabinet, comprising a Prime Minister and 8 other members of the Assembly. The Prime Minister, appointed by the Head of State, must have the support of a majority in the Assembly. Cabinet decisions may be reviewed by the Executive Council, comprising the Head of State, the Prime Minister and some other Ministers.

Western Samoa joined the Commonwealth on 28 Aug. 1970.
Telephones: 5857 (1982).
Radio: 50 000 (1975).
TV: 2800 (1973).
Length of roadways: 1119 miles *1800 km.*
Adult illiteracy: 2·2% (males 2·2%; females 2·1%) in 1971.
Expectation of life: Males 60·8 years; females 65·2 years (1961–66).
Cinemas: 8 (seating capacity 4200) in 1975.
Foreign tourists: 34 538 in 1982.

The Yemen Arab Republic

Official name: Al-Jamhuriya al-'Arabiya al-Yamaniya.
Population: 8 500 000 (census of 1 Feb. 1981).
Area: 75 290 miles² *195 000 km².*
Language: Arabic.
Religion: Muslim.
Capital city: Sana'a, population 277 817 (1980).
Other principal towns: Hodeida; Ta'iz.
Highest point: Jebel Hadhar, 12 336 ft *3760 m.*
Principal mountain range: Yemen Highlands.
Head of State: Col 'Ali Abdullah Saleh (b. 1942), President.
Prime Minister: Dr 'Abd ul Aziz Abdulghani.
Climate: Very hot (up to 54°C *130°F*) and extremely humid on semi-desert coastal strip. Cooler on highlands inland (average maximum of 22°C *71°F* in June) with heavy rainfall and winter frost. Desert in the east.
Labour force: 1 676 000 (mid-1970): Agriculture, forestry and fishing 79·2%; Services 11·8% (ILO estimates).
Gross domestic product: 3709·7 million riyals in

1973: Agriculture, forestry and fishing 62·9%; Trade, restaurants and hotels 14·9% (trade 13·8%).
Exports: $7·7 million in 1976: Food and live animals 32·5% (coffee 19·5%); Hides and skins 20·1% (sheep skins 13·8%); Raw cotton 33·4%.
Monetary unit: Yemeni riyal. 1 riyal = 100 fils.
Denominations:
Coins 1, 5, 10, 25, 50, 100 fils.
Notes 1, 5, 10, 20, 50, 100 riyals.
Exchange rate to £ sterling: 6·53 (14 Jan. 1985).
Political history and government: Formerly a monarchy, ruled by an hereditary Imam. Army officers staged a *coup* on 26–27 Sept. 1962, declared the Imam deposed and proclaimed a republic. Civil war broke out between royalist forces, supported by Saudi Arabia, and republicans, aided by Egyptian troops. The republicans gained the upper hand and Egyptian forces withdrew in 1967. A Republican Council, led by a Chairman, took power on 5 Nov. 1967 and announced a new constitution (which did not permit political parties) on 28 Dec. 1970. This provided for a unicameral legislature, the Consultative Council of 179 members (20 appointed by the Republican Council and 159 directly elected for 4 years by general franchise on 27 Feb.–18 Mar. 1971). On 13 June 1974 power was seized by army officers who suspended the constitution and established a Military Command Council. On 19 June 1974 the new régime published a provisional constitution which, for a transitional period, gave full legislative and executive authority to the Command Council, whose Chairman was granted the powers of Head of State. The Consultative Council was dissolved after the *coup*, later reinstated but dissolved again on 22 Oct 1975. The first Chairman of the Command Council, Lt-Col Ibrahim al-Hamadi, was assassinated on 11 Oct. 1977. The remaining three members of the Command Council formed a Presidential Council, under Lt-Col Ahmad Husain al-Ghashmi, and imposed martial law.

On 6 Feb. 1978 the Command Council issued a decree providing for the formation of a Constituent People's Assembly, with 99 members appointed by the Council for 2 to 3 years. The new Assembly first met on 25 Feb. 1978. On 22 Apr. it elected Ghashmi to be President for a 5-year term. The Command Council was then dissolved. President Ghashmi was assassinated on 24 June 1978 and the Assembly formed a four-man provisional Presidential Council. On 17 July 1978 the Assembly elected a member of the Presidential Council to be President and he was sworn in on 18 July. On 8 May 1979 the President signed a constitutional declaration which provided that the Assembly would be expanded to 159 members, with a two-year term of office. On the same day 60 new members were selected. The President rules with the assistance of an appointed Cabinet, led by a Prime Minister. Yemen comprises eleven provinces.
Telephones: 90 350 (1981).
Daily newspapers: 6 (1970).
Total circulation: 56 000.
Radio: 110 000 (1983).
TV: 25 000 (1983).
Length of roadways: 1192 miles *1924 km.*
Universities: 1.
Adult illiteracy: 97·5% (males 95%; females 100%) in 1962 (UNESCO estimates).
Expectation of life: Males 37·3 years; females 38·7 years (UN estimates for 1970–75).
Defence: Military service: 3 years; total armed forces 22 100 (1984); defence expenditure, 1981: $212 million.
Cinemas: 14 (seating capacity 16 900) in 1975.
Foreign tourists: 25 000 in 1978.

The People's Democratic Republic of Yemen

Official name: Jumhuriyat al-Yaman al-Dimuqratiya ash-Sha'abiya.
Population: 2 030 000 (1981 estimate).
Area: 128 560 miles² *332 968 km².*

Language: Arabic.
Religion: Muslim.
Capital city: Aden, population 264 326 (1981 estimate).
Other principal town: Al Mukalla, population 100 000.
Highest point: Qaured Audilla, 8200 ft *2499 m.*
Head of State: 'Ali Nasir Muhammad (b. 1939), Chairman of the Presidium of the People's Supreme Assembly; also Prime Minister and Secretary-General of the Yemen Socialist Party.
Climate: Summer extremely hot (temperatures over 54°C *130°F*) and humid. Very low rainfall (average less than 76 mm *3 in* per year). Winter can be very cold in high areas.
Labour force: 338 220 (excluding 71 522 unemployed) aged 7 and over (1973 census): Agriculture, forestry and fishing 52·0%; Community, social and personal services 24·9%.
Gross domestic product: 320 million dinars in 1982: Agriculture, forestry and fishing 19·4%; Manufacturing 25·2%; Trade, restaurants and hotels 12·7%.
Exports: 269 million dinar in 1980: Petroleum products 74·4% (motor spirit 13·7%; lamp oil and white spirit 17·7%; distillate fuel oils 43·0%).
Monetary unit: Yemeni dinar. 1 dinar = 1000 fils.
Denominations:
Coins 1, 5, 25, 100, 250 fils.
Notes 250, 500 fils; 1, 5, 10 dinars.
Exchange rate to £ sterling: 0·387 (14 Jan. 1985).
Political history and government: Formerly the British colony of Aden and the Protectorate of South Arabia. Became independent, outside the Commonwealth, on 30 Nov. 1967 as the People's Republic of Southern Yemen. Power was held by a revolutionary movement, the National Liberation Front, renamed the National Front (NF). The interim legislative authority was the NF's Supreme General Command. On 22 June 1969 the country's first President was replaced by a Presidential Council. Salim Rubayyi 'Ali became Chairman of the Council on 24 June 1969. A new constitution, adopted on 30 Nov. 1970, gave the country its present name and provided for the establishment of a unicameral legislature, the Supreme People's Council (SPC). A Provisional SPC, inaugurated on 14 May 1971, had 101 members, including 86 elected by the NF's General Command and 15 by trade unions. It was empowered to appoint members of the Presidential Council and the Cabinet. In Oct. 1975 the ruling NF merged with two smaller parties to form the United Political Organisation-National Front (UPO-NF).

On 26 June 1978 the Head of State, Rubayyi 'Ali, was ousted from power and executed by opponents within the UPO-NF. The Prime Minister, 'Ali Nasir Muhammad, became interim Head of State. It was announced on 28 June that the three parties within the UPO-NF had agreed to form a Marxist-Leninist 'vanguard' party. The constituent congress of the new party, the Yemen Socialist Party (YSP), was held on 11–14 Oct. 1978. Constitutional amendments providing for a new form of legislature and the abolition of the Presidential Council were approved on 31 Oct. 1978. A 111-member People's Supreme Assembly (PSA), replacing the SPC, was elected on 16–18 Dec. At its first session, on 27 Dec. 1978, the PSA elected an 11-member Presidium (to replace the Presidential Council) and elected as Chairman of the Presidium (and thus as Head of State) 'Abd al-Fattah Isma'il, Secretary-General of the YSP, the sole legal party. On 21 Apr. 1980 Isma'il relinquished his positions as Head of State and YSP leader, being replaced in both offices by the Prime Minister, previously Deputy Chairman of the PSA Presidium. A YSP Congress on 12–14 Oct. 1980 elected a new Central Committee, which in turn elected a seven-member Political Bureau.

The country, also called Democratic Yemen, is divided into 8 governorates.
Telephones: 9876 (1973).
Daily newspapers: 4 (1976).
Total circulation: 12 000 (2 dailies).
Radio: 150 000 (1983).

TV: 26 000 (1983).
Length of roadways: 1150 miles *1851 km.*
Universities: 1.
Adult illiteracy: 72·9% (males 52·3%; females 92·1%) in 1973 (population aged 10 and over).
Expectation of life: Males 40·6 years; females 42·4 years (UN estimates for 1970–75).
Defence: Military service: 2 years; total armed forces 26 000 in 1984; defence expenditure, 1980: $127 million.
Cinemas: 21 (seating capacity 20 900) in 1977.
Foreign tourists: 17 996 in 1976.

Yugoslavia

Official name: Socijalistička Federativna Republika Jugoslavija (Socialist Federal Republic of Yugoslavia).
Population: 22 424 711 (census of 31 Mar. 1981); 22 800 000 (estimate for mid-1983).
Area: 98 766 miles² *255 804 km².*
Languages: Serbo-Croatian/Croato-Serbian, Slovenian, Macedonian.
Religions: Serbian Orthodox, Roman Catholic, Muslim, Macedonian Orthodox and smaller Protestant groups.
Capital city: Beograd (Belgrade), population 1 470 075 at 1981 census.
Other principal towns (1981): Zagreb 855 568; Skopje 504 932; Sarajevo 448 519; Ljubljana 305 211; Novi Sad 257 685; Priština 210 040; Titograd 132 290.
Highest point: Triglav, 9396 ft *2864 m.*
Principal mountain ranges: Slovene Alps, Dinaric Mts. Šar-Pindus and Rhodope ranges, Carpathian and Balkan Mts.
Principal rivers: Dunav (Danube) (1700 miles *2848 km* total length, in Yugoslavia 368 miles *588 km*) and tributaries (Drava, Sava (590 miles *945 km*), Morava), Vardar.
Head of State: Veselin Djuranović (b. 17 May 1925), President of the Presidency of the SFRY for 1984/85.
Head of Government: Milka Planinc (b. 20 November 1924), President of the Federal Executive Council.
Climate: Mediterranean climate on Adriatic coast (dry, warm summers; mild, rainy winters). Continental climate (cold winters) in hilly interior. In Belgrade, average maximum 3°C *37°F* (January) to 29°C *85°F* (July), minimum −3°C *27°F* (January, February) to 16°C *61°F* (July). Rainiest months are April, May, June, December (each 9 days). In Split, average maximum 14°C *57°F* (January) to 30°C *87°F* (July, August), minimum 4°C *39°F* (January, February) to 20°C *68°F* (July), rainiest month is December (11 days). Absolute maximum temperature 46,2°C *115·2°F*, Mostar, 31 July 1901; absolute minimum −37,8°C *−36·0°F*, Sjenica, 26 Jan. 1954.
Labour force: 8 779 735 (excluding 625 069 persons working abroad temporarily) at 1981 census: Agriculture, forestry and fishing 30·3%; Mining and manufacturing (excluding crafts) 26·1%; Services, construction, banking,

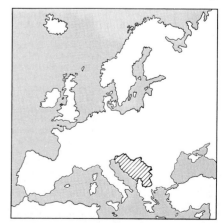

YUGOSLAVIA

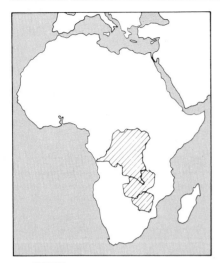

top: **ZAIRE**
centre: **ZAMBIA**
below: **ZIMBABWE**

education and social insurance 34·5%. Figures exclude unemployed dependants.

Gross material product: 2 924 794 million dinars in 1982: Agriculture, forestry and fishing 15·2% (agriculture 14%); Industry 42·1%; Construction 9·1%; Trade, restaurants, etc. 21·8%.

Exports: $9913·4 million in 1983; Machinery and transport equipment 29·5% (non-electric machinery 8·9%, transport equipment 12·3%).

Monetary unit: 1 dinar = 100 para.

Denominations:
Coins 5, 10, 20, 25, 50; 1, 2, 5, 10 dinars.
Notes 10, 20, 50, 100, 500, 1000 dinars.

Exchange rate to £ sterling: 299 (24 April 1985).

Political history and government: Yugoslavia was formed by a merger of Serbia, Croatia, Slovenia, Montenegro and Bosnia-Herzegovina. A pact between Serbia and other South Slavs was signed on 20 July 1917 to unite all the territories in a unitary state under the Serbian monarchy. The Kingdom of Serbs, Croats and Slovenes was proclaimed on 1 Dec. 1918. It was renamed Yugoslavia on 3 Oct. 1929. The Kingdom was invaded by German and Italian forces on 6 Apr. 1941. Resistance was divided between royalists and Partisans, led by the Communist Party under Marshal Tito (né Josip Broz). Their rivalry led to civil war, won by the Partisans, who proclaimed the Federal People's Republic of Yugoslvia, with Tito as Prime Minister, on 29 Nov. 1945. A Soviet-type constitution, establishing a federation of 6 republics, was adopted on 31 Jan. 1946. Yugoslav leaders followed independent policies and the country was expelled from the Soviet-dominated Cominform in June 1948. At its 6th Congress, on 2–7 Nov. 1952, the Communist Party was renamed the League of Communists of Yugoslvia (LCY). A new constitution was adopted on 13 Jan. 1953 and Tito sworn in as President the next day.

Another constitution, promulgated on 7 Apr. 1963, introduced the country's present name. Since 29 July 1971 national leadership has been held by a Collective Presidency. Tito was elected 'President for life' on 16 May 1974. With his death, on 4 May 1980, the office of President was terminated.

The present constitution, which increased decentralisation, was adopted on 21 Feb. 1974. Legislative power is vested in the bicameral Federal Assembly, comprising a Federal Chamber of 220 members (30 from each of the 6 republics and 20 each from the two autonomous provinces within Serbia) and a Chamber of Republics and Provinces, with 88 members (12 from each Republican Assembly and 8 from each Provincial Assembly). Members are elected for four years by communal assemblies which have been chosen by about 1 million delegates, themselves elected by universal adult suffrage, with voters grouped according to their place of work.

The Collective Presidency has nine members: the President of the Presidium of the LCY's Central Committee (*ex officio*) and eight others (one each from the republics and provinces) elected by the Federal Assembly for five years. The posts of President and Vice-President of the Collective Presidency rotate annually in a fixed sequence among the members. The Federal Assembly also elects the Federal Executive Council, led by a President and five Vice-Presidents (one from each of the six republics), for a four-year term as the administrative branch of government.

The only authorised political party is the LCY, which controls political life through the Socialist Alliance of the Working People of Yugoslavia. The LCY's highest authority is the Congress. The 12th Congress, held on 26–29 June 1982, elected a Central Committee of 163 members (equal number of members from each republic, and a corresponding number of members from the provinces and from the Army) to supervise the LCY's work. The Committee elected a Presidium of 23 members to direct its policy. Since the death of Tito, the President of the Presidium is chosen annually on a rotation basis among the republics and provinces. The Presidium had decided on 15 May 1979 that the post of Presidium Secretary (previously nominated by Tito) should be similarly filled by rotation, though for a two-year term.

Each constituent republic has its own government, with an indirectly elected assembly and an executive.

Telephones: 2 796 000 (1983).

Daily newspapers: 28 (1983).
Total circulation: 2 393 000.

Radio: 4 689 000 (1983).

TV: 4 001 000 (1983).

Length of roadways: 72 757 miles *116 411 km.*

Length of railways: 5870 miles *9399 km.*

Universities: 18.

Adult illiteracy: 9·5% (males 4·1%; females 14·7%) in 1981.

Expectation of life: Males 67·7 years; females 73·2 years (1980–1).

Defence: Military service: 15 months (12 months for the sole supporter of the family); total armed forces 252 000 (154 000 conscripts) in 1981: defence expenditure in 1983: $2438·5 million.

Cinemas: 1278 (seating capacity 424 000) (1982).

Foreign tourists: 5 947 000 plus 21 149 000 excursionists (1983).

Zaire

Official name: La République du Zaïre (the Republic of Zaire).

Population: 31 944 000 (estimate 1983).

Area: 905 365 miles² *2 344 885 km².*

Languages: French (official), Lingala, Kiswahili, Tshiluba, Kikongo.

Religions: Animist, Roman Catholic, Protestant.

Capital city: Kinshasa (formerly Léopoldville), population 2 443 876 (1976).

Other principal towns (1976): Kananga (Luluabourg) 704 211; Lubumbashi (Elisabethville) 451 332; Mbuji-Mayi 382 632; Kisangani (Stanleyville) 339 210; Bukavu (Costermanville) 209 051.

Highest point: Ngaliema (Mt Stanley), 16 763 ft *5109 m* (first climbed 1900), on the border with Uganda.

Principal mountain ranges: Chaîne des Mitumba, Ruwenzori.

Principal rivers: Zaïre (Congo), Ubangi, Kasai.

Head of State: Lt-Gen Mobutu Sese Seko Kuku Ngbendu wa Za Banga (b. Joseph-Désiré Mobutu, 14 Oct. 1930), President.

Head of Government: N'Singa Udjuu Ongwabeki Untube (b. Joseph N'Singa, 1934), First State Commissioner.

Climate: Tropical. Hot and humid in Congo basin, cool in highlands. In Kinshasa, March and April hottest (22°C *71°F* to 32°C *89°F*), July coolest (18°C *64°F* to 27°C *81°F*) and driest, April and November rainiest (16 days each).

Absolute maximum temperature 41,0°C *105·8°F* at Yahila; absolute minimum −1,5°C *29·3°F*, Sakania, 11 Jan. 1949.

Labour force: 9 719 000 (mid-1970): Agriculture, forestry and fishing 79·3%; Industry 10·8% (ILO estimates).

Gross domestice product: 3874·0 million zaires in 1977: Agriculture, forestry and fishing 26·5%; Trade 22·3%; Public administration and defence 12·1%.

Exports: 2360·9 million zaires in 1981: Copper 47%; Cobalt 16%; Coffee 15%; Diamonds 7%.

Monetary unit: Zaire. 1 zaire = 100 makuta (singular: likuta) = 10 000 sengi.

Denominations:
Coins 10 sengi; 1, 5 makuta.
Notes 10, 20, 50 makuta; 1, 5, 10 zaires.

Exchange rate to £ sterling: 46·6635 (14 Jan. 1985).

Political history and government: Formerly the Belgian Congo, independent as the Republic of the Congo on 30 June 1960. Renamed the Democratic Republic of the Congo on 1 Aug. 1964. Power was seized on 24 Nov. 1965 by army officers, led by Maj-Gen (later Lt-Gen) Joseph-Désiré Mobutu (from January 1972 called Mobutu Sese Seko). The new régime, with Mobutu as President, was approved by Parliament on 28 Nov. 1965. A new constitution approved by referendum, was adopted on 24 June 1967. Mobutu was elected President by popular vote on 31 Oct.–1 Nov. 1970 and inaugurated for a 7-year term on 5 Dec. 1970. The country's present name was introduced on 27 Oct. 1971. A unicameral National Legislative Council of 244 members, led by Mobutu, was elected by acclamation for 5 years on 2 Nov. 1975. The President appoints and leads the National Executive Council, a cabinet of State Commissioners with departmental responsibilities. On 6 July 1977 the President appointed a First State Commissioner, equivalent to a Prime Minister. Direct elections for a new Legislative Council were held on 15–16 Oct. 1977, when 268 members were elected (from 2080 candidates) to serve a 5-year term. Mobutu was re-elected President (unopposed) and sworn in on 5 Dec. 1977.

Since 1970 the only authorised political party has been the *Mouvement populaire de la révolution* (MPR) or People's Revolutionary Movement. The highest policy-making body is the MPR's Political Bureau. In 1979 the Bureau had 38 members, including 20 appointed by the President and 18 elected (two from each region and two from Kinshasa). The Bureau has a 7-member Permanent Committee. On 14 Feb. 1980 the Legislative Council approved constitutional changes, including the dissolution of the MPR's executive secretariat and the replacement of elected members of the MPR's Political Bureau, when their terms expired in 1982, by presidential nominees. A meeting of the Political Bureau on 31 July–4 Aug. 1980 agreed on the establishment of a central committee (114 members appointed by the President on 2 Sept.) and the creation of a new executive secretariat.

Zaire comprises eight regions, each headed by an appointed Commissioner, and the capital district of Kinshasa, under a Governor.

Telephones: 30 284 (1980).

Daily newspapers: 6 (1976).
Total circulation: 45 000 (2 dailies).

Radio: 245 000 (1979).

TV: 7700 (1979).

Length of roadways: 90 100 miles *145 000 km* (31 Dec. 1979).

Length of railways: 3212 miles *5169 km* (1978).

Universities: 1 (three campuses).

Adult illiteracy: 84·6% (males 70·8%; females 97·2%) in 1955–58.

Expectation of life: Males 41·9 years; females 45·1 years (UN estimates for 1970–75).

Defence: Military service voluntary; total armed forces 26 000 (1984); defence expenditure, 1979: $50·5 million.

Cinemas: 91 (seating capacity 23 400) and 1 drive-in (capacity 2000) in 1974.

Foreign tourists: 2525 plus 51 151 excursionists (1977).

Zambia

Official name: The Republic of Zambia.
Population: 5 679 808 (census of 1 Sept. 1980); 6 242 000 (1982 estimate).
Area: 290 586 miles² *752 614 km²*.
Languages: English (official), Nyanja, Bemba, Tonga, Lozi, Lunda, Luvale.
Religions: Roman Catholic, Protestant, Animist.
Capital city: Lusaka, population 538 469 (1980).
Other principal towns (1980): Kitwe 314 794; Ndola 282 439; Mufulira 149 778; Chingola 145 869; Kabwe 143 035.
Highest point: 6210 ft *1893 km*.
Principal mountain range: Muchinga Mts.
Principal rivers: Zambezi and tributaries (Kafue, Luangwa), Luapula.
Head of State: Dr Kenneth David Kaunda (b. 28 Apr. 1924), President.
Prime Minister: Nalumino Mundia (b. 1927).
Climate: Hot season September–November, rainy season November–April, winter May–September. Day temperatures 27°C *80°F* to 38°C *100°F* in hot season, sharp fall at night. Average annual rainfall from 635 mm *25 in* in south to 1270 mm *50 in* in north. In Lusaka, average annual minimum 18°C *64°F*, maximum 31°C *88°F*, average rainfall 8382 mm *33 in*.
Labour force: 363 800 in 1983: Agriculture, forestry and fisheries 9·4%; Mining and quarrying 16·6%; Manufacturing 13·2%; Construction 11·6%; Transport and communications 7%.
Gross domestic product: 4205·6 million kwacha in 1983.
Exports: 985 million kwacha in 1982: Copper and other non-ferrous metals 95%.
Monetary unit: Zambian kwacha. 1 kwacha = 100 ngwee.
Denominations:
Coins 1, 2, 5, 10, 20, 50 ngwee.
Notes 50 ngwee; 1, 2, 5, 10, 20 kwacha.
Exchange rate to £ sterling: 2·50 (14 Jan. 1985).
Political history and government: Formerly the British protectorate of Northern Rhodesia. On 24 Oct. (UN Day) 1964 the territory became an independent republic, as Zambia (named from the Zambezi river), and a member of the Commonwealth. A one-party state was proclaimed on 13 Dec. 1972 and inaugurated by a new constitution on 25 Aug. 1973. Legislative power is held by the unicameral National Assembly, with 135 members (10 nominated by the President and 125 elected for five years by universal adult suffrage, with up to three candidates per constituency). There is also an advisory House of Chiefs (27 members) to represent traditional tribal authorities. Executive power is held by the President, elected by popular vote at the same time as the Assembly. He appoints a Cabinet, led by a Prime Minister, to conduct the administration. The sole authorised party is the United National Independence Party (UNIP), led by the President. The highest policy-making body is UNIP's Central Committee (25 members), to which the Cabinet is subordinate. Zambia is divided in 9 provinces, each administered by a Cabinet Minister.
Telephones: 37 834 (1984).
Daily newspapers: 2 (1983).
Total circulation: 110 000.
Radio: 115 000 (1977).
TV: 25 000 (1976).
Length of roadways: 22 627 miles *36 415 km* (31 Dec. 1979).
Length of railways: 1360 miles *2188 km*.
Universities: 1.
Adult illiteracy: 52·4% (males 38·5%; females 65·4%) in 1969.
Expectation of life: Males 44·3 years; females 47·5 years (UN estimates for 1970–75).
Defence: Military service voluntary; total armed forces 15 500 (1984); defence expenditure, 1979: $388 million.
Cinemas: 12 (seating capacity 4100) and 1 drive-in (capacity 1200) in 1976.
Foreign tourists: 56 165 in 1976.

Zimbabwe

Population: 7 532 000 (1982 census).
Area: 150 804 miles² *390 580 km²*.
Languages: English (official), Sindebele, Chishona.
Religions: Tribal beliefs, Christian minority.
Capital city: Harare (Salisbury), population 656 000 (1982 census).
Other principal towns (1982): Bulawayo 414 000; Chitungwiza 175 000; Gweru (Gwelo) 79 000; Mutara (Umtali) 70 000; Kwekwe (Que Que) 48 000; Kadoome (Gatooma) 45 000; Hwange (Wankie) 39 000; Masvingo (Fort Victoria) 31 000.
Highest point: Mount Inyangani, 8503 ft *2592 m*.
Principal mountain ranges: Enyanga, Melsetter.
Principal rivers: Zambezi and tributaries (Shangani, Umniati), Limpopo and tributaries (Umzingwani, Nuanetsi), Sabi and tributaries (Lundi, Odzi).
Head of State: Rev. Canaan Sodindo Banana (b. 5 Mar. 1936), President.
Prime Minister: Robert Gabriel Mugabe (b. 21 Feb. 1924).
Climate: Tropical, modified by altitude. Average temperature 18°C *65°F* to 24°C *75°F*. In Salisbury, average daily maximum 21°C *70°F* (June, July) to 28°C *83°F* (October), minimum 7°C *44°F* (June, July) to 15°C *60°F* (November–February), January rainiest (18 days).
Labour force: 2 500 000 in 1983: 30% peasant cultivators; 40% employed in the formal sector of the economy.
Gross domestic product: Z$2219·9 million in 1977: Agriculture, forestry and fishing 16·5%; Manufacturing 21·8%; Trade, restaurants and hotels 11·8%; Community, social and personal services (including business services) 21·8%.
Exports: Z$1118 million in 1982: Tobacco 23%; Gold 12%; Ferrochrome 8%; Asbestos 8%; Cotton lint 6%; Nickel and nickel alloys 5%; Raw sugar 5%; Iron and steel 4%; Maize 4%.
Monetary unit: Zimbabwe dollar (Z$). 1 dollar = 100 cents.
Denominations:
Coins ½, 1, 2½, 5, 10, 20, 25 cents.
Notes 1, 2, 5, 10 dollars.
Exchange rate to £ sterling: 1·759 (14 Jan. 1985).
Political history and government: The British South Africa Company was granted a Royal Charter over the territory on 29 Oct. 1889. On 12 Sept. 1923 Southern Rhodesia (as it was known) was transferred from the Company to the British Empire and became a colony. It was granted full self-government (except for African interests and some other matters) on 1 Oct. 1923. Administration was controlled by European settlers as African voting rights were severely restricted. The colony became part of the Federation of Rhodesia and Nyasaland (the Central African Federation), proclaimed on 1 Aug. 1953. A new constitution, which removed most of the UK's legal controls (except for foreign affairs), was promulgated on 6 Dec. 1961 and made fully operative on 1 Nov. 1962. This constitution provided for a limited African franchise and could have led to ultimate majority rule. The Federation was dissolved on 31 Dec. 1963.

African nationalists campaigned for an end to discrimination and more rapid progress to full democracy. On 17 Dec. 1961 leaders of the banned National Democratic Party formed the Zimbabwe African People's Union (ZAPU), using the site of an ancient African ruin as the name of the whole country. The party split on 9 July 1963 and a breakaway group formed the Zimbabwe African National Union (ZANU) on 8 Aug. 1963.

Ian Smith became Prime Minister on 13 Apr. 1964. After Northern Rhodesia achieved independence as Zambia on 24 Oct. 1964, Southern Rhodesia became generally (although not officially) known as Rhodesia. Following unsuccessful negotiations with the British Government, a state of emergency was declared on 5 Nov. 1965 and Ian Smith made a unilateral declaration of independence (UDI) on 11 Nov. 1965. The British-appointed Governor announced the Cabinet's dismissal but no effective steps were taken to remove it from power. The Smith régime abrogated the 1961 constitution and proclaimed its own, naming the country Rhodesia. The British Government regarded UDI as unconstitutional and having no legal validity, and no other country formally recognised the territory's independence.

A new constitution was approved by referendum on 20 June 1969, adopted on 29 Nov. 1969 and took effect on 2 Mar. 1970, when a republic was proclaimed. The constitution provided for a bicameral Legislative Assembly, comprising a 23-member Senate (having only limited powers) and a House of Assembly with 66 members: 50 Europeans (whites), elected by non-African voters, and 16 Africans. The President was given no formal powers and Smith remained Prime Minister.

Attempts to reach a constitutional settlement acceptable to all parties proved unsuccessful. ZAPU and ZANU had both taken up arms against the illegal régime and a full-scale guerrilla war was begun by African nationalists in Dec. 1972. Following internal dissension in ZANU in 1975–76, the party's secretary-general, Robert Mugabe, emerged as leader of an 'external wing' committed to gaining power by armed struggle. After a meeting with the US Secretary of State on 19 Sept. 1976, Smith announced that his régime had agreed to proposals leading to majority rule within two years. On 9 Oct., in preparation for negotiations, ZAPU and the Mugabe faction of ZANU announced the formation of an alliance as the Patriotic Front (PF). A conference was held in Geneva (28 Oct. to 14 Dec. 1976) but no agreement was reached. In 1977 Smith began negotiations with three African parties within Rhodesia, although the main guerrilla groups (based in neighbouring countries) did not participate. An agreement was signed on 3 Mar. 1978 for an 'internal settlement' (not internationally recognised), providing for a transition to majority rule by 31 Dec. 1978. A transitional administration, comprising Europeans and Africans, was formed but the elections leading to majority rule were postponed.

A 'majority rule' constitution, changing the name of the country to Zimbabwe Rhodesia, was approved by the House of Assembly on 20 Jan. 1979. It vested legislative authority in a bicameral Parliament, comprising a 100-member House of Assembly (in which 72 seats were reserved for Africans and 28, including 20 directly elected, were to be held by Europeans for at least 10 years) and a Senate of 30 members.

The constitution, which included entrenched provisions safeguarding the position of whites, was approved by European voters in a referendum on 30 Jan. 1979. Elections to the new House of Assembly (the country's first by universal adult suffrage) were held in two stages: on 10 Apr. for 20 European members and on 17–20 Apr. for the 72 African members (chosen by the whole electorate). The existing white-dominated Legislative Assembly was dissolved on 4 May. Members of the new House of Assembly were sworn in on 8 May and the Senate was constituted on 23 May. The President was elected by Parliament on 28 May. He and the first African Prime Minister, Bishop Abel Muzorewa, were sworn in on 29 May and the constitution became effective on 1 June. The House of Assembly was opened on 26 June 1979. In accordance with the constitution, the first African majority government was one of 'national unity' (a coalition of parties, including European members). The new constitution was not accepted by the United Kingdom and the new régime did not gain international recognition.

At the meeting of Commonwealth heads of government in Lusaka, Zambia, on 1–7 Aug. 1979, agreement was reached on proposals for a fresh attempt to secure legal independence for the country. As a result, a constitutional conference was held in London from 10 Sept. to 15 Dec. 1979 between the British government, the

Muzorewa régime and the PF. It was announced on 19 Oct. that all parties had agreed on the terms of a new constitution for an independent republic of Zimbabwe. On 15 Nov. agreement was reached on transitional arrangements for the pre-independence period, including the restoration of British rule and elections for a new government. On 5 Dec. the conference agreed 'in principle' on a cease-fire to end the guerrilla war. Details of the procedure for implementing the cease-fire were agreed on 17 Dec. The final agreement (covering constitutional, transitional and cease-fire arrangements) was signed on 21 Dec. 1979.

Meanwhile, inside the country, the House of Assembly voted on 11 Dec. to renounce independence and to revert to the status of a British colony as Southern Rhodesia. Illegal rule ended on the next day, when Parliament was dissolved, the President, Prime Minister and Cabinet resigned, and the British-appointed Governor, Lord Soames, arrived to hold executive and legislative authority during the transition to legal independence. The cease-fire became effective from 29 Dec. 1979.

The independence constitution provided for the establishment of a republic under the name of Zimbabwe. Legislative power is vested in a bicameral Parliament, comprising a Senate (40 members), with delaying powers only, and a House of Assembly (100 members). Members of both houses serve a term of five years (subject to dissolution). Of the Senators, 14 are chosen by those members of the House elected by Africans; 10 are chosen by those members of the House elected by non-Africans; 10 are African chiefs elected by the Council of Chiefs (five from Mashonaland, five from Matabeleland); and six are appointed by the President on the advice of the Prime Minister. Members of the House are directly elected by adult suffrage in single-member constituencies: 80 by Africans and 20 by non-Africans. Executive power is vested in the President, a constitutional Head of State elected by Parliament for a six-year term, but is

exercised in almost all cases on the advice of the Executive Council (Cabinet), led by the Prime Minister. The President appoints the Prime Minister and, on the latter's recommendation, other Ministers. The Executive Council is responsible to the House of Assembly.

On 2 Jan. 1980 the two parties in the PF announced that they would contest the elections to the new House of Assembly separately: as ZANU (PF), led by Mugabe, and as the Patriotic Front (ZAPU). The elections were again held in two stages: on 14 Feb. for non-African members and on 27–29 Feb. for African members. ZANU (PF) won an overall majority and Mugabe was appointed Prime Minister by the Governor. The 34 elective seats in the Senate were filled on 19 Mar. and the six nominated Senators appointed on 11 Apr. ZANU (PF)'s nominee for President was the sole candidate. Zimbabwe became legally independent, and a member of the Commonwealth, on 18 Apr. 1980, when the constitution entered into force and the President and Prime Minister were sworn in. The Emergency Powers Act of 1965 remained in force.

Telephones: 242 252 (1982).
Daily newspapers: 2 (1976).
Total circulation: 78 000.
Radio: 170 000 (1982).
TV: 82 000 (1982).
Length of roadways: 49 045 miles *78 930 km.*
Length of railways: 2110 miles *3394 km.*
Universities: 1.
Adult illiteracy: 95·3% (males 94·4%; females 96·3%) in 1962 (Africans only).
Expectation of life: Males 49·8 years; females 53·3 years (UN estimates for 1970–75). Europeans: Males 66·9 years; females 74·0 years (1961–63).
Defence: Military service selective; total armed forces 5300 (1984); defence expenditure, 1980/81: US$ 444 million.
Cinemas: 72 (capacity 51 000) in 1971.
Foreign tourists: 327 261 in 1981.

SOURCES
Population: Primarily *de facto* but for some countries the figures cover *de jure* population. *Source:* mainly UN, *Population and Vital Statistics Report.*
Area, Capital city and Principal towns: *Source:* national data; also UN, *Demographic Yearbook.*
Labour force: Figures refer to the total economically active population. The categorisation of the labour force is, in most cases, according to the International Standard Industrial Classification of all Economic Activities (ISIC). *Sources:* ILO, *Year Book of Labour Statistics* and *Labour Force Estimates and Projections, 1950–2000.*
Gross domestic product: Unless otherwise indicated, GDP is given in terms of purchasers' values (market prices), i.e. GDP at factor cost (producers' values) plus indirect taxes net of subsidies. Net domestic product is GDP less consumption (depreciation) of fixed capital. Gross national product (GNP) is GDP plus net income from abroad. National income is net national product, i.e. GNP less capital consumption. Net material product (NMP) comprises the net value of goods and 'material' services produced, i.e. gross output (including turnover taxes) minus intermediate material (including capital) consumption. Gross material product (GMP) is NMP plus consumption of fixed capital. *Source:* UN, *Yearbook of National Accounts Statistics* and *Monthly Bulletin of Statistics;* International Bank for Reconstruction and Development, *World Bank Atlas.*
Exports: Total merchandise exports, valued f.o.b. (free on board). *Source:* mainly UN, *Yearbook of International Trade Statistics.*
Exchange rate: In most cases the rate given is the mid-point quotation (i.e. half way between the buying and selling rates). *Sources:* International Monetary Fund; *Financial Times.*
Telephones: Figures refer to instruments in use. *Source:* mainly American Telephone and Telegraph Company, *The World's Telephones.*
Daily newspapers, Radio and TV, Cinemas: Figures for newspapers refer to general-interest periodicals published at least four times per week. Circulation figures refer to the combined average circulation per issue. Data on radio and television refer, wherever possible, to the estimated number of receivers in use. Where no such estimate is available, figures are given for radio and/or TV licences issued. *Source:* UNESCO, *Statistical Yearbook.*
Length of roadways: Source: mainly International Road Federation, *World Road Statistics.*
Length of railways: *Source:* mainly *Railway Directory and Yearbook* (Railway Gazette International, IPC Transport Press).
Adult illiteracy: Unless otherwise stated, figures refer to persons aged 15 years and over. Literacy is defined as the ability to both read and write, so semi-literates are treated as illiterate. *Sources:* UNESCO, *Statistical Yearbook;* UN, *Demographic Yearbook.*
Expectation of life: *Source:* mainly UN, *Demographic Yearbook.*
Defence: *Source:* International Institute for Strategic Studies, *The Military Balance.*
Foreign tourists: Unless otherwise indicated, figures refer to visits for leisure or business and cover persons staying at least 24 hours or making at least one overnight stay. *Source:* UN, *Statistical Yearbook* (quoting World Tourism Organisation, Madrid).

United Kingdom

Physical and Political Geography

The various names used for the islands and parts of islands off the north-west coast of Europe geographically known as the British Isles are confusing. Geographical, political, legal and popular usages unfortunately differ, thus making definition necessary.

The British Isles is a convenient but purely *geographical* term to describe that group of islands lying off the north-west coast of Europe, comprising principally the island of Great Britain and the island of Ireland. There are four political units: the United Kingdom of Great Britain and Northern Ireland; the Republic of Ireland; the Crown dependencies of the Isle of Man and, for convenience, also the Channel Islands.

Area: 121 689 miles² *315 173 km².*
Population (latest estimate): 60 082 000

The United Kingdom (UK) (of Great Britain and Northern Ireland)
The political style of the island of Great Britain, with its offshore islands and, since the partition of Ireland (see below), the six counties of Northern Ireland. The term United Kingdom, referring to Great Britain and (the whole island of) Ireland, first came into use officially on 1 Jan. 1801 on the Union of the two islands. With the coming into force of the Constitution of the Irish Free State as a Dominion on 6 Dec. 1922, the term 'United Kingdom of Great Britain and Ireland' had obviously become inappropriate. It was dropped by Statute from the Royal style on 13 May 1927 in favour of 'King of Great Britain, Ireland and of, etc.'. On the same date Parliament at Westminster adopted as its style 'Parliament of the United Kingdom of Great

Britain and Northern Ireland'. On 29 May 1953 by Proclamation the Royal style conformed to the Parliamentary style – Ireland having ceased to be a Dominion within the Commonwealth on 18 Apr. 1949.
Area: 94 220 miles² *244 030 km².*
Population (mid-1983 estimate): 56 376 800.

Great Britain (GB) is the geographical and political name of the main or principal island of the solely geographically named British Isles group. In a strict geographical sense, off-shore islands, for example the Isle of Wight, Anglesey, or Shetland, are not part of Great Britain. In the political sense Great Britain was the political name used unofficially from 24 Mar. 1603, when James VI of Scotland succeeded his third cousin twice removed upwards, Queen Elizabeth of England, so bringing about a Union of the Crowns, until on 1 May 1707 the style was formally adopted with the Union of the Parliaments

of England and Scotland and was used until 1 Jan. 1801. The government of Great Britain is unitary, but in 1975 plans for separate Scottish and Welsh assemblies were first published.
Area: 88 799 miles² *229 988 km²*.
Population (mid-1983): 54 804 100.

England is geographically the southern and greater part of the island of Great Britain. The islands off the English coast, such as the Isle of Wight and the Isles of Scilly, are administratively part of England. Politically and geographically England (historically a separate Kingdom until 1707) is that part of Great Britain governed by English law which also pertains in Wales and, since 1746, in Berwick-upon-Tweed.
The term 'England' is widely (but wrongly) used abroad to mean the United Kingdom or Great Britain.
Area: 50 366 miles² *130 477 km²*.
Population (mid-1983 estimate): 46 845 900.

Isles of Scilly
Area: 4041 acres *1 635 ha* (6·31 miles² *16,35 km²*).
Population: 2006 (1981 estimate). There are five populated islands (1981 estimates) – Bryher (pop. 155), St Agnes (pop. 60), St Martin's (pop. 80), St Mary's (pop. 1650) and Tresco (pop. 155). There are 19 other islands and numerous rocks and islets.
The islands are administered by 25 councillors, which is a unique type of local government unit set up by an Order made under the Local Government Act, 1974. For some purposes the Isles are administered in company with the Cornwall County Council. The islands form part of the St Ives electoral division.

Wales (The principality of) now comprises eight instead of twelve counties. The area was incorporated into England by Act of Parliament in 1536. The former county of Monmouthshire, though for all administrative intents and purposes part of Wales, only became an integral part of Wales on 1 Apr. 1974. The other boundaries between England and Wales expressly could not be altered by the ordinary processes of local government reorganisation.
Wales may not, by Statute, be represented by fewer than 35 MPs at Westminster.
Area: 8018 miles² *20 766 km²*.
Population (mid-1983 estimate): 2 807 800.

Scotland consists of the northern and smaller part of the island of Great Britain. The separate Kingdom of Scotland ceased on 24 March 1603 when King James VI of Scotland (ascended 1567) became also King James I of England. Both countries continued, however, to have their separate Parliaments until the Union of the Parliaments at Westminster, London, on 1 May 1707. Scotland continues to have its own distinctive legal system. By Statute Scotland may not be represented by less than 71 MPs at Westminster. Proposals for a separate Scottish Assembly of some 140 seats were published in 1975. On 16 May 1975 the 33 traditional counties were reduced to 9 geographical regions and 3 island authorities.
Area: 30 415 miles² *78 774 km²*.
Population (mid-1983 estimate): 5 150 400.

Ireland is the name of the second largest island in the geographical British Isles. Henry VIII assumed the style 'King of Ireland' in 1542, although Governors of Ireland (the exact title varied) ruled on behalf of the Kings of England from 1172. The viceroyalty did not disappear until 1937. The Union of the Parliaments of Great Britain and Ireland occurred on 1 Jan. 1801.

Northern Ireland consists of six counties in the north-eastern corner of the island. County government has been replaced by 26 districts. They are all within the larger ancient province of Ulster which originally consisted of nine counties. The government's relationship to the Imperial Parliament in England was federal in

nature. Certain major powers were reserved by the Imperial Parliament, the sovereignty of which was unimpaired. There is a provision in the Ireland Act of 1949 that Northern Ireland cannot cease to be part of the United Kingdom, or part of the Queen's Dominions without the express consent of her Parliament. This Parliament, known as Stormont and established in 1921, was however abolished by the Northern Ireland Constitution Act, 1973. Devolved government came into effect on 1 Jan. 1974, but the Northern Ireland Assembly was prorogued on 29 May 1974 after the Executive collapsed. Arrangements for a Constitutional Convention, under the Northern Ireland Constitution Act 1974, which came into force in July 1974, collapsed in February 1976. Northern Ireland is represented by the fixed number of twelve Members of the Imperial Parliament at Westminster.

UNITED KINGDOM MOUNTAIN AND HILL RANGES

Scotland

Range	Length (miles)	Length (km)	Culminating peak	Height (ft)	Height (m)
Grampian Mountains	155	250	Ben Macdhui, Grampian	4300	1310
North West Highlands	140	225	Càrn Eige, Highland	3877	1181
*Southern Uplands (Scottish Lowlands)	125	200	Merrick, Dumfries & Galloway	2764	842
Liath Mountains	35	55	Càrn Dearg, Highland	3093	942

England

Range	Length (miles)	Length (km)	Culminating peak	Height (ft)	Height (m)
Pennines	120	195	Cross Fell, Cumbria	2930	893
North Downs	85	135	Leith Hill, Surrey	965	294
Cotswold Hills	60	95	Cleeve Hill, Gloucestershire	1083	330
South Downs	55	85	Butser Hill, Hampshire	888	271
Cheviot Hills	45	70	The Cheviot, Northumberland	2676	815
Chiltern Hills	45	70	Coombe Hill, Buckinghamshire	852	259
Berkshire Downs (White Horse Hills)	35	55	Walbury Hill, Berkshire	974	296
Cumbrian Mountains	30	50	Scafell Pike, Cumbria	3210	978
Exmoor	30	50	Dunkery Beacon, Somerset	1706	519
North Yorkshire Moors (Cleveland and Hambleton Hills)	30	50	Urra Moor, Bottom Head North Yorkshire	1491	454
Hampshire Downs	25	40	Pilot Hill, Hampshire	938	285
Yorkshire Wolds	22	35	Garrowby Hill, Humberside	808	246

Wales

Range	Length (miles)	Length (km)	Culminating peak	Height (ft)	Height (m)
Cambrian Mountains	110	175	Snowdon (Yr Wyddfa), Gwynedd	3560	1085
Berwyn Mountains	40	65	Aran Fawddwy, Gwynedd	2972	905

Northern Ireland

Range	Length (miles)	Length (km)	Culminating peak	Height (ft)	Height (m)
Sperrin Mountains	40	65	Sawel Mt, Londonderry-Tyrone	2240	682
Mountains of Mourne	30	50	Slieve Donard, County Down	2796	852
Antrim Hills	25	40	Trostan, Antrim	1817	553

* Includes: Lammermuir Hills (Lammer Law, Lothian 1733 ft *528 m*); Lowther Hills (Green Lowther, Strathclyde, 2403 ft *732 m*); Pentland Hills (Scald Law, Lothian, 1898 ft *578 m*) and the Tweedsmuir Hills (Broad Law, Borders, 2754 ft *839 m*).

BRITISH ISLES EXTREMITIES

Island of Great Britain
Great Britain, the eighth largest island in the world, has extreme (mainland) dimensions thus:

Most Northerly Point	Easter Head, Dunnet Head, Highland	Lat	58° 40′ 24″ N
Most Westerly Point	Corrachadh Mor, Ardnamurchan, Highland	Long	6° 14′ 12″ W
Most Southerly Point	Lizard Point, Cornwall	Lat	49° 57′ 33″ N
Most Easterly Point	Lowestoft Ness, Lowestoft, Suffolk	Long	1° 46′ 20″ E

Other extreme points (mainland) in its 3 constituent countries are:

Most Southerly Point in Scotland	Gallie Craig, Mull of Galloway, Dumfries & Galloway	Lat	54° 38′ 27″ N
Most Easterly Point in Scotland	Keith Inch, Peterhead, Grampian	Long	1° 45′ 49″ W
Most Northerly Point in England	Meg's Dub, Northumberland	Lat	55° 48′ 37″ N
Most Westerly Point in England	Dr Syntax's Head, Land's End, Cornwall	Long	5° 42′ 15″ W
Most Northerly Point in Wales	Point of Air, Clwyd	Lat	53° 21′ 08″ N
Most Westerly Point in Wales	Porthtaflod, Dyfed	Long	5° 19′ 43″ W
Most Southerly Point in Wales	Rhoose Point, South Glamorgan	Lat	51° 22′ 40″ N
Most Easterly Point in Wales	Lady Park Wood, Gwent	Long	2° 38′ 49″ W

Island of Ireland (20th largest island in the world)

Most Northerly Point in Ireland	Malin Head, Donegal	Lat	55° 22′ 30″ N
Most Northerly Point in Northern Ireland	Benbane Head, Moyle, Antrim	Lat	55° 15′ 0″ N
Most Westerly Point in Ireland	Dunmore Head, Kerry	Long	10° 28′ 55″ W
Most Westerly Point in Northern Ireland	Cornaglah, Fermanagh	Long	8° 10′ 30″ W
Most Southerly Point in Ireland	Brow Head, Cork	Lat	51° 26′ 30″ N
Most Southerly Point in Northern Ireland	Cranfield Point, Newry and Mourne, Down	Lat	54° 01′ 20″ N
Most Easterly Point in Ireland (Northern)	Townhead, Ards Peninsula, Down	Long	5° 26′ 52″ W
Most Easterly Point in Republic of Ireland	Wicklow Head, Wicklow	Long	5° 59′ 40″ W

Area: 5452 miles² *14 120 km².*
Population (mid-1983 estimate): 1 572 700.

The Republic of Ireland
This State came into being on 15 Jan. 1922 and consists of 26 of the pre-partition total of 32 Irish counties. The original name was 'The Irish Free State' (or in Irish Gaelic 'Saorstát Eireànn') and the country had Dominion status within the British Commonwealth. A revised Constitution, which became operative on 29 Dec. 1937, abolished the former name and substituted the title 'Eire', which is the Gaelic word for 'Ireland'. On 18 Apr. 1949 the official description of the State became 'The Republic of Ireland' (Poblacht na h-Eireann), but the name of the State remains 'Ireland' in the English and 'Eire' in the Irish Gaelic language. On the same date the Republic of Ireland ceased to be a member of the British Commonwealth.
Area: 27 136 miles² *70 282 km².*
Population (mid-1984 estimate): 3 535 000.

The Crown Dependencies

The Isle of Man
The Isle of Man (Manx-Gaelic, *Ellan Vannin*) is a Crown dependency.
Area: 141 440 acres *57 200 ha* (221 miles² *572 km²*).
Population: 64 679 (1981 census).
Administrative headquarters: Douglas 19 897. The ancient capital was Castletown (2788).

History: Habitation of the island has been traced to the Mesolithic period. The island was converted to Christianity in the 5th or 6th century probably by monks from Ireland. At this time the island's people spoke Gaelic. Norsemen from Scandinavia plundered the island towards the end of the 8th century but became settled around the middle of the 9th century. During the ensuing period of Norse rule, Tynwald was established as the national Parliament. In 1266 the island was sold by Norway to Scotland, but the island alternated between English and Scottish rule until 1333 when it came under England. The island was held by a succession of English noblemen until 1405, when Henry IV granted it to the Stanley family who ruled until 1736 apart from the period 1651 to 1660 when it was under the rule of the English Commonwealth. The Stanleys became the Earls of Derby in 1485 and adopted the title Lord of Mann and the Isles. The Stanleys were succeeded by the Dukes of Atholl who sold the Lordship of Mann to the British Crown in 1765, when the island became a Crown dependency, although it has never been part of the United Kingdom. A period of rule under English officialdom followed. In 1866 the House of Keys became a popularly elected legislature for the first time since the rule of the Norse and women in the Isle of Man got the right to vote in 1881. More recent times have seen the Isle of Man gaining increasing independence from the United Kingdom. Tynwald is the oldest continuous national Parliament in the world and celebrated its millenium in 1979.

Legislature: Her Majesty the Queen as Lord of Mann appoints the Lieutenant Governor who is the nominal head of the Isle of Man Government. The island's legislative assembly is the Court of Tynwald which comprises the Legislative Council and the House of Keys. The upper house, the Legislative Council, consists of 8 members elected by the House of Keys and 2 ex-officio members, the Lord Bishop of Sodor and Man and the Attorney-General. The House of Keys is made up of 24 members who are elected from the island's 13 constituencies.
Highest point above sea-level: Snaefell (2034 ft *619 m*).
Leading Industries: Finance, agriculture, manufacturing, tourism.
Events and Attractions: Tynwald Hill, St John's; Peel Castle; Castle Rushen; Castletown; Laxey waterwheel; steam railway; electric railway; TT motor-cycle races.

THE CHANNEL ISLANDS
The Channel Islands (French: *Iles Anglo-Normandes*) are a Crown dependency. There is a Channel Isle department in the Home Office, Whitehall, London.
Area: 48 083 acres *19 458 ha* (75·13 miles² *194,6 km²*).
Guernsey (French: *Guernesey*) – 15 654 acres *6334 ha* (24.46 miles² *63,3 km²*).
Jersey – 28 717 acres *11 621 ha* (44·87 miles² *116,2 km²*).
Dependencies of Guernsey:
Alderney (French: *Aurigny*) – 1962 acres *794 ha* (3·07 miles² *7,9 km²*).

WATERFALLS
The principal waterfalls of the British Isles are:

Height (ft)	Height (m)	Name
658	*200*	Eas-Coul-Aulin, Highland
370	*112*	Falls of Glomach, Highland
350	*106*	Powerscourt Falls, County Wicklow
>300	*>90*	Pistyll-y-Llyn, Powys-Dyfed
240	*73*	Pistyll Rhaiadr, Clwyd
205	*62*	Foyers, Highland
204 (total)	*62*	Falls of Clyde, Strathclyde (comprises Bonnington Linn (30 ft *9 m*), Corra Linn (84 ft *25 m*), Dundaff Linn (10 ft *3 m*) and Stonebyres Linn (80 ft *24 m*) cataracts
200	*60*	Falls of Bruar, Tayside (upper fall)
200	*60*	Cauldron (or Caldron) Snout, Cumbria
200	*60*	Grey Mare's Tail, Dumfries & Galloway

DEPRESSIONS
A very small area of Great Britain is below sea-level. The largest such area is in the Fenland of East Anglia, and even here a level of 9 ft *2,7 m* below sea-level is not exceeded in the Holme Fen near Ely, Cambridgeshire. The beds of three Lake District lakes are below sea-level with the deepest being part of the bed of Windermere, Cumbria at −90 ft *−27 m.* The bed of Loch Morar, Highland, Scotland reaches 987 ft *301 m* below sea-level.

CAVES
Large or deep caves are few in Great Britain. Great Britain's deepest cave is Ogof Ffynnon Ddu (1010 ft *308 m*) in Powys, Wales. The largest system is the Easegill system with 46,3 km *28·8 miles* of surveyed passages. England's deepest cave is Giant's Hole, Oxlow Caverns, Derbyshire which descends 702 ft *214 m.* Scotland's largest cave is Great Smoo, Highland. The Republic of Ireland's deepest is Carrowmore Cavern, County Sligo being 459 ft *140 m* deep. Northern Ireland's deepest is Reyfad Pot, Fermanagh being 587 ft *179 m* deep.

UK LOCHS AND LAKES

Area (miles²)	Area (km²)	Name and Country	Max. Length (miles)	Max. Length (km)	Max. Breadth (miles)	Max. Breadth (km)	Max. Depth (ft)	Max. Depth (m)
Northern Ireland								
147·39	*381,7*	Lough Neagh, Antrim, Down, Armagh, Tyrone, Londonderry	18	*28*	11	*17*	102	*31*
40·57	*105,0*	Lower Lough Erne, Fermanagh	18	*28*	5·5	*8,8*	226	*68*
12·25	*31,7*	Upper Lough Erne, Fermanagh – Cavan	10	*16*	3·5	*5,6*	89	*27*
Scotland (Fresh-water (inland) lochs, in order of size of surface area)								
27·5	*71,2*	Loch Lomond, Strathclyde-Central	22·64	*36,4*	5	*8*	623	*189*
21·87	*56,6*	Loch Ness, Highland	22·75	*36,6*	2	*3,2*	751	*228*
14·95	*38,7*	Loch Awe, Strathclyde	25·5	*41,0*	2	*3,2*	307	*93*
11·0	*28,4*	Loch Maree, Highland	13·5	*21,7*	2	*3,2*	367	*111*
10·3	*26,6*	Loch Morar, Highland	11·5	*18,5*	1·5	*2,4*	1017	*309*
10·19	*26,3*	Loch Tay, Tayside	14·55	*23,4*	1·07	*1,7*	508	*154*
8·70	*22,5*	Loch Shin, Highland	17·35	*27,7*	1	*1,6*	162	*49*
7·56	*19,5*	Loch Shiel, Highland	17·5	*28,1*	0·9	*1,4*	420	*128*
7·34	*19,0*	Loch Rannoch, Tayside	9·75	*15,6*	1·1	*1,7*	440	*134*
7·18	*18,5*	Loch Ericht, Highland–Tayside	14·6	*23,4*	1·1	*1,7*	512	*156*
6·25	*16,1*	Loch Arkaig, Highland	12·0	*19,3*	0·9	*1,4*	359	*109*
5·9	*15,2*	Loch Lochy, Highland	9·9	*15,9*	1·25	*2,0*	531	*161*

England (Lake District lakes in order of size of surface area)
(all in Cumbria)

Area (miles²)	Area (km²)	Name	Max. Length (miles)	Max. Length (km)	Max. Breadth (yd)	Max. Breadth (km)	Max. Depth (ft)	Max. Depth (m)
5·69	*14,7*	Windermere	10·50	*16,8*	1610	*1,47*	219	*66*
3·44	*8,9*	Ullswater	7·35	*11,8*	1100	*1,0*	205	*62*
2·06	*5,3*	Bassenthwaite Water	3·83	*6,1*	1300	*1,18*	70	*21*
2·06	*5,3*	Derwentwater	2·87	*4,6*	2130	*1,94*	72	*21*
1·89	*4,8*	Coniston Water	5·41	*8,7*	870	*0,79*	184	*56*
1·12	*2,9*	Ennerdale Water	2·40	*3,8*	1000	*0,9*	148	*45*
1·12	*2,9*	Wastwater	3·00	*4,8*	880	*0,8*	258	*78*
0·97	*2,5*	Crummock Water	2·50	*4,0*	1000	*0,9*	144	*43*
0·54	*1,3*	Haweswater	2·33	*3,7*	600	*0,54*	103	*31*
0·36	*0,9*	Buttermere	1·26	*2,0*	670	*0,61*	94	*28*
Wales								
1·69	*4,3*	Bala Lake (Llyn Tegid), Gwynedd	3·8	*6,1*	850	*0,53*	125	*38*
3·18	*8,2*	Lake Vyrnwy (dammed), Powys	4·7	*7,5*	1000	*0,06*	120	*36*

Sark (Sercq) – 1274 acres *515 ha* (1·99 miles² *5,1 km²*). (Greak Sark, 1035 acres *419 ha 4,2 km²*; Little Sark 239 acres *96 ha 0,9 km²*).
Herm – 320 acres *129 ha 1,29 km²*.
Brechou (Brecqham) – 74 acres *30 ha 0,3 km²*.
Jethou – 44 acres *18 ha*.
Lihou (Libon) – 38 acres *15 ha*.
Other islands include Ortach, Burhou, the Casquets, Les Minquiers (including Maîtresse Ile) and the Ecrehou Islands (including Marmaoutier, Blanche Ile, and Maître Ile).
Population: 132 500.

Jersey – 76 050   Alderney – 2090.
Guernsey – 53 300   Sark – 600.

Administrative headquarters: Jersey – St Helier, Guernsey and dependencies – St Peter Port.
History: The islands are known to have been inhabited by Acheulian man (before the last Ice Age) and by Neanderthal man. Continuously inhabited since Iberian settlers, who used flint implements, arrived in the 2nd millennium BC. The islands were later settled by the Gauls, and after them the Romans; Christian missionaries came from Cornwall and Brittany in the 6th century AD. The Vikings began raiding the islands in the 9th century. Rollo, the Viking nobleman, established the duchy of Normandy in AD 911. His son, the second duke, William I 'Longsword' annexed the Channel Islands in 933. Jethou was ceded to England in 1091. The other islands were annexed by the crown in 1106. Normandy was conquered by France, and the King (John) was declared to have forfeited all his titles to the duchy. The islanders, however, remained loyal to John. Administration has since been under the control of his successors, while maintaining a considerable degree of home rule and, until 1689, neutrality. Before the Reformation the islands formed part of the diocese of Coutances, but were later placed under the bishops of Winchester. From the 9th

century everyone in the islands spoke Norman French, but English became dominant by the mid-19th century. The islands were occupied by Nazi Germany on 30 June–1 July 1940, and fortified for defence. They were relieved by British forces on 9 May 1945.
Administration: The islands are divided into two Bailiwicks, the States of Jersey and the States of Guernsey. The two Bailiwicks each have a Lieutenant-Governor and Commander-in-Chief, who is the personal representative of the Monarch and the channel of communication between HM Government and the Insular Governments. The Crown appoints Bailiffs, who are both Presidents of the Assembly of the States (the Legislature) and of the Royal Court. In Jersey the States consists of elected senators, *connétables* (constables) and deputies; in Guern-

sey, *conseillers* (councillors), elected by an intermediate body called the States of election, people's deputies, representatives of the *douzaines* (parish councils) and representatives of Alderney.
Highest points above sea-level:
Jersey – 453 ft *138 m*
Guernsey – 349 ft *106 m*
Alderney – 281 ft *85,5 m*
Sark – 375 ft *114 m*
Herm – 235 ft *71,5 m*
Jethou – 267 ft *81 m*
Lihou – 68 ft *21 m*
Leading Industries: Agriculture, chiefly cattle, potatoes, tomatoes, grapes, and flowers; tourism; finance and industry.
Places of Interest: The Museum of the Société Jersiaise; the church of St Peter Port.

New Towns

There are **28 New Towns built by government-appointed Development Corporations in England (21), Wales (2) and Scotland (5). When development of a New Town in England and Wales is substantially completed it is transferred to the** *Commission for the New Towns.* **Between 1862 and April 1985 this stage was reached in 11 towns (*below).**

Population (1984).
*Stevenage, Herts. (1946) – 75 700
Crawley, Sussex. (Jan. 1947) – 72 900
Hemel Hempstead, Herts. (Feb. 1947) – 77 100
*Harlow, Essex. (May 1947) – 78 000
Aycliffe, Durham. (July 1947) – 25 500
East Kilbride, Strathclyde. (Aug. 1947) – 70 500
Peterlee, Durham. (Mar. 1948) – 23 400
*Welwyn Garden City, Herts. (June 1948) – 40 500
*Hatfield, Herts. (June 1948) – 25 200
Glenrothes, Fife. (Oct. 1948) – 37 500

Basildon, Essex. (Feb. 1949) – 101 800
*Bracknell, Berks. (Oct. 1949) – 50 800
Cwmbran. Gwent. (Nov. 1949) – 45 600
*Corby, Northants. (1950) – 48 500
Cumbernauld, Strathclyde. (1956) – 49 500
*Skelmersdale, Lancashire. (1962) – 41 800
Livingston, Lothian. (1962) – 39 300
Telford, Shropshire. (1963) – 107 400
Runcorn, Cheshire. (1964) – 66 000
*Redditch, Hereford & Worcester. (1964) – 70 000
Washington, Tyne & Wear. (1964) – 55 000
Irvine, Strathclyde. (1966) – 57 150
Milton Keynes, Buckinghamshire. (1967) – 115 000
Newtown, Powys. (1967) – 10 000
*Northampton. (1968) – 160 000
Peterborough. (1968) – 125 400
Warrington, Cheshire. (1968) – 140 000
Central Lancashire New Town. (1970)
Stonehouse, Strathclyde was scheduled in 1973 but development plans were abandoned in 1976.

HIGHEST PEAKS IN THE BRITISH ISLES

Though the eighth largest island in the world, Great Britain does not possess any mountains of great height.

In only two Scottish regions, those of Grampian and Highland, does the terrain surpass a height of 4000 ft *1219 m*. In Great Britain there are seven mountains and five subsidiary points (tops) above 4000 ft *1219 m* all in Scotland, and a further 283 mountains and 271 tops between 3000 ft and

4000 ft *914–1219 m* of which only 21 (see below) are in England or Wales. South of the border, 3000 ft *914 m* is only surpassed in Gwynedd and Cumbria, Scotland possesses 54 mountains higher than Snowdon and 165 higher than the Scafell Pike. Ben Nevis was probably first climbed about 1720 and Ben Macdhui was thought to be Great Britain's highest mountain until as late as 1847.

Scotland's ten highest peaks	ft	m
1. Ben Nevis, Highland	4406	*1392*
2. Ben Macdhui, Grampian	4300	*1310*
3. Braeriach, Grampian-Highland border	4248	*1294*
North top (Ben Macdhui)	*4244*	*1293*
4. Cairn Toul, Grampian	4241	*1292*
South Plateau (Braeriach) (also c. 4160 ft 1268 m)	*4149*	*1264*
Sgor an Lochan Uaine (Cairn Toul)	*4116*	*1254*
Coire Sputan Dearg (Ben Macdhui)	*4095*	*1248*
5. Cairngorm, Grampian-Highland border	4084	*1244*
6. Aonach Beag, Highland	4060	*1237*
Coire an Lochain (Braeriach)	*4036*	*1230*
7. Càrn Mòr Dearg, Highland	4012	*1222*
8. Aonach Mòr, Highland	3999	*1218*
Carn Dearg (Ben Nevis)	*3990*	*1216*
Coire an t-Saighdeir (Cairn Toul)	*3989*	*1215*
9. Ben Lawers, Tayside	3984	*1214*
Cairn Lochan (Cairngorm)	*3983*	*1214*
10. Beinn a'Bhùird (North Top), Grampian	3924	*1196*

Wales' ten highest peaks (all in Gwynedd)	ft	m
1. Snowdon (Yr Wyddfa)	3560	*1085*
Garnedd Ugain or Crib Y Ddisg (Yr Wyddfa)	*3493*	*1065*
2. Carnedd Llewelyn	3484	*1062*
3. Carnedd Dafydd	3426	*1044*
4. Glyder Fawr	3279	*999*
5. Glyder Fâch	3262	*994*
Pen Yr Oleu-wen (Carnedd Dafydd)	*3210*	*978*
Foel Grach (Carnedd Llewelyn)	*3195*	*974*
Yr Elen (Carnedd Llewelyn)	*3151*	*960*
6. Y Garn	3104	*946*
7. Foel Fras	3091	*942*
8. Elidir Fawr	3029	*923*
Crib Goch (Yr Wyddfa)	*3023*	*921*
9. Tryfan	3010	*917*
10. Aran Fawddwy	2970	*905*

Ireland's ten highest peaks	ft	m
1. Carrauntual (or Carrauntoohil), Kerry	3414	*1041*
2. Beenkeragh, Kerry	3314	*1010*
3. Caher, Kerry	3200	*975*
4. Ridge of the Reeks (*two other tops of the same height, a third of 3141 ft 957 m, and a fourth of c. 3050 ft 930 m*), Kerry	3200	*c. 975*
5. Brandon, Kerry	3127	*953*
Knocknapeasta (Ridge of the Reeks)	*3062*	*933*
6. Lugnaquillia, Wicklow	3039	*926*
7. Galtymore, Tipperary	3018	*920*
8. Slieve Donard, County Down	*2796	*852*
9. Baurtregaum, Kerry	2796	*852*
10. Mullaghcleevaun, Wicklow	2788	*849*

* Highest peak in Northern Ireland.

England's ten highest peaks (all in Cumbria)	ft	m
1. Scafell Pike	3210	*978*
2. Sca Fell	3162	*963*
3. Helvellyn	3116	*950*
Broad Crag (Scafell Pikes)	*3054*	*930*
4. Skiddaw	3053	*930*
Lower Man (Helvellyn)	*3033*	*922*
Ill Crags (Scafell Pikes)	*c. 3025*	*c. 922*
Great End (Scafell Pikes)	*2984*	*909*
5. Bow Fell	2960	*902*
6. Great Gable	2949	*898*
7. Cross Fell	2930	*893*
8. Pillar Fell	2927	*892*
Catstye Cam (Helvellyn)	*2917*	*889*
9. Esk Pike	2903	*884*
Raise (Helvellyn)	*2889*	*880*
10. Fairfield	2863	*872*

LONGEST RIVERS IN THE UNITED KINGDOM

Specially compiled maps issued by the Ordnance Survey in the second half of the last century are still the authority for the length of the rivers of the United Kingdom. It should, however, be noted that these measurements are strictly for the course of a river bearing the one name; thus for example where the principal head stream has a different name its additional length is ignored – unless otherwise indicated.

Length (miles)	Length (km)	Names	Remotest source	Mouth	Area of basin (miles²)*	Area of Basin (km²)	Extreme Discharge (cusecs)†
220	354	Severn (for 158 miles)	Lake on E side of Plinlimmon, Powys	Bristol Channel	4409·7	11 421	23 100 (1937)
215	346	Thames (for 111 miles) – Isis (43 miles) – Churn	Severn Springs, Gloucestershire	North Sea (The Nore)	3841·6	9 948	27 900 (1894)
185	300	Trent (147) – Humber (38)	Biddulph Moor, Staffs	North Sea (as Humber)	4029·2	10 436	5 510
161	260	Aire (78) – (Yorkshire) Ouse (45) and Humber (38)	NW of North Yorks	North Sea (as Humber)	4388·4	11 366	4 580 (Aire only)
143	230	Ouse (Great or Bedford)	nr Brackley, Northamptonshire	The Wash	3313·6	8 582	11 000
135	215	Wye (or Gwy)	Plinlimmon, Powys	Into Severn 2½ miles S of Chepstow, Gwent	1615·3	4 184	32 000
117	188	Tay (93·2) – Tummel	(Tay) Beinn Oss' Tayside	North Sea	1961·6	5 080	49 000
100	161	Nene (formerly Nen)	nr Naseby, Northants	The Wash	914·5	2 369	13 500
98·5	158	Clyde (inc. Daer Water)	nr Earncraig Hill, Extreme S Strathclyde	Atlantic Ocean (measured to Port Glasgow)	1173·8	3 040	20 200
98·0	157,5	Spey	Loch Spey, Highland	North Sea	1153·5	2 988	34 200
96·5	155,3	Tweed	Tweed's Well, Borders	North Sea	1992·3	5 160	21 400
85·2	137,1	Dee (Aberdeenshire)	W of Cairn Toul, Grampian	North Sea	817·2	2 116	40 000
85	136,7	Avon (Warwickshire or Upper)	nr Naseby, Northants	Into Severn at Tewkesbury	(part of Severn Basin)		8 560
80·5	129,5	Don (Aberdeenshire)	Carn Cuilchathaidh, Grampian	North Sea	515·7	1 336	Not available
79	127	Tees	Cross Fell, Cumbria	North Sea	863·6	2 237	13 600
76	122	Bann (Upper Bann – Lough Neagh – Lower Bann)	Mountains of Mourne, SW Down	Atlantic Ocean	—	—	—
73	117,5	Tyne (34) – North Tyne (39)	Cheviots between Peel Fell and Carter Fell	North Sea	1126·4	2 917	42 000
70	112,5	Dee (Cheshire)	Bala Lake, Gwynedd	Irish Sea	818·1	2 119	16 000
69	111	Eden (Cumberland)	Pennines, SE of Kirby Stephen	Solway Firth, Irish Sea	926·7	2 400	—
65	104,5	Usk	Talsarn Mt, Powys	Bristol Channel	672·0	1 740	23 700
65	104,5	Wear	W of Wearhead, Northumberland	North Sea	462·6	1 198	6 130
65	104,5	Wharfe	7½ miles S of Hawes, North Yorks	Into York Ouse, nr Cawood	(part of Yorks Ouse Basin)		15 300
64·5	103,5	Forth	Duchray Water (13½ miles), Ben Lomond	Firth of Forth, North Sea	627·9	1 626	—

* This column gives the hydrometric area of the whole river system as per *The Surface Water Survey*.
† This column gives the highest recorded discharge in cubic feet per second (*note*: 1 cusec = 0·0283168 m³/sec 538 170 gallons per day) taken at the lowest sited gauging on the name river.

UNITED KINGDOM'S LARGEST ISLANDS

A unique check list of more than 1000 islands of Great Britain will appear in the forthcoming *Guinness Book of British Islands*.

England (12 largest)

	mile²	km²
Isle of Wight	147·09	380,99
*Sheppey	36·31	94,04
*Hayling	10·36	26,84
*Foulness	10·09	26,14
*Portsea	9·36	24,25
*Canvey	7·12	18,45
*Mersea	6·96	18,04
*Walney	5·01	12,99
*Isle of Grain	4·96	12,85
*Wallasea	4·11	10,65
St Mary's, Isles of Scilly	2·43	6,29
*Thorney	1·91	4,96

Scotland (12 largest)

	mile²	km²
Lewis with Harris	859·19	2225,30
Skye	643·28	1666,08
Mainland, Shetland	373·36	967,00
Mull	347·21	899,25
Islay	246·64	614,52
Mainland, Orkney	206·99	536,10
Arran	168·08	435,32
Jura	142·99	370,35
North Uist	135·71	351,49
South Uist	128·36	332,45
Yell, Shetland	82·69	214,16
Hoy, Orkney	52·84	136,85

Wales (12 largest)

	mile²	km²
*Anglesey (Ynys Mon)	275·60	713,80
Holy I	15·22	39,44
Skomer	1·12	2,90
Ramsey	0·99	2,58
Caldey	0·84	2,79
Bardsey	0·76	1,99
Skokholm	0·41	1,06
Flat Holm	0·13	0,33
*Llanddwyn I	0·12	0,31
Puffin Island	0·11	0,28
The Skerries	0·06	0,15
Cardigan Island	0·06	0,15

Crown Dependencies:

	mile²	km²
Isle of Man	220·72	571,66
Calf of Man	0·96	2,49

The principal Channel Isles comprise

	mile²	km²
Jersey	44·87	116,21
Guernsey	24·46	63,34
Alderney	3·07	7,94
Sark	1·99	5,15
Herm	0·50	1,29

Northern Ireland's principal offshore island is Rathlin Island (5·56 mile² *14,41 km²*)

* Bridged or causewayed to the mainland

The 58 cities of the United Kingdom

The term City as used in the United Kingdom is a title of dignity applied to 58 towns of varying local Government status by virtue of their importance as either archiepiscopal or episcopal sees or former sees, or as commercial or industrial centres. The right has been acquired in the past by (1) traditional usage – for example, the Doomsday Book describes Coventry, Exeter and Norwich as *civitas*; by (2) statute; or by (3) royal prerogative, and in more recent times solely by royal charter and letters patent – the most recent examples are Lancaster (1937), Cambridge (1951). Southampton (1964), Swansea (1969), the extension of the City of Westminster to include the former Metropolitan Boroughs of Paddington and St Marylebone in 1965 and Derby (1977).

Name of City with Geographical County or Region	First Recorded Charter	Title of Civic Head
Aberdeen, Grampian, Scotland	1179	Lord Provost
Bangor, Gwynedd, Wales	1883	Mayor
Bath, Avon	1590	Mayor
Belfast, Antrim, Northern Ireland	1613	Lord Mayor*
Birmingham, West Midlands	1838	Lord Mayor
Bradford, West Yorkshire	1847	Lord Mayor
Bristol, Avon	1188	Lord Mayor
Cambridge, Cambridgeshire	1207	Mayor
Canterbury, Kent	1448	Mayor
Cardiff, South Glamorgan, Wales	1608	Lord Mayor
Carlisle, Cumbria	1158	Mayor
Chester, Cheshire	1506	Mayor
Chichester, West Sussex	1135–54	Mayor
Coventry, West Midlands	1345	Lord Mayor
Derby, Derbyshire	1154 (present charter 1977)	Mayor
Dundee, Tayside, Scotland	c.1179	Lord Provost
Durham, Durham	1602	Mayor
Edinburgh, Lothian, Scotland	c.1124	Lord Provost
Elgin, Grampian, Scotland	1234	Lord Provost
Ely, Cambridgeshire	no charter	Chairman
Exeter, Devon	1156	Mayor
Glasgow, Strathclyde, Scotland	1690	Lord Provost*
Gloucester, Gloucestershire	1483	Mayor
Hereford, Hereford and Worcester	1189	Mayor
Kingston upon Hull, Humberside	1440	Lord Mayor
Lancaster, Lancashire	1193	Mayor
Leeds, West Yorkshire	1626	Lord Mayor
Leicester, Leicestershire	1589	Lord Mayor
Lichfield, Staffordshire	1549	Mayor
Lincoln, Lincolnshire	1154	Mayor
Liverpool, Merseyside	1207	Lord Mayor
London, Greater London	1066–87	Lord Mayor*
Londonderry, Londonderry, Northern Ireland	1604	Mayor
Manchester, Greater Manchester	1838	Lord Mayor
Newcastle upon Tyne, Tyne and Wear	1157	Lord Mayor
Norwich, Norfolk	1194	Lord Mayor
Nottingham, Nottinghamshire	1155	Lord Mayor
Oxford, Oxfordshire	1154–87	Lord Mayor
Perth, Tayside, Scotland	1210	Lord Provost
Peterborough, Cambridgeshire	1874	Mayor
Plymouth, Devon	1439	Lord Mayor
Portsmouth, Hampshire	1194	Lord Mayor
Ripon, North Yorkshire	886	Mayor
Rochester, Kent	1189	Mayor
St Albans, Hertfordshire	1553	Mayor
Salford, Greater Manchester	1835	Mayor
Salisbury, Wiltshire	1227	Mayor
Sheffield, South Yorkshire	1843	Lord Mayor
Southampton, Hampshire	1447	Mayor
Stoke-on-Trent, Staffordshire	1874 (present charter 1910)	Lord Mayor
Swansea, West Glamorgan, Wales	1169 (present charter 1969)	Mayor
Truro, Cornwall	1589	Mayor
Wakefield, West Yorkshire	1848	Mayor
Wells, Somerset	1201	Mayor
Westminster, Greater London	1256 (present charter 1965)	Lord Mayor
Winchester, Hampshire	1155	Mayor
Worcester, Hereford & Worcester	1189	Mayor
York, North Yorkshire	1396	Lord Mayor*

* Is styled 'Rt Hon'.

Cities, towns and districts in the United Kingdom with a population of over a quarter of a million

Since the recent reform of local government the definition of many towns has been difficult: a few new districts show an improved delineation of towns, but many new districts have Borough status, although the towns from which they take their nomenclature may represent but a fraction of their population. Also, some urban districts, usually with Borough status, do not bear the name of the principal town; e.g. the Borough in which West Bromwich is the main town is called Sandwell.

These figures are those officially estimated by the Registrar-General for mid 1983:

1.	London	Greater London	6 754 500
2.	Birmingham	West Midlands	1 012 900
3.	Glasgow City	Strathclyde	774 068
4.	Leeds	West Yorkshire	716 100
5.	Sheffield	South Yorkshire	542 700
6.	Liverpool	Merseyside	502 500
7.	Bradford	West Yorkshire	463 900
8.	Manchester	Greater Manchester	457 500
9.	Edinburgh City	Lothian	446 165
10.	Bristol	Avon	399 300
11.	Kirklees	West Yorkshire	377 300
12.	Wirral	Merseyside	338 600
13.	Belfast City	N. Ireland	322 600
14.	Coventry	West Midlands	315 900
15.	Wakefield	West Yorkshire	312 100
16.	Wigan	Greater Manchester	308 200
17.	Sandwell	West Midlands	307 300
18.	Dudley	West Midlands	300 900
19.	Sefton	Merseyside	299 800
20.	Sunderland	Tyne and Wear	299 400
21.	Doncaster	South Yorkshire	289 800
22.	Stockport	Greater Manchester	288 900
23.	Leicester	Leicestershire	282 300
24.	Newcastle-upon-Tyne	Tyne and Wear	281 200
25.	Cardiff	South Glamorgan	279 800
26.	Nottingham	Nottinghamshire	277 100
27.	Kingston-upon-Hull	Humberside	269 100
28.	Walsall	West Midlands	265 300
29.	Bolton	Greater Manchester	261 800
30.	Wolverhampton	West Midlands	255 400
31.	Plymouth	Devon	255 200
32.	Rotherham	South Yorkshire	253 200
33.	Stoke-on-Trent	Staffordshire	250 400

The United Kingdom counties

The United Kingdom of Great Britain and Northern Ireland's traditional 91 counties were in 1974 and 1975 reduced to 66 in Great Britain and six in Northern Ireland.

England has 46 *geographical* counties (formerly 40)
Scotland has 9 *geographical* regions and 3 island authorities (formerly 33 counties)
Wales has 8 *geographical* counties (formerly 12)

Northern Ireland has 6 *geographical counties (divided into 26 districts)*

Names of the counties: For some counties there are alternatives such as Devon and Devonshire. We however have generally only added the suffix 'shire' where there is a town of the same name as its county. This occurs in 17 cases but to these must be added four others which traditionally

(but not statutorily) use 'shire': Berkshire, Cheshire, Lancashire, and Wiltshire. 'Hampshire' was adopted in 1959 in place of the County of Southampton.

County worthies by birth: The term 'worthy' is used in its sense of famous man or woman and in some cases fame includes notoriety.

* Metropolitan Counties to be abolished in 1986.

Avon

First recorded name and derivation: 1973. From the river of that name. (Afon is Welsh for river.)
Area: 332 453 acres *134 539 ha.*
Population: 929 000.
Density: 2·78 per acre *6,87 per ha.*
Administrative HQ: Avon House, The Haymarket, Bristol.
Highest point above sea-level: Nett Wood, East Harptree – 825 ft *251 m.*

Road lengths:	miles	km
motorway and trunk	76·44	122,31
principal	248·3	399,6
other	2567·5	4132,0

Schools and colleges: Nursery 17; Primary 392; Secondary 62; Special 31; Colleges of further education 8; College of education 1; Polytechnic 1.
Places of interest: Bath (Roman remains); Bath Abbey; Clevedon Court; Bristol Cathedral; Stanton Drew (standing stones); Clifton Suspension Bridge.
County worthies by birth: John Locke (1632–1704); Thomas Chatterton (1752–70); Robert Southey (1774–1843); Samuel Plimsoll (1824–98); W G Grace (1848–1915).

Bedfordshire

First recorded use of name and derivation: 1011 (Bedanfordscir), Beda's ford, or river crossing.
Area: 305 088 acres *123 465 ha.*
Population: 512 900.
Density: 1·65 per acre *4,07 per ha.*
Administrative HQ: County Hall, Cauldwell St, Bedford.
Highest point above sea-level: Dunstable Downs 798 ft *243 m.*

Road lengths:	miles	km
motorway	16·0	25,7
trunk	70·0	112,6
principal	133·0	214,0
others	1150·0	1850,7

Schools and colleges: Nursery 12; Lower/primary 217; Middle 43; Upper/secondary 33; Sixth form college 1; Special 15; Colleges of higher education 2; Colleges of further education 2.
Places of interest: Woburn Abbey; Whipsnade Park (Zoo); Luton Hoo; Elstow Moot Hall; Dunstable Priory Church; Wrest Park; Old Warden Shuttleworth Collection.
County worthies by birth: John Bunyan (1628–88); John Howard (1726–90); Sir Joseph Paxton (1801–65); Thomas Tompion (1638–1713).

Berkshire

First recorded use of name and derivation: AD 860, wooded hill district named after Bearruc hill.
Area: 311 080 acres *125 890 ha.*
Population: 705 800.
Density: 2·16 per acre *5,6 per ha.*
Administrative HQ: Shire Hall, Shinfield Park, Reading.
Highest point above sea-level: Walbury Hill, 974 ft *296 m.*

Road lengths:	miles	km
motorway	69·1	111,3
trunk	22·9	37,0
principal	205·6	331,0
others	1639·7	2639,0

Schools and colleges: Nursery 18; Primary (various) 293; Secondary 65; Special 17; Establishments of further education 19.
Places of interest: Windsor Castle (St George's Chapel); Reading Abbey (ruin); Sandhurst; Eton College.
County worthies by birth: Edward III (1312–77); Henry VI (1421–71); Archbishop William Laud (1628–88); Sir John Herschel (1792–1871).

Borders

First recorded use of name and derivation: 1975, from the district bordering on the boundary between England and Scotland from the Middle English word *bordure*; Term 'border' used in Act of the English Parliament, 1580.
Area: 1 154 349 acres *467 158 ha.*
Population: 101 202.
Density: 0·09 per acre *0,21 per ha.*
Administrative HQ: Regional Headquarters, Newtown St Boswells.
Highest point above sea-level: Broad Law (Southern summit) 2756 ft *840 m.*
Districts: Berwickshire 18 370; Ettrick and Lauderdale 33 249; Roxburgh 35 210; Tweeddale 14 373.

Road lengths:	miles	km
trunk	113·6	182,8
principal	270·7	385,1
classified	836·5	1346,2
unclassified	640·3	1030,4

Schools and colleges: Primary 84; Secondary 9; Colleges of further education 2.
Places of interest: Dryburgh Abbey; Jedburgh Abbey; Kelso Abbey; Condingham Priory; Jedburgh Castle; Cessford Tower; Drochill Castle.
County worthies by birth: Johannes Duns Scotus (*c.* 1266–1308); James Thomson (1700–48); James Hogg (1770–1835); Mungo Park (1711–1806); Dr John Leyden (1775–1811); Sir David Brewster (1781–1868); Henry Lyte (1793–1847); James Parish Lee (1831–1904); Sir James Murray (1837–1915).

Buckinghamshire

First recorded use of name and derivation: 1016 (Buccingahamscir) the hamm (watermeadow) of Bucca's people.
Area: 465 358 acres *188 287 ha.*
Population: 608 700.
Density: 1·30 per acre *3,38 per ha.*
Administrative HQ: County Hall, Aylesbury.
Highest point above sea-level: Nr. Aston Hill 876 ft *267 m.*

Road lengths:	miles	km
motorway	35·0	56,3
trunk	38·0	61,1
principal	251·0	403,9
classified	690·0	1110,4
unclassified	1262·0	2030,9

Schools and colleges: Nursery 5; First 134; Middle 72; Combined 96; Secondary 52; Special 20; Colleges of further education 4.
Places of interest: Claydon House; Cliveden House; Hughenden Manor; Stowe House; Chequers; Hellfire Caves (West Wycombe); Chiltern Open Air Museum; Milton's Cottage; Waddesdon Manor; Ascott House.
County worthies by birth: Edmund Waller (1605–87); Sir William Herschel (1792–1871); James Brudenell, 7th Earl of Cardigan (1797–1868); Sir (George) Gilbert Scott (1811–78); William Grenfell, Baron Desborough (1855–1945); William Malcolm, Baron Hailey (1872–1969).

Cambridgeshire

First recorded use of name and derivation: 1010 (Grantabricscir), a Norman corruption of Grantabrice (bridge over River Granta).
Area: 842 433 acres *340 921 ha.*
Population: 606 000 (county) 100 700 (City of Cambridge).
Density: 1·39 per acre *0,56 per ha.*
Administrative HQ: Shire Hall, Castle Hill, Cambridge.
Highest point above sea-level: 300 yd *275 m* south of the Hall, Great Chishill, 478 ft *145 m.*

Road lengths:	miles	km
motorway	44	70,8
trunk	181	291,2
principal	280	450,6
others	2417	3889,7

Schools and colleges: Nursery and Primary 28; Secondary 49; Special 18; Colleges of further education 6.
Places of interest: Burghley House; Cambridge University; The Backs, Cambridge; Ely Cathedral; Peterborough Cathedral; Sawston Hall, near Cambridge; Peckover House and The Brinks, Wisbech; Kimbolton Castle, near Huntingdon; Imperial War Museum, Duxford; Cromwell Museum, Huntingdon; Wimpole Hall, near Cambridge; Fitzwilliam Museum, Cambridge.
County worthies by birth: Orlando Gibbons (1583–1625); Oliver Cromwell (1599–1658); Jeremy Taylor (1613–67); Octavia Hill (1838–1912); Lord Keynes (1883–1946).

Central Scotland

First recorded use of name and derivation: self-explanatory, pertaining to the centre, the word *central*, first recorded in this sense, 1647.
Area: 651 732 acres *263 747 ha.*
Population: 272 662.
Density: 0·42 per acre *1,03 per ha.*
Administrative HQ: Central Region Offices, Viewforth, Stirling.
Highest point above sea-level: Ben More, 3852 ft *1174 m.*
Districts (with population): Clackmannan 47 875; Falkirk 143 921; Stirling 80 866.

Road lengths:	miles	km
motorway	42·9	68,9
trunk	70·1	112,9
principal	207·8	334,5
classified	379·9	611,5
unclassified	564·7	908,8

Schools and colleges: Nursery 121; Primary 121; Secondary (various) 22; Colleges of further education 2.
Places of interest: Stirling Castle; Old Stirling Bridge; Cambuskenneth Abbey; Field of Bannockburn; Loch Lomond (east side); Doune Castle; Castle Campbell; Dunblane Cathedral; Wallace Monument.
County worthies by birth: George Buchanan (1506–82); Rob Roy McGregor (1671–1734); Sir George Harvey (1806–76); Marshal of the RAF Lord Tedder (1890–1967).

Cheshire

First recorded use of name and derivation: AD 980 (Legeceastersir), corrupted from the camp (*castra*) of the legions (*legiones*).
Area: 575 372 acres *232 845 ha.*
Population: 933 200.
Density: 1·62 per acre *4,01 per ha.*
Administrative HQ: County Hall, Chester.
Highest point above sea-level: Shining Tor 1834 ft *559 m.*

Road lengths:	miles	km
motorway	120·5	194,0
trunk	127·3	205,0
principal	427·5	688,4
classified	860·7	1386,0
unclassified	1851·4	2981,4

Schools and colleges: Nursery 8; Primary 482; Secondary 79; Special 26; Colleges of further education 8.
Places of interest: Roman remains within walled city of Chester; Chester Cathedral; Gawsworth Hall; Jodrell Bank; Tatton Hall.
County worthies by birth: John Bradshaw (1602–59); Emma, Lady Hamilton (*c.* 1765–1815); Rev Charles Dodgson (Lewis Carroll) (1832–98).

Cleveland

First recorded use of name and derivation: 1110, *Clivelanda*, 'the hilly district'.
Area: 144 677 acres *58 550 ha.*
Population: 565 400.
Density: 3·91 per acre *9,66 per ha.*
Administrative HQ: Municipal Buildings, Middlesbrough.
Highest point above sea-level: Hob on the Hill 1078 ft *328 m.*

Road lengths:	miles	km
trunk	34	55,5
principal	167	268,57
others	1183	1905,50

Schools and colleges: Nursery 4; Primary 218; Secondary 57; Special 22; Colleges of further education 6; Polytechnic 1.
Places of interest: Church of St Hilda (Hartlepool); Capt James Cooke Museum (Marton); Guisborough Priory; Preston Hall; Ormesby Hall.
County worthies by birth: Capt James Cook (1728–79); Thomas Sheraton (1751–1806); John Walker (1781–1859); Sir Compton Mackenzie (1823–1972).

Clwyd

First recorded use of name and derivation: 1973 from the river of that name.
Area: 599 481 acres *242 602 ha.*
Population: 395 300.
Density: 0·64 per acre *1,58 per ha.*
Administrative HQ: Shire Hall, Mold.
Highest point above sea-level: Moel Sych 2713 ft *826 m.*

Road lengths:	miles	km
trunk	119·0	191,5
principal	263·0	423,2
classified	1190·0	1915,1
unclassified	1255·0	2019,7

Schools and colleges: Nursery 5; Primary 257; Secondary 33; Special 14; Colleges of further education 6; College of education 1.
Places of interest: Denbigh Castle; Valle Crucis (Cistercian Abbey); Rhuddlan Castle (ruins); Bodrhyddan Hall; Wrexham Church; Erddig Hall; Brenig Reservoir.
County worthies by birth: William Salisbury (c. 1520–84); Sir Hugh Myddleton (1560–1631); Judge George Jeffreys (1648–1689); Sir Henry M Stanley (1841–1904).

Cornwall

First recorded use of name and derivation: 884 (Cornubia) and 981 (Cornwalum), possibly the territory of the Welsh tribe Cornovii.
Area: 876 370 acres *354 654 ha.*
Population: 408 790.
Density: 0·47 per acre *1,15 per ha.*
Administrative HQ: County Hall, Truro.
Highest point above sea-level: Brown Willy 1375 ft *419 m.*

Road lengths:	miles	km
trunk	147	236,5
principal	293	471,4
classified	1894	3047,4
unclassified	2212	3559,1

Schools and colleges: Nursery 2; Primary 257; Secondary 33; Special 4; Colleges of further education 4.
Places of interest: Chun Castle (ring-fort); Chysauster (Iron Age village); Cotehele House (Tudor house); Land's End; Lanhydrock House (17th century house); Lanyon Quoit; The Lizard; Rame Head; Restormel (moated castle); St Buryan (Bronze Age stone and 15th century church); St Michael's Mount; St Neot church (stained glass); Tintagel (ruins); Kynance Cove; Truro Cathedral.
County worthies by birth: Samuel Foote (1720–77); John Opie (1761–1807); Richard Trevithick (1771–1833); Sir Humphrey Davy (1778–1829); Richard (1804–34) and John (1807–39) Lander; Sir Arthur Quiller-Couch (1863–1944); Robert Fitzsimons (1862–1917).

Cumbria

First recorded use of name and derivation: AD 935 Cumbra land, land of the Cumbrians from the Welsh *Cymry.*
Area: 1 701 455 acres *688 555 ha.*
Population: 483 000.
Density: 0·28 per acre *0,69 per ha.*
Administrative HQ: The Courts, Carlisle.
Highest point above sea-level: Scafell Pike 3 210 ft *978 m.*

Road lengths:	miles	km
motorway	60·2	97,0
trunk	217·4	349,0
principal	399·4	643,0
others	3895·2	6268,0

Schools and colleges: Nursery 8; Primary 329; Secondary 44; Special 12; Colleges of further education 4; Other colleges 2; College of education 1.
Places of interest: Hadrian's Wall; Lake District; Grasmere (Wordsworth monuments – museum, cottage, grave); Levens Hall; Carlisle Cathedral.
County worthies by birth: John Dalton (1766–1844); William Wordsworth (1770–1850); John Peel (1776–1854); Sir William H Bragg (1862–1942); George Romney (1734–1802); Queen Catherine Parr (c. 1512–48).

Derbyshire

First recorded use of name and derivation: 1049 (Deorbyscir), village with a deer park.
Area: 650 149 acres *263 106 ha.*
Population: 911 100.
Density: 1·40 per acre *3,46 per ha.*
Administrative HQ: County Offices, Matlock.
Highest point above sea-level: Kinder Scout 2088 ft *636 m.*

Road lengths:	miles	km
motorway	21·3	34,3
trunk	159·7	257,0
principal	331·7	533,9
classified	1129·2	1817,2
unclassified	1873·0	3014,2

Schools and colleges: Nursery 14; Primary 460; Middle 2; Secondary 79; Special 28; Colleges of further education 6; College of higher education 1.
Places of interest: Peak District; Chatsworth House; Repton School; Haddon Hall; Hardwick Hall; Melbourne Hall; Dove Dale.
County worthies by birth: Samuel Richardson (1689–1761); Marquess Curzon of Kedleston (1859–1925); James Brindley (1716–72); Thomas Cook (1808–92).

Devon

First recorded use of name and derivation: AD 851 (Defenascir), territory of the Dumonii (an aboriginal Celtic tribal name adopted by the Saxons).
Area: 1 658 294 acres *671 088 ha.*
Population: 973 000.
Density: 0·59 per acre *1,45 per ha.*
Administrative HQ: County Hall, Exeter.
Highest point above sea-level: High Willhays 2038 ft *621 m.*

Road lengths:	miles	km
motorway	23·3	37,5
trunk	187·0	301,0
principal	562·0	905,0
classified	3188·0	5131,0
unclassified	4191·0	6744,0

Schools and colleges: Nursery 2; Primary 447; Secondary 85; Special 23; Establishments of further education 9; Polytechnic 1.
Places of interest: Exeter Castle (ruins); Exeter Cathedral; Devonport dockyard; Dartmoor; Buckfast Abbey; Clovelly; Powderham Castle; Dartmouth (port, castle and Royal Naval College).
County worthies by birth: St Boniface (c. 680–755); Sir John Hawkins (1532–95); Sir Francis Drake (c. 1540–96); Sir Walter Raleigh (?1552–1618); 1st Duke of Albermarle (George Monk) (1608–70); 1st Duke of Marlborough (1650–1722); Thomas Newcomen (1663–1729); Sir Joshua Reynolds (1723–92); Samuel Taylor Coleridge (1772–1834); Sir Charles Kingsley (1819–75); William Temple (1881–1944); Dame Agatha Christie (1891–1976).

Dorset

First recorded use of name and derivation: AD 940 (Dorseteschire), (suggested meaning) dwellers (*saete*) of the place of fist-play (*Dorn-gweir*).
Area: 655 790 acres *265 388,5 ha.*
Population: 609 100.
Density: 0·88 per acre *2,18 per ha.*
Administrative HQ: County Hall, Dorchester.
Highest point above sea-level: Pilsdon Pen 909 ft *277 m.*

Road lengths:	miles	km
trunk	59·0	94,9
principal	286·0	460,7
classified	979·0	1575,5
unclassified	1563·0	2514,9

Schools and colleges: Primary/First 193; Middle 26; Secondary/Upper 45; Special 14; Colleges of further/higher education 5.
Places of interest: Corfe Castle; Sherborne Abbey; Wimborne Minster; Maiden Castle; Clouds Hill (Nat. Trust); Cerne Giant; Forde Abbey; Milton Abbey; Poole Harbour; Christchurch Priory; Compton Acres Gardens.
County worthies by birth: John, Cardinal Morton (c. 1420–1500); 1st Earl of Shaftesbury (1621–83); Sir James Thornhill (1676–1734); Thomas Love Peacock (1785–1866); William Barnes (?1800–86); Thomas Hardy (1840–1928); Sir Frederick Treves (1853–1923).

Dumfries and Galloway

First recorded use of name and derivation: Dumfries c. 1183, Fort *Dum*, of the Welsh *prys* (copse). Galloway: c. 990, Gall-Gaidheal, the foreign Gael.
Area: 1 574 400 acres *637 138 ha.*
Population: 145 078.
Density: 0·09 per acre *0,23 per ha.*
Administrative HQ: Regional Headquarters, Dumfries.
Highest point above sea-level: Merrick, 2770 ft *844 m.*
Districts (with population): Annandale and Eskdale 35 338; Nithsdale 56 493; Stewartry 23 138; Wigtown 30 109.

Road lengths:	miles	km
trunk	216	347,5
principal	309	497,2
classified	1121	1803,7
unclassified	1004	1615,4

Schools and colleges: Nursery 2; Primary 119; Secondary 17; Special 18; Establishments of further education 5.
Places of Interest: Stranraer Castle; Dunskey Castle; St Ninian's Cave; Glenluce Abbey; Threave Castle (ruins); Glentrool National Park; The Ruthwell Cross; Caerlaverock Castle; Drumlanrig Castle; Burns' House and Muasoleum (Dumfries); Gretna Green; Dundrennan Abbey; Costume Museum, New Abbey.
County worthies by birth: John Dalrymple, 1st Earl of Stair (1646–95); William Paterson (1660–1719); Thomas Telford (1757–1834); Sir John Ross (1777–1856); Thomas Carlyle (1795–1881); John Paul Jones (1747–1792); Hugh MacDiarmid (1892–1978).

Durham

First recorded use of name and derivation: c. 1000 (Dunholme), the hill (old English, *dun*) crowning a holm or island.
Area: 601 939 acres *243 596 ha.*
Population: 606 800.
Density: 1·00 per acre *2,48 per ha.*
Administrative HQ: County Hall, Durham.
Highest point above sea-level: Mickle Fell 2591 ft *798 m.*

Road lengths:	miles	km
motorway	26·5	42,76
trunk	51·4	82,87
principal	236·1	380,01
classified	727·2	1170,40
unclassified	1330·6	2141,50

Schools and colleges: Nursery 5; Primary 347; Secondary 50; Special 21; Colleges of further education 4; College of education 1; agricultural college.
Places of interest: Durham Cathedral, Bowes Museum, Raby Castle.
County worthies by birth: Earl of Avon (Anthony

Eden) (1897–1977); Elizabeth Barrett Browning (1806–61).

Dyfed

First recorded use of name and derivation: The name of an ancient 5th century province.
Area: 1 424 668 acres *576 543 ha.*
Population: 330 000.
Density: 0·22 per acre *0,56 per ha.*
Administrative HQ: County Hall, Carmarthen.
Highest point above sea-level: Carmarthen Fan Foel 2500+ ft *762+ m.*

Road lengths:	miles	km
trunk	237	381,6
principal	260	418,3
classified	2410	3877,7
unclassified	1979	3184,2

Schools and colleges: Nursery 4; Primary 356; Secondary 36; Special 6; Colleges of further education 3; other colleges 3.
Places of interest: Cardigan Castle (ruins); Aberystwyth Castle (ruins); Strata Florida Abbey; Nanteos Mansion; Kidwelly Castle; Carreg-Cennen Castle, Talley Abbey; Pendine Sands, Laugharne; St David's Cathedral and Bishop's Palace; Pentre Ifan (burial chamber), near Newport; Pembroke Castle; Carew Castle; Bishop's Palace, Lamphey; Manorbier Castle; Cilgerran Castle; Pembrokeshire Coast National Park.
County worthies by birth: Griffith Jones of Llanddowror (1683–1761); Henry VII (1457–1509); Giraldus Cambrensis (c. 1147–c. 1223); John Dyer (1701–1757); Sir Lewis Morris (1833–1907); Dafydd ap Gwilym (c. 1340–1370); Sir John Rhys (1840–1915); St David (d. 601?); Bishop Asser (d. 909 or 910); Augustus John (1878–1961); Robert Recorde (1510?–58).

East Sussex

First recorded use of name and derivation: AD 722 (Suth Seaxe), the territory of the southern Saxons or suthseaxa.
Area: 443 634 acres *179 532 ha.*
Population: 673 800.
Density: 1·52 per acre *3,75 per ha.*
Administrative HQ: Pelham House, St Andrew's Lane, Lewes.
Highest point above sea-level: Ditchling Beacon 813 ft *248 m.*

Road lengths:	miles	km
trunk	62·2	100,08
principal	245·6	394,92
classified	635·44	1022,78
unclassified	1254·4	2018,5

Schools and colleges: Nursery 3; Primary 222; Secondary 37; Sixth form colleges 3; Special 20; Colleges of further education 5; Polytechnic 1.
Places of interest: Pevensey Castle; Bodiam Castle; Brighton Pavilion; Lewes Castle; Herstmonceux (Royal Observatory); Bentley Wildfowl; Battle Abbey.
County worthies by birth: John Fletcher (1579–1625); Aubrey Beardsley (1872–98).

Essex

First recorded use of name and derivation: AD 604 (East Seaxe), territory of the eastern Saxons.
Area: 907 331 acres *367 192 ha.*
Population: 1 491 700.
Density: 1·60 per acre *3,96 per ha.*
Administrative HQ: County Hall, Chelmsford.
Highest point above sea-level: In High Wood, Langley 480 ft *146 m.*

Road lengths:	miles	km
motorway	58·0	94,0
trunk	88·0	141,0
principal	401·0	645,8
classified	1465·0	2357,5
unclassified	2600·0	4183,4

Schools and colleges: Nursery 2; Primary 601; Secondary 116; Sixth form colleges 2; Special 40; Colleges of further education 10; College of education 1.

Places of interest: Waltham Abbey; Colchester Castle; Epping Forest (part of); Thaxted Church and Guildhall; Hadleigh Castle; Castle Hedingham Keep; St Osyth Priory.
County worthies by birth: Dick Turpin (1705–39); Field Marshal Lord Wavell (1883–1950).

Fife

First recorded use of name and derivation: AD c. 590, from Fibh (disputed), possibly one of the seven sons of Cruithne, British patriot.
Area: 322 560 acres *130 536 ha.*
Population: 340 341.
Density: 1·05 per acre *2,60 per ha.*
Administrative HQ: The Regional Council meets at: Fife House, North Street, Glenrothes.
Highest point above sea-level: West Lomond 1713 ft *522 m.*
Districts (with population): Dunfermline 127 484, Kirkcaldy 149 491, North East Fife 65 851.

Road lengths:	miles	km
motorway ⎫ trunk ⎬	86·9	139,9
principal	204·3	328,8
classified	339·8	546,9
unclassified	727·0	1170,0

Schools and colleges: Nursery 69; Primary 149; Secondary 20; Special 6; Establishments of further education 4.
Places of interest: St Andrew's; Dunfermline; Falkland Palace; Isle of May; Culross; Inchcolm; Dysart; East Neuk Villages; Aberdour Castle.
County worthies by birth: Sir David Lyndsay (c. 1486–1555); David, Cardinal Beaton (1494–1546); Charles I (1600–49); Alexander Selkirk (1676–1721); Adam Smith (1723–90); Robert (1728–92) and James (1730–94) Adams; Dr Thomas Chalmers (1780–1847); Sir David Wilkie (1785–1841); Sir Joseph Noel Paton (1821–1901); Andrew Carnegie (1835–1919).

Gloucestershire

First recorded use of name and derivation: AD 1016 (Gleawcestrescir), the shire around the fort (*ceaster*) at the splendid place (Old Welsh, *gloiu*).
Area: 653 010 acres *264 266 ha.*
Population: 508 400.
Density: 0·8 per acre *1,9 per ha.*
Administrative HQ: Shire Hall, Gloucester.
Highest point above sea-level: Cleeve Cloud 1083 ft *330 m.*

Road lengths:	miles	km
motorway	30·4	49,0
trunk	121·7	196,0
principal	286·2	459,0
classified	1118·5	1800,0
unclassified	1505·6	2423,0

Schools and colleges: Primary 273; Secondary 51; Special 7; Colleges of further education 4.
Places of interest: Tewkesbury Abbey; Gloucester Cathedral; Roman remains at Chedworth and Cirencester; Berkeley Castle; Sudeley Castle; Forest of Dean; The Cotswolds; Prinknash Abbey.
County worthies by birth: Edward Jenner (1749–1823); Rev. John Keble (1792–1866); Ralph Vaughan Williams (1872–1958); Gustav Theodore Holst (1874–1934).

Grampian Region

First recorded use of name and derivation: 1526 derivation uncertain, perhaps from Gaelic *greannich* 'gloomy or rugged', or from the Celtic root *grug* 'curved, rounded' and related to the old Welsh *crwb* 'a haunch or hump'.
Area: 2 150 798 acres *870 389 ha.*
Population: 494 491.
Density: 0·22 per acre *0,57 per ha.*
Administrative HQ: Woodhill House, Ashgrove Road West, Aberdeen AB9 2LU.
Highest point above sea-level: Ben Macdhui 4300 ft *1310 m.*
Districts (with population): Aberdeen (city)

214 100; Banff and Buchan 83 086; Gordon 67 344; Kincardine and Deeside 44 314; Moray 85 647.

Road lengths:	miles	km
trunk	213·0	342,7
principal	525·0	844,7
classified	1931·0	3107,0
unclassified	2062·0	3317,8

Schools and colleges: Nursery 19; Primary 278; Secondary 39; Special 20; Colleges of further education 5.
Places of interest: Balmoral Castle (near Crathie); Kildrummy Castle (ruins); Aberdeen University; Braemar (annual Highland games); Findlater Castle; Duff House (Banff); Maiden Stone; Haddo House; Leith Hall; Huntly Castle; Elgin Cathedral (ruins); Cairngorms (National Nature Reserve).
County worthies by birth: John Barbour (c. 1316–95); James Sharp (1618–79); Alexander Cruden (1701–1770); James Ferguson (1710–76); Sir James Clark (1788–1870); James Gordon Bennett (1795–1872); William Dyce (1806–64); Mary Slessor (1848–1915); James Ramsay Macdonald (1866–1937); John Charles Walsham Reith, 1st Baron (1889–1971).

Greater London*

First recorded use of name and derivation: AD 115 (*Londinium*), possibly from the Old Irish *Londo*, a wild or bold man.
Area: 390 287 acres *157 944 ha.*
Population: 6 754 500.
Density: 17·55 per acre *43,36 per ha.*
Administrative HQ: County Hall, London SE1.
Highest point above sea-level: 809 ft *246 m* 33 yd *30 m* South-east of Westerham Heights (a house) on the Kent-GLC boundary.

London Boroughs in order of population

1.	Croydon	319 300	20.	Hounslow	201 600
2.	Bromley	290 300	21.	Harrow	196 600
3.	Barnet	289 200	22.	Hackney	191 000
4.	Ealing	283 100	23.	Camden	186 400
5.	Wandsworth	271 900	24.	Islington	169 700
6.	Lambeth	262 200	25.	Sutton	167 000
7.	Enfield	259 700	26.	Merton	160 800
8.	Brent	249 800	27.	Richmond	160 000
9.	Havering	239 900		upon Thames	
10.	Lewisham	238 200	28.	Hammersmith	158 300
11.	Hillingdon	230 500	29.	Barking	149 200
12.	Redbridge	225 700	30.	Tower	149 000
13.	Newham	222 600		Hamlets	
14.	Haringey	221 400	31.	Kensington	148 600
15.	Southwark	219 700		and Chelsea	
16.	Waltham	217 800	32.	Kingston	135 500
	Forest			upon Thames	
17.	Bexley	213 200	33.	City of London	5300
18.	Westminster,	210 400		(not a London	
	City of			Borough)	
19.	Greenwich	205 400			

Road Lengths:	miles	km
motorway	44	70,81
trunk	129·2	208,0
principal	879·6	1415,6
classified	909·1	1463,1
unclassified	6046·7	9731,2

Schools and colleges: (including ILEA). Nursery 89; Primary and Middle 2177; Secondary and Middle 535; Sixth form Colleges 6; Special 231; Establishments of further education 78.
Places of interest: Buckingham Palace; Houses of Parliament; St Paul's Cathedral; Tower of London; Westminster Abbey; British Museum; National Gallery; Trafalgar Square; Port of London; Hampton Court Palace; Syon House, Isleworth; Chiswick House, W4; Osterley Park, Osterley; Harrow School; London Airport (Heathrow); Kew Gardens; Tower Bridge; Greenwich (Cutty Sark, Maritime Museum and Royal Observatory); South Kensington Museums; Westminster Cathedral; Post Office Tower.
County worthies by birth:
The following 18 Kings and Queens (see separate section for details): Mathilda, Edward I, Edward V, Henry VIII, Edward VI, Mary I, Elizabeth I, Charles II, James II, Mary II, Anne, George III, George IV, William IV, Victoria, Edward VII, George V, Elizabeth II.
The following 15 Prime Ministers (see separate

section for details): Earl of Chatham, Duke of Grafton, Lord North, William Pitt, Henry Addington, Spencer Perceval, George Canning, Viscount Goderich, Viscount Melbourne, Lord John Russell, Benjamin Disraeli, Earl of Rosebery, Earl Attlee, Harold Macmillan, Lord Home of the Hirsel.

Thomas à Becket (1118–70); Geoffrey Chaucer (c. 1340–1400); Sir Thomas More (1478–1535); Thomas Cromwell, Earl of Essex (c. 1485–1540); Edmund Spenser (1552–99); Sir Francis Walsingham (c. 1530–90); Francis Bacon (1561–1626); Ben Jonson (1572–1637); Inigo Jones (1573–1652); Earl of Stafford, Thomas Wentworth (1593–1641); John Hampden (c. 1595–1643).

Sir Thomas Browne (1605–82); John Milton (1608–74); Samuel Pepys (1633–1703); William Penn (1644–1718); Edmond Halley (1656–1742); Henry Purcell (c. 1658–95); Daniel Defoe (1660–1731); Viscount Bolingbroke (1678–1751); Alexander Pope (1688–1744); Earl of Chesterfield (1694–1773).

Thomas Gray (1716–71); Horace Walpole (1717–97); Richard Howe (1726–99); Edward Gibbon (1737–94); Charles James Fox (1749–1806); John Nash (1752–1835); Joseph Turner (1775–1851); Sir Charles Napier (1782–1853); Viscount Palmerston (1784–1865); Viscount Stratford de Redcliffe (1786–1880); George Gordon, Lord Byron (1788–1824); Michael Faraday (1791–1867); John Keats (1795–1821); Thomas Hood (1799–1855).

John Stuart Mill (1806–73); Robert Browning (1812–89); Anthony Trollope (1815–82); George F. Watts (1817–1904); John Ruskin (1819–1900); Lord Lister (1827–1912); Dante Gabriel Rossetti (1828–82); William Morris (1834–96); Sir William Gilbert (1836–1911); Algernon Charles Swinburne (1837–1909); Sir Arthur Sullivan (1842–1900); Lord Baden-Powell (1857–1941); Marquess of Reading (1860–1935); Gerard Manley Hopkins (1844–89); H G Wells (1866–1946); John Galsworthy (1867–1933); Sir Max Beerbohm (1873–1956); G K Chesterton (1874–1936); Virginia Woolf (1882–1941); Sir Charles Chaplin (1889–1978); Evelyn Waugh (1903–66).

Greater Manchester*

First recorded use of name and derivation: AD 923 *Mameceaster*, first element reduced from the Old British *Mamucion* to which was added the Old English *ceaster*, a camp.
Area: 317 960 acres *128 674 ha*.
Population: 2 597 800.
Density: 8·17 per acre *20,2 per ha*.
Administrative HQ: County Hall, Piccadilly Gardens, Manchester.
Highest point above sea-level: Featherbed Moss 1774 ft *540 m*.

Road lengths:	miles	km
motorway	105·0	169,0
trunk	26·7	43,0
principal	506·4	815,0
classified	502·6	809,0
unclassified	3733·1	6008,0

Schools and colleges: Nursery 59; Primary 1203; Middle 16; Secondary 238; Sixth form Colleges 9; Special 99; Establishments of further education 35; Polytechnic 1.
Places of interest: Castlefield (Britain's first urban heritage park); Foxdenton Hall; Haigh Hall; Peel Tower; Salford Art Gallery and Museum; Manchester: Chethams School and Library, Cathedral, Ship Canal, Bramhall Hall; Dunham Massey Hall; Heaton Hall; Lyme Hall and Park.
County worthies by birth: Samuel Crompton (1753–1827); Sir Robert Peel (1788–1850); William Harrison Ainsworth (1805–82); John Bright (1811–89); James Prescott Jowle (1818–89); Emmeline Pankhurst (1858–1928); 1st Earl Lloyd-George of Dwyfor (1863–1945); L S Lowry (1887–1976); John William Alcock (1892–1919); Gracie Fields (1898–1979); Sir William Walton (b. 1902).

Gwent

First recorded use of name and derivation: The name of an ancient province dating from 5th century.
Area: 340 102 acres *137 632 ha*.
Population: 439 900.
Density: 1·29 per acre *3,19 per ha*.
Administrative HQ: County Hall, Cwmbran.
Highest point above sea-level: Chwarel-y-Fan. 2228 ft *679 m*.

Road lengths:	miles	km
motorway	31·16	50,1
trunk	96·72	155,6
principal	131·42	211,5
classified unclassified }	1831·60	2947,0

Schools and colleges: Nursery 17; Primary 254; Secondary 35; Special 7; Colleges of further education 7.
Places of interest: Tintern Abbey; Caldicot Castle; Caerleon (Roman remains); Chepstow Castle; Wye Valley; Raglan Castle; Bit Pit; Blaenavon, Sirhowy Ironworks; Penhow Castle; Tredegar House.
County worthies by birth: Henry V (1387–1422); Bertrand Russell (1872–1970); Charles S Rolls (1877–1910); W H Davies (1877–1940); Aneurin Bevan (1897–1960); Neil Kinnock (b. 1942).

Gwynedd

First recorded use of name and derivation: The name of an ancient kingdom or principality dating from the 5th century.
Area: 955 517 acres *386 684 ha*.
Population: 232 000.
Density: 0·24 per acre *0,59 per ha*.
Administrative HQ: County Offices, Caernarfon (formerly Caernarvon).
Highest point above sea-level: Snowdon. 3560 ft *1085 m*.

Road lengths:	miles	km
trunk	208·0	334,7
principal	258·0	415,2
classified	1192·0	1918,3
unclassified	1292·0	2079,3

Schools and colleges: Primary 198; Secondary 24; Special 7; Establishments of further education 4.
Places of interest: Castles: Harlech, Beaumaris, Caernafon, Conwy (Conway), Criccieth, Dolbadarn (Llanberis), Dolwyddelan, Penrhyn, Gwydyr; Snowdonia National Park (840 sq miles); Bryn Celli Ddu; Portmeirion; Lloyd George Memorial and Museum, Llanystumdwy; Snowdon Mountain Railway; Ffestiniog Narrow Gauge Railway.
County worthies by birth: Edward II* (1284–1327); Lewis Morris (1700–65); Goronwy Owen (1723–69); Sir Hugh Owen (1804–81); T E Lawrence (1888–1935).

Hampshire

First recorded use of name and derivation: AD 755 (Hamtunscir), the shire dependent on Hamtun (*hamm*, a meadow; *tun*, a homestead).
Area: 933 276 acres *377 684 ha*.
Population: 1 491 800.
Density: 1·57 per acre *3,88 per ha*.
Administrative HQ: The Castle, Winchester.
Highest point above sea-level: Pilot Hill 937 ft *285 m*.

Road lengths:	miles	km
motorway	71·0	114,0
trunk	119·0	191,5
other	5450·0	8760,0

Schools and colleges: Primary 603; Secondary 100; Sixth form colleges 10; Special 49; Colleges of Further education 14; Polytechnic 1.
Places of interest: Winchester Cathedral; Beaulieu Palace House and Motor Museum; New Forest; Art Gallery, Southampton; Portsmouth dockyard (with HMS Victory).
County worthies by birth: Henry III (1207–72); William of Wykeham (1324–1404); Gilbert

White (1720–93); Jane Austen (1775–1817); Isambard Kingdom Brunel (1806–59); Charles Dickens (1829–70); Sir John Everett Millais (1829–96); Admiral Lord Jellicoe (1859–1935); Lord Denning (b. 1899); James Callaghan MP (b. 1912).

Hereford and Worcester

First recorded use of name and derivation: AD c. 1038 Hereford, *herepaeth*, military road, meaning ford, a river crossing and AD 889 *Uuegorna ceastre*, the fort (Latin *caester*) of the Weogoran tribe, probably named from the Wyre Forest.
Area: 970 292 acres *392 672 ha*.
Population: 640 400.
Density: 0·16 per acre *1,63 per ha*.
Administrative HQ: County Hall, Worcester.
Highest point above sea-level: In Black Mountains 2306 ft *702 m*.

Road lengths:	miles	km
motorway	56·4	90,8
trunk	110·8	178,4
principal	474·4	763,8
other	3888·9	6260,9

Schools and colleges: Primary 279; Middle 54; Secondary 45; Special 27; Sixth form colleges 2; Colleges of further education 10; College of education 1.
Places of interest: Offa's Dyke; Hereford Cathedral; Worcester Cathedral; Malvern Priory; Pershore Abbey; Dinmore Manor; Symond's Yat and Wye Valley; Brockhampton Court; Goodrich Castle; Bulmer Railway Centre; Hereford Museum of Cider; Hergest Croft Gardens; Eastnor Castle; Croft Castle; Severn Valley Railway; West Midlands Safari Park; Avoncroft Museum of Buildings; Hagley Hall; Hanbury Hall; Harvington Hall; Hartlebury Castle; County Museum; Elgar's Birthplace; National Needle Museum.
County worthies by birth: Richard Hakluyt (1553–1616); Robert Devereux, Earl of Essex (1567–1601); Samuel Butler (1612–80); David Garrick (1717–79); Sir Rowland Hill (1795–1879); Sir Edward Elgar (1857–1934); A E Housman (1859–1936); Stanley Baldwin (1867–1947).

Hertfordshire

First recorded use of name and derivation: AD 866 (Heortfordscir), the river crossing (ford) of the stags (harts).
Area: 403 800 acres *163 415 ha*.
Population: 975 400.
Density: 2·40 per acre *6,00 per ha*.
Administrative HQ: County Hall, Hertford.
Highest point above sea-level: Hastoe 802 ft *244 m*.

Road lengths:	miles	km
motorway	64·0	102,0
trunk	81·0	129,0
principal	227·0	363,0
other	2314·0	3703,0

Schools and colleges: Primary and Nursery 474; Secondary and Middle 102; Special 35; Further education establishments 13; Polytechnic 1.
Places of interest: St Albans Cathedral, Roman remains of Verulamium (now at St Albans); Hatfield House; Knebworth House; Salisbury Hall.
County worthies by birth: Nicholas Breakspear (Pope Adrian IV) (1100–59); Sir Henry Bessemer (1813–98); Henry Manning (1808–92); Queen Elizabeth, the Queen Mother (b. 1900); Third Marquess of Salisbury (1830–1903); William Cowper (1731–1800); Cecil Rhodes (1853–1902); Sir Richard Fanshawe (1608–66).

Highland Region

First recorded use of name and derivation: c. 1425 (implied in *hielandman*) from adjective *high*, noun *land*.
Area: 6 274 278 acres *2 539 122 ha*.
Population: 196 079.

Density: 0·03 per acre *0,07 per ha.*
Administrative HQ: Regional Buildings, Glenurquhart Road, Inverness. Regional Council meets at County Buildings, Dingwall.
Highest point above sea-level: Ben Nevis 4406 ft *1342 m.*
Districts (with population): Badenoch and Strathspey 10 003; Caithness 27 494; Inverness 57 526; Lochaber 19 561; Nairn 10 039; Ross and Cromarty 47 351; Skye and Lochalsh 10 963; Sutherland 13 142.

Road lengths:	miles	km
trunk	484	*778,9*
principal	1006	*1619*
classified	1522	*2450*
other	1637	*2535*

Schools and colleges: Primary 219; Secondary 29; Special 7; Establishments of further education 3.
Places of interest: St Mary's Chapel (Forse Thurso); Site of John O'Groat's House (Pentland Firth); Girnigoe Castle; Dunrobin Castle; Culloden Battlefield; Glenfinnan Monument (raising of Prince Charles Stewart's standard); Loch Ness; Eilean Donan Castle; Dunvegan Castle (Skye); Cawdor Castle (Nairn); Castle Tioram; Beauly Priory (Inverness); Clava Cairns (Inverness); Fortrose Cathedral; Glenelg Brochs; Highland Folk Museum; Strathnaver Museum.
County worthies by birth: Hugh Mackay (?1640–92); Simon Fraser, Lord Lovat (?1667–1749); Duncan Forbes (1685–1746); Flora MacDonald (1722–90); Gen Arthur St Clair (1734–1818); Sir John Sinclair (1754–1835); Sir Alexander Mackenzie (1755–1820); Hugh Miller (1802–56); Alexander Bain (1810–77); Sir Hector MacDonald (1853–1903); William Smith (1854–1914).

Humberside

First recorded use of name and derivation: AD *c.* 730 *humbri*, the British river name, side.
Area: 867 560 acres *351 099 ha.*
Population: 857 900.
Density: 0·99 per acre *2,44 per ha.*
Administrative HQ: County Hall, Beverley, N. Humberside.
Highest point above sea-level: Cot Nab 808 ft *246 m.*

Road lengths:	miles	km
motorway	70·8	*114,0*
trunk	80·2	*129,0*
principal	343·6	*553,0*
other	3031·8	*4879,0*

Schools and colleges: Nursery 9; Primary 350; Junior high 74; Comprehensive 64; Special 18; Colleges of further and higher education 8.
Places of interest: Kingston upon Hull: Trinity House, Wilberforce House, Town Docks Museum; Beverley Minster; Thornton Abbey; St Mary's Church; Museum of Army Transport; Burton Agnes Hall; Burton Constable Hall; Elsham Hall; Old Rectory, Epworth; Danes Dyke, Flamborough; Humber Bridge; Sandtoft Transport Centre; Normanby Hall, Scunthorpe; Spurn Point.
County worthies by birth: John Fisher (*c.* 1469–1535); Andrew Marvell (1621–78); John (1703–91) and Charles (1707–88) Wesley; William Wilberforce (1759–1833); Amy Johnson (1903–41); Sir Mark Sykes (1879–1919); Henry Frederick Lindley, 1st Earl of Halifax (1881–1959).

Isle of Wight

First recorded use of name and derivation: The Celtic name Ynys-yr-Wyth, from which the Romans derived Vectis predates the Roman conquest.
Area: 94 146 acres *38 100 ha.*
Population: 120 000.
Density: 1·27 per acre *3,15 per ha.*
Administrative HQ: County Hall, Newport.
Highest point above sea-level: St Boniface Down 787 ft *240 m.*

Road lengths:	miles	km
trunk	nil	*nil*
principal	76	*122,3*
classified	167	*268,7*
unclassified	218	*350,8*

Schools and colleges: Primary 47; Middle 16; Secondary 5; Special 2; College of further education 1.
Places of interest: Osborne House; Carisbrooke Castle; Brading and Newport (Roman Villas); Blackgang Chine Fantasy Theme Park.
County worthies by birth: Sir Thomas Fleming (1544–1613); Dr Thomas James (1580–1629); Robert Hooke (1635–1703); Dr Thomas Arnold (1795–1842).

Kent

First recorded use of name and derivation: *c.* 308 BC Celtic *canto*, a rim or coastal area.
Area: 922 076 acres *373 151 ha.*
Population: 1 487 100.
Density: 1·59 per acre *3,92 per ha.*
Administrative HQ: County Hall, Maidstone.
Highest point above sea-level: Betsom's Hill, Westerham 824 ft *251 m.*

Road lengths:	miles	km
motorway	86·9	*139,9*
trunk	123	*198,0*
principal	483·4	*777,8*
non-principal	4538	*7303,0*

Schools and colleges: Nursery and primary 602; Middle 10; Secondary 143; Special 39; Colleges of further and higher education 12.
Places of interest: Canterbury Cathedral; Dover Cliffs; Pilgrim's Way; North Downs; Knowle; Penshurst Place; Deal Castle; Chartwell; Rochester Castle and Cathedral; Leeds Castle.
County worthies by birth: Christopher Marlow (1564–93); Sir William Jenner (1815–98); Sir William Harvey (1578–1657); Robert Bridges (1844–1930); General James Wolfe (1727–59); William Caxton (*c.* 1422–91); Edward Richard George Heath (b. 1916); William Hazlitt (1778–1830).

Lancashire

First recorded use of name and derivation: the shire around *Lancastre* AD 1087; camp, (*castrum*) on the River Lune.
Area: 756 980 acres *306 346 ha.*
Population: 1 377 600.
Density: 1·8 per acre *4,45 per ha.*
Administrative HQ: County Hall, Preston.
Highest point above sea-level: Greygarth Hill 2058 ft *627 m.*

Road lengths:	miles	km
motorway	82·0	*132,0*
trunk	118·8	*180,0*
principal	369·0	*594,0*
classified	1109·1	*1785,0*
unclassified	2818·5	*4536,0*

Schools and colleges: Nursery 38; Primary 675; Secondary 125; Special 49; Establishments of further education 12; Polytechnic 1.
Places of interest: Blackpool Tower; Gawthorpe Hall; Lancaster Castle; Browsholme Hall.
County worthies by birth: Sir Richard Arkwright (1732–92); James Hargreaves (?1745–78); Sir Ambrose Fleming (1849–1945).

Leicestershire

First recorded use of name and derivation: 1086 (Domesday Book) Ledecestrescire. From the camp (*castra*) of the *Ligore*, dwellers on the River Legra (now the R Soar).
Area: 630 843 acres *255 293 ha.*
Population: 863 700.
Density: 1·324 per acre *3,31 per ha.*
Administrative HQ: County Hall, Glenfield, Leicester.
Highest point above sea-level: Bardon Hill 912 ft *277 m.*

Road lengths:	miles	km
motorway	51·6	*83,0*
trunk	109·4	*176,0*
principal	257·2	*414,0*
classified	1023·5	*1647,0*
unclassified	1674·8	*2695,0*

Schools and colleges: Nursery 1; Primary 347; Secondary 79; Sixth form colleges 4; Special 21; Colleges of further education 7; other colleges 5; Polytechnic 1.
Places of interest: Belvoir Castle; Ashby-de-la-Zouche Castle; Kirby Muxloe Castle; Stanford Hall; Battlefield of Bosworth; Oakham Castle; Rutland Water; Stapleford Park.
County worthies by birth: Queen Jane (1537–54); George Fox (1624–91); Thomas Babington Macaulay (1800–59); George Villiers, Duke of Buckingham (1592–1628); Hugh Latimer (?c. 1485–1555); Titus Oates (1649–1705); Francis Beaumont (1584?–1616); Robert Burton (1577–1640); Robert Hall (1764–1831); C. P. Snow (1905–1980).

Lincolnshire

First recorded use of name and derivation: 1016 (Lincolnescire), a colony (*colonia*) by the *lindum* (a widening in the river, i.e. River Witham).
Area: 1 461 560 acres *491 485 ha.*
Population: 550 750.
Density: 0·38 per acre *0,94 per ha.*
Administrative HQ: County Offices, Lincoln.
Highest point above sea-level: Normanby-le-Wold 548 ft *167 m.*

Road lengths:	miles	km
motorway	nil	*nil*
trunk	221·4	*355,10*
principal	475·2	*765,29*
classified	2204	*3549,05*
unclassified	2410·0	*3877,69*

Schools and colleges: Nursery 5; Primary 326; Secondary 70; Special 21; Establishments of further education 7.
Places of interest: Lincoln: Cathedral, Castle, Art Gallery; Tattershall Castle; Boston Stump.
County worthies by birth: Henry IV (1367–1413); John Foxe (1516–87); William Cecil, Lord Burghley (1520–98); Sir Isaac Newton (1642–1727); Sir John Franklin (1786–1847); Alfred, Lord Tennyson (1809–92); Sir Malcolm Sargent (1895–1967); Margaret Thatcher (b. 1925).

Lothian

First recorded use of name and derivation: *c.* AD 970 from personal name, possibly a Welsh derivative of Laudinus.
Area: 425 783 acres *172 308 ha.*
Population: 744 802.
Density: 1·75 per acre *4,32 per ha.*
Administrative HQ: Regional Headquarters, George IV Bridge, Edinburgh.
Highest point above sea-level: Blackhope Scar 2137 ft *651 m.*
Length of coastline: 63 miles *101 km.*
Districts (with population): East Lothian 80 838; Edinburgh (city) 440 902; Midlothian 82 362; West Lothian 140 700.

Road lengths:	miles	km
motorway	30	*48,3*
trunk	64	*103,0*
principal	272	*438,0*
classified	573	*922,0*
unclassified	1184	*1905,0*

Schools and colleges: Primary 244; Secondary 51; Special 26; Establishments of further education 5.
Places of interest: Dunbar Castle; Tantallon Castle (ruins); Muirfield Golf Centre (Gullane); Aberlady (bird sanctuary); Rosslyn chapel; Borthwick Castle; Newbattle Abbey; Dalkeith Palace; Edinburgh Castle; St Giles Cathedral; Crichton Castle; Palace of Holyrood House; Craigmillar Castle; Linlithgow Palace; Dundas Castle; The Binns (near Queensferry); Torphichen Church; Hopetoun House; The Forth Bridges.
County worthies by birth: John Knox (*c.* 1505–72); Mary, Queen of Scots (1542–87); John Napier (1550–1617); James VI of Scotland and I of England (1566–1625); David Hume (1711–76); James Boswell (1740–95); Sir Walter Scott

(1771–1832); George Gordon, 4th Earl of Aberdeen (1784–1860); James Nasmyth (1808–90); Alexander Melville Bell (1819–1905); Sir Herbert Maxwell (1845–1937); Alexander Graham Bell (1847–1922); Arthur James Balfour (1848–1930); Robert Louis Stevenson (1850–94); Sir Arthur Conan Doyle (1859–1930); Field Marshal Douglas Haig (1861–1928).

Merseyside*

First recorded use of name and derivation: AD 1002 *Maerse* from Old English *Maeres-ea* boundary river (between Mercia and Northumbria).
Area: 161 118 acres *65 202 ha*.
Population: 1 500 800.
Density: 9·39 per acre *23,20 per ha*.
Administrative HQ: Metropolitan House, Old Hall St, Liverpool.
Highest point above sea-level: Billinge Hill 588 ft *179 m*.
Length of coastline: 56 miles *93 km*.

Road lengths:	miles	km
motorway	30·26	48,71
trunk	41·44	66,70
principal	225·13	362,3
classified	301·19	484,7
unclassified	2220·44	3573,4

Schools and colleges: Nursery 9; Primary 693; Combined 10; Middle 56; Secondary 171; Special 76; Establishments of further and higher education 24; Polytechnic 1.
Places of interest: Liverpool: Roman Catholic Cathedral and Anglican Cathedral, Speke Hall, Croxteth Hall; Walker Art Gallery; Sudley Art Gallery; Merseyside: County Museum, Maritime Museum; Pilkington Glass Museum; Knowsley Safari Park; Ainsdale Nature Reserve; Albert Dock Village; Festival Gardens; Beatle City Museum.
County worthies by birth: George Stubbs (1724–1806); William Ewart Gladstone (1809–98); 1st Earl of Birkenhead (1872–1930); Edward Stanley, 14th Earl of Derby (1799–1869); Sir Thomas Beecham (1879–1961).

Mid-Glamorgan

First recorded use of name and derivation: 1242 (Gwlad Morgan) the terrain of Morgan, a 10th century Welsh Prince.
Area: 251 706 acres *101 861 ha*.
Population: 536 400.
Density: 2·13 per acre *5,26 per ha*.
Administrative HQ: County Hall, Cathays Park, Cardiff, South Glamorgan (i.e. outside the county).
Highest point above sea-level: Near Craig-y-Llyn 1919 ft *585 m*.

Road lengths:	miles	km
motorway and trunk	104·4	167,9
principal	299·1	481,5
classified	470·5	797,5
unclassified	1782·5	2869,8

Schools and colleges: Nursery 23; Primary 314; Secondary 42; Special 10; Colleges of higher and further education 7; Polytechnic 1.
Places of interest: Ewenny Priory; Caerphilly Castle; Brecon Mountain Railway; Dare Valley Country Park; Stuart Crystal Glassworks, Aberdare; Llanharan House; Ogmore Castle; Kenfig Nature Reserve; Glyncornel Environmental Centre.
County worthies by birth: Richard Price (1723–91); Dr William Price (1800–93); Joseph Parry (1841–1903); Sir Geraint Evans (b. 1922); Stuart Burrows (b. 1933).

Norfolk

First recorded use of name and derivation: AD 1043 (Norfolk), the territory of the *nor* (northern) *folk* (people) of East Anglia.
Area: 1 326 412 acres *536 781 ha*.
Population: 711 300.
Density: 0·536 per acre *1,325 per ha*.

Administrative HQ: County Hall, Martineau Lane, Norwich NR1 2DH.
Highest point above sea-level: Sandy Lane, east of Sheringham 335 ft *102 m*.

Road lengths:	miles	km
trunk	241·0	388,01
principal	660·0	1062,0
classified	3853·0	6203,0
unclassified	4528·0	7290,0

Schools and colleges: Nursery 4; Primary and middle 272; Secondary 64; Special 19; Colleges of further education 2.
Places of interest: The Broads; Sandringham House; Blickling Hall; Holkham Hall; Breckland; Scolt Head; Norwich Cathedral; The Castle, Norwich; Maddermarket Theatre, Norwich; Castle Acre; Grimes Graves; Walsingham.
County worthies by birth: Sir Edward Coke (1552–1634); 2nd Viscount Townshend (1674–1738); Sir Robert Walpole (1676–1745); Thomas Paine (1737–1809); Fanny Burney (1752–1840); 1st Viscount Nelson (1758–1805); Elizabeth Fry (1780–1845); George Borrow (1803–81); 1st Earl of Cromer (1841–1917); H Rider Haggard (1856–1925); Edith Cavell (1865–1915); George VI (1895–1952).

Northamptonshire

First recorded use of name and derivation: c. AD 1011 (Hamtunscir) [see Hampshire], the northern homestead.
Area: 585 009 acres *236 745 ha*.
Population: 538 500.
Density: 0·90 per acre *2,22 per ha*.
Administrative HQ: County Hall, Northampton.
Highest point above sea-level: Arbury Hill, 734 ft *223 m*.

Road lengths:	miles	km
motorway	28·0	45,1
trunk	129·3	208,1
principal	246·6	397,0
classified	719·4	1157,8
unclassified	1197·0	1926,5

Schools and colleges: Nursery 34; Primary 271; Middle and secondary 67; Special 21; Establishments of further education 5.
Places of interest: Earls Barton Church; Sulgrave Manor; Fotheringhay; Brixworth Church.
County worthies by birth: Richard III (1452–85); John Dryden (1631–1700); Christopher Hatton (1540–91).

Northumberland

First recorded use of name and derivation: AD 895 (Norohymbraland), the land to the north of the Humber.
Area: 1 242 817 acres *503 165 ha*.
Population: 302 000.
Density: 0·24 per acre *0,60 per ha*.
Administrative HQ: County Hall, Morpeth.
Highest point above sea-level: The Cheviot 2676 ft *815 m*.

Road lengths:	miles	km
trunk	140	224,0
primary	181·2	290,0
secondary	351·9	563,0
local district	225·6	361,0
access	2176·9	3483,0

Schools and colleges: First 146; Middle 46; Secondary 16; Special 13; Establishments of further education 2.
Places of interest: Hadrian's Wall; Lindisfarne Priory; Alnwick Castle; Warkworth Castle; Hexham Abbey; Bamburgh Castle; Norham Castle; Chillingham Castle (wild cattle); Blanchland.
County worthies by birth: William Turner (1508–68); Lancelot ('Capability') Brown (1716–83); Thomas Bewick (1753–1828); 2nd Earl Grey (1764–1845); George Stephenson (1781–1848); Grace Darling (1815–42); Robert ('Bobby') Charlton (b. 1937).

North Yorkshire

First recorded use of name and derivation: c. AD 150 Ebórakon (Ptolemy); AD 1050 *Eoferwicscir*, land possessed by Eburos.
Area: 2 053 940 acres *831 218 ha*.
Population: 684 700.
Density: 0·33 per acre *0,82 per ha*.
Administrative HQ: County Hall, Northallerton.
Highest point above sea-level: Whernside 2419 ft *737 m*.

Road lengths:	miles	km
motorway	6·5	10,4
trunk	254·0	408,7
principal	446·7	718,7
other	5015·1	8069,3

Schools and colleges: Nursery 5; Primary 416; Secondary (various) 68; Special 18; Establishments of further and higher education 11.
Places of interest: Richmond Castle; Scarborough Castle; City of York (the Minster and the Five Sisters Windows); Byland Abbey; Castle Howard; Rievaulx Abbey; Fountains Abbey; Bolton Priory (ruins); Ripon Cathedral; The Yorkshire Dales; The North York Moors; Selby Abbey.
County worthies by birth: Alcuin (735–804); Henry I (1068–1135); Miles Coverdale (1488–1568); Roger Ascham (1515–68); Guy Fawkes (1570–1606); Thomas Fairfax (1612–71); Sir George Cayley (1773–1857); John Flaxman (1755–1826); William Etty (1787–1849); William Powell Frith (1819–1909); William Stubbs (1825–1901); Sir William Harcourt (1827–1904); Frederick, Lord Leighton (1830–78); Edith Sitwell (1887–1964); Sir Herbert Read (1893–1968); Wystan Hugh Auden (1907–73).

Nottinghamshire

First recorded use of name and derivation: 1016 (Snotingahamscir), the shire around the dwelling (ham) of the followers of Snot, a Norseman.
Area: 534 650 acres *216 365 ha*.
Population: 992 200.
Density: 1·86 per acre *4,59 per ha*.
Administrative HQ: County Hall, West Bridgford, Nottingham.
Highest point above sea-level: Herrod's Hill, 652 ft *198 m*.

Road lengths:	miles	km
motorway	9·32	15,0
trunk	134·2	216,0
principal	304·4	490,0
classified	683·5	1100,0
unclassified	1710·6	2753,0

Schools and colleges: Nursery 7; Primary 428; Secondary 92; Special 29; Further education establishments 10; Polytechnic 1.
Places of interest: Southwell Cathedral; Sherwood Forest; The Dukeries; Wollaton Hall; Newstead Abbey.
County worthies by birth: Thomas Cranmer (1489–1556); Edmund Cartwright (1743–1823); Richard Bonington (1801–28); Gen William Booth (1829–1912); Samuel Butler (1835–1902); D H Lawrence (1885–1930).

Orkney

First recorded use of name and derivation: c. 308 BC as Orcas (Pytheas) from Celtic Innse Orc, islands of the Boars, the Boars being a Pictish tribe; later altered to the Norse Orkneyjar, islands of the Young Seals.
Area: 240 848 acres *97 468 ha*. Consists of 54 islands.
Population: 19 314.
Density: 0·07 per acre *0,18 per ha*.
Administrative HQ: Council Offices, Kirkwall.
Highest point above sea level: Ward Hill, Hoy 1570 ft *478 m*.

Road lengths:	miles	km
principal	100	160,9
classified	225	362,0
unclassified	252	405,5

Schools and colleges: Primary 20; Secondary 6;

Special 1; College of further education 1.
Places of interest: Noltland Castle (ruins); the prehistoric village of Skara Brae; the stone circle at Brogar; Old Man of Hoy; Kirkwall Cathedral; Scapa Flow.
County worthies by birth: John Rae (1813–93); Sir Robert Strange (1721–92).

Oxfordshire

First recorded use of name and derivation: AD 1010 (Oxnfordscir), the shire around Oxford (a river ford for oxen). The town (city) was first recorded (as Osnaforda) in AD 912.
Area: 644 418 acres *260 782 ha*.
Population: 553 800.
Density: 0·85 per acre *2,12 per ha*.
Administrative HQ: County Hall, New Road, Oxford.
Highest point above sea-level: White Horse Hill, 856 ft *260 m*.

Road lengths:	miles	km
motorway	8·5	13,6
trunk	169·0	272,0
principal	242·9	391,0
classified	950·0	1529,0
unclassified	1060·0	1706,0

Schools and colleges: Nursery 7; First/primary 246; Middle and secondary 49; Special 16; Establishments of further education 6; Polytechnic 1.
Places of interest: Oxford University; Blenheim Palace, nr Woodstock; Rollright Stones; Broughton Castle; Radcliffe Camera; Bodleian Library, Oxford; Christ Church Cathedral, Oxford; Iffley Road running track; White Horse of Uffington.
County worthies by birth: Alfred (849–99); St Edward the Confessor (c. 1004–66); Richard I (1157–99); John (1167–1216); Sir William D'Avenant (1606–68); Warren Hastings (1732–1818); Lord Randolph Churchill (1849–95); Sir Winston Churchill (1874–1965); William Morris, 1st Viscount Nuffield (1877–1963).

Powys

First recorded use of name and derivation: The name of an ancient province probably dating from c. 5th century AD.
Area: 1 254 656 acres *507 742 ha*.
Population: 111 000.
Density: 0·09 per acre *0,22 per ha*.
Administrative HQ: County Hall, Llandrindod Wells.
Highest point above sea-level: Pen-y-Fan (Cadet Arthur) 2907 ft *885 m*.

Road lengths:	miles	km
trunk	262	421,6
principal	155	249,4
classified	1607	2585,7
unclassified	1464	2355,6

Schools and colleges: Primary 119; Secondary 13; Special 3; Colleges of further education 3.
Places of interest: Brecon Beacons; Elan Valley Reservoirs; Brecon Cathedral; Powis Castle and gardens; Lake Vyrnwy; Montgomery Castle; Gregynog Hall; Dan-y-Ogof Caves.
County worthies by birth: Owain Glyndwr (c. 1354–fl 1416); George Herbert (1593–1633); Robert Owen (1771–1858).

Shetland

First recorded use of name and derivation: 1289, land of Hjalto (Old Norse personal name c.f. Scots, Sholto) or hilt-shaped land.
Area: 352 337 acres *142 586 ha*. Consists of 117 islands.
Population: 22 797.
Density: 0·06 per acre *0,16 per ha*.
Administrative HQ: Town Hall, Lerwick.
Highest point above sea-level: Ronas Hill, Mainland, 1475 ft *449 m*.

Road lengths:	miles	km
principal	140·0	225,3
classified	210·0	337,9

unclassified	200·0	*321,9*

Schools and colleges: Primary 37; Secondary 9; Further Education Centre 1.
Places of interest: Scalloway Castle; Jarlshof; Broch of Mousa; Broch of Clickimin; St Ninian's Isle; Lerwick Museum; Muckle Flugga lighthouse. Sullem Voe Terminal; Lerwick Town Hall.
County worthies by birth: Arthur Anderson (1792–1868); Sir Robert Stout (1844–1930).

Shropshire

First recorded use of name and derivation: AD 1006 *Scrobbesbyrigscir* from Scrobbesbyrig or Shrewsbury.
Area: 862 426 acres *349 019 ha*.
Population: 387 000.
Density: 0·45 per acre *1,11 per ha*.
Administrative HQ: Shirehall, Abbey Foregate, Shrewsbury.
Highest point above sea-level: Brown Clee Hill 1790 ft *545 m*.

Road lengths:	miles	km
motorway	5·0	11,6
trunk	154·0	247,8
principal	262·0	421,6
classified	1513·0	2434,4
unclassified	1467·0	2360,4

Schools and colleges: Nursery 2; Primary 223; Secondary (various) 44; Special 10; Colleges of further and higher education 5.
Places of interest: Offa's Dyke; Ludlow Castle; Stokesay Castle; Coalbrookdale and Ironbridge; The Wrekin; Hodnet Hall Gardens; Severn Valley Railway; Bridgnorth; Acton Scott Working Farm Museum; Buildwas Abbey; Wenlock Priory; Wroxeter.
County worthies by birth: Lord Clive of Plassey (1725–74); Thomas Minton (1766–1836); Charles Darwin (1809–82); Capt Matthew Webb (1848–83); Mary Webb (1881–1927).

Somerset

First recorded use of name and derivation: AD 878 *Sumorsaete*, the people who looked to Somerton (Sumortun) as the tribal capital of the 'land of summer' (Welsh *gwlad yr haf*).
Area: 852 762 acres *345 100 ha*.
Population: 434 800.
Density: 0·51 per acre *1,26 per ha*.
Administrative HQ: County Hall, Taunton.
Highest point above sea-level: Dunkery Beacon 1705 ft *519 m*.

Road lengths:	miles	km
motorway	33·0	53,1
trunk	60·0	96,6
principal	393·0	632,5
classified	1575·0	2534,7
unclassified	1861·0	2995,0

Schools and colleges: Nursery 1; Primary 239; Middle 9; Secondary 29; Special 8; Colleges of further and higher education 6.
Places of interest: Cheddar Gorge; Wookey Hole; Wells Cathedral; Exmoor National Park; Glastonbury Abbey (ruins).
County worthies by birth: St Dunstan (c. 925–88); Roger Bacon (1214–94); John Pym (1584–1643); Robert Blake (1599–1657); Henry Fielding (1707–54); Sir Henry Irving (1838–1905); John Hanning Speke (1827–64); Ernest Bevin (1881–1951).

South Glamorgan

First recorded use of name and derivation: 1242 (Gwlad Morgan) the terrain of Morgan, a 10th century Welsh Prince.
Area: 102 790 acres *41 629*.
Population: 391 600.
Density: 3·87 per acre *9,56 per ha*.
Administrative HQ: County offices, Newport Road, Cardiff.
Highest point above sea-level: Near Lisvane 866 ft *264 m*.

Road lengths:	miles	km
motorway and trunk	38·3	61,70
principal	61·2	98,60
other	968·9	1559,44

Schools and colleges: Nursery 12; Primary 162; Secondary 29; Special 17; Establishments of further and higher education 4.
Places of interest: Cardiff: Castle, National Museum of Wales, The Welsh Industrial and Maritime Museum; Llandaff Cathedral; St Fagan's Castle (Welsh Folk Museum); St Donat's Castle; Fonmon Castle; Llantwit Major.

South Yorkshire*

First recorded use of name and derivation: c. AD 150 Ebórakon (Ptolemy). 1050 (Eoferwicscir), land possessed by Eburos.
Area: 385 598 acres *156 049 ha*.
Population: 1 301 500.
Density: 3·37 per acre *8,34 per ha*.
Administrative HQ: County Hall, Barnsley.
High point above sea-level: Margery Hill, 1793 ft *546 m*.

Road lengths:	miles	km
motorway	73·3	118,0
trunk	82·6	133,0
classified	832·0	1339,0
unclassified	2120·7	3413,0

Schools and colleges: Nursery 10; Primary 571; Secondary 116; Special 43; Establishments of further education 31; Polytechnic 1.
Places of interest: Sheffield: Cathedral Church of ss Peter and Paul, Cutler's Hall, Abbeydale Industrial Hamlet, Bishops House, Kelham Island Industrial Museum, Cusworth Hall; Conisbrough Castle, Doncaster; Roche Abbey, Rotherham (ruins); Barnsley: Cannon Hall, Cawthorne Victoria Jubilee, Monk Bretton Priory, Worsborough Mill.
County worthies by birth: Thomas Osborne, Earl of Danby (1631–1712); Gordon Banks (b. 1938).

Staffordshire

First recorded use of name and derivation: 1016 (Staeffordscir), the shire around a ford by a *staeth* or landing place.
Area: 671 175 acres *271 621 ha*.
Population: 1 018 800.
Density: 1·49 per acre *3,69 per ha*.
Administrative HQ: County Buildings, Stafford.
Highest point above sea-level: Oliver Hill, near Flash, 1684 ft *513 m*.

Road lengths:	miles	km
motorway	43·04	69,30
trunk	178·04	286,70
principal 'A'	343·39	552,96
class II	209·02	336,59
class III	850·37	1369,35
unclassified	2 147·78	3458,59

Schools and colleges: Nursery 27; Primary/Infants 430; Middle 36; Secondary 83; Special 32; Sixth form college 1; Establishments of further and higher education 14; Polytechnic 1.
Places of interest: Lichfield Cathedral; Croxden Abbey; Cannock Chase; Alton Towers; Blithfield Hall; Tamworth Castle; Shugborough Hall and County Museum; Stafford Castle; Gladstone Pottery Museum.
County worthies by birth: Isaak Walton (1593–1683); Dr Samuel Johnson (1709–84); Josiah Wedgwood (1730–95); Admiral Earl of St Vincent (1735–1823); Arnold Bennett (1867–1931); Havergal Brian (1876–1972).

Strathclyde

First recorded use of name and derivation: c. AD 85 Clota, the river (per Tacitus) AD 875 Straecled Wenla cyning.
Area: 3 408 942 acres *1 379 580 ha*.
Population: 2 418 820.
Density: 0·71 per acre *1,75 per ha*.
Administrative HQ: Strathclyde House, 20 India St, Glasgow G2 4PF.

Highest point above sea-level: Bidean nam Bian 3766 ft *1147 m.*

Districts (with population): Argyll and Bute 64 290; Bearsden and Milngavie 39 180; Clydebank 51 870; Clydesdale 56 730; Cumbernauld and Kilsyth 64 620; Cumnock and Doon Valley 45 820; Cunninghame 135 980; Dumbarton 79 570; East Kilbride 82 760; Eastwood 51 940; Glasgow (city) 781 700; Hamilton 107 520; Inverclyde 100 860; Kilmarnock and Loudoun 81 560; Kyle and Carrick 112 360; Monklands 109 360; Motherwell 150 760; Renfrew 214 570; Strathkelvin 87 360.

Road lengths:	miles	km
regional motorway	28·5	46,0
trunk motorway	60·8	98,0
trunk	447·3	727,0
principal	1042·6	1678,0
non principal	2269·2	3652,0
unclassified	4180·5	6728,0

Schools and colleges: Nursery 207; Primary 924; Secondary 191; Special 57; Establishments of further education 21.

Places of interest: Fingal's Cave (Isle of Staffa); Iona; Loch Lomond: Rossdhu House; Cameron House; Dumbarton Rock and Castle; Newark Castle; Glasgow Cathedral; Bothwell Castle (ruins); Culzean Castle (National Trust for Scotland); Burns' Cottage and Museum (Alloway); Inveraray Castle; Brodick Castle; Rothesay Castle (Isle of Bute); Paisley Abbey; Kelvin grove Art Galleries and Museum, Burmell Collection, Glasgow; Livingstone Memorial, Blantyre.

County worthies by birth: Sir William Wallace (1274–1305); James Watt (1736–1819); William Murdoch (1754–1839); Robert Burns (1759–96); David Livingstone (1813–73); John Boyd Dunlop (1840–1921); James Chalmers (1841–1901); Sir Alexander Fleming (1881–1955); John Logie Baird (1888–1946).

Suffolk

First recorded use of name and derivation: AD 895 (Suthfolchi), the territory of the southern folk (of East Anglia).
Area: 938 174 acres *379 665 ha.*
Population: 608 400.
Density: 0·64 per acre *1,59 per ha.*
Administrative HQ: County Hall, Ipswich.
Highest point above sea-level: Rede, 420 ft *128 m.*

Road lengths:	miles	km
trunk	157·4	253,3
principal	293·0	471,6
classified	1539·7	2478,0
unclassified	1879·9	3025,4

Schools and colleges: Nursery 2; Primary 283; Middle 41; High 39; Special 10; Colleges of further education 5.

Places of interest: Flatford Mill and Willy Lott's Cottage; Framlingham Castle; Kyson Hill; Saxtead Green Windmill; Gainsborough's House; Lavenham (Guild Hall, Wool Hall); Long Melford Church; Newmarket; Bury St Edmunds (Abbey ruins) and Cathedral (nave); Ickworth Mansion; The Maltings, Snape.

County worthies by birth: Sir Joseph Hooker (1817–1911); John Constable (1776–1837); Cardinal Thomas Wolsey (*c.* 1475–1530); Edward Fitzgerald (1809–83); Thomas Gainsborough (1727–88); Robert Bloomfield (1766–1823); Benjamin Britten (1913–76).

Surrey

First recorded use of name and derivation: AD 722 (Suthrige), from the Old English, *suthergé* or southern district.
Area: 414 949 acres *167 928 ha.*
Population: 1 110 800.
Density: 2·68 per acre *6,61 per ha.*
Administrative HQ: County Hall, Kingston upon Thames (i.e. outside the county). The traditional county town is Guildford.
Highest point above sea-level: Lieth Hill 965 ft *294 m.*

Road lengths:	miles	km
motorway	47·0	75,6
trunk	38·0	61,1
principal	354·0	569,7
classified	604·0	972,0
unclassified	1607·0	2586,2

Schools and colleges: Nursery 6; Primary and middle 400; Secondary 70; Special 35; Establishments of further and higher education 11.

Places of interest: Guildford Cathedral; Waverley Abbey; Royal Horticultural Soc Gardens, Wisley; Box Hill, Polesden Lacey; Loseley House.

County worthies by birth: William of Ockham (d. 1349?); Thomas Malthus (1766–1834); Aldous Huxley (1894–1936); Sir Lawrence Olivier (b. 1907); John Evelyn (1620–1706); William Cobbett (1762–1835); Matthew Arnold (1822–88).

Tayside

First recorded use of name and derivation: *c.* AD 85 *Taus* or *Tanaus* (Tacitus).
Area: 1 894 080 acres *766 507 ha.*
Population: 394 895.
Density: 0·21 per acre *0,51 per ha.*
Administrative HQ: Tayside House, Dundee.
Highest point above sea-level: Ben Lawers 3984 ft *1214 m.*
Length of coastline: 76 miles *122 km.*
Districts (with population): Angus 93 163, Dundee 180 748; Perth and Kinross 120 984.

Road lengths:	miles	km
motorway	28·5	46,0
trunk	137·3	221,0
principal	433·7	698,0
classified	1163·8	1873,0
unclassified	1199·2	1930,0

Schools and colleges: Nursery 16; Primary 200; Secondary 32; Special 16; Establishments of further education 4.

Places of interest: Glamis Castle; Arbroath Abbey (ruins); Brechin Cathedral and Round Tower; Scone Palace; Bridge of Dun (near Montrose); Guthrie Castle; Blair Castle; Edzell Castle; Loch Leven Castle; Queen's View, Loch Tummel; Pitlochry Ladder and Fish Dam.

County worthies by birth: Pontius Pilate *fl* AD 36; James Chalmers (1822–53); Sir James Barrie (1860–1937); John Buchan 1st Baron Tweedsmuir (1875–1940); HRH The Princess Margaret, Countess of Snowdon (b. 1930).

Tyne and Wear*

First recorded use of name and derivation: *c.* AD 150 Tina (river) (Ptolemy) and *c.* AD 720 Wirus (river) (Bede).
Area: 133 449 acres *54 006 ha.*
Population: 1 145 300.
Density: 8·58 per acre *21,2 per ha.*
Administrative HQ: Sandyford House, Newcastle-upon-Tyne.
Highest point above sea-level: Leadgate near Chopwell 851 ft *259 m.*

Road lengths:	miles	km
motorway	5·5	9,0
trunk	39·1	63,0
principal	198·8	320,0
classified	283·3	456,0
unclassified	1982·1	3190,0

Schools and colleges: (administered at District Council level) Nursery 35; Primary 516; Middle 33; Secondary 88; Special 65; Colleges of further education 7; Polytechnics 2.

Places of interest: Church of St Andrew's Byker; Monkwearmouth (ruins); Tynemouth Castle and Priory; Washington Old Hall Plummer Tower; South Shields Roman Fort.

County worthies by birth: The Venerable Bede (673–735); Admiral (1st) Lord Collingwood (1750–1810); Sir Joseph Swann (1828–1914); Owen Brannigan (1908–73); Cardinal Basil Hume, Archbishop of Westminster (b. 1923).

Warwickshire

First recorded use of name and derivation: the name was recorded in 1001 and means dwellings by the weir.
Area: 489 405 acres *198 055 ha.*
Population: 477 800.
Density: 0·98 per acre *2,41 per ha.*
Administrative HQ: Shire Hall, Warwick.
Highest point above sea-level: Ilmington Downs 854 ft *260 m.*

Road lengths:	miles	km
motorway	29·1	46,91
trunk	145·7	234,5
principal	186·9	300,8
classified	730·7	1175,8
unclassified	1105·0	1778,1

Schools and colleges: Nursery 9; Primary 252; Secondary 41; Special 17; Establishments of further and higher education 5.

Places of interest: Warwick Castle; Kenilworth Castle; Stratford-upon-Avon (Shakespeare's birthplace); Compton Wynyates; Charlecote; Coughton Court; Ragley Hall; Arbury Hall.

County worthies by birth: William Shakespeare (1564–1616); Joseph Arch (1826–1919); Walter Savage Landor (1775–1864); Marion Evans (George Eliot) (1819–80); Rupert Brooke (1887–1915); Michael Drayton (1563–1631); Sir William Dugdale (1605–1686); Sir Fulke Greville, 1st Baron Brooke (1554–1628); Francis Willughby (1635–1672).

West Glamorgan

First recorded use of name and derivation: 1242 (Gwlad Morgan) the terrain of Morgan, a 10th century Welsh Prince.
Area: 202 228 acres *81 839 ha.*
Population: 366 600.
Density: 1·81 per acre *4,48 per ha.*
Administrative HQ: County Hall, Swansea.
Highest point above sea-level: Cefnffordd 1969 ft *600 m.*

Road lengths:	miles	km
motorway	23·0	37,0
trunk	29·0	46,7
principal	126·0	202,8
classified	199·0	320,2
unclassified	676·0	1088,0

Schools and colleges: Nursery 2; Primary 176; Secondary 26; Special 7; Colleges of further education 3; Other college 1; Institute of higher education.

Places of interest: Neath Abbey (ruins); Penrice Castle; Gower Peninsula; Margam Park; Aberdulais Falls and Basin; Afan Argoed Forest Park; Cefn Coed Coal and Steam Museum.

County worthies by birth: Dylan Thomas (1914–53); Wynford Vaughan Thomas (b. 1908); Daniel Jones (b. 1912); Harry Secombe CBE (b. 1921); Richard Burton (1925–1984).

West Midlands*

First recorded use of name and derivation: 1555 mydlande, mid lands (applied to the middle counties of England).
Area: 222 250 acres *89 941 ha.*
Population: 2 657 600.
Density: 12·0 per acre *29,5 per ha.*
Administrative HQ: County Hall, Lancaster Circus, Birmingham.
Highest point above sea-level: Turner's Hill 876 ft *267 m.*

Road lengths:	miles	km
motorway	43·5	70,0
trunk	42·6	68,5
principal	370·9	596,9
classified	455·5	732,8
unclassified	3135·4	5045,6

Schools and colleges: Nursery 19; Primary 962; Middle 34; Secondary 236; Special 97; Establishments of further and higher education 28; Polytechnics 3.

Places of interest: Dudley Castle; Birmingham: Aston Hall, City Museum and Art Gallery,

Museum of Science and Industry; Coventry Cathedral.

County worthies by birth: Sir Edward Burne-Jones (1833–98); George Cadbury (1839–1922); Sir Henry Newbolt (1862–1938); Neville Chamberlain (1869–1940); Sir Frank Whittle (b. 1907).

West Sussex

First recorded use of name and derivation: AD 722 (*Suth Seaxe*), the territory of the southern Saxons or *suthseaxa*.
Area: 491 589 acres *198 939 ha*.
Population: 681 600.
Density: 1·38 per acre *3,41 per ha*.
Administrative HQ: County Hall, West St, Chichester.
Highest point above sea-level: Blackdown Hill 919 ft *280 m*.

Road lengths:	miles	km
motorway	4·3	6,9
trunk	54·6	87,9
principal	299·3	481,7
classified	697·4	1122,3
unclassified	1164·3	1873,7

Schools and colleges: Nursery 4; Primary 237; Middle 17; Secondary 44; Sixth form colleges 3; Special 14; Colleges of further and higher education 6.
Places of interest: Chichester Cathedral; Arundel Castle; Goodwood House; Petworth House; Uppark; Fishbourne Roman Palace.
County worthies by birth: John Selden (1584–1654); William Collins (1721–59); Percy Bysshe Shelley (1792–1822); Richard Cobden (1804–65).

West Yorkshire*

First recorded use of name and derivation: c. AD 150 Ebórakon (Ptolemy), 1050 (Eoferwicscir), land possessed by Eburos.
Area: 503 867 acres *203 912 ha*.
Population: 2 063 000.
Density: 4·04 per acre *9,99 per ha*.
Administrative HQ: County Hall, Wakefield.
Highest point above sea-level: Black Hill 1908 ft *581 m*.
Districts (with population): Bradford 464 700; Calderdale 191 800; Kirklees 377 100; Leeds 716 100; Wakefield 313 400.

Road lengths:	miles	km
motorway	39·1	63,0
trunk	62·1	100,0

	principal	310·0	499,0
	classified	377·7	608,0
	unclassified	2206·4	3551,0

Schools and colleges: Nursery 79; Primary and middle 940; Secondary (various) 160; Sixth form colleges 3; Special 80; Establishments of further and higher education 33; Polytechnics 2.
Places of interest: Bronte Museum (Haworth); Kirkstall Abbey; Ilkley Moor; Temple Newsam House; Harewood House; Wakefield Cathedral.
County worthies by birth: Sir Martin Frobisher (*c.* 1535–94); Thomas Fairfax (1612–71); Thomas Chippendale (1718–79); Joseph Priestley (1733–1804); Charlotte Bronte (1816–55); Anne Bronte (1820–49); Emily Bronte (1818–48); Henry Herbert, Lord Asquith (1852–1928); Frederick Delius (1862–1934); Barbara Hepworth (1903–75); John Boynton Priestley (1894–1984); Wilfred Rhodes (1877–1973); James Harold Wilson (b. 1916).

Western Isles

First recorded use of name and derivation: Possibly 14th century (during the reign of David II the style 'Lord of the Isles' appears, whereas in the Treaty of Perth, 1266, the Norse name *sudreys* is used).
Area: 716 800 acres *290 079 ha*.
Population: 31 456.
Density: 0·04 per acre *0,11 per ha*.
Administrative HQ: Council Offices, Stornoway, Isle of Lewis.
Highest point above sea-level: Clisham, Harris 2622 ft *799 m*.
Main Islands: The largest islands in the Long Island archipelago.

	miles²	km²
Lewis with Harris	859·19	2225
North Uist	135·71	351
South Uist	128·36	332

Road lengths:	miles	km
principal	197	316,9
classified	229	368,5
unclassified	271	436

Schools and colleges: Nursery 3; Primary 45; Secondary 16; College of further education 1.
Places of interest: Kisimul Castle (Isle of Barra); Kilpheder (South Uist); Callanish – stone circle and cairn (Isle of Lewis); St Kilda, Rockall; St Clement's Church, Rodel (Isle of Harris).
Islands worthies by birth: Flora Macdonald (1722–90).

Wiltshire

First recorded use of name and derivation: AD 878 (Wiltunscire), the shire around *Wiltun* (tun, town) on the River Wylye.
Area: 860 099 acres *348 070 ha*.
Population: 522 800.
Density: 0·61 per acre *1,50 per ha*.
Administrative HQ: County Hall, Trowbridge.
Highest point above sea-level: Milk Hill and Tan Hill (or St Anne's Hill) 964 ft *293 m*.

Road lengths:	miles	km
motorway	33·0	53,1
trunk	84·0	135,2
principal	402·0	647,0
classified	1218·0	1960,2
unclassified	1187·0	1910,3

Schools and colleges: Primary 302; Middle and Secondary 51; Special 13; Establishments of further education 7.
Places of interest: Salisbury Cathedral; Longleat; Stonehenge; Avebury Stone Circle; Wilton House; Stourhead; Windmill Hill.
County worthies by birth: 1st Duke of Somerset (*c.* 1500–52); Edward (Hyde) 1st Earl of Clarendon (1609–74); Sir Christopher Wren (1632–1723); Joseph Addison (1672–1719); William H F Talbot (1800–77); Sir Isaac Pitman (1813–97); Thomas Hobbes (1588–1679).

England's Regises

The use of the suffix 'Regis' – meaning 'of the King' – is used in the names of 12 places in England. In most cases the term has arisen from local usage to distinguish a Royal Manor, rather than from any exercise of prerogative by the sovereign.

	Earliest Mention
Bere Regis, Dorset	1244
Bognor Regis, West Sussex (1929)†	680
Grafton Regis, Northamptonshire	1204
Houghton Regis, Bedfordshire	1353
Kingsbury Regis, Somerset	1200
Letcombe Regis, Berkshire	1136
Lyme Regis, Dorset	1285
Lynn Regis, Norfolk (1537)†	1085
Melcombe Regis, Dorset	1280
Milton Regis, Kent	
Rowley Regis, West Midlands (1933)†	1173
Wyke Regis, Dorset	998

† By royal prerogative.

Northern Ireland

Area: 3 489 150 acres *1 412 010 ha*. (5452 miles² *14 120 km²*).
Population: 1 572 700 (mid-1983).
Density: 0·44 per acre *1,09 per ha*.
Administrative HQ: Belfast.
Districts: The province is now divided into 26 districts, whose councils have similar functions to English district councils. The six geographical counties no longer exist as administrative units. Northern Ireland is divided into nine areas: five education and library areas plus four health and social services areas (other functions such as police, planning, roads, water, housing, fire services, etc., are run centrally from Stormont. The area boards are not directly elected: about a third of their members are district councillors while the rest are persons appointed by the appropriate United Kingdom minister. The six traditional geographic counties of Northern Ireland in order of size are:

COUNTY TYRONE
First recorded use of name and derivation: From Tir Eoghan, land of Eoghan (Owen, son of Niall).
Area: 806 918 acres *326 548 ha*.

Former capital: Omagh on the river Strule.
Highest point: Sawel (in Sperrin Mts) 2240 ft *683 m*.
Coastline length: nil.

COUNTY ANTRIM
First recorded use of name and derivation: From the 5th century monastery of Aentrebh.
Area: 718 257 acres *290 668 ha*.
Former capital: City of Belfast on the river Lagan.
Highest point: Trostan 1817 ft *544 m*.
Coastline length: 90 miles *145 km*.

COUNTY DOWN
First recorded use of name and derivation: From Dun, Irish gaelic for fort (i.e. St Patrick's fort).
Area: 609 439 acres *246 631 ha*.
Former capital: Downpatrick on the river Quoile.
Highest point: Slieve Donard 2796 ft *852 m*.
Coastline length: 125 miles *201 km*.

COUNTY LONDONDERRY
First recorded use of name and derivation: From the charter granted by James I in 1613 to the City of London (England) livery companies. 'Derry' is a corruption of the celtic *doire*, an oak grove c. AD 500.
Area: 514 376 acres *208 161 ha*.
Former capital: City of Londonderry on the river Foyle.
Highest point: Sawel 2240 ft *683 m*.
Coastline length: 18 miles *29 km*.

COUNTY FERMANAGH
First recorded use of name and derivation: From Fir Mhanach, territory of the men of Managh.
Area: 457 376 acres *185 094 ha*.
Former capital: Enniskillen.
Highest point: Cuilcagh 2188 ft *667 m*.
Coastline length: nil.

COUNTY ARMAGH
First recorded use of name and derivation: From Queen Macha c. 3rd century BC.
Area: 312 767 acres *126 572 ha*.
Former capital: Armagh on the Blackwater tributary Callan.
Highest point: Slieve Gullion 1894 ft *577 m*.
Coastline length: 2 miles *3,2 km*.

Education and library areas: BELFAST AREA (HQ Belfast): Nursery 27; Primary 108; Secondary Intermediate 33; Grammar 18; Special 10; Colleges of further education 3. NORTH-EASTERN AREA (HQ Ballymena): Nursery 17; Primary 248; Secondary Intermediate 42; Grammar 18; Special 5; Colleges of further education 8. SOUTH-EASTERN AREA (HQ Belfast): Nursery 16; Primary 168; Secondary Intermediate 33; Grammar 11; Special 5; Colleges of further education 5. SOUTHERN AREA (HQ Armagh): Nursery 14; Primary 284; Secondary Intermediate 39; Grammar 18; Special 1; Colleges of further education 6. WESTERN AREA (HQ Omagh): Nursery 10; Primary 209; Secondary Intermediate 36; Grammar 13; Special 4; Colleges of further education 4.

Health and social services: EASTERN AREA (HQ Belfast); NORTHERN AREA (HQ Ballymena); WESTERN AREA (HQ Londonderry); SOUTHERN AREA (HQ Craigavon).

Highest point above sea-level: Slieve Donard (in Newry and Mourne District) 2796 ft *852 m*.

Places of interest: Lakes of Fermanagh; Mourne Mountains; Armagh Cathedrals; Florence Court; Antrim Coast Road; Giant's Causeway; Mount Stewart; Carrickfergus Castle; Sperrin Mountains; Downpatrick Cathedral.

Worthies by birth: St Malachy (*c.* 1095–1148); Sir Hans Sloane (1660–1753); Robert Stewart, Lord Castlereagh (1769–1822); Thomas Andrews (1813–85); Thomas Mayne Reid (1818–83); John Nicholson (1822–57); Lord Kelvin (1824–1907); Lord Alexander of Tunis (1891–1969).

NORTHERN IRELAND: THE 26 DISTRICTS

District	HQ	Pop.	Area acres	Area hectares
Antrim	Antrim	45 500	139 001	56 289
Ards	Newtownards	59 700	89 277	36 949
Armagh	Armagh	49 900	166 691	67 249
Ballymena	Ballymena	55 400	157 306	63 837
Ballymoney	Ballymoney	23 400	103 246	41 871
Banbridge	Banbridge	30 600	110 029	44 423
Belfast	Belfast	322 600	32 397	13 111
Carrickfergus	Carrickfergus	28 400	19 017	8 687
Castlereagh	in Belfast, i.e. out of the district	59 800	20 868	8 479
Coleraine	Coleraine	47 400	119 708	48 218
Cookstown	Cookstown	29 300	153 973	62 311
Craigavon	Lurgan and Portadown	73 400	95 924	38 164
Down	Downpatrick	54 000	159 612	64 528
Dungannon	Dungannon	45 700	192 731	77 906
Fermanagh	Enniskillen	51 600	463 505	187 557
Larne	Larne	29 300	83 982	33 821
Limavady	Limavady	28 000	145 621	58 662
Lisburn	Lisburn	87 900	110 369	44 376
Londonderry	Londonderry	96 100	92 498	37 433
Magherafelt	Magherafelt	34 200	138 902	56 213
Moyle	Ballycastle	14 500	122 090	49 543
Newry and Mourne	Newry	83 400	220 637	89 289
Newtownabbey	Newtownabbey	71 900	37 468	15 163
North Down	Bangor	66 800	18 174	7 355
Omagh	Omagh	46 900	277 973	112 874
Strabane	Strabane	37 000	212 884	86 642
Total		1 572 700		1 412 026

Note: The name Ulster is sometimes (but mistakenly) used as an alternative for the Province of Northern Ireland. Ulster is in fact one of the four ancient provinces of the island of Ireland [viz Connaught (5 counties), Leinster (12 counties), Munster (6 counties) and Ulster (9 counties)] and comprised the six counties of Northern Ireland and the three of the 26 counties (viz Cavan, Donegal and Monaghan) in the Republic of Ireland.

Britain's pre-history

British history starts with the earliest written references dating from *c.* 525 BC by Himilco of the Tunisian city of Carthage. Events prior to that belong to pre-history – a term invented by Daniel Wilson in 1851.

Pre-historic events are subject to continuous reassessment as new dating methods are advanced. Most notable among these has been radiocarbon dating invented by Dr Willard F Libby (US) in 1949. This is based upon the decay rate of the radioactive carbon isotope C14, whose half-life is 5730 years (formerly thought to be 5568 years). Other modern methods include dendrochronology (calibration by study of tree-rings), developed by Professor C W Ferguson since 1969 and thermoluminescence, pollen analysis and amino-acid testing.

BC
c. 400 000
Disputed evidence for *Homo erectus*, predecessor of *H. sapiens* in paleolithic hand-axes found 1975 near Westbury-sub-Mendip, Somerset.

? 285 000–240 000
Anglian glaciation possibly contemporary with the alpine Mindel glaciation with ice sheets reaching the Thames valley. Human occupation (known as pre-Hoxnian) may have occurred during a warmer interstadial phase of this glaciation, e.g. course hand-axe culture at Fordwich, Kent (published 1968) and Kents Cavern, near Torquay, Devon (reassessed 1971).

? 240 000–130 000
Hoxnian interglacial (so named after Hoxne site, Suffolk, disc. 1797). Clactonian flake assemblages followed by Acheulian hand-axe industry, which latter yielded earliest British human remains at Swanscombe, Kent found by Marston in 1935–6. Sea level 30–35 m *98–114 ft* above present datum.

130 000–105 000
Wolstonian glaciation, probably contemporary with the alpine Riss glaciation.

105 000–75 000
Ipswichian interglacial – sea level 8 m *26 ft* above present datum.

75 000–19 000
Last or Devensian glaciation, contemporary with the alpine Würm glaciation, reaching to the latitude of York. Britain probably discontinuously unpopulated but populated during the warmer Chelford interstadial of 59 000 BC and during a further interstadial of 40 000 to 36 000 BC.

26 700 ± 450
Earliest upper palaeolithic radiocarbon dating from Kents Cavern.

18 000–14 000
Maximum extension of ice-sheets. Sea-level fall of 100–150 m *328–492 ft*.

10 500–8000
Mesolithic Creswellian period and the close of the late Upper Palaeolithic era.

c. 9050
Irish Sea land-bridge breached.

8400
Start of the present Flandrian post-glacial period. Earliest (Maglemosian) to latest (Lussa, Jura) datings of Mesolithic finds. Mesolithic man may have had herds by 4300 BC.

c. 6850
The North Sea land bridge between East Yorkshire and Holland breached by rising sea-level.

c. 6450
The English Channel attained its current width under the impact of the Flandrian transgression.

6100
Earliest dated habitation in Scotland, microlithic industry at Morton in Fife.

4580
Earliest dated habitation in Ireland – neolithic site at Ballynagilly, Tyrone two centuries earlier than England's earliest neolithic sites at Broome Heath, Norfolk; Findon, West Sussex and Lambourne, Berkshire.

4210–3990
Earliest dated British farming site at Hembury, Devon (first excavated 1934–5).

3795
Earliest dated pottery at Ballynagilly (see above).

3650–3400
Avebury Stone Circle building, Wiltshire.

2930–2560
Giant Silbury Hill round barrow, Wiltshire.

2760
Earliest Bronze Age dating with Beaker pottery from Ballynagilly (see above), four centuries before earliest English datings at Chippenham, Cambridge and Mildenhall, Suffolk.

2285–2075
Phase I at Stonehenge (ditch construction).

1260
Earliest dated hill-fort, Ivinghoe, Buckinghamshire.

c. 750
Introduction of iron into Britain from Hallstatt by the Celts. Hill-forts proliferate.

c. 308
First circumnavigation of Great Britain by Pytheas the Greek sea-captain from Massilia (Marseille).

c. **125**
Introduction of Gallo-Belgic gold coinage via
Kent from the Beauvais region of France.

c. **90**
Earliest British coinage – Westerham gold
staters so named after the hoard find in Kent in
1927.

55 (26 Aug.)
Julius Caesar's exploratory expedition with 7th
and 10th legions and 98 ships from Boulogne
and Ambleteuse.

54 (18 or 21 July)
Second Julian invasion with five legions and
2000 cavalry.

AD
43
Claudian invasion and the start of the Roman
Occupation.

Roman Era, 55 BC–AD 410

Caesar arrived off Dover from Boulogne with 98
transports and two legions in the early hours of
26 Aug. 55 BC. He landed against beach opposition between Deal and Walmer. Repeated
skirmishing prevented the reconnaisance being
a success and Caesar withdrew. He returned in
54 BC (variously on 18 or 21 July) with five
legions and 800 vessels, and encamped on the
Kentish shore and crossed the Thames near
Brentford. He was much harried by the British
leader, Cassivellaunus, based on the old Belgic
capital of St Albans (*Verulamium*). The occupation was not sustained.

It was nearly a century later in AD 43 when the
third Roman landing was made with some
20 000 men in three waves under the command
of Plautius. This invasion is referred to as the
Claudian Invasion, after the Roman emperor of
that time. The British leader, Cunobelinus, was
aged but resistance remained bitter. Roman
cruelties against the king of the Iceni tribe and
his family in East Anglia fired a native 'death or
liberty' revolt under his widow, Queen Bodicca
(Boadicea) in AD 61. Colchester (*Camulodunum*),
London (*Londinium*) and St Albans were in turn
sacked. The total death roll was put at 70 000 by
Tacitus. Boadicea's horde of some 80 000 was
met by Suetonius' 14th and 20th Legions of
10 000 men on a battlefield perhaps near Hamp-
stead Heath, North London. For the loss of only
about 400 of the fully-armed Romans, 70 000
Britons were claimed to have been killed.
Subjugation, however, was not achieved until
AD 83, when Agricola, the Roman Governor,
won the Battle of Mons Graupius, suggested by
some to be the Pass of Killiecrankie, Tayside.

For nearly 300 years the Roman régime
brought law, order, peace, food, and even
unknown warmth and cleanliness for the few
who aspired to villas. The legions recruited
locally to maintain 40 000 troops, garrisoned at
Chester, Caerleon-on-Usk, York, and Hadrian's
Wall. Hadrian arrived in Britain in 122 after the
annihilation of the 9th Legion by the Picts. The
74½-mile-long *120 km* wall across the Tyne-
Solway isthmus was built between AD 122 and
129. The 37-mile-long *59,5 km* Forth-Clyde or
Antonine Wall was built *c.*150, but was abandoned within 40 years. Emperor Severus re-
established military order in the period 208–11,
but by the time of Carausius, who ruled in 287–
93, raids by the Saxons (*Seax*, short, one-handed
sword) from the Schleswig-Holstein area were
becoming increasingly troublesome. Demands
were made by the Saxons, Scots and Picts that
Emperor Valentinian send his general, Theodosius, in 367 to restore order in the Province. In
400 Theodosius in turn sent his general, Stilicho,
to deliver the Province from the ever-increasing
pressure of the barbarians, but by 402 he was
forced to recall the Roman garrison to help resist
the incursions in Northern Italy of the Visigoths
under Alaric. In 405 there was mutiny in the
remaining garrison in Britain, who elected
Gratianus, a Briton, as rival emperor. In 410
Emperor Honorius told the Britons from Rome
that they must 'defend themselves' against the
Saxons, Picts, and Scots.

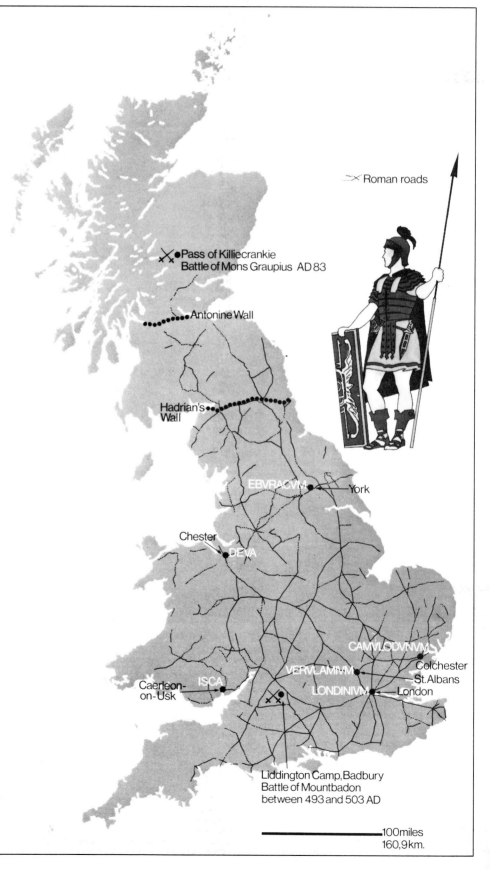

Roman roads

Pass of Killiecrankie
Battle of Mons Graupius AD 83

Antonine Wall

Hadrian's
Wall

EBVRACVM — York

Chester
DEVA

CAMVLODVNVM
Colchester
St. Albans
VERVLAMIVM
LONDINIVM — London

Caerleon-
on-Usk
ISCA

Liddington Camp, Badbury
Battle of Mountbadon
between 493 and 503 AD

100 miles
160,9 km.

AD 410–1066

British rulers between the end of the Roman occupation (AD 410) and the Norman conquest (1066)

By 449 a Jutish Kingdom had been set up in Kent by Hengist and Horsa. The 5th and 6th centuries were a period of utter confusion and misery with conflict between English and the remaining Britons, whose last champion was reputedly King Arthur. Some time between 493 and 503 Arthur fought the Battle of Mountbadon against the cruel Saxon invaders on an uncertain site, now ascribed to Liddington Camp, Badbury, near Swindon, Wiltshire.

England (excluding Cumbria) did not again become a unified state before AD 954. Some earlier kings exercised direct rule over all England for intermittent periods during their reigns. Edward the Elder (899–924 or 925), son of Alfred (871–99) the most famous of the Kings of the West Saxons, had suzerainty over the whole of England though he did not directly rule the Danish kingdom of York, which was not finally extinguished until 954.

The following nine kingdoms existed in England before it became a unified kingdom. All existed contemporaneously during the first half of the 7th century (c. AD 604 to 654), but became absorbed in each other until the Kings of Wessex established overall authority.

1. Kings of Kent	c. 455 to 825, conquered by West Saxons.
2. Kings of the South Saxons	477–c. 786, absorbed by Wessex.
3. Kings of West Saxons	519–954, established authority over all England.
4. Kings of Bernicia	547–670, annexed by Northumbria.
5. Kings of Northumbria	c. 588–?878, reduced by the Danish Kingdom of York.
6. Kings of Mercia	c. 595–ante 883, first acknowledged overlordship of West Saxons 829.
7. Kings of Deira	599 or 560 to 654, annexed by Bernicia.
8. Kings of the East Angles	c. 600–870, conquest by Danes.
9. Kings of the East Saxons	ante 604–825, submitted to West Saxons.
Danish Kingdom of York	875 or 876–954, expulsion by Edred, the King of West Saxons.

The West Saxon King Egbert (802–39), grandfather of King Alfred, is often quoted as the first King of All England from AD 829, but in fact he never reduced the Kingdom of Northumbria ruled by Eanred (808 or 810 to 840 or 841).

Kings of All England

Athelstan, eldest son of the eldest son of King Alfred of the West Saxons, acceded 924 or 925. The first to establish rule over all England (excluding Cumbria) in 927. d. 27 Oct. 939 aged over 40 years.

Edmund, younger half-brother of Athelstan; acceded 939 but did not regain control of all England until 944–45. Murdered, 26 May 946 by Leofa at Pucklechurch, near Bristol, Avon.

Edred, younger brother of Edmund; acceded May 946. Effectively King of All England 946–48, and from 954 to his death, on 23 Nov. 955. Also intermittently during the intervening period.

Edwy, son of Edmund, b. c. 941; acceded November 955 (crowned at Kingston, Greater London); lost control of Mercians and Northumbrians in 957. d. 1 Oct. 959 aged about 18.

Edgar, son of Edmund, b. 943; acceded October 959, as King of All England (crowned at Bath, 11 May 973). d. 8 July 975, aged c. 32.

Edward the Martyr, son of Edgar by Aethelflaed, b. c. 962; acceded 975. d. 18 Mar. 978 or 979, aged 16 or 17.

Ethelred (*Unraed*, i.e. ill-counselled), second son of Edgar by Aelfthryth, b. ?968–69; acceded 978 or 979 (crowned at Kingston, 14 Apr. 978 or 4 May 979); dispossessed by the Danish king, Swegn Forkbeard, 1013–14. d. 23 Apr. 1016, aged c. 47 or 48.

Swegn Forkbeard, King of Denmark 987–1014, acknowledged King of All England from about September 1013 to his death, 3 Feb. 1014.

Edmund Ironside, prob. 3rd son of Ethelred, b. c. 992; chosen King in London, April 1016. In summer of 1016 made agreement with Cnut whereby he retained dominion only over Wessex. d. 30 Nov. 1016.

Cnut, younger son of King Swegn Forkbeard of Denmark, b. c. 995. Secured Mercia and Danelaw, summer 1016; assumed dominion over all England December 1016; King of Denmark 1019–35. King of Norway 1028–1035; overlord of the King of the Scots and probably ruler of the Norse-Irish kingdom of Dublin. d. 12 Nov. 1035, aged c. 40 years.

Harold Harefoot, natural son of Cnut by Aelfgifu of Northampton, b. ?c. 1016–17; chosen regent for half-brother, Harthacnut, late 1035 or early 1036; sole King 1037, d. 17 Mar. 1040, aged c. 23 or 24 years.

Harthacnut, son of Cnut by Emma, widow of King Ethelred (d. 1016) b. ?c. 1018; titular King of Denmark from 1028; effectively King of England from June 1040. d. 8 June 1042, aged c. 24 years.

Edward the Confessor, senior half-brother of Harthacnut and son of King Ethelred and Emma, b. 1002–05; resided with Harthacnut from 1041, acceded 1042, crowned 3 Apr. 1043. d. 5 Jan. 1066, aged between 60 and 64. Sanctified.

Harold Godwinson, brother-in-law of Edward the Confessor and brother of his Queen Edith, son of Godwin, Earl of Wessex, b. ?c. 1020; acceded 6 Jan. 1066, d. or k. 14 Oct. 1066.

Edgar Etheling, chosen by Londoners as king after the Battle of Hastings. Oct. 1066; not apparently crowned, submitted to William I before 25 Dec. 1066; believed still living c. 1125.

Rulers in Wales (844–1289)

Province of Gwynedd (North Wales) (844–1283) last prince executed for treason by Edward I.

Province of Deheubarth (Dyfed) (South Central and South West Wales) (844–1231), last of line imprisoned in Norwich.

Province of Powys (North Central Wales) (1063–1160), split into Southern and Northern Powys. Southern Powys (1160–1277), dispossessed, Northern Powys (1160–ante 1289) became marcher lordship.

Kings of Scotland (1005–1603)

The chronology of the early kings of Alba (north of the Clyde and the Forth) before the 10th century is highly obscure.

Malcolm II (1005–34), b. c. 954. d. 25 Nov. 1034, aged c. 80 years. Formed the Kingdom of Scotland by annexing Strathclyde, c. 1016.

Duncan I (1034–40), son of Malcolm II's daughter, Bethoc.

Macbeth (1040–57), ?son of Malcolm II's daughter, Donada. d. aged c. 52 years.

Lulach (1057–8), stepson of Macbeth and son of his wife Gruoch. d. aged c. 26.

Malcolm III (Canmore) (1058–93), son of Duncan I. d. aged c. 62.

Donald Bane (1093–94 and 1094–97), son of Duncan I, twice deposed.

Duncan II (May to October 1094), son of Malcolm III. d. aged c. 34.

Edgar (1097–1107), son of Malcolm III, half-brother of Duncan II. d. aged c. 33.

Alexander I (1107–24), son of Malcolm III, brother of Edgar. d. aged c. 47.

David I (1124–53), son of Malcolm III and brother of Edgar. d. aged c. 68.

Malcolm IV (1153–65), son of Henry, Earl of Northumberland. d. aged c. 24.

William I (*The Lion*) (1165–1214), brother of Malcolm IV. d. aged c. 72 (from 1174 to 1189 King of England, acknowledged as overlord of Scotland).

Alexander II (1214–49), son of William I. d. aged 48.

Alexander III (1249–1286), son of Alexander II. d. aged 44.

Margaret (*Maid of Norway*) (1286–90), daughter of Margaret, daughter of Alexander III by King Eric II of Norway. Never visited her realm. d. aged 7.

First Interregnum 1290–92.

John (*Balliol*) (1292–96), son of Dervorguilla, a great-great-granddaughter of David I, awarded throne from 13 contestants by adjudication of Edward I who declared after four years that John would have to forfeit his throne for contumacy.

Second Interregnum 1296–1306.

Robert I (1306–29), son of Robert Bruce and grandson of a 1291 competitor. d. aged c. 55.

David II (1329–71), son of Robert I. d. aged 46. *Note*: Edward Balliol, son of John, was crowned King in 1332, acknowledged Edward III of England as overlord in 1333 and surrendered all claims to Scottish crown to him in 1356.

Robert II (1371–90), founder of the Stewart dynasty, son of Walter the Steward and Marjorie Bruce. d. aged 74.

Robert III (1390–1406), legitimated natural son of Robert II. d. aged c. 69.

James I (1406–37), son of Robert III, captured by English 13 days before accession and kept prisoner in England till March 1424. d. aged 42.

James II (1437–60), son of James 1. d. aged 29.

James III (1460–88), son of James II. d. aged 36.

James IV (1488–1513), son of James III and Margaret of Denmark, married Margaret Tudor. d. aged 40.

James V (1513–42), son of James IV and Margaret Tudor. d. aged 30.

Mary (*Queen of Scots*) (1542–67), daughter of James V and Mary of Lorraine, acceded aged 6 or 7 days, abdicated 24 July 1567 and was succeeded by her son (James VI) by her second husband, Henry Stuart, Lord Darnley. She was executed, 8 Feb. 1587, aged 44.

James VI (1567–1625), son of Mary and Lord Darnley (see above), succeeded to the English throne as James I on 24 Mar. 1603, so effecting a personal union of the two realms. d. aged 58.

The eleven royal houses of England since 1066

A royal dynasty normally takes its house name

from the family's patronymic. It does not change by reason of a Queen Regnant's marriage – for example, Queen Victoria, a member of the House of Hanover and Brunswick, did not become a member of the House of Saxe-Coburg and Gotha (her husband's family) but her son, Edward VII, and her grandson, George V (until renamed in 1917), were members of the house of their respective fathers.

The House of Normandy (by right of conquest) **(69 years)**
The house name derives from the fact that William I was the 7th Duke of Normandy with the style William II. This was despite the fact that he was illegitimate because his father, Duke Robert II, had him formally instituted as his legal heir.
William I (1066–87); William II (1087–1100); Henry I (1100–35) and Matilda.

The House of Bois (19 years)
The house name derives from the fact that the father of King Stephen was Stephen (sometimes called Henry), Count of Blois.
Stephen (1135–54).

The House of Anjou (331 years)
The house name derives from the fact that the father of King Henry II was Geoffrey V, 10th Count of Anjoy and Maine. This family was alternatively referred to as the Angevins, the name deriving from Angers, the town and diocese within the boundaries of Anjou.
Henry II (1154–89) and the next thirteen kings down to and including Richard III (1483–5).
Note: (1) This house, but only since the mid-15th century, and in fact less than 50 years before its male line became extinct, has been referred to as The House of Plantagenet. This name originates from Count Geoffrey's nick-name 'Plantagenet', which in turn derived, it is said, from his habit of wearing a sprig of broom (*Planta genista*) in his cap during a crusade.
(2) The House of Anjoy (or Plantagenet) may be sub-divided after the deposing of Richard II in 1399 into The House of Lancaster with Henry IV (1399–1413); Henry V (1413–22); Henry VI (1422–61 and 1470–1), and The House of York with Edward IV (1461–83 – except 1470–1); Edward V (1483); Richard III (1483–5).
(3) The names Lancaster and York derived respectively from the titles of the 4th and 5th sons of Edward III; John of Gaunt (1340–99) was 1st Duke of Lancaster (of the second creation), and the father of Henry IV, and Edmund of Langley (1341–1402) was 1st Duke of York and a great-grandfather of Edward IV.

The House of Tudor (118 years)
This house name derives from the surname of Henry VII's father, Edmund Tudor, Earl of Richmond, and son of Sir Owen Tudor, by Catherine, widow of King Henry V.
Henry VII (1485–1509); Henry VIII (1509–47); Edward VI (1547–53); after the reign of Queen Jane, Mary I (1553–8); Elizabeth I (1558–1603).

The House of Grey (14 days)
This house name derives from the family and surname of the 3rd Marquess of Dorset, the father of Lady Guil(d)ford Dudley, who reigned as Queen Jane from 6 July, 1553 for 14 days until 19 July when the House of Tudor regained the throne.

The House of Stuart and the House of Stuart and Orange (98 years and 5 years)
This house name is derived from the family and surname of Henry Stuart, Lord Darnley and Duke of Albany, the eldest son of Matthew, 4th Earl of Lennox. Lord Darnley was the second of three husbands and cousin of Mary Queen of Scots and the father of James VI of Scotland and I of England.
James I (1603–25); Charles I (1625–49); Charles II (*dejure* 1649 but *de facto* 1660–85); James II (1685–8).

The house name became The House of Stuart and Orange when in 1689 William III, son of William II, Prince of Orange, became the sovereign conjointly with his wife, Mary II, the 5th Stuart monarch.
The House of Stuart resumed from 1702 to 1714 during the reign of Queen Anne.

The House of Orange
William III reigned alone during his widowerhood from 1694 to 1702. William in fact possessed the sole regal power during his entire reign from 1689.

The House of Hanover and Brunswick-Lüneburg (187 years)
This house name derives from the fact that George I's father, Ernest Augustus, was the Elector of Hanover and a duke of the House of Brunswick-Lüneburg.
George I (1714–27); George II (1727–60); George III (1760–1820); George IV (1820–30); William IV (1830–7); Queen Victoria (1837–1901).

The House of Saxe-Coburg and Gotha (16 years)
This house name derives from the princely title of Queen Victoria's husband, Prince Albert, later Prince Consort.
Edward VII (1901–10); George V (1910–1917); on 17 July 1917 King George V declared by Royal Proclamation that he had changed the name of the royal house to the House of Windsor.

The House of Windsor (65 years to date)
George V (1917–36); Edward VIII (1936); George VI (1936–52); Elizabeth II (from 1952).
In the normal course of events Prince Charles, Prince of Wales, on inheriting the throne would become the first monarch of the House of Mountbatten but by further Proclamations the Queen first declared in 1952 that her children and descendants will belong to the House of Windsor, and later in 1960 that this Declaration would only affect her descendants in the male line who will bear a royal style and title. Descendants outside this class will bear the surname 'Mountbatten-Windsor'.

Titles of the Royal House

Husbands of Queens Regnant
The husband of a queen regnant derives no title from his marriage. Philip II of Spain, husband of Queen Mary I, was termed 'King Consort'. Prince George of Denmark, husband of Queen Anne, was created Duke of Cumberland. Prince Albert of Saxe-Coburg-Gotha was created 'Royal Highness' and seventeen years after his marriage 'Prince Consort'. The Duke of Edinburgh, husband of Queen Elizabeth II, is HRH and a prince of the United Kingdom of Great Britain and Northern Ireland.

Queens Consort
A queen consort ranks with and shares the king's titles. In the event of her being widowed she cannot continue to use the title 'The Queen'. She must add to it her christian name or use the style additionally, or by itself, of 'Queen Mother' (if she has children), or, as in the case of the widow of King William IV, 'Queen Dowager'.
In the event of her re-marriage, which can only be with the consent of the Sovereign, she does not forfeit her royal status. The last such example was when Queen Catherine (Parr) married, as her fourth husband, Lord Seymour of Sudeley, KG, in 1547.

The Heir to the Throne
The Heir Apparent to the throne can only be the son or grandson (as in the case of the Prince of Wales from 1751 to 1760) of the reigning Sovereign. Should the first person in the order of succession bear any relationship other than in the direct male line, they are the Heir (or Heiress) Presumptive. The last Heiress Presumptive to the Throne was HRH the Princess Elizabeth (1936–52). A female could be an

Heiress Apparent if she were the only or eldest daughter of a deceased Heir Apparent who had no male issue.
The eldest surviving son of a reigning Sovereign is born The Duke of Cornwall, The Duke of Rothesay, the Earl of Carrick and The Baron Renfrew, together with the styles of Lord of the Isles, Prince and Great Steward (or Seneschel) of Scotland. The titles Prince of Wales and Earl of Chester are a matter of creation and not of birthright. The Prince of Wales is a part of the establishment of The Order of the Garter. If, however, a Prince of Wales died, as in 1751, his eldest son would automatically succeed to that title and the Earldom of Chester but not to the Dukedom of Cornwall and the other honours because they are expressly reserved for the son (and not the grandson) of a Sovereign.

Princes, Princesses and Royal Highnesses
Since 1917 the style HRH Prince or Princess has been limited to the children of the Monarch and the children of the sons of the Monarch and their wives. Grand-children of a Prince of Wales also would enjoy this style. In practice the sons of a Sovereign have a dukedom bestowed upon them after they become of age. Such 'Royal Dukedoms' only enjoy their special precedence (i.e. senior to the two Archbishops and other dukes) for the next generation. A third duke would take his seniority among the non-royal dukes according to the date of the original creation.
The title 'Princess Royal' is conferred (if vacant) for life on the eldest daughter of the Sovereign.

The order of Succession to the Crown

The order of succession is determined according to ancient Common Law rules but these may be upset by an enactment of the Crown in Parliament under powers taken in the Succession to the Crown Act of 1707, provided always (since 1931) that the parliaments of all the Members of the Commonwealth assent. At Common Law the Crown descends lineally to the legitimate issue of the sovereign, males being preferred to females, in their respective orders of age. In the event of failure of such issue (e.g. King Edward VIII in 1936) the Crown passes to the nearest collateral being an heir at law. The common law of descent of the Crown specifically departs from the normal feudal rules of land descent at two points. First, in the event of two or more sisters being next in succession the eldest alone (e.g. The Princess Elizabeth from 1936 to 1952) shall be the heiress and shall not be merely a coparcener with her sister or sisters. Secondly, male issue by a second or subsequent marriage takes precedence over half sisters (e.g. King Edward VI, son of King Henry VIII's third wife, took precedence over Queen Mary I, daughter of his first marriage, and Queen Elizabeth I, daughter of his second marriage).
Below is set out the Order of Succession to the Crown.

1 The heir apparent is HRH The Prince CHARLES Philip Arthur George, KG, KT, The Prince of Wales, The Duke of Cornwall, The Duke of Rothesay, The Earl of Carrick, and the Baron Renfrew, Lord of the Isles and Great Steward of Scotland, born 14 Nov. 1948, then follows his son:

2 HRH The Prince WILLIAM Arthur Philip Louis, born 21 June 1982, then his brother:

3 HRH The Prince HENRY Charles Albert David, born 15 Sept. 1984, then his uncle:

4 HRH The Prince ANDREW Albert Christian Edward, born 19 Feb. 1960, then his brother:

5 HRH The Prince EDWARD Antony Richard Louis, born 10 Mar. 1964, then his sister:

6 HRH The Princess ANNE Elizabeth Alice

Louise, Mrs Mark Phillips, born 15 Aug. 1950, then her son:

7 PETER Mark Andrew Phillips, born 15 Nov. 1977, then his sister:

8 Miss ZARA Anne Elizabeth Phillips, born 15 May 1981, then her great aunt:

9 HRH The Princess MARGARET Rose, CI, GCVO, The Countess of Snowdon, born 21 Aug. 1930, then her son:

10 DAVID Albert Charles Armstrong-Jones, commonly called Viscount Linley, born 3 Nov. 1961, then his sister:

11 The Lady SARAH Frances Elizabeth Armstrong-Jones, born 1 May 1964, then her cousin, once removed:

12 HRH Prince RICHARD Alexander Walter George, Duke of Gloucester, born 26 Aug. 1944, then his son:

13 Lord ALEXANDER Patrick George Richard, Earl of Ulster, born 24 Oct. 1974, then his sister:

14 The Lady DAVINA Elizabeth Alice Benedikte Windsor, born 19 Nov. 1977, then her sister:

15 The Lady ROSE Victoria Birgitte Louise WINDSOR, born 1 Mar. 1980, then her cousin once removed:

16 HRH Prince EDWARD George Nicholas Paul Patrick, GCVO, the (2nd) Duke of Kent, the Earl of St Andrews and the Baron Downpatrick, born 9 Oct. 1935, then his son:

17 Lord GEORGE Philip Nicholas WINDSOR, commonly called Earl of St Andrews, born 26 June 1962, then his brother:

18 Lord NICHOLAS Charles Edward Jonathan WINDSOR, born 25 July 1970, then his sister:

19 The Lady HELEN Marian Lucy WINDSOR, born 28 Apr. 1964, then her cousin:

20 Lord FREDERICK Michael George David Louis WINDSOR, born 6 Apr. 1979, (his father, HRH Prince MICHAEL George Charles Franklin of Kent, born 4 July 1942, having forfeited his claim to the Throne by his marriage (30 June 1978) to a Roman Catholic, Baroness Marie-Christine von Reibnitz), then his sister:

21 The Lady GABRIELA Marina Alexandra Ophelia WINDSOR, born 23 Apr. 1981, then her aunt:

22 HRH Princess ALEXANDRA Helen Elizabeth Olga Christabel of Kent, GCVO, the Hon Mrs Angus J B Ogilvy, born 25 Dec. 1936, then her son:

23 JAMES Robert Bruce Ogilvy, Esq, born 29 Feb. 1964, then his sister:

24 Miss MARINA Victoria Alexandra Ogilvy, born 31 July 1966, then her second cousin, once removed upwards.

Factors affecting the order
Two further factors should be borne in mind in determining the order of succession. First, no person may unilaterally renounce their right to succeed. Only an Act of Parliament can undo what another Act of Parliament (the Act of Settlement, 1701) has done. Secondly, some marriages among the descendants of George II are null and void and hence the descendants are not heirs at law, by failure to obtain the consent to marry as required by the Royal Marriage Act of 1772. In some cases this failure, prior to 1956, may have been inadvertent because it was only then confirmed by the House of Lords that every such descendant, born before 1948, is by a statute of 1705 deemed a British subject. So the escape from the requirements of the Royal Marriage Act accorded to all female descendants of George II who apparently married into *foreign* families is not so readily available as was once thought.

The Act of Settlement
On 6 Feb. 1701 the Act of Settlement came into force. It laid down that failing issue from HRH The Princess (later Queen Anne) George (of Denmark) and/or secondly from any subsequent marriage by her first cousin and brother-in-law, the widower King William III, the crown would vest in Princess Sophia, Dowager Electress of Hanover (1630–1714), the granddaughter of King James I, and the heirs of her body, with the proviso that all Roman Catholics, or persons marrying Roman Catholics, were for ever to be excluded, as if they 'were naturally dead'.

The Duke of Windsor
The only subsequent change in statute law was on 11 Dec. 1936 by His Majesty's Declaration of Abdication Act, 1936, by which the late HRH The Prince Edward, MC (later HRH The Duke of Windsor), and any issue he might subsequently have had were expressly excluded from the succession.

Conditions of tenure
On succeeding to the Crown the Sovereign must (1) join in Communion with the established Church of England; (2) declare that he or she is a Protestant; (3) swear the oaths for the preservation of both the Established Church of England and the Presbyterian Church of Scotland, and (4), and most importantly, take the coronation oath, which may be said to form the basis of the contract between Sovereign and subject, last considered to have been broken, on the Royal side, by King James II in 1688.

'The King never dies'
The Sovereign can never be legally a minor, but in fact a regency is provided until he or she attains the age of 18.

There is never an interregnum on the death of a Sovereign. In pursuance of the common law maxim 'the King never dies' the new Sovereign succeeds to full prerogative rights instantly on the death of his or her predecessor.

Notes on the British peerage

There are five ranks in the British temporal peerage – in ascending order they are: 1. Barons or Baronesses; 2. Viscounts or Viscountesses; 3. Earls or Countesses; 4. Marquesses (less favoured, Marquises) or Marchionesses; 5. Dukes or Duchesses.

The British spiritual peerage is of two ranks, Archbishops (of Canterbury and of York) who rank between Royal Dukes and dukes, and twenty-four of the bishops (but always including the Bishops of London, Durham, and Winchester with the Bishop of Sodor and Man always excluded), based on their seniority, who rank between Viscounts and Barons.

A few women hold peerages in their own right and since The Peerage Act, 1963, have become peers of Parliament. The remaining category of membership of the House of Lords is life peers. These are of two sorts: (a) The Lords of Appeal in Ordinary, who are appointed by virtue of the Appellate Jurisdiction Act, 1876. Their number has been increased from the original four to six in 1913, to seven in 1929, and to nine since 1947; (b) by virtue of The Life Peerages Act, 1958, both men and women may be appointed for life membership of The House of Lords. Such creations so far have been confined to the fifth and junior temporal rank of baron or baroness.

1. Peerages of England, i.e. those created prior to the union with Scotland on 1 May 1707.
2. Peerages of Scotland, i.e. those created before the union with England.
3. Peerages of Ireland (the last creation was in 1898 and no further ones are at present likely).
4. Peerages of Great Britain, i.e. those created between the union with Scotland (1707) and the union with Ireland (2 July 1800).
5. Peerages of the United Kingdom of Great Britain and (Northern) Ireland, i.e. those created since 2 July 1800.

All holders of peerages of England, Great Britain and the United Kingdom and (only since The Peerage Act, 1963) also of Scotland, are also peers of Parliament provided they are over 21 and are not unpardoned major felons, bankrupts, lunatics or of alien nationality. Peers who are civil servants may sit but neither speak nor vote.

The single exception to the rule concerning minors is that the Duke of Cornwall (HRH The Prince of Wales) has been technically entitled to a seat from the moment of his mother's accession, when he was only three years of age.

The peers (and peeresses in their own right) of Ireland are not peers of Parliament but they are entitled to stand for election to the House of Commons for any seat in the United Kingdom. The previous system by which this category of peer could elect 28 of its number to sit in the House of Lords has now fallen into disuse because since the Partition of Ireland in 1922 there has been no machinery available to carry out that election and all the representative peers elected prior to that date have since died.

Only the holder of a substantive peerage can be described as noble. In the eyes of the law the holder of a courtesy title is a commoner. For example, the Duke of Marlborough's son is known by courtesy as Marquess of Blandford. Note the omission of the definite article 'the'. The reason is that the Duke of Marlborough is also *the* Marquess of Blandford and his secondary peerage style is merely lent to this son.

Life Peers
The Crown in the past used on occasions to grant life peerages, both to men and women. The Wensleydale peerage case of 1856 acknowledged the Crown's right to do this but denied the consequent right of a seat in the House of Lords to such a peer. The two current categories of life peers are treated above. It should be noted that there is no provision for these non-hereditary peers or peeresses to disclaim their peerages.

Widows of Peers
The only correct style for the widow of a peer is 'The Dowager' prefixed to her peerage title of duchess, marchioness, countess, viscountess, or lady (note: 'baroness' is only normally used by a peeress in her own right). But in fact most widowed peeresses dislike this title because of its association with advanced age, so they prefix their Christian name to their title. In the event of a widow remarrying, she should forfeit her previous title but some, quite unjustifiably, retain it.

The Effect of Divorce
Some peeresses who divorce their husbands or have been divorced by them continue to bear their former husband's style though in strict English law they are probably no longer peeresses. If a new wife appears they adopt the practice of most widows and prefix their christian name to their title. With Scottish peerages, however, the position of a divorced peeress is exactly the same as if her husband were dead and hence she takes her legal rights as a widow.

Courtesy Titles
According to the preamble of The Peerage Act, 1963, 'Courtesy titles are, by definition, not matters of law'. They are governed by custom and fall into two categories – those borne by all the children of a peer and those reserved for the heir. The children (except the eldest son) of a duke or marquess take the title 'Lord' or 'Lady' before their christian name and the family name (e.g. Lord Charles Cavendish). The same applies to the daughters of an earl but not, oddly enough, to the younger sons who take the style 'Honourable' which is borne by *all* the children of a viscount, a baron and a temporal life peer. When male holders of this title marry, their wives also become 'The Honourable'. The heir to a

dukedom is given the courtesy style 'Marquess', provided, of course, his father has a marquessate, which failing he takes the title 'Earl' but enjoys the precedence of a duke's eldest son. Likewise, the heir to a marquessate takes the courtesy style of 'Earl' (if available) and similarly the heir of an earldom takes the title of his father's viscountcy (if any) or barony.

In the Scottish peerage the term 'Master of' is used by the male heir to many peerages as of right. If he is married, his wife is styled 'The Hon Mrs'.

Courtesy titles in the second generation extend only to the grandchildren who are the children of an elder son.

The Signature of Peers
A peer's signature, whether on a formal or informal document, is simply his title without any qualification of rank or the use of a christian name. This also applies to peeresses in their own right. Members of the Royal Family who hold peerages, however, sign with their principal Christian name.

The Prefix 'Lady'
This title causes more confusion than any other, simply because of the wide range of its use. It can be used as a less formal alternative by marchionesses, countesses, viscountesses and the wives of barons. It is never used by duchesses. It is used, but only with the addition of their christian names, by the daughters of dukes, marquesses and earls. It is also used by the wives of the younger sons of dukes and marquesses, e.g. Lady Charles Cavendish. It is used, but never with the definite article, by the wives of baronets and knights. There is one baroness.

Special Remainders
The Crown has power to create what are termed 'special remainders' so that a peerage can, for example, pass to an elder brother or some other relative. An example is that the earldom of Mountbatten of Burma passed to the first earl's elder daughter and her male issue.

Dormant Peerages
A peerage is deemed dormant when there is no discoverable heir but there is a reasonable presumption that there may be an heir if he or she could be found. The Crown will not permit the use of a name of a peerage for a subsequent creation unless there is absolute certainty that the former creation is truly extinguished.

The Descent of Peerages
Usually a peerage descends in the male line. Illegitimate offspring are, of course, excluded. If the direct male line fails, then the succession may go back to the male line in an earlier cadet branch of the family. The ancient category of English baronies by writ provides its own rules of descent. These peerages date back to the time when the original holder was deemed to be a peer solely by virtue of receiving a Writ of Summons to attend Parliament. The invariable practice since those days has been to grant a peerage specifically by Letters Patent.

Kings and Queens of England and Great Britain

The precise dates of all the main events in the lives of the earlier monarchs are not known, and probably now never will be. Where recognised authorities are in dispute, as quite frequently occurs in the first twenty or so reigns, we have adhered to the dates given by the Royal Historical Society's *Handbook of British Chronology* (second edition, 1961). This work includes the fruits of recent researches based on only acceptable evidence.

King or Queen Regnant Date of Accession and Final Year of Reign; Style	Date and Place of Birth and Parentage	Marriages and No. of Children	Date, Cause and Place of Death, and Place of Burial	Notes and Succession
1. **WILLIAM I** 25 Dec. 1066–87 'The Bastard' 'The Conqueror' *Style:* 'Willielmus Rex Anglorum'	1027 or 1028 at Falaise, north France; illegitimate son of Robert I, 6th Duke of Normandy, and Herleva, dau. of Fulbert the Tanner	m. at Eu in 1050 or 1051 MATILDA (d. 1083), d of Baldwin V, Count of Flanders. 4s 5d	d., aged 59 or 60, 9 Sept. 1087 of an abdominal injury from his saddle pommel at the Priory of St Gervais, nr. Rouen. The Abbey of St Stephen at Caen (remains lost during French Revolution).	William I succeeded by right of conquest by winning the 'Battle of Hastings', 14 Oct. 1066, from Harold II, the nominated heir of Edward III ('The Confessor'). Succeeded as King of England by his third, but second surviving, son, William
2. **WILLIAM II** 26 Sept. 1087–1100 'Rufus' *Style:* 'Dei Gratia Rex Anglorum'	between 1056 and 1060 in Normandy; third son of William I and Matilda	unmarried. Had illegitimate issue	d., aged between 40 and 44, 2 Aug. 1100 (according to tradition) of impalement by a stray arrow while hunting in the New Forest nr. Brockenhurst, Hants. Winchester Cathedral	Succeeded by his younger brother, Henry
3. **HENRY I** 5 Aug. 1100–35 'Beauclerc' *Style:* As No. 2 but also Duke of Normandy from 1106	in the latter half of 1068 at Selby, Yorks; fourth son of William I and Matilda	m. (1) at Westminster Abbey, 11 Nov. 1100 EADGYTH (Edith), known as MATILDA (d. 1118), d of Malcolm III, King of the Scots, and Margaret (grand-d of Edmund 'Ironside') 1s, 1d and a child who died young. m. (2) 29 Jan 1121 ADELA (d. 1151), d of Godfrey VII, Count of Louvain. No issue	d., aged 67, 1 Dec. 1135, from a feverish illness at St Denis-le-Ferment, nr. Grisors. Reading Abbey	Succeeded by his nephew, Stephen (the third, but second surviving, son of Adela, the fifth d of William I) who usurped the throne from Henry's only surviving legitimate child and d, Matilda (1102–67)
4. **STEPHEN** 22 Dec. 1135–54 *Style:* As No. 2.	between 1096 and 1100 at Blois, France; third son of Stephen (sometimes called Henry), Count of Blois, and Adela	m. 1125, MATILDA (d. 1151), d of Eustace II, Count of Boulogne, and Mary, sister of Queen Matilda, wife of Henry I. 3s 2d	d., aged between 54 and 58, 25 Oct. 1154, from a heart attack at St Martin's Priory, Dover. Faversham Abbey	Succeeded by his first cousin once removed downwards, Henry. Between April and November 1141 he was not *de facto* King and was imprisoned in Bristol Castle
5. **MATILDA** April–Nov. 1141 'Empress Maud' *Style:* 'Imperatrix Henrici Regis filia et Anglorum domina'	Feb. 1102 in London, only legitimate d of Henry I	m. (1) 1114 Henry V, Emperor of Germany (d. 1125). No issue. m. (2) 1130 GEOFFREY V, Count of Anjou (d. 1151). 3s	d., aged 65, 10 Sept. 1167 of uncertain cause, nr. Rouen in Normandy. Fontevraud(?), France	Succeeded by her cousin, Stephen, whom she had deposed

King or Queen Regnant Date of Accession and Final Year of Reign; Style	Date and Place of Birth and Parentage	Marriages and No. of Children	Date, Cause and Place of Death, and Place of Burial	Notes and Succession
6. **HENRY II** 19 Dec. 1154–1189 *Style:* 'Rex Angliae, Dux Normaniae et Aquitaniae et Comes Andigaviae'	5 Mar. 1133 at Le Mans, France; eldest son of Geoffrey V, Count of Anjou (surnamed Plantagenet), and Matilda (only d of Henry I)	m. at Bordeaux, 18 May, 1152, ELEANOR (c. 1122–1204), d of William X, Duke of Aquitaine, and divorced wife of Louis, later Louis VII, King of France, 5s 3d	d., aged 56, 6 July 1189, of a fever at the Castle of Chinon, nr. Tours, France. Fontevraud abbey church in Anjou Reburied Westminster Abbey	Succeeded by his third and elder surviving son, Richard. On 14 June 1170, Henry II's second and eldest surviving son Henry was crowned and three years later recrowned with his wife at Winchester as King of England. Contemporaneously he was called King Henry III. He predeceased his father, 11 June 1183
7. **RICHARD I** 3 Sept. 1189–99 'Coeur de Lion' *Style:* As No. 6	8 Sept. 1157 at Oxford; third son of Henry II and Eleanor	m. at Limassol, Cyprus, 12 May 1191, BERENGARIA (d. soon after 1230), d of Sancho VI of Navarre. No issue	d., aged 41, 6 Apr. 1199 from a mortal arrow wound while besieging the Castle of Châlus in Limousin, France. Fontevraud abbey church in Anjou. Reburied Westminster Abbey	Succeeded by his younger brother, John, who usurped the throne from his nephew Arthur, the only son of Geoffrey, Duke of Brittany (1158–86); and from his niece, Eleanor (1184–1241). Arthur (b, post-humously 1187) was murdered (unmarried) 3 Apr. 1203 in his 17th year
8. **JOHN** 27 May 1199–1216 'Lackland' *Style:* 'Joannes Rex Angliae et Dominus Hiberniae' etc.	24 Dec. 1167 at Beaumont Palace, Oxford; fifth son of Henry II and Eleanor	m. (1) at Marlborough, Wilts, 29 Aug. 1189, ISABEL (d. 1217). No issue. m. (2) at Angoulême, 24 Aug. 1200, ISABELLA (d. 1246), d of Aimir, Count of Angoulême. 2s 3d	d., aged 48, 18–19 Oct. 1216, of dysentery at Newark Castle, Notts. Worcester Cathedral	In late 1215 the Crown was offered to Louis, son of Philip II of France but despite a visit in 1216 the claim was abandoned in Sept. 1217. Succeeded by his elder son, Henry
9. **HENRY III** 28 Oct. 1216–72 *Style:* 'Rex Angliae, Dominus Hiberniae et Dux Aquitaniae'	1 Oct. 1207 at Winchester; elder son of John and Isabella	m. at Canterbury, 20 Jan 1236, ELEANOR (d. 1291) d of Raymond Berengar IV, Count of Provence. 2s 3d at least 4 other children who died in infancy	d., aged 65, 16 Nov. 1272, at Westminster. Westminster abbey church	The style 'Dux Normaniae' and Count of Anjou was omitted from 1259. Succeeded by Edward, his first son to survive infancy (probably his third son)
10. **EDWARD I** 20 Nov. 1272–1307 'Longshanks' *Style:* As the final style of No. 8	17/18 June 1239 at Westminster; eldest son to survive infancy (probably third son) of Henry III and Eleanor	m. (1) at the monastery of Las Huelgas, Spain, 13–31 Oct. 1254, ELEANOR (d. 1290), d of Ferdinand III, King of Castille. 4s 7d m. (2) at Canterbury, 10 Sept. 1299, MARGARET (1282–1317), d of Philip III, King of France. 2s 1d	d., aged 68, 7 July 1307, at Burgh-upon-the-Sands, nr. Carlisle. Westminster Abbey	Succeeded by the fourth, and only surviving, son of his first marriage, Edward (created Prince of Wales, 7 Feb. 1301)
11. **EDWARD II** 8 July 1307 (deposed 20 Jan. 1327) 'of Caernarfon' *Style:* As the final style of No. 8	25 Apr. 1284 at Caernarfon Castle; fourth and only surviving son of Edward I and Eleanor	m. at Boulogne, c. 25 Jan. 1308, ISABELLA (1292–1358), d of Philip IV, King of France, 2s 2d	murdered, aged 43, 21 Sept. 1327 (traditionally by disembowelling with red-hot iron) at Berkeley Castle. The abbey of St Peter (now the cathedral), Gloucester	Succeeded by his elder son, Edward of Windsor. Edward II was deposed by Parliament on 20 Jan. 1327, having been imprisoned on 16 Nov. 1326
12. **EDWARD III** 25 Jan. 1327–1377 *Style:* As No. 10, until 13th year when 'Dei Gratiâ, Rex Angliae, et Franciae et Dominus Hiberniae'	13 Nov. 1312 at Windsor Castle; elder son of Edward II and Isabella	m. at York, 24 June 1328, PHILIPPA (c. 1314–69), d of William I, Count of Holland and Hainault. 7s 5d	d. peacefully, aged 64, 21 June 1377 at Sheen (now in Greater London). Westminster Abbey	Succeeded by his grandson Richard, the second and only surviving son of his eldest son Edward, the Black Prince
13. **RICHARD II** 22 June 1377–99 *Style:* As final style of No. 12	6 Jan. 1367 at Bordeaux; second, but only surviving, son of Edward, the Black Prince, and Joane, commonly called The Fair Maid of Kent (grand-d of Edward I)	m. (1) at St Stephen's Chapel, Westminster, 20 Jan. 1382, ANNE of Bohemia (1366–94), d of Emperor Charles IV. No issue. m. (2) at St Nicholas' Church, Calais, probably 4 Nov. 1396, ISABELLE (1389–1409), d of Charles VI of France. No issue	d., aged 33, probably 14 Feb. 1400, a sufferer from neurasthenia at Pontefract Castle, Yorks. Westminster Abbey	He was a prisoner of Henry, Duke of Lancaster, later Henry IV, from 19 Aug. 1399 until death. He was deposed 30 Sept. 1399. Henry usurped the throne from the prior claims of the issue of his father John of Gaunt's deceased elder brother, Lionel of Antwerp

King or Queen Regnant Date of Accession and Final Year of Reign; Style	Date and Place of Birth and Parentage	Marriages and No. of Children	Date, Cause and Place of Death, and Place of Burial	Notes and Succession
14. **HENRY IV** 30 Sept. 1399–1413 *Style:* As No. 12	probably Apr. 1366 at Bolingbroke Castle, nr. Spilsby, Lincs.; eldest son of John of Gaunt, 4th son of Edward III, and Blanche, great-great-grand-d of Henry III	m. (1) at Rochford, Essex, between July 1380 and Mar. 1381, Lady MARY de Bohun (?1368/70–94), younger d of Humphrey, Earl of Hereford. 5s 2d. m. (2) at Winchester, 7 Feb. 1403, JOAN (c. 1370–1437), second d of Charles II, King of Navarre. No issue	d., aged probably 46, 20 Mar. 1413, of pustulated eczema and gout in the Jerusalem Chamber, Westminster. Canterbury Cathedral	Succeeded by his second, but eldest surviving, son, Henry of Monmouth
15. **HENRY V** 21 Mar. 1413–1422 *Style:* As No. 13, until 8th year when 'Rex Angliae, Haeres, et Regens Franciae, et Dominus Hiberniae'	probably 16 Sept. 1387 at Monmouth; second and eldest surviving son of Henry IV and the Lady Mary de Bohun	m. at the church of St John, Troyes, 2 June 1420, CATHERINE of Valois (1401–37), youngest d of Charles VI of France. 1s	d., aged probably 34, 31 Aug./Sept. 1422, of dysentery at Bois de Vincennes, France. Chapel of the Confessor, Westminster Abbey	Succeeded by his only child Henry
16. **HENRY VI** 1 Sept. 1422–1461 and 6 Oct. 1470–1471 *Style:* 'Dei Gratiâ Rex Angliae et Franciae et Dominus Hiberniae'	6 Dec. 1421 at Windsor; only son of Henry V and Catherine	m. at Tichfield Abbey, 23 Apr. 1445, MARGARET (1430–82), d of René, Duke of Anjou. 1s	murdered by stabbing, aged 49, 21 May 1471 at Tower of London. Windsor	Succeeded by the usurpation of his third cousin, Edward IV
17. **EDWARD IV** 4 Mar. 1461–1470 and 11 April 1471–1483 *Style:* As No. 16	28 Apr. 1442 at Rouen; eldest son of Richard, 3rd Duke of York ('The Protector') and the Lady Cecily Nevill	m. at Grafton, Northants, 1 May 1464, ELIZABETH (c. 1437–92), eldest d of Sir Richard Woodville. 3s 7d	d., aged 40, 9 Apr. 1483, of pneumonia at Westminster. Windsor	Edward IV was a prisoner of the Earl of Warwick in Aug. and Sept. of 1469; he fled to the Netherlands 3 Oct. 1470; returned to England 14 Mar. 1471, and was restored to kingship 11 Apr. 1471. Succeeded by his eldest son, Edward
18. **EDWARD V** 9 Apr.–25 June 1483 *Style:* As No. 16	2 Nov. 1470 in the Sanctuary at Westminster; eldest son of Edward IV and Elizabeth Woodville	unmarried	d. (traditionally murdered), possibly in 1483 or in 1486, at the Tower of London. A body of the stature and dentition of a 12 year old male discovered at the Tower on 6 July 1933	Edward V was deposed 25 June 1483, when the throne was usurped by his uncle, Richard III (the only surviving brother of his father)
19. **RICHARD III** 26 June 1483–5 *Style:* As No. 16	2 Oct. 1452 at Fotheringay Castle, Northants; fourth and only surviving son of Richard, 3rd Duke of York ('The Protector'), and the Lady Cecily Nevill	m. 12 July 1472, the Lady ANNE (1456–85), younger d of Richard Nevill, Earl of Warwick ('The King Maker') and widow of Edward, Prince of Wales, only child of Henry VI. 1s	killed aged 32, 22 Aug. 1485, at the battle of Bosworth Field. The Abbey of the Grey Friars, Leicester	Richard III was succeeded by his third cousin once removed downwards, Henry Tudor, 2nd Earl of Richmond
20. **HENRY VII** 22 Aug. 1485–1509 *Style:* As No. 16	27 Jan. 1457 at Pembroke Castle; only child of Edmund Tudor, 1st Earl of Richmond, and Margaret Beaufort, great-great-grand-d of Edward III	m. at Westminster, 18 Jan. 1486, ELIZABETH (1466–1503) d of Edward IV. 3s and 4d, of whom 2 died in infancy	d., aged 52, 21 Apr. 1509, had rheumatoid arthritis and gout at Richmond. In his own chapel at Westminster	Succeeded by his second and only surviving son, Henry
21. **HENRY VIII** 22 Apr. 1509–47 *Style:* (from 35th year) 'Henry the eighth, by the Grace of God, King of England, France, and Ireland, Defender of the Faith and of the Church of England, and also of Ireland, on earth the Supreme Head'	28 June 1491 at Greenwich; second and only surviving son of Henry VII and Elizabeth	m. (1) secretly at the chapel of the Observant Friars, 11 June 1509, CATHERINE of Aragon (1485–1536), d of Ferdinand II, King of Spain and widow of Arthur, Prince of Wales. 2s 2d and a child who died young *Subsequent marriages of HENRY VIII:*	d., aged 55, 28 Jan. 1547, had chronic sinusitis and periostitis of the leg at the Palace of Westminster. Windsor · m. (2) secretly 25 Jan. 1533, ANNE Marchioness of Pembroke (b. 1507, beheaded 1536), d of Sir Thomas Boleyn, the Viscount Rochford. A daughter and possibly another child	Henry was the first King to be formally styled with a post nominal number, i.e. VIII. Succeeded by his only surviving son, Edward · m. (3) in the Queen's Closet, York Place, London, 30 May 1536, JANE (d. 1537), eldest d of Sir John Seymour. 1s

King or Queen Regnant Date of Accession and Final Year of Reign; Style	Date and Place of Birth and Parentage	Marriages and No. of Children	Date, Cause and Place of Death, and Place of Burial	Notes and Succession
		m. (4) at Greenwich, 6 Jan. 1540, ANNE (1515–57), second d of John, Duke of Cleves. No issue.	m. (5) at Oatlands, 28 July 1540, CATHERINE (beheaded 1542), d of Lord Edmund Howard. No issue	m. (6) at Hampton Court, 12 July 1543, CATHERINE (c. 1512–48), d of Sir Thomas Parr and widow of 1. Sir Edward Borough and 2. John Neville, 3rd Lord Latimer. No issue
22. **EDWARD VI** 28 Jan. 1547–53 *Style:* As No. 21	12 Oct. 1537 at Hampton Court; only surviving son of Henry VIII, by Jane Seymour	unmarried	d., aged 15, 6 July 1553, of pulmonary tuberculosis at Greenwich. Henry VII's Chapel, Westminster Abbey	Succeeded briefly by Lady Guil(d)ford Dudley (Lady Jane Grey), his first cousin once removed
23. **JANE** 6 July (proclaimed 10 July) 1553 (deposed 19 July)	Oct. 1537 at Bradgate Park, Leics.; eldest d of Henry Grey, 3rd Marquess of Dorset, and Frances (d of Mary Tudor, sister of Henry VIII)	m. at Durham House, London, 21 May 1553, Lord GUIL(D)FORD DUDLEY (beheaded 1554), 4th son of John Dudley, Duke of Northumberland. No issue	beheaded, aged 16, 12 Feb. 1554, in the Tower of London. St Peter ad Vincula, within the Tower	Succeeded by her second cousin once removed upwards, Mary
24. **MARY I** 19 July 1553–8 *Style:* As No. 21 (but supremacy title was dropped) until marriage then as footnote	18 Feb. 1516 at Greenwich Palace; only surviving child of Henry VIII and Catherine of Aragon	m. at Winchester Cathedral, 25 July 1554, PHILIP (1527–98), King of Naples and Jerusalem, son of Emperor Charles V and widower of Maria, d of John III of Portugal. No issue	d., aged 42, 17 Nov. 1558 of endemic influenza at London. Westminster Abbey	Philip was styled, but not crowned, king. Mary was succeeded by her half sister, Elizabeth, the only surviving child of Henry VIII
25. **ELIZABETH I** 17 Nov. 1558–1603 *Style:* 'Queen of England, France and Ireland, Defender of the Faith' etc.	7 Sept. 1533 at Greenwich; d of Henry VIII and Anne Boleyn	unmarried	d., aged 69, 24 Mar. 1603, of sepsis from tonsillar abscess at Richmond. Westminster Abbey	Succeeded by her first cousin twice removed, James
26. **JAMES I** 26 Mar. 1603–25 and VI of Scotland from 24 July 1567 *Style:* 'King of England, Scotland, France and Ireland, Defender of the Faith' etc.	19 June 1566 at Edinburgh Castle; only son of Henry Stuart, Lord Darnley, and Mary, Queen of Scots (d of James V of Scotland, son of Margaret Tudor, sister of Henry VIII)	m. 20 Aug. 1589 (by proxy) ANNE (1574–1619), d of Frederick II, King of Denmark and Norway. 3s 4d	d., aged 58, 27 Mar. 1625, of Bright's disease at Theobalds Park, Herts. Westminster Abbey	Succeeded by his second and only surviving son, Charles
27. **CHARLES I** 27 Mar. 1625–49 *Style:* As No. 26	19 Nov. 1600 at Dunfermline Palace, second and only surviving son of James I and Anne	m. in Paris, 1 May 1625 (by proxy) HENRIETTA MARIA (1609–69) d of Henry IV of France. 4s 5d	beheaded, aged 48, 30 Jan. 1649, in Whitehall. Windsor	The Kingship was *de facto* declared abolished 17 Mar. 1649
28. **CHARLES II** 29 May 1660 (but *de jure* 30 Jan. 1649) to 1685 *Style:* As No. 26	29 May 1630 at St James's Palace, London; eldest surviving son of Charles I and Henrietta Maria	m. at Portsmouth, 21 May 1662, CATHERINE (1638–1705), d of John, Duke of Braganza. No legitimate issue	d., aged 54, 6 Feb. 1685, of uraemia and mercurial poisoning at Whitehall. Henry VII's Chapel, Westminster Abbey	Succeeded by his younger and only surviving brother, James
29. **JAMES II** 6 Feb. 1685–8 *Style:* As No. 26	14 Oct. 1633 at St James's Palace, London; only surviving son of Charles I and Henrietta Maria	m. (1) at Worcester House, The Strand, London, 3 Sept. 1660, ANNE (1637–71), eldest d of Edward Hyde. 4s 4d. m. (2) At Modena (by proxy), 30 Sept. 1673, MARY D'Este (1658–1718), only d of Alfonso IV, Duke of Modena. 2s 5d	d., aged 67, 6 Sept. 1701, of a cerebral haemorrhage at St Germains, France. His remains were divided and interred at five different venues in France. All are now lost except for those at the parish church of St Germains	James II was deemed by legal fiction to have ended his reign 11 Dec. 1688 by flight. A Convention Parliament offered the Crown of England and Ireland 13 Feb. 1689 to Mary, his eldest surviving d, and her husband, his nephew, William Henry of Orange
30. **WILLIAM III** 13 Feb. 1689–1702	4 Nov. 1650 at The Hague; only son of William II, Prince of Orange, and Mary (Stuart), d of Charles I	They were married at St James's Palace, London, 4 Nov. 1677. No issue	d., aged 51, 8 Mar. 1702, of pleuro-pneumonia following fracture of right collarbone, in Kensington	The widower, King William III, was succeeded by his sister-in-law, Anne, who was also his first cousin

and *(see over)*

King or Queen Regnant Date of Accession and Final Year of Reign; Style	Date and Place of Birth and Parentage	Marriages and No. of Children	Date, Cause and Place of Death, and Place of Burial	Notes and Succession
MARY II 13 Feb. 1689–94 *Style:* 'King and Queen of England, Scotland, France and Ireland, Defenders of the Faith etc.'	30 Apr. 1662 at St James's Palace, London; elder surviving d of James II and Anne Hyde		d., aged 32, 28 Dec. 1694, of confluent haemorrhagic smallpox with pneumonia, at Kensington. They were buried in Henry VII's Chapel, Westminster Abbey	
31. **ANNE** 8 Mar. 1702–14 *Style:* Firstly as No. 25; secondly (after Union with Scotland 6 Mar. 1707) 'Queen of Great Britain, France and Ireland, Defender of the Faith' etc.	6 Feb. 1665 at St James's Palace, London; only surviving d of James II and Anne Hyde	m. at the Chapel Royal, St James's Palace, 28 July 1683, GEORGE (1653–1708), second son of Frederick III, King of Denmark. 2s 3d from 17 confinements	d., aged 49, 1 Aug. 1714, of a cerebral haemorrhage and possibly chronic Bright's disease at Kensington. Henry VII's Chapel, Westminster Abbey	Succeeded in the terms of the Act of Settlement (which excluded all Roman Catholics and their spouses) by her second cousin, George Lewis, Elector of Hanover
32. **GEORGE I** 1 Aug. 1714–27 *Style:* 'King of Great Britain, France and Ireland, Duke of Brunswick-Lüneburg, etc., Defender of the Faith'	28 May 1660 at Osnabrück; eldest son of Ernest Augustus, Duke of Brunswick-Lüneburg and Elector of Hanover, and Princess Sophia, 5th and youngest d and 10th child of Elizabeth, Queen of Bohemia, the eldest d of James I	m. 21 Nov. 1682 (div. 1694), SOPHIA Dorothea (1666–1726), only d of George William, Duke of Lüneburg-Celle. 1s 1d	d., aged 67, 11 June 1727, of coronary thrombosis, at Ibbenbüren or Osnabrück. Hanover	The Kings of England were Electors of Hanover from 1714 to 1814. Succeeded by his only son, George Augustus
33. **GEORGE II** 11 June 1727–60 *Style:* As No. 32	30 Oct. 1683 at Hanover; only son of George I and Sophia Dorothea	m. 22 Aug. (O.S.), 2 Sept. (N.S.), 1705, Wilhelmina Charlotte CAROLINE (1683–1737), d of John Frederick, Margrave of Brandenburg-Ansbach. 3s 5d	d., aged 76, 25 Oct. 1760, of coronary thrombosis at the Palace of Westminster. Henry VII's Chapel, Westminster Abbey	Succeeded by his elder son's eldest son, George William Frederick
34. **GEORGE III** 25 Oct. 1760–1820 *Style:* As No. 31 (until Union of Great Britain and Ireland, 1 Jan. 1801), whereafter 'By the Grace of God, of the United Kingdom of Great Britain and Ireland, King, Defender of the Faith'	24 May (O.S.) 1738 at Norfolk House, St James's Square, London; eldest son of Frederick Lewis, Prince of Wales (d. 20 Mar. 1751) and Princess Augusta of Saxe-Gotha	m. at St James's Palace, London, 8 Sept. 1761, CHARLOTTE Sophia (1744–1818), youngest d of Charles Louis Frederick, Duke of Mecklenburg-Strelitz. 9s 6d	d., aged 81 years 239 days, 29 Jan. 1820, of senility at Windsor. St George's Chapel, Windsor	His eldest son became Regent owing to his insanity 5 Feb. 1811. Hanover was made a kingdom in 1814. Succeeded by his eldest son, George Augustus Frederick
35. **GEORGE IV** 29 Jan. 1820–30 *Style:* As later style of No. 34	12 Aug. 1762 at St James's Palace, London; eldest son of George III and Charlotte	m. (2)* at the Chapel Royal, St James's Palace, 8 Apr. 1795, CAROLINE Amelia Elizabeth (1768–1821), his first cousin, second d of Charles, Duke of Brunswick-Wolfenbüttel. 1d. *First married Maria FitzHerbert	d., aged 67, 26 June 1830, of rupture of the stomach blood vessels; alcoholic cirrhosis; and dropsy at Windsor. St George's Chapel, Windsor	Succeeded by his eldest surviving brother, William Henry (George's only child, Princess Charlotte, having died in child-birth 6 Nov. 1817)
36. **WILLIAM IV** 26 June 1830–7 *Style:* As No. 34	21 Aug. 1765 at Buckingham Palace; third and oldest surviving son of George III and Charlotte	m. at Kew, 11 July 1818, ADELAIDE Louisa Theresa Caroline Amelia (1792–1849), eldest d of George, Duke of Saxe-Meiningen. 2d	d., aged 71, 20 June 1837, of pleuro-pneumonia and alcoholic cirrhosis at Windsor. St George's Chapel, Windsor	On William's death the crown of Hanover passed by Salic law to his brother, Ernest, Duke of Cumberland. Succeeded by his niece, Alexandrina Victoria
37. **VICTORIA** 20 June 1837–1901 *Style:* As (except for 'Queen') No. 34 until 1 May 1876, whereafter 'Empress of India' was added	24 May 1819 at Kensington Palace, London; only child of Edward, Duke of Kent and Strathearn, 4th son of George III, and Victoria, widow of Emich Charles, Prince of Leiningen and d of Francis, Duke of Saxe-Coburg-Saafeld	m. at St James's Palace, London, 10 Feb. 1840, her first cousin Francis ALBERT Augustus Charles Emmanuel (1819–61), second son of Ernest I, Duke of Saxe-Coburg-Gotha. 4s 5d	d., aged 81 years 243 days, 22 Jan. 1901 of senility at Osbourne, I.o.W. Frogmore	Assumed title Empress of India 1 May 1876. Succeeded by her elder surviving son, Albert Edward

King or Queen Regnant Date of Accession and Final Year of Reign; Style	Date and Place of Birth and Parentage	Marriages and No. of Children	Date, Cause and Place of Death, and Place of Burial	Notes and Succession
38. **EDWARD VII** 22 Jan. 1901–10 *Style:* 'By the Grace of God, of the United Kingdom of Great Britain and Ireland and of the British Dominions beyond the Seas, King, Defender of the Faith, Emperor of India'	9 Nov. 1841 at Buckingham Palace, London; elder surviving son of Victoria and Albert	m. at St George's Chapel, Windsor, 10 Mar. 1863, ALEXANDRA Caroline Maria Charlotte Louisa Julia (1844–1925), d of Christian IX of Denmark. 3s 3d	d., aged 68, 6 May, 1910, of bronchitis at Buckingham Palace. St George's Chapel, Windsor	Succeeded by his only surviving son, George Frederick Ernest Albert
39. **GEORGE V** 6 May 1910–36 *Style:* As for No. 37 until 12 May 1927, whereafter 'By the Grace of God, of Great Britain, Ireland, and of the British Dominions beyond the Seas, King, Defender of the Faith, Emperor of India'	3 June 1865 at Marlborough House, London; second and only surviving son of Edward VII and Alexandra	m. at St James's Palace, London, 6 July 1893, Victoria MARY Augusta Louise Olga Pauline Claudine Agnes (1867–1953), eldest child and only d of Francis, Duke of Teck. 5s 1d	d., aged 70, 20 Jan. 1936, of bronchitis at Sandringham House, Norfolk. St George's Chapel, Windsor	Succeeded by his eldest son, Edward Albert Christian George Andrew Patrick David
40. **EDWARD VIII** 20 Jan. 1936–11 Dec. 1936 *Style:* As for No. 39	23 June 1894 at the White Lodge, Richmond Park; eldest son of George V and Mary	m. at the Château de Candé, Monts, France, 3 June 1937, Bessie Wallis Warfield (b. 1896), previous wife of Lt. Earl Winfield Spencer, USN (div. 1927) and Ernest Simpson (div. 1936). No issue	d., aged 77, 28 May, 1972, of cancer of the throat at 4, Route du Champ, D'Entrainement, Paris XVIᵉ, France	Edward VIII abdicated for himself and his heirs and was succeeded by his eldest brother, Albert Frederick Arthur George
41. **GEORGE VI** 11 Dec. 1936–52 *Style:* As for No. 39 until the Indian title was dropped 22 June 1947	14 Dec. 1895 at York Cottage, Sandringham; second son of George V and Mary	m. at Westminster Abbey, 26 Apr. 1923, Lady ELIZABETH Angela Marguerite Bowes-Lyon (b. 1900), youngest d of 14th Earl of Strathmore and Kinghorne. 2d	d., aged 56, 6 Feb. 1952, of lung cancer at Sandringham House, Norfolk. St George's Chapel, Windsor	Succeeded by his elder d, Elizabeth Alexandra Mary
42. **ELIZABETH II** Since 6 Feb. 1952 *Style:* (from 29 May 1953) – By the Grace of God, of the United Kingdom of Great Britain and Northern Ireland and of Her other Realms and Territories, Queen, Head of the Commonwealth, Defender of the Faith'	21 Apr. 1926 at 17 Bruton Street, London, W1; elder d of George VI and Elizabeth	m. at Westminster Abbey, 20 Nov. 1947, her third cousin PHILIP (b. Corfu, Greece, 10 June 1921), only son of Prince Andrea (Andrew) of Greece and Princess Alice (great-grand-d of Queen Victoria). 3s 1d	—	The Heir Apparent is Charles Philip Arthur George, Prince of Wales, b. 14 Nov. 1948

UK Legislature

THE COMPOSITION OF THE TWO HOUSES OF PARLIAMENT

House of Lords

Peers of the Blood Royal	3
Archbishops of Canterbury and York	2
Dukes	27
Marquesses	36
Earls	171
Countesses in their own right	5
Viscounts	110
Anglican Bishops (by seniority)	23
Barons and Scots Lords (hereditary)	428
Baronesses in their own right (hereditary)	13
Life Peers (Barons)	312
Life Peeresses (Baronesses)	46
	1176

House of Commons

The size of the House of Commons has frequently been altered:

1885 By a Representation of the People Act (RPA) membership was increased by 12 to total 670.

1918 By an RPA, membership was increased by 37 to an all-time high point of 707.

1922 By two Acts of Parliament (the Partition of Ireland) membership was reduced by 92 to 615. (*Note:* Irish representation was reduced from 105 to 13 members representing Northern Ireland.)

1945 By an RPA, membership was increased by 25 to 640.

1948 By an RPA, membership was decreased by 15 to 625. (*Note:* This took effect in 1950 and involved the abolition of the 12 university seats and 12 double-member constituencies.)

1955 By an Order in Council under the House of Commons (Redistribution of Seats) Act, membership was increased by five to a total of 630.

1974 By an Order in Council membership was increased by 5 to a total of 635.

1983 By an Order in Council membership was increased by 15 to the present total of 650.

The results of the 23 general elections 1900–1983

No.	Election and Date	Total Seats	Conservatives	Liberals	Labour	Others	% Turn-out of Electorate
					Result (and % share of Total Poll)		
1	1900 (28 Sept.–24 Oct.)	670	**402**(51·1)	184(44·6)	2 (1·8)	82 (2·5)	74·6% of 6 730 935
2	1906 (12 Jan.–7 Feb.)	670	157(43·6)	**400**(49·0)	30 (5·9)	83 (1·5)	82·6% of 7 264 608
3	1910 (14 Jan.–9 Feb.)	670	273(46·9)	275(43·2)	40 (7·7)	82 (2·2)	86·6% of 7 694 741
4	1910 (2–19 Dec.)	670	272(46·3)	272(43·8)	42 (7·2)	84 (2·7)	81·1% of 7 709 981
5	1918 (14 Dec.)	707	**383**(38·7)	161(25·6)	73(23·7)	90(12·0)	58·9% of 21 392 322
6	1922 (15 Nov.)	615	**345**(38·2)	116(29·1)	142(29·5)	12 (3·2)	71·3% of 21 127 663
7	1923 (6 Dec.)	615	**258**(38·1)	159(29·6)	191(30·5)	7 (1·8)	70·8% of 21 281 232
8	1924 (29 Oct.)	615	**419**(48·3)	40(17·6)	151(33·0)	5 (1·1)	76·6% of 21 731 320
9	1929 (30 May)	615	260(38·2)	59(23·4)	**288**(37·1)	8 (1·3)	76·1% of 28 850 870
10	1931 (27 Oct.)	615	**521**(60·5)	37 (7·0)	52(30·6)	5 (1·7)	76·3% of 29 960 071
11	1935 (14 Nov.)	615	**432**(53·7)	20 (6·4)	154(37·9)	9 (2·0)	71·2% of 31 379 050
12	1945 (5 July)	640	213(39·8)	12 (9·0)	**393**(47·8)	22 (2·8)	72·7% of 33 240 391
13	1950 (23 Feb.)	625	298(43·5)	9 (9·1)	**315**(46·4)	3 (1·3)	84·0% of 33 269 770
14	1951 (25 Oct.)	625	**321**(48·0)	6 (2·5)	295(48·7)	3 (0·7)	82·5% of 34 465 573
15	1955 (25 May)	630	**344**(49·8)	6 (2·7)	277(46·3)	3 (1·2)	76·7% of 34 858 263
16	1959 (8 Oct.)	630	**365**(49·4)	6 (5·9)	258(43·8)	1 (0·9)	78·8% of 35 397 080
17	1964 (15 Oct.)	630	303(43·4)	9(11·1)	**317**(44·2)	1 (1·3)	77·1% of 35 894 307
18	1966 (31 Mar.)	630	253(41·9)	12 (8·5)	**363**(47·9)	2 (1·7)	75·9% of 35 965 127
19	1970 (18 June)	630	**330**(46·4)	6 (7·5)	288(43·0)	6 (3·1)	72·0% of 39 247 683
20	1974 (28 Feb.)	635	297(38·2)	14(19·3)	**301**(37·2)	23 (5·3)	78·8% of 39 752 317
21	1974 (10 Oct.)	635	277(35·8)	13(18·3)	**319**(39·3)	26 (6·6)	72·8% of 40 083 286
22	1979 (3 May)	635	**339**(43·9)	11(13·8)	268(36·9)	17 (5·4)	75·9% of 41 093 262
23	1983 (9 June)	650	**397**(42·4)	17(25·4) (Alliance)	209(27·6)	21 (4·6)	72·7% of 42 197 344

The 23 General Elections of 1900 to 1983

1900 Lord Salisbury's Conservative Government exercised its undoubted constitutional right to cash in on the apparently victorious (Mafeking and Pretoria) outcome of the Boer War two years before its 7 years of life was expired. The Liberal opposition called these tactics immoral and dubbed the election the 'Khaki Election'. The Government were given the most triumphant encore seen since the Reform Act of 1832 with an overall majority of 134 compared with the Dissolution figure of 128. The Liberal opposition was divided into the 'pro-Boers', comprising Gladstonians with the young Lloyd George, and the followers of Asquith, Haldane and Grey, who were Empire men.

1906 By December 1905 A J Balfour, who had succeeded his uncle as Prime Minister in 1902, had his majority reduced to 68 because of losses in by-elections. Feeling out of tune with the objects of the Tariff Reform League, he resigned. The King asked Campbell-Bannerman to form a government which he did and then immediately went to the country. The result was a landslide victory for the Liberals, who won an overall majority of 130. The Conservatives lost support mainly because of alarm over Chamberlain's Tariff Reform campaign and State support for Church of England schools, which offended nonconformist opinion. Liberal policy was the trinity of Free Trade, Home Rule for Ireland, and Humanitarianism.

1910 (Jan./Feb.) Asquith took over the premiership in 1908 shortly before the death of Campbell-Bannerman. The stock of the Tories rose because of Liberal pacifism in the face of the 'German Menace' and the Government lost 10 by-elections. The Liberal hopes of securing a second term rested on their taking advantage of the Conservative peers' inevitable rejection of Lloyd George's deliberately provocative budget. The government were thus handed on a plate the priceless slogan 'Lords versus the People'. The Liberals, however, only ended up with 125 seats fewer than their 1906 highwater mark. More seriously, they were now at the mercy of the jubilant 82 Irish Nationalists and 40 Labourites.

1910 (Dec.) The Government's House of Lords policy was: (1) abolition of Lords' power to veto over certified Money Bills; (2) a delaying power only of three sessions for other Bills, and (3) the life of a Parliament to be reduced from seven to five years. The ostensible reason for another

General Election was that the country should vote on these policies. But the real reason was that secretly King George V, who had succeeded his father that May, had insisted on a second appeal to the nation before giving his promise to create if necessary the required number of Liberal peers to vote the Parliament Bill through. The result of the election was almost a carbon copy of that eleven months previously.

1918 The victorious wartime premier, Lloyd George, at the head of the Coalition which had superseded Asquith's Liberal administration in 1916, went to the country in December 1918. The election was called by the opposition the 'coupon election'. This was because Lloyd George (Lib.) and Bonar Law (Con.) jointly signed letters (nicknamed 'coupons') giving support to those they regarded as loyal supporters of the Coalition. The Government's election policy in terms of slogans was 'Hang the Kaiser'; make the Germans pay for the war 'until the lemon pips squeak'; and make the country 'fit for heroes to live in'. Women over 30 were first given the vote. The Coalition won a crushing victory on a very low (58·9 per cent) poll.

1922 The Coalition Government under Lloyd George progressively lost the confidence of its predominant Conservative wing. The Conservatives disliked the Liberal Prime Minister's vacillating and extravagant domestic policies, especially in regard to agriculture and what they regarded as naïve foreign policies. Left-wing opinion was displeased with the rate of social progress on the home front. Many major strikes were organised. In Oct. 1922 the Conservatives resolved to fight the next election as an independent party. Lloyd George promptly resigned. Bonar Law formed a Government and went to the country. The Conservatives, with Bonar Law's policy of 'Tranquillity', won a majority of 75 over all other parties. The Labour Party overtook the divided Liberals by nearly doubling their representation to 142 and became the official Opposition.

1923 Bonar Law, who had started his premiership a sick man, retired in May 1923, and died shortly afterwards. His successor, in preference to Lord Curzon, was Stanley Baldwin. The main domestic problem was unemployment. Baldwin took the view that protective tariffs would alleviate it: but he was bound by Bonar Law's promise not to introduce such a measure. The only way out was to appeal to the country. The election saw a tiny change from the 1922

percentages but a dramatic loss of 87 seats by the Conservatives. Baldwin, although now in a minority of 99, waited to face the new Parliament and was inevitably defeated by a Labour-Liberal alliance and then resigned in favour of Ramsay MacDonald (Labour).

1924 MacDonald found himself embarrassingly short of talented Ministers and under intense pressure and scrutiny from the National Executive of the Labour Party. His greatest success was to sort out the Franco-German squabble over war reparation payments. The Government were brought down when their often unwilling allies, the Liberals, voted with the Tories for a motion for enquiry into the circumstances under which a journalist, J R Campbell, was to have his prosecution by the Attorney General for sedition (he advocated British soldiers disobeying orders if confronted with strikers) withdrawn. The Labour Party lost 40 seats and the Conservatives, profiting from there being fewer Liberal candidates, won an overall majority of 225 seats under Baldwin.

1929 Despite Baldwin's Government's surviving overall majority of 185 seats, Labour won this election with 288 seats, but could not command an absolute majority (Conservatives 260, Liberals 59, Others 8 = 327). Over 5 million women between the ages of 21 and 30 were eligible to vote for the first time. The Conservatives had adopted the uninspiring slogan 'Safety First'. The Labour Party, with the slogan 'Socialism In Our Time', had a three-pronged policy of world peace, disarmament, and a desire to deal more energetically with unemployment. The Liberals also based their appeal on unemployment remedies. The Liberal leader, Mr Lloyd George, decided to support Labour in office.

1931 The Labour Government committed themselves to increased expenditure and the unemployment figures rose alarmingly. A loss of confidence in sterling caused a summer crisis and Ramsay MacDonald suggested to his Cabinet an economy scheme which included the reduction of unemployment insurance benefits. The National Executive of the Labour Party and the TUC characteristically flatly refused to support any such measure. On 24 Aug. the Labour Government resigned and MacDonald formed a National Government which went to the polls on 27 Oct. The extent of their victory amazed contemporary opinion as the National Government won 554 seats, including 13 by National Labour candidates, while the opposition was reduced to 52 Labour and 4 Liberal Members.

1935 Ramsay MacDonald (National Labour) resigned his premiership in June 1935 and was logically succeeded by Stanley Baldwin (Conservative), who held a snap November General Election by dissolving Parliament two days short of the fourth anniversary of the 1931 election. The main issue was simply, did the nation approve of the work of the National Government in restoring the economy after the slump and want it to continue, or did the Nation want to revert to a Labour Government? The result was a massive vote of confidence in the National (predominantly Conservative) Government which won an overall majority of 249 seats. The Labour Party's main attack was over the 'Means Test' for unemployment assistance ('the dole'), although their own 1929 Government had accepted the principle of it, and the National Government had quickly withdrawn the new unsatisfactory regulations introduced earlier that year. Broadcasting for the first time played a significant rôle in the campaign with the public listening to a series of speeches made by the various Party Leaders every night during the first part of the election campaign.

1945 During the ten years since the previous election the country underwent the traumatic total war of 1939–45. Baldwin resigned in 1937 and was succeeded by Neville Chamberlain who resigned in 1940 at the nadir of our wartime fortunes. For the remaining five years Winston Churchill gave dynamic leadership which secured victory over Nazi Germany in May 1945. In that month the wartime Coalition broke up and was replaced by a predetermined Conservative administration. This Government, despite Churchill's premiership, was defeated by a Labour landslide. The new Government had Labour's first overall majority – 146 seats.

1950 Mr Attlee's administration launched the 'Welfare State' along the lines set out by various wartime White Papers, but his nationalisation measures, especially as regards steel, met fierce resistance. A balance of payments crisis in the autumn of 1949 compelled the Government to devalue the pound against the dollar and make drastic economies. The result of the February election was a narrow Labour victory with an overall majority of only 5.

1951 After 20 months of precarious administration, during which time the Conservatives ceaselessly harried the Government ranks, especially over the nationalisation of steel, Mr Attlee resigned. The last straw was another balance of payments crisis in September following the earlier resignation of Aneurin Bevan (Minister of Labour) and Harold Wilson (Pres., Board of Trade). The nation's reply to Mr Attlee's appeal over the radio for a larger majority was to elect the Conservatives with an overall majority of 17. Winston Churchill returned as Prime Minister.

1955 In April 1955, after 4½ years of government with a small majority, Sir Winston Churchill resigned as Prime Minister in favour of Sir Anthony Eden, who seven weeks later went to the country for a vote of confidence. The Conservatives had succeeded in restoring the nation's finances, had denationalised steel and road haulage, and twice reduced the standard rate of income tax by 6d. The Government's majority rose to 58 and the five years of near deadlock in the House was broken.

1959 In Jan. 1957, following the strain of the Suez crisis, Eden resigned and Harold Macmillan became Prime Minister. The Government had been losing support, largely owing to some unpopularity over the Rent Act. The new Prime Minister, despite a number of difficulties, managed to repair Conservative fortunes. His 1959 visit to the USSR and the further reduction of income tax in April added to general content-

ment. The election was fought on the Conservative theme 'life is better with us' while Labour got into difficulties with Mr Gaitskell's promises of no higher taxes, yet very expensive projects. The result was that the Government again increased their overall majority to 100 seats.

1964 The Conservative Government, after 13 consecutive years of rule, went to the country in October, as required every five years by the Parliament Act of 1911. After the post-war high water mark of 1959 (majority 100) Conservative fortunes declined owing notably to the Profumo scandal and a public wrangle over the successorship to Mr Macmillan who resigned in Oct. 1963 owing to ill health. The nation wanted a change: the Conservatives were however defeated by a rise in the Liberal vote from 5·9 per cent to 11·2 per cent rather than the Labour vote which was less than their 1959 total. Labour won by an overall majority of only 4.

1966 After 20 months in power, Mr Wilson became convinced (on the death of the Member for Falmouth in February) of the danger of continuing with his hairline majority. Labour fought the campaign on the slogan 'You Know Labour Government Works'. The Conservatives fought on a policy of entering the Common Market, reforming the 'over-mighty' Trade Unions and making the Welfare State less indiscriminate. Mr Wilson increased his overall majority from 3 to 97 and declared his intention to govern for five years to achieve 'a juster society'.

1970 Having completed four of the five years of his second term in power, Mr Wilson called the Labour Party to action in a bid for his hat-trick in May 1970. Remembered as the General Election most dominated by the pollsters, their findings consistently showed strong leads for Labour. Wages rates had risen in an unrestrained way in the five month run-up but prices levels were also just beginning to erode the reality of these monetary gains. Within six days of polling NOP showed a massive Labour lead of 12·4 per cent. In reality, however, the voters gave the Conservatives a 3·4 per cent lead, thus an overall majority of 30 seats.

1974 (Feb.) This was the first 'crisis' election since 1931. It was called to settle 'Who governs Britain?' under the duress of the National Union of Mineworkers' coal strike against the restraints of Stage III of the Incomes Policy. The situation was exacerbated by the Arab decision the previous November to raise the price of oil fourfold. A three-day week for most industries was decreed under Emergency Powers to start on 1 Jan. A ballot inviting the miners to give the NUM authority to call a strike was announced on 4 Feb., an election was called on 7 Feb., and a strike began on 10 Feb. after 81 per cent of the miners had voted in favour of giving the NUM Executive the authority they sought. Mr Wilson spoke of conciliation in place of confrontation and the alternative possibilities under a 'Social Contract' agreed between the Labour Party and the TUC on 18 Feb. 1973. The electorate, largely due to the impact of a successful Liberal campaign, spoke equivocally, giving Labour a majority of four over the Conservatives but 10 less than the combined Conservatives and Liberals. The Liberals rejected a coalition and appealed for a government of National Unity. Two hours after Mr Heath's resignation on 4 Mar., the Queen sent for Mr Wilson for a third time.

1974 (Oct.) For the first time since 1910 there were two elections within the same year. On 11 Mar. the miners returned to full working accepting a National Coal Board offer to raise their wage bill by 29 per cent. In June and July HM Opposition, with Liberal support, defeated Mr Wilson's precarious lobby strength 29 times, notably on the Trade Union and Labour Relation Bill. An election was called by Mr Wilson on 18 Sept. The campaign was fought mainly on

the issue of inflation statistics, unemployment prospects and the promise by Labour to hold an EEC ballot. Though less than 29 out of each 100 persons eligible to vote cast votes for Labour candidates, only 27 such voters supported Conservative candidates. Thus Mr Wilson won his fourth General Election, with an overall majority of three seats, but with a secure working majority of 42 over the Conservatives, who were by far the largest party in a fragmented Opposition. Mr Wilson resigned and was replaced by Mr Callaghan, who had been elected leader of the Labour Party on 5 Apr. 1976.

1979 (May) During the 1974–79 Parliament all three parties had changed their leaders: Callaghan for Wilson; Steel for Thorpe; and Mrs Thatcher for Heath. The period was one of falling living standards due in part to oil prices and inflation which reached a peak of 26·9% in August 1975 and was painfully reduced by a £6 pay increase limit in 1975–76, followed by a Phase II 5% limit in 1976–77 and an attempted 10% limit in 1977–78. The 5% 'guideline' in 1978–79 precipitated on 2 Jan. a prolonged lorry drivers strike and a winter of public service strikes causing much frustration and anger. On 28 March 1979 the Government was brought down by 1 vote on the issue of Scottish Devolution. The Conservatives fought the ensuing general election on trade union reform, cutting public expenditure, reducing taxation and Whitehall intervention. Mrs Thatcher gained 51 seats from Labour in a 5·2% swing mainly in the Midlands and South East to win a 44 overall majority. She became Britain's first and the world's 4th woman Prime Minister and had the largest margin of the popular vote since 1935.

1983 (June) Mrs Thatcher's success was only the second time a Conservative Prime Minister has ever been re-elected after a full term (Lord Salisbury in 1900 was the other). The Conservatives' increase of 58 seats over the 1979 result was also the largest ever by an incumbent government although allowance should be made for an estimated 21 seats gained through boundary changes. By contrast, Labour lost more than a quarter of its previous vote – the lowest ever share won by the principal party of opposition. That the Conservatives could win such a landslide victory with only 42·2 per cent of the national vote was mainly due to a divided opposition, with the Liberal/SDP Alliance, under David Steel and Roy Jenkins, securing 25·4 per cent compared to Labour's 27·6 per cent. The fact that Labour obtained 9 times as many seats as the Alliance, with only 2 per cent more of the vote, triggered new pressure for voting by proportional representation. Election issues included the abolition of the GLC and Metropolitan County Councils, unilateral nuclear disarmament and unemployment. The Conservatives capitalised on the first two and held off Labour's challenge on the third.

Prime Ministers of Great Britain and the United Kingdom

Below is complete compilation of the 51 Prime Ministers of Great Britain and the United Kingdom. The data run in the following order: final style as Prime Minister (with earlier or later styles); date or dates as Prime Minister with party affiliation; date and place of birth and death and place of burial; marriage or marriages with number of children; education and membership of Parliament with constituency and dates.

1. The Rt Hon, Sir Robert **WALPOLE**, KG (1726) KB (1725, resigned 1726), (PC 1714), cr. 1st Earl of Orford (of the 2nd creation) in the week of his retirement; ministry, 3 April 1721 to 8 Feb. 1742, (i) reappointed on the accession of George II on 11 June 1727, (ii) Walpole's absolute control of the Cabinet can only be said to have dated from 15 May 1730; Whig; b. 26

Aug. 1676 at Houghton, Norfolk; d. 18 Mar. 1745 at No. 5 Arlington St, Piccadilly, London; bur. Houghton, Norfolk m. 1 (1700) Catherine Shorter (d. 1717), m. 2ndly (1738) Maria Skerrett (d. 1738); children, 1st, 3s and 2d; 2nd, 2d (born prior to the marriage); ed. Eton and King's, Camb. (scholar); MP (Whig) for Castle Rising (1701–2); King's Lynn (1702–42) (expelled from the House for a short period 1712–13).

2. The Rt Hon, the Hon Sir Spencer Compton, 1st and last Earl of **WILMINGTON**, KG (1733), KB (1725, resigned 1733), (PC 1716), cr. Baron Wilmington 1728; cr. Earl 1730; ministry, 16 Feb. 1742 to 2 July 1743; Whig; b. 1673 or 1674; d. 2 July 1743; bur. Compton Wynyates, Warwickshire; unmarried; no legitimate issue; ed. St Paul's School, London, and Trinity, Oxford; MP (originally Tory until about 1704) for Eye (1698–1710); East Grinstead (1713–15); Sussex (Whig) (1715–28); Speaker 1715–27.

3. The Rt Hon, the Hon Henry **PELHAM** (PC 1725); prior to 1706 was Henry Pelham, Esq.; ministry 27 Aug. 1743 to 6 Mar. 1754 (with an interregnum 10–12 Feb. 1746); Whig; b. c. 1695; d. 6 Mar. 1754 at Arlington St, Piccadilly, London; bur. Laughton Church, nr. Lewes, E. Sussex; m. (1726) Lady Catherine Manners; children, 2s and 6d; ed. Westminster School and Hart Hall, Oxford; MP Seaford (1717–22); Sussex (1722–54).

4. The Rt Hon Sir William Pulteney, 1st and last Earl of **BATH** (cr. 1742) PC (1716) (struck off 1731); kissed hands 10 Feb. 1746 but unable to form a ministry; Whig; b. 22 Mar. 1684 in London; d. 7 July 1764; bur. Westminster Abbey; m. Anna Maria Gumley; ed. Westminster School and Christ Church, Oxford; MP Hedon (or Heydon) 1705–34; Middlesex 1734–42.

5. His Grace the 1st Duke of **NEWCASTLE** upon Tyne and 1st Duke of Newcastle under Lyme (The Rt Hon, the Hon Sir Thomas Pelham-Holles), Bt, KG (1718). (PC 1717); added the surname Holles in July 1711; known as Lord Pelham of Laughton (1711–14); Earl of Claire (1714–15); cr. Duke of Newcastle upon Tyne 1715 and cr. Duke of Newcastle under Lyme 1756; ministry, (a) 16 Mar. 1754 to 26 Oct. 1756, (b) 2 July 1757 to 25 Oct. 1760, (c) 25 Oct. 1760 to 25 May 1762; Whig; b. 21 July 1693; d. 17 Nov. 1768 at Lincoln's Inn Field, London; bur. Laughton Church, nr. Lewes, E. Sussex; m. (1717) Lady Henrietta Godolphin (d. 1776); no issue; ed. Westminster School and Claire Hall, Camb.

6. His Grace the 4th Duke of **DEVONSHIRE** (Sir William Cavendish, KG (1756), (PC 1751, but struck off roll 1762)); known as Lord Cavendish of Hardwick until 1729 and Marquess of Hartington until 1755; ministry, 16 Nov. 1756 to May 1757; Whig; b. 1720; d. 2 Oct. 1764 at Spa, Belgium; bur. Derby Cathedral; m. (1748) Charlotte Elizabeth, Baroness Clifford (d. 1754); children, 3s and 1d; ed. privately; MP (Whig) for Co. Derby (1741–51). Summoned to Lords (1751) in father's Barony Cavendish of Hardwick.

7. The Rt Hon James **WALDEGRAVE**, 2nd Earl of Waldegrave (pronounced Wallgrave) from 1741, PC (1752), KG (1757); kissed hands 8 June 1757 but returned seals 12 June being unable to form Ministry; b. 14 Mar. 1715; d. 28 Apr. 1763; m. Marion Walpole (niece of No. 1); children 3d; ed. Eton; took seat in House of Lords, 1741.

8. The 3rd Earl of **BUTE** (The Rt Hon, the Hon Sir John Stuart, KG (1762), KT (1738, resigned 1762), (PC 1760)); until 1723 was The Hon John Stuart; ministry, 26 May 1762 to 8 April 1763; Tory; b. 25 May 1713 at Parliament Square, Edinburgh; d. 10 Mar. 1792 at South Audley St, Grosvenor Square, London; bur. Rothesay, Bute; m. (1736) Mary Wortley-Montagu later

(1761) Baroness Mount Stuart (d. 1794); children, 4s and 4d (with other issue); ed. Eton.

9. The Rt Hon, the Hon George **GRENVILLE** (PC 1754); prior to 1749 was G. Grenville Esq; ministry, 16 Apr. 1763 to 10 July 1765; Whig; b. 14 Oct. 1712 at? Wotton, Bucks; d. 13 Nov. 1770 at Bolton St, Piccadilly, London; bur. Wotton, Bucks; m. (1749) Elizabeth Wyndham (d. 1769); children, 4s and 5d; ed. Eton and Christ Church, Oxford; MP for Buckingham (1741–70).

10. The Most Hon The 2nd Marquess of **ROCKINGHAM** (The Rt Hon Lord Charles Watson-Wentworth), KG (1760), (PC 1765); known as Hon Charles Watson-Wentworth until 1739; Viscount Higham (1739–46); Earl of Malton (1746–50); succeeded to Marquessate 14 Dec. 1750; ministry, (a) 13 July 1765 to July 1766, (b) 27 March 1782 to his death on 1 July 1782; Whig; b. 13 May 1730; d. 1 July 1782; bur. York Minster; m. (1752) Mary Bright (her father was formerly called Liddell) (d. 1804); no issue; ed. Westminster School (and possibly St John's Camb.). Took his seat in House of Lords 21 May 1751.

11. The 1st Earl of **CHATHAM** (The Rt Hon William Pitt (PC 1746)); cr. Earl 4 Aug. 1766; ministry, 30 July 1766 to 14 Oct. 1768; Whig; his health in 1767 prevented his being PM in other than name; b. 15 Nov. 1708 at St James's, Westminster, London; d. 11 May 1788 at Hayes, Kent; bur. Westminster Abbey; m. (1754) Hon. Hester Grenville*, later (1761) cr. Baroness Chatham in her own right (d. 1803); children, 3s and 2d; ed. Eton, Trinity, Oxford (took no degree owing to gout), and Utrecht; MP (Whig) Old Sarum (1735–47); Seaford (1747–54); Aldborough (1754–6); Okehampton (1756–7) (also Buckingham (1756), Bath (1757–66)).

12. His Grace the 3rd Duke of **GRAFTON** (The Rt Hon Sir Augustus Henry FitzRoy) KG (1769), (PC 1765); prior to 1747 known as the Hon. Augustus H. FitzRoy; 1747–57 as Earl of Euston; succeeded to dukedom in 1757; ministry, 14 Oct. 1768 to 28 Jan. 1770; Whig; he was virtually PM in 1767 when Lord Chatham's ministry broke down; b. 28 Sept. 1735 at St Marylebone, London; d. 14 Mar. 1811 at Euston Hall, Suffolk; bur. Euston, Suffolk; m. 1st (1765) Hon. Anne Liddell (sep. 1765, mar. dis. by Act of Parl. 1769) (d. 1804), m. 2ndly (1769) Elizabeth Wrottesley (d. 1822); children, 1st, 2s and 1d; 2nd, 6s and 6d (possibly also another d. who died young); ed, private school at Hackney, Westminster School, and Peterhouse, Camb; MP (Whig) Bury St Edmunds (1756–7).

13. Lord **NORTH** (The Rt Hon, the Hon Sir Frederick North), KG (1772), (PC 1766); succ. (Aug. 1790) as 2nd Earl of Guildford; ministry 28 Jan. 1770 to 20 Mar. 1782; Tory; b. 13 Apr. 1732 at Albermarle St, Piccadilly, London; d. 5 Aug. 1792 at Lower Grosvenor Street, London; bur. All Saints' Church, Wroxton, Oxfordshire; m. (1756) Anne Speke (d. 1797); children, 4s and 3d; ed. Eton; Trinity, Oxford, and Leipzig; MP (Tory) for Banbury (1754–90) (can be regarded as a Whig from 1783). Took his seat in the House of Lords 25 Nov. 1790.

14. The 2nd Earl of **SHELBURNE** (Rt Hon, the Hon Sir William Petty, KG (1782) (PC 1763); formerly, until 1751, William Fitz-Maurice; Viscount Fitz-Maurice (1753–61); succeeded to Earldom 10 May 1761; cr. The 1st Marquess of Lansdowne (6 Dec. 1784); Col. 1760: Maj. Gen. 1765; Lt. Gen. 1772, and Gen. 1783; ministry, 4 July 1782 to 24 Feb. 1783; Whig, b. 20 May 1737 at Dublin, Ireland, d. 7 May 1805 at Berkeley Square, London; bur. High Wycombe, Bucks; m. 1st (1765) Lady Sophia Carerett (d. 1771), 2ndly (1779) Lady Louisa FitzPatrick (d.

1789); children, 1st, 2s, 2nd, 1s and 1d; ed. local school in S. Ireland, private tutor, and Christ Church, Oxford; MP Chipping Wycombe (1760–1). Took seat in House of Lords (as Baron Wycombe) 3 Nov. 1761.

15. His Grace the 3rd Duke of **PORTLAND** (The Most Noble Sir William Henry Cavendish Bentinck, KG (1794) (PC 1765)); assumed additional name of Bentinck in 1775; assumed by Royal Licence surname of Cavendish-Bentinck in 1801; Marquess of Titchfield from birth until he succeeded to the dukedom on 1 May 1762; ministry (a) 2 April 1783 to Dec. 1783, (b) 31 Mar. 1807 to Oct. 1809; (a) coalition and (b) Tory; b. 14th Apr. 1738; d. 30 Oct. 1809 at Bulstrode, Bucks; bur. St Marylebone, London; m. (1766) Lady Dorothy Cavendish (d. 1794); children, 4s and 1d; ed. Westminster or Eton and Christ Church, Oxford, MP (Whig) Weobley, Herefordshire (1761–2).

16. The Rt Hon, the Hon William **PITT** (PC 1782) prior Aug. 1766 was William Pitt, Esq.; ministry (a) 19 Dec. 1783 to 14 Mar. 1801, (b) 10 May 1804 to his death on 23 Jan. 1806; Tory; b. 28 May 1759 at Hayes, nr. Bromley, Kent; d. 23 Jan. 1806 at Bowling Green House, Putney, Surrey; bur. Westminster Abbey; unmarried, ed. privately and Pembroke Hall, Cambridge, MP (Tory) Appleby.

17. The Rt Hon Henry **ADDINGTON** (PC 1789); cr. 1st Viscount Sidmouth 1805; ministry, 17 Mar. 1801 to 30 April 1804; Tory; b. 30 May 1757 at Bedford Row, London; d. 15 Feb. 1844 at White Lodge, Richmond Park, Surrey; bur. Mortlake; m. 1st (1781) Ursula Mary Hammond (d. 1811), 2ndly (1823) Hon Mrs Marianne Townshend (née Scott) (d. 1842); children, 1st, 3s and 4d, 2nd, no issue; ed. Cheam, Winchester Col., Lincoln's Inn, and Brasenose, Oxford (Chancellor's Medal for English Essay); MP (Tory) Devizes (1783–1805). Speaker 1789–1801. As a peer he supported the Whigs in 1807 and 1812 administration.

18. The Rt Hon the 1st Baron **GRENVILLE** of Wotton-under-Bernewood (William Wyndham Grenville (PC(I) 1782; PC 1783)); cr. Baron 25 Nov. 1790; ministry, 10 Feb. 1806 to Mar. 1807; b. (the son of No. 9) 25 Oct. 1759; d. 12 Jan. 1834 at Dropmore Lodge, Bucks; bur. Burnham, Bucks; m. (1792) Hon Anne Pitt (d. 1864 aged 91); no issue; ed. Eton, Christ Church, Oxford (Chancellor's prize for Latin Verse), and Lincoln's Inn; MP Buckingham (1782–4), Buckinghamshire (1784–90). Speaker Jan.–June 1789.

19. The Rt Hon, the Hon Spencer **PERCEVAL** (PC 1807), KC (1796); ministry, 4 Oct. 1809 to 11 May 1812; b. 1 Nov. 1762 at Audley Sq., London; murdered 11 May 1812 in lobby of the House; bur. at Charlton; m. (1790) Jane Spencer-Wilson (later Lady Carr) (d. 1844); children, 6s and 6d; ed. Harrow, Trinity, Camb., and Lincoln's Inn; MP (Tory) Northampton (1796–and 1797).

20. The Rt Hon the 2nd Earl of **LIVERPOOL** (Sir Robert Banks Jenkinson, KG (1814) (PC 1799)); from birth to 1786 R B Jenkinson, Esq.; from 1786–96 The Hon R B Jenkinson; from 1796–1808 (when he succeeded to the earldom) Lord Hawkesbury; ministry, (a) 8 June 1812 to 29 Jan. 1820, (b) 29 Jan. 1820 to 17 Feb. 1827; Tory; b. 7 June 1770; d. 4 Dec. 1828 at Coombe Wood, near Kingston-on-Thames; bur. at Hawkesbury; m. 1st (1795) Lady Louisa Theodosia Hervey (d. 1821), 2ndly (1822) Mary Chester (d. 1846); no issue; ed. Charterhouse and Christ Church, Oxford; summoned to House of Lords in his father's barony of Hawkesbury 15 Nov. 1803 (elected MP (Tory) for Appleby (1790) but did not sit as he was under age); Rye (1796–1803).

21. The Rt Hon George **CANNING** (PC 1800); ministry, 10 Apr. 1827 to his death; Tory; b. 11

---

* This lady had the extraordinary distinction of being the wife, the mother, the sister and the aunt of four British Prime Ministers. They were Nos. 11, 16, 9, and 18 respectively.

Apr. 1770 in London; d. 8 Aug. 1827 at Chiswick Villa, London; m. (1800) Joan Scott (later, 1828, cr. Viscountess) (d. 1837); children, 3s and 1d; ed. in London; Hyde Abbey (nr. Winchester); Eton; Christ Church, Oxford (Chancellor's prize, Latin Verse), and Lincoln's Inn; MP (Tory) Newton, I.o.W. (1793–6); Wendover (1796–1802); Tralee (1802–6); Newton (1806–7); Hastings (1807–12); Liverpool (1812–23); Harwich (1823–6); Newport (1826–7), and Seaford (1827).

22. The Viscount **GODERICH** (Rt Hon, the Hon Frederick John Robinson (PC 1812, PC (I) c. 1833); cr. Earl of Ripon 1833; ministry 31 Aug. 1827 to 8 Jan. 1828; Tory; b. 1 Nov. 1782 in London; d. 28 Jan. 1859 at Putney Heath, London; bur. Nocton, Lincs; m. (1814) Lady Sarah Albinia Louisa Hobart (d. 1867); children, 2s and 1d; ed. Harrow; St John's Col., Camb., and Lincoln's Inn; MP Carlow (1806–7); Ripon (1807–27).

23. His Grace The 1st Duke of **WELLINGTON** (The Most Noble, The Hon Sir Arthur Wellesley, KG (1813), GCB (1815), GCH (1816), (PC 1807, PC (I) (1807); known as The Hon Arthur Wesley until 1804; then as The Hon Sir Arthur Wellesley, KB, until 1809 when cr. The Viscount Wellington; cr. Earl of Wellington Feb. 1812; Marquess of Wellington Oct. 1812 and Duke May 1814. Ensign (1787); Lieut. (1787); Capt. (1791); Major (1793); Lt-Col (1793); Col (1796); Maj. Gen. (1802); Lt. Gen. (1808); Gen. (1811); Field Marshal (1813); ministry, (a) 22 Jan. 1828 to 26 June 1830, (b) 26 June 1830 to 21 Nov. 1830, (c) 17 Nov. to 9 Dec. 1834; Tory; b. 1 May 1769 at Mornington House, Upper Merrion St., Dublin; d. 14 Sept. 1852 at Walmer Castle, Kent; bur. St Paul's Cathedral; m. (1806) the Hon Catherine Sarah Dorothea Pakenham (d. 1831); children, 2s; ed. Browns Seminary, King's Rd., Chelsea, London; Eton; Brussels, and The Academy at Angiers; MP Rye (1806); St Michael (1807); Newport, Isle of Wight (1807–9). Took seat in House of Lords as Viscount, Earl, Marquess, and Duke 28 June 1814. Physical height: 5 ft 9½ in 1,76 m.

24. The 2nd Earl **GREY** (The Rt Hon, the Hon Sir Charles Grey, Bt (1808), KG (1831), (PC 1806); styled Viscount Howick 1806–7 and previously The Hon Charles Grey; ministry, 22 Nov. 1830 to July 1834; Whig; b. 13 Mar. 1764 at Fallodon, Northumberland; d. 17 July 1845 and bur. at Howick House, Northumberland; m. (1794) Hon Mary Elizabeth Ponsonby (d. 1861); children, 8s and 5d; ed. at a private school in Marylebone, London; Eton; Trinity, Camb., and Middle Temple; MP (Whig) Northumberland (1786–1807); Appleby (1807); Tavistock (1807).

25. The 3rd Viscount **MELBOURNE** (The Rt Hon, The Hon Sir William Lamb, Bt (PC (UK & I) 1827)); ministry, (a) 16 July 1834 to Nov. 1834, (b) 18 April 1835 to 20 June 1837, (c) 20 June 1837 to Aug. 1841; Whig; b. (of disputed paternity) 15 March 1779 Melbourne House, Piccadilly, London; d. 24 Nov. 1848 at Brocket; bur. at Hatfield; m. (1805) Lady Caroline Ponsonby, separated 1824 (d. 1828); only 1s survived infancy; ed. Eton; Trinity, Cambridge; Glasgow University, and Lincoln's Inn; MP (Whig) Leominster (1806); Haddington Borough (1806–7); Portarlington (1807–12); Peterborough (1816–19); Herts (1819–26); Newport, Isle of Wight (1827); Bletchingley (1827–8). Took his seat in House of Lords 1 Feb. 1829.

26. The Rt Hon Sir Robert **PEEL**, Bt (PC 1812); prior to May 1830 he was Robert Peel, Esq., MP, when he succeeded as 2nd Baronet; ministry, (a) 10 Dec. 1834 to 8 Apr. 1835, (b) 30 Aug. 1841 to 29 June 1846; Conservative; b. 5 Feb. 1788 prob. at Chamber Hall, nr. Bury, Lancashire; d. 2 July 1850 after fall from horse; bur. at Drayton Bassett; m. (1820) Julia Floyd (d. 1859); children, 5s and 2d; ed. Harrow; Christ Church, Oxford (Double First in Classics

and Mathematics), and Lincoln's Inn; MP (Tory) Cashel (Tipperary) (1809–12); Chippenham (1812–17); Univ. of Oxford (1817–29); Westbury (1829–30); Tamworth (1830–50).

27. The Rt Hon Lord John **RUSSELL** (PC 1830), and after 30 July 1861 1st Earl **RUSSELL**, KG (1862), GCMG (1869); ministry, (a) 30 June 1846 to Feb. 1852, (b) 29 Oct. 1865 to June 1866; (a) Whig and (b) Liberal; b. 18 Aug. 1792 in Hertford St, Mayfair; d. 28 May 1878 at Pembroke Lodge, Richmond Park, Surrey; bur. Chenies, Bucks; m. 1st (1835) Adelaide (née Lister), Dowager Baroness Ribblesdale (d. 1838), 2ndly (1841) Lady Frances Anna Maria Elliot-Murray-Kynynmound (d. 1898); children, 1st, 2d, 2nd 3s and 3d; ed. Westminster School and Edinburgh University; MP (Whig) Tavistock (1813–17, 1818–20 & 1830–1); Hunts (1820–6); Bandon (1826–30); Devon (1831–2); S. Devon (1832–5); Stroud (1835–41); City of London (1841–61). Took seat in the House of Lords on 30 July 1861.

28. The 14th Earl of **DERBY**, Rt Hon Sir Edward Geoffrey Smith-Stanley, Bt, KG (1859), GCMG (1869), PC 1830, PC (I) (1831); prior to 1834 known as the Hon E G Stanley, MP; then known as Lord Stanley MP until 1844; ministry, (a) 23 Feb. 1852 to 18 Dec. 1852, (b) 20 Feb. 1858 to 11 June 1859, (c) 28 June 1866 to 26 Feb. 1868; Tory and Conservative; b. 19 March 1799 at Knowsley, Lancs; d. 23 Oct. 1869 and bur. at Knowsley, Lancs; m. (1825) Hon Emma Caroline Wilbraham-Bootle (d. 1876); 2s, 1d; ed. Eton; Christ Church Oxford (Chancellor's prize for Latin Verse); MP (Whig) Stockbridge (1822–6); Preston (1826–30); Windsor (1831–2); North Lancs (1832–44). Summoned 1844 to House of Lords as Lord Stanley (of Bickerstaffe); succeeded to Earldom 1851; became a Tory in 1835.

29. The Rt Hon Sir George Hamilton Gordon, Bt, 4th Earl of **ABERDEEN**, KG (1855), KT (1808), (PC 1814); prior to Oct. 1791 known as the Hon G Gordon; from 1791 to Aug. 1801 known as Lord Haddo; assumed additional name of Hamilton Nov. 1818; ministry, 19 Dec. 1852 to 5 Feb. 1855; Peelite; b. 28 Jan. 1784 in Edinburgh; d. 14 Dec. 1860 at Argyll House, St James's, London; bur. at Stanmore, G. London; m. 1st (1805) Lady Catherine Elizabeth Hamilton (d. 1812), 2ndly (1815) to her sister-in-law Harriet (née Douglas), Dowager Viscountess Hamilton (d. 1833); children, 1st, 1s and 3d, 2nd 4s and 1d; ed. Harrow and St John's, Camb.; House of Lords 1814.

30. The Rt Hon Sir Henry John Temple, 3rd and last Viscount **PALMERSTON** (a non-representative peer of Ireland), KG (1856), CGB (1832), (PC 1809); known (1784–1802) as the Hon H J Temple; ministry, (a) 6 Feb. 1855 to 19 Feb. 1858, (b) 12 June 1859 to 18 Oct. 1865; Liberal; b. 20 Oct. 1784 at Broadlands, nr. Romsey, Hants (or possibly in Park St, London); d. 18 Oct. 1865 at Brocket Hall, Herts; bur. Westminster Abbey; m. (1839) Hon. Emily Mary (née Lamb), the Dowager Countess Cowper (d. 1869); no issue; ed. Harrow; Univ. of Edinburgh, and St John's Camb.; MP (Tory) Newport, Isle of Wight (1807–11); Camb. Univ. (1811–31); Bletchingley (1831–2); S. Hants. (1832–4); Tiverton (1835–65); from 1829 a Whig and latterly a Liberal.

31. The Rt Hon Benjamin **DISRAELI**, 1st and last Earl of **BEACONSFIELD**, KG (1878), (PC 1852); prior to 12 Aug. 1876 Benjamin Disraeli (except that until 1838 he was known as Benjamin D'Israeli); ministry, (a) 27 Feb. 1868 to November 1868, (b) 20 Feb. 1874 to Apr. 1880; Conservative; b. 21 Dec. 1804 at either the Adelphi, Westminster, or at 22 Theobald's Rd, or St Mary Axe; d. 19 Apr. 1881 at 19 Curzon St, Mayfair, London; bur. Hughenden Manor, Bucks (monument in Westminster Abbey); m. (1839) Mrs Mary Anne Lewis (née Evans) later (1868) Viscountess (in her own

right) Beaconsfield; no issue; ed. Lincoln's Inn; MP (Con.) Maidstone (1837–41); Shrewsbury (1841–7); Buckinghamshire (1847–76), when he became a peer.

32. The Rt Hon William Ewart **GLADSTONE** (PC 1841); ministry, (a) 3 Dec. 1868 to February 1874, (b) 23 April 1880 to 12 June 1885, (c) 1 Feb. 1886 to 20 July 1886, (d) 15 Aug. 1892 to 3 March 1894; Liberal; b. 29 Dec. 1809 at 62 Rodney St, Liverpool; d. 19 May 1898 (aged 88 yr 142 days) at Hawarden Castle, Clwyd; bur. Westminster Abbey; m. (1839) Catherine Glynne (d. 1900); children, 4s and 4d; ed. Seaforth Vicarage; Eton and Christ Church, Oxford (Double First in Classics and Mathematics); MP Tory, Newark (1832–45); Univ. of Oxford (1847–65) (Peelite to 1859, thereafter a Liberal); S. Lancs. (1865–8); Greenwich (1868–80); Midlothian (1880–95).

33. The Rt Hon Robert Arthur Talbot Gascoyne-Cecil, the 3rd Marquess of **SALISBURY**, KG (1878), GCVO (1902), (PC 1866); known as Lord Robert Cecil till 1865; and as Viscount Cranbourne, MP, from 1865 to 1868; ministry, (a) 23 June 1885 to 28 Jan. 1886, (b) 25 July 1886 to Aug. 1892, (c) 25 June 1895 to 22 Jan. 1901, (d) 23 Jan. 1901 to 11 July 1902; Conservative; b. 3 Feb. 1830 at Hatfield House, Herts; d. 22 Aug. 1903 at Hatfield House; bur. at Hatfield; m. (1857) Georgiana Charlotte (née Alderson), Lady of the Royal Order of Victoria and Albert and C.I. (1899) (d. 1899); Children, 4s and 3d; ed. Eton and Christ Church, Oxford (Hon. 4th Cl. Maths.); MP (Con.) for Stamford (1853–68).

34. The Rt Hon Sir Archibald Philip Primrose, Bt, 5th Earl of **ROSEBERY**, KT (1895), VD (PC 1881); b. the Hon A P Primrose; known as Lord Dalmeny (1851–68); Earl of Midlothian from 1911 but style not adopted by him; ministry, 5 Mar. 1894 to 21 June 1895; Liberal; b. 7 May 1847 at Charles St, Berkeley Square, London; d. 21 May 1929 at 'The Durdans', Epsom, Surrey; bur. at Dalmeny; m. (1878) Hannah de Rothschild (d. 1890); children, 2s and 2d; ed. Eton and Christ Church, Oxford.

35. The Rt Hon Arthur James **BALFOUR** (PC 1885), PC (I) 1887); KG (1922), later (1922) the 1st Earl of Balfour, OM (1916); ministry, 12 July 1902 to 4 Dec. 1905; Conservative; b. 25 July 1848 at Whittingehame, E. Lothian, Scotland; d. 19 Mar. 1930 at Fisher's Hill, Woking, Surrey; bur. at Whittingehame; unmarried; ed. Eton and Trinity, Camb; MP (Con.) Hertford (1874–85); E. Manchester (1885–1906); City of London (1906–22).

36. The Rt Hon Sir Henry **CAMPBELL-BANNERMAN**, GCB (1895), (PC 1884); known as Henry Campbell until 1872; ministry, 5 Dec. 1905 to 5 Apr. 1908; Liberal; b. 7 Sept. 1836 at Kelvinside House, Glasgow; d. 22 Apr. 1908 at 10 Downing Street, London; bur. Meigle, Scotland; m. (1860) Sarah Charlotte Bruce (d. 1906); no issue; ed. Glasgow High School; Glasgow Univ. (Gold Medal for Greek); Trinity, Camb. (22nd Sen. Optime in Maths Tripos; 3rd Cl. in Classical Tripos); MP (Lib.) Stirling District (1868–1908).

37. The Rt Hon Herbert Henry **ASQUITH** (PC 1892, PC (I) 1916); later (1925) 1st Earl of **OXFORD AND ASQUITH**, KG (1925); ministry, (a) 7 Apr. 1908 to 7 May 1910, (b) 8 May 1910 to 5 Dec. 1916 (coalition from 25 May 1915); Liberal; b. 12 Sept. 1852 at Morley, W. Yorks; d. 15 Feb. 1928 at 'The Wharf', Sutton Courtney, Berks; bur. Sutton Courtney Church; m. 1st (1877) Helen Kelsall Melland (d. 1891), 2ndly (1894) Emma Alice Margaret Tennant; children, 1st, 4s and 1d, 2nd 1s and 1d; ed. City of London School; Balliol, Oxford (Scholar, 1st Class Lit. Hum.); MP (Lib.) East Fife (1886–1918); Paisley (1920–4).

38. The Rt Hon (David) Lloyd **GEORGE**, OM (1919), (PC 1905); later (1945) 1st Earl **LLOYD-GEORGE** of Dwyfor; ministry, 7 Dec. 1916 to 19 Oct. 1922; Coalition; b. 17 Jan. 1863 in Manchester; d. 26 Mar. 1945 at Ty Newydd, nr. Llanystumdwy; bur. on the bank of the river Dwyfor; m. 1st (1888) Margaret Owen, GBE (1920) (d. 1941), 2ndly (1943) Frances Louise Stevenson, CBE; children, 1st 2s and 3d, 2nd no issue; ed. Llanystumdwy Church School and privately; MP Caernarvon Boroughs (1890–1945) (Lib. 1890–1931 and 1935–45; Ind. Lib. 1931–5). Physical height: 5 ft 6 in *1,67 m*.

39. The Rt Hon (Andrew) Bonar **LAW** (PC 1911); ministry, 23 Oct. 1922 to 20 May 1923; Conservative; b. 16 Sept. 1858 at Kingston, nr. Richibucto, New Brunswick, Canada; d. 30 Oct. 1923 at 24 Onslow Grdns., London; bur. Westminster Abbey; m. (1891) Annie Pitcairn (d. 1909); children, 4s and 2d; ed. Gilbertfield School, Hamilton; Glasgow High School; MP (Con.) Blackfriars Div. of Glasgow (1900–6); Dulwich Div. of Camberwell (1906–10); MP Bootle Div. of Lancs (1911–18); Central Div. of Glasgow (1918–23). Physical height: 6 ft 0 in *1,83 m*.

40. The Rt Hon Stanley **BALDWIN** (PC 1920, PC (Can.) 1927); later (1937) 1st Earl Baldwin of Bewdley, KG (1937); ministry, (a) 22 May 1923 to 22 Jan. 1924 (Con.), (b) 4 Nov. 1924 to 4 June 1929 (Con.), (c) 7 June 1935 to 20 Jan. 1936 (Nat.), (d) 21 Jan. 1936 to 11 Dec. 1936 (Nat.), (e) 12 Dec. 1936 to 28 May 1937 (Nat.); b. 3 Aug. 1867 at Bewdley; d. Astley, 14 Dec. 1947; bur. Worcester Cathedral; m. (1892) Lucy Ridsdale, GBE (1937) (d. 1945); children, 2s and 4d; ed. Harrow and Trinity, Camb.; MP (Con.) Bewdley Div. of Worcestershire (1908–37). Physical height: 5 ft 8½ in *1,74 m*.

41. The Rt Hon (James) Ramsay **MACDON-ALD** (PC 1924, PC (Canada) 1929); ministry, (a) 22 Jan. 1924 to 4 Nov. 1924 (Labour), (b) 5 June 1929 to 7 June 1935 (Labour and from 1931 National Coalition); b. 12 Oct. 1866 at Lossiemouth, Grampian; d. 9 Nov. 1937 at sea, mid-Atlantic; bur. Spynie Churchyard, nr. Lossiemouth, Scotland; m. (1896) Margaret Ethel Gladstone (d. 1911); children, 3s and 3d; ed. Drainie Parish Board School; MP (Lab.) Leicester (1906–18); (Lab.) Aberavon (1922–9); (Lab.) Seaham Div. Co. Durham (1929–31); (Nat. Lab.) (1931–5); MP for Scottish Univs. (1936–7). Physical height: 5 ft 10½ in *1,79 m*.

42. The Rt Hon (Arthur) Neville **CHAMBER-LAIN** (PC 1922); ministry, 28 May 1937 to 10 May 1940; National; b. 18 Mar. 1869 at Edgbaston, Birmingham; d. 9 Nov. 1940 at High Field Park, Hickfield, nr. Reading; ashes interred Westminster Abbey; m. (1911) Annie Vere Cole (d. 12 Feb. 1967); children, 1s and 1d; ed. Rugby School; Mason College (later Birmingham Univ.) (Metallurgy & Engineering Design); MP (Con.) Ladywood Div. of Birmingham (1918–29); Edgbaston Div. of Birmingham (1929–40). Physical height: 5 ft 10 in *1,77 m*.

43. The Rt Hon Sir Winston (Leonard **SPEN-CER-)CHURCHILL**; KG (1953) OM (1946), CH (1922), TD (PC 1907); ministry, (a) 10 May 1940 to 26 July 1945 (Coalition but from 23 May 1945 Conservative), (b) 26 Oct. 1951 to 6 Feb. 1952 (Conservative), (c) 7 Feb. 1952 to 5 Apr. 1955 (Conservative); b. 30 Nov. 1874 at Blenheim Palace, Woodstock, Oxon; d. 24 Jan. 1965 Hyde Park Gate, London; bur. Bladon, Oxfordshire; m. (1908) Clementine Ogilvy Hozier, GBE (1946), cr. 1965 (Life) Baroness Spencer-Churchill (d. 13 Dec. 1977); children, 1s and 4d; ed. Harrow School and Royal Military College; MP (Con. until 1904, then Lib.) Oldham (1900–6); (Lib.) N.-W. Manchester (1906–8); (Lib.) Dundee (1908–18 and (Coalition Lib.) until 1922); Epping Div. of Essex (1924–45); Woodford Div. of Essex (1945–64); Physical height: 5 ft 8½ in *1,74 m*.

44. The Rt Hon Clement (Richard) **ATTLEE** CH (1945), (PC 1935); created 1955 1st Earl Attlee, KG (1956), OM (1951); ministry, 26 July 1945 to 26 Oct. 1951; Labour; b. 3 Jan. 1883 at Putney, London; d. Westminster Hospital, 8 Oct. 1967; m. (1922) Violet Helen Millar, children, 1s and 3d; ed. Haileybury College and Univ. College, Oxford (2nd Cl. Hons. (Mod. Hist)); MP Limehouse Div. of Stepney (1922–50); West Walthamstow (1950–5). Physical height: 5 ft 8 in *1,73 m*.

45. The Rt. Hon Sir (Robert) Anthony **EDEN**, KG (1954), MC (1917), (PC 1934); cr. 1961 1st Earl of Avon; ministry, 6 Apr. 1955 to 9 Jan. 1957; Conservative; b. 12 June 1897 Windlestone, Durham; d. Alvediston, Wilts. 14 Jan. 1977; m. 1st (1923) Beatrice Helen Beckett (m. dis. 1950) (d. 1957), 2ndly (1952) Anne Clarissa Spencer-Churchill, children, 1st, 2s 2nd, no issue; ed. Eton and Christ Church, Oxford (1st Cl. Hons (Oriental Langs)); MP Warwick and Leamington (1923–57). Physical height: 6 ft 0 in *1,83 m*.

46. The Rt Hon (Maurice) Harold **MACMIL-LAN** OM (1976) (PC 1942); ministry, 10 Jan. 1957 to 18 Oct. 1963; Conservative; b. 10 Feb. 1894, 52 Cadogan Place, London; m. (1920) Lady Dorothy Evelyn Cavendish, GBE; children, 1s and 3d; ed. Eton (Scholar); Balliol, Oxford ((Exhibitioner) 1st Class Hon Mods.); MP Stockton-on-Tees (1924–9 and 1931–45); Bromley (1945–64). Physical height: 6 ft 0 in *1,83 m*.

47. The Rt Hon Sir Alexander (Frederick) **DOUGLAS-HOME**, KT (1962) (PC 1951); known until 30 April 1918 as the Hon A F Douglas-Home; thence until 11 July 1951 as Lord Dunglass; thence until his disclaimer of 23 Oct. 1963 as the (14th) Earl of Home, Lord Home of the Hirsel; ministry, 19 Oct. 1963 to 16 Oct. 1964; Conservative; b. 2 July 1903, 28 South St, London; m. (1936) Elizabeth Hester Alington; children, 1s and 3d; ed. Eton; Christ Church, Oxford; MP South Lanark (1931–45); Lanark (1950–1); Kinross and West Perthshire (1963–74). Physical height: 5 ft 11 in *1,80 m*.

48. The Rt Hon Sir (James) Harold **WILSON**; KG (1976) OBE (civ.) (1945) (PC 1947); ministry, (a) 16 Oct. 1964 to 30 Mar. 1966 (b) 31 Mar. 1966 to 17 June 1970, (c) 4 Mar. 1974 to 10 Oct. 1974, (d) 10 Oct. 1974 to 5 Apr. 1976; Labour; b. Linthwaite, W. Yorks, 11 Mar. 1916; m. (1940) Gladys Mary Baldwin; children, 2s; ed. Milnsbridge C.S.; Royds Hall S.; Wirral G.S.; Jesus College, Oxford (1st Cl. Philosophy, Politics and Economics); MP Ormskirk (1945–50); Huyton (1950 to date). Physical height: 5 ft 8½ in *1,74 m*.

49. The Rt Hon Edward Richard George **HEATH**, MBE (mil.) (1946), (PC 1955); ministry, 18 June 1970 to 3 Mar. 1974; Conservative; b. 9 July 1916 at Broadstairs, Kent; unmarried; ed. Chatham House School, Ramsgate and Balliol College, Oxford; MP Bexley (1950–74); Bexley-Sidcup from 1974. Physical height: 5 ft 11 in *1,80 m*.

50. The Rt Hon (Leonard) James **CAL-LAGHAN** (PC 1964); ministry 5 Apr. 1976 to 4 May 1979; Labour; b. 27 Mar. 1912 at 38 Funtingdon Rd, Portsmouth, Hampshire; m. (1938) Audrey Elizabeth Moulton, children 1s and 2d; ed. Portsmouth Northern Secondary Sch.; MP South Cardiff (1945–50); Southeast Cardiff (1950 to date). Physical height: 6 ft 1½ in *1,87 m*.

51. The Rt Hon Mrs Margaret (Hilda) **THATCHER** *née* Roberts (PC 1970); ministry (a) 4 May 1979 to 9 June 1983 (b) 10 June 1983 to date; Conservative; b. 13 Oct. 1925, Grantham, Lincolnshire; m. (13 Dec. 1951) Denis Thatcher MBE (b. 10 May 1915, he prev. m. Margaret D. Kempson, who in 1948 m. Sir Howard Hickman 3rd Bt.); 1s 1d (twins); ed. Kesteven & Grantham Girls' Sch.; Somerville Coll., Oxford (MA, BSc); MP Finchley (1959–74); Barnet, Finchley (1974 to date). Physical height: 5 ft 5 in *1,65 m*.

Authorised Post nominal letters in their correct order

There are 72 Orders, Decorations, and Medals which have been bestowed by the Sovereign that carry the entitlement to a group of letters after the name. Of these, 54 are currently awardable. The order (*vide London Gazette*, supplement 27 Oct. 1964) is as follows:

1	VC	Victoria Cross.
2	GC	George Cross.
3	KG	(but *not* for Ladies of the Order), Knight of the Most Noble Order of the Garter.
4	KT	(but *not* for Ladies of the Order), Knight of the Most Ancient and Most Noble Order of the Thistle.
5	GCB	Knight Grand Cross of the Most Honourable Order of the Bath.
6	OM	Member of the Order of Merit.
7*	GCSI	Knight Grand Commander of the Most Excellent Order of the Star of India.
8	GCMG	Knight (or Dame) Grand Cross of the Most Distinguished Order of St Michael and St George.
9*	GCIE	Knight Grand Commander of the Most Eminent Order of the Indian Empire.
10*	CI	Lady of The Imperial Order of the Crown of India.
11	GCVO	Knight (or Dame) Grand Cross of the Royal Victorian Order.
12	GBE	Knight (or Dame) Grand Cross of the Most Excellent Order of the British Empire.
13	CH	Member of the Order of Companions of Honour.
14	KCB	(but *not* if also a GCB) Knight Commander of the Most Honourable Order of the Bath.
15	DCB	(but *not* if also a GCB) Dame Commander of the Most Honourable Order of the Bath.
16*	KCSI	(but *not* if also a GCSI), Knight Commander of the Most Excellent Order of the Star of India.
17	KCMG	(but *not* if also a GCMG), Knight Commander of the Most Distinguished Order of St Michael and St George.
18	DCMG	(but *not* if also a GCMG) Dame Commander of the Most Distinguished Order of St Michael and St George.
19*	KCIE	(but *not* if also a GCIE), Knight Commander of the Most Eminent Order of the Indian Empire.
20	KCVO	(but *not* if also a GCVO), Knight Commander of the Royal Victorian Order.
21	DCVO	(but *not* if also a GCVO), Dame Commander of the Royal Victorian Order.
22	KBE	(but *not* if also a GBE), Knight Commander of the Most Excellent Order of the British Empire.
23	DBE	(but *not* if also a GBE), Dame Commander of the Most Excellent Order of the British Empire.
24	CB	(but *not* if also a GCB and/or a KCB), Companion of the Most Honourable Order of the Bath.
25*	CSI	(but *not* if also a GCSI and/or a KCSI), Companion of the Most

26	CMG	Excellent Order of the Star of India. (but *not* if also a GCMG and/or a KCMG or DCMG), Companion of the Most Distinguished Order of St Michael and St George.
27*	CIE	(but *not* if also a GCIE and/or a KCIE), Companion of the Most Eminent Order of the Indian Empire.
28	CVO	(but *not* if also a GCVO and/or a KCVO or DCVO), Commander of the Royal Victorian Order.
29	CBE	(but *not* if also a GBE and/or a KBE or DBE), Commander of the Most Excellent Order of the British Empire.
30	DSO	Companion of the Distinguished Service Order.
31	MVO	(but *not* if also either a GCVO and/or a KCVO or a DCVO, and/or a CVO), Lieutenant of the Royal Victorian Order.
32	OBE	(but *not* if also either a GBE and/or a KBE or DBE and/or a CBE), Officer of the Most Excellent Order of the British Empire.
33	QSO	Queen's Service Order (NZ only).
34	ISO	Companion of the Imperial Service Order.
	MVO	(but *not* if also either a GCVO and/or a KCVO or a DCVO, and/or a CVO and/or an LVO), Member of the Royal Victorian Order.
35	MBE	(but *not* if also a GBE and/or a KBE or DBE and/or a CBE and/or an OBE), Member of the Most Excellent Order of the British Empire.
36*	IOM	(if in Military Division), Indian Order of Merit.
37*	OB	Order of Burma (when for gallantry).
38	RRC	Member of the Royal Red Cross.
39	DSC	Distinguished Service Cross.
40	MC	Military Cross.
41	DFC	Distinguished Flying Cross.
42	AFC	Air Force Cross.
43	ARRC	(but *not* if also an RRC), Associate of the Royal Red Cross.

44*	OBI	Order of British India.
*	OB	Order of Burma (when for distinguished service).
45	DCM	Distinguished Conduct Medal.
46	CGM	(both the Naval and the Flying decorations), Conspicuous Gallantry Medal.
47	GM	George Medal.
48*	KPM	King's or Queen's Police Medal.
49*	KPFSM	or Police & Fire Services Medal
50	QPM	for Gallantry.
51	QFSM	
*	DCM	(if for Royal West African Frontier Force), Distinguished Conduct Medal.
*	DCM	(if for the King's African Rifles), Distinguished Conduct Medal.
52*	IDSM	Indian Distinguished Service Medal.
53*	BGM	Burma Gallantry Medal.
54	DSM	Distinguished Service Medal.
55	MM	Military Medal.
56	DFM	Distinguished Flying Medal.
57	AFM	Air Force Medal.
58	SGM	Medal for Saving Life at Sea (Sea Gallantry Medal).
*	IOM	(if in Civil Division), Indian Order of Merit.
59*	EGM	Empire Gallantry Medal (usable only in reference to pre-1940 honorary awards unexchangeable for the GC)
60	CPM	Colonial Police Medal for Gallantry.
61	QGM	Queen's Gallantry Medal.
62	QSM	Queen's Service Medal (NZ only).
63	BEM	British Empire Medal, for Gallantry, or the British Empire Medal.
64*	CM	(or for French speakers M du C, Medaille du Canada), Canada Medal.
*	KPM	See 48–51 above, but for distinguished or good service.
*	KPFSM	
	QPM	
	QFSM	
65*	MSM	(but only if awarded for Naval service prior to 20 July 1928), Medal for Meritorious Service.
66	ERD	Emergency Reserve Decoration (Army).

67	*VD	Volunteer Officers' Decoration (1892–1908); for India and the Colonies (1894–1930) and the Colonial Auxiliary Forces Officers' Decoration (1899–1930).
68	TD	(for either the obsolescent Territorial Decoration (1908–30) or for the current Efficiency Decoration (inst. 1930) when awarded to an officer of the (*Home*) Auxiliary Military Forces and the TAVR (inst. 1969)).
69	ED	(if for the current Efficiency Decoration (inst. 1930) when awarded to an officer of *Commonwealth* or Colonial Auxiliary Military Forces).
70	RD	Decoration for Officers of the Royal Naval Reserve.
71*	VRD	Decoration for Officers of the Royal Naval Volunteer Reserve.
72	CD	Canadian Forces Decoration.

* This distinction is no longer awarded, but there are surviving recipients.

Any of the above post nominal letters precede any others which may relate to academic honours or professional qualifications. The unique exception is that the abbreviation 'Bt.' (or less favoured 'Bart.'), indicating a Baronetcy, should be put before *all* other letters, e.g. The Rt Hon Sir John Smyth, Bt., VC, MC.

The abbreviation PC (indicating membership of the Privy Council), which used to be placed after KG, is now not to be used, except possibly with peers, because in their case the style 'Rt Hon' cannot be used to indicate membership of the Privy Council, since Barons, Viscounts and Earls already enjoy this style *ipso facto* and Marquesses and Dukes have the superior styles 'Most Hon' and 'Most Noble' respectively.

Obsolete post nominal letters include: KP Knight of St Patrick; KB Knight of the Bath (prior to its division into 3 classes in 1815); GCH, KCH and KH Knights Grand Cross, Knight Commanders or Knights of the Order of the Guelphs (1815–1837); KSI Knights of the Star of India (1861–1866); CSC Conspicuous Service Cross (1901–1914); AM Albert Medal; EM Edward Medal; VD Volunteer Decoration.

UK Economics

British Isles – Progressive populations for Great Britain and Ireland combined

Date	Estimate
c. 400 000BC	200
c. 250 000BC	1000
12 000BC	3000
2000BC	50 000
1000BC	100 000
200BC	500 000
AD 43	800 000
600	900 000
1068[1]	2 250 000
1348[2]	5 000 000
1355	3 500 000
1500	5 500 000
1600[3]	6 250 000
1650	7 500 000
1700	9 250 000
1750	10 000 000
1800	16 000 000

[1] Partly on the evidence of the Domesday Book.
[2] Prior to onset of the Black Death.
[3] Of which 4 811 000 in English parishes.

Expectation of life

(Average expectation at birth)

	Male	*Female*
1900	46	50
1910	52	55
1920	56	60
1930	59	63
1938	61	66
1950	66	72
1958	68	74
1969–71	69·2	75·2
1975–77	69·8	75·9
1980–82	71·1	77·1
1981–83	71·3	77·4

Decennial Censuses*

Date	Total
1801	11 944 000
1811	13 368 000
1821	15 472 000
1831	17 835 000
1841	20 183 000
1851	22 259 000
1861	24 525 000
1871	27 431 000
1881	31 015 000
1891	34 264 000
1901	38 237 000
1911	42 082 000
1921	44 027 000
1931	46 038 000
1951	50 225 000
1961	52 676 000
1971	55 515 000
1981	55 633 683

* These figures are in respect of the United Kingdom (i.e. the figures for the present area of the Republic of Ireland are excluded). The 1921 and 1931 figures for Northern Ireland are estimates only but were based on censuses subsequently held in 1926 and 1937 respectively.

Birth and Death Rates – Rates for 1000 of population

	1871	*1901*	*1911*	*1921*	*1931*	*1951*	*1961*	*1971*	*1980*	*1981*	*1982*	*1983*
Birth Rate	35·0	28·6	24·6	23·1	16·3	15·7	17·8	16·2	13·2	12·8	12·6	12·7
Death Rate	22·1	17·3	14·1	12·7	12·2	12·6	12·0	11·6	11·8	11·7	11·8	—
Rate of Natural Increase	12·9	11·3	10·5	10·4	4·1	3·2	5·8	4·6	1·4	1·1	0·8	—
Illegitimacy	60	43	45	48	48	48	55	82				

National Employment and Unemployment

	Working Population (Thousands)	Unemployment Excluding School Leavers and Students	Percentage Rate		Working Population (Thousands)	Unemployment Excluding School Leavers and Students	Percentage Rate
1965	25 504	338 200	1·4%	1978	26 433	1 375 700	5·2%
1970	25 293	602 000	2·6%	1979	26 443	1 307 300	4·9%
1971	25 124	775 800	3·4%	1980	26 324	1 667 600	6·3%
1972	25 234	855 000	3·7%	1981	26 079	2 464 300	9·4%
1973	25 578	611 000	2·6%	1982	23 373	2 687 900	11·5%
1974	25 515	600 100	2·6%	1983	24 013	3 025 700	12·6%
1975	25 665	929 000	3·6%	1984	24 108	3 013 600	12·5%
1976	25 886	1 273 500	4·9%	1985 (Mar)	24 204	3 146 600	13·0%
1977	26 310	1 378 200	5·2%				

DISTRIBUTION OF WORK FORCE OF THE UK AS AT JUNE 1983

Agriculture, forestry and fishing	349 000
Energy and water supply industries	662 000
Extractive industries, metal and mineral products and chemicals	821 000
Metal goods, engineering and vehicles	2 651 000
Other manufacturing industries	2 170 000
Construction	1 016 000
Distribution, hotels, catering and repairs	4 209 000
Transport and communication	1 332 000
Banking, finance, insurance, business services and leasing	1 837 000
Other services	6 164 000
All industries and Services	**21 210 000**
Self-employed	2 199 000
Public corporations	1 700 000
Central and local government	5 200 000
Total employed labour force	**23 700 000**

Strikes

	Working Days Lost	Workers Involved
1960	3 024 000	814 000
1965	2 933 000	867 800
1970	10 980 000	1 793 000
1973	7 197 000	1 513 000
1974	14 750 000	1 622 000
1975	6 012 000	789 000
1976	3 284 000	666 000
1977	10 142 000	1 155 000
1978	9 405 000	1 001 000
1979	29 116 000	4 432 000
1980	11 910 000	789 400
1981	4 266 000	1 513 000
1982	5 313 000	2 103 000
1983	3 754 000	574 000
1984	26 564 000	1 405 000

Standard of living – in 21·31 mil. households

	1983
TV (Colour 81%)	98%
Refrigerator	94%
Washing machine	80%
Telephone	77%
Central heating	64%
Car	43% with one, 16% with two or more, 59% with one or more

Average from Weekly Earnings mid-1984 — £159·3 (£8,183 p.a.)

[1] There were 16 401 000 cars in Britain by Dec. 1984 of which 47% were foreign made

The United Kingdom's National Debt

The National Debt is the nominal amount of outstanding debt chargeable on the Consolidated Fund of the United Kingdom Exchequer only, i.e. the debt created by the separate Northern Ireland Exchequer is excluded.

The National Debt became a permanent feature of the country's economy as early as 1692. The table below shows how the net total Debt has increased over the years (data being for 31 March of year shown):

Year	National Debt (£ million)	Year	National Debt (£ million)	Year	National Debt (£ million)	Year	National Debt (£ million)
1697	14	1910	713·2	1944	18 562·2	1965	30 440
1727	52	1914	649·8	1945	21 365·9	1966	31 340
1756	75	1915	1 105·0	1946	23 636·5	1967	31 985
1763	133	1916	2 133·1	1947	25 630·6	1968	34 193
1775	127	1917	4 011·4	1948	25 620·8	1969	33 984
1781	187	1918	5 871·9	1949	25 167·6	1970	33 079
1784	243	1919	7 434·9	1950	25 802·3	1971	33 441
1793	245	1920[1]	7 828·8	1951	25 921·6	1972	35 839
1802	523	1921	7 574·4	1952	25 890·5	1973	36 884
1815	834	1923	7 742·2	1953	26 051·2	1974	40 124
1828	800	1931	7 413·3	1954	26 538	1975	45 886
1836	832	1934	7 822·3	1955	26 933	1976	56 577
1840	827	1935[2]	6 763·9	1956	27 038	1977	54 041
1854	802	1936	6 759·3	1957	27 007	1978	79 000
1855	789	1937	6 764·7	1958	27 232	1979	82 597
1857	837	1938	6 993·7	1959	27 376	1980	91 245
1860	799	1939	7 130·8	1960	27 732	1981	112 780
1899	635	1940	7 899·2	1961	28 251	1982	117 959
1900	628·9	1941	10 366·4	1962	28 674	1983	127 072
1903	770·8	1942	13 041·1	1963	29 847	1984	142 545
1909	702·7	1943	15 822·6	1964	30 226	1985	158 101

[1] Beginning 1920, total excludes bonds tendered for death duties and held by the National Debt Commissioner.
[2] Beginning 1935, total excludes external debt, then £1036·5 million, arising out of the 1914–18 war.

Balance of Payments

(Expressed in £, million)

	Visible Exports	Visible Imports	Visible Balance	Invisible Balance	Current Balance (− Deficit + surplus)		Visible Exports	Visible Imports	Visible Balance	Invisible Balance	Current Balance (− Deficit + surplus)
1965	4848	5071	−223	+198	−27	1977	32 148	33 892	−1744	+2037	+293
1970	8121	8163	−42	+818	+776	1978	35 432	36 607	−1175	+2207	+1032
1971	9060	8799	+261	+889	+1150	1979	40 678	44 136	−3458	+2595	−863
1972	9450	10 172	−722	+930	+208	1980	47 389	46 211	+1178	+2028	+3206
1973	12 115	14 498	−2383	+1508	−875	1981	50 977	47 325	+3652	+3620	+7272
1974	16 538	21 773	−5235	+1928	−3307	1982	55 565	53 181	+2384	+3167	+5551
1975	19 463	22 699	−3236	+1615	−1621	1983	60 658	61 158	−500	+2549	+2049
1976	25 441	29 012	−3601	+2759	−842	1984	[1]70 377	74 632	−4255	+4879	+624

[1] Provisional.

Internal purchasing power of the £

The worth of the £ at various periods compared with its worth in mid 1985 may be regarded thus:

1870	£1	worth	£26·76
1886	£1	worth	£36·51
1896	£1	worth	£35·30
1909	£1	worth	£31·66
1925	£1	worth	£17·17
1931	£1	worth	£23·65
1949	£1	worth	£12·30
1957	£1	worth	£8·00
1967	£1	worth	£6·99
1970	£1	worth	£5·35
1976	£1	worth	£2·76
1977	£1	worth	£2·31
1978	£1	worth	£1·92
1979	£1	worth	£1·68
1980	£1	worth	£1·40
1985 (mid)	£1	worth	£1·00

Sterling – US Dollar Exchange Rates

$4·50–$5·00	Post War of Independence	1776
$12·00	All-time Peak (Civil War)	1864
$4·86 21/32	Fixed parity	1880–1914
$4·76 7/16	Pegged rate World War I	Dec. 1916
$3·40	Low point after £ floated, 19 May 1919	Feb. 1920
$4·86 21/32	Britain's return to gold standard	28 Apr. 1925
$3·14½	Low point after Britain forced off Gold Standard (20 Sept. 1931 [$3·43])	Nov. 1932
$5·20	High point during floating period	Mar. 1934
$4·03	Fixed rate World War II	4 Sept. 1939
$2·80	First post-war devaluation	18 Sept. 1949
$2·40	Second post-war devaluation	20 Nov. 1967
$2·42	Convertibility of US dollar into gold was suspended on	15 Aug. 1971
$2·58	£ Refloated	22 June 1972
$1·99	£ broke $2 barrier	5 Mar. 1976
$1·56	£ at new all-time low	28 Oct. 1976
$1·76	Bank of England buying pounds	10 Oct. 1977
$2·00	£ breaks back to $2 level (1978 av. $1·91)	15 Aug. 1978
$2·26	Dollar weakens	June 1979
$2·19	Iranian crisis unresolved	8 Dec. 1979
$1·99	£ again falls below $2	3 June 1981
$1·90	One year of 'Reaganomics'	20 Jan. 1982
$1·04	Strength of dollar against all currencies	6 Mar. 1985
$1·21	Recovery after Ohio Bank anxiety	11 Apr. 1985

Imports

Principal Imports into the UK (1984)	£ millions c.i.f.*
Petroleum, petroleum products and related materials	8078·4
Road vehicles (including air cushion vehicles)	5958·3
Office machines and automatic data processing equipment	4112·3
Electrical machinery, apparatus and appliances and electrical parts thereof	3848·1
Miscellaneous manufactured articles	3235·1
Textile yarn, fabrics, made-up articles and related products	2706·2
Paper, paperboard and articles of paper pulp, of paper or of paperboard	2281·5
Non-metallic mineral manufactures	2269·2
General industrial machinery and equipment and machine parts	2249·7
Coal, coke, gas and electric current	2114·2
Machinery specialised for particular industries	2072·0
Articles of apparel and clothing accessories	2013·1
Non-ferrous metals	1996·6
Vegetables and fruit	1931·1
Organic chemicals	1874·4
Telecommunications and sound recording and reproducing apparatus and equipment	1848·6
Power generating machinery and equipment	1782·6
Artificial resins and plastic materials, and cellulose ester and ethers	1609·6
Professional scientific and controlling instruments and apparatus	1592·8
Iron and steel	1487·2
Manufactures of metal	1385·2
Other transport equipment	1362·7
Metalliferous ores and metal scrap	1344·2
Meat and meat preparations	1342·4

Exports

Principal Exports from the UK (1984)	f.o.b.*
Petroleum, petroleum products and related materials	14909·8
Road vehicles (including air cushion vehicles)	3311·9
Office machines and automatic data processing equipment	3046·2
Miscellaneous manufactured articles	2921·4
Electrical machinery, apparatus and appliances and electrical parts thereof	2804·9
Other transport equipment	2763·9
Power generating machinery and equipment	2686·4
Machinery specialised for particular industries	2678·6
General industrial machinery and equipment and machine parts	2572·1
Organic chemicals	2381·7
Non-metallic mineral manufactures	2298·7
Commodities and transactions not specified elsewhere	1795·3
Professional, scientific and controlling instruments and apparatus	1778·7
Non-ferrous metals	1656·6
Iron and steel	1529·1
Textile yarn, fabrics, made up articles and related products	1484·8
Manufactures of metal	1464·6
Medicinal and pharmaceutical products	1222·4
Chemical materials and products, not elsewhere specified	1183·7
Artificial resins and plastic materials and cellulose esters and ethers	1179·9
Beverages	1157·0
Telecommunications and sound recording and reproducing apparatus and equipment	1117·1
Articles of apparel and clothing accessories	996·4

* c.i.f., cost, insurance and freight. f.o.b., free on board.

25 Top Nations – Imports into UK: (1984)

	£ million	% of total UK imports
West Germany	1 090·2	14·1
United States	9489·8	12·1
Netherlands	6147·3	7·8
France	5885·7	7·5
Norway	3852·7	4·9
Italy	3814·2	4·8
Japan	3768·0	4·8
Belgium & Luxemburg	3691·8	4·7
Irish Republic	2635·0	3·3
Switzerland	2490·6	3·2
Sweden	2416·4	3·1
Spain	1667·4	2·1
Denmark	1660·4	2·1
Canada	1617·5	2·1
Hong Kong	1267·0	1·6
Finland	1248·6	1·6
Soviet Union	854·3	1·1
South Africa	725·6	0·9
Portugal	644·5	0·8
Brazil	637·7	0·8
Australia	612·1	0·8
Taiwan	585·2	0·7
India	571·5	0·7
Saudi Arabia	545·1	0·7
Austria	529·6	0·7

25 Top Nations – Exports from UK: (1984)

	£ million	% of total exports
United States	10 225·8	14·5
West Germany	7458·0	10·6
France	7082·4	10·0
Netherlands	6128·0	8·7
Irish Republic	3393·5	4·8
Belgium & Luxemburg	3051·7	4·3
Italy	2902·7	4·1
Sweden	2888·6	4·1
Switzerland	1549·5	2·2
Saudi Arabia	1387·2	2·0
Spain	1322·4	1·9
South Africa	1205·1	1·7
Denmark	1197·4	1·7
Australia	1186·5	1·7
Canada	1183·2	1·7
Norway	968·4	1·4
Japan	925·3	1·3
Hong Kong	897·4	1·3
India	781·0	1·1
Nigeria	768·5	1·1
Soviet Union	735·2	1·0
Iran	703·1	1·0
Finland	684·5	1·0
Singapore	556·4	0·8
Egypt	427·7	0·6

GROSS NATIONAL PRODUCT

The economic power of a nation is reflected in its Gross National Product (GNP) and its National Income.

Gross National Product is derived from Gross Domestic Product at factor cost plus net property income from overseas. National Income is GNP less capital consumption.

Gross Domestic Product at factor cost can be determined in two ways, (A) by the expenditure generating it, or (B) the incomes, rent and profits which enable the expenditure. The components in any year are thus:

A	B
Consumers' expenditure	Income from employment
Public authority current spending	Income from self-employment
Gross fixed capital formation	Gross trading profits of companies
Value of work in progress	Gross profits and surpluses of public corporations
Value of physical increase in stocks	Rent *less* stock appreciation
Exports *less* imports	
Income from abroad *less* payments abroad	
Subsidies *less* taxes on expenditure	
= Gross Domestic Product	= Gross Domestic Product

MINIMUM LENDING RATE

The Bank Rate was maintained at its record low level of 2 per cent for 12 years 13 days from 26 Oct. 1939 to 7 Nov. 1951, throughout World War II and the post-war period of the Cheap Money Policy under the Attlee government. The only previous occasion that such a low rate had been available was in 1852.

On 13 Oct. 1972 the Bank Rate was more descriptively named Bank of England Minimum Lending Rate when standing at 7¼ per cent. On 13 Nov. 1973 the MLR attained its then all-time peak of 13 per cent with the Arab Oil Price crisis. The devaluation crisis of October 1976 produced a new record rate of 15 per cent. By 14 Oct. 1977 this had subsided to 5 per cent. On 25 May 1978 MLR was fixed by administrative decision. By 8 Feb. 1979 it was back up to 14%. An all-time record of 17% was announced on 15 Nov. 1979. On 20 Aug. 1981 MLR was discontinued and was for practical purposes replaced by the London Clearing Banks base rate.

AVERAGE WEEKLY HOUSEHOLD EXPENDITURE

The average household weekly income in 1983 was £142·59. The breakdown of the average expenditure was as follows:

Food	29·56
Housing	23·99
Transport and vehicles	20·96
Services	16·09
Other Goods	10·81
Durable household goods	10·26
Clothing and footwear	10·00
Fuel, light and power	9·22
Alcoholic drink	6·91
Tobacco	4·21
Miscellaneous	0·58

The Judicial System

The supreme judicial court for the United Kingdom is the House of Lords as an ultimate court of appeal from all courts, except the Scottish criminal courts. Leave to appeal to it is not as of right and is usually reserved for important points of law. The work is executed by the Lord High Chancellor and nine Lords of Appeal in Ordinary. Only one case in 40,000 ever reaches them.

The Supreme Court of Judicature consists of the Court of Appeal under the Master of the Rolls and 21 Lord Justices of Appeal and The High Court of Justice with (a) the Chancery Division with 13 judges (b) the Queen's Bench Division under the Lord Chief Justice of England and 49 judges (c) the Court of Appeal (Criminal Division) with all the foregoing judges excepting the Chancery Division judges (d) the Family Division with a President and currently 13 male and 3 female judges.

On 1 January 1972 the Crown Court replaced Assizes and Quarter Sessions. Under the Courts Service, First tier centres deal with both civil and criminal cases and Second tier centres with only criminal cases. Both are served by High Court (see above) and Circuit Judges. Third tier centres deal with criminal cases only but are served by Circuit Judges only. There are six circuits in England and Wales viz.

Northern Circuit	(46 Judges)
North Eastern Circuit	(40 Judges)
Midland and Oxford	(52 Judges)
Wales and Chester	(22 Judges)
South Eastern Circuit	(181 Judges)
Western Circuit	(31 Judges)

There are in addition 422 Recorders.

Major urban areas have courts presided over by whole-time salaried magistrates known as Stipendiaries thus –
London
Bow Street (Chief Metropolitan Stipendiary and

Public expenditure

£s million cash

Programme	1978–79	1979–80	1980–81	1981–82	1982–83	1983–84	1984–85
Social security	16 934	20 006	24 145	29 435	33 440	36 431	38 391
Health and personal social services	9 227	11 057	14 084	15 817	17 179	18 283	19 217
Education and science, arts and libraries	9 856	11 372	13 837	15 100	16 181	17 009	16 600
Housing	4 503	5 665	5 687	4 193	3 762	3 912	3 604
Environmental services	2 818	3 362	3 875	3 957	4 469	4 812	4 452
Transport	3 263	3 962	4 773	5 146	5 309	5 547	5 324
Employment services	981	1 159	1 842	2 152	2 252	2 762	3 009
Law, order, and protective services	2 438	3 076	3 780	4 434	4 937	5 519	5 806
Defence, overseas aid, and other overseas services	9 342	11 304	12 793	14 289	16 571	18 010	19 314
Other expenditure on programmes	6 391	6 958	8 210	10 075	9 767	9 443	9 784
Total public expenditure on programmes	65 752	77 921	93 028	104 597	113 865	121 728	125 503
Of which, expenditure by local authorities	17 995	21 613	25 103	26 690	29 232	32 780	32 127

Income, Expenditure and Savings

	Population Mid-Year	Gross National Product GNP (at factor cost)	Total Personal Income Pre-tax	Real Personal Disposable Income at 1980 prices	Consumer Expenditure at prices current	Personal Saving as % of Disposable Income
	Thousands	£ millions	£ millions	£ millions	£ millions	
1955	51 199	£17 240	£15 609	£79 708	£13 177	3·9
1960	52 508	£23.097	£21 324	£94 453	£17 124	7·3
1965	54 218	£31 934	£30 581	£110 942	£23 110	9·8
1970	55 421	£44 528	£43 853	£122 845	£31 935	9·8
1975	55 900	£96 575	£97 239	£143 924	£65 216	13·3
1976	55 886	£115 154	£112 401	£143 146	£75 712	12·6
1977	55 852	£129 226	£125 573	£140 943	£86 537	11·6
1978	55 836	£149 291	£144 138	£151 197	£99 486	13·1
1979	55 883	£171 999	£170 605	£159 821	£117 912	14·1
1980	55 901	£199 156	£201 118	£161 364	£136 789	15·2
1981	55 671	£219 076	£220 912	£158 106	£152 125	13·5
1982	56 258	£236 924	£240 868	£158 554	£166 477	12·9
1983	56 376	£259 437	£258 360	£161 578	£182 427	10·9

4 Stipendiaries); Camberwell Green (4); Clerkenwell (3); Greenwich and Woolwich (3); Highbury Corner (4); Horseferry Road (3); Marlborough Street (2); Marylebone (4); Old Street (2); South Western (3); Thames (2); Tower Bridge (3); Wells Street (4); West London (2).

Other Stipendiaries operate in Kingston-upon-Hull, Leeds, Greater Manchester, Merseyside, Merthyr Tydfil, Mid Glamorgan, South Glamorgan, South Yorkshire and West Midlands.

In Scotland the Court of Session (established 1532) has an Inner House of 8 Judges (in which the Lord President presides over the First Division and the Lord Justice Clerk over the Second Division) and an Outer House of 12 Judges. The country is divided into 6 Sheriffdoms, each with a Sheriff Principal, Sheriffs and Procurators Fiscal: these are Grampian, Highland and Islands; Tayside, Central and Fife; Lothian and Borders; Glasgow and Strathkelvin; North Strathclyde; and South Strathclyde and Dumfries and Galloway.

Criminal Statistics

ENGLAND AND WALES

Offences recorded by the Police – 1984

Offences	Number of Offences 1984
VIOLENCE AGAINST THE PERSON:	
Murder	
Manslaughter } Homicide	620
Infanticide	
Attempted murder	156
Threat or conspiracy to murder	836
Child destruction	Nil
Causing death by dangerous driving	222
Wounding or other act endangering life	5 276
Endangering railway passenger	40
Endangering life at sea	Nil
Other wounding, etc.	106 352
Assault	587
Abandoning child under two years	15
Child stealing	56
Procuring illegal abortion	1
Concealment of birth	24
SEXUAL OFFENCES:	
Homosexual offences	4 003
Rape	1 433
Indecent assault on a female	10 837
Incest	290
Procuration	102
Abduction	99
Bigamy	94
BURGLARY:	
Burglary in a dwelling	475 787
Burglary in a building other than a dwelling	415 078
ROBBERY:	
Robbery	24 890
THEFT AND HANDLING STOLEN GOODS:	
Theft from the person of another	30 107
Theft or unauthorised taking from mail	2 134
Theft from vehicle	454 943
Theft from shops	248 792
Theft or unauthorised taking of motor vehicle	344 806
Handling stolen goods	45 046
FRAUD AND FORGERY:	
Fraud and forgery	126 093
CRIMINAL DAMAGE:	
Arson	18 889
Criminal damage	478 264
OTHER OFFENCES:	
Blackmail	653
Kidnapping	131
High treason	Nil
Treason felony	Nil
Riot	5
Unlawful assembly	31
Other offence against the State or public order	778
Perjury	304
Criminal libel	3
Aiding suicide	11
Perverting the course of justice	331
Absconding from lawful custody	1 434

SCOTLAND

Crimes and Offences recorded by the Police – 1983

TOTAL CRIMES	448 260
NON-SEXUAL CRIMES OF VIOLENCE	13 025
Serious assault etc.	4 985
Handling offensive weapons	3 097
Robbery	4 170
Other	771
CRIMES OF INDECENCY	5 474
Sexual assault	1 262
Lewd and libidinous practices	2 450
Other	1 762
CRIMES OF DISHONESTY	342 452
Housebreaking	108 520
Theft by opening lockfast places	50 693
Theft of a motor vehicle	29 888
Shoplifting	24 041
Other theft	101 533
Fraud	17 317
Other	10 460
FIRE-RAISING, VANDALISM ETC.	73 060
Fire-raising	3 683
Vandalism etc.	69 377
OTHER CRIMES	14 251
Crimes against public justice	10 856
Drugs	3 227
Other	168
TOTAL OFFENCES	351 308
MISCELLANEOUS OFFENCES	114 807
Petty assault	30 329
Breach of the peace	51 305
Drunkenness	15 046
Other	18 127
MOTOR VEHICLE OFFENCES	236 501
Reckless and careless driving	25 352
Drunk driving	15 373
Speeding	37 674
Unlawful use of vehicle	90 710
Vehicle defect offences	29 412
Other	37 980

The 46 United Kingdom universities

There are 46 institutions of university or degree-giving status in the UK.
The list below is given in order of seniority of date of foundation, and the data run as follows: name, year of foundation, location, and population full-time as at 1 January 1984.

1. The University of Oxford 1249*
Oxford OX1 2JD
11 708
Colleges, Halls and Societies: University (1249), Balliol (1263), Merton (1264), Exeter (1314), Oriel (1326), Queen's (1340), New College (1379), Lincoln (1427), All Souls (1438), Magdalen (1458), Brasenose (1509), Corpus Christi (1517), Christ Church (1546), Trinity (1554), St John's (1555), Jesus (1571), Wadham (1612), Pembroke (1624), Worcester (1714), Hertford (1874), St Edmund Hall (1270), Keble (1868), St Catherine's (1962), Campion Hall (1962), St Benet's Hall (1947), St Peter's (1929), St Antony's (1950), Nuffield (1937), Linacre House (1962), Mansfield (1886), Regent's Park (1810), Greyfriars Hall (1910), St Cross (1965), and Wolfson (1965). Lady Margaret Hall (1878), Somerville (1879), St Hugh's (1886), St Hilda's (1893), St Anne's (1952) [originally 1893].

2. The University of Cambridge 1284*
Cambridge
11 598
Peterhouse (1284), Clare (1326), Pembroke (1347), Gonville and Caius (1348), Trinity Hall (1350), Corpus Christi (1352), King's (1441), Queen's (1448), St Catherine's (1473), Jesus (1496), Christ's (1505), St John's (1511), Magdalene (1542), Trinity (1546), Emmanuel (1584), Sidney Sussex (1596), Downing (1800), Selwyn (1882), Churchill (1960), Fitzwilliam House (1896), Girton (1869), Newnham (1871), Hughes Hall (1885), New Hall (1954).

3. The University of St Andrews 1411
St Andrews KY16 9AJ
3 454
Colleges: United College of St Salvator and St Leonard; College of St Mary; Queen's College, Dundee.

4. The University of Glasgow 1451
Gilmorehill, Glasgow G12 8QQ
10 043

5. The University of Aberdeen 1495
Aberdeen AB9 1FX
5 470

6. The University of Edinburgh 1583
South Bridge, Edinburgh EH8 9YL
9 866

7. The University of Durham 1832
Old Shire Hall, Durham DH1 3HP
4 704
Colleges: University, Hatfield, Grey, St Chad's, St John's, St Mary's, St Aidan's, Bede, St Hild's, Neville's Cross, St Cuthbert's Society, Van Mildert, Trevelyan, Collingwood, Ushaw, Graduate Society.

8. The University of London 1836
Greater London
40 764
Schools: Bedford College, Birkbeck College, Chelsea College, Imperial College of Science and Technology, King's College, London School of Economics, Queen Elizabeth College, Queen Mary College, Royal Holloway College, Royal Veterinary College, School of Oriental and African Studies, School of Pharmacy, University College, Westfield College, Wye College.
Medical Schools: Charing Cross Hospital, Guy's Hospital, King's College Hospital, The London Hospital, The Middlesex Hospital, Royal Dental Hospital of London, Royal Free Hospital, St Bartholomew's Hospital, St George's Hospital, St Mary's Hospital, St Thomas's Hospital, University College Hospital, Westminster Hospital, British post-graduate Medical Federation, London School of Hygiene and Tropical Medicine, Royal post-graduate Medical School, and

numerous post-graduate teaching hospitals; and various training colleges.

Institutes: Courtauld Institute of Art, Institute of Advanced Legal Studies, Institute of Archaeology, Institute of Classical Studies, Institute of Commonwealth Studies, Inter-collegiate Computer Science, Institute of Education, Institute of Germanic Studies, Institute of Historical Research, Institute of Latin American Studies, Institute of United States Studies, School of Slavonic and East European Studies, Warburg Institute, British Institute, Paris.

9. The University of Manchester[1]   1851
Oxford Road, Manchester M13 9PL
15 438

10. The University of Newcastle upon Tyne   1852
Newcastle upon Tyne NE1 7RU
7 538

11. The University of Wales   1893
see colleges
18 735
Colleges: Aberystwyth, Bangor, Cardiff, Swansea, National School of Medicine (Cardiff), Institute of Science and Technology (Cardiff), St David's College, Lampeter.

12. The University of Birmingham   1900
P.O. Box 363, Birmingham B15 2TT
8 736

13. The University of Liverpool   1903
P.O. Box 147, Liverpool L69 3BX
7 519

14. The University of Leeds   1904
Leeds LS2 9JT
10 569

15. The University of Sheffield   1905
Sheffield S10 2TN
7 648

16. The Queen's University of Belfast   1908
Belfast BT7 1NN
6 645
College: Magee University College (1865), Londonderry.

17. The University of Bristol   1909
Bristol BS8 1TH
6 907

18. The University of Reading   1926
London Road, Reading RG6 2AH
5 576

19. The University of Nottingham   1948
University Park, Nottingham NG7 2RD
6 829

20. The University of Southampton   1952
Southampton SO9 5NH
6 416

21. The University of Hull   1954
Kingston upon Hull HU6 7RX
5 025

22. The University of Exeter   1955
Exeter EX4 4QJ
4 758

23. The University of Leicester   1957
Leicester LE1 7RH
4 668

24. The University of Sussex   1961
Brighton BN1 9RH
4 360

25. The University of Keele   1962
Keele, Staffordshire ST5 5BG
2 729

26. The University of Strathclyde†   1964
George Street, Glasgow G1 1XQ
7 163

27. The University of East Anglia   1963
Norwich NR4 7TJ
4 031

28. The University of York   1963
Heslington, York YO1 5DD
3 338

29. The University of Lancaster   1964
Bailrigg, Lancaster LA1 4YW
4 438

30. The University of Essex   1964
Wivenhoe Park, Colchester CO4 3SQ
3 188

31. The University of Warwick   1965
Coventry CV4 7AL
5 377

32. The University of Kent   1965
Canterbury CT2 7NZ
4 159

33. New University of Ulster   1965
Coleraine, Co. Londonderry BT52 1SA, Northern Ireland
2 226

34. Heriot-Watt University   1966
Edinburgh EH14 4AS
3 185

35. Loughborough University of Technology   1966
Loughborough, Leicestershire LE11 3TU
5 232

36. The University of Aston in Birmingham   1966
Gosta Green, Birmingham B4 7ET
4 054

37. The City University   1966
London, EC1V 0NB
2 798

38. Brunel University   1966
Uxbridge UB8 3PH
2 654

39. University of Bath   1966
Claverton Down, Bath BA2 7AY
3 730

40. University of Bradford   1966
Bradford BD7 1DP
4 574

41. University of Surrey   1966
Guildford GU2 5XH
3 240

42. University of Salford   1967
Salford M5 4WT
3 835

43. University of Dundee   1967
Dundee DD1 4HN
3 198

44. University of Stirling   1967
Stirling FK9 4LA
2 470

45. The Open University   1969
Walton Hall, Milton Keynes MK7 6AA
76 140

46. University of Buckingham§   1976
Buckingham MK18 1EG
518

* Year of foundation of oldest constituent college
† Formerly the Royal College of Science and Technology, founded 1796
‡ Tuition mainly by correspondence
§ Financed independently from the University Grants Committee and HM Treasury
[1] Includes Manchester Business School and Manchester Institute of Science and Technology
[2] Excludes short courses

Note: The Royal College of Art (1837) Kensington Gore, London (568 post graduates) and The Cranfield Institute of Technology (1969), Cranfield, Bedford (575 post graduates, 2500 short course students) grant degrees.

Basic educational statistics

ENGLAND AND WALES 1982/83

PUBLIC SECTOR SCHOOLS	Number of Schools	Number of Pupils	Number of Teachers	Pupil Teacher Ratio
Nursery	1 259	56 300	2 600	21·8
Primary	25 755	4 659 000	211 100	22·1
Secondary	5 437	4 493 600	277 000	16·2
NON-MAINTAINED SCHOOLS	2 637	583 400	47 800	12·2
SPECIAL SCHOOLS	1 989	142 200	19 400	7·3
ALL SCHOOLS	37 077	9 934 200	558 000	17·8

FURTHER EDUCATION (1982/3) (Excluding Universities)

	No. of Establishments	Course Enrolments[1]	Full-time Teachers[2]
Polytechnics	30	204 803	16 699
Other Major Establisments	563	1 685 637	75 301
Adult Education Centres	4 542	1 847 464	1 654

[1] All Modes of attendance
[2] Full-time only

SCOTLAND 1982/83

SCHOOLS	Number of Schools	Number of Pupils	Number of Teachers
Education Authority Nursery	537	34 700	700
Education Authority Primary	2 489	468 000	23 000
Education Authority Secondary	442	399 100	27 900
Education Authority Special	320	10 300	1 500
Grant Aided	55	17 900	1 200
All Schools	3 843	930 000	53 600

POST-SCHOOL	Number of Colleges	Number of Students	Number of Teachers
Colleges of Vocational Further Education	175 ⎫		
Education Authority Colleges/Centres	161 ⎬	206 800	7 100
Central Institutions	14 ⎭		
Voluntary Bodies	—		
Colleges of Education	7	7 200	900

The 30 Polytechnics of England and Wales

City of Birmingham Polytechnic 1971
Perry Bar, Birmingham B42 2BU
9 419

Brighton Polytechnic 1970
Moulsecomb, Brighton BN2 4AT
6 700

Bristol Polytechnic 1969
Coldharbour Lane, Frenchay, Bristol BS16 1QY
9 345

Polytechnic of Central London 1970
309 Regent Street, London W1R 8AL
9 530

City of London Polytechnic 1970
Administrative Headquarters, 117 Houndsditch, London EC3A 7BU
11 294

Hatfield Polytechnic 1970
P.O. Box 109, Hatfield, Herts AL10 9AB
5 681

Huddersfield Polytechnic 1970
Queensgate, Huddersfield HD1 3DH
6 347

Kingston Polytechnic 1970
Penrhyn Road, Kingston-upon-Thames, Surrey KT1 2EE
6 538

Lanchester Polytechnic 1970
Priory Street, Coventry CV11 5FB
6 565

Leeds Polytechnic 1970
Calverty Street, Leeds LS1 3HE
10 218

Leicester Polytechnic 1969
P.O. Box 143, Leicester LE1 9BH
8 496

Liverpool Polytechnic 1970
Richmond House, Rumford Place, Liverpool L3 9RH
9 222

Manchester Polytechnic 1970
All Saints, Manchester M18 6BH
14 403

Middlesex Polytechnic 1973
114 Chase Side, London N14 5PN
9 340

Newcastle upon Tyne Polytechnic 1969
Ellison Building, Ellison Place, Newcastle upon Tyne NE1 8ST
9 807

North East London Polytechnic 1970
Romford Road, London E15 4LZ
8 230

Polytechnic of North London 1971
Holloway Road, London N7 8DB
7 085

Oxford Polytechnic 1970
Gypsy Lane, Headington, Oxford OX3 0BP
5 219

Plymouth Polytechnic 1970
Drake Circus, Plymouth PL4 8AA
5 196

Portsmouth Polytechnic 1969
Museum Road, Portsmouth PD1 2QQ
7 015

Preston Polytechnic 1972
Corporation Street, Preston PR1 2TQ
6 020

Sheffield Polytechnic 1969
Pond Street, Sheffield S1 1WB
11 682

Polytechnic of the South Bank 1970
Borough Road, London SE1 0AA
8 433

Sunderland Polytechnic 1969
Langham Tower, Ryhope Road, Sunderland SR2 7EE
5 290

North Staffordshire Polytechnic 1970
College Road, Stoke-on-Trent, Staffordshire ST4 2DE
6 373

Teesside Polytechnic 1970
Middlesbrough, Cleveland TS1 3BA
5 088

Thames Polytechnic 1970
Wellington Street, Woolwich, London SE18 6PF
5 337

Trent Polytechnic 1971
Burton Street, Nottingham NG1 4BU
10 424

The Polytechnic – Wolverhampton 1969
The Molineux, Molineux Street, Wolverhampton WV1 1SB
7 642

WALES
The Polytechnic of Wales 1970
Llantwit Road, Treforest, Pontypridd, Mid-Glamorgan CF37 1DL
5 120

Economics and meaning of terms used

Among the history of sciences, economics has a relatively modern development.

The word *economics* was earlier (since 1393) used for the art of housekeeping. Its modern sense of the practical and theoretical science of the production and distribution of wealth first came in the context of rural economics in 1792. The earliest attempt at a rigorous treatment however dates from Galiani's *Della Moneta* published in 1751.

The first major landmark in the history of economic thought was in 1776 with the publication of *An Enquiry into the Nature and Causes of the Wealth of Nations* by Adam Smith (1723–90), the Scottish professor of Logic and Moral Philosophy. He propounded the theory that a whole community achieves the benefit of the largest possible total wealth through the delicate market balance of free competition and man's conflicting self-interests. In the next two centuries economic landmarks included:

1776 Smith, Adam (1723–90) *An Enquiry into the Nature and Causes of the Wealth of Nations*. Argued that wealth arose out of labour (especially the division of labour). The handbook of the industrial revolution.

1798 Malthus, Thomas (1766–1834) *An Essay on the Principle of Population*. Over-population was the death knell of economic growth and prosperity.

1848 Mill, John Stuart (1806–73) *Principles of Political Economy*. Value of any commodity depended upon the amount of all factors going into its production.

1848 Marx, Karl (1818–83). *The Communist Manifesto*. Written with Friedrich Engels.

1867 Marx (see above). *Das Kapital* (Vol 2, 1885, Vol 3, 1894). Theory of 'surplus value' accruing to the insatiable capitalist. Free enterprise system is self-destructive and a 'dictatorship of the proletariat' would follow.

1890 Marshall, Alfred (1842–1924). *Principles of Economics*. Utility and costs are the joint determinants of value.

1936 Keynes, John Maynard (1883–1946). *The General Theory of Employment, Interest and Money*. Duty of state to dispel depressions by higher public expenditure even at the price of persistent inflation.

1962 Friedman, Milton (b. 1912). *Capitalism and Freedom*. Duty of states with large inflationary public sector economies to restore prosperity by cutting public spending and borrowing.

A–Z of Economic Terminology

Arbitrage — Process of making a buying or selling margin out of differences in commodity prices or currency values in different markets.

Assets — Resources employed within an enterprise to conduct its business.

Asset Stripping — Purchasing a business with the motive of selling off its assets at a profit above the purchase price instead of perpetuating it.

Austrian School — A group of University of Vienna deductive economists led by Carl Menger (1840–1921), von Wieser (1851–1926) and von Böhm-Bawerk (1851–1914). Followed in the 20th century by Ludwig von Mises (1881–1973) and Friedrich Hayek (b. 1899) who oppose the Keynesian ascendancy of macro-economics.

Backwardation — A percentage charge paid by the seller of stock for the right to delay delivery.

Balance of Payments — Balance of international transactions and transfers for goods (imports and exports) and services (invisibles).

Balance of Trade — The solely *current* account sector of the balance of payments. This latter embraces also the capital account.

Bank Rate — The rate at which a central bank will lend to its national banking system. In Britain this rate was pivotal to interest levels until replaced by Minimum Lending Rate or MLR.

Banks, Joint Stock — Banks whose principal function is to receive deposits and make short term loans, mainly for working capital. Also described as commercial banks.

Bear — A speculator who sells on a falling market in the hope that he may buy back at a lower level.

Bill of Exchange — A transferable and unconditional order drawn by a creditor on a debtor for discharge on an agreed fixed date – hence a 90 day bill.

Bridging Loan — Often applied to bank or other loans where the borrower is prepared to bear interest for a fixed period, to avoid

	losing an intended new investment, while anticipating the sale of another.
Bull	A speculator who buys stock in the belief that he will be able to sell it at a profit (see Bear).
Capitalism	A social system in which work is undertaken for individual reward, under a system of free contract, and capital is ownable by private persons.
Cartels	Associations which limit competition by price-fixing and/or market-sharing.
C.I.F.	Cost, insurance, freight. The inclusion of these on-costs in the quoted price.
Communism	The official doctrine, originating from Lenin's interpretation of the writings of Marx, which controls the USSR, China, Eastern European and other countries. A system under which property is owned by the state and the community is provided for each according to his need.
Demurrage	Payment by a shipper to a shipowner for discharging or loading delays beyond the stipulated time contracted.
Depreciation	The decrease in the value of an asset due to wear and tear, age, obsolesence or fall in market price.
Devaluation	Reducing the value of the nation's currencies thereby cheapening exports and raising the price of imports.
Discounted Cash Flow	The discounting of cash flows to present value to determine or compare the viability of a project.
Disinflation	Measures to relieve inflationary stress such as running a budget surplus, credit squeezes or hire purchase controls.
Dividend	Money yield per share from the profits or reserves of a company.
Elasticity of demand	Responsiveness or sensitivity of demand to a change in price. Inelastic demand is insensitive.
Entrepreneur	One who risks his own capital in an enterprise.
Equity	Ordinary (as opposed to preference) shares holding in a limited company.
Exports	Sales overseas or abroad of a country's goods (visible exports) or services (invisible exports).
Fiduciary Issues	Issue of notes 'in faith' unbacked by gold or tangible assets.
Floating Exchange Rate	Exchange rates which are not fixed and which fluctuate according to foreign exchange market supply or demand.
Foreign Exchange Market	Financial centres in which foreign currency is bought and sold by dealers. In Britain these include banks, finance houses and exchange brokers.
Free Trade	Trade which flows freely and without tariffs or other distortions so that the benefit of international specialisation is globally maximised.
Funded Debt	Perpetual loans or debts with no fixed repayment date.
General Agreement on Tariffs and Trade (GATT)	Established in Geneva in 1947 it aims to eliminate all barriers to trade through non-discrimination and a negotiated reduction in tariffs.
Gilt-edged Securities	Those considered absolutely safe for purposes of interest and redemption at par when they mature.
Gold Standard	A monetary system in which the gold value of the currency is fixed by law.
Gresham's Law	Tendency for money of lower intrinsic value to circulate more freely than money of higher intrinsic and equal nominal value.
Gross National Product	*See page 244.*
Hard Currency	Currency is 'hard' if it has an underlying strength based on internal stability and external surplus on balance of trade.
Hyper-inflation	Inflation so rapid that contracts can be shortened no further and flight from the currency is total, thus leading to a total economic breakdown, e.g. Germany (1922–23), Hungary (1946), China (1948–49).
Indexed Pension	Pension rates annually or periodically adjusted to preserve value by allowing for rises (and falls) in the Retail Price Index.
Indirect Taxes	Taxes on goods and services collected indirectly through traders or manufacturers (as opposed to direct collection as in case of income tax).
Inflation	A fall in the value of money caused by expansion of money supply, high public spending, credit creation, high wage settlements etc.
Interest	The price payable for the use of loanable funds or credit.
Keynesianism	The doctrine of the macro-economist Lord Keynes (1883–1946), adopted by the British Government in 1944, that generation of demand by public spending (or budget deficit) will promote faster expansion, more private investment and higher employment levels.
Liquidity	The ease and speed with which an asset can be exchanged. Cash has 'perfect' liquidity whereas a deposit account requiring notice of withdrawal has not.
M1	Total money supply in its most liquid form (coin, banknotes, and immediately encashable assets).
M2	(Not used since 1972) M1 plus clearing bank and discount house deposits.
M3	M1 plus assets liquefiable in the short term, *viz* Building Society deposits and shares encashable within the account period.
Market Economy	Conditions of competitive, non-centralised supply and demand that operates like a continuous referendum, between consumers and manufacturers, buyers and sellers, and lenders and borrowers.
Marxism	The doctrine of the co-author of the *Communist Manifesto* (1848), Karl Marx (1818–1883). He maintained that any free enterprise capitalist system would inevitably result in revolution because the owners of the means of production had an insatiable thirst for profit.
Monetarism	The doctrine that the avoidance of inflation and deflation is better achieved by monetary rather than fiscal methods, i.e. by control over money supply (*via* interest rates, hire purchase and other credit creations, and levels of public spending and borrowing).
National Income	The total of incomes of all residents, companies and government bodies derived from goods and services produced through economic activity.
Negative Income Tax	A device for alleviating poverty by 'topping up' the lowest band of incomes by fiscal rebate rather than by conventional social benefits.
Overmanning	The employment of more labour than required to achieve efficient production due to unfulfilled expectations of rising demand, anxiety to deny skilled workers to a competitor, or trade union pressure to prevent job losses.
PAYE	Pay As You Earn system of collection of income tax from current earnings. Developed from a German model by Sir Paul Chambers. Introduced into Britain in 1944.
Public Sector Borrowing Requirement (PSBR)	The amount by which the revenue of public sector organisations falls short of expenditure. This deficit, by central and local authorities and nationalised industries, is financed by sales of securities, increases in currency, borrowing from overseas and bank lending to the public sector.
Reflation	The initial and temporary phase in the upturn from a slump in which extra spending is matched by increased supply. Reflation ends and inflation starts if demand continues or grows to the point of raising prices.
Reverse Income Tax	*See* Negative Income Tax.
Stagflation	A simultaneous presence of rises in prices and rises in unemployment levels once thought by economists to be mutually exclusive.
Syndicalism	A doctrine whereunder industry is controlled by workers.
Treasury Bills	Bills issued by the Treasury (originating in 1873) in multiples of £5000 for short term (3 months) funding of Government debt.
Value Added Tax	A tax levied on the basis of the cost of 'inputs' of materials and labour as opposed to a turnover or sales tax.
Zero Price	Economists jargon for a state service supplied at no cost to the eligible recipient at the time. The tax-price, paid by most people, is paid only later and indirectly.

INDEX

INDEX

INDEX

INDEX

INDEX

PLANT KINGDOM

See pages 63–64

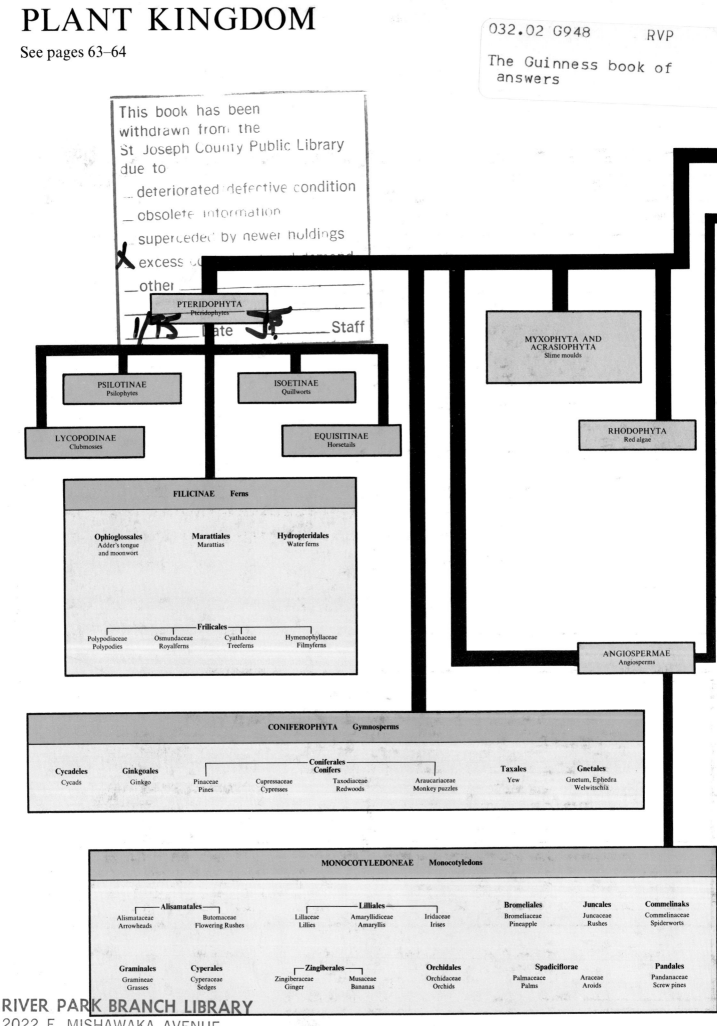